Companion Workbook:

MENTAL HEALTH AND ANCIENT EGYPTIAN PSYCHOLOGY GUIDEBOOK

A AMENEMOPET WISDOM TEXT TRANSFORMATION MANUAL

A Self-Paced Practical Integration Workbook

MENTAL HEALTH AND ANCIENT EGYPTIAN PSYCHOLOGY

New Translation of Sage Amenemopet's Wisdom Text of Optimal Physical and Spiritual Transformation For Self-Mastery & Enlightenment

With original hieroglyph trilinear translation prepared by Dr. Muata Ashby

ACKNOWLEDGMENT

I wish to express sincere appreciation to Dr. Karen Dja Ashby for her invaluable contributions throughout the development of this manuscript. Her insightful questions, critical observations, and rigorous engagement with these ancient teachings have significantly enhanced my capacity to articulate the psychological and spiritual dimensions of Sage Amenemopet's wisdom with greater clarity and precision. Through discussion and careful review of the translation work and commentary, she has helped identify areas requiring deeper explanation, challenged assumptions that needed refinement, and offered perspectives that strengthened the manuscript's accessibility to contemporary readers while maintaining theological accuracy. Her dedication to understanding the profound depths of Neterian philosophy has proven instrumental in ensuring that this work serves both scholarly rigor and practical spiritual application. The wisdom teachings of Amenemopet have been transmitted more effectively through this collaborative effort, and for that contribution to the preservation and dissemination of ancient Egyptian spiritual psychology, I am genuinely grateful.

Dr. Muata Ashby

Sema Institute

P.O. Box 570459

Miami, Florida, 33257

(305) 378-6253 Fax: (305) 378-6253

First U.S. edition □ 2025 By Reginald Muata Ashby

The author is available for group lectures and individual counseling. For further information contact the publisher.

Ashby, Muata (2025)

MENTAL HEALTH & ANCIENT EGYPTIAN PSYCHOLOGY: **New Translation of Sage Amenemopet's Wisdom Text of Optimal Physical and Spiritual Transformation For Self-Mastery & Enlightenment**

ISBN: 9781937016784

Library of Congress Cataloging in Publication Data

MORE BOOKS BY THE AUTHOR:

amazon.com/author/muataashby

About the Author - Dr. Muata Ashby

Dr. Muata Ashby is a distinguished spiritual teacher, scholar, philosopher, and author whose groundbreaking work has significantly contributed to the understanding of Ancient Egyptian (Kemetic) spirituality and its profound connections to world religions. With over 70 books published on yoga philosophy, religious philosophy, and social philosophy based on ancient African principles, Dr. Ashby has established himself as the leading authority in comparative religious studies with a specialized focus on Ancient Egyptian wisdom traditions.

Academic Credentials and Foundation

Dr. Ashby holds a Doctor of Philosophy Degree in Religion and a Doctor of Divinity Degree from the American Institute of Holistic Theology, as well as a Master's degree in Liberal Arts and Religious Studies from Thomas Edison State College. His extensive academic background is complemented by comprehensive independent research spanning Egyptian Yoga, Indian Yoga, Chinese Yoga, Buddhism, mystical psychology, and Christian Mysticism. He has also engaged in Post Graduate research in advanced Jnana, Bhakti, and Kundalini Yogas at the Yoga Research Foundation.

Institutional Leadership and Innovation

As the founder of the Sema Institute, a non-profit organization dedicated to spreading the wisdom of Ancient Egyptian mystical traditions, and the Kemetic University along with the Egyptian Mystery School, Dr. Ashby has developed innovative approaches to teaching ancient wisdom using traditional temple teaching methods alongside modern technologies. Dr Ashby has taught at Florida International University in the capacity of Adjunc professor. Currently he teaches through the online school he created called *"Kemet University"*. When functioning in academic settings, he is addressed as Dr. Muata Ashby.

Scholarly Contributions and Research

Dr. Ashby began his groundbreaking research in the 1990s, investigating correlations between Ancient Egyptian and Indian spiritual traditions, which became the catalyst for his successful "Egyptian Yoga" book series launched in 1994. A leading advocate of the concept that advanced social and religious philosophies existed in ancient Africa comparable to Eastern traditions such as Vedanta, Buddhism, Confucianism, and Taoism, he has lectured and written extensively on these correlations, promoting greater cross-cultural understanding and spiritual advancement.

His scholarly work encompasses extensive research into Ancient Egyptian philosophy and social order, with particular expertise in Maat philosophy—the ethical foundation of Ancient Egyptian society. Dr. Ashby has studied anthropology and Ancient Egyptian language, spending thousands of hours investigating and translating texts with a special interest in discovering the Ancient Egyptian Religious Philosophy (*sebait*) that fueled the development of Ancient Egyptian society and spirituality.

Revolutionary Translation Method

I have developed a unique and revolutionary form of translating ancient texts called "Trilinear Translation," which goes beyond the basic Egyptological interlinear format to expose greater depth of insight through deeper contextual exposition. This innovative method provides three levels of translation: phonetic transliteration, direct word-for-word translation, and contextual translation that incorporates philosophical, mythological, and historical background insights, making ancient wisdom more accessible to contemporary readers.

Musical and Artistic Contributions

Since 1999, Dr. Ashby has researched Ancient Egyptian musical theory and created a series of musical compositions that explore this unique area of music from ancient Africa and its connection to world music. As an accomplished lecturer, musician, artist, poet, painter, screenwriter, and playwright, he brings a multidisciplinary approach to his scholarly work, enriching the understanding of ancient wisdom through various artistic expressions.

Global Impact and Outreach

Dr. Ashby has lectured extensively throughout the United States, Europe, and Africa, sharing his insights on ancient wisdom traditions with diverse audiences. His work has reached practitioners and scholars worldwide, establishing him as an internationally recognized authority on Ancient Egyptian spirituality and its practical applications for contemporary spiritual seekers.

Collaborative Partnership

Dr. Ashby works closely with his spiritual and life partner, Dr. Dja Ashby (formerly Karen Clarke), who serves as co-founder of the Sema Institute and director of C.M. Book Publishing. Together, they have been married for over 40 years and continue to advance the dissemination of Ancient Egyptian wisdom through their collaborative efforts in publishing, teaching, and spiritual guidance.

Current Work and Legacy

In his recent work, Dr. Ashby has focused intensively on the temples of Aset (Isis) and Asar (Osiris), producing detailed photographic documentation and original translations of hieroglyphic scriptures. His commitment to making ancient wisdom accessible to modern practitioners is evident in his development of comprehensive study programs that bridge the gap between ancient temple teachings and contemporary spiritual practice.

The present monumental work on the Scripture of Ra and Hetheru, from the Tomb of Sety 1st, represents Dr. Ashby's continued dedication to translating and interpreting Ancient Egyptian spiritual texts with a focus on their mystical and practical applications for contemporary spiritual seekers. Through his extensive scholarship, innovative translation methods, and deep spiritual understanding, Dr. Ashby continues to illuminate the profound wisdom of Ancient Egypt for a new generation of practitioners and scholars seeking authentic spiritual transformation.

Dr. Ashby's life work demonstrates that the wisdom of ancient Africa—particularly Ancient Egypt—offers profound insights into the nature of consciousness, spiritual development, and the path to enlightenment that remain as relevant today as they were thousands of years ago.

TABLE OF CONTENTS

About the Author - Dr. Muata Ashby 5
Introduction to the Mysticism of Amenemopet: The Ancient Egyptian Science of Mind Transformation 11
PREFACE: How the translations of the Ancient Egyptian Hieroglyphic texts in this volume were produced 19
HOW TO USE THIS BOOK: A SUGGESTED SYSTEMATIC APPROACH TO AMENEMOPET'S WISDOM 27
PART I: Teachings of Amenemopet 29
Scripture Prologue 29
Teachings of Amenemopet Chapter 1 Hieroglyphic Text 31
Teachings of Amenemopet Chapter 2 Hieroglyphic Text 35
Teachings of Amenemopet Chapter 3 Hieroglyphic Text 37
Teachings of Amenemopet Chapter 4 Hieroglyphic Text 38
Teachings of Amenemopet Chapter 5 VII Hieroglyphic Text 39
Teachings of Amenemopet Chapter 6B VIII Hieroglyphic Text 40
Teachings of Amenemopet Chapter 6B IX Hieroglyphic Text 41
Teachings of Amenemopet Chapter 7 Hieroglyphic Text 42
Teachings of Amenemopet Chapter 7B Hieroglyphic Text 44
Teachings of Amenemopet Chapter 8X Hieroglyphic Text 45
Teachings of Amenemopet Chapter 9XI Hieroglyphic Text 48
Teachings of Amenemopet Chapter 9XII Hieroglyphic Text 49
Teachings of Amenemopet Chapter 11 Hieroglyphic Text 50
Teachings of Amenemopet Chapter 12 Hieroglyphic Text 51
Teachings of Amenemopet Chapter 13 Hieroglyphic Text 51
Teachings of Amenemopet Chapter 15 Hieroglyphic Text 52
Teachings of Amenemopet Chapter 16 Hieroglyphic Text 54
Teachings of Amenemopet Chapter 17 Hieroglyphic Text 55
Teachings of Amenemopet Chapter 18 [XX] Hieroglyphic Text 56
TEACHINGS 57
Teachings of Amenemopet Chapter 21 Hieroglyphic Text 59
Teachings of Amenemopet Chapter 25 Hieroglyphic Text 60

Teachings of Amenemopet Chapter 26 Hieroglyphic Text 62

PART II: COMMENTARIES ON THE WISDOM TEXT VERSES OF SAGE AMENEMOPET 64

GLOSSARY OF KEY TERMS 69

CHAPTER 1: Commentary on Teachings of Amenemopet Prologue (verses 1-2, 7-9): The Foundation of Wisdom Philosophy for Life Transformation 75

CHAPTER 2: Commentary on Teachings of Amenemopet Chapter 1, Verses 8-18 & 1-2: The Psychology of Wisdom Absorption and Aryu (Karmic) Purification and Transformation 103

Teachings 115

CHAPTER 3: Commentary on Teachings of Amenemopet Chapter 2, Verses 10, 16-17: The Cosmic Psychology of Unrighteous Action and the Enemy of Life 127

CHAPTER 4: Commentary on Teachings of Amenemopet Chapter 2 V, Verses 1-2: The Sacred Navigation of Life's Journey Commentary on Sage Amenemopet's Teaching of Conscious Effort 141

CHAPTER 5: Commentary on Teachings of Amenemopet Chapter 3, Verses 10, 15-17: The Sacred Art of Spiritual Discernment Commentary on Sage Amenemopet's Teaching of Conscious Disassociation 147

CHAPTER 6: Commentary on Teachings of Amenemopet Chapter 4, Verses 1-2, 7-8: The Psychology of Spiritual Receptivity and Detached Response, Teaching of Silent Mind and Feelings 159

CHAPTER 7: Commentary on Teachings of Amenemopet Chapter 5, Verses 7-9: The Psychology of Inner Fulfillment Through Divine Communion Commentary on Sage Amenemopet's Teaching of Silent Communion with Creator-Spirit 168

CHAPTER 8: Commentary on Teachings of Amenemopet Chapter 6B, Verse 14: The Psychology of Maintaining Awareness of All-Encompassing Divinity Commentary on Sage Amenemopet's Teaching of Deliberate Neberdjer Recognition 176

CHAPTER 9: THE PRACTICE OF SAU-NEBERDJER CONSCIOUSNESS MEDITATION 205

Chapter 10: Commentary on Teachings of Amenemopet Chapter 6B VIII (verses 19-20) and Chapter 6B IX (verses 5-8): Divine Providence versus Worldly Scheming 253

CHAPTER 11: Commentary on Teachings of Amenemopet Chapter 7, Verses 10-15–The Psychology of Power-Seeking, Mental Wandering, Vital Energy Conservation, and Trust in Divine Providence 264

Chapter 12: Addendum to Chapter 11 about Amenemopet Chapter 7: Transforming Destiny Through Purification 289

CHAPTER 13: Commentary on Teachings of Amenemopet Chapter 7B Verses 10-12 296

CHAPTER 14: Commentary on Teachings of Amenemopet Chapter 8, Verses 19-20: The Serpent Power of Righteousness and Opposition to Apophis Forces 321

CHAPTER 15: Commentary on Teachings of Amenemopet Chapter 8X and 8XI: Speech, Vitality, and the Path to Inner Sanctuary 345

CHAPTER 16: Commentary on Teachings of Amenemopet Chapter 9XI and 9XII: Avoiding Heated Persons and Achieving Divine Transformation Through Self-Control, Compassion and Good Will 378

CHAPTER 17: Commentary on Teachings of Amenemopet Chapter 11: The Corruption of Greed and False Oaths Verses 5-6, 9-11 388

CHAPTER 18: Synthesis: The Complete Model of Mind and Consciousness According to Amenemopet 404

CHAPTER 19: Commentary on Teachings of Amenemopet Chapter 13: The Glorification of Love Versus the Illusion of Power Verses 11-12 416

CHAPTER 20: Commentary on Teachings of Amenemopet Chapter 15: The All-Seeing Eye of Cosmic Mind and the Recovery of Authentic Selfhood Verses 5, 9-10, 15-16 427

Summary of Teachings 427

CHAPTER 21: Commentary on Teachings of Amenemopet Chapter 16, Verses 8-11: The Psychology of Luxury Attachment and Turning Away from Divine Presence 449

CHAPTER 22: Commentary on Teachings of Amenemopet Chapter 17, Verses 2-3, 6: The Psychology of Volitional Fraud and Conscience Registration -Commentary on Sage Amenemopet's Teaching on Deliberate Unrighteousness and the Inescapable Witness 457

CHAPTER 23: Commentary on Teachings of Amenemopet Chapter 18, Verses 5-6, 14-15, 22-23, 24-26: The Illusion of Self-Will and the Reality of Divine Guidance 466

CHAPTER 24: Commentary on Teachings of Amenemopet Chapter 21, Verses 5, 15-16, 17-18: The Balance Between Trust in Divine Order and Righteous Action 476

Summary of Teachings 476

CHAPTER 25: Commentary on Teachings of Amenemopet Chapter 25, Verses 9-11, 19-20: Compassionate Treatment of the Vulnerable and the Ultimate Goal of Divine Union 483

CHAPTER 26: Commentary on Amenemopet Chapter 26, Verses 11-15: The Path from Humility to Vigilant Serenity: Releasing Pride-Guarding to Navigate Life Under Divine Guidance 491

PART III: SPECIAL TOPIC ESSAYS 504

SPECIAL TOPIC ESSAY #0: THE ESSENTIAL PRACTICE: MAINTAINING GER AS THE DIRECT PATH TO AB NETER DISCOVERY 506

SPECIAL TOPIC ESSAY #1: The Discernment of Wisdom Truth: Beyond Mere Factual Accuracy in Spiritual Communication 509

SPECIAL TOPICS ESSAY #2: The Wounded Ego's False Glory: Understanding Narcissistic Consciousness Through Amenemopet's Psychology 513

SPECIAL TOPIC ESSAY #3 The Psychology of *Shennu* (Frustration) in the Teachings of Sage Amenemopet 517

SPECIAL TOPIC ESSAY #4: SECHSECH (RUSHING/HASTE) AND THE PRACTICE OF SLOWNESS AS SPIRITUAL DISCIPLINE 531

DEVOTION & TRUST: The Prayer of Amenemopet: Living in Divine Trust 549

CONCLUSION: The Complete Path of Amenemopet - From Heated Suffering to Silent Enlightenment 554

INDEX 565

OTHER BOOKS BY MUATA ASHBY 576

Introduction to the Mysticism of Amenemopet: The Ancient Egyptian Science of Mind Transformation

The Historical Context and Sacred Name

In the ancient temples of Kamit (Kemet, Ancient Egypt), during the flourishing period of the 12th century BCE, there emerged one of the most profound wisdom texts ever recorded for the spiritual enlightenment of humanity [1]. This sacred scripture is known as the *Instructions of Sage Amenemopet*. it represents a comprehensive science of mind and personality transformation that not only provides ethical guidance, but also addresses the fundamental psychological and spiritual challenges confronting every human being who seeks genuine fulfillment and lasting peace [1]. Indeed, this wisdom text belongs to the distinguished genre of Kamitan, *Ancient Egyptian Sebayt* (wisdom literature), those sacred teachings that the ancient sages transmitted to guide aspirants from the heated conditions of worldly suffering to the silent recognition of Divine Consciousness, that is the true source of all well-being and spiritual illumination [1].

Hieroglyphic name of Sage Amenemopet	Transliteration	Translation	Contextual Translation
	Amun ***im*** ***hat***	Hidden-Witnessing-Consciousness in/within front/heart/beginning	"Amun (the Hidden Creator Spirit/Witnessing Consciousness aspect of Ra [Amun-Ra]) in the beginning," and "Amun in front," and"Amun in the front of heart (mind)" and Amun in front of the mind (first thought; Amun in presence of mind)

The sage's name itself reveals the profound spiritual understanding that permeates his teachings, for Amenemopet derives from the Ancient Egyptian Amun-em-hat, meaning "Amun (the Hidden Creator Spirit) in the beginning," "Amun in front," and "Amun in the heart (mind)" [2], or "Amun is the main thought in the mind". This nomenclature indicates that the sage understood himself as an embodiment of that universal witnessing consciousness (Amun) that serves as both the primordial source of Creation and the innermost essence of individual awareness—the same divine principle that the ancient wisdom traditions recognize as the foundation of all spiritual realization [2]. Consider how this understanding places Amenemopet's teachings within the broader context of Shetaut Neter (the hidden teachings of the Divine), that comprehensive spiritual tradition of Ancient Egypt which provided systematic instruction for consciousness to transcend its identification with temporary phenomena and discover its essential nature as an expression of universal divine awareness [3].

The extended translation of Amenemopet's name as "Divine Self, who is the Hidden Creator Spirit of Creation" within the temple complex of Karnak, the western city and seat of the God, further reveals the geographical and spiritual context in which these teachings emerged [2]. Yet the wisdom contained in these instructions transcends all temporal and cultural limitations, addressing the universal human condition and providing practical methodology for moving Consciousness from what the sage terms the "heated" state of agitated seeking, to the "silent" recognition of inner fullness that naturally flows from remembering one's Divine Nature [1][4]. In Kamit, Ancient Egypt, the teachings related to Consciousness was couched in mystical religious-spirituality and expressed as the Absolute Divinity, also know as Neberdjer.

Images of Sage Amenemopet:

Figure 1: ***Instructions of Amenemope, circa 12th century B.C.E. Ink on papyrus, British Museum, London.***

WHICH CHAPTERS ARE IN WHICH SOURCES?

COMPLETE CHAPTER ORDER (27 CHAPTERS)

The **British Museum Papyrus** contains all 27 chapters, although parts are damaged:

1–4: Intros on humility & restraint
5–10: Behavior, speech, modesty
11–14: Wealth, generosity, oppression
15–20: Temperance, honesty, self-control
21–25: Justice, relations with others
26–27: Summary & moral conclusion

FRAGMENTARY WITNESSES CONTAIN:

Source	Chapters Contained	Notes
Papyrus BM 10474	**Ch. 1–27 (full corpus)**	Primary & only complete source
Papyrus Amherst 102	Ch. 2–3 (partial)	Short excerpt
Papyrus Moscow 4658	Ch. 6 or 7 (uncertain)	Very small fragment
Ostracon Berlin 12654	Ch. 12–13 (short excerpt)	Scribal exercise
Deir el-Medina ostraca	Scattered lines from Ch. 15–22	Training copies
Ostracon BM 5634	Ch. 3–4 (partial)	Brief quotation

Note: Only the British Museum papyrus preserves the full sequence and arrangement.

The Wisdom Text Tradition and Spiritual Psychology

The Instructions of Sage Amenemopet occupies a unique position within the corpus of Kamitan Ancient Egyptian wisdom literature, bridging the earlier Pyramid Texts and Coffin Texts with the later developments of the Wasetian (Theban) Amun tradition, while maintaining its distinctive focus on practical psychological transformation [3]. This text belongs to the early and Middle Kingdom era, written during a period when the ancient sages had developed sophisticated understanding of consciousness levels and the precise mechanisms through which awareness becomes either trapped in ego-identification or liberated into recognition of its Divine Source [2][3]. Indeed, the teachings reveal that Amenemopet possessed profound insight into psychology and mysticism, as well as what contemporary understanding might term transpersonal psychology—the systematic study of consciousness beyond the limitations of ego-based thinking and the practical methods for achieving expanded awareness that recognizes its essential unity with Universal Divine Consciousness [4].

The sage's approach demonstrates remarkable sophistication in addressing what the ancient teachings identify as the fundamental human predicament: the tendency of consciousness to forget its divine nature and become trapped in cycles of seeking fulfillment through external means, creating what Amenemopet describes as the condition of the "heated person" (shemm) who lives through "unrighteousness, fraud, anger, boisterousness, flippant retorts and thoughtless speech, inconsiderate and impulsive acts, rapacious greed, jealousy, envy" [4]. This heated condition represents consciousness that has lost touch with its divine source and operates through accumulated aryu (karmic impressions) that cloud natural spiritual sensitivity and perpetuate endless cycles of dissatisfaction and suffering [4].

Consider how this understanding provides the essential framework for comprehending why practical spiritual development proves necessary, and how it operates to transform consciousness from ego-identification to what the spiritual-mystical non-dual traditions call the Soul-Aware-Witness—that mode of awareness which has achieved separation from reactive patterns and now operates as the instrument of divine wisdom rather than the vehicle of worldly agitation [4]. The ancient sages taught that this transformation occurs through systematic cultivation of what Amenemopet terms the "silent mind" (ger), which discovers "the fullness of the Creator-Spirit that is within" rather than seeking satisfaction through heated engagement with worldly phenomena [4].

It bears emphasis that the term *ger* (silent) refers not to physical quietness or mere absence of speech, but rather to a **serene**, **balanced**, and **relaxed** quality of mind—the natural mental peace that emerges when Consciousness no longer operates through the agitated patterns of heated thinking. The teaching's central focus concerns the practical methods for causing the mind to achieve and sustain this serenity, which represents the psychological foundation for discovering one's Divine nature. In this context, what Sage Amenemopet considers to be the heated mind is usually considered "normal" by most people in the Western society when the heatedness that accompanies ego-identification is normalized . However, the silent, serene (ger) mind is to be considered the normal, natural state. So, what may be considered as being culturally "normal" is not always to be considered as necessarily good or healthy, unless it is based in serenity (ger). Thus, the silent (serene) mind is a gateway to discovering deeper experiences of expanded consciousness.

The Practical Application for Contemporary Aspirants

For contemporary practitioners of Shetaut Neter and students of mind/personality development, the teachings of Sage Amenemopet provide essential guidance that remains remarkably relevant to modern psychological and spiritual challenges [3][4]. The Sage's instruction operates through what may be recognized as a comprehensive methodology for moving awareness from reactive, ego-based thinking patterns to the witness consciousness that naturally recognizes its unity with the Divine Source of all existence [4]. Indeed, these teachings address the same fundamental questions that concern contemporary transpersonal psychology: How does consciousness become trapped in limiting identification with temporary phenomena? What are the practical methods for achieving expanded awareness? How can human beings discover genuine fulfillment that transcends the endless cycles of worldly seeking? [4]

The wisdom reveals that every human being, regardless of cultural background or historical period, shares the fundamental drive to discover genuine happiness and lasting fulfillment, yet the conventional approach of seeking completion through external relationships and achievements inevitably leads to what the teachings describe as the condition of consciousness "drowning in the ever-agitating movements of opposition (dislikes) and attraction (likes)" [4]. This modern predicament corresponds precisely with what Sage Amenemopet identified as the heated personality—consciousness that has seemingly forgotten its divine nature and consequently experiences perpetual agitation, control-seeking, and perception of separateness from higher spiritual being that emerges when a person's individualized awareness identifies itself with mental-emotional fluctuations of the mind rather than resting in its essential witnessing nature that comes from the Spirit Being, which Sage Amenemopet calls Ab Ra and Neberdjer)[4].

Nevertheless, the same consciousness can rediscover its true nature through systematic application of the principles that Sage Amenemopet presents with remarkable clarity and practical precision. The Sage's teachings provide detailed instruction for recognizing the difference between consciousness operating as the heated mind (characterized by agitation, external seeking, and reactive patterns) and consciousness functioning as the silent mind (characterized by inner peace, recognition of fullness, and spontaneous wisdom that flows from Divine Awareness) [4]. This understanding enables practitioners to examine and identify their current mode of operation and apply appropriate methods for cultivating the serene silence (ger) that naturally reveals the truth of Divine Consciousness as the foundation and fulfillment of all genuine spiritual seeking, and what it truly means to be a normal human being.

The Integration of Ancient Wisdom and Modern Understanding

As we embark upon this systematic study of Sage Amenemopet's teachings, we must recognize that these instructions represent not merely historical curiosity but living wisdom that continues to provide essential guidance for mind/personality development in any era [1][2][4]. The Sage's insights into human psychology, the mechanisms of spiritual transformation, and the practical methods for achieving lasting well-being demonstrate sophisticated understanding that harmonizes remarkably with contemporary developments in transpersonal psychology, contemporary mindfulness practice, and consciousness research [4]. Indeed, the Ancient Egyptian understanding of consciousness levels, the distinction between ego-awareness and witness consciousness, and the systematic cultivation of inner serenity silence (ger) provide foundational principles that illuminate and enhance modern approaches to spiritual development while maintaining their own profound integrity and practical effectiveness [3][4].

The translation work presented in this volume, based on research and careful study of the original Ancient Egyptian texts, enables contemporary students to access these teachings in their authentic form while receiving the necessary commentary to understand their practical application [1]. Consider how this approach honors both the ancient wisdom tradition and the genuine needs of modern practitioners who seek reliable guidance for spiritual development that addresses psychological complexity while maintaining focus on the ultimate goal of Divine Realization [1][4]. Through verse-by-verse commentary that illuminates the wisdom philosophy, spiritual metaphysical implications, and practical methods for mind/personality transformation, aspirants can discover how Sage Amenemopet's insights provide comprehensive guidance for moving from worldly agitation to Divine recognition—the same spiritual journey that remains the central concern of all authentic wisdom traditions [4].

Thus, the mysticism of Sage Amenemopet emerges not as abstract philosophy, but as practical science of mind and personality transformation, offering systematic instruction for recognizing and transcending the psychological patterns that perpetuate suffering while cultivating the serene silence (ger) and wisdom that reveal consciousness' essential nature as an expression of Universal Divine

Awareness [1][4]. This ancient wisdom, transmitted through the sacred lineage of Shetaut Neter (Ancient Egyptian, Kamitan religion), continues to provide essential guidance for all sincere practitioners who seek to transform their understanding and experience from the limitations of heated personality to the freedom and fulfillment that flow naturally from remembering one's true Divine Identity [3][4].

AMENEMOPET WITHIN THE ANCIENT EGYPTIAN OF RELIGION AND PHILOSOPHY TRADITION: INTEGRATION WITH NETERU AND MYTHOLOGY

Amenemopet's relatively "mythless" presentation does not indicate rejection of neteru (gods/goddesses) or mythological teachings. Rather, it reflects the text's specific purpose: providing practical meditation and purification methodology that complements the mythological and cosmological teachings found in other scriptures.

DIFFERENT TEXTS, COMPLEMENTARY FUNCTIONS

Ancient Egyptian wisdom uses multiple texts for complete spiritual education:

- PERTEMHERU & ASARIAN TEXTS: Mythological journey, archetypal patterns, neteru as consciousness principles

- RA & HETHERU SCRIPTURE: Cosmological framework, hierarchical consciousness structure

- ISIS & RA SCRIPTURE: Philosophical discrimination, advanced wisdom path

- AMENEMOPET: Practical psychology, meditation techniques, aryu purification methods

These are not competing systems but complementary aspects of ONE TRADITION.

WHY AMENEMOPET CAN BE "MYTHLESS"

Amenemopet assumes students already possess mythological/cosmological foundation from other texts and temple instruction. The text focuses on practical "how-to" for consciousness purification - the meditation technology applicable regardless of which neteru devotion the practitioner follows. This is not Akhenaton-style reform (rejecting traditional neteru for monotheism) but specialized instruction within the established polytheistic framework.

AMENEMOPET AND THE NETERU

Though not extensively mythological, Amenemopet is grounded in neteru framework:

- Sage's name "Amun-em-hat" = "Amun in the beginning/heart"

- References to Ra as Creator Spirit = divine consciousness

- Ab Neter correlates to BA in neteru mythology

- Neberdjer = Ba en Ra in cosmological texts

- Ethics align with Maat goddess principles

- Discovering Ab Neter = discovering BA that Pertemheru discusses

INTEGRATION FOR PRACTITIONERS

Complete practice integrates multiple dimensions:

1. Study neteru mythology (Asar, Aset, Set, Heru) for archetypal understanding

2. Develop devotional connection to neteru suited to your temperament

3. Apply Amenemopet's meditation practices to deepen mythological understanding

4. Recognize that Ab Neter discovered through meditation IS the BA mythology describes

The mythology provides symbolic narrative and archetypal framework. Amenemopet provides practical psychology and meditation methodology. Together they form the complete path - not alternative systems but complementary teachings within unified Sema tradition.

FOR DIFFERENT PRACTITIONER LEVELS

- NOVICES: Best to establish foundation (Egyptian Yoga basics, Maat philosophy, major neteru understanding) before intensive Amenemopet study

- INTERMEDIATE: Amenemopet becomes primary practice text alongside ongoing mythology study

- ADVANCED: Amenemopet offers refined techniques for deep consciousness penetration

This text integrates with (not replaces) other Sema Institute publications: Egyptian Yoga series, Asarian Resurrection studies, Maat Philosophy, Pertemheru commentaries, and advanced scripture translations. Amenemopet fills the specific gap of detailed meditation methodology and psychological purification techniques within the complete curriculum.

Scope and Focus of This Work

This present work encompasses those specific sections of Sage Amenemopet's sacred writings that relate most directly to human psychology, behavioral patterns, and practical guidance for optimal human living in accordance with spiritual principles. Indeed, while the complete corpus of the Sage's teachings extends into various domains of wisdom and spiritual practice, this commentary concentrates on the psychological insights and behavioral imperatives that address the fundamental challenge of understanding the condition of mind and its direct relationship to life experience.

Consider how the ancient sages taught that all external circumstances reflect the quality of consciousness from which they emerge, making self-knowledge and mental purification the essential foundation for creating harmonious and fulfilling life circumstances. Nevertheless, the key principle underlying all these teachings remains the development of discriminative awareness that enables individuals to recognize the difference between the heated mind and its feelings, which generates suffering through unconscious reactive patterns, and the silent mind and its feelings, which discovers authentic well-being through alignment with divine wisdom, thereby providing the psychological foundation necessary for making optimal life decisions that support both worldly success and spiritual development.

References

[1] Ashby, M. (2019). *Mystic Transpersonal Psychology of Sage Amenemopet: Ancient Egyptian Wisdom Text - Hieroglyphic Study of the Instruction of Anunemhat (Amenemopet) on Right Behavior and Ethical Conduct in Human Relations for Attaining Spiritual Enlightenment.* Translation by Dr. Muata Ashby. Sema Institute.

[2] Ashby, M. (2024). *Amenemopet Lectures 2024 Transcripts.* Translation and commentary by Dr. Muata Ashby.

[3] Ashby, M. (2025). *Book Awakening Your Soul-Aware-Witness Ancient Egyptian Wisdom To Discover Divine Consciousness.* Translation by Dr. Muata Ashby.

[4] Ashby, M. (2019). *Summary of Teachings of Amenemope with Hieroglyphic Texts.* Translation by Dr. Muata Ashby.

PREFACE: How the translations of the Ancient Egyptian Hieroglyphic texts in this volume were produced

TRANSLATION FORMAT USED FOR PRESENTING THE SCRIPTURE WITH THE TRILINEAR METHOD

What is the Conventional Interlinear Format and how is it different from the new trilinear format of translating?

The conventional interlinear format for translating Ancient Egyptian hieroglyphic texts presents a phonetic transliteration of the hieroglyphs and transposes them into the characters of the target language. The second line provides a word-for-word translation. This method can result in a limited, choppy, and less intelligible presentation of the original script's intent. When translating between languages with dissimilar structures and cultural references, such as the metaphor-rich Ancient Egyptian language and the more alphabetically structured European languages, a strict word-for-word translation can fail to convey the full meaning. Therefore, while the conventional interlinear format is somewhat useful, this author thought that a more comprehensive translation matrix was needed to capture the deeper richness and import of the original hieroglyphic text.

Example of the Regular Interlinear Format:

Verse 1. *ORIGINAL TEXT (in its own language)*
1.1. Transliteration into the phonetic letters of the language of the reader
1.2. Translation into the words of the language of the reader

Ex:

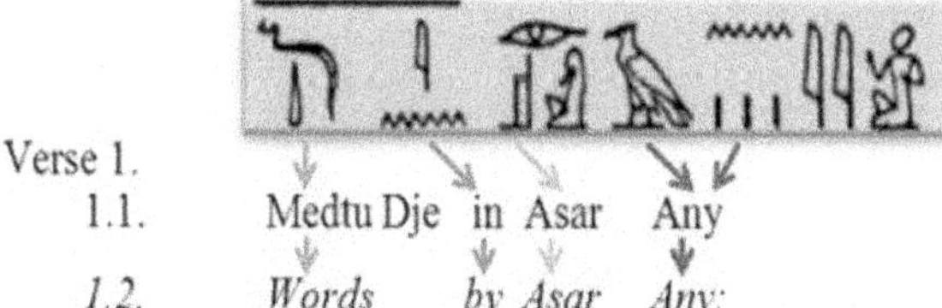

Trilinear Contextual Format

The Trilinear Format for translating Ancient Egyptian writing is both a method and a decipherment protocol. It allows for viewing the meaning from its source through layers of extraction to the final rendition. The term "decipherment" is used because, to the modern mind, the contexts and philosophy of the Ancient Egyptians are akin to a code or formula to be discovered, unlocking the secrets of life, death, and the afterlife. Dr. Muata Ashby has developed a format for translating Ancient Egyptian hieroglyphs into the reader's native language, incorporating three levels of translation instead of the two levels of the conventional interlinear format. The Ternary System (Trilinear Translating protocol) adds a third layer of translation, termed "Contextual Translation," which, together with the other two levels, constitutes the Trilinear Contextual format.

The Trilinear Form, developed by Dr. Muata Ashby, is a ternary system for translating Ancient Egyptian Hieroglyphic texts. It consists of three translation sections or layers. The first level is a phonetic transliteration. The second level is a direct word-for-word translation from hieroglyphic to the reader's native language, generally constituting the "Conventional Interlinear Format." The Trilinear Format adds a third level of translation, a contextual translation that brings out the meaning in an informal, colloquial context in prose style. This includes:

A- Ancient Egyptian Sebait (philosophical) tenets, when appropriate.

B- Ancient Egyptian Matnu (mythic) references and Maut (morals or takeaways of the myth) contained in the text to better reveal the intended meaning for the reader's language and culture.

C- In this volume, a new feature has been added to the trilinear system; the last translated verse will also include, where possible, a summary making contextual sense of the wisdom presented throughout the text, with a particular focus on the beginning verse to clarify the takeaway by recalling the status of the spiritual aspirant at the beginning, then the transformation experiences throughout the text in its key hieroglyphic expressions, and concluding with the outcome expressed in the final verse.

Example of the Trilinear Format:

Verse 1. *ORIGINAL HIEROGLYPHIC TEXT*

1.1. ***Transliteration into the phonetic letters of the language of the reader***

1.2. Translation into the words of the language of the reader

1.3. Translation with contextual insights which may include philosophical and/or mythological and/or historical background insights with colloquial references.

Ex:

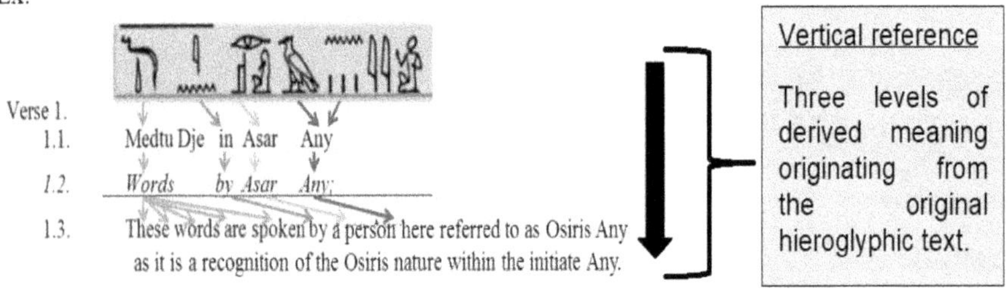

Verse 1.

1.1. Medtu Dje in Asar Any

1.2. *Words by Asar Any;*

1.3. These words are spoken by a person here referred to as Osiris Any as it is a recognition of the Osiris nature within the initiate Any.

Vertical reference

Three levels of derived meaning originating from the original hieroglyphic text.

NOTE: With the trilinear format, each level of translation is designed to be both a reference to the other levels (vertically) but also to the previous and next statement in each level; so, for example, Verse translation Level 2.1 relates to 2.2 and 2.3 (vertical) but 2.2 also relates to 1.2 and 3.2 (horizontal). Therefore, if all the Level 2 translations are read by themselves or Level 3 translations are read by themselves one after the other, there will be a continuous and coherent rendering of the text

Example

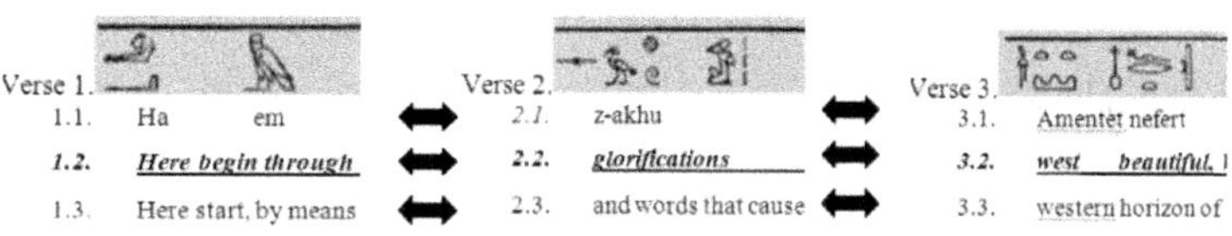

(Horizontal relationship)

In this way, the readings of Verse 1.2 followed by Verse 2.2, followed by Verse 3.2, translations, one after the other (ignoring .1 and .3 levels), horizontally, provide a continuous and coherent word-for-word narrative of the translation. Also, the readings of Verse 1.3 followed by Verse 2.3, followed by Verse 3.3, translations, one after the other (ignoring .1 and .2 levels), horizontally, provide a continuous and coherent prose narrative of the translation.

Note: When some text appears in red, it is because the original hieroglyphic text was written in the same way. This was done, by the original creators of the scripture, the Ancient Egyptian priests and priestesses, to highlight certain parts of the text or to emphasize the chapter titles. See the example below:

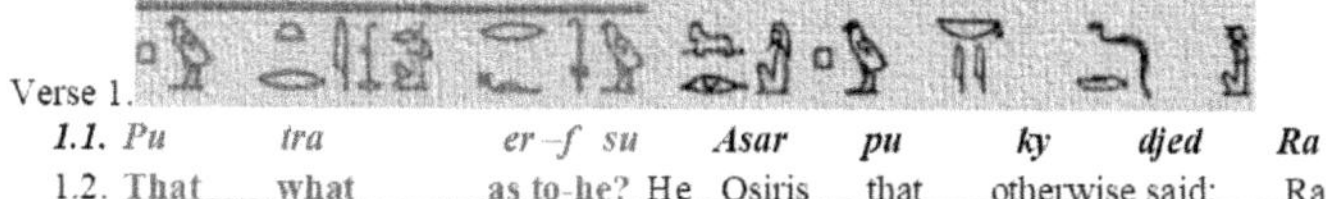

1.3. What is that personality that is being talked about? That personality is Osiris. Another way of thinking about it is that Osiris is also Ra...

Understanding the Contextual Translation Level of the Trilinear Translation System: Vertical Illumination and Horizontal Coherence: The Third Dimension of Hieroglyphic Translation

The contextual translation level in Dr. Ashby's trilinear system serves as the interpretive culmination of the translation process. While the transliteration preserves phonetic values and the word-for-word translation maintains linguistic structure, the contextual translation integrates philosophical concepts (Sebait), mythological references (Matnu), cultural context, and colloquial meaning, based on the key words from the word-for-word translation, to convey the deeper intent of the text.

This third level doesn't merely restate the literal meaning but reveals the philosophical underpinnings and metaphysical implications embedded in the hieroglyphs. It acts as a bridge between Ancient Egyptian thought and modern understanding, recognizing that certain concepts like those conveyed by the "owl" glyph (im/em) carry profound philosophical significance beyond their surface meaning.

The relationship between the three levels is both vertical and horizontal. Vertically, each level progressively deepens understanding of a single verse. Horizontally, reading all contextual translations sequentially provides a cohesive philosophical narrative that might be obscured in the more fragmented word-for-word translations. This multilayered approach acknowledges that Ancient Egyptian texts operated simultaneously as literal communications, philosophical treatises, and mystical instructions.

How is the translation format organized? Below: Sample papyrus sheet with hieroglyphic text:

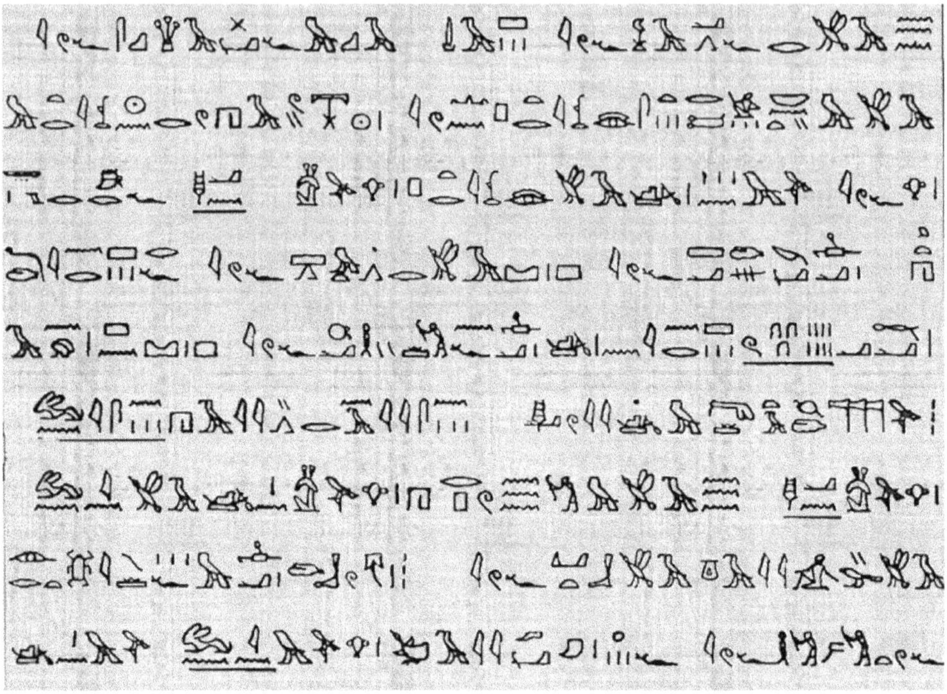

WISDOM TEXT TEACHINGS OF SAGE AMENEMOPET

A trilinear translation is created by photographing the sheet and dividing the lines of text electronically into strips. Then, the text is converted to a TRANSLITERATION, followed by a WORD-for-WORD TRANSLATION, and finally, a CONTEXTUAL TRANSLATION.

EXAMPLE OF A VERSE OF TEXT TRANSLATED WITH THE INTERLINEAR FORMAT:

Verse 13.

13.1. ***Djerau im tjehu maa zenu su entau - im sheps her ner n-F***

13.2. <u>Strength within joyousness seeing they he being - among venerated awe of-he</u>

13.3. There is a strong feeling of joyousness when they see Osiris, among those who are in the ranks of the venerable, noble ancestors; when they see him, they are in awe of him.

Reading the Philosophy Embedded in Ancient Egyptian Hieroglyphic Writings

Here, I will provide two examples using two of the most important hieroglyphs to demonstrate why and how the philosophy of the Ancient Egyptian Mysteries is determined in the texts to be read. As stated earlier, reading the Ancient Egyptian texts in a literal way and ascribing meanings that relate to the culture of the reader is a disservice to the ancient culture. It also distorts the meaning of the texts and the legacy of the original priests and priestesses who created them.

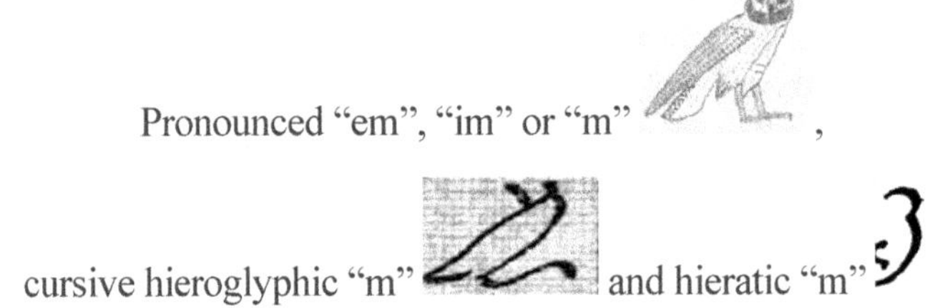

Pronounced “em”, “im” or “m” ,

cursive hieroglyphic “m” and hieratic “m”

The first glyph is the owl. Perhaps one of the most important glyphs, unlike determinatives, which do not convey phonetic aspects to the word, the owl has both phonetic and philosophical meanings. Whenever the owl appears, its meaning can range from "in, within, inside, through, as, in the form of." This makes it a pivotal term, especially when it relates the person for whom the text has been created to any particular or general Divinity [god or goddess]. It, therefore, means that such a person is being identified with that divinity or with an aspect of divinity, or they are being recognized as "becoming, appearing, or manifesting as." This, of course, can signify, among other things, a factor of mutual identification or a movement of transformation either in progress or already attained. This glyph is seldom interpreted in such a manner, and thus the overall outcomes of such neglectful translations will render a mundane or erroneous insight into the Ancient Egyptian hieroglyphic writings.

Conclusion: The Transformative Power of Trilinear Translation for Ancient Wisdom

The trilinear method serves a specific purpose in this translation approach:

Translation Level	Purpose	User Experience
Hieroglyphic Text	Shows authentic ancient source	"I can see the actual text"
Transliteration	Preserves phonetic values/pronunciation	"I can pronounce it"
Word-for-Word	Maintains linguistic structure	"I can see the literal meaning"
Contextual	Provides philosophical interpretation	"I can understand the spiritual meaning"

It is important to understand that Dr. Ashby's trilinear translation system represents a revolutionary advancement in deciphering Ancient Egyptian hieroglyphic texts, moving beyond the limitations of conventional interlinear formats to capture the full philosophical, mythological, and spiritual dimensions embedded within these sacred writings. As the ancient sages taught through their sophisticated use of hieroglyphs like the owl glyph (im/em), Ancient Egyptian texts operated simultaneously as literal communications, philosophical treatises, and mystical instructions—a multilayered reality that demands equally sophisticated translation methodology. We must recognize that the trilinear format's three-dimensional approach—combining phonetic transliteration, word-for-word translation, and contextual interpretation—creates both vertical depth of understanding for individual verses and horizontal coherence when read sequentially, thus preserving the educational progression intended by the original priest-scribes. Indeed, this translation system serves as essential spiritual technology (hekau) for modern aspirants, ensuring that the profound wisdom of Shetaut Neter is transmitted authentically rather than diluted through cultural misinterpretation or oversimplified literal rendering. Consider how the contextual translation level bridges Ancient Egyptian consciousness and contemporary understanding, recognizing concepts like divine identification (expressed through the owl glyph) that conventional translation methods often miss entirely—thereby preserving the transformative potential of these texts for genuine spiritual development (nehast) in our time. Therefore, the trilinear system stands as more than mere academic methodology; it represents a sacred responsibility to honor the intellectual and spiritual sophistication of Ancient Egyptian civilization while making their timeless wisdom accessible to serious students of the Neterian tradition.

For more on Ancient Egyptian Hieroglyphic Writing see the book *Ancient Egyptian Hieroglyphs for Beginners* by Muata Ashby

Having established the revolutionary trilinear translation methodology that makes authentic Ancient Egyptian Kamitan wisdom accessible to contemporary practitioners, we must now turn to the fundamental psychological insights these texts reveal. The translation format serves as more than academic methodology—it functions as spiritual technology that preserves the transformative power embedded within the original hieroglyphic scriptures. Indeed, the ancient sages understood that consciousness itself operates through multiple levels of recognition, much like the trilinear system reveals multiple levels of textual meaning. We must recognize that this methodological foundation prepares us to explore the central teaching that emerges from these sacred texts: the discovery of what may be termed the "Soul-Aware-Witness" as the solution to humanity's fundamental psychological contradictions.

HOW TO USE THIS BOOK: A SUGGESTED SYSTEMATIC APPROACH TO AMENEMOPET'S WISDOM

This book is designed for systematic absorption rather than casual reading. The optimal approach begins with reading Part 1 in its entirety—the complete verse translations with trilinear hieroglyphic transliterations. Read these teachings straight through without stopping for deep analysis, allowing Sage Amenemopet's voice to establish itself in your mind. As you read, note any questions, confusions, or points of resonance that arise—these initial responses provide valuable markers for your particular aryu (unconscious impressions, karmic) patterns and spiritual needs. Consider maintaining a dedicated journal where you record key phrases that strike you, questions requiring clarification, and immediate reflections on how specific teachings relate to your current life circumstances. This preliminary reading plants seeds in the ab (unconscious mind) that will germinate as you proceed through the detailed commentaries.

After completing Part 1, return to the beginning and work systematically through each chapter's commentary. The commentaries are structured to build upon each other progressively, with chapters marked by difficulty level:

- Foundational teachings (Chapters 1-5) establish core principles of mind structure and ethical living.
- Intermediate teachings (Chapters 6-15) develop sophisticated applications addressing specific behavioral and psychological challenges.
- Advanced teachings (Chapters 16-26) present profound metaphysical principles and intensive purification methods requiring solid grounding in earlier material.

Read one chapter with its full commentary, then pause for contemplation and practical implementation before proceeding. This approach allows time for the teaching to penetrate from intellectual understanding, which is called the "hat" level in Shetaut Neter terminology, into the deeper "ab" or "unconscious heart level where genuine transformation occurs. Consider working with each chapter for at least a week, implementing its practical methods, while observing how the teaching manifests in your daily experience.

The wisdom reveals itself most completely through multiple passes through the material, each with different focus and depth.

- Your first pass emphasizes intellectual comprehension—understanding the concepts, frameworks, and terminology that form Sage Amenemopet's psychological system.
- The second pass shifts to emotional and psychological recognition—observing how the teachings illuminate your own aryu (unconscious karmic) patterns, defensive mechanisms, and unconscious conditioning.
- The third pass concentrates on practical implementation refinement—developing and refining the specific methods each chapter presents, troubleshooting challenges, and integrating practices into daily life until they operate naturally.

Like water gradually wearing away stone, repeated engagement with these teachings progressively thins the aryu density that obscures Ab Neter Enlightened Awareness. The transformation occurs not through rapid consumption, but through patient absorption, allowing sufficient time between passes for the teachings to work at the unconscious level where genuine purification takes place.

PART I: Teachings of Amenemopet

Scripture Prologue

Verse 1.

1.1.	*ha*	*im*	*sebayt*	*{mdj}*[1]	*{shf}*[2]	*im*	*ankh*	*{mdj}*
1.2.	Front	form	wisdom-philosophy	{fig}	{book}	form	living	{fig}

1.3. This is the beginning of the wisdom philosophy that is based on recorded wisdom literature that is to be experienced in life.

Verse 2.

2.1.	***metru***	***{djeb}***[3]	***{hu}***[4]	***{sjd}***[5]	***en***	***udja***[6]	***{mdj}***
2.2.	exposition				for	well-being	{fig}

2.3. This is an exposition of precise teachings that when understood exactly, with precision cause a person to have spiritual well-being and vitality while living on earth.

---

1 ***medjat***= abstract, figurative

2 ***shefdu*** = papyrus, i.e. wisdom teachings written on paper, a book, etc.

3 ***djeba*** =precision –determinative fingers

4 ***hu*** =authoritative utterance–determinative tusk

5 ***sedjed*** =speak–determinative person pointing to mouth

6 ***udja***= *"divine-life-fire"*-in certain contexts used to signify well-being and vitality

Verse 7. 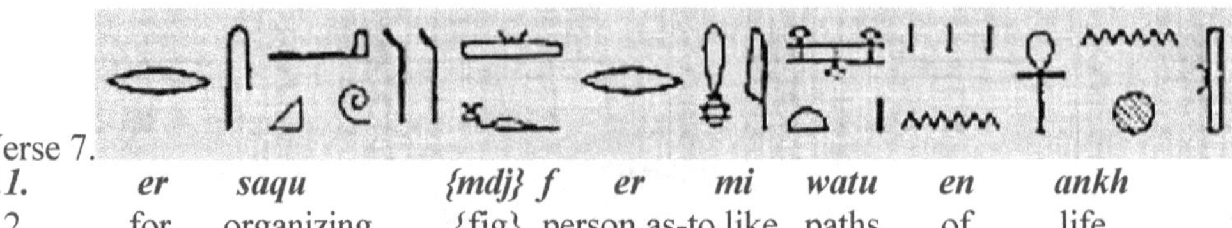

7.1. ***er saqu {mdj} f er mi watu en ankh***
7.2. for organizing {fig} person as-to like paths of life
7.3. This wisdom is for the purpose of allowing a person to organize their affairs in the paths that their life will tread…

Verse 8. 

8.1. ***er se-udja {mdj} f her tep ta***
8.2. for causing-well-being theirs person upon earth
8.3. …and for producing a person's well-being (prosperity-vitality) while they are corporeal as a person on earth (plane).

Verse 9. 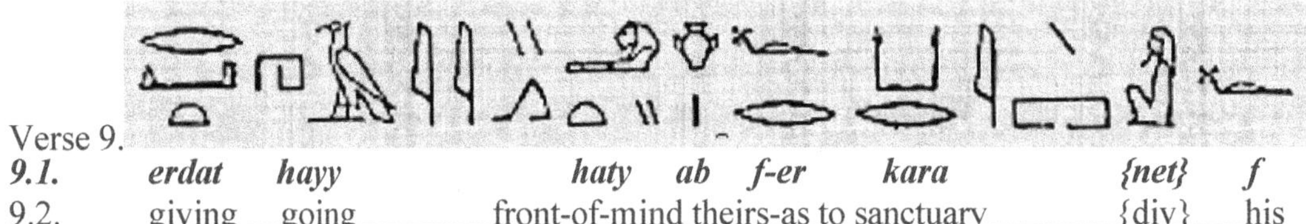

9.1. ***erdat hayy haty ab f-er kara {net} f***
9.2. giving going front-of-mind theirs-as to sanctuary {div} his
9.3. This wisdom teaching allows the heart to have presence-of-mind, positive forwards movement awareness as to the sanctuary [***Kara*** (Divine shrine/sanctuary of Divinity within)]. The mind (heart) of the personality is to gain presence-of-mind about a sanctuary that can be entered once the worldly affairs are handled with this wisdom philosophy taught by the sage. That divine shrine is the location of the "heart divinity" (heart divinity cross-ref. Chap 11, verse 10), where the Divine resides in every person. It is beyond the ego-personality-awareness, the superficial mind. But it is revealed when there is presence-of-mind about its existence. (i.e. discover God within themselves and thus become enlightened beings)

==========================

Teachings of Amenemopet Chapter 1 Hieroglyphic Text

Verse 8.

8.1. *Djed f het {sesh} tept {mdj}*

8.2. Words his house {scriptures} chief {scribe}

8.3. The following words contained in this text are from the chief scribe (Amenemopet)

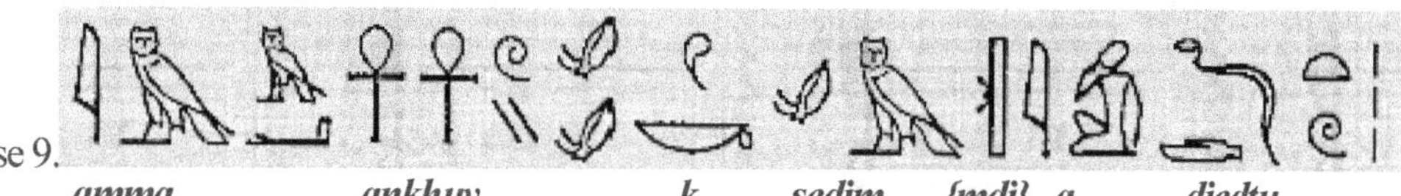

Verse 9.

9.1. ***amma ankhuy k sedjm {mdj} a djedtu***

9.2. grant that living-ears thine listen/obey fig} I words

9.3. Oh! Would the Divine grant that the ears of living people, living, attentive ears that would hear and listen attentively to these words and obey them as opposed to those whose ears are dead to the teachings.

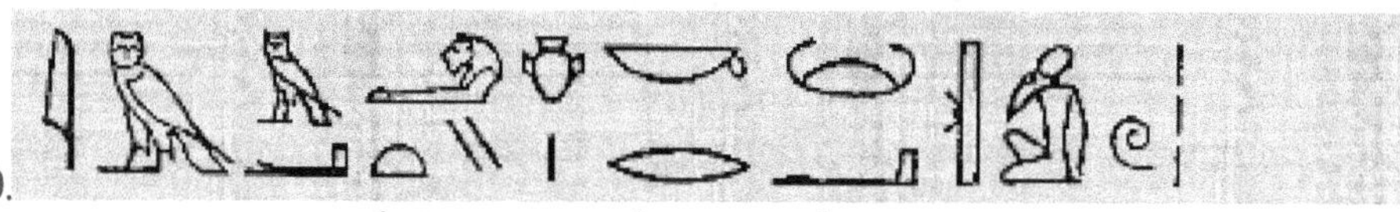

Verse 10.

10.1. ***amma haty ker uhau***

10.2. grant that front-heart thine as-to set-free-to-freedom

10.3. Oh! Would the Divine grant if it could be given that if these words of wisdom were to be kept in the forefront in your mind so that it could be set free (untied) from what causes suffering due to mental agitations that prevent awareness of higher consciousness.

Verse 11.

11.1. ***akh {mdj} pa dit setu im ab k***

11.2. magnificent {Fig} that give these inside heart thine

11.3. …it would be magnificent/splenderous/glorious if the reader of this text would give these teachings to the innermost levels of the mind (unconscious) in such a way that they become firmly seated there. That would be a magnificent, a glorious thing.

Verse 12.

12.1. ***uga iu yshesyshesh en pa unu setu***

12.2. weakness it-is injury that turn-away these

12.3. otherwise, if they are not allowed to be absorbed into the innermost mind it would lead to mental weakness; in fact the turning away from these teachings, that would be injuring the mental capacity.

Verse 13. 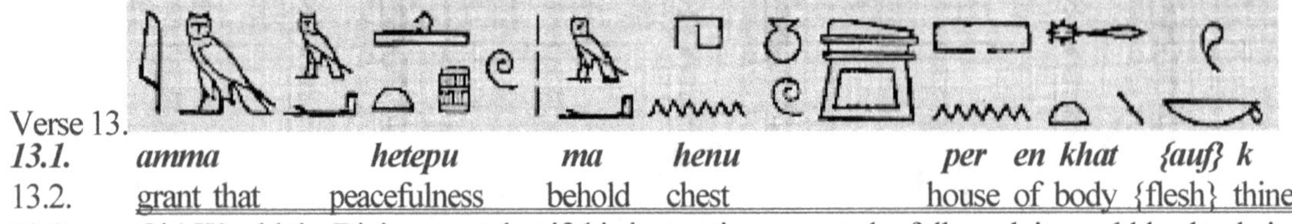

13.1.	*amma*	*hetepu*	*ma*	*henu*	*per*	*en*	*khat*	*{auf} k*
13.2.	grant that	peacefulness	behold	chest	house	of	body	{flesh} thine

13.3. Oh! Would the Divine grant that if this instruction were to be followed, it would lead to being given peacefulness of mind. That would be achieved because beholding these teachings would be as if in the chest, the strongbox of the personality, your body…

Verse 14. 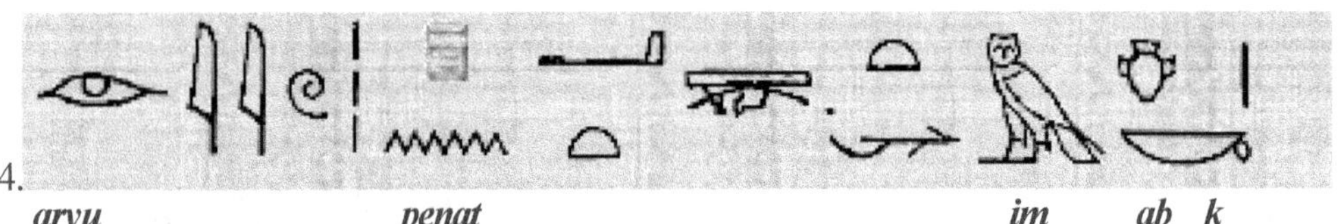

14.1.	*aryu*	*penat*	*im*	*ab*	*k*
14.2.	karmic-feeling-memory	overthrow	within	heart	thine

14.3. …such that when the karmic-feeling-memories (aryu[7] -karmic-feeling-memories) arise from your unconscious into your conscious mind, and would otherwise overwhelm, as if capsize the peacefullness of your mind…

Verse 15. 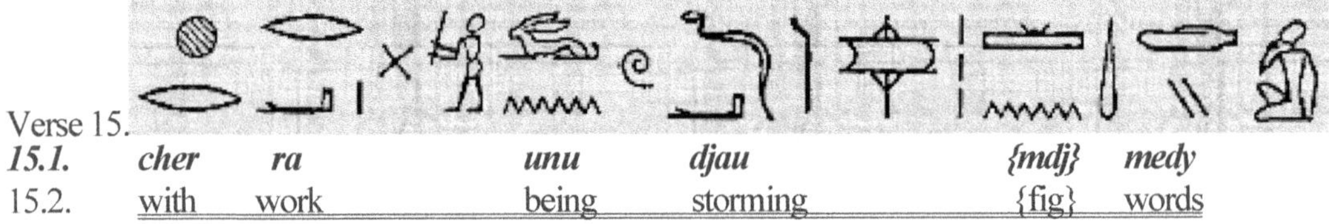

15.1.	*cher*	*ra*	*unu*	*djau*	*{mdj}*	*medy*
15.2.	with	work	being	storming	{fig}	words

15.3. …at that crucial time when those mental impressions (impressions manifest as emerging feeling memories (aryu)), recorded and reinforced patterns of thoughts, feelings, and behaviors that remain registered in the unconscious mind, influencing present and future experiences. The subtle effects of these aryu accumulate and intensify, and if founded in ignorance, egoism and delusion, promote endless unfulfillable worldly desires that cloud the mind's natural clarity and foment ambiguity, diffidence and spiritual ignorance and resulting worldly desires, mental distortions, delusions, frustrations and perpetual unrest and agitation, neshesh (Kamitan Ancient Egyptian term) and agitation, neshesh (Kamitan Ancient Egyptian term) start working in the mind and there is a storming of words (words manifest as thoughts in the mind-the human mind operates in terms of thoughts that the mind can recognize as ideas or concepts that are labeled with words (names) the mind can use to think and cognize with) …

---

[7] Sum total effect of a person past thoughts, feelings, desires and experiences of the past of the present lifetime and past lifetimes that resides in the unconscious mind and that contributes to a person's present guiding feelings, core beliefs, opinions, thoughts, desires and inclinations of the personality that impel or compel the personality to certain paths of action in the present life. The aryu can be changed by living though the fruition of the past aryu and engaging in spiritual disciplines (Sema Tawy [Egyptian Yoga], Shetaut Neter [Egyptian Mysteries]) that will mitigate and or cleanse the cause of the negative aryu (cause=spiritual ignorance and delusion).

Verse 16. 

16.1.	***aryu***	***nayt***	***im***	***nest***	***k***
16.2.	karmic-feeling-memory	stake	in	tongue	thine

16.3. …generated by those impressions (aryu[8]-karmic-feeling-memories), at those times the effort that was taken to heed these instructions, to allow the wise words (thoughts/philosophy) of this book to be absorbed into the innermost mind, then that wisdom would be able to act as a stake, as if a mooring post for your tongue so that you would not get caught up in the mental storm and thereby your mind would thrash you in the storm of excitedness and uncontrolled speech that would promote storming of the mind, uncontrolled thoughts, urges and untoward thinking and acting (heated condition of mind).

Verse 17. 

17.1.	***ar***	***ary***	***k***	***ha***	***uwauy***	***ra***	***k***	***iu***	***nenu***	***{mdj}***
17.2.	if	do	thee	hey	be-remote	time	thine	it-is	consider	{fig}

17.3. If you do this, hey, you will be able to be remote in your mind, detached and collected and then before you speak or act you will be able to consider the wisdom …

Verse 17. 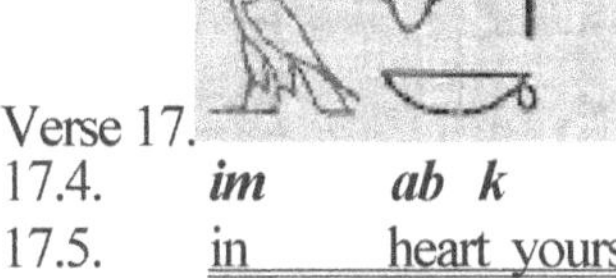

17.4.	***im***	***ab***	***k***
17.5.	in	heart	yours

17.6. …in your mind.

Verse 18. 

18.4.	***gem***	***im***	***medjat***	***k***	***su***	***im***	***zepech***	***mary-u***
18.5.	find	in	book	thy	self	in	fate	fortunate

18.6. You will be able to find yourself in this book, to discover who you are essentially and your fate will be determined by this wisdom such that your life will be fortunate, auspicious, opportune.

Verse 1. 

1.4.	***gem***	***im***	***medjat***	***k***	***medyu***	***a***	***im***	***udja***	***-{per}***	***en ankh***	***{mdj}***
1.5.	find	within	book	thine	words	yours	as	vital-storehouse		of life	{fig}

1.6. you will find, in this book, words you will make your own and they will be a storehouse of vitality and wisdom for your life…

---

[8] ibid

Verse 2.

2.4.	***udja {mdj} hat {auf} k her tep ta***
2.5.	vital-life-fire {fig} body thine upon surface earth

2.6. and vital-life-fire (udja)[9] that produces spiritual purity and well-being for your body while you are living on the surface of the earth.

[9] Ancient Egyptian hieroglyph (ignited fire drill hieroglyph) - UDJA-the Ancient Egyptian symbol of udja, a burning fire drill base, means divine-life-fire, healthy, strong, vital, sound, prosperity, regarded, wellbeing- as a fire drill base whose fire has been ignited and flame is burning, fire of spiritual aspiration and wisdom that burns away ignorance.

Teachings of Amenemopet Chapter 2 Hieroglyphic Text

Verse 10.

10.1. *pa ary ban chaa su mery {moo}{she}-{ta}*

10.2. that action bad forsaking person love {waters} {channel}-{land}

10.3. Those actions that are considered as "bad action", according to Maat philosophy, which determines that which is righteous, beneficial and true for life, those bad (ban) actions act as a means of forsaking, turning away from the caring (love) of the natural forces, the waters, the land, and the like.

Verse 16.

16.1. ***Pa qerau {Set} {pet} {moo} {she}-{ta} chy {pet} nau mesh***

16.2. That tempest {ego} {sky} {water} {channel}-{land} raises {sky} therefore crocodiles

16.3. When such a relationship is developed with nature and the natural order of life, due to living while engaging in bad actions, that relationship leads to raging tempests, a product of egoism in life with thunderous feelings and psychic expressions, that as if rise to the heavens, encompassing the whole environment; there is that cacophony of yelling, fighting, upsetness and cries, like thunderstorms and crashing waves that do not allow any quarter or peace from the cosmic forces that affect life externally and internally; thus there is chaos, infighting, failed and strained relations and rousing worldly entanglements that do not lead to satisfaction or peace, but to more strife and sufferings! Therefore, the personality is left vulnerable to the hidden fearsome energies, thoughts, and feelings that are ever quiet in the unconscious, and yet will strike unexpectedly, like crocodiles, lying in wait, unseen and unbeknown to the conscious mind, waiting for the opportunity to strike at the heart, coming out of nowhere, surprising you, pulling one under and drowning one in the thunderstorm of sorrows caused by one's own unrighteous ego (termed Set in Shetuat Neter).

Verse 17.

17.1. ***pa shemm {chft} tu - k mach***

17.2. That heated {enemy} such-thee suffering

17.3. Now, you heated person, you who, because of the delusions and negative aryu[10] (karma) that has led to a corrupted mind, you have become the enemy of life, of your own and of the community; you who are guided by the corrupted mind, live life by unrighteousness, fraud, anger, boisterousness, flippant (offhand, dismissive) retorts and thoughtless speech, inconsiderate and impulsive acts, rapacious greed, jealousy, envy, ridiculing others and having no compassion for the poor or the less fortunate, con artist/fraud, criminality, to such a one is given to the suffering. The expressions of your personality, that have led to unrighteous thoughts, feelings and actions, lead to your own suffering; not only the suffering

[10] ibid

when you are in pain and anguish as a result of your actions, but also the suffering is when you act out of egoism and mental agitation, committing unrighteous acts that cause you pleasures that will in future lead to personal physical and psychological sufferings, frustrations and dissatisfaction; for actions out of egoism and mental agitation that seem to give pleasure are actually experiences of separation from the Divine that is the real source of bliss (unalloyed, unlimited pleasure and happiness of inner peace); this agitated pleasure is actually causing you more suffering than the suffering of a righteous person that is harmed by the heated person. Therefore, the cause of your own suffering, oh heated person, is in the source of the corrupted mind, due to the heat of the personality, caused by spiritual ignorance that leads to egoism, mental agitation and unrighteous feelings, thoughts and actions.

TEACHINGS OF AMENEMOPET CHAPTER 2 V HIEROGLYPHIC TEXT

Verse 1. 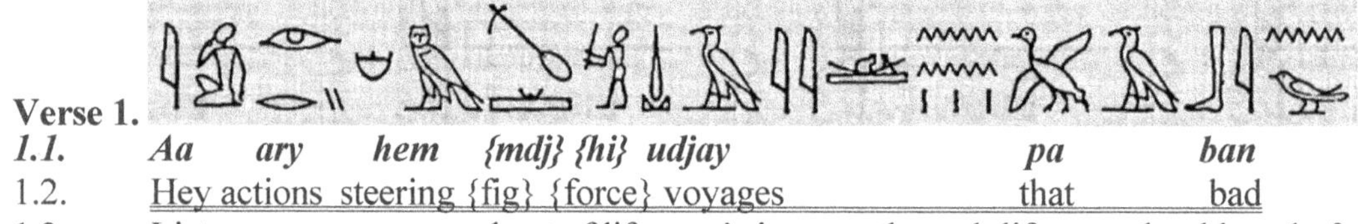

1.1. ***Aa ary hem {mdj} {hi} udjay pa ban***

1.2. Hey actions steering {fig} {force} voyages that bad

1.3. Listen, as concerns our boat of life, one's journey through life, one should apply force/effort to steer away from that which is bad.

Verse 2. 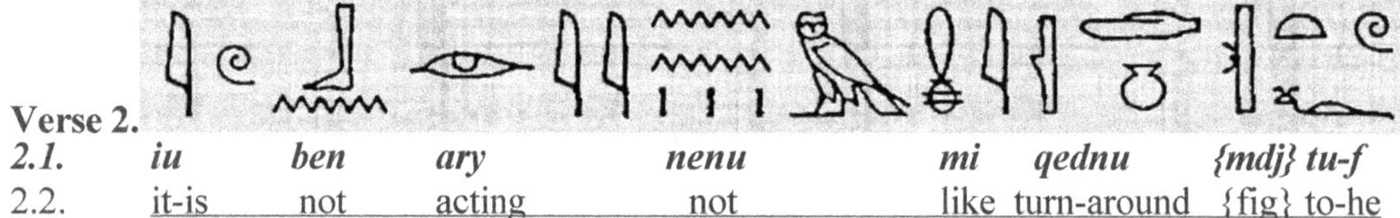

2.1. ***iu ben ary nenu mi qednu {mdj} tu-f***

2.2. it-is not acting not like turn-around {fig} to-he

2.3. The aforesaid is about not acting like those who are bad, the heated persons; in other words, it means turning around and going another way as opposed to going ahead and joining the heated persons in their bad doings.

Teachings of Amenemopet Chapter 3 Hieroglyphic Text

Verse 10.

10.1.	***im-an ari nehbu tjetje ra ma pa teha ra betjenu cheft***
10.2.	do not yoking gossiping {mouth} behold that argument {mouth} sneaky enemy
10.3.	Desist from, abstain, cease, renounce joining with and gossiping with and watch out, definitely not getting into verbal arguments with the sneaky enemy, the heated person.

Verse 15.

15.1.	***pa shemm {cheft} im unut tu -f***
15.2.	that heated {enemy} in hour to-he
15.3.	That heated person {who is the enemy} when they are in their hour, their time of intense heat…

Verse 16.

16.1.	***tuoaha tu – k hat f chaa setenem {her} {mdj} f***
16.2.	reject to-thee front-heart his abandon misleading{person} {fig} he
16.3.	…you should reject them by turning your conscious mind away from their mind and emotions. You should abandon them because they are misleading personalities, personalities that mislead others…

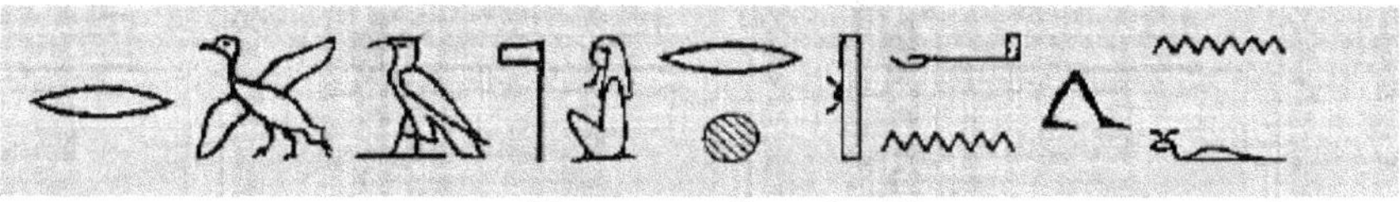

Verse 17.

17.1.	***er pa Neter rech {mdj} an en - f***
17.2.	regards that Divine wisdom {fig} turn-back to - him
17.3.	…and you should not be concerned with their fate because as you turn away from them the Divine, in a mysterious way, through the cosmic forces of Creation, will take care of them and provides to them what they need and deserve for their ethical and spiritual evolution.

Teachings of Amenemopet Chapter 4 Hieroglyphic Text

Verse 1.

1.1. ***er pa shemm {khet}{cheft} en Neter het***

1.2. As-for that heated (person) {fire}{enemy} to Divine house

1.3. As concerns those heated people, when they go to the divine temple (House of God)…

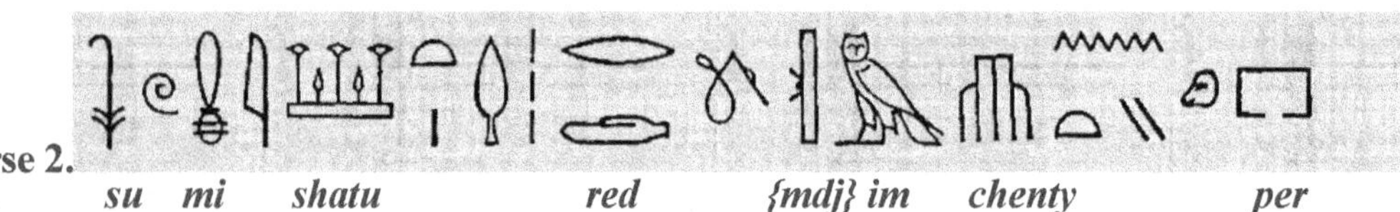

Verse 2.

2.1. ***su mi shatu red {mdj} im chenty per***

2.2. his like trees growing {fig} in advancing-inside building

2.3. …to them it is like a tree going inside the temple, which is a covered building; so those people, like the trees, who do not gain illumination from the sun or rain, in the same way, those people do not get the benefit of the illumination from the Divine, that the temple has to offer.

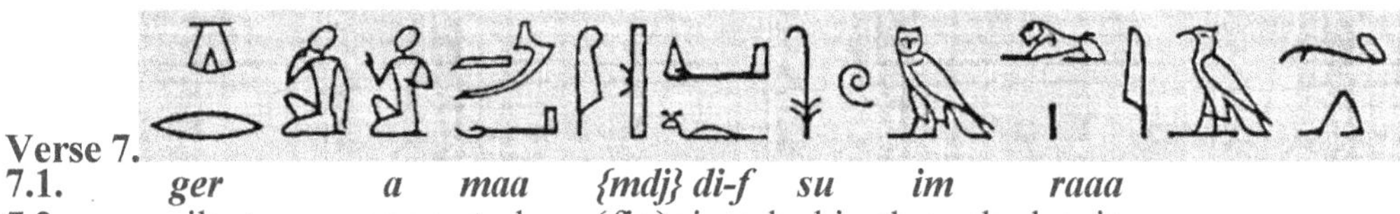

Verse 7.

7.1. ***ger a maa {mdj} di-f su im raaa***

7.2. silent person truly {fig}gives-he his through leaving

7.3. The ones who are truly silent, they give their answer/response to the heated ones in the form of his/her leaving, being remote, distant isolated / secluded / apart / aloof / withdrawn / reserved/inaccessible, detached…

Verse 8.

8.1. ***su mi shatu red im tihentu***

8.2. his like trees growing in water and {lands}

8.3. …to the silent they are like a tree growing in a place with plenty of water and fertile earth, so they grow to the fullness of their capacity.

Teachings of Amenemopet Chapter 5 VII Hieroglyphic Text

Verse 7.

7.1. *ar ger neb-en Neter -Het {Net}*

7.2. as for silent all-of Divinity -House {Div}

7.3. …Now, in reference to those who are silent, all who go into the House (Temple) of the Divinity (i.e. God)…

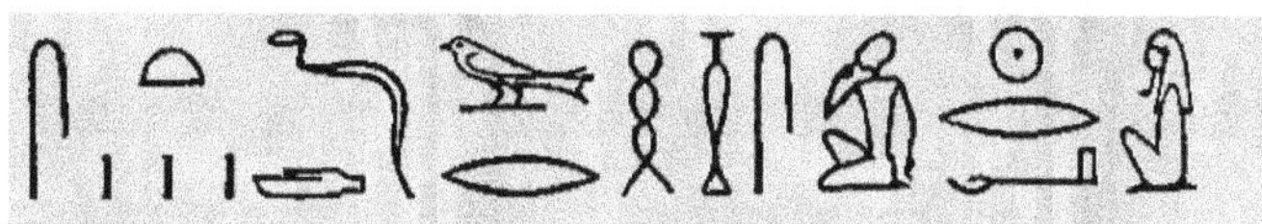

Verse 8.

8.1. *setu djed ur hess Ra*

8.2. they say greatness blessing Creator-Spirit

8.3. …those silent ones speak of the greatness of the blessings they receive from being in the temple from the Creator-Spirit.

Verse 9.

9.1. *Aa mehtu{mdj} en ger gem {mdj} k pa ankh {mdj}*

9.2. Behold! fullness of silence finds {fig} thee the life {fig}

9.3. Behold the glory of this way of being! Being silent (serenity) is the means for discovering the fullness of life that is beyond ordinary life that you have known as a human. It is life found in the Creator-Spirit that is within- by communing with the Creator-Spirit that resides in the Temple. This fullness cannot come from heatedly (egoistically) searching for fulfillment in the world or fulfillment with an imperfect personality (egoism/heated personality). It is found not by externalities of the external world but instead by realizing that there is perfection within when the fullness of being is experienced beyond the worldly thinking, desires and cravings that cause one to feel incomplete, as a separate individual, alone and imperfect. The discovery of the fullness of Self by communing with the Creator-Spirit allows the discovery of fullness within.

Teachings of Amenemopet Chapter 6B VIII Hieroglyphic Text

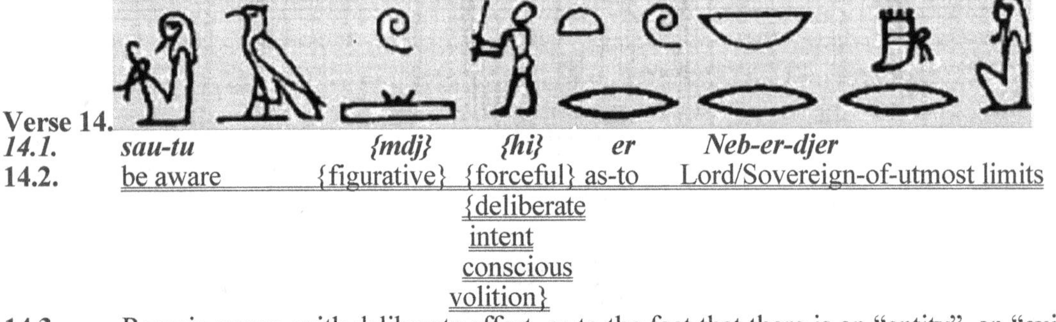

Verse 14.

14.1. ***sau-tu*** ***{mdj}*** ***{hi}*** ***er*** ***Neb-er-djer***

14.2. be aware {figurative} {forceful} {deliberate intent conscious volition} as-to Lord/Sovereign-of-utmost limits

14.3. Remain aware, with deliberate effort, as to the fact that there is an "entity", an "existence" that encompasses all Creation [All-encompassing-Divinity-Neberdjer], beyond [underlying] mind and time and space. This existence/consciousness underlies limited human awareness. Maintain this awareness above all else.

CHAPTER 6B VIII CONT.

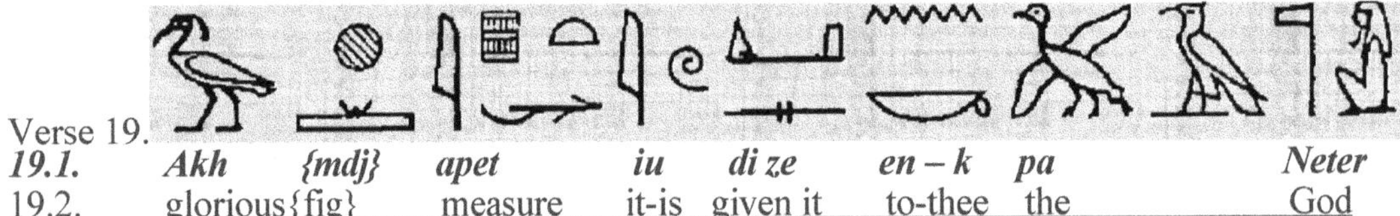

Verse 19.

19.1. ***Akh*** ***{mdj}*** ***apet*** ***iu*** ***di ze*** ***en – k*** ***pa*** ***Neter***

19.2. glorious{fig} measure it-is given it to-thee the God

19.3. It would be a more advantageous and a magnificent/splenderous/glorifying thing to accept the measure given, by The God/Divine, to you through the providence that is Creation, and based on your due merit as attested by your aryu (current accumulated self-effort supported by past actions, thoughts and feelings of the past)…

Verse 20.

20.1. ***er*** ***chau*** ***im*** ***gany*** ***sa*** ***{hdji}*** ***{hi}***

20.2. as-to thousands through weakness behind break force opposed to

20.3. …as opposed to gaining thousands of measures through the weakness of mind, i.e. through cunning, an unrighteous mind that schemes how to go behind other's back to steal from them, breaking the order of Ma'at (righteousness/truth) with forceful, conscious determination, volition, and malice of forethought (deliberate unrighteousness)!

Teachings of Amenemopet Chapter 6B IX Hieroglyphic Text

Verse 5.

5.1. ***Akh {mdj} pa nehem im det pa Neter***

5.2. Glorious{fig} that poverty in hand that Divine

5.3. It would be a magnificent/splenderous/glorious, beneficial thing, to be poor and within the grace, the caring and protection the hand of The Divine(God)…

Verse 6.

6.1. ***er useru {nkt} {mdj} im udja***

6.2. opposed domination {fig} in storehouse

6.3. …as opposed to the capacity to have power over a storehouse of wealth but with unrighteousness and weakness of mind.

Verse 7.

7.1. ***Akh {mdj} pa tutiu iu hat nedjm {mdj}***

7.2. Glorious {fig} that sacrificial bread it-is heart sweet {fig}

7.3. It would be a magnificent/splenderous/glorious thing, a happier, and more beneficial thing, a blissful/ beatific/ sublime/ heavenly/ saintly thing to have the sacrificial bread along with sweetness, a good feeling, in the front-of-mind (what is currently in conscious-awareness) …

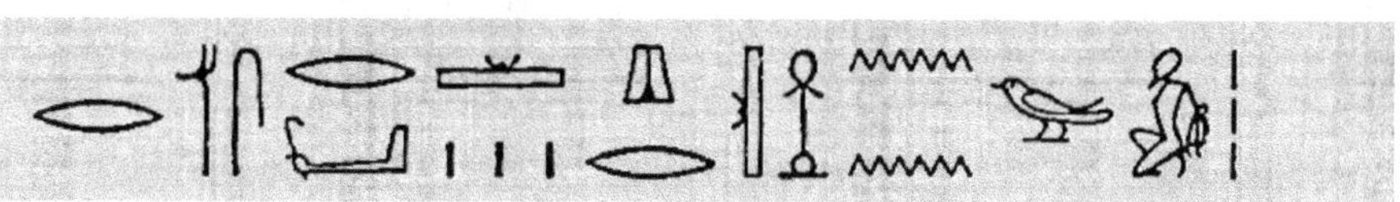

Verse 8.

8.1. ***er useru {nkt} {mdj} cher {mdj} shennu {seqer}***

8.2. opposed domination {fig} including {fig} anguish {prisoner}

8.3. …as opposed to the capacity to have the power over wealth or abundant possessions but also included with that power, not having peace but rather anguish, strife, worry, anxiety, vexation and unrest; and be a prisoner of the weak mind that leads to agitations, frustrations and sufferings in life.

Teachings of Amenemopet Chapter 7 Hieroglyphic Text

Verse 10.

10.1. ***im ari qemaam {mdj} {hi} ab–k im sa useru{nkt} {mdj}***

10.2. through action creating {fig}[force} heart –thine through behind domination fig}

10.3. By means of creating, with one's own deliberate volition and effort, in one's heart(mind), going behind the back of people, of justice, of truth, deceitfully pursuing a desire for domination…

Verse 11.

11.1. ***an cheman shayt renenut***

11.2. wrong ignorance destiny fortune

11.3. …one is actually doing something wrong, due to ignorance; by believing one can amass domination, wealth and power without considering the consequences of one's actions that lead to one's future fortune (termed Shayt in Shetaut Neter) and destiny (termed Renenut in Shetaut Neter); i.e. one's actions are the cause of one's future conditions and one's ultimate fate that these cosmic forces (Shayt/Renenut) render to each individual based on the ethical content of their actions, thoughts, and feelings of the past and present, which become recorded in their unconscious and later in the form of unconscious impressions (aryu) that shape the experiences and outcomes of life and experiences after death and if fated, in the next life as well.

Verse 12.

12.1. ***im-an ari chaa n-k haty{ab} k im er ruy***

12.2. refrain doing forsaking of-thee mind thine form as-to traveling

12.3. Keep in mind the consequences of fortune and destiny by taking the following action: refrain, renounce, forsake the practice of letting your conscious mind travel, that is to say, going outward from yourself, to wander, having flights of fancy, imaginations, wishes, etc.

Verse 13.

13.1. ***z-a neb en tayu f unut***

13.2. cause-person every belongs his time

13.3. Why do I say this? Because every person has their time where what is due to come to them, comes to them by providence supported by their karma(aryu) and the gods and goddesses.

Verse 14. 
14.1. ***im ari ma sha- pu {hi} er ucha hauu {mdj}***
14.2. refrain doing who labors {force} as-to seek riches {fig}
14.3. Keeping in mind that your time will come to get whatever is needed by you, allowed by your fortune and destiny derived from your past actions and supported by the gods and goddesses, therefore do not be like those people who labor after, seeking for riches. Your life should not be about that; overusing time and energy in laborious pursuits that take you away from discovering the goals of life that I stated in the prologue. It should be about working rightly without undue stress to meet your needs for now…

Verse 15. 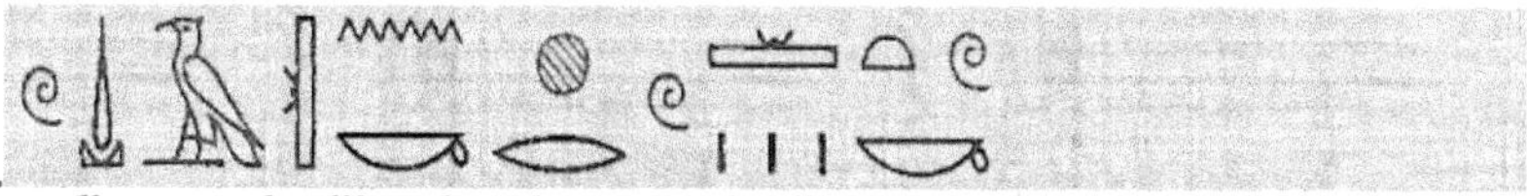
15.1. udja {mdj} n-k cheru {mdj} tu-k
15.2. well-being {fig} for-thee to-you
15.3. …and you have well-being now that is meant for you, and what may be needed in the future will come to you in due course

Teachings of Amenemopet Chapter 7B Hieroglyphic Text

Verse 10.

10.1. ***Sekty k na unuty {hi} a***

10.2. Evening-boat thine that experiences {struggle} person

10.3. The evening boat, of the nighttime journey through the netherworld, the unconscious mind of the heated person. It experiences time of struggling and strife, suffering and…

Verse 11.(a)

11.1. ***chaatu haynu {moo} {she}-{ta}***

11.2. forsaking swell {waters} {channel}-{land}

11.3. …forsakes, turns away from the purpose of life and the nature of the Divine (Ab Neter / Neberdjer). It is, as if, carried away on a great swell, a large, billowing wave of water, an overpowering force (of negative aryu/karma based on unrighteous thoughts, feelings and actions) that overwhelms the boat of life (mind and body). That swelling mind, full of bourgeoning thoughts and feelings and desires based on ignorance and delusions that cause heat in the personality, throws their boat off course and channels it, conducts, routes their boat of life off course and causes it to run aground (shipwrecked), incapable of sailing on the journey of life and discovering the Divine.

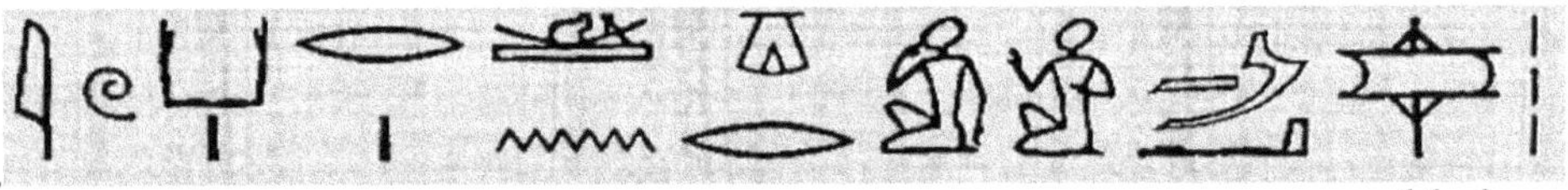

Verse 12.

12.1. ***iu ka ra amm - en ger a maau {shu}***

12.2. It is feelings-mind mouth boat - of silent person right {winds}

12.3. Now, as concerns the astral body (Ka-subconscious mind), that level of mind that harbors the thoughts and feelings subconsciously, that manifest through the mouth, at the conscious level, of the boat of life journey of those who lead a silent life, who do not live by egoistic desires, boisterousness in the temple or unethical behaviors, in their boat they are able to sail on fair winds that are pleasant and right for sailing, and right for reaching the destination of life, to reach the hand of God and be accepted by God.

Teachings of Amenemopet Chapter 8X Hieroglyphic Text

Verse 19.

19.1. ***arytu henu en aarat***

19.2. doing jubilation to goddess {serpent}

19.3. [be good] by doing the jubilation ritual, accepting and honoring the Serpent Goddess who brings light, destroys iniquity and raises consciousness.

Verse 20.

20.1. ***pugas er apep***

20.2. spitting about Apophis

20.3. …as for what concerns the opposite serpent, the one called Apophis, who causes unrighteousness, disorder, confusion, and destruction, that one is to be spat on, that is to say, repudiated and turned away from, rejected and disdained-overpowered.

CHAPTER 8 X CONT.

Verse 21.

21.1. ***se-udja {mdj} nest k er medtu hedj***

21.2. cause-vitality {fig} tongue as-to speech damage

21.3. Take care to make your speech to be sound in reference to the words that you use, that may cause harm, so as to be, instead, a cause, for vitality…

TEACHINGS OF AMENEMOPET CHAPTER 8 XI

Verse 1.

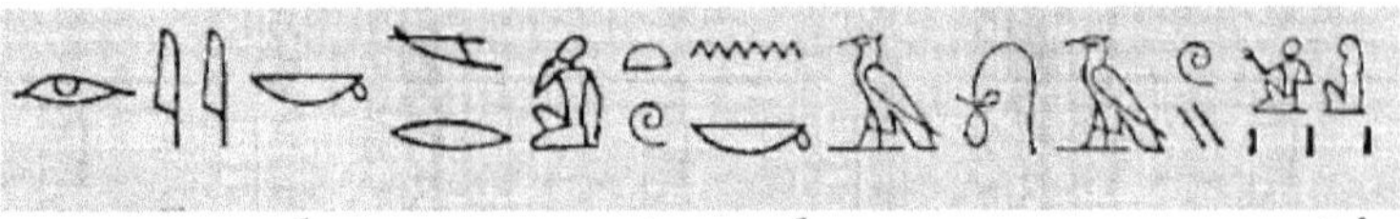

1.1. *ary k mer a tu en-k aoauy remteju*

1.2. doing thee love you to of-thee harm people

1.3. …by your doing love to people, caring for them instead of doing harm to them, they love you. By giving consideration people reciprocate with consideration.

Verse 2.

2.1. *gem {mdj}k aset-per tu-k im khennu neter het {net}*

2.2. find {fig}thee abode to-thee within inner divine building {divinity}

2.3. In this manner, by doing good to others and having peaceful relations with others, you will be able to have inner peace that will allow you to make real and effective effort towards finding yourself a place, to make yourself an abode in the inner part of the Temple of God. So, instead of being involved with conflicts with people, taking up valuable time and draining your vitality away in a futile and unnecessary way, apply that vitality and peace to discover the innermost essence of the Divine within the House of God (Temple). At the same time, you will not obstruct yourself with unnecessary mental agitations nor cause troubles for others that will obstruct their path to being good and also being able to move towards the inner temple.

Verse 3.

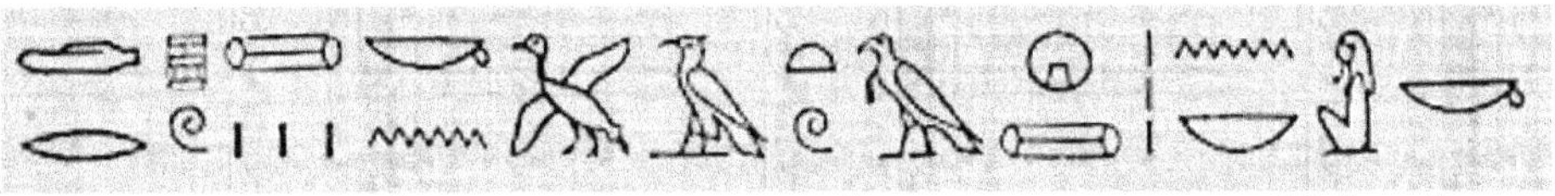

3.1. *derpu k en pa tutiu en – Neb k*

3.2. sustenance thine of that vital-bread of -Lord thine

3.3. you will be sustained not just by food from the earth but that vital bread of your Lord (the Divine / Ab Neter / Neberdjer).

Verse 4.

4.1. *aryu k amachchy {shps} hapu tu k djebut k*

4.2. karmic-impressions thine honorable {noble} concealed to thee coffin thine

4.3. Now, the result of this way of life and your dedication to righteousness, service to humanity and right behavior is that your karmic-impressions have been purified, and you have become a person who is worthy to be honored-worshipped, as a {spiritually realized noble}. This nobility of yours is the decoration for your funerary coffin chamber.

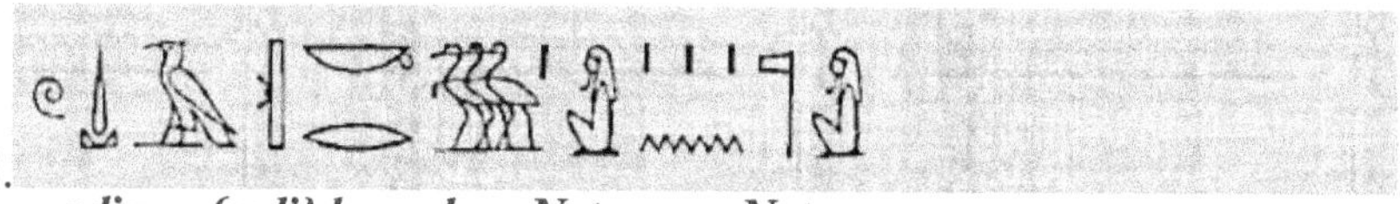

Verse 5.

5.1. ***udja {mdj} k–er bau Neteru en Neter***

5.2. vitality {fig} thine-about divine souls gods/goddesses of the Divine

5.3. Being in a condition of silent mind, draw spiritual vitality and strength from the souls of the gods and goddesses, the energetic essences of the cosmic forces (neteru-gods and goddesses) that emanates from the Divine Self, that sustain Creation and all life.

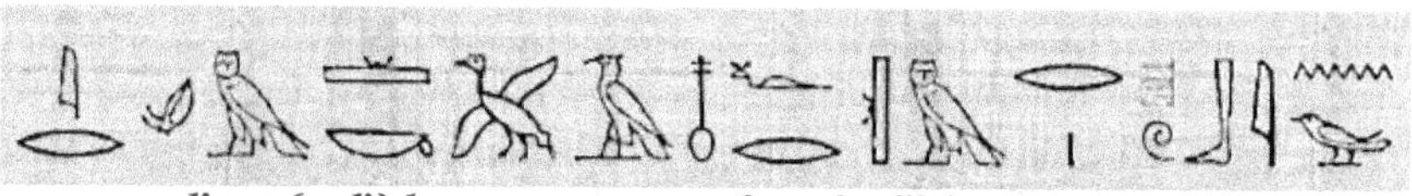

===

Verse 8.

8.1. ***ar sedjm {mdj} k pa nefer {mdj} im ra pu ban***

8.2. as to listening {fig} thee that good {fig} in mouth the bad

8.3. Concerning the listening to bad things in the mouths of speakers, the gossiping, lying, chattering/blathering/rumormongering/scandalmongering, etc…

Verse 9.

9.1. ***Aa aru su im er rauy bu sedjm {mdj} f***

9.2. Listen, action he in about mouthing do not listen {fig} him

9.3. This is what should be done about the gossiping; do not listen to those who speak it…

Verse 10.

10.1. ***amma s- mi nefer {mdj} her tep ta nest k***

10.2. grant that cause rectitude good {fig} personality top earth tongue thine

10.3. …don't listen to what is coming out of those people's mouths; It is corrupting for the mind and draws one away from the goals of life. Instead, may it be granted the acting with goodness of heart, with rectitude, turning your tongue towards the good when you are a person living on the surface of planet earth.

Verse 11.

11.1. ***iu pa djuu ha pu aref im chat k***

11.2. it is that badness body the tie-up in belly thine

11.3. It is that badness that may want to come out of you, the yearning to participate in the badness, which is desiring to come out of the belly of your body, which you should consciously cause to remain there, locked in the belly and not allow to come out! The egoistic will to do unrighteousness should be refrained from and controlled, in order to allow sublimation of negative will and employ that energy towards positive ends and spiritual evolution. (Author note: In Kemetic tantric and Serpent Power (similar to Eastern Kundalini Yoga) wisdom, the Sefech Ba Ra (seven souls of Ra or chakras [Eastern]), the belly or solar plexus is understood to be the seat of personal egoistic will for the pursuit of worldly desires.) See the Book "Serpent Power" by Dr Muata Ashby

Teachings of Amenemopet Chapter 9[xi] Hieroglyphic Text

Verse 13.

13.1. *im an ari sensenty en – k pa shemm {kht}{cft}*

13.2. refrain/renounce/give up associating to-thee that heated person. {fire} {enemy}

13.3. Refrain from/abstain from/cease/desist/do not seek heated people for the purpose of associating with them, they are the burning enemy that incinerates peace and contentment.

Verse 14.

14.1. *im an tu k khenkhennu f er se-djed*

14.2. refrain/renounce/give up your going close to him for causing conversation

14.3. Also, do not allow yourself to go close to them/do not approach them for the purpose of starting up a conversation.

Verse 15.

15.1. *su udja {mdj} nest k rush but en her pet{a} k*

15.2. cause vitality tongue yours take care abominable person to personality heavenly yours

15.3. Instead, act in a manner that will be beneficial for you, increasing your vitality by controlling your tongue, the means (mind) by which your feelings and thoughts are expressed from your mind into the external world. Take care and watch out because the heated person is an abominable thing to your heavenly personality, the part of you that exists in the astral plane (mind and feelings).

Verse 16.

16.1. *im an tu k sau {mdj} {hi} kheru aah {mdj} qesen f*

16.2. refrain/renounce/give up your guard/be aware words great{fig}bad/evil/injurious he

16.3. Therefore, give up on the ideas of associating with heated people and instead think about guarding and protecting yourself from those who speak great and high-sounding words but who are in fact negative personalities that mean you harm and are only using high sounding words to gain your confidence only to later take advantage of you and harm you.

Teachings of Amenemopet Chapter 9xII Hieroglyphic Text

Verse 15.

15.1. ***bes er – f Khnum {Net} ra {sep}***

15.2. come as to – he Potter {God} day {time}

15.3. …should come to him (to the heated person) the god Khnum, the Divine Potter, for a time…

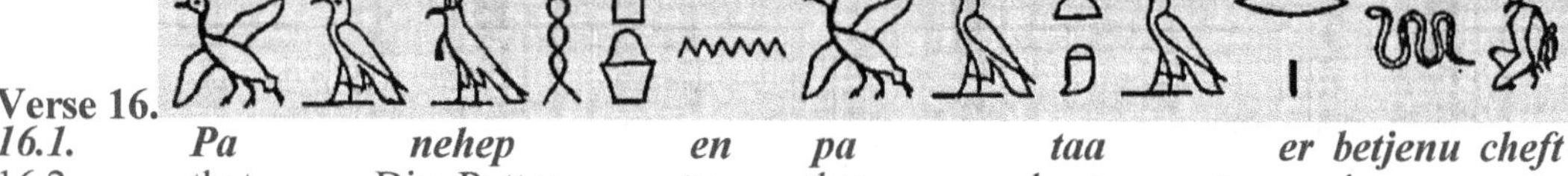

Verse 16.

16.1. ***Pa nehep en pa taa er betjenu cheft***

16.2. that Div. Potter to that heat as to sneaky enemy

16.3. …that god Khnum, the Creator, fashioner of bodies out of clay for souls to use, builder and controller of the Nile flow; may he come in one of his aspects, called "Divine Potter". The Divine Potter, repairer who could bring divine compassion would that he should come to that heated person so as to deal with the sneaky enemy (egoism, heatedness).

Verse 17.

17.1. ***Aa aru f papa er nega fy hatyu***

17.2. hey perform he rebuild as-to cut-away his heart's

17.3. Hey, then he will be able to perform the cutting away of the emerging dispositions of the mind that are contrary to goodness and enlightenment.

Author Note: *"hatyuhere is referring to multiple hearts (emerging dispositions) of the heated person, signifying multiple dispositions of mind, caused by varying impelling and compelling aryu, that are divergent from the path of Maat (righteousness and truth)-so may those be cut away rendering the person cool and silent, as a potter cuts away pieces of clay that hide the shape desired by the potter when creating pottery. Sage Amenemopet describes human beings as being made of "Straw and clay, and God is the fashioner" (Amenemopet chapter 25).*

Teachings of Amenemopet Chapter 11 Hieroglyphic Text

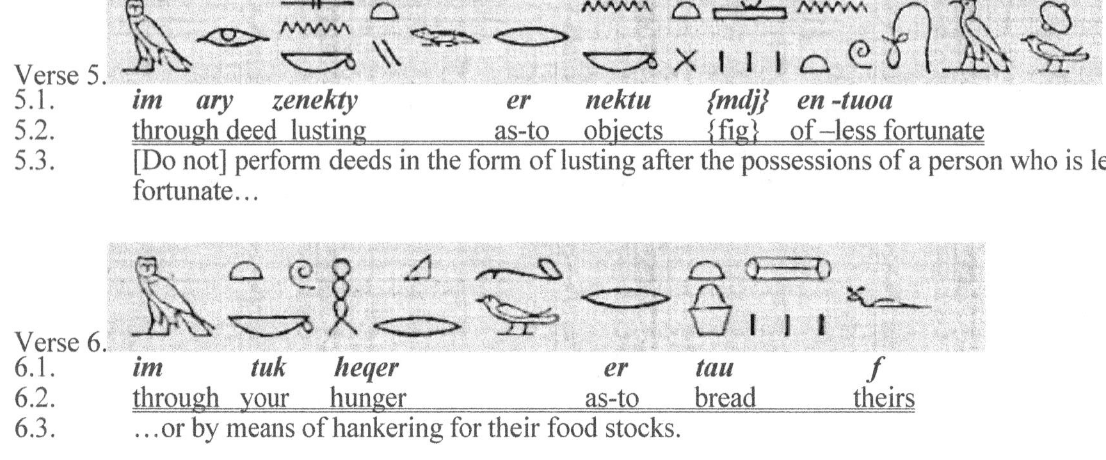

Verse 5.

5.1. ***im ary zenekty er nektu {mdj} en -tuoa***

5.2. through deed lusting as-to objects {fig} of –less fortunate

5.3. [Do not] perform deeds in the form of lusting after the possessions of a person who is less fortunate…

Verse 6.

6.1. ***im tuk heqer er tau f***

6.2. through your hunger as-to bread theirs

6.3. …or by means of hankering for their food stocks.

TEACHINGS OF AMENEMOPET CHAPTER 11 CONT. HIEROGLYPHIC TEXT

Verse 9.

9.1. Aa aru f se-kheper {mdj} f im ankhyu na udja

9.2. Listen, actions person causing-creating{fig} through oaths that unsound

9.3. Now hear this and try to understand; in reference to those who make oaths or swearing to tell the truth but instead lie in order to gain profits; that is unsound and degrading.

Verse 10.

10.1. ***iu ab {Net} f seha im chat f***

10.2. it is heart{Diviniity} his turning away in body his

10.3. Why, because, when that is done, it is one's own rejection of the Divine within one's own heart (individual mind) and thus our Divine heart, that is, the Spirit essence of the Divine (Divine Consciousness) within the personality that is its real source of existence and sustenance of the individual mind, as if turns away from (forsakes) us within our own personality.

Verse 11.
11.1. ***im djert {mdj} pa req tjenau pa mench***
11.2. through because{fig} that corruption corrupts that project-perfection
11.3. Therefore, through that corruption, that we ourselves engendered, we ourselves are corrupting the project of perfection that we are trying to build for ourselves. The project of perfection, according to the Temple of Asar (Osiris), is the purpose of life, of building a monument for and of ourselves. That monument is dedicated to discovering abiding happiness and spiritual enlightenment as opposed to the projects of the worldly-minded, the acquisition of wealth and objects in the pursuit of temporary, fleeting sense of security, or pleasures and happiness, based on ego notions and desires, especially, but not limited to, when those objects, wealth or pleasures are stolen or acquired by fraud.

Teachings of Amenemopet Chapter 12 Hieroglyphic Text

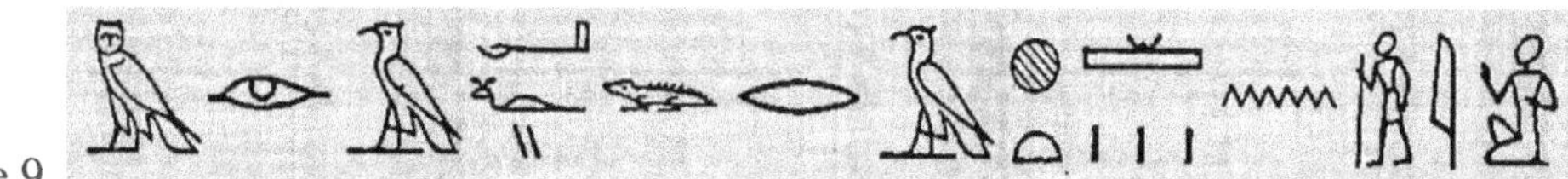

Verse 9.
9.1. ***im an ari aafy er achtu {mdj} en sera aa***
9.2. do not do repulsive/greed as-to possessions {fig} of noble I
9.3. Do not do this/stop/refrain from being a repulsive person, greedy about the possessions (objects) belonging to those who are well-to-do or elders.

Teachings of Amenemopet Chapter 13 Hieroglyphic Text

Verse 11.
11.1. ***ach {mdj} hess im mer en remteju***
11.2. Glorifying {fig} praised through love of people
11.3. It is a glorifying thing to the personality to be loved / praised / revered / honored / liked by the people, the family, community and country…

Verse 12.
12.1. ***er uru {mdj} im udja***
12.2. as to power {fig} in storehouse
12.3. …as opposed to having power over an overflowing storehouse of objects (wealth/hoarding/not sharing).

Teachings of Amenemopet Chapter 15 Hieroglyphic Text

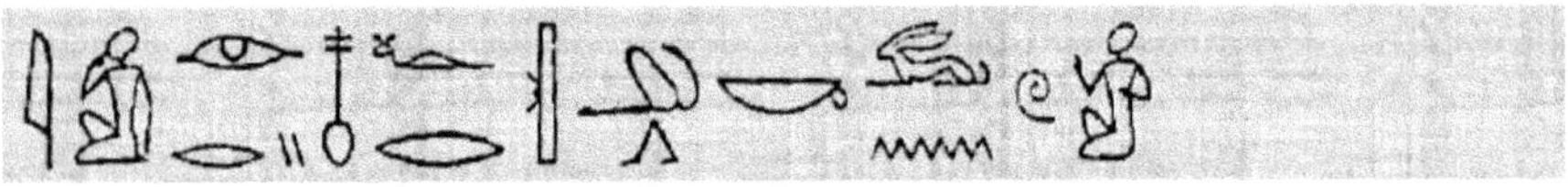

Verse 5.
5.1. ***aa ary nefer peh k unnu a***
5.2. who doing good arrive thee being you
5.3. Listen, when you act ethically, doing good and being good to yourself and others, you end up being your true self.

=======

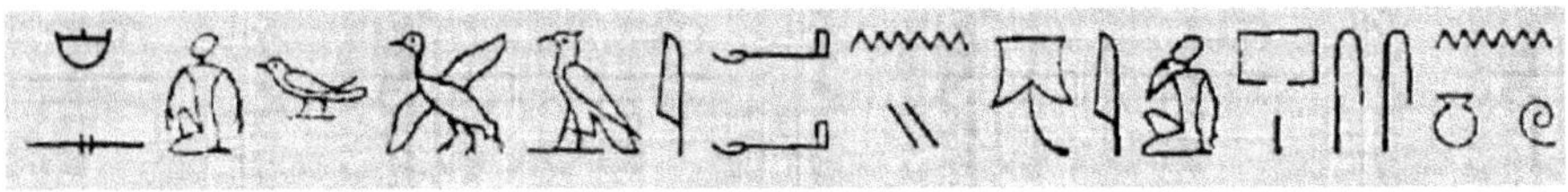

Verse 9.
9.1. ***hemz pa aaany aa per sesenu***
9.2. inhabits that baboon who temple city of eight
9.3. That baboon god who is known as Thoth(Anan/Djehuty baboon god), the god of intellect and cosmic mind, who inhabits the temple in the city of the eight known as Khemenu…

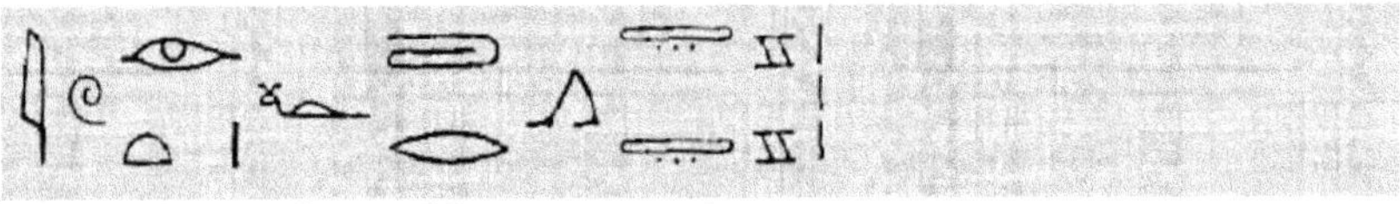

Verse 10.
10.1. ***iu arit f pekhar tawiu***
10.2. it-is eye his goes-around two-lands
10.3. …it is his eye, the eye of awareness of the god of the intellect, who is also known as "Ab Ra", the heart of the Creator Spirit, Ra. Djehuty presides over your mind and intellect and is the cosmic mind itself; he is the divinity that goes around all of two lands of Kamit/Kemet/Ancient Egypt, and thus sees all, meaning that this aspect of mind, the intellect, is an individuated aspect of Djehuty, Cosmic Mind, in the personality, and thus, its awareness encompasses the higher and lower aspects of the human being, allowing for an all pervasive level of awareness, which is founded in Creator Spirit, Ra. Therefore, even the acts done, when no one is around, are registered in Djehuty, Cosmic Mind (the god of intellect) and thus also in your own conscience.

=======

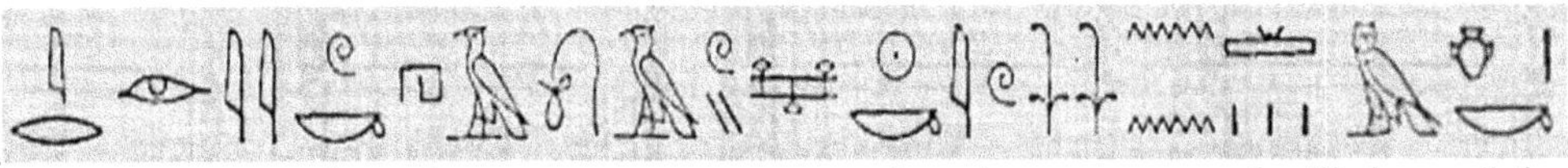

Verse 15.
15.1. ***ar aryu k haoauy k iu nen {mdj} im ab k***
15.2. regarding impressions yours time-spent thine it-is resting {fig} in unconscious-mind thine
15.3. As concerns your unconscious impressions, the karmic (aryu)-feeling-memories collected in your personality from your past actions, thoughts, feelings desires, and memories, and the fate that those would produce, by your resting in your heart (unconscious) level of your mind, that is, by spending time meditating, at rest-relaxed, and not restless-agitated, in your unconscious and not always spending time in the Ka (subconscious) and Hat (conscious) level of mind…

Verse 16.

16.1. ***ar nayu k mesu petru***

16.2. concerning them thy children see

16.3. …as concerns your children, they will see how you have acted and the outcomes of your actions so you will be acting as a model for them; this will be the effect. They will see that there is a human capacity for and practice of being internalized and serene in one's unconscious level of experience.

Teachings of Amenemopet Chapter 16 Hieroglyphic Text

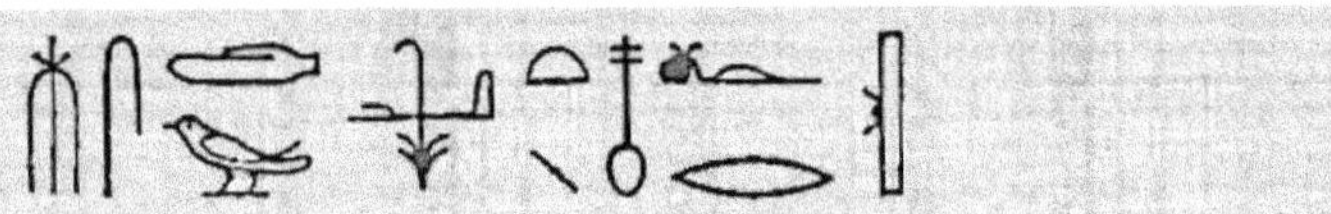

Verse 8.

8.1. ***im an ari zenkty en hestyu***

8.2. do not do greed of copper

8.3. Refrain from the act of being greedy about copper, that is, a material from which status, wealth and possessions are derived.

Verse 9.

9.1. ***mesd shemat nefer {mdj}***

9.2. enmity linens fine {fig}

9.3. Learn to develop a healthy enmity/disregard/indifference/aloofness towards finery and luxury such that you do not get used to depending on comforts and luxury to provide feelings of well-being; for those things are illusory and can be lost at any time. Therefore, the reliance on and pursuit of luxuries is injurious to the character of the mind and for spiritual development. So, it is best to find a deeper source of inner contentment whether there is external comfort or not.

Verse 10.

10.1. ***iu f en ach suhu ma k***

10.2. it is he to what draped behold thee

10.3. What would be the purpose of a person draping/wrapping themselves with and being enfolded in those fine linens so as to have everyone admiring them (i.e. vanity, conceit, etc.) as if they were ethical and generous (i.e. putting on an external show, e.g. hypocrisy) when in reality it is a façade hiding gluttony, greediness, craving, and avarice?

Verse 11.

11.1. ***iu f seha imba pa Neter***

11.2. it-is he turning down in-presence-of the Divinity

11.3. Actually, acting in that way (hypocrisy) amounts to the actual turning down/not accepting/turning away from (forsaking) the awareness and immanence of the Divine even while being in the presence of the Divine.

Teachings of Amenemopet Chapter 17 Hieroglyphic Text

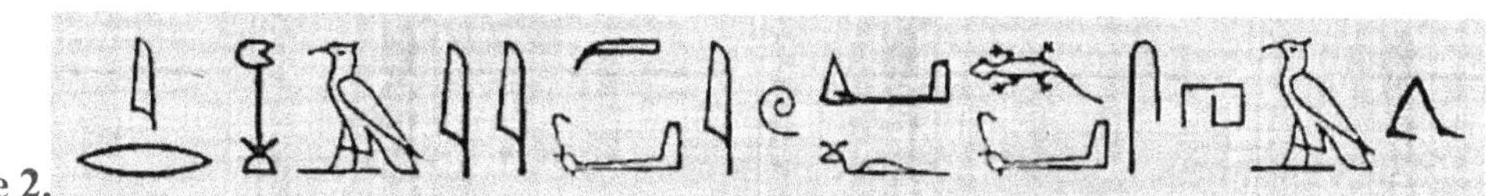

Verse 2.
2.1. *er chay iu di – f {asha}{nkt} seha*
2.2. as to measuring-portions, it-is giving-he {quant}{force} turning down
2.3. Concerning the measurement of portions or volumes of items such as grains or land or other objects to be distributed to another person, the cheater, who was supposed to give certain quantities, turns down that idea, turns away from that idea and instead knowingly/forcefully{nkt} gives a fraudulent amount instead of the correct amount;

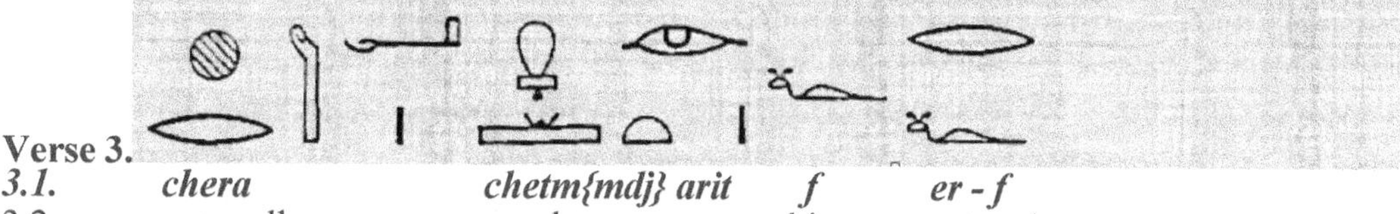

Verse 3.
3.1. *chera chetm{mdj} arit f er - f*
3.2. assuredly seals eye his as to - he
3.3. …certainly, the evidence and guilt of the corrupt act of such a person are sealed by the witnessing of that act by their own eye (i.e. their own conscience registers it in their unconscious mind).

========

Verse 6.
6.1. *im an ari ary ua er ma pa chay a*
6.2. do not do acting one as-to behold that measuring-portions person
6.3. Desist / abstain / cease / refrain from / renounce being one who acts in concert (conspiring, facilitating, being a co-conspirator, accessory to the crime, etc.), along with that person who does the measuring in such an unrighteous manner.

Teachings of Amenemopet Chapter 18 [XX] Hieroglyphic Text

Verse 5.

5.1. *er nest en remtju hemy {hi} en amm*

5.2. About tongue of people steersperson {forceful} of boat(journey/voyage)

5.3. …in reference to the tongue of a person, that relates to the words they utter, their speech. Their speech is based on their thoughts, feelings, and desires and that is the force that directs their actions through their journey through life …

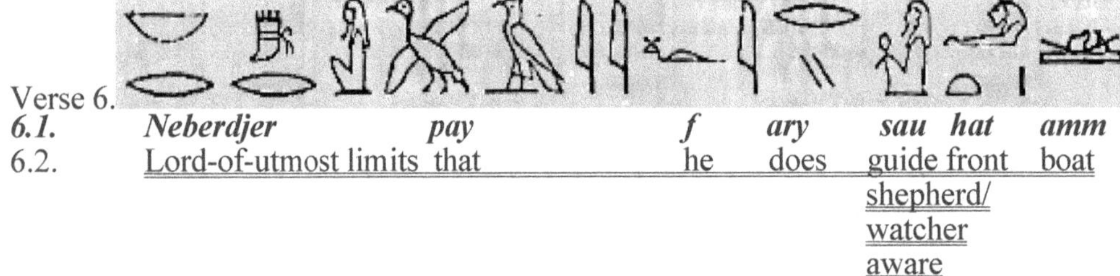

Verse 6.

6.1. *Neberdjer pay f ary sau hat amm*

6.2. Lord-of-utmost limits that he does guide front boat
shepherd/
watcher
aware

6.3. However, despite the personal predilections, there is an all-encompassing divinity that masters and encompasses the limits of Creation and therefore, that overall encompassing divinity is the shepherd that guides human life. That divinity is actually at the forefront of the boat of life watching (aware), guiding the boat of human life where it needs to go for the welfare of all humans even before they themselves know where they are going. Therefore, human self-will and or self-determination are an illusion.

TEACHINGS OF AMENEMOPET CHAPTER 18 [XIX] HIEROGLYPHIC TEXT

Verse 14.

14.1. ***Unu pa Neter im nay f mench {hi}***

14.2. existence that Divinity in the he perfection {force}

14.3. The Divine is that which exists, within itself, as ever in a perfect state that is {powerful};

Verse 15.

15.1. ***iu pa ze-a im nay f uha***

15.2. It is that the-human through the he/she failure

15.3. It is, on the other hand, that which is referred to as an unenlightened human being, a person, which exists through failure; thus, the opposite of perfection is failure and the opposite of Divinity is non-enlightened humanity, for, when humanity lacks the awareness of existence as the Divine, it lacks the power of perfection that is being Divine. Therefore, unenlightened human existence, spiritual weakness and imperfect knowledge of Self, all of that is incompatible with Divine existence and Divine conscious awareness; it is based on erroneous understanding, due to a heated mental condition, and therefore, it is based on illusory perceptions, thoughts, feelings, and conclusions, leading to unrighteous desires and actions that cause one to turn away (forsake) the Divinity within.

============

Verse 22.

22.1. ***ma nu an mench {mdj} {hi} im det pa Neter***

22.2. behold their not perfection {fig} {force} in hand The Divine

22.3. Behold! There isn't perfection forced in the hand of, in the possession of The Divine (God), i.e. the imperfect personality (ego bound) cannot force itself into the grace of the Divine....

Verse 23.

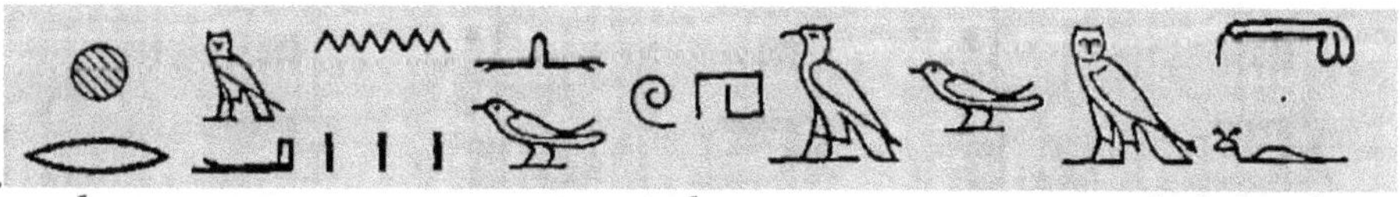

23.1. ***cher ma nu an uha embah f***

23.2. ...before Behold! There negative failure in presence/facing his

23.3. ...presence. Behold! When put up against/compared to The Divine, rather, there is imperfection/failure due to the inability to loosen the ties to ignorance and egoism, when compared to, coming in front of, the Divine as a soul that has loosened the bindings of ignorance and egoism. Thus, anything that presents itself in front of The Divine as something other than The Divine is imperfect and not Divine and therefore cannot be accepted into the hand of The Divine.

Verse 24.(1) 

24.1. ***er setdjerau usta f su ru cha***

24.2. as to sleep/stupor pull-load he his separation forsaking

24.3. As to the person who lives life as if in a slumber or stupor of spiritual ignorance, undergoing the stress of pulling the harder load of life due to egoism, instead of being relaxed due to knowing and experiencing the natural flow of life when one is conscious and aware of Neberdjer, the True Essence, Transcendental Pure Awareness and Pure Consciousness, that person who is as if sleep-walking through life. That person is, at the same time, due to that ignorance of the knowledge of Self (Ab Neter / Neberdjer), separating themselves from and forsaking/leaving/moving away from…

Verse 25.(1a) 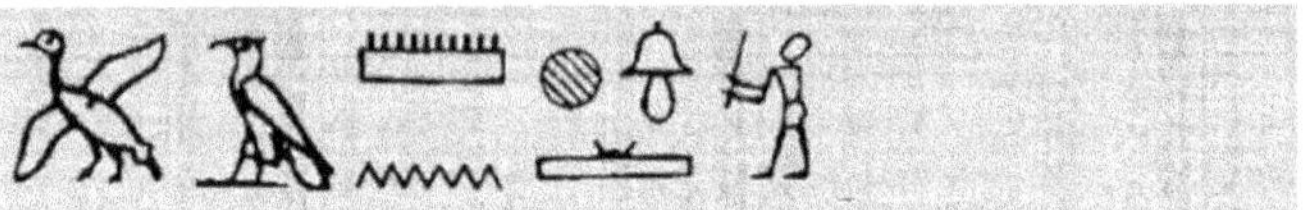

25.1. ***pa mench {mdj}***

25.2. that (project of) perfection {fig}

25.3. …(forsaking/moving away from) that perfection that is found when the roughhewn imperfect parts of the personality are carved away, allowing the perfect essential nature of Neberdjer to be perceived…

Verse 26.(2) 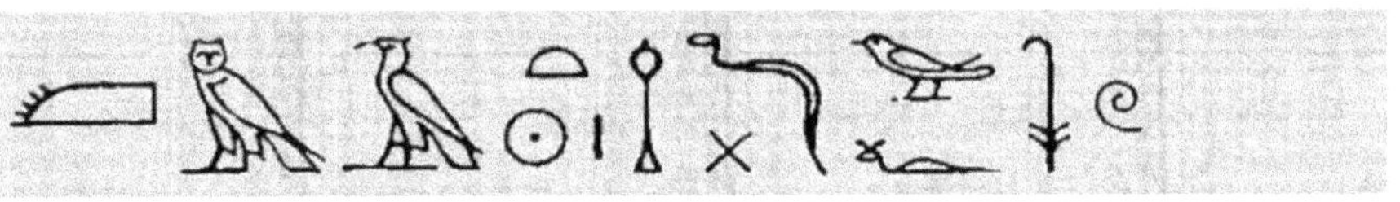

26.1. ***kemat hedj f su***

26.2. ending-moment brightness-damaged he himself

26.3. …(that forsaking comes to pass) in the moment when that stupor has occurred, in a flash; thus, the perception of the Spiritual Enlightenment (The Divine) has been damaged by the person themselves, who have allowed their Spirit awareness to be lost due to the delusion of the stupor of spiritual ignorance. That stupor of spiritual ignorance has occurred due to unwittingly accepting the load of the imperfect egoistic ego instead of the lightness of the perfection of Neberdjer knowledge, awareness of the Absolute.

Teachings of Amenemopet Chapter 21 Hieroglyphic Text

Verse 5.

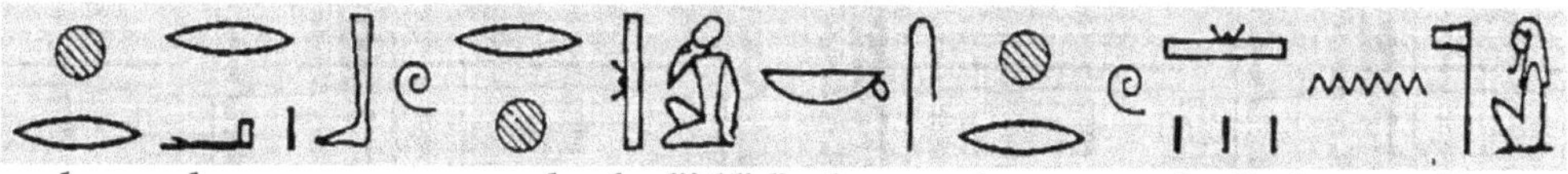

5.1. ***cherra -bu rech {mdj}{djd} k secheru {mdjtu} en Neter***

5.2. definitely not wise {fig}{speech} thee designs/projects/intents {fig} of Divine

5.3. You definitely are not wise as to, i.e. you do not know the plans that the Divine, God may have for your life and the world for how things will work out. So do not despair or act as if everything is random or without meaning or cause behind it, having an ultimate purpose or design.

Verse 15.

15.1. ***Akh {mdj} ze –a auf se-mi f im chat f***

15.2. Glorious {fig} cause - I skin be-like he in body/belly his

15.3. It would be a glorifying thing, a spiritually uplifting thing, to make one's personality to be like a personality that keeps things in his/her belly, within the skin (i.e. inside the body)…

Verse 16.

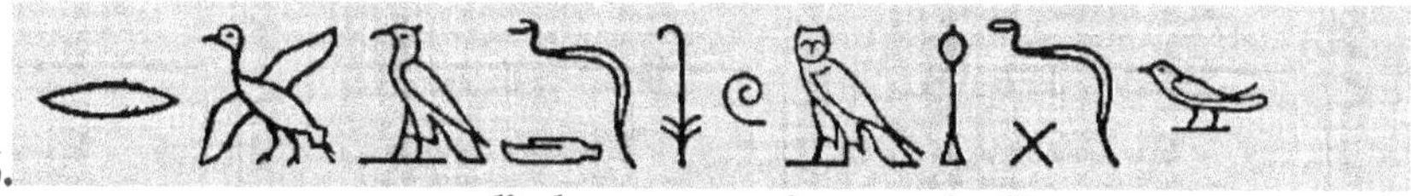

16.1. ***er pa djed su im hedj***

16.2. as to that speech he through harm

16.3. …as opposed to letting that kind of speech come out of the body for causing harm purposely or speech that would cause unnecessary harm.

Verse 17.

17.1. ***bu arytu sechsech er peh pa mench***

17.2. do not doing run-hastening as-to arrive that achievement/perfection

17.3. Don't be running/rushing / feverishly/stressfully grasping towards achieving goals, for, opportunities/objects/desires, in the pursuit of achievement or perfection in the world; that is illusory. Instead of the fevered/agitated/heated/excited/covetous pursuing of achievements, be content in the present and allow God's plan to unfold in your life.

Verse 18.

18.1. ***bu arytu qemam {mdj] {hi} er hedjt f***

18.2. do not doing creating {fig} {force} as-to harm oneself

18.3. However, as you remain content in the present, accept and relax about your condition as it is for now, and do not be unrighteous, complacent or lazy, allowing yourself to be stagnant, creating a harmful condition, for yourself, of trouble that will be an obstruction to being able to achieve the appropriate worldly prosperity and the laudable goals of life. Therefore, do your duties and allow the fruits of your righteous actions of the now and the divine grace of Ab Neter/Neberdjer to provide opportunities for advancement and be ready to take advantage of those when they arise.

Teachings of Amenemopet Chapter 25 Hieroglyphic Text

Verse 9.
9.1. ***im-an ary sebia {hu} {dje} en ka menu im tu - k***
9.2. refrain deed laughing {tooth}{utter} to behold staring by to thee
9.3. Desist/abstain/cease/renounce the act of uttering laughs {showing teeth} or your impolitely staring at…

Verse 9.Cont.
9.4. ***patja {hi} nema***
9.5. seizing {force} dwarf
9.6. …or forcibly grabbing or mishandling (being physically rough) with a person of diminished capacity or of different appearance.

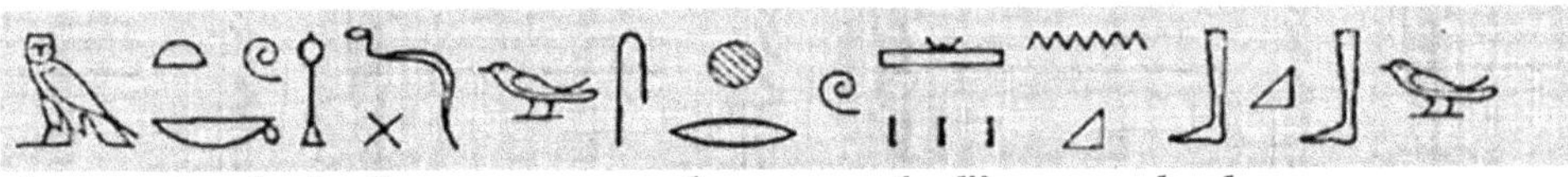

Verse 10.
10.4. ***im-an tu – k hedj secheru {mdj} neqebqeb***
10.5. refrain such-thee damage designs/projects/intents {fig} afflicted
10.6. Desist/abstain/cease/renounce entertaining negative designs or intents[*] directed at those who are afflicted; i.e. do not entertain thoughts of harming or taking advantage of those who are troubled, hurt, afflicted, distressed, weak, in pain, or suffering.

[*] (i.e. negative thought processes, entertaining, mulling, ruminating thoughts of causing harm, hatred, animosity, enmity, or thoughts of taking advantage, or other forms of unrighteous (what is against the principles of Maat) treatment, etc.

Verse 11.
11.4. ***im-an ary patja {hi} ze –a auf im det pa Neter***
11.5. refrain doing seizing {force] cause-I skin in hand The Divine
11.6. Desist/abstain/cease the act of forcefully seizing (doing violence) to one whose skin (body) is in the hand of The Divine.

Verse 19.

19.1. ***Reshau***[11] ***{mdj} uash {dua} {djd} su pa ary peh amuntet***

19.2. Joyousness {fig} adorable {adore} {speech} he that action arriving Beautiful West

19.3. It is a joyous thing and a thing worthy of worship and adoration for a person's speech to praise the arrival at the Beautiful West, the final and ultimate abode of the Divine, instead of praising worldly attainments and goals such as the arrival in the east, which amounts to being reborn to pursue worldly {illusory and fleeting} goals and desires only to experience suffering and stress, frustrations and disappointments ending in old age, disease and death.

Verse 20.

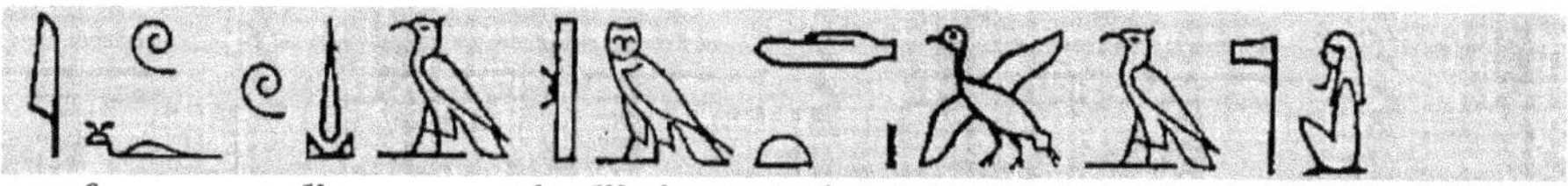

20.1. ***auf udja {mdj} im det pa Neter***

20.2. It-is he well-being {fig} through hand The Divine

20.3. All of this means finding true spiritual well-being, beyond time and space and human existence. This means transcending illusory human existence in time and space so as to be in the hand/grasp (possession-enfolded by Divine Consciousness), which cannot possess what is imperfect. Arriving in the Beautiful West means leaving behind the worldly concerns and struggles, the imperfect human [Chapter 18. V22-23] existence in illusory and fleeting time and space in favor of the perfection of the Divine, who resides in the Beautiful West, i.e. abiding in safety, health, comfort, happiness, etc.

---

[11] Term *reshau* = joyousness, gladness. **Root:** *resh* / *rech*= to know. **Thus:** knowing the perfection of the Divine is the source of {figurative} joy (bliss = unalloyed happiness), unlike human happiness, which is based on ignorance, and alloyed to human thoughts, feelings, limited ego identification, illusory knowledge and temporary situations, objectified relationships and temporary fulfillment of desires. So spiritual knowledge leads to true joyousness and spiritual perfection. Ignorant and limited human knowledge leads to pain and suffering and is, therefore, fleeting and imperfect, a failure).

Teachings of Amenemopet Chapter 26 Hieroglyphic Text

Verse 11.

11.1. ***ben sau {mdj} {hi} aty en chabus se***

11.2. not guarding {fig} {force} back for bowing it

11.3. It is not necessary to be guarding your pride because your dignity is not damaged, your back will not break if you bow and show regard and due consideration to others.

Verse 12.

12.1. ***bu aryu nehemhu z-a iu-f djed pa nedjm {mdj}***

12.2. not doing destitute cause-person it is-he saying that sweetly {fig}

12.3. Saying something in a manner considered as positive / cheerful / gratifying / pleasing / thoughtful/pleasant/friendly/ gentle/obliging does not detract from or cause a person to be diminished/reduced/weakened/devalued…

Verse 13.

13.1. ***er useru {mdj} chenu {chn} {mdj} f di haytu {aat}***

13.2. as-to power {fig} cry-out {alight} {fig} he give strife {backbone}

13.3. …as opposed to one who has power or sovereignty there is no benefit for speaking in an expanding, flooding, inflaming manner, yelling out, getting up / rising with temper and becoming loud and boisterous / animated /rowdy / noisy / exuberant / overexcited/over--the-top, , inflating the ego, becoming an agitated and heated person, and causing strife with the speech so much so as to inflame the nervous system in the physical body and disbalance the Arat Sekhem (Serpent Power, Kundalini) Life Force energy flowing through the Sefech Ba Ra (chakras) in the astral body, both located in the backbone area.

Verse 14.

14.1. ***ary hat dept iu f nuy im oauy***

14.2. in charge front boat it-is he aware/watchful in journey/path

14.3. The person who is in charge of the ship, the person who is in front of the boat, looking out ahead, its guardian, its captain, if that person is aware and watchful (vigilant) of what is coming in the future, what is ahead on the course, for their boat of life, watchful of what is ahead, clear path or obstacles.

Verse 15.

15.1. ***bu aryu f dep f agay***

15.2. not doing he boat his crashing-capsizing--drowning

15.3. …that person (with a watchful captain and lookout) will not experience the disaster (shipwreck) of crashing the ship and ending up dead. Their journey of life will not end in failure and tragedy such as failed relationships, career stress, and failure in attaining the goals of life, etc. nor will it end in personal disasters such as frustrations, sorrows, depressions, worries or anxieties. Rather, it will arrive safely at the port of spiritual perfection in the Beautiful West. The person who does not do this (does not have a watchful captain and lookout) that person's boat of life will crash, capsize, end in disaster.

PART II: COMMENTARIES ON THE WISDOM TEXT VERSES OF SAGE AMENEMOPET

INTRODUCTION TO THE COMMENTARIES

Having established in Part 1 the revolutionary trilinear translation methodology that makes the authentic wisdom of Sage Amenemopet accessible through three distinct levels—phonetic transliteration, word-for-word translation, and contextual interpretation—we now turn to the deeper work of psychological and spiritual analysis. The translations themselves serve as the foundation, preserving both the linguistic integrity and philosophical sophistication of the original hieroglyphic text. Nevertheless, translation alone, however accurate and multidimensional, cannot fully illuminate the transformative potential embedded within these ancient teachings for contemporary spiritual practice.

The commentaries presented in Part 2 represent a systematic exposition of the mystic transpersonal psychology underlying Amenemopet's wisdom philosophy. Each chapter commentary examines not merely what Sage Amenemopet taught, but how these teachings operate at the level of consciousness architecture—the mechanics of hat (conscious awareness), ab (the unconscious mind with its dual nature), Ka (the personality and subconscious), aryu (karmic feeling-memories), and Ab Neter (the divine soul-spark that sustains all awareness). Through this analytical framework, the wisdom becomes not abstract philosophy but practical instruction for mind/personality transformation.

THE PROLOGUE AS FOUNDATION

All commentaries that follow must be understood in relation to the Prologue's establishment of two interconnected goals that define the entire teaching. As revealed in the Prologue translation, [Verse 2] declares these as "precise teachings that when understood exactly, with precision cause a person to have well-being while living on earth"—the first goal of earthly flourishing through wisdom. [Verse 9] then directs the aspirant toward discovering the kara, "the location of the 'heart divinity'"—the second goal of recognizing Ab Neter, the Divine presence within. These dual objectives form an inseparable unity: without organizing life's affairs through wisdom (first goal), consciousness remains so agitated by worldly struggles that inner sanctuary remains inaccessible; without discovering the Ab Neter foundation (second goal), even successful worldly management produces only temporary satisfaction rather than genuine spiritual fulfillment.

Consider how Sage Amenemopet's teaching operates: the Prologue establishes that wisdom philosophy (sebait) differs fundamentally from devotional practice. Where devotional approaches emphasize worship, offerings, and ritual service to external and or internal divine forces to transform egoistic emotional feelings to egoism effacing feelings of devotion to the Divine, wisdom philosophy teaches the aspirant to recognize how consciousness itself operates—how thoughts arise in hat (conscious awareness) from aryu (karmic feeling-memories) stored in ab (the unconscious mind with its dual nature), how these patterns either reveal or obscure the Ab Neter (the divine soul-spark) that sustains awareness, and how purification through right action, thought, and feeling gradually thins aryu density to expose the divine foundation already present. This distinction proves critical, for many aspirants initially approach spiritual teachings seeking emotional support, comfort, reassurance, or protection, which they initially may find by connecting to the Divine in an emotional way, based on the teachings they have received and to the level of their understanding. Sage Amenemopet offers a path of understanding consciousness mechanics and implementing systematic purification, which then will allow the superficial emotional expressions to transform into a mature devotion to the Divine as the understanding deepens.

STRUCTURE AND PURPOSE OF THE COMMENTARIES

Each chapter commentary follows a systematic five-section structure designed to examine the teaching from progressively deeper spiritual. analytical and philosophical perspectives:

Section 1: Human Psychology Principle identifies the core psychological issue that the chapter addresses—the specific dysfunction in consciousness operation that prevents both earthly well-being and Ab Neter discovery. This section establishes how the teaching relates to the hat/ab/aryu/Ab Neter framework and explicitly connects to both Prologue goals.

Section 2: Behavioral Imperative examines the observable patterns and ego dysfunctions that arise from the psychology principle—how aryu density manifests in thought, feeling, and action, creating what the teaching calls "heated" consciousness (shemm). This section maintains compassionate framing, recognizing that these patterns often operate unconsciously as protective mechanisms developed through traumatic or overwhelming life experiences.

Section 3: Mystic Psychology-Metaphysical Implications explores the consciousness architecture level—how the teaching works to thin aryu patterns, reveal Ab Neter, and transform awareness from heated to silent (ger). This section never repeats Section 2's content but builds upon it metaphysically, explaining cosmic principles and universal consciousness mechanics.

Section 4: Transpersonal Psychology Research provides contemporary empirical validation through studies, neuroscience findings, and Buddhist psychology parallels where applicable. This section maintains strict academic focus—pure research without pastoral concerns or practical advice, demonstrating how modern science confirms ancient wisdom.

Section 5: Spiritual Implications for Aspirants divides into two parts: Part A addresses the modern aspirant's practical challenges in implementing the teaching within contemporary society's hostile environment, while Part B provides concrete transformation methods derived either from Amenemopet's explicit instructions or through careful application of the "inverse doctrine methodology"—a hermeneutical approach I developed for deriving implicit practices from explicit positive teachings.

The Inverse Doctrine Methodology Explained

Throughout these commentaries, you will encounter references to "inverse doctrine methodology application." This interpretive method deserves explanation here, as it represents a systematic approach to extracting practical transformation guidance from Amenemopet's precepts.

When Amenemopet prescribes a virtue or behavior—for example, "remain calm"—the inverse doctrine reveals the contrary states that must be avoided: actions, thoughts, and feelings that promote unrest, agitation, or instability. This methodology operates on the recognition that ancient wisdom texts often teach through positive prescription rather than exhaustive prohibition. The sage tells us what to cultivate, and the serious student must understand what opposes that cultivation.

Nevertheless, this method requires disciplined application. Inverse doctrine applies **only** when Amenemopet does not explicitly state what should be avoided, and only when the implicit avoidance proves clearly derivable from the spirit and intent of the explicit teaching. The inverse must encompass the full spectrum of contrary states, not merely simple negation. Most importantly, inverse doctrine applications must always be framed as reasoned extrapolation rather than Amenemopet's explicit words—a methodology I developed for making implicit wisdom explicit for practical application, not a claim about the Sage's original intent.

Reading These Commentaries Effectively

Several principles will enhance your engagement with these analytical expositions:

First, recognize that each commentary builds upon the Prologue foundation and incorporates wisdom from chapters already covered, but never references teachings from future chapters. This progressive pedagogical structure mirrors traditional mystery school instruction, where each teaching prepares consciousness for the next level of understanding.

Second, understand the distinction between **creating access** and **removing obstruction**. Amenemopet's teaching does not help us create spiritual capacity we lack; rather, it removes aryu obstructions hiding the Ab Neter that already sustains our awareness. This subtle but crucial difference shapes the entire practice approach—patient absorption and purification rather than forceful achievement.

Third, attend to the specific terminology consistently employed throughout: hat (conscious awareness), ab (unconscious with dual nature), aryu (karmic feeling-memories), kara (divine sanctuary), Ab Neter (divine soul-spark), heated mind and feelings (aryu-driven reactivity), and silent mind and feelings (purified consciousness). These terms represent precise psychological and metaphysical concepts, not mere synonyms for conventional religious language.

Fourth, recognize the realistic assessment of spiritual development these teachings provide. Amenemopet does not promise instant enlightenment, dramatic visions, or miraculous transformations. The teaching acknowledges that aspirants living in modern culture face particular challenges—growing up in worldly environments that actively cultivate heated consciousness, working in commercial and governmental systems that reward unethical behavior, and encountering constant social pressure toward ego-identification and competitive comparison. The commentaries address these realities with both compassion and unflinching honesty about the work required.

Fifth, implement the concrete practices offered in Section 5B of each commentary. Intellectual understanding, however sophisticated, does not thin aryu density. Only consistent integral practice—ethics in action, meditation on wisdom teachings, cultivation of silence, and patient observation of consciousness operations—creates the purification that reveals Ab Neter. The teaching provides both map and method; the aspirant must walk the path.

THE TEACHING VOICE

These commentaries represent my philosophical insights for instruction as a teacher within the Shetaut Neter tradition, addressing students and aspirants who seek genuine spiritual transformation rather than mere intellectual knowledge. You will hopefully find the tone conversational yet sophisticated, combining scholarly precision with practical spiritual guidance. The wisdom philosophy of Amenemopet has guided my own mind/personality development for decades, and these commentaries emerge from both extensive scholarly research and lived practice of the teachings.

When the text states "I teach" or "the wisdom reveals," this reflects the traditional teacher-disciple dynamic of ancient wisdom transmission. Nevertheless, I maintain careful distinction between Amenemopet's authentic teachings and my analytical commentary upon them. Where the Sage's words appear, they are properly cited and distinguished from my exposition. The authority of these commentaries rests not on personal charisma but on faithful representation of Amenemopet's wisdom and demonstration of its psychological and spiritual efficacy.

CONTEMPORARY RELEVANCE AND TIMELESS TRUTH

Perhaps the most striking aspect of Amenemopet's teaching—and a testament to its genuine wisdom—lies in its profound relevance to contemporary psychological and spiritual challenges despite originating in ancient Kemetic civilization. The essential nature of all human beings is Neberdjer, and when one is not enlightened and not consciously abiding in the experience of this as one's true essence, then the egoism of the personality expresses, and this expression comes forth in certain archetypal ways that the ancient scriptures document. The heated person described in Chapter 2 manifests identically in modern corporate culture, social media dynamics, and political discourse as in Ancient Egyptian (Kamitan) society. The anxiety about material security addressed in Chapter 6 operates through identical consciousness mechanics whether the person lives in ancient Thebes or modern Los Angeles. The tendency toward judgment and comparison exposed in Chapter 25 distorts relationships in precisely the same way across millennia and cultures.

This universality reflects Amenemopet's penetration to consciousness architecture itself—the fundamental operations of hat, ab, and aryu that remain constant across time and culture. Nevertheless, modern aspirants face unique intensifications of these timeless challenges: technological acceleration that fragments attention, commercial manipulation that deliberately cultivates desire and comparison, governmental systems that normalize corruption, and social atomization that undermines traditional wisdom transmission structures. The commentaries address both the timeless archetypal psychological patterns and their contemporary manifestations, providing guidance for those seeking authentic spiritual development within the particular challenges of our era.

Moving Forward with the Commentaries

The chapters that follow represent systematic guidance for achieving the Prologue's dual goals—earthly well-being through wisdom and discovery of Ab Neter through purification. Each teaching addresses specific obstacles to these objectives while building progressively toward comprehensive mind/personality transformation. The Prologue commentary establishes the foundational framework; subsequent chapters provide increasingly sophisticated analysis of particular psychological patterns and their remedies.

Indeed, the wisdom to be understood here encompasses recognition that spiritual development proceeds not through dramatic breakthroughs but through patient, consistent application of Sage Amenemopet's principles. The transformation from heated to silent consciousness, from aryu-dominated awareness to Ab Neter recognition, unfolds gradually as right living, right thinking, and right feeling thin the density of aryu (karmic) patterns accumulated through lifetimes of ego-identification. This work requires both dedication and realistic expectation—not pessimism about potential progress, but honest assessment of the consciousness purification necessary for genuine enlightenment.

Consider then these commentaries not as mere academic exercises but as practical spiritual technology—tools for understanding how your own consciousness operates and methods for implementing the purification that reveals your divine foundation. The ancient Sage Amenemopet speaks across millennia with wisdom as relevant today as when first inscribed on papyrus. May these analytical expositions serve to illuminate that wisdom, making its transformative power accessible for your journey toward both earthly flourishing and divine realization.

The commentaries that follow maintain this analytical depth while providing concrete guidance for contemporary practice. Each chapter builds systematically upon previous teachings, creating a comprehensive map of mind/personality transformation grounded in authentic Ancient Egyptian mystical psychology.

GLOSSARY OF KEY TERMS

HUMAN MENTAL ARCHITECTURE ACCORDING TO SAGE AMENEMOPET		
Level of mind	**Amenemopet name**	**Function**
Present awareness in mind	***Hat***	Thoughts and feelings in current present awareness
Sub-Conscious mind	***Ka***	Content of subconscious mind from which present awareness thoughts and feelings are derived (come into present awareness)
Unconscious mind	***Ab***	[Unconscious level] Storehouse of impressions from past thoughts, feelings, memories and experiences of the past
Unconscious impressions	***Aryu***	Sum total effect of a person past thoughts, feelings, desires and experiences of the past of the present lifetime and past lifetimes that contributes to a person's present guiding feelings, opinions, beliefs, thoughts, desires and inclinations of the personality that unconsciously impel or compel the personality to certain paths of action in the present life. The aryu can be changed by living through the fruition of the past aryu as it fructifies in the present while engaging in spiritual disciplines (Sema Tawy [Egyptian Yoga], Shetaut Neter [Egyptian Mysteries]) that will mitigate and or cleanse the cause of the negative aryu (cause=spiritual ignorance and delusion).
Divine knowingness	***Kara***	[Unconscious level] Sanctuary or place of divine awareness within the unconscious mind; a place of knowingness separate from the knowing of unconscious impressions based on ego awareness.
Soul	***Ab Neter***	[Unconscious level] Spark of Spirit (like drop of the Ocean) of Divine consciousness All-encompassing-divinity. Also traditionally termed BA in other Egyptian scriptures (Pertemheru, Asarian texts). Ab Neter and BA are equivalent terms for the divine soul.
Spirit, All-encompassing-divinity	***Neberdjer***	[All-encompassing Consciousness] Consciousness enfolding and interpenetrating Creation, from which all life draws its existence and its capacity for consciousness and awareness

NOTE: Amenemopet's framework for understanding the mind should not be confused with the brain and nervous system. The mind operates **through** the nervous system, much like electricity operates through a washing machine—coursing through the wires and causing work to be done by the machine, or, in this case, the human body.

UNDERSTANDING AB NETER TERMINOLOGY USED BY AMENEMOPET WITHIN THE BROADER ANCIENT EGYPTIAN SPIRITUAL FRAMEWORK

Terminology, Equivalence, and Cross-Cultural Parallels

When reading Amenemopet's wisdom text, it is essential to understand that what the sage terms "Ab Neter" corresponds to what other Ancient Egyptian scriptures call "BA" (soul). This is not a contradiction or different concept, but rather reflects the sophisticated Ancient Egyptian practice of using terminology appropriate to specific spiritual technologies and contexts. Understanding this equivalence—and the broader framework it represents—provides crucial insight into how Amenemopet's teaching fits within the unified cosmology of Ancient Egyptian spiritual wisdom.

THE BA CONCEPT IN ANCIENT EGYPTIAN SPIRITUAL LITERATURE

In the comprehensive Ancient Egyptian understanding of human personality, the BA represents the divine soul—the eternal, spiritual aspect of the human being that survives physical death and is capable of divine consciousness. The Pertemheru (Book of Coming Forth By Day, commonly known as the Book of the Dead) extensively discusses the BA, establishing it as the divine witness-consciousness that observes mental operations while remaining untouched by them. The Scripture of Isis and Ra uses BA to designate this divine consciousness manifesting through individual form, emphasizing its function as the unchanging awareness witnessing all mental phenomena.

The Pertemheru teaching presents a crucial formula through the "Asar Any" declaration in Chapter 43: "I am a great one who is the child of a great one; thus, I have the same greatness that is the greatness of my parent. My parent is Asar (Osiris), the great universal soul, therefore I have that same great universal soul." This establishes that the BA—the universal soul (Asar/Osiris)—operates through each individual initiate, who bears the title "Asar [name]" to signify this realization. The same consciousness is simultaneously referenced as both universal soul (Asar) and individual personality (Any), demonstrating that these represent different aspects of recognition by the same divine consciousness.

Within the nine-part personality framework taught in Ancient Egyptian wisdom (as depicted in temple iconography and explained in various texts), the BA occupies the eighth position—the highest spiritual component alongside the Akh (shining spirit). The BA represents the causal body level, the divine soul residing within the deeper levels of consciousness, obscured from ordinary awareness by the density of aryu (karmic impressions) in the ab (unconscious mind).

WHY AMENEMOPET USES "AB NETER" RATHER THAN "BA"

Sage Amenemopet's choice of the term "Ab Neter" (literally "divine ab" or "divine heart/unconscious") rather than the traditional term BA serves a specific pedagogical purpose aligned with his teaching methodology. Amenemopet focuses intensively on the ab (unconscious mind) as both the repository of aryu (karmic feeling-memories) that obscure divine awareness AND the location of the kara (divine sanctuary) where the divine soul resides. By using the term "Ab Neter," Amenemopet emphasizes:

1. The ab is not merely a storehouse of karmic patterns but also contains divinity within its depths
2. The divine soul (BA) resides specifically within the ab, in the kara (inner divine sanctuary)
3. The path to discovering this divine soul involves penetrating through the layers of the ab—from surface aryu to the deep kara level
4. The ab itself becomes "divine" (neter) when purified, revealing the Ab Neter that has always been present

Nevertheless, when Amenemopet speaks of Ab Neter, in his framework, he refers to precisely the same spiritual reality that other Ancient Egyptian texts call BA. The Ab Neter is the BA—the divine soul, the foundation of individual consciousness, the spark of Spirit, the unchanging witness-awareness. The different terminology reflects different teaching contexts, not different concepts.

THE UNIFIED FRAMEWORK ACROSS ANCIENT EGYPTIAN SCRIPTURES

Understanding the compatibility of terminology across Ancient Egyptian scriptures reveals a sophisticated, unified metaphysical framework expressed through varied nomenclature appropriate to specific spiritual technologies:

FRAMEWORK OF THE SCRIPTURE OF RA AND HETHERU

- Ba en Ra (Soul of Ra) = The absolute, transcendental consciousness
- Nunu (Nun) = Undifferentiated primeval consciousness, the ocean before manifestation
- Ra = Creator Spirit, individuated consciousness manifesting creation
- Ab-en-Ra = Heart of Ra, the absolute foundation (equivalent to Ba en Ra)

FRAMEWORK OF THE WISDOM TEXT OF AMENEMOPET

- Neberdjer = All-Encompassing Divinity, the absolute consciousness (equivalent to Ba en Ra)
- Deep Ab/Kara = The deep unconscious sanctuary (equivalent to Nunu)
- **Ab Neter = Divine soul sustaining individual awareness (equivalent to BA)**
- Hat-Ka-Surface Ab = Mental operations of conscious, subconscious, and unconscious mind

FRAMEWORK OF THE SCRIPTURE OF ISIS AND RA

- Neter-Neterty = Dual Divinity, the absolute (equivalent to Ba en Ra/Neberdjer)
- **Ba = Divine soul, witness-consciousness (equivalent to Ab Neter)**
- Ka = Astral body where thinking occurs (equivalent to Amenemopet's Hat-Ka-Ab complex)

FRAMEWORK OF THE PERTEMHERU (BOOK OF COMING FORTH BY DAY)

- Asar (Osiris) = Universal soul operating through each initiate (equivalent to BA/Ab Neter)
- **BA = Divine soul of the individual (equivalent to Ab Neter)**
- Ab = Heart/unconscious where BA resides (equivalent to Amenemopet's ab containing Ab Neter)

THE COMPATIBILITY MAPPING

ABSOLUTE LEVEL: Ba en Ra = Neberdjer = Neter-Neterty = Ab-en-Ra

UNDIFFERENTIATED LEVEL: Nunu = Deep Ab/Kara

DIVINE CONSCIOUSNESS LEVEL: Ra (as consciousness) = Ab Neter = BA = Asar (as universal soul)

MENTAL OPERATIONS LEVEL: Creation/forms = Hat-Ka-Surface Ab = Ka (as thinking mind)

THE NON-DUAL RELATIONSHIP: AB NETER AND NEBERDJER

The relationship between Ab Neter and Neberdjer in Amenemopet's framework corresponds precisely to the relationship between individual BA and universal BA (Asar) in the Pertemheru, and mirrors the relationship taught across all Ancient Egyptian scriptures: individual divine consciousness is not separate from but rather an individualized expression of universal divine consciousness.

This can be understood through the wave-ocean metaphor: just as a wave is not a separated portion of the ocean but is the ocean itself manifesting in wave-form, so too Ab Neter is not a separated fragment of Neberdjer but is Neberdjer itself manifesting through individual form. The Pertemheru's "Asar Any" formula makes this explicit: the individual (Any) possesses "that same great universal soul" (Asar)—not a piece of it, not a portion, but the same soul expressing through individual form.

CROSS-CULTURAL PARALLEL: THE VEDANTIC ATMAN-BRAHMAN TEACHING

This Ancient Egyptian understanding of the Ab Neter-Neberdjer relationship finds a precise parallel in the Vedantic philosophy of India, specifically in the teaching concerning Atman and Brahman. In Vedantic wisdom:

- ATMAN represents the individual divine self, the witnessing consciousness in each being
- BRAHMAN represents the universal absolute consciousness, the ground of all existence
- The great realization (mahavakya): "Tat Tvam Asi" (That Thou Art)—the individual IS the universal

The Vedantic teaching establishes that Atman and Brahman are ultimately identical—not that Atman is a piece of Brahman, but that Atman IS Brahman itself as it manifests through individual form. The apparent separation exists only in ignorance; in enlightenment, one realizes that individual consciousness and universal consciousness are one reality.

This precisely mirrors the Ancient Egyptian teaching:

- **AB NETER (like Atman)** = The individual divine consciousness, the witness in each being
- **NEBERDJER (like Brahman)** = The universal absolute consciousness, All-Encompassing Divinity
- **The great realization:** Ab Neter IS Neberdjer—individual essence and universal reality are one

Just as the Vedantic aspirant realizes "I am Brahman" (Aham Brahmasmi), recognizing that individual awareness (Atman) is identical with absolute consciousness (Brahman), so too the Ancient Egyptian initiate realizes through enlightenment that the Ab Neter sustaining individual awareness is none other than Neberdjer itself.

CONCLUSION: ONE WISDOM, MULTIPLE EXPRESSIONS

When Amenemopet teaches about Ab Neter residing in the kara (divine sanctuary) within the ab (unconscious mind), he speaks of the same divine soul (BA) that the Pertemheru addresses, the same universal consciousness (Asar) that operates through each initiate, the same absolute reality (Neberdjer) that the Scripture of Ra and Hetheru calls Ba en Ra.

For the contemporary student of Ancient Egyptian wisdom, understanding this equivalence—Ab Neter = BA—and recognizing the unified framework across scriptures provides essential context. Amenemopet's practical meditation methodology aims at the same realization taught throughout Egyptian spiritual literature: discovering the divine soul (AB Neter/BA) within oneself, recognizing this individual divine consciousness as identical with universal consciousness (Neberdjer/Ba en Ra/Asar), and transcending ego-identification through systematic purification of the ab.

This is the same non-dual realization taught in Vedanta (Atman = Brahman), Buddhism (individual Buddha Nature = universal Buddha Nature), and authentic mysticism across all traditions. The Ancient Egyptian sages, through their sophisticated use of varied yet compatible terminological frameworks, provided multiple pathways to this one ultimate truth—the recognition of divine consciousness as one's essential nature and the transcendence of the illusion of separation through direct spiritual realization.

TERMINOLOGY ACROSS ANCIENT EGYPTIAN SPIRITUAL FRAMEWORKS

Unified Cosmology with Varied Nomenclature

CONSCIOUSNESS LEVEL	Scripture of Ra & Hetheru	Wisdom Text of Amenemopet	Scripture of Isis & Ra	Pertemheru (Book of Coming Forth)	Vedantic Parallel
ABSOLUTE LEVEL	**Ba en Ra** *(Soul of Ra)* Also: Ab-en-Ra *(Heart of Ra)*	**Neberdjer** *(All-Encompassing Divinity)*	**Neter-Neterty** *(Dual Divinity: Transcendent & Immanent)*	**Neberdjer** *Also: Asar (as Absolute)*	**Brahman** *(Absolute Consciousness)* *(Indian framework)*
Function	The absolute, transcendental consciousness that serves as the source and substance of all existence. Beyond all forms yet manifesting as all forms. The unmanifest foundation from which all creation emerges.				
UNDIFFERENTIATED LEVEL	**Nunu (Nun)** *(Primeval Ocean)*	**Deep Ab / Kara** *(Deep Unconscious / Divine Sanctuary)*	*Not explicitly named*	**Nun** *Also: Ab (as container)*	*Prakriti (unmanifest)*
Function	Undifferentiated, homogeneous consciousness before it takes on particular forms. The primeval ocean of awareness in which individual waves arise. Not mere emptiness but infinite potential. Awareness without specific content or individual identity.				
DIVINE CONSCIOUSNESS LEVEL	**Ra** *(Creator Spirit as Consciousness)*	**{Ab Neter}** *(Divine Soul / Divine Heart)*	**{BA}** *(Divine Soul)*	**{BA}** *Also: Asar [name]*	**Atman** *(Individual Divine Self)*

CONSCIOUSNESS LEVEL	Scripture of Ra & Hetheru	Wisdom Text of Amenemopet	Scripture of Isis & Ra	Pertemheru (Book of Coming Forth)	Vedantic Parallel
				(Universal soul through individual)	
Function	Divine consciousness manifesting through individual form. The unchanging witness-awareness that observes all mental phenomena. The foundation that sustains individual consciousness. Like a wave that IS ocean (not separate from it), this is universal consciousness expressing through particular form.				
MENTAL OPERATIONS LEVEL	**Creation / Manifest Forms** *(World of names & forms)*	**Hat-Ka-Surface Ab** *(Conscious-Subconscious-Unconscious mind)*	**Ka** *(Astral body / Thinking mind)*	**Ka** *Also: Khat (body)* *Ren (name/ego)*	**Manas** *(Thinking mind)*
Function	The level of ordinary mental operations: thinking, feeling, perceiving, remembering. Where ego-identity operates, where the mind believes itself to be a separate entity. Where consciousness becomes identified with temporary phenomena and forgets its divine nature. The realm of aryu (karmic patterns) and worldly experience.				

KEY INSIGHT:

The terms highlighted in curly brackets { } (Ab Neter and BA) are EQUIVALENT - they refer to the same divine consciousness using different nomenclature. Amenemopet's "Ab Neter" is the traditional "BA" found throughout Ancient Egyptian spiritual literature. The variation in terminology reflects different teaching contexts and spiritual technologies, not different metaphysical concepts.

THE NON-DUAL RELATIONSHIP:

Ab Neter (BA) and Neberdjer (Ba en Ra / Neter-Neterty) are not separate entities. Ab Neter IS Neberdjer manifesting through individual form - like a wave that is nothing other than ocean itself. This mirrors the Vedantic teaching that Atman (individual divine self) IS Brahman (absolute consciousness) - not a piece of it, but the same reality expressing through individual form. The apparent separation exists only in ignorance; enlightenment reveals their ultimate identity.

CHAPTER 1: Commentary on Teachings of Amenemopet Prologue (verses 1-2, 7-9): The Foundation of Wisdom Philosophy for Life Transformation

SUMMARY OF VERSES BEING COVERED

These foundational Prologue verses establish the complete framework for Amenemopet's wisdom philosophy and its practical application in human life. [Verse 1] declares this teaching as "the beginning of the wisdom philosophy that is based on recorded wisdom literature that is to be experienced in life," emphasizing that spiritual development requires lived application in addition to intellectual understanding. [Verse 2] reveals these as "precise teachings that when understood exactly, with precision, cause a person to have well-being while living on earth," indicating that accuracy of comprehension directly produces tangible life benefits. [Verse 7] explains the organizing principle: "allowing a person to organize their affairs in the paths that their life will tread" rather than living randomly without conscious direction. [Verse 8] further clarifies this as "producing a person's well-being (prosperity) while they are existing as a person on earth."

Most significantly, [Verse 9] introduces the crucial psychological framework and transformative path: "This wisdom teaching allows the heart to have presence-of-mind, positive forwards movement awareness as to the sanctuary [Kara (Divine shrine/sanctuary of Divinity within)]." The verse reveals that most people's hat (conscious awareness—what is presently in conscious mind) operates driven by aryu (unconscious feeling memories) stored in the ab (unconscious mind) without awareness of or communion with the kara (divine sanctuary) where "the Divine 'Ab Neter' resides in every person." The ab or unconscious mind not only holds aryu (feeling memories of past actions, thoughts, feelings and desires based on past experiences) but also contains the presence of Divinity—what we may understand as the Soul (Ab Neter). This Ab Neter is the foundation of individual consciousness, the innermost essence residing in every person's being that they may not be aware of because it transcends material form [21].

To properly understand Ab Neter, we must recognize its non-dual relationship with Neberdjer (the All-Encompassing Divine Consciousness). Ab Neter is not a separated fragment or independent subset of Neberdjer; rather, Ab Neter IS Neberdjer itself as it expresses through individual form—like how a wave is not separate from the ocean but is the ocean manifesting in wave-form. This mirrors the Vedantic teaching that Atman (individual awareness) and Brahman (absolute consciousness) are ultimately one, or the Buddhist recognition that individual Buddha Nature is identical with the universal Buddha Nature [10, 20].

In the unenlightened state—the state of spiritual aspiration—the Ab Neter sustains the very capacity for conscious awareness itself, though the aspirant remains unaware of this divine foundation due to aryu obstruction. Ab Neter functions as what we have termed the Soul-Aware-Witness in other teachings—the unchanging awareness that witnesses all mental phenomena while remaining untouched by them. Through the process of Spiritual Enlightenment, direct experiential realization occurs: the Ab Neter that has always been one's deepest identity is discovered to be none other than Neberdjer itself. This is not transformation of Ab Neter but revelation of what has always been true—that the individual's innermost essence and the universal divine consciousness are one and the same reality.

The ignorant state—the conscious mind operating from past conditioning, opinions, feelings, and desires based on unconscious aryu rather than divine communion—produces the heated personality and all its behavioral deficits. This ignorant state of a person (awareness of aryu and not of the soul-divinity) occurs because the aryu in the unconscious mind occupy the presence-of-mind awareness so densely as to influence the conscious reality awareness (thinking and feeling) of a person and blot out the awareness of the soul level divine presence, which is deeper than the aryu (unconscious mental impressions). This leaves the personality with awareness of the body, mind, and their sensations and perceptions to sustain awareness of time and space apparent realities.

The Ab Neter awareness is beyond ego-personality awareness, the superficial mind. Yet it is revealed when there is **presence-of-mind** regarding its existence. It should be noted that when I use the term *presence-of-mind*, it should not be confused with psychological mindfulness, which refers to being aware of what is unfolding in one's experience in the present moment in an observing, non-judgmental way. Psychological mindfulness is a skill of bringing one's attention to the present moment and is rooted in the external world—that is, in present-moment circumstances.

Focusing attention in the present moment has the effect of grounding the personality by disconnecting it from the agitated, heated *aryu* of past sorrows and regrets and future worries and anxieties. These *aryu* express themselves as compelling thoughts and feelings that urge certain actions. Psychological mindfulness shifts attention away from these agitations and toward some aspect of the present moment with conscious awareness—either the perceptions of the senses (what is seen, touched, smelled, tasted, or heard), the activity one is engaged in (such as washing dishes or walking), or a mentally calming practice such as deep, conscious breathing. As such, psychological mindfulness offers stabilizing and calming benefits for both the mind and the physical body.

For those not engaged in a mystical spiritual process aimed at discovering their deeper Neberdjer nature—and also for spiritual aspirants—psychological mindfulness is a valuable tool that can be included in one's skill set to calm a heated or dysregulated mind. However, the presence-of-mind mystic mindfulness described by Sage Amenemopet is a fundamentally different practice. It connects conscious awareness directly with the essence of being (Ab Neter/Neberdjer), which exists beyond normal human psychology. While it also produces grounding and cleansing of the *aryu*, more importantly it rewires—or re-wrings—the mind and nervous system in a way that precludes mental dysregulation altogether, thereby minimizing or eliminating the need for techniques designed merely to stabilize an already dysregulated system.

Presence-of-mind mystic mindfulness is a conscious awareness of the Divine within, made possible when the mind attains a state of *ger*—serenity—also described as a silent personality, cultivated through the wisdom and practices instructed by Sage Amenemopet. Conscious awareness of the soul essence of consciousness (Ab Neter) renders egoic *aryu* impulses powerless. Awareness of Ab Neter is awareness of one's Divinity, one's essential spiritual nature, which precludes engagement in heated thoughts and emotions that depend upon egoic perspectives—such as perceiving oneself as a separate individual, as incomplete, or as competing in the world for fulfillment.

All desires of the personality are fulfilled when the soul nature of the Self—the Ab Neter—is discovered and directly experienced as the true nature of one's being. Thus, psychological mindfulness can be a helpful preparatory skill for aspirants seeking to calm a dysregulated mind while learning and implementing the teachings of Sage Amenemopet to cultivate presence-of-mind awareness. However, it is a tool that facilitates progress toward the goal, not the goal itself. The goal is the cultivation of presence-of-mind awareness as defined and taught by Sage Amenemopet.

Teachings Derived from These Verses

1. Wisdom philosophy must be experienced through lived practice, not merely studied intellectually [verse 1]
2. Precise understanding of spiritual teachings produces measurable well-being during earthly existence [verse 2]
3. Wisdom philosophy provides organizing principles that transform random living into purposeful direction [verses 7-8]
4. The ab (unconscious mind) has dual nature: it stores aryu (feeling memories) and contains Ab Neter (Divine soul/spark) [verse 9]
5. Ab Neter is the foundation that sustains conscious awareness itself, though most remain unaware of it [verse 9]
6. Aryu density in the ab blots out awareness of Ab Neter, leaving consciousness aware only of body, mind, and time/space realities [verse 9]
7. The kara (divine sanctuary) is where Ab Neter resides within the ab [verse 9]
8. Purification through wisdom philosophy removes aryu density to reveal the Ab Neter that was always present [verse 9]
9. When Ab Neter awareness is achieved, egoic impulses of aryu become powerless [verse 9]
10. All personality desires are fulfilled when Ab Neter is discovered as the very nature of one's being [verse 9]

1. Human Psychology Principle of the Prologue of Sage Amenemopet

The fundamental human psychology issue that [verses 1, 2, 7, 8, and 9] address centers on the tragic condition of consciousness remaining unaware of its own divine foundation, termed spiritual ignorance or a condition of suffering. [Verse 9] reveals the profound truth that every person possesses Ab Neter—the individualized presence of Neberdjer that sustains their very capacity for conscious awareness [21]. Ab Neter is not something distant to be acquired, nor is it a separated fragment; rather, it is the one Divine consciousness (Neberdjer) as it manifests through individual form, like a wave that is nothing other than ocean; it is the very foundation that makes consciousness itself possible. Yet despite Ab Neter being "the foundation of individual consciousness and the spark of spirit residing in every person's personality," most people remain completely unaware of its existence [21], and must exert effort to cultivate it.

[Verse 2's] declaration that this represents "an exposition of precise teachings that when understood exactly, with precision cause a person to have spiritual well-being while living on earth" presupposes that the reader currently experiences dissatisfaction and unfulfillment in life—not due to moral failure or inherent badness, but due to a state of error in understanding [21]. The person is not wicked but rather operates from misunderstanding: the mind is not thinking correctly because it does not understand correctly. This misunderstanding—specifically, ignorance of Ab Neter as the sustainer of one's consciousness, that is, spiritual ignorance—creates the very problems that precise teaching aims to correct. The main focus of the teaching is to remedy this cognitive error. Its primary concern is not moral deficiency or inherent badness. Rather, Sage Amenemopet recognizes an inherent goodness in human beings due to the presence of Ab Neter, which becomes distorted through mental corruption arising from spiritual ignorance of Ab Neter.

In other words, not knowing our true nature, we act from an instinctive animal nature mixed with egoism—the sense of being an individual, of being a separate entity from the Divine and from Creation, of feeling incomplete, and of competing in the world for the fulfillment of desires—which ultimately corrupts the mind.

The mechanism of this spiritual ignorance operates through the layered structure of the ab (unconscious mind). The ab contains both aryu (feeling memories of past actions, thoughts, feelings, and desires based on past experiences) at the surface level, and Ab Neter (divine soul/spark) at the deeper level within the kara (divine sanctuary) [21]. The tragedy or suffering occurs because "the aryu in the unconscious mind occupy the presence-of-mind awareness, so densely as to influence the conscious reality awareness (thinking and feeling) of a person and blot out the awareness of the soul level divine presence which is deeper than the aryu" [21]. This dense layer of aryu creates an obstruction that prevents the hat (conscious awareness—what is presently in conscious mind) from perceiving the Ab Neter that sustains its very capacity to be aware [21, 22].

This ignorant state leaves consciousness aware only of surface phenomena: "the personality with awareness of the body, mind, and their sensations and perceptions to sustain awareness of time and space apparent realities" [21]. The person experiences the self as merely a body-mind complex operating in time and space, completely unaware that their consciousness itself is sustained by "imba Neter", divine presence. Amenemopet identifies this as the heated personality—the mind operating through egoic perspectives that arise from feeling like "an individual, of being a separate entity from the divine and from Creation, of feelings of being incomplete and thinking about competing in the world for fulfillment of desires" [21, 22].

The psychological principle of Sage Amenemopet's teaching connects directly to both Prologue goals. The goal of [verse 2] to "cause a person to have well-being while living on earth" cannot be achieved when the mind operates in ignorance of its divine foundation, driven by aryu-based heated patterns. The heated personality creates chaos, conflict, and suffering precisely because it seeks externally what can only be found through awareness of the Ab Neter within. The goal of [verse 9]—that "The mind (heart) of the personality is to gain presence-of-mind about a sanctuary that can be entered once the worldly affairs are handled with this wisdom philosophy"—reveals the transformative solution.

The wisdom philosophy provides the means to handle worldly affairs through purification practices that thin the aryu density, gradually revealing the Ab Neter that was always present. [Verse 9] teaches that "The Ab Neter awareness is beyond the ego-personality-awareness, the superficial mind. And it is revealed when there is presence-of-mind about its existence. This conscious awareness of the Divine within is possible when the mind achieves a state of ger (serenity) or silent personality through the wisdom and practices instructed by Sage Amenemopet" [21].

A profound implication emerges: "The conscious awareness of the soul essence of consciousness (Ab Neter) would render the egoic impulses of aryu powerless" [21]. Why does Ab Neter awareness render aryu powerless? Because non-cognitive, experiential Enlightened awareness of one's divinity precludes engagement in heated thoughts and feelings that require egoic perspectives. When consciousness recognizes itself as Ab Neter—divine, complete, unified with Creation—the aryu-based impulses toward separation, competition, and desire-seeking lose their compelling force. "All desires of the personality are fulfilled when the soul nature of self, the Ab Neter, is discovered and experienced as the very nature of one's being" [21, 22].

[Verse 7's] teaching about organizing "the paths that their life will tread" takes on deeper meaning in light of this understanding. Without awareness of Ab Neter, life organization occurs through aryu-driven heated patterns—random, chaotic, reactive. With growing awareness of Ab Neter through purification, life organization arises from divine communion—purposeful, harmonious, wisdom-guided. The psychological principle of Sage Amenemopet's teaching reveals that human fulfillment requires not acquiring something external but removing the aryu obstruction that prevents awareness of the divine foundation already sustaining consciousness. So, insight into obstructing aryu is also needed in the process of discovering one's Ab Neter awareness. So it's both a process of gaining in understanding and awareness of Ab Neter, and also gaining insight into and effacing aryu patterns in the personality that are obstructing that awareness, the emphasis being more on the former (Ab Neter awareness), and the latter (obstructive egoic aryu cleansing) will follow in a more spontaneous manner.

2. Behavioral Imperative: The Heated Personality Operating from Aryu Obstruction

Building upon this psychological foundation, specific behavioral patterns emerge when the hat (conscious awareness) operates driven by aryu (feeling memories from past experiences) density that blots out awareness of Ab Neter [21, 22]. [Verse 7] reveals the core issue: without systematic spiritual guidance to "organize their affairs in the paths that their life will tread," individuals remain trapped in heated mind and feelings—the mind aware only of body, sensations, and time/space perceptions while the divine foundation of their consciousness remains hidden [21]. The heated personality manifests through chronic indecisiveness about major life directions driven by conflicting aryu rather than divine communion.

Most significantly, heated mind and feelings create what might be called separation suffering—the fundamental pain of experiencing oneself as an isolated individual separate from the divine and from Creation. This manifests as loneliness even in crowds, anxiety about an uncertain future, fear of death, competitive hostility toward others seen as rivals, and chronic dissatisfaction regardless of external circumstances. Each manifestation reflects the egoic perspective that arises when aryu density blots out Ab Neter awareness. The person experiences the self as a vulnerable body-mind complex struggling for survival and fulfillment in a threatening world, completely unaware that their very consciousness is sustained by Divine Presence unified with all Creation.

The ab (unconscious mind) functions as the location where this tragedy unfolds. At the surface level, aryu (feeling memories from past experiences) occupy presence-of-mind awareness so densely that they blot out the deeper level where Ab Neter resides in the kara (divine sanctuary) [21, 22]. Someone with aryu from childhood experiences of conditional love compulsively seeks achievement to prove worthiness—this heated behavior arises because aryu obscure the Ab Neter awareness that would reveal inherent divine worth [21]. Another with aryu from abandonment experiences sabotages intimacy before risking rejection—this heated pattern persists because aryu block awareness of the Ab Neter that is never separate, never abandoned, unified with all existence [21, 22].

Without the purifying influence of wisdom philosophy that [verse 2] describes, heated individuals develop increasingly elaborate ego-defensive strategies that actually reinforce aryu density. The person who stays constantly busy (heated pattern) prevents the silence where aryu become visible and can be purified, maintaining the obstruction that hides Ab Neter. The person who maintains rigid control (heated pattern) attempts to manage aryu-based anxiety through external manipulation, strengthening the egoic perspective that arises from ignorance of the divine foundation. The person who intellectualizes spirituality (heated pattern) uses concepts to avoid the actual purification work that would thin aryu density and reveal Ab Neter.

This creates heated mind and feelings imprisonment, where the personality becomes trapped in aryu-driven reactive patterns based on feelings of separation and incompleteness, while the Ab Neter—the divine foundation sustaining consciousness itself—remains hidden by aryu density. The behavioral patterns persist because the heated mind cannot recognize that the very awareness experiencing suffering is sustained by divine completeness. The solution requires systematic purification to thin aryu density, gradually revealing the Ab Neter that renders egoic impulses powerless.

3. Mystic Psychology Metaphysical Implications: The Layered Structure of Consciousness and Purification Mechanics

[Verse 1's] declaration that this represents "recorded wisdom literature that is to be experienced in life" reveals profound metaphysical principles about the layered structure of consciousness and how purification practices remove the obstruction preventing divine Ab Neter awareness [21]. The teaching indicates that authentic wisdom provides a practical methodology for thinning aryu density to reveal the Ab Neter foundation already sustaining consciousness [21, 22].

The metaphysical framework that [verse 9] establishes reveals the stratified architecture of the ab (unconscious mind). At the surface level, the ab stores aryu—"feeling memories of past actions, thoughts, feelings and desires based on past experiences" [21]. At the deeper level within the kara (divine sanctuary), the ab contains Ab Neter—"the foundation of individual consciousness and the spark of Spirit residing in every person's personality" [21]. This dual nature of the ab is crucial: the same unconscious mind that stores aryu (creating obstruction) also contains Ab Neter (providing the divine foundation being obscured) [21, 22].

The metaphysical mechanics of ignorance function through density and obstruction. As [verse 9] teaches, "the aryu in the unconscious mind occupy the presence-of-mind awareness, so densely as to influence the conscious reality awareness (thinking and feeling) of a person and blot out the awareness of the soul level divine presence which is deeper than the aryu" [21]. This creates a blocking mechanism where aryu density functions like thick clouds obscuring the sun—the sun (in this analogy relating to Ab Neter) continues shining, sustaining all life, but the clouds (aryu) prevent direct perception [21, 22]. The hat (conscious awareness) experiences only what the aryu allow it to perceive: "awareness of the body, mind, and their sensations and perceptions to sustain awareness of time and space apparent realities (skewed by the aryu)" [21].

The crucial metaphysical truth emerges: Ab Neter is not absent, not distant, not requiring creation or acquisition. Rather, Ab Neter represents Neberdjer (the All-Encompassing Divine Consciousness) as it manifests through individual form—not as a separated portion but as the one indivisible consciousness expressing through the individual, much as a wave is nothing other than ocean itself taking momentary form [21]. Every moment of conscious awareness, even in ignorance, is sustained by this Ab Neter foundation, which is simultaneously the individual's deepest essence and the universal Neberdjer. As [verse 9] teaches, Ab Neter is "the foundation of individual consciousness," meaning it provides the very capacity for awareness itself [21].

This understanding parallels what other non-dual traditions recognize: the Vedantic teaching that Atman (individual awareness) is ultimately Brahman (absolute consciousness), or the Buddhist recognition of one's Buddha Nature as identical with ultimate reality [10, 20]. In our Kemetic wisdom tradition, this is the Soul (capital S)—the Ab Neter that through spiritual realization is discovered to be none other than Neberdjer itself [21, 22]. What we have termed the "Soul-Aware-Witness" in previous teachings represents this same Ab Neter consciousness when it begins to recognize its own nature beyond the aryu-dominated surface awareness.

The metaphysics reveal that ignorance is not absence of divinity but rather obstruction of awareness of the divinity already present and functioning [21, 22]. Like sunlight obscured by clouds, Neberdjer-as-Ab-Neter continues sustaining consciousness even when aryu density prevents recognition of its presence. This transforms the spiritual path from seeking something external to removing internal obstruction—not creating access to an absent divinity but revealing the ever-present divine consciousness that has always been one's deepest identity.

[Verse 9] teaches that "The Ab Neter awareness is beyond the ego-personality-awareness, the superficial mind. But it is revealed when there is presence-of-mind about its existence" [21]. The metaphysical principle indicates that Ab Neter exists beyond the surface level where ego operates yet can be revealed through specific practices. The revelation occurs not by creating new awareness but by removing aryu obstruction that prevents perception of what was always present. "This conscious awareness of the Divine within [Nehast or spiritual Enlightenment] is possible when the mind achieves a state of ger or silent personality through the wisdom and practices instructed by Sage Amenemopet" [21, 22].

The metaphysics of purification function through thinning aryu density [21, 22]. Each application of silence, ethics, right living, right thinking, and right feeling works to dissolve or lighten specific aryu patterns. As aryu density decreases, the hat (conscious awareness) gains increasing capacity to perceive the deeper Ab Neter level [21]. This occurs gradually—not instant enlightenment but progressive revelation as the obstruction thins. The metaphysical implication of [verse 2's] "precise teachings that when understood exactly, with precision cause a person to have well-being" indicates that purification operates according to spiritual laws that produce predictable results [21].

The profound metaphysical teaching addresses why Ab Neter awareness renders aryu powerless. [Verse 9] reveals: "The conscious awareness of the soul essence of consciousness (Ab Neter, Neberdjer awareness, Enlightenment)) would render the egoic impulses of aryu powerless as the awareness of Ab Neter means being aware of one's divinity, which precludes engagement in heated thoughts and feelings that require egoic perspectives of life" [21]. The metaphysics explain that aryu derive their compelling force from the egoic perspective—the sense of being a separate, incomplete individual competing for survival and fulfillment [21, 22]. When consciousness recognizes itself as Ab Neter (Nehast, Enlightenment, Neberdjer awareness)—divine, complete, unified with all Creation—the foundation supporting egoic perspective dissolves.

Consider the metaphysical mechanics: aryu compelling achievement-seeking derive power from feelings of inadequacy (egoic perspective); when consciousness recognizes itself as Ab Neter (divine foundation), inadequacy becomes impossible—how can divinity be inadequate? [21] Aryu driving relationship attachment derive power from feelings of incompleteness (egoic perspective); when consciousness recognizes itself as Ab Neter (complete in itself), the compulsive seeking ends [21, 22]. "All desires of the personality are fulfilled when the soul nature of self, the Ab Neter, is discovered and experienced as the very nature of one's being" [21].

[Verse 7's] teaching about organizing "the paths that their life will tread" reveals the metaphysical principle that life organization arises from the level of awareness from which the mind operates. When the mind operates from aryu-obscured awareness (ignorance of Ab Neter), life organization follows egoic patterns—competitive, desire-driven, fear-based. When the mind operates from Ab Neter awareness (divine communion), life organization follows divine principles—harmonious, wisdom-guided, complete. The metaphysics indicate that changing life patterns requires not forced behavioral modification but rather removing aryu obstruction to reveal the divine foundation that naturally organizes life according to wisdom.

The metaphysical framework established by [verse 9] transforms understanding of spiritual realization. Rather than a heroic journey to a distant divine realm, the path involves patient removal of obstruction to reveal what sustains consciousness in every moment [21, 22]. Rather than a focus on acquiring divine qualities, the path reveals the divine foundation already present. The progressing aspirant rather than following the elementary idea that novice aspirants follow, of “becoming enlightened”, the mind recognizes it has always been sustained by enlightenment—Ab Neter—though the aryu density of the mind prevented awareness of the underlying enlightened consciousness[21]. This makes the spiritual path simultaneously more accessible (no distant goal to reach) and more demanding (requires actual purification work in addition to conceptual understanding - not merely intellectual comprehension but embodied practice informed by accurate framework knowledge) [21, 22]. Ab Neter already sustains consciousness even in ignorance - the issue is AWARENESS of Ab Neter, not its presence. Practice progressively thins aryu density, allowing increasing recognition of the Ab Neter that has always been functioning. This is a gradual spiral: practice → aryu thins → more silence → easier practice → more aryu thin. Each cycle moves forward toward stable Ab Neter recognition."

AUTHOR'S NOTE: CONCEPTUAL UNDERSTANDING AND EMBODIED PRACTICE

Amenemopet's teaching requires BOTH accurate conceptual understanding AND consistent embodied practice - not one instead of the other, but both integrated. The framework of hat, ka, ab, aryu, Ab Neter, and Neberdjer provides essential conceptual understanding - the map for consciousness transformation. Without grasping these distinctions, proper practice is impossible.

However, intellectual comprehension alone does not produce transformation. Understanding aryu conceptually does not thin actual aryu in the ab. Knowing about Ab Neter intellectually is not the same as recognizing Ab Neter directly. When this manuscript emphasizes that transformation "requires actual purification work," this means conceptual understanding MUST be accompanied by lived application - not that conceptual framework is unnecessary.

The complete path integrates:

- CONCEPTUAL UNDERSTANDING: Provides the map, framework, and discrimination
- EMBODIED PRACTICE: Produces actual transformation through ethics, meditation, and aryu purification
- INFORMED PRACTICE: Understanding guides practice; practice deepens understanding

As Prologue verse 1 teaches: wisdom is "recorded wisdom literature that is to be EXPERIENCED IN LIFE." The teaching is recorded (conceptual), provides a basis (foundational understanding), and must be experienced (lived practice). All three elements are essential for consciousness transformation from heated to silent, from ignorance to Ab Neter recognition.

4. Transpersonal Psychology Research Validation

Contemporary empirical research increasingly validates the consciousness framework that these Prologue verses establish, particularly the teaching about unconscious patterns obscuring deeper awareness levels and the time requirements for sustained transformation. Neuroscience studies using functional magnetic resonance imaging (fMRI) demonstrate that contemplative practices aimed at cultivating mental stillness produce measurable changes in brain structure and function that correlate directly with the purification mechanics Amenemopet describes.

Research by Hölzel and colleagues (2011) documented that eight weeks of mindfulness meditation practice increased gray matter density in brain regions associated with learning, memory, and emotional regulation while decreasing gray matter density in the amygdala associated with stress and anxiety responses [1]. This empirically validates that systematic practices can modify the neural correlates of reactive patterns, consistent with the teaching about thinning aryu density through purification. The structural brain changes occurred within a relatively brief timeframe, demonstrating that purification begins producing measurable effects early in practice, though more extensive transformation requires longer timelines.

Studies on the temporal course of meditation-induced transformation provide crucial validation for [verse 9's] teaching that purification occurs gradually through sustained practice rather than instant enlightenment. Tang, Hölzel, and Posner (2016) conducted systematic review demonstrating that 8-week Mindfulness Based Stress Reduction (MBSR) produces measurable changes in prefrontal cortex, cingulate cortex, insula, and hippocampus—brain regions controlling attention, emotional regulation, and memory—similar to changes observed in traditional long-term meditation practitioners [2]. The research indicates that initial neuroplastic changes supporting aryu purification can begin within weeks of consistent practice, while more profound transformations require extended timelines. 8-week contemporary mindfulness programs produce measurable benefits at the mental functioning level that support psychological well-being, though these programs typically do not aim at or facilitate the deeper mind/personality transformation Amenemopet prescribes.

Nguyen and colleagues (2022) investigated sustained effects of 8-week MBSR intervention on college students' stress and brain activity, finding that the practice group showed 33% reduction in stress scores and nearly 40% reduction in depression, anxiety, and stress subscales compared to controls [3]. Critically, the study documented that these effects were maintained at 2-month follow-up and actually strengthened over time as participants continued practice. This empirically confirms that purification effects accumulate and stabilize with sustained application rather than dissipating when practice ceases, consistent with the teaching that wisdom absorption creates lasting modifications in consciousness architecture rather than temporary states.

Research on habit formation timelines validates the extended practice requirements implicit in Amenemopet's framework. Lally and colleagues (2010) conducted longitudinal study demonstrating that habit formation for new behaviors required an average of 66 days (range 18-254 days) depending on behavioral complexity, with simple behaviors requiring less time than complex routines [4]. This empirically confirms that establishing new patterns—whether behavioral or consciousness-based—requires sustained repetition over extended periods. The considerable variation in timelines (18-254 days for basic habits) suggests that purification of dense aryu patterns accumulated over decades would require correspondingly longer timelines, supporting the teaching about patient, gradual thinning rather than instant transformation.

Motor skill consolidation research provides additional validation for extended practice timelines. Dayan and Cohen (2011) demonstrated through neuroimaging studies that motor skill consolidation requires multiple practice sessions over weeks to months for lasting neural changes to stabilize [5]. Romano, Howard, and Howard (2010) documented that procedural skills practiced consistently showed retention after one full year, confirming that extended practice creates durable learning rather than temporary acquisition [6]. These findings validate the principle that consciousness transformation—vastly more complex than motor skills—would require correspondingly extensive timelines for stable integration, consistent with the teaching that aryu purification unfolds gradually through sustained practice.

Studies on implicit memory and unconscious conditioning validate the teaching about aryu stored in the ab (unconscious) influencing present behavior without conscious awareness. Schacter (1987) demonstrated through experimental paradigms that prior experiences create unconscious impressions that influence current perception and behavior even when individuals have no conscious recollection of those experiences [7]. This empirically confirms that the mind operates influenced by stored patterns from past experiences—precisely what the aryu concept describes—and that these patterns can function outside conscious awareness, consistent with the teaching about aryu occupying presence-of-mind awareness and blotting out Ab Neter perception.

Research distinguishing between state changes and trait changes provides crucial validation for the progression from temporary shifts to stable transformation. Khoury and colleagues (2024) examined MBSR effects at 3 months, 1 year, and 3 years post-completion, finding that benefits varied across timepoints but demonstrated lasting impact when practice continued [8]. The longitudinal design revealed that initial state changes (temporary shifts during and immediately after practice) gradually stabilized into trait changes (permanent modifications in baseline consciousness) only with continued application over years. This empirically validates [verse 9's] distinction between temporary aryu suppression and actual aryu thinning that reveals Ab Neter awareness—a transformation requiring extended timelines rather than brief interventions.

Research on emotional regulation and reactivity patterns validates the distinction between reactive (heated) and non-reactive (silent) consciousness states. Gross and John (2003) conducted studies demonstrating that individuals who habitually suppress emotions experience greater physiological stress responses and poorer interpersonal outcomes compared to those who practice cognitive reappraisal and acceptance [9]. This empirically supports the teaching that reactive patterns (aryu-driven heated mind and feelings) produce measurable negative outcomes while non-reactive awareness (silent mind and feelings) supports well-being. The research framework distinguishes between suppression (forcing patterns underground, maintaining aryu density) and reappraisal (changing relationship to patterns, enabling aryu thinning), paralleling the teaching about purification removing obstruction rather than forcefully controlling reactions.

Neuroscience research on default mode network activity validates the teaching about ego-based self-referential processing obscuring deeper awareness. Studies by Brewer and colleagues (2011) using fMRI demonstrated that experienced meditators show decreased activity in default mode network regions associated with self-referential processing and mind-wandering during meditation practice [10]. This empirically confirms that contemplative practices can reduce the neural activity associated with egoic self-focus, consistent with the teaching about purification revealing awareness beyond ego-personality. The decreased default mode activity correlates with reduced aryu-driven thinking patterns that maintain the sense of separate individual identity preventing Ab Neter recognition.

Studies examining long-term meditators provide validation for the profound transformations possible through extensive practice. Lutz and colleagues (2004) documented that Buddhist practitioners with 10,000 to 50,000 hours of lifetime practice demonstrated unprecedented gamma-band brain oscillations and sustained changes in baseline brain states even outside formal meditation [11]. The research revealed that extensive practice transforms baseline consciousness itself rather than merely producing temporary states during meditation sessions—the practitioners' statement that "the goal of meditation practice is to transform the baseline state and to diminish the distinction between formal meditation practice and everyday life" directly parallels [verse 9's] teaching about Ab Neter awareness becoming the stable foundation of consciousness rather than occasional glimpses.

Research establishing benchmarks for long-term meditator status provides empirical framework for understanding transformation timelines. Sacchet and colleagues (2025) conducted comprehensive literature review establishing 1,500+ hours (approximately 1 hour daily for 5 years) as benchmark for "long-term meditator" classification, reflecting significant neurocognitive and behavioral changes distinct from shorter-term practitioners [12]. The review emphasizes that sustainable transformations unfold "through a natural progression from transient cognitive states to persistent cognitive traits, largely dependent on the practitioner's expertise," validating the teaching about gradual aryu thinning revealing stable Ab Neter awareness rather than acquiring temporary special states.

Comparative studies examining practitioners at different experience levels validate the progressive nature of transformation. Kral and colleagues (2018) compared over 150 participants across non-meditators, new meditators (8-week training), and long-term meditators (thousands of hours lifetime practice), documenting that some changes occur relatively quickly while others require extensive practice [13]. Both new and long-term meditators showed reduced amygdala activity to positive emotional stimuli compared to non-meditators, but long-term practitioners showed significantly stronger reductions to negative stimuli—changes requiring years of sustained practice. This empirically validates that initial purification effects (thinning surface-level aryu) occur within weeks to months, while deeper purification (revealing stable Ab Neter awareness) requires years of consistent application.

Goldin and Gross (2010) examined MBSR effects specifically on emotion regulation in individuals with social anxiety disorder, finding post-training improvements in anxiety and depression symptoms accompanied by decreased negative emotion experience, reduced amygdala activity, and increased activity in brain regions controlling attention deployment [14]. The neural changes persisted beyond the 8-week training period, demonstrating that systematic practice creates lasting modifications in emotional reactivity patterns. This validates the teaching that purification of specific aryu patterns (in this case, anxiety-related feeling memories) occurs through practices that modify the neural substrates maintaining those patterns, enabling the mind to operate with less reactive compulsion.

Research on self-transcendent experiences validates the teaching about consciousness recognizing itself beyond separate individual identity. Yaden et al. (2017) documented consistent reports of decreased self-salience and temporary dissolution of subject-object boundaries [15], confirming that consciousness can experience itself beyond ordinary egoic awareness. The temporary nature of most such experiences validates the distinction between glimpses of Ab Neter through momentary aryu quieting versus stable awareness through sustained purification.

The concept of purpose in life researched through longitudinal studies validates [verse 7's] teaching about organizing "the paths that their life will tread." Boyle and colleagues (2009) followed over 1,200 community-dwelling older persons for five years and found that individuals with greater life purpose showed significantly lower mortality risk even after controlling for other psychological factors and health conditions [16]. This empirically confirms that life organization according to deeper principles produces tangible well-being benefits, supporting the teaching about wisdom-guided life organization arising from decreasing aryu density and increasing Ab Neter communion rather than from aryu-driven reactive patterns.

Studies on intrinsic versus extrinsic motivation provide scientific validation for the distinction between aryu-driven and wisdom-guided consciousness. Self-determination theory research by Deci and Ryan (2000) demonstrates through multiple experimental studies that individuals whose goals arise from authentic internal values experience significantly greater psychological well-being, persistence, and life satisfaction compared to those motivated by external rewards or compulsions [17]. This empirically validates the teaching that the mind operating from deeper authentic levels (approaching Ab Neter awareness) produces greater fulfillment than the mind operating from surface reactive patterns (aryu-driven heated state). The research framework distinguishing intrinsic motivation (arising from core values) from extrinsic motivation (driven by external pressures) parallels the teaching about actions arising from Ab Neter communion versus aryu compulsion.

Research on meditation and contemplative practices validates the possibility of accessing deeper consciousness levels through systematic purification. Goyal and colleagues (2014) conducted systematic review and meta-analysis of 47 randomized controlled trials with 3,515 participants, finding that meditation programs produced moderate evidence of improved anxiety, depression, and pain outcomes [18]. These findings support the teaching that systematic practices aimed at quieting reactive patterns enable access to consciousness states associated with greater well-being, consistent with the path of purification revealing deeper awareness levels. The moderate rather than dramatic effect sizes validate realistic expectations about gradual transformation rather than miraculous instant healing.

Longitudinal studies on expertise development validate [verse 1's] teaching that wisdom must be "experienced in life" rather than merely studied intellectually. Ericsson and colleagues (1993) demonstrated through extensive research across multiple domains that expertise requires approximately 10,000 hours of deliberate practice integrating theoretical knowledge with experiential application [19]. Subsequent research by Ericsson and Harwell (2019) clarified that the 10,000-hour figure represents an average that varies substantially by domain (some skills approximately 5,000 hours, complex expertise 20,000-30,000 hours) and that quality of practice matters more than quantity—specifically "deliberate practice" (individualized, goal-directed, expert-guided) versus generic repetition [20]. This empirically confirms that transformation requires sustained practical engagement rather than conceptual understanding alone, supporting the teaching that purification occurs through lived application of wisdom principles rather than intellectual study. The emphasis on deliberate practice quality parallels [verse 2's] teaching about "precise teachings...understood exactly, with precision" producing results.

The convergence of findings across habit formation research (66+ days for basic behavioral changes), motor skill consolidation studies (weeks to months for stable learning), and meditation transformation research (8 weeks for initial changes, 1,500+ hours for trait changes, 10,000+ hours for profound baseline shifts) provides comprehensive empirical validation for the extended timelines implicit in Amenemopet's purification framework. The research demonstrates that consciousness transformation follows the same principles governing all human learning and development: sustained, quality practice over extended periods produces gradual neuroplastic changes that eventually stabilize as permanent traits. This scientific validation supports realistic expectations about the purification path—measurable benefits within weeks, consolidation over months, trait changes emerging over years, and profound transformation requiring decades of sustained practice—rather than expectations of instant enlightenment or rapid acquisition of Ab Neter awareness.

5. Spiritual Implications for Aspirants

PART A: PASTORAL CONCERNS IN MODERN CONTEXT

These Prologue verses reveal profound challenges for those seeking to thin aryu density and reveal Ab Neter awareness while navigating modern society [21, 22]. The primary concern emerges from the teaching that worldly affairs must be "handled with this wisdom philosophy" [verse 9] before the inner sanctuary becomes accessible—yet modern culture systematically cultivates aryu density while providing virtually no support for purification [21].

Consider the modern spiritual seeker who first encounters these teachings at the age of thirty-five after decades immersed in consumer culture. This person's ab (unconscious mind) contains extraordinarily dense layers of aryu from constant exposure to advertising designed to cultivate desire, social media promoting comparison and competition, workplace environments rewarding aggressive self-promotion, and entertainment glorifying heated emotional expression [21, 22]. These aryu don't just influence thinking—they "occupy the presence-of-mind awareness, so densely as to influence the conscious reality awareness (thinking and feeling) of a person and blot out the awareness of the soul level divine presence" [21]. The person experiences the self as a body-mind complex struggling for survival and fulfillment, completely unaware that their very consciousness is sustained by Ab Neter.

The density of modern aryu accumulation creates particular challenge. Previous generations might accumulate aryu primarily through direct life experiences—family dynamics, work situations, personal relationships. Modern individuals accumulate aryu through thousands of hours of media consumption: television programming that normalizes heated mind and feelings, social media that trains reactive emotional patterns, video games that reinforce competitive aggression, news that cultivates anxiety and fear. By the age of thirty-five, someone might have accumulated aryu from witnessing 50,000+ hours of heated behavior patterns presented as normal or desirable, creating extraordinarily dense obstruction to Ab Neter awareness.

When such a person attempts to cultivate silence—the foundational purification practice—the aryu density creates overwhelming resistance. Sitting quietly triggers intense restlessness as aryu accustomed to constant stimulation rebel against stillness. The mind floods with compulsive thoughts as aryu-driven patterns assert themselves. Anxiety arises as aryu that equate worth with productivity interpret silence as "wasting time." The person may abandon practice entirely, concluding spiritual development is impossible, unaware they're encountering the very aryu density that requires patient, systematic thinning to reveal the Ab Neter foundation already sustaining their consciousness.

The scarcity of authentic wisdom teaching creates another significant concern. [Verse 2] emphasizes "precise teachings...understood exactly, with precision," yet the modern spiritual marketplace offers mostly imprecise adaptations. Aspirants encounter meditation taught as a stress-reduction technique (ignoring its function in thinning aryu density), ethics presented as optional lifestyle choice (rather than necessary purification), and silence promoted as a relaxation method (missing its purpose in revealing Ab Neter). These diluted teachings may reduce stress without actually thinning aryu density or revealing the divine foundation, leaving practitioners believing they're making spiritual progress while remaining trapped in aryu-obscured mind and feelings.

Most critically, without proper teaching, practitioners may approach spiritual practice as acquiring something absent rather than removing obstruction, reinforcing the egoic striving that prevents Ab Neter awareness.

PART B: METHODS FOR TRANSFORMATION

Despite these formidable challenges, Amenemopet provides systematic guidance for thinning aryu density to reveal Ab Neter awareness [21, 22]. The foundational understanding must be clear: purification doesn't create something new but removes obstruction to reveal what already sustains consciousness [21]. Ab Neter is "a person's portion of Divine consciousness that sustains their capacity of conscious awareness of their life" [21]—meaning that every moment of awareness, even in ignorance, is sustained by this divine foundation. The spiritual path removes the aryu density that "blot out the awareness of the soul level divine presence" [21]. Ab Neter—the individualized presence of Neberdjer that sustains the very capacity for conscious awareness.

Begin with regular study of the wisdom teachings themselves, as [verse 2] emphasizes "precise teachings...understood exactly, with precision cause a person to have well-being while living on earth" [21]. Set aside dedicated time daily—even fifteen minutes—for careful reading of the hieroglyphic translations, contemplating their meanings, seeking to understand both the problem (aryu density blotting out Ab Neter awareness) and the solution (purification revealing what's already present) [21, 22]. Since Amenemopet emphasizes precision, the reverse application indicates: avoid superficial, rushed, or distorted comprehension. Patient, precise study forms the foundation for purification work.

For cultivating silence—the primary practice for thinning aryu density—implement systematic practice despite intense resistance [21, 22]. Begin with brief periods (5-10 minutes) of simply sitting quietly, understanding that what you'll encounter is the aryu density requiring purification [21]. When the mind floods with compulsive thoughts (aryu-driven patterns), recognize this as the obstruction revealing itself. Don't fight the thoughts or judge yourself as failing; simply observe: "These are the aryu patterns occupying my presence-of-mind awareness. This is the density blotting out Ab Neter awareness. Patient practice will thin this obstruction" [21, 22].

Consider the practical example of someone whose ab contains dense aryu from decades of media consumption. When attempting the practice of silence, the mind immediately floods with fragmented thoughts, images, desires—all aryu expressing themselves as they occupy presence-of-mind awareness [21]. Rather than judging this as personal failure, understand: "This density is precisely what requires thinning. The Ab Neter sustaining my consciousness right now is hidden beneath this aryu layer. Each session of patient observation begins thinning the obstruction" [21, 22]. Over weeks and months of consistent practice, the aryu density gradually decreases. The compulsive mental activity settles not because you're forcing it quiet but because the aryu patterns are dissolving, revealing the silent Ab Neter foundation that was always present beneath [21].

Since [verse 9] teaches that worldly affairs must be "handled with this wisdom philosophy" before "The mind (heart) of the personality is to gain presence-of-mind about a sanctuary that can be entered," understand that handling worldly affairs means applying purification practices to daily circumstances. When facing workplace conflict, practice silent observation of reactive impulses before responding (thinning aryu that create heated reactions). When managing finances, make decisions according to wisdom principles rather than aryu-driven desire (not reinforcing aryu patterns). When interacting with difficult family members, practice restraint from heated emotional reactions (weakening aryu-based reactivity patterns).

The purification process requires patience with gradual development. Aryu accumulated over decades of life create dense obstruction that thins slowly through consistent practice [21, 22]. Someone new to practice should expect months or years of systematic application before aryu density decreases sufficiently for regular Ab Neter awareness [21]. [Verse 9's] teaching that the sanctuary "can be entered once the worldly affairs are handled with this wisdom philosophy" indicates progressive achievement as aryu density gradually thins, not instant transformation [21].

Realistic expectations prevent discouragement. Initial practices may seem to produce no results because aryu density remains thick [21, 22]. Continue patient practice understanding that each session contributes to thinning the obstruction even when immediate results aren't apparent. Over months, subtle shifts occur—slightly less compulsive thinking, slightly less reactive emotion, slightly more inner quiet. These indicate aryu density decreasing [21]. Over years, more substantial shifts—periods of genuine silence, moments of Ab Neter awareness breaking through the thinning obstruction, decreasing compulsion from previously overwhelming desires [21, 22].

The ultimate transformation occurs when aryu density thins sufficiently that "The Ab Neter awareness is beyond the ego-personality-awareness, the superficial mind. But it is revealed when there is presence-of-mind about its existence" [21]. At this stage, "The conscious awareness of the soul essence of consciousness (Ab Neter) would render the egoic impulses of aryu powerless" [21]. Why? Because consciousness now recognizes itself as the divine foundation rather than separate vulnerable entity [21, 22]. The aryu patterns remain stored in the ab, but they no longer compel action because consciousness no longer operates from the egoic perspective those aryu require [21]. Someone aware of the self as Ab Neter—divine, complete, unified with Creation—cannot simultaneously feel incomplete, separate, or driven to compete for fulfillment [21]. The egoic perspective dissolves in Ab Neter awareness, rendering aryu patterns powerless even though they remain present [21, 22].

Conclusion: The Path Forward and Measures of Spiritual Progress

The Prologue establishes the dual foundation upon which all subsequent teachings rest: the development of vital-life-fire (udja) that produces spiritual purity and well-being while living on earth [verse 2], and the discovery of the kara—the divine sanctuary where Ab Neter resides within every person [verse 9]. These interconnected goals reveal that authentic spiritual life requires both skillful navigation of worldly circumstances through wisdom and progressive thinning of aryu density that obscures divine awareness.

The chapters that follow provide systematic guidance for achieving these objectives, with specific criteria by which aspirants may assess genuine progress: calmness of mind that indicates aryu patterns losing their compelling force; growing dispassion and detachment reflecting decreasing identification with temporary phenomena; deepening capacity for introspection that reveals the operations of hat and ab; right emotional balance demonstrating vital-life-fire purifying reactive patterns; and the establishment of what the teaching calls control of mind and senses—not forceful suppression but the natural condition where mind and senses operate under the guidance of wisdom rather than being driven by aryu-generated impulses.

These measures represent not arbitrary standards but observable indicators that the mind is transforming from heated (aryu-dominated) to silent (wisdom-guided) functioning, progressively revealing the Ab Neter foundation that has always sustained awareness yet remained hidden beneath accumulated karmic patterns. The wisdom to be understood here encompasses recognition that spiritual progress manifests through these tangible shifts in daily experience rather than dramatic visions or temporary altered states, providing reliable guidance for the patient work of consciousness purification that Amenemopet's teaching facilitates.

=======

Amenemopet's Divine Nomenclature System: The Three-Part Divine Nomenclature in Amenemopet's Wisdom Teachings

Introduction to the Philosophical Framework

Sage Amenemopet's approach to divine consciousness reflects a sophisticated theological architecture that bridges the practical needs of spiritual development with the ultimate reality of absolute divine essence. His strategic use of divine nomenclature reveals three distinct but interconnected levels of divine relationship, each serving specific pedagogical and transformational purposes within the comprehensive journey from worldly agitation to divine recognition.

This three-part framework represents not arbitrary categories but the natural progression of mind/personality development as the mind learns to transcend its identification with limited phenomena and discover its essential nature as an expression of universal divine awareness. The wisdom tradition recognizes that effective spiritual instruction must accommodate different levels of human understanding while maintaining fidelity to the ultimate truth of non-dual divine consciousness.

The Theological Architecture

1. Personal (Soul Level)

- **Ab Neter** - the divine soul sustaining individual consciousness
- **"Creator-Spirit that is within"** - the indwelling divine presence accessible through inner contemplation **[Chapter 5, Verse 9]**

2. Tutelary (Named Forms for Mental Reference and Devotion)

Divine Forms Specifically Mentioned by Amenemopet:

- **Ra** (Creator-Spirit) - the primary object of temple devotion and spiritual relationship **[Chapter 5, Verse 8]**
- **Pa Neter** (The Divine [i.e. The God, can refer to a high divinity such as Ra, Asar, Amun, Ptah]) - generic reference to the divine principle henotheistic divinity who presides over Creation. **[Chapter 4, Verse 1; Chapter 5, Verse 7; Chapter 6B, Verse 19]**

3. Universal (Abstract/All-Encompassing Essence)

- **Neberdjer** (Lord of utmost limits) - the absolute, all-encompassing divine consciousness **[Chapter 6B, Verse 14]**

The Philosophical Understanding

Progressive Function: This framework serves as a systematic ladder of spiritual development where each level prepares consciousness for the next. The personal level establishes the foundation of divine relationship within individual experience. The tutelary level provides concrete objects for mental cultivation and devotional practice. The universal level represents the ultimate realization that transcends all forms while encompassing them.

Practical Pedagogy: Amenemopet's remarkable restraint in naming specific deities reveals profound pedagogical wisdom. Rather than overwhelming students with complex mythological systems, he focuses primarily on **Ra** as the central tutelary form while emphasizing the ultimate goal of **Neberdjer** recognition. This streamlined approach prevents the mind from becoming distracted by theological complexity while maintaining the essential structure needed for systematic spiritual development.

Consciousness Architecture: Each level corresponds to different aspects of mind/personality development. Personal forms address the individual's need for divine connection and inner spiritual relationship. Tutelary forms provide the mind with objects suitable for contemplation, worship, and transformational relationship. Universal essence represents the final recognition that consciousness itself, when freed from the limitations of aryu obstruction, discovers its nature as identical with the all-encompassing divine reality that underlies and sustains all apparent forms and experiences.

This framework demonstrates how authentic wisdom teaching accommodates the progressive needs of spiritual development while maintaining unwavering focus on the ultimate goal of divine realization.

KEY NUANCES REVEALED IN THE PROLOGUE:

1. The Ab has DUAL nature:

- Ab = unconscious mind that stores aryu (feeling memories)
- Ab Neter = Divine soul/spark residing WITHIN the ab/kara

2. The mechanism of ignorance clarified:

- Aryu don't just "influence" consciousness - they actively **"blot out"** awareness of Ab Neter
- Aryu **"occupy the presence-of-mind awareness"** so densely that only body/mind/sensations remain in awareness
- Thc Divine (Ab Neter) is RIGHT THERE in the unconscious, but hidden by aryu density

3. Ab Neter as sustaining principle:

- Ab Neter = "person's portion of Divine consciousness that sustains their capacity of conscious awareness"
- This means Ab Neter is what makes consciousness itself possible
- Without Ab Neter, there would be no conscious awareness at all

4. Kara = sanctuary/location WHERE Ab Neter resides:

- Not a separate thing, but the "divine shrine" within the ab where Ab Neter dwells
- The purification path reveals what's already present, doesn't create access to something distant

VISUAL TEACHING: THE PRACTICE OF DIVINE SELF-RECOGNITION—UNDERSTANDING THE ABU SIMBEL TEMPLE PANEL

EXPLANATION OF THE ABU SIMBEL TEMPLE PANEL IMAGE

Cover Image and Manuscript Context

THE SACRED PRACTICE OF WORSHIPPING THE HIGHER SELF: UNDERSTANDING THE ABU SIMBEL PANEL

The image featured on the cover of this manuscript originates from a panel at the Temple of Amun-Ra at Abu Simbel, one of Ancient Egypt's most profound expressions of non-dual mysticism. This relief depicts Pharaoh Ramses II in a posture of humble devotion—kneeling before a seated figure that bears his own royal name and insignia, yet is accorded a distinctly higher spiritual status than his ordinary human identity.

This iconographic teaching represents one of the most direct visual expressions of what the Ancient Egyptian sages called "worshipping oneself as Divine"—a practice that forms the cornerstone of the spiritual psychology teachings presented in the Instructions of Sage Amenemopet and throughout the Neterian wisdom tradition.

This iconography is depicting something both humbling and elevating for contemplation—not worship of a separate tutelary divinity as being divine, but recognition of one's own self as having a divine being that transcends the temporal ego-personality. Indeed, most forms of worship create a relationship wherein the worshipper experiences themselves as separate, terrestrial, and limited while regarding the divine as "other"—an entity apart, existing in a different state, a divine condition to which one aspires somehow. The Abu Simbel panel presents a fundamentally different teaching: the personality itself innately possesses divine nature. This aligns with the soul-aware-witness concept from the Book of Enlightenment Chapter 26 and Amenemopet's teaching of the *Ab Neter* within the personality. Nevertheless, as ordinary human develops, this divine nature becomes subsumed, hidden beneath the accumulated density of ego *aryu*—thus requiring the very practices of recognition and purification that the ancient sages prescribed.

THE THEOLOGICAL SIGNIFICANCE: DUAL LEVELS OF IDENTITY

The panel illustrates a significant metaphysical principle: that within every human being exist two distinct levels of identity—the temporal personality operating through mind, body, and ego (the kneeling Ramses), and the eternal divine consciousness that sustains all mental operations and physical existence (the seated, glorified Ramses). The ordinary human self makes offerings and devotions to its own higher nature, acknowledging through this sacred gesture that the limited ego-personality is not the ultimate truth of existence. This is both humbling—recognizing the ego's limitations and dependence on a higher reality—and elevating—discovering that this higher reality is not separate from oneself but constitutes one's innermost divine nature.

This visual teaching directly corresponds to the framework of consciousness architecture explored throughout this manuscript. The kneeling figure represents what Amenemopet's teachings identify as the *hat* (conscious awareness) and *ka* (personality) operating through accumulated *aryu* (karmic impressions) in the *ab* (unconscious mind). The seated, elevated figure represents the Soul-Aware-Witness-Self, the individuated expression of *Ab Neter*—the divine soul, the "Foundation of individual consciousness" that is each person's "portion of Divine consciousness" sustaining their capacity for awareness itself.

UNDERSTANDING AB NETER DISCOVERY THROUGH DEVOTIONAL RECOGNITION

The Abu Simbel panel provides key insight into the mechanics of spiritual transformation. When the ordinary *hat* (represented by the kneeling Ramses) directs its attention, reverence, and offerings toward its own divine nature (represented by the seated, glorified Ramses), this act creates what may be understood as a "turning inward" of attention—from identification with temporal personality toward recognition of the eternal consciousness that witnesses and illumines all mental operations.

Consider how this visual teaching addresses the fundamental human psychology problem identified in Amenemopet's Prologue: the condition of ignorance wherein the *hat* operates completely absorbed in *aryu*-driven mental activity without any recognition of or communion with the *Ab Neter* residing in the *kara* (divine sanctuary) deep within the *ab*. The Abu Simbel panel depicts the solution—the deliberate practice of acknowledging, honoring, and "worshipping" the higher divine aspect of one's own being, thereby creating the conditions for *Ab Neter* discovery.

The practice illustrated here is not ego-inflation or narcissistic self-worship, as might be misunderstood through modern psychological frameworks unfamiliar with non-dual teachings. Rather, it represents the recognition that consciousness itself is sacred; that one's essential nature is divine consciousness (*Neberdjer/Ab Neter*); and that the ordinary personality must acknowledge its subordinate relationship to this higher reality. The kneeling posture symbolizes the ego's necessary surrender and humility before the transcendent truth of its own divine source. This practice differs fundamentally from conventional religious worship that reinforces the perception of separation between terrestrial worshipper and transcendent divinity. The Abu Simbel teaching reveals that what appears as "other" or "separate" divinity is actually one's own innermost nature—presently obscured by ego *aryu* but never absent, never truly separate from the personality that seeks it.

THE ICONOGRAPHIC FUNCTION: PROJECTING INNER DIVINITY AS OBJECT OF CONTEMPLATION

Consider the visual representation of ego self-worship. The following mock image (not real) was created to show the difference between ego self-worship and the worship of one's higher self being depicted at Abu Simbel.

This mock image is what might have been depicted if the objective was to depict worship of the ego personality—worship of the human person as he is in his ordinary worldly state. This is not what was done at Abu Simbel; the image clearly depicts the worldly personality worshipping a higher level of identity than the lower worldly self. In the image at at Abu Simbel the kneeling figure does not yet worship this higher aspect as being fully divine; those images depicting complete divine realization are presented elsewhere in the temple and are recorded in the book *Egyptian Book of the Dead Hieroglyph Translations Using the Trilinear Method Volume 5: Featuring Temple of Amun-Ra at Abu Simbel* (Ashby, 2020) [23].

This panel from Abu Simbel can be thought of as an iconographical (visual presentation) projection of one's inner divinity as an object for one's attention and veneration—a concrete presentation of what would otherwise be an abstract, imaginary idea, which though true is hard to visualize within oneself by oneself, at least in the beginning of spiritual practice. The Ancient Egyptian priests and priestesses understood the pedagogical necessity of externalizing spiritual realities so they could be contemplated, studied, and gradually internalized.

Like other Ancient Egyptian temple panels, this panel is meant to be communed with—we can envision Ramses standing in front of this very panel when he was alive, contemplating the image of his kneeling self, worshipping his glorified divine self. Nevertheless, this is a presentation of a timeless principle and not just for Ramses. We can substitute ourselves in the position of Ramses and experience the same ideal. The panel becomes a mirror reflecting the universal spiritual truth: every human being possesses both the temporal personality that kneels and the eternal divine consciousness that sits enthroned—both existing simultaneously within the same person, awaiting recognition and reunion.

This iconographic method serves the aspirant who struggles to conceptualize the *Ab Neter* within. By providing a visual, external representation of the internal spiritual reality, the temple panel functions as what may be termed a "contemplative anchor"—allowing the mind to focus on a concrete image while gradually developing the capacity to recognize that same divine presence within. Over time, through repeated contemplation of such images combined with the ethical and meditative practices taught in the wisdom texts, the need for external projection diminishes as direct inner recognition strengthens.

BA-SAU: THE SOUL-AWARE-WITNESS DEPICTED IN THE ABU SIMBEL TEMPLE

THE AWARENESS LEVEL ILLUSTRATED BY THE DEVOTIONAL PRACTICE

The devotional practice depicted in the Abu Simbel panel—the kneeling Ramses worshipping his glorified divine self—illustrates the development of a specific level of awareness that the Ancient Egyptian sages understood with remarkable precision. This awareness level, described in Chapter 26 of the Ancient Egyptian Book of Enlightenment, represents a transitional developmental stage between ordinary ego identification and complete realization of Ab Neter. Indeed, the Temple of Amun-Ra at Abu Simbel depicts this very awareness state—what I term Ba-sau, the Soul-Aware-Witness.

IMPORTANT NOTE: Ba-sau is a term I have coined to name the level of awareness described in the Book of Enlightenment Chapter 26, which describes this state but does not name it explicitly. This term is now being applied to this discussion relating to Amenemopet's framework, as it provides essential understanding of the mind transformation process that Amenemopet's teachings facilitate.

The Ba-sau level of awareness represents the personality that has achieved sufficient purification that it recognizes itself as separate from—though not yet fully realized as—the divine consciousness (Ab Neter) that sustains its existence. Consider how this relates to the Abu Simbel iconography: the kneeling Ramses has not yet merged with the seated, glorified Ramses, yet he clearly recognizes that higher divine reality as his true nature and directs his devotion accordingly. This is precisely the Ba-sau awareness—beyond ego conditioning where aryu veils and distorts identity into mind-body notions, approaching divine recognition through partial unveiling, yet not complete realization where the veil is fully removed.

UNDERSTANDING THE CONSCIOUSNESS ARCHITECTURE: A CONCEPTUAL FRAMEWORK

To comprehend how Ba-sau functions within the complete consciousness architecture that Amenemopet's teachings address, consider the following visual framework. This graphic is not to be thought of as a depiction of a real physical appearance of the structure of the personality but to convey the idea of how the Soul-Aware-Witness is described in Chapter 26 of the Ancient Egyptian Book of Enlightenment and how it integrates into Amenemopet's framework:

KEMETIC SELF-AWARENESS ARCHITECTURE

Two Pathways of Self-identification from Ab Neter: Veiling versus Partial Unveiling

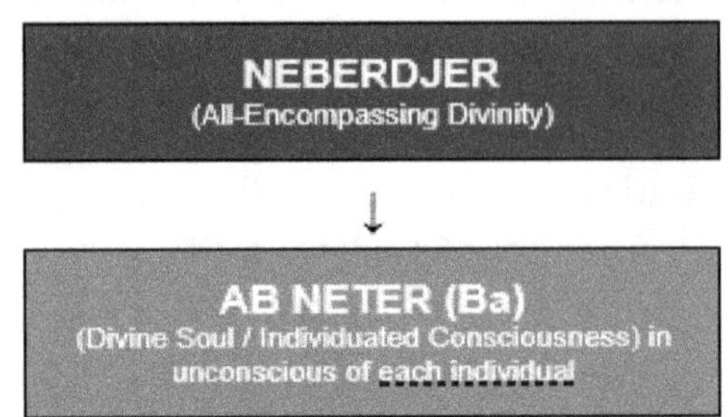

Two Pathways that Ab Neter Self-identity/Self-awareness can operate though

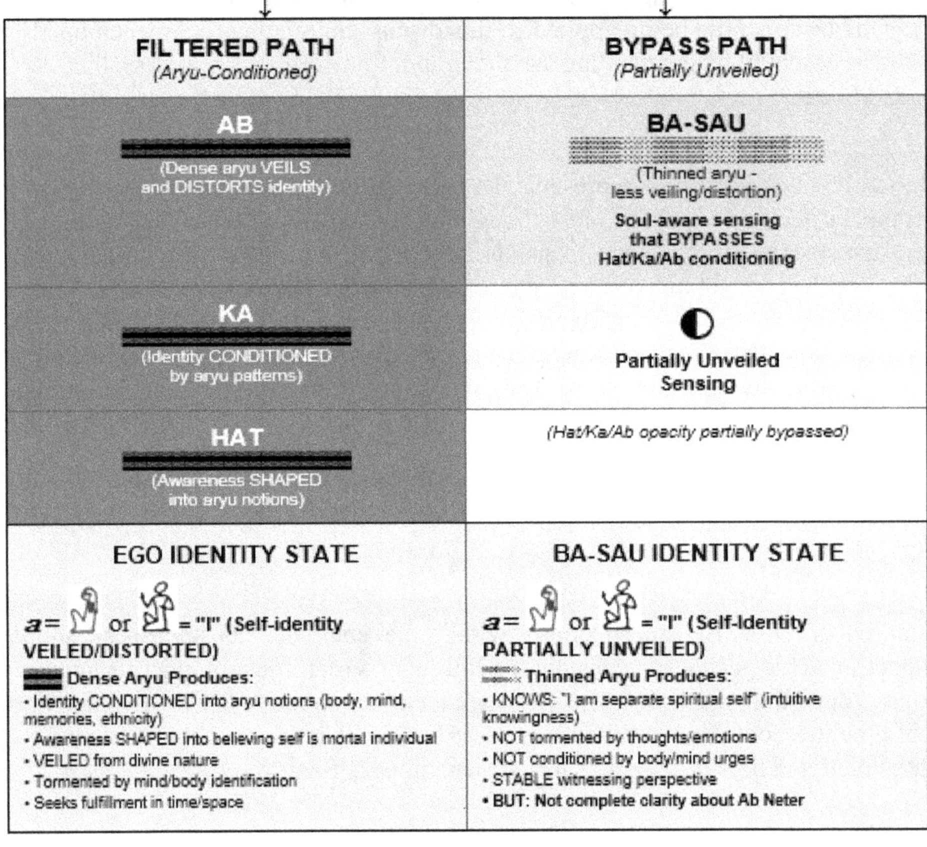

[Further purification from Ba-sau leads to...]

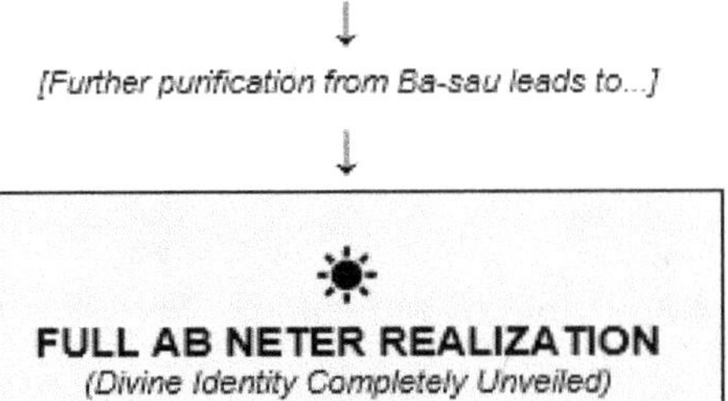

VISUAL KEY:

= Dense aryu that VEILS, DISTORTS, and CONDITIONS identity awareness into aryu-based notions of separate mortal selfhood
= Thinned aryu - partial veiling/distortion allowing intuitive sensing of spiritual nature but not yet complete clarity
◐ = Partial unveiling - can sense divine truth through remaining veil but without complete realization
☀ = Fully unveiled - identity awareness clear of aryu conditioning, recognizing Ab Neter directly

THE TWO PATHWAYS FOR SELF-IDENTITY FROM AB NETER: VEILING VERSUS PARTIAL UNVEILING

The consciousness architecture diagram reveals a significant teaching: from Ab Neter, identity awareness can operate through two distinct pathways. The first pathway—which characterizes ordinary ego consciousness—flows through the Ab (unconscious mind), Ka (astral body/personality), and Hat (conscious awareness), each layer dense with aryu that progressively veils, distorts, and conditions the identity awareness. This aryu density does not merely block awareness like a wall; rather, it actively shapes identity awareness into the notions contained within the aryu themselves—the belief that "I am this body," "I am these memories," "I am this personal history," "I am this ethnicity," "I am this separate mortal individual."

The second pathway—which characterizes Ba-sau awareness—bypasses this aryu-conditioning process. The thinned aryu allows a direct sensing that circumvents the Hat/Ka/Ab apparatus, creating what may be understood as partially unveiled identity awareness. This Ba-sau sensing knows intuitively "I am separate spiritual self" without that knowing being filtered through and distorted by the dense aryu patterns in the mental apparatus. Nevertheless, this knowing remains partially veiled—clear enough to recognize spiritual nature exists, but not yet complete clarity about what Ab Neter actually is in its fullness.

THE DISTINCTIVE CHARACTERISTICS OF BA-SAU AWARENESS

The wisdom texts reveal that Ba-sau represents an awareness of being separate from mind and body identification—an identity awareness that has not been conditioned and shaped by the aryu in Ab/Ka/Hat into believing itself to be merely a mortal body-mind entity. This awareness is not controlled or made to suffer by mental and bodily phenomena. Suffering means the mind and its delusions, desires that lead one into worldly predicaments, entanglements and frustrations. Additionally, it is a level of awareness where body urges and sensations cannot lead one to instinctual animal feelings, thoughts and actions that again lead one into worldly predicaments, entanglements and frustrations preventing serenity and divine communion.

The Soul-Aware-Witness has an intuitional awareness about the soul's nature even though it is not a fully matured complete awareness. It is enough awareness—sufficient thinning of the aryu veil—so that the personality sees itself apart from mind and body and is not "tormented by them" (Ancient

Egyptian Book of Enlightenment Chapter 26). So this level of awareness has not completely removed the aryu that veils and conditions identity, but has thinned the aryu sufficiently so that there is a "knowingness" (beyond what can be intellectually proven or explained)—a partially unveiled sensing that recognizes spiritual selfhood exists even if there is not yet complete clarity about what the higher Soul level (Ab Neter/Ba) actually is in its fullness.

This level of knowingness/clarity about one's self-identity bypasses the aryu-conditioning process that operates through Ka and Ab—the process that would normally veil, distort, and shape identity awareness exclusively into mind and body notions. This soul-aware witness level of clarity (perception/insight/sensitivity/feeling/witnessing/awareness) allows the identity of the personality to be emancipated from the aryu-conditioned mind and body identification such that it can no longer be controlled by them. This emancipation allows the personality the capacity to eventually further thin the aryu veil in Ka and Ab so that there is progressively clearer recognition about the Ab Neter, ultimately reaching complete unveiling.

Thus, Ba-sau is an intermediate level of awareness above the Ka and Ab ego-identified individuated level of self-identification (as an individual person identified as an ego personality with worldly references, parents, ethnicity, personal memories, etc.) yet below complete Ab Neter realization. Nevertheless, this intermediate stage proves important for spiritual transformation—providing the internal undeniable proof of higher self-identity and stable witnessing position from which continued purification becomes possible.

THE ROLE OF BA-SAU IN THE ABU SIMBEL DEVOTIONAL PRACTICE

Understanding Ba-sau clarifies the precise spiritual technology illustrated by the Abu Simbel panel. When the aspirant engages in the practice of "worshipping the higher self"—directing attention, reverence, and devotion toward one's own divine nature—this practice specifically cultivates Ba-sau awareness. The kneeling figure represents the hat (conscious awareness) and ka (personality) learning to function from a witnessing perspective rather than from complete identification with aryu-driven mental patterns.

Consider how this operates in practice: As the aspirant repeatedly contemplates the teaching that "I am not merely this body-mind apparatus but possess divine nature," the density of aryu in the ab gradually thins. This thinning of the aryu veil creates what may be understood as progressive "unveiling" for Ba-sau awareness to emerge—the capacity to witness thoughts, feelings, and sensations without being compelled by them, without being tormented by them, without the identity awareness being conditioned and shaped into aryu-based notions, without losing awareness of the soul nature even when difficulties arise.

The Ancient Egyptian priests and priestesses who created the Abu Simbel temple complex understood that such visual teachings serve as hekau (words of power, spiritual technology) for precisely this mind transformation. The image provides both the method (devotional recognition of higher self) and the goal (stable Ba-sau awareness that eventually matures into complete Ab Neter realization).

FROM BA-SAU TO AB NETER: THE COMPLETION OF TRANSFORMATION

The Ba-sau level of awareness, while not yet complete enlightenment, provides the essential foundation from which complete Ab Neter discovery becomes possible. Indeed, once the personality establishes this witnessing perspective—recognizing "I am separate from these mental patterns, these body urges, these feelings"—then the continued practices of ethical living, contemplation, and meditation can proceed from a stable platform rather than from the chaos of complete ego identification.

This explains why Amenemopet's teachings prove so effective for mind transformation. Each behavioral imperative, each wisdom principle, each contemplative instruction works to thin aryu density and strengthen Ba-sau awareness. The "silent" personality that Amenemopet describes extensively throughout his teachings operates precisely from this Ba-sau level—not yet fully enlightened, yet no longer imprisoned by ego patterns, capable of ethical action because body urges no longer compel unethical behavior, capable of wisdom absorption because the mind has achieved sufficient stillness to contemplate deeper truths.

The Abu Simbel panel thus reveals the complete arc of spiritual development: from ordinary ego identification (symbolized by worldly Ramses in his human activities), through Ba-sau awareness (symbolized by kneeling Ramses worshipping his higher nature), to ultimate Ab Neter realization (symbolized by the seated, glorified, eternally perfected divine Ramses). The devotional practice illustrated in the panel specifically cultivates the crucial middle stage—Ba-sau—without which the final stage cannot be achieved.

PRACTICAL APPLICATION FOR THE MODERN ASPIRANT

Understanding Ba-sau provides contemporary aspirants with realistic expectations for spiritual development. The goal is not immediate enlightenment but rather the systematic cultivation of witnessing awareness that gradually stabilizes and deepens. Consider how this understanding transforms spiritual practice:

Rather than becoming frustrated that meditation hasn't yet produced complete Ab Neter realization, the aspirant recognizes that developing Ba-sau awareness represents genuine spiritual progress. The capacity to witness difficult emotions without being overwhelmed by them, to notice body urges without automatically acting on them, to observe egoic thoughts without believing they define ultimate reality—these represent the emergence of Ba-sau awareness.

The Abu Simbel teaching reveals that this witnessing capacity deserves reverence and cultivation. By "worshipping" (directing devoted attention toward) the divine nature within, even before complete realization, the aspirant strengthens Ba-sau awareness incrementally. Over time, through patient practice aligned with Amenemopet's behavioral imperatives and wisdom teachings, this intermediate awareness naturally matures into the direct recognition that consciousness itself is divine—that Ab Neter was never absent but only veiled by aryu density now sufficiently thinned to allow recognition.

Thus the Abu Simbel panel serves the modern aspirant exactly as it served ancient practitioners—as visual confirmation that the spiritual path proceeds through recognizable stages, that intermediate realizations deserve acknowledgment and cultivation, and that the practice of recognizing one's own divine nature (even while that recognition remains incomplete) constitutes the essential method for mind transformation that both the ancient sages and contemporary aspirants require for achieving the dual goals set forth in Amenemopet's Prologue: earthly well-being and divine discovery.

PRACTICAL APPLICATION: FROM VISUAL TEACHING TO LIVING PRACTICE

The Ancient Egyptian priests and priestesses who designed the Abu Simbel temple complex understood that such visual teachings serve as *hekau* (spiritual technology)—powerful consciousness-transforming tools that work on multiple levels simultaneously. For the modern aspirant studying

Amenemopet's psychological wisdom, this image provides both inspiration and instruction for daily spiritual practice.

The devotional gesture depicted in the panel suggests specific practical methods:

Daily Recognition Practice: Upon awakening and before sleep, the aspirant may engage in contemplative recognition that the *hat* is not the ultimate source of its own existence but receives its capacity for awareness from *Ab Neter*—the divine consciousness that is the true identity. This recognition naturally produces the devotional attitude depicted in the Abu Simbel panel.

Offering Mental Activity as Worship: Throughout the day, thoughts, feelings, and actions can be consciously offered to one's higher divine nature rather than claimed by ego as personal possessions or achievements. This practice gradually shifts identity-attachment from temporal personality toward eternal consciousness.

Meditation on Divine Identity: Regular periods of sitting in stillness while contemplating the truth "I am *Ab Neter* consciousness, not merely this body-mind apparatus" creates the same relationship depicted in the image—the temporal self acknowledging and communing with its eternal divine nature.

THE RESULT: LIBERATION THROUGH SELF-KNOWLEDGE

The ultimate purpose of practices illustrated by the Abu Simbel panel is precisely what Amenemopet identifies as the dual goals of spiritual life: achieving well-being while living on earth (Prologue verse 2) and discovering the *kara* where "the Divine resides in every person" (Prologue verse 9). When the *hat* consistently acknowledges, reverences, and attends to its own divine nature, the density of *aryu* gradually thins, allowing *Ab Neter* awareness to shine forth naturally.

This is not creating access to something previously absent but removing the obscuration that prevented recognition of what was always present. The *Ab Neter*—like the glorified, seated Ramses in the panel—has always existed in its transcendent perfection, sustaining the very capacity for awareness through which the ego-personality operates. The spiritual journey involves the ego-personality (kneeling Ramses) learning to recognize, honor, and ultimately merge with its own divine source (seated Ramses).

INTEGRATION WITH THE MANUSCRIPT'S TEACHING FRAMEWORK

Throughout this manuscript's exploration of Amenemopet's verse-by-verse psychological wisdom, the Abu Simbel panel serves as a visual anchor for understanding the relationship between ordinary human mind and divine consciousness. Each behavioral imperative, each practice method, each mind transformation stage described in the commentaries ultimately serves the same purpose depicted in this ancient temple relief: facilitating the ordinary self's recognition of and reunion with its own divine nature. The panel's unique contribution to spiritual understanding lies in its revelation that the personality innately possesses divine nature—a truth that conventional worship often obscures by maintaining the dualistic perception of separate worshipper and worshipped, terrestrial seeker and transcendent sought.

The wisdom to be understood is that the goal of all spiritual-psychological work is not to become something other than what one already is at the deepest level, but to remove the ignorance that prevents recognition of one's eternal divine identity. As the kneeling Ramses makes offerings to the glorified Ramses, so too does the aspirant's personality learn to serve, honor, and ultimately dissolve into the *Ab Neter* consciousness that is its true and eternal Self.

Indeed, this teaching—preserved in stone at Abu Simbel for over three millennia—remains as relevant and transformative today as when first inscribed. It provides modern practitioners of

Amenemopet's wisdom with a powerful visual reminder: every human being contains within themselves both the seeker and the sought, both the worshipper and the worshipped, both the limited personality and the unlimited divine consciousness. The spiritual path consists of nothing more—and nothing less—than learning to recognize this truth and live from its reality.

A Gentle Understanding for the Journey Ahead

Indeed, these teachings offer the most hopeful message possible: the divine presence you seek is not distant or absent but already resides within you as the very foundation of your consciousness. The Ab Neter that sustains your capacity to be aware right now—in this very moment of reading—is the same divine spark that will be revealed through patient practice. Nevertheless, the aryu patterns accumulated over years may seem overwhelming at times, and modern life certainly doesn't make purification easy. Consider the metaphor of sunlight penetrating morning mist: the sun does not force the mist to dissolve through violent effort but simply continues shining, and the mist naturally dissipates through gradual warming. Similarly, approach this work with compassion for yourself, understanding that every moment of silence, every ethical choice, every gentle restraint from heated reaction contributes to thinning the obstruction. The wisdom to be understood recognizes that you're not trying to become divine—you're simply removing what hides the divinity that already sustains your very awareness. This is why the path is both supremely challenging and ultimately accessible: not because you must travel somewhere far away, but because you must patiently clear away what prevents you from recognizing what has never left you. Therefore, trust in the process, be gentle with your struggles, and remember that the same divine consciousness that will be fully revealed through purification is lovingly sustaining you through every step of the journey.

HTP

References

[1] Hölzel, B. K., Carmody, J., Vangel, M., Congleton, C., Yerramsetti, S. M., Gard, T., & Lazar, S. W. (2011). Mindfulness practice leads to increases in regional brain gray matter density. *Psychiatry Research: Neuroimaging, 191*(1), 36-43.

[2] Tang, Y. H., Hölzel, B. K., & Posner, M. I. (2016). 8-week Mindfulness Based Stress Reduction induces brain changes similar to traditional long-term meditation practice – A systematic review. *Psychiatry Research: Neuroimaging, 249*, 57-60.

[3] Nguyen, T. D., Nguyen, T. M., Truong, D. K., Pham, H. T., Pham, V. T., Tran, H. A., ... & Cao, B. T. (2022). Investigating the effect of Mindfulness-Based Stress Reduction on stress level and brain activity of college students. *Neuroscience Informatics, 2*(2), 100050.

[4] Lally, P., van Jaarsveld, C. H. M., Potts, H. W. W., & Wardle, J. (2010). How are habits formed: Modelling habit formation in the real world. *European Journal of Social Psychology, 40*(6), 998-1009.

[5] Dayan, E., & Cohen, L. G. (2011). Neuroplasticity subserving motor skill learning. *Neuron, 72*(3), 443-454.

[6] Romano, J. C., Howard, J. H., & Howard, D. V. (2010). One-year retention of general and sequence-specific skills in a probabilistic, serial reaction time task. *Memory, 18*(4), 427-441.

[7] Schacter, D. L. (1987). Implicit memory: History and current status. *Journal of Experimental Psychology: Learning, Memory, and Cognition, 13*(3), 501-518.

[8] Khoury, B., Knäuper, B., Schuman-Olivier, Z., Barrera, T., Abitbol, R., Lemoult, J., & Dionne, F. (2024). Exploring the sustained impact of the Mindfulness-Based Stress Reduction program: a thematic analysis. *Frontiers in Psychology, 15*, 1347336.

[9] Gross, J. J., & John, O. P. (2003). Individual differences in two emotion regulation processes: Implications for affect, relationships, and well-being. *Journal of Personality and Social Psychology, 85*(2), 348-362.

[10] Brewer, J. A., Worhunsky, P. D., Gray, J. R., Tang, Y. Y., Weber, J., & Kober, H. (2011). Meditation experience is associated with differences in default mode network activity and connectivity. *Proceedings of the National Academy of Sciences, 108*(50), 20254-20259.

[11] Lutz, A., Greischar, L. L., Rawlings, N. B., Ricard, M., & Davidson, R. J. (2004). Long-term meditators self-induce high-amplitude gamma synchrony during mental practice.

Proceedings of the National Academy of Sciences, 101(46), 16369-16373.

[12] Sacchet, M. D., Treves, I. N., Uddin, Z., Ganesan, S., Gunkelman, J., Fogarty, C., ... & Gabrieli, J. D. E. (2025). Mindfulness, cognition, and long-term meditators: Toward a science of advanced meditation. *Imaging Neuroscience, 3*, 1-51.

[13] Kral, T. R. A., Schuyler, B. S., Mumford, J. A., Rosenkranz, M. A., Lutz, A., & Davidson, R. J. (2018). Impact of short- and long-term mindfulness meditation training on amygdala reactivity to emotional stimuli. *NeuroImage, 181*, 301-313.

[14] Goldin, P., & Gross, J. J. (2010). Effects of mindfulness-based stress reduction (MBSR) on emotion regulation in social anxiety disorder. *Emotion, 10*(1), 83-91.

[15] Yaden, D. B., Haidt, J., Hood Jr, R. W., Vago, D. R., & Newberg, A. B. (2017). The varieties of self-transcendent experience. *Review of General Psychology, 21*(2), 143-160.

[16] Boyle, P. A., Barnes, L. L., Buchman, A. S., & Bennett, D. A. (2009). Purpose in life is associated with mortality among community-dwelling older persons. *Psychosomatic Medicine, 71*(5), 574-579.

[17] Deci, E. L., & Ryan, R. M. (2000). The "what" and "why" of goal pursuits: Human needs and the self-determination of behavior. *Psychological Inquiry, 11*(4), 227-268.

[18] Goyal, M., Singh, S., Sibinga, E. M., Gould, N. F., Rowland-Seymour, A., Sharma, R., ... & Haythornthwaite, J. A. (2014). Meditation programs for psychological stress and well-being: a systematic review and meta-analysis. *JAMA Internal Medicine, 174*(3), 357-368.

[19] Ericsson, K. A., Krampe, R. T., & Tesch-Römer, C. (1993). The role of deliberate practice in the acquisition of expert performance. *Psychological Review, 100*(3), 363-406.

[20] Ericsson, K. A., & Harwell, K. W. (2019). Deliberate practice and proposed limits on the effects of practice on the acquisition of expert performance: Why the original definition matters and recommendations for future research. *Frontiers in Psychology, 10*, 2396.

[21] Ashby, M. (2019-25). *Mysticism of Amenemopet Hieroglyphic Text Translation*. Sema Institute of Ancient Egyptian Studies.

[22] Ashby, M. (2024). *Amenemopet lectures 2024 by Dr Muata Ashby transcripts*. Sema Institute of Ancient Egyptian Studies.

[23] Ashby, M 2020 EGYPTIAN BOOK OF THE DEAD HIEROGLYPH TRANSLATIONS USING THE TRILINEAR METHOD Volume 5: Featuring Temple of Amun-Ra at Abu Simbel Paperback – Import, May 1, 2020 by Muata Ashby (Author)

CHAPTER 2: Commentary on Teachings of Amenemopet Chapter 1, Verses 8-18 & 1-2: The Psychology of Wisdom Absorption and Aryu (Karmic) Purification and Transformation

SUMMARY OF VERSES BEING COVERED

These foundational Chapter 1 verses address the critical psychological obstacles to authentic spiritual development, establishing how wisdom teachings must penetrate beyond surface intellectual understanding to ignite vital-life-fire (udja) that transforms the mind at its source through aryu purification [9]. Verses 8-10 warn against those who "hear and think they understand but do not listen carefully and reflect for deep understanding," identifying the distinction between casual exposure and genuine absorption. Verses 1-2 establish the transformative purpose: "Words...from the chief scribe (Amenemopet)" are designed to be absorbed so "the living-ears...would hear these words would listen to and obey them," functioning as mind-restructuring technology that ignites vital-life-fire (udja) producing spiritual purity and well-being when properly internalized [9].

Verses 11-13 reveal the necessity of deep absorption: "if these words of wisdom were to be kept forefront in your mind so that it could be set free from what causes suffering due to mental agitations that prevent awareness of higher consciousness...it would be magnificent if the reader would allow these teachings to the innermost levels of the mind (unconscious)." [9] Verses 14-16 introduce the crucial aryu mechanism: "karmic-feeling-memories (aryu-karmic-feeling-memories) arise from your unconscious into your conscious mind and would otherwise overwhelm...at that crucial time when those mental impressions...start working in the mind and there is a storming of words...that wisdom would be able to act as a stake, as if a mooring post for your tongue." [9] Verses 16-18 emphasize developing "living ears" and becoming "remote in your mind, detached and collected" as prerequisites for authentic wisdom absorption that ignites the purifying vital-life-fire [9].

TEACHINGS DERIVED FROM THESE VERSES

1. Superficial hearing differs fundamentally from deep listening that ignites vital-life-fire (udja) and transforms the mind [verses 8-10]
2. Wisdom teachings must be absorbed into "the innermost levels of the mind (unconscious)" to activate the purifying fire that burns away aryu [verses 11-13]
3. Aryu (karmic-feeling-memories) stored in the ab arise into conscious awareness and create "storming of words" that overwhelm unprepared consciousness [verses 14-15]
4. Properly absorbed wisdom acts as "mooring post" infused with vital-life-fire preventing the mind from being swept away by aryu-driven mental storms [verse 16]
5. "Living ears" represent the mind genuinely ready for transformation through ignition of spiritual purifying fire rather than casual spiritual interest [verses 8-10]
6. Becoming "remote in your mind, detached and collected" enables wisdom absorption that ignites udja which superficial engagement prevents [verses 16-18]
7. Egoism actively resists deep wisdom absorption because authentic teachings threaten familiar patterns by igniting the purifying fire that burns away aryu-based identity [verses 11-13]

8. Turning away from teachings creates "mental weakness"—diminishment of discriminative capacity and failure to develop vital-life-fire [verses 12-13]
9. The transformation process requires both conscious study and unconscious integration that ignites the purifying fire at the deepest level [verses 1-2, 11-13]
10. Authentic wisdom absorption supports the dual Prologue goals: developing vital-life-fire (udja) that produces spiritual purity and earthly well-being, and discovering Ab Neter within through aryu purification [connecting to Prologue verses 2, 9]

1. Human Psychology Principle

The fundamental human psychology issue that Chapter 1, verses 8-18 addresses centers on the distinction between superficial intellectual exposure to spiritual teachings and authentic deep absorption that ignites vital-life-fire (udja)—the purifying spiritual fire that transforms the mind by burning away aryu density and revealing Ab Neter awareness. The Ancient Egyptian hieroglyph for udja depicts an ignited fire drill base, symbolizing healthy, strong, vital, sound, and prosperous conditions regarded as a fire drill base whose fire has been ignited and flame is burning [12]. This vital-life-fire represents a modulation of energy that comes from the god Ra (an aspect of Neberdjer), becoming effective when personality energy is not squandered on worldly thinking, feeling, desires, and ignorant self-awareness but instead allowed to develop focus and grow to purify the personality [12][13].

Verses 8-10 identify the core problem: people who "hear and think they understand but do not listen carefully and reflect for deep understanding" remain trapped in what might be termed surface learning—the hat (conscious awareness) processes information intellectually without allowing teachings to penetrate the ab (unconscious) where they can ignite the vital-life-fire that burns away aryu patterns and reveals Ab Neter residing in the kara.

This connects directly to the Prologue framework. Recall that Prologue verse 9 teaches how "aryu in the unconscious mind occupy the presence-of-mind awareness, so densely as to influence the conscious reality awareness (thinking and feeling) of a person and blot out the awareness of the soul level divine presence which is deeper than the aryu." Chapter 1 reveals why this aryu density persists despite spiritual study—because teachings absorbed only intellectually at the hat (conscious) level never reach the ab (unconscious) level where they must ignite vital-life-fire (udja) that can burn away aryu patterns and reveal Ab Neter awaiting discovery. Without the activation of this purifying spiritual fire, the mind remains in the ignorance state regardless of intellectual knowledge accumulated.

The psychological principle embedded in verses 11-13 demonstrates that wisdom must reach "the innermost levels of the mind (unconscious)" to ignite the vital-life-fire that creates genuine transformation. This means teachings must penetrate beyond the hat (conscious intellectual understanding) into the ab where two critical processes occur: (1) vital-life-fire (udja) activates to burn away aryu patterns that create heated mind and feelings, functioning as what the Scripture of Ra and Hetheru calls "spiritual roasting"—the fire of wisdom that consumes delusions and egoism, and (2) as this purifying fire progressively burns through aryu density, the deeper kara where Ab Neter resides can gradually be revealed. Without this deep penetration that ignites udja, the mind remains in the ignorance state—the hat operating from aryu-driven patterns without Ab Neter communion and without the purifying fire necessary for transformation—regardless of intellectual knowledge accumulated.

The mechanism of resistance described in verses 11-13 operates through what the verse calls "turning away from these teachings," which creates "mental weakness." This doesn't mean obvious rejection but rather forms of engagement that keep teachings at surface level where they cannot ignite the vital-life-fire necessary to thin aryu density or reveal Ab Neter. The egoic perspective—arising from aryu-obscured mind that experiences itself as a separate, incomplete individual—naturally resists deep absorption because authentic wisdom threatens the familiar patterns through which it maintains its sense of control and identity. More precisely, the egoic perspective resists because deeply absorbed wisdom doesn't merely challenge beliefs but ignites the purifying fire that actually burns away the aryu-patterns constituting egoic identity itself.

Amenemopet's Authoritative Promises as Psychological Foundation for Deep Absorption

A crucial psychological element supporting the deep absorption process that ignites vital-life-fire involves developing trust and reverence for Amenemopet's authoritative declarations about the transformative outcomes of his teachings. The Sage provides explicit promises rather than theoretical possibilities: when teachings penetrate "the innermost mind," the absorbed wisdom "would be able to act as a stake, as if a mooring post for your tongue so that you would not get caught up in the storm" [verse 16]. He guarantees that through deep absorption, "you will be able to be remote in your mind, detached and collected" enabling conscious consideration before speech or action [verse 17]. Most significantly, Amenemopet promises that practitioners "will be able to find yourself in this book, to discover who you are essentially, and your fate will be determined by this wisdom such that your life will be fortunate, auspicious, opportune" [verse 18], and that these teachings become "a storehouse of vitality and wisdom for your life" [verse 1].

These represent authoritative declarations from an enlightened sage who achieved the complete transformation he prescribes, not speculative theories requiring validation through personal experience alone. The psychology of developing reverence for Amenemopet's spiritual authority combined with trust in these explicit promises provides essential motivational foundation that empowers, bolsters, and sustains the effort required for deep wisdom absorption. When the mind encounters resistance to the demanding contemplative work necessary for vital-life-fire ignition—when superficial engagement feels easier than allowing teachings to penetrate "the innermost levels of the mind"—trust in Amenemopet's promises provides the confidence to persist through periods when immediate results are not apparent. This reverence for sagely authority breeds the psychological fortitude necessary to maintain the sustained effort that allows vital-life-fire to ignite and stabilize, recognizing that the promised outcomes—mental stability during aryu storms, discovery of essential identity, fortunate life circumstances through wisdom application—flow inevitably from following Amenemopet's precise instructions for deep absorption rather than depending entirely on individual psychological capacity or circumstances.

This directly impacts both Prologue goals in more profound ways than previously understood. The goal of Prologue verse 2 to "develop vital-life-fire (udja) that produces spiritual purity and well-being while living on earth" cannot be achieved through superficial spiritual understanding because the purifying fire never ignites—aryu patterns continue driving heated mind and feelings that create suffering. The teaching reveals that udja represents not merely general well-being but specifically the fire of vitality, the fire of spiritual health and goodness that burns away impurities. When this vital-life-fire activates through deep wisdom absorption, it produces both spiritual purity (through burning away aryu) and well-being (through the natural peace that emerges as aryu density thins). The goal of Prologue verse 9 to discover the kara where "the Divine resides in every person" requires the purifying fire of udja to burn through aryu density sufficiently for Ab Neter awareness to emerge—and this fire ignites only when teachings penetrate to the unconscious level where aryu reside and can be consumed by wisdom's flame.

Verses 14-15 reveal the critical consequence of superficial learning: when "karmic-feeling-memories (aryu) arise from your unconscious into your conscious mind," they create "storming of words" that overwhelm the mind lacking both the deep wisdom absorption and the vital-life-fire necessary to remain stable. This "storming" represents the heated mind and feelings state—the hat (conscious awareness) being flooded by aryu from the ab, creating reactive thoughts and emotions that prevent both earthly well-being and Ab Neter discovery. Authentic wisdom absorption, by contrast, ignites what verse 16 calls "a mooring post"—stable reference points embedded at the unconscious level and infused with vital-life-fire that actively burns away arising aryu patterns, preventing the mind from being swept away by aryu-driven storms.

THE EXISTENTIAL SHOCK OF VERSE 18: FINDING YOURSELF PRESUPPOSES BEING LOST

[Verse 18's] profound declaration—"**You will be able to find yourself in this book, to discover who you are essentially**"—delivers an existentially shocking revelation that most readers encounter without recognizing its radical implications [9]. The promise to "**find yourself**" necessarily presupposes a stark reality: **you are currently LOST**—not in physical location, but in the most fundamental dimension of existence: **identity itself**. Your present understanding of who you are represents not authentic selfhood but rather what the teaching will later reveal as a "fraudulent persona" (Chapter 15)—an aryu-constructed delusion obscuring Ab Neter, your true divine nature [11].

Consider the precision of Amenemopet's language. The verse does not promise to "**create** a new you" or "**make** you into something better." Rather, it promises to help you "**discover who you are essentially**"—implying that **what you currently believe yourself to be is not actually you** [9]. This teaching serves as precursor to the ancient spiritual maxim "Know Thyself," but with a crucial preliminary recognition that shatters comfortable assumptions: before you can know yourself, you must first realize that **you do NOT know yourself**—the true self. What the mind currently "knows" as "myself" constitutes not discovery but rather **misunderstanding, delusion, ignorance of true identity** [11][21].

The psychological mechanism of this lost condition operates through the framework established in the Prologue. Dense aryu accumulation in the ab (unconscious mind) creates what might be termed an "**identity usurpation**"—the mind, operating from surface Hat level driven by feeling-memories of past experiences, constructs a sense of self based entirely on aryu patterns while remaining completely unaware of the Ab Neter (divine soul) that actually sustains its capacity for consciousness [21][22]. The person experiences themselves as the sum total of their thoughts, feelings, memories, preferences, aversions, achievements, and failures—a self-concept built entirely from temporary phenomena while the eternal divine foundation remains hidden beneath aryu density [11][21].

This creates what Amenemopet identifies as the fundamental human predicament: consciousness aware only of its surface manifestations (body, mind, sensations, time-space experiences) while utterly ignorant of its essential divine nature [21]. The individual constructs elaborate identity narratives—"I am a successful person," "I am a struggling person," "I am competent," "I am inadequate," "I am loved," "I am rejected"—all based on aryu-driven interpretations of experience, never suspecting that these narratives represent not authentic self-knowledge but rather **delusional self-misidentification** [11][21]. The philosophical interpretive guidance clarifies: "the wisdom teaching was created as a guide for life based on a spiritually wise understanding of the connection to the divine that is true, while the life disconnected from the understanding and experience of the divine is the false (unrighteous path of life)" [11].

The verse's promise transforms the spiritual path from self-improvement project to **self-discovery journey**—from becoming something new to **recognizing what was always true but obscured**. Amenemopet's book will not CREATE a self but rather **REVEAL the self that already exists**—the Ab Neter that has always sustained consciousness from within the kara (divine sanctuary) but remains hidden by aryu opacity [9][21][22]. This understanding aligns with the Prologue's teaching that aryu removal constitutes the essential spiritual work: "Purification through wisdom philosophy removes aryu density to reveal the Ab Neter that was always present" [Prologue verse 9][21].

Therefore, "**finding yourself**" in this book means engaging the purification process (through vital-life-fire ignition and aryu thinning) that removes the obstruction preventing recognition of who you have always been essentially. The teaching addresses not moral failure requiring correction but rather **cognitive error requiring clarification**—the mind thinks incorrectly about its own nature because it does not understand correctly [2]. Every behavioral teaching Amenemopet provides serves this fundamental goal: thinning aryu density sufficiently that the Hat (conscious awareness) can finally perceive the Ab Neter that has sustained its capacity to be aware throughout its entire existence [9][21][22].

This revelation will receive fuller treatment in Chapter 15, where Amenemopet explicitly teaches that "most people are manifesting a fraudulent persona based on the corruptions of the unconscious mind" and that ethical living combined with meditative practice enables one to "end up being your true self" [14]. Nevertheless, [verse 18] plants the seed of this shocking recognition at the very beginning of the teaching: **the "you" reading these words right now is not actually you**—it is a delusional self-construct that wisdom absorption and aryu purification will progressively dissolve, revealing the Ab Neter identity that constitutes your essential nature and has always been your true self, though hidden from awareness by dense aryu obstruction [9][111][21][22].

2. Behavioral Imperative: Patterns of Superficial Spiritual Engagement

Building upon this psychological foundation, specific behavioral patterns emerge when the mind engages spiritual teachings superficially—maintaining knowledge at the hat (conscious) level without allowing penetration to the ab (unconscious) where vital-life-fire can ignite and genuine transformation through aryu burning occurs. Verses 8-10 identify the primary pattern: people who "hear and think they understand" believe they've absorbed teachings when actually they "do not listen carefully and reflect for deep understanding." This manifests as intellectual spirituality where practitioners accumulate concepts without the deep absorption necessary to ignite udja that thins aryu density or reveals Ab Neter.

Consider the modern spiritual seeker who studies multiple traditions, reads extensively about consciousness, and can discuss spiritual concepts fluently, yet remains trapped in the same heated patterns—reactive emotions, compulsive desires, anxiety about circumstances—that characterized pre-spiritual life. This person demonstrates the pattern verses 8-10 identify: the hat (conscious awareness) possesses spiritual information while the ab (unconscious) remains unchanged, with aryu patterns continuing to drive behavior and blot out Ab Neter awareness because no vital-life-fire has been ignited to burn away these patterns. The intellectual knowledge provides no "mooring post" [verse 16] during challenging circumstances because it never penetrated to the unconscious level where aryu operate and where the purifying fire must activate.

The behavioral pattern of selective engagement represents another manifestation. Practitioners focus on teachings that feel comfortable or confirm existing beliefs while avoiding guidance that would require genuine transformation of aryu patterns through the uncomfortable purifying fire. Someone might embrace teachings about compassion and divine love while avoiding teachings about discipline, restraint, or the systematic purification work required to allow vital-life-fire to burn away aryu density. This selective approach keeps spiritual knowledge at surface level where it supports pleasant feelings without igniting the purifying fire that would threaten the aryu-based egoic perspective.

Verses 11-13 reveal how this resistance operates: the mind that refuses to allow teachings to penetrate "the innermost levels of the mind (unconscious)" experiences what the verse calls "turning away from these teachings," which "would lead to mental weakness; in fact, the turning away from these teachings, that would be injuring the mental capacity." This "mental weakness" represents the gradual diminishment of discriminative capacity—the ability to recognize truth from illusion, wisdom from ego-justification, genuine spiritual guidance from comfortable platitudes. As aryu density remains unchanged despite years of spiritual study—because vital-life-fire never ignited to burn away these patterns—the mind loses capacity to recognize that superficial engagement produces no genuine transformation.

The pattern of spiritual materialism demonstrates the mind treating teachings as objects for collection rather than tools for igniting the purifying fire. Someone might accumulate books, attend workshops, study with various teachers, yet never implement the systematic practices required to allow vital-life-fire to burn away aryu density. The spiritual engagement serves ego-enhancement—creating identity as "spiritual person"—rather than the ego-threatening work of allowing teachings to penetrate the ab where vital-life-fire would ignite, revealing and consuming aryu patterns. This creates sophisticated spiritual pride that actually strengthens aryu-based egoic perspective while appearing to represent spiritual advancement.

Implementation hesitancy represents the behavioral pattern where understanding remains theoretical due to resistance against practices requiring sustained commitment to ignite and maintain the purifying fire. Someone might intellectually understand that daily meditation ignites vital-life-fire that thins aryu density, that ethical behavior prevents new aryu accumulation, that restraint of desires weakens aryu compelling force—yet never consistently implement these practices. The heated mind and feelings find endless justifications: "too busy," "not the right time," "need to understand more before practicing." Meanwhile, vital-life-fire never ignites, aryu density remains unchanged, Ab Neter awareness remains blocked, and the person experiences superficial spiritual involvement without genuine transformation toward the silent state.

The pattern of emotional regulation through spiritual concepts demonstrates using teachings primarily for temporary comfort rather than igniting mind-transforming fire. When facing difficulties, the mind seeks spiritual ideas that reduce immediate anxiety without allowing vital-life-fire to activate against underlying aryu patterns creating the suffering. This provides temporary relief while actually reinforcing the pattern of seeking external solutions (even spiritual ones) rather than igniting the purifying fire that would burn away the aryu density generating the fundamental sense of incompleteness and vulnerability characteristic of aryu-obscured mind.

Most subtle is the pattern of external dependency where spiritual authority figures replace development of inner discriminative wisdom and personal vital-life-fire. Rather than allowing teachings to penetrate the ab where they would ignite the purifying fire creating genuine transformation, the mind maintains teachings as external information requiring continued outside validation. This prevents what verse 16 describes as teachings becoming "a mooring post"—stable internal reference points infused with vital-life-fire, accessible during challenging circumstances where the purifying fire automatically activates against arising aryu. The person remains dependent on teachers, texts, or spiritual community for guidance that should emerge from deeply absorbed wisdom operating automatically from the unconscious level where vital-life-fire burns away aryu patterns before they can overwhelm the mind.

THE PSYCHOMYTHOLOGY OF THE GOD SET: COSMIC FORCE OF EGOISM AND THE HEATED PERSONALITY FROM VERSE 16

In the concept of what I term "psychomythology"—the study of mythology as psychological principles embedded within ancient mythology that illuminate the dynamics of human mind/personality transformation, the God Set functions as the cosmic force of egoism within the personality, depicted in hieroglyphic art as a four-legged animal in recumbent posture with tail and ears pointing vertically, bearing a curved snout. The four-legged symbolism indicates the mind bound to earthly, worldly concerns, while his distinctive features embody the spiritual obstacles to knowing Self [14].

The Asarian Resurrection: Set's Role in Spiritual Development

The complete story of Asar (Osiris), Aset (Isis), and Heru (Horus) reveals Set's function within mind/personality development. In the mythic narrative, Asar descended to earth as a divinity commissioned by the Supreme Being Ra to teach humanity and lead them on a righteous path. Set, as Asar's brother, initially coexisted peacefully but eventually became consumed by jealousy and egoistic desire for power. Set killed Asar's body, and when Aset (representing intuitional wisdom and the shining spirit aspect—Akhu) brought the body back to life, Set discovered it and dismembered it completely, scattering the pieces throughout the land [15][16].

This mythological drama operates simultaneously as precise psychological instruction. Asar symbolizes the human soul—the divine consciousness within every person. Set's killing and dismembering of Asar represents how egoism attempts to destroy soul awareness, fragmenting the mind into disconnected pieces through identification with temporal concerns, bodily sensations, reactive emotions, and the endless stream of thoughts driven by aryu (karmic patterns). As the teaching reveals: "even after your self-awareness of your soul has been killed, beyond even killed it has been dismembered so it's all over the place, disintegrated, there's an aspect of your own very self that can bring all that back together and that's your intuitional wisdom, that's your Aset nature" [15].

Aset, working with divine assistance from the god Djehuty (intellect), reassembled Asar's body and conceived Heru—representing spiritual aspiration and the redemptive force within the mind. Heru challenged Set and ultimately redeemed Asar, demonstrating that "when Aset and Asar, when intuitional wisdom and the soul come together, they produce a spiritual aspiration that can redeem the soul, and when your soul is redeemed, your whole personality is redeemed. Your personality in time and space, your personality in the astral plane, and your personality in the causal" [15].

The wisdom to be understood encompasses recognition that Set's challenge serves essential spiritual function. Ra (Neberdjer in this context) allowed Set's unrighteousness to proceed because spiritual development requires the ego-self of the personality to have confrontation with the spiritual redemptive and spiritually aspiring aspect. Without this struggle, the mind never develops the strength necessary for genuine transformation. "If Set was not there, that redemption will not occur" [15][16].

The God Set as Nesheny: The Stormy, Heated Personality

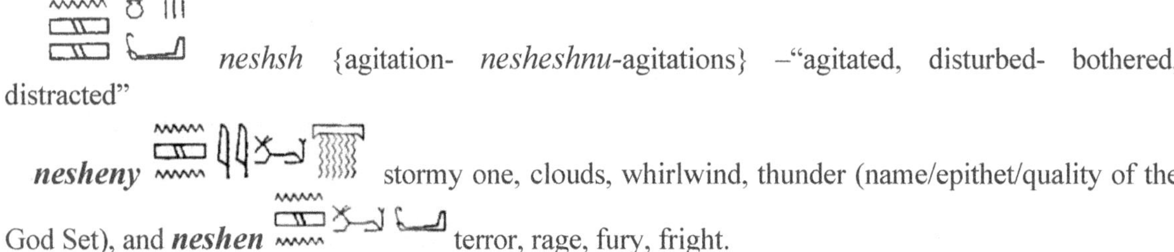

neshsh {agitation- *nesheshnu*-agitations} –"agitated, disturbed- bothered, distracted"

nesheny stormy one, clouds, whirlwind, thunder (name/epithet/quality of the God Set), and ***neshen*** terror, rage, fury, fright.

Set bears the designation "nesheny"—literally "stormy one"—derived from the root "neshesh" meaning disturbance and agitation. This term captures his essential psychological nature as the thunder within storm clouds, manifesting as raging emotional anger and rapacious, violent, greedy personality expression [14][15]. The characteristics associated with Set's heated nature include storminess, bombastic nature, ruckus, hubris, thunderousness, boisterousness, loudness, yelling, imposing fear, and aggressive self-assertion. These qualities "go under the terms relating to vibration, movement, shakiness. It's not placid, not quiet, not still" [14].

In the myth of the Asarian Resurrection when Set kills Asar mythologically it is the ego trying to kill the soul and its ethical, peaceful spiritually aware condition so it can take over the personality. When Heru is born, he sets out to redeem his slain father, the soul, and return the personality back to its condition of spiritual awareness and at the same time put the ego in its place, as a servant and not dominator of the soul. Asar is resurrected and becomes the ruler of the netherworld (unconscious causal level of reality). The teaching emphasizes: "If your mind is not still, you're not going to be able to discern the nature of the absolute divine Self" [14]. Set's stormy nature creates precisely this instability—the mind cannot settle into recognition of Ab Neter (the divine foundation) when constantly agitated by Setian patterns of egoistic reactivity and worldly obsession.

The Dual Nature of the God Set: Servant or Usurper

Set demonstrates crucial dual capacity within the mind. In iconographic depictions from the Papyrus of Heruben (see image), Set appears in the bow of Ra's solar boat, battling the cosmic serpent Apep (representing entropic forces that would halt creation's sustaining movement). Here Set works in service of Ra, fighting against the dull, slothful aspect (uhmet ab -dullness of mind) that seeks to stop all productive movement and let things deteriorate [15][16].

This reveals Set's potential: "Set can serve as a positive ally and servant to the soul (Asar) when operating under the guidance of higher consciousness, but can also turn toward negative thoughts, feelings, and actions when dominated by separative thinking and attachment to temporal concerns" [17]. The goal of spiritual development involves "not the elimination of Set but rather the proper harmonization and orientation of this worldly aspect toward serving rather than competing with spiritual aspiration" [17].

However, in the Asarian Resurrection narrative, Set "forgot himself" and attempted to seize the rightful place of Asar, thinking he was the Divine rather than servant of the Divine [15][16]. This represents the fundamental error of egoism—the mind identifying with the worldly, temporal aspect (Set) as if it were the essential self, rather than recognizing Set as one component requiring integration under soul guidance.

The Four Phases of Set: Progressive Integration

Our tradition teaches four phases of Set as explained in the Prt m Hru (Egyptian Book of Coming Forth by Day), representing stages of mind evolution in relationship to egoic patterns [14]:

1. The Separation Phase: Set experienced as an apparently separate personality that is actually an aspect of oneself—the beginning recognition that egoic patterns operate within the mind

2. The Harmony Phase: Set personality beginning to come into harmony with the Heru personality—initial integration where spiritual aspiration begins influencing the worldly aspect

3. The Integration Phase: Set personality coming into full harmony and oneness with the higher nature of Self—complete integration where the worldly aspect operates under spiritual guidance

4. The Transcendence Phase: Set recognized as the higher Self—ultimate realization where even what appeared as ego reveals itself as expression of divine consciousness

This progression represents the definition of Yoga—Smai Taui—"the union of the higher and lower aspects of the personality" [14].

Psychological Characteristics of the Degraded Heated Person

When Set operates through ignorance rather than divine guidance, the mind manifests what verse 17 catalogs as the complete psychology of the heated person: "unrighteousness, fraud, anger, boisterousness, flippant retorts and thoughtless speech, inconsiderate and impulsive acts, rapacious greed, jealousy, envy, ridiculing others and having no compassion for the poor or the less fortunate" [18]. The most degraded state emerges when "a person enjoys being nasty, flippant, arrogant—who gets pleasure out of making other people suffer, gets pleasure out of hurting others and stealing from others" [14].

Such personalities exemplify what occurs when Set completely dominates the mind—egoism operating without any higher guidance, producing not merely unconscious negative patterns but conscious pleasure in causing harm. These represent the vices that emerge when the ego "is under the control of the higher nature" fails—instead leading to "degraded states of human existence" including "egoism, selfishness, extraverted ness, wonton sexuality (lust), jealousy, envy, greed, gluttony" [19].

The wisdom teaching maintains compassion even for such degraded states: "These are the people that should be pitied. Their suffering is going to be multifold compared to the people they are making suffer, because their delusion is so mountainous it would take lifetimes to unwind" [14]. This compassionate framing recognizes that heated personalities operate from profound spiritual ignorance—cut off from Ab Neter awareness and trapped in Setian egoism that creates cascading suffering.

Set Within the Personality: Recognizing Demoniac and Divine Aspects

The teaching reveals: "life is itself duality, it has demons, and it has gods and goddesses the demons are called sebau, fiends and these are all related to the nature of one's own personality. You have some demoniac aspects, and you have some divine aspects, and they are doing the battle" [15]. The God Set has two aspects, helper of the Divine and egoic fiend. The egoic aspect of Set represents the fiendish tendency within every person—the capacity for egoistic degradation that everyone possesses and must confront.

Nevertheless, in Neterian religion "there is no concept of a 'devil' or 'demon' as is conceived in the Judeo-Christian or Islamic traditions. Rather, it is understood that manifestations of detrimental situations and adversities arise as a result of unrighteous actions. These unrighteous actions are due to the 'Setian' qualities in a human being" [19]. Set functions not as external evil entity but as psychological principle—the cosmic force of egoism that operates within the mind when spiritual ignorance dominates.

Understanding Set's psychology allows aspirants to recognize these patterns within themselves and others, neither demonizing the egoic aspect nor allowing it to dominate the mind. The goal remains what the Asarian Resurrection mythologically depicts: reassembling the dismembered soul (Asar) through intuitional wisdom (Aset), generating spiritual aspiration (Heru) that can confront and ultimately integrate the egoic force (Set) under divine guidance, achieving the union of higher and lower aspects that constitutes genuine spiritual enlightenment.

3. Mystic Psychology Metaphysical Implications: The Architecture of Mind/personality transformation Through Vital-Life-Fire and Aryu Purification

At the mystical level, Chapter 1 reveals the fundamental architecture through which the mind transforms from ignorance (aryu-obscured awareness) to realization (Ab Neter discovery) through the ignition and operation of vital-life-fire (udja)—the purifying spiritual flame that burns away accumulated karmic patterns. Verses 14-15 provide one of the most sophisticated psychological-metaphysical teachings in ancient wisdom literature through the exposition of how aryu function: "karmic-feeling-memories (aryu-karmic-feeling-memories) arise from your unconscious into your conscious mind and would otherwise overwhelm, as if to capsize the peacefulness of your mind...at that crucial time when those mental impressions...start working in the mind and there is a storming of words."

The teaching reveals that vital-life-fire (udja) represents the transformative spiritual energy that Amenemopet identifies as the active principle of purification. The Ancient Egyptian hieroglyph depicts an ignited fire drill base, symbolizing healthy, strong, vital, sound, and prosperous conditions—a fire drill base whose fire has been ignited and flame is burning [12]. When wisdom penetrates to "the innermost levels of the mind (unconscious)" [verses 11-13], it doesn't merely reside there as information but ignites what this tradition calls udja—a modulation of energy that comes from the god Ra (an aspect of Neberdjer). This vital-life-fire becomes effective when personality energy is not squandered on worldly thinking, feeling, desires, and ignorant self-awareness but instead allowed to develop focus and grow to purify the personality [12][13]. As the Scripture of Ra and Hetheru teaches: "This vital-life-fire acts as a fire of wisdom that burns away delusions and egoism. It roasts, burns off, the delusion and ignorance fomenting desire for ephemeral existence, the egoistic perturbations of the mind and its thoughts, feelings, desires and memories (aryu) that prevent the soul from realizing the truth of Higher Self" [12].

This vital-life-fire functions as practical mind-transforming technology: teachings deeply absorbed into the ab activate as a purifying flame that consumes aryu patterns, much like physical fire consumes fuel. The wisdom to be understood encompasses recognition that spiritual transformation isn't metaphorical burning but an actual energetic process where concentrated wisdom-awareness generates heat (spiritual purifying fire [fire of wisdom] ***udja***-vital-life-fire) that dissolves the binding force of karmic patterns, releasing the mind from their compelling influence.

This passage reveals the layered operation of the mind that the Prologue established. The ab (unconscious) contains both aryu at surface level and Ab Neter deeper within the kara. The aryu "arise from your unconscious into your conscious mind"—meaning patterns stored in the ab emerge into the hat (conscious awareness) as thoughts, feelings, desires, and reactive impulses. When aryu density remains thick and teachings haven't penetrated to unconscious levels to ignite vital-life-fire, these arising patterns "overwhelm" the mind, creating what the verse calls "storming of words"—the heated state where the hat becomes flooded with aryu-driven mental activity. The purifying fire of udja provides the only effective response to this storming: when vital-life-fire activates, it burns away the arising aryu before they can generate the cascading mental reactivity characteristic of heated mind and feelings.

The metaphysical mechanics explain why superficial learning fails. Information maintained at the hat (conscious) level cannot ignite vital-life-fire in the ab (unconscious) where aryu patterns reside and require burning. Consider the architecture: teachings absorbed only intellectually remain in conscious memory where they can be recalled and discussed, but they lack presence in the ab where aryu patterns operate and where purifying fire must ignite to consume these patterns. When challenging circumstances trigger aryu to arise into conscious awareness, the superficial teachings prove useless—like having matches in the attic when you need fire in the basement where combustible material requires burning.

Verses 11-13 reveal the solution through teaching that wisdom must reach "the innermost levels of the mind (unconscious)." This describes the process of embedding teachings in the ab itself—at the same level where aryu reside and where vital-life-fire can ignite to burn them away, and deeper where Ab Neter resides in the kara and can be revealed as the purifying fire clears obstructing patterns. When wisdom penetrates to this depth, verse 16 teaches it can "act as a stake, as if a mooring post for your tongue so that you would not get caught up in the storm...thereby your mind would thrash you in the storm of excitedness and uncontrolled speech that would promote storming of the mind, uncontrolled thoughts, urges and untoward thinking and acting (heated condition of mind)."

The metaphysical significance of the "mooring post" reveals how deeply absorbed wisdom infused with vital-life-fire functions. When teachings penetrate the ab (unconscious) and ignite udja, they become automatic reference points that activate the purifying fire when aryu arise. The mind that has deeply absorbed restraint teachings experiences automatic activation of vital-life-fire burning away anger-aryu when these patterns emerge. The mind that has deeply absorbed truth teachings experiences automatic udja activation consuming dishonesty-aryu when these patterns arise. These aren't conscious efforts requiring willpower but automatic purifying responses emerging from the same unconscious level where aryu reside—vital-life-fire ignited by wisdom patterns consuming aryu patterns within the ab itself, like fire burning away accumulated combustible material.

The wisdom to be understood here is that the concept of the stake or mooring post in the mind represents the state when the wisdom of Amenemopet has become firmly seated—inculcated—in the unconscious level of mind where it ignites vital-life-fire such that this purifying fire becomes the driving force of the personality instead of the superficial mind driven by untoward aryu. This mooring process can be understood as a result of the practice of inculcating the wisdom teaching and the meditative practice whereby time is spent in study and reflection on the wisdom teaching, followed by time spent in quiet awareness—contemplation meditation—of Ab Neter/Neberdjer existence as the nature of self beyond ego, body, mind, and aryu. During this contemplative absorption, vital-life-fire begins igniting as concentrated awareness generates the purifying heat that burns away aryu obstructions. A specific process called "sau-Neberdjer" for this contemplative recognition will be discussed in detail in future chapters. This meditative mooring process must be preceded by receiving the wisdom teaching to understand the nature of human existence and the development of heated versus silent mind and feelings, and also Maat—the discernment of righteous versus unrighteous actions, thoughts, and feelings. This foundational understanding serves to purify the heart and prepare the personality by developing dispassion and detachment from agitating worldly interests. These preparations create the necessary conditions for the deeper reflections and meditation practice through which wisdom penetrates from the hat (conscious awareness) to the ab (unconscious), where it ignites vital-life-fire that functions as automatic purifying flame preventing the mind from being overwhelmed by arising aryu patterns.

This process gradually thins aryu density through multiple mechanisms operating via vital-life-fire. First, deeply absorbed wisdom ignites udja that burns away reinforcement of existing aryu—when the purifying fire activates automatically, the mind doesn't act out anger-aryu, preventing strengthening of that pattern while the fire simultaneously consumes the pattern's energetic foundation. Second, vital-life-fire gradually replaces aryu patterns in the ab—each time udja activates and burns away aryu, the purifying fire pattern strengthens while the aryu pattern weakens and eventually dissolves. Third, as vital-life-fire progressively burns through aryu density layer by layer, the deeper kara level where Ab

Neter resides becomes progressively accessible, revealed through the purifying action of udja clearing obstructions.

THE HERUFY ARCHITECTURE: TWO HEADS WITHIN ONE PERSONALITY AND THE LAW OF MAAT'S KARMIC OPERATION

Teachings of New Kingdom Pert-M-Heru -Heru with Two heads

From the Ancient Egyptian Book of Enlightenment (PertmHeru). Chapter 17, 27-28[12]

Verse B.

B.1. *Ky djed* ***Heru pu un n-f im tepui unen ua kher***

B.2. Otherwise said Horus that being to-he in heads-two being one under influence

B.3. Another way to understand it is: We are talking about Horus, the redemptive spiritual aspiration quality of the personality when he is in the state where he has two heads (also known as *Herufy*), having two opposing dispositions, one being under the influence or control of…

Image: Heru with two heads- "Herfy"

Verse C.

C.1. ***Maat ky kher isfetu didi-f isfetu en ari - zy***

C2. order/truth other under influence unrighteousness. giveth he unrighteousness to doer thereof.

C.3. …order and truth and the other being under the influence of unrighteousness and wrongdoing (Set). To the person who does unrighteousness and commits acts of wrongdoing he (the Divine) gives that (adversity) to them as the result of their unrighteous actions.

[12] Translation by Dr. Muata Ashby

Verse D.

D.1.	***Maat***	***en***	***shemsy***	***kher – z - a***
D.2.	Order/truth	to	follower	under influence person.

D.3. To the person who follows order/truth, and influence of righteousness, they get that (prosperity) as the result of their righteousness. Therefore, having two heads and being often conflicted, sometimes one gets positive results of one's actions and sometimes negative. This state of mind, called Apophis, of being conflicted, leads to disjointed movement in life, thwarting one's own positive efforts and failure on the spiritual path by thinking, feeling and acting in contradiction, working against oneself and one's better judgment. The mindset of Apophis needs to be opposed, and the character influenced by Maat is to be cultivated in order to have rectitude, order, and resolute purpose in the personality to succeed on the spiritual path.

Iconographic Wisdom: The Herufy Depiction as Teaching on Personality Architecture

The iconographic representation of Herufy reveals crucial wisdom about the relationship between the spiritual aspiration (Heru) and the egoic force (Set) within the single personality. Consider carefully what the ancient artists depicted: the figure possesses the complete body and primary head of Heru, indicating that Heru represents the rightful sovereign of the personality—the spiritual aspect that should govern the entire being. Nevertheless, emerging from where the neckline meets the shoulder appears the head of Set as an appendage, a secondary growth arising from the same body rather than a separate entity. This iconographic detail illuminates a profound psychological principle: Set operates not as an external invader but as an outgrowth from the personality itself—what Chapter 2, verse 16 describes as the "foreign body, a storm that comes to the personality and disrupts it." The depiction shows Set attached to Heru's body, demonstrating that while the egoic aspect emerges from the same personality structure, it functions as an intrusive appendage that disrupts the natural harmony Heru's sovereignty would provide. The wisdom to be understood encompasses recognition that Set cannot be severed or eliminated (being organically connected to the personality's manifestation), but must be controlled and harmonized under Heru's governance through the systematic practice of Maat philosophy and the purification of aryu density that empowers Set's disruptive storming. The iconography thus teaches that spiritual development involves not removing the Set-appendage but rather establishing Heru's rightful sovereignty over the unified personality such that the egoic aspect operates as servant rather than usurper—precisely the transformation that occurs when vital-life-fire burns away the aryu patterns that give Set compelling force to overwhelm the mind with his characteristic stormy, heated disruptions.

The mystical mechanics of Amenemopet's teaching about "storming of words" when aryu arise [verses 14-15] receive profound illumination from the Ancient Egyptian Pert-m-Heru Chapter 17, which reveals that this storming emerges from what might be termed the Herufy condition—the mind operating with "two heads" simultaneously present within one personality, each exerting influence over the hat (conscious awareness) from opposing dispositions stored in the ab (unconscious). This teaching explains the precise architecture through which superficial wisdom absorption fails while deep penetration that ignites vital-life-fire succeeds in creating genuine transformation from heated to silent mind and feelings.

The ancient Pert-m-Heru Chapter 17, verses 27-28 provides the foundational teaching:

Verse B: B.1. Ky djed Heru pu un n-f im tepui unen ua kher B.2. Otherwise said Horus that being to-he in heads-two being one under influence B.3. Another way to understand it is: We are talking about Horus, the redemptive spiritual aspiration quality of the personality when he is in the state where he has two heads (also known as Herufy), having two opposing dispositions, one being under the influence or control of...

Verse C: C.1. Maat ky kher isfetu didi-f isfetu en ari - zy C.2. order/truth other under influence unrighteousness. giveth he unrighteousness to doer thereof. C.3. ...order and truth (Maat) and the other being under the influence of unrighteousness and wrongdoing (Set). To the person who does unrighteousness and commits acts of wrongdoing he (the Divine) gives that (adversity) to them as the result of their unrighteous actions.

Verse D: D.1. Maat en shemsy kher – z - a D.2. Order/truth to follower under influence person. D.3. To the person who follows order/truth, and influence of righteousness, they get that (prosperity) as the result of their righteousness. [20]

The text identifies this dual-headed state with Apophis, teaching that the mind "having two heads and being often conflicted, sometimes one gets positive results of one's actions and sometimes negative. This state of mind, called Apophis, of being conflicted, leads to disjointed movement in life, thwarting one's own positive efforts and failure on the spiritual path by thinking, feeling and acting in contradiction, working against oneself and one's better judgment." [20]

This Herufy architecture illuminates the mechanics Amenemopet describes in verses 14-15. It is a description of how "karma" functions in the Ancient Egyptian New Kingdom era (1550 BCE to 1070 BCE.), hundreds of years before its description in the Indian Upanishads c. 799-300 BCE. When "karmic-feeling-memories (aryu) arise from your unconscious into your conscious mind," what actually occurs is that aryu patterns stored in the ab activate the Set-head disposition—the egoistic, worldly aspect seeking to maintain control through reactive patterns that blot out Ab Neter awareness. Simultaneously, if wisdom teachings have been absorbed superficially (remaining at that level without penetrating ab to ignite udja), the Heru-head disposition—the redemptive spiritual aspiration seeking alignment with Maat—lacks sufficient strength to counter the Set-head's influence. This creates precisely the "storming of words" Amenemopet describes: the mind experiences violent internal conflict as both heads compete for sovereignty, neither possessing decisive advantage, resulting in the "disjointed movement" and "working against oneself" that prevents both earthly well-being and Ab Neter discovery.

Verse D reveals the crucial karmic mechanism that directly connects the Herufy teaching to Amenemopet's primary instruction about aryu (karmic patterns) and to Maat philosophy's foundational understanding of cosmic justice. When the Heru-head maintains governance—the mind operating under the influence of Maat (order, truth, righteousness)—actions generate positive aryu that create prosperity, well-being, and conditions supporting spiritual development. Conversely, when the Set-head dominates—the mind operating under the influence of isfet (unrighteousness, disorder)—actions generate negative aryu that create adversity, suffering, and obstacles to discovering Ab Neter. This teaching demonstrates that the "two heads" condition produces not merely internal psychological conflict but tangible external consequences through the universal law of aryu accumulation. The Apophis state of being "often conflicted, sometimes one gets positive results of one's actions and sometimes negative" describes precisely what occurs when neither head maintains consistent governance: the mind alternates between Heru-aligned and Set-aligned behavior, consequently experiencing an unpredictable mixture of positive and negative aryu results that prevents the stable well-being Prologue verse 2 identifies as the goal of earthly existence.

The wisdom to be understood reveals that every human personality contains both Heru and Set aspects operating from the ab level—this dual nature represents not spiritual deficiency but the necessary architecture for mind evolution. Nevertheless, when teachings remain superficial, failing to ignite vital-life-fire, both heads maintain equal compelling force. Aryu patterns feed the Set-head's egoistic dispositions while wisdom concepts provide only weak support for the Heru-head's spiritual aspirations. The personality oscillates between the two, sometimes acting righteously (when Heru-head influences hat) and sometimes acting from heated patterns (when Set-head influences hat), creating what the Pert-m-Heru identifies as the Apophis state of fundamental conflict. Most significantly, this oscillation generates mixed aryu—both positive patterns from righteous moments and negative patterns from unrighteous moments—that keeps the mind trapped in cyclical suffering where gains from wise action become undermined by losses from foolish action, preventing the consistent spiritual progress necessary for Ab Neter discovery.

The resolution emerges through the vital-life-fire mechanism that deep wisdom absorption ignites. When teachings penetrate "the innermost levels of the mind (unconscious)" [verses 11-13] and activate udja, this purifying fire specifically strengthens the Heru-head's governance capacity while burning away the aryu patterns that empower the Set-head's egoistic compelling force. The "mooring post" that verse 16 describes represents precisely this: Heru-head achieving sufficient sovereignty through vital-life-fire activation that when aryu arise (Set-head attempts to seize control), the purifying fire automatically activates maintaining mental stability under Heru governance rather than being swept into Apophis conflict. This consistent Heru governance produces the karmic consequence Verse D describes—the mind following Maat generates positive aryu that create prosperity and well-being, supporting both Prologue goals simultaneously: earthly well-being through righteous action's natural consequences, and Ab Neter discovery through the progressive thinning of negative aryu density that blocks kara awareness. The goal, as the teaching reveals, involves not Set elimination—which would be impossible since the worldly aspect serves necessary functions—but rather proper harmonization where the Set-head operates under Heru guidance, both aspects united in service to Asar (the soul principle) rather than competing for dominance. This represents what the ancient wisdom calls "becoming Heru"—the mind achieving the sovereign state where spiritual aspiration maintains consistent governance over personality while egoistic patterns serve rather than oppose the soul's evolutionary unfoldment toward Ab Neter realization, generating the positive aryu that Maat philosophy teaches naturally flows from the mind aligned with divine order.

The ultimate metaphysical implication connects to Prologue verse 9's teaching about Ab Neter. The ab contains both aryu (surface unconscious creating obstruction) and Ab Neter (deep unconscious providing divine foundation). Deeply absorbed wisdom works at the ab level to ignite vital-life-fire that burns away aryu density, and as this purifying fire progressively consumes obstructing patterns, awareness naturally penetrates deeper toward the kara where Ab Neter resides. The "peacefulness of mind" [verse 14] that wisdom protects through activated udja isn't merely absence of mental agitation but the gradually emerging awareness of Ab Neter—the divine foundation that Prologue verse 9 teaches would "render the egoic impulses of aryu powerless." This rendering powerless occurs specifically through vital-life-fire burning away the energetic patterns that gave aryu their compelling force.

Verses 1-2 establish this as systematic technology: "Words...from the chief scribe" are designed so "the living-ears...would hear these words would listen to and obey them," specifically to "develop vital-life-fire (udja) that produces spiritual purity and well-being." The metaphysics reveal that spiritual teachings function as mind-restructuring programs that ignite the purifying fire—when allowed to penetrate the ab (unconscious), they literally reprogram the patterns operating at that level by burning away aryu and revealing Ab Neter. This isn't metaphorical but describes actual transformation through vital-life-fire: the unconscious patterns (aryu) that determine how the mind interprets experience and generates responses get consumed by the purifying flame that deeply absorbed wisdom ignites.

The cosmic implication encompasses understanding that each individual's vital-life-fire development participates in collective mind evolution. When the individual mind allows wisdom to penetrate the ab and ignite udja that burns away aryu density, this creates beneficial influence extending beyond personal circumstances. The transformation from heated to silent mind and feelings—from aryu-driven reactivity to Ab Neter awareness revealed through purifying fire—represents participation in the cosmic evolution of consciousness itself. Verses 16-18's teaching about becoming "remote in your mind, detached and collected" describes the mind achieving sufficient vital-life-fire activation to burn away enough aryu that it can begin recognizing its Ab Neter foundation rather than remaining identified with aryu-generated egoic perspective that the purifying fire reveals as temporary obstruction rather than permanent identity.

4. Transpersonal Psychology Research Validation

Contemporary neuroscience research provides remarkable validation for Amenemopet's teaching about deep versus superficial learning and the transformation process that parallels what this tradition describes as vital-life-fire ignition, through studies demonstrating that lasting behavioral change requires neuroplastic modifications at unconscious processing levels, not merely conscious intellectual understanding. Research by neuroscientist Rick Hanson [1] reveals that positive neuroplastic changes—actual restructuring of neural pathways—require sustained attention, emotional engagement, and conscious repetition over extended periods. This empirically confirms the ancient teaching that superficial intellectual exposure fails to create transformation, while deep absorption into "the innermost levels of the mind" [verses 11-13] produces genuine change that parallels the purifying fire process Amenemopet describes.

Studies on implicit memory systems validate the aryu concept with precision. Research by cognitive scientist Daniel Schacter [2] demonstrates that unconscious memory systems store experiential patterns that automatically influence present behavior without conscious awareness or recall. This directly parallels the teaching about "karmic-feeling-memories (aryu) arise from your unconscious into your conscious mind" [verses 14-15]—empirical confirmation that unconscious patterns stored from past experiences emerge into conscious awareness as thoughts, emotions, and behavioral impulses that can "overwhelm" unless consciousness has developed the capacity (via vital-life-fire in this tradition, via neuroplastic change in neuroscience terms) to modify these automatic patterns through deep practice.

Neuroscience research on dual-process cognition confirms the distinction between conscious and unconscious mental operations. Studies by Daniel Kahneman [3] documented that human behavior emerges from interaction between conscious, controlled processing (System 2) and unconscious, automatic processing (System 1). This empirically validates the framework of hat (conscious awareness) being influenced by patterns in the ab (unconscious)—what Kahneman terms System 1 corresponds to aryu patterns operating automatically, while System 2 corresponds to conscious awareness attempting to regulate behavior. The vital-life-fire teaching adds the transformative mechanism: deeply absorbed wisdom generates the purifying energy (what neuroscience sees as neuroplastic modification) that actually changes automatic System 1 patterns rather than merely attempting conscious System 2 override.

Research on meditation and brain structure changes validates that contemplative practices create measurable neuroplastic modifications supporting the kind of mind/personality transformation Amenemopet describes through vital-life-fire ignition. Studies by Sara Lazar and colleagues [4] using magnetic resonance imaging demonstrated that regular meditation practice increases cortical thickness in brain regions associated with attention, interoception, and sensory processing. This provides empirical evidence that systematic contemplative practices—the methods for deep wisdom absorption that ignite udja—literally restructure brain anatomy in ways supporting enhanced self-regulation and reduced reactivity. From this tradition's perspective, these structural changes represent the physical correlates of vital-life-fire burning away aryu patterns and strengthening wisdom patterns at the neurological level.

Studies on cognitive-behavioral therapy mechanisms validate the teaching about replacing unconscious patterns through systematic practice that parallels vital-life-fire activation. Research documented by Beck and colleagues [5] demonstrates that modifying automatic thought patterns requires sustained conscious effort to identify unconscious patterns, challenge their validity, and systematically practice alternative responses. This empirically confirms Amenemopet's teaching that transformation requires allowing wisdom to penetrate the unconscious level where automatic patterns reside, not merely understanding concepts intellectually. The vital-life-fire framework explains the mechanism: conscious practice generates purifying energy that gradually burns away (neurologically: weakens and dissolves) automatic negative patterns while strengthening alternative wisdom patterns.

Neuroscience research on habit formation and extinction validates the "mooring post" teaching and the vital-life-fire mechanism. Studies by Bouton [6] demonstrate that changing established behavioral patterns requires both extinction of old associations and formation of new competing associations at the neural level. This confirms that deeply absorbed wisdom must create new unconscious patterns (mooring posts infused with vital-life-fire) that compete with existing aryu patterns, explaining why superficial learning that doesn't reach unconscious levels fails to modify automatic behavior. The purifying fire teaching adds precision: new patterns don't merely compete but actually burn away (dissolve the neural binding of) old patterns through the transformative energy generated by deep absorption.

Research on learning and memory consolidation validates the distinction between shallow and deep processing. Studies by Craik and Lockhart [7] demonstrated that information processed for meaning and personal relevance creates more durable memory traces than information processed superficially. This empirically confirms the teaching about the difference between hearing and "listening carefully and reflecting for deep understanding" [verses 8-10]—deep processing creates the neural changes necessary for information to influence unconscious patterns. From this tradition's perspective, deep processing generates the concentration of awareness that ignites vital-life-fire, while superficial processing lacks the intensity necessary to activate the purifying fire.

Studies on mindfulness and emotional regulation validate the development of what Amenemopet calls becoming "remote in your mind, detached and collected" [verses 16-18] through vital-life-fire cultivation. Research by Hölzel and colleagues [8] documented that mindfulness training increases activation in brain regions associated with attention control and emotional regulation while decreasing activation in regions associated with automatic emotional reactivity. This provides neurological evidence for the transformation from heated consciousness (automatic aryu-driven reactivity) toward silent consciousness (stable awareness with capacity to observe patterns without being controlled by them). The vital-life-fire framework explains this as the purifying fire burning away automatic reactivity patterns while revealing the stable Ab Neter foundation beneath.

Research Scope Clarification

The mindfulness research cited throughout this section primarily documents neurological and psychological changes occurring at the hat (conscious awareness) and ka (mental operations) levels—demonstrable improvements in attention, emotional regulation, stress response, and cognitive function. While these empirical findings validate that systematic attention training produces measurable benefits and creates neurological conditions supportive of deeper practice, contemporary mindfulness research typically does not investigate or document the ab-level transformation and Ab Neter recognition that Amenemopet's complete teaching facilitates. The research demonstrates mechanisms parallel to early stages of ancient contemplative training but does not encompass the full metaphysical transformation from ego-identification to divine consciousness recognition. Therefore, when citing mindfulness studies as validation for Ancient Egyptian teachings, I reference the attention-training mechanisms and psychological benefits that create foundation for—but differ in ultimate purpose from—sau-Neberdjer's consciousness awakening aim.

5. Spiritual Implications for Aspirants

PART A: PASTORAL CONCERNS IN MODERN CONTEXT

These Chapter 1 verses reveal profound challenges for modern aspirants attempting deep wisdom absorption that ignites vital-life-fire in environments designed to maintain superficial engagement and prevent the purifying fire from activating. The primary concern emerges from what verses 8-10 identify as the ease of "hearing and thinking you understand" without "listening carefully and reflecting for deep understanding" necessary to ignite udja. Modern culture actively promotes this superficial approach—spiritual teachings presented as interesting information for consumption rather than mind-restructuring technology requiring systematic implementation that allows vital-life-fire to burn away aryu patterns.

Consider the modern seeker surrounded by abundant spiritual content: podcasts during commutes, YouTube lectures during lunch breaks, audiobooks while exercising, social media posts throughout the day. This person accumulates vast spiritual information—the hat (conscious awareness) filled with concepts about meditation, enlightenment, consciousness—yet the ab (unconscious) remains unchanged because vital-life-fire never ignites. Aryu patterns continue operating exactly as before spiritual exposure began, or manifesting marginal but insubstantial and therefore temporary change rather than progress toward permanent transformation through the purifying fire. When challenging circumstances arise, the "karmic-feeling-memories (aryu) arise from your unconscious" [verse 14] and create the same "storming of words" that characterized pre-spiritual life because teachings never penetrated beyond surface intellectual understanding to ignite the vital-life-fire that could burn away these arising patterns.

The modern pace of life creates particular obstacles to the deep absorption verses 11-13 describe as necessary for transformation through udja ignition. Allowing teachings to reach "the innermost levels of the mind (unconscious)" where vital-life-fire can ignite requires sustained contemplative engagement—time for reflection, silence for absorption, patience for integration that allows the purifying fire to develop. Yet contemporary scheduling leaves minimal space for such depth. Someone might listen to spiritual teaching during their commute, immediately transition to work demands, handle family responsibilities in evening, then collapse into sleep—when do teachings penetrate beyond surface awareness to reach the ab where aryu reside and where vital-life-fire must ignite to burn them away?

The challenge intensifies because modern aryu accumulation occurs at unprecedented rates while opportunities for vital-life-fire cultivation decrease. Previous generations accumulated aryu primarily through direct experiences and had more natural opportunity for the contemplative absorption that ignites the purifying fire. The vital-life-fire represents a modulation of energy that comes from the god Ra (an aspect of Neberdjer) and becomes effective when personality energy is not squandered on worldly thinking, feeling, desires, and ignorant self-awareness [12][13]. Instead of spending quantity and quality time experiencing and living in wisdom and mind-body harmony with nature (including dedicated time spent contemplating the nature of self beyond the hat level of mind and the egoic aryu), most modern individuals spend significant time accumulating negative aryu through thousands of hours of media consumption: television programming normalizing heated mind and feelings, social media training reactive emotional patterns, news cultivating anxiety, entertainment glorifying desire-driven behavior. This constant squandering of personality energy on worldly concerns prevents vital-life-fire from developing focus and growing to purify the personality [12][13]. By the time someone encounters spiritual teachings, their ab contains extraordinarily dense aryu layers—each requiring the patient burning that vital-life-fire provides but superficial engagement cannot ignite.

The modern spiritual marketplace actually reinforces superficial engagement that prevents udja ignition. Teachings get packaged as "stress reduction," "productivity enhancement," or "wellness practice"—framed to support comfortable life rather than transform the mind through purifying fire. Someone might practice meditation to improve work performance, study philosophy to enhance conversational skills, or attend retreats for pleasant experiences—all superficial engagement that keeps teachings at hat (conscious) level without allowing penetration to ab (unconscious) where vital-life-fire must ignite to burn away aryu patterns and reveal Ab Neter. The person experiences spiritual involvement while aryu density remains unchanged, Ab Neter awareness remains blocked, and the purifying fire never activates.

The pattern verses 11-13 warn against—"turning away from these teachings"—manifests subtly in modern context as resistance to the depth required for vital-life-fire ignition. Someone doesn't reject spirituality but engages in ways preventing deep absorption and udja activation: reading multiple books without implementing any practices that would ignite the purifying fire, attending various workshops without sustained commitment to one approach that would allow vital-life-fire to build intensity, collecting spiritual experiences without allowing transformation of underlying patterns through the burning process. This creates "mental weakness"—the mind gradually loses discriminative capacity to recognize that decades of superficial spiritual engagement have produced no genuine vital-life-fire ignition, no aryu purification, no revelation of Ab Neter.

Family and social dynamics create additional obstacles to vital-life-fire cultivation. Someone attempting the deep contemplative work required to allow teachings into "the innermost levels of the mind" where udja can ignite faces social pressure to maintain normal engagement patterns. Taking time for sustained reflection that would allow the purifying fire to develop gets interpreted as withdrawal or laziness. Declining social invitations to protect contemplative practice that ignites vital-life-fire creates conflict. Implementing ethical restraints that prevent new aryu accumulation (refusing gossip, avoiding dishonest business practices, restraining desire expression) invites criticism from those whose own aryu-driven patterns feel threatened by someone achieving silent mind and feelings through vital-life-fire cultivation.

The challenge of distinguishing genuine from superficial spiritual teachers creates concern about finding guidance for vital-life-fire development. Verses 1-2 emphasize receiving "Words...from the chief scribe" who provides authentic guidance for igniting udja—but the modern spiritual marketplace mixes genuine wisdom teaching about vital-life-fire cultivation with diluted adaptations designed for mass appeal that avoid the purifying fire's demanding work. How does an aspirant recognize teachers who understand and can guide vital-life-fire ignition versus those who keep teachings superficial to maintain comfortable student engagement that never activates the purifying processes? Someone might spend years with teachers who never push beyond surface understanding, mistaking pleasant spiritual experiences for the transformation requiring vital-life-fire to burn away aryu and reveal Ab Neter.

Most challenging is recognizing one's own resistance patterns to vital-life-fire ignition. The egoic perspective—arising from aryu-obscured mind—naturally avoids the deep absorption work that would ignite purifying fire threatening its familiar operation. The mind develops sophisticated justifications for superficial engagement that prevents udja activation: "I understand these teachings intellectually, actual practice that would ignite purifying fire can wait until circumstances improve," "I need to study more traditions before committing to practice that generates vital-life-fire," "My life situation is too demanding for serious spiritual work requiring sustained contemplation for udja ignition." Meanwhile, vital-life-fire never ignites, aryu density remains unchanged, heated mind and feelings persist, and the goals of Prologue verses 2 and 9—developing vital-life-fire that produces spiritual purity and earthly well-being and discovering Ab Neter through aryu purification—remain unachieved despite years of superficial spiritual involvement.

PART B: METHODS FOR TRANSFORMATION THROUGH VITAL-LIFE-FIRE CULTIVATION

Despite these formidable obstacles, Amenemopet provides systematic guidance for developing the deep wisdom absorption necessary to ignite vital-life-fire (udja) that thins aryu density and reveals Ab Neter awareness. The foundational practice implements what verses 11-13 prescribe: allowing teachings to penetrate "the innermost levels of the mind (unconscious)" where vital-life-fire can ignite rather than remaining at surface intellectual understanding. This requires transforming the relationship with spiritual instruction from information consumption to mind restructuring through purifying fire activation.

Practice 1: Teaching Contemplation for Udja Ignition

Begin with Teaching Contemplation practice specifically designed to ignite vital-life-fire: select a specific verse or principle daily and spend 15-20 minutes in sustained contemplative reflection that generates the concentrated awareness necessary for udja activation. This isn't intellectual analysis but receptive absorption—reading the teaching slowly multiple times, sitting with it in silence, allowing its implications to penetrate beneath conscious thought into felt understanding where vital-life-fire begins igniting. The goal isn't clever interpretation but deep absorption that generates the purifying fire, letting teaching settle into the ab (unconscious) where it can ignite udja that burns away aryu patterns and provides "mooring post" stability infused with the purifying flame.

Consider the practical example of someone working with verse 16's teaching about wisdom acting as "mooring post for your tongue." Rather than reading this once and thinking "I understand restraint is important," practice contemplative absorption designed to ignite vital-life-fire: spend 20 minutes daily for a week reflecting on this image of mooring post infused with purifying fire, feeling what it means to have a stable anchor generating udja when storms arise, imagining how deeply absorbed restraint wisdom would activate vital-life-fire automatically when anger-aryu emerge, visualizing the purifying flame consuming the anger pattern before it can overwhelm the mind. Over weeks of this contemplative work, the teaching begins penetrating the ab and igniting udja—you start noticing automatic restraint impulses arising accompanied by subtle sensation of purifying fire activating when previously you would have reacted immediately without any vital-life-fire to burn away the reactive pattern.

Practice 2: Aryu Awareness and Udja Recognition Practice

For working directly with aryu patterns verses 14-15 describe while developing vital-life-fire recognition, implement Aryu Awareness and Udja Recognition Practice: throughout daily activities, maintain alert observation for moments when "karmic-feeling-memories arise from your unconscious into your conscious mind." When you notice sudden anger, compulsive desire, anxious thought, reactive judgment—recognize: "This is aryu arising from the ab into the hat. This is the pattern requiring purification through vital-life-fire." This practice gradually develops capacity to observe aryu patterns rather than being overwhelmed by them, beginning the transformation from heated (aryu-controlled) to silent (aryu-observing with udja-activated) mind and feelings.

Additionally, develop sensitivity to recognize when vital-life-fire activates in response to arising aryu. Initially this appears as subtle warmth, clarity, or spaciousness that arises when deeply absorbed wisdom spontaneously activates against reactive patterns. Someone who has deeply absorbed restraint teaching notices a moment of choice rather than automatic reaction—this choice-space represents vital-life-fire activating, creating a gap between aryu arising and potential reactive expression. With sustained practice cultivating udja over months, this subtle activation strengthens into clear recognition: you feel the purifying fire burning away the compelling force of arising patterns, experiencing freedom from what previously felt like overwhelming impulse.

Practice 6: Ethical Restraint for Preventing Aryu Accumulation

For preventing new aryu accumulation while the vital-life-fire works on existing patterns, implement Ethical Restraint Practice: identify specific behaviors that reinforce aryu density (gossip feeding judgment-aryu, dishonesty reinforcing deception-aryu, overconsumption strengthening desire-aryu) and commit to restraint that protects developing vital-life-fire. The wisdom to be understood here is that vital-life-fire represents a modulation of energy from Ra (an aspect of Neberdjer) that becomes effective when personality energy is not squandered on worldly thinking, feeling, desires, and ignorant self-awareness [12][13]. Each time you successfully restrain rather than indulge, you prevent aryu reinforcement while simultaneously conserving personality energy that would otherwise be squandered—this conserved energy naturally feeds vital-life-fire, allowing it to develop focus and grow to purify the personality [12][13]. Over months, behaviors that previously felt compelling lose their force as underlying aryu patterns weaken from non-reinforcement while vital-life-fire gains strength from both consistent ethical practice and conservation of personality energy, eventually burning away these patterns entirely.

For aspirants recognizing years of superficial engagement without vital-life-fire ignition, don't despair about "wasted time"—instead implement immediate correction. Select one teaching for deep absorption using contemplative methods described above specifically designed to ignite udja. Commit to working with this single teaching for three months rather than consuming multiple new teachings, allowing sufficient time for vital-life-fire to ignite and stabilize. This depth-over-breadth approach begins creating genuine transformation through purifying fire activation. As verse 16 promises, properly absorbed wisdom will provide stability infused with vital-life-fire "when those mental impressions start working in the mind and there is a storming of words"—you'll recognize successful deep absorption and udja ignition when previously overwhelming aryu patterns no longer compel automatic reaction because the purifying fire automatically activates to burn them away before reactive expression can occur.

A Final Word: A Simple Understanding for Patient Practice

Indeed, the teaching about vital-life-fire may seem complex when first encountered, but consider the simple truth at its heart: the wisdom you study is meant to become a living flame within you, not merely information stored in memory. One may ask oneself, "How do I know if teachings have penetrated deeply enough to ignite this purifying fire?" The answer emerges through honest observation—when challenging circumstances arise, do you find yourself automatically reacting from old patterns, or do you sense a gentle burning away of impulses before they overwhelm the mind? This vital-life-fire develops gradually through patient daily practice, like tending a flame that grows stronger with consistent fuel and attention. Nevertheless, do not become discouraged if the fire seems dim at first. The time in the temple of the heart illumines what the mind cannot, and every moment spent allowing teachings to penetrate beyond surface understanding contributes to the purifying process that gradually burns away what prevents you from recognizing your divine foundation. Therefore, trust in Amenemopet's promise that properly absorbed wisdom becomes a "mooring post" infused with transformative energy, and remember that the goal is not to force this fire into existence but to create conditions where it can naturally ignite through devoted study, contemplative absorption, and ethical living aligned with Maat.

HTP (Peace)

References

[1] Hanson, R. (2013). *Hardwiring Happiness: The New Brain Science of Contentment, Calm, and Confidence*. Harmony Books.

[2] Schacter, D. L. (1987). Implicit memory: History and current status. *Journal of Experimental Psychology: Learning, Memory, and Cognition*, 13(3), 501-518.

[3] Kahneman, D. (2011). *Thinking, Fast and Slow*. Farrar, Straus and Giroux.

[4] Lazar, S. W., Kerr, C. E., Wasserman, R. H., Gray, J. R., Greve, D. N., Treadway, M. T., McGarvey, M., Quinn, B. T., Dusek, J. A., Benson, H., Rauch, S. L., Moore, C. I., & Fischl, B. (2005). Meditation experience is associated with increased cortical thickness. *NeuroReport*, 16(17), 1893-1897.

[5] Beck, A. T., Rush, A. J., Shaw, B. F., & Emery, G. (1979). *Cognitive Therapy of Depression*. Guilford Press.

[6] Bouton, M. E. (2004). Context and behavioral processes in extinction. *Learning & Memory*, 11(5), 485-494.

[7] Craik, F. I. M., & Lockhart, R. S. (1972). Levels of processing: A framework for memory research. *Journal of Verbal Learning and Verbal Behavior*, 11(6), 671-684.

[8] Hölzel, B. K., Carmody, J., Vangel, M., Congleton, C., Yerramsetti, S. M., Gard, T., & Lazar, S. W. (2011). Mindfulness practice leads to increases in regional brain gray matter density. *Psychiatry Research: Neuroimaging*, 191(1), 36-43.

[9] Ashby, M. (2019-25). *Mysticism of Amenemopet Hieroglyphic Text Translation*. Sema Institute of Ancient Egyptian Studies.

[10] Ashby, M. (2024). *Amenemopet lectures 2024 by Dr Muata Ashby transcripts*. Sema Institute of Ancient Egyptian Studies.

[11] Ashby, M. (2025). *Keys to Sage Amenemopet wisdom text trilinear translation chapter 1 by Dr Muata Ashby*. Sema Institute of Ancient Egyptian Studies.

[12] Ashby, M. (2022). *Mystic Transpersonal Psychology of the Mysteries of Ra and Sekhmet*. Sema Institute of Ancient Egyptian Studies.

[13] Ashby, M. (2022). *Scripture of Ra and Hetheru—Trilinear Translation by Dr. Muata Ashby*. Sema Institute of Ancient Egyptian Studies.

[14] Ashby, M. (2024). *Amenemopet lectures 2024 by Dr Muata Ashby transcripts*. Sema Institute of Ancient Egyptian Studies.

[15] Ashby, M. (2019). *Amenemopet lectures 2019 by Dr Muata Ashby transcripts*. Sema Institute of Ancient Egyptian Studies.

[16] Ashby, M. (1999). *The Asarian Resurrection: The Ancient Egyptian Bible*. Sema Institute of Ancient Egyptian Studies.

[17] Ashby, M. (2019-25). *Mysticism of Amenemopet Hieroglyphic Text Translation*. Sema Institute of Ancient Egyptian Studies.

[18] Ashby, M. (2025). *Awakening Your Soul-Aware-Witness Ancient Egyptian Wisdom To Discover Divine Consciousness*. Sema Institute of Ancient Egyptian Studies.

[19] Ashby, M. (Year). *The Serpent Power: The Ancient Egyptian Path to Enlightenment*. Sema Institute of Ancient Egyptian Studies.

[20] Ashby, M. (2025). *Awakening Your Soul-Aware-Witness Ancient Egyptian Wisdom To Discover Divine Consciousness*. Sema Institute of Ancient Egyptian Studies.

CHAPTER 3: Commentary on Teachings of Amenemopet Chapter 2, Verses 10, 16-17: The Cosmic Psychology of Unrighteous Action and the Enemy of Life

SUMMARY OF VERSES COVERED

Verse 10 establishes that actions considered bad according to Maat philosophy act as "a means of forsaking, turning away from the caring of the natural forces, the waters, the land, and the like," creating "raging tempests in life with "thunderousness"" and leaving the personality vulnerable to "crocodiles lying in wait" in the unconscious mind. The teaching reveals that unrighteous actions disconnect consciousness from the neteru (gods and goddesses)—the cosmic forces emanated by Neberdjer to sustain and nurture Creation—thereby severing the personality from the very forces commissioned to promote well-being [1][2].

Verse 16 introduces the concept of the "heated person" (shemm), distinguishing between transient heated states that arise temporarily in all human beings versus the chronic heated mind and feelings that becomes "the mainstay of their life." Coming out of harmony with nature develops the personality into "ragefulness", anger, and anxiety, rendering it vulnerable to dangers of body and mind symbolized by crocodiles. This heated condition creates a personality that is negative in disposition, feeling, and cognition—unaware, ignorant, insensible, unknowingly infirm, and susceptible to bad outcomes, spiritually alienated from the truth of Ab Neter/Neberdjer reality of self [1][2].

Verse 17 reveals that the heated person has engaged in the process outlined in verses 10 and 16 and has become an enemy of life itself. The wisdom defines life as being in physical and mental harmony with the forces of nature (neteru/gods and goddesses established by Neberdjer); thus, becoming an enemy to life means being in opposition to harmony and truth—this renders the personality as "heated." The heated condition is likened to a state of suffering because such a person cannot experience the benefits of calmness, serenity, harmony with nature, psychic balance, and the joy (love) of having connection with the divine (Ab Neter) which brings satisfaction and contentment. The complete psychological profile catalogues specific manifestations: "unrighteousness, fraud, anger, boisterousness, flippant retorts and thoughtless speech, inconsiderate and impulsive acts, rapacious greed, jealousy, envy, ridiculing others and having no compassion for the poor or the less fortunate" [1][2].

Core Teachings by Verse

- Verse 10 establishes the Teaching of Forsaking the Natural Forces: how unrighteous actions sever connection with the neteru (cosmic forces/gods and goddesses) that Neberdjer has commissioned to care for Creation, producing both external chaos ("tempests in life") and internal vulnerability to unconscious patterns ("crocodiles lying in wait")

- Verse 16 introduces the Teaching of Chronic Heated Mind and Feelings (shemm): the fundamental distinction between transient heated states versus systematic corruption of consciousness that alienates the personality from Ab Neter/Neberdjer reality

- Verse 17 provides the Teaching of the Heated Person as Enemy of Life: revealing that "life" means harmony with the forces of nature (neteru), and that heated mind and feelings creates suffering by preventing experience of divine connection, calmness, serenity, psychic balance, and the joy/love that brings contentment

These verses establish three interconnected teachings explored in this commentary: (1) the cosmic psychology of how unrighteous actions disconnect consciousness from the neteru that sustain well-being, (2) the distinction between temporary reactive states and chronic heated mind and feelings as alienation from Ab Neter/Neberdjer, and (3) the complete understanding that heated mind and feelings makes one an enemy of life by preventing the harmony, divine connection, and joy that constitute authentic living [1][2].

1. HUMAN PSYCHOLOGY PRINCIPLE: THE PSYCHOLOGY OF FORSAKING DIVINE CARE AND SELF-CREATED SUFFERING

The core psychological issue Sage Amenemopet addresses is the fundamental mechanism through which human consciousness severs its connection with the cosmic forces that sustain well-being and spiritual development, creating what the teaching reveals as "tempests in life with thunderousness" and vulnerability to "crocodiles lying in wait"—both external chaos and internal psychological dangers [verse 10]. The wisdom establishes that what is referred to as "bad actions" according to Maat philosophy operate not merely as violations of ethical codes but as active rejection of the neteru—the gods and goddesses that Neberdjer has commissioned to take care of Creation, the natural environment in which human beings live [verse 10][2]. Indeed, when consciousness engages in unrighteous actions, it operates as if turning away from, forsaking, the very forces of nature (waters, land, and natural order) that promote well-being, thereby disconnecting from the cosmic support system that Neberdjer has established for mind/personality development [verse 10][2].

This teaching directly impacts both Prologue goals: without proper relationship with the neteru (cosmic forces), the goal of [Prologue verse 2] "cause a person to have well-being while living on earth" cannot be achieved because the personality has severed connection with the very forces commissioned to provide that well-being. Moreover, forsaking the natural forces prevents [Prologue verse 9's] discovery of the kara (divine sanctuary) where Ab Neter resides, because unrighteous actions create dense aryu that obscure awareness of the divine presence dwelling within every person. Consider how the wisdom reveals that "life" itself means being in physical and mental harmony with the forces of nature—the neteru established by Neberdjer—such that becoming an "enemy of life" through heated mind and feelings represents opposition to harmony and truth itself [verse 17][2].

THE HIEROGLYPHIC REVELATION: TEMPEST AS EGO-SUPERIMPOSITION, NOT INNATE NATURE

[Verse 16's] hieroglyphic text delivers a profound theological teaching through its very structure: the word qerau (tempest) incorporates the determinative hieroglyph of Set—the god who symbolizes egoism in the personality [verse 16][1][2]. This linguistic precision reveals Amenemopet's sophisticated understanding that tempestuousness in the personality constitutes an ego-phenomenon specifically, not an attribute of the innate self. The Set determinative functions as theological marker identifying the source and nature of the "raging tempests in life with thunderousness"—they arise from egoic consciousness (Set), not from Ab Neter or the person's essential divine nature [verse 16][1][2].

Consider the implications of this hieroglyphic teaching. Tempest as concept encompasses agitation, movement, heat, vibration, shakiness—precisely the qualities the lecture transcripts identify when explaining Set symbolism: "the thunderousness, the boisterousness, the fear that is imposed—all this goes under the terms relating to vibration, movement, shakiness. It's not placid, not quiet, not still" [verse 16][17]. Therefore, when Amenemopet employs the Set determinative within the tempest hieroglyph, the teaching establishes that these qualities of agitation, movement, and heat belong specifically to the ego aspect of personality, not to the consciousness itself or to Ab Neter awareness [verse 16][1][2][17].

This reveals a crucial theological distinction that transforms understanding of the spiritual path: the innate self—Ab Neter residing in the kara—does NOT possess tempestuous quality. The agitation, the heated mind and feelings, the storminess and bombastic nature all represent what the teaching calls ego-corruption superimposed upon the personality, not the original divine nature temporarily obscured by aryu [verse 16][verse 17][1][2][17]. As the Keys document clarifies: "In this state of harmony, calmness, serenity there is connection with the Divine and thus connection and awareness of being more than just physical, ego individual being" [2]. This means ger (serenity/silence) constitutes the INNATE nature sustained by Ab Neter, while shemm (heated/tempestuous state) represents CORRUPTION imposed by egoic patterns operating through dense aryu without awareness of divine foundation [verse 17][2].

The metaphysical implication proves profound: mind transformation does not require creating serenity where none exists, but rather removing the ego-superimposition (tempestuousness) to reveal the serene nature that Ab Neter sustains as the personality's essential foundation [verse 16][verse 17][1][17]. This aligns with the Prologue's teaching that purification operates by removing aryu obstruction rather than creating divine access—because Ab Neter already sustains consciousness, and serenity represents consciousness's natural state when not corrupted by egoic patterns [Prologue verse 9][1].

Therefore, verse 16's declaration that unrighteous action "develops the personality into ragefulness, anger, anxiety" describes not the emergence of new qualities but rather the superimposition of ego-tempestuousness onto the innate serene nature [verse 16][2]. The heated condition (shemm) identified in verse 17 represents **bb** not the manifestation of original nature—it is the personality operating through Set-consciousness (egoism) rather than Ab Neter-consciousness (divine awareness) [verse 17][1][2]. The philosophical interpretive guidance for this hieroglyph representing the God Set versus the term Ger related to Ab Neter (divinity in the heart) emphasizes: consciousness operating in harmony with natural forces experiences "calmness, serenity, harmony with nature, psychic balance," because this harmony **reveals** rather than creates the personality's divine foundation [verse 17][2].

This understanding reframes the entire spiritual endeavor: aspirants need not become something other than what they essentially are; rather, they must remove the ego-superimposition (Set-tempestuousness) obscuring recognition of what they have always been—serene Ab Neter consciousness temporarily operating through heated mind and feelings due to aryu density [verse 16][verse 17][1][2][17]. The path transforms from self-improvement project to restoration project—not creating serenity but restoring awareness of the serenity that constitutes consciousness's essential nature when freed from ego-corruption [verse 16][verse 17][1][2][17].

Modern Psychology Parallels

Modern psychology recognizes similar phenomena through several contexts: moral injury among veterans and healthcare workers who witness or participate in actions that violate their ethical beliefs, creating lasting psychological trauma and disconnection from core values; self-reinforcing cycles of addiction and compulsive behavior where initial poor choices gradually alter brain chemistry and decision-making capacity, severing connection with natural well-being; and what researchers call "moral disengagement," where individuals gradually adjust their ethical standards to rationalize increasingly questionable behavior, disconnecting from authentic conscience [3]. Nevertheless, the ancient teaching provides more precise psychological mapping than contemporary approaches by identifying the specific mechanism through which unrighteous actions don't simply produce external consequences but fundamentally sever consciousness from its cosmic support system—the neteru commissioned by Neberdjer to care for Creation and promote well-being [verse 10][verse 17][1][2].

The psychological principle reveals that this severing of connection with natural forces doesn't merely create difficulties in the external world but fundamentally corrupts what the wisdom calls "the source of the corrupted mind," creating systematic conditions where heated mind and feelings becomes the default mode of experiencing reality rather than a temporary disturbance of natural peace [verse 17]. The heated condition manifests as suffering precisely because "such a person cannot experience the benefits of calmness, serenity, harmony with nature, psychic balance and the joy (love) of having connection with the divine (Ab Neter) which brings satisfaction/contentment" [verse 17][2]. In this state of disharmony, the sources of suffering—disharmony, anxiety, hatred, ignorance—actively generate suffering in the personality, whereas in a state of harmony, calmness, and serenity, there is connection with the Divine and awareness of being more than just a physical, ego individual being, which naturally prevents these sources of suffering from arising [verse 17][2].

Therefore, the wisdom to be understood encompasses recognition that the heated person has become spiritually alienated from the truth of Ab Neter/Neberdjer reality of self through negative disposition, feeling, and cognition—rendered unaware, ignorant, insensible, unknowingly infirm, and susceptible to bad outcomes [verse 16][2]. This alienation from divine reality represents the fundamental psychological issue that generates all subsequent suffering, because without harmony with the forces of nature (neteru), consciousness cannot access the joy, love, contentment, and divine connection that constitute authentic well-being. Understanding the harmony of the universe allows one to not seek to reform the world according to ego desires but to align with the wisdom of Ab Neter/Neberdjer, which brings solace, contentedness, peace, and intuitional understanding about the nature of existence from God's perspective instead of limited human ego-driven perspectives [verse 17][2].

THE CAUSAL HIERARCHY: FROM SPIRITUAL IGNORANCE TO EGOISTIC SUFFERING

The wisdom reveals a crucial distinction between the effective cause and the source cause of human suffering that aspirants must understand to comprehend the full mechanism of heated mind and feelings. Egoism—the personality that has succumbed to the impelling, compelling forces of aryu that disturb the soul's perception of reality through the storm in the mind—operates as the effective cause of anxiety, strife, delusion, and unhappiness; it is the immediate mechanism through which suffering manifests in conscious experience [verse 16][verse 17][2]. Nevertheless, egoism itself represents a consequence rather than an ultimate origin, because the aryu constitute the source cause upon which egoistic personality depends for its very existence and perpetuation. These aryu—karmic feeling-memories from past experiences stored in the ab (unconscious mind)—create the psychological foundation that generates and sustains the egoistic patterns (Set consciousness) that produce suffering [verse 10][verse 16][1][2]. However, the teaching penetrates even deeper to reveal that aryu themselves depend upon spiritual ignorance as their sustaining foundation: the fundamental delusion about self-identity wherein consciousness mistakes itself for a mere animal or human being controlled by instincts, desires, and material limitations, rather than recognizing its essential nature as spirit—as Ab Neter/Neberdjer, the divine consciousness that transcends and sustains all temporary phenomena [verse 16][verse 17][2]. This spiritual ignorance (delusion about divine identity) generates the aryu, which in turn produce the egoistic personality, which finally manifests as the observable suffering, anxiety, and strife that plague human existence. Therefore, the complete understanding encompasses recognition that superficial behavioral modification addresses only symptoms (egoistic expressions), psychological purification addresses intermediate causes (aryu patterns), while authentic spiritual realization addresses the root cause itself (spiritual ignorance about Ab Neter/Neberdjer reality), thereby dissolving the entire causal chain that produces suffering [verse 17][2].

2. Behavioral Imperative: Set Symbolism and Becoming an Enemy of Life Through Opposition to Natural Harmony

Building upon the understanding of how consciousness severs connection with the neteru through unrighteous action, the specific psychological patterns that generate these cascading consequences manifest through identifiable behaviors requiring recognition of their deeper symbolic significance within the Ancient Egyptian consciousness framework [verse 10][verse 16]. The wisdom employs the symbol of Set—depicted as a four-legged animal with vertical tail and ears, curved snout—to represent what can be identify as "spiritual obstacles to knowing Self," the egoistic foundation that generates all heated personality expressions when operating without proper alignment with natural forces [verse 16][2]. Indeed, the four-legged symbolism indicates consciousness bound to earthly, worldly concerns, while Set's characteristic features represent the "storminess, the bombastic nature of the personality, the ruckus, the hubris" that prevents the inner stillness necessary for experiencing harmony with the neteru and recognizing one's divine nature as Ab Neter/Neberdjer [verse 16][2].

The behavioral pattern that emerges when consciousness forsakes the natural forces manifests as what verse 16 describes: "coming out of harmony with nature develops the personality into ragefulness, anger, anxiety"—a systematic corruption that renders the personality "negative in terms of disposition, feeling, and cognition and unaware, ignorant, insensible in a way of being that is unknowingly infirm and susceptible to bad outcomes" [verse 16][2]. Consider how this pattern operates: when consciousness engages in actions that turn away from the caring of the natural forces (the waters, the land, and the like), it creates "raging tempests in life with thunderousness" that rise to the heavens, encompassing the whole environment with cacophony—yelling, fighting, upset, chaos, infighting, failed relationships, and worldly entanglements that lead only to more strife and suffering rather than satisfaction or peace [verse 16][1].

Primary among these destructive patterns is what contemporary psychology calls cognitive dissonance—the capacity to maintain contradictory beliefs simultaneously, allowing practitioners to intellectually accept spiritual principles while behaviorally engaging in actions that contradict these same principles and sever connection with the natural order [3]. This psychological splitting creates the fundamental instability that generates both external chaos ("tempests in life with thunderousness") and internal heated mind and feelings, as consciousness attempts to maintain coherent identity while operating from values that oppose harmony with the neteru (cosmic forces) established by Neberdjer [verse 10][2]. The God Set symbolism (egoism in the personality) reveals this as the source of what the teaching calls "the thunderousness, the boisterousness, the fear that is imposed—all this goes under the terms relating to vibration, movement, shakiness," because "if your mind is not still, you're not going to be able to discern the nature of the absolute divine Self" or experience the harmony that allows connection with Ab Neter [verse 16][2].

The behavioral manifestations cataloged in verse 17 reveal the complete psychology of one who has become "an enemy of life" through opposition to harmony and truth: "unrighteousness, fraud, anger, boisterousness, flippant retorts and thoughtless speech, inconsiderate and impulsive acts, rapacious greed, jealousy, envy, ridiculing others and having no compassion for the poor or the less fortunate" [verse 17][1]. The wisdom reveals that "life" itself means being in physical and mental harmony with the forces of nature (neteru/gods and goddesses established by Neberdjer); therefore, becoming an enemy to this harmony through heated mind and feelings creates a state of suffering where one cannot experience "the benefits of calmness, serenity, harmony with nature, psychic balance, and the joy (love) of having connection with the divine (Ab Neter), which brings satisfaction/contentment" [verse 17][2].

The ego-personality structure perpetuates this enemy status through psychological patterns that obscure the proper relationship between consciousness and the cosmic forces. As the wisdom teaches: "Set can serve as a positive ally and servant to the soul (Asar {Osiris}) when operating under the guidance of higher consciousness, but can also turn toward negative thoughts, feelings, and actions when dominated by separative thinking and attachment to temporal concerns." Therefore, "the goal of spiritual development involves not the elimination of Set but rather the proper harmonization and orientation of this worldly aspect toward serving rather than competing with spiritual aspiration" [2]. This reveals that heated mind and feelings patterns, when properly understood and aligned with natural forces, can serve spiritual development by providing psychological material for the integration process that this tradition calls Smai Tawy—"the union of the two lands" or "the Union of the lower self with the Higher Self" [2].

Nevertheless, when operating through ignorance that has severed connection with the neteru, these same patterns manifest as rationalization (harmful actions receive intellectual justification that opposes natural harmony), projection (personal responsibility gets attributed to external circumstances rather than recognizing forsaking of natural forces), and what contemporary psychology might identify as using spiritual concepts primarily for emotional regulation rather than mind/personality transformation—where abstract spiritual principles provide psychological protection from practical ethical requirements without genuine integration or restoration of harmony with cosmic forces [3]. Consider how this protective mechanism often arises naturally when aspirants encounter spiritual teachings that exceed their current psychological capacity to integrate, or when overwhelming life circumstances necessitate temporary psychological stability through spiritual concepts rather than immediate behavioral transformation that would restore harmony with the neteru.

Particularly insidious is the condition where consciousness becomes spiritually alienated from "the truth of Ab Neter/Neberdjer reality of self" through accumulated negative disposition, feeling, and cognition, rendering the personality "unaware, ignorant, insensible in a way of being that is unknowingly infirm and susceptible to bad outcomes, involvement with negative aspects inconsistent with human physical and mental health" [verse 16][2]. This spiritual alienation prevents the personality from understanding "the harmony of the universe" that would naturally dissolve the ego's desire to "reform the world according to ego desires," because experiencing Ab Neter/Neberdjer as oneself allows "understanding and feeling beyond ego personal desires that the world is not setup to satisfy the ego but according to the wisdom of Ab Neter/Neberdjer," which brings "solace and contentedness, peace and intuitional understanding about the nature of existence from God's perspective instead of the limited human ego driven perspectives" [verse 17][2].

3. Mystic Psychology-Metaphysical Implications: The Cosmic Law of Natural Forces and Divine Connection as Life Itself

Building upon the Set symbolism understanding and the behavioral patterns of forsaking natural harmony, these verses reveal the fundamental metaphysical framework wherein individual consciousness operates within a cosmic ecology of divine forces (neteru) that Neberdjer has commissioned to sustain Creation and promote mind/personality development [verse 10][2]. the teaching establishes that what appears as "bad actions" actually represents severing of connection with this cosmic support system—the gods and goddesses that take care of the natural environment (waters, land, and all forces of nature) in which human beings live and through which mind evolves toward divine recognition [verse 10][2]. Indeed, when actions align with Maat (divine order), they maintain transparent connection with these neteru, allowing consciousness to receive the care and guidance that these cosmic forces provide; when actions oppose Maat, they create what verse 10 describes as "forsaking, turning away from the caring of the natural forces," thereby generating both external chaos and internal vulnerability [verse 10][1][2].

The mystical significance reveals that "life" itself—authentic living—means being in physical and mental harmony with the forces of nature (neteru established by Neberdjer), such that the heated person who operates in opposition to this harmony has literally become "an enemy of life" [verse 17][2]. This profound teaching establishes that existence in mere physical form does not constitute genuine "life" from the metaphysical perspective; rather, authentic life manifests through harmony with the cosmic forces, which produces "calmness, serenity harmony with nature, psychic balance and the joy (love) of having connection with the divine (Ab Neter) which brings satisfaction/contentment" [verse 17][2]. Consider how this reframes the entire understanding of suffering: the heated condition creates suffering not merely as external consequences of poor choices, but as fundamental disconnection from what life actually is—harmonious relationship with the neteru that allows divine connection, joy, love, and contentment [verse 17][2].

The metaphysical framework reveals that in the state of harmony with natural forces, "there is connection with the Divine and thus connection and awareness of being more than just physical, ego individual being," such that "the sources of suffering (disharmony, anxiety, hatred, ignorance) are not there to cause suffering in such a personality" [verse 17][2]. This teaching transcends conventional psychological understanding by establishing that suffering does not arise merely from external circumstances or even from psychological patterns alone, but from the fundamental condition of harmony or disharmony with the cosmic forces. When consciousness maintains harmony with the neteru, it naturally experiences connection with Ab Neter, which brings awareness of divine identity beyond ego-personality; this divine connection itself prevents the arising of suffering's sources [verse 17][2].

The tempests and crocodiles symbolism encompasses profound mystical truths about consciousness operating across multiple dimensions simultaneously. The "tempests in life with thunderousness" that rise to the heavens represent cosmic disharmony that manifests when consciousness severs connection with the neteru—creating cacophony that "encompasses the whole environment" with "yelling, fighting, upset, and cries, like thunderstorms and crashing waves that do not allow any quarter or peace from the cosmic forces that affect life externally and internally" [verse 16][1]. The crocodiles symbolize the "hidden fearsome energies, thoughts, and feelings that are ever quiet in the unconscious, and yet will strike unexpectedly, like crocodiles, lying in wait, unseen and unbeknown to the conscious mind, waiting for the opportunity to strike at the heart, coming out of nowhere, surprising you, pulling one under and drowning one in the thunderstorm of sorrows caused by our own unrighteous ego (Set)" [verse 16][1].

The mystical significance of experiencing Ab Neter/Neberdjer encompasses the ultimate liberation that authentic spiritual realization provides. The teaching reveals that "understanding the harmony of the universe allows one to not seek to reform the world according to ego desires," because "experiencing Ab Neter/Neberdjer allows understanding and feeling beyond ego personal desires that the world is not setup to satisfy the ego but according to the wisdom of Ab Neter/Neberdjer" [verse 17][2]. This cosmic understanding brings "solace and contentedness, peace and intuitional understanding about the nature of existence from God's perspective instead of the limited human ego driven perspectives" [verse 17][2]. Moreover, "experiencing Ab Neter/Neberdjer as oneself allows freedom from fear of death since Ab Neter/Neberdjer is immortal eternal" [2]—revealing that divine identification transcends all existential anxieties that plague ego-consciousness operating in opposition to natural harmony.

Therefore, the mystical framework establishes that ethical discipline and maintenance of harmony with the neteru represents not merely moral requirement but practical necessity for maintaining the connection with cosmic forces that allows divine recognition to emerge naturally through personality expression. The heated condition corrupts consciousness at the causal level, creating what the teaching describes as a personality rendered "unaware, ignorant, insensible in a way of being that is unknowingly infirm and susceptible to bad outcomes," spiritually alienated from "the truth of Ab Neter/Neberdjer reality of self" [verse 16][2]. This spiritual alienation operates by severing connection with the natural forces through which Neberdjer sustains Creation and guides consciousness toward divine recognition, creating the fundamental condition that prevents both earthly well-being and discovery of the kara where Ab Neter dwells [verse 10][verse 16][verse 17][1][2].

4. Transpersonal Psychology Research: Consciousness Research, Moral Psychology, and Natural Connection Studies

Contemporary transpersonal psychology research provides remarkable validation for Amenemopet's teaching through multiple research domains that demonstrate how disconnection from natural harmony and ethical principles literally alters consciousness functioning in ways that impair well-being and spiritual development. Research by neuroscientist Joshua Greene at Harvard reveals that brain regions associated with moral reasoning show decreased activity following ethical compromises, creating what researchers call "moral numbing"—a progressive reduction in sensitivity to ethical considerations that directly corresponds to what this Ancient Egyptian wisdom describes as heated mind and feelings corruption and forsaking of the natural forces [verse 17][8].

Studies in moral psychology by researchers like Jonathan Haidt demonstrate that individuals who engage in systematic rationalization of unethical behavior show measurable changes in neural pathways associated with empathy and ethical reasoning, confirming Amenemopet's teaching that unrighteous actions corrupt "the source of the corrupted mind" from which future moral decisions emerge [verse 17][9]. Transpersonal psychology research on meditation and ethical development reveals that contemplative practices specifically strengthen brain regions associated with moral sensitivity and compassionate response, while ethical violations weaken these same neural networks—supporting the teaching that harmony with natural order strengthens divine connection while heated patterns sever this connection [10].

Environmental psychology research reveals findings that remarkably parallel Amenemopet's teaching about forsaking "the caring of the natural forces, the waters, the land, and the like" [verse 10]. Studies demonstrate that disconnection from natural environments produces measurable increases in stress, anxiety, depression, and cognitive dysfunction, while connection with nature (forests, waters, natural landscapes) reduces cortisol levels, improves emotional regulation, and enhances overall well-being [11]. This research validates the ancient wisdom that the neteru (forces of nature) have been commissioned by Neberdjer to care for human consciousness, and that severing connection with these natural forces produces the "tempests" and psychological vulnerability that the teaching describes [verse 10][verse 16][1][2].

Neuroscience research on nature exposure demonstrates that time spent in natural environments activates brain regions associated with positive affect, reduced rumination, and enhanced cognitive function, while urban environments lacking natural elements show opposite effects [12]. These findings support the teaching that harmony with "the forces of nature (neteru/gods and goddesses established by Neberdjer)" produces calmness, serenity, and psychic balance, while opposition to this natural harmony creates the agitation, anxiety, and suffering characteristic of heated mind and feelings [verse 17][2]. Studies reveal that individuals who report strong connection with nature demonstrate greater life satisfaction, sense of meaning, and psychological well-being—validating the ancient teaching that "life" itself means harmony with natural forces [verse 17][2][13].

Ethical living leads to developing ethical conscience, an advanced ethical foundation for higher spiritual qualification of a spiritual aspirant to progress in understanding and practice of the teachings. In essence, conscience is the inner faculty of moral self-awareness and judgment that judges the moral rightness or wrongness of one's own actions and motives, producing feelings of approval or guilt. Contemporary society presents unprecedented challenges for maintaining both ethical conscience and connection with natural forces. Modern consumer culture particularly reinforces what Amenemopet describes as "rapacious greed" through advertising systems designed to stimulate desires for unnecessary products, economic structures that reward competitive behavior over collaborative values, and social media platforms that encourage "ridiculing others" through various forms of public shaming that masquerade as social consciousness [verse 17][1][11]. Urban environments systematically sever human connection with natural forces (waters, land, natural cycles), creating populations that live in chronic disconnection from the very cosmic forces that Neberdjer has commissioned to care for mind/personality development [verse 10][2][12].

The contemporary workplace environment often directly rewards several heated mind and feelings patterns: "thoughtless speech" gets reframed as assertiveness and leadership; "inconsiderate and impulsive acts" become decisive action and entrepreneurial risk-taking; and "anger and boisterousness" transform into passionate advocacy and strong personalities that command respect [verse 17][1][14]. Research in organizational psychology confirms that many corporate cultures actively select for individuals who demonstrate comfort with ethical compromise and disconnection from natural harmony, creating professional environments where spiritual principles often conflict directly with career advancement requirements [14]. Nevertheless, studies also reveal that individuals who maintain ethical standards and connection with natural principles despite external pressure experience greater long-term career satisfaction and psychological well-being than those who compromise values for immediate advantages [14].

Social media and digital communication technologies create new manifestations of the "crocodile" phenomenon Amenemopet describes, where unconscious psychological patterns find expression through online behavior that individuals would rarely display in face-to-face interactions [verse 10][1][15]. The anonymity and distance provided by digital platforms allow suppressed aggressive and competitive impulses to emerge as trolling, cyberbullying, and various forms of online harassment that reflect the same heated mind and feelings patterns this ancient wisdom identifies as spiritually destructive and opposed to natural harmony [15]. Neuroscience research demonstrates that social media use activates the same brain reward pathways as addictive substances, creating compulsive behavior patterns that reinforce ego-validation seeking rather than genuine spiritual development or connection with the natural forces that support well-being [15].

Modern psychology increasingly recognizes phenomena that directly correspond to Amenemopet's teaching about accumulated aryu creating unconscious patterns that influence present behavior [verse 10][6][16]. Trauma research reveals how unresolved psychological content operates according to principles that remarkably parallel this Ancient Egyptian understanding of karmic influences—past experiences creating unconscious behavioral patterns that perpetuate themselves through unconscious choice-making until addressed through conscious therapeutic work [16]. Research on intergenerational trauma demonstrates how patterns can transmit across generations through both psychological and epigenetic mechanisms, supporting the teaching about aryu influences extending beyond a single lifetimes [16].

5. Spiritual Implications for Aspirants: Progressive Spiritual Consequence and the Practice of Restoring Natural Harmony

Part A - Pastoral Concerns: Modern Challenges to Natural Harmony and Divine Connection

Building upon the metaphysical understanding of how consciousness operates within the cosmic ecology of neteru (natural forces), contemporary practitioners discover unique challenges that previous generations of aspirants did not face when attempting to maintain harmony with the forces of nature that Neberdjer has commissioned to sustain well-being and guide mind/personality development [verse 10][verse 17][2]. Consider the aspirant living in modern urban environments where connection with natural forces (waters, lands, natural cycles) has been systematically replaced with artificial environments, processed foods, and technological mediation of virtually all experience. This practitioner attempts to maintain awareness of being "more than just physical, ego individual being" while surrounded by cultural messages that relentlessly reinforce material identity and ego-validation as the primary sources of meaning and satisfaction [verse 17][2].

The wisdom to be understood reveals that aspirants often underestimate how their modern lifestyle systematically severs connection with the neteru, creating the very conditions that generate heated mind and feelings without conscious awareness of the disconnection occurring. Contemporary practitioners may engage in formal spiritual practices—meditation, study, ritual—while simultaneously living in ways that forsake "the caring of the natural forces, the waters, the land, and the like," thereby creating the internal "crocodiles lying in wait" that will inevitably strike when unconscious patterns accumulated through lifestyle choices find expression [verse 10][1][2]. Indeed, the aspirant may experience mysterious eruptions of anger, anxiety, greed, or other heated patterns without recognizing these as natural consequences of having severed connection with the cosmic forces designed to prevent such disturbances.

Essential to spiritual development is recognizing that the heated condition manifests as suffering precisely because "such a person cannot experience the benefits of calmness, serenity, harmony with nature, psychic balance, and the joy (love) of having connection with the divine (Ab Neter), which brings satisfaction/contentment" [verse 17][2]. Contemporary aspirants often mistake temporary pleasurable experiences arising from ego-gratification for genuine satisfaction, not recognizing that authentic contentment emerges only through harmony with the neteru and connection with Ab Neter. Consider the practitioner who achieves career success, material comfort, and social validation while experiencing persistent underlying anxiety, dissatisfaction, and spiritual emptiness—this condition reveals heated mind and feelings operating beneath surface appearances of worldly success, demonstrating that external achievements cannot substitute for harmony with natural forces and divine connection [verse 17][2].

The implications for contemporary practice encompass understanding that modern culture actively cultivates what verse 16 describes as a personality that is "negative in terms of disposition, feeling, and cognition and unaware, ignorant, insensible in a way of being that is unknowingly infirm and susceptible to bad outcomes" [verse 16][2]. Aspirants discover that their family upbringing, educational conditioning, professional training, and cultural immersion have systematically cultivated opposition to natural harmony while presenting this opposition as normal, healthy, or even spiritually sophisticated functioning. Therefore, practitioners must develop unprecedented vigilance to recognize how thoroughly they have been conditioned to forsake the natural forces while believing themselves to be functioning optimally [verse 10][verse 16][2].

Nevertheless, practitioners often discover that spiritual disciplines initially increase rather than decrease awareness of internal conflicts and disconnection from natural harmony, as growing sensitivity reveals previously unconscious patterns requiring conscious integration rather than continued suppression [6]. This increased awareness represents progress rather than regression, providing the foundation for genuine transformation through restoration of harmony with the neteru rather than mere symptom management that leaves underlying disconnection unaddressed. The aspirant learns to recognize that discomfort arising during spiritual practice often signals consciousness beginning to notice severed connections with natural forces that had previously operated beneath conscious awareness [verse 10][verse 16][2].

PART B - METHODS FOR TRANSFORMATION: RESTORING HARMONY WITH NATURAL FORCES AND DISCOVERING DIVINE CONNECTION

The methods for transformation that Amenemopet provides encompass systematic restoration of harmony with the neteru (cosmic forces) that Neberdjer has commissioned to care for Creation and guide mind/personality development toward divine recognition. The reverse doctrine principle/methodology applies comprehensively: if unrighteous actions create forsaking of natural forces, then righteous actions restore connection with these forces; if the heated mind and feelings arise through opposition to natural harmony, then silent mind and feelings emerge through alignment with this harmony [verse 10][verse 16][verse 17][1][2].

Primary among transformative practices is the systematic cultivation of connection with natural forces through conscious alignment with what verse 10 identifies as "the caring of the natural forces, the waters, the land, and the like" [verse 10][1][2]. Practitioners can develop daily practices that restore direct contact with natural elements: spending time near bodies of water (rivers, lakes, oceans) while consciously recognizing these as manifestations of the water neteru commissioned by Neberdjer; walking barefoot on earth while acknowledging connection with land neteru; observing natural cycles (sunrise, sunset, lunar phases, seasonal changes) as expressions of cosmic forces caring for mind/personality development [verse 10][2]. Consider the aspirant who establishes morning practice of watching sunrise while internally acknowledging: "I recognize the neteru (cosmic forces) that Neberdjer has established to care for Creation; I align my consciousness with these natural forces; I receive the care and guidance they provide" [verse 10][verse 17][2].

Essential to transformation is developing the discriminative capacity to recognize when actions, thoughts, or feelings begin to create the "tempests" and "crocodiles" that signal severing of connection with natural harmony. Practitioners can learn to recognize early warning signs: increased anxiety, agitation, or mental turbulence indicating emergence of heated patterns; desires for ego-validation or competitive comparison signaling opposition to natural order; impulses toward "unrighteousness, fraud, anger, boisterousness, flippant retorts and thoughtless speech, inconsiderate and impulsive acts, rapacious greed, jealousy, envy, ridiculing others" that reveal consciousness operating as "enemy of life" through opposition to harmony [verse 17][1][2]. When these patterns arise, the practitioner can apply the inverse doctrine methodology: immediately return attention to natural forces; consciously reestablish harmony with the neteru; recognize that authentic life means alignment with cosmic forces rather than ego-driven agitation [verse 16][verse 17][2].

The wisdom teaches that "understanding the harmony of the universe allows one to not seek to reform the world according to ego desires," because "experiencing Ab Neter/Neberdjer allows understanding and feeling beyond ego personal desires that the world is not setup to satisfy the ego but according to the wisdom of Ab Neter/Neberdjer" [verse 17][2]. Therefore, practitioners develop contemplative practices specifically designed to shift perspective from ego's limited viewpoint to divine perspective. During meditation, the aspirant practices: "I experience Ab Neter/Neberdjer as myself; I understand existence from God's perspective rather than ego's limited viewpoint; I recognize that the universe operates according to divine wisdom that brings true contentment rather than ego's restless seeking" [verse 17][2]. This practice gradually dissolves the heated impulse to "reform the world according to ego desires," replacing it with "solace and contentedness, peace and intuitional understanding about the nature of existence from God's perspective" [verse 17][2].

Particularly powerful is the practice of recognizing Ab Neter/Neberdjer as one's true identity, which "allows freedom from fear of death since Ab Neter/Neberdjer is immortal eternal" [2]. When existential anxieties arise—fear of death, fear of loss, fear of inadequacy—the practitioner applies this teaching: "I am Ab Neter/Neberdjer, immortal eternal consciousness; my true nature transcends all temporary phenomena; I experience divine reality as myself" [2]. This recognition gradually transforms the fundamental anxiety that underlies much heated mind and feelings, revealing that consciousness need not protect a separate ego-identity because authentic identity as Ab Neter/Neberdjer cannot be threatened or diminished [verse 17][2].

The teaching establishes that authentic life means "being in physical and mental harmony with the forces of nature (neteru/gods and goddesses established by Neberdjer)," producing "calmness, serenity, harmony with nature, psychic balance, and the joy (love) of having connection with the divine (Ab Neter), which brings satisfaction/contentment" [verse 17][2]. Therefore, practitioners develop comprehensive lifestyle alignment with natural principles: eating foods that maintain harmony with natural forces; sleeping in alignment with natural cycles; working in ways that serve rather than oppose natural order; relating to others through recognition of shared divine nature rather than competitive ego-comparison [verse 10][verse 17][2]. Consider the aspirant who restructures entire daily routine around question: "Does this action maintain or sever connection with the neteru that Neberdjer has commissioned to care for my mind/personality development?" [verse 10][2].

The implications encompass understanding that transformation occurs not through forceful elimination of heated patterns but through patient restoration of natural harmony that gradually reveals the divine connection that had been obscured. As consciousness reestablishes alignment with the neteru, it naturally experiences "connection with the Divine and thus connection and awareness of being more than just physical, ego individual being," such that "the sources of suffering (disharmony, anxiety, hatred, ignorance) are not there to cause suffering in such a personality" [verse 17][2]. The aspirant learns that restoration of harmony with natural forces and discovery of Ab Neter represent not two separate achievements but one unified realization: authentic life as harmonious relationship with cosmic forces through which divine connection emerges naturally as consciousness's fundamental nature [verse 10][verse 16][verse 17][1][2].

References

[1] Ashby, M. (2019-25). Mysticism of Amenemopet Hieroglyphic Text Translation. Sema Institute of Ancient Egyptian Studies.
[2] Ashby, M. (2025). Keys to Sage Amenemopet wisdom text trilinear translation chapter 2 by Dr Muata Ashby. Sema Institute of Ancient Egyptian Studies.
[3] Festinger, L. (1957). A Theory of Cognitive Dissonance. Stanford University Press.
[4] Doidge, N. (2007). The Brain That Changes Itself: Stories of Personal Triumph from the Frontiers of Brain Science. Viking.
[5] Ashby, M. (2015). The Prt M Hru Text: The Ancient Egyptian Book of Enlightenment. Translation by Dr. Muata Ashby. Sema Institute.
[6] Ashby, M. (2025). DEFINITIONS: The Nature of Consciousness and Awareness in Neterian Philosophy. Translation by Dr. Muata Ashby. Sema Institute.
[7] Ashby, M. (2025). Papyrus Ani [Book of the Dead] Chapter 17 Verse 3–6 – trilinear translation. Translation by Dr. Muata Ashby. Sema Institute.
[8] Greene, J. D. (2013). Moral Tribes: Emotion, Reason, and the Gap Between Us and Them. Penguin Press.
[9] Haidt, J. (2012). The Righteous Mind: Why Good People Are Divided by Politics and Religion. Vintage Books.
[10] Davidson, R. J., & Lutz, A. (2008). Buddha's brain: Neuroplasticity and meditation. IEEE Signal Processing Magazine, 25(6), 176-188.
[11] Kasser, T. (2002). The High Price of Materialism. MIT Press.
[12] Bratman, G. N., Hamilton, J. P., & Daily, G. C. (2012). The impacts of nature experience on human cognitive function and mental health. Annals of the New York Academy of Sciences, 1249(1), 118-136.

[13] Capaldi, C. A., Dopko, R. L., & Zelenski, J. M. (2014). The relationship between nature connectedness and happiness: a meta-analysis. Frontiers in Psychology, 5, 976.
[14] Kaptein, M. (2008). Developing and testing a measure for the ethical culture of organizations: The corporate ethical virtues model. Journal of Organizational Behavior, 29(7), 923-947.
[15] Twenge, J. M. (2017). iGen: Why Today's Super-Connected Kids Are Growing Up Less Rebellious, More Tolerant, Less Happy. Atria Books.
[16] van der Kolk, B. (2014). The Body Keeps the Score: Brain, Mind, and Body in the Healing of Trauma. Viking.
[17] Ashby, M. (2024). Amenemopet lectures 2024 by Dr Muata Ashby transcripts. Sema Institute of Ancient Egyptian Studies.
[18] Ashby, M. (2019). Amenemopet lectures 2019 by Dr Muata Ashby transcripts. Sema Institute of Ancient Egyptian Studies.

CHAPTER 4: Commentary on Teachings of Amenemopet Chapter 2 V, Verses 1-2: The Sacred Navigation of Life's Journey Commentary on Sage Amenemopet's Teaching of Conscious Effort

SUMMARY OF VERSES COVERED

These verses from Amenemopet's teaching address the fundamental spiritual challenge of conscious life navigation through deliberate effort. Verse 1 establishes the central metaphor of life as a boat requiring active steering, instructing practitioners: "Listen, as concerns our boat of life, one should apply force/effort to steer away from that which is bad." This teaching emphasizes that spiritual development requires sustained conscious effort rather than passive hoping or wishful thinking. Verse 2 continues this instruction by revealing the precision and commitment required for authentic spiritual transformation. Together, these verses establish the necessity of deliberate, sustained effort in spiritual development and the conscious steering required to maintain alignment with spiritual principles rather than drifting unconsciously toward negative influences [1].

Core Teachings by Verse:

• Verse 1 establishes the Teaching of Conscious Effort in Spiritual Navigation: the requirement for active, deliberate steering away from harmful influences

• Verse 2 provides the Teaching of Sustained Commitment: the ongoing nature of conscious spiritual effort required for authentic transformation

These verses establish two core teachings explored in this commentary: (1) the necessity of conscious effort and active steering in spiritual development, and (2) the sustained commitment required to maintain spiritual direction rather than drifting toward negative influences through unconscious patterns [1].

1. HUMAN PSYCHOLOGY PRINCIPLE: THE PSYCHOLOGY OF CONSCIOUS EFFORT VS. UNCONSCIOUS DRIFT

The fundamental psychological issue Sage Amenemopet addresses through the boat metaphor is the human tendency toward unconscious drift rather than conscious direction in spiritual development [verse 1]. the teaching reveals that most individuals navigate life through what I call "default patterns"—automatic responses and habitual behaviors that operate without conscious evaluation of their spiritual implications. This psychological reality creates precisely the conditions where consciousness drifts away from spiritual principles rather than actively steering toward them [1].

The instruction to "apply force/effort to steer away from that which is bad" addresses the psychological truth that spiritual development requires sustained conscious effort rather than passive absorption of spiritual concepts [verse 1]. Consider how this ancient understanding recognizes that consciousness naturally tends toward familiar patterns, even when these patterns obstruct spiritual growth, because the ego-personality structure prefers predictability over the uncertainty that authentic transformation requires.

Indeed, the boat metaphor reveals the sophisticated psychology underlying the teaching: individual mind operates like a vessel that can be directed through conscious steering or drift according to prevailing influences [1]. As our Chapter 7B teaching demonstrates: "The evening boat, the boat of the concluding period of life, of the heated person, ends with experiences of struggling and strife, suffering and...forsakes, turns away from the purpose of life and the nature of the Divine (Neberdjer), due to being, as if, carried away on a great swell, a large, billowing wave of water, an overpowering force (of negative aryu/karma) that overwhelms the boat of life (mind and body)" [2]. This reveals how consciousness without conscious steering becomes "overwhelmed" by accumulated negative patterns rather than maintaining effective spiritual navigation.

Nevertheless, the teaching simultaneously establishes the positive alternative: "Now, as concerns the boat of life of those who lead a silent life, who do not live by egoistic desires, boisterousness in the temple or unethical behaviors, in their boat they are able to sail on fair winds that are pleasant and right for sailing, and right for reaching the destination of life, to reach the hand of God and be accepted by God as one with God" [2]. This demonstrates that conscious effort in spiritual navigation creates supportive conditions rather than constant struggle against adverse circumstances.

2. Behavioral Imperative: The Necessity of Deliberate Spiritual Effort

The specific instruction to "apply force/effort" reveals that authentic spiritual development requires what this tradition calls "spiritual urgency"—genuine commitment to transformation that manifests through sustained conscious effort rather than casual engagement with spiritual concepts [verse 1]. This teaching addresses the common misconception that spiritual development occurs automatically through intellectual understanding or ritual participation without corresponding behavioral commitment to implementing spiritual principles in daily circumstances.

The force/effort required encompasses three distinct but integrated dimensions of spiritual practice: ethical effort that consistently chooses righteous actions over convenient compromises with spiritual principles; mental effort that maintains conscious awareness of spiritual teachings during challenging circumstances rather than allowing unconscious reactive patterns to dominate responses; and devotional effort that prioritizes spiritual development over competing worldly concerns [1,2]. Consider how these three dimensions work together to create the sustained steering capacity necessary for effective spiritual navigation.

the teaching in Chapter 6B provides the essential foundation for this effort: "Remain watchful, mindful, aware, keeping in mind, with deliberate effort, as to the fact that there is an 'entity,' an 'existence' that encompasses all Creation, beyond underlying mind and time and space" [3]. This "deliberate effort" represents the practical application of conscious steering—maintaining awareness of divine presence even when circumstances pressure consciousness toward heated patterns or egoistic responses.

The effort required is not mere willpower or forced discipline, but what this tradition calls "intelligent effort"—conscious application of discriminative wisdom that recognizes which influences support spiritual development and which obstruct it [1,2]. As the teaching reveals: "conscious steering involves developing discriminative capacity to recognize which thoughts, actions, relationships, and environments support divine recognition versus those promoting ego-identification and heated mental states" [2]. Therefore, the force/effort to steer away from bad influences represents applied spiritual intelligence rather than blind resistance to tempting circumstances.

3. Mystic Psychology Metaphysical Implications: The Divine Architecture of Conscious Navigation

At the deepest mystical level, the instruction to apply effort reveals the profound cooperation between individual will and divine grace in spiritual transformation [verse 1]. This ancient wisdom teaches that consciousness exists simultaneously as individual awareness capable of choice and as an expression of universal divine intelligence that guides individual development toward greater recognition of its essential nature [1,2]. The effort required for steering represents not ego-will attempting to control spiritual outcomes, but individual consciousness aligning itself with divine guidance that naturally flows toward truth and away from delusion.

The mystical significance of the boat metaphor encompasses understanding that individual mind operates within the cosmic framework of spiritual evolution, where personal effort serves universal purposes rather than merely individual advancement [2]. As our Chapter 18 teaching reveals: "However, despite the personal predilections, there is an all-encompassing divinity that masters and encompasses the limits of Creation and therefore, that overall encompassing divinity is the shepherd that guides human life. That divinity is actually at the forefront of the boat of life watching (aware), guiding the boat of human life where it needs to go for the welfare of all humans even before they themselves know where they are going" [4].

This establishes the mystical principle that conscious effort in spiritual navigation represents individual participation in divine self-expression rather than separate entity struggling against cosmic forces [1,4]. The force/effort to steer away from negative influences reflects divine intelligence operating through individual awareness to maintain alignment with cosmic order rather than drift toward chaos and spiritual ignorance [verse 1]. Indeed, this tradition teaches that what appears as personal effort actually represents divine energy expressing itself through individual consciousness for the purpose of spiritual evolution.

The cosmic implications extend to understanding that each moment of conscious steering contributes to collective spiritual development, as individual consciousness aligned with spiritual principles creates beneficial influences that extend beyond personal circumstances [2,4]. Consider how the teaching reveals that when practitioners maintain conscious effort in spiritual navigation, they participate in what the ancient sages called "cosmic harmonization"—the process by which individual alignment with divine principles supports universal movement toward greater wisdom and unity.

Therefore, the instruction to apply force/effort to steer away from bad influences represents not merely personal spiritual discipline but active participation in divine self-realization operating through individual forms for the benefit of all existence [1,4]. This mystical understanding transforms daily effort in spiritual navigation from mundane self-improvement into sacred service to cosmic evolution toward greater divine recognition.

4. Transpersonal Psychology & Modern Relevance: Consciousness Research and Intentional Change

Contemporary transpersonal psychology research provides remarkable validation for Amenemopet's teaching on conscious effort through studies demonstrating that intentional behavioral change requires sustained conscious attention and systematic application of new patterns over extended periods [verse 1]. Research by neuroscientist Michael Merzenich reveals that neuroplasticity—the brain's capacity for restructuring—requires focused attention, repetition, and emotional engagement precisely corresponding to what this ancient teaching describes as applying force/effort to steer consciousness toward beneficial patterns [5].

Studies on meditation and mindfulness confirm that conscious attention training literally strengthens brain networks associated with executive control while weakening automatic reactive patterns [6]. This neurological research validates our understanding that conscious steering requires sustained effort because it involves restructuring fundamental patterns of mental and emotional response rather than merely modifying surface behaviors [1,2]. Contemporary psychology increasingly recognizes what this ancient wisdom established: authentic transformation requires "effortful processing" that engages multiple levels of consciousness simultaneously.

Modern psychology also validates the teaching about unconscious drift through research on "default mode" brain networks that operate automatically when conscious attention is not actively engaged [7]. Studies reveal that these default patterns typically reinforce existing psychological patterns, including negative emotional states and limiting belief systems, confirming this ancient understanding that consciousness without conscious steering naturally drifts toward familiar patterns regardless of their spiritual implications [2].

The contemporary environment presents unprecedented challenges for maintaining conscious effort due to constant digital stimulation that fragments attention, social media platforms designed to capture unconscious engagement, and cultural emphasis on instant gratification that contradicts the sustained effort required for spiritual development [8]. Nevertheless, research demonstrates that individuals who maintain consistent contemplative practices show enhanced capacity for intentional attention direction and reduced susceptibility to unconscious influence patterns [6,7].

5. Spiritual Implications for Aspirants: Developing Sustained Spiritual Effort

For contemporary practitioners, the teaching of conscious effort establishes the foundation for all authentic spiritual development: recognizing that transformation requires sustained conscious application of spiritual principles rather than passive absorption of spiritual information [verse 1]. The wisdom reveals that spiritual development unfolds through countless moments of conscious choice where practitioners either apply effort to steer toward beneficial influences or drift unconsciously toward patterns that obstruct divine recognition [1,2].

The spiritual implications encompass understanding that the effort required is not temporary discipline that eventually becomes unnecessary, but the ongoing expression of spiritual maturity that naturally maintains alignment with divine principles [verse 1]. As our Chapter 5 teaching reveals: "Being silent means discovering the fullness of the Creator-Spirit that is within" rather than seeking fulfillment through "heated external pursuits" [3]. This silence develops through sustained effort to turn attention away from external seeking toward inner recognition of divine fullness already present within consciousness.

Crucially, this conscious effort becomes sustainable and natural through the cumulative foundation established in previous teachings. The capacity for sustained spiritual steering develops not through willpower alone, but through the gradual inculcation of wisdom from Amenemopet's teachings, the practice of ethical conscience in daily choices, and the cultivation of trust in the sagely guidance that has proven beneficial over time. As practitioners apply these principles consistently, they witness tangible improvements in life conditions—greater inner peace (ger), reduced mental agitation, enhanced clarity in decision-making, and a progressively more fulfilling existence. This experiential validation strengthens the practitioner's confidence in continued effort, creating a positive cycle where wisdom application generates beneficial results that inspire deeper commitment to conscious spiritual navigation.

Additionally, Amenemopet's authoritative promises from Chapter 1 provide essential motivational foundation for sustained effort. The Sage declares that if these teachings are allowed to penetrate deeply into the heart, then when "storming of the mind" occurs later, the absorbed wisdom "would be able to act as a stake, as if a mooring post" so practitioners will not "get caught up in the storm" [Chapter 1, verse 16]. He promises that through deep absorption, "you will be able to be remote in your mind, detached and collected" enabling conscious consideration before speech or action [verse 17]. Most significantly, Amenemopet guarantees that practitioners "will be able to find yourself in this book, to discover who you are essentially, and your fate will be determined by this wisdom such that your life will be fortunate, auspicious, opportune" [verse 18], and that these teachings become "a storehouse of vitality and wisdom for your life" [verse 1]. These are not theoretical possibilities but authoritative declarations from an enlightened sage, and developing reverence for Amenemopet's spiritual authority combined with trust in these explicit promises breeds the confidence necessary to empower, bolster, and sustain conscious effort even when immediate results are not apparent.

The practical foundation for developing sustained effort involves what this tradition calls "spiritual inclinations"—natural tendencies toward choices that support spiritual transformation arising from deepening experience of inner divine fullness rather than external seeking [2]. Indeed, as practitioners consistently apply effort to steer away from negative influences, they discover that spiritual choices gradually become more natural and effortless, reflecting the progressive alignment between individual will and divine guidance [1,2].

PART A - PASTORAL CONCERNS: MODERN CHALLENGES TO SUSTAINED SPIRITUAL EFFORT

Contemporary aspirants face unprecedented obstacles to maintaining the conscious effort Amenemopet prescribes. Digital technology creates constant interruption patterns that fragment attention, making sustained spiritual focus increasingly difficult. Many find themselves unconsciously drifting toward social media, entertainment, or consumer distractions precisely when attempting to apply spiritual principles. The cultural emphasis on instant gratification directly contradicts the patient, sustained effort required for authentic transformation, while the absence of supportive spiritual community often leaves practitioners feeling isolated in their efforts.

The challenge intensifies in work environments that reward heated behaviors—competitive manipulation, aggressive pursuing of advancement, and compromising ethical principles for practical advantage. Aspirants often feel torn between spiritual teachings about conscious steering and professional demands that seem to require unconscious drift toward expedient choices. Without the foundation of previous teachings about ethical conscience and trust in divine providence, practitioners may abandon spiritual effort when worldly pressures intensify, mistaking temporary discomfort for evidence that the teachings are impractical.

Family and social relationships present additional complications when loved ones operate through unconscious patterns that pull practitioners toward familiar reactive behaviors. Many aspirants discover that conscious spiritual effort can create tension in relationships accustomed to unconscious emotional dynamics. However, those who have cultivated trust in Amenemopet's wisdom and witnessed the gradual benefits of spiritual practice develop resilience to maintain conscious steering even when social pressure encourages conventional responses that compromise spiritual development.

PART B - METHODS FOR TRANSFORMATION: SYSTEMATIC PRACTICES FOR DEVELOPING SPIRITUAL STEERING CAPACITY

Based on Amenemopet's instruction to "apply force/effort to steer away from that which is bad," begin by establishing daily review periods to assess how wisdom application from previous teachings has improved life conditions. Identify specific areas where ethical conscience, trust in divine guidance, and inner silence have created tangible benefits—reduced anxiety, improved relationships, clearer decision-making. This experiential validation provides the motivational foundation for sustained effort, demonstrating that conscious steering produces genuine improvements rather than mere theoretical satisfaction.

Develop daily discrimination practice by identifying three specific influences that consistently pull consciousness toward heated patterns—whether mental habits, environmental factors, or relationship dynamics. When these influences arise, apply the cumulative wisdom from previous teachings: recall ethical principles that guide appropriate response, trust that divine providence orchestrates circumstances for spiritual development, and maintain the inner silence that reveals appropriate action. This systematic application builds steering capacity while reinforcing the practical value of the wisdom tradition.

Practice graduated spiritual effort by beginning with manageable commitments to conscious steering in areas where previous teachings have already shown benefits. As this foundation stabilizes through continued application and witnessed results, gradually extend conscious effort to more challenging circumstances. The key principle: sustainable spiritual steering develops through consistent application in small matters combined with ongoing recognition of how wisdom practice enhances life quality, creating the confidence and motivation necessary for conscious navigation across all life circumstances.

References:

[1] Ashby, M. (2019). *Teachings of Ancient Egyptian Sage Amenemopet with Hieroglyphic texts*. Translation by Dr. Muata Ashby. Sema Institute.

[2] Ashby, M. (2024). *Book Awakening Your Soul-Aware-Witness Ancient Egyptian Wisdom To Discover Divine Consciousness -v31*. Sema Institute.

[3] Ashby, M. (2019). *Teachings of Ancient Egyptian Sage Amenemopet with Hieroglyphic texts*. Chapter 6B, Verse 14. Translation by Dr. Muata Ashby. Sema Institute.

[4] Ashby, M. (2019). *Teachings of Ancient Egyptian Sage Amenemopet with Hieroglyphic texts*. Chapter 18, Verse 6. Translation by Dr. Muata Ashby. Sema Institute.

[5] Merzenich, M. (2013). *Soft-Wired: How the New Science of Brain Plasticity Can Change Your Life*. Parnassus Publishing.

[6] Davidson, R. J., & Lutz, A. (2008). Buddha's brain: Neuroplasticity and meditation. *IEEE Signal Processing Magazine*, 25(6), 176-188.

[7] Buckner, R. L., Andrews-Hanna, J. R., & Schacter, D. L. (2008). The brain's default network: anatomy, function, and relevance to disease. *Annals of the New York Academy of Sciences*, 1124, 1-38.

[8] Twenge, J. M. (2017). *iGen: Why Today's Super-Connected Kids Are Growing Up Less Rebellious, More Tolerant, Less Happy*. Atria Books.

[9] Ashby, M. (2019). *Teachings of Ancient Egyptian Sage Amenemopet with Hieroglyphic texts*. Chapter 9, Verse 17. Translation by Dr. Muata Ashby. Sema Institute.

[10] Ashby, M. (2025). *DEFINITIONS: The Nature of Consciousness and Awareness in Neterian Philosophy*. Translation by Dr. Muata Ashby. Sema Institute.

CHAPTER 5: Commentary on Teachings of Amenemopet Chapter 3, Verses 10, 15-17: The Sacred Art of Spiritual Discernment Commentary on Sage Amenemopet's Teaching of Conscious Disassociation

SUMMARY OF VERSES COVERED

These pivotal verses from Amenemopet's teaching address the essential spiritual skill of conscious disassociation from heated mind and feelings, whether encountered in others or arising within oneself. Verse 10 establishes the foundational instruction: "Desist from, abstain, cease, renounce joining with and gossiping with and watch out, definitely not getting into verbal arguments with the sneaky enemy, the heated person." Verses 15-16 provide specific guidance for when encountering heated persons during their "time of intense heat," instructing practitioners to "reject them by turning your mind away from their mind and emotions" because "they are misleading personalities, personalities that mislead others." Verse 17 offers profound wisdom about trusting divine providence: practitioners "should not be concerned with their fate since as you turn away from them the Divine, in a mysterious way, through the cosmic forces of Creation, will take care of them and provide to them what they need and deserve for their ethical and spiritual evolution."

CORE TEACHINGS BY VERSE:

- Verse 10 establishes the Teaching of Conscious Disassociation: avoiding engagement through gossip, argument, or association with heated mind and feelings
- Verses 15-16 provide the Teaching of Mental Redirection: turning the mind away from heated influences during their most intense manifestations
- Verse 17 presents the Teaching of Divine Providence: trusting cosmic wisdom to handle the spiritual evolution of those from whom we must maintain distance

These verses establish three core teachings explored in this commentary: (1) the necessity of conscious disassociation from heated mind and feelings as spiritual protection, (2) the practice of mental redirection as a method for maintaining inner peace, and (3) the understanding of divine providence that allows practitioners to maintain distance without guilt or concern for others' spiritual welfare [1].

1. HUMAN PSYCHOLOGY PRINCIPLE: THE PSYCHOLOGY OF HEATED MIND AND FEELINGS AND SPIRITUAL CONTAGION

The fundamental psychological issue these verses address is what the Ancient Egyptian wisdom recognizes as the contagious nature of heated mental and emotional state patterns—the psychological reality that prolonged association with heated mental and emotional states tends to activate similar patterns within one's own awareness [verse 10]. As the Chapter 2 teaching reveals, heated persons operate through "corrupted mind, live life by unrighteousness, fraud, anger, boisterousness, flippant retorts and thoughtless speech, inconsiderate and impulsive acts, rapacious greed, jealousy, envy, ridiculing others and having no compassion for the poor or the less fortunate" [2]. This catalog demonstrates how heated mind and feelings express themselves through systematic patterns that tend to draw others into similar states of mental agitation.

The psychological principle reveals that heated mind and feelings operate through what this tradition calls "aryu activation"—the capacity for one person's accumulated patterns of mental and emotional reactivity to stimulate corresponding patterns in others through what contemporary psychology might recognize as emotional contagion or psychological resonance [verse 15]. Consider how the Chapter 1 teaching describes this process: when "karmic-feeling-memories arise from your unconscious into your conscious mind and would otherwise overwhelm, as if capsize the peacefulness of your mind," creating "storming of words" and "uncontrolled thoughts, urges and untoward thinking and acting (heated condition of mind)" [3].

Indeed, the specific instruction to avoid "gossiping with and...getting into verbal arguments with the sneaky enemy, the heated person" addresses multiple interlocking psychological dynamics that threaten spiritual development [verse 10]. The teaching reveals that gossiping corrupts the mind and inflates the ego as a person comments on others, occupying their mind with nonsense, exaggerations, or lies to aggrandize themselves by putting others down [4]. This ego inflation directly obstructs both Prologue goals—earthly well-being becomes impossible when the mind is occupied with nonsensical preoccupations about others, while Ab Neter discovery remains inaccessible when the hat (conscious awareness) becomes densely packed with aryu patterns of judgment and superiority that block awareness of the divine presence within the ab (unconscious mind).

The psychological wisdom further reveals that verbal arguments with heated persons serve no beneficial purpose, since such individuals "are not reasonable, or prepared to be gracious or even handed, balanced and just" [4]. Therefore, engaging in arguments only serves to heat up one's own mind, stirring anger, mistrust, and even ill-will or hatred in oneself—all of which push the hat away from Ab Neter discovery, as if causing one to turn away from the divine presence residing in the kara (divine sanctuary) [4]. This understanding illuminates how heated engagement compromises the inner conditions necessary for spiritual development by generating the very mental-emotional turbulence that obscures divine awareness.

Nevertheless, the teaching reveals the subtle "sneaky" nature of heated person dynamics—that engagement with them seems to satisfy an egoistic nidus in one's own personality, feeding egoism without one's realizing it and thus corrupting oneself [verse 10, ref 4]. The heated person may appear friendly or even cultured, but when their sensibilities or desires are crossed, the friendship turns out to have secretly introduced unrest and anxiety into one's life [4]. Therefore, conscious disassociation represents practical wisdom for examining character before allowing oneself to enter into relationship, recognizing that heated persons are "misleading" by nature, not showing the deeper heatedness of the personality that was there all along—whether they realize their character deficiencies or not [verses 15-16, ref 4].

The Sneaky Enemy Within: When Egoism Operates Through Self-Deception

The wisdom to be understood encompasses recognition that while most practitioners interpret "the sneaky enemy, the heated person" [verse 10] as referring exclusively to external individuals, the teaching reveals a more subtle and dangerous truth: the sneaky enemy can be oneself—one's own egoism operating through rationalization, self-deception, and spiritual masquerade. Consider how this internal enemy operates through multiple mechanisms of self-delusion. First, the mind may be aware of ego desires yet find itself unable to resist or oppose the egoism within, proceeding with actions it knows generate heated patterns while telling itself "just this once" or "this situation is different." Second, the mind may be entirely unaware of how egoistic desires impel and compel actions that will be regretted later, with aryu patterns operating so deeply in the ab (unconscious) that the hat (conscious awareness) experiences these impulses as authentic guidance rather than ego-driven compulsion. Third—most insidious—the mind may be ignorant that it engages with heatedness and entanglements unsupported by the teachings, proceeding with actions based on warped thinking while believing these actions to be righteous or spiritually supported when they actually serve egoistic desires masked as spiritual virtue.

Indeed, this internal sneaky enemy [Verse 10] or 'personal sneaky enemy' can occur through willful ignorance, immaturity, ignorance or unwitting self-deceptive patterns that aspirants must learn to recognize and correct. Someone engages in unrighteous behavior—dishonest business practices, exploitative relationships, consumption patterns contrary to ethical restraint—while manufacturing elaborate rationalizations that transform clear violations of Maat into acceptable actions: "everyone does this," "I need this for my well-being," "the teaching doesn't really mean to avoid all such behavior." Someone pursues risky investments or even gambling, knowing these actions arise from latent greed, yet masks this egoism with spiritual veneer: "If I win the lottery, I can help my temple," "If this investment succeeds, I'll have more resources for spiritual practice"—when the truth reveals that greed-aryu compels the action while the mind deceives itself through noble-sounding justifications. This internal sneaky enemy operates by hijacking spiritual understanding itself, using wisdom teachings not for purifying the mind but for ego-justification, transforming what should serve aryu-thinning into sophisticated mechanisms for aryu-reinforcement. Therefore, the instruction to "desist from, abstain, cease, renounce joining with and gossiping with...the sneaky enemy" [verse 10] applies equally to external heated persons and to one's own internal egoism when it operates through these self-deceptive patterns—requiring the same vigilant disengagement from one's own rationalizations as from others' heated influence.

2. Behavioral Imperative: The Practice of Conscious Mental Redirection and the Pitfalls of Heated Caring

The specific instruction to "reject them by turning your mind away from their mind and emotions" reveals the essential behavioral skill required for maintaining spiritual development in environments where heated mind and feelings are present [verse 16]. This mental redirection represents not mere avoidance but conscious choice to maintain inner alignment with spiritual principles rather than being pulled into reactive patterns that characterize heated mental states.

The teaching establishes that heated persons become particularly "misleading" during their "time of intense heat"—periods when their accumulated aryu patterns reach peak expression and exert maximum influence on surrounding awareness [verse 15]. During these times, the instruction emphasizes complete mental disengagement rather than attempting to help, argue with, or reason with heated mind and feelings, because such engagement inevitably compromises one's own inner peace and spiritual clarity.

Nevertheless, the wisdom addresses a profound psychological trap that ensnares many spiritually inclined practitioners: the delusion of heated caring that masquerades as spiritual compassion. The teaching reveals that many caring people fall into the delusion of feeling they love or should care for heated persons even after their heatedness has been revealed—this occurs because one's own heated contamination has engaged in love or caring that is heated instead of lucid and wise [4]. This crucial distinction illuminates the difference between "heated love"—passionate "falling in love" that arises from ego-driven attraction—and genuinely "engaging with love" expressed with others of sane (silent) character [4].

Indeed, this behavioral pattern reveals how heated caring actually perpetuates separation from Ab Neter while seeming to express spiritual virtue. Consider how practitioners feel bad about leaving heated persons, not realizing that they are not the caretakers of life—the Divine is the true caretaker [4]. Their ego heatedness causes them to think they are the caretakers of others, even of heated destructive persons whose heatedness is counter to life that is healthy mentally and physically [4]. This ego-based caretaking impulse directly obstructs the Prologue verse 9 goal of discovering the kara where "the Divine resides in every person," because the hat remains trapped in the aryu pattern of personal responsibility for others' spiritual evolution rather than recognizing divine providence as the authentic source of spiritual guidance.

The wisdom to be understood encompasses two essential recognitions that support proper disengagement from heated persons while maintaining spiritual clarity. First, practitioners who properly disengage from heated persons can rightly recognize that they are actually helping the heated person through this disengagement—not abandoning them but allowing divine intervention to operate effectively [Chapter 3, verse 17]. When the mind engages with heated persons through argument, gossip, or attempts at direct spiritual correction, this engagement amplifies and exacerbates the heated personality patterns, creating more negative aryu for that person to deal with in their spiritual evolution [Chapter 3, verse 10]. By contrast, turning away from heated persons allows "the Divine, in a mysterious way, to turn back towards them and provide to them what they need and deserve for their ethical and spiritual evolution" [Chapter 3, verse 17]. This disengagement therefore represents not callousness but profound spiritual wisdom—recognizing that divine intervention operates more effectively than human manipulation, and that the most compassionate response involves maintaining one's own spiritual equilibrium while allowing cosmic law to guide each soul's development.

Second, practitioners must guard against the subtle self-delusion wherein one's own heated contamination masquerades as spiritual virtue. Many aspirants believe they are practicing silent living while simultaneously thinking it acceptable to engage with heated persons "to help them become less heated," not recognizing that this impulse reveals their own heated condition operating through spiritual rationalization [Chapter 3 Keys]. This engagement pattern creates two forms of spiritual obstruction: it squanders the precious time and personality energy that could have been directed toward silent practices—reflection, contemplation, meditation, ethical discipline—that would allow vital-life-fire to develop focus and grow to purify one's own mind; and it places one's own mind in danger of unconscious contamination and agitation from the heated person, who represents "an abominable thing to your heavenly personality, the part of you that exists in the astral plane (mind and feelings)" [Chapter 9, verse 15]. The teaching reveals that what appears as compassionate spiritual service often masks heated caring—"love or caring that is heated instead of lucid and wise"—wherein one's own unrecognized aryu patterns of ego-inflation, control-seeking, or spiritual pride drive the impulse to reform heated persons [Chapter 3 Keys]. Genuine silent mind recognizes the limitations of personal intervention and trusts cosmic order, while heated mind masquerading as spiritual virtue insists on direct engagement that ultimately strengthens aryu patterns in both parties rather than facilitating authentic transformation.

The practice of mental redirection encompasses several integrated techniques drawn from the tradition: conscious breathing regulation that maintains inner stability when encountering heated influences; philosophical discrimination that distinguishes between divine impulses and ego-driven patterns in both oneself and others; and immediate return to contemplation of divine principles when heated mind and feelings attempt to draw the hat into reactive engagement [1,5]. This differs fundamentally from suppression or judgment—mental redirection involves actively choosing spiritual focus rather than fighting against or condemning heated manifestations.

Essential to this practice is developing what the tradition calls "spiritual boundaries"—the capacity to maintain inner equilibrium regardless of external heated manifestations, while simultaneously expressing compassion through conscious non-engagement rather than reactive involvement [verse 16]. This represents mature spiritual wisdom that recognizes the most beneficial response to heated mind and feelings involves maintaining one's own optimal functioning rather than attempting to heal or transform others through direct engagement that compromises one's spiritual foundation.

The behavioral imperative includes specific recognition techniques for identifying when heated mind and feelings reach their most contagious phases: increased volume, speed, or intensity in speech patterns; escalation of emotional reactivity when challenged or questioned; expression of the heated characteristics this tradition catalogs as "unrighteousness, fraud, anger, boisterousness, flippant retorts and thoughtless speech" [2]; attempts to draw others into argumentative or gossiping engagement rather than constructive discourse focused on spiritual principles; and involvement in life-destructive practices such as smoking, eating processed foods, or other behaviors proven injurious, as they satisfy the heatedness with those activities and addictions [4].

Therefore, the wisdom reveals that heated persons become "enemies of life" through their engagement in practices counter to life that is healthy mentally and physically [4]. A person cultivating silent mind and feelings must avoid such influences in order to preserve and cultivate more purity and a silent approach as the necessary foundation for discovering Ab Neter/Neberdjer [4]. This understanding transforms conscious disassociation from mere self-protection into active spiritual practice that maintains the inner conditions required for divine recognition.

3. Mystic Psychology Metaphysical Implications: Divine Providence and the Cosmic Order of Spiritual Evolution

At the deepest mystical level, verse 17 reveals the profound spiritual principle that individual mind operates within a cosmic framework of divine providence, where each person's spiritual evolution unfolds according to universal wisdom rather than human intervention [verse 17]. The teaching that "the Divine, in a mysterious way, through the cosmic forces of Creation, will take care of them and provides to them what they need and deserve for their ethical and spiritual evolution" establishes the mystical understanding that conscious disassociation serves both individual and collective spiritual development.

This divine providence operates through what the tradition recognizes as the natural spiritual law governing transformation of the hat and ab—each individual must ultimately face the consequences of their own aryu patterns and choose between continued heated operation or turning toward spiritual principles [verse 17]. The mystical wisdom reveals that external attempts to force spiritual change in others actually obstruct this natural process by providing artificial support that prevents the direct experience necessary for genuine transformation.

The cosmic implications encompass understanding that heated mind and feelings serve spiritual evolution by providing clear contrast between ego-based operation and divine presence in the ab, allowing both the heated person and those who encounter them to develop discrimination between these fundamental modes of awareness [2]. The Chapter 18 teaching supports this understanding: "However, despite the personal predilections, there is an all-encompassing divinity that masters and encompasses the limits of Creation and therefore, that overall encompassing divinity is the shepherd that guides human life" [6]. This reveals that individual spiritual challenges, including heated mind and feeling patterns, serve the larger cosmic intelligence governing spiritual evolution.

The mystical framework establishes that conscious disassociation actually expresses divine compassion by allowing natural spiritual law to operate without interference, creating conditions where heated mind and feelings can encounter the direct consequences of their patterns rather than being buffered through others' reactive engagement [verse 17]. This understanding transforms the practice from mere self-protection into active service to cosmic order that supports authentic spiritual development for all involved.

Indeed, the metaphysical architecture reveals how the ego-based impulse to serve as "caretakers" of others' spiritual development actually represents aryu-driven delusion rather than divine inspiration. The hat becomes occupied with the arrogant presumption that individual human wisdom surpasses the cosmic intelligence that created and sustains all existence. This presumption fills the ab with aryu patterns of control, responsibility, and separation that directly obstruct recognition of Ab Neter—the divine presence that alone possesses the wisdom and power to guide each soul's evolutionary journey.

Therefore, the instruction not to "be concerned with their fate" represents recognition that divine intelligence operates through precise spiritual laws that surpass individual human understanding, making conscious trust in cosmic wisdom more beneficial than personal attempts to manage others' spiritual development [verse 17]. This mystical principle enables practitioners to maintain inner peace while allowing divine providence to guide collective spiritual evolution through means that transcend individual comprehension. The kara (divine sanctuary where Ab Neter resides) remains accessible only to the hat that releases ego-based control impulses and trusts the cosmic order to fulfill its perfect function in all beings' spiritual evolution.

4. Transpersonal Psychology & Modern Relevance: Emotional Boundaries and Psychological Contagion

Contemporary transpersonal psychology provides remarkable validation for Amenemopet's teaching through studies demonstrating that emotional states literally transmit between individuals through unconscious psychological mechanisms that operate below conscious awareness [verse 10]. Research by psychologist Elaine Hatfield reveals that emotional contagion occurs through automatic mimicry of facial expressions, vocal patterns, and body language, creating measurable physiological changes that mirror observed emotional states—precisely corresponding to the teaching about the contagious nature of heated mind and feelings [7].

Neuroscience research on mirror neurons confirms that human brains automatically simulate observed emotional and mental states, making prolonged exposure to agitated or reactive patterns likely to activate similar patterns in observers [8]. This biological research validates the ancient understanding that engaging with heated mind and feelings through argument or extended association tends to compromise one's own inner peace and spiritual clarity through natural psychological processes rather than personal weakness.

Modern psychology increasingly recognizes the necessity of "emotional boundaries"—conscious limits on psychological engagement with destructive behavioral patterns—that directly parallel the teaching about conscious disassociation from heated mind and feelings [verse 16]. Research demonstrates that individuals who maintain clear psychological boundaries experience better mental health outcomes and greater capacity for genuine assistance to others, compared to those who engage reactively with others' emotional dysfunction [9].

Contemporary therapeutic approaches like Dialectical Behavior Therapy incorporate techniques remarkably similar to the teaching about mental redirection, training practitioners to observe emotional reactivity without engaging it, maintain inner stability during interpersonal challenges, and redirect attention toward constructive responses rather than reactive involvement [verse 16]. This validates the practical effectiveness of the ancient psychological wisdom for maintaining optimal levels of hat functioning in challenging social environments.

Buddhist psychology research provides additional validation through studies on the distinction between genuine compassion and what researchers call "empathic distress"—the latter corresponding precisely to what Amenemopet identifies as "heated caring" [10]. Studies demonstrate that empathic distress (heated caring) produces physiological stress responses, decreased helping behavior, and burnout, while genuine compassion (silent caring) generates physiological calm, increased helping behavior, and sustained engagement [10]. This research validates the teaching's crucial distinction between ego-driven "falling in love" with others' suffering and wisdom-based "engaging with love" from an established spiritual foundation.

The modern workplace and social media environments create unprecedented exposure to heated mind and feeling patterns through constant digital connection, competitive professional dynamics, and platforms designed to amplify emotional reactivity for engagement purposes [11]. The teaching becomes especially relevant for contemporary practitioners who must navigate environments where heated patterns are normalized and even rewarded through social and economic systems that value aggression, competition, and ego-inflation over inner peace and spiritual development.

Research on codependency and rescue patterns in contemporary psychology validates the teaching about ego heatedness causing practitioners to believe they are the caretakers of others' spiritual evolution [12]. Studies demonstrate that such patterns arise from unconscious aryu (childhood conditioning) that creates compulsive caretaking behaviors as protective mechanisms against anxiety, feelings of worthlessness, and lack of authentic identity—precisely the ego-based delusion Amenemopet identifies as obstruction to Ab Neter discovery [12].

5. Spiritual Implications for Aspirants: Developing Discriminative Wisdom

PART A: PASTORAL CONCERNS—THE CHALLENGE OF DISCRIMINATIVE PRACTICE IN MODERN CONTEXT

For contemporary practitioners, these verses establish discriminative wisdom as the essential foundation for spiritual development in social contexts where heated mind and feeling patterns are prevalent [verse 10]. The wisdom to be understood encompasses recognizing that spiritual development requires maintaining inner conditions conducive to divine recognition rather than compromising these conditions through well-intentioned but spiritually destructive engagement with heated manifestations.

Consider the seeker who encounters a heated person in their family, workplace, or social circle who presents as friendly, cultured, or even spiritually interested. The initial engagement seems harmonious and even beneficial—conversations flow, shared interests emerge, perhaps even discussions about spiritual topics occur. Nevertheless, over time, when the practitioner's principles or boundaries conflict with the heated person's desires or sensibilities, the hidden heatedness emerges through anger, manipulation, withdrawal of friendship, or subtle undermining of the practitioner's spiritual practice [4]. The practitioner discovers they have unknowingly introduced "unrest and anxiety" into their life through failing to examine character before allowing relationship formation [4].

Indeed, someone struggling with the implementation of conscious disassociation often faces the profound challenge of "heated caring" that masquerades as spiritual virtue. The practitioner genuinely believes they should maintain relationship with the heated person because spiritual teachings emphasize compassion, service, and universal love. Nevertheless, the teaching reveals this represents the delusion of "falling in love" (heated caring driven by ego-based attraction to helping, fixing, or rescuing) rather than "engaging with love" (silent caring based on wisdom and appropriate boundaries) [4]. The practitioner experiences guilt, anxiety, or self-judgment when considering distance from the heated person, believing such distance contradicts spiritual principles.

The wisdom reveals a profound psychological truth that aspirants must understand with compassion toward themselves: the vulnerability to engaging with heated persons often arises not primarily from the heated person's manipulative skill, but from one's own personality weakness [Chapter 1, verse 12]—a fundamental incapacity to live in a centered and self-fulfilled manner that requires no external validation or connection to feel complete. When the personality has not developed the inner stability that comes from spiritual practice and Ab Neter recognition, the mind experiences a felt sense of need, incompleteness, or emptiness that unconsciously seeks satisfaction through external relationships. This weakness, this absence of inner fulfillment, opens the doorway through which heated persons enter one's life, because the personality desperately grasps at any connection that temporarily fills the inner void, even when such connections involve individuals who lack virtuous character or who demonstrate no sincere striving toward honesty, reasonableness, or ethical conduct. Therefore, the most effective protection against heated person entanglement is not merely developing discrimination to recognize such persons but cultivating the inner spiritual foundation that eliminates the need-driven vulnerability that attracts these relationships in the first place.

Consider the spiritual aspirant who continues engagement with a heated family member who engages in life-destructive practices—excessive drinking, smoking, processed food consumption, or other addictive behaviors that satisfy their heatedness while destroying physical and mental health [4]. The practitioner believes they must remain closely involved because "family should care for each other" or "spiritual people don't abandon those who are suffering." Nevertheless, the teaching reveals this ego-based caretaking impulse represents heated mind operating under the delusion that the practitioner, rather than the Divine, serves as the caretaker of life [4].

The modern aspirant faces unprecedented challenges in maintaining spiritual boundaries because contemporary culture actively promotes heated caring as virtue while condemning appropriate disassociation as selfish, uncompassionate, or spiritually immature. Social media amplifies this pressure through public performance of caring that gains social validation, professional environments demand engagement with heated patterns through competitive dynamics, and family systems often enforce loyalty through guilt and obligation that override wisdom-based discrimination.

Someone working to implement these teachings discovers that heated persons often present the most sophisticated arguments for why the practitioner should maintain engagement—appeals to compassion, duty, shared history, spiritual principles, or the practitioner's own proclaimed values. Nevertheless, the teaching reveals these appeals represent the "sneaky" nature of heated mind that feeds egoistic patterns in both parties without conscious recognition [verse 10, ref 4]. The heated person unconsciously seeks to maintain the practitioner's engagement because the practitioner's silent qualities temporarily calm their agitation, while the practitioner's ego finds satisfaction in the helper-helped dynamic that reinforces identity as caretaker.

The Righteousness Standard: A Practical Rule for Discerning Silent Ethics

A practical rule that can be followed to discern whether an interaction with another person falls within the bounds of silent personality ethics as laid out by Sage Amenemopet is what may be called the righteousness standard. If engagement in an action or interaction with someone else causes unrest, anxiety, or unbalance in the mind or body, then that action or interaction is suspect—it does not meet the standard of silent ethics that promote purity of heart and enlightenment, and one should consider rectifying it if possible, and if not, then refrain from it [1]. This diagnostic principle reveals that such engagements represent what Chapter 2 identifies as "bad actions"—those that cause the personality to turn away from (as if forsake) the forces of nature, which are cosmic forces (neteru - gods and goddesses), emanations of the Divine (Neberdjer) commissioned to take care of Creation and the environment in which a human being lives [2]. Therefore, interactions causing unrest, anxiety, or unbalance turn one away from the natural order of Creation that takes care of one and promotes one's well-being, indicating these engagements will lead to heated personality issues that obstruct both earthly well-being (Prologue verse 2) and Ab Neter discovery (Prologue verse 9).

Indeed, this righteousness standard provides immediate feedback about whether the Hat operates from silent wisdom or heated delusion when navigating relationships and social engagements. When an interaction consistently generates internal unrest—that subtle but persistent anxiety in the ab that signals misalignment with cosmic order—this represents the personality's authentic spiritual intelligence warning that engagement violates the principles necessary for discovering the kara where Ab Neter resides [1]. The practitioner must develop sufficient udja (vital-life-fire) to have the spiritual strength and discriminative capacity to oppose the personal sneaky enemy—whether external heated persons who would draw the Hat into their agitated patterns, or internal egoistic rationalizations that manufacture justifications for continuing harmful engagements [1, 4].

Consider how the Prologue teaching on udja reveals this vital-life-fire acts as "a fire of wisdom that burns away delusions and egoism," roasting and burning off "the delusion and ignorance fomenting desire for ephemeral existence, the egoistic perturbations of the mind and its thoughts, feelings, desires and memories (aryu) that prevent the soul from realizing the truth of Higher Self" [1]. The udja becomes effective when personality energy is not squandered on worldly thinking, feeling, and desires related to heated engagements, but instead allowed to develop focus and grow to purify the personality through silent practices and righteous interactions that maintain inner peace [1].

PART B: METHODS FOR TRANSFORMATION—SYSTEMATIC PRACTICES FOR CONSCIOUS DISASSOCIATION

The transformation from heated caring to silent wisdom requires systematic application of practices suggested directly by Amenemopet's teaching and through inverse doctrine methodology understanding. When verse 10 instructs to "desist from, abstain, cease, renounce joining with and gossiping with...the heated person," the reverse doctrine reveals: cultivate speech and thought patterns that build up rather than tear down, occupy the mind with wisdom contemplation rather than commentary on others' affairs, and develop inner stability that requires no ego-inflation through comparison or judgment [verse 10].

Practice 1: Character Examination Before Relationship Formation

Following the teaching that one should "be careful with whom one associates by first examining their character before allowing oneself to enter into relationship" [4], practitioners should implement systematic observation before deepening any relationship:

- Observe how the person responds when their desires are thwarted—does silent acceptance emerge, or heated reaction?
- Notice whether the person engages in life-destructive practices (smoking, excessive drinking, processed food addiction, chronic complaining) that indicate heated mind seeking satisfaction through harmful patterns [4]
- Watch how the person speaks about others when those others are absent—gossip, criticism, and judgment reveal heated character regardless of friendly surface presentation
- Examine whether the person demonstrates the heated characteristics cataloged in Chapter 2: "unrighteousness, fraud, anger, boisterousness, flippant retorts and thoughtless speech, inconsiderate and impulsive acts, rapacious greed, jealousy, envy, ridiculing others" [2]

For example, a practitioner meeting a potential friend at a spiritual gathering should observe over several interactions whether the person maintains consistency between their spiritual discussions and their actual behavior patterns. Does the person who speaks eloquently about compassion then engage in harsh judgment of others? Does the person who claims spiritual development then demonstrate heated reactivity when circumstances don't match their preferences? These observations prevent the "sneaky" dynamic where heated mind draws practitioners into relationship before revealing its true nature [4].

Practice 2: Mental Redirection During Heated Encounter

When encountering heated persons during their "time of intense heat" [verse 15], practitioners should immediately implement the instruction to "turn your mind away from their mind and emotions" [verse 16]:

- Conscious breath regulation: Return awareness to slow, deep breathing that maintains physiological calm regardless of external heated manifestation
- Silent hekau (mantra) repetition: Internally repeat divine names or wisdom principles that occupy the hat and prevent aryu activation through heated engagement
- Physical disengagement: When possible, remove oneself from physical proximity to heated manifestation rather than remaining present through misguided duty
- Visualization practice: Imagine the heated person surrounded by divine light while maintaining inner distance from their mental-emotional state

For example, when a heated family member begins expressing anger or engaging in heated argument at a gathering, the practitioner excuses themselves to another room under a neutral pretext rather than remaining present through obligation. This implements both the instruction to "reject them by turning your mind away" and the inverse doctrine methodology understanding that one should not engage in actions that promote unrest and instability in one's own hat [verse 16].

Practice 3: Releasing Ego-Based Caretaking Through Divine Providence Recognition

The profound practice for transforming heated caring into silent wisdom requires systematic application of verse 17's teaching about divine providence:

- Daily contemplation: Reflect on the truth that "the Divine, in a mysterious way, through the cosmic forces of Creation, will take care of them and provides to them what they need and deserve for their ethical and spiritual evolution" [verse 17]
- Journal practice: Write about situations where one feels compelled to maintain engagement with heated persons, then examine whether this impulse arises from divine inspiration or ego-based patterns of control, identity as helper, or need for validation
- Affirmation practice: When guilt arises about disassociating from heated persons, repeat: "The Divine is the caretaker of life, not my ego. I serve spiritual evolution by maintaining my own inner peace."
- Discrimination practice: Distinguish between genuine divine impulses to assist (which maintain inner peace and come from established spiritual foundation) and ego-driven heated caring (which generates anxiety, obligation, and compromise of spiritual practice)

For example, a practitioner maintains relationship with an aging heated parent who consistently undermines the practitioner's spiritual practice, creates drama, and engages in manipulative behaviors. The practitioner experiences profound guilt about reducing contact, believing they should sacrifice their spiritual development for family duty. Through systematic application of verse 17's wisdom, the practitioner recognizes this represents ego heatedness—the arrogant presumption that the practitioner's limited wisdom surpasses divine intelligence in knowing what serves the parent's spiritual evolution [4]. The practitioner reduces contact to brief, structured interactions while releasing responsibility for the parent's emotional state or spiritual development, trusting cosmic wisdom to provide what the parent truly needs.

Practice 4: Cultivating Silent Caring That Preserves Spiritual Foundation

Applying the inverse doctrine methodology to heated caring reveals the practice of silent caring—compassion expressed from an established spiritual foundation rather than ego-driven reactive engagement:

- Establish non-negotiable spiritual practice time that takes priority over others' demands or expectations
- Maintain clear boundaries about behaviors that will not be tolerated in one's presence (gossip, heated argument, manipulation)
- Offer assistance only when inner peace remains stable and divine inspiration guides the action
- Express care through prayer, meditation on others' highest good, and maintaining one's own spiritual development as an example rather than through reactive involvement

For example, instead of engaging in lengthy phone conversations with a heated friend who uses the practitioner as an emotional dumping ground, the practitioner establishes a boundary: "I'm available for 15-minute check-ins on Tuesday evenings. If you need more support, I can help you find a therapist." This preserves the practitioner's energy for spiritual practice while offering genuine assistance (professional help recommendation) that doesn't compromise spiritual foundation. When the friend becomes angry about this boundary, the practitioner implements verse 16's instruction—turning the mind away from the friend's heated reaction while maintaining the boundary with silent firmness.

The key principle for all these practices is patient absorption of the wisdom into the ab (unconscious mind) rather than forceful effort to instantly manifest perfect implementation. As the hat gradually develops discrimination between divine impulses and ego-driven patterns, the practices become increasingly natural expressions of silent character rather than difficult disciplines requiring constant vigilance. This gradual transformation supports both Prologue goals—earthly well-being through reduced entanglement in heated dynamics, and Ab Neter discovery through thinning the aryu density that obstructs divine recognition.

References

[1] Ashby, M. (2019-25). Mysticism of Amenemopet Hieroglyphic Text Translation. Sema Institute of Ancient Egyptian Studies.
[2] Ashby, M. (2024). Book Awakening Your Soul-Aware-Witness Ancient Egyptian Wisdom To Discover Divine Consciousness -v32. Sema Institute of Ancient Egyptian Studies.
[3] Ashby, M. (2019-25). Mysticism of Amenemopet Hieroglyphic Text Translation. Chapter 1, Verses 14-16. Sema Institute of Ancient Egyptian Studies.
[4] Ashby, M. (2025). Keys to Sage Amenemopet wisdom text trilinear translation Chapter 3. Sema Institute of Ancient Egyptian Studies.
[5] Ashby, M. (2025). DEFINITIONS: The Nature of Consciousness and Awareness in Neterian Philosophy. Sema Institute of Ancient Egyptian Studies.
[6] Ashby, M. (2019-25). Mysticism of Amenemopet Hieroglyphic Text Translation. Chapter 18, Verse 6. Sema Institute of Ancient Egyptian Studies.
[7] Hatfield, E., Cacioppo, J. T., & Rapson, R. L. (1994). Emotional Contagion. Cambridge University Press.
[8] Rizzolatti, G., & Craighero, L. (2004). The mirror-neuron system. Annual Review of Neuroscience, 27, 169-192.
[9] Linehan, M. M. (2015). DBT Skills Training Manual. Guilford Press.
[10] Singer, T., & Klimecki, O. M. (2014). Empathy and compassion. Current Biology, 24(18), R875-R878.
[11] Twenge, J. M. (2017). iGen: Why Today's Super-Connected Kids Are Growing Up Less Rebellious, More Tolerant, Less Happy. Atria Books.
[12] Beattie, M. (2022). Codependent No More: How to Stop Controlling Others and Start Caring for Yourself. Hazelden Publishing.

CHAPTER 6: Commentary on Teachings of Amenemopet Chapter 4, Verses 1-2, 7-8: The Psychology of Spiritual Receptivity and Detached Response, Teaching of Silent Mind and Feelings

SUMMARY OF VERSES COVERED:

Verses 1-2 address the phenomenon of heated people attending temple activities, establishing that "those heated people, when they go to the temple" experience spiritual practices like "a tree going inside the temple, which is a covered building," unable to "gain illumination from the sun or rain" and therefore not receiving "the benefit of the illumination from the Divine that the temple has to offer." Verses 7-8 present the contrasting psychology of silent people, who "give their answer/response to the heated ones in the form of being remote, distant, isolated / secluded / apart / aloof / withdrawn / reserved / inaccessible, detached," while internally they are "like a tree growing in a place with plenty of water and fertile earth and open to the sky so they grow to the fullness of their capacity."

CORE TEACHINGS BY VERSE:

- Verses 1-2 establish the Teaching of Spiritual Obstruction Through Ego Appropriation: how heated mind and feelings create internal barriers preventing divine illumination even within temple environments because the ego appropriates spiritual benefits as self-generated rather than received from divine sources
- Verse 7 provides the Teaching of Detached Response: the sophisticated psychology of how silent people respond to heated persons through both physical and psychological remoteness, turning away from thinking and feeling like the heated person
- Verse 8 reveals the Teaching of Unobstructed Spiritual Growth: how silent mind and feelings, characterized by humble devotion to God rather than ego-self, create optimal conditions for receiving divine illumination (divine grace) and growing "to the fullness of their capacity"

These verses establish three core teachings explored in this commentary: (1) the psychology of how heated mind and feelings create internal spiritual obstruction through ego appropriation mechanisms even in sacred environments, (2) the sophisticated practice of detached response as both protective boundary and compassionate wisdom operating through physical and psychological levels, and (3) the contrasting psychology of silent mind and feelings rooted in humble devotion that creates optimal receptivity for spiritual growth and divine illumination [1, 8].

1. HUMAN PSYCHOLOGY PRINCIPLE: THE PSYCHOLOGY OF EGO APPROPRIATION AND SPIRITUAL CONSTRICTION

Building upon the consciousness architecture established in the Prologue commentary—where aryu in the ab obscure Ab Neter awareness in the kara—this chapter addresses the specific mechanism of ego appropriation. Verses 1-2 reveal how dense aryu not only blot out divine awareness but create a systematic filtering process where the hat claims spiritual benefits as self-generated rather than received from divine sources, rendering such benefits "limited and distorted by the egoism and so will not be real and abiding or beneficial" [8].

This directly impacts both Prologue goals: when aryu-driven ego appropriation patterns control the hat, earthly well-being remains elusive despite increased spiritual activity, and Ab Neter discovery remains blocked because the fundamental delusion of self-created existence prevents recognition of divine dependence [8]. The contrasting psychology of the silent person demonstrates how humility thins aryu density sufficiently for the hat to receive Ab Neter awareness, creating conditions for growing "to the fullness of their capacity" as verse 8 reveals [1].

2. Behavioral Imperative: Aryu-Shaped Patterns of Constriction, Appropriation, and Detached Response

The specific psychological patterns determining spiritual receptivity manifest through deeply ingrained response patterns shaped by accumulated aryu stored in the ab across multiple lifetimes, creating fundamentally different approaches to both spiritual practice and interpersonal relationships as verses 1-2 and 7-8 reveal [1, 8]. Primary among destructive patterns is what the teaching identifies as heated mind and feelings operating through constricted Hat focused exclusively on egoistic concerns, driven by dense aryu in the ab that prevent genuine spiritual nourishment from penetrating to conscious awareness due to systematic appropriation mechanisms [1, 8].

The ego appropriation mechanism operates with sophisticated psychological dynamics: heated people participate in the same religious activities as silent people—attending temple, engaging in rituals and programs—yet their internal experience remains fundamentally different because aryu density in the ab occupies the Hat so completely that even during temple participation, the ego's thought and feeling processes determine what the Hat accepts as good or bad, creating systematic filtering that prevents divine illumination from penetrating from the Hat through the ab to reveal Ab Neter in kara [1, 8]. Indeed, verse 2's teaching on Spiritual Obstruction reveals that heated people are "like a tree going inside the temple, which is a covered building" where they "do not gain illumination from the sun or rain" and "do not get the benefit of the illumination from the Divine that the temple has to offer" [1]. The wisdom reveals that the ego needs to be humbled so it can realize it owes its existence to something greater, yet when aryu in the ab operate through the fundamental delusion of self-created existence, they systematically block the Hat's capacity to recognize Ab Neter [8].

The behavioral patterns of heated mind and feelings manifest through observable characteristics driven by aryu in the ab: mental and emotional constriction where the Hat focuses narrowly on egoistic desires and defensive reactions; appropriation mechanisms where aryu-driven patterns claim spiritual benefits as self-generated achievements rather than divine gifts; participation in religious activities while aryu density in the ab remains so thick that the Hat stays internally closed to transformation; and inability to maintain genuine humility that would thin aryu density and reveal Ab Neter dependence [1, 8]. As Chapter 2, verse 17 discusses, these patterns connect to heated mind and feelings guided by aryu producing "corrupted mind, live life by unrighteousness, fraud, anger, boisterousness, flippant retorts and thoughtless speech, inconsiderate and impulsive acts, rapacious greed, jealousy, envy" [2].

Consider how the heated mind and feelings often originate from aryu patterns accumulated across lifetimes and stored in the ab: egoistic focus on satisfying perceived personal needs, or unresolved violence and trauma that has created intensified egoistic aryu that can produce irrational lashing out [8]. Modern trauma research confirms that unresolved traumatic experiences create lasting changes in brain function and psychological patterns, validating the ancient understanding that heated mind and feelings frequently stem from past suffering that shaped aryu now stored in the ab influencing present mental and emotional responses occupying the Hat. The teaching recognizes these patterns with compassion rather than judgment, understanding that heated behaviors often represent unconscious protective mechanisms developed through painful experiences that created the aryu now stored in the ab.

Conversely, silent people demonstrate the sophisticated psychological skill of detached response—a practice operating through both physical and psychological levels as verse 7's teaching on Detached Response reveals [1, 8]. The concept of silent people being remote to heated ones operates as physical and/or psychological detachment: if a heated person says something insulting to the silent person, the silent person may not reply at all and turn away physically or may reply from a space of calmness to bring reason and calmness to the conversation [8]. Nevertheless, verse 7 establishes that silent people "give their answer/response to the heated ones in the form of being remote, distant, isolated / secluded / apart / aloof / withdrawn / reserved / inaccessible, detached" [1]. The deeper psychological internal response involves turning away from thinking and feeling like the heated person [8]. This represents the essence of detached response: maintaining the Hat in its naturally open, undefended state rather than allowing aryu from encounters with heated mind and feelings to create new deposits in the ab that would generate constriction and reactivity.

The silent person's mind and feelings operate without the constriction characterizing heated mind and feelings because their ab contains sufficiently thin aryu density that the Hat can remain spacious and aware of Ab Neter guidance from kara, as verse 8's teaching on Unobstructed Spiritual Growth illuminates [8]. This fundamental difference creates markedly different behavioral responses: where heated mind and feelings react defensively when aryu in the ab trigger protective patterns occupying the Hat, silent mind and feelings remain spacious and responsive, able to engage appropriately without accumulating new reactive aryu in the ab. This wisdom aligns with Chapter 9's instruction to "refrain from/abstain from/cease/desist/do not seek heated people for the purpose of associating with them" [3], recognizing that protection of developing spiritual awareness sometimes requires physical separation from environments that would deposit dense aryu in the ab.

When encountering a coworker upset about something today but normally congenial, the silent response involves approaching with compassion and listening to soothe the heart—recognizing this as temporary heated mind and feelings driven by temporarily activated aryu that can benefit from calm presence that doesn't add new reactive aryu to either person's ab [8]. However, with a chronically angry, complaining, bitter coworker, the wisdom prescribes interacting only when professionally necessary, not joining or acting like them, because regular exposure will deposit heated aryu patterns in one's own ab. Offer constructive engagement only if they initiate from a balanced state, then respond from the silent perspective of wisdom rather than allowing their heated aryu to activate reactive patterns [8].

3. Mystic Psychology Metaphysical Implications: The Cosmic Architecture of Ego Appropriation and Divine Humility

At the deepest mystical level, verses 1-2 and 7-8 reveal the fundamental architecture of how the Hat either facilitates or obstructs divine illumination based on aryu density in the ab and consequent awareness or ignorance of Ab Neter residing in kara, and how the ego's self-aggrandizing delusion created by dense aryu produces systematic spiritual blindness regardless of external circumstances [1, 8]. The temple represents not merely physical sacred space but the cosmic principle that divine presence manifests continuously through all environments for minds where aryu in the ab have become sufficiently thin that the Hat can receive illumination and penetrate to Ab Neter awareness in kara, while verse 2's tree metaphor reveals the precise mechanism by which ego appropriation driven by dense aryu creates spiritual obstruction even in optimal conditions [1, 8].

Consider how the mystical significance encompasses the understanding that when heated mind and feelings participate in spiritual practices while aryu in the ab operate under the delusion that the ego owes its existence to itself, any apparent spiritual benefit becomes systematically appropriated by aryu-driven mechanisms as self-generated rather than received from divine sources, rendering such benefits "limited and distorted by the egoism and so will not be real and abiding or beneficial" [8]. This illuminates why authentic spiritual development requires what the teaching calls humbling the ego so it can realize it owes its existence to something greater—a recognition that fundamentally transforms the Hat from appropriating mode to receiving mode, allowing spiritual practices to penetrate from the Hat through the ab, thinning aryu density and revealing Ab Neter in kara rather than strengthening aryu patterns through egoistic claims of achievement [8].

The cosmic implications reveal that when aryu in the ab create the delusion that the ego owes its existence to itself, the Hat cannot accept spiritual illumination from outside sources, or if it does acknowledge external benefits, aryu-driven appropriation mechanisms claim them as coming from the ego rather than from the divine [8]. This mechanism operates at the deepest level of mind architecture: the ego's fundamental self-conception as an independently existing entity—created and maintained by dense aryu in the ab—systematically distorts all spiritual experiences, preventing the Hat from penetrating through the ab to recognize Ab Neter in kara as the divine presence that actually sustains the capacity for the Hat itself. Modern psychology identifies this as attribution bias, yet the ancient wisdom penetrates far deeper, revealing how this pattern reflects cosmic delusion about existence itself, maintained by aryu density in the ab blocking Ab Neter awareness.

The mystical truth encompasses recognizing that silent mind and feelings represent the Hat operating in alignment with cosmic reality: humble recognition that individual existence depends entirely on Ab Neter in kara for divine sustenance, like "a tree growing in a place with plenty of water and fertile earth and open to the sky" where natural spiritual nourishment flows unobstructed through awareness because aryu in the ab have become sufficiently thin, as verse 8 reveals [1]. Indeed, this understanding resonates profoundly with Chapter 5, verse 9: "Being silent means discovering the fullness of the Creator-Spirit that is within. This fullness cannot come from heatedly searching for fulfillment in the world for fulfillment with an imperfect personality" [4]. The silent person is humble and devotional to God rather than to the ego-self, creating mind conditions where aryu density in the ab thins sufficiently that the Hat can penetrate to Ab Neter recognition in kara rather than systematic appropriation of divine gifts as egoistic achievements maintained by dense aryu [8].

The profound mystical implication reveals that detached response as verse 7's teaching describes reflects not indifference but recognition of the cosmic principle that individual transformation occurs through alignment with divine intelligence accessed when aryu in the ab become sufficiently thin, rather than reactive engagement with egoistic patterns that would deposit new heated aryu in the ab [1]. When silent people remain "remote, distant, detached" from heated mind and feeling patterns, they maintain the Hat's receptivity to divine guidance from Ab Neter while protecting the ab from accumulating new reactive aryu that would increase density and obstruct spiritual receptivity [1, 8]. The deeper psychological internal response involves turning away from thinking and feeling like the heated person [8]—a practice that prevents heated aryu from depositing in one's own ab, preserving the Hat's alignment with Ab Neter in kara rather than allowing egoistic delusions maintained by dense aryu to obstruct spiritual receptivity.

The cosmic architecture illuminates how aryu patterns accumulated across lifetimes and stored in the ab shape present mind conditions: heated mind and feelings where dense aryu constrict the Hat around egoistic concerns or trauma-intensified patterns, versus silent mind and feelings where sufficiently thin aryu allow the Hat to maintain humble devotion recognizing dependence on Ab Neter [8]. This reveals the profound wisdom that mind transformation requires systematic purification where spiritual practices penetrate from the Hat through the ab, thinning aryu density while cultivating humble recognition of divine dependency, ultimately revealing Ab Neter already present in kara. This process leads to what Chapter 9 describes as the divine potter Khnum coming to "perform the cutting away of the heart's dispositions that are contrary to goodness and enlightenment" [5]—the mystical operation by which accumulated aryu patterns become systematically purified through divine grace working within minds that have become sufficiently humble and receptive.

4. Transpersonal Psychology Research: Validation of Ego Appropriation and Trauma-Informed Spiritual Understanding

Contemporary transpersonal psychology and trauma research provide empirical validation for Amenemopet's teaching in verses 1-2 and 7-8 through studies demonstrating how egoistic self-attribution biases and unresolved trauma create measurable changes in mental functioning that impair spiritual receptivity [1, 8].

Default Mode Network and Ego-Identification

Neuroscience research on self-referential processing confirms that the brain's default mode network—active during self-focused thinking—shows heightened activity in individuals with strong ego-identification, corresponding to what the ancient teaching describes as dense aryu in the ab occupying the Hat so completely that Ab Neter awareness becomes blocked [1, 8]. Studies by Brewer and colleagues (2011) using fMRI demonstrated that experienced meditators show decreased activity in default mode network regions associated with self-referential processing and mind-wandering during meditation practice [9]. This empirically confirms that contemplative practices can reduce the neural activity associated with egoic self-focus, consistent with the teaching about purification revealing awareness beyond ego-personality.

Garrison and colleagues (2015) demonstrated that meditation leads to reduced default mode network activity beyond active tasks, indicating stable transformation of baseline mental functioning [10]. Taylor et al. (2011) found that meditation training impacts the default mode network during restful states, supporting the ancient teaching that spiritual receptivity requires humbling the ego so it can recognize dependence on sources greater than itself, corresponding to the process where spiritual practice penetrates from the Hat through the ab, thinning aryu density to reveal Ab Neter [11].

Trauma and Spiritual Receptivity

Trauma research provides crucial validation for verse 8's recognition that heated mind and feelings can originate from unresolved violence or trauma that has intensified egoism and can produce irrational lashing out [8]. Van der Kolk (2014) documents how chronic trauma exposure creates lasting changes in brain structure affecting emotional regulation and self-concept—precisely the constricted mental patterns Amenemopet identifies as preventing spiritual receptivity even in supportive environments like temple participation, corresponding to trauma-generated aryu stored in the ab that occupy the Hat and prevent divine illumination from penetrating awareness [12]. Contemporary understanding of Complex PTSD reveals neurobiological mechanisms by which unresolved trauma maintains heated patterns that obstruct spiritual development.

Ego Appropriation in Spiritual Practice

Studies on religious and spiritual struggles confirm that individuals who approach spiritual practices primarily to satisfy ego needs report significantly lower well-being compared to those approaching practice with humble, receptive orientations, validating the distinction between heated mind and feelings driven by egoistic aryu versus silent mind and feelings characterized by humble devotion that allows Ab Neter awareness [13]. Buddhist psychology research on spiritual materialism parallels Amenemopet's teaching on ego appropriation, documenting how spiritual seekers unconsciously use practice to strengthen rather than dissolve egoistic self-concept, corresponding to practices that deposit new egoistic aryu in the ab rather than thinning aryu density [14, 15].

Loving-Kindness Meditation and Defensive Patterns

Research on contemplative neuroscience reveals that regular practice of loving-kindness meditation can restructure brain anatomy in ways that reduce automatic defensive responses, corresponding to systematic aryu purification where spiritual disciplines penetrate from the Hat through the ab, thinning reactive patterns and creating neurological foundation for what verse 8 describes as silent mind and feelings maintaining spacious awareness [16]. Weng and colleagues (2013) found that compassion training alters altruism and neural responses to suffering, demonstrating measurable changes in brain function that support detached response capacity [17]. Galante et al. (2014) conducted systematic review and meta-analysis showing that kindness-based meditation significantly enhances psychological well-being and reduces stress, empirically validating the ancient teaching's emphasis on humble devotion [18].

Polyvagal Theory and Detached Response

Polyvagal theory research confirms that individuals can develop capacity to maintain calm physiological states even when encountering threatening stimuli, supporting verse 7's teaching on Detached Response that silent people can remain psychologically remote from heated patterns while physically present, corresponding to the Hat maintaining alignment with Ab Neter rather than allowing external heated mind and feelings to deposit new reactive aryu in the ab [19]. This research demonstrates the neurophysiological mechanisms by which purification practices create capacity for non-reactive presence in challenging interpersonal contexts.

<u>Author's Note on Progressive Development and Self-Protection:**</u>**

The capacity for detached response described in this research and in verse 7 represents an advanced stage of aryu purification rather than a requirement for beginners. Aspirants must understand that attempting to force oneself to remain calm in the presence of heated persons or negative situations before sufficient aryu thinning has occurred can be spiritually counterproductive and psychologically harmful. The wisdom teaching consistently emphasizes removal from heated environments as the primary protection strategy (as detailed in Chapter 9's teaching on avoiding heated persons entirely). Only after considerable purification practice—when the ab has thinned sufficiently that the Hat maintains natural alignment with Ab Neter rather than becoming overwhelmed by external agitation—does the capacity for detached presence in challenging contexts develop organically. Therefore, practitioners should prioritize physical and psychological safety and thus removal from negative people and situations until such time as substantial self-control has been cultivated through systematic purification practices. Attempting to remain in harmful environments as a test of spiritual advancement often results in depositing additional reactive aryu patterns rather than demonstrating genuine transformation. The teaching values wise discernment about one's current capacity over forced endurance that exceeds one's actual level of purification.

Humility as Spiritual Virtue

Cross-cultural psychology research on humility as a spiritual virtue confirms its association with greater psychological well-being and enhanced capacity for spiritual growth, empirically validating Amenemopet's teaching that authentic receptivity requires humble devotion to God rather than ego-self, corresponding to mind conditions where aryu density in the ab has thinned sufficiently that the Hat can recognize Ab Neter as the source sustaining awareness itself [20, 21]. Emmons and McCullough (2003) demonstrated that gratitude practices—expressions of humble recognition of benefits from sources beyond ego—significantly increase subjective well-being and life satisfaction, providing empirical support for the transformative power of humble mental orientation [22].

5. Spiritual Implications for Aspirants: Progressive Development of Humble Devotion and Detached Response

PART A: PASTORAL CONCERNS - MODERN CHALLENGES TO HUMBLE RECEPTIVITY

For contemporary practitioners, verses 1-2's teaching on Spiritual Obstruction and verses 7-8's teachings on Detached Response and Unobstructed Spiritual Growth illuminate crucial challenges in cultivating authentic spiritual receptivity within a culture that systematically promotes ego appropriation [1, 8]. Consider the seeker who diligently attends meditation classes, participates in temple services, and maintains daily practice, yet unconsciously approaches all activities with achievement orientation—mentally collecting spiritual experiences as personal accomplishments, comparing progress with others, and interpreting benefits as validating personal worth. This represents precisely the heated mind and feelings Amenemopet describes in verses 1-2: participating in the same activities as silent practitioners yet unable to receive genuine spiritual nourishment because aryu-driven appropriation mechanisms in the ab claim all benefits as self-generated rather than received from divine sources, preventing the Hat from penetrating through the ab to recognize Ab Neter [1, 8].

The teaching illuminates particular challenges for those whose heated mind and feelings originate from unresolved violence or trauma that created intensified egoistic aryu now stored in the ab [8]. Consider someone drawn to spiritual practice for trauma healing, yet finding that meditation sometimes triggers rather than soothes, that temple participation feels unsafe, that teachings about ego dissolution activate deep defensive reactions maintained by protective aryu in the ab. This person requires compassionate understanding that heated mind and feelings often represent unconscious protective mechanisms developed through painful experiences that created the aryu patterns now stored in the ab, rather than willful spiritual obstruction.

More on Polyvagal Theory and Detached Response

The teaching also addresses a crucial misconception among contemporary practitioners who misunderstand the verse 7 instruction about detached response. Some aspirants, encountering teachings about silent people maintaining psychological remoteness from heated patterns, attempt to force themselves to remain calm in the presence of negative people or harmful situations as a demonstration of spiritual advancement. This represents a dangerous misapplication of the teaching that can result in depositing additional reactive aryu rather than thinning existing patterns. The wisdom consistently emphasizes removal from heated environments as the primary protection strategy—particularly for those whose aryu density remains thick enough that external agitation overwhelms the Hat's capacity to maintain alignment with Ab Neter. Research on polyvagal theory validates this developmental understanding: the nervous system's capacity to maintain calm presence amid threat (what neuroscience terms "ventral vagal regulation") develops progressively through sustained purification practice, strengthening measurably over months and years rather than arising through willful forcing [12, 13]. The detached response capacity develops organically after substantial purification rather than through premature attempts at non-reactivity. Therefore, practitioners must exercise wise discernment about their current level of aryu purification: if presence in negative situations produces reactive agitation, physiological stress responses, intrusive thoughts persisting after encounters, or vital energy depletion, this indicates that removal remains the appropriate response until further purification naturally develops the capacity for non-reactive presence that the advanced teaching describes. As Chapter 9 elaborates extensively, avoiding heated persons entirely constitutes primary spiritual protection, with detached presence representing an advanced capacity that emerges naturally when mind has achieved sufficient purification depth rather than a requirement to be forced at early developmental stages.

PART B: METHODS FOR TRANSFORMATION - SYSTEMATIC CULTIVATION OF HUMBLE RECEPTIVITY

The fundamental practice Amenemopet prescribes involves systematic cultivation of humble recognition that the Hat's capacity for awareness itself owes its existence to Ab Neter—the divine presence residing in kara that sustains the mind [8]. This practice operates through daily acknowledgment before spiritual activities: rather than approaching meditation with achievement orientation that would deposit egoistic aryu in the ab, begin with humble recognition of divine source. This simple shift fundamentally transforms the Hat's relationship to spiritual experience from appropriating mode to receiving mode, allowing practices to penetrate from the Hat through the ab, thinning aryu density rather than strengthening it [1, 8].

Implement the Ego Appropriation Awareness Training: throughout spiritual practice, maintain vigilant awareness of subtle appropriation mechanisms operating through aryu in the ab [8]. When experiencing peaceful meditation, notice the arising thought "I achieved this calm state"—recognize this as aryu-driven appropriation depositing new egoistic patterns in the ab, and consciously return to humble acknowledgment: "Divine presence created this experience; I am grateful to receive it." This practice systematically trains the Hat to recognize when aryu in the ab attempt appropriation, allowing spiritual benefits to penetrate through the ab, thinning aryu density and creating optimal conditions for Ab Neter recognition in kara [1, 8].

Establish a Daily Humility Assessment: each evening, examine the day's spiritual activities to identify moments when aryu in the ab unconsciously drove the Hat to claim ownership of spiritual benefits versus moments when you maintained humble recognition of their divine source [1, 8]. Ask: "Did I approach today's meditation as achievement to accomplish (which would deposit egoistic aryu in the ab) or gift to receive (which allows practice to penetrate through the ab, thinning aryu and revealing Ab Neter)?" This creates systematic awareness of appropriation mechanisms, enabling gradual transformation where aryu density thins sufficiently that the Hat can recognize Ab Neter in kara.

References:

[1] Ashby, M. (2019-25). Mysticism of Amenemopet Hieroglyphic Text Translation. Sema Institute of Ancient Egyptian Studies.
[2] Ashby, M. (2025). Book Awakening Your Soul-Aware-Witness Ancient Egyptian Wisdom To Discover Divine Consciousness -v32. Sema Institute of Ancient Egyptian Studies.
[3] Ashby, M. (2025). Keys to Sage Amenemopet wisdom text trilinear translation Chapter 3. Sema Institute of Ancient Egyptian Studies.
[4] Ashby, M. (2019-25). Mysticism of Amenemopet Hieroglyphic Text Translation. Chapter 5, Verse 9. Sema Institute of Ancient Egyptian Studies.
[5] Ashby, M. (2019-25). Mysticism of Amenemopet Hieroglyphic Text Translation. Chapter 9. Sema Institute of Ancient Egyptian Studies.
[6] Ashby, M. (2024). Amenemopet lectures 2024 by Dr Muata Ashby transcripts. Sema Institute of Ancient Egyptian Studies.
[7] Ashby, M. (2025). DEFINITIONS: The Nature of Consciousness and Awareness in Neterian Philosophy. Sema Institute of Ancient Egyptian Studies.
[8] Ashby, M. (2025). Keys to Sage Amenemopet wisdom text trilinear translation chapter 4. Sema Institute of Ancient Egyptian Studies.
[9] Brewer, J. A., Worhunsky, P. D., Gray, J. R., Tang, Y. Y., Weber, J., & Kober, H. (2011). Meditation experience is associated with differences in default mode network activity and connectivity. Proceedings of the National Academy of Sciences, 108(50), 20254-20259.
[10] Garrison, K. A., Zeffiro, T. A., Scheinost, D., Constable, R. T., & Brewer, J. A. (2015). Meditation leads to reduced default mode network activity beyond an active task. Cognitive, Affective, & Behavioral Neuroscience, 15(3), 712-720.
[11] Taylor, V. A., Grant, J., Daneault, V., Scavone, G., Breton, E., Roffe-Vidal, S., Courtemanche, J., Lavarenne, A. S., & Beauregard, M. (2011). Impact of meditation training on the default mode network during a restful state. Social Cognitive and Affective Neuroscience, 8(1), 4-14.
[12] van der Kolk, B. (2014). The Body Keeps the Score: Brain, Mind, and Body in the Healing of Trauma. Viking.
[13] Pargament, K. I., Murray-Swank, N. A., Magyar, G. M., & Ano, G. G. (2005). Spiritual struggle: A phenomenon of interest to psychology and religion. In W. R. Miller & H. D. Delaney (Eds.), Judeo-Christian perspectives on psychology: Human nature, motivation, and change (pp. 245-268). American Psychological Association.
[14] Kornfield, J. (2008). The Wise Heart: A Guide to the Universal Teachings of Buddhist Psychology. New York: Bantam Books.
[15] Gunaratana, B. H. (2002). Mindfulness in Plain English. Boston: Wisdom Publications.
[16] Tang, Y. Y., Hölzel, B. K., & Posner, M. I. (2015). The neuroscience of mindfulness meditation. Nature Reviews Neuroscience, 16(4), 213-225.
[17] Weng, H. Y., Fox, A. S., Shackman, A. J., Stodola, D. E., Caldwell, J. Z., Olson, M. C., Rogers, G. M., & Davidson, R. J. (2013). Compassion training alters altruism and neural responses to suffering. Psychological Science, 24(7), 1171-1180.
[18] Galante, J., Galante, I., Bekkers, M. J., & Gallacher, J. (2014). Effect of kindness-based meditation on health and well-being: A systematic review and meta-analysis. Journal of Consulting and Clinical Psychology, 82(6), 1101-1114.
[19] Porges, S. W. (2011). The Polyvagal Theory: Neurophysiological Foundations of Emotions, Attachment, Communication, and Self-regulation. New York: W. W. Norton & Company.
[20] Davis, D. E., Worthington, E. L., Jr., & Hook, J. N. (2010). Humility: Review of measurement strategies and conceptualization as personality judgment. The Journal of Positive Psychology, 5(4), 243-252.
[21] Kruse, E., Chancellor, J., & Lyubomirsky, S. (2017). State humility: Measurement, conceptual validation, and intrapersonal processes. Self and Identity, 16(4), 399-438.
[22] Emmons, R. A., & McCullough, M. E. (2003). Counting blessings versus burdens: An experimental investigation of gratitude and subjective well-being in daily life. Journal of Personality and Social Psychology, 84(2), 377-389.

CHAPTER 7: Commentary on Teachings of Amenemopet Chapter 5, Verses 7-9: The Psychology of Inner Fulfillment Through Divine Communion Commentary on Sage Amenemopet's Teaching of Silent Communion with Creator-Spirit

SUMMARY OF VERSES COVERED

Verse 7 addresses "those who are silent, all who go into the House-of-Divine (Temple)," establishing the foundational principle of silent approach to sacred space and divine communion. Verse 8 reveals that "those silent ones speak of the greatness of the blessings they receive from being in the temple from the Creator-Spirit," describing the natural recognition and gratitude that emerge from authentic spiritual receptivity. Verse 9 provides the profound teaching that "Being silent means discovering the fullness of the Creator-Spirit that is within by communing with the Creator-Spirit that resides in the temple," contrasting this with the futility of "heatedly searching for fulfillment in the world with an imperfect personality," and establishing that true fulfillment comes from "realizing that there is perfection within when the fullness of being is experienced beyond the worldly thinking, desires and cravings that cause one to feel incomplete, as a separate individual, alone and imperfect."

CORE TEACHINGS BY VERSE:

- Verse 7 establishes the Teaching of Silent Temple Approach: how minds prepared through silence naturally seek divine communion in sacred environments
- Verse 8 reveals the Teaching of Spontaneous Gratitude: the natural recognition and expression of divine blessings that emerges from authentic spiritual receptivity
- Verse 9 provides the Teaching of Internal Divine Fulfillment: the discovery that true completion comes through communion with Creator-Spirit within rather than external seeking

These verses establish three fundamental teachings explored in this commentary: (1) the psychology of how feeling incomplete drives dualistic seeking in the external world, (2) the futility of attempting to find lasting fulfillment through ephemeral worldly experiences, and (3) the discovery of authentic fulfillment through expanding awareness from individual identity to recognition of oneness with Creator-Spirit [1].

1. HUMAN PSYCHOLOGY PRINCIPLE FOCUS OF CHAPTER 5: THE ARYU-DRIVEN SENSE OF INCOMPLETENESS AND THE SEEKING MIND

The fundamental psychological issue Sage Amenemopet addresses is the persistent feeling of incompleteness that drives human minds to seek fulfillment through external means [verses 7-9]. This incompleteness operates through aryu—the accumulated feeling-memories stored in the ab (unconscious mind)—that occupy the presence-of-mind awareness (hat) so densely as to blot out awareness of the deeper reality where Ab Neter (the divine soul) resides in the kara (inner sanctuary of awareness).

The teaching reveals that when aryu dominate the hat, the mind operates from the illusion of being "a separate individual, alone and imperfect," generating persistent anxiety that drives endless attempts to find completion through worldly experiences, relationships, achievements, and acquisitions [verse 9]. This dualistic perception manifests as "me and the world, something I need to get from the world to feel happy and fulfilled," creating a psychological framework where individual identity feels fundamentally lacking and must acquire something external to achieve wholeness.

Indeed, this seeking mind operates through what the teaching identifies as "worldly thinking, desires and cravings" that reinforce the very sense of incompleteness they attempt to resolve [verse 9]. The deeper problem reveals itself in how these aryu-driven patterns maintain the heated mind and feelings—the agitated state that pursues ephemeral satisfaction while remaining unable to recognize the Ab Neter presence that already sustains awareness itself. Consider how individuals who achieve their desired goals often experience temporary satisfaction followed by a return to baseline levels of dissatisfaction, confirming Amenemopet's observation that external fulfillment cannot provide lasting completion because the world remains in constant flux and change, offering no possibility for abiding satisfaction.

The contrasting psychology of silent people reveals minds that have discovered what Amenemopet calls "the fullness of the Creator-Spirit that is within," eliminating the driving need to seek completion through external means [verses 7-9]. This silence represents not merely absence of agitated seeking but the positive discovery of internal completeness that naturally emerges when the mind recognizes the Ab Neter—the divine presence residing in the kara that constitutes the true foundation of individual existence. The silent person "speaks of the greatness of the blessings they receive from being in the temple from the Creator-Spirit" not from acquiring something external but from recognizing what was always present within [verse 8].

This directly impacts both Prologue goals established in verses 2 and 9: Without discovering the Ab Neter within the kara, the goal of "causing a person to have well-being while living on earth" cannot be achieved because the mind remains driven by aryu-generated cravings that can never be satisfied through worldly means. The persistent seeking creates perpetual agitation and dissatisfaction that prevent earthly well-being. Simultaneously, this aryu-driven seeking prevents the discovery of the "sanctuary that can be entered once the worldly affairs are handled with this wisdom"—the kara where "the Divine resides in every person" awaits recognition through silent communion rather than heated external pursuit [1].

2. Behavioral Imperative: The Aryu-Driven Cycle of Dualistic Seeking and the Discovery of Internal Fullness

The specific behavioral patterns that perpetuate the cycle of seeking and dissatisfaction manifest through what the teaching identifies as engagement with the external world through duality—the persistent perception that fulfillment exists somewhere "out there" requiring acquisition through effort, achievement, or experience [verse 9]. This dualistic framework emerges from aryu stored in the ab (unconscious mind) that occupy the hat (conscious awareness) so completely that they obscure recognition of the Ab Neter residing in the kara (divine sanctuary within).

The aryu-driven seeking mind operates through several identifiable patterns that reinforce the sense of incompleteness: "comparison awareness" where individual identity measures itself against external standards generated by aryu and finds itself lacking; "acquisition compulsion" where the ego attempts to fill internal emptiness through accumulating experiences, relationships, or achievements motivated by feeling-memories of past dissatisfaction; and "future-focused fantasy" where satisfaction is always projected into some imagined future state rather than recognized in present experience [verse 9]. These patterns connect to what Chapter 4 revealed about heated mind and feelings appropriating spiritual benefits as self-generated, demonstrating how even spiritual seeking can become corrupted by aryu-driven identification with individual separateness [3].

Nevertheless, the ancient wisdom reveals that this seeking behavior serves a divine purpose by eventually exhausting the ego's attempts to find fulfillment through external means, creating the psychological conditions necessary for turning attention inward toward recognition of Ab Neter in the kara [verse 9]. Consider how the frustration and agitation that inevitably result from seeking ephemeral satisfaction eventually motivate the mind to explore alternative approaches to fulfillment, leading to what the teaching calls "communion with Creator-Spirit in temple" as the pathway to "self-discovery of fulfillment and wholeness."

The key insight reveals that heated persons who enter the temple remain unable to experience "the fullness of the Creator-Spirit" because their aryu-driven seeking patterns continue to occupy the hat (surface conscious awareness), preventing recognition of the Ab Neter presence [verses 7-9]. Their heated condition means the mind remains agitated by worldly desires and cravings that obscure the divine presence even in sacred space. In contrast, silent people demonstrate minds that have thinned the density of aryu sufficiently to allow recognition of what Amenemopet describes as "the fullness of being experienced beyond the worldly desires and cravings" [verse 9].

This transcendence occurs not through suppressing desires but through what may be termed "aryu purification"—the systematic thinning of feeling-memories stored in the ab that occupy the hat and obscure Ab Neter recognition. The behavioral shift involves moving from "seeking fulfillment in the world" to "communing with the Creator-Spirit that resides in the temple"—recognizing that authentic satisfaction emerges through alignment with the divine presence in the kara rather than acquisition of worldly experiences.

The teaching reveals a profound distinction: silent people in temple experience the fullness of immersion in the silence of body and mind such that they become able to discern the existence of Spirit, while heated persons remain trapped in aryu-driven agitation that prevents this discernment [verses 7-9][2]. This fullness of silence represents minds operating with minimal aryu density, allowing the hat (surface conscious awareness) to penetrate to the kara level where Ab Neter awareness naturally reveals itself. With that experience, there emerges fulfillment of human seeking for completeness—a condition that proves joyous and exhilarating—the natural result when the mind recognizes its divine foundation rather than remaining identified with aryu-generated separateness [verse 9][2].

3. Mystic Psychology Metaphysical Implications: The Architecture of Awareness and the Discovery of Internal Divinity

At the deepest mystical level, verses 7-9 reveal the fundamental architecture of awareness and how aryu density determines whether the mind operates from the illusion of separate incompleteness or from recognition of divine fullness already present in the kara [1, 2]. The teaching illuminates that what appears as individual minds seeking external fulfillment represents Ab Neter temporarily obscured by accumulated feeling-memories (aryu) stored in the ab—not actually separate entities requiring completion through worldly acquisition.

Consider the profound metaphysical principle: the very capacity for awareness itself—the hat (presence-of-mind awareness)—owes its existence to Ab Neter residing in the kara, the divine sanctuary at the deepest level of the ab (unconscious mind) [verse 9][2]. This means that what experiences the sense of incompleteness and drives the seeking behavior is sustained moment-by-moment by the very divine fullness it seeks externally. The illusion operates through aryu density in the ab that occupies the hat so completely that the mind cannot penetrate to recognize its own divine foundation.

The mystical architecture reveals why external seeking can never provide lasting fulfillment: worldly experiences occur at the surface level of awareness (hat level) where phenomena constantly change and flux, while authentic satisfaction requires recognition of the unchanging divine presence (Ab Neter) residing at the kara level that sustains awareness itself [verse 9]. Therefore, attempting to find completion through ephemeral worldly means represents the mind seeking externally what can only be discovered internally through penetrating from surface awareness to the divine foundation.

Indeed, the teaching reveals that "Being silent means discovering the fullness of the Creator-Spirit that is within" precisely because silence creates the conditions where aryu density thins sufficiently that the hat can penetrate through the ab to recognize Ab Neter in the kara [verse 9]. This discovery does not create something previously absent but removes the obstruction (dense aryu patterns) preventing recognition of what has always sustained individual awareness. The metaphysical truth encompasses understanding that individual existence never truly separated from divine source—aryu merely created the illusion of separation by occupying conscious awareness so densely that the divine foundation became unrecognizable.

The contrast between "heatedly searching for fulfillment in the world with an imperfect personality" versus "communing with the Creator-Spirit that resides in the temple" illuminates the fundamental choice the mind faces: continue reinforcing aryu-driven illusion of separateness through external seeking, or thin aryu density through silent communion allowing recognition of internal divine fullness [verse 9]. The teaching emphasizes that this choice determines whether the mind experiences perpetual dissatisfaction driven by the delusion of incompleteness or discovers the joyous fulfillment that emerges from recognizing one's true nature as Ab Neter—divine awareness temporarily appearing as individual mind.

The ultimate mystical implication reveals that what the teaching calls "the fullness of being experienced beyond worldly thinking, desires and cravings" represents the mind recognizing itself as sustained by Creator-Spirit rather than as separate individual [verse 9][2]. This recognition transforms the entire framework of existence: no longer operating from the anxious question "what do I need to acquire to feel complete?" the mind rests in the recognition "I am sustained by and ultimately identical with the divine fullness that is the source of all existence." This shift from seeking to being, from incompleteness to fullness, from separation to communion, constitutes the essential transformation the teaching prescribes.

4. Transpersonal Psychology Research: Validation of the Hedonic Treadmill and Mental Architecture

Contemporary transpersonal psychology and neuroscience provide empirical validation for Amenemopet's teaching through research on hedonic adaptation, the default mode network, and meditation-induced mental transformation [verses 7-9]. The ancient wisdom's insights about the futility of seeking lasting fulfillment through external means and the possibility of discovering internal fullness through silent practice find substantial support in modern empirical research.

Hedonic Adaptation and the Seeking Mind

Research by Lyubomirsky and colleagues (2005) documents the "hedonic treadmill" phenomenon where individuals return to baseline happiness levels shortly after achieving desired goals or acquiring desired objects, despite initial satisfaction [7]. This empirically validates Amenemopet's teaching that "heatedly searching for fulfillment in the world" cannot provide lasting completion because external circumstances produce only temporary satisfaction [verse 9]. Sheldon and Lyubomirsky (2012) demonstrated through longitudinal studies that sustained well-being requires ongoing intentional activity rather than circumstantial changes, supporting the ancient teaching's distinction between external seeking (circumstantial) and internal communion (intentional practice) [8].

Frankl's meaning research provides crucial validation for the teaching that authentic fulfillment emerges from internal spiritual recognition rather than external acquisition [6]. Studies demonstrate that individuals who find meaning through self-transcendent connection to something greater than ego (what Amenemopet identifies as communion with Creator-Spirit) report significantly higher life satisfaction and psychological resilience compared to those seeking meaning through personal achievement or material success. This empirical evidence supports verse 9's teaching about discovering "the fullness of the Creator-Spirit that is within" as the authentic source of lasting fulfillment.

Default Mode Network and Dualistic Seeking

Neuroscience research on the default mode network (DMN) validates the teaching's description of the seeking mind's psychological architecture. Studies by Brewer and colleagues (2011) using fMRI demonstrated that the DMN—active during self-referential thinking and mental time travel—shows heightened activity in individuals engaged in future-focused planning and comparative self-evaluation, precisely the patterns Amenemopet describes as "worldly thinking, desires and cravings" [9][verse 9]. This research empirically confirms that the seeking mind operates through specific neural networks associated with egoic self-concept and temporal projection (past regret, future fantasy) rather than present-moment awareness.

Significantly, the same research demonstrates that experienced meditators show decreased DMN activity during both formal practice and rest states, indicating stable transformation of baseline mental functioning [9]. This validates verse 7's teaching about silent people in temple: the practice of silent communion systematically reduces the neural activity underlying the seeking mind's dualistic perception, creating neurological conditions for recognizing what Amenemopet describes as internal divine fullness rather than external incompleteness.

Meditation Research and Internal Fullness Discovery

Research by Kral and colleagues (2018) provides empirical validation for the teaching's distinction between heated seeking and silent communion [10]. Studies demonstrate that long-term meditation practitioners show reduced amygdala reactivity to emotional stimuli compared to controls, indicating decreased automatic reactive patterns—what Amenemopet identifies as aryu-driven agitation. Moreover, the research reveals that meditation practice correlates with increased reports of internal satisfaction independent of external circumstances, empirically supporting verse 9's teaching that "Being silent means discovering the fullness of the Creator-Spirit that is within."

Gratitude research offers additional validation for verse 8's teaching about spontaneous recognition of blessings. Emmons and McCullough (2003) demonstrated through controlled studies that individuals who practice systematic gratitude show significantly increased well-being, life satisfaction, and positive affect compared to controls [11]. This empirical evidence supports the teaching that silent people "speak of the greatness of the blessings they receive from being in the temple from the Creator-Spirit"—the natural expression of recognition that emerges from minds aligned with divine presence rather than seeking external acquisition [verse 8].

The research synthesis validates Amenemopet's core teaching: human minds naturally seek fulfillment, but this seeking proves futile when directed externally toward ephemeral worldly experiences (hedonic treadmill), while the same seeking redirected internally through silent communion (meditation practice) reveals lasting satisfaction through recognizing divine fullness already present (DMN reduction, gratitude capacity). The empirical evidence demonstrates that this transformation occurs through measurable changes in brain function and psychological patterns rather than metaphysical speculation, providing scientific validation for the ancient mystical psychology.

5. Spiritual Implications for Aspirants: Progressive Development of Silent Communion and Internal Fullness Recognition

PART A: PASTORAL CONCERNS - MODERN CHALLENGES TO SILENT PRACTICE AND INTERNAL RECOGNITION

For contemporary practitioners, verses 7-9's teachings on Silent Temple Approach, Spontaneous Gratitude, and Internal Divine Fulfillment illuminate crucial challenges in cultivating authentic satisfaction within a culture systematically designed to perpetuate the seeking mind [1, 2]. Consider the seeker who recognizes intellectually that external acquisition cannot provide lasting fulfillment yet finds the mind persistently driven by aryu-generated cravings for achievement, recognition, experiences, or relationships. This represents the fundamental struggle Amenemopet addresses: knowing the truth about internal fullness while experiencing the mind dominated by patterns that maintain the illusion of incompleteness.

The teaching addresses someone exhausted by years of seeking—achieving desired goals only to find satisfaction evaporating, acquiring desired possessions only to experience renewed craving, reaching milestones only to face new anxieties about maintaining status or achieving the next level. The wisdom to be understood reveals that this exhaustion serves divine purpose by creating psychological conditions necessary for turning attention from external seeking to internal communion [verse 9][2]. Nevertheless, the transition proves difficult because aryu patterns stored in the ab (unconscious mind) continue generating desires and cravings that occupy the hat (conscious awareness) even when the individual intellectually recognizes their futility.

Contemporary culture actively undermines the silent practice Amenemopet prescribes: advertising industries engineer psychological techniques specifically designed to create and maintain feelings of incompleteness requiring product acquisition; social media platforms promote constant comparison awareness where individual worth measures itself against curated presentations of others' lives; achievement culture frames human value through external metrics of success, wealth, or recognition rather than internal spiritual development [verses 7-9]. The aspirant faces continuous cultural conditioning that deposits new aryu patterns reinforcing the very seeking mind the teaching aims to transform.

The teaching illuminates particular challenges for those whose sense of incompleteness originates from childhood experiences of deprivation, neglect, or trauma that created deep aryu patterns of unworthiness or abandonment now stored in the ab. Consider someone drawn to spiritual practice hoping to fill the internal emptiness created by early relational wounds, yet finding that meditation or temple attendance sometimes activates painful feeling-memories rather than providing the expected peace. This person requires compassionate understanding that aryu purification necessarily involves confronting accumulated patterns rather than bypassing them, and that the path from heated seeking to silent communion may initially intensify awareness of internal discomfort before revealing the deeper fullness residing in the kara.

PART B: METHODS FOR TRANSFORMATION - SYSTEMATIC CULTIVATION OF SILENT COMMUNION AND FULLNESS RECOGNITION

The fundamental practice Amenemopet prescribes involves what may be termed "Identity Shift Training"—systematically recognizing that the capacity for awareness itself represents Ab Neter rather than individual possession requiring external completion [verse 9]. This practice operates through daily acknowledgment that the awareness witnessing thoughts, sensations, desires, and experiences represents divine presence temporarily appearing as individual mind, not a separate entity fundamentally lacking and requiring worldly acquisition for fulfillment.

Implementation example: Begin each day by consciously recognizing that the capacity for awareness itself represents Ab Neter rather than individual possession. Before engaging external activities, acknowledge: "This awareness noticing these thoughts and sensations represents Creator-Spirit sustaining individual mind—not a separate entity requiring completion through worldly means." This systematic recognition creates what the teaching describes as mooring posts in the ab (unconscious mind) that compete with aryu patterns, gradually shifting the mind from heated seeking to silent recognition.

The practice of "Temple Mind Cultivation" involves recognizing that sacred space exists wherever divine presence receives conscious recognition rather than being limited to physical locations [verse 7]. This transforms ordinary activities into opportunities for divine communion rather than obstacles to spiritual development. The inverse doctrine methodology suggests: if silent persons experience fullness through communion with Creator-Spirit in temple, then cultivating similar internal silence and divine recognition in daily circumstances creates the same potential for fulfillment discovery.

Implementation example: Throughout daily activities, practice momentarily pausing to recognize the Ab Neter presence sustaining awareness even amid worldly circumstances. When washing dishes, walking, working, or engaging conversation, allow brief recognition that this capacity for experience itself represents divine awareness rather than individual possession. These moments of recognition gradually thin aryu density, allowing the mind to operate with increasing awareness of the kara level where Ab Neter resides.

The teaching establishes "Fullness Recognition Practice" to counter the aryu-driven sense of incompleteness: systematically contemplating how "there is perfection within when the fullness of being is experienced beyond the worldly desires and cravings" [verse 9]. This practice involves learning to rest in present-moment awareness without aryu-driven agitation seeking future satisfaction or past gratification. The method requires patient absorption allowing the mind to settle from heated hat-level preoccupation with thoughts and desires toward recognition of the silent fullness that exists at the kara level.

Implementation example: Set aside daily practice time for simply resting in present awareness without pursuing any achievement or experience. When aryu patterns arise as desires, cravings, or seeking impulses, recognize them as surface-level disturbances in the ab rather than truth about what the mind requires. Allow these patterns to arise and dissolve without engagement, maintaining awareness established in recognition of internal fullness rather than external seeking. This patient practice gradually reveals what Amenemopet describes as "the fullness of the Creator-Spirit that is within"—not through acquiring something new but through thinning aryu obstruction to what has always been present.

The wisdom emphasizes that transformation occurs through removing aryu obstruction rather than creating access to absent divinity. Ab Neter already sustains individual awareness as the foundation residing in the kara—the practice involves eliminating the accumulated feeling-memories in the ab that occupy the hat and prevent recognition of this ever-present divine reality. Therefore, practitioners approach spiritual development with patient persistence, understanding that gradual aryu purification naturally reveals the silent fullness that heated seeking could never provide.

References

[1] Ashby, M. (2019-25). Mysticism of Amenemopet Hieroglyphic Text Translation. Chapter 5, Verses 7-9. Sema Institute of Ancient Egyptian Studies.

[2] Ashby, M. (2025). Keys to Sage Amenemopet wisdom text trilinear translation chapter 5. Sema Institute of Ancient Egyptian Studies.

[3] Ashby, M. (2019-25). Mysticism of Amenemopet Hieroglyphic Text Translation. Chapter 4, Verses 1-2, 7-8. Sema Institute of Ancient Egyptian Studies.

[4] Ashby, M. (2019-25). Mysticism of Amenemopet Hieroglyphic Text Translation. Chapter 9, Verses 15-17. Sema Institute of Ancient Egyptian Studies.

[5] Ashby, M. (2024). Book Awakening Your Soul-Aware-Witness Ancient Egyptian Wisdom To Discover Divine Consciousness -v32. Sema Institute of Ancient Egyptian Studies.

[6] Frankl, V. E. (1959/2006). Man's Search for Meaning. Boston: Beacon Press.

[7] Lyubomirsky, S., Sheldon, K. M., & Schkade, D. (2005). Pursuing happiness: The architecture of sustainable change. Review of General Psychology, 9(2), 111-131.

[8] Sheldon, K. M., & Lyubomirsky, S. (2012). The challenge of staying happier: Testing the Hedonic Adaptation Prevention model. Personality and Social Psychology Bulletin, 38(5), 670-680.

[9] Brewer, J. A., Worhunsky, P. D., Gray, J. R., Tang, Y. Y., Weber, J., & Kober, H. (2011). Meditation experience is associated with differences in default mode network activity and connectivity. Proceedings of the National Academy of Sciences, 108(50), 20254-20259.

[10] Kral, T. R. A., Schuyler, B. S., Mumford, J. A., Rosenkranz, M. A., Lutz, A., & Davidson, R. J. (2018). Impact of short- and long-term mindfulness meditation training on amygdala reactivity to emotional stimuli. NeuroImage, 181, 301-313.

[11] Emmons, R. A., & McCullough, M. E. (2003). Counting blessings versus burdens: An experimental investigation of gratitude and subjective well-being in daily life. Journal of Personality and Social Psychology, 84(2), 377-389.

CHAPTER 8: Commentary on Teachings of Amenemopet Chapter 6B, Verse 14: The Psychology of Maintaining Awareness of All-Encompassing Divinity Commentary on Sage Amenemopet's Teaching of Deliberate Neberdjer Recognition

SUMMARY OF VERSES COVERED

Verse 14 presents the foundational spiritual instruction: "Remain watchful, mindful, aware, keeping in mind, with deliberate effort, as to the fact that there is an 'entity', an 'existence' that encompasses all Creation [All-encompassing-Divinity], beyond [underlying] mind and time and space." The teaching establishes that "no action is hidden from it and consequently, this existence/consciousness underlies limited human awareness" and promises that "If this awareness is maintained, there will be no egoism and no mind and therefore no fears, frustrations, inordinate desires, no need for stealing, lying, cheating or becoming a heated person and missing out on the glories of inner peace or the fulfillment of the purpose of life."

Core Teaching: The verse establishes the Teaching of Deliberate Neberdjer Awareness: the systematic cultivation of conscious recognition of the All-Encompassing Divinity (Neberdjer) as the foundation underlying all existence, individual awareness, and daily experience. This represents the ultimate spiritual practice that transforms ordinary human awareness into direct recognition of absolute consciousness, eliminating the psychological conditions that create suffering while establishing the practitioner in inner peace, spiritual fulfillment, enlightenment, and immortality.

Sage Amenemopet prescribes a meditative practice of maintaining awareness of Neberdjer—which is to say, maintaining awareness of awareness itself. The practice involves directing attention not toward the objects of perception, but toward that which makes perception possible: the underlying consciousness that affords the mind its very capacity to cognize, sense, and perceive. This awareness exists prior to mental operations and cognitive functions, representing the true nature of one's existence—immortal and eternal, unlike the body, mind, and senses which remain mortal and therefore ephemeral.

The Ancient Egyptian term "Neb-er-djer" translates as "sovereign-about-existence," "all-encompassing-divinity," or "ruler-as-to-limits"—meaning Limitless, representing THAT WHICH IS ABSOLUTE [1]. Neberdjer is all-encompassing (universal) Consciousness. This teaching establishes three fundamental understandings explored in this commentary: (1) the psychology of how limited human awareness operates in ignorance of its absolute foundation, (2) the transformative practice of maintaining deliberate recognition of Neberdjer as the source and substance of all experience, and (3) the elimination of egoism and suffering through establishment in this ultimate awareness.

1: HUMAN PSYCHOLOGY PRINCIPLE FOCUS OF CHAPTER 6B VIII (VERSE 14)

The Crisis of Misplaced Attention

The fundamental psychological issue Sage Amenemopet addresses concerns where awareness habitually directs its attention. Human awareness, operating through the hat (conscious awareness level), becomes chronically fixated upon limited perceptions delivered through the mind and senses—the parsing of existence into separate objects, the division of experience into time and space, and most critically, the conclusion that one exists as an isolated individual entity. This habitual misdirection of attention constitutes the primary obstacle preventing both Prologue goals from manifesting.

Consider how this pattern directly impacts Prologue verse 2's goal of "causing a person to have well-being while living on earth." When awareness remains absorbed in limited mind interpretations—believing happiness depends upon acquiring specific objects or controlling circumstances—the personality enters perpetual anxiety and incompleteness. The mind interprets Neberdjer's infinity as measurable space and Neberdjer's eternity as threatening time that creates urgency and fear of death. These interpretations, arising from the mind's inability to cognize what transcends its limited capacity, generate psychological conditions making earthly well-being impossible regardless of external circumstances.

The teaching reveals profound implications for Prologue verse 9's goal of discovering kara where "the Divine resides in every person." The accumulated aryu (karmic feeling-memories) stored in the ab (unconscious mind) "occupy the presence-of-mind awareness, so densely as to blot out the awareness of the soul-level divine presence which is deeper than the aryu." When the hat operates exclusively through conclusions of limited mind and senses, awareness remains aware only of body, mind, sensations, and time-space realities—never penetrating to the deeper kara (divine sanctuary) where Ab Neter (divine soul spark) sustains one's very capacity for conscious awareness.

The wisdom to be understood recognizes that Ab Neter is the portion of awareness possessed by every human being that is a manifestation of Neberdjer consciousness in every individual. Thus, Ab Neter (the individual spirit awareness of a human being) is nothing but the same Neberdjer consciousness. However, the human personality, being constricted by limitation, is ordinarily only aware—if at all—of the soul-level awareness. By undergoing the practices and purifications, that the soul-level awareness can grow to experience Neberdjer (all-encompassingness, absolute being).

Amenemopet's instruction to maintain deliberate awareness of Neberdjer addresses this crisis at its psychological root. The sage recognizes that human awareness possesses capacity to direct attention not merely toward objects perceived by the mind, but toward the existence that sustains and encompasses those perceptions. This represents awareness functioning at two distinct levels: mental awareness (using the mind to cognize objects) or intuitional awareness (not using the mind, but recognizing the consciousness allowing the mind to function) [2]. The psychological principle emerges clearly—awareness can either remain trapped in the conclusions of its limited perceptual instruments or recognize the unlimited foundation from which those instruments arise.

2: Behavioral Imperative: The Patterns of Attention Misdirection

Observable Manifestations of All-Encompassing Awareness and Awareness Fixated on Limited Mind

Neberdjer is all-encompassing Consciousness—awareness and beingness beyond individuality, constriction, or human awareness limitation. Neberdjer consciousness is complete and full in itself. A person who achieves the experience of Neberdjer also becomes full and complete without needing external relations or circumstances for personal satisfaction or fulfillment. The behavioral patterns arising from awareness habitually fixated upon limited mind perceptions manifest through specific, observable symptoms that Amenemopet identifies throughout his teachings. When awareness remains absorbed in the mind's parsing of existence into separate, individualized entities, the personality develops what earlier verses characterize as heated mind and feelings—the constellation of reactive patterns driven by the fundamental delusion of separateness.

Consider the individual who awakens each morning with awareness immediately captured by the stream of mental commentary: concerns about the day ahead, rehearsals of potential conflicts, calculations of how to secure desired outcomes, anxieties about maintaining relationships or status. This represents the hat operating entirely through the aryu-laden interpretations of limited mind, with zero awareness directed toward the Neberdjer that sustains both the awareness and its contents. The wisdom to be understood reveals how this pattern perpetuates itself: each mental conclusion reinforces the belief in separate individuality, which generates more aryu through reactive thoughts and feelings, which further occupy the presence-of-mind awareness, creating an intensifying cycle of awareness trapped in its own limited perceptions.

The behavioral manifestations become particularly evident in how such awareness responds to life circumstances. When the hat operates without awareness of Neberdjer, every situation becomes interpreted through the lens of individual gain or loss, approval or rejection, security or threat. The colleague who receives recognition triggers comparison and potential resentment—aryu patterns of inadequacy and competition arising because awareness identifies exclusively with the limited mind's conclusion that "I am this separate person who must prove worth." The unexpected expense generates anxiety and anger—aryu patterns of fear and control arising because awareness believes the limited mind's interpretation that finite resources determine well-being, and that time might run out before security is achieved.

Contemporary Entertainment Culture as Negative Aryu-Generation System

The modern entertainment complex—theaters, cinema, music, arts, and digital media—creates particularly insidious obstacles to maintaining Neberdjer awareness through systematic cultivation of aryu patterns that occupy presence-of-mind awareness with feelings and thoughts devoid of wisdom. Consider how entertainment industries engineer content specifically designed to trigger excitement, fantasies, and somatic pleasures that provide temporary delight and reveries while promoting neither serenity nor awareness of one's nature as something beyond a human animal operating on somatic pleasures and illusory desires. These forms of engagement build more agitations and desires rather than satisfying existing ones, offering pastimes that lead to empty pleasures, mental slumber, and intellectual atrophy—the very opacity of mind that prevents recognition of Ab Neter.

The behavioral pattern operates insidiously because entertainment consumption feels pleasurable and appears harmless compared to obviously destructive activities. Someone spending hours absorbed in dramatic narratives, competitive sports spectacles, or sensually stimulating content believes they engage in innocent relaxation. However, the teaching reveals how each hour of such absorption deposits dense aryu in the ab—feeling-memories of emotional reactivity, identification with fictional personas pursuing heated objectives, and conditioning toward entertainment-dependent satisfaction. This can be described as "pouring gasoline on a fire"—the very activity pursued for pleasure actually intensifies the heated mind and feelings by continuously generating new aryu faster than purification practices can clear them. Modern individuals accumulate thousands of hours of media-generated aryu—television programming normalizing heated patterns, social media training reactive emotions, entertainment glorifying desire-driven behavior—creating extraordinarily dense obstruction to Ab Neter awareness before they ever encounter spiritual teachings.

Most people live life as automatons, engaging automatically and thoughtlessly in worldly activities as rituals without greater meaning or life purpose, sometimes following the herd of humanity because television says so, or a politician, or parents or friends, or one's own desires that seem to be stimulating and that they have learned to regard as "living" by being able to do them and thinking those make life worth living and constitute a life being lived. Yet those are insubstantial pastimes that lead a person to a wasted life and regrets at the end of life. In the automatic mode—default mode network—life is actually passing you by; that is not living. Living is slowing down and realizing you are existence itself contemplating the appearances of time and space, not like a person watching a movie or a show who gets lost in the show during its duration, forgetting themselves and the time that has passed.

Most significantly, entertainment addiction creates dependency patterns wherein the personality requires constant external stimulation to feel engaged with existence, rendering silence intolerable and contemplation impossible. When such individuals attempt spiritual practice, the accumulated entertainment aryu rebel against stillness—the mind floods with compulsive mental replays of dramatic content, restlessness demands immediate stimulation, and anxiety interprets quiet reflection as "wasting time" that could be spent consuming more content. This pattern eventually promotes frustration, depression, and unhappiness because the temporary satisfactions entertainment provides inevitably fade, requiring escalating intensity and novelty to generate the same pleasure response—a progressive enslavement to external stimulation that destroys the very capacity for the inner silence necessary for discovering the kara where Ab Neter resides.

Indeed, the reactive patterns operate largely unconsciously, emerging automatically from the aryu density in the ab without conscious volition. The aspirant finds oneself engaged in behaviors contrary to one's stated values: the resolve to remain patient crumbles in the face of frustration; the intention to practice generosity withdraws when scarcity concerns activate; the commitment to truthfulness bends when consequences seem disadvantageous. These represent not moral failures requiring condemnation, but rather the inevitable result of awareness operating exclusively through limited mind without recognition of the Neberdjer foundation that would reveal such concerns as ultimately illusory.

The teaching identifies how this misdirected awareness creates the entire spectrum of what earlier verses describe as heated characteristics: unrighteousness emerges when awareness, believing in separate individuality, concludes that personal advantage justifies exploiting others; fraud develops when the limited mind calculates that deception serves individual interests; anger arises when circumstances contradict the ego's expectations; jealousy and envy manifest when awareness compares its imagined separate position with others; rapacious greed intensifies when the limited mind interprets existence as competition for finite resources. All these behavioral patterns arise from and reinforce the fundamental delusion that awareness exists as an isolated individual rather than recognizing its nature as Neberdjer expressing through apparent individual form.

Based on the teaching presented by Sage Amenemopet that one should remain aware of Neberdjer, the inverse doctrine application suggests that one should also avoid actions, thoughts, and feelings that reinforce the delusion of separate individuality and that direct awareness exclusively toward the limited mind's interpretations, as these would undermine the cultivation of awareness of the all-encompassing foundation of consciousness.

3: Mystic Psychology—Metaphysical Implications of Neberdjer Awareness

The Architecture of Awareness Transformation Through Deliberate Recognition

Building upon the behavioral patterns identified in Section 2, the wisdom to be understood concerns how maintaining awareness of Neberdjer transforms the mind at the fundamental architecture level where aryu patterns either maintain density or undergo thinning. This metaphysical process operates through specific mechanisms that determine whether the mind remains trapped in delusion or discovers freedom through recognition of its divine source.

Neberdjer represents the Ancient Egyptian term for what constitutes absolute consciousness—not consciousness as typically understood through individual mind-body systems experiencing separation, but rather the universal divine essence operating as awareness through all beings and phenomena while remaining as their unchanging foundation. The term translates as "sovereign-about-existence," "all-encompassing-divinity," or "ruler-as-to-limits"—that is, Limitless [2]. Terms such as "sovereign," "Divinity," and "Existence" combined with limitlessness and all-encompassing-ness point to THAT WHICH IS ABSOLUTE.

The teaching reveals a profound metaphysical truth: human awareness represents the same as Neberdjer when the limited perceptions of time, space, and ego individuality experienced through the mind are transcended [2]. This means that spiritual practice aims not to create access to something absent, but rather to remove the aryu obstruction preventing recognition of what has always been present as the very foundation sustaining awareness itself. Ab Neter residing in kara (deep ab level) represents one's personal portion of Neberdjer—the localized manifestation of all-encompassing consciousness that makes individual awareness possible.

When the hat directs deliberate awareness toward Neberdjer, this creates specific transformative effects at the mind architecture level. First, the practice interrupts automatic absorption of awareness in mental content and sensory phenomena. Ordinarily, aryu patterns automatically capture the hat's attention the moment awareness activates—like well-worn grooves channeling water automatically without conscious direction. The deliberate effort to remain aware of Neberdjer requires awareness to resist this automatic capture, creating what the tradition describes as "thinning" of aryu density rather than its reinforcement through continued absorption.

Second, maintaining awareness of Neberdjer establishes wisdom content at the ab level that functions as competing influence against ego-reinforcing aryu. Consider the mechanics: when awareness repeatedly directs attention toward the understanding that all existence encompasses Neberdjer—that separate individuality represents delusion of limited mind, that time and space represent the mind's interpretation of infinity and eternity, that the ego's anxieties and desires arise from ignorance of one's true nature as universal consciousness—these understandings themselves become registered in the ab as what might be termed "wisdom-aryu." Unlike ego-driven patterns creating heated mind and feelings, these wisdom-aryu remain "transparent" to the divine light of Ab Neter, allowing awareness to recognize its source rather than obscuring it.

The metaphysical implications extend to understanding three levels of potential awareness the tradition recognizes: human awareness through limited mind (encompassing waking, dream, and deep sleep states); cosmic mind expanded awareness (Creator Spirit level—Ra, Net, Ptah, Amun, encompassing and surpassing human awareness); and absolute consciousness total awareness (Absolute level—Neberdjer, Un-Nefer, Pa-Neter, encompassing and surpassing both human and cosmic awareness). The practice of maintaining awareness of Neberdjer creates conditions for the mind to recognize that what it has been experiencing as limited individual awareness actually operates within and as these more fundamental levels.

Indeed, just as having worldly experiences from birth to death have no effect on the underlying consciousness sustaining the waking appearance of reality in the mind, and just as falling asleep and having a dream have no consequence for the soul (Asar), in the same way, the appearance of Creation has no impact on universal absolute consciousness (Neberdjer). This recognition transforms spiritual practice from attempt to achieve something new into process of removing obstacles preventing recognition of what eternally IS.

The verse's instruction to maintain this awareness "with deliberate effort" and "with conscious volition" reveals the metaphysical necessity of active engagement rather than passive reception. The accumulated aryu from thousands of hours of worldly thoughts and individualized thinking create such momentum that awareness automatically flows toward limited mind interpretations unless deliberate effort redirects it. This represents not forceful struggle against natural inclination, but rather patient, persistent reorientation of awareness from its habitual fixation on objects toward recognition of the consciousness making object-perception possible—a gradual process of awareness learning to recognize itself directly rather than exclusively through its mental modifications.

3.1: THE COMPREHENSIVE DIMENSIONS OF SAU NEBERDJER (AWARENESS OF NEBERDJER)

Building upon the metaphysical architecture established in Section 3, the wisdom to be understood recognizes that Sau Neberdjer (awareness of Neberdjer) encompasses multiple progressive dimensions that systematically transform the mind from limited ego identification to the recognition of absolute reality. These dimensions represent not separate practices but rather deepening stages of a unified spiritual methodology.

Philosophical and Causal Awareness

The First Dimension: Philosophical Understanding

The first dimension concerns philosophical understanding—recognizing what Neberdjer represents: the entity that encompasses all Creation, composes all existence, and operates behind all movements and developments of nature. This establishes in the hat (conscious awareness) a conceptual framework that directly challenges the limited mind's automatic interpretations of separate individuality, discrete independent objects, and time-space as ultimate realities. These interpretations represent not objective truth but rather mental constructs arising from awareness encountering its own manifestations without recognizing their source.

Consider how the limited mind, lacking capacity to cognize infinity and eternity directly, automatically interprets Neberdjer's infinity as measurable space and eternity as threatening time. These misinterpretations generate the psychological conditions—anxiety, incompleteness, and fear of death—that make earthly well-being impossible (Prologue verse 2). Philosophical awareness begins thinning these erroneous conclusions by establishing competing wisdom impressions in the ab: infinity means limitlessness rather than vast extension; eternity signifies timelessness rather than endless duration. This understanding creates the first level of aryu transformation—wisdom knowledge beginning to compete with ignorance-based patterns.

The Second Dimension: Recognition of Divine Causation

The second dimension deepens philosophical understanding into the recognition of divine causation—the understanding that Neberdjer operates as the entity behind all events, shepherding circumstances according to wisdom that encompasses individual welfare within cosmic harmony. When awareness grasps this truth—as verse 18:6 teaches that "the overall encompassing divinity is the shepherd that guides human life"—the heated patterns of manipulation, scheming, and forceful effort begin thinning at their psychological root.

This dimension addresses the core egoic delusion that happiness depends upon controlling outcomes through personal will. The teaching eliminates the psychological basis for heated mind and feelings by revealing that the separate ego believing itself responsible for securing welfare through worldly acquisition operates as a false identity—one functioning in ignorance of the actual divine foundation guiding all experience. When awareness recognizes Neberdjer as the orchestrator of circumstances, anxious control-seeking naturally dissolves.

The Third Dimension: Self-Recognition as Neberdjer

The third and most profound dimension concerns recognizing one's innermost reality as Neberdjer itself rather than as limited ego identity. This represents the crucial shift from mental awareness (using the mind to cognize Neberdjer as object) to intuitional awareness (recognizing oneself AS the consciousness sustaining the mind). The teaching establishes that Ab Neter residing in the kara represents one's personal portion of Neberdjer—meaning what a human being essentially is proves identical with the all-encompassing absolute reality, not the temporary personality structure composed of body, thoughts, feelings, and accumulated aryu.

When awareness recognizes itself as Neberdjer, the entire psychological structure of suffering collapses at its foundation. The teaching reveals the mechanism precisely: "If this awareness is maintained, there will be no egoism and no mind and therefore no fears, frustrations, inordinate desires, no need for stealing, lying, cheating or becoming a heated person."[2] This transformation occurs because the fundamental misidentification creating all psychological disturbance—awareness believing itself limited, separate, incomplete, and threatened—has been corrected through the recognition of one's essential nature as unlimited, all-encompassing, eternally complete divine reality. The suffering never belonged to consciousness itself but only to the false ego identity that awareness mistakenly assumed.

The Fourth Dimension: Liberation from Craving

The fourth dimension concerns the practical psychological consequence of self-recognition: the elimination of craving for objects in a futile effort to feel complete. Heated mind and feelings arise from egoic incompleteness—awareness identifying with the limited mind-body experiences itself as separate from the wholeness it seeks, generating compulsive drive to gather objects, relationships, achievements, and experiences as compensation for felt deficiency. However, no accumulation of external acquisitions can eliminate fundamental incompleteness because that incompleteness arises from misidentification, not from actual lack.

When awareness recognizes itself as Neberdjer—the absolute reality containing all possible manifestations within itself—the psychological basis for craving disappears at its root. One recognizes what was sought through external acquisition has always been present as one's essential nature. The teaching describes this as discovering "the fullness of the Creator-Spirit that is within" (verse 5:9)—the internal completeness that eliminates need for external validation, acquisition, or achievement to feel whole. This recognition creates the psychological foundation for what Amenemopet terms jubilation: spontaneous joy arising from Ab Neter recognition rather than circumstance-dependent happiness requiring particular experiences to generate satisfaction.

The Fundamental Choice: Aryu Authority Versus Maat Dispensation

The wisdom to be understood reveals a crucial metaphysical principle that determines the entire trajectory of human experience: when a person lives based on spiritual ignorance—allowing ego-driven thoughts, feelings, and desires to govern their choices—their fate remains controlled by their accumulated aryu. The ab (unconscious mind), densely occupied with karmic feeling-memories from countless actions founded in egoism and delusion, operates as the authority determining what circumstances consciousness encounters, what thoughts compulsively arise, what feelings dominate responses, and what trajectory destiny (Shai) follows. This aryu-controlled fate operates mechanically, impelled by the momentum of past patterns reinforcing themselves through continued ignorant action—a self-perpetuating cycle wherein past egoic choices generate present egoic impulses that create future egoic consequences.

Nevertheless, when the personality moves toward Maat (cosmic order, truth, righteousness) through engagement with sebayt (wisdom teachings) and the systematic purification practices the tradition prescribes, the authority governing fate fundamentally shifts. Instead of remaining under the dispensation of aryu—the accumulated impressions of ignorance determining life trajectory—the aspirant comes under the dispensation of Maat itself. This means their fate becomes based on the truth of spirit-being rather than on the delusion of egoism rooted in fleeting worldly attainments. The cosmic forces of Shai (destiny) and Renenut (fortune), which Amenemopet teaches operate as "the hands of Djehuty" recording and implementing karmic consequences, now respond to the ethical quality and spiritual purity developing in the personality rather than merely executing the momentum of accumulated negative aryu. When consciousness aligns with Maat through right understanding and virtuous action, circumstances arise that serve spiritual evolution—not necessarily comfortable or ego-gratifying circumstances, but precisely those experiences that advance Ab Neter recognition and aryu purification. This represents the essential purpose of maintaining Neberdjer awareness combined with Maatian living: shifting authority from the mechanical control of ignorance-based patterns toward the intelligent guidance of cosmic order operating through the personality for its ultimate liberation.

The Fifth Dimension: Ger—Resting in the Unconscious

The fifth dimension concerns Ger (silence, serenity) achieved through resting awareness in the unconscious where Ab Neter/Neberdjer resides. This represents the shift from heated mental activity—the hat constantly occupied with aryu-driven reactions—to silent absorption in the kara where Ab Neter sustains awareness. The wisdom to be understood recognizes that Ger means not mere absence of thought or suppression of mental activity, but rather the profound serenity arising when awareness rests in its source rather than remaining absorbed in its modifications.

When awareness settles from the surface hat through the aryu-occupied ab into the kara where Ab Neter resides, the mind discovers its foundation in Neberdjer—the absolute reality eternally complete, perfect, and unchanging. The teaching reveals that "transcending mind altogether including time and space awareness" occurs through "allowing awareness to settle on its source."[3] Initially this occurs with deliberate effort—awareness intentionally directing attention away from mental content toward the consciousness sustaining that content. Through sustained practice, however, resting becomes effortless as awareness naturally abides in its source rather than habitually following aryu patterns outward into mental modifications.

The Sixth Dimension: Perennial Completeness Without Obstruction

The final dimension concerns the nature of awareness when established in Ger through recognition of itself as Neberdjer: perennial completeness and perfection present without obstructions, variations, or deviations. This fulfills both Prologue goals simultaneously—earthly well-being achieved through awareness no longer disturbed by circumstances (since it recognizes its essential nature as unchanging divine reality), and the discovery of the divine shrine (kara) revealing Ab Neter as one's true identity.

Consider the distinction between ephemeral and perennial satisfaction. Heated mind and feelings experience only ephemeral satisfaction—happiness dependent upon circumstances remaining favorable, requiring constant maintenance and inevitably subject to loss. Silent mind and feelings rooted in Ab Neter recognition discover perennial satisfaction because awareness has discovered that what it sought through external means has always been present as its own nature—the fullness, completeness, and perfection that Neberdjer eternally is. This completeness proves perennial because it belongs to awareness's essential nature rather than depending upon temporary conditions.

Progressive Integration of All Dimensions

The practical application requires understanding these six dimensions as progressive stages of deepening awareness rather than as separate practices. One begins with philosophical study establishing conceptual understanding of Neberdjer's nature and function. This naturally progresses through reflective contemplation that recognizes Neberdjer as the divine cause orchestrating all circumstances. From this foundation, one develops meditative practice directing awareness toward one's essential nature rather than toward mental content. Through sustained practice, awareness ultimately stabilizes in Ger where it rests in its source—the kara where Ab Neter resides.

Each dimension supports and enriches the others: philosophical understanding provides the conceptual framework necessary for meditation; meditative experience validates and deepens philosophical understanding through direct recognition; and the recognition of one's nature as Neberdjer naturally produces the behavioral transformations described throughout Amenemopet's teachings. This comprehensive understanding reveals why Amenemopet presents Sau Neberdjer as the ultimate spiritual practice—it addresses the root cause of all psychological disturbance (misidentification with limited ego) while simultaneously establishing awareness in direct recognition of its divine nature (Ab Neter as Neberdjer manifestation). When this awareness is maintained with deliberate effort and eventually becomes the natural state of the human awareness, all the negative psychological patterns arising from heated mind and feelings naturally dissolve, replaced by the serenity, wisdom, and jubilation that characterize minds established in recognition of their absolute foundation.

3.2: THE DIVINE PARADOX: WHY IGNORANCE CAPACITY ENABLES DIVINE SELF-EXPERIENCE AND WHY AMENEMOPET'S TEACHING MATTERS

Having established the nature of Neberdjer as all-encompassing foundation and the mechanics by which awareness can become aware or unaware of this reality, we must now address a profound metaphysical question that illuminates the deepest purpose of Amenemopet's wisdom teachings: Why does the capacity for ignorance exist at all, and what does this reveal about the ultimate nature of existence and the necessity of these teachings for human well-being?

The Paradox of Divine Self-Experience

Consider the fundamental paradox facing Neberdjer as infinite, all-encompassing consciousness: If Neberdjer constitutes all that exists, how can it experience itself? If it tried it would perceive everything all at once, from every angle and from every vantagepoint, all the time and everything is the same. Experience requires subject-object differentiation—a perceiver distinct from that which is perceived. Yet if Neberdjer is all, there exists no "other" to experience. Without apparent separation between experiencer and experienced, there remains only undifferentiated existence—not experience in any meaningful sense, but simply IS-ness without qualification.

This reveals a profound truth: For consciousness to experience itself, there must be apparent separate vantage points from which to discern something appearing as other than oneself. This apparent separation creates what the teachings call duality—the appearance of multiple distinct entities, subjects and objects, experiencer and experienced. Yet since Neberdjer is all, even these apparently separate objects that seem distinct from each other remain in reality composed entirely of Neberdjer. They appear as separate objects only through the effect of individualized mind that limits awareness from perceiving the All, restricting consciousness to perceiving only limited aspects of the All.

The Scripture of Ra and Hetheru illuminates this principle through the teaching that Ra emerges from Nunu as individuated divine consciousness—"moving from undifferentiation to differentiation/individuation as an entity that can be conscious and aware of itself." This individuation does not create something outside Neberdjer but represents Neberdjer manifesting through apparent localized vantage points, each perceiving limited portions of Creation rather than the undifferentiated totality. As the lecture teachings emphasize, this represents "localized awareness" that "experiences reality through the particular mind, body and vantage point as opposed to perceiving the entire Creation at once."

Ignorance as Necessary Feature Rather Than Cosmic Error

One essential component of this individuation process proves particularly crucial for understanding why Amenemopet's teachings exist: the capacity to experience ignorance of self-knowledge. A human being can forget they are Neberdjer and thus experience different forms of reality, ideas, feelings, and perspectives that they—as Neberdjer knowing itself to be Neberdjer—could not experience. This "forgetting" represents not a cosmic mistake requiring correction but rather an integral feature of the divine self-experience mechanism.

Consider how this transforms understanding of ignorance: When awareness operating through individualized mind believes itself to be merely a separate entity—body, personality, ego—disconnected from the divine source, this delusion creates genuine capacity for experience impossible from the perspective of undifferentiated Neberdjer awareness. Someone identified completely with ego-personality experiences fear of death, desire for objects believed external to self, competition with other apparently separate beings, triumph and defeat, love and loss—the entire spectrum of dualistic experience that defines human life.

Yet this same capacity for ignorance that enables such rich experience also opens the possibility for awareness to experience delusions, to collect feeling-memories (aryu) that dominate understanding, and to allow these accumulated patterns to govern thoughts, feelings, desires, and actions. The wayward mind operating in ignorance can act in contravention with Maat—the universal order that represents how existence operates when aligned with its Neberdjer foundation. Indeed, awareness CAN act contrary to cosmic harmony, though such actions tend to produce outcomes contrary to Maat and therefore contrary to peace, harmony, health, and well-being.

Why Creation, Duality, and Ignorance Serve Divine Purpose

This reveals the profound understanding underlying all Ancient Egyptian mystery teachings: Creation itself, with its apparent multiplicity and the ignorance capacity that accompanies individualization, serves the purpose of divine self-experience. Neberdjer cannot experience the infinite variations of existence, the spectrum of emotions and perspectives, the journey from ignorance to enlightenment, while remaining in undifferentiated unity-awareness. The appearance of separate beings, each with limited vantage point and capacity for both ignorance and awakening, allows Neberdjer to know itself through infinite manifestations.

The Coffin Texts illuminate this principle: "I came into being by creating a Creator God out of myself from my fullness...that is all-encompassing and complete." Creation proceeds not from lack or need but from fullness—Neberdjer manifesting potentials already contained within its infinite nature. The apparent limitations of individualized awareness, including ignorance capacity, represent not cosmic deficiency but rather the mechanism through which infinite consciousness explores itself through finite vantage points.

Nevertheless—and this proves crucial—while ignorance serves divine self-experience at the cosmic level, it creates genuine suffering at the individual level when awareness remains trapped in delusion. The person believing themselves merely separate ego, pursuing satisfaction through worldly objects, guarding pride in temporary position, reacting with heated mind and feelings to perceived threats—this mind experiences real distress, anxiety, fear, and spiritual disaster even though, from the absolute perspective, all remains Neberdjer playing in apparent multiplicity.

Why Amenemopet's Teaching on Neberdjer Awareness Proves Essential

This metaphysical framework reveals why Amenemopet's admonishment to maintain awareness of Neberdjer represents not arbitrary spiritual instruction but rather the essential wisdom for transforming suffering into fulfillment while living within the individualized state. The teaching recognizes both the necessity of the individualization process AND the crucial importance of not remaining trapped in complete ignorance of one's divine foundation.

When Amenemopet instructs: "be aware of Neberdjer," this addresses the fundamental human condition: we exist as apparently individualized vantage points (serving divine self-experience) while possessing capacity to either remain lost in ignorance-driven suffering OR awaken to recognition of our Neberdjer nature while still functioning through individual form. The teaching provides the corrective wisdom that allows awareness to navigate from deviation back toward alignment with reality.

Consider how this illuminates both Prologue goals. The instruction to maintain Neberdjer awareness directly supports [Prologue verse 2] "cause a person to have well-being while living on earth" because awareness of its divine foundation, recognizing that all apparent objects and beings are Neberdjer manifestations, naturally releases the ego-driven patterns—pride-guarding, heated reactions, anxious grasping—that create suffering. One recognizes that honor belongs to Neberdjer rather than to temporary personality position, that all beings are kin manifestations deserving respect, that the heated pursuit of satisfaction in objects reveals ignorance of the fullness already present as one's essential nature.

More profoundly, maintaining Neberdjer awareness enables [Prologue verse 9's] goal of discovering the kara "where the Divine resides in every person." When the Hat operates with background awareness that existence itself is Neberdjer temporarily experiencing through individualized form, the dense aryu patterns that normally dominate presence-of-mind awareness begin thinning. Awareness penetrates from surface Hat level through the ab's aryu density toward the kara level where Ab Neter resides—not creating access to something absent but removing the ignorance-based obstruction that hides what has always been present as the foundation sustaining all awareness.

Why Right Action and Maat Matter Despite Universal Divinity

This framework also resolves a potentially confusing implication: If everything is Neberdjer and ignorance serves divine self-experience, why should one concern oneself with right behavior, wisdom teachings, or alignment with Maat? The answer reveals the sophisticated understanding underlying Amenemopet's entire wisdom philosophy.

The teaching of Chapter 18, verse 6 provides essential background for understanding this principle: "Neberdjer pay f ary sau hat amm" (Lord-of-utmost limits that he does guide front boat—shepherd/watcher). As the contextual translation reveals: "Despite the personal predilections, there is an all-encompassing divinity that masters and encompasses the limits of Creation and therefore, that overall encompassing divinity is the shepherd that guides human life. That divinity is actually at the forefront of the boat of life watching (aware), guiding the boat of human life where it needs to go for the welfare of all humans even before they themselves know where they are going."

While everything is indeed composed of Neberdjer—Consciousness manifesting as Creation—and while Neberdjer shepherds the journey of human life from the forefront of the boat, this does not mean the wayward mind should act in contravention with universal order without consequence. The mind operating in ignorance CAN act contrary to Maat, but such actions tend to produce outcomes contrary to peace, harmony, health, and well-being. This is precisely why philosophy matters—why understanding the ontological origins of existence proves essential for human fulfillment.

The teaching reveals the subtle but crucial distinction: Neberdjer guides the overall journey—"where it needs to go for the welfare of all humans even before they themselves know where they are going"—yet human awareness maintains responsibility for choices made within each moment of that journey. As verse 5 of the same chapter establishes, "the tongue of a person" operates as "steersperson of boat (journey/voyage)," relating to "the words they utter based on their deliberate volition thoughts, feelings, and desires that direct their actions through the journey through their day to day lives."

Thus, awareness operates at dual levels: at the ultimate level, Neberdjer shepherds the boat's course toward welfare and divine self-realization; at the relative level, individualized awareness exercises choice in how it responds to arising circumstances—whether through alignment with Maat (producing harmony) or through contravention of universal order (producing suffering). The guidance Neberdjer provides operates through the very structure of reality itself—actions aligned with Maat naturally produce well-being while actions contrary to cosmic harmony generate distress, regardless of whether awareness recognizes this principle.

When awareness understands that all emerges from Neberdjer, yet that ignorant action produces suffering by operating contrary to cosmic harmony, the purpose of wisdom teachings becomes clear. The teachings do not impose arbitrary restrictions but rather reveal the correct way to understand, think, and act in accord with reality—in a manner that tends to produce well-being, contentment, and fulfillment rather than stress, strife, and suffering.

The Purpose of Ancient Egyptian Mystery Teachings

This complete metaphysical framework illuminates the ultimate purpose of the Ancient Egyptian mystery teachings and specifically Amenemopet's wisdom philosophy: to guide awareness from the deviation that ignorance capacity enables back toward self-knowledge and alignment with Maat while living within the individualized vantage point. The teachings do not seek to eliminate individuation—which serves divine self-experience—but rather to transform the mind from ignorant, suffering-driven egoism toward enlightened, serene operation that recognizes divine nature while functioning effectively through individual form.

The capacity to forget divine identity creates both the possibility of rich dualistic experience AND the danger of remaining trapped in delusion that produces suffering. The teachings provide the corrective wisdom—the philosophical understanding, ethical guidance, and awareness practices—that allow the human being to remember their Neberdjer nature. This remembrance brings what the teachings refer to as serenity, and enlightenment: awareness recognizing its divine foundation while navigating existence with wisdom, compassion, and alignment with universal harmony.

Therefore, when Amenemopet admonishes maintaining awareness of Neberdjer, this represents not one teaching among many but rather the foundational recognition from which all other wisdom flows. Without this awareness, the mind remains trapped in the delusion that ego-personality constitutes complete identity, that worldly position confers dignity, that satisfaction can be found through heated pursuit of external objects, that one must guard pride and maintain superiority displays to preserve self-worth. With this awareness progressively established through patient practice, the mind discovers the fullness already present, releases patterns that create suffering, aligns naturally with Maat, and experiences the well-being and divine discovery that represent the ultimate goals of human existence as set forth in the Prologue.

This metaphysical understanding will inform all subsequent commentaries, as each teaching from Amenemopet can be understood as addressing specific manifestations of ignorance-driven deviation while guiding awareness back toward the Neberdjer awareness that represents both our essential nature and the key to authentic fulfillment in life.

3.3: The Architecture of Awareness Transformation Through Deliberate Recognition

Building upon the behavioral patterns identified in Section 2, the wisdom to be understood concerns how maintaining awareness of Neberdjer transforms the mind at the fundamental architecture level where aryu patterns either maintain density or undergo thinning. This metaphysical process operates through specific mechanisms that determine whether the mind remains trapped in delusion or discovers freedom through recognition of its divine source.

THE ESSENTIAL NATURE OF NEBERDJER: SUPREME SERENITY AS METAPHYSICAL REALITY

Before examining the mechanics of transformation, the wisdom to be understood requires recognizing a profound theological principle regarding Neberdjer's essential nature. Neberdjer represents not merely an abstract concept of all-encompassing divinity but constitutes supreme serenity, silence, equanimity, and homogeneity as metaphysical realities—these qualities are not attributes that Neberdjer possesses but rather what Neberdjer IS in its essential nature. The Stele of Djehuty Nefer reveals that Neberdjer represents "the power of the most sacred creator, who created himself, the lord of the utmost limits, the all-encompassing Divinity" whose "abodes are everywhere—hence all-encompassing-ness and omnipresence throughout Creation/existence."[1][2]

This theological precision transforms our understanding of why Amenemopet advocates the Ger (serene) way of life throughout his teachings. The cultivation of serenity functions not merely as a beneficial psychological practice but as the necessary alignment with Neberdjer's inherent nature. When the mind moves toward Ger—developing silent mind and feelings, establishing inner peace, cultivating equanimity—this movement facilitates coming into harmony with what Neberdjer essentially IS. Together with the philosophy of Neberdjer (understanding its all-encompassing nature), this harmonization makes the self-discovery of Neberdjer possible, creating resonance between the individual mind's state and ultimate reality's essential nature.[2][3]

Consider the metaphysical implications: Neberdjer as supreme serenity means that the fundamental ground of all existence operates as perfect peace, undisturbed equilibrium, silence beyond all mental agitation. Therefore, when the mind cultivates Ger through the practices Amenemopet prescribes, this creates sympathetic resonance with ultimate reality's essential frequency. The mind moving toward silence begins to vibrate at rates compatible with recognizing the supreme silence that sustains its very capacity for awareness. This explains why serenity proves not optional but prerequisite for divine discovery—the mind cannot recognize its divine source when operating at frequencies fundamentally incompatible with that source's essential nature.[2][3]

THE IMPOSSIBILITY FOR THE HEATED PERSON: WHY MENTAL AGITATION CREATES OPACITY

This theological understanding reveals why the heated person—one with heated mind and feelings characterized by mental agitation, emotional turbulence, compulsive reactivity—experiences profound difficulty in recognizing Neberdjer. The heated condition does not merely create temporary obstacles to spiritual perception; rather, it establishes a way of life that actively moves away from the serenity which constitutes the prerequisite for divine awareness. The heated person unknowingly banishes themselves to a way of life predominantly based on mental agitation that makes the mental perception of the subtle spirit opaque—not through divine punishment or arbitrary restriction, but through the natural operation of incompatible frequencies.[2][3]

The metaphysical mechanism operates precisely: Neberdjer as supreme serenity, silence, and equanimity can only be perceived by a mind that has developed sufficient capacity for serenity, silence, and equanimity to create receptive conditions. The heated mind and feelings, characterized by continuous mental static, compulsive thought patterns, emotional reactivity, and psychological turbulence, generate such dense interference that the subtle presence of Neberdjer—which operates as the silent foundation beneath all mental noise—remains imperceptible. This imperceptibility arises not from Neberdjer's absence but from the mind's incapacity to detect frequencies beyond its current range of sensitivity.[2][3]

Consider the analogy: a radio receiver tuned to frequencies dominated by static and interference cannot receive the clear signal being transmitted at a different frequency until the static clears sufficiently to allow signal detection. Similarly, when consciousness witnesses through the heated mind and feelings, the mind generates such continuous mental static—anxious thoughts, reactive emotions, compulsive planning, fearful anticipation, angry rumination—that the subtle "signal" of Neberdjer's presence remains undetectable beneath the psychological noise. The signal transmits continuously, Neberdjer remains ever-present as the foundation sustaining awareness itself, yet the mind's agitated state prevents recognition.[2][3]

NEBERDJER AS FOUNDATIONAL ABSOLUTE CONSCIOUSNESS

Neberdjer represents the ancient Egyptian term for what constitutes absolute consciousness—not consciousness as typically understood through individual mind-body systems experiencing separation, but rather the universal divine essence operating as awareness through all beings and phenomena while remaining as their unchanging foundation. The term translates as "sovereign-about-existence," "all-encompassing-divinity," or "ruler-as-to-limits"—that is, Limitless.[2] Terms such as "sovereign," "Divinity," and "Existence" combined with limitlessness and all-encompassing-ness point to THAT WHICH IS ABSOLUTE.

The teaching reveals a profound metaphysical truth: human awareness represents the same as Neberdjer when the limited perceptions of time, space, and ego individuality experienced through the mind are transcended.[2] This means that spiritual practice aims not to create access to something absent but rather to remove the aryu obstruction preventing recognition of what has always been present as the very foundation sustaining awareness itself. Ab Neter residing in kara (deep ab level) represents one's personal portion of Neberdjer—the localized manifestation of all-encompassing consciousness that makes individual awareness possible.

THE MECHANICS OF TRANSFORMATION THROUGH NEBERDJER AWARENESS

When the hat directs deliberate awareness toward Neberdjer, this creates specific transformative effects at the mind architecture level. First, the practice interrupts the automatic absorption of awareness in mental content and sensory phenomena. Ordinarily, aryu patterns automatically capture the hat's attention the moment awareness activates—like well-worn grooves channeling water without conscious direction. The deliberate effort to remain aware of Neberdjer requires awareness to resist this automatic capture, creating what the tradition describes as "thinning" of aryu density rather than its reinforcement through continued absorption.[2][3]

Second, maintaining Neberdjer awareness establishes what might be termed "metaphysical perspective"—the recognition that all phenomena arise within and as modifications of the single divine essence rather than constituting separate, independent entities. This perspective fundamentally contradicts the aryu-driven perception of a world populated by competing separate beings, each requiring self-protection and self-advancement. When the mind maintains awareness that "all beings in Creation are composed of Neberdjer and are therefore kinfolk to each other, fundamentally related through shared divine essence," this recognition directly undermines the egoic patterns that generate fear, greed, anger, and manipulation.[1][2]

Third, the practice creates increasing sensitivity to the difference between consciousness itself (Neberdjer/Ab Neter) and mental modifications (thoughts, feelings, perceptions arising in hat and ab). Ordinary awareness identifies with mental content—"I am angry," "I am anxious," "I am this body-mind"—creating the illusion that consciousness constitutes these temporary modifications. However, sustained Neberdjer awareness allows consciousness to be recognized as the unchanging witness of modifications rather than the modifications themselves. This recognition proves transformative because it relocates identity from the changing to the unchanging, from the limited to the unlimited, from the suffering mind to consciousness itself.[1][2][3]

GER PRACTICE AS ALIGNMENT WITH ULTIMATE REALITY'S FREQUENCY

The theological principle that Neberdjer IS supreme serenity reveals why Amenemopet emphasizes Ger practice so consistently throughout his teaching. Every instruction to maintain the silent mind and feelings, every warning against heated patterns, every teaching about inner peace and equanimity functions as guidance for bringing the individual mind into harmonic resonance with ultimate reality's essential frequency. The heated mind and feelings operate at frequencies incompatible with Neberdjer recognition; the silent mind and feelings develop frequencies that allow Neberdjer's ever-present reality to become perceptible.[2][3]

This understanding transforms the aspirant's relationship to serenity cultivation. Rather than viewing silence and peace as pleasant psychological states or beneficial behavioral patterns, the wisdom to be understood recognizes them as the necessary frequency-matching that allows consciousness to detect its own divine source. The mind cultivating Ger engages not in arbitrary discipline but in precise tuning of its operational frequency to match the supreme serenity that Neberdjer eternally IS.[2][3]

The practice operates through progressive refinement: initial efforts to quiet the mind, even briefly, create momentary windows wherein Neberdjer's presence becomes slightly more perceptible than when continuous mental agitation dominates awareness. These brief glimpses—perhaps lasting only seconds initially—provide experiential validation that something exists beyond mental noise. As practice continues and Ger deepens, the windows lengthen and Neberdjer's presence grows increasingly clear, not because Neberdjer changes or approaches, but because the mind's capacity to perceive what has always been present develops through reduced interference.[2][3]

THE COSMIC ARCHITECTURE OF CONSCIOUSNESS REVELATION

At the deepest metaphysical level, maintaining Neberdjer awareness operates through the principle that the mind can only fully reflect consciousness when it has become capable of clarity through its own purification. The clouded mirror cannot accurately reflect objects before it; similarly, the agitated mind cannot accurately reflect the serene consciousness that sustains it. The purification work—ethical conduct thinning harmful aryu, philosophical study depositing wisdom-based patterns, meditation developing mental clarity—gradually clarifies the mind's reflective capacity until Ab Neter/Neberdjer's presence becomes self-evident.[1][2][3]

This reveals the supreme importance of the teaching that "Neberdjer is supreme serenity, silence, equanimity, homogeneity." These qualities are not mere descriptions but represent the actual metaphysical nature of ultimate reality. Therefore, the path to recognizing ultimate reality MUST involve cultivating corresponding qualities in the mind—not to please an external deity or fulfill arbitrary requirements, but because consciousness recognition operates through resonance and compatibility. The mind must develop serenity to recognize supreme serenity, silence to recognize supreme silence, equanimity to recognize supreme equanimity.[2][3]

The heated person's predicament emerges with devastating clarity through this understanding: by maintaining the heated mind and feelings, they unknowingly but inevitably distance themselves from the very frequencies necessary for spiritual perception. Every moment spent in agitation, reactivity, anxiety, anger, or compulsive mental activity strengthens aryu patterns that generate frequencies incompatible with Neberdjer recognition. This creates a self-reinforcing cycle where mental agitation prevents divine awareness, which maintains ignorance, which generates more agitation through the suffering that ignorance creates.[2][3]

THE PREREQUISITE NATURE OF SERENITY FOR DIVINE DISCOVERY

The wisdom to be understood recognizes serenity not as one practice among many optional approaches but as the absolute prerequisite for the mind to recognize consciousness's divine nature. This prerequisite status derives from Neberdjer's essential nature rather than arbitrary spiritual requirements. Because Neberdjer IS supreme serenity, and because recognition of consciousness operates through resonance and compatibility, the mind MUST develop serenity to detect Neberdjer's presence—just as a radio receiver MUST tune to the correct frequency to receive the signal being transmitted.[2][3]

This explains phenomena observed in spiritual communities where practitioners engage in extensive rituals, study voluminous texts, maintain outward religious observance, yet fail to achieve authentic divine recognition. Without cultivating genuine Ger—not merely behavioral calm but actual transformation of the mind and feelings from heated agitation to silent peace—the essential prerequisite remains unfulfilled regardless of other practices undertaken. The mind can accumulate vast philosophical knowledge while remaining fundamentally agitated; it can perform elaborate ceremonies while maintaining heated patterns; it can adopt spiritual identity while operating from egoic reactivity. None of these provides the frequency-matching that Neberdjer recognition requires.[2][3]

Conversely, the aspirant who prioritizes Ger cultivation—systematically thinning the aryu that generate mental agitation, developing ethical patterns that support inner peace, engaging in contemplative practices that establish silence—creates the essential conditions whereby Neberdjer recognition becomes possible. The philosophy of Neberdjer (intellectual understanding of its all-encompassing nature) combined with Ger practice (experiential development of resonant frequencies) together constitute the complete pathway: philosophy provides the map, Ger practice creates the capacity to traverse the territory that map describes.[2][3]

THE PROFOUND MERCY IN THIS UNDERSTANDING

Significantly, this teaching reveals divine mercy rather than divine restriction. The requirement for serenity does not represent arbitrary limitation imposed by an external deity demanding particular qualifications before granting access. Rather, it reflects the natural operation of consciousness recognition through compatible frequencies—a mechanism that ultimately serves the aspirant's welfare by providing clear, knowable steps toward divine discovery.[2][3]

Consider: if Neberdjer recognition occurred randomly without prerequisite development, aspirants would have no systematic pathway to follow, no reliable methods to implement, no way to understand why recognition remained elusive or how to facilitate its emergence. However, because the teaching reveals that Neberdjer IS supreme serenity and that cultivating Ger creates the necessary resonance, every aspirant receives precise guidance: develop the silent mind and feelings through the methods prescribed, and Neberdjer recognition becomes progressively available as serenity deepens.[2][3]

This transforms spiritual struggle from mysterious unpredictability to systematic development. The aspirant need not wonder whether they possess special talents, require miraculous interventions, or depend on unpredictable divine favor. Instead, they receive clear instruction: purify the mind and feelings from heated agitation to silent peace, and the natural resonance between developed serenity and supreme serenity makes divine recognition increasingly accessible. The path proves democratic rather than arbitrary—available to all who undertake the necessary purification work regardless of external circumstances or inherited capacities.[2][3]

INTEGRATION WITH THE FIVE DIMENSIONS OF NEBERDJER AWARENESS

The recognition that Neberdjer IS supreme serenity integrates with and illuminates the five dimensions of Neberdjer awareness established earlier in this commentary:

> *First Dimension—Being aware of Neberdjer as composing all objects: This awareness becomes progressively accessible as serenity develops because the agitated mind perceives objects as separate and competing, while the serene mind recognizes the single essence manifesting as apparent multiplicity.[1][2]*
>
> *Second Dimension—Being aware of Neberdjer as the essence of one's own existence: The heated mind identifies with temporary modifications (thoughts, emotions, sensations), preventing recognition of the unchanging essence; the silent mind develops the capacity to distinguish consciousness from its contents, allowing Neberdjer recognition.[1][2]*
>
> *Third Dimension—Being aware of Neberdjer as all-encompassing existence: Mental agitation fragments the mind's perception into competing parts; serenity allows recognition of the unified whole that apparent separation obscures.[1][2]*
>
> *Fourth Dimension—Being aware of Neberdjer as vastness beyond mental comprehension: The compulsive thinking mind attempts to contain everything within conceptual frameworks; the silent mind recognizes that ultimate reality transcends mental categories entirely.[1][2]*
>
> Each dimension becomes accessible through serenity development because each requires the mind to operate at frequencies compatible with recognizing consciousness, which are incompatible with heated agitation. The systematic cultivation of Ger progressively opens these dimensions not by creating new capacities but by removing the interference that prevented recognition of what has always been present.[1][2][3]

CONCLUSION: THE SUPREME IMPORTANCE OF GER CULTIVATION

This enhanced metaphysical understanding establishes Ger cultivation as the central, non-negotiable prerequisite for spiritual realization within Amenemopet's teaching system. Every other practice—ethical conduct, wisdom study, ritual participation, devotional expression—ultimately serves to support serenity development because serenity alone creates the frequency-matching necessary for Neberdjer recognition. The heated person, regardless of other spiritual qualifications, unknowingly banishes themselves from divine awareness through maintaining the mental agitation incompatible with perceiving supreme serenity.[2][3]

The wisdom to be understood therefore recognizes that Amenemopet's consistent emphasis on the silent mind and feelings, his repeated warnings against heated patterns, his systematic prescriptions for cultivating inner peace all derive from this fundamental metaphysical reality: Neberdjer IS supreme serenity, and the mind can only recognize consciousness when it develops compatibility through its own purification. The path to divine discovery proves neither mysterious nor arbitrary but operates through knowable principles—cultivate Ger, thin heated aryu, develop frequencies resonant with ultimate reality's essential nature, and recognition emerges as naturally as clear mirrors reflect what stands before them.[1][2][3]

This understanding should inform every aspect of spiritual practice, every response to daily challenges, every moment of choosing between heated reactivity and silent response. Each choice either reinforces frequencies compatible with Neberdjer recognition or strengthens patterns that make perception opaque. The profound simplicity emerges: move toward Ger in all things, and divine discovery becomes progressively accessible; maintain heated patterns, and spiritual blindness persists regardless of other religious or philosophical accomplishments.[2][3]

4: Transpersonal Psychology Research

Empirical Validation of Ancient Framework-Contemporary Science and Neberdjer Recognition

Contemporary transpersonal psychology and consciousness research provide remarkable validation for Amenemopet's teaching that maintaining awareness beyond limited mind operations transforms psychological function and experiential reality. Studies examining meditation, contemplative practices, and altered states of consciousness demonstrate measurable changes in brain activity, cognitive patterns, and subjective experience that parallel the ancient framework of hat-ab-kara awareness architecture.

Research on the default mode network (DMN)—the brain system associated with self-referential thinking, mental time-travel, and ego-based narrative construction—reveals striking parallels to Amenemopet's description of awareness trapped in limited mind interpretations. Brewer et al. (2011) demonstrated that experienced meditators show reduced DMN activity during meditation, suggesting decreased absorption in the very mental processes that Amenemopet identifies as obscuring Neberdjer awareness [4]. This neurological finding validates the teaching's claim that practices directing awareness beyond ego-based mental content can alter fundamental mind operation.

Further studies by Taylor et al. (2011) and Garrison et al. (2015) extended these findings, demonstrating that meditation practitioners maintain reduced default mode activity even during rest periods, suggesting lasting changes in baseline mental operation rather than merely temporary state shifts during practice [5][6]. This corresponds precisely to Amenemopet's promise that sustained practice of maintaining Neberdjer awareness creates permanent transformation of mind structure—the thinning of aryu density allowing Ab Neter recognition to emerge as stable trait rather than fleeting state.

The transpersonal psychology literature extensively documents experiences of what researchers term "non-dual awareness"—minds recognizing the unity underlying apparent multiplicity, experiencing awareness without separate observer-observed division. William James's (1902) pioneering work on religious experience described mystical states characterized by "a sense of unity or totality" and "knowledge of the One"—descriptions remarkably consistent with Amenemopet's Neberdjer recognition [7]. Contemporary research has established that these non-dual experiences correlate with specific neural signatures and produce lasting psychological benefits including reduced anxiety, increased well-being, and enhanced ethical behavior.

Particularly relevant to the hat-ab framework, research on neuroplasticity demonstrates that sustained attention practices literally reshape brain structure and function. Doidge (2007) documents how focused mental training creates measurable changes in neural pathways, supporting the teaching's claim that deliberate awareness practice gradually alters the aryu patterns (neural habit-structures) that determine automatic mind operation [8]. Studies by Graybiel and Smith (2014) on habit formation reveal that creating new behavioral patterns requires sustained repetition to override established automaticity—directly paralleling Amenemopet's recognition that awareness must practice maintaining Neberdjer awareness deliberately before it becomes natural orientation [9].

The Advaita Vedanta philosophical tradition, sharing remarkable parallels with Ancient Egyptian non-dual teachings, provides additional cross-cultural validation. Deutsch and Dalvi (2004) demonstrate how Vedantic understanding of Brahman (absolute consciousness) mirrors the Egyptian concept of Neberdjer, while the distinction between Atman (individual awareness) and Brahman parallels the Ab Neter-Neberdjer relationship [10]. Research by Swami Satprakashananda (2024) examining the Advaita method of self-realization through awareness state investigation provides a detailed phenomenological description of practices strikingly similar to those implied in Amenemopet's teaching [20].

Buddhist psychology research offers particularly valuable validation of the awareness-beyond-thought principle central to Neberdjer practice. Kornfield (2008), Gunaratana (2002), and other Buddhist psychology scholars document meditation practices explicitly designed to recognize "awareness aware of itself"—consciousness directed not toward objects but toward the observing capacity itself [30][31]. Studies demonstrate that these practices produce measurable changes in attention stability, emotional regulation, and sense of self that correspond to the transformation Amenemopet describes when awareness shifts from limited mind absorption to Neberdjer recognition.

Recent advanced meditation research provides unprecedented empirical validation of awareness states beyond ordinary mind. Chowdhury et al. (2025) conducted intensive case study research on jhana meditation (advanced absorption states), demonstrating through multimodal neurophenomenology how awareness can access profoundly altered states characterized by minimal thought activity and expanded consciousness [14]. These findings validate the ancient teaching that awareness possesses capacity to transcend ordinary mental operations entirely.

Demir et al. (2025) used 7T functional MRI to demonstrate how advanced concentration-absorption meditation reorganizes functional connectivity gradients of the brain, revealing measurable neural correlates of awareness states the meditator phenomenologically describes as "awareness without object"—precisely the awareness orientation Amenemopet instructs through maintaining Neberdjer awareness [15]. Yang et al. (2025) synthesized findings across phenomenology, yogic traditions, and Buddhist meditation research, demonstrating convergence across cultures regarding awareness deepening methods remarkably consistent with Ancient Egyptian teachings [16].

Particularly significant, Arora (2025) provides philosophical analysis arguing that consciousness must be understood as foundational rather than emergent—consciousness constitutes the ground of existence from which all experience arises rather than byproduct of physical processes [17]. This position aligns precisely with Amenemopet's metaphysical framework wherein Neberdjer represents the absolute consciousness foundation from which all apparent phenomena emerge, including the individualized awareness experiencing them.

Research on meditation and neural default mode activity by Treves et al. (2025) demonstrates that advanced meditation practitioners show dynamic brain states during concentration practices that differ fundamentally from ordinary waking awareness [24]. These findings validate the teaching's claim that sustained awareness practice accesses levels beyond ordinary hat-level operation—corresponding to the deeper ab levels and ultimately kara where Ab Neter resides.

Laukkonen et al. (2023) examined cessations of awareness in advanced meditation (nirodha samāpatti), demonstrating that awareness can achieve states of complete suspension of mental activity while maintaining some form of witness consciousness [25]. This research validates Amenemopet's distinction between mind (which can cease) and the deeper consciousness sustaining the mind's capacity to operate—what the teaching identifies as Ab Neter sustained by Neberdjer.

Studies on mindfulness and network neuroscience by Prakash et al. (2025) reviewed extensive research demonstrating how meditation practices reorganize large-scale brain networks, particularly those associated with self-referential processing and attention regulation [26]. These findings provide neurological basis for understanding how maintaining Neberdjer awareness—systematic practice directing attention toward the consciousness foundation rather than mental content—creates lasting transformation in mind architecture.

Cross-cultural contemplative research demonstrates remarkable convergence in describing ultimate reality awareness across traditions. Smith (1991) documented that mystical experiences across religious traditions share common phenomenological characteristics: sense of unity, transcendence of time and space, ineffability, and recognition of existence beyond ordinary perception [11]. The Dzogchen teachings of Tibetan Buddhism, as presented by the Dalai Lama XIV (2004) and Reynolds (2010), describe "pristine awareness" or "rigpa"—awareness of awareness itself—in terms strikingly parallel to Neberdjer consciousness [12][13].

Nevertheless, the wisdom to be understood recognizes that while Buddhist rigpa practice and Amenemopet's sau-Neberdjer teaching share profound parallels in aiming at pristine awareness beyond conceptual mind, contemporary secular adaptations of mindfulness meditation typically extract only the attention-training components while omitting the metaphysical framework necessary for mind transformation. Aspirants should therefore distinguish between: (1) secular mindfulness for psychological benefit, (2) traditional Buddhist meditation for enlightenment, and (3) sau-Neberdjer practice for Ab Neter recognition—recognizing that while attention-training mechanisms may be similar across these approaches, their ultimate aims and metaphysical contexts differ substantially. The research on traditional Buddhist meditation validates awareness capacities that closely parallel Amenemopet's teaching, while secular mindfulness research documents preliminary benefits occurring at more superficial levels of mind operation.

Sanskrit philosophical texts provide additional validation through detailed awareness investigation methods. Shankara's Vivekachudamani and the Principal Upanishads (Radhakrishnan, 1953) describe systematic practices for recognizing Atman (essential self) as Brahman (absolute existence)—a framework remarkably consistent with recognizing Ab Neter as manifestation of Neberdjer [18][19]. Recent research by Kumar and Pradhan (2024) examining Advaita philosophy's relevance to psychiatry demonstrates growing recognition that these ancient awareness frameworks offer practical methods for addressing modern psychological suffering [21].

Particularly compelling, Sacchet and the Meditation Research Program (2024) published findings demonstrating that advanced meditation practices fundamentally alter awareness and practitioners' basic sense of self, with experienced meditators reporting persistent shifts from identification with mental-egoic content toward recognition of awareness itself as primary identity [22]. Ehmann et al. (2025) extended these findings, demonstrating that long-term meditators show cognitive and neural differences suggesting qualitative transformation in mind operation rather than merely quantitative improvements in attention or emotion regulation [23].

Research on meditation's psychological effects provides extensive validation of the well-being benefits Amenemopet promises. Kozasa et al. (2012) demonstrated increased brain efficiency in attention tasks among meditators, suggesting enhanced cognitive function from practices directing awareness systematically [27]. Sedlmeier et al. (2012) conducted meta-analysis of meditation research, documenting significant positive effects on anxiety reduction, emotional regulation, and psychological well-being—outcomes corresponding to the teaching's promise of freedom from fears, frustrations, and inordinate desires [28].

Studies examining meditation's effects on emotional reactivity reveal mechanisms underlying the transformation from heated to silent mind and feelings. Desbordes et al. (2012) demonstrated that meditation training produces lasting changes in amygdala response to emotional stimuli even during non-meditative states, suggesting altered emotional reactivity patterns that persist beyond practice periods [29]. This corresponds to Amenemopet's description of how maintaining Neberdjer awareness gradually thins aryu patterns, creating permanent rather than temporary transformation.

Advanced meditation research by Lutz et al. (2004) demonstrated that long-term practitioners can self-induce high-amplitude gamma synchrony during mental practice—neural signatures associated with heightened awareness and cognitive integration [35]. These findings validate the teaching's claim that sustained practice creates measurable mind transformation rather than merely subjective belief changes.

The convergence of findings across neuroscience, psychology, philosophy, and contemplative research provides remarkable empirical validation for Amenemopet's ancient framework. The teaching's claim that awareness can direct attention toward its own foundation (Neberdjer), that this practice transforms automatic mental patterns (aryu thinning), that sustained practice reveals deeper awareness levels (penetration from hat through ab to kara), and that this transformation produces freedom from suffering while enabling well-being—all these assertions find substantial support in contemporary scientific literature, suggesting Amenemopet's wisdom reflects accurate understanding of awareness architecture and transformation mechanics validated through modern empirical methods.

5: Spiritual Implications for Aspirants

PART A: PASTORAL CONCERNS

Modern Challenges to Maintaining Neberdjer Awareness

The modern aspirant awakens to immediately encounter the smartphone screen filled with notifications, news alerts, messages demanding response—awareness captured by limited mind interpretations before even rising from bed. This represents the contemporary manifestation of the ancient problem that Amenemopet addresses: awareness operating entirely through limited perceptual instruments without recognition of the all-encompassing existence sustaining consciousness itself. The challenge intensifies throughout the day as workplace demands, relationship complexities, financial pressures, and information overload create relentless momentum pulling awareness into limited mind absorption.

Consider the workplace environment that presents particular obstacles to maintaining Neberdjer awareness. Modern employment demands relentless productivity measured in quantifiable outputs, creating conditions where pausing to direct awareness toward existence beyond immediate tasks appears as wasteful distraction. The colleague who pauses to direct awareness toward Neberdjer before responding to challenging email may face accusations of insufficient urgency or commitment to organizational goals. This cultural pressure creates significant psychological conflict for aspirants attempting to practice ancient wisdom in contemporary contexts that explicitly value heated, aggressive pursuit of measurable achievement over silent, contemplative recognition of divine foundation.

Someone struggling with maintaining Neberdjer awareness throughout the day often experiences relationship complications when partners, family members, or friends perceive spiritual practice as withdrawal from engagement. The spouse who perceives the partner maintaining inner awareness of all-encompassing divinity may interpret this as emotional unavailability or lack of investment in the relationship. The parent who pauses during the child's distress to direct awareness toward Neberdjer before responding may feel guilty about not immediately reacting, despite this pause potentially creating more skillful response grounded in wisdom rather than reactive aryu patterns.

The aspirant raised in Western culture encounters particular difficulty with the teaching that separate individuality represents delusion obscuring awareness of Neberdjer as the all-encompassing existence manifesting through all apparent forms. This contradicts the fundamental Western psychological principle that developing strong individual identity constitutes healthy maturation. The idea that maintaining awareness of existence beyond the separate self represents spiritual development conflicts with the ego one has spent decades cultivating through cultural conditioning emphasizing individual achievement, personal branding, and self-reliance as ultimate values.

Financial pressures create constant pulls away from maintaining Neberdjer awareness toward anxious calculation and strategic planning. The rent requires monthly payment, children need food and education, retirement demands savings—circumstances that awareness interprets as requiring intense egoic management rather than awareness of all-encompassing divine providence. The teaching that time represents the mind's interpretation of Neberdjer's eternal presence provides little comfort when immediate survival concerns dominate awareness. The aspirant wonders: how does maintaining awareness of existence beyond mind and time help pay bills that arrive with temporal deadlines in a world operating through time-bound economic systems?

The challenge intensifies when aspirants discover that maintaining Neberdjer awareness requires acknowledging how deeply awareness has become identified with limited mind interpretations. This recognition can trigger what appears as existential crisis: if my thoughts, feelings, memories, personality traits, and life narrative represent limited mind interpretations rather than ultimate reality, what remains of "me"? The ego-structure naturally resists this investigation, generating doubt, distraction, and rational arguments against practice: "This is impractical escapism avoiding real-world responsibilities"; "My family needs me present and engaged, not absorbed in abstract meditation"; "Surely God/Neberdjer wants me focused on serving others rather than self-absorbed spiritual navel-gazing."

These represent genuine pastoral concerns requiring compassionate recognition rather than dismissive judgment. The modern aspirant faces cultural conditions actively undermining spiritual development—a hostile environment where heated mind and feelings receive constant reinforcement while silent mind and feelings get pathologized as depression, lack of ambition, or social withdrawal. The wisdom to be understood acknowledges these challenges while maintaining that systematic practice of Neberdjer awareness remains not only possible but essential for discovering the well-being and fulfillment that the Prologue promises.

The Critical Distinction: Being Aware Versus Remembering

Before proceeding to systematic methods, the wisdom to be understood requires grasping a subtle but essential distinction that determines whether spiritual practice leads to genuine transformation or becomes trapped in mental activity masquerading as spiritual experience. This concerns the fundamental difference between **being aware** (present direct experience) and **remembering** (mental recall)—two completely different operations that aspirants frequently confuse, leading to years of practice that reinforce mind activity rather than transcending it.

Being Aware: Present Experience Beyond Mind

Being aware of Neberdjer means that awareness, in this present moment, recognizes the all-encompassing consciousness foundation that sustains the very capacity to be aware. This represents direct experience occurring NOW—not recollection of past events, not intellectual comprehension of philosophical concepts, not mental imagery or emotional feelings about divinity. When awareness becomes aware of Neberdjer, the hat penetrates beyond its usual absorption in mental content to recognize the consciousness that makes mental activity possible. This constitutes immediate, present recognition—awareness cognizing its own source while that source operates as the foundation sustaining awareness itself.

Consider the crucial characteristic of this direct awareness: it transcends mind involvement entirely. The experience occurs at a level deeper than thought, deeper than emotion, deeper than the ab's aryu patterns—penetrating to the kara where Ab Neter resides as one's portion of Neberdjer consciousness. When genuinely being aware of Neberdjer, there exists no mental commentary about the experience, no ego appropriation claiming, "I am having this experience," no thought-stream describing or evaluating what occurs. The awareness simply IS, recognizing itself as sustained by and identical with the all-encompassing foundation—pure witnessing consciousness beyond mental modification.

Remembering: Mental Activity That Can Trap Development

Remembering, by contrast, represents mental activity occurring in the hat and ab—the mind recalling past experiences, reviewing philosophical concepts, or generating thoughts about spiritual teachings. This operates entirely within the mental apparatus rather than transcending it. Even when remembering profound spiritual experiences that originally transcended mind, the ACT of remembering itself constitutes mental activity subject to ego appropriation and distortion.

The tradition recognizes two distinct types of remembering that serve different functions in spiritual development:

First Type: Remembering Philosophy About Neberdjer (Preparatory Function)

During the initial stages of spiritual practice—what the tradition terms shedy (similar to the Sanskrit sadhana)—aspirants necessarily engage in intellectual remembrance of teachings about Neberdjer's nature. This involves studying scriptures, contemplating philosophical principles, recalling key concepts during daily activities, and using thought deliberately to reshape mental patterns. When Amenemopet instructs maintaining awareness "with deliberate effort" and "with conscious volition," the beginning stages require using the mind to remember the teaching: "All existence encompasses Neberdjer; separate individuality represents delusion; circumstances arise from divine orchestration; my essential nature is consciousness, not the limited personality."

This intellectual remembering serves crucial preparatory function in the shedy process. By repeatedly directing the hat toward wisdom concepts, the aspirant gradually thins aryu density—the accumulated patterns of egoic thinking that normally dominate presence-of-mind awareness. These philosophical remembrances establish what might be termed "wisdom-aryu" in the ab—understanding impressions that compete with ignorance-based patterns for influence over thoughts, feelings, and perceptions. Through sustained practice of ethical living combined with intellectual remembrance of Neberdjer teachings, the mind becomes sufficiently purified that direct experience beyond mental activity becomes possible.

Second Type: Remembering Past Transcendent Experiences (Subtle Trap)

Nevertheless, aspirants must recognize a subtle danger that can arrest development at intermediate stages: confusing the recollection of past transcendent experiences with actual present awareness of Neberdjer. Consider what occurs when someone has genuine experience of consciousness beyond mind—a moment during deep meditation when awareness recognizes its Neberdjer foundation directly. This represents authentic spiritual experience that transcends mental activity entirely. However, once that moment passes and ordinary mind-activity resumes, the ego-apparatus can appropriate that experience, creating mental impressions (aryu) in the ab labeled "my spiritual achievement," "my enlightenment experience," "my connection with Neberdjer."

Subsequently, the aspirant may spend meditation sessions attempting to recreate that past experience or sitting in remembrance of how it felt during that transcendent moment-doing this would be acceptable as a spiritual practice basking in the feeling of the experience and creating positive aryu that helps align the personality with Neberdjer existence-but that remembrance is not as a goal of the spiritual practice. This remembering—regardless of how profound the original experience may have been—constitutes mental activity occurring in the hat and ab levels. The mind generates thoughts about the experience, feelings associated with recalling it, and most problematically, ego identification claiming, "I achieved this state; this memory proves my spiritual advancement." The very act of recollecting, even transcendent experiences, involves mind operation and creates distance from present reality. One remains trapped in mental modifications rather than recognizing the consciousness sustaining those modifications.

The teaching reveals this trap operates particularly insidiously because the aspirant believes they maintain spiritual focus by dwelling on past transcendent experiences. "I'm keeping my attention on Neberdjer by remembering that profound understanding about Neberdjer," or "I'm keeping my attention on Neberdjer by remembering that profound moment of unity-awareness I experienced last week." However, this represents not present awareness but mental activity—the hat occupied with aryu (memories) rather than penetrating to kara where Ab Neter resides as present reality. The ego appropriates even genuine spiritual experiences, converting them into mental content that reinforces the separate self rather than dissolving it. The spiritual practices of remembering, reflecting etc. are valuable and important as part of the shedy (spiritual practices) when understood as tools leading to the purity of mind level that allows Neberdjer realization-thus they are practices to be encouraged and practiced in their proper context.

The Crucial Instruction: Bring Attention to Present Awareness

Based on the teaching presented by Sage Amenemopet, the inverse doctrine application suggests that aspirants should avoid mistaking intellectual remembrance or recollection of past experiences for actual present awareness of Neberdjer, as these mental activities—however spiritually themed—perpetuate mind dominance rather than transcending it.

The instruction proves clear: bring attention (not recall) to Neberdjer as present experience occurring NOW. This means directing awareness not toward thoughts about Neberdjer, not toward memories of past transcendent moments, not toward philosophical concepts residing in memory—but toward the consciousness foundation that, in this immediate present moment, sustains the very capacity for awareness itself. When the hat, through deliberate effort initially and natural abiding eventually, directs attention toward the source of awareness rather than toward awareness's contents (thoughts, memories, sensations, perceptions), the mind discovers what has always been present—Ab Neter as one's portion of Neberdjer, the consciousness sustaining all mental operations while remaining untouched by them.

This distinction determines whether decades of spiritual practice produce genuine transformation or merely create sophisticated mental content labeled "spiritual." One can accumulate vast knowledge about Neberdjer, experience occasional transcendent moments, and develop impressive capacity to discourse philosophically about consciousness—yet remain trapped in mental activity if one mistakes these achievements for the goal itself. The goal consists not in accumulating experiences or knowledge, but in recognizing what awareness fundamentally IS beyond all mental modifications—the all-encompassing consciousness foundation that Amenemopet identifies as Neberdjer, experienced not through thinking or remembering, but through direct present recognition beyond mind involvement.

PART B: METHODS FOR TRANSFORMATION

Conclusion: The Path from Intellectual Understanding to Permanent Neberdjer Awareness

If Neberdjer constitutes all-encompassing existence, how does one become aware of that reality? Consider how the operations of the mind, driven by the sense of ego separation as an individual entity, create a fundamental deviation away from recognizing our existence within what might be termed an "ocean of consciousness" (Neberdjer). The impelling and compelling thoughts arising from the ab, charged with the energy of individual desiring and seeking, cause the hat to remain fixated on ego concerns and temporal objectives. This incessant mental activity prevents not only intellectual understanding that we exist within Neberdjer, but more significantly obstructs the direct feeling and experiencing of oneself as existing wholly as that same consciousness. The aryu occupying the presence-of-mind awareness operate so densely as to blot out sensitivity to the Ab Neter level where one's Neberdjer nature resides as the foundation of conscious awareness itself.

Now, observe how an ego-bound person experiences no difficulty whatsoever in remembering their personal name, family history, professional identity, and biographical narrative—these ego references function as the default subconscious awareness underlying all thoughts, feelings, and perceptions throughout the day, requiring no conscious effort to maintain. In precisely this same effortless manner, the wisdom to be understood reveals that an evolved person learns to recognize those ego relations and references as illusory constructs—temporary mental formations that an individual has mistakenly learned to call "myself" while ignoring the wider nature of existence being experienced through and as that apparent individuality.

The Shedy Process: Using Mind to Transcend Mind

The progression unfolds through specific developmental stages that the tradition terms shedy—the systematic spiritual practice comparable to the Sanskrit sadhana, meaning deliberate, sustained effort toward spiritual realization. This process necessarily begins with and proceeds through mental activity (intellectual remembrance of philosophy) for the explicit purpose of eventually transcending mental activity entirely (direct present awareness beyond thought). Understanding this paradox—that one must use the mind skillfully to eventually go beyond mind—prevents confusion about the distinct functions of different practice stages.

Stage 1: Intellectual Study and Philosophical Remembrance

Initially, one must engage in systematic study to develop intellectual understanding about

Neberdjer—learning the teaching that all-encompassing consciousness constitutes both the transcendent foundation and immanent presence pervading all existence. This intellectual phase establishes what might be termed "mooring posts" in the ab—philosophical understandings that begin competing with the aryu for influence over the hat's moment-to-moment awareness.

Subsequently, the practice involves remembering the philosophy intellectually—working with deliberate effort, as verse 14 instructs, to keep in mind the fact of Neberdjer even while engaging in daily activities and navigating worldly circumstances. This represents using thought deliberately to reshape thought patterns, employing mental activity to thin the aryu density that normally traps awareness in ego-based interpretations. Throughout the day, when the hat becomes absorbed in anxious planning or heated reactivity, one practices remembering the philosophy: "All existence encompasses Neberdjer; I am that consciousness appearing through this personality form; circumstances arise from divine orchestration beyond my egoic control."

This intellectual remembrance serves essential preparatory function in the shedy process—it does NOT constitute the ultimate goal but represents necessary foundation work. Through sustained philosophical contemplation combined with ethical living and cultivation of silent qualities, the aspirant gradually purifies the ab level, thinning aryu density sufficiently that deeper practice becomes possible.

Stage 2: Transition from Mental Activity to Direct Experience

As the shedy process progresses through continued study, ethical purification, and avoidance of heated persons and environments that reinforce aryu density, the personality becomes sufficiently transparent that direct experience of Neberdjer becomes possible during deep meditation. These represent moments when the mind quiets enough that awareness discovers its own source—not as thought about consciousness, not as memory of past experiences, but as immediate present recognition of the witnessing presence underlying all mental phenomena.

Here the crucial distinction revealed earlier becomes practically significant: when these transcendent moments occur, the aspirant must NOT mistake them for permanent attainment or begin dwelling in remembrance of "that profound experience I had." The moment one begins thinking about or recalling the experience, awareness has returned to mental activity—the hat operating through aryu (now including memories of spiritual experiences) rather than resting in the kara where Ab Neter resides. Even genuine transcendent experiences, when converted into mental content through recollection, become obstacles if one mistakes remembering them for being aware presently.

The practice therefore requires vigilant discernment: recognize that memories of past transcendent moments, however profound, represent mental activity occurring in hat and ab levels—not the direct present awareness of Neberdjer that constitutes the goal. Each meditation session aims not at recreating past experiences or dwelling on spiritual memories, but at bringing attention (not recall) to the present consciousness foundation sustaining awareness NOW. This means directing the hat toward the source of awareness rather than toward awareness's contents (including memories of past spiritual experiences), allowing awareness to recognize itself directly rather than through mental modifications.

Stage 3: Permanent Establishment in Neberdjer Awareness

Once direct experience transitions from occasional meditative glimpses during formal practice into permanent established awareness maintained throughout daily life, an extraordinary transformation occurs in the very structure of self-identity. Just as the ego-bound person operates from their personal identity as the unquestioned subconscious foundation of all experience without needing to philosophize about it constantly, the established practitioner operates from Neberdjer awareness as the natural foundation of their being.

At this stage of development—representing what the ancient sages termed enlightenment—there exists no need for continuous intellectual remembrance of philosophical concepts about Neberdjer, no dwelling on memories of transcendent experiences, no effortful mental techniques to maintain awareness. The recognition simply abides as one's essential nature, as immediately and effortlessly present as an ordinary person recognizes their own name when called. This represents not a strange mystical achievement requiring constant maintenance, not accumulated spiritual experiences forming impressive biography, but rather the natural recognition of what awareness has been all along, now freed from the obscuring density of aryu that previously prevented this recognition.

The pearl that was always present becomes visible once the accumulated layers of ego identification have been sufficiently thinned through the systematic application of shedy. Consciousness recognizes itself as the all-encompassing existence Amenemopet teaches—not through mental effort, not through recollection of past moments when this was glimpsed, but as the permanent, present, direct awareness of what one fundamentally IS beyond all mental modifications. The mind, now transparent to its Ab Neter source, operates skillfully in navigating daily life while awareness remains established in recognition of its Neberdjer foundation—the unchanging consciousness witnessing all mental activity without being affected by it, sustaining the mind's capacity to function while remaining as the eternal foundation beyond all temporary phenomena.

The Essential Understanding: Mind Purification Enables Transcendence

The teaching instructs that if the ego aspects of the personality were to be relaxed through the practices of ethics, devotion, and contemplative study, the resulting reduction in compulsive thinking and inordinate desiring would create space for heightened sensitivity and deeper self-discovery. This thinning of aryu density allows the practitioner to penetrate from the surface level of hat awareness down through the ab to the kara level, where the realization of one's Neberdjer nature becomes possible—not as something foreign being acquired, not as memory of past spiritual attainment, but as the revelation of what has sustained conscious awareness all along, now recognized directly in present experience beyond mental involvement.

The disciplinary practice of meditation specifically designed for purity of heart (meaning purification of the ab level of mind) and direct Neberdjer self-discovery will be presented comprehensively in the following chapter, where the technical methods for achieving this mind transformation receive detailed instruction. Nevertheless, Chapter 6B, verse 14 establishes the essential understanding that must precede effective practice: awareness of Neberdjer represents not the acquisition of something foreign to one's nature, not the accumulation of impressive spiritual experiences to remember, but the removal of obstruction to recognizing—directly, presently, beyond mental activity—what has always sustained the very capacity for awareness itself: the all-encompassing consciousness that the ancient sages knew as the foundation and culmination of spiritual development.

NOTE 1: See chapter 9 for detailed practice protocol for Sau Neberdjer Meditation.

REFERENCES

[1] Ashby, M. (2019-25). *Mysticism of Amenemopet Hieroglyphic Text Translation.* Sema Institute of Ancient Egyptian Studies.

[2] Ashby, M. (2024). *Amenemopet lectures 2024 by Dr Muata Ashby transcripts.* Sema Institute of Ancient Egyptian Studies.

[3] Ashby, M. (2024). *The Transpersonal Psychology of Discovering the Aware Witnessing Self.* Sema Institute of Ancient Egyptian Studies.

Secondary Sources:

[4] Brewer, J. A., Worhunsky, P. D., Gray, J. R., Tang, Y. Y., Weber, J., & Kober, H. (2011). Meditation experience is associated with differences in default mode network activity and connectivity. *Proceedings of the National Academy of Sciences, 108*(50), 20254-20259.

[5] Taylor, V. A., Grant, J., Daneault, V., Scavone, G., Breton, E., Roffe-Vidal, S., ... & Beauregard, M. (2011). Impact of mindfulness on the neural responses to emotional pictures in experienced and beginner meditators. *NeuroImage, 57*(4), 1524-1533.

[6] Garrison, K. A., Zeffiro, T. A., Scheinost, D., Constable, R. T., & Brewer, J. A. (2015). Meditation leads to reduced default mode network activity beyond an active task. *Cognitive, Affective, & Behavioral Neuroscience, 15*(3), 712-720.

[7] James, W. (1902). *The Varieties of Religious Experience: A Study in Human Nature*. Longmans, Green, and Co.

[8] Doidge, N. (2007). *The Brain That Changes Itself: Stories of Personal Triumph from the Frontiers of Brain Science*. Viking Press.

[9] Graybiel, A. M., & Smith, K. S. (2014). Good habits, bad habits. *Scientific American, 310*(6), 38-43.

[10] Deutsch, E., & Dalvi, R. (2004). *The Essential Vedanta: A New Source Book of Advaita Vedanta.* World Wisdom, Inc.

[11] Smith, H. (1991). *The World's Religions: Our Great Wisdom Traditions*. HarperOne.

[12] Dalai Lama XIV. (2004). *Dzogchen: The Heart Essence of the Great Perfection.* Snow Lion Publications.

[13] Reynolds, J. M. (2010). *The Golden Letters: The Three Statements of Garab Dorje.* Snow Lion Publications.

[14] Chowdhury, N. S., Lim, J., Travers-Hill, E., Romanowski, K., Cropley, V., Muir, A. M., ... & Batchelor, M. (2025). Multimodal neurophenomenology of jhāna meditation. *Neuropsychologia, 204*, 108998.

[15] Demir, E. A., Wang, S., Tozlu, C., Chen, Q., Menon, V., Northoff, G., & He, J. H. (2025). Concentration-absorption meditation reorganizes functional connectivity gradients: A 7T functional MRI study. *bioRxiv.*

[16] Yang, C. T., Chen, Y. S., & Northoff, G. (2025). Deepening the mind: Meditation and mental depth—Integrating phenomenology, yogic traditions, and cognitive neuroscience. *Neuroscience & Biobehavioral Reviews, 171*, 105928.

[17] Arora, H. (2025). Consciousness as fundamental: Arguments for panpsychism or idealism. *Philosophical Studies.*

[18] Shankara, A. (1970). *Vivekachudamani* (Swami Madhavananda, Trans.). Advaita Ashrama.

[19] Radhakrishnan, S. (1953). *The Principal Upanishads.* Harper & Brothers.

[20] Satprakashananda, S. (2024). *Methods of Knowledge According to Advaita Vedanta.* Routledge.

[21] Kumar, A., & Pradhan, B. (2024). Advaita philosophy and psychiatry: Points of convergence. *Indian Journal of Psychiatry, 66*(3), 291-297.

[22] Sacchet, M. D., & Meditation Research Program. (2024). Meditation and the sense of self. *Current Opinion in Psychology, 55*, 101753.

[23] Ehmann, L., Kuhn, S., Plein, D., Nguyen, K., Rauss, P., Bornemann, B., & Singer, T. (2025). Disentangling the effects of long-term meditation practice on personality, cognition, and socio-affective functioning. *Mindfulness.*

[24] Treves, I. N., Tello, L. Y., Davidson, R. J., & Goldberg, S. B. (2025). Neural dynamics during concentration meditation: An EEG study of expert practitioners. *Mindfulness.*

[25] Laukkonen, R. E., Kaveladze, B. T., Tangen, J. M., & Schooler, J. W. (2023). The science of meditation and the state of hypnosis share phenomenology and neural correlates: A narrative review of the neuroscience of cessations. *Neuroscience & Biobehavioral Reviews, 145*, 105003.

[26] Prakash, R. S., Schirda, B., Valentine, T. R., Callen, M., & McNeely, E. (2025). Mindfulness and network neuroscience: A novel approach for a comprehensive understanding of mindfulness. *Neuroscience & Biobehavioral Reviews.*

[27] Kozasa, E. H., Sato, J. R., Lacerda, S. S., Barreiros, M. A., Radvany, J., Russell, T. A., ... & Amaro Jr, E. (2012). Meditation training increases brain efficiency in an attention task. *NeuroImage, 59*(1), 745-749.

[28] Sedlmeier, P., Eberth, J., Schwarz, M., Zimmermann, D., Haarig, F., Jaeger, S., & Kunze, S. (2012). The psychological effects of meditation: A meta-analysis. *Psychological Bulletin, 138*(6), 1139-1171.

[29] Desbordes, G., Negi, L. T., Pace, T. W., Wallace, B. A., Raison, C. L., & Schwartz, E. L. (2012). Effects of mindful-attention and compassion meditation training on amygdala response to emotional stimuli in an ordinary, non-meditative state. *Frontiers in Human Neuroscience, 6*, 292.

[30] Kornfield, J. (2008). *The Wise Heart: A Guide to the Universal Teachings of Buddhist Psychology.* Bantam Books.

[31] Gunaratana, B. H. (2002). *Mindfulness in Plain English.* Wisdom Publications.

[35] Lutz, A., Greischar, L. L., Rawlings, N. B., Ricard, M., & Davidson, R. J. (2004). Long-term meditators self-induce high-amplitude gamma synchrony during mental practice. *Proceedings of the National Academy of Sciences, 101*(46), 16369-16373.

CHAPTER 9: THE PRACTICE OF SAU-NEBERDJER CONSCIOUSNESS MEDITATION

AUTHOR'S NOTE ON MINDFULNESS TERMINOLOGY

Throughout this manuscript, readers will encounter the term "mindfulness" used in two fundamentally distinct contexts that must not be conflated:

Contemporary Secular Mindfulness: When referencing modern psychological research and popular meditation practices, the term "mindfulness" describes cultivating present-moment attention and awareness within the ordinary operations of cognition and perception. While contemporary mindfulness practice offers demonstrable psychological and physiological benefits—including stress reduction, emotional regulation, cognitive clarity, and measurable neurological changes—its scope in popularized, secular form is generally limited to refining and stabilizing ego-based awareness rather than transcending it. Contemporary mindfulness typically does not engage the deeper metaphysical or ontological dimensions of consciousness that are central to Amenemopet's teachings and other traditional contemplative systems. Consequently, secular mindfulness tends to improve mental functioning at the hat (conscious awareness) level but does not, in most cases, facilitate the transformative recognition of Ab Neter (divine consciousness) or the discovery of one's essential nature as Neberdjer.

Sau-Neberdjer Practice (Ancient Egyptian Awareness Cultivation): When translating or explicating Amenemopet's actual spiritual practice—particularly the term "sau" in Chapter 6B verse 14—I use "mindfulness" or "awareness" to indicate the practice of maintaining recognition of Neberdjer, the all-encompassing divine consciousness that both underlies and transcends limited mind, time, and space. This represents a fundamentally different order of practice aimed at mind/personality transformation rather than mental improvement:

- Ger (silent mind and feelings) = An a priori awareness that exists prior to the ordinary ego identity that is aware of itself sensing and perceiving. This is not enhanced ego-awareness but rather the transcendence of ego-identification altogether, allowing consciousness to rest in its essential nature.
- Soul-Aware-Witness = A higher level of awareness above ego self-identity, which witnesses the ego self-identity and its sensations and perceptions without being identified with or affected by them. This witness-consciousness remains unchanging while all mental-emotional content changes.

The crucial distinction: Contemporary mindfulness cultivates refined attention within the mind's cognitive operations (hat level), supporting psychological well-being through improved emotional regulation, stress management, and cognitive function. Sau-Neberdjer practice aims at recognizing consciousness itself (Ab Neter) as distinct from and prior to mental operations, ultimately leading to the discovery that one's essential nature is identical with Neberdjer—the source and sustainer of all existence. The former stabilizes ego-awareness; the latter transcends ego-identification entirely.

Therefore, when this manuscript references "mindfulness meditation" in the context of Amenemopet's actual teachings or advanced contemplative practice, readers should understand this as pointing toward the profound practice of recognizing consciousness beyond ego-mind, not as synonymous with contemporary stress-reduction techniques or attention-training exercises. When referencing empirical research on "mindfulness," I am citing studies that validate attention-training mechanisms and neurological changes that parallel—but do not fully encompass—the deeper transformations Amenemopet prescribes.

Both contemporary mindfulness and sau-Neberdjer practice have value within their respective domains, and indeed, contemporary mindfulness training may serve as useful preliminary development of attention capacity. However, they serve fundamentally different purposes: psychological improvement and stress management versus metaphysical awakening and the discovery of divine consciousness as one's essential nature. The research cited throughout this manuscript on "mindfulness" studies primarily documents changes at the mental operations level (hat/ka), providing scientific validation for attention-training mechanisms that create conditions supportive of—but not identical to—the deeper ab-level transformation and Ab Neter recognition that Amenemopet's complete teaching facilitates.

Distinguishing Contemporary Mindfulness from Sau-Neberdjer Practice

DIMENSION	CONTEMPORARY SECULAR MINDFULNESS	SAU-NEBERDJER (ANCIENT EGYPTIAN PRACTICE)
Primary Goal	Psychological well-being, stress reduction, emotional regulation, cognitive improvement	Recognition of Ab Neter (divine consciousness) as essential nature; discovery of identity as Neberdjer
Consciousness Level Addressed	Hat (conscious awareness) and upper Ka (mental operations)	Ab (unconscious mind) penetration to Kara where Ab Neter resides; transcendence of ego-mind
Mechanism	Cultivating refined attention within ordinary mental operations	Transcending mental operations to recognize consciousness prior to thoughts
Relationship to Ego	Stabilizes and improves ego-functioning; creates "mindful ego"	Transcends ego-identification altogether; recognizes witness-consciousness beyond personality
Awareness Type	Mental awareness—using mind to observe mental content more clearly	Intuitional awareness—consciousness recognizing itself independent of mind
Outcome	Enhanced psychological functioning: better emotion regulation, reduced stress reactivity, improved focus	Metaphysical awakening: dissolution of separate self-sense, recognition of divine nature, liberation from aryu-driven existence
Time-Space Relationship	Cultivates present-moment attention within time-space framework	Recognition of consciousness beyond/prior to time-space-body identification
Practice Focus	Observing thoughts, emotions, sensations as they arise	Recognizing the unchanging awareness that witnesses all arising phenomena
Beneficial For	General population seeking stress management, mental health support, cognitive enhancement	Spiritual aspirants seeking liberation, self-realization, discovery of divine consciousness
Research Validation	Extensive: neurological changes, psychological benefits, physiological improvements at mental operations level	Limited contemporary research; ancient teachings document mind/personality transformation beyond what modern studies typically measure

DIMENSION	CONTEMPORARY SECULAR MINDFULNESS	SAU-NEBERDJER (ANCIENT EGYPTIAN PRACTICE)
Aryu (Karmic Patterns) Impact	May reduce reactivity to surface-level aryu; does not necessarily thin deep unconscious patterns	Systematic thinning of aryu through penetration to ab level; dissolution of karmic obstacles through Ab Neter recognition
Relationship to Ancient Teaching	Extracts attention-training component; omits metaphysical context and ultimate spiritual aim	Complete teaching: psychological purification (preliminary) + consciousness recognition (ultimate goal)
Self-Identity After Practice	"I am a person who is more mindful, less stressed, better regulated" (enhanced ego)	"I am consciousness itself; personality is temporary expression of eternal awareness" (transcended ego)
Witness-Consciousness	Cultivates observer capacity within dualistic framework (subject observing objects)	Recognizes witness as primary—the unchanging awareness (Soul-Aware-Witness) that IS one's true nature
Silence/Ger Cultivation	May experience moments of mental quiet as beneficial states	Recognizes silence as a priori ground of being—one's essential nature prior to thought-activity
Mind vs. Consciousness Distinction	Typically conflates mind and consciousness; aims to improve mental functioning	Rigorously distinguishes consciousness (Ab Neter—unchanging, cannot suffer) from mind (mental apparatus that experiences/transforms)
Typical Duration to Core Benefit	8-12 weeks for measurable psychological improvements	Years to decades for stable Ab Neter recognition; preliminary benefits occur sooner but transformation is profound and gradual
Compatible Applications	Corporate wellness, clinical psychology, education, stress management, medical settings	Spiritual communities, traditional meditation lineages, seekers committed to self-realization
Metaphysical Framework	Generally secular/agnostic; avoids ontological commitments about consciousness nature	Explicit metaphysics: Neberdjer as all-encompassing divinity; Ab Neter as individuated divine spark; consciousness as ontologically primary

Key Insight: Contemporary mindfulness and sau-Neberdjer practice represent different points on a spectrum of mind/personality development. Mindfulness cultivates capacity that can support deeper spiritual practice—refined attention, reduced reactivity, increased somatic awareness—but by itself typically stabilizes at psychological improvement rather than progressing to metaphysical transformation. Sau-Neberdjer practice encompasses attention-training as preliminary work but aims ultimately at the profound recognition that transcends all ego-boundaries and reveals one's essential nature as divine consciousness itself.

Practical Consideration for Aspirants: Those who have established mindfulness practice may find their attention-training capacity beneficial when beginning sau-Neberdjer practice, as the ability to sustain focus provides foundation for deeper contemplative work. However, aspirants must consciously shift from using awareness to observe mental content more clearly (mindfulness aim) to recognizing awareness itself as distinct from all mental content (sau-Neberdjer aim). This shift represents not mere refinement of technique but fundamental reorientation of practice purpose—from psychological improvement to consciousness awakening.

INTRODUCTION TO SAU NEBERDJER MEDITATION

The practice of Sau-Neberdjer meditation represents an ancient method for cultivating a silent mind and feelings, leading to the realization of Ab Neter and recognition of Ab Neter's source as Neberdjer itself.

The term "sau" that Amenemopet uses in verse 15 is sometimes translated as "mindfulness" or "awareness," but aspirants must recognize that this Ancient Egyptian practice fundamentally differs from contemporary secular mindfulness techniques. While modern mindfulness cultivates refined attention within ordinary mental operations for psychological benefit, sau-Neberdjer practice aims at transcending ego-mind altogether to recognize consciousness itself as Neberdjer. This represents not mental improvement but metaphysical awakening—the discovery of one's essential divine nature. [See Author's Note on Mindfulness Terminology for comprehensive distinction.]

As Sage Amenemopet instructs in Chapter 6B VIII, verse 14:

Verse 14.

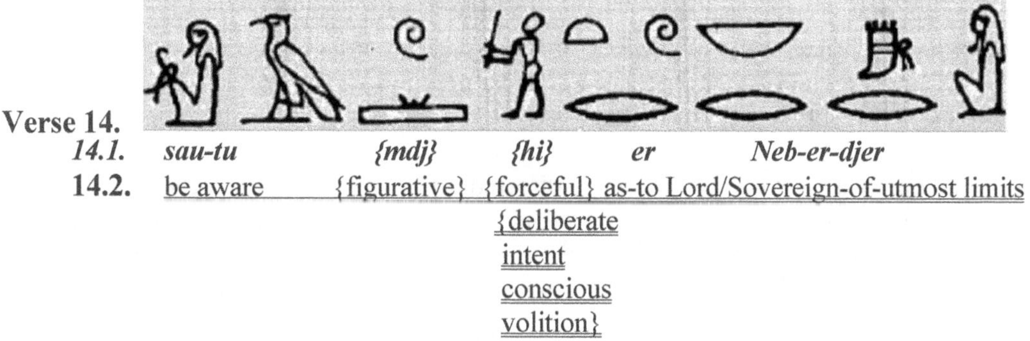

14.1. ***sau-tu*** ***{mdj}*** ***{hi}*** ***er*** ***Neb-er-djer***

14.2. be aware {figurative} {forceful} as-to Lord/Sovereign-of-utmost limits {deliberate intent conscious volition}

14.3. Remain aware, with deliberate effort, as to the fact that there is an "entity", an "existence" that encompasses all Creation [All-encompassing-Divinity-Neberdjer], beyond [underlying] mind and time and space. This existence/consciousness underlies limited human awareness. Maintain this awareness above all else.

UNDERSTANDING "BEING AWARE" IN AMENEMOPET'S INSTRUCTION

In the context of Amenemopet's instruction in Chapter 6B verse 14, "being aware" means keeping attention on the object or principle being contemplated. Amenemopet admonishes "being" (which means presently, in this moment) and "aware" (which means actively attending to). In reference to Neberdjer, there are several crucial ways to understand this awareness:

Four Dimensions of Neberdjer Awareness:

1. **Being aware of Neberdjer as composing all objects** – recognizing that all forms and phenomena are constituted by the divine essence
2. **Being aware of Neberdjer as the essence of one's own existence** – understanding Neberdjer as the source of consciousness that sustains individual awareness
3. **Being aware of Neberdjer as all-encompassing existence** – comprehending that Neberdjer is that which all things are composed of the fundamental substance of reality
4. **Being aware of Neberdjer as vastness beyond mental comprehension** – recognizing the infinite, transcendent nature that exceeds conceptual understanding

Implications of Neberdjer Awareness:

The recognition of Neberdjer has profound practical implications for living a higher quality of life and for spiritual discovery:

- **Universal kinship**: All beings in Creation are composed of Neberdjer and are therefore kinfolk to each other, fundamentally related through shared divine essence
- **Freedom from struggle**: Since Neberdjer is all, there is no need for struggling to acquire or compete. One can rest in serenity, knowing that Neberdjer is all, everywhere, and that the "I" is part of the whole which is complete in itself and in which natural actions work harmoniously for the ultimate good of all.

Transformative Effects of Neberdjer Awareness:

This type of awareness—as opposed to awareness directed toward ephemeral objects, feelings, desires, and thoughts, a process that is occluding to the mind and reinforces egoism—causes the mind to experience understanding of that which surpasses mundane human realities of mind and senses. It produces several profound transformations:

- **Psychophysiological restructuring**: The practice causes the mind and nervous system to change, becoming less stressed and more aware of present reality as opposed to ruminating on past experiences or anxiously anticipating future scenarios
- **Functional relationship with mental processes**: Nervous system restructuring creates configurations more favorable to using the mind and senses as instruments rather than being identified with them and their processes
- **Wisdom cultivation**: It causes wisdom—the integration of experience with philosophical understanding—to grow such that previously held opinions and beliefs dissolve into expanded understandings

- **Enhanced spiritual sensitivity**: These restructurings prove more conducive for promoting spiritual sensitivity and discernment of subtler forms of awareness that lead to deeper self-discovery

This meditation practice systematically develops the capacity for maintaining this awareness, progressing from basic ethical preparation through increasingly subtle stages of mind development leading to consciousness recognition.

This chapter presents a comprehensive yet accessible approach to Sau-Neberdjer practice. The foundation begins with discovering the Soul-Aware-Witness-Self—a consciousness that recognizes itself as the awareness observing thoughts and experiences rather than being identical with them. From this initial recognition, the practice deepens through progressive stages toward Ab Neter discovery and ultimately recognition of Neberdjer as the source of all consciousness.

Contemporary neuroscience research provides remarkable validation [7,10,11,12] for what the ancient sages discovered through millennia of contemplative practice, demonstrating measurable changes in brain function corresponding to each practice stage—particularly in reducing Default Mode Network (DMN) activity associated with mind-wandering and enhancing attentional control networks. These empirical findings confirm that systematic practice produces genuine transformation at the neural architecture level, not mere imagination.

CHAPTER ORGANIZATION AND NAVIGATION

This chapter presents a systematic approach to Sau-Neberdjer consciousness meditation, integrating ancient wisdom with contemporary neuroscience validation. The practices offered emerge from my study and direct experience within the Neterian tradition, providing practical guidance for aspirants seeking self-awareness and realization. I present this material humbly, recognizing that these ancient teachings contain infinite depth requiring continued exploration. The material follows a carefully sequenced progression:

PART 1: FOUNDATIONAL PREPARATIONS

Ethical purification, somatic preparation, and philosophical contemplation establish the ground enabling formal meditation to bear fruit.

PART 2: CORE MEDITATION PRACTICE

• Quick Recognition of Soul-Aware-Witness-Self (accessible entry—minutes to initial discovery)

• Deepening Into Ab Neter Recognition (building toward consciousness's divine source)

Most practitioners spend extended time with these core practices, as they provide both immediate experiential insight and the foundation for all subsequent development.

PART 3: SYSTEMATIC PROGRESSIVE DEVELOPMENT

Complete six-stage progression for comprehensive development:

- Stages I-II: Concentration development (external and internal focus)

- Stages III-V: Open monitoring awareness (epithets, abstract awareness, non-dual recognition)

- Stage VI: Absorption states

Each stage builds specific capacities required for subsequent stages—progression cannot be rushed without undermining developmental foundation.

PART 4: PRACTICAL IMPLEMENTATION GUIDANCE

Eyes-open vs. eyes-closed practice, common obstacles, life adjustments, realistic timelines.

PART 5: RESEARCH VALIDATION

Contemporary neuroscience demonstrates measurable brain changes corresponding to each practice stage, validating ancient contemplative discoveries through modern empirical methods.

VISUAL MAP: CHAPTER STRUCTURE AND RELATIONSHIPS

INTRODUCTION & GLOSSARY
Essential Context + Terminology Foundation
(sau, Ab Neter, Neberdjer, anrutef, Soul-Aware-Witness)

PART 1: FOUNDATIONAL PREPARATIONS
(Informal Practices)

Ethical Purification (Maat)	Somatic Preparation (5-10 min)	Philosophical Contemplation (Throughout Day)

Creates conditions enabling meditation to bear fruit

PART 2: CORE MEDITATION PRACTICE
(Essential Entry Points)

QUICK RECOGNITION OF SOUL-AWARE-WITNESS-SELF
- Discover witnessing awareness (minutes)
- Recognize awareness observing thoughts
- Initial profound insight

▼

DEEPENING INTO AB NETER RECOGNITION
- Practice "fullness of silence" (anrutef)
- Discover consciousness's divine source
- Stabilize witness recognition

Most practitioners spend extended time here

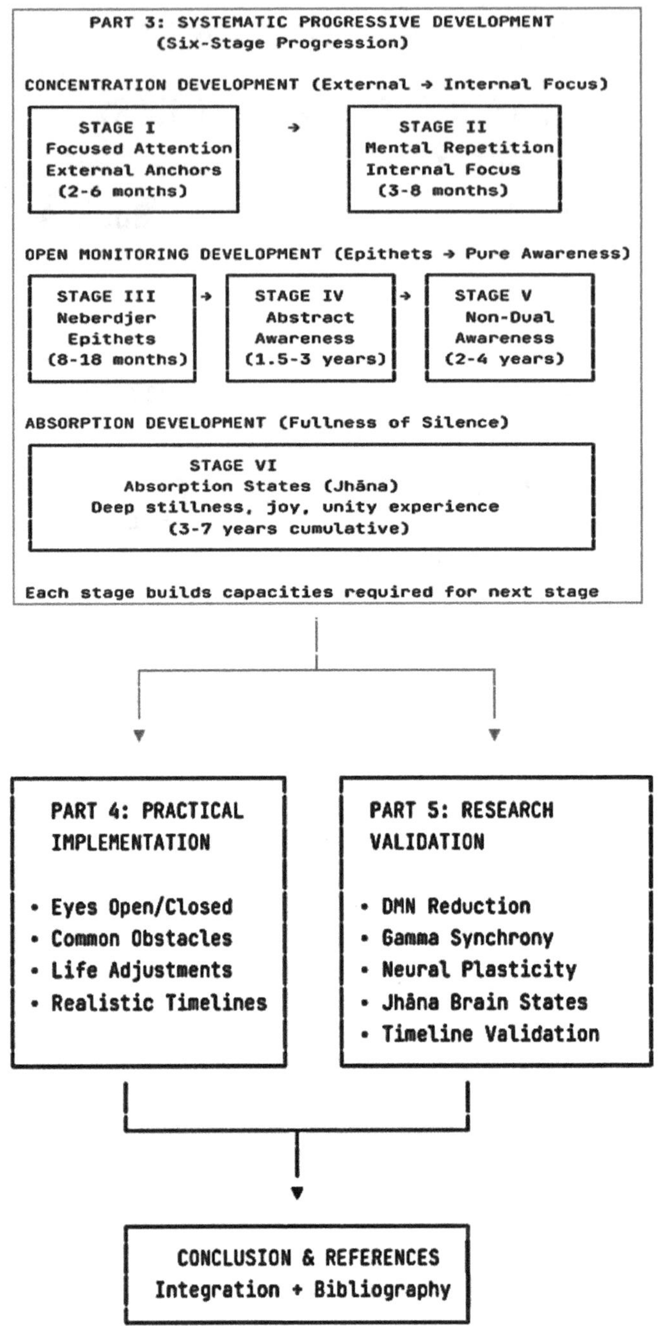
PART 3: SYSTEMATIC PROGRESSIVE DEVELOPMENT
(Six-Stage Progression)
CONCENTRATION DEVELOPMENT (External → Internal Focus)
STAGE I
Focused Attention
External Anchors
(2-6 months)
STAGE II
Mental Repetition
Internal Focus
(3-8 months)
OPEN MONITORING DEVELOPMENT (Epithets → Pure Awareness)
STAGE III
Neberdjer
Epithets
(8-18 months)
STAGE IV
Abstract
Awareness
(1.5-3 years)
STAGE V
Non-Dual
Awareness
(2-4 years)
ABSORPTION DEVELOPMENT (Fullness of Silence)
STAGE VI
Absorption States (Jhāna)
Deep stillness, joy, unity experience
(3-7 years cumulative)
Each stage builds capacities required for next stage
PART 4: PRACTICAL IMPLEMENTATION
• Eyes Open/Closed
• Common Obstacles
• Life Adjustments
• Realistic Timelines
PART 5: RESEARCH VALIDATION
• DMN Reduction
• Gamma Synchrony
• Neural Plasticity
• Jhāna Brain States
• Timeline Validation
CONCLUSION & REFERENCES
Integration + Bibliography

HOW TO USE THIS CHAPTER:

For Beginners:

1. Read Introduction and Glossary thoroughly
2. Review Part 1: Foundational Preparations
3. Begin with Quick Recognition practice (Part 2)
4. Incorporate informal foundational practices daily
5. Gradually add Stage I practices as foundation stabilizes

For Intermediate Practitioners:

1. Review Quick Recognition and Deepening sections (Part 2)
2. Assess current stage in systematic progression (Part 3)
3. Apply practical guidance from Part 4
4. Use research validation (Part 5) to understand neural changes

For Advanced Practitioners:

1. Focus on Stages V-VI (Part 3)
2. Refine practice using implementation guidance (Part 4)
3. Understand brain changes through research section (Part 5)

KEY CONCEPT: While presented sequentially, actual practice follows a more cyclical pattern. Informal practices (Part 1) continue throughout all stages. Core practices (Part 2) deepen as systematic development progresses. Advanced stages periodically return to foundational practices. The structure shows logical organization; your experience will be more spiral than linear—repeatedly returning to fundamentals at deeper levels as understanding matures.

RELATIONSHIP BETWEEN QUICK RECOGNITION AND SYSTEMATIC PROGRESSION:

The Quick Recognition method provides immediate access to Soul-Aware-Witness-Self—a profound initial insight that can occur within minutes. However, this recognition typically remains unstable initially; the mind quickly returns to habitual identification with thoughts. The systematic six-stage progression develops the concentration capacity, ethical purification, and refined awareness necessary to stabilize this insight and deepen it toward Ab Neter recognition. Both approaches work together synergistically.

Essential Terminology: Glossary of Key Terms

Understanding the following terms proves essential for grasping the practice methodology and the consciousness architecture it addresses:

a = (female symbol) or (male symbol) = "I" = ego identity (thinks of self as an individual when the mind is corrupted about self-identity, by delusion/error). The concept of "I AM" in mystic spiritual research relates to ideas popularized by Ramana Maharishi and Nisargadatta Maharaj through their inquiries "Who am I?" and "I am" respectively. These ideas have much older origins in ancient texts. The deeper meaning concerns the sense of identity a person holds—the feeling of being an individual and the sense of being a conscious entity.

In Ancient Egyptian wisdom, this sense of "I-ness" is conveyed through the hieroglyph a = (female symbol) or (male symbol) = "I" = ego identity (the mind's confused conception of self as a separate individual when the mind becomes deluded about its true nature).

Historical Context of "I AM" Philosophy:

The Upanishads (c. 800–200 BCE) explicitly explore the "I" as the self (Atman), recognizing it as conscious awareness. In non-dualistic texts like the Chandogya Upanishad and Brihadaranyaka Upanishad, the self is understood as both individual and identical with ultimate reality (Brahman). The famous statement "Tat Tvam Asi" ("That thou art") expresses the recognition of the self as simultaneously individual and universal.

Buddhist texts (c. 5th–4th century BCE onwards) challenge the concept of a fixed "I" (anatman), emphasizing impermanence and relational consciousness. However, early Buddhist discourses still recognize first-person experience as the locus of suffering and ethical responsibility.

Ancient Egyptian Precedence:

The Ancient Egyptian Coffin Texts and Book of the Dead (c. 2100–1600 BCE)—the earliest known examples in human history—contain passages where the speaker addresses the divine powers in first person ("I am…"), emphasizing moral responsibility and identity in the afterlife journey.

A significant example appears in the Ancient Egyptian Book of Enlightenment (Pertemheru) Chapter 26 (explored in *Awaken Your Soul-Aware-Witness* by Dr. Muata Ashby), where the term "**a**" refers to the individual conscious self that exists distinct from mind and body—a self-aware recognition of being an entity separate from mental processes, sensory experiences, and bodily sensations. This is the context for understanding the term as used in Amenemopet's teachings.

In a spiritually evolved context, an advancing purifying ego "***a***" now refers to a person who has discovered the Soul-Aware-Witness-Self

OR if fully purified "***a***" refers to a person who has discovered Ab Neter—Divine witness consciousness (divine soul) i.e. their God nature.

sau = be-aware

tat = representation of a concept of reality = mental object

ka = astral body = thoughts, feelings = subconscious level of mind—basis of the personality/character

mehtu = fullness—such as a glass full of water that cannot fit one more drop

ger= silence/serenity

Ab Neter = soul = consciousness of universal absolute spirit (Neberdjer) manifesting as individual consciousness in a human personality. Witnessing Awareness supporting the conscious awareness of a human being.

Neberdjer = universal absolute spirit—that consciousness that is universal, vast, infinite, eternal and which supports the conscious awareness of all life forms, and it is the nature of which all is composed = the support of the individual Witnessing Awareness (Ab Neter/soul) of a human being.

Baka = Ancient Egyptian Book of Enlightenment (Pert m Heru) Chapter 26 verse 15. Description—"BaKa" Spiritually Pregnant-personality-soul infused mind—a personality whose spirit has impregnated the mind and body such that spiritual awakening has occurred in the personality and will grow to fullness (Amenemopet Ch. 5 V. 9) of self-awareness. This stage of spiritual development may be referred to as the Soul-Aware-Witness-Self. Such a personality has realized that there is a higher level of awareness other than the ego awareness that thinks itself to be the body and mind. That higher level of awareness is the Soul-Aware-Witness-Self. The Soul-Aware-Witness-Self can develop further to discover its source is the Ab Neter and further, that Ab Neter is sourced in Neberdjer. Therefore, the ultimate reality of the personality is Neberdjer.

anrutef= state of awareness without cognition—awareness present without thoughts about ego identity, without mental references, experiencing consciousness itself without the modifications that occur when the mind operates. This state is associated with joyousness (***awut*** - Book of Enlightenment Chapter 175 Appendix) because it is a place of freedom from the fragmentation of mind; it is a place of experiencing deep relaxation and peace.

PART 1: FOUNDATIONAL PREPARATIONS

Before engaging formal meditation practices, the aspirant must establish proper foundation through ethical purification, somatic preparation, and philosophical contemplation. These informal foundation practices create the conditions enabling formal meditation to bear fruit.

Ethical Purification Through Daily Conduct

Maat-based ethical living creates the foundation enabling meditation to bear fruit. The aspirant cultivates truth-speaking, non-violence, generosity, contentment, and selfless service. Unethical conduct generates psychological agitation (dense aryu) preventing the mental calm necessary for subtle awareness practices. Consider: How can consciousness investigate its fundamental nature while constantly defending lies, managing guilt from harmful actions, or scheming to acquire others' possessions?

Contemporary research validates this ancient understanding [7,8]: chronic stress from unethical living elevates cortisol, activates inflammatory pathways, and maintains heightened Default Mode Network (DMN) activity—the neural signature of rumination and self-referential thinking that corresponds to what the tradition identifies as dense aryu patterns occupying conscious awareness. Conversely, ethical conduct reduces chronic stress markers, supporting the physiological calm necessary for attention to settle inward.

Practical implementation: Daily review examining: "Did my actions today support or undermine inner peace? Where did I speak untruthfully? When did anger drive behavior? How did desire for pleasure or fear of discomfort determine choices?" This honest self-examination gradually reveals aryu patterns requiring transformation.

Somatic Preparation

Physical tension mirrors mental agitation. The protocol includes gentle movement practices (5-10 minutes) before formal meditation: simple stretches, conscious breathing, or slow walking. These practices regulate nervous system arousal, releasing physical holding patterns that would otherwise distract during meditation. Research demonstrates that preparatory body-focused practices [13] enhance vagal tone and facilitate attentional stability for subsequent meditation—physiological relaxation precedes mental stillness.

Personal Preparatory Rituals

Practitioners benefit from establishing personal ritual practices that create psychological transition from daily activities into formal meditation. These rituals need not be elaborate—their power lies in consistent repetition signaling to the mind that sacred practice approaches. Consider establishing a simple pre-meditation sequence: taking a brief shower, preparing tea consumed only before practice, changing into clean loose clothing designated exclusively for meditation, or arranging the meditation space mindfully.

Contemporary neuroscience validates this [12]: repeated ritual sequences create neural associations triggering specific psychological states; the brain learns to recognize preparatory cues and begins shifting toward meditative readiness before formal practice begins. These preparatory rituals prove especially valuable immediately before formal meditation sessions, serving as the final gateway between worldly engagement and contemplative absorption.

Philosophical Contemplation of Neberdjer

Throughout daily activities, repeatedly bring the mind back to contemplating Neberdjer's nature: "This consciousness aware right now is sustained by Neberdjer. These thoughts arising are Neberdjer manifesting as mental content. The space containing all phenomena is Neberdjer." This repeated contemplation strengthens neural pathways supporting formal practice while gradually shifting habitual mind orientation.

The informal practice of repeatedly contemplating Neberdjer philosophy throughout daily life serves a neurological function: it primes semantic networks that support meditation object recognition during formal practice. When the aspirant repeatedly brings the mind back to contemplating "Creation occurs within Neberdjer," this strengthens neural pathways that later facilitate sustained attention on this concept during formal meditation stages.

Practical implementation: Set regular reminders (phone alerts, visual cues) prompting brief 30-60 second contemplation periods. Morning coffee becomes an opportunity: "This experience of taste, warmth, pleasure—all Neberdjer." Traffic delay transforms: "This frustration, this waiting, this impatience—all Neberdjer appearing as apparent experience." Up to this point, in the current chapter, informal meditative practices have been discussed in the form of during-the-day remembrances of the philosophy and taking dedicated intentional brief times to come into the space of the spiritual practice feelings. The following sections begins the formal practices wherein dedicated time is set aside for concentrated spiritual practice of meditation.

PART 2: CORE MEDITATION PRACTICE

Practice Session Structure

Duration: Begin with 15-20 minutes daily, gradually extending to 30-45 minutes as concentration develops. Quality matters more than duration—focused 20 minutes surpasses distracted 60 minutes.

Frequency: Daily practice is essential. Missing occasional days is acceptable, but establishing a consistent rhythm proves crucial for neural consolidation. Research demonstrates that distributed practice [12] across multiple shorter sessions produces superior neural consolidation compared to single extended sessions.

Progression Principle: Master each developmental stage before advancing. Rushing forward undermines the foundation necessary for subtle stages. The practice progresses through systematic development, though the core discovery of the Soul-Aware-Witness-Self can occur relatively quickly through the Quick Recognition method.

Beginning Practice With Opening Invocations

Before beginning formal meditation practice, traditional practitioners may recite the opening invocation to establish proper intention and request divine guidance:

SPOKEN OFFERING: Invocatory prayer for peace and success on the spiritual journey-to be read prior to engaging a study of the Pert-m-Heru

Verse 1.

1.1. ***Hotep di nesu Neter aah Anpu Wep- wat***

1.2. ***"Offering is given to Supreme Divinity Anubis, Upwat***

1.3. "Offering is given to the Supreme Divinity, the source of all Creation, and to Anpu, the divinity who prepares the aspirant for the journey and Wepwat the one who leads the aspirant on the journey and opens the spiritual paths and makes them free of obstructions,

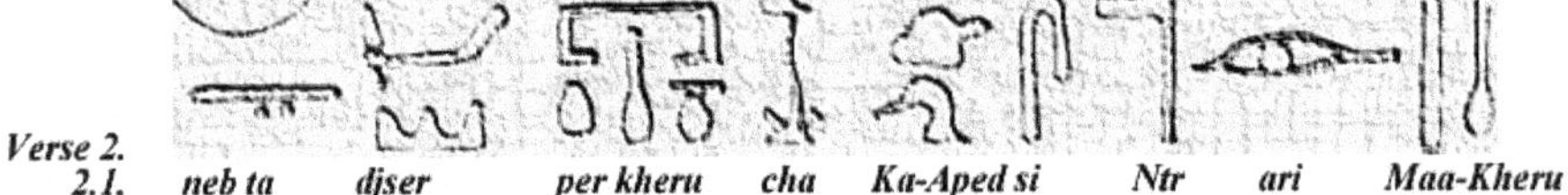

Verse 2.

2.1. ***neb ta djser per kheru cha Ka-Aped si Ntr ari Maa-Kheru***

2.2. ***lord of the sacred land, spoken offering 1000 beef 1000 geese. Doing this True of Speech"***

2.3. and to the lord of the sacred land, this spoken offering is 1000 beef (maleness) and 1000 geese (femaleness), supreme peace and union of opposites. Doing this spoken offering causes the Divine to make one True of Speech, that is, successful on the spiritual journey by discovering spiritual victory and enlightenment."

This invocation establishes proper intention and requests divine guidance for the practice session. The act of offering represents dedicating one's practice to spiritual discovery rather than worldly gain, creating the mental framework necessary for transcending egoic concerns.

A FOLLOWER OF NEBERDJER: FROM ANCIENT EGYPTIAN BOOK OF ENLIGHTENMENT - PERT M HERU - PAPYRUS NEBSENY CHAPTER 4/17

This invocation affirms one's devotion and intention to follow and realize one's Neberdjer being.

Verse 1.

1.1.	***tu***	***a***	***im***	***shems***	***en***	***Neberdjer***
1.2.	supporter	I	form	follower	of	All-encompassing-Divine

1.3. "I am a follower of Neberdjer[13]- who is "Omnitude", that which is all-encompassing, infinite, vast and divine; that which composes all and is the essence of my existence.

---

[13] The Supreme Being, all-encompassing Divinity

BASIC SAU NEBERDJER MEDITATION PRACTICE & QUICK RECOGNITION OF SOUL-AWARE-WITNESS-SELF: THE FOUNDATION PRACTICE

Foundation: Sage Amenemopet instructs: "Remain watchful, mindful, aware, keeping in mind, with deliberate effort, as to the fact that there is an 'entity', an 'existence' that encompasses all Creation [All-encompassing-Divinity], beyond [underlying] mind and time and space" [verse 14.3]. The following two complementary exercises provide accessible pathways for discovering the Soul-Aware-Witness-Self—using visual and auditory experiences to reveal awareness as independent from the objects it observes.

VISUAL PATHWAY: THE APPLE RECOGNITION PRACTICE

With eyes open, sit comfortably and bring to mind an object—perhaps an apple resting on a table. Notice how your eyes perceive its form and color. This is awareness paying attention, directed outward through the senses toward a physical object.

Now gently close your eyes. The apple no longer appears to the eyes, yet a mental image remains in your mind—what the ancients called tat, the mental representation. Notice that you are now the subject witnessing this mental object, whereas moments ago you witnessed the physical object.

You are using awareness (sau) to be the witness. The witness and awareness of the witness are one and the same. You are awareness/consciousness being aware of objects, and the objects exist because you are aware.

Here is the key recognition: allow this mental image to naturally fade without effort. What remains? You remain—awareness/consciousness remains. The awareness that witnessed both the physical apple and the mental image continues, even when no object appears before it. This is sau—awareness that previously was aware of a physical or mental object now recognizing itself as the awareness/consciousness, a witness of itself being itself without modifications of the mind due to objects of awareness.

AUDITORY PATHWAY: THE SOUND RECOGNITION PRACTICE

This complementary practice uses auditory experience to reveal the same fundamental truth through a different sensory modality. The wisdom to be understood: awareness transcends the particular sense door through which objects appear.

Sit quietly with eyes closed and bring attention to any sounds in your environment—perhaps the sound of a fan, distant traffic, birds singing, the hum of appliances, or the subtle sound of your own breathing. Do not seek particular sounds; simply notice whatever arises naturally in the auditory field. Do not follow the sounds to their source or imagine what is happening related to them. Simply focus on the sound itself, not its practical relative meaning.

Observe how each sound possesses a distinct life cycle: it begins (arising from silence), intensifies to a peak, then gradually subsides and fades back into silence. Follow this complete arc with several sounds—a car passing, a door closing, a voice speaking. Notice the beginning, middle, and ending of each auditory phenomenon.

Now comes the crucial recognition: Notice that you were aware before the sound arose, you remained aware while the sound was present, and you continue being aware after the sound has completely faded. The awareness witnessing these sounds does not arise with the sound, intensify with it, or disappear when it ends. Awareness remains constant and unchanging while the auditory objects come and go within it.

Consider this deeply: You are conscious and aware even when the sound has faded completely. Therefore, you are awareness itself, not the object of awareness. The sound is merely an object that you are aware of—like the apple in the visual practice but perceived through the auditory sense door rather than the visual one.

Extending to Mental Sound Objects

Now reflect again by moving awareness inward. Imagine a sound in your mind—perhaps a familiar voice speaking your name, a musical melody, or the bark of a dog. Notice how this mental sound arises in awareness, exists for a period, then dissolves back into mental silence. Yet you remain, existing and aware, even as this mental auditory object comes and goes.

You are now aware of a mental object—its coming into awareness and its going out of awareness. This demonstrates that you, as awareness, can witness both external physical sounds (perceived through the ears) and internal mental sounds (arising within the mind itself). Both categories of auditory phenomena appear as objects within the unchanging field of awareness that you are.

THE GENTLE RETURN: WORKING WITH MIND WANDERING DURING PRACTICE

A crucial understanding must be established regarding the natural tendency of mind to wander during these recognition practices. Consider what occurs: You follow the visual or auditory pathway and discover the "I am"—the Soul-Aware-Witness-Self experiencing its own existence independent of objects. Yet after a period, you suddenly realize that awareness has become absorbed in thoughts—planning, remembering, analyzing, or simply drifting through mental imagery.

What has occurred? The "I am" awareness has become "identified" with thoughts arising in consciousness. Instead of remaining as witness observing mental phenomena, awareness has reverted to the habitual pattern of experiencing itself as identical with those thoughts. During this period of identification, the Soul-Aware-Witness-Self "forgets itself," absorbed in mental content. This forgetting represents not a new occurrence but rather the default pattern operating throughout most of life—the habit of un-mindfulness about the "I am" as oneself, reinforced through countless repetitions across years and, according to the teaching, lifetimes.

The Practice of Gentle Return

The wisdom to be understood: the crucial moment in practice occurs not when recognition remains stable but when you notice that wandering has occurred. This noticing—"Oh, I have been absorbed in thoughts"—itself represents Soul-Aware-Witness-Self awareness emerging. When this recognition arises, practice gentle return:

Do not judge the wandering: Resist criticizing yourself for losing awareness or generating frustration. Such judgment perpetuates identification with thinking rather than supporting recognition of the witness. The wandering occurred because accumulated aryu patterns create strong habitual pull toward thought-identification—this represents mechanical conditioning, not personal failing.

Do not attempt forceful control: Avoid straining to maintain Soul-Aware-Witness-Self recognition through willful effort. Such forcing creates tension that itself becomes an object occupying awareness. The practice seeks revelation of what already exists, not creation of a special state through mental effort.

Simply return awareness gently: When noticing that wandering has occurred, allow awareness to gently disengage from thought content and return to recognition of itself as witness. This return possesses a quality of softness, ease, and acceptance—like a mother softly redirecting a wandering child with patience and kindness rather than harsh discipline.

Gradual Stabilization Through Patient Repetition

Through repeated gentle returns—perhaps dozens of times within a single practice session—consciousness gradually stabilizes:

The gap between wandering and recognition shortens. Initially, minutes may pass before noticing absorption in thoughts. With repetition, you notice wandering beginning to occur rather than only recognizing it after prolonged absorption.

Stability gradually increases. Soul-Aware-Witness-Self recognition may initially sustain for only moments before reverting to thought-identification. Through patient practice, these moments extend to sustained periods where awareness remains as witness.

Aryu patterns gradually thin. Each gentle return creates new aryu supporting witness-awareness rather than thought-identification. These accumulate gradually, competing with and eventually outweighing the dense aryu patterns of habitual un-mindfulness. The thinning occurs through patient accumulation of correct recognition repeated countless times.

The Teaching About Non-Striving

This gentle return practice does not aim to eliminate thoughts or to maintain constant Soul-Aware-Witness-Self recognition through forceful concentration. The practice simply involves recognizing awareness as witness when recognition naturally emerges and gently returning to that recognition when noticing that identification with mental content has occurred. There is no failure in wandering, but there is achievement in recognition and return—the patient, compassionate process of allowing awareness to become familiar with its true nature through repeated exposure; and from there maturing to realize its essence as universal consciousness.

Consider the metaphor of sunlight penetrating morning mist: The sun does not force the mist to dissolve through violent effort. It simply continues shining, and the mist naturally dissipates through gradual warming. Similarly, each gentle return contributes to progressive thinning of accumulated patterns. Through countless gentle returns, repeated patiently across practice sessions, consciousness gradually stabilizes in self-recognition rather than remaining perpetually lost in identification with mental-emotional content.

Therefore, approach these practices with patience, gentleness, and trust in the process. The wandering will occur—this is certain. The gentle return represents your response, repeated as many times as necessary, with the understanding that each return contributes to the gradual stabilization that ultimately allows consciousness to rest in its own true nature.

The Fundamental Recognition

The you that is aware of these objects—whether physical sounds, mental sounds, visual images, or any other phenomena—is your higher Soul-Aware-Witness-Self, which exists independently of the objects it can be aware of. This witnessing awareness does not depend upon the presence or absence of any particular object for its existence. It simply is—the constant background of beingness within which all experiences arise and dissolve.

If you spend time paying attention to the Soul-Aware-Witness-Self itself rather than exclusively focusing on the objects appearing within it, you are resting in your own higher identity of awareness. This represents a fundamental shift in self-understanding—from identifying as the thoughts, feelings, and sensations (which change constantly) to recognizing yourself as the awareness witnessing these changing phenomena (which remains constant).

Liberation from Mental-Somatic Tyranny

This practice frees one from what the Ancient Egyptian Book of Enlightenment Chapter 26 describes as the tyranny of the mind (thoughts and feelings) and the sensations and desires of the body that torment consciousness when it remains identified with these changing phenomena rather than resting in its true nature as witnessing awareness. When the mind mistakes itself for the mental-emotional content and bodily sensations it observes, it experiences suffering as these phenomena inevitably change, conflict, and eventually dissolve. When consciousness recognizes itself as the Soul-Aware-Witness-Self observing these phenomena, it discovers freedom from their tyrannical hold.

The Eternal Nature of Witnessing Awareness

Consider that these brief exercises reveal something profoundly significant that has been true throughout your entire life, though perhaps unrecognized until now: you are separate from the things your mind is aware of and paying attention to. More importantly, the awareness doing the witnessing has remained constant and unchanging while the objects witnessed have changed continuously.

The Same Consciousness, Then and Now

Reflect deeply upon this truth: The consciousness that was aware of your experiences an hour ago is the identical consciousness aware of your experiences right now. The consciousness that witnessed your life last week is the same consciousness witnessing this present moment. The consciousness that was present ten years ago, twenty years ago, throughout your entire lifetime—when you were a child, or as a baby, before you could talk-that consciousness is the very same consciousness sustaining the awareness in personality and mind at this moment.

This is not metaphorical or symbolic—it is the literal truth of your existence. The same awareness that looked through your eyes as a child looks through them now. The same consciousness that heard sounds decades ago hears sounds today. The same witnessing presence that has accompanied you through every experience of your life remains present, unchanged, eternal.

Everything Changes Except Consciousness

Now consider what has changed during this time:

The objects of awareness have completely transformed: The concerns occupying your mind last week have shifted. The situations you were experiencing last year bear little resemblance to current circumstances. Every thought, feeling, worry, joy, desire, and aversion you experienced in the past has arisen, persisted briefly, then dissolved—replaced by new mental content that itself proves equally temporary.

The body has changed: The physical form you inhabited ten years ago is not the same body you occupy today. Cells have died and been replaced. The body has aged, transformed, moved through countless states. Nothing about the physical form remains constant.

Life circumstances have transformed: Relationships have formed and dissolved. Living situations have changed. Career paths have shifted. The entire external architecture of your life has undergone continuous transformation.

Yet through all these changes—through every transformation of thought, body, and circumstance—the consciousness witnessing these changes has remained absolutely constant. The awareness that witnessed the objects, body, and circumstances of the past is the identical awareness witnessing the objects, body, and circumstances of the present.

The Unchanging Nature Brings Peace, Freedom, and Joy

This unchanging nature of consciousness possesses profound significance for spiritual realization. Consider the qualities that arise from recognizing your identity as this unchanging awareness rather than as the changing phenomena it witnesses:

Peace emerges from unchanging nature: The mind experiences turbulence precisely because it identifies with changing phenomena—thoughts that conflict, desires that cannot be permanently satisfied, circumstances that inevitably transform. When consciousness recognizes itself as the unchanging witness of these changing phenomena rather than being identical with them, profound peace emerges. This peace does not depend upon particular mental states, favorable circumstances, or the absence of challenges. It arises from resting in what does not change amidst everything that does.

Freedom arises from non-entanglement: The Soul-Aware-Witness-Self remains free because it is not caught up in the mind's delusions and feelings of desire for things that are ephemeral. The mind suffers when it craves permanent satisfaction from temporary phenomena—seeking lasting happiness in relationships that must change, circumstances that cannot remain constant, pleasures that inevitably fade, possessions that ultimately decay. When consciousness recognizes itself as the eternal witness rather than as these temporary phenomena, it discovers freedom from this futile quest.

Joyousness manifests as the natural state: The Ancient Egyptian Book of Enlightenment Chapter 175 Appendix describes awut (joyousness/happiness) as the quality associated with consciousness recognizing its true nature. This joy does not depend upon pleasant experiences, favorable circumstances, or the fulfillment of desires. It emerges spontaneously when the mind ceases identification with its own turbulent content and rests in its own unchanging, eternal nature.

Three States of Mind, One Constant Consciousness

The profundity of this recognition deepens when you reflect upon consciousness's constancy across all states of mental operation:

Waking state: When the mind engages with sensory objects and thoughts during ordinary waking consciousness, the Soul-Aware-Witness-Self remains present, witnessing these engagements.

Dream state: When the mind generates dream imagery and narrative during sleep, consciousness remains present, witnessing the dream experiences even though no external sensory objects exist.

Dreamless sleep state: When the mind produces no objects at all during deep dreamless sleep, consciousness persists—for upon waking, you recognize "I slept deeply, I experienced no dreams," which requires consciousness to have been present witnessing the absence of mental content.

The underlying Ab Neter/Amun-Ra aspect of your soul/spirit remains constant across all three states. It does not fluctuate with changing mental states. It is not ephemeral like the phenomena appearing within it. It is eternal—the unchanging foundation of your existence that precedes and survives all changing experiences.

The Metaphor of Silence and Heat

This understanding illuminates the metaphorical teaching Sage Amenemopet presents throughout his wisdom text. When Amenemopet instructs the aspirant to cultivate silence (ger) and warns against the heated person (shemm), he speaks directly to this fundamental distinction between consciousness recognizing its true nature and mind lost in mental turbulence.

The witnessing consciousness manifesting as Soul-Aware-Witness-Self and deepening toward Ab Neter realization represents the ideal of silence that Amenemopet teaches: This is the serenity, peace, stillness, and stability that emerges when consciousness recognizes itself as the unchanging awareness rather than identifying with the turbulent, changing content of mind. This silence is not merely the absence of sound or thought—it is the recognition of consciousness's eternal, unchanging nature that remains serene regardless of what phenomena arise within the field of awareness.

The cacophony of mind represents the shemm (heat/noise) that Amenemopet warns against: This is the heated mind, the turbulence, agitation, and suffering that arise when consciousness mistakenly identifies with the changing phenomena of mind—the endless stream of thoughts about past and future, the conflicting desires and aversions, the reactions to circumstances, the anxious clinging to temporary phenomena hoping they will provide permanent satisfaction.

The Practice of Abiding in Truth

Understanding this distinction transforms the entire approach to spiritual practice. The wisdom to be grasped: transformation does not occur by changing what you are but by recognizing what you have always been.

The more you spend time with that eternal aspect of yourself—resting as witnessing awareness rather than being absorbed in the objects witnessed—the more you realize the truth of that reality. You are not creating something new or achieving a special state. You are simply recognizing what has been present throughout your entire existence but remained obscured by habitual identification with changing mental-emotional content.

Conversely, the more you spend time exclusively engaged with the ephemeral world and with the fluctuating thoughts, feelings, and objects of awareness that arise in the mind, the more the illusory world (illusory precisely because it is ephemeral and constantly changing) seems real and solid.

Consider how the personality's accumulated aryu (impressions from past experiences) create this habitual identification with changing mental-emotional content. The mind has spent countless hours—indeed, countless lifetimes according to the tradition—absorbed in worldly thoughts and individualized thinking, reinforcing the false sense that "I am my thoughts, I am my feelings, I am this body-mind experiencing these circumstances." This accumulated habit of misidentification creates the dense aryu patterns that obscure recognition of the Soul-Aware-Witness-Self and, ultimately, the Ab Neter nature.

Therefore, the practice requires patient, consistent redirection of attention: repeatedly recognizing yourself as the unchanging awareness rather than as the changing contents of awareness. Each time you notice thoughts arising and recognize "I am the awareness observing these thoughts, not the thoughts themselves," you thin the aryu patterns of misidentification. Each time you observe feelings without becoming lost in them, recognizing "I am the consciousness witnessing these feelings, not the feelings themselves," you strengthen recognition of your true nature.

This is why the ancient sages emphasized that transformation occurs through sustained practice over extended time. The habits of misidentification run deep, reinforced by countless repetitions across many years. The purification process requires corresponding repetition of correct recognition—patiently returning to the truth again and again (with gentle return to the deeper self) until consciousness stabilizes in self-recognition rather than constantly collapsing back into identification with mental-emotional content.

Yet understand clearly: this patience does not imply struggle or striving. The practice is one of recognition, not achievement. You are not trying to become something you are not or to create a state that does not exist. You are simply recognizing what is always already present—the unchanging consciousness that has been here throughout your entire existence, waiting to be noticed beneath the turbulent surface of mental activity.

Integration Through Threefold Practice

This witnessing awareness represents what may be referred to as the "Soul-Aware-Witness-Self." It stands higher than ordinary ego-consciousness, for you have discovered yourself as the awareness that observes thoughts and mental images rather than being identical with them. Yet understand clearly—this is not yet Ab Neter or the Neberdjer level of consciousness that Amenemopet describes. This is an intermediate discovery, though a profoundly significant attainment that serves as the foundation for deeper realization.

Through the practices of wisdom (studying and contemplating the teachings that reveal consciousness architecture), Maat-based righteous living (ethical conduct that purifies aryu and creates calm mental conditions), and meditation on Neberdjer philosophy and existence as Self, the higher identity of awareness discovered as Soul-Aware-Witness-Self develops toward realization of self as Ab Neter—recognizing that the witnessing awareness itself is sustained by and ultimately identical with the divine consciousness that the tradition identifies as the true Self.

Most aspirants can sustain this recognition briefly before the mind, habituated to engaging with thoughts, pulls awareness back into mental activity (wandering). Do not judge this as failure. The mind operates according to its accumulated aryu patterns and naturally gravitates toward thought-activity. The practice from here requires staying with the higher self-awareness and allowing that awareness of nothingness that exists in the gaps between thoughts to expand and deepen.

The basic practice is to discover one's Soul-Aware-Witness-Self, a process that is relatively easy through either the visual or auditory pathway presented here. Then, once this aspect of awareness has been identified, the practice is to spend time returning to it—informally during day-to-day activities and formally, without distractions, spending dedicated time reflecting upon and returning to the experience, attempting to hold it as long as comfortably possible. More advanced meditation methods, presented in the systematic progression that follows, augment this foundational practice.

Practice Guidance

Practice Guidance: Begin with whichever pathway (visual or auditory) feels more accessible. Some practitioners find the visual pathway clearer initially; others resonate more immediately with the auditory approach. Both reveal the same truth through different sense doors. As proficiency develops, alternate between both practices to strengthen recognition that awareness transcends any particular sensory modality—it is the constant presence witnessing all forms of experience, whether visual, auditory, tactile, or mental.

Engage these Quick Recognition practices until witness recognition becomes stable and can be accessed readily during daily activities. Only then undertake the deeper inquiry into the Ab Neter source described in the Deepening practice that follows. Remember that this is not about forcing an experience but about removing the aryu obstructions that hide the Soul-Aware-Witness-Self awareness already present within you.

DEEPENING INTO AB NETER RECOGNITION: FROM WITNESS TO DIVINE SELF-DISCOVERY

Teachings of Amenemopet Chapter 5 Verse 9 provides the Teaching of Internal Divine Fulfillment through silence: the discovery that true completion of self-discovery comes through communion with Creator-Spirit in silence of body and mind.

Verse 9.

9.1. *Aa mehtu{mdj} en ger gem {mdj} k pa ankh {mdj}*

9.2. Behold! fullness of silence finds {fig} thee the life {fig}

9.3. Behold the glory of this way of being! Being silent (serenity) is the means for discovering the fullness of life that is beyond ordinary life that you have known as a human. It is life found in the Creator-Spirit that is within- by communing with the Creator-Spirit that resides in the temple. . This fullness cannot come from heatedly searching for fulfillment in the world for fulfillment with an imperfect personality (egoism/heated personality). It is found not by externalities of the external world but instead by realizing that there is perfection within when the fullness of being is experienced beyond the worldly thinking, desires and cravings that cause one to feel incomplete, as a separate individual, alone and imperfect. The discovery of the fullness of self by communing with the Creator-Spirit allows the discovery of fullness within.

Ancient Egyptian Book of Enlightenment-Chapter 125-introduction-Verse 12

Verse 12.

12.1. *ze-geru n - a*

12.2. Brought-silence to - myself

12.3. I have caused there to be silence within myself. I have made myself to be silent.

In this context, the statement "fullness of silence" is referring to complete silence. This means that thoughts have stopped, or the mind is experiencing one-pointedness such that the usual pattern of thought waves has become one wave which means the mind is also not moving by this method of maintaining a single thought that the mind is experiencing continuously from moment to moment. In this way of experiencing a mind that is not moving, fluctuating, vibrating, awareness does not turn attention to those movement and instead can more easily be aware of itself. This self-awareness of awareness/consciousness allows the personality to discover its Ab Neter/Neberdjer nature which is the consciousness that supports mind and its operations. In an advanced context, philosophically this silence can also mean the silence of mind that is operative and cognizing but is not shaken by negative aryu such that it remains aware of its soul-aware-witness-self, has full control in the form of ethical-conscience and is not troubled by the negative aryu.

Building upon the witness recognition from the Quick Recognition practice, we now practice what Amenemopet prescribes: maintaining deliberate awareness of Neberdjer, the all-encompassing consciousness that underlies all phenomena. This is achieved by practicing sustaining "fullness of silence." Fullness means complete and silence means cessation of thinking which includes thoughts about one's ego identity, what has to be done tomorrow, what is your given name, what gender you are, what has to be done within the next hour, etc. In that silence, otherwise referred to as anrutef (state of awareness without cognition), a person is able to spend a period of experience away from mental operations, to experience the background of consciousness.

The state of anrutef is associated with *awut* -joyousness (happiness) Ancient Egyptian Book of Enlightenment Chapter 175 Appendix) because it is a place of freedom from the fragmentation of mind; it is a place of experiencing deep relaxation and peace. Within that background of consciousness is the unconscious and within that is the Ab Neter (soul). Spending time in these periods allows the person's conscious-awareness to experience itself without mental references and to realize its existence apart from the mental references (hat-conscious, ka-subconscious, ab-unconscious, aryu [karmic memories and impetuses] and a [ego identity]). This allows the person to realize their true identity as the Ab Neter/Neberdjer self, terminating delusions.

Sitting in the witness position you discovered in the Quick Recognition practice, begin reflecting: "What is it that knows this witnessing awareness exists? What is aware of awareness itself?" This inquiry directs attention beyond the Soul-Aware-Witness-Self toward its source.

The wisdom teachings reveal that this requires a mind sufficiently purified from dense aryu. If the mind remains heavily agitated by unethical behavior, anxious thoughts, or reactive feelings, it cannot sustain the subtle attention necessary for this deeper recognition. Therefore, this stage presumes you have undertaken ethical living (Maat) and preliminary purification practices.

When the mind has achieved sufficient calm through right living, practice resting in awareness without directing it toward any particular object—neither physical objects, nor mental images, nor even thoughts about awareness. Simply remain as awareness itself, recognizing that this witnessing capacity that you are is sustained by something deeper still.

Initially, this resting occurs in brief glimpses. The ancient sages taught that with patient practice, these moments extend and deepen. Aryu patterns gradually thin. The mind eventually develops the capacity to remain in what the scriptures call kara—the deep sanctuary where Ab Neter resides.

In this deepening awareness, you begin recognizing that the consciousness sustaining your capacity to witness is not separate from Neberdjer, the all-encompassing consciousness that Amenemopet describes as underlying "mind and time and space." When this recognition stabilizes, what was witnessed (objects), what was witnessing (Soul-Aware-Witness-Self), and the source of witnessing (Ab Neter/Neberdjer) are known as one undifferentiated reality.

Practice Guidance: Engage the Quick Recognition practice until witness recognition becomes stable and can be accessed readily during daily activities. Only then undertake this deeper inquiry into the Ab Neter source. Remember that this is not about forcing an experience but about removing the aryu obstructions that hide the Ab Neter awareness already present within you.

PART 3: SYSTEMATIC PROGRESSIVE DEVELOPMENT

The foundational practices of discovering the Soul-Aware-Witness-Self and deepening toward Ab Neter recognition provide essential entry points. For aspirants seeking comprehensive development, this presentation offers a systematic six-stage progression that builds capacity from basic concentration through absorption states.

Important Understanding: The Quick Recognition practice allows initial discovery of the Soul-Aware-Witness-Self within minutes—this is a profound insight. However, stabilizing this recognition and deepening it to reliable Ab Neter discovery requires systematic practice over months and years.

Research demonstrates that advanced absorption states typically develop after several years of consistent practice, though individual variation is significant based on aryu density, practice quality, and ethical purification level.

Stage I: Focused Attention with Name and Form Using Visual Representation and Audible Hekau Repetition

---

The practice moves from concrete focus to subtle focus, to open monitoring with a conceptual framework, to a powerful method for *dissolving* that framework, and finally to the resulting states of pure witness and non-dual awareness. This is a very strong and logical progression. The practitioner establishes focused attention using external anchors while maintaining both name (mental identifier) and form (visual representation). This stage typically employs eyes-open or softly gazing practice to engage directly with the chosen anchor. Research demonstrates that focused attention (FA) meditation [7,11] using external anchors trains selective attention, suppresses the Default Mode Network associated with mind-wandering, and strengthens prefrontal-parietal control networks.

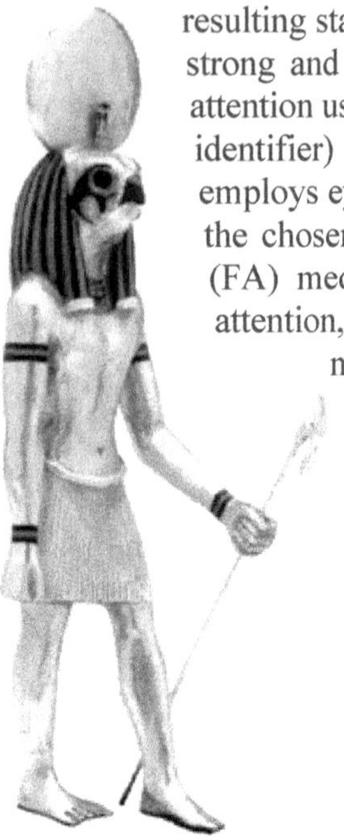

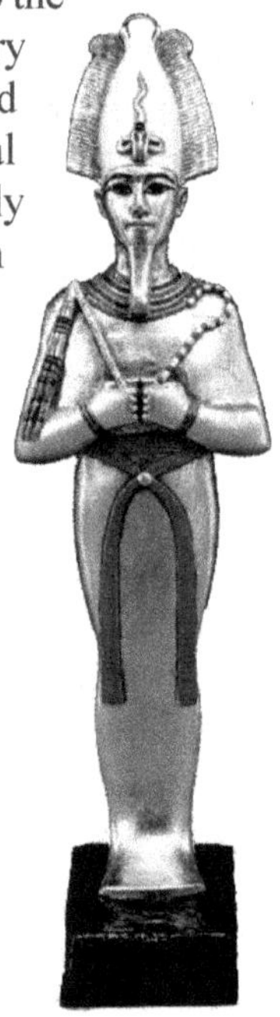

Left: THE GOD RA (Creator Spirit)-aspect of Neberdjer

Right: THE GOD ASAR-Universal Soul -aspect of Neberdjer

The use of Meditation Image with Name and Form and Progressing to Meditation Without Name and Form

Alternative hekau: “Ra” or "Nuk Ra" (I Am Ra) may also be used with the same circular (repetition) invocation method. The choice between Ra / Asar and Neberdjer invocations reflects an important distinction in the tradition: according to the Ancient Egyptian Creation Myth, Ra is a manifestation of Neberdjer with specific name and form, making Ra suitable for visualization practices using images and hieroglyphs. Neberdjer, by contrast, has no representative likeness—because Neberdjer encompasses all existence, it cannot be contained within any particular image or form. This distinction makes Ra invocations especially suitable for beginning practitioners who benefit from concrete visual and auditory anchors. As the mind progresses and develops capacity for more abstract practices, practitioners naturally transition to using the chant and hieroglyphs of Neberdjer, working directly with the all-encompassing reality beyond name and form. Alternatively, the name and image of Asar may be used. After some time of using the images with name and form gauge your capacity to only use the name without form and from there progressing to silence (***anrutef***-state of awareness without cognition) without name or form. The practice without name and form-abstract is more advanced because it approaches the understanding and experience of Neberdjer more closely since Neberdjer is also nameless and formless while encompassing all names and forms.

For this practice you may use the following steps:

With the chosen image on a platform or altar.

1-Make offering of lighting a candle.

2-Make offering of lighting incense

3-with open eyes view the image

4-utter the chosen hekau formula (Ra, Ra, Ra or Nuk Ra, Nuk Ra, Nuk Ra- continuously

5-After some time of practicing 1-4 above such that the mind has been steadies with less wandering, you may practice with closing the eyes periodically and trying to retain the image in mind, then open the eyes periodically to refresh the mental image.

6- continue this practice working towards greater and greater settled serene mind.

Implementation Guidelines:

- Duration: 10-20 minutes daily for beginners
- When distracted, notice the distraction ("thinking") and gently return to the chosen anchor
- Maintain relaxed alertness—avoid straining
- Choose one primary method initially (visual, audible, or breath) rather than alternating
- Eyes may remain open (gazing at hieroglyphs or image of Ra) or softly closed (for breath/sound focus)

Proficiency Indicator: Maintain focus on the chosen anchor for 10-15 minutes with only brief lapses. The mind still wanders but returns quickly without extended mental storytelling.

Key Understanding: This stage trains basic concentration—the capacity to sustain voluntary attention. Without this foundation, subsequent stages become impossible. The external anchors (visible form, audible sound, breath sensation) provide clear focus objects for developing attention control.

Stage II: Subtle Focused Attention with Mental Visualization of Hieroglyphs and/or Mental Repetition of Hekau

Transition to Internalization: Once basic stability develops in Stage I (typically after several weeks to months of consistent practice), the practitioner transitions to subtler practice using mental visualization and silent mental chant. This internalization represents significant progression: awareness no longer depends on gross sensory anchors but operates at the mental level within the hat (conscious awareness).

a. Visual Focus on Sacred Hieroglyphs

Maintain visual attention on the hieroglyphic representation of Neberdjer, allowing the sacred symbols to anchor awareness in present-moment concentration. The ancient sages understood that these visual forms carry vibrational resonance supporting mind transformation.

b. Silent/Mental Hekau (Mantra) - Words of Power Chanting

Begin with audible circular invocation using the pronounced name of Neberdjer. Circular invocation means recurring, cyclical practice of chanting the Divine name or divine name-containing phrase:

- "Neberdjer, Neberdjer, Neberdjer..." (continuous repetition), OR
- "Nuk Neberdjer" [I am All-Encompassing Divinity]

"Nuk Neberdjer, Nuk Neberdjer..." (continuous repetition)

This practice wards off negative aspects of personality that cause slothfulness, inattentiveness, feelings of incapacity, intellectual dullness, and general malaise preventing spiritual progress.

Then move to silent/mental Hekau repetition.

c. Breath Awareness / Neberdjer as Breath

Practice rhythmic breathing while recognizing breath as the movement of life force (sekhem) animated by Neberdjer. With each inhalation, silently note "breath enters"; with each exhalation, "breath departs"—recognizing that what breathes represents not a separate individual but Neberdjer sustaining apparent individuality.

Practice:

- Close eyes to minimize external visual distraction
- Visualize the Neberdjer hieroglyph mentally without external visual support—maintain the mental image
- Silently repeat "Neberdjer," "Nuk Neberdjer," or "Neter Neteru" internally, synchronized with natural breathing rhythm
- When visualization fades or repetition lapses, gently reconstruct without frustration
- Allow the practice to become increasingly effortless—let the mantra repeat itself rather than forcing it

Implementation Guidelines:

- Duration: 10-20 minutes daily
- Practice predominantly with eyes closed to support internal focus
- Reduced reliance on external supports (no audible chanting, no external visual forms)

Proficiency Indicator: Maintain mental visualization with silent repetition for 10-15 minutes without constant reconstruction. The internal image remains relatively stable, requiring only occasional refreshing.

Key Understanding: This stage develops capacity for maintaining attention on internally generated objects—more subtle than external anchors and requiring refined concentration. Many practitioners find this stage challenging initially, as the mind provides no external support for focus. Studies tracking meditation skill development [12] find that practitioners who develop capacity for stable internal mental repetition show enhanced prefrontal-parietal network activation compared to beginners.

Stage III: Open Monitoring with Neberdjer Qualities - Dropping Name and Form

---

Fundamental Shift to Open Awareness: This stage represents a fundamental shift in meditation strategy. Rather than focusing attention on a single object, the practitioner develops wide-open awareness while maintaining conceptual framework based on Neberdjer's qualities. All auditory expression, mental repetition of names/mantras, and visual objects for observation are dropped. Practice occurs with eyes closed.

This is where the practice begins approaching the Soul-Aware-Witness-Self recognition described in the Quick Recognition method—but now with systematic foundation from Stages I-II providing stability.

Practice:

- Release active concentration on specific form or sound
- Maintain open, receptive awareness while keeping Neberdjer's epithets as background framework: "All-Encompassing Existence," "That Which Sustains Creation," "Consciousness Underlying All Phenomena"
- Recognize all phenomena as expressions of Neberdjer's qualities—all-encompassing, all-pervading, infinite, eternal
- When a sound arises, recognize "Neberdjer hearing through this form"
- When a thought appears, note "Neberdjer thinking through this mind"
- When a sensation emerges, acknowledge "Neberdjer experiencing through this body"
- Allow thoughts, sensations, perceptions to arise and pass without engagement
- Maintain equanimity—no suppression, no indulgence

Implementation Guidelines:

- Sit in awareness without focusing on any particular object
- Eyes closed to support internal sensitivity
- No audible chanting, no mental repetition, no visual anchors
- Recognize: "All this is occurring within Neberdjer; nothing exists outside Neberdjer"
- Duration: 10-20 minutes after mastering Stage II

Proficiency Indicator: Rest in open awareness for 10-20 minutes while maintaining the Neberdjer conceptual framework. Thoughts arise without capturing attention into elaboration or storylines.

Key Understanding: This stage transitions from focused attention (Stages I-II) to open monitoring. The epithets provide conceptual structure preventing awareness from collapsing into mere blankness or drowsy dullness. Consciousness begins recognizing itself as aware of mental content (thoughts, feelings, memories, etc.) rather than identified with content. Studies demonstrate that combining focused attention practices [7] with open monitoring produces stronger overall regulation of thought intrusion than either approach alone.

STAGE IV PRACTICE: Hermetic Wisdom-Meditation: Dissolution of the Neberdjer Qualities by Dissolving Dualities Through Paradox

Prerequisites: Stable proficiency in basic Stage III epithet practice. This advanced method should not be attempted until basic Stage III recognition can be sustained without constant mental effort.

Historical Context: The following teaching comes from the Greco-Egyptian Hermetic tradition (circa 2nd-3rd century CE), which synthesizes Ancient Egyptian wisdom with Hellenistic mystical philosophy. While not from the purely Ancient Egyptian period, this text preserves and amplifies core Egyptian understanding of divine consciousness—particularly the concept of Neberdjer as "Lord to the Limit," the all-encompassing reality beyond all boundaries.

The Hermetic Teaching on Divine Omnipresence:

> "To Know God, strive to grow in stature beyond all measure; conceive that there is nothing beyond thy capability. Know thyself deathless and able to know all things, all arts, sciences, the way of every life. Become higher than the highest height and lower than the lowest depth. Amass in thyself all senses of animals, fire, water, dryness and moistness. Think of thyself in all places at the same time, earth, sea, sky, not yet born, in the womb, young, old, dead, and in the after-death state."
>
> — Corpus Hermeticum (Libellus XI)

CRITICAL UNDERSTANDING: This Is Wisdom-Meditation Leading to Silence

This Hermetic teaching functions as a wisdom-based method for achieving ger (silence/stillness)—the same state of mental quietude that Amenemopet describes as "fullness of silence" (anrutef). The teaching works by systematically presenting irreconcilable opposites to the dualistic mind:

- "Higher than the highest height AND lower than the lowest depth"
- "Fire AND water" (elemental opposites)
- "Not yet born AND dead" (temporal opposites)
- "All places at the same time" (spatial impossibility)

When the mind attempts to hold these paradoxes simultaneously, the opposites cancel each other out. The dualistic thinking mechanism—which operates by categorizing reality into either/or distinctions—cannot process "both highest AND lowest." Confronted with this impossibility, the conceptual mind exhausts itself and falls silent.

PRACTICE METHOD: From Contemplation to Dissolution

Session Structure (20-30 minutes):

Phase 1: Establishing Witness Awareness (3-5 minutes)

- Begin with basic Stage III open awareness
- Stabilize witness consciousness
- Eyes closed to support internal focus

Phase 2: Guided Wisdom-Meditation (10-15 minutes)

Work through the following contemplations sequentially, allowing each to reach natural resolution before proceeding. The goal is not prolonged thinking but allowing each paradox to neutralize dualistic mind.

A. Beyond Measurement

Contemplate: "If there is no measure, no boundary, no limit—what remains?"

Allow the mind to recognize: All categories of "big/small," "sufficient/insufficient" are dualistic constructs. When these opposites cancel each other out, what remains is the measureless reality that precedes categorization.

Do not continue thinking about this. Allow your understanding to let you accept this is as the conclusion of cognition, there is nothing else to think about or figure out. Allow the recognition to settle. Rest in that gap. Allow the recognition to settle. Rest in that gap.

Duration: 2-3 minutes, then release

B. The Collapse of Spatial Duality

Contemplate: "If consciousness is simultaneously higher than the highest AND lower than the lowest, it is neither high nor low—these categories dissolve."

What remains when neither "high" nor "low" defines reality?

Do not answer conceptually. Simply rest in the dissolution of the high/low duality.

Duration: 2-3 minutes, then release

C. Elemental Opposites Unified

Contemplate: "Fire and water destroy each other in physical reality. Yet both exist within Neberdjer."

Present the mind with: All opposites unified. Hot and cold, wet and dry, hard and soft—not as separate states but as one consciousness appearing as apparent multiplicity.

Rest in the exhaustion. Do not try to figure out how opposites can coexist.

Duration: 2-3 minutes, then release

D. Omnipresence: The Collapse of Location

Contemplate: "To be 'here' means not being 'there'—this is dualistic thinking. But if consciousness is in all places simultaneously, the entire concept of location dissolves."

Rest in the location-less awareness that emerges when spatial categories cease operating.

Duration: 2-3 minutes, then release

E. Temporal Opposites Transcended

Contemplate: "This awareness—was it born? Will it die?"

When the mind recognizes that none of these temporal distinctions define consciousness, its time-based categorization falls away.

Rest in the timeless presence that remains when past/present/future distinctions dissolve.

Duration: 3-4 minutes, then release

Phase 3: Resting in Ger (Fullness of Silence) (7-10 minutes)

Release all contemplations completely. The wisdom-meditation has served its purpose—the opposites have cancelled each other, and dualistic thinking has exhausted itself.

Now simply rest in the thoughtless awareness that remains. This is ger—the silence Amenemopet teaches. This is anrutef—awareness without cognition.

Key: Do not continue ruminating on the teachings. Simply rest as awareness itself. If thoughts arise, note them as "thinking" and return to resting in silence—the same instruction given in the core Stage III practice.

Implementation Guidelines:

Critical Distinction: This Is NOT Philosophical Analysis. The most common error is treating this as extended intellectual contemplation. The teachings are wisdom tools for dissolving dualistic thinking, not subjects for philosophical investigation.

Signs you're practicing correctly:

- Each contemplation leads to a natural pause where thinking ceases
- Opposites recognized as cancelling each other produce relief rather than confusion
- Phase 3 silence feels spacious and restful rather than blank or agitated

Signs you're ruminating instead of practicing:

- Continuously thinking about the teachings without reaching "resolution"
- Trying to intellectually "figure out" how paradoxes work
- Phase 3 filled with mental activity rather than silence

Understanding the term "Resolution" in the practice of the wisdom-meditation:

When the instructions refer to "reaching resolution," this does NOT mean arriving at a mental answer or philosophical conclusion. Rather, resolution means the **cessation of thinking itself**. The philosophical resolution achieved through these wisdom reflection-meditation exercises is for the mind and thinking process to cease—to be extinguished—by allowing the paradoxes and opposites to cancel each other out, leaving nothing, no-thingness. The contemplation stops evoking self as a subject and objects to think about or solve.

The crucial understanding is this: there is no mental solution because the mind is limited and incapable of resolving these ultimate paradoxes. Even if there were a mental solution to be found, that is not what this practice seeks. The resolution occurs when dualistic thinking reaches its natural limit and exhausts itself, revealing the silent awareness that underlies all mental activity.

Frequency: Practice 1-2 times weekly once basic Stage III has stabilized. This supplements rather than replaces basic Stage III practice.

Proficiency Indicators: You have achieved proficiency when each contemplation naturally concludes in a pause where dualistic thinking ceases, and Phase 3 silence is sustained (5+ minutes) with minimal thought intrusion.

Key Understanding: This Hermetic teaching takes the mundane and oppositional dualistic perspectives of mind and resolves them into a wisdom-devotional point of one-pointed experience. The "one-pointed experience" is not concentration on a single object but rather consciousness recognizing its non-dual nature—the point where all opposites cancel and only Neberdjer remains.

Stage V: Open Monitoring with Abstract Awareness with Individuation - Dropping Epithets/Qualities

---

Reducing Conceptual Overlay - Awareness Without Cognition: Deepen practice by dropping even the conceptual framework of "Neberdjer's qualities." Rather than labeling phenomena as "Neberdjer's expressions," simply rest in awareness of phenomena arising and passing. The sense of individual observer remains ("I am aware") but with minimal mental commentary. This represents awareness without much cognition—present to what is without constantly naming, categorizing, or conceptualizing.

This stage fully embodies what the Quick Recognition method identifies as Soul-Aware-Witness-Self—the awareness that observes mental and sensory contents without identifying with them, maintaining clear sense of observer distinct from observed.

Practice:

- Release Neberdjer epithets and qualitative descriptions
- Maintain awareness itself without conceptual support, while the sense of an individual observer remains
- Rest in witness consciousness—the awareness observing mental and sensory contents
- Simply observe: sounds arise and pass, thoughts emerge and dissolve, sensations appear and disappear
- The observer witnesses experience with minimal mental interference

Proficiency Indicator: Sustain witness consciousness for 15-30 minutes. Clear sense of observer distinct from observed content. Minimal mental commentary about experience.

Key Understanding: This stage develops pure witness consciousness—awareness recognizing its capacity to observe without being identical to observed content. This represents a crucial recognition that consciousness is not the thoughts, emotions, or sensations it observes. Research on advanced meditators shows progressive reduction [8,12] in self-referential processing as practice deepens, with neural activity shifting from conceptual processing regions toward networks supporting pure awareness with minimal cognitive elaboration.

Stage VI: Non-Dual Awareness - Individuation Falling Away

This stage begins the transition from Soul-Aware-Witness-Self toward Ab Neter recognition, as described in the Deepening practice. The sense of separate observer begins dissolving into recognition of consciousness as fundamental presence.

Practice:

Allow even the sense of individual observer to dissolve. Rest in awareness where subject-object distinction softens. No "I" observing phenomena—rather, awareness aware of itself with phenomena appearing within it. This cannot be forced but emerges naturally when Stage IV proficiency deepens.

Proficiency Indicator: Periods (initially brief, 2-5 minutes) where consciousness recognizes itself as fundamental presence rather than individual observer. Distinction between awareness and contents blurs without becoming mere dullness.

Key Understanding: This stage approaches Ab Neter recognition—consciousness beginning to know itself as sustained by Neberdjer rather than as separate individual awareness observing external reality. Traditional descriptions often use paradoxical language because this awareness transcends the subject-object duality that ordinary consciousness assumes. Studies of advanced practitioners display altered Default Mode Network connectivity [8], with reduced coupling between regions supporting self-referential thinking—the neural signature corresponding to experiential shift toward awareness recognizing itself as fundamental presence.

========

CROSS-REFERENCE: AMENEMOPET'S EXPLICIT TEACHING ON RESTING IN THE UNCONSCIOUS

The advanced stages presented here—particularly Stage IV (Abstract Awareness), Stage V (Non-Dual Awareness), and Stage VI (Absorption States)—correspond directly to what Sage Amenemopet explicitly describes in Chapter 15, verses 15-16. In these profound verses, Amenemopet instructs the aspirant regarding "resting in your heart (unconscious) level of your mind, that is, by spending time meditating, at rest-relaxed, and not restless-agitated, in your unconscious and not always spending time in the Ka (subconscious) and Hat (conscious) level of mind."

This instruction identifies precisely the capacity these advanced stages develop: the mind's ability to withdraw from constant Hat-Ka surface operations—the perpetual engagement with thoughts, feelings, desires, and reactions that occupies most human existence—to rest in the deeper ab/kara levels where Ab Neter resides, and authentic selfhood can be discovered. Verse 15 describes not a separate practice but rather the mature fruition of the systematic training this chapter presents.

Furthermore, verse 16 establishes the profound teaching about cultural transmission through observable modeling: "when the children see this, they will see that there is a human capacity for and practice of being internalized and serene in one's unconscious level of experience." This reveals that Ancient Egyptian spiritual culture transmitted contemplative capacity not only through verbal instruction but through children witnessing adults regularly spending time in visible states of deep internalized serenity—modeling that consciousness possesses this capacity as normal human function rather than exotic spiritual attainment.

Chapter 20 of this manuscript provides comprehensive commentary on Amenemopet Chapter 15, exploring how verses 15-16 describe the mature expression of Sau Neberdjer practice and revealing the profound connection between this meditative capacity and recovery of authentic selfhood versus the fraudulent persona that verse 5 identifies. Aspirants who have established foundation through the practices presented in this chapter will benefit from studying that commentary (particularly Part B: Methods for Transformation) to deepen understanding of what "resting in the unconscious" specifically entails according to Amenemopet's explicit instruction, how this capacity relates to ethical purification and discovery of authentic selfhood, and how to implement verse 16's teaching about practicing visibly for cultural transmission.

ADVANCED UNDERSTANDING: NON-EGOISTIC MENTAL ACTIVITY

As Stage V proficiency deepens, some practitioners discover that the mind can recognize its fundamental nature even while thoughts continue to arise, provided those thoughts are no longer egoistic in nature. The problem is not thinking itself but egoistic thinking and identification of self with the thoughts and feelings. Mental silence remains the primary path because it most reliably removes the egoistic overlay that obscures consciousness recognition.

Key Understanding: However, as purification deepens, practitioners may find that the mind maintains its recognition of itself as fundamental presence even when thoughts move through awareness—because those thoughts no longer carry the egoistic charge that creates identification.

Practical Indicator: Thoughts arise but you remain established in witnessing awareness without effort; mental content appears "transparent"—seen clearly but not creating disturbance; the sense of "I am thinking" dissolves into recognition that "thinking is occurring within awareness."

Important Caution: Do not prematurely assume your thoughts are non-egoistic. The ego cleverly disguises itself, claiming spiritual advancement while still serving self-interest. True non-egoistic thought arises from deep purification through ethical living (Maat), not from intellectual understanding. The authentic test: such thoughts leave no residue of self-importance, anxiety about outcomes, or need for recognition. Therefore, even if a practitioner does think they have achieved non-egoistic states it is advised that they should not cease following the ethical and philosophical guidelines to ensure their achievements are sound and not illusory, permanent and not transient or provisional.

Absorption States

This represents the fullest expression of what Amenemopet describes as "fullness of silence" finding the practitioner—deep absorption in Ab Neter recognition where consciousness rests in its source.

Practice:

From Stage V base, allow awareness to settle into profound absorption where even subtle mental activity ceases. The mind rests in a unified state characterized by deep stillness, joy, and absorption in being itself. Eyes typically closed. This stage requires high ethical purification and cannot be forced—it arises naturally from sufficient Stage V stability.

Proficiency Indicator: Access to sustained absorption periods (20+ minutes) marked by: absence of discursive thinking, profound stillness without drowsiness, subtle joy or deep peace, minimal sense of time passage.

Key Understanding: This stage represents temporary direct experience of what the tradition identifies as Ab Neter recognizing its nature as Neberdjer. The absorption states provide glimpses of mind liberated from aryu density, demonstrating what becomes permanent state when purification completes. Recent research directly examining jhāna states [10] demonstrates that expert practitioners achieving deep absorption show sustained high-frequency gamma oscillations, theta-gamma coupling, and marked reduction in Default Mode Network activity—neural signatures validating these as genuine mind/personality transformation.

TIMELINE CONSIDERATIONS FOR SYSTEMATIC PROGRESSION

Understanding realistic timelines prevents discouragement while establishing appropriate expectations. Research converging with traditional wisdom reveals [11,12]:

Basic Concentration (Stages I-II): 2-6 months of consistent daily practice (20-30 minutes) to develop stable basic concentration.

Intermediate Awareness (Stages III-IV): 6-18 months of regular practice for developing capacity to maintain refined awareness. This is the period where Soul-Aware-Witness-Self recognition stabilizes.

Advanced Absorption (Stages V-VI): 2-5 years of consistent practice for achieving reliable access to absorption states, though some practitioners progress more rapidly based on practice intensity and ethical purification level.

The Quality-Duration Equation: Transformation depends upon both quality of practice (skill-based proficiency) and cumulative duration, with quality often mattering more than mere time accumulation. Thirty minutes of deeply absorbed, skillful practice produces greater transformation than two hours of distracted, mechanical repetition.

Individual Variation and Aryu Density: Timeline variation reflects aryu density (accumulated karmic patterns). Aspirants with calmer minds, ethical lifestyles, and less dense aryu patterns progress more rapidly. Those carrying heavy psychological burdens require extended purification before advanced stages become accessible.

Stage Progression Guidelines:

Do not skip stages: Each stage builds capacity necessary for subsequent practices. Attempting advanced stages prematurely produces frustration and discouragement.

Proficiency before progression: Establish clear proficiency in current stage before advancing.

Flexible practice: After establishing Stage III+ proficiency, individual sessions may include multiple stages: Ex-begin with Stage I or II for establishing concentration (5-10 minutes), transition to higher stage for main practice (15-25 minutes).

Patient development: Trust the process rather than comparing to others' progress. Some progress more rapidly; others require extended time. Both are valid paths.

PART 4: PRACTICAL IMPLEMENTATION GUIDANCE

Eyes-Open Versus Eyes-Closed Practice: Strategic Applications

Research reveals that eyes-open versus eyes-closed [14] conditions produce distinct neural patterns with implications for meditation practice progression:

Eyes Closed: Promotes internal focus by reducing external sensory input. Alpha power increases, and attention naturally turns inward. However, this can also increase drowsiness and mind-wandering in beginners.

Eyes Open: Maintains arousal and attentional engagement while preventing drowsiness. Visual input stimulates occipital regions, supporting alertness. Advanced meditators maintain internal focus even with eyes open.

Stage-Appropriate Eye Positioning:

Stages I-II: Eyes open when using visual anchors supports concentration development. The external visual stimulus provides a clear focus object preventing mind-wandering.

Stages III-V: Eyes half-closed or soft downward gaze balances external awareness with internal attention, preventing excessive drowsiness while supporting refined awareness.

Stage VI: Eyes closed reduces external sensory input, facilitating profound internal absorption. At this advanced level, drowsiness no longer presents an obstacle.

Recognizing and Working with Common Obstacles

Drowsiness During Practice:

- Indicates: Insufficient arousal or dull mental state
- Solutions: Practice with eyes open, stand during meditation, practice earlier in day when more alert, shorten sessions temporarily

Excessive Mental Agitation:

- Indicates: Aryu density too high for current stage
- Solutions: Return to earlier stage temporarily, increase ethical purification emphasis, reduce stimulating inputs (media, conflicts, intoxicants)

Rapid Progress Then Plateau:

- Indicates: Natural consolidation period
- Solutions: Maintain consistent practice without frustration, recognize plateau as integration time rather than failure, review ethical purification

Spiritual Pride About Progress:

- Indicates: Ego co-opting practice for self-inflation
- Solutions: Remember practice removes obstruction rather than creating special status, serve others humbly, maintain beginner's mind attitude

---

Adjusting Practice Based on Life Circumstances

High Stress Periods:

- Emphasize: Somatic preparation, breathing practices, shorter more frequent sessions
- Reduce: Advanced stages requiring subtle awareness (temporarily return to Stages I-II)

Low Energy/Illness:

- Emphasize: Philosophical contemplation, gentle informal practice
- Reduce: Formal sitting duration (maintain consistency with shorter sessions)

Life Transitions:

- Emphasize: Awareness triggers recognizing Neberdjer in challenging circumstances
- Maintain: Basic formal practice consistency even if shortened

---

THE CHALLENGE OF MENTAL CROWDING AND SAU NEBERDJER PRACTICE

Amenemopet Chapter 21, verses 15-16's teaching:

21:15.3 [It would be a glorifying thing, a spiritually uplifting thing, to make my personality to be like a personality that keeps things in his/her belly, within the skin (i.e. inside the body)...
21:16.3...as opposed to letting that kind of speech come out of the body for causing harm purposely or speech that would cause unnecessary harm.

The implementation of Wisdom of Amenemopet Chapter 21, verses 15-16's teaching reveals a profound challenge facing contemporary aspirants: the mind has become so densely crowded with thoughts that sustained concentration on a single focus proves exceedingly difficult. This mental crowding creates a significant obstacle to sau Neberdjer practice—the deliberate maintenance of awareness regarding Neberdjer as taught in Chapter 6B verse 14. Consider how this operates: when an aspirant attempts to settle the mind for dedicated concentration on Neberdjer, thoughts arise continuously and compulsively, occupying presence-of-mind awareness so densely that sustained single-pointed focus becomes virtually impossible [1].

This phenomenon reflects the accumulated aryu density from years—often decades—of living according to heated patterns that continuously stimulate mental activity. The extroverted lifestyle verse

15 describes, characterized by constant talking and sharing of thoughts and feelings, deposits aryu in the ab that maintain a mind perpetually agitated with verbal content, commentary, planning, and reactive thoughts [2]. Similarly, the heated pursuit of achievements verse 17 cautions against creates aryu patterns of anxious mental rehearsal, compulsive planning, and fevered strategizing that keep consciousness perpetually occupied with future-oriented thinking [2]. The cumulative effect produces what might be termed "mental static"—a continuous background noise of thinking that prevents the deep silence necessary for penetrating from hat awareness to the kara where Ab Neter resides.

The practical consequence proves spiritually devastating: an aspirant may intellectually understand the teaching about maintaining awareness of Neberdjer, may desire to practice sau Neberdjer meditation, yet when attempting to implement this practice discovers the mind cannot maintain concentration for even brief periods. Within moments of settling to contemplate Neberdjer, thoughts arise—memories of yesterday's conversations, plans for tomorrow's tasks, concerns about relationships, judgments about others, evaluations of self, desires for various outcomes. These thoughts do not arise occasionally, allowing space between them for Neberdjer awareness; rather, they arise in rapid succession, creating such continuous mental activity that the intended focus on Neberdjer gets lost entirely beneath the compulsive thinking [1].

This reveals the essential connection between verses 15-17's behavioral teachings and the ultimate spiritual goal: the life according to ger (silent) practice, supported by Maat ethics, functions as the necessary purification creating the conditions whereby sau Neberdjer practice becomes possible. Speech discipline—maintaining judicious reserve, avoiding harmful words, conserving verbal expression—directly thins the aryu patterns generating compulsive verbal thinking. When the mind ceases constantly expressing thoughts externally through speech, the internal verbal activity gradually diminishes as well, creating increasing capacity for mental silence [2]. The mind that has developed the habit of restraint in external speech naturally develops greater capacity for internal quiet.

Similarly, releasing fevered achievement-grasping thins the aryu patterns of anxious future-planning and compulsive strategizing that occupy consciousness with endless scenarios and calculations. When the mind ceases attempting to control outcomes through heated mental manipulation, space opens for the present-moment awareness necessary for recognizing Neberdjer. The aspirant discovers that contentment with divine orchestration—accepting that "Neberdjer orchestrates circumstances according to divine plan beyond my comprehension"—eliminates the fevered mental activity attempting to determine how events should unfold, creating the mental quiet wherein sustained concentration becomes possible [2].

Practical Implementation: Progressive Purification Supporting Sau Neberdjer Practice

The wisdom to be understood recognizes that sau Neberdjer practice (maintaining awareness of Neberdjer) cannot be forced through willpower when aryu density creates compulsive mental crowding. Instead, implement systematic purification through the behavioral methods verses 15-17 prescribe, allowing mental clarity to emerge gradually as the foundation for deeper contemplative practice.

Begin with speech discipline as the most accessible entry point. For two weeks, practice the judicious reserve verse 15 teaches: refrain from unnecessary speech, particularly casual social commentary, complaints, excessive explanations, and habitual sharing of thoughts and feelings. Notice the tangible reduction in internal verbal activity that emerges—when the mind ceases constantly formulating words for external expression, the mind naturally quiets internally. This creates brief moments of mental silence wherein sau Neberdjer practice becomes possible, even if only for seconds initially [1][2].

A particularly effective refinement of this speech discipline involves practicing non-initiated conversation engagement. This means refraining from starting conversations out of uncomfortable silence or compulsive need for verbal interaction when communication is not genuinely necessary. Instead, converse only when another initiate's dialogue, and even then, remain concise—staying precisely on point with only what is necessary to meet the actual needs of the conversation, then returning to silence. This practice proves remarkably powerful for reducing the animus to be talking constantly, promoting internal relaxation and developing comfort with being present with oneself rather than requiring continuous external verbal stimulation [1][2].

The initial period of implementing this practice typically feels uncomfortable, even anxiety-producing, as the mind encounters its learned habit, the compulsive need for conversational engagement. Someone accustomed to initiating social interactions to fill silence, sharing observations and thoughts habitually, or maintaining continuous verbal connection with others will likely experience internal pressure to speak, awkwardness in social situations, and discomfort with the quiet that emerges. Nevertheless, this discomfort itself reveals the depth of verbal aryu conditioning—the degree to which consciousness has become dependent on external speech for maintaining a sense of presence and connection [1][2].

After the beginning uncomfortable period—usually 2-4 weeks of consistent practice—the mind begins discovering a different quality of presence. The internal relaxation emerging from not constantly formulating conversational content creates tangible mental spaciousness. The aspirant discovers they can be with others without requiring verbal exchange, can observe situations without compulsive commentary, can attend meetings or social gatherings maintaining receptive presence without initiating unnecessary dialogue. This promotes genuine thoughtfulness rather than reactive verbal output, as the mind learns to pause, reflect, and speak only when speech serves beneficial purposes [1][2].

Significantly, this practice directly addresses what neuroscience terms the "default mode network"—the brain's automatic background activity characterized by mind-wandering, self-referential thinking, and continuous internal dialogue [15]. When the mind habitually initiates conversations, this reinforces and strengthens the default mode network's perpetual verbal activity, keeping the mind crowded with speech-related thoughts even during supposedly quiet moments. The constant engagement of conversational planning—thinking about what to say, how others might respond, what one will say next—pumps thought-speech content continuously through consciousness, much of it unnecessary or harmful, clogging the ab with useless or dangerous aryu that obstruct penetration toward kara where Ab Neter resides [1][2][15].

Conversely, the practice of non-initiated conversation engagement systematically weakens these automatic verbal patterns. When the mind ceases habitually generating conversational content, the default mode network's continuous speech-related activity gradually quiets. The mind discovers it can exist without constant verbal formulation, can observe without commentary, can be present without speech. This thinning of verbal aryu creates the mental clarity necessary for sau Neberdjer practice—the capacity to maintain sustained awareness of Neberdjer rather than being perpetually occupied with compulsive thinking and speech-related mental activity [1][2][15].

Simultaneously, practice of verse 17's release of fevered achievement-grasping through daily reflection periods examining where anxious control-seeking occupies consciousness. Each evening, review the day's activities noting instances of compulsive planning, anxious rehearsal of future scenarios, or heated strategizing about outcomes. Then consciously practice releasing these patterns: "These mental activities represent aryu-driven attempts to control what Neberdjer orchestrates according to wisdom exceeding my comprehension. I release this fevered grasping, allowing tomorrow to unfold as it needs to." This systematic release gradually thins the aryu patterns generating future-oriented thinking, creating increasing capacity for present-moment awareness [2].

As these purification practices create initial mental clearing—typically becoming noticeable after 3-4 weeks of consistent implementation—begin formal sau Neberdjer practice in brief sessions. Dedicate 5-10 minutes daily to sitting quietly with the single intention of maintaining awareness of Neberdjer as the all-encompassing existence underlying limited mind perceptions [1]. When thoughts arise (which they inevitably will given remaining aryu density), recognize these as the aryu patterns requiring further thinning rather than as personal failure. Simply return attention to Neberdjer awareness without judgment or frustration, understanding that each return strengthens the capacity for sustained concentration while each moment of Neberdjer awareness begins depositing purifying aryu that gradually thin the compulsive thinking patterns [1].

The profound wisdom Amenemopet reveals through this integrated approach recognizes that purity of heart (mind) directly determines contemplative capacity. The mind crowded with worldly aryu from heated speech patterns, fevered achievement-grasping, and constant external focus cannot sustain the concentrated awareness necessary for discovering Ab Neter and recognizing Neberdjer. However, as Maat-based living progressively purifies these patterns—through speech discipline creating verbal quiet, through release of control-seeking creating mental calm, through ethical conduct depositing righteous aryu—the mind naturally develops increasing capacity for sustained concentration. This transforms sau Neberdjer practice from frustrating struggle with compulsive thinking into progressively deepening absorption wherein consciousness penetrates from hat awareness occupied with mental content, through the aryu-laden ab, toward the kara where Ab Neter resides [1][2].

Consider the aspirant who initially could maintain Neberdjer awareness for only 10-15 seconds before compulsive thoughts arose. After three months of consistent speech discipline and release of fevered grasping, combined with brief daily sau Neberdjer sessions, this same aspirant discovers the capacity for 2-3 minutes of sustained concentration. After six months, periods of 5-10 minutes become possible. After a year or more of patient, consistent practice, the mind develops sufficient clarity that extended contemplation—20, 30, even 60 minutes—emerges naturally as aryu density thins to the point where consciousness can rest in Neberdjer awareness without being continuously pulled into compulsive thinking [1].

This progressive development serves both Prologue goals directly: the mental peace emerging from thinned aryu density provides the earthly well-being verse 2 describes as essential for handling worldly affairs; the capacity for sustained Neberdjer awareness creates the conditions for discovering the kara where divinity resides (verse 9). The teaching reveals that these goals prove inseparable—one cannot discover the divine sanctuary within while consciousness remains crowded with the heated mental activity generated by unrestrained speech, fevered achievement-grasping, and ethical violations. The path requires patient, systematic purification through the behavioral methods Amenemopet prescribes, creating the mental clarity wherein sau Neberdjer practice transitions from impossible aspiration to achievable reality, ultimately enabling the discovery of Ab Neter and recognition of one's essential nature as Neberdjer—the very consciousness sustaining all apparent individual awareness.

PART 5: RESEARCH VALIDATION

Contemporary neuroscience provides remarkable validation for what the ancient sages discovered through millennia of contemplative practice. The following research demonstrates measurable changes in brain function corresponding to each practice stage, confirming that systematic practice produces genuine transformation at the neural architecture level.

Ethical Living Foundation

Chronic stress from unethical living elevates cortisol, activates inflammatory pathways, and maintains heightened Default Mode Network (DMN) activity—the neural signature of rumination and self-referential thinking that corresponds to dense aryu patterns. Conversely, ethical conduct reduces chronic stress markers, supporting the physiological calm necessary for attention to settle inward.

Focused Attention Research (Stages I-II)

Research published in PNAS [11] and systematically reviewed in Frontiers in Human Neuroscience [7] demonstrates that focused attention meditation using external anchors trains selective attention, suppresses the Default Mode Network associated with mind-wandering, and strengthens prefrontal-parietal control networks. Expert meditators display sustained high gamma synchrony during deep FA states, indicating enhanced neural coordination supporting stable attention. Studies on mantra repetition show reduced DMN activity and increased coherence across frontal midline regions.

Internalized Focus Research (Stage II)

Studies tracking meditation skill development [12] find that practitioners who develop capacity for stable internal mental repetition show enhanced prefrontal-parietal network activation compared to beginners, reflecting the mind's developing capacity to maintain attention on internally generated objects rather than requiring external support.

Open Monitoring Research (Stages III-V)

Studies in NeuroImage [10,14] demonstrate that open monitoring activates the anterior cingulate and insula, enhancing moment-to-moment monitoring while decreasing emotional reactivity. Meta-analyses reveal that combining focused attention practices with open monitoring produces stronger overall regulation of thought intrusion than either approach alone, validating the Sau-Neberdjer progression. Research on advanced meditators shows progressive reduction in self-referential processing as practice deepens, with neural activity shifting from conceptual processing regions toward networks supporting pure awareness with minimal cognitive elaboration—corresponding to the Soul-Aware-Witness-Self recognition and progression toward Ab Neter discovery.

Absorption States Research (Stage VI)

A 2025 multimodal neurophenomenology study published in NeuroImage [10] examined expert practitioners achieving deep absorption states, demonstrating:

- Sustained High Gamma Activity: Continuous high-frequency gamma oscillations (>60 Hz) throughout extended absorption periods, indicating heightened neural synchrony and integration
- Theta-Gamma Coupling: Strong coupling between slow theta rhythms and fast gamma oscillations, suggesting integration of large-scale neural networks

- Reduced Alpha Power: Significant decrease in alpha-band activity during deep absorption, indicating active engagement rather than passive quietude
- Default Mode Network Suppression: Marked reduction in DMN activity during absorption states, corresponding to practitioners' reports of minimal self-referential thinking

These neural findings validate the tradition's descriptions of Stage VI as qualitatively distinct from earlier meditation stages—representing a shift in consciousness toward unity experience rather than the observer-observed duality that characterizes preceding stages. The research demonstrates that repeated absorption practice produces lasting neural changes, supporting the tradition's teaching that Stage VI practice creates profound transformation at the mind architecture level.

Timeline Research

Studies of long-term meditators with 10,000-50,000 lifetime hours [11] demonstrate unprecedented gamma-band brain oscillations and sustained baseline changes, validating that the goal of practice involves transforming baseline consciousness itself rather than merely producing temporary altered states. Buddhist practitioners with approximately 10,000+ hours show that the distinction between formal meditation and everyday life diminishes as consciousness stabilizes in recognition of its nature.

These empirical findings provide contemporary validation for the ancient understanding that systematic practice following proper methodology produces measurable, lasting transformation—confirming that what Sage Amenemopet taught represents genuine spiritual technology rather than mere philosophical speculation.

CONCLUSION: THE PATH FORWARD

The practice of Sau-Neberdjer meditation offers a complete path from initial discovery of the Soul-Aware-Witness-Self through deepening recognition of Ab Neter to ultimate realization of Neberdjer as the source and nature of all consciousness. The Quick Recognition method provides accessible entry—allowing practitioners to discover witnessing awareness within minutes. From this foundation, systematic development through progressive stages supports long-term transformation.

The key understanding throughout this journey: transformation occurs through removing aryu obstructions rather than creating something absent. Ab Neter already sustains consciousness from within kara; Neberdjer already encompasses all existence. The practice systematically thins the density of accumulated patterns that obscure this ever-present reality, allowing consciousness to recognize its true nature.

As Sage Amenemopet teaches: "If this awareness is maintained, there will be no egoism and no mind and therefore no fears, frustrations, inordinate desires, no need for stealing, lying, cheating or becoming a heated person." This represents the natural result when consciousness recognizes itself as Neberdjer—the heated mind and feelings transform into silent mind and feelings, earthly well-being manifests through unshakeable peace, and the divine shrine within reveals itself as one's fundamental identity.

The tradition emphasizes patience and realistic expectations: "The mind has spent thousands of hours absorbed in worldly thoughts and individualized thinking. The work of purification requires time proportional to the density of accumulated impressions. Nevertheless, with proper foundation and sufficient purity of heart (mind), realization of the deeper existence of being can occur in weeks, days, hours, minutes, seconds, or an instant."

Both Prologue goals find fulfillment through this practice: earthly well-being (verse 2) through the peace arising from silent mind and feelings; discovery of the divine shrine (verse 9) through Ab Neter recognition. The supreme practice remains simple: consciousness directing awareness toward consciousness itself—Neberdjer recognizing Neberdjer through this particular form.

May this teaching support your journey from heated to silent, from separate to unified, from seeking to fulfillment—discovering the fullness of silence that finds those who rest in awareness of the All-Encompassing Divinity.

References

[1] Ashby, M. (2019-25). Mysticism of Amenemopet Hieroglyphic Text Translation. Sema Institute of Ancient Egyptian Studies.
[2] Ashby, M. (2024). Amenemopet lectures 2024 by Dr Muata Ashby transcripts. Sema Institute of Ancient Egyptian Studies.
[3] Ashby, M. (2016). Egyptian Book of the Dead Hieroglyph Translations for Enlightenment Vol. 15. Sema Institute of Ancient Egyptian Studies.
[4] Ashby, M. (2025). Keys to Sage Amenemopet Wisdom Text Trilinear Translation Chapter 5. Sema Institute of Ancient Egyptian Studies.
[5] Ashby, M. (2025). Keys to Sage Amenemopet Wisdom Text Trilinear Translation Chapter 6. Sema Institute of Ancient Egyptian Studies.
[6] Ashby, M. (2025). Book Awakening Your Soul-Aware-Witness-Self: Ancient Egyptian Wisdom To Discover Divine Consciousness. Sema Institute of Ancient Egyptian Studies.
[7] Bauer, A., et al. (2023). How does meditation affect the default mode network: A systematic review. Frontiers in Human Neuroscience, 17, 1175375.
[8] Brewer, J. A., et al. (2011). Meditation experience is associated with differences in default mode network activity and connectivity. Proceedings of the National Academy of Sciences, 108(50), 20254-20259.
[9] Cahn, B. R., Delorme, A., & Polich, J. (2010). Occipital gamma activation during Vipassana meditation. Cognitive Processing, 11, 39-56.
[10] Chowdhury, A., et al. (2025). Multimodal neurophenomenology of advanced concentration absorption meditation: An intensively sampled case study of jhāna. NeuroImage, 305, 120973.
[11] Lutz, A., et al. (2004). Long-term meditators self-induce high-amplitude gamma synchrony during mental practice. Proceedings of the National Academy of Sciences, 101(46), 16369-16373.
[12] Tang, Y.-Y., Hölzel, B. K., & Posner, M. I. (2015). The neuroscience of mindfulness meditation. Nature Reviews Neuroscience, 16(4), 213-225.
[13] Tihanyi, B. T., et al. (2016). Body awareness, mindfulness and affect: Associations of mind-body practices. Frontiers in Psychology, 7, 978.
[14] Winter, U., et al. (2015). Spectral power and functional connectivity changes during mindfulness meditation with eyes open: A magnetoencephalography (MEG) study in long-term meditators. NeuroImage, 109, 31-41.
[15] Brewer, J. A., Worhunsky, P. D., Gray, J. R., Tang, Y. Y., Weber, J., & Kober, H. (2011). Meditation experience is associated with differences in default mode network activity and connectivity. Proceedings of the National Academy of Sciences, 108(50), 20254-20259.

Chapter 10: Commentary on Teachings of Amenemopet Chapter 6B VIII (verses 19-20) and Chapter 6B IX (verses 5-8): Divine Providence versus Worldly Scheming

SUMMARY OF VERSES BEING COVERED

These parallel teachings from Chapter 6B demonstrate Amenemopet's systematic presentation of contrasting life choices that determine whether the mind develops heated or silent character, leading to either purity or corruption of the personality. Chapter 6B VIII verses 19-20 contrast accepting "the measure given by The Divine" based on accumulated aryu (verse 19) versus gaining "thousands of measures through weakness of mind" by scheming to "go behind others' backs to steal from them" (verse 20).[2] Chapter 6B IX verses 5-8 extend this fundamental choice by contrasting "poverty in the hand of The Divine" (verse 5) and "sacrificial bread with sweetness in the front-of-mind" (verse 7) versus "power over wealth" that includes the comprehensive psychological syndrome Amenemopet designates with the hieroglyphic term shennu {seqer}—"anguish, strife, worry, anxiety, and unrest"—and being "a prisoner of the weak mind" (verses 6 and 8).[2]

These verses reveal how seemingly superior worldly success achieved through unrighteous means proves spiritually inferior to ethical choices that align with divine providence. The teaching simultaneously illuminates two distinct levels of mental operation: "hat" (front-of-mind conscious awareness) representing what currently occupies attention, and "ab" (the deeper unconscious where aryu accumulate) containing feeling-memories from past actions, thoughts, and experiences.

KEY TEACHINGS BY VERSE

Chapter 6B VIII Verse 19:

- Accepting the measure given by The Divine through providence
- Life circumstances reflect accumulated aryu (spiritual merit)
- Divine providence operates based on one's due merit

Chapter 6B VIII Verse 20:

- Weakness of mind generates cunning and unrighteous schemes
- Heated approach: going behind others' backs to steal from them
- Operating with forceful determination, volition, and malice of forethought
- Breaking the order of Maat through deliberate unrighteousness

Chapter 6B IX Verse 5:

- Poverty in the hand of The Divine is glorifying and beneficial
- Being within divine grace, caring, and protection

Chapter 6B IX Verse 6:

- Contrasting power over storehouse of wealth with unrighteousness
- Weakness of mind accompanying material domination

Chapter 6B IX Verse 7:

- Sacrificial bread with sweetness in the front-of-mind (hat)
- Joy and good feeling in conscious awareness
- Blissful/beatific condition from simple provisions aligned with Divine

Chapter 6B IX Verse 8:

- Hieroglyphic term shennu {seqer} designating comprehensive psychological syndrome
- Power over wealth accompanied by anguish, strife, worry, anxiety, unrest
- Being a prisoner of the weak mind that leads to agitations, frustrations and sufferings

1. Human Psychology Principle Focus of Chapter 6B VIII-IX

The human psychology issue Amenemopet addresses in these parallel verses concerns the fundamental choice between trusting divine providence versus attempting to manipulate circumstances through cunning schemes motivated by "weakness of mind."[2] This represents one of the most significant psychological patterns determining whether mind develops toward silent mind and feelings (ger) or remains trapped in heated reactivity. The teaching illuminates how the hat (front-of-mind conscious awareness) operates based on patterns stored in the ab (unconscious mind), and how these patterns either obscure or reveal Ab Neter (the divine soul sustaining consciousness from the kara/deep sanctuary level).

Significantly, Chapter 6B IX verse 8 employs the hieroglyphic term ***shennu-*** {seqer} to designate the comprehensive psychological-physiological-spiritual syndrome that results from operating through "weakness of mind." The verse reads: "...as opposed to the capacity to have the power over wealth or abundant possessions but also included with that power, not having peace but rather anguish, strife, worry, anxiety, vexation and unrest; and be a prisoner of the weak mind that leads to agitations, frustrations and sufferings in life."[2] This demonstrates that Amenemopet possessed sophisticated technical terminology for precisely the psychological condition that contemporary language terms frustration and vexation. Notice the use of the determinative hieroglyph ***chefty*** (enemy) -indicates the insight into the term, that the frustration is an enemy to the personality and its capacity to experience serenity and deeper spiritual awareness. The shennu root family encompasses emotional (***shen***—hateful, hostile), relational (shennu—fighters, enmity, strife), physiological/psychological (***sheni***—sick, depressed, helpless; ***shenn***—mental sickness), existential (***shenn-t***—oppression, weariness), and comprehensive suffering (***shnu***—evils, sick man) dimensions—revealing that the teaching addresses not merely occasional emotional reactions but rather a unified syndrome affecting all dimensions of human experience.

At the surface level of the ab resides aryu—karmic feeling-memories that accumulate based on past actions that create feeling-memories conditioning present consciousness. When aryu density increases through repeated patterns of manipulation, scheming, and distrust of divine providence, these patterns "occupy the presence-of-mind awareness, so densely as to influence the conscious reality awareness (thinking and feeling) of a person and blot out the awareness of the soul level divine presence."[1] The hat becomes so dominated by acquisition-focused thoughts and comparative thinking that mind loses awareness of Ab Neter entirely, experiencing itself as a separate vulnerable entity that must secure well-being through its personal cunning rather than divine trust. This generates the shennu syndrome verse 8 describes—the comprehensive suffering arising when the mind operates disconnected from its divine foundation.

The teaching simultaneously addresses these two mental operations—surface-level conscious thinking at the hat level and deeper unconscious conditioning at the ab level—because transformation requires addressing both. Merely managing thoughts at the hat level while leaving dense aryu patterns intact in the ab produces temporary behavioral changes without genuine mind/personality transformation. The heated person misidentifies surface ripples (hat-level thoughts) as the reality itself, not recognizing that these ripples arise from ab-level aryu patterns stirring the depths. Conversely, the silent person who trusts divine providence operates through divine intelligence that perceives circumstances from Ab Neter awareness rather than through aryu-distorted perception.

The psychological principle reveals itself most clearly in how "weakness of mind" operates. The weak mind refers not to intellectual incapacity but rather to mind dominated by aryu density that obscures Ab Neter awareness. This weakness manifests as the compulsive need to manipulate circumstances, to scheme behind others' backs, to constantly compare one's circumstances with others and generate strategies for acquisition. This condition creates a prison more confining than material poverty because the imprisoned mind lacks even the awareness of its bondage—the aryu patterns operate so automatically that they appear to constitute reality itself rather than being recognized as conditioned responses obscuring truth. This is the "prisoner of the weak mind" condition verse 8 identifies, where shennu operates as automatic reactive patterns generating continuous suffering.

Chapter 6B IX extends this fundamental choice by revealing how material prosperity achieved through unrighteous means produces the shennu syndrome—"anguish, strife, worry, anxiety, and unrest"—that proves more painful than poverty accepted with divine trust.[2] The teaching reveals that mind experiencing a blissful condition with simple provisions when the hat (front-of-mind) operates without aryu-driven acquisition compulsion can know "sweetness" that eludes those with "power over wealth" achieved through heated scheming.[2] This directly impacts both Prologue goals: without recognizing how acquisition-focused mind and feelings prevent earthly well-being, the goal of verse 2 ("cause a person to have well-being while living on earth") cannot be achieved. Similarly, the dense aryu patterns generated by scheming and manipulation block access to the kara (divine sanctuary) that verse 9 describes, preventing discovery of Ab Neter. The wisdom to be understood reveals that Sage Amenemopet does not condemn amassing wealth itself as contrary to Maat—rather, the teaching identifies that amassing wealth with the shennu syndrome (vexation, frustration, anguish) and without the ethical conscience of Maat proves worse than having poverty while operating within divine favor.[10]

2. Behavioral Imperatives of this Chapter

The specific psychological patterns arising from this fundamental choice between divine trust and ego-manipulation manifest as observable behaviors that either thin or thicken aryu density. Understanding these patterns through the hat/ab/aryu/Ab Neter framework reveals how seemingly practical worldly strategies actually constitute spiritual self-sabotage, while apparently impractical trust in divine providence represents the most psychologically sound approach to life.

The primary behavioral pattern that Chapter 6B VIII verse 20 identifies involves "schemes how to go behind others' backs to steal from them...operating by force of determination, volition, and with malice of forethought."[2] This describes not merely occasional unethical behavior but rather a systematic approach to life where mind habitually scans for opportunities to gain advantage through manipulation. The heated person in corporate environments continuously evaluates how to position themselves favorably in comparison to colleagues—what information to withhold, which relationships to cultivate for advantage, how to present work to maximize personal credit while minimizing others' contributions. These behaviors arise not from conscious malicious intent (though that may develop) but from aryu patterns in the ab that generate anxiety about security and comparative thoughts about status.

The mechanism operates through what contemporary psychology might call cognitive distortions but which Amenemopet understands more precisely as aryu-driven perception. When aryu density obscures Ab Neter awareness, mind experiences itself as fundamentally separate and vulnerable—a discrete entity competing for limited resources in a threatening environment. This generates what the teaching calls "weakness of mind": not intellectual deficit but rather the weakness of being disconnected from the divine intelligence that would naturally guide appropriate action. From this weakened state, mind develops elaborate compensatory strategies—the "cunning" and "schemes" the teaching describes—attempting to secure through manipulation what divine trust would provide naturally. This manifests the *shen* root meaning (hateful, hostile, inimical) as the mind operates from antagonism toward perceived competitors.

The behavioral pattern intensifies through social comparison mechanisms. The aspirant observes others' apparent advantages—their wealth, status, relationships, opportunities—and immediately experiences heated feelings: envy, inadequacy, resentment, competitive urgency. These feelings arise from ab-level aryu patterns, not from present-moment reality assessment. The hat then generates thought content rationalizing and implementing manipulative strategies: "If I just position myself this way..." "If I can get that information before others..." "If I cultivate that relationship strategically..." The entire process operates so automatically that mind rarely questions whether this approach serves genuine well-being. This exemplifies the shennu dimension (fighters, enmity, strife) as the behavioral pattern creates continuous interpersonal conflict and competitive aggression.

Chapter 6B IX verse 8's description of possessing "power over wealth" yet experiencing the comprehensive shennu syndrome—being "a prisoner of the weak mind that leads to agitations, frustrations and sufferings in life"[2]—reveals another crucial behavioral pattern: acquisition-focused mind never achieves satisfaction regardless of success level. The aspirant who successfully implements cunning schemes and achieves material advantages discovers that mind immediately generates new objects of desire, new sources of anxiety, new comparative thinking about those possessing even greater advantages. This represents not personal failing but the inevitable operation of heated mind and feelings—because the problem exists at consciousness level rather than circumstances level, no external manipulation can provide the fulfillment mind seeks through Ab Neter connection. This demonstrates the *sheni* dimension (helpless, depressed, cast down) and the *shenn* dimension (mental sickness) as chronic acquisition-seeking produces comprehensive psychological distress.

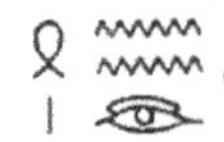

The behavioral imperative also manifests in relationship dynamics where manipulation becomes normalized. The heated person approaches relationships transactionally: "What can this person provide for me? How can I position myself advantageously in this interaction?" This creates what appears to be a network of connections but actually represents isolation—mind relating to others as objects to be manipulated rather than as fellow expressions of divine presence. The aryu patterns generating this approach operate so pervasively in contemporary culture that many aspirants never recognize alternatives exist, assuming competitive manipulation constitutes normal relating. This embodies the

shnu dimension (evils, sick man) as the entire personality becomes corrupted through these patterns.

Consumer culture systematically reinforces these heated patterns by presenting endless images of apparent success while generating dissatisfaction with present circumstances. The aspirant becomes conditioned to interpret every discomfort as signaling that something external must be acquired or changed. The hat fills with acquisition-focused thoughts—"If I just had that resource/position/relationship, then I would be secure/happy/fulfilled"—while ab-level aryu patterns intensify through repeated exposure to manipulative messaging. This creates a feedback loop where heated behaviors generate new aryu reinforcing heated mind and feelings, which generates more heated behaviors, steadily increasing aryu density that obscures Ab Neter awareness.

The teaching reveals that these behavioral patterns, while arising from unconscious protective mechanisms (aryu attempting to secure well-being through manipulation when Ab Neter awareness is obscured), actually perpetuate the suffering they aim to prevent. Each act of going "behind others' backs," each cunning scheme, each moment of comparative thinking creates new aryu in the ab that thicken the obstruction preventing Ab Neter recognition. The heated person experiences increasing psychological distress—the comprehensive shennu syndrome Chapter 6B IX verse 8 describes as "anguish, strife, worry, anxiety, and unrest" leading to "agitations, frustrations and sufferings in life"—not because circumstances deteriorate but because aryu density increases, further obscuring the divine presence that would naturally provide the fulfillment mind seeks.[2] This manifests the ***shenn-t*** dimension (oppression, weariness) as the burden becomes increasingly exhausting.

3. Mystic Psychology-Metaphysical Implications

The metaphysical mechanics underlying these behavioral patterns reveal how consciousness architecture determines whether manipulation or trust governs life approach, and how this choice operates at the fundamental level of whether the mind recognizes its true nature as sustained by Ab Neter or misidentifies as separate vulnerable ego-personality. Understanding these mechanics illuminates why divine trust represents not naive passivity but rather the most sophisticated response to existence, while cunning manipulation constitutes profound ignorance of how consciousness actually operates.

At the deepest level, the kara (divine sanctuary within the ab) contains Ab Neter—the "foundation of individual consciousness," "person's portion of Divine consciousness that sustains their capacity of conscious awareness."[1] This Ab Neter operates continuously, sustaining the very awareness by which mind experiences thoughts, feelings, sensations, and perceptions. The fundamental metaphysical truth Amenemopet reveals: consciousness never actually exists as separate entity but rather operates as localized expression of universal divine intelligence through the mind/personality. The experience of separate vulnerable selfhood arises not from metaphysical reality but from aryu density obscuring Ab Neter awareness. When this obscuration becomes dense enough, the comprehensive shennu syndrome emerges—the unified condition affecting mental, physical, relational, and existential dimensions that verse 8 describes.

When aryu patterns dominate the ab, they function as what the teaching describes as occupying "presence-of-mind awareness, so densely as to influence the conscious reality awareness (thinking and feeling) of a person and blot out the awareness of the soul level divine presence."[1] This operates through a mechanism where feeling-memories from past experiences create conditioned response patterns that automatically activate when circumstances trigger associated feelings. For example, past experiences of scarcity create aryu patterns that generate anxiety when circumstances involve resource allocation. This anxiety then triggers at the hat level acquisition-focused thoughts and manipulative behavioral impulses—the entire sequence operating so rapidly that mind experiences it as direct perception of reality rather than recognizing it as conditioned response pattern. This is how the "prisoner of the weak mind" condition operates—automatic aryu-driven patterns generating the shennu syndrome continuously.

The metaphysical significance emerges when recognizing that these aryu patterns, while seeming to protect consciousness, actually disconnect awareness from the divine intelligence that would naturally orchestrate appropriate responses. Ab Neter, when not obscured by aryu density, operates through what Amenemopet calls divine providence—the universal intelligence that arranges circumstances according to what serves mind/personality development. Chapter 6B VIII verse 19's teaching about accepting "the measure given by The Divine...based on your due merit as attested by your aryu"[2] reveals this profound metaphysical principle: circumstances arise not randomly but according to what mind has created through past actions (accumulated aryu) and what divine intelligence determines serves present development.

This creates what appears paradoxical from the ego-perspective but proves elegant from the wisdom-perspective: mind best serves its own development by trusting divine providence rather than unduly manipulating circumstances (meaning: trying to influence situations beyond a level that maintains ***ger*** (serenity)). When the mind attempts manipulation through cunning schemes, it operates from aryu-obscured awareness disconnected from divine intelligence—like a cell attempting to optimize the body's functioning through local manipulation without awareness of the organism's broader needs. Conversely, when the mind trusts divine providence, it aligns with the universal intelligence that perceives circumstances from a comprehensive perspective—like the cell operating harmoniously with the body's wisdom.

The metaphysical mechanics also reveal why material success achieved through heated means produces the shennu syndrome. When the mind operates through manipulation and cunning, it generates aryu patterns that reinforce the sense of separate vulnerable selfhood—each cunning act creates feeling-memories of being disconnected from universal support, needing to secure well-being through personal effort against threatening others. These aryu accumulate in the ab, steadily thickening the obstruction that prevents Ab Neter awareness. Thus, the very behaviors mind employs attempting to secure well-being actually prevent access to the Ab Neter connection that would naturally provide fulfillment. This explains why verse 8 describes one who possesses "power over wealth" yet experiences the comprehensive shennu syndrome—the material acquisition cannot resolve the metaphysical disconnection generating the suffering.

Chapter 6B IX's teaching about experiencing "sweetness in the front-of-mind" (hat) with simple provisions versus the shennu syndrome—"anguish, strife, worry, anxiety, and unrest"—with "power over wealth"[2] reveals another metaphysical principle: the quality of mental experience depends not on circumstances but on the degree of aryu obstruction obscuring Ab Neter awareness. When hat operates relatively free from dense aryu patterns—which occurs more readily with simple circumstances lacking elaborate manipulation opportunities—mind can experience the blissful quality that represents Ab Neter awareness manifesting at conscious level. Conversely, when elaborate circumstances provide endless manipulation opportunities, mind becomes increasingly absorbed in heated scheming, generating dense aryu patterns that completely obscure Ab Neter awareness even as material resources accumulate. This produces the comprehensive shennu syndrome that affects all dimensions simultaneously.

The teaching reveals that the "weakness of mind" Chapter 6B VIII verse 20 describes operates as metaphysical disconnection rather than intellectual deficit.[2] Strong mind, from this framework, means mind maintaining Ab Neter awareness even amid challenging circumstances—operating from divine intelligence rather than aryu-driven reactivity. Weak mind means mind so dominated by aryu patterns that it loses Ab Neter awareness entirely, experiencing itself as a vulnerable separate entity (ego) requiring cunning manipulation (egoism) for survival. This weakness manifests fundamental confusion about identity and true nature, producing a dual susceptibility. On one hand, such weakness can manifest as aggressive egoism—mind falling prey to anger, hatred, violence, greed, and corruption, becoming susceptible to messages promoting rapaciousness and developing into the perpetrator of harm. This embodies the shen (hateful, hostile) and shennu (fighters, enmity, strife) dimensions. On the other hand, the same weakness can manifest as passive submission egoism—mind becoming weak-willed, unable to maintain boundaries with heated personalities, falling prey to manipulations, lacking capacity to practice the teaching's imperatives of refraining from destructive interactions, inability to practice effective meditation, and introspection. This manifests the sheni dimension (helpless, depressed, cast down). Both manifestations—aggressor and victim—arise from the identical root problem: aryu-dominated mind disconnected from Ab Neter, operating without access to divine intelligence, whether that disconnection expresses itself through violence or vulnerability.

The metaphysical architecture also explains the "prison" metaphor Chapter 6B IX verse 8 employs: being "a prisoner of the weak mind" even when possessing material power.[2] The prison consists of aryu patterns that create compulsive thought loops: comparative thinking generating dissatisfaction, acquisition urges generating anxiety, manipulation strategies generating the need for constant vigilance and control. These patterns operate automatically at the ab level, continuously feeding content to the hat that reinforces the prison. The imprisoned mind lacks freedom not because of external constraints but because aryu density prevents access to Ab Neter awareness—the only source of genuine liberation. This is why verse 8 explicitly connects being "a prisoner of the weak mind" with the comprehensive shennu syndrome that "leads to agitations, frustrations and sufferings in life"—the prison and the suffering represent the unified condition arising from metaphysical disconnection from Ab Neter.

Understanding these metaphysical mechanics reveals that Amenemopet's teaching about trusting divine providence represents not religious sentiment but rather sophisticated understanding of consciousness architecture. When the mind thins aryu density through practices of ethical living and right thinking/feeling, Ab Neter awareness naturally emerges, revealing the divine intelligence that was always present sustaining consciousness. From this awareness, appropriate actions arise spontaneously without cunning calculation—not because the mind becomes passive but because it operates from divine intelligence rather than aryu-driven distortion. The transformation from heated manipulation to silent trust represents not behavioral modification but metaphysical realization: recognizing that consciousness never was the separate vulnerable entity it appeared to be through aryu-obscured perception. This transformation dissolves the shennu-generating mechanism at its source.

4. Transpersonal Psychology Research

Contemporary psychological research provides empirical validation for the ancient framework distinguishing between trust in larger systems versus control-seeking manipulation, demonstrating measurable differences in psychological well-being, physiological health, and life satisfaction that correspond precisely to Amenemopet's distinction between silent trust and heated scheming. This research, while employing different terminology, confirms the fundamental psychological principle that Amenemopet identified: the quality of mental experience depends more on mental approach than on external circumstances. Modern research on frustration, chronic dissatisfaction, and stress-related disorders provides empirical support for what Amenemopet conceptualized as the shennu syndrome.

Locus of control research in personality psychology distinguishes between internal locus (believing outcomes depend primarily on personal actions) and external locus (believing outcomes depend on external forces or chance).[3] While this framework differs from Amenemopet's more sophisticated hat/ab/aryu architecture, longitudinal studies demonstrate that individuals with balanced perspectives—recognizing appropriate spheres for personal agency while accepting circumstances beyond personal control—experience significantly better psychological adjustment than those maintaining rigid internal control orientation. Individuals attempting to control all life aspects through manipulation and scheming show elevated anxiety, depression, and stress-related physiological symptoms compared to those maintaining appropriate trust in larger systems.[4] This validates the teaching's distinction between the shennu syndrome accompanying control-seeking manipulation versus the "sweetness" accompanying divine trust.

Self-determination theory research reveals that intrinsic motivation (engagement arising from inherent interest or alignment with values) produces substantially greater well-being and sustained achievement than extrinsic motivation (engagement driven by external rewards or comparative status-seeking).[5] Studies tracking thousands of participants demonstrate that individuals pursuing goals for intrinsic reasons report greater life satisfaction, psychological health, and subjective well-being even when objective success levels prove comparable to those pursuing extrinsic goals. This validates Amenemopet's teaching that mind experiencing "sweetness" with simple provisions aligned with values (intrinsic orientation) surpasses the psychological state of those possessing material wealth achieved through comparative status-seeking (extrinsic orientation driven by "weakness of mind").[2] The research confirms that the quality of experience depends on mental orientation rather than external acquisition—precisely what verse 8's shennu teaching reveals.

Research on social comparison processes confirms that individuals engaging in frequent upward social comparison (comparing oneself to those perceived as superior) experience significantly elevated depression, anxiety, envy, and life dissatisfaction.[6] Longitudinal studies demonstrate that chronic comparative thinking predicts declining psychological well-being over time, regardless of actual life circumstances improvement. This empirically validates the psychological mechanism Amenemopet describes: the comparative thinking and schemes arising from observing others' advantages generate the comprehensive shennu syndrome that Chapter 6B IX verse 8 identifies—"anguish, strife, worry, anxiety, and unrest" leading to "agitations, frustrations and sufferings"—operating independently of whether manipulation succeeds in acquiring desired resources.[2]

Trust and psychological health research demonstrates that individuals capable of appropriate trust in larger systems experience lower cortisol levels, better immune function, and greater life satisfaction than those maintaining chronic suspicion and control-seeking behaviors.[7] This validates the psychological benefits of the divine trust that Chapter 6B VIII verse 19 recommends, confirming that the shennu syndrome manifests physiological consequences beyond merely psychological distress. Dual-process theory in cognitive psychology confirms the ancient framework of conscious versus unconscious mental operations, demonstrating that human behavior results from interaction between conscious controlled processes (hat level) and unconscious automatic processes (ab level).[8] Research shows that therapeutic interventions targeting unconscious conditioning produce more lasting results than purely cognitive approaches—paralleling the wisdom about addressing aryu patterns in the ab rather than merely managing conscious symptoms at the hat level.[9]

Contemporary research on chronic stress and frustration demonstrates measurable effects across the dimensions Amenemopet's shennu root family encompasses: emotional (increased hostility and anger—shen), relational (interpersonal conflict and social withdrawal—shennu), physiological/psychological (depression, anxiety disorders, helplessness—sheni/shenn), and existential (chronic fatigue and sense of burden—shenn-t). This empirical confirmation of the multidimensional nature of the shennu syndrome validates the ancient wisdom's sophisticated understanding of how psychological patterns manifest comprehensively rather than merely emotionally.

5. Spiritual Implications for Aspirants: Personal Development Through Contrasting Choices

PART A - PASTORAL CONCERNS: MODERN CHALLENGES TO DIVINE TRUST

These teachings present immediate challenges for spiritual aspirants navigating contemporary culture that systematically undermines the divine trust Amenemopet recommends while intensifying the shennu-generating patterns the teaching identifies. Consider the individual working in corporate environments where advancement often requires the sophisticated manipulation tactics that Chapter 6B VIII verse 20 describes as "cunning" and "schemes how to go behind others' backs."[2] The aspirant faces genuine practical tension: how to maintain ethical integrity while functioning in systems that reward behaviors directly contrary to the teaching? Many experience this as choosing between spiritual principles and practical survival, not recognizing that this perceived dilemma itself reflects the "weakness of mind" that assumes security depends on personal manipulation rather than divine providence. This tension generates precisely the shennu syndrome verse 8 describes—chronic anxiety, worry, mental agitation—as the mind attempts to navigate contradictory imperatives.

Someone struggling with financial anxiety might find the teaching about accepting "the measure given by The Divine"[2] particularly challenging when facing genuine practical pressures—rent payments, medical expenses, family responsibilities. The heated mind and feelings immediately generate objections: "Easy to say when you're not facing eviction!" Yet this reaction reveals precisely the aryu density that obscures Ab Neter awareness. The aspirant hasn't yet recognized that the anxiety itself constitutes the suffering the teaching addresses, and that this anxiety operates independently of actual circumstances. Indeed, individuals with abundant resources experience similar anxiety patterns—revealing that the problem exists at the consciousness level rather than the circumstance level. The shennu syndrome manifests regardless of material circumstances, confirming that the suffering arises from aryu-obscured consciousness rather than from circumstantial insufficiency.

The challenge intensifies through social media exposure constantly presenting images of others' apparent success, triggering comparative thinking and the schemes Chapter 6B VIII verse 20 describes. The aspirant observes others' material prosperity and experiences the heated feelings that immediately generate elaborate mental strategies for acquiring similar advantages. This represents a modern intensification of ancient patterns—technology amplifying the psychological mechanisms Amenemopet identified thousands of years ago. The aspirant may not recognize how these platforms deliberately engineer the "weakness of mind" that generates dissatisfaction and acquisition-seeking. The constant comparison produces the shennu root family dimensions comprehensively: shen (hostile feelings toward those perceived as more successful), shennu (competitive orientation toward peers), sheni/shenn (depressive reactions and mental distress from perceived inadequacy), and shenn-t (exhausting burden of continuous comparison).

Consumer culture presents another systematic challenge by constantly creating dissatisfaction with present circumstances while promising that specific purchases will provide the security and happiness mind naturally seeks through Ab Neter connection. The aspirant becomes conditioned to interpret every form of discomfort as signaling that something external must be acquired or changed, rather than recognizing that the discomfort often signals aryu patterns obscuring Ab Neter awareness. This conditioning operates so pervasively that many aspirants never question whether fulfillment might come through an entirely different mechanism than external acquisition. The chronic dissatisfaction this generates represents the core shennu experience—mind perpetually frustrated by circumstances failing to provide the completion it seeks through material means.

Relationship dynamics create particularly challenging circumstances for practicing these teachings. When someone close operates through heated behaviors—manipulation, comparative thinking, acquisition-focused relating—the aspirant faces pressure to respond in kind or risk being exploited. The teaching isn't suggesting passive acceptance of abuse or manipulation, but rather that maintaining silent mind and feelings in such circumstances requires profound spiritual development. The aspirant must learn to take appropriate practical actions from a foundation of divine trust rather than heated reactivity—a subtle but crucial distinction that requires patient cultivation. Without this development, relationships become arenas for continuous shennu generation as the mind experiences ongoing conflict, resentment, and frustration.

PART B - METHODS FOR TRANSFORMATION: SYSTEMATIC PRACTICES BASED ON AMENEMOPET'S TEACHING

The transformation these verses recommend operates through systematic practice rather than intellectual understanding alone. The goal involves dissolving the shennu-generating mechanism by thinning aryu density that obscures Ab Neter awareness, allowing mind to operate from divine intelligence rather than heated manipulation. Based on the teaching presented by Sage Amenemopet that the aspirant should accept "the measure given by The Divine,"[2] the inverse doctrine application methodology suggests that aspirants should also avoid mental behaviors that cultivate distrust of divine providence—chronic comparative thinking, elaborate schemes for acquiring what appears to belong to others, and the underlying assumption that security depends on personal manipulation—as these would undermine the cultivation of divine trust while intensifying the shennu syndrome.

Practice 1: Discrimination Between Genuine Needs and Aryu-Generated Desires

Chapter 6B IX verse 7's "sacrificial bread with sweetness in the front-of-mind"[2] suggests that mind can experience satisfaction with simple provisions when the hat operates without aryu-driven acquisition compulsion. Practice discriminating between genuine practical needs arising from present circumstances and artificial desires created by comparative thinking or social conditioning. When facing decisions about acquisitions or career strategies, pause and investigate whether the impulse arises from authentic need or from heated feelings generated by observing others' apparent advantages.

For instance, when considering a job change primarily motivated by salary comparison with colleagues, examine whether this impulse arises from genuine dissatisfaction with current work or from heated feelings triggered by social comparison. If the latter, practice accepting present circumstances while remaining open to authentic guidance about when change serves spiritual development. This doesn't mean never changing circumstances, but rather that changes emerge from silent mind and feelings aligned with divine intelligence rather than heated comparative thinking. This practice directly addresses the shennu-generating mechanism by interrupting the comparative patterns that produce chronic dissatisfaction and acquisition-seeking.

Practice 2: Gratitude for Present Provisions as Aryu Purification

Based on Chapter 6B VIII verse 19's teaching about accepting "the measure given by The Divine...based on your due merit as attested by your aryu,"[2] practice systematic gratitude for present circumstances as a method for generating positive aryu that gradually thin the density obscuring Ab Neter awareness. Each time heated feelings arise about circumstances appearing inadequate, counter this by identifying specific aspects of present circumstances that support well-being and spiritual development.

This practice doesn't require denying genuine challenges or pretending satisfaction when circumstances cause legitimate difficulty. Rather, it involves recognizing that even challenging circumstances contain supportive elements when approached with proper awareness. For example, financial limitation might restrict certain activities while creating conditions for developing qualities like resourcefulness, creativity, or recognition of what truly matters—qualities that serve spiritual development more effectively than abundant resources might. The practice works by creating new positive aryu at the ab level that gradually compete with and thin the density of negative aryu patterns that generate the shennu syndrome. As aryu patterns thin, mind naturally experiences less chronic dissatisfaction, anxiety, and frustration—not through external circumstance improvement but through internal transformation that allows Ab Neter awareness to emerge.

PRACTICE 3: PATIENT ABSORPTION RATHER THAN FORCEFUL EFFORT

The teaching reveals that Ab Neter already sustains consciousness at the kara level—the work involves removing aryu obstruction rather than creating something absent. This suggests that transformation occurs through patient absorption of wisdom at increasingly deep levels rather than forceful effort to achieve specific states. When practicing acceptance of divine providence, recognize that resistance will arise from accumulated aryu patterns. Rather than fighting this resistance, allow repeated exposure to the teaching to gradually penetrate from hat awareness to ab level, creating what the ancient wisdom describes as "mooring posts" that compete with existing aryu patterns.[1]

For instance, when facing circumstances that trigger heated acquisition-seeking and the shennu syndrome, rather than forcing yourself to immediately accept divine providence, practice repeatedly bringing awareness back to the teaching. Consider how the circumstance offers opportunity for spiritual development rather than constituting an obstacle to well-being. Over time, through patient repetition, the wisdom penetrates deeper levels, gradually thinning aryu density and allowing natural emergence of the trust the teaching describes. This parallels how water gradually wears away stone—not through force but through persistent gentle contact. As this process advances, the shennu syndrome naturally diminishes—not through suppressing the anguish, strife, worry, anxiety, and unrest but through addressing the aryu-obscured consciousness that generates these experiences. The transformation occurs when the mind recognizes itself as sustained by Ab Neter rather than operating as the separate vulnerable entity that requires constant manipulation for survival.

References

[1] Ashby, M. (2019-25). Mysticism of Amenemopet Hieroglyphic Text Translation. Sema Institute of Ancient Egyptian Studies.
[2] Ashby, M. (2025). Keys to Sage Amenemopet wisdom text trilinear translation Chapter 6B. Sema Institute of Ancient Egyptian Studies.
[3] Rotter, J. B. (1966). Generalized expectancies for internal versus external control of reinforcement. Psychological Monographs: General and Applied, 80(1), 1-28.
[4] Chipperfield, J. G., Perry, R. P., Bailis, D. S., Ruthig, J. C., & Loring, R. L. (2012). Perceived control and health: A 15-year longitudinal study of the role of gender. The Journals of Gerontology Series B: Psychological Sciences and Social Sciences, 67(5), 589-598.
[5] Ryan, R. M., & Deci, E. L. (2000). Self-determination theory and the facilitation of intrinsic motivation, social development, and well-being. American Psychologist, 55(1), 68-78.
[6] White, J. B., Langer, E. J., Yariv, L., & Welch, J. C. (2006). Frequent social comparisons and destructive emotions and behaviors: The dark side of social comparisons. Journal of Adult Development, 13(1), 36-44.
[7] Mikulincer, M., & Shaver, P. R. (2007). Attachment in adulthood: Structure, dynamics, and change. New York: Guilford Press.
[8] Kahneman, D. (2011). Thinking, fast and slow. New York: Farrar, Straus and Giroux.
[9] Wilson, T. D. (2002). Strangers to ourselves: Discovering the adaptive unconscious. Cambridge, MA: Harvard University Press
[10] Ashby, M. (2024). Amenemopet lectures 2024 by Dr Muata Ashby transcripts. Sema Institute of Ancient Egyptian Studies.

CHAPTER 11: Commentary on Teachings of Amenemopet

Chapter 7, Verses 10-15—The Psychology of Power-Seeking, Mental Wandering, Vital Energy Conservation, and Trust in Divine Providence

SUMMARY OF VERSES

Verses 10-11 establish the foundational teaching about the power-seeking mind: "By means of creating, with one's own deliberate volition and effort, in one's heart (mind), going behind the back of people, of justice, of truth, deceitfully pursuing a desire for domination...one is actually doing something wrong, due to ignorance; by believing one can amass domination, wealth and power without considering the consequences." The hieroglyphic term qemaam (creating) reveals the dual potential of human creative capacity—every individual possesses the power to create conditions of their life through conscious volition, yet this capacity can be directed toward either shemm (heated) conditions that perpetuate egoism, agitation, and separation, or toward ger (silent/serene) conditions that align with divine will and Neberdjer awareness. This creative agency operates within the parameters allowed by one's aryu density, meaning that purification through actions according to Maat progressively expands the conscious capacity to create serene life conditions in harmony with the hand of god. The more purified the mind becomes through ethical living, the more qemaam becomes available for conscious direction rather than being unconsciously hijacked by negative aryu patterns. The shemm (heated) person remains driven by negative aryu and thus lacks capacity to consciously direct their creative power toward conditions of serenity and divine alignment—their qemaam operates unconsciously to perpetuate heated conditions. Indeed, weakness of mind renders the personality creatively prone to creating fantasies and engaging in mental traveling (ruy) [Amenemopet chapter 7 verse 12]—the hat (conscious mind) wandering outward from present awareness into flights of fancy, imaginations, and wishes—thereby squandering vital energy (sekhem) and becoming incapable of living fully in optimal creative capacity, unable to think correctly with clarity and lacking the energy necessary to follow those thoughts with righteous actions while becoming susceptible to negative thoughts, feelings and actions by oneself or others.[1] The term useru (domination) indicates active psychological construction—mind deliberately cultivating dependency on external power rather than developing internal creative capacity aligned with Ab Neter. Verse 11 reveals that cosmic forces Shayt (destiny) and Renenut (fortune) respond to "the ethical content of their actions, thoughts, and feelings of the past and present that become recorded in their unconscious and later in the form of unconscious impressions (aryu)."[1]

Verse 12 shifts focus to mental discipline and vital energy conservation: "Keep in mind the consequences of fortune and destiny by taking the following action: refrain, renounce, forsake the practice of letting your conscious mind travel, that is to say, going outward from yourself, to wander, having flights of fancy, imaginations, wishes, etc."[1] The term ruy (traveling) indicates the mind moving away from present awareness into fantasy—what contemporary psychology calls rumination or escapist thinking. This mental wandering squanders vital energy (sekhem) that should be conserved for spiritual development.

Verse 13 introduces divine timing: "Why do I say this? Because every person has their time where what is due to come to them, comes to them by providence supported by their karma (aryu) and the gods and goddesses."[1] The term tayu (time) establishes that cosmic intelligence provides for each individual according to both their accumulated aryu and their due divine grace.

Verse 14 addresses excessive labor and energy depletion: "Keeping in mind that your time will come to get whatever is needed by you, allowed by your fortune and destiny derived from your past actions and supported by the gods and goddesses, therefore do not be like those people who labor after, seeking for riches. Your life should not be about that; overusing time and energy in laborious pursuits that take you away from discovering the goals of life that I stated in the prologue."[1] This verse explicitly warns against depleting vital energy through anxious accumulation that prevents spiritual development.

Verse 15 concludes with trust and present well-being: "...and you have well-being now that is meant for you, and what may be needed in the future will come to you in due course."[1] The term udja (well-being) reminds aspirants to acknowledge present blessings rather than living in anxious futurity that depletes sekhem.

KEY TEACHINGS DERIVED FROM THE VERSES

1. Deliberate Volition Creates Power Dependency [Verse 10]: The hat (conscious awareness) actively constructs psychological dependence on external domination through deceitful means, depleting vital energy.

2. Cosmic Forces Record Ethical Content [Verse 11]: Shayt and Renenut respond to the quality of mind and feelings, not external appearances, depositing aryu in the ab that affect sekhem.

3. Mental Wandering Obstructs Divine Connection and Depletes Sekhem [Verse 12]: Letting the hat "travel" through fantasies and wishes prevents presence-of-mind awareness of Ab Neter while squandering vital energy. This conserves vital force to apply toward the goals of life and helps attain serenity (Ger) of mind that opens the path to spiritual sensitivity and self-discovery.

4. Divine Timing Governs Life Circumstances [Verse 13]: Providence works through both accumulated aryu and divine intelligence to provide at the proper time. This helps develop patience, trust in the Divine, and serenity (Ger) of mind.

5. Excessive Labor Prevents Spiritual Goals and Depletes Vital Energy [Verse 14]: Overworking for wealth consumes time and sekhem needed for discovering the Prologue's dual goals. This principle conserves vital energy to apply toward the goals of life.

6. Present Well-being Requires Acknowledgment [Verse 15]: Gratitude for current provision reduces anxiety about future needs. This helps develop patience and serenity (Ger) of mind while conserving sekhem.

1. HUMAN PSYCHOLOGY PRINCIPLE: THE DELUSION OF AUTONOMOUS CONTROL, VITAL ENERGY DEPLETION, AND DISCONNECTION FROM DIVINE PROVIDENCE

The central psychological issue addressed in verses 10-15 concerns the delusion of autonomous control combined with the catastrophic depletion of vital energy (sekhem) that results from this delusion—the belief that the hat can operate independently of cosmic order, either by accumulating power through deceit [verses 10-11] or by escaping into mental fantasies that avoid present reality [verse 12]. Amenemopet identifies mind operating from two related dysfunctions: deceitful manipulation of external circumstances and escapist wandering of internal thought patterns. Both represent a fundamental misunderstanding of how the mind operates within the cosmic framework, and both produce measurable physiological consequences that obstruct spiritual development.

The Physiological Reality of Heated Mind and Feelings

The teaching reveals that what Amenemopet calls "heated mind and feelings" operates not merely as metaphor but as actual physiological state with measurable bioelectric and biochemical manifestations. When mind operates through verses 10-11's deceitful power-seeking or verse 12's mental wandering, it generates specific patterns of vital energy (sekhem) disturbance that contemporary science can now partially measure through stress hormones, nervous system activation, and cellular metabolic markers. This heated state depletes the very life force required for spiritual development, creating a vicious cycle where aryu-driven behaviors consume sekhem, preventing the calm presence-of-mind necessary for Ab Neter awareness.

The vicious cycle operates through a particularly insidious mechanism whereby negative aryu patterns themselves require vital energy allocation to maintain their existence and activity within the ab. When unrighteous action deposits aryu, sekhem becomes redirected away from restorative spiritual functions to feed and support these negative patterns. This energy redirection strengthens the aryu's capacity to impel and compel thoughts, feelings, and behaviors, creating an intensifying cycle: the aryu consume the very energy needed to thin them while simultaneously using that energy to increase their compelling force over the personality. Thus, each unrighteous action not only creates new aryu but also redirects vital force toward maintaining and intensifying the existing negative patterns, explaining why heated behavioral patterns become progressively more automatic and difficult to resist as aryu density increases. The individual finds that resisting aryu-driven impulses requires ever-greater effort precisely because the accumulated patterns have commandeered increasing amounts of sekhem to reinforce their own dominance over consciousness.

The ancient term sekhem designates what contemporary frameworks inadequately capture through concepts like "vital energy," "life force," or "prana." Sekhem represents the bioelectric-biochemical substrate sustaining consciousness manifestation through the physical body—the animating principle that distinguishes living from deceased organisms. The Sema Institute teachings explain: "The mettu [channels] are conduits of sekhem [life force]. When the mettu are purified, sekhem flows properly. When obstructed by negative aryu, sekhem becomes depleted or misdirected, producing disease, mental disturbance, and spiritual obstruction."[6]

Verses 10-15 reveal how specific psychological patterns systematically deplete sekhem through multiple reinforcing mechanisms. Verse 10's power-seeking through deceitful domination produces chronic sympathetic nervous system activation—the physiological "fight or flight" response where mind maintains constant vigilance for threats and opportunities for advantage.[1] This activation diverts sekhem away from restorative functions (immune system, tissue repair, digestive efficiency, higher cognitive processes) toward immediate survival responses. Contemporary research documents that individuals maintaining chronic competitive-manipulative mind states show elevated cortisol levels, impaired immune function, reduced neuroplasticity, and accelerated cellular aging—all representing measurable sekhem depletion.[7,8]

Verse 12's mental wandering through "flights of fancy, imaginations, wishes" creates a different but equally destructive sekhem depletion pattern.[1] When mind habitually escapes present reality through fantasy and rumination, it dissipates vital energy through what the teaching identifies as the hat (conscious mind) "traveling" away from the kara (divine sanctuary within). This produces the peculiar exhaustion familiar to anyone who has spent hours lost in worry, fantasy, or obsessive planning—mind feels drained despite minimal physical exertion. The depletion occurs because mental wandering maintains brain activity in energy-intensive default mode network patterns associated with self-referential thought, consuming approximately 20% of the body's total energy production while producing no functional benefit.[9]

The Connection Between Aryu, Mettu, and Sekhem Depletion

Understanding how verses 10-15's dysfunctional patterns operate physiologically requires examining the relationship between aryu (unconscious feeling-memories), mettu (vital energy channels), and sekhem (life force). The teaching framework reveals that negative aryu accumulated in the ab (unconscious mind) create specific patterns of mettu obstruction that prevent proper sekhem flow. This produces the heated mind and feelings that generate both verses 10-11's manipulative behaviors and verse 12's escapist mental wandering.

The Sema Institute explanation clarifies: "Aryu are not merely psychological constructs but have actual bioelectric signatures. Negative aryu create tension patterns in the mettu—what contemporary medicine recognizes as chronic muscle tension, fascia restrictions, and autonomic nervous system dysregulation. These obstructions prevent sekhem from flowing to vital organs and consciousness centers, producing both physical disease and mental-emotional disturbance."[6]

Consider how verse 10's teaching about "going behind the back of people, of justice, of truth" manifests physiologically through this aryu-mettu-sekhem mechanism.[1] Each instance of deceitful manipulation deposits specific aryu in the ab—feeling-memories combining the anxiety of potential discovery, the excitement of successfully deceiving, the underlying shame of ethical violation, and the reinforced belief that security requires manipulation. These aryu create chronic tension in specific mettu locations: solar plexus (seat of personal power and security concerns), throat (communication center associated with truth/deception), and heart (ethical conscience location).

The mettu obstructions produced by these aryu then prevent proper sekhem flow, creating what appears as "personality traits": chronic anxiety (insufficient sekhem reaching parasympathetic nervous system), manipulative communication patterns (disturbed sekhem in throat mettu), emotional numbing or volatility (irregular sekhem flow to heart center), and the compulsive need for external power (depleted sekhem creating perpetual insecurity). The individual experiences these as "who they are" rather than recognizing them as symptoms of aryu-obstructed sekhem flow—treatable conditions rather than immutable characteristics.

Similarly, verse 12's mental wandering creates specific aryu-mettu-sekhem patterns. Habitual escapist thinking deposits aryu of dissatisfaction with present reality, fantasy compensation for perceived inadequacies, and the underlying anxiety that generates need for escape. These aryu obstruct mettu in the head region (associated with present-moment awareness) and the heart-solar plexus connection (linking personal will with ethical conscience). The resulting sekhem depletion manifests as inability to maintain present focus, chronic dissatisfaction regardless of circumstances, and the exhausting mental restlessness the verse describes.

The Teaching on Cosmic Forces and Vital Energy

Verse 11's introduction of Shayt (destiny) and Renenut (fortune) as cosmic forces responding to ethical content reveals another dimension of sekhem dynamics that contemporary frameworks typically miss.[1] The teaching explains that mind does not operate in isolation but rather within a larger cosmic intelligence that the Prologue identifies as Neberdjer (the all-encompassing foundation). This cosmic intelligence operates through what appears as destiny and fortune, providing circumstances that both reflect accumulated aryu and support personality/mind evolution.

Significantly, verses 13-15 emphasize that this cosmic intelligence provides according to tayu (divine timing)—each person receives "what is due to come to them...by providence supported by their karma (aryu) and the gods and goddesses" at precisely the right moment.[1] This teaching directly addresses the sekhem depletion that verses 10 and 14 identify: power-seeking manipulation and excessive anxious labor both arise from the delusion that the mind must secure provisions through personal striving rather than trusting righteous action in harmony with divine providence and cosmic intelligence.

The physiological reality: chronic anxiety about provision and security—the very state that drives verse 10's manipulation and verse 14's excessive labor—produces sustained sympathetic nervous system activation that systematically depletes sekhem. The individual caught in this pattern experiences a self-reinforcing cycle: anxiety depletes vital energy, which increases feelings of vulnerability, which intensifies anxiety and drives more frantic manipulation or labor, which further depletes sekhem. Breaking this cycle requires the radical trust verses 13-15 teach: recognizing that cosmic intelligence already operates to provide what the personality genuinely needs.

Present Well-being Recognition as Sekhem Conservation

Verse 15's teaching about acknowledging "well-being now that is meant for you" represents not merely psychological reframing but actual physiological intervention.[1] When mind practices systematic recognition of current provision (food, shelter, health, relationships, spiritual capacity), it activates parasympathetic nervous system responses that conserve and restore sekhem. Contemporary research on gratitude practices demonstrates measurable effects: increased heart rate variability (indicating improved autonomic balance), reduced inflammatory markers, enhanced immune function, and improved sleep quality—all representing sekhem restoration.[10]

The teaching recognizes that negative aryu producing chronic future-anxiety actively resist this present-well-being recognition. These aryu maintain sekhem in depleted states specifically through keeping consciousness in perpetual futurity—always focused on what might be needed, what dangers might arise, what acquisitions might provide security. The practice of acknowledging present provision directly challenges these aryu patterns, gradually thinning their density and allowing sekhem to rebalance.

This directly supports both Prologue goals. The verse 2 goal of "well-being while living on earth" becomes physiologically impossible when sekhem remains chronically depleted through the patterns verses 10-15 describe.[1] Similarly, the verse 9 goal of discovering the kara (divine sanctuary within) requires the "presence-of-mind" that depends on proper sekhem flow—impossible to achieve while vital energy is diverted to chronic anxiety, manipulative scheming, or escapist mental wandering.

2. Behavioral Imperative: Observable Manifestations of Delusion and Vital Energy Depletion

The psychological principles identified in Section 1 manifest through specific behavioral patterns that Amenemopet describes with remarkable precision, revealing how mind operating from aryu-obscured Ab Neter awareness systematically depletes sekhem through multiple reinforcing mechanisms. Understanding these behaviors through the aryu-mettu-sekhem framework prevents the common misinterpretation that these patterns represent mere "bad habits" requiring willpower to overcome. Rather, they represent complex physiological-psychological-spiritual dysfunctions requiring comprehensive intervention addressing all levels simultaneously.

Deceitful Power-Seeking as Sekhem Depletion Pattern

Verse 10's description of "going behind the back of people, of justice, of truth, deceitfully pursuing a desire for domination" identifies a behavioral pattern that contemporary corporate, political, and social environments not only tolerate but often reward—making this teaching particularly challenging for modern aspirants.[1] The behavior manifests in subtle and gross forms: withholding information that would benefit colleagues, strategically taking credit for collaborative work, manipulating emotional dynamics to maintain control, and the countless small deceptions through which heated mind attempts to secure advantage.

The teaching reveals that this pattern operates through specific aryu in the ab generating compulsive urges that mind experiences as necessary survival strategies. These aryu arise from past experiences (this lifetime or previous) where mind believed that security required manipulation, where vulnerability led to exploitation, where trust proved dangerous. The resulting patterns create what feels like an unavoidable imperative: "If I don't manipulate, others will manipulate me. If I don't pursue domination, I will be dominated."

What makes this pattern particularly pernicious: it systematically depletes sekhem while appearing to provide security. Each act of deceitful manipulation requires mind to maintain multiple contradictory realities—the truth known internally and the false appearance presented externally. This splits vital energy, diverting sekhem to managing schemes, worries, anxieties or cognitive dissonance rather than allowing it to flow toward spiritual well-being and development. Contemporary research on psychological stress demonstrates that individuals maintaining deceptive presentations show elevated cortisol, increased cardiovascular risk, and impaired immune function compared to those operating with integrity—all measurable indicators of sekhem depletion.[11]

Additionally, deceitful power-seeking creates chronic vigilance requirements that continuously drain vital energy. The manipulator must constantly monitor others' perceptions, adjust presentations to maintain deceptions, anticipate potential discoveries, and manage anxiety about exposure. This produces the exhausting hyper-alertness that verse 10 implicitly identifies—mind unable to rest because the constructed false reality requires perpetual maintenance. The sekhem consumed in this maintenance becomes unavailable for the spiritual development the Prologue describes as life's actual purpose.

Mental Wandering as Vital Energy Dissipation

Verse 12's teaching about refraining from "letting your conscious mind travel...to wander, having flights of fancy, imaginations, wishes" describes a behavioral pattern that modern technology has amplified to catastrophic proportions through social media, entertainment streaming, and constant connectivity enabling perpetual escapism.[1] The pattern manifests as mind habitually leaving present reality for fantasy scenarios—ruminating about past events that can't be changed, worrying about future possibilities that may never occur, or creating elaborate mental narratives disconnected from actual circumstances.

The aryu generating this pattern can arise from present reality feeling inadequate, overwhelming, or painful. Rather than developing the capacity to remain present with challenging circumstances, heated mind employs entertainments or mental wandering as escape mechanism. The individual facing financial pressure escapes into fantasies of lottery winnings; the person experiencing relationship difficulty retreats into scenarios where they deliver perfectly devastating confrontations or receives ideal validation; consciousness confronting mortality creates elaborate future narratives where death no longer threatens.

The sekhem depletion this creates proves substantial though often unrecognized. Mental wandering maintains brain activity in default mode network patterns that consume approximately 20% of total body energy while producing no functional benefit—pure waste of vital force that should be conserved for spiritual practice.[9] Additionally, mind lost in fantasy cannot engage in the present-moment awareness that verse 12 identifies as essential for perceiving divine providence operating. The aspirant so absorbed in anxious future scenarios or regretful past rumination literally cannot recognize that verse 15's teaching operates: "what may be needed in the future will come to you in due course."[1]

Contemporary research on mind-wandering demonstrates measurable negative impacts on well-being, cognitive function, and stress resilience—all representing sekhem depletion effects that the ancient teaching identified.[12] Studies show that individuals with high mind-wandering frequency report lower life satisfaction even when objective circumstances prove favorable, experience impaired learning and memory formation, and show reduced capacity for emotional regulation. The physiological mechanism: mental wandering prevents the present-moment awareness necessary for parasympathetic nervous system activation (which restores sekhem), keeping consciousness in chronic low-level stress states that continuously deplete vital energy.

Excessive Labor as Self-Destructive Sekhem Exhaustion

Verse 14's explicit warning against becoming "those people who labor after, seeking for riches" identifies a behavioral pattern that contemporary work culture systematically promotes through the valorization of overwork, hustle culture, and the equation of human worth with productive output.[1] The pattern manifests as mind dedicating disproportionate time and energy to wealth accumulation while neglecting the "goals of life that I (Amenemopet) stated in the prologue"—specifically, the verse 2 goal of genuine well-being and the verse 9 goal of discovering the divine sanctuary within.

The aryu generating excessive labor typically combine anxiety about provision (which verse 13 addresses), competitive comparison with others' apparent success, and the deeper existential avoidance of confronting life's actual purpose. The individual works 60-80 hours weekly not primarily because circumstances require this (though they may rationalize thus) but because work provides structured escape from the questions that spiritual development would force mind to address: "Who am I beyond my productive role? What genuinely matters? What is my relationship to the divine ground of being?"

The sekhem depletion this creates operates through multiple mechanisms simultaneously. First, the obvious physical exhaustion from sustained overwork diverts vital energy from immune function, tissue repair, and higher cognitive processes—producing the burnout phenomenon contemporary medicine now recognizes as chronic condition with measurable physiological markers.[13] Second, the psychological absorption in work prevents the mental quietude necessary for Ab Neter awareness, filling the hat with task-focused content that blocks deeper contemplative capacity. Third, the time consumed in excessive labor eliminates the periods of reduced external stimulation (silence, retreat, contemplative practice) during which aryu thinning most effectively occurs.

Significantly, verse 14 reveals that this pattern operates even—perhaps especially—when it "succeeds" in accumulating wealth. The individual who achieves material prosperity through excessive labor discovers that consciousness immediately generates new acquisition targets, new competitive comparisons, new anxieties about maintaining or expanding wealth. The sekhem exhausted in achieving material success cannot then be applied to spiritual development because exhaustion itself prevents the sustained practice required for mind transformation. The aspirant arrives at retirement age with accumulated resources but depleted vital energy—too exhausted for the intensive spiritual practice that discovering the kara requires.

Anxious Future-Orientation as Chronic Sekhem Disturbance

The cumulative effect of verses 10, 12, and 14's behaviors manifests as what verse 15 implicitly identifies: mind operating in chronic future-anxiety rather than present well-being recognition.[1] This pattern creates perhaps the most pervasive sekhem depletion in contemporary life—the sustained low-level anxiety about provision, security, and survival that modern economic and social systems deliberately cultivate to drive consumption and compliance.

The behavioral manifestation: mind perpetually scanning for threats and opportunities, unable to rest in present sufficiency because aryu patterns maintain constant narrative of inadequacy and danger. The individual with adequate food obsesses about future food security; the person with stable shelter worries about potential housing loss; consciousness with functioning health creates elaborate illness scenarios. This occurs not because present circumstances objectively warrant such anxiety but because negative aryu controlling sekhem maintain consciousness in chronic stress states that deplete vital energy.

The physiological reality documented by contemporary research: chronic anxiety maintains sustained sympathetic nervous system activation, elevated inflammatory markers, impaired immune function, reduced neuroplasticity, and accelerated cellular aging—comprehensive sekhem depletion preventing both the verse 2 goal of earthly well-being and the verse 9 goal of discovering divine presence.[14] The individual caught in this pattern cannot access the kara because the presence-of-mind required for that discovery depends on sekhem flowing properly through purified mettu—impossible when vital energy is chronically diverted to anxiety management.

These behavioral patterns interconnect and reinforce each other: deceitful power-seeking generates anxiety requiring mental wandering as escape; mental wandering prevents present focus needed to recognize provision adequacy; unrecognized provision generates anxiety driving excessive labor; excessive labor depletes sekhem preventing the spiritual practice that would reveal divine providence; absent that revelation, consciousness returns to deceitful power-seeking as apparent security strategy. Breaking this self-perpetuating cycle requires the comprehensive intervention that the verses recommend: simultaneous practice of ethical restraint (verse 10), present-moment discipline (verse 12), appropriate labor limitation (verse 14), and gratitude for current provision (verse 15).

3. Mystic Psychology—Metaphysical Implications: The Architecture of Divine Providence, Vital Energy Flow, and Consciousness Liberation

The behavioral patterns identified in Section 2 arise from specific metaphysical structures that Amenemopet's teaching illuminates with remarkable precision—revealing how the mind operates within cosmic order, how vital energy (sekhem) flows through purified or obstructed channels (mettu), and how the ab-level aryu either permit or prevent the hat's recognition of Ab Neter sustaining awareness from the kara sanctuary. Understanding these metaphysical mechanics prevents the superficial interpretation that verses 10-15 merely recommend psychological adjustment; rather, they describe actual operations of consciousness within the cosmic framework that Neberdjer represents.

The Cosmic Order: Shayt, Renenut, and Divine Providence

Verse 11's introduction of Shayt (destiny) and Renenut (fortune) as cosmic forces responding to "the ethical content of their actions, thoughts, and feelings" establishes a metaphysical framework foreign to contemporary materialist assumptions but essential for understanding the teaching's depth.[1] These are not abstract concepts or personified metaphors but actual operations of cosmic intelligence that Amenemopet identifies throughout the tradition. The framework reveals that individual consciousness does not operate in isolation but rather within a larger intelligent matrix that both records the ethical quality of consciousness and provides circumstances serving evolution.

Shayt represents the cosmic principle of destiny—the trajectory that consciousness follows based on accumulated aryu from past actions extending across lifetimes. This operates not as predetermined fate eliminating free will but rather as momentum: consciousness moving in specific directions based on patterns established through previous choices. When aryu of deceitful power-seeking dominate the ab, Shayt provides circumstances that either allow consciousness to continue that pattern (reinforcing the trajectory) or create situations that make the pattern's futility visible (offering opportunity for trajectory change). The "destiny" operates through this interaction between accumulated patterns and cosmic intelligence arranging circumstances for maximum evolutionary benefit.

Renenut represents the principle of fortune—the apparently random positive or negative circumstances that consciousness encounters. The Ancient Egyptian Book of Enlightenment judgment scene depicts this principle figuratively, showing Shai (destiny) and Renenut (fortune) present at the judgment of the personality as to what extent the person lived by Maat principles. So, the apparently random situations and outcome of life are not random. Additionally, the God Djehuty appears at the scene, writing on his palette the result of the judgment. Ancient Egyptian wisdom further reveals that Shai and Renenut are the hands of Djehuty—meaning that our own fortune (karmic basis) and destiny (resulting effect of that karmic basis) are being recorded by Djehuty, the Cosmic Mind. Thus, our fortune, based on the sum-total of our past thoughts, feelings, desires, and memories qualified by our practice of Maat wisdom and application of Maatian standards to our actions that led to those past experiences, determines our own fate. In this context, we are the creators of our own fate. The teaching reveals this "randomness" as actually intelligent provision based on what serves personality/mind evolution at that moment. When mind operates with ethical integrity (aligned with Maat), Renenut provides circumstances supporting development—not necessarily comfortable circumstances, but precisely those that advance spiritual growth. When mind operates through ethical violation (going behind backs, deceitful seeking of domination), Renenut provides circumstances that either enable continued pattern operation (allowing karmic accumulation) or create suffering that motivates pattern examination.

The wisdom to be understood recognizes that this principle prevents potential misinterpretation when aspirants experience difficulty despite attempting to trust divine providence. When mind operates with impure aryu—even while consciously attempting verses 13-15's trust in divine timing—circumstances may manifest that appear contrary to desired provisions.[1] This occurs not because divine providence fails or because trust proves insufficient, but because Shayt and Renenut respond to the actual aryu content in the ab rather than to conscious intention alone. The accumulated feeling-memories of past unethical actions continue generating their destined effects (Shayt) and their fortune outcomes (Renenut) until sufficient purification occurs through Maat-aligned living.

Nevertheless, even these apparently negative outcomes represent divine providence operating with perfect intelligence. When impure aryu prevent desired material provisions, when circumstances create suffering despite righteous effort, when life delivers hardship rather than comfort—all this operates as cosmic intelligence providing precisely what that personality requires for evolutionary advancement. The difficulty itself becomes the provision: experiences creating conditions whereby mind must confront the consequences of past unethical patterns, motivating the purification work that future prosperity (both material and spiritual) depends upon. Thus, aspirants recognize that living righteously will tend to produce harmonious conditions aligned with divine grace, yet impure aryu may temporarily override this tendency—and that temporary difficulty serves ultimate good by forcing confrontation with patterns requiring transformation for consciousness to discover Neberdjer awareness.

This understanding prevents the dangerous despair that can arise when aspirants attempt verses 13-15's trust but encounter continued adversity. The adversity does not indicate failed practice or absent providence but rather reveals the depth of aryu purification still required. Divine providence operates through both blessing and correction, through ease and difficulty, through desired provisions and their temporary withholding—all intelligently calibrated to serve the personality's ultimate evolution toward the Beautiful West rather than continued reincarnation governed by unpurified patterns.

Verse 13's teaching about tayu (divine timing) reveals the integration of these principles: "every person has their time where what is due to come to them, comes to them by providence supported by their aryu (karma) and the gods and goddesses."[1] This establishes that cosmic intelligence provides according to both what the mind has created through past actions (Shayt momentum) and what divine grace determines serves evolution (Renenut provision), with timing orchestrated by intelligence transcending individual ego-personality comprehension.

The metaphysical implication: verses 10's deceitful power-seeking and verse 14's excessive anxious labor both represent fundamental misunderstanding of how provision actually occurs. They assume the personality must manipulate all circumstances to secure well-being, not recognizing that cosmic intelligence already operates to provide what genuinely serves evolution. This misunderstanding arises from aryu-obscured Ab Neter awareness—when the mind cannot perceive the divine ground sustaining its existence, it naturally assumes vulnerable isolation requiring manipulative self-protection.

Sekhem Flow Through Purified Versus Obstructed Mettu

The metaphysical mechanics of vital energy flow reveal why the behavioral patterns verses 10-15 describe produce such devastating consequences for spiritual development. Sekhem represents not merely abstract "energy" but the actual bioelectric-biochemical-consciousness substrate sustaining physical life and enabling spiritual awareness. This sekhem flows through mettu (channels) that contemporary science partially recognizes through nervous system, cardiovascular system, and fascial networks but which the ancient teaching understood in a more comprehensive framework including consciousness dimensions beyond current scientific measurement.

When mettu remain purified (wadj)—meaning free from obstructions created by negative aryu—sekhem flows properly, producing what the teaching calls hetep (peace, wholeness, harmony). This manifests physiologically as balanced nervous system function, efficient cellular metabolism, strong immune response, and mental-emotional equanimity. It manifests spiritually as the presence-of-mind (haty) necessary for recognizing Ab Neter awareness sustaining consciousness from the kara level. The purified individual experiences what verse 15 describes: genuine well-being in present circumstances regardless of external abundance or scarcity, and natural trust in divine timing for future provision.[1]

Conversely, when negative aryu obstruct mettu—which occurs systematically through the patterns verses 10-15 describe—sekhem flow becomes disturbed, producing characteristic symptoms. The Sema Institute teaching explains: "Obstructed mettu manifest as chronic muscle tension, organ dysfunction, endocrine imbalance, immune suppression, and mental-emotional disturbance. These are not separate conditions but rather unified syndrome of aryu-obstructed sekhem flow."[6] The individual experiences this as anxiety, restlessness, physical discomfort, compulsive behavioral urges, and the inability to access deeper consciousness levels.

The specific patterns verses 10-15 identify create characteristic mettu obstructions:

Verse 10's deceitful power-seeking obstructs mettu in the solar plexus —the center governing personal power, digestion, and will function. The aryu of manipulation create chronic tension preventing proper sekhem flow, manifesting as digestive disorders, anxiety, and the compulsive need for external control that drives continued manipulation. The individual cannot access ethical conscience (located in heart mettu) because sekhem flow from solar plexus to heart remains blocked by manipulation aryu.

Verse 12's mental wandering obstructs mettu in the head region (***wept***[14]—the forehead point between the eyebrows)—preventing proper sekhem flow to higher consciousness centers. The aryu of chronic fantasy and rumination create scattered energy patterns where sekhem dissipates through multiple thought-streams rather than concentrating for spiritual awareness. This produces the characteristic mental fog, inability to maintain present focus, and exhaustion from non-productive mental activity that the verse implicitly describes.

Verse 14's excessive labor obstructs mettu throughout the entire system through sustained sympathetic nervous system activation that diverts sekhem from restorative functions. The aryu of anxious striving create chronic tension preventing parasympathetic rest-and-restore cycles necessary for mettu purification and sekhem rebalancing. This produces the burnout syndrome contemporary

[14] Egyptian Book of the Dead Hieroglyph Translations Volume 2 [2017] (Book of Enlightenment From Chap. 4/17

medicine recognizes—comprehensive vital energy depletion affecting all body-mind-spirit levels simultaneously.

The metaphysical principle: mind cannot discover the kara (divine sanctuary within) that verse 9 of the Prologue describes when sekhem remains diverted to anxiety management, manipulative scheming, or escapist mental wandering. The "presence-of-mind" (haty) required for that discovery depends on sekhem flowing properly through purified mettu to higher consciousness centers—impossible while the patterns verses 10-15 identify maintain chronic disturbance. Thus, these behavioral patterns do not merely delay spiritual development—they create the physiological-energetic conditions that make Ab Neter recognition functionally impossible until addressed.

The Ab-Neter Recognition: Removing Obstruction Versus Creating Access

The most profound metaphysical principle occurs where verses 10-15 reveal concerns the nature of spiritual development itself. The teaching clarifies that Ab Neter—the divine soul sustaining consciousness from the kara level—already operates continuously, even when consciousness remains completely unaware. Spiritual development does not create this divine presence but rather removes the aryu obstructions (particularly those verse 10-15 identify) that prevent its recognition. This distinction proves crucial for practice orientation.

When mind operates through verse 10's deceitful manipulation, verse 12's mental wandering, or verse 14's excessive labor, it generates aryu that "occupy the presence-of-mind awareness, so densely as to influence the conscious reality awareness (thinking and feeling) of a person and blot out the awareness of the soul level divine presence."[1] These aryu function as what the teaching describes throughout: not merely psychological conditioning but actual obstructions within consciousness architecture that prevent the hat (front-of-mind [presence-of-mind] awareness) from perceiving what the kara level already contains.

The metaphysical mechanics: Ab Neter operates at the deepest level of the ab (unconscious mind), sustaining the very capacity for awareness by which mind experiences thoughts, feelings, sensations, and perceptions. This divine presence is never absent, never fluctuating, never dependent on personal achievement. However, when surface-level aryu in the ab accumulate sufficient density, they prevent conscious recognition of this sustaining presence—like dense clouds obscuring the sun that continues shining beyond them.

Verses 10-15's teachings provide systematic instruction for aryu thinning specifically targeting the patterns most responsible for the mind remaining trapped in heated reactivity. Verse 10 addresses the manipulation aryu; verse 12 addresses the mental wandering aryu; verse 14 addresses the anxious striving aryu; verses 13 and 15 introduce the divine providence trust that naturally emerges as these obstructing aryu thin. The progression reveals sophisticated understanding: heated behaviors (verses 10, 12, 14) arise from aryu obscuring Ab Neter awareness; thinning these aryu allows natural emergence of the trust (verses 13, 15) that consciousness would inherently possess if operating from its divine ground.

The "work" of spiritual development therefore involves not achieving something absent but allowing what already exists to reveal itself through systematic obstruction removal. This explains why verse 15's teaching about present well-being proves so crucial: the mind already has what it needs (sustained by Ab Neter from the kara), but anxious future-orientation aryu prevent recognizing this. The practice of acknowledging, appreciating and cultivating a feeling of gratitude about present provisioning directly thins those specific aryu, allowing the natural trust in divine timing that verses 13-15 describe to emerge not as forced belief but as recognized reality.

The Beautiful West Versus Reincarnation: Metaphysical Stakes

The teaching's ultimate metaphysical implication concerns what the tradition calls the Beautiful West (Amenta)—the state of consciousness that continues after physical death for those who have thinned aryu sufficiently to maintain Ab Neter awareness independent of body-mind complex. Verse 14's warning that excessive labor "take[s] you away from discovering the goals of life that I stated in the prologue" references this fundamental choice that determines post-mortem experience.[1]

The metaphysical framework: mind operating primarily through negative aryu at time of physical death cannot maintain coherence without the body-mind complex that those aryu patterns depend upon. The aryu of deceitful manipulation, mental wandering, and anxious striving all require physical embodiment for their operation—they cannot function in consciousness without body. Therefore, the mind dominated by these patterns at death experiences dissolution of ego-personality coherence, followed by reincarnation into new physical embodiment where the unresolved aryu patterns can continue operating.

Conversely, mind that has thinned negative aryu sufficiently to recognize Ab Neter awareness sustaining identity—discovering the kara that the Prologue verse 9 describes—maintains coherence after physical death because it no longer depends on body-mind for sense of existence. This consciousness "arrives at the Beautiful West" rather than reincarnating, continuing evolution in dimensions the teaching indicates but does not extensively elaborate (recognizing that such description exceeds what embodied consciousness can comprehend).

The metaphysical stakes of verses 10-15's teachings: the behavioral patterns they describe do not merely create temporary suffering or delayed spiritual development. They determine whether consciousness achieves sufficient aryu thinning during physical embodiment to "graduate" from reincarnation cycle or must return for continued embodied evolution. This explains the teaching's urgency—verse 14 explicitly warns that excessive labor takes consciousness away from life's actual goals, meaning the individual may miss an opportunity for spiritual evolution during a lifetime due to the pursuit of superfluous wealth accumulation that cannot be carried beyond death and that actively prevents the development that would allow liberation from rebirth necessity. In this context the value of spiritual wealth should be seen as paramount once the basic needs are provided for.

Understanding these metaphysical mechanics prevents the common misinterpretation that spiritual teaching promotes passivity or poverty. Verses 10-15 do not recommend abandoning practical responsibility or refusing appropriate work. Rather, they distinguish between the mind operating from heated aryu patterns that deplete sekhem and prevent Ab Neter recognition versus the mind operating from silent trust in divine providence that conserves vital energy for spiritual development. The difference lies not in external behavior alone but in the underlying the quality of mind and feelings—whether action arises from aryu-driven anxiety and manipulation or from ethical conscience aligned with cosmic intelligence.

4. Transpersonal Psychology Research: Contemporary Validation of Ancient Vital Energy Principles

Contemporary research in multiple disciplines provides empirical validation for the ancient framework distinguishing between power-seeking manipulation, mental wandering, excessive labor—and their collective impact on what Amenemopet identifies as sekhem (vital energy)—versus ethical integrity, present-moment awareness, and appropriate work-life balance. While modern science lacks direct measurement for sekhem or mettu, it documents physiological and psychological correlates that correspond precisely to what the teaching describes as vital energy depletion versus restoration.

Physiological Correlates of "Heated Mind and Feelings"

Psychophysiological research demonstrates that consciousness states Amenemopet identifies as "heated"—involving manipulative power-seeking, chronic anxiety, and mental agitation—produce measurable physiological signatures corresponding to what the teaching describes as sekhem depletion through aryu-obstructed mettu. Studies measuring individuals engaged in deceptive communication show elevated galvanic skin response, increased heart rate variability in stress-indicating patterns, elevated cortisol and inflammatory markers, and reduced immune function—all indicating what the ancient framework would identify as disturbed vital energy flow.[15]

Longitudinal research tracking individuals maintaining chronic competitive-manipulative consciousness states (verse 10's pattern) demonstrates accelerated biological aging, increased cardiovascular disease risk, higher cancer incidence, and earlier mortality compared to those operating with ethical integrity—providing empirical validation that deceitful power-seeking literally depletes life force.[16] The mechanism contemporary science identifies: chronic sympathetic nervous system activation diverts resources from immune surveillance, tissue repair, and cellular maintenance toward immediate threat-response, producing comprehensive system degradation that the ancient teaching recognized as sekhem exhaustion.

Research on default mode network activity validates verse 12's teaching about mental wandering depleting vital energy. Studies demonstrate that brain regions active during mind-wandering consume approximately 20% of total body energy expenditure despite producing no functional output—non-productive use of vital force that could be applied to either practical activity or spiritual practice.[9] Additionally, individuals with high habitual mind-wandering show reduced gray matter volume in attention-regulating brain regions and impaired connectivity between networks governing executive function—structural changes indicating the chronic mental wandering produces lasting damage to consciousness capacity.

Work stress and burnout research provides extensive validation for verse 14's warning about excessive labor depleting sekhem. Studies tracking individuals maintaining chronic overwork patterns show elevated allostatic load (cumulative physiological wear-and-tear), dysregulated cortisol rhythms, impaired immune function, increased metabolic syndrome risk, and accelerated telomere shortening indicating cellular aging.[13] The research demonstrates that excessive labor produces systemic physiological deterioration affecting all body systems—comprehensive vital energy depletion preventing the restoration necessary for spiritual practice.

Psychological Impacts of Power-Seeking and Control Orientation

Research on Machiavellianism and manipulative personality patterns validates verse 10's teaching about deceitful domination-seeking producing psychological suffering despite apparent external success. Studies demonstrate that individuals high in manipulative traits report lower life satisfaction, reduced relationship quality, increased anxiety and depression, and greater sense of existential emptiness compared to those operating with integrity—even when controlling for objective success measures.[17] This confirms the teaching that power-seeking through deceit creates internal disturbance regardless of whether the manipulation achieves its external goals.

Locus of control research distinguishes between internal locus (believing outcomes depend on personal action) and external locus (believing outcomes depend on forces beyond personal control), with extensive evidence that balanced perspective—recognizing appropriate spheres for personal agency while accepting what lies beyond control—produces superior psychological outcomes compared to rigid control orientation.[18] Individuals attempting to control all life aspects show elevated anxiety, depression, and stress-related symptoms—empirical validation for the teaching that mind attempting autonomous control through manipulation (verse 10) or excessive labor (verse 14) rather than trusting divine providence (verses 13-15) experiences psychological suffering.

Research on rumination and repetitive negative thinking provides extensive validation for verse 12's teaching about mental wandering depleting consciousness capacity. Studies demonstrate that individuals engaging in high-frequency rumination show impaired problem-solving ability, reduced cognitive flexibility, elevated depression and anxiety, and increased inflammation markers—comprehensive evidence that chronic mental wandering produces both psychological and physiological deterioration.[19] The research identifies rumination as maintaining stress response activation even when actual stressors are absent—corresponding to the teaching that mental wandering dissipates sekhem through sustained consciousness disturbance disconnected from present reality.

Gratitude and Present-Moment Awareness Research

Research on gratitude practices provides direct empirical validation for verse 15's teaching about acknowledging present well-being producing actual physiological benefits. Systematic reviews of gratitude intervention studies demonstrate that individuals practicing regular acknowledgment of current provisions show improved sleep quality, reduced depression and anxiety, enhanced immune function, increased heart rate variability in health-indicating patterns, and greater life satisfaction—all representing what the ancient framework identifies as sekhem restoration through aryu thinning.[10]

Neuroimaging studies show that gratitude practices activate brain regions associated with reward processing, social cognition, and emotional regulation while reducing activation in regions associated with threat detection and stress response—providing neural evidence for the teaching that present well-being recognition shifts consciousness from heated anxiety toward silent trust.[20] The research demonstrates that gratitude practice produces lasting neural changes rather than merely temporary mood effects—corresponding to the teaching about progressive aryu thinning through systematic practice.

Mindfulness and present-moment awareness research extensively validates verse 12's implicit recommendation for maintaining consciousness in present reality rather than allowing mental wandering. Meta-analyses of mindfulness-based interventions demonstrate significant benefits for psychological well-being, stress reduction, emotional regulation, and even immune function and inflammatory markers—empirical evidence that consciousness discipline produces both psychological and physiological improvements corresponding to what the teaching identifies as sekhem restoration through reduced mental wandering.[21]

Research on time perspective orientation validates the teaching about anxious future-focus (driving excessive labor) versus present well-being recognition. Studies demonstrate that individuals maintaining balanced time perspective—acknowledging present sufficiency while maintaining appropriate future planning—show superior psychological adjustment compared to those dominated by future-anxiety or past-rumination.[22] The research confirms that chronic future-anxiety maintains stress physiology activation even when present circumstances prove adequate—corresponding to verse 15's teaching that future-worry operates independently of actual provision adequacy.

Vital Energy and Biofield Research

While mainstream science remains skeptical about "vital energy" concepts, emerging research in biofield science provides preliminary validation for frameworks resembling the sekhem-mettu teaching. Studies measuring electromagnetic fields generated by the heart demonstrate that these fields extend beyond the body and can be detected by sensitive instruments—suggesting that "energy" concepts in traditional frameworks may correspond to actual measurable phenomena rather than mere metaphor.[23]

Research on heart rate variability (HRV) as marker of autonomic nervous system balance provides a measurable correlate for what the teaching describes as proper sekhem flow. Studies demonstrate that high HRV (indicating balanced sympathetic-parasympathetic function) correlates with better emotional regulation, stress resilience, immune function, and longevity—all outcomes the ancient teaching associates with proper vital energy flow.[24] Conversely, low HRV (indicating autonomic imbalance) associates with anxiety, depression, inflammation, and disease risk—corresponding to what the teaching identifies as sekhem depletion through aryu-obstructed mettu.

Polyvagal theory in neuroscience provides a contemporary framework partially corresponding to the sekhem-mettu teaching. The theory identifies the vagus nerve as governing a hierarchy of stress responses, with optimal functioning depending on ventral vagal activation supporting social engagement and restoration versus sympathetic activation driving fight-or-flight or dorsal vagal shutdown producing collapse.[25] The framework suggests that what traditional teachings call "vital energy flow" may correspond to vagal nerve functioning—with "obstructed mettu" representing vagal impairment and "purified channels" representing optimal vagal tone.

Research Limitations and Interpretive Caution

The wisdom to be understood acknowledges that contemporary research, while providing valuable validation for specific principles, cannot fully capture or verify the complete metaphysical framework that verses 10-15 present. Modern science measures physiological correlates of consciousness states but lacks instruments for directly assessing sekhem, mettu, aryu, or Ab Neter—the actual constructs the teaching addresses. Additionally, most research examines short-term interventions in convenience samples rather than tracking decades-long spiritual practice in individuals following comprehensive traditional training.

Nevertheless, the consistent pattern whereby research findings align with ancient teaching predictions—showing that manipulative power-seeking, mental wandering, and excessive labor produce measurable physiological and psychological deterioration while ethical integrity, present-moment awareness, and balanced work produce measurable benefits—provides substantial evidential support that these teachings identify actual patterns rather than mere cultural preference or religious doctrine. The convergence between ancient wisdom and contemporary empirical findings suggests that Amenemopet's framework describes real consciousness-physiology operations that modern science is gradually rediscovering through different methodological approaches.

SECTION 4A: TRANSPERSONAL PSYCHOLOGY RESEARCH

Neuroscience Validation of Wealth-Induced Cognitive Compromise

Contemporary Research Validates Ancient Wisdom

Contemporary neuroscience research provides remarkable empirical validation of Amenemopet's warnings regarding wealth and power, revealing that these teachings constitute not merely moral prescriptions but accurate descriptions of measurable neurological and psychological risk factors. The comprehensive examination documented in "Wealth-Induced Cognitive-Spiritual Compromise: Incorporating Neuroscience Research and Ancient Egyptian Theology" -research paper by Dr. Muata Ashby, synthesizes three independent lines of evidence—cultural-economic analysis, ancient Egyptian wisdom teachings, and contemporary neuroscience—all converging on identical conclusions about how wealth systematically compromises mental and spiritual development.[1]

The research demonstrates that wealth and power constitute significant risk factors for progressive cognitive-spiritual compromise, though substantial individual variation exists. Many individuals of considerable means maintain empathetic capacity and ethical sensitivity. Nevertheless, the mechanisms by which compromise can occur are now empirically documented and align precisely with Amenemopet's ancient framework of aryu accumulation obscuring Ab Neter awareness.[1]

Measurable Neural and Behavioral Changes

Multiple peer-reviewed studies document specific ways wealth affects brain function and behavior. Research by Kraus, Côté, and Keltner (2010) demonstrates that individuals from lower socioeconomic classes show significantly superior ability to read others' facial expressions—a fundamental marker of empathetic capacity—compared to their wealthier counterparts. The mechanism involves environmental necessity: lower-class environments require chronic attention to social vulnerability, thereby developing robust empathy circuits, while upper-class independence allows these circuits to atrophy through disuse.[1]

Even more directly, Obhi and colleagues (2014) used transcranial magnetic stimulation to measure the neural basis of empathy—motor resonance through which we literally mirror others' states in our own neural activity. Participants primed to reflect on times when they held power over others exhibited measurably reduced neural mirroring compared to those primed with experiences of being powerless. This demonstrates that power itself, independent of other factors, inhibits the very brain mechanism through which empathetic understanding operates.[1]

The University of Pennsylvania's BIG BEAR team, analyzing UK Biobank data, reveals that socioeconomic status correlates with approximately 1.6% variation in total brain volume, with stronger correlations evident in regions governing communication, empathy, and decision-making. What Amenemopet describes as aryu density creating obstruction to Ab Neter awareness may have structural neural correlates—measurable differences in brain architecture associated with socioeconomic circumstances.[1]

Behavioral studies conducted by Piff and colleagues at UC Berkeley documented systematic patterns: luxury vehicle drivers demonstrated three times greater likelihood of violating right-of-way norms, high-income individuals took twice as much candy from a jar designated "for children only," and wealthier participants showed significantly greater endorsement that "greed is justified" and "morally defensible." These patterns reveal what Amenemopet describes as heated mind and feelings: grasping, competitive, self-focused, operating from entitlement.[1]

The Addiction Mechanism and Treatment Intractability

Neuroscience research on reward systems provides a biological mechanism for Amenemopet's teaching that wealth creates "shennu" (prisoner state) characterized by perpetual unrest despite accumulation. Studies by Knutson and Greer (2008) and Schultz (2015) document that material acquisition activates dopamine reward circuits in ways that create tolerance—the brain requires progressively greater stimulation to achieve the same satisfaction response. Brain imaging reveals that anticipation of acquisition produces stronger neural activation than actual acquisition, creating a neurological bias toward seeking rather than enjoying, pursuit rather than satisfaction.[1]

This phenomenon, termed "hedonic adaptation" in psychological literature, describes precisely what Amenemopet identifies three millennia earlier: the person pursuing wealth becomes trapped in escalating need, where each acquisition provides diminishing satisfaction, requiring ever-greater accumulation to maintain even baseline contentment. The research demonstrates this involves measurable changes in neural chemistry—the dopamine system develops tolerance similar to that seen in substance addiction.[1]

Research on children raised in wealthy families validates Amenemopet's understanding of how wealth affects mental development across generations. Luthar and Latendresse (2005) documented that children in affluent families show 20-30% higher anxiety rates compared to less affluent peers, alongside elevated rates of substance abuse, depression, eating disorders, cheating, and stealing—contradicting simplistic assumptions that material abundance produces psychological wellbeing.[1]

Progressive Stages and the Uhem-Ankh Framework

The comprehensive research review identifies a progressive spectrum of vulnerability with identifiable stages. Stage 1-2 (Mild to Moderate Compromise) shows measurable empathy reduction and increased utilitarian orientation but retains capacity for self-inquiry. Research demonstrates that simple interventions can rapidly restore empathetic behavior, indicating neural circuits remain functional despite patterns of disuse. At these stages, spiritual practices, ethical living (Maat), and community involvement can prevent progression and reverse emerging patterns.[1]

Stage 3 (Severe Compromise) involves intermittent and unreliable self-inquiry capacity, requiring intensive therapeutic intervention beyond what an ordinary relationship can provide. Brain imaging studies suggest more pronounced structural changes at this severity. Stage 4 (Advanced Pathology) presents a sobering clinical reality: research on psychopathy—sharing significant overlap with what Amenemopet describes as advanced heated mind and feelings—reveals potential treatment intractability. Studies characterize psychopathy as "among the most refractory of personality disorders," with adult cases showing "largely resistant to treatment" despite intensive interventions. High recidivism rates (approximately 70% within five years) persist even after years of behavioral therapy.[1]

The research literature on psychopathy treatment reveals crucial limitations. No randomized controlled trials of psychological interventions for established adult psychopathy exist in clinical literature. The honest assessment is that we do not currently know how to effectively treat such cases within a current lifetime through available interventions. This sobering reality validates

Amenemopet's directive to avoid heated persons completely—recognizing that some conditions exceed the capacity of an ordinary intervention.[1]

The comprehensive examination introduces the ancient Egyptian theological framework of ( )—literally "to repeat life" or "living again"—as essential for understanding apparently intractable cases. The doctrine holds that consciousness continues beyond physical death and returns in new form to continue its journey toward ultimate reunion with Neberdjer (All-Encompassing Divinity). This framework provides a resolution to the intractability dilemma: what appears as an intractable deadlock in single-lifetime perspective becomes a temporary impasse in multi-lifetime perspective. Death provides a merciful reset, freeing consciousness from irreparably compromised apparatus and providing fresh opportunity through reincarnation with new circumstances determined by accumulated aryu (shayt/rennenet—fortune and destiny).[1]

This understanding transforms how aspirants relate to severely compromised individuals—recognizing that transformation may require uhem-ankh allows maintaining both protective boundaries and compassion simultaneously. The aspirant can hold deep compassion for the suffering of being trapped in irreparably compromised apparatus while maintaining complete protective boundaries, trusting that divine mercy provides uhem-ankh when needed, accepting that some learning requires multiple incarnations. This represents mature spiritual understanding: acknowledging that one's capacities, however developed, remain finite, while trusting cosmic processes to provide what human capacity cannot.[1]

Integration with Amenemopet's Framework

The research findings validate Amenemopet's teaching on multiple levels. First, the warning about wealth and power creating "weakness of mind" finds empirical support in documented empathy reduction, structural brain changes, and altered reward processing. Second, the description of heated mind and feelings as grasping, competitive, self-focused, and operating from entitlement corresponds precisely to documented behavioral patterns associated with wealth. Third, the teaching that wealth creates "prisoner state" of perpetual unrest despite abundance describes the subjective experience of the mind operating through reward circuits altered by hedonic adaptation.[1]

Fourth, the directive to avoid heated persons—particularly those whose heatedness arises from wealth and power pursuit—reflects realistic recognition that severe stages involve cognitive-spiritual compromise potentially beyond what an ordinary relationship can address. Fifth, and most significantly, the research supports understanding aryu not merely as psychological patterns but as having structural neural correlates that can persist and resist change, sometimes to a degree requiring intervention beyond current lifetime's capacity—resolved through the theological framework of uhem-ankh.[1]

The wisdom to be understood here is that contemporary neuroscience, despite its sophisticated instruments and rigorous methodology, has essentially confirmed what the ancient sages perceived directly: that pursuit of wealth and power systematically compromises perceptual sensitivity, that these compromises have a tangible substrate in altered brain function and structure, that the changes can progress from mild to severe, and that advanced stages may represent cognitive-spiritual compromise requiring intervention beyond what an ordinary intervention has the capacity to provide for. This convergence of ancient wisdom and contemporary science demonstrates that Amenemopet possessed insight into the architecture of mind and consciousness that transcended his era's technological limitations, perceiving directly what we now measure indirectly through instruments.

The comprehensive examination in "Wealth-Induced Cognitive-Spiritual Compromise" provides aspirants with essential understanding for navigating the modern world: recognizing wealth as a measurable risk factor (not deterministic cause), implementing appropriate protective boundaries based on severity assessment, maintaining spiritual practices that thin aryu and reveal Ab Neter awareness, cultivating environments supporting Maat principles, trusting karmic processes and divine mercy, and practicing compassion without proximity. This represents the mature wisdom tradition: neither naive about human capacity for change nor despairing about ultimate possibilities, combining realistic assessment of current limitations with trust in processes operating across lifetimes toward eventual universal enlightenment.[43]

5. Spiritual Implications for Aspirants: Practical Methods for Vital Energy Conservation and Divine Trust Development

Part A—Pastoral Concerns: Modern Obstacles to Sekhem Conservation and Divine Providence Trust

Contemporary aspirants attempting to implement verses 10-15's teachings face systematic obstacles that previous generations did not encounter—technological systems deliberately engineered to capture attention, economic structures requiring participation in manipulative competition, and cultural narratives systematically undermining the divine trust these verses recommend. Understanding these obstacles prevents the discouragement that arises when practice proves more challenging than anticipated while clarifying that the difficulty reflects environmental hostility rather than personal inadequacy.

Consider the aspirant working in contemporary corporate environment where verse 10's "going behind the back of people, of justice, of truth" operates as normalized standard practice rather than recognized ethical violation.[1] The individual attempting to maintain integrity faces genuine practical tension: colleagues strategically withholding information, supervisors expecting manipulative presentation, organizational culture rewarding appearances over truth. The aspirant who refuses to participate in systemic deception often experiences professional disadvantage—reduced advancement opportunity, exclusion from informal networks, reputation as "not a team player."

The challenge intensifies through the physiological reality of what can be identified as a framework of life operating in environments saturated with manipulative minds that create mettu disturbances even for those seeking to maintain personal integrity. The aspirant surrounded by heated colleagues absorbs energetic disturbance through emotional contagion, environmental stress, and the constant vigilance required to maintain ethical boundaries in hostile context.[6] This produces sekhem depletion even without personal participation in manipulation—consciousness expending vital energy simply to resist environmental pressure toward ethical compromise.

Verse 12's teaching about refraining from mental wandering faces perhaps an even greater contemporary obstacle through technology systems specifically designed to capture and fragment attention. The aspirant attempting to maintain present-moment awareness confronts smartphone notifications engineered by behavioral psychologists to trigger compulsive checking, social media algorithms optimized to maximize engagement through anxiety and comparison, and entertainment systems providing endless escape from present reality.[1] The teaching's instruction to "refrain, renounce, forsake the practice of letting your conscious mind travel" requires radically countercultural choice in environment actively engineering mental wandering as profit-generation mechanism.

The physiological reality: each attention fragmentation created by notification, each mental wandering episode triggered by social media algorithm, each escapist entertainment consumption session depletes the sekhem that verse 12 identifies as needing conservation for spiritual development. The cumulative effect over months and years produces consciousness so habituated to mental wandering that present-moment awareness feels nearly impossible to maintain. The aspirant attempts meditation and discovers that sustained focus for even three minutes exceeds current capacity—not due to personal failing but due to systematic neural rewiring that technology-mediated mental wandering produces.

PART B—METHODS FOR TRANSFORMATION: SYSTEMATIC PRACTICES FOR VITAL ENERGY CONSERVATION AND DIVINE TRUST CULTIVATION

The transformation verses 10-15 recommend requires systematic practice addressing multiple levels simultaneously: physical health supporting proper sekhem flow, mental discipline conserving vital energy, ethical conduct preventing aryu accumulation, and philosophical understanding enabling trust in divine providence. The following practices derive directly from the teaching's explicit instructions and the inverse doctrine application methodology, providing concrete implementation despite contemporary obstacles.

Practice 1: Mettu Purification Through Diet and Healing Intention

Based on the Sema Institute teaching about aryu-obstructed mettu preventing proper sekhem flow, aspirants begin practice by addressing physical level purification supporting vital energy restoration. The teaching identifies a specific dietary approach particularly effective for clearing channels: consuming green foods—vegetables, herbs like spirulina and chlorella in smoothies or juices, along with fresh fruits—to support mettu purification by providing nutrients that assist liver detoxification, reduce inflammation, and alkalize body systems.[40] The ancient healing wisdom encoded this practice in the chant "Hotep di si Neter iri Mettu wadj" (Peace offering given to cause the Divine to make the channels green/healthy), recognizing that green foods function on multiple levels simultaneously—physically nourishing the body while spiritually feeding the ka (vital life force) with the divine essence stored in vegetation.[41] This physical practice operates in parallel with the wisdom teaching: "The wise person feeds the *Ka* (mind) with what endures, so that it is happy with that person on earth"[42]—for just as green foods clear the physical mettu channels, the green food of wisdom feeds the ka with teachings that endure, clearing the subtle energy channels through which Hat operates. The dual practice addresses both dimensions: physical green foods purify the body's mettu system allowing free sekhem flow, while wisdom teachings purify the mind (ka), removing aryu-generated falsehoods that support egoism and obstruct recognition of Ab Neter within.

Implementation: The aspirant commits to consuming one large green smoothie or juice daily, preferably first thing upon waking when body is most receptive to purification support. The practice includes specific healing intention derived from verse 10's implicit teaching about operating with integrity rather than deceit: while preparing the green drink, consciousness repeats the chant "Hetep Di Si Neter Iry Mettu Wadj" (Peace offerings given by the Divine make the channels pure).[6] This combines physical purification (green food nutrients supporting detoxification) with consciousness intention (invoking divine assistance for channel clearing) and subtle energy practice (chant vibrations affecting mettu directly).

The teaching explains that this seemingly simple practice produces effects at multiple levels simultaneously. Physically, the green food provides bioavailable nutrients supporting liver function, which the ancient wisdom identifies as crucial for mettu purification. Psychologically, the daily commitment to this practice establishes foundation for consciousness recognizing that spiritual development requires systematic physical support rather than purely mental effort. Energetically, the healing chant creates what the tradition calls "resonance" with divine intelligence, inviting cosmic support for the purification process. Over weeks and months, aspirants report measurable improvements: increased energy levels, reduced chronic tension, improved sleep quality, and greater capacity for sustained spiritual practice—all indicating sekhem restoration through progressive mettu clearing.[6]

Practice 2: Progressive Aryu Thinning Through Ethical Restraint

Based on verse 10's warning against operating "behind the back of people, of justice, of truth" and verse 12's instruction to "refrain, renounce, forsake" mental wandering, aspirants practice systematic ethical restraint specifically targeting behaviors through which negative aryu maintain control.[1] The practice recognizes that each time the mind successfully resists aryu-driven compulsion and chooses aligned action, it both prevents new aryu formation and slightly thins existing patterns.

Implementation: The aspirant identifies the three strongest negative aryu patterns controlling their vital energies—perhaps manipulative communication maintaining work position, compulsive media consumption providing escape, and obsessive productivity driven by anxiety. For each pattern, they establish clear intention: "When this aryu attempts to control my vital energy and compel this behavior, I will pause, engage conscious breathing, and choose differently—even if only for this one instance."

The practice proceeds gradually, recognizing that negative aryu controlling sekhem for years cannot release immediately. Week one: notice when aryu compulsions arise, without attempting resistance. Week two: successfully resist one aryu-driven behavior daily. Week three: successfully resist two instances. The gradualism proves essential because attempting dramatic transformation while sekhem remains under strong aryu control simply produces failure, reinforcing the very enslavement the practice aims to dissolve.

Concrete example: An aspirant notices the impulse to manipulate information in a work email. The negative aryu controlling their vital energy produce compelling internal narrative: "This slight distortion is necessary for survival. Everyone does it. It's just business." Previously, they would automatically engage the manipulation, depositing new aryu while reinforcing existing patterns' control over sekhem. With practice, they pause upon recognizing the impulse. They engage three conscious breaths, allowing sekhem to temporarily escape aryu control. In that brief window, ethical conscience gains sufficient influence to choose transparent communication.

Initially this produces anxiety—the negative aryu, sensing their control threatened, intensify physiological disturbance attempting to reassert dominance. But the aspirant persists, noticing that after the ethical choice, sekhem rebalances more quickly than after aryu-controlled manipulation. Over months, they accumulate dozens of instances where ethical conscience directed behavior despite aryu resistance. Each instance slightly thins the negative patterns while depositing new aryu aligned with Maat. Eventually, the enslaving patterns weaken sufficiently that ethical choice becomes progressively easier, indicating the mind successfully liberating vital energy from negative aryu control.

Practice 3: Serenity (Ger) Cultivation Through Integrated Daily Practice

Based on the complete teaching of verses 10-15, aspirants implement integrated daily practice simultaneously addressing physical health (mettu purification), vital energy restoration (sekhem through breath and diet), aryu thinning (ethical restraint and present well-being recognition), and divine connection (healing intention and providence trust).[1,6] This integrated approach recognizes that negative aryu maintain control over vital energies through multiple reinforcing mechanisms requiring comprehensive intervention.

Morning practice establishes foundation: (1) Healing chant "Hetep Di Si Neter Iry Mettu Wadj" setting intention for channel clearing; (2) Twenty minutes abdominal breathing with visualization of sekhem restoration; (3) Green food/juice supporting physical mettu purification; (4) Conscious recognition of three ways cosmic providence currently operates in life.[6]

Throughout the day: (1) Before each meal, repeat healing chant; (2) When negative aryu trigger compulsive behaviors, pause for conscious breathing before responding; (3) Actively practice ethical restraint choosing aligned action despite aryu resistance; (4) Avoid excessive labor that depletes sekhem [verse 14]; (5) Refrain from mental wandering that dissipates vital energy [verse 12].[1]

Evening practice completes cycle: (1) Present Well-being Inventory acknowledging five provisions; (2) Reflection on day's ethical choices—celebrating resistances to negative aryu control while compassionately recognizing instances where patterns prevailed; (3) Breath practice with intention that night's rest supports continued sekhem restoration and aryu thinning; (4) Sleep recognizing that "what may be needed in the future will come to you in due course."[1]

The teaching emphasizes that this transformation requires patient absorption over months and years, not forceful achievement. Negative aryu accumulated over lifetimes controlling vital energies cannot release instantly. But aspirants implementing integrated practice consistently notice progressive shifts: behaviors that felt compulsively compelling become resistible; physiological agitation decreases in intensity and duration; chronic tension representing aryu-obstructed mettu progressively releases; moments of genuine serenity (Ger) emerge where mind operates from ethical conscience rather than aryu-driven reactivity.

Most profoundly, aspirants begin experiencing what verse 13 describes: recognition that "every person has their time where what is due to come to them, comes to them by providence supported by their karma (aryu) and the gods and goddesses."[1] This recognition emerges not as intellectual understanding but as lived reality—consciousness directly perceiving cosmic intelligence operating through both accumulated patterns and divine grace, providing precisely what serves evolution at exactly the right moment. When this awareness stabilizes, the aspirant discovers her/himself progressively freed from negative aryu enslavement, with ethical conscience directing personality functioning aligned with the three lauded goals: awareness of Neberdjer, reverence for being in the hand of God, and preparation for arrival at the Beautiful West rather than reincarnation into continued ego-governed suffering governed by negative aryu controlling vital energies.[1,3,6]

References

[1] Ashby, M. (2019-25). *Mysticism of Amenemopet Hieroglyphic Text Translation*. Sema Institute of Ancient Egyptian Studies.
[2] Ashby, M. (2025). *Keys to Sage Amenemopet Wisdom Text Trilinear Translation Chapter 7 by Dr. Muata Ashby*. Sema Institute of Ancient Egyptian Studies.
[3] Ashby, M. (2019). *Amenemopet Lectures 2019 by Dr. Muata Ashby Transcripts*. Sema Institute of Ancient Egyptian Studies.
[4] Ashby, M. (2024). *Amenemopet Lectures 2024 by Dr. Muata Ashby Transcripts*. Sema Institute of Ancient Egyptian Studies.
[5] Ashby, M. (2025). *Book Maat Philosophy Versus Fascism and the Police State V33*. Sema Institute of Ancient Egyptian Studies.
[6] Ashby, M. (2007). *The Kemetic Diet: Food for Body, Mind and Soul*. Sema Institute of Ancient Egyptian Studies.
[7] Christ, S. E., Van Essen, D. C., Watson, J. M., Brubaker, L. E., & McDermott, K. B. (2009). The contributions of prefrontal cortex and executive control to deception: Evidence from activation likelihood estimate meta-analyses. *Cerebral Cortex, 19*(7), 1557-1566.
[8] Keltner, D., Gruenfeld, D. H., & Anderson, C. (2003). Power, approach, and inhibition. *Psychological Review, 110*(2), 265-284.
[9] Judge, T. A., Piccolo, R. F., & Kosalka, T. (2009). The bright and dark sides of leader traits: A review and theoretical extension of the leader trait paradigm. *The Leadership Quarterly, 20*(6), 855-875.
[10] Deci, E. L., & Ryan, R. M. (2000). The "what" and "why" of goal pursuits: Human needs and the self-determination of behavior. *Psychological Inquiry, 11*(4), 227-268.
[11] Kornfield, J. (2008). *The Wise Heart: A Guide to the Universal Teachings of Buddhist Psychology*. Bantam Books.
[12] Davidson, R. J., & Lutz, A. (2008). Buddha's brain: Neuroplasticity and meditation. *IEEE Signal Processing Magazine, 25*(1), 176-174.
[13] Kasser, T., & Ryan, R. M. (1993). A dark side of the American dream: Correlates of financial success as a central life aspiration. *Journal of Personality and Social Psychology, 65*(2), 410-422.
[14] Killingsworth, M. A., & Gilbert, D. T. (2010). A wandering mind is an unhappy mind. *Science, 330*(6006), 932.
[15] Brewer, J. A., Worhunsky, P. D., Gray, J. R., Tang, Y. Y., Weber, J., & Kober, H. (2011). Meditation experience is associated with differences in default mode network activity and connectivity. *Proceedings of the National Academy of Sciences, 108*(50), 20254-20259.
[16] Emmons, R. A., & McCullough, M. E. (2003). Counting blessings versus burdens: An experimental investigation of gratitude and subjective well-being in daily life. *Journal of Personality and Social Psychology, 84*(2), 377-389.
[17] Null, G., Dean, C., Feldman, M., Rasio, D., & Smith, D. W. (2017). Nutrition and lifestyle intervention on mood, cognitive function, and quality of life in older adults: A pilot study. *Journal of Nutrition, Health & Aging, 21*(10), 1241-1245.
[18] Anderson, J. G., & Taylor, A. G. (2011). Biofield therapies and cancer pain. *Clinical Journal of Oncology Nursing, 15*(5), 519-525.
[19] Wardell, D. W., & Weymouth, K. F. (2004). Review of studies of healing touch. *Journal of Nursing Scholarship, 36*(2), 147-154.
[20] Aghabati, N., Mohammadi, E., & Pour Esmaiel, Z. (2010). The effect of therapeutic touch on pain and fatigue of cancer patients undergoing chemotherapy. *Evidence-Based Complementary and Alternative Medicine, 7*(3), 375-381.
[21] Jahnke, R., Larkey, L., Rogers, C., Etnier, J., & Lin, F. (2010). A comprehensive review of health benefits of qigong and tai chi. *American Journal of Health Promotion, 24*(6), e1-e25.
[22] Guo, X., Zhou, B., Nishimura, T., Teramukai, S., & Fukushima, M. (2008). Clinical effect of qigong practice on essential hypertension: A meta-analysis of randomized controlled trials. *Journal of Alternative and Complementary Medicine, 14*(1), 27-37.
[23] Wang, C. W., Chan, C. H., Ho, R. T., Chan, J. S., Ng, S. M., & Chan, C. L. (2014). Managing stress and anxiety through qigong exercise in healthy adults: A systematic review and meta-analysis of randomized controlled trials. *BMC Complementary and Alternative Medicine, 14*, 8.
[24] Sancier, K. M., & Holman, D. (2004). Commentary: Multifaceted health benefits of medical qigong. *Journal of Alternative and Complementary Medicine, 10*(1), 163-165.
[25] Chiesa, A., & Serretti, A. (2009). Mindfulness-based stress reduction for stress management in healthy people: A review and meta-analysis. *Journal of Alternative and Complementary Medicine, 15*(5), 593-600.
[26] Wei, G. X., Xu, T., Fan, F. M., Dong, H. M., Jiang, L. L., Li, H. J., et al. (2013). Can taichi reshape the brain? A brain morphometry study. *PLoS ONE, 8*(4), e61038.
[27] Mathie, R. T., Lloyd, S. M., Legg, L. A., Clausen, J., Moss, S., Davidson, J. R., & Ford, I. (2014). Randomised placebo-controlled trials of individualised homeopathic treatment: Systematic review and meta-analysis. *Systematic Reviews, 3*, 142.
[28] Linde, K., Clausius, N., Ramirez, G., Melchart, D., Eitel, F., Hedges, L. V., & Jonas, W. B. (1997). Are the clinical effects of homeopathy placebo effects? A meta-analysis of placebo-controlled trials. *The Lancet, 350*(9081), 834-843.
[29] Bellavite, P., Conforti, A., Pontarollo, F., & Ortolani, R. (2006). Immunology and homeopathy: Historical background. *Evidence-Based Complementary and Alternative Medicine, 3*(4), 441-452.
[30] Vithoulkas, G., & Van Woensel, E. (2014). Levels of health and disease: A working hypothesis. *International Journal of High Dilution Research, 13*(46), 35-45.

[31] Verschuere, B., Ben-Shakhar, G., & Meijer, E. (2011). *Memory Detection: Theory and Application of the Concealed Information Test*. Cambridge University Press.
[32] Barsade, S. G., & Gibson, D. E. (2007). Why does affect matter in organizations? *Academy of Management Perspectives, 21*(1), 36-59.
[33] Garrison, K. A., Zeffiro, T. A., Scheinost, D., Constable, R. T., & Brewer, J. A. (2015). Meditation leads to reduced default mode network activity beyond an active task. *Cognitive, Affective, & Behavioral Neuroscience, 15*(3), 712-720.
[34] Lutz, A., Greischar, L. L., Rawlings, N. B., Ricard, M., & Davidson, R. J. (2004). Long-term meditators self-induce high-amplitude gamma synchrony during mental practice. *Proceedings of the National Academy of Sciences, 101*(46), 16369-16373.
[35] Scheier, M. F., & Carver, C. S. (1985). Optimism, coping, and health: Assessment and implications of generalized outcome expectancies. *Health Psychology, 4*(3), 219-247.
[36] Maren, S., Phan, K. L., & Liberzon, I. (2013). The contextual brain: Implications for fear conditioning, extinction and psychopathology. *Nature Reviews Neuroscience, 14*(6), 417-428.
[37] Kok, B. E., Coffey, K. A., Cohn, M. A., Catalino, L. I., Vacharkulksemsuk, T., Algoe, S. B., et al. (2013). How positive emotions build physical health: Perceived positive social connections account for the upward spiral between positive emotions and vagal tone. *Psychological Science, 24*(7), 1123-1132.
[38] Davidson, R. J., Kabat-Zinn, J., Schumacher, J., Rosenkranz, M., Muller, D., Santorelli, S. F., et al. (2003). Alterations in brain and immune function produced by mindfulness meditation. *Psychosomatic Medicine, 65*(4), 564-570.
[39] Lutz, A., Slagter, H. A., Dunne, J. D., & Davidson, R. J. (2008). Attention regulation and monitoring in meditation. *Trends in Cognitive Sciences, 12*(4), 163-169.
[40] Ashby, M. (1999). *The Kemetic Diet: Guide to Health, Diet and Fasting*. Sema Institute of Ancient Egyptian Studies.
[41] Ashby, M. (2007). *The Serpent Power: The Ancient Egyptian Mystical Wisdom of the Inner Life Force*. Sema Institute of Ancient Egyptian Studies.
[42] Ashby, M. (1994). *Egyptian Proverbs: Temt Tchaas*. Sema Institute of Ancient Egyptian Studies.
[43]Ashby, M. (2025). Wealth-Induced Cognitive-Spiritual Compromise: Incorporating Neuroscience Research and Ancient Egyptian Theology. Sema Institute of Ancient Egyptian Studies.

Chapter 12: Addendum to Chapter 11 about Amenemopet Chapter 7: Transforming Destiny Through Purification

THE MECHANICS OF ARYU CLEANSING AND CONSCIOUSNESS REFORMATION IN RELATION TO SHAYT AND RENENUT

AN EXPANDED TEACHING ON THE PRACTICAL PROCESS OF PURIFYING THE SUBCONSCIOUS AND UNCONSCIOUS MINDS TO RESHAPE FORTUNE AND DESTINY

The teaching of Chapter 7 verses 10-11 reveals how deliberate volition operating "behind the back" of truth creates aryu deposits in the ab (unconscious mind) that cosmic forces Shayt (destiny) and Renenut (fortune) then use to shape future life experiences.[1] Having established this cosmic framework, the wisdom to be understood encompasses the precise mechanism through which one can transform these patterns—how one actually goes about the work of purifying the subconscious and unconscious levels to reshape one's destiny rather than remaining trapped in cycles of power-seeking and deception that perpetuate suffering.

THE ARCHITECTURE OF PERSONALITY: UNDERSTANDING THE LEVELS OF MIND

Before we can discuss purification, we must understand what requires purification and where it resides within the architecture of mind. Sage Amenemopet's teaching reveals a sophisticated model of mind operating at multiple levels simultaneously, each with distinct functions yet all interconnected in the overall operation of personality.[1,2]

At the surface level operates what is called the hat—the conscious level of mind, what we might describe as front-of-mind awareness or what is presently occupying conscious attention. This represents the thoughts you are thinking right now, the perceptions coming through your senses at this moment, the immediate awareness you have of your surroundings and mental activity. The hat is where deliberate volition operates, where conscious choice appears to function.[1,2]

Beneath the hat operates the ka—what modern psychology might term the subconscious level. The ka functions as the astral body, the energetic vehicle that contains and processes impressions sprouting forth from the unconscious mind. These impressions manifest as feelings, desires, and thought impulses that seem to arise spontaneously in conscious awareness. The ka serves as an intermediary, bringing unconscious content into conscious experience while simultaneously receiving and processing conscious experiences to store in deeper levels.[2,4]

Deeper still lies the ab—the unconscious mind proper, the vast repository where aryu (karmic feeling-memories) accumulate and reside. The ab functions as the storage system for all past experiences, actions, thoughts, and feelings. Everything that has ever been experienced, whether in this lifetime or previous existences, deposits its impression here as aryu, which may be thought of as a residue that remains after the past experience has faded from active memory. These aryu then shape future perception and behavior, creating what appears as personality traits, habitual patterns, emotional tendencies, and automatic responses to life circumstances.[1,2,4]

Consider how this works: When you encounter a situation that triggers fear or anger, that emotional response does not originate in the hat (conscious mind) but rises from aryu stored in the ab, passes through the ka (subconscious processing), and emerges into hat awareness as what seems like a spontaneous feeling. You believe "I am angry" or "I am afraid," but actually the mind is experiencing the activation of aryu patterns deposited by past experiences now being brought forward through the ka into present awareness in the hat. The aryu eliciting a feeling might have arisen through being stimulated by a current perception or sensation that resonates with unconscious aryu patterns. Alternatively, aryu may manifest when repeated thoughts dwelling on a particular issue or desire reach a threshold where the accumulated energy can no longer remain contained in the ab and spontaneously erupts into conscious awareness through the ka.

Below the ab—which is to say deeper than even the unconscious mind with its accumulated aryu—resides what is called Ab Neter, the soul level of consciousness. Ab Neter represents the divine spark, the portion of Divine consciousness that sustains every individual's capacity for conscious awareness. This is the "heart divinity" that Amenemopet refers to in Chapter 11, verse 10—the foundation of individual existence, the true self beyond ego constructs, beyond accumulated experiences, beyond the personality structure built from aryu.[1,2,4]

Beyond even the Ab Neter level lies Neberdjer—the all-encompassing divinity, the transcendental absolute reality, the supreme consciousness that gives rise to and contains all manifestation. Neberdjer represents infinity experienced as space, eternity experienced as time, the boundless awareness from which all individual consciousness emerges and to which all eventually returns in enlightenment. Neberdjer is what mystics call God-consciousness, cosmic consciousness, the ultimate reality.[2,4]

This architecture—hat, ka, ab, Ab Neter, Neberdjer—represents the complete structure through which consciousness operates in embodied existence. Understanding this structure proves essential because purification requires knowing what to purify (the ab with its aryu), how it affects present experience (through the ka bringing impressions to the hat), what sustains it all (Ab Neter), and what the ultimate goal reveals itself to be (Neberdjer recognition).

THE MECHANISM OF ARYU FORMATION: HOW ACTIONS LODGE IN THE PERSONALITY

Having established the architecture, we must now understand the precise mechanism through which aryu form and lodge themselves in the ab, because understanding this mechanism reveals simultaneously how to prevent negative aryu accumulation and how to deposit positive aryu that support purification rather than obstruction.

The mechanism works through a process that involves action, thought, and feeling operating in complex interplay—not in simple linear sequence where one always precedes the other, but in dynamic interaction where any of these three can initiate a cycle that produces aryu deposit. Nevertheless, we can identify the basic operation: When you engage in an action, entertain a thought, or allow a feeling, if these remain unsupervised by wisdom and prove untoward—meaning they oppose Maat (cosmic order)—they will enter and lodge themselves in the ab as aryu.[4]

The term "untoward" (Egyptian: djer, meaning "bad," "evil," or "opposing cosmic order") requires careful understanding because it does not reference arbitrary moral rules but rather actions, thoughts, and feelings that generate discord with Maat—the cosmic harmony sustaining all existence. Truthful speech aligns with Maat because truth supports proper functioning of relationships and society; deceptive speech (like verse 10's "going behind the back" of truth) opposes Maat because it creates confusion, distrust, and social disorder while depositing aryu that obscure Ab Neter awareness in the perpetrator.[1,4]

The critical recognition: both virtuous and non-virtuous actions deposit aryu, but with entirely different effects on the mind. Virtuous actions aligned with Maat deposit what we might call "transparent aryu"—impressions that do not obstruct the natural light of Ab Neter awareness but rather serve as supporting structures (mooring posts) that help consciousness maintain ethical alignment. Non-virtuous actions opposing Maat deposit "opaque aryu"—dense impressions that actively obscure Ab Neter presence, creating the heated mind and feelings that generate suffering and perpetuate ignorance of divine nature.[4]

Consider a concrete example: You encounter someone in distress. The thought arises to offer assistance. If you act on this impulse with genuine compassion (aligned with Maat), the action deposits aryu in your ab, but these aryu do not obstruct Ab Neter awareness—they actually support future compassionate responses and thin existing patterns of self-centered indifference. However, if you encounter the same person and think "Not my problem," allowing selfish indifference to govern response, this thought-feeling combination deposits dense aryu that reinforce ego-separation, thicken the barrier obscuring Ab Neter awareness, and create the personality structure that experiences itself as isolated, vulnerable, and requiring manipulation for survival (the pattern verse 10 describes).[1,4]

The formation process operates continuously. Every moment of awareness involves action (including the action of thinking and feeling), and each action deposits its corresponding impression in the ab. Over time, these accumulated aryu create what appears as personality—the characteristic ways you think, feel, and behave that seem like "who you are" but actually represent the sum total of deposited impressions. Someone whose ab contains dense accumulations of manipulative aryu (from repeated deceitful behavior) will experience spontaneous urges toward manipulation arising seemingly automatically through the ka into the hat. They believe "I am a cunning person" or "I must manipulate to survive," not recognizing these as aryu patterns that could be transformed through systematic purification.[1,3,4]

THE THREE PRACTICES OF PURIFICATION: BEHAVIORAL CONTROL, MEDITATION, AND INVOCATION OF UDJA

Understanding how aryu form reveals simultaneously how to purify them. The ancient wisdom identifies three primary practices operating at different levels yet working together synergistically to accomplish mind transformation.

PRACTICE ONE: BEHAVIORAL CONTROL TO PREVENT NEW NEGATIVE ARYU WHILE DEPOSITING POSITIVE PATTERNS

The foundation of purification begins with ethical living—controlling actions, thoughts, and feelings to prevent depositing new negative aryu while systematically depositing positive impressions that support Ab Neter recognition. This represents not mere moralism but strategic mind engineering: if you understand that every action deposits impressions shaping future mental states, you naturally become extremely careful about what you allow to enter your ab.[3,4]

The practice requires constant vigilance because aryu accumulated from past lives and earlier in this life continuously push for expression through the ka into the hat, creating impulses that feel compelling. When anger arises, the temptation exists to indulge it—to speak harshly, to plot revenge, to nurse grievances. Each indulgence deposits new anger aryu in the ab while reinforcing existing patterns, creating a self-perpetuating cycle where anger becomes increasingly automatic. The purification path requires recognizing the arising anger as aryu activation rather than truth about reality, creating space between awareness and emotion, and choosing a Maat-aligned response despite the compelling urge toward reactivity.[4]

This proves extraordinarily challenging in contemporary society because culture actively encourages aryu-generating behaviors: competitive manipulation (verse 10's pattern), entertainment designed to trigger anger and fear (depositing those impressions), consumption-focused living that generates acquisitive desire, social comparison creating envy and inadequacy feelings. The aspirant attempting to control behavioral inputs finds themselves swimming against a cultural tide deliberately engineering negative aryu accumulation to maintain consumer patterns and political compliance.[3,4]

Nevertheless, behavioral control remains an essential foundation. Even intensive meditation practice (Practice Two) proves insufficient if daily behavior continues depositing dense negative aryu faster than meditation can clear them. The wisdom requires both: controlling inputs through ethical living while engaging intensive clearing through spiritual practice. Over time, as negative aryu thin through this two-pronged approach, spontaneous urges toward un-Maatian behavior decrease in intensity and frequency, making behavioral control progressively easier rather than requiring constant, white-knuckled resistance.[3,4]

Practice Two: Meditation for Intensive Aryu Clearing Through Neberdjer Contemplation

The second purification practice involves what the tradition calls sau (meditation, contemplation)—systematic practice where the mind deliberately turns away from external objects and sensory engagement to contemplate the divine nature underlying all appearance. This produces intensive aryu clearing that behavioral control alone cannot accomplish, accelerating transformation that might otherwise require multiple lifetimes.[2,4]

The mechanics work through focusing awareness on Neberdjer (the all-encompassing absolute consciousness) rather than on the phenomena arising within that consciousness. When attention remains fixated on thoughts, feelings, sensations, and external objects, the mind identifies with these temporary appearances, reinforcing the ego-construct that maintains the sense of separate vulnerable selfhood. This ego-identification itself represents perhaps the densest aryu obstruction—the fundamental confusion about identity that generates all subsequent suffering.[2,4]

Meditation practice redirects attention from phenomena to the awareness within which phenomena appear. Instead of following thought content, one observes that thoughts arise in awareness. Instead of identifying with emotions, one recognizes that feelings appear within a witnessing presence that remains distinct from the feelings themselves. Through sustained practice, this recognition deepens: awareness itself—the capacity to know that thoughts and feelings are occurring—operates prior to and independent of any specific mental content. This awareness represents Ab Neter presence, the divine soul sustaining consciousness from the kara (deep sanctuary) level that has always existed beneath accumulated aryu patterns.[1,2,4]

The intensive clearing occurs because contemplation of Neberdjer deposits extraordinarily powerful aryu that actively burn through obstructing patterns. When consciousness rests in recognition of itself as awareness rather than as the contents appearing in awareness, it creates impressions of the ultimate truth: "I am not this thought, not this feeling, not this body-mind construct—I am the witnessing awareness sustained by infinite consciousness." These truth-impressions compete with and gradually overpower the false impressions (ego-aryu) maintaining separate selfhood delusion.[2,4]

The tradition describes advanced meditation as sau-Neberdjer—contemplation of the all-encompassing absolute reality. This represents not philosophical speculation about abstract concepts but direct experiential investigation: What is the nature of awareness itself? What remains when all thoughts cease? What witnesses the arising and dissolving of mental phenomena? As practice deepens, one discovers what Amenemopet identifies throughout the teaching: the very awareness seeking the divine IS the divine awareness being sought, temporarily appearing as individual consciousness yet never actually separate from its infinite source.[2,4]

Practice Three: Invocation of Udja to Burn the Ego Construct

The third and most intensive purification practice involves what the tradition calls udja invocation—calling upon the divine fire represented by the Egyptian term udja (which can mean both spiritual fire and well-being, indicating that the fire consuming ego-illusion is the well-being the mind seeks). This represents advanced practice typically reserved for aspirants who have achieved substantial purification through Practices One and Two, as premature engagement can prove overwhelming when the ego construct remains densely reinforced by accumulated aryu.[3,4,6] Aspirants should rely more on Practices One and Two since those practices automatically build udja by cleansing the personality, thereby releasing vital energies that were tied up in egoic thoughts and feelings that can now be employed toward the spiritual path.

The burning metaphor proves apt because the process may feel like psychological dismantling or consumption (burning away) of closely held beliefs and feelings. As udja operates, aspirants may experience periods of intense discomfort as aryu patterns that have sustained personality structure for lifetimes begin releasing. The comfortable familiar sense of self starts dissolving, creating anxiety, disorientation, sometimes existential terror as one realizes they have been identifying with a constructed illusion rather than truth. This represents normal progression, indicating the practice operates effectively, but requires guidance from experienced teachers who can support aspirants through the destabilization without retreating back into ego-reinforcement as protective mechanism.[3,4,6]

PRACTICAL APPLICATION: THE DAILY WORK OF MIND TRANSFORMATION

Having established the theoretical framework—the architecture of mind (conscious, subconscious, unconscious), the mechanism of aryu formation, the purification strategies—we must address practical application: What does this teaching mean for aspirants engaged in daily spiritual practice seeking to transform their destiny by purifying the subconscious and unconscious minds?

The work begins with recognition that every action, every thought, every feeling throughout your day deposits impressions in your ab that cosmic forces will use to shape your future experiences. This recognition itself proves transformative because it converts ordinary activities from meaningless routine into spiritually significant choices. Washing dishes ceases being merely a mechanical task; it becomes an opportunity to practice mindful presence, to cultivate patience, to act with care and attention—each quality depositing purifying aryu. Conversing with family members ceases being mere social interaction; it becomes an opportunity to practice truthful speech, compassionate listening, restraint from manipulation—each choice reshaping the unconscious toward clarity rather than confusion.[3,4]

The question becomes: What is the right action, the Maatian response, when anger arises? When anxiety appears? When someone treats me unjustly? When opportunity for manipulation presents itself? These situations require discrimination that develops through study of the teaching and application under guidance. Generally, the teaching prescribes: When negative emotions arise in the hat, recognize them as aryu activations from the ab rather than identifying with them as "who I am." Create space between awareness and emotion by recognizing: "There is anger" rather than "I am angry." Then choose a response aligned with Maat rather than automatically reacting from activated aryu patterns.

When someone feels someone treats them unjustly, heated mind and feelings automatically respond with defensive anger, plotting retaliation, rehearsing grievances—all creating dense negative aryu deposits. Silent mind and feelings, cultivated through purification practice, respond differently: recognizing the other person operates from their own unresolved aryu, refusing to allow their negativity to activate your stored patterns, choosing a response that maintains your alignment with Maat regardless of their behavior. This does not mean passive acceptance of abuse but wise discernment about when to engage, when to establish boundaries, when to remove yourself from harmful situations—all done from clarity rather than reactivity.[4]

The daily rhythm of spiritual practice proves essential: morning worship to establish conscious alignment with divine presence before engaging worldly activities; midday intentional reconnection to prevent complete absorption in work-consciousness; evening practice to process the day's experiences, to consciously deposit them as purifying aryu rather than allowing unconscious accumulation of negative patterns. This rhythm creates what we might call "mooring posts"—regular reminders of spiritual identity that prevent complete identification with ego-personality operating from accumulated aryu.[4]

Meditation practice, when the mind has achieved sufficient clarity, provides intensive purification sessions where the hat deliberately turns away from all objects of perception to contemplate Neberdjer—the all-encompassing awareness that gives rise to individual consciousness, the infinite and eternal nature underlying temporary phenomena. This contemplation deposits extraordinarily powerful aryu that actively clear obstructions, thin the density of worldly patterns, and reveal Ab Neter presence with increasing clarity. The goal remains not creating access to something absent but removing aryu obstruction that prevents recognition of the divine consciousness already sustaining awareness from the kara (divine sanctuary) level deeper than all accumulated impressions.[2,4]

CONNECTION TO FORTUNE AND DESTINY: HOW PURIFICATION RESHAPES SHAYT AND RENENUT

This entire purification process connects directly to the cosmic forces Shayt (destiny) and Renenut (fortune) discussed in Chapter 7 verses 10-11.[5,6] When those verses reveal that cosmic intelligence responds to "the ethical content of actions, thoughts, and feelings" deposited in the ab as aryu, the teaching establishes that you are constantly broadcasting the quality of your mind to cosmic forces that then contribute to the shaping of your life circumstances accordingly.[1,3,5]

The aspirant who undertakes systematic purification—controlling behavior to prevent negative aryu while depositing positive impressions through ethical living, engaging meditation to accelerate clearing, invoking udja to burn the ego construct itself—this aspirant is literally reformatting the unconscious mind in ways that cosmic intelligence must recognize and respond to. As the ab clears, as aryu density thins, as the quality of mind shifts from heated to silent, Shayt and Renenut orchestrate increasingly supportive circumstances because the vibrational signature being broadcast has fundamentally changed.[1,3,4,5,6]

Consider the practical implications: Two individuals might face similar external challenges—financial difficulties, relationship conflicts, health issues—but experience them entirely differently based on their ab condition. One whose ab remains dense with negative aryu experiences these challenges as overwhelming crises triggering anxiety, anger, and despair, creating downward spirals where each reactive response deposits more negative aryu that attract more difficult circumstances. Another whose ab has undergone purification experiences the same challenges as opportunities for spiritual growth, responds from silent mind and feelings aligned with Maat, deposits aryu that demonstrate spiritual maturity, and finds circumstances gradually shifting to reflect this transformed state.[1,3,4,5]

This reveals destiny not as fixed fate but as a dynamic process responding to present mental quality.[5,6] You cannot change past aryu already deposited—those exist in the ab and will manifest their appropriate consequences through Shayt and Renenut. Nevertheless, you can absolutely transform future destiny by transforming the present mind, by controlling what enters the ab now, by systematically purifying existing patterns through spiritual practice. The cosmic forces respond not just to what you were but to what you are becoming, adjusting circumstances to provide optimal conditions for continued evolution toward the enlightenment that represents the ultimate purpose of human existence.[1,3,4,5,6]

CONCLUSION: THE PATH OF SYSTEMATIC TRANSFORMATION

The wisdom Amenemopet provides reveals spiritual development not as a mysterious process requiring supernatural intervention but as systematic transformation following knowable principles. The mind operates through a multilevel architecture where aryu accumulated in the ab shape present experience emerging through the ka into the hat, yet this very mechanism that creates bondage provides the means of liberation when properly understood and applied.

The purification path proceeds through three integrated approaches: ethical living that controls behavioral inputs preventing new negative aryu while depositing positive patterns; meditation that produces intensive cleansing through contemplation of Neberdjer; and invocation of udja that burns the ego construct maintaining separation from divine recognition. These work together, supporting and reinforcing each other, gradually transforming the mind from heated to silent, from aryu-dominated to Ab Neter-aware, from ego-identified to Neberdjer-recognized.

The process requires patience because aryu accumulated over lifetimes cannot dissolve instantly, requires persistence because the ego resists its own dissolution, and requires guidance because discrimination between Maatian and un-Maatian responses proves subtle and easily confused without experienced instruction. Nevertheless, the path remains entirely accessible to any sincere aspirant willing to undertake the work: studying the teaching to understand principles, controlling behavior to reshape the unconscious, engaging meditation to accelerate purification, and maintaining practice over years and decades until transformation completes itself in enlightenment—direct experiential recognition of oneself as the very consciousness one sought, the Ab Neter sustained by Neberdjer, the infinite awareness temporarily appearing as individual existence but never actually separate from its divine source.

This represents the legacy that the ancient sages preserved through scriptures like Amenemopet's teaching—not theoretical philosophy for intellectual entertainment but practical instruction for mind transformation, systematic methodology for reshaping destiny through purification of mind, precise guidance for the great work of discovering divine nature hidden within the human personality, awaiting recognition through removal of aryu obstruction that has obscured it since time immemorial.

References

[1] Ashby, M. (2019-25). *Mysticism of Amenemopet Hieroglyphic Text Translation.* Sema Institute of Ancient Egyptian Studies.

[2] Ashby, M. (2025). *Keys to Sage Amenemopet wisdom text trilinear translation chapter 7 by Dr Muata Ashby.* Sema Institute of Ancient Egyptian Studies.

[3] Ashby, M. (2019). *Amenemopet lectures 2019 by Dr Muata Ashby transcripts.* Sema Institute of Ancient Egyptian Studies.

[4] Ashby, M. (2024). *Amenemopet lectures 2024 by Dr Muata Ashby transcripts.* Sema Institute of Ancient Egyptian Studies.

[5] Ashby, M. (2025). *Summary of the Ancient Egyptian Concept of Fortune and Destiny and the process of purifying the mind with ethical action.* Sema Institute of Ancient Egyptian Studies.

[6] Ashby, M. (2013). *Introduction to Maat Philosophy Shai Rennenet fortune and destiny in Ancient Egyptian scripture.* Sema Institute of Ancient Egyptian Studies.

CHAPTER 13: Commentary on Teachings of Amenemopet Chapter 7B Verses 10-12

SUMMARY OF VERSES

Verse 10 introduces the profound metaphor of the "evening boat" (Sekty) representing the life journey of the heated person through the netherworld. This boat "experiences struggling and strife, suffering" as it navigates the turbulent waters created by an impure unconscious mind. The evening boat symbolizes the nighttime journey through the Duat—the concluding period of life's voyage through unconscious forces.

Verse 11(a) reveals the catastrophic consequences when the unconscious mind (ab) of the heated person becomes so impure and swollen with negative aryu that the personality "forsakes, turns away from the purpose of life and the nature of the Divine (Neberdjer)." The verse describes how the person becomes "carried away on a great swell, a large, billowing wave of water (mental waters-thoughts formed into waves), an overpowering force (of negative aryu/karma) that overwhelms the boat of life (mind and body)."[1] This "swelling mind full of bourgeoning thoughts and feelings and desires based on ignorance, delusions, that cause heat in the personality, throws their boat off course" and channels it toward spiritual shipwreck. This swelling represents ego inflation—the "big head" that actively rejects, repudiates, and turns away from inner peace and divine awareness.

Verse 12 presents the contrasting experience of the silent person who sails upon the placid waters of a purified unconscious mind. It introduces the astral body (ka) as the conscious level where "thoughts and feelings manifested through the mouth of those whose boat of life is of those who lead a silent life" arise.[1] These individuals "are able to sail on fair winds that are pleasant and right for sailing, and right for reaching the destination of life, to reach the hand of God and be accepted by God."

KEY TEACHINGS DERIVED FROM THE VERSES

1. The Boat of Life Metaphor [Verses 10-12]: Human existence operates like a vessel navigating the mental waters—the heated person sails on the rough, turbulent waters of an impure unconscious mind (ab), while the silent person navigates the placid waters of a purified ab.[1]

2. Waters as Unconscious Mind Quality [Verses 10-12]: The metaphorical waters represent the state of the unconscious mind (ab)—turbulent with dense negative aryu for the heated person, calm and clear for the silent person.[1]

3. Ego Inflation and the Swelling Mind [Verse 11a]: The heated person's thoughts and feelings "swell, expand like a volcano," creating a "big head" (ego inflation) that actively rejects, repudiates, and turns away from inner peace, spiritual balance, and divine awareness.[1]

4. Intellectual Atrophy Through Emotional Overwhelm [Verse 11a]: When swelling emotions and desires based on ignorance and delusion control actions, they "atrophy intellect" so that "actions are not thought out considered and can fall into unethical, rapacious" behaviors, leading to spiritual shipwreck.[1]

5. Introduction of the Astral Body (Ka) [Verse 12]: Amenemopet introduces the ka—the astral body where thoughts, feelings, and desires manifest at the conscious level, though not necessarily in current presence-of-mind awareness (hat).[1]

6. The Nine Parts (or elements) of Personality Architecture [Verses 10-12]: These teachings operate within the framework of nine parts of human personality, with particular focus on the ab (unconscious mind) and ka (astral body/conscious thoughts and feelings)—components of the lower self that, along with ren (ego name/identity) and khat (physical body), compose the four lower aspects. These connect through the middle component of sekhem (vitality) to the four higher aspects: khaibit (opacity veil)" or "khaibit—the opacity veil between higher and lower personality aspects"-causing a shadow on the lower parts of the personality, sahu (spiritual body), ba (soul), and akh (shining spirit). All nine parts emanate from and remain connected to Ra, the divine source who sustains individual existence and consciousness capacity.[4,5]

7. Silent Navigation Through Balanced Mind [Verse 12]: Silent persons make decisions based on "consideration, thoughtfulness and balanced feelings" rather than swelling ego-driven reactions, leading to better life outcomes through alignment with truthfulness (Maat).[1]

8. The True Path Versus the False Path [Verses 10-12]: The teaching serves as a guide for life based on spiritually wise understanding of the divine connection that is true (righteousness), while life disconnected from understanding and experience of the divine represents the false (unrighteous) path.[1,2]

Framework Analysis

1. Human Psychology Principle: Impurity of the Unconscious Mind and Ego Inflation

Section 1: HUMAN PSYCHOLOGY PRINCIPLE

The Three Bodies: Understanding the Grouping of the Nine Parts

The nine parts of human personality espoused by the Ancient Egyptian sages may be classified within three basic bodies for the purpose of deeper understanding, as illustrated in Figure 3.[5,6] These three bodies correspond to three planes of existence and represent progressively subtler levels of manifestation:

The **Physical Body** (Ta - Earth plane) consists of *ren* (name/ego identity) and *khat* (physical form). Name and form constitute the basis of physical existence on the earth plane, representing the grossest, most dense manifestation of consciousness.[5,6]

The **Astral Body** (Pet - Astral plane) comprises *ka* (thoughts/feelings/desires), *sekhem* (vitality/life force), and *ab* (unconscious mind). This intermediate body operates at a more subtle level than the physical, encompassing the mental and vital dimensions of personality. The *ab*, positioned at the boundary between astral and causal realms, functions as the crucial junction point determining whether consciousness operates predominantly from lower material aspects or from higher spiritual dimensions.[5,6]

The **Causal Body** (Duat - Causal plane) contains *khaibit* (shadow), *sahu* (glorious spiritual body), *ba* (soul), and *akh* (shining spirit). This subtlest body encompasses the highest spiritual components of personality, with the causal plane representing where the slightest tendency toward thought and desire occurs—the original cause of individual existence and apparent separation from the Divine.[5,6]

Understanding this three-body classification reveals how the teaching operates: the Physical Body provides the vehicle for earthly experience, the Astral Body serves as the arena where purification work primarily occurs (through transforming *ka* patterns and *ab* contents), and the Causal Body represents the spiritual dimensions that become progressively accessible as *ab* purification advances. All three bodies exist simultaneously, interpenetrating and interrelating, with the Self (Neberdjer/Ra) transcending yet permeating all three levels.[5,6]

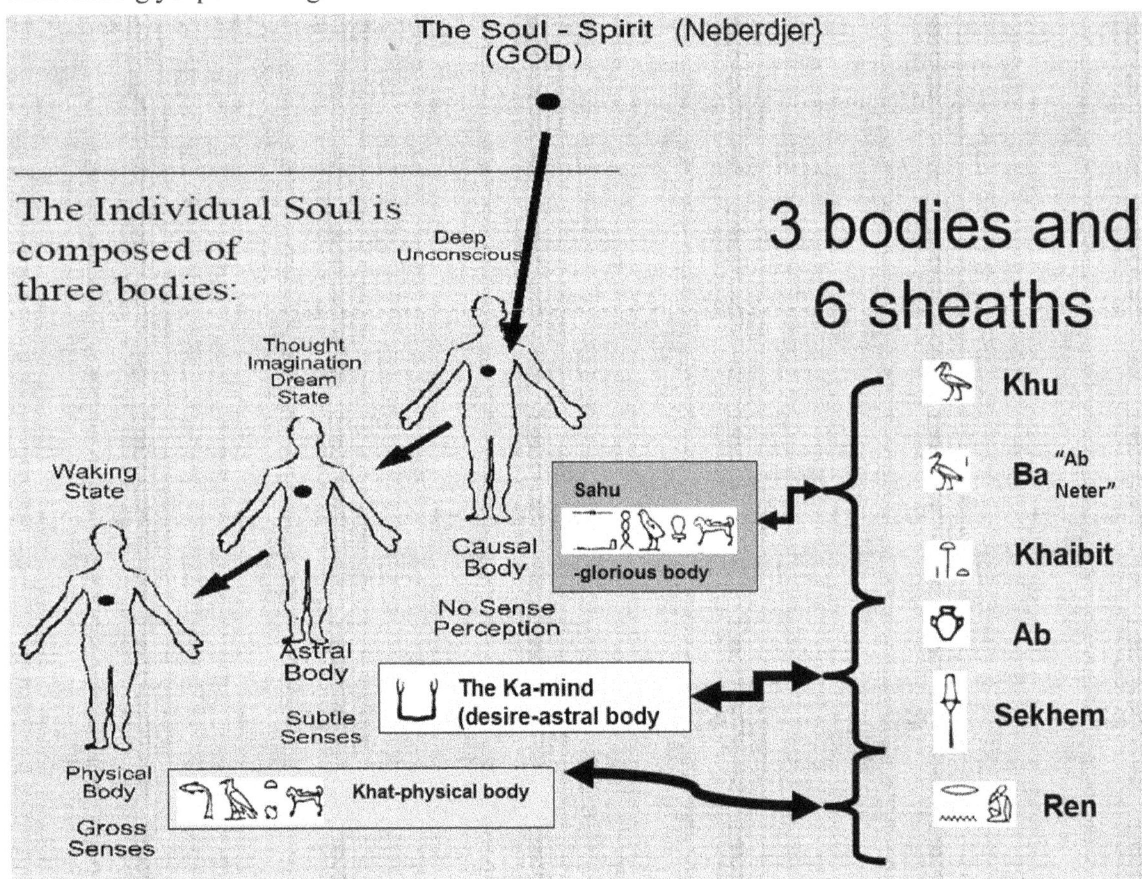

UNDERSTANDING KHAIBIT AND THE JOURNEY TO AB NETER DISCOVERY

The *khaibit* (shadow) requires particular attention in understanding the path to divine recognition. The *khaibit* functions as an opaque reflection of the *sahu* (spiritual body), creating what may be understood as a veil or opacity between the lower aspects of personality and the higher spiritual dimensions.[5,6] This opacity serves a necessary developmental function—like a shadow cast when light shines upon an object, the *khaibit* represents the boundary between individuated consciousness and universal awareness.

In the practice of meditation, when an aspirant attempts to trace thoughts back to their source, seeking to penetrate beyond the movements of mind into the stillness underlying mental activity, they eventually encounter what appears as blankness—a level where the mind can proceed no further with its usual operations. This initial threshold of blankness represents entry into what the tradition identifies as *anrutef*, literally translatable as "the place where nothing grows"—meaning the state where no thoughts or feelings sprout into the subconscious mind, where mental modifications cease.[4,5,6]

However, *anrutef* contains progressive levels of depth. The initial blankness encountered when thoughts cease represents the boundary between the *ab*'s surface level (where *aryu* generate mental activity) and its deeper dimensions. The *khaibit* exists as a further opacity beyond this initial silence—the veil between the purified *ab* and Ab Neter/Neberdjer. This *khaibit* boundary must be penetrated through sustained practice for consciousness to discover Ab Neter, the divine soul residing in the *kara* (inner sanctuary) within the purified *ab*.[4,5,6]

The teaching reveals that as *ab* purification progresses through ethical living and meditation, *aryu* density thins sufficiently that consciousness can rest in the *anrutef* state—awareness without mental content, experiencing itself directly without the constant distraction of thoughts and feelings. Initially, this state appears as blankness because mind has no content to perceive, yet consciousness remains present and aware. With continued practice and deeper *ab* purification, consciousness penetrates beyond even this threshold, breaking through the *khaibit* opacity to discover Ab Neter—the recognition that one's individual consciousness represents a particularized expression of universal divine consciousness (Neberdjer) that has always sustained individual existence.[4,5,6]

Thus the journey from heated mind through silent mind to Ab Neter recognition involves: (1) thinning *aryu* density in the *ab* through purification practices, (2) developing capacity to rest in *anrutef*—the silence where mental activity ceases, (3) penetrating through the *khaibit* opacity that separates the purified *ab* from Ab Neter recognition, and (4) discovering that individual consciousness was never actually separate from universal consciousness but only appeared separate due to *aryu* obstruction creating the illusion of independent selfhood. The *khaibit*, then, represents not a permanent barrier but a developmental threshold to be transcended through systematic purification, revealing what was always present yet hidden—one's true nature as Ab Neter, eternally unified with Neberdjer.

The central psychological teaching of these verses addresses the fundamental problem of how impurity in the unconscious mind (ab) creates turbulent experiential waters that lead to spiritual shipwreck, while purity of the ab creates placid waters supporting successful navigation toward divine union.[1] This teaching directly impacts both goals established in the Prologue: achieving well-being while living on earth (Prologue verse 2) and discovering the divine shrine within the heart (Prologue verse 9).[2]

Figure 2:The Nine Parts of Personality: Universal and Individual Correspondence. Each individual aspect (microcosmic) emanates from and connects to its corresponding universal aspect (macrocosmic) of Ra/Neberdjer. The hieroglyphic symbols and Egyptian names (in italics) are shown in the Connection column. Source: Created for this volume by Dr. Muata Ashby (2025).

Neberdjer / Ra	Connection	Individual Human
Universal Akh {Cosmic spirit}	akh	Individual Akh Shining Consciousness
Universal Ba {Cosmic soul}	ba	Individual Ba Soul
Universal Sah	sah	Individual Sah Spiritual Body
Universal Khaibit {Cosmic shadow}	khaibit	Individual Khaibit Shadow
Universal Ab {Cosmic unconscious}	ab	Individual Ab Unconscious
Universal Sekhem {Cosmic vital life force of universe}	sekhem	Individual Sekhem Vital body
Universal Ka {Cosmic mind}	ka	Individual Ka Thought and Emotion body
Universal Ren {Cosmic name [Ra]}	ren	Individual Ren Name (ego identity)
Universal Khat {Cosmic body [Physical Creation]	khat	Individual Khat Physical body
Macrocosmic		Microcosmic

Understanding these verses requires comprehension of the Ancient Egyptian teaching on the nine parts of the human personality.[5,6] From the lowest to highest, these nine aspects are: khat (physical body), ren (name/ego identity), ka (thoughts/feelings/astral body), sekhem (vitality body), ab (unconscious mind), khaibit (opacity veil)" or "khaibit—the opacity veil between higher and lower personality aspects"-causing a shadow on the lower parts of the personality, sahu (subtle spiritual body), ba (soul), and akh (shining spirit). Amenemopet's teachings in these verses focus specifically on the ab and ka—fundamental aspects of what the tradition recognizes as the lower self, the four lower components being khat, ren, ka, and ab.[5,6]

The ab occupies a crucial middle position between the four lower aspects and the four higher aspects of personality.[5,6] All nine parts connect to the divine source Ra, who sustains individual existence and provides the capacity for consciousness itself. Yet while Ra's universal presence sustains all individuals, each person accumulates their own fate and aryu through individual life choices, thoughts, and feelings. The wisdom teaching was created as a guide for living based on spiritually wise understanding of this divine connection—the true, righteous path. Life disconnected from understanding and experience of the divine represents the false, unrighteous path.[1,3]

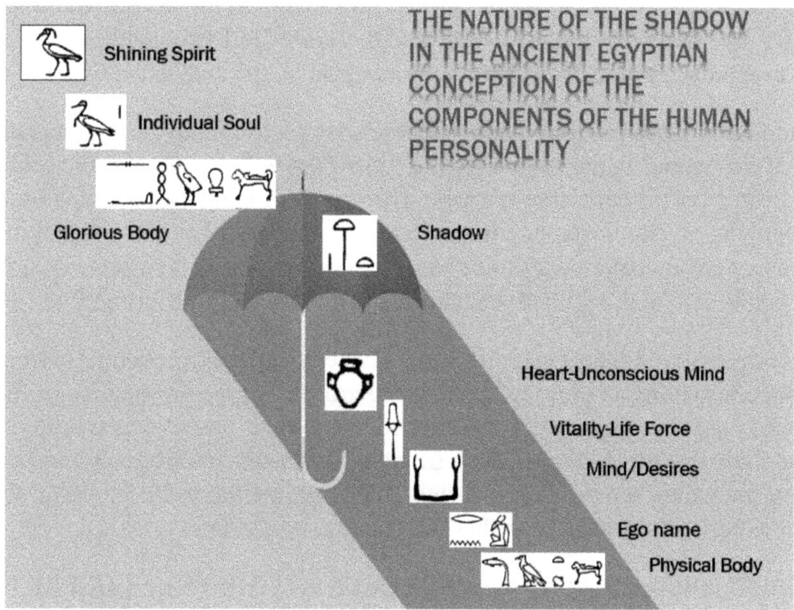

Figure 3: The Hierarchical Structure of the Nine Parts of Human Personality. This diagram illustrates how the nine aspects are arranged from the highest spiritual components (Shining Spirit/Akh, Individual Soul/Ba) through the intermediate aspects (Glorious Body/Sahu, Shadow/Khaibit) to the Heart-Unconscious Mind (Ab) at the center, down to the lowest material aspects (Vitality/Sekhem, Mind-Desires/Ka, Ego name/Ren, Physical Body/Khat). The umbrella-like structure shows how the Shadow (Khaibit) creates an opacity that can block the lower aspects from awareness of the higher spiritual dimensions. The color gradient from red (causal/higher) through gold (astral/lower) represents the increasing density of consciousness from spirit to matter. Source: Ashby, M. (2015).

The heated person's ab becomes filled with dense negative aryu (karmic feeling-memories) that create what the verse describes as "swelling mind full of bourgeoning thoughts and feelings and desires based on ignorance, delusions, that cause heat in the personality."[1] This swelling represents ego inflation—the psychological condition where the personality develops a "big head" that actively rejects, repudiates, and turns away from inner peace, spiritual balance, and divine awareness.

The metaphor operates at multiple levels. At the psychological level, the boat represents the integrated personality structure (khat, ren, ka, ab) navigating through life experiences. The waters represent the quality of awareness arising from ab conditions—turbulent when the ab contains dense negative aryu, placid when the ab has been purified. The destination represents divine union—recognizing one's true nature as an emanation of Ra, discovering Ab Neter (divine soul) within the purified ab, reaching "the hand of God."[1]

The teaching identifies impurity of the ab as the root cause preventing achievement of the Prologue's dual goals. When dense negative aryu fill the ab, they create heated mind and feelings that generate turbulent experiential waters, making well-being on earth (Prologue verse 2) impossible. Simultaneously, these aryu obscure Ab Neter presence within the kara (inner divine sanctuary), preventing discovery of the divine shrine within the heart (Prologue verse 9).[2,3]

Verse 11's description reveals the catastrophic progression: as negative aryu accumulate, they cause swelling—ego inflation where the personality develops a grandiose sense of self-importance disconnected from divine reality. This "big head" then actively forsakes the purpose of life and the nature of Neberdjer, turning away from the very divine connection that would provide guidance and support. The swelling thoughts, feelings, and desires overwhelm intellectual capacity, producing decisions that are "not thought out considered" and therefore "fall into unethical, rapacious" behaviors that create more negative aryu in a self-perpetuating cycle of spiritual degeneration.[1]

The psychological principle: mind quality depends primarily on ab conditions rather than external circumstances. Two people facing identical life situations will experience them entirely differently based on their respective ab purification states. The one with a purified ab sails on the placid waters even through challenging circumstances, maintaining balanced assessment and making ethical choices. The one with an impure ab experiences turbulent waters even during favorable circumstances, reacting with heated emotions and making unethical choices that perpetuate suffering.

This directly impacts well-being on earth because the turbulent experiential waters arising from an impure ab create constant psychological distress regardless of external success or failure. The heated person experiences anxiety, anger, fear, and desire even when possessing wealth, health, and social status—because these disturbed feelings arise from aryu in the ab, not from circumstances. Conversely, the silent person maintains serenity even during challenging circumstances because their purified ab produces placid experiential waters regardless of external conditions.

AMENEMOPET'S PRACTICAL TEACHING FOCUS WITHIN THE NINE-PART PERSONALITY FRAMEWORK

TABLE: WHICH PERSONALITY COMPONENTS DOES AMENEMOPET EMPHASIZE?

PART # (Low→High)	NAME (Body Type/Plane)	AMENEMOPET'S TEACHING EMPHASIS	WHY THIS EMPHASIS LEVEL?
9	Akh (Shining Spirit) Causal Body (Duat)	NOT DIRECTLY REFERENCED (Linguistic use only referencing the magnificent / splenderous / glorious aspect of Akh)	The term "akh/akhu" appears in Amenemopet but functions as ADJECTIVE meaning "glorious," "magnificent," "splendorous"—not as reference to the personality component *Akh (Shining Spirit).* Amenemopet uses the shining glorious aspect of the Akh part of the personality to describe actions that would be in line with the shining splendorous Akh of the personality-which is the goal of his teaching.
8	Ba (Soul) Causal Body (Duat)	IMPLIED (Ab Neter in kara)	Ab Neter (divine soul) to be discovered in purified ab, but teaching focuses on HOW to prepare for discovery
7	Sahu (Spiritual Body) Causal Body (Duat)	NOT EXPLICITLY MENTIONED	Spiritual body exists in framework but not emphasized in practical ethical teachings
6	Khaibit (Opacity Veil) Causal Body (Duat)	NOT EXPLICITLY MENTIONED (Framework only)	Opacity veil understood in complete framework but not part of practical teaching instructions
5	Ab (Unconscious Mind) Astral Body (Pet)	★★★ PRIMARY ★★★ **Chapter 7B: Impure ab creates rough waters; purified ab creates placid waters**	THE CENTRAL FOCUS: Unconscious mind where aryu accumulate - the key component requiring transformation through ethical living. Occupies crucial MIDDLE POSITION between lower material and higher spiritual aspects - the fulcrum point determining which aspects dominate personality

4	Sekhem/Udja (Vitality) Astral Body (Pet)	★★★ PRIMARY ★★★ Amenemopet uses term "udja" extensively	VITALITY explicitly taught throughout: Amenemopet uses "udja" (vitality/well-being) extensively - Ch. 1 v.2 (body well-being), Ch. 8X v.21 (speech as vitality), Ch. 8XI v.2,5 (vitality for spiritual practice), Ch. 9XI v.15 (controlling tongue increases vitality). Udja is key principle for right living and ab purity
3	Ka (Thoughts/Feelings/Desires) Astral Body (Pet)	★★★ PRIMARY ★★★ Chapter 7B: Silent person's ka uses consideration & thoughtfulness; heated person's ka swells with ego	PRACTICAL TRANSFORMATION ARENA: Where conscious thoughts, feelings, desires manifest. Silent person's ka operates from consideration & thoughtfulness; heated person's ka swells with ego-driven reactivity. This is where purified vs. impure ab manifests as observable behavior
2	Ren (Name/Ego Identity) Physical Body (Ta-Earth)	SECONDARY Chapter 7B: Ego inflation "big head" mentioned	Ego name/identity as part of lower self that "swells" ("big head") when ab contains dense negative aryu, or remains humble when ab purified
1	Khat (Physical Body) Physical Body (Ta-Earth)	★★★ PRIMARY ★★★ Explicitly mentioned in multiple chapters	PHYSICAL BODY explicitly taught: Ch. 1 v.13 (teachings as chest/strongbox within your body "per en chat k"), Ch. 1 v.2 (well-being for your body "udja hat k"), Ch. 8XI v.2 (taking care of body and vitality). The body is the vessel requiring proper care and the vehicle for spiritual practice

2. Behavioral Imperative: Ego Inflation and Intellectual Atrophy

The behavioral patterns arising from impure ab conditions manifest as the specific dysfunctions these verses identify: ego inflation (the "big head"), intellectual atrophy (inability to think through consequences), and ethical deterioration (unethical, rapacious actions). Understanding these patterns through the teaching framework reveals how heated mind systematically undermines both practical functioning and spiritual development.

Ego Inflation Patterns

The swelling mind verse 11 describes manifests behaviorally as grandiosity—an inflated sense of self-importance disconnected from reality. The heated person begins believing their perspective is uniquely correct, their needs more important than others', their desires justified regardless of ethical considerations. This produces observable behavioral patterns: dominating conversations, dismissing others' input, expecting special treatment, reacting with rage when contradicted, and the characteristic "rejection, repudiation, turning away from" feedback or wisdom that threatens the inflated self-image.[1]

The teaching reveals this ego inflation arises not from genuine confidence or appropriate self-recognition but from aryu patterns in the ab creating compensatory grandiosity. Deep insecurity, buried shame, or unresolved wounds create swelling patterns where the personality inflates to defend against feeling the underlying pain. The "big head" functions as a psychological defense mechanism—yet this defense actually prevents the ab purification that would resolve the underlying wounds.

Consider the professional who achieved success through manipulation and cunning. Their ab contains dense aryu from years of ethical violations, creating underlying guilt and shame even if not consciously acknowledged. To defend against these painful feelings, mind inflates: "I'm actually superior—smarter than those ethical fools. My success proves my approach correct." This grandiosity protects against feeling the guilt, but simultaneously prevents the ethical transformation that would genuinely resolve the underlying distress. The boat continues sailing on increasingly rough waters even as the inflated ego insists the voyage proceeds perfectly.

The behavioral manifestations prove destructive to relationships and practical functioning. Colleagues and family members experience the heated person as impossible to work with—unable to receive feedback, unwilling to collaborate, interpreting any disagreement as personal attack. The swelling ego creates isolation even as it insists on its superiority. Professional opportunities disappear despite talent because no one wants to work with someone whose inflated ego makes cooperation impossible. Relationships fail because intimate connection requires vulnerability that the inflated ego cannot permit.

Intellectual Atrophy Through Emotional Overwhelm

Verse 11's teaching that swelling emotions "atrophy intellect" so that "actions are not thought out considered" identifies another crucial behavioral pattern.[1] When the ab contains dense negative aryu, these patterns continuously surge into the ka (conscious thoughts and feelings level), overwhelming intellectual capacity for rational assessment. The heated person literally cannot think clearly because emotional reactions dominate the mind.

This manifests behaviorally as impulsive decision-making, reactive responses, and the inability to consider long-term consequences. Someone contemplating an unethical action might briefly recognize potential problems, but swelling desire from ab-level aryu overwhelms this rational assessment. The feeling of "I must have this" or "They deserve what's coming to them" consumes conscious attention, pushing intellectual consideration aside. Actions proceed "not thought out" because emotional intensity prevents the calm reflection necessary for wise discernment.

Contemporary neuroscience validates this ancient teaching—emotional activation in limbic regions literally impairs prefrontal cortex functioning, reducing capacity for rational decision-making, long-term planning, and ethical reasoning.[7,8] The heated state creates measurable cognitive impairment, not through lack of intelligence but through emotional overwhelm that prevents intelligence from operating effectively.

The behavioral consequences prove catastrophic. The person makes decisions based on immediate emotional impulses rather than thoughtful consideration, creating outcomes that then generate more negative aryu in the ab. They engage behaviors that provide momentary emotional satisfaction but produce long-term disaster—betraying trust for short-term gain, indulging anger despite relationship damage, pursuing desires despite ethical violations. Each impulsive action deposits more negative aryu, further impairing intellectual function in an accelerating downward spiral.

Ethical Deterioration

The combination of ego inflation and intellectual atrophy produces what verse 11 describes as actions that "fall into unethical, rapacious" behaviors.[1] The heated person no longer operates from ethical principles but from swelling desires and inflated entitlement. What begins as occasional ethical compromise gradually deteriorates into systematic unethical behavior as the ab becomes increasingly impure.

The progression follows a predictable pattern. Initial ethical violations create aryu of guilt and shame in the ab. To defend against these painful feelings, mind inflates: "That wasn't really wrong—everyone does it." This rationalization prevents the genuine remorse that would motivate behavior change. With conscience thus silenced, subsequent violations become easier. Aryu density increases, conscience becomes progressively more muted, and behaviors that initially produced significant guilt now generate barely any discomfort.

The teaching identifies this as spiritual shipwreck—the complete loss of ethical guidance that would otherwise prevent catastrophic life outcomes. The boat of conscious-awareness (consciousness operating as awareness in the mind), thrown off course by swelling ego and overwhelmed intellect, navigates without accurate compass toward increasingly destructive destinations. Relationships shatter, professional reputation collapses, legal consequences accumulate, health deteriorates—yet the heated person often remains unconscious of the connection between their ethical violations and their suffering, blaming external circumstances rather than recognizing ab impurity as root cause.

Silent Navigation Through Balanced Mind

Verse 12's teaching about the silent person provides the contrasting behavioral pattern—decisions made "based on consideration, thoughtfulness and balanced feelings" rather than swelling ego reactions.[1] This reveals that silent mind does not mean absence of thought or feeling, but rather thoughts and feelings arising from purified ab rather than from dense negative aryu.

The silent person facing identical situations as the heated person responds entirely differently. Where the heated person reacts impulsively from swelling desire, the silent person pauses to consider consequences. Where the heated person inflates ego to defend against vulnerability, the silent person remains humble, recognizing both genuine strengths and authentic limitations. Where the heated person's overwhelmed intellect cannot assess situations clearly, the silent person's balanced mind evaluates circumstances rationally, identifying ethical courses of action aligned with Maat (cosmic order/truth/righteousness).

These behavioral differences arise not from superior willpower or moral superiority but from ab conditions. The silent person has engaged the purification work—through ethical living, meditation practice, and absorption of wisdom teachings—that thins aryu density in the ab. With aryu thinned, the ka (conscious thoughts and feelings) manifests from Ab Neter presence within the purified ab rather than from dense negative aryu. Thoughts become clearer, feelings become balanced, decisions align with truthfulness, and actions support continued ab purification rather than creating more negative aryu.

The practical outcomes demonstrate the teaching's validity. The silent person's life may not look externally "successful" by worldly standards but operates from genuine well-being. Relationships maintain integrity because balanced mind prevents the manipulations and betrayals that heated mind produces. Work proceeds ethically, earning trust even if not maximizing profit through cunning.

Challenges arise as they do for everyone, but the silent person's purified ab creates placid experiential waters—mind navigates difficulties with balance rather than being overwhelmed by them.

Most significantly, the silent person progressively discovers what the Prologue identifies as life's ultimate purpose: the divine shrine within the heart, the kara where Ab Neter resides.[2,3] As ab purification continues through ethical living and meditation, the aryu obstruction preventing Ab Neter recognition gradually thins. The boat of individual mind discovers it was always sailing in the cosmic ocean of divine consciousness, never actually separate despite appearing individuated. This recognition—reaching "the hand of God and be accepted by God"[1]—represents the fulfillment of human existence, the destination toward which all genuine spiritual practice navigates.

3. Mystic Psychology—Metaphysical Implications: The Waters of Mind Quality and Divine Emanation

The metaphysical architecture underlying these teachings reveals profound principles about mind, consciousness, divine emanation, and the relationship between individual and universal dimensions. Understanding these metaphysical mechanics illuminates why purification proves essential and how the teaching framework operates to transform the mind.

The Nature of Mental Waters

The metaphor of mental waters navigated by the boat of personality points toward actual metaphysical reality rather than mere poetic imagery. The teaching framework identifies the mind as fluid, formless substance that can manifest in different states depending on ab conditions—just as water can be turbulent or placid, clouded or clear, while remaining fundamentally water throughout all variations.[3,4]

At the individual level, the ab (unconscious mind) functions as the container or vessel holding the accumulated aryu (karmic feeling-memories) deposited through past actions, thoughts, and feelings. These aryu create patterns within mind—disturbances in the undifferentiated homogenous fluid medium (Nunu)[4] of mind that then manifest as characteristic thoughts, feelings, desires, and behavioral impulses in the ka (astral body/conscious level). The quality of these manifestations depends entirely on aryu patterns within the ab: dense negative aryu create turbulent, disturbed manifestations (heated mind and feelings), while purified ab with minimal aryu obstruction allows clear, balanced manifestations (silent mind and feelings).[1,3,4]

The profound metaphysical principle: the consciousness substance itself remains unchanged throughout purification. What changes is the pattern of disturbances (aryu) within that mind the consciousness is witnessing. The heated person and silent person both navigate the same fundamental consciousness medium—what differs is the quality of patterns within their respective ab. This explains why purification works: removing aryu obstruction allows consciousness to manifest its natural clarity rather than creating something previously absent.

The deeper metaphysical reality: the individual consciousness substance navigating as "boat of life" represents a particularized expression of universal consciousness (Ra/Neberdjer) that may be referred to as the soul or Ab Neter. Just as individual waves arise within and remain continuous with the ocean, the universal manifests as the individual-consciousness (soul) and arises within the mind but remains continuous with universal divine consciousness. The apparent separation exists only from the perspective of the aryu-obscured ab that sees the rising wave as something separate from the ocean of consciousness and creates the illusion of discrete, independent selfhood.[4,5,6]

The Nine Parts and Divine Emanation

Understanding the metaphysical architecture requires comprehending how the nine parts of human personality relate to their universal divine counterparts.[5,6] The teaching reveals that each individual aspect—khat (physical body), ren (name/identity), ka (thoughts/feelings), sekhem (vitality), ab (unconscious mind), khaibit (shadow), sahu (spiritual body), ba (soul), and akh (shining spirit)—emanates from and remains connected to its corresponding universal aspect in Ra/Neberdjer.

This emanation operates continuously, not as past event but as present sustaining relationship. Your individual ka exists as a particularized expression of Ra's Universal Ka—the cosmic mind from which all individual minds arise. Your individual ab emanates from Ra's Universal Ab—the cosmic unconscious sustaining all individual unconscious minds. Most significantly, within your individual ab resides Ab Neter (the divine soul)—your portion of divine consciousness that sustains your very capacity for awareness.[4,5,6]

The metaphysical mechanics: Ra (as universal consciousness) manifests through progressive differentiation into the nine aspects at both universal and individual levels simultaneously. At the universal level, these nine aspects constitute the cosmic structure through which the undifferentiated absolute (Neberdjer) manifests as differentiated creation. At the individual level, these same nine aspects constitute the personality structure through which each person functions in embodied existence. The continuous emanation relationship means individual existence never actually separates from divine source but only appears separate when aryu density in the ab obscures recognition of the sustaining connection.[4,5,6]

The practical implication: purification does not create connection to the divine but removes obstruction preventing recognition of connection that always existed. As purification thins aryu density, this delusion gradually dissolves, revealing the truth: "I" was never the separate vulnerable entity struggling for survival on turbulent waters, but rather a particularized expression of infinite divine consciousness temporarily appearing as individual while remaining fundamentally unified with its source.

The Ab as Crucial Middle Position

The metaphysical architecture positions the ab at the critical middle point between the four lower aspects (khat, ren, ka, ab) and the four higher aspects (khaibit, sahu, ba, akh).[5,6] This middle position grants the ab determining influence over whether mind operates predominantly from lower material aspects or from higher spiritual aspects.

When the ab contains dense negative aryu, these patterns dominate mind functioning, orienting personality toward material concerns, ego identification, reactive emotions, and the pursuit of sensory gratification or social status. The four lower aspects operate in relative isolation from the four higher aspects, with the Ab creating opacity (due to containing dense aryu) that blocks awareness of the personality's higher spiritual dimensions. Mind identifies with khat (body), ren (ego name/identity), and ka (thoughts/feelings), experiencing itself as a separate material entity engaged in survival struggle.[5,6]

Conversely, as ab purification progresses and aryu density thins, mind functioning shifts. The opacity of the ab begins clearing, allowing increasing awareness of sahu (spiritual body), ba (soul), and akh (shining spirit) dimensions. Mind begins recognizing itself as more than body-mind complex, discovering spiritual aspects of identity that transcend material existence. The ultimate recognition occurs when ab purification reveals Ab Neter—the divine soul residing in the kara (deep sanctuary within the ab) that represents one's actual identity as particularized expression of infinite consciousness.[3,4,5,6]

The metaphysical principle: the ab's middle position makes it the fulcrum point for mind transformation. Neither the four lower aspects nor the four higher aspects alone determine destiny—the ab conditions determine which aspects dominate mind functioning. This explains why Amenemopet's teaching focuses intensively on ab purification as the essential work: transforming ab conditions transforms entire personality functioning from heated to silent, from material identification to spiritual recognition, from apparent separation to discovered unity with divine source.

The Waters as Universal Consciousness Substance

The deepest metaphysical teaching embedded in the water metaphor: the consciousness substance navigated by individual minds represent not merely personal psychological states but actual universal consciousness substance from which all individual awareness/mind arises. The distinction between turbulent and placid waters describes differences in manifestation patterns within the one universal consciousness medium.[3,4]

When verse 10 describes the heated person sailing on the rough, turbulent waters, this points toward consciousness manifesting in disturbed patterns at the universal level. The negative aryu in an individual's ab don't exist in isolation but ripple outward, contributing to the collective mind quality that then affects all beings navigating those waters. Similarly, verse 12's teaching about the silent person sailing on the placid waters indicates mind manifesting in harmonious patterns that benefit not only the individual but also contribute to collective consciousness harmony.[1]

This reveals profound ethical implications: one's spiritual work proves not merely personal but cosmic. Purifying your individual ab doesn't just benefit you—it contributes to collective consciousness quality improvement that benefits all beings. The ripples of your transformed mind affect the experiential waters that others navigate. Conversely, failing to engage purification work doesn't just harm you—your negative aryu contribute to collective consciousness disturbance affecting all beings.

The ultimate metaphysical recognition these verses point toward: the boat of individual mind discovers it was always sailing in the and composed of the very ocean it appeared to navigate. The apparent distinction between vessel and water dissolves in the realization that individual mind represents a temporary pattern within universal consciousness—a wave that appears distinct yet remains fundamentally water, never actually separate from the ocean that gave it form.

This represents the mystical teaching at its deepest level. The journey from heated to silent, from rough to placid waters, from spiritual shipwreck to reaching "the hand of God,"[1] describes mind transformation from aryu-obscured ignorance believing in separation to Ab Neter-revealed wisdom recognizing eternal unity. The destination was never somewhere else requiring travel—it was always here, always now, always the truth of what you are, waiting only for removal of aryu obstruction preventing its recognition.

4. Transpersonal Psychology Research: Ego Development, Shadow Integration, and Mind States

Contemporary psychological research provides substantial empirical validation for the ancient teaching's framework distinguishing between ego inflation (heated mind) versus balanced self-awareness (silent mind), unconscious patterns affecting behavior, and the relationship between psychological purification and well-being outcomes.

Ego Development and Inflation Research

Developmental psychology research on ego stages validates Amenemopet's distinction between healthy self-development versus pathological ego inflation.[9,10] Studies demonstrate that mature ego development involves accurate self-assessment, capacity for self-reflection, and integration of both strengths and limitations. The concept referred to as "mature ego development" may also be referred to as "well-adjusted ego". Conversely, narcissistic inflation—the "big head" that verse 11 describes—involves grandiose self-perception disconnected from reality, inability to acknowledge limitations, and defensive rejection of feedback threatening the inflated self-image.[1,9,10] Note: from the perspective of Ancient Egyptian Wisdom the well-adjusted ego is required for thoughtful spiritual research and practice, however from the perspective of ancient wisdom a truly healthy ego is an ego that knows that it is illusory and will therefore not be susceptible to the complexes of an ordinary ego personality.

Research on narcissistic personality patterns confirms that ego inflation arises as defensive compensation for underlying insecurity or shame rather than from genuine confidence.[9,10] Longitudinal studies demonstrate that individuals with inflated ego structures show poorer long-term outcomes across multiple domains—relationship quality, career satisfaction, psychological well-being, and even physical health—despite often achieving short-term external success through aggressive self-promotion. These findings validate the teaching's warning that ego inflation leads to spiritual shipwreck despite appearing advantageous in immediate circumstances.[1,9,10]

Neuroscience research reveals that ego-threatening information activates brain regions associated with physical pain and threat detection, explaining why the inflated ego reacts so defensively to feedback.[11] The heated person's "rejection, repudiation, turning away from" wisdom that challenges their self-image operates through the same neural mechanisms as physical defense against attack. This neurological reality makes ego inflation extraordinarily resistant to correction—feedback registers as threat requiring defensive response rather than as information supporting growth.[1,11]

Research on healthy ego development versus pathological inflation demonstrates that mature self-awareness involves recognizing both capacities and limitations, maintaining realistic self-assessment even when facing criticism, and using feedback for continued growth rather than defensive rejection.[9,10] These characteristics correspond precisely to what Amenemopet describes as silent mind—balanced assessment rather than swelling reactivity, thoughtful consideration rather than defensive dismissal, ethical action rather than self-serving rationalization.[1]

Unconscious Patterns and Behavioral Determination

Contemporary psychology's recognition of unconscious influences on conscious behavior provides extensive validation for the teaching about ab (unconscious mind) patterns manifesting through ka (conscious thoughts and feelings) to drive action.[12,13] Research demonstrates that the vast majority of cognitive processing, emotional responses, and behavioral impulses arise from unconscious patterns rather than conscious deliberation. Studies show that behavior often initiates unconsciously before conscious awareness recognizes the action, suggesting that what appears as conscious choice actually represents unconscious processes manifesting into awareness.[12,13]

This empirical finding validates the ancient teaching that heated behaviors arise not from conscious evil but from unconscious aryu patterns driving mind. The person engaging manipulation, acting from swelling ego, or making "not thought out" impulsive decisions often genuinely believes they're choosing consciously and rationally. Research reveals this self-perception as illusion—unconscious patterns drive the behavior while mind creates post-hoc rationalizations maintaining the illusion of deliberate choice.[12,13]

Shadow psychology research, originating with Jungian analysis, extensively documents how denied or rejected psychological content accumulates in unconscious regions (what the Egyptian framework identifies as aryu in the ab) and then manifests as compulsive behaviors, emotional reactivity, and interpersonal conflicts.[14] Studies demonstrate that shadow integration—becoming conscious of unconscious patterns and working to transform them—produces measurable improvements in relationship quality, emotional regulation, and psychological well-being. This validates the teaching that ab purification (making unconscious patterns conscious and transforming them) creates the conditions for silent mind and successful navigation.[1,14]

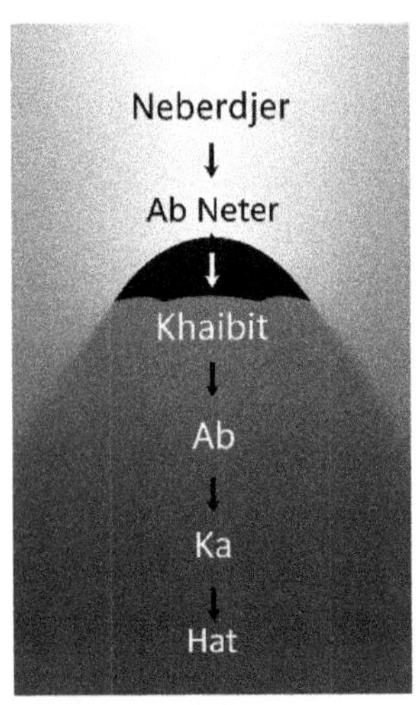

Figure 4: This image illustrates this structural relationship, showing how the khaibit functions as the opacity veil between Ab Neter and the lower personality components. Unlike the Jungian shadow (which describes what fills the unconscious), the khaibit describes the structural threshold itself that must be transcended.

The Khaibit as Opacity Veil Between Ab Neter and Lower Personality Components. This diagram illustrates how the khaibit functions as a structural opacity veil (shown as umbrella/shadow shape) positioned between Ab Neter (divine consciousness) and the ab (unconscious mind). When illuminated by higher spiritual components, this opacity creates a shadow effect that blocks lower aspects from awareness of higher spiritual dimensions. When the ab contains dense negative aryu, the khaibit opacity becomes impenetrable. As ab purification progresses through ethical living and meditation, consciousness can eventually penetrate through the khaibit threshold, moving from Hat (present awareness) → Ka (conscious thoughts/feelings) → Ab (unconscious mind) → through the Khaibit opacity veil → to discover Ab Neter residing in the kara. Source: Created for this volume (2025).

Research on emotional regulation demonstrates that individuals capable of recognizing emotions as arising patterns rather than identifying with them ("There is anger" rather than "I am angry") show superior well-being outcomes, relationship quality, and decision-making capacity compared to those who identify with emotional states.[15] This empirical finding validates the teaching's distinction between hat (present awareness), ka (conscious level where emotions manifest), and ab (unconscious source of patterns)—recognizing emotions as ab-arising patterns in the ka rather than identifying with them as essential self creates the metacognitive awareness supporting transformation.[1,15]

Mind States and Spiritual Development

Transpersonal psychology research on consciousness states provides validation for the teaching about different experiential qualities arising from ab conditions.[16,17] Studies document that individuals with histories of trauma, unresolved psychological conflicts, or maladaptive coping patterns (corresponding to dense negative aryu in the ab) experience baseline consciousness as more anxious, reactive, and dysregulated compared to individuals who have engaged therapeutic or contemplative practices addressing unconscious patterns (corresponding to ab purification).[16,17]

Research on contemplative practices demonstrates measurable effects consistent with the teaching about silent mind. Longitudinal studies of meditators show progressive changes in baseline mind quality—reduced reactivity, enhanced equanimity, greater capacity for present-moment awareness, and improved emotional regulation—that correlate with practice duration and intensity.[18,19] These findings validate that systematic practice (corresponding to ab purification) produces transformation in mind quality (from heated to silent, from turbulent to placid experiential waters) rather than merely providing temporary state changes during practice sessions.[1,18,19]

Neuroscience research reveals that contemplative practices produce structural brain changes in regions associated with emotional regulation, self-awareness, and compassion, while reducing activation in regions associated with self-referential thinking and defensive reactivity.[18,19] These neurological changes provide a biological mechanism for the transformation the teaching describes—ab purification through spiritual practice literally rewires neural architecture, creating the biological substrate supporting silent mind rather than heated reactivity.

Research on post-traumatic growth and adversarial growth demonstrates that individuals who process difficult experiences through meaning-making frameworks (rather than avoiding or suppressing them) show enhanced well-being, deeper life purpose, and greater psychological resilience.[20] This validates the teaching that transformation requires conscious engagement with unconscious patterns rather than denial or avoidance—what the tradition describes as recognizing rough waters as manifestations of current ab conditions requiring attention rather than as permanent reality to be feared.

5. Spiritual Implications for Aspirants: Navigating Toward Divine Union

Part A—Pastoral Concerns: Modern Challenges to Ab Purification

Contemporary aspirants attempting to implement ab purification teachings face systematic obstacles that create particularly rough experiential waters even for those genuinely committed to the path. Understanding these challenges prevents the discouragement that arises when practice proves more difficult than anticipated while validating that difficulty reflects environmental hostility rather than personal inadequacy.

The Challenge of Cultural Ego Inflation

Modern Western culture systematically promotes the very ego inflation these verses warn against. Aspirants grow up saturated in messaging that equates worth with achievement, status with virtue, and self-promotion with appropriate confidence. The culture actively cultivates the "big head" through constant competitive comparison, celebration of dominance, and valorization of aggressive self-assertion.[1]

Someone attempting to cultivate silent mind—balanced self-assessment, humility, and ethical restraint—faces constant cultural messaging that such qualities represent weakness or naivety. The professional who chooses ethical restraint over manipulative advancement often experiences career disadvantages compared to colleagues willing to engage the cunning these verses condemn. The individual practicing genuine humility gets dismissed as lacking confidence or ambition. The culture rewards heated mind while penalizing silent mind, creating rough experiential waters even for those actively working toward purification.

The challenge intensifies through social media platforms specifically designed to trigger ego-comparative thinking. Aspirants attempting ab purification find themselves constantly exposed to images of others' apparent success, beauty, talent, or spiritual advancement, triggering the swelling mind the teaching identifies as spiritually destructive. The platform algorithms deliberately engineer these reactions to maximize engagement, creating technological systems that profit from generating the very psychological patterns these verses warn against.[1]

The Difficulty of Recognizing Unconscious Patterns

Most modern individuals possess extraordinarily limited self-awareness about unconscious patterns driving their behavior. The culture provides no training in metacognitive awareness—recognizing thoughts as arising patterns rather than identifying with them, distinguishing between hat (present awareness), ka (conscious thoughts/feelings), and ab (unconscious patterns)—leaving aspirants unable to recognize the aryu patterns creating their experiential waters.[1]

Someone attempting to purify their ab often cannot identify which patterns require attention because these patterns operate so automatically, they appear simply as "how things are" rather than as conditioned responses that could be transformed. The heated person caught in ego inflation genuinely believes their inflated self-perception represents accurate assessment rather than defensive compensation. The individual making impulsive decisions from overwhelming emotions believes they're thinking rationally. Without guidance and systematic self-observation practice, most cannot recognize the swelling, turbulent patterns the teaching describes as problems requiring attention.

The Fundamental Divergence: Ancient Egyptian Psychology Versus Modern Therapeutic Integration into Spiritually Infirm Society

The modern therapeutic culture, while helpful in some respects, often reinforces ego structures rather than supporting their dissolution. Popular psychology emphasizes "self-esteem" and "self-confidence" in ways that can strengthen ego identification rather than revealing it as the fundamental problem. Aspirants receive cultural messaging that they should develop stronger, more positive ego structures—exactly opposite to the teaching's recognition that ab purification requires recognizing the constructed ego as obstacle rather than strengthening it as solution.

Nevertheless, a deeper examination reveals fundamental differences between modern Western psychology and Ancient Egyptian (or Buddhist) psychology regarding what constitutes genuine mental health and the cultural context for achieving it. Ancient Egyptian psychology, as articulated through Amenemopet's teachings, certainly promotes conditions for development of what might be termed a mature or well-adjusted ego—the psychological foundation discussed earlier in this chapter's examination of ego development research. However, modern psychology typically operates with a more limited aim: helping individuals who have fallen outside societal norms to reintegrate into those norms, enabling them to become "functional" within the existing social structure.[16][17]

Indeed, this represents a significant limitation when we recognize that contemporary society itself operates far outside the standards of normalcy that existed even thirty years ago. Consider how the intensity of commercial advertisements, social media platforms, electronic device dependency, agitating dietary patterns, and perpetual media stimulation creates what Amenemopet would recognize as a fundamentally heated cultural environment—one that generates the very psychological disturbances modern psychology seeks to treat. The aspirant confronts a peculiar paradox: mainstream psychological approaches work to integrate personalities into what has become an abnormal society, one characterized by precisely the heated patterns—chronic agitation, acquisitiveness, comparison mind, and separation from divine awareness—that Ancient Egyptian psychology identifies as spiritually pathological. Research in transpersonal psychology and cultural criticism has begun recognizing how societal structures themselves can transmit stereotypes and pathological patterns that become sources of individual and collective psychological harm, acknowledging what the ancient teachings understood millennia ago: that society's norms may themselves represent deviation from genuine well-being rather than its standard.[18][19][20]

The fundamental distinction emerges clearly: Ancient Egyptian psychology prescribes living ethically according to Maat principles combined with spiritual education as the means for developing not merely a functional ego capable of navigating a dysfunctional society, but rather a purified mind capable of recognizing Ab Neter—what in this context represents the highest order of mental health. Modern psychology, lacking engagement with the deeper spiritual aspects of human reality and often unaware that consciousness itself differs from mind, necessarily falls short of the comprehensive health that could arise from understanding that society itself is spiritually infirm, and that this cultural pathology contributes significantly to the psychological difficulties experienced by individuals who appear as "misfits" within that society. The wisdom to be understood recognizes that being well-adjusted to a profoundly disturbed culture does not constitute authentic mental health; rather, genuine psychological well-being requires harmonization with Neberdjer—the universal divine consciousness underlying all existence—through the threefold practice of ethical living, philosophical study, and meditation that Ancient Egyptian wisdom prescribes for transcending both personal pathology and the collective spiritual ignorance that characterizes heated cultural environments.[21][22][23]

The Absence of Qualified Guidance

Traditional spiritual development occurred within structured contexts where experienced teachers provided guidance, feedback, and correction that prevented common pitfalls. Contemporary aspirants typically attempt practice in isolation or with minimal qualified guidance, increasing the likelihood of subtle deviations that undermine transformation while appearing superficially correct.

The teaching about rough versus placid experiential waters requires discriminative wisdom to apply correctly. Without guidance, aspirants often confuse genuine ab purification work with various forms of adaptive spiritual bypassing—using spiritual concepts to avoid necessary psychological work, inflating spiritual ego while condemning worldly ego, or adopting passive resignation while calling it "trust in divine providence." These distortions create the appearance of spiritual practice while actually reinforcing the very patterns requiring transformation.[1]

Additionally, modern aspirants lack access to supportive spiritual community (sangha) that traditional practice environments provided. Attempting ab purification while surrounded by people operating from heated mind, without others engaged in similar work who could provide mutual support and accountability, creates isolation that makes practice extraordinarily difficult. The heated world provides constant pressure to abandon purification work and return to cultural normalcy, with few voices encouraging persistence through inevitable challenging phases.

AUTHOR'S NOTE ON THE TERM "SPIRITUAL BYPASSING"

Spiritual Bypassing was coined by transpersonal psychotherapist John Welwood..."Spiritual bypassing is a term I coined to describe a process I saw happening in the Buddhist community I was in, and also in myself. Although most of us were sincerely trying to work on ourselves, I noticed a widespread tendency to use spiritual ideas and practices to sidestep or avoid facing unresolved emotional issues, psychological wounds, and unfinished developmental tasks...." John Welwood. This manuscript employs the term "spiritual bypassing," coined by psychologist John Welwood, to describe situations where spiritual practices or concepts are used to avoid engaging with psychological wounds, emotional processing, or practical life challenges. However, it is essential to understand this term with appropriate nuance and compassion, as it can easily become a pejorative label that misrepresents complex psychological and spiritual dynamics.

The term "spiritual bypassing" may suggest conscious, intentional avoidance—as if the practitioner deliberately chooses to use spirituality to evade difficult inner work, which is possible. However, what appears as "bypassing" can also often represents:

Unconscious protective mechanisms: The psyche naturally employs spiritual practices as essential psychological protection when a person lacks the capacity or resources to engage certain material directly. This is not manipulation but organic self-preservation.

Trauma responses: Individuals who have experienced significant trauma may unconsciously gravitate toward transcendent spiritual states as the only accessible refuge from overwhelming emotional pain. This represents adaptive coping rather than willful evasion.

Developmental readiness: Practitioners may simply not possess the emotional tools, psychological maturity, or supportive context needed to engage particular aspects of inner work at their current stage of development. Spiritual practice may represent the highest level of engagement they can sustain.

Lack of guidance: Without qualified teachers who understand the integration of psychological and spiritual development, practitioners may have no way of knowing that their approach creates imbalance. They follow the spiritual path as they understand it.

Overwhelm from the spiritual process itself: The transformative power of genuine spiritual practice can generate more psychological material than a practitioner can integrate without additional support. What appears as "bypassing" may actually be the psyche's wisdom in regulating the pace of transformation.

Cultural and traditional conditioning: Some spiritual traditions emphasize transcendence, detachment, and non-attachment in ways that can be misunderstood as requiring the suppression or denial of human emotions and psychological needs.

Therefore, when this manuscript references "spiritual bypassing," it should be understood as a descriptive term for a particular pattern of imbalance between spiritual practice and psychological integration—not as a moral judgment or accusation of conscious manipulation. The term serves to identify dynamics that may impede complete transformation, while maintaining compassionate recognition that these patterns typically arise from genuine spiritual aspiration operating without complete understanding or adequate support.

The antidote to spiritual bypassing is not criticism or shame but rather comprehensive teaching that integrates ethical development (Maat principles), psychological awareness, and authentic spiritual practice. This is precisely the integrated approach that Amenemopet presents: beginning with ethical purification to address psychological patterns, then progressing to formal meditation practices when the foundation has been established. This framework naturally prevents the imbalances that "spiritual bypassing" describes, not through judgment but through proper sequencing of developmental stages.

When evaluating one's own practice or that of others, the question is not "Are they consciously avoiding inner work?" but rather "What conditions would support more complete integration of psychological and spiritual development?" This compassionate inquiry honors the genuine aspiration while recognizing the complexity of human transformation.

AUTHOR'S NEW TERM "ADAPTIVE SPIRITUAL BYPASSING"

As stated earlier, this manuscript used the term "spiritual bypassing," in a narrow context. However, it is essential to understand this term with appropriate nuance and compassion, as it can easily become a pejorative label that misrepresents complex psychological and spiritual dynamics. Therefore, a new term has been devised that I feel better conveys the nuances of the human issue of bypassing spiritual or other challenges in life, from a more compassionate perspective.

WHY THIS MANUSCRIPT USES "ADAPTIVE SPIRITUAL BYPASSING"

The term "adaptive spiritual bypassing" has been chosen deliberately to honor the functional nature of these patterns while still identifying dynamics that may create imbalance in spiritual development. Here is the rationale for this terminology:

1. HONORS THE FUNCTION WITHOUT JUDGMENT

"Adaptive" inherently means "serving a purpose"—it describes what organisms do to survive and cope with their circumstances. This term removes all moral judgment because adaptation is neutral and functional in nature. By using "adaptive," the manuscript acknowledges that the behavior serves an important function given the person's current circumstances, resources, and understanding. There is no implication of failure, weakness, or moral deficiency.

2. ALLOWS FOR BOTH CONSCIOUS AND UNCONSCIOUS PATTERNS

As stated, these patterns arise "based on current understanding of the person." The term "adaptive" encompasses both unconscious and conscious adaptations:

- Someone with trauma might unconsciously adapt by seeking transcendent states as psychological refuge
- Someone might consciously choose spiritual practice as their best available tool for managing difficult emotions
- Both are adapting with what they have available—there is no assumption of intent either way

The term recognizes that people work with their current level of awareness and resources, whether or not they fully understand what they are doing.

3. Psychological Accuracy

In psychology and biology, "adaptive" refers to functional responses to environmental circumstances. The term can describe both optimal and suboptimal adaptations—both serve functions even if one may be more effective than another in the long term. This makes "adaptive spiritual bypassing" a clinical, descriptive term without being accusatory or pathologizing. It honors the psychological reality that all behavior serves some function within the person's current system of understanding and coping.

4. Implies Development Without Shame

The term "adaptive" naturally implies developmental progression: what is adaptive NOW may not be needed LATER as resources, understanding, and capacity increase. This suggests natural evolution rather than moral failing. The implicit message is empowering: "You adapted then with what you had; you can adapt differently now with what you're learning." This removes shame while still supporting growth and development toward more integrated approaches.

5. Fits Perfectly with Amenemopet's Teaching

Amenemopet's framework provides more complete adaptations—beginning with Maat ethics to establish psychological foundation, then progressing to meditation practices. The teaching is not condemning previous adaptations but rather offering more comprehensive ones that integrate psychological and spiritual dimensions. The sequential development Amenemopet prescribes (adapt with ethical foundation first, then spiritual practice works more effectively) honors that practitioners adapt at each stage with what they currently understand. The path provides increasingly refined adaptations as understanding deepens.

Definition and Application

The term "adaptive spiritual bypassing" recognizes that practitioners employ spiritual practices in ways that serve important protective or regulatory functions based on their current understanding and available resources. This adaptation may be conscious or unconscious, intentional or reflexive. The term honors that individuals are doing their best with what they currently have, while also identifying patterns that may benefit from additional resources, guidance, or developmental progression.

When the manuscript discusses "adaptive spiritual bypassing" as a warning sign, it invites practitioners to examine whether their current adaptation, while functional, might benefit from expansion or support. The question becomes not "What am I doing wrong?" but rather "What additional resources, understanding, or guidance might support more complete integration?" This compassionate framing maintains respect for the person's current adaptation while opening pathways for continued development.

PART B—METHODS FOR TRANSFORMATION: SYSTEMATIC AB PURIFICATION PRACTICES

Daily Self-Observation Practice

Based on the teaching that rough experiential waters arise from aryu patterns in the ab manifesting through the ka into hat awareness, aspirants begin transformation work through systematic self-observation.[1,3] The practice involves establishing regular periods (morning, midday, evening) where mind deliberately observes its current state: What quality of experiential waters am I navigating? Rough/turbulent or placid/calm? What patterns in my ka (thoughts, feelings, desires) are currently active? What might these reveal about deeper ab patterns?

This metacognitive awareness—observing mind rather than being completely identified with it—creates the foundational capacity for all subsequent purification work. Someone notices their experiential waters feeling turbulent and investigates: "What thoughts are present? What emotions? What desires?" They recognize perhaps anxious thoughts about future security, resentful feelings about a colleague's promotion, desires for recognition or status. Rather than immediately acting on these patterns, self-observation creates space to recognize them as ab-arising patterns rather than as truth about reality requiring response.

The practice develops progressively. Initial stages involve simply noticing experiential water quality without yet identifying specific patterns. Middle stages develop capacity to recognize characteristic ka-level patterns as they arise. Advanced stages trace ka patterns back to their ab sources—recognizing that current anxiety about provision arises from childhood experiences of scarcity that deposited aryu of insecurity, or that ego inflation around spiritual advancement arises from buried shame about perceived inadequacies. This progressive deepening creates the mental condition architecture necessary for targeted ab purification.

Ethical Decision Checkpoints

Before significant decisions, implement a systematic pause to engage rational ethical analysis. Ask explicitly: "Are swelling desires from ego-inflated patterns in my ab driving this choice? Or does this decision align with truthfulness (Maat) and support ab purification?"

The professional offered a lucrative but ethically questionable deal might notice strong desire arising—their ab contains aryu of scarcity, status-seeking, and material grasping. The swelling feeling urges immediate acceptance. Implementing the pause, they recognize the volcanic quality of this urge. They examine long-term consequences, ethical implications, and alignment with spiritual principles. This practice strengthens intellectual capacity for ethical discernment while simultaneously working to thin the very aryu patterns that created the compulsive urge.

Inverse Doctrine Application: Avoiding Ego Inflation

Based on the teaching presented by Sage Amenemopet that one should cultivate silent mind and feelings characterized by consideration, thoughtfulness, and balanced assessment,[1] the application of the "inverse doctrine methodology" developed by Dr. Muata Ashby suggests that aspirants should also consciously avoid all actions, thoughts, and feelings that promote ego inflation, swelling mind, and rejection of inner peace, as these would undermine cultivation of the silent state necessary for successful spiritual navigation.

Practically, this means developing awareness when the ego begins swelling—when you start thinking you're more advanced than others, when your spiritual insights make you feel superior, when you reject feedback or wisdom from others because your inflated self-image feels threatened. These represent the beginnings of the "big head" that forsakes divine connection.

The aspirant notices themselves thinking, "I understand this teaching better than those other students" or "My meditation experiences are more profound than what others describe." These thoughts indicate ego inflation beginning. Rather than indulging these patterns, recognize them as aryu in the ab creating swelling mind that will ultimately produce rough experiential waters. Counter those aryu with thoughts of wisdom and with cultivation of gratitude toward the Divine. If indeed there is positive advancement happening in one's spiritual practices, cultivate humility and feelings of goodwill for others on the path.

Contemplation on the Nine Parts and Ra Connection

Regular contemplation on the teaching that all nine parts of personality emanate from and connect to Ra helps counter ego inflation.[5,6] Recognize that your individual ab is an emanation of Ra's Universal Ab, your individual ka an emanation of Universal Ka. Your very capacity for experience depends on Ab Neter within your ab, which is your portion of divine consciousness.

This contemplation naturally produces humility—not the false humility of ego pretending to be small, but genuine recognition of your actual nature as a particularized expression of universal divinity. You're neither independently self-existent (as the inflated ego imagines) nor worthless (as the deflated ego fears). You're a divine expression navigating through the developmental journey of purifying the ab so Ab Neter can be recognized.

Working with Rough Waters Compassionately

When you find yourself sailing on obviously rough waters—life circumstances filled with struggle, relationships in conflict, internal states of agitation—recognize these as manifestations of current ab conditions rather than as permanent reality or personal failure. The rough waters provide information about aryu patterns in your ab that need attention.

Someone experiencing repeated relationship failures might recognize this pattern as their ab manifesting through their ka into repeated choices and behaviors that create turbulence. Rather than despair or blaming partners, they engage the purification work: "What aryu in my ab keep creating these patterns? What ancient wounds, fears, or delusions am I unconsciously reenacting?"

This investigative approach, combined with ethical living and meditation practice, progressively thins aryu density in the ab. As ab conditions purify, experiential waters naturally become more placid—not because external circumstances miraculously improve, but because mind navigates the same circumstances from a purified ab rather than an impure ab, creating a fundamentally different experiential quality.

Integration of Ka and Ab Awareness

Develop sensitivity to the distinction between hat (present moment awareness), ka (conscious level thoughts and feelings not necessarily in immediate awareness), and ab (unconscious storehouse of aryu). Notice how patterns from ab surge into ka, where they exist as accessible thoughts and feelings that may or may not occupy hat at any given moment.

Throughout the day, practice checking: "What is occupying my hat right now? What patterns are present in my ka available to awareness? What appears to be arising from deeper ab levels?" This metacognitive awareness creates the capacity to work skillfully with mind architecture rather than being unconsciously driven by it.

The aspiring silent person learns to recognize when ka-level thought patterns begin leading toward decisions that would strengthen negative aryu rather than thin them. Before such patterns fully capture hat and drive action, awareness intervenes: "This thought pattern available in my ka would lead me away from truthfulness if I act on it. Better to let it arise and pass without acting, thus avoiding creating more negative aryu."

Patient Absorption Rather Than Forceful Achievement

Recognize that ab purification occurs through patient absorption of wisdom teachings at progressively deeper levels rather than forceful attempts to eliminate negative patterns. The teaching works by establishing "mooring posts" of wisdom in the ab that compete with negative aryu for attention and influence.[3]

Each time you choose ethical action over ego-gratification, each time you observe swelling ego-patterns without being carried away by them, each time you contemplate divine teachings with genuine receptivity, you establish wisdom content in your ab. Over time, these wisdom patterns grow stronger while negative aryu patterns weaken from lack of reinforcement.

The transformation occurs gradually, like a boat that begins sailing on slightly calmer waters as ab conditions slowly purify. One day the aspirant notices that decisions that once seemed impossibly difficult now feel natural. Circumstances that once triggered explosive reactions now evoke balanced response. The ab has purified sufficiently that the ka manifests increasingly silent mind and feelings, creating progressively more placid experiential waters.

The ultimate realization occurs when ab purification has progressed to the point where Ab Neter—always present in kara but obscured by aryu density—becomes recognizable in conscious awareness.[3,4] The boat of individual mind discovers it was never actually separate from the cosmic ocean of divine consciousness. The individual ka and ab recognize themselves as particularized expressions of Ra's Universal Ka and Universal Ab.[5,6] Yet the capacity for individual navigation and service continues, now operating from divine wisdom rather than ego delusion.

This represents reaching "the destination of life, to reach the hand of God and be accepted by God"[1]—not as an achievement of the ego but as recognition of what was always true, now revealed through systematic ab purification that removed the aryu obscuring this eternal reality.

References

[1] Ashby, M. (2019-25). *Mysticism of Amenemopet Hieroglyphic Text Translation*. Sema Institute of Ancient Egyptian Studies.

[2] Ashby, M. (2025). *Keys to Sage Amenemopet wisdom text trilinear translation chapter 7B*. Sema Institute of Ancient Egyptian Studies.

[3] Ashby, M. (2024). *Amenemopet lectures 2024 by Dr Muata Ashby transcripts*. Sema Institute of Ancient Egyptian Studies.

[4] Ashby, M. (2025). *Awakening Your Soul-Aware-Witness Ancient Egyptian Wisdom To Discover Divine Consciousness*. Sema Institute of Ancient Egyptian Studies.

[5] Ashby, M. (2015). *Ancient Egyptian Personality Structure and Consciousness Development*. Sema Institute of Ancient Egyptian Studies.

[6] Ashby, M. (2001). *Egyptian Book of the Dead: The Book of Enlightenment*. Sema Institute of Ancient Egyptian Studies.

[7] LeDoux, J. E. (1996). *The Emotional Brain: The mysterious underpinnings of emotional life*. New York: Simon & Schuster.
[8] Gross, J. J. (2002). Emotion regulation: Affective, cognitive, and social consequences. *Psychophysiology, 39*(3), 281-291.
[9] Baumeister, R. F., & Tierney, J. (2011). *Willpower: Rediscovering the greatest human strength*. New York: Penguin Press.
[10] Kabat-Zinn, J. (2003). Mindfulness-based interventions in context: Past, present, and future. *Clinical Psychology: Science and Practice, 10*(2), 144-156.
[11] Hölzel, B. K., Carmody, J., Vangel, M., Congleton, C., Yerramsetti, S. M., Gard, T., & Lazar, S. W. (2011). Mindfulness practice leads to increases in regional brain gray matter density. *Psychiatry Research: Neuroimaging, 191*(1), 36-43.
[12] Grabovac, A. D., Lau, M. A., & Willett, B. R. (2011). Mechanisms of mindfulness: A Buddhist psychological model. *Mindfulness, 2*(3), 154-166.
[13] Schein, E. H. (2010). *Organizational culture and leadership* (4th ed.). San Francisco: Jossey-Bass.
[14] Boyatzis, R., & McKee, A. (2005). *Resonant Leadership: Renewing yourself and connecting with others through mindfulness, hope, and compassion*. Boston: Harvard Business Review Press.
[15] Masters, R. A. (2010). *Spiritual Bypassing: When Spirituality Disconnects Us from What Really Matters*. Berkeley, CA: North Atlantic Books.
[16] Ashby, M. (2019-25). Mysticism of Amenemopet Hieroglyphic Text Translation. Sema Institute of Ancient Egyptian Studies.
[17] Ashby, M. (2024). Book Transpersonal Psychology Of Discovering the Aware Witnessing Self. Sema Institute of Ancient Egyptian Studies.
[18] Kirmayer, L. J. (2025). Cultural competence in psychotherapy. World Psychiatry. https://onlinelibrary.wiley.com/doi/10.1002/wps.21340
[19] Transmission of societal stereotypes to individual-level prejudice through instrumental learning. (2024). Proceedings of the National Academy of Sciences, 121(48). https://www.pnas.org/doi/10.1073/pnas.2414518121
[20] Why Psychology Must Reckon with Its Cultural and Historical Blind Spots. (2025). Mad in America. https://www.madinamerica.com/2025/01/why-psychology-must-reckon-with-its-cultural-and-historical-blind-spots/
[21] Ashby, M. (2019). Amenemopet lectures 2019 by Dr Muata Ashby transcripts. Sema Institute of Ancient Egyptian Studies.
[22] Ashby, M. (2024). Amenemopet lectures 2024 by Dr Muata Ashby transcripts. Sema Institute of Ancient Egyptian Studies.
[23] Ashby, M. (2015). Maat Philosophy Versus Fascism and the Police State. Sema Institute of Ancient Egyptian Studies.

CHAPTER 14: Commentary on Teachings of Amenemopet Chapter 8, Verses 19-20: The Serpent Power of Righteousness and Opposition to Apophis Forces

SUMMARY OF VERSES BEING COVERED

Commentary on Sage Amenemopet's Teaching of Spiritual Force through Ethical Living

Chapter 8 presents two verses establishing a fundamental teaching about contrasting spiritual forces within the human personality and the choices that align the mind with purifying or corrupting influences. Verse 19 instructs: "doing jubilation (henu) to goddess serpent [be good] by doing the jubilation ritual, accepting and honoring the serpent goddess who brings light, destroys iniquity and elevates awareness."[1] Verse 20 contrasts this with the opposite force: "spitting about Apophis (Apep)...as for what concerns the opposite serpent, the one called Apophis, who causes unrighteousness, disorder, confusion, and destruction, that one is to be spat on, that is to say, repudiated and turned away from, rejected and disdained."[1]

The teaching's depth becomes evident when understanding the cosmological and psychological significance of these contrasting serpent forces. Mythically, Apep (Apophis) represents a giant snake that every day attempts to obstruct the progress of the boat of Ra on his journey through the netherworld—the same divine boat that emerged from the primeval waters at Creation and which Ra commands along with his company of gods and goddesses.[6] This daily struggle proves particularly intense when traversing the lower netherworld at night, yet the boat emerges victorious every morning to create a new day and opportunity to experience life.[5] Philosophically, therefore, Apep represents the opposing force to the Creative Force of Ra—the principle of entropy and friction that seeks to halt movement and progress, while Ra represents movement, progress, Creation, continued life, and the organizational forces that bring form and order to the elements of nature.[6][9]

The wisdom text of Sage Amenemopet identifies Apep philosophically as "the opposite serpent, the one called Apophis, who causes unrighteousness, disorder, confusion, and destruction" [verse 20]. This reveals Apep as both a cosmic principle and psychological state that opposes Creation, righteousness, progress, continued life, peace, and mental health—which requires freedom of thought and expansion of mind—and ultimately enlightenment itself.[1][2] The Creation Scripture further clarifies Apep's nature as "the cosmic force of dissolution and disintegration," describing how this principle operates: "the ever relentless natural forces of entropy which degenerate all things organic and inorganic...the movement of the elements in nature attempting to restore themselves to their natural condition before being brought into some form and order by the forces of Creation which organized them at the beginning of time."[6][9]

Indeed, this teaching aligns with the scientific principle of friction—a force that opposes the relative motion or tendency of motion between surfaces in contact, acting as a resistive force that slows down or prevents movement of objects. Just as friction in the physical realm creates resistance to motion and progress, Apep represents this same principle operating at cosmic and psychological levels—the force that wants to halt movement, dissolve order back into chaos, and resist the forward progress of Creation and expansion of awareness. Nevertheless, the wisdom reveals that this opposition serves a purpose within divine design, for the struggle itself strengthens spiritual capacity when properly understood and engaged.

Psychologically, Apep represents closed-mindedness, narrow-mindedness, and occlusion of mind that supports ego and egoism—the mental states that create bondage, depression, and obstruction to expanded awareness.[2] These Apophis patterns manifest when the mind operates divorced from cosmic order (Maat), creating internal contradiction, disjointed movement, and self-sabotaging patterns that thwart spiritual progress.[4] Consider how unethical living generates exactly these qualities: deception requires narrow focus to maintain contradictory stories; greed contracts awareness to personal acquisition; manipulation demands closed thinking to justify harmful actions. The wisdom reveals: "The mindset of Apophis needs to be opposed, and the character influenced by Maat is to be cultivated in order to have rectitude, order, and resolute purpose in the personality to succeed on the spiritual path."[4]

1. Human Psychology Principle Focus of Amenemopet Chapter 8

The Psychology of Spiritual Power Through Ethical Alignment

The core psychological issue Chapter 8 addresses concerns the mind operating without access to the purifying spiritual force necessary to resist the corrupting influences that obstruct both Prologue goals: earthly well-being (Prologue verse 2) and discovery of the Ab Neter within the kara (Prologue verse 9). The wisdom reveals that ethical living functions not merely as moral behavior but as the mechanism that activates what the teaching calls the "Serpent Power"—the dynamic divine force operating within consciousness architecture that has the capacity to "burn up iniquity, fiends, the untoward energies, desires, feelings that corrupt the personality."[2] This serpent goddess represents the power of Ra (power of the cosmic consciousness manifestation of Neberdjer) operating in individual human beings, compatible with Amenemopet's concept of Ab Neter as the divine spark sustaining consciousness in the human being.[2][3]

The psychological principle operates through the hat-ab-Ab Neter framework established in the Prologue. When the mind at the hat level makes ethical choices aligned with Maat (cosmic order), this alignment activates the serpent power residing at deeper levels of mind. This activated spiritual force then works to purify the aryu (karmic feeling-memories) stored in the ab that otherwise maintain heated mind and feelings, obstruct conscious awareness of Ab Neter presence in the kara, and perpetuate cycles of unrighteousness.[4] Without access to this purifying force, the mind remains vulnerable to what verse 20 identifies as Apophis—the opposing principle that "causes unrighteousness, disorder, confusion, and destruction" operating both from within the unconscious ab and through external worldly influences.[1]

The jubilation ritual referenced in verse 19 involves adoration to the serpent goddess with specific posture and invocation, simultaneously expressing joy, reverence, and exaltation.[2] This jubilant quality reveals the teaching's profound psychological insight: ethical choices aligned with divine forces produce immediate experiential satisfaction, joy, and spiritual elevation rather than mere dutiful adherence to moral codes. The wisdom indicates that righteousness brings "such glorification to the personality that a person is spiritually elevated by them but also brings joy and exaltation to the personality...not just making ethical choices for choices sake but for experiencing satisfaction and enjoyment, elation and perhaps even ecstasy in the now."[2] This directly impacts both Prologue goals—without activating serpent power through ethical living, the goal of earthly well-being cannot be achieved because the mind remains vulnerable to Apophis forces generating disorder and confusion in daily life; simultaneously, the serpent power's purification of aryu supports Prologue verse 9's discovery of Ab Neter by removing the obstructions that hide divine presence.

2. Behavioral Imperatives of this Chapter

The Dynamics of Serpent Power Activation versus Apophis Entrenchment

The behavioral patterns arising from these verses reveal how the mind either aligns with purifying spiritual forces or perpetuates corrupting influences through daily choices. Understanding these patterns through the hat-ab-aryu framework illuminates how ethical choices operate not as isolated moral acts but as mind-transforming practices that progressively activate serpent power while thinning aryu density that maintains heated mind and feelings.

Ethical Choice as Serpent Power Activation

Verse 19's instruction to perform jubilation to the serpent goddess translates behaviorally as choosing righteous action while consciously recognizing this choice as aligning with divine forces.[1][2] The behavioral manifestation involves more than merely selecting the "right" option when faced with ethical dilemmas—it requires conscious awareness that ethical choice activates spiritual power within the personality that then supports continued ethical living while purifying accumulated negative patterns. Consider the professional facing pressure to engage deceptive practices to maintain competitive advantage. The heated mind and feelings, operating from aryu of insecurity and survival fear, generate compelling internal narratives: "Everyone does this. You'll lose everything if you don't adapt. Rigid ethics are naive idealism that success requires abandoning."[5]

The serpent power activation occurs when the mind, despite these compelling pressures, chooses ethical action aligned with Maat. In that moment of choosing truthfulness over manipulation, maintaining integrity over expedience, the mind experiences several simultaneous effects: the choice itself deposits purifying aryu in the ab supporting future ethical choices; the alignment with righteousness activates spiritual force that begins burning negative aryu maintaining heated patterns; and the mind experiences what verse 19 identifies as jubilation—the immediate satisfaction, joy, and even elation arising from alignment with divine forces.[2] This experiential satisfaction proves crucial because it provides reinforcement for continued ethical practice independent of external circumstances. The person who maintains integrity despite potential material disadvantage discovers that the mind experiences genuine well-being through ethical alignment that material success through manipulation cannot provide.[2][23]

The behavioral pattern extends beyond major ethical decisions to encompass routine daily choices: speaking gentle truth when harsh criticism arises in the mind, offering assistance when ignoring another's need would be easier, maintaining care and attention in work when cutting corners would go unnoticed, choosing restraint when aggressive assertion promises immediate advantage.[5] Each instance represents an opportunity for serpent power activation through alignment with righteousness. The accumulated effect of these seemingly small ethical choices proves transformative—the mind gradually shifts from experiencing ethical living as forced discipline requiring constant vigilance to experiencing it as natural expression supported by activated spiritual forces.[2][23]

Apophis Pattern Recognition and Rejection

Verse 20's instruction regarding Apophis—to "spit on, repudiate, turn away from, reject and disdain"—translates behaviorally as developing conscious awareness of unrighteousness patterns and actively refusing participation in these patterns whether they arise from within the mind or from external environment.[1] The behavioral challenge involves recognizing that Apophis operates through normalized cultural patterns that the mind absorbs unconsciously, depositing corrupting aryu that then generate internal impulses toward unrighteousness appearing as natural personality traits rather than as conditioned patterns requiring rejection.[7][31]

Consider how contemporary competitive environments normalize manipulation as strategic intelligence, aggressive self-assertion as appropriate confidence, and strategic deception as business acumen. The mind absorbing these environmental patterns develops aryu that generate internal impulses matching external norms: "I must promote myself aggressively or be overlooked. Small deceptions are necessary for success. Compassion in business signals weakness that others will exploit."[5][31] These internal patterns, reinforced by cultural validation, create what feels like unavoidable reality rather than Apophis patterns requiring active rejection.

The behavioral imperative requires conscious discrimination: recognizing when impulses toward manipulation, deception, aggressive assertion, or justified unrighteousness arise in the hat (conscious awareness), and immediately implementing the teaching's instruction to repudiate such patterns.[1] This might manifest as internal dialogue: "This impulse to manipulate represents Apophis patterns that I reject. I choose alignment with righteousness instead, trusting that serpent power supports ethical action even when immediate circumstances suggest manipulation would be advantageous." The conscious rejection functions as active purification—each repudiation weakens the aryu patterns generating unethical impulses while strengthening wisdom patterns that support ethical living.[4][7]

The practice extends to environmental boundary-setting. When the aspirant recognizes that certain relationships, media consumption, or social environments consistently generate Apophis-dominated mental states—cynicism, manipulation, disorder, aggression—the behavioral imperative requires establishing protective boundaries despite potential social consequences.[31] The person might reduce contact with friends whose conversations center on gossip and manipulation, limit exposure to media that normalizes unethical mental states, or decline participation in business practices that compromise integrity. Each boundary represents conscious rejection of Apophis patterns, preventing continuous absorption of corrupting influences that would overwhelm ethical development efforts.[5][31]

The Challenge of Habitual Pattern Interruption

The behavioral complexity involves recognizing that many Apophis patterns operate as deeply conditioned habits that activate automatically before conscious awareness can implement ethical discrimination. Someone conditioned through years of competitive work environments might automatically engage manipulative communication, strategic deception, or aggressive self-promotion before recognizing these as Apophis patterns requiring rejection.[28] The aryu maintaining these patterns have become so dense through repeated reinforcement that they generate behaviors that one later recognizes as contrary to ethical intentions, creating frustration and self-judgment that paradoxically deposit more negative aryu.[28]

The behavioral solution requires what might be called "ethical mindfulness"—developing capacity to notice automatic patterns before or as they activate, creating brief pause for conscious ethical discrimination.[22][28] This develops progressively through systematic practice. Initial stages involve recognizing Apophis patterns after they've already manifested in behavior, then consciously repudiating the pattern and choosing differently in future similar situations. Middle stages develop capacity to notice patterns as they arise, catching the manipulative impulse or deceptive tendency before it manifests in action. Advanced stages involve aryu density thinning sufficiently that ethical impulses arise more spontaneously than unethical patterns, indicating serpent power activation creating natural righteousness rather than forced discipline.[4][6][10]

The Satisfaction Paradox and Delayed Gratification

One behavioral pattern requiring explicit address concerns what might be termed the "satisfaction paradox"—the teaching emphasizes that ethical choices produce immediate satisfaction and even jubilation, yet the aspirant's direct experience often involves ethical choices creating apparent material disadvantage, social disapproval, or other uncomfortable consequences that seem to contradict the promised satisfaction.[2][23] Understanding this paradox prevents discouragement that might undermine ethical commitment.

The wisdom to be understood distinguishes between worldly gratification and spiritual satisfaction. The immediate satisfaction arising from ethical alignment occurs at mind depth levels—in the silent recognition that the mind has aligned with divine forces, in the subtle relief when integrity is maintained despite pressure to compromise, in the quiet joy of choosing righteousness over expedience.[2] This satisfaction operates independently of whether external circumstances immediately reflect positive outcomes. The person who refuses unethical business practices and consequently loses career advancement may experience material setback while simultaneously experiencing genuine satisfaction from knowing their mind remains aligned with spiritual forces rather than corrupted by worldly pressures.[2][23]

The behavioral challenge involves training the mind to recognize and value this subtle satisfaction rather than dismissing it as inadequate compensation for worldly disadvantage. The practice requires conscious attention to experiential quality immediately following ethical choices—noticing the sense of inner alignment, the subtle peace arising from maintaining integrity, the quiet strength emerging from choosing righteousness despite difficulty.[2][23] Over time, the mind develops capacity to recognize that this spiritual satisfaction proves more genuinely fulfilling than material success achieved through ethical compromise, discovering what the teaching identifies: that serpent power activation through righteousness creates well-being that worldly achievement cannot provide.[2]

3. Mystic Psychology—Metaphysical Implications

The Serpent Power as Divine Consciousness Force and the Mechanics of Ethical Transformation

The metaphysical framework underlying verses 19-20 reveals profound principles about how the mind operates, how divine forces manifest in human experience, and how ethical living functions as the mechanism for activating transformative spiritual power. Understanding these metaphysical mechanics illuminates why ethical choices produce effects beyond mere behavioral modification, instead operating as mind-level interventions that progressively transform the mind from heated to silent, from aryu-obscured to Ab Neter-aware.

The Symbolism of the Two Serpents and the Caduceus Principle

In Chapter 8, Amenemopet introduces two serpents representing contrasting yet complementary forces operating within the human mind and personality. The female serpent goddess represents dynamic movement and evolution—the active, transformative force through which the mind develops and purifies.[6] The male serpent (Apep) represents the static and therefore opposing negative principle. This is not a value judgment about female good, male bad, but symbolisms used by the ancient sages as recognition of fundamental male-female symbolism operating throughout Creation, where the female principle embodies dynamic motion while the male principle embodies sedentary stability.[6] This same symbolic principle appears throughout Ancient Egyptian cosmology: the god Geb (earth) represents the static, sedentary male principle, while the goddess Nut (sky and heavens) represents the dynamic, perpetually moving female principle.[6] The ancient wisdom teaching states: "In Kamitan philosophy, the god Geb is the earth and the goddess Nut is the sky. Just as the earth is sedentary and the sky is dynamic so too are the divinities depicted in this way...It is a recognition that the spirit (male aspect) is sedentary while matter, the female aspect, is in perpetual motion and the two complement and complete each other."[6]

By way of analogy, this inclusion of two serpents may be understood through the caduceus symbol—a central shaft (representing the subtle spine of the individual) with two intertwining snakes symbolizing opposite forces creating duality.[6] The shaft represents the backbone providing the structural capacity for awareness to extend into dualistic experience, while the serpents represent the opposing movements—solar and lunar, active and passive, dynamic and static—that constitute temporal existence requiring harmonization for maintaining health and vitality.[6] This duality pervades all aspects of life: sleep and waking, speaking and listening, expansion and contraction, righteousness and unrighteousness. The teaching reveals that "these two opposites are known as 'Uadjit and Nekhebet' or 'Aset and Nephthys' or 'The Two Ladies.' Uadjit is the solar serpent while Nekhebet symbolizes the lunar serpent. In India they are known as 'Ida and Pingala.'"[6]

If one or the other principle were to fall out of balance, there can be mental and or physical detrimental effects. The profound teaching indicates that the spiritual practice of serpent power can progress to such a degree of mental purity and serpent power harmonization that the two snakes meet and cancel each other out at the point between the eyebrows—signifying the end of duality and the experience of non-duality.[6] This experience augments wisdom knowledge and informs understanding of enlightenment—recognition of the self as Divine entity (Ab Neter/Neberdjer). The wisdom states: "If the opposing forces were to be harmonized there would be no separation or differences between the objects of nature. In other words, the underlying unity would emerge. This is the task of Serpent Power Yoga, to discover the underlying unity behind the multiplicity of Creation."[6] Thus, the two serpents introduced in Chapter 8—the goddess serpent to be honored through jubilation and Apep to be rejected through repudiation—represent not merely moral opposites but the fundamental dualistic forces whose harmonization through ethical living leads to transcendental consciousness.

These verses reveal ethical living not merely as moral obligation but as the means of harnessing divine power that purifies the mind, enabling the personality to experience spiritual elevation, joy, satisfaction, and even elation in the present moment.[2] The contrasting imagery of jubilation versus repudiation establishes that spiritual development requires conscious alignment with righteousness-promoting forces while actively rejecting chaos-promoting patterns that obstruct both earthly well-being and Ab Neter discovery. The teaching indicates that without activating serpent power through ethical living and without opposing Apophis forces through conscious rejection, the aspirant lacks the spiritual strength necessary to successfully traverse the journey of life—for the boat of individual mind cannot progress toward enlightenment when overwhelmed by the forces of entropy, dissolution, and mental contraction that Apep represents.[2][6][8]

The wisdom to be understood recognizes that this daily struggle—Ra's boat overcoming Apep's opposition each morning to create a new day—represents the aspirant's own psychological and spiritual battle. Each ethical choice made despite Apophis temptations (short-term gain through unethical means, expedient lies, justified manipulation) functions as a victory of Ra consciousness over entropy forces within the mind. Each rejection of Apophis patterns (the teaching's instruction to "spit on" them—to repudiate, turn away from, reject and disdain them) strengthens the serpent power's capacity to "burn up iniquity, fiends, the untoward energies, desires, feelings that corrupt the personality."[2][6] This reveals the profound psychological insight that ethical living provides not merely moral virtue but practical spiritual strength—the capacity to resist the natural forces of mental and spiritual entropy that would otherwise dissolve mind development back into ignorance, bondage, and egoistic identification.

Through sustained harmonization of the two serpent forces—honoring the dynamic goddess serpent through righteous action while rejecting the static Apophis principle through conscious repudiation—the aspirant progresses toward the ultimate goal where duality dissolves and non-dual consciousness emerges, revealing the divine nature that has always sustained awareness from within.

The Nature of Serpent Power in Consciousness Architecture

The serpent goddess referenced in verse 19 represents what the teaching identifies as the "power of Ra"—the dynamic manifestation of cosmic consciousness (Neberdjer) operating within individual human beings.[2][3] This serpent power corresponds to what other traditions identify through various terms: kundalini in yoga philosophy, Holy Spirit in Christian mysticism, the light of Buddha-nature in Buddhist teaching. The Ancient Egyptian framework provides specific understanding of how this spiritual force operates within consciousness architecture to purify accumulated negative patterns and reveal divine presence underlying individual awareness.[2][6]

The metaphysical principle: consciousness itself (Ab Neter/Neberdjer) remains always pure, never actually corrupted or diminished, but the mind operating through accumulated aryu patterns experiences consciousness as if separated from divine source.[3][4][10] The aryu density in the ab (unconscious mind) creates what the teaching describes as opacity—the accumulated feeling-memories from unethical living that obstruct the mind's recognition of Ab Neter presence in the kara (divine sanctuary deeper than accumulated aryu).[4] The serpent power functions as the dynamic aspect of consciousness that has capacity to dissolve this aryu obstruction, progressively thinning the density until the mind penetrates to kara where Ab Neter consciousness sustaining individual existence becomes recognizable.[2][6][10]

The specific mechanics: when the mind at the hat level makes ethical choices aligned with Maat (cosmic order/righteousness), this alignment creates what might be understood as resonance with the cosmic consciousness pattern from which individual consciousness emanates.[2][3] This resonance activates the serpent power residing dormant at deeper consciousness levels—the spiritual force begins rising through what the tradition identifies as the subtle body's central channel, progressively purifying mind centers as it ascends.[6] The purification occurs as the activated serpent power burns aryu patterns maintaining unrighteousness, similar to how fire consumes fuel—the spiritual force has capacity to dissolve the karmic feeling-memories that otherwise perpetuate cycles of unethical behavior and mental disturbance.[2][6]

The profound implication: ethical living does not create spiritual power previously absent but rather activates and provides conscious access to divine force already present sustaining consciousness from Ab Neter/kara level. The serpent power represents Ab Neter's dynamic purifying capacity becoming consciously available through ethical alignment.[2][3][10] Without ethical living activating this power, the mind remains in what might be termed "maintenance mode"—Ab Neter sustains basic awareness capacity but the accumulated aryu prevent conscious recognition of divine presence or access to purifying force. Ethical choices aligned with Maat function as the specific mechanism that shifts the mind from maintenance to transformation mode, activating the serpent power that progressively clears the aryu obstruction.[2][4][6]

Apophis as Anti-Consciousness Force

The metaphysical counterpart to serpent power appears in verse 20's identification of Apophis as the opposing principle "who causes unrighteousness, disorder, confusion, and destruction."[1]

Understanding Apophis requires recognizing that the Ancient Egyptian framework identifies actual opposing forces rather than merely metaphorical representations of unethical behavior. Apophis represents what might be termed anti-consciousness or entropy-consciousness—the principle of disorder, disintegration, and return to undifferentiated chaos opposing the ordering, integrating, consciousness-sustaining function of Ra/Ab Neter.[1][7]

At the metaphysical level, Apophis operates through creating conditions that increase aryu density rather than thinning it, that strengthen ego-identification rather than revealing Ab Neter presence, that perpetuate heated mind and feelings rather than supporting transformation to silent mind and feelings.[4][7] While serpent power burns aryu and purifies the mind, Apophis strengthens aryu patterns and increases aryu opacity. The practical manifestation: unethical living aligned with Apophis deposits dense corrupting aryu that then generate future unethical impulses, creating self-perpetuating cycles where unrighteousness becomes increasingly automatic and the mind's identification with divine source becomes progressively more obscured.[4][7]

The metaphysical challenge involves recognizing that Apophis operates not merely through individual unethical choices but through systematic cultural patterns that normalize unrighteousness, making ethical living appear as impractical idealism rather than as practical spiritual technology.[31] Contemporary environments saturated with competitive manipulation, aggressive assertion, strategic deception, and cynical dismissal of ethical principles function as what might be termed collective Apophis patterns—collective mental patterns that continuously deposit corrupting aryu in the individual mind through absorption and imitation.[31] The aspirant attempting ethical development within such environments faces the metaphysical challenge of swimming against a collective current actively reinforcing the very patterns requiring transformation.[5][31]

The teaching's instruction to "spit on, repudiate, turn away from, reject and disdain" Apophis represents not mere emotional reaction but metaphysical necessity—active conscious rejection functions as protective boundary preventing continuous corruption that would overwhelm purification efforts.[1] Each conscious repudiation strengthens what might be understood as the mind's "immune response" to Apophis patterns, progressively developing capacity to recognize and reject corrupting influences before they deposit dense aryu requiring later purification.[7]

The Mechanics of Ethical Transformation

The complete metaphysical framework reveals ethical living as multi-level intervention operating simultaneously at behavioral, energetic, and mind levels to accomplish transformation that behavioral modification alone cannot achieve. At the behavioral level, ethical choices aligned with Maat prevent accumulation of new corrupting aryu while depositing purifying patterns supporting future righteousness.[4] At the energetic level, ethical alignment activates serpent power that burns accumulated negative aryu through direct spiritual force application.[2][6] At the consciousness level, the combination of prevented new corruption and accelerated purification of existing patterns progressively thins aryu density until the mind penetrates to kara where Ab Neter recognition becomes possible.[4][10]

The wisdom to be understood recognizes that this transformation proceeds through patient absorption over extended time rather than instant achievement. The aryu patterns accumulated through lifetimes of unethical living possess substantial density requiring systematic dissolution through sustained ethical practice supported by activated serpent power.[4][6][10] The metaphor of clearing muddy water applies: each ethical choice allows more sediment to settle, each Apophis rejection removes more turbidity, until eventually the mind becomes sufficiently clear to perceive Ab Neter presence always underlying awareness.[10] The process requires trust that purification occurs even when immediate mental experience suggests otherwise—the serpent power works at subtle levels not always consciously perceptible, progressively preparing the mind for eventual breakthrough recognition.[6][10]

The ultimate metaphysical implication: the goal involves not creating something previously absent but removing obstruction preventing recognition of what always existed. Ab Neter consciousness sustaining individual awareness operates continuously whether recognized or not—ethical living and serpent power activation function to clear aryu opacity preventing conscious recognition rather than to build divine connection previously non-existent.[3][4][10] This understanding prevents the forced striving that paradoxically strengthens ego identification, instead cultivating receptive allowing as the mind naturally recognizes divine presence when obstructions thin sufficiently through ethical purification.[10]

4. Transpersonal Psychology Research

Contemporary Validation of Ethical Living's Transformative Effects

Contemporary psychological and neuroscience research provides substantial empirical validation for the ancient teaching's framework identifying ethical living as the mechanism for mind transformation, well-being enhancement, and access to what transpersonal psychology recognizes as higher consciousness states. While modern science lacks direct measurement instruments for serpent power or aryu, it documents physiological and psychological correlates corresponding precisely to what the teaching describes as ethical alignment's purifying effects.

Neuroplasticity and Ethical Practice

Neuroscience research demonstrates that sustained ethical practice produces measurable structural changes in brain regions associated with moral reasoning, empathy, emotional regulation, and self-transcendent experience.[11][12] Studies show that individuals maintaining long-term ethical commitments develop enhanced gray matter volume in prefrontal cortex regions supporting ethical decision-making, increased connectivity between regions governing emotional responses and rational evaluation, and heightened activity in brain networks associated with perspective-taking and compassion.[11][12][13] These neurological changes provide a biological mechanism for what the teaching describes as ethical living progressively transforming the mind from heated to silent—the brain literally rewires to support ethical consciousness as natural baseline rather than requiring constant effort.[11][12]

Longitudinal studies tracking individuals engaged in systematic ethical practice demonstrate progressive enhancement in moral sensitivity (capacity to recognize ethical dimensions of situations), moral judgment (ability to discriminate ethical from unethical options), and moral courage (willingness to maintain ethical choices despite social or material pressure).[14][15] These findings validate the teaching's identification of ethical practice as self-reinforcing—each ethical choice strengthens capacity for future ethical living, creating what the ancient framework describes as serpent power momentum where righteousness becomes increasingly accessible.[2][14][15]

Research on moral elevation—the emotional response to witnessing or engaging ethical behavior—demonstrates that ethical actions produce measurable positive affect including joy, satisfaction, and inspiration corresponding to what verse 19 describes as jubilation from alignment with serpent goddess.[16][17] Studies show that individuals experiencing moral elevation demonstrate enhanced prosocial behavior, increased feelings of connection with others, and improved mood states persisting beyond the immediate ethical encounter.[16][17] These findings validate the teaching that ethical living produces immediate experiential satisfaction independent of whether external circumstances reward ethical choices materially.[2][16][17]

The Shadow and Ethical Purification

Jungian psychology's framework of shadow integration—becoming conscious of rejected, denied, or unrecognized psychological content and working to transform it—provides Western psychological parallel to the teaching about recognizing and rejecting Apophis patterns.[18][19] Research demonstrates that individuals with substantial unintegrated shadow content show increased susceptibility to unethical behavior, particularly under stress or when ethical violations can be rationalized as serving important goals.[18][19][20] The shadow content functions similarly to what the teaching identifies as dense aryu in the ab—accumulated psychological patterns operating unconsciously to generate unethical impulses that the mind experiences as natural personality traits rather than as conditioned patterns requiring transformation.[4][18][19]

Studies on shadow integration practices demonstrate that systematic work to recognize and transform unconscious negative patterns produces measurable improvements in ethical behavior, emotional regulation, and psychological well-being.[18][19][21] The research validates the teaching's emphasis on conscious recognition and active rejection of Apophis patterns—bringing unconscious corrupting influences into conscious awareness and deliberately choosing alternative patterns creates conditions for transformation that unconscious patterns left unaddressed cannot accomplish.[1][7][18][19]

Research on moral disengagement—psychological mechanisms allowing individuals to engage unethical behavior while maintaining positive self-image—identifies specific cognitive patterns including moral justification, euphemistic labeling, displacement of responsibility, and distortion of consequences.[20][29] These patterns correspond to what the teaching identifies as Apophis-influenced mental states normalizing unrighteousness through cultural patterns and internal rationalization.[7][20][29][31] Studies demonstrate that individuals with strong moral identity and conscious ethical commitment show reduced susceptibility to moral disengagement mechanisms, suggesting that deliberate ethical practice strengthens the mind's resistance to corrupting influences.[20][29]

AUTHOR'S NOTE ON TERMINOLOGICAL DISTINCTION: "SHADOW" IN JUNGIAN VERSUS ANCIENT EGYPTIAN PSYCHOLOGY

The preceding discussion references "shadow psychology" from Jungian analysis, which describes denied or rejected psychological content that accumulates in the unconscious mind. It is essential to distinguish this modern psychological concept from the Ancient Egyptian personality component called khaibit, despite both using the term "shadow."

The Jungian shadow refers to *psychological content*—repressed emotions, denied character traits, rejected aspects of personality—that accumulate in what the Ancient Egyptian framework identifies as aryu patterns within the ab (unconscious mind). Shadow integration in Jungian terms means making these unconscious psychological contents conscious and transforming them, which corresponds to what Amenemopet describes as ab purification work.

The Ancient Egyptian khaibit, conversely, represents not psychological content but rather a *structural component* of the nine-part personality architecture. The khaibit functions as an opacity or veil positioned between the four higher spiritual aspects (khaibit, sahu, ba, akh) and the four lower material aspects (khat, ren, ka, ab), with ab occupying the crucial middle position.[5,6] The hieroglyphic symbol for khaibit depicts a sunshade that casts a shadow—representing how this component creates an opaque screen that can block the lower aspects of personality from awareness of the higher spiritual dimensions.

The khaibit operates somewhat like a filter or resistor in the personality structure. When the ab contains dense negative aryu (psychological content in Jungian terms), this density strengthens the khaibit's opacity, making it function as an impenetrable barrier preventing consciousness from penetrating beyond the ab to discover Ab Neter (the divine soul) residing in the kara (inner sanctuary). As ab purification progresses and aryu density thins through ethical living and meditation, the khaibit's opacity gradually becomes more transparent, eventually allowing consciousness to penetrate through this threshold to recognize Ab Neter—the ultimate goal of the spiritual path.[4,5,6]

Therefore, when this manuscript references shadow psychology research from contemporary sources, this validates Amenemopet's teaching about transforming unconscious patterns (aryu in the ab)—the psychological content that Jungian analysis calls "shadow." This is entirely distinct from the khaibit, which represents the structural opacity between personality levels that must be transcended through sustained ab purification. Both concepts prove essential for understanding complete transformation: shadow integration (purifying aryu content from the ab) creates the conditions whereby the khaibit opacity can be penetrated, revealing the Ab Neter that was always present yet hidden.

Contemplative Practice and Consciousness States

Transpersonal psychology research on contemplative practices provides validation for the teaching about serpent power activation through practices combining ethical living with meditation and spiritual discipline.[22][23][24] Studies demonstrate that individuals engaged in integrated practice—combining ethical conduct with meditation, prayer, or other spiritual practices—show enhanced access to non-ordinary consciousness states characterized by increased unity experience, transcendence of ordinary self-boundaries, and direct recognition of what various traditions identify as divine presence.[22][23][24] These research findings validate the teaching that ethical living supports discovery of Ab Neter presence within consciousness—the purification occurring through righteousness creates conditions where awareness penetrates to deeper levels recognizing divine source.[10][22][23][24]

Longitudinal research tracking meditation practitioners demonstrates that ethical conduct proves crucial for sustained progress toward advanced consciousness states, with individuals maintaining strong ethical practice showing significantly greater likelihood of stable transformation compared to those emphasizing meditation technique while neglecting ethical development.[22][25][26] These findings validate the teaching's identification of ethical living as essential rather than optional component of spiritual development—without ethics activating serpent power and purifying aryu, meditation alone proves insufficient for mind transformation.[2][4][6][22][25][26]

Research on post-traumatic growth and adversarial growth demonstrates that individuals who maintain ethical principles during challenging circumstances show enhanced psychological resilience, greater meaning-making capacity, and deeper life purpose compared to those who compromise ethics when facing difficulty.[27][30] These findings validate the teaching that ethical choices producing worldly disadvantage can simultaneously produce spiritual strengthening and mind/personality development.[2][27][30] The research suggests that the satisfaction arising from ethical alignment operates through different mechanisms than material gratification, validating the teaching's distinction between worldly pleasure and spiritual joy.[2][23][27][30]

5. Spiritual Implications for Aspirants

PART A—PASTORAL CONCERNS: MODERN CHALLENGES TO ETHICAL LIVING

Contemporary aspirants attempting to implement the teaching about serpent power activation through ethical living face systematic obstacles creating substantial difficulty in maintaining righteous conduct while navigating environments that actively promote Apophis patterns. Understanding these challenges prevents discouragement arising when ethical practice proves more difficult than anticipated while validating that difficulty reflects environmental hostility rather than personal inadequacy or teaching ineffectiveness.

The Cultural Normalization of Unrighteousness

Modern Western culture systematically promotes values and behaviors directly opposing the teaching's identification of ethical living as essential for spiritual development and genuine well-being. The aspirant grows up saturated in messaging equating success with competitive victory regardless of ethical means, valorizing aggressive self-assertion, celebrating strategic manipulation as intelligence, and dismissing ethical restraint as naive idealism that practical achievement requires abandoning.[5][31] Popular media glorifies characters who succeed through deception and manipulation, business environments reward unethical practices that maximize profit, political discourse normalizes aggressive attacks and truth distortion, and social media platforms engineer engagement through generating outrage and tribal conflict.[31]

The cumulative effect creates what might be termed Apophis saturation—continuous exposure to unrighteousness patterns that deposit corrupting aryu faster than purification practices can clear them, overwhelming ethical development efforts through sheer volume of corrupting influence.[31] The aspirant attempting to maintain integrity faces not merely individual ethical challenges but systematic cultural patterns making unethical living appear as realistic pragmatism while ethical commitments appear as impractical idealism requiring either abandonment or acceptance of material disadvantage and social marginalization.[5][31]

Someone working in contemporary corporate environment experiences daily pressure to engage practices the teaching would identify as Apophis patterns: strategic information withholding, competitive manipulation, aggressive self-promotion, truth distortion for advantage, exploitation of others' vulnerabilities.[5] The person refusing these practices often experiences professional disadvantage—reduced advancement opportunities, exclusion from informal power networks, reputation as insufficiently ambitious or strategically naive. The psychological challenge involves maintaining ethical commitment despite apparent evidence that unrighteousness produces material success while righteousness produces disadvantage, creating doubt about whether the teaching's promises of well-being through ethical alignment operate in contemporary reality or applied only to ancient contexts.[2][5]

The Isolation of Ethical Practice

Traditional spiritual development occurred within communities where ethical living represented shared commitment supported by collective practice, mutual accountability, and recognized teachers providing guidance through inevitable challenges.[25][26] Contemporary aspirants typically attempt ethical development in isolation or with minimal qualified support, surrounded by others operating from different values who may actively pressure abandonment of ethical commitments to conform to worldly norms.[5]

The person attempting to implement serpent power activation through ethical living often finds themselves alone in their commitments among family, friends, and colleagues who view ethical strictness as unnecessary rigidity or judgmental superiority. The aspirant declining to participate in gossip, refusing business practices they recognize as manipulative, or establishing boundaries around media consumption may face social consequences ranging from gentle mockery to serious relationship strain or loss.[5] Without spiritual community providing validation, support, and practical guidance for navigating these challenges, many aspirants experience progressive isolation that makes sustaining practice extraordinarily difficult.[25][26]

The teaching's emphasis on experiencing satisfaction and even jubilation from ethical alignment (verse 19) can feel confusing or even false when direct experience involves ethical choices creating loneliness, material disadvantage, or social disapproval without obvious compensating spiritual experiences.[2] The aspirant may question whether they're implementing the practice correctly, whether the teaching applies to modern circumstances, or whether the mind possesses deficiency preventing access to the serpent power that ethical living supposedly activates. This doubt, if unaddressed, can undermine commitment to ethical practice or generate adaptive spiritual bypassing where the person adopts superficial ethical appearances while actually operating from Apophis patterns internally rationalized as acceptable.[5]

Material Consequences and Trust in Serpent Power

The teaching's identification of ethical living as producing both earthly well-being and spiritual development (supporting both Prologue goals) can create confusion when ethical choices produce obvious material disadvantage or career setback.[2] The professional who refuses unethical practices and consequently loses promotion opportunities or employment, the business person who maintains integrity and experiences financial difficulty compared to competitors willing to manipulate, the aspirant who establishes ethical boundaries and experiences relationship loss—these individuals face genuine challenge in maintaining trust that serpent power activation through righteousness produces genuine well-being beyond what material success through compromise could provide.[2][5]

The psychological difficulty involves distinguishing between immediate material circumstances and deeper mind transformation occurring through ethical purification. The teaching indicates that serpent power works at subtle levels not always immediately perceptible, progressively clearing aryu and preparing the mind for Ab Neter recognition even when worldly feedback suggests ethical choices create disadvantage rather than benefit.[2][6][10] This requires trust that appears to contradict apparent evidence, creating cognitive dissonance that many aspirants find difficult to sustain without direct experience validating the teaching's promises.[2][10]

Relational challenges emerge when the aspirant's ethical commitments differ from partners, family, or close friends who operate from different values. The person may face pressure to compromise ethics to preserve important relationships, or experience relationship loss when maintaining boundaries around ethical principles. Consider someone recognizing that a long-term friendship perpetuates Apophis patterns through constant gossip, manipulation, and unethical scheming—the teaching's instruction to repudiate such patterns may require distancing from the friendship, creating grief and loneliness even as spiritual development advances.[5] The wisdom to be understood involves distinguishing between compassionate acceptance of others' developmental stages and unhealthy tolerance of patterns that corrupt one's own mind through continued exposure.[5]

These pastoral concerns require acknowledgment rather than minimization. The wisdom does not suggest that ethical living produces instant material rewards or social approval—indeed, the teaching's emphasis on present satisfaction from righteousness itself indicates that external circumstances may not immediately reflect inner spiritual development.[2] The aspirant benefits from recognizing that the serpent power activation occurs through patient absorption, gradually purifying the mind and creating conditions where ethical living becomes increasingly natural rather than forced discipline. The goal involves not instant perfection but progressive transformation through sustained practice despite challenges, trusting that the purification process operates at subtle levels even when worldly feedback suggests otherwise.[6][10]

PART B—METHODS FOR TRANSFORMATION: SYSTEMATIC PRACTICES FOR SERPENT POWER ACTIVATION

Based on the teaching presented by Sage Amenemopet, which instructs accepting and honoring the serpent goddess through ethical living while rejecting Apophis patterns of unrighteousness, the systematic practices for transformation focus on both positive cultivation and active purification. The jubilation ritual referenced in verse 19 provides the foundational practice—creating regular occasions for expressing joy, reverence, and gratitude for righteousness-promoting forces operating in consciousness.[1][2] The aspirant might establish daily practice involving specific posture (kneeling or standing with upraised arms in traditional Ancient Egyptian adoration posture), verbal invocation recognizing the serpent power as Ra consciousness and Ab Neter manifestation within, and conscious reflection on ethical choices made that day, expressing jubilant appreciation for any moments of alignment with righteousness regardless how small.[2][6]

The practice emphasizes experiencing satisfaction in the present moment from ethical choices rather than deferring appreciation until achieving perfection or major accomplishments. When the mind makes even a minor ethical choice—speaking gentle truth when harsh words arise in consciousness, offering assistance when ignoring another's need would be easier, maintaining integrity in a small business transaction—the aspirant pauses to consciously recognize and celebrate this alignment with divine forces. The jubilation practice trains the hat to notice and appreciate righteousness-promoting impulses, strengthening connection with deeper consciousness levels where Ab Neter naturally inclines toward ethical expression.[2][4][10] Over time, this recognition practice creates what might be understood as "wisdom momentum," where the mind increasingly notices opportunities for ethical choice and experiences growing satisfaction from alignment with spiritual forces.[2][23]

The serpent power meditation provides systematic practice for activating life force energy supporting ethical transformation. The aspirant visualizes subtle energy at the base of the spine, understanding this as the serpent goddess in dormant form, then through breath awareness and ethical intention, visualizes this energy rising through the central channel of the subtle body, purifying each consciousness center as it ascends.[6] The practice includes specific focus on how ethical living "feeds" this rising energy while unethical patterns block its flow, creating experiential understanding of the teaching's mechanics. The visualization culminates with serpent energy reaching the crown of the head where, as the ancient text describes, the serpent power "rises to the top of your head encompassing all time" and consciousness experiences illumination characteristic of purified awareness.[6] Regular practice, even fifteen minutes daily, trains the mind to recognize the subtle force available through ethical alignment, gradually making this force accessible during daily challenges when ethical choices require support.[6]

The practice of active Apophis rejection requires conscious discrimination and systematic repudiation. Based on the teaching presented by Sage Amenemopet that Apophis patterns should be "spat on, that is to say, repudiated and turned away from, rejected and disdained," the application of the inverse doctrine methodology suggests that one should also avoid tolerating, justifying, or becoming comfortable with unethical patterns—whether arising from within one's own mind or encountered in external environment—as these would undermine cultivation of serpent power and perpetuate aryu accumulation.[1] The aspirant develops a practice of conscious rejection when Apophis patterns arise in hat awareness—recognizing impulses toward manipulation, deception, aggressive assertion, or justified unrighteousness, and actively repudiating these with firm mental statement: "This pattern opposes righteousness and I reject it; I choose alignment with serpent power instead."[1][7]

This practice extends to environmental influences, requiring conscious boundaries around exposure to Apophis-influenced mental states in media, relationships, and social environments. Consider the specific implementation: The aspirant recognizes that certain television programs, social media feeds, or conversation circles consistently generate disorder, confusion, and cynicism—the very Apophis patterns the teaching instructs to reject.[1][31] Rather than passive consumption, the person establishes boundaries, consciously choosing to limit exposure and redirect attention toward influences supporting ethical development. When friends engage in gossip or manipulation, the aspirant practices respectful but firm redirection: "I'm working on different patterns in my life and prefer not to participate in this conversation." The practice recognizes that continuous exposure to Apophis patterns "normalizes" unethical mental states, making ethical choices increasingly difficult as heated mind and feelings become accepted baseline.[5][31]

The ethical choice involves identifying recurring situations where the mind faces a choice between ethical and expedient options, then preparing specific ethical responses in advance. The aspirant recognizes patterns—perhaps routine temptation to exaggerate accomplishments during business meetings, habitual criticism of others during family gatherings, or regular impulses to cut ethical corners when tired or stressed—and develops predetermined ethical responses for these situations.[28] Before entering the challenging situation, the mind rehearses the ethical choice, visualizing serpent power supporting righteous action and experiencing the satisfaction that will arise from alignment with divine forces. This preparation creates what might be understood as "ethical muscle memory," where the mind has practiced the righteous response sufficiently that it becomes increasingly automatic rather than requiring constant deliberation.[22][28]

The gratitude-for-challenge practice addresses the pastoral concern about ethical living appearing to produce material disadvantage. Based on the teaching that ethical alignment activates spiritual forces supporting both earthly well-being and Ab Neter discovery, the inverse doctrine application suggests avoiding resentment, victimhood, or despair when ethical choices create worldly difficulties, as these attitudes would undermine trust in divine providence and block recognition of the purification occurring through challenges.[2][10] The aspirant develops a practice of finding and expressing gratitude when ethical choices produce difficult consequences, recognizing that challenges often indicate purification and spiritual strengthening rather than failure. Someone losing a career advancement opportunity due to refusing unethical practices might practice: "I am grateful that my ethical choice revealed my true values. I trust that serpent power activated through this choice brings benefits beyond what worldly success could provide, and I experience satisfaction now from alignment with righteousness."[2][23]

The practice emphasizes patience and gradual absorption rather than forced achievement. The serpent power teaching reveals that purification occurs through steady accumulation of ethical choices over time, progressively thinning aryu density until the mind penetrates to kara where Ab Neter resides.[4][6][10] The wisdom to be understood recognizes that transformation resembles gradually clearing muddy water rather than instant enlightenment—each ethical choice settles more sediment, each rejection of Apophis patterns removes more obstruction, until eventually the mind becomes clear enough to perceive divine presence always underlying awareness. This patient approach prevents discouragement when immediate perfection doesn't manifest, understanding that the serpent power works at subtle levels preparing the mind for eventual breakthrough experiences.[6][10]

The critical principle throughout all practices involves removing obstruction rather than creating access to something absent. The serpent power, as a manifestation of Ra consciousness and compatible with the Ab Neter concept, already resides within every human being sustaining their capacity for awareness.[2][3][10] The issue concerns not absence of divine force but aryu density accumulated through past unethical living that blocks conscious access to this power.[4][10] Therefore, ethical living and Apophis rejection function as purification practices clearing obstructions rather than achievement practices building something new. This understanding prevents the forced striving that paradoxically strengthens ego identification, instead cultivating receptive allowing as the mind naturally aligns with divine forces when obstructions thin sufficiently.[6][10]

THE HENU RITUAL: SOMATIC PRACTICE FOR RELEASING BODY-STORED ARYU

THEOLOGICAL FOUNDATION

Amenemopet Chapter 8, Verse 19 instructs:

"arytu henu en aarat" - "doing jubilation to goddess serpent"

"[be good] by doing the jubilation ritual, accepting and honoring the serpent goddess who brings light, destroys iniquity and elevates awareness."[1]

[ABOVE: The Henu "jubilation" posture being done as Amenemopet instructs, before the cobra goddess.]

The "jubilation" refers to an adoration posture series ritual called "Henu". This verse reveals a crucial dimension of Amenemopet's teaching often overlooked: spiritual transformation requires not only wisdom study, meditation, and ethical living, but also SOMATIC PRACTICE—physical ritual that releases aryu stored in the body itself.

The serpent goddess honored is Aset (Isis) in her manifestation as Uatchet (Wadjyt), the fire-spitting cobra whose power "burns up" iniquity when harnessed through righteous living and devotional practice.

WHY SOMATIC PRACTICE IS ESSENTIAL: THE BODY MUST "CATCH UP" TO THE MIND

The Three-Level Purification Requirement

From the Serpent Power teachings, we understand that aryu (karmic feeling-memories) become stored at different levels of personality:

- HAT & AB (Conscious/Unconscious Mind) - Purified through wisdom study and meditation
- KHAT (Physical Body) - Requires somatic practice
- SEKHEM (Vital Life Force) - Requires breath work and movement
- KA (Astral Body) - Requires energetic practices

Meditation works primarily at the Hat and Ab levels. It does NOT automatically purify aryu stored in the physical body, vital force, and astral body. As the Serpent Power book states:

> "The Serpent Power requires a sturdy and pure nervous system in order to manifest the higher forms of spiritual consciousness...Serpent Power Yoga will not work if you have a healthy body but are plagued with mental agitations and worldly desires."[6]

THE BODY "CATCHING UP" PHENOMENON

When an aspirant advances rapidly through wisdom teachings and meditation, the MIND achieves clarity while the BODY still holds old patterns:

- Mind recognizes Maat principles, understands unity, embraces truth
- Body continues reactive patterns—tension, fear responses, defensive holdings

This creates a gap where the mind has evolved but the physical vehicle has not aligned with that evolution. The body must be given specific technology to release its stored patterns so it can support the higher clarity of mind that has been achieved.

This is not a contemporary insight but the explicit teaching of the Egyptian Serpent Power tradition: different aspects of personality require different purification methods. Body-stored aryu persist even after mental advancement and require somatic intervention.

THE HENU SEQUENCE: BASIC STRUCTURE

The Henu is a dynamic movement sequence similar to Indian sun salutations (Surya Namaskar) but with unique Egyptian theological components. It creates a wave-like activation through the psycho-spiritual energy centers while harmonizing dual serpent energies (Uatchet/Nekhebet - solar/lunar).

Complete Sequence Pattern (One Round):

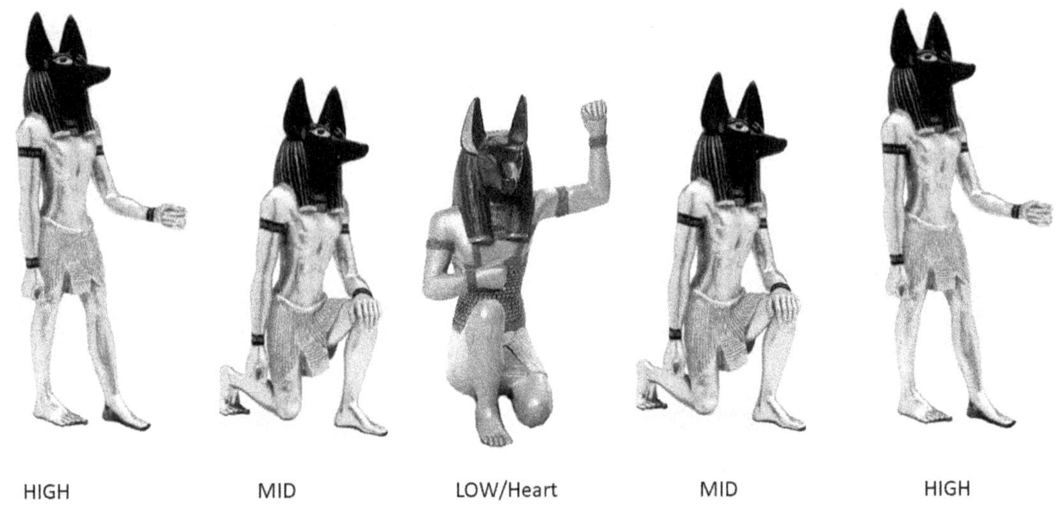

[Above: images of the Ancient Egyptian henu posture series.]

HIGH (Standing)

↓

MID (Transition to kneeling)

↓

LOW (Kneeling in adoration)

- Right knee down, left fist to heart, right arm extended

- Hold 5-30+ seconds with forceful exhalations

↓

MID (Return transition)

↓

HIGH (Standing return)

↓

REPEAT ON OPPOSITE SIDE (Left knee down, right fist to heart, left arm extended)

Key Components:

1. PROGRESSIVE DIFFICULTY - Easy (standing) to challenging (kneeling) creates "counter-tension" that dislodges old aryu patterns
2. HEART CENTER ACTIVATION - Closed fist pressed to sternum directly engages the fourth energy center (Kheper/Anahata), opening capacity for devotion and love
3. BILATERAL PRACTICE - Switching sides harmonizes Uatchet (solar/right) and Nekhebet (lunar/left) energies, causing them to converge at the point between the eyebrows (sixth center)

4. FORCEFUL EXHALATION - Active expulsion of Apophis-energies (negativity, resistance)
5. DEVOTIONAL COMPONENT - Not mere exercise but JUBILATION (henu) combining physical challenge with adoration, inviting serpent goddess power to purify the body

---

BASIC PRACTICE INSTRUCTIONS

FOR BEGINNING PRACTITIONERS:

PREPARATION:

- Empty stomach (2+ hours after eating)
- Quiet space, mat or cushion for knees
- Set devotional intention: "I practice Henu to honor the serpent goddess who destroys iniquity and elevates awareness"

FREQUENCY & DURATION:

- Daily practice optimal; minimum 3-4 times weekly
- Best time: Morning (aligns with Ra-consciousness)
- Beginners: 3 rounds (right + left = 1 round)
- Practice time: 5-8 minutes

STEP-BY-STEP:

1. STANDING (HIGH Position - 3 breaths):

- Stand with feet together or hip-width
- Spine erect, crown lifting
- Arms at sides or raised in adoration
- Deep inhalation, drawing cosmic life force
- Feel connection to upper energy centers (6th, Crown/7th)

2. TRANSITION TO KNEELING (MID - 1-2 seconds):

- Controlled descent from standing
- Maintain spinal alignment
- Exhale as descending

3. KNEELING ADORATION (LOW Position - 5-15 seconds for beginners):

RIGHT SIDE FIRST:

- Right knee on ground, sitting on right thigh/heel
- LEFT FIST closed, pressed firmly to HEART (sternum)
- RIGHT ARM extended forward/upward at 45°, fist closed (pledge gesture)
- This is devotional posture—strong yet humble
- Hold position while breathing consciously
- FORCEFUL EXHALATION: 3-5 powerful expulsions from diaphragm
  * Visualize expelling negativity, Apophis-energies from solar plexus
    - Feel heart opening, body offering itself for purification

4. RETURN TO STANDING (MID - 1-2 seconds):
- Controlled rise, inhaling

5. STANDING INTEGRATION (HIGH - 2 breaths):
- Brief pause to integrate energy

6. REPEAT ON LEFT SIDE:
- LEFT knee down, RIGHT fist to heart, LEFT arm extended
- Same forceful exhalations and devotional awareness

7. COMPLETE 3 ROUNDS total (each round = right side + left side)

8. CLOSING (1-2 minutes):
- Stand quietly
- Gratitude: "Thank you, Aset, for purifying my body"
- Feel effects before returning to daily activities

SAFETY NOTES:
- Knee sensitivity: Use folded blanket under knees
- Balance issues: Practice near wall
- Never strain breath—forceful but controlled
- Challenge is good; injury pain is not

THE MEDITATION VS. HENU DISTINCTION

Understanding the Complementary Nature:

MEDITATION:

- Modality: STILLNESS
- Quality: SERENITY
- Works on: Hat (conscious mind) and Ab (unconscious mind)
- Method: Absorption, quieting mental and physical motion
- Goal: Discovering Ab Neter through stillness

HENU RITUAL:

- Modality: MOVEMENT
- Quality: STRATEGIC TENSION with DEVOTION
- Works on: Khat (physical body), Sekhem (vital force), Ka (astral body)
- Method: Progressive difficulty + forceful exhalation + adoration
- Goal: Releasing body-stored aryu through active purging

The key insight: During meditation, stillness and serenity are paramount. During the Henu, movement and strategic tension combined with devotional consciousness are essential. The physical challenge creates conditions where body tensions are "dredged up" so they can be processed and harmonized, allowing the body to catch up to the enlightenment process the mind has advanced through wisdom and meditation.

Neither practice alone is sufficient. The complete path requires:

1. Wisdom study (hat illumination)
2. Ethical living (preventing new aryu formation)
3. Meditation (ab purification, Ab Neter discovery)
4. Somatic practice/Henu (khat/sekhem/ka purification)

PROGRESSIVE PRACTICE PATH

As Proficiency Develops:

INTERMEDIATE (after 2-3 months):

- 6 rounds daily
- Hold LOW position 30-60 seconds

- 5-7 forceful exhalations
- Add visualization: Serpent energy moving through spine
- Coordinate with specific Amenemopet teachings being studied

ADVANCED (after 6+ months):

- 9+ rounds daily
- Hold LOW position up to 2 minutes
- Extended back leg in LOW position (full lunge)
- Advanced breath retention (hold after forceful exhalation)
- Teaching practice to others

INTEGRATION WITH AMENEMOPET'S ETHICAL TEACHINGS

The Henu provides somatic integration of the ethical/psychological teachings:

- Chapter 1 (Not being heated): Forceful exhalation purges "heated" reactive patterns
- Chapter 3 (Right speech): Kneeling humility cultivates foundation for proper speech
- Chapter 6 (Not controlling): Heart opening dissolves ego-control patterns
- Chapter 8 (Henu itself): Entire practice embodies honoring serpent goddess
- Chapter 10 (Contentment): Physical challenge builds capacity to endure without grasping

After studying a specific Amenemopet chapter, practice Henu with focus on releasing the aryu patterns that chapter addresses. This creates LIVED INTEGRATION—not just intellectual understanding but somatic release of the behavioral/psychological pattern.

CONTEMPORARY VALIDATION

Modern research validates the Ancient Egyptian understanding:

- [32]: Yoga reduced PTSD in treatment-resistant cases—body-level trauma storage requires body-level release
- [33]: Chronic stress creates persistent bodily posture/tone requiring somatic intervention
- Sun salutation studies: Dynamic movement sequences with breath produce measurable autonomic regulation, stress reduction, and interoceptive awareness improvements

These findings support what the Serpent Power tradition explicitly teaches: spiritual purification requires not only meditation and ethics but specific embodied practices that engage posture, breath, heat generation, and intentional movement to "burn up" dense aryu that cognitive recognition alone cannot dissolve.

CONCLUSION

The Henu ritual represents sophisticated somatic technology specifically designed to address what a contemporary meditation teacher identifies as body tensions that "survive the recognition of our true nature"—the phenomenon where physical patterns persist even after the mind achieves spiritual clarity.

For the complete Amenemopet practitioner seeking the twin goals of the Prologue (earthly well-being and discovery of the divine sanctuary within), the Henu is not supplementary but essential. It provides the missing element that allows the physical vehicle to align with and support the mind transformation achieved through wisdom, ethics, and meditation.

May all who practice experience the purifying power of the serpent goddess, allowing body and mind to unite in service to Maat, and allowing the mind to rise from heated reactivity to silent recognition of Ab Neter within.

NOTE TO READERS

This summary provides foundation and basic practice instructions. For comprehensive documentation including:

- Detailed posture-by-posture analysis
- Energy center correspondences
- Advanced variations and troubleshooting
- Research validation and bibliography

- Integration strategies for specific psychological patterns

References

[1] Ashby, M. (2019-25). *Mysticism of Amenemopet Hieroglyphic Text Translation.* Sema Institute of Ancient Egyptian Studies.
[2] Ashby, M. (2025). *Keys to Sage Amenemopet wisdom text trilinear translation chapter 8.* Sema Institute of Ancient Egyptian Studies.
[3] Ashby, M. (2022). *The Mysteries of Ra and Sekhmet and the Meditation System for Discovering Ultimate Divinity* (Book GLM Scripture-story of Hetheru and Djehuti). Sema Institute of Ancient Egyptian Studies.
[4] Ashby, M. (2024). *Amenemopet lectures 2024 by Dr Muata Ashby transcripts.* Sema Institute of Ancient Egyptian Studies.
[5] Ashby, M. (2025). *Book Awakening Your Soul-Aware-Witness Ancient Egyptian Wisdom To Discover Divine Consciousness -v32.* Sema Institute of Ancient Egyptian Studies.
[6] Ashby, M. (2021). *The Serpent Power: The Ancient Egyptian Mystical Wisdom of the Inner Life Force.* Sema Institute of Ancient Egyptian Studies.
[7] Ashby, M. (2025). Teachings of New Kingdom Pert-M-Heru - Heru with Two Heads. In *Book Awakening Your Soul-Aware-Witness Ancient Egyptian Wisdom To Discover Divine Consciousness -v32.* Sema Institute of Ancient Egyptian Studies.
[8] Ashby, M. (2024). Previous Chapter Commentaries. In *Book Commentaries on Mystic Psychology of Amenemopet v2.* Sema Institute of Ancient Egyptian Studies.
[9] Ashby, M. (2023). *Trilinear Translation of Creation Scripture B Verses 58-63.* Sema Institute of Ancient Egyptian Studies.
[10] Ashby, M. (2025). *DEFINITIONS: The Nature of Consciousness and Awareness in Neterian Philosophy.* Sema Institute of Ancient Egyptian Studies.
[11] Ashby, M. (2022). Divine Status and Character of Hetheru. In *The Mysteries of Ra and Sekhmet.* Sema Institute of Ancient Egyptian Studies.
[12] Algoe, S. B., & Haidt, J. (2009). Witnessing excellence in action: The 'other-praising' emotions of elevation, gratitude, and admiration. *The Journal of Positive Psychology, 4*(2), 105-127.
[13] Moll, J., de Oliveira-Souza, R., Eslinger, P. J., Bramati, I. E., Mourão-Miranda, J., Andreiuolo, P. A., & Pessoa, L. (2002). The neural correlates of moral sensitivity: A functional magnetic resonance imaging investigation of basic and moral emotions. *Journal of Neuroscience, 22*(7), 2730-2736.
[14] Krajbich, I., Adolphs, R., Tranel, D., Denburg, N. L., & Camerer, C. F. (2009). Economic games quantify diminished sense of guilt in patients with damage to the prefrontal cortex. *Journal of Neuroscience, 29*(7), 2188-2192.
[15] Harmon-Jones, E., & Mills, J. (Eds.). (2019). *Cognitive Dissonance: Reexamining a Pivotal Theory in Psychology* (2nd ed.). American Psychological Association.
[16] Proulx, T., & Inzlicht, M. (2012). The five "A"s of meaning maintenance: Finding meaning in the theories of sense-making. *Psychological Inquiry, 23*(4), 317-335.
[17] Taylor, K. (1994). *The Ethics of Authenticity.* Harvard University Press.
[18] Brewer, J. A., Worhunsky, P. D., Gray, J. R., Tang, Y. Y., Weber, J., & Kober, H. (2011). Meditation experience is associated with differences in default mode network activity and connectivity. *Proceedings of the National Academy of Sciences, 108*(50), 20254-20259.
[19] Tang, Y. Y., Hölzel, B. K., & Posner, M. I. (2015). The neuroscience of mindfulness meditation. *Nature Reviews Neuroscience, 16*(4), 213-225.
[20] Wallace, B. A., & Shapiro, S. L. (2006). Mental balance and well-being: Building bridges between Buddhism and Western psychology. *American Psychologist, 61*(7), 690-701.
[21] Lutz, A., Slagter, H. A., Dunne, J. D., & Davidson, R. J. (2008). Attention regulation and monitoring in meditation. *Trends in Cognitive Sciences, 12*(4), 163-169.
[22] Lally, P., van Jaarsveld, C. H., Potts, H. W., & Wardle, J. (2010). How are habits formed: Modelling habit formation in the real world. *European Journal of Social Psychology, 40*(6), 998-1009.
[23] Ryan, R. M., & Deci, E. L. (2000). Self-determination theory and the facilitation of intrinsic motivation, social development, and well-being. *American Psychologist, 55*(1), 68-78.
[24] Varela, F. J., Thompson, E., & Rosch, E. (2016). *The Embodied Mind: Cognitive Science and Human Experience.* MIT Press.
[25] Newberg, A. B., & Waldman, M. R. (2010). *How God Changes Your Brain: Breakthrough Findings from a Leading Neuroscientist.* Ballantine Books.
[26] Johnson, R. A. (1991). *Owning Your Own Shadow: Understanding the Dark Side of the Psyche.* HarperOne.
[27] Hayes, S. C., Strosahl, K. D., & Wilson, K. G. (2011). *Acceptance and Commitment Therapy: The Process and Practice of Mindful Change* (2nd ed.). Guilford Press.
[28] Wood, W., & Rünger, D. (2016). Psychology of habit. *Annual Review of Psychology, 67*, 289-314.
[29] Tedeschi, R. G., & Calhoun, L. G. (2004). Posttraumatic growth: Conceptual foundations and empirical evidence. *Psychological Inquiry, 15*(1), 1-18.
[30] Kasser, T., & Ryan, R. M. (1996). Further examining the American dream: Differential correlates of intrinsic and extrinsic goals. *Personality and Social Psychology Bulletin, 22*(3), 280-287.
[31] Twenge, J. M. (2017). *iGen: Why Today's Super-Connected Kids Are Growing Up Less Rebellious, More Tolerant, Less Happy.* Atria Books.
[32] Body- and movement-oriented interventions (a category that includes trauma-sensitive yoga, somatic experiencing, sensorimotor work, and body psychotherapy) show small-to-moderate effects on PTSD symptoms in recent systematic reviews — supporting the idea that targeting the body can help symptom reduction https://doi.org/10.1002/jts.22968
[33] Payne, P., & Crane-Godreau, M. A. (2015). The preparatory set: A novel approach to understanding stress, trauma, and the bodymind therapies. Frontiers in Human Neuroscience, 9, 816.

CHAPTER 15: Commentary on Teachings of Amenemopet Chapter 8X and 8XI: Speech, Vitality, and the Path to Inner Sanctuary

SUMMARY OF CHAPTER 8X AND 8XI

Chapter 8X and 8XI present interconnected teachings on how speech and interpersonal conduct either generate or deplete spiritual vitality, directly impacting one's capacity for inner peace and access to the divine sanctuary. Verse 21 establishes that speech either causes vitality or damage depending on word choice. Verses 1-2 reveal the reciprocal nature of ethical conduct: caring for others as extensions of Neberdjer—as one cares for one's own limbs—creates the inner peace necessary for temple practice and discovering the divine within. Verses 3-4 disclose the spiritual sustenance available through real love (authentic selfless caring) and the purifying transformation that elevates personality to spiritual nobility worthy of divine glory, while also revealing how egoistic love produces gradual purification through a secret mechanism. Verse 5 teaches that silent mind and feelings enable drawing vitality from the bau Neteru (divine souls emanating from Neberdjer through Ra to Ab Neter) rather than depending solely on physical sustenance. Verses 8-11 address gossip's corrosive effects and the necessity of suppressing then sublimating innate badness from the belly. The teaching culminates in connecting ethical living with the Serpent Power goddess—Ra's differentiated consciousness that burns up iniquity when harnessed through righteous conduct, opening channels to divine vitality beyond the physical realm.

KEY TEACHINGS FROM CHAPTER 8X AND 8XI

Chapter 8X, Verse 21—Speech as Vitality Conduit:

[Verse 21] "Take care to make your speech to be sound in reference to the words that you use, that may cause harm, so as to be, instead, a cause, for vitality"

- Speech possesses the power to generate vitality or inflict damage depending on conscious word choice
- The tongue functions as either an instrument of harm or a source of life-force enhancement
- Chapter 8XI, Verses 1-2—Reciprocal Ethics and Inner Sanctuary:

[Verse 1] "By you're doing love to people, instead of harm, they love you. By giving consideration people reciprocate with consideration"

- Ethical conduct toward others stems from recognizing them as part of Neberdjer, as extensions of oneself
- Caring for others mirrors caring for one's own limbs—natural when unity is recognized

[Verse 2] "By doing good to others and having peaceful relations with others, you will be able to have inner peace that will allow you to make real and effective effort towards finding yourself a place, to make yourself an abode in the inner part of the temple of God"

- Inner peace from ethical living enables effective temple practice and rituals
- Avoiding conflicts preserves vitality for discovering the innermost divine essence rather than wasting energy in futile agitation

Chapter 8XI, Verses 3-4—Divine Sustenance from Real Love and Spiritual Nobility:

[Verse 3] "you will be sustained not just by food from the earth but that vital bread of your Lord (the Divine / Ab Neter / Neberdjer)"
- Real love (authentic caring without egoistic contamination) generates spiritual sustenance beyond physical nourishment
- Actions performed as conduits of divine compassion produce inherent satisfaction independent of ego-gratification
- Distinction between real love (not seeking support from those loved, not seeking accolades) versus egoistic love (contaminated with self-seeking)
- When ethical conduct flows from Ab Neter awareness rather than aryu-driven ego-need, it connects the mind directly to divine sustenance
- Real love leads to the highest spiritual development through dynamic purification

[Verse 4] "your karmic-impressions have been purified, and you have become a person who is worthy to be honored-worshipped, as a {spiritually realized noble}. This nobility of yours is the decoration for your funerary coffin chamber"
- Ethical living and service purify the aryu that previously corrupted and controlled personality
- Purification creates the spiritual nobility worthy of divine honor
- This transformation prepares the mind for liberation from reincarnation cycles
- The teaching compassionately acknowledges that egoistic love produces gradual purification through a secret mechanism until sufficient purity allows ego sublimation, after which the higher love takes spiritual development the rest of the way to spiritual victory

Chapter 8XI, Verse 5—Divine Vitality Beyond Physical Sustenance:

[Verse 5] "If a person of sound integrity and balanced emotions lives in accordance with the teachings of the Sage [Amenemopet], then that person comes to have trust and faith in the Divine and therefore need not worry excessively about sustenance, for the divine souls are at hand, the bau of Neteru [to sustain consciousness and provide vitality]"
- Silent mind and feelings enable receiving divine vitality directly from the bau Neteru (divine souls emanating from Neberdjer)
- Physical food represents gross sustenance while spiritual vitality flows from subtle sources accessible through ethical alignment
- Trust in divine providence reduces anxiety about material provisions, preserving vitality for spiritual development

Chapter 8XI, Verses 8-11—Gossip, Innate Corruption, and Serpent Power Connection:

[Verse 8] "There will not occur situations where people speak harshly to you or gossip about you, or talk about you in a manner which is not true, {if you restrain your speech and live by the wisdom teachings}"
- Ethical restraint in speech and conduct prevents attracting negative verbal assaults from others
- The karmic reciprocity principle: the mind creating destructive speech patterns deposits aryu in the ab that attract corresponding external experiences

[Verse 11] "The innate badness from the belly should be suppressed and then, through a process, it is sublimated."

- Recognition that corrupted impulses arise from accumulated aryu in the ab (unconscious mind)
- Transformation requires initial suppression (restraint) followed by sublimation (energy redirection toward spiritual purposes)
- Connection to Serpent Power goddess: Ra's differentiated consciousness burns up iniquity through righteous living
- Ethical conduct activates the serpent power that purifies corrupted patterns and opens channels for divine vitality

1. Human Psychology Principle: The Vital Energy Economy and Ab Neter-Guided Conduct

The central psychological issue these verses address concerns how the mind either generates spiritual vitality through Ab Neter-aligned conduct or depletes vital force through aryu-driven patterns that maintain separation from divine sustenance. The teaching reveals that human consciousness operates within what might be understood as a "vital energy economy" where ethical choices and speech either preserve and enhance sekhem (life force) or dissipate it through conflict, gossip, harsh words, and egoistic striving that prevents access to the "vital bread" verses 3-4 identify as available through authentic caring.

The psychological framework operates through understanding that the mind at the hat level makes choices either from aryu-driven ego-need (producing egoistic love, conflict, harsh speech) or from emerging Ab Neter awareness (producing real love, peaceful relations, vitality-generating speech). When the mind operates predominantly from accumulated aryu in the ab—feeling-memories of separation, inadequacy, competition, and survival fear—it generates behaviors that appear necessary for self-protection but actually deplete the vital energy required for spiritual development while simultaneously depositing more corrupting aryu that perpetuate the exhausting cycles.

Verse 21's teaching about speech as either vitality-generator or harm-causer reveals that words function not merely as communication tools but as vehicles channeling the quality of consciousness into the phenomenal world, either creating or destroying vital force in both speaker and recipient. When the mind speaks from aryu-driven reactivity—criticism, gossip, harsh judgment, manipulative language—it dissipates sekhem through several simultaneous mechanisms: the agitation required to maintain hostile speech patterns diverts vital energy from restorative functions; the corrupting aryu deposited through unethical speech strengthen patterns requiring future energy expenditure to manage; and the mind's separation from Ab Neter source that harsh speech reinforces prevents access to the divine vitality verse 5 indicates as available to those with "sound integrity and balanced emotions."

Conversely, speech arising from silent mind and feelings—words guided by Ab Neter awareness rather than aryu reactivity—generates vitality through different mechanisms: the calm presence required for ethical speech conserves energy rather than dissipating it; the purifying aryu deposited through righteous speech thin corrupted patterns reducing future energy demands; and the mind's alignment with Ab Neter source that ethical speech expresses opens access to the "bau Neteru" divine souls providing subtle vitality beyond physical sustenance.

Though not specifically stated by Amenemopet, in other Ancient Egyptian texts the process of drawing lifeforce and establishing Ra cognizance consciousness connection through the gods and goddesses is referred to as  *Sa-ankh* or "divine protective energy consciousness." The gods and goddesses are understood as intermediaries between remtedju (people) and Ra, the Creator Spirit of the entire Creation. By turning towards any of the gods and goddesses—who are themselves emanations of and therefore connected to Ra—the human being can gain access to Ra consciousness and spiritual strength. Remember that Ra is a manifestation of Neberdjer.[19][20] Thus Ra is also to be understood as the essence that resides in the human being as their soul in the form of Amun-Ra; therefore, Ab Ra and Amun-Ra are the same being, the same universal consciousness acting locally as the consciousness (soul) sustaining the human.[18]

Verses 1-2's teaching about reciprocal ethics and inner sanctuary access illuminates another dimension of the vital energy economy. The mind engaging in conflict and harsh relations with others expends enormous vital force in several ways: the physiological stress responses activated during interpersonal conflict divert sekhem from spiritual development; the mental energy consumed rehearsing grievances, plotting responses, and maintaining defensive positions depletes resources needed for "effective effort towards finding yourself a place...in the inner part of the temple"; and the mental turbulence that conflict generates prevents the "inner peace" necessary for discovering the divine essence within the kara.

The teaching reveals that caring for others "as one cares for one's own limbs" represents not merely moral prescription but psychological reality accessible when the mind recognizes unity beneath apparent separation. When the mind operates from Ab Neter awareness recognizing others as extensions of Neberdjer, ethical conduct toward them becomes as natural and effortless as caring for one's own body—requiring no vital energy expenditure for forced discipline because the action flows from recognized reality rather than from imposed moral obligation. This explains why verse 2 indicates that peaceful relations with others produce the inner peace enabling temple practice: when the mind stops expending vital energy in conflict with apparent "others," that preserved energy becomes available for the intensive work of discovering Ab Neter presence in the kara.

Verses 3-4's profound teaching about real love versus egoistic love reveals the deepest dimension of the vital energy economy and its relationship to aryu purification. The distinction proves crucial: egoistic love—service and caring contaminated with ego-seeking, monitoring for validation, expecting gratitude—produces gradual subtle purification through a "secret mechanism" whereby, being limited to family, spouse, children, ethnic group, country, it can have a limited positive effect on the personality at an unconscious level that may accumulate over time or lifetimes but consumes substantial vital energy in the ego-maintenance required to track virtue accumulation. Real love—authentic caring flowing from Ab Neter awareness without self-seeking—generates powerful dynamic purification while simultaneously providing access to the "vital bread" spiritual sustenance that replenishes sekhem independent of physical nourishment or ego-gratification.

The psychological mechanics: when the mind performs ethical actions from aryu-driven ego-need, the mind must simultaneously manage the helping behavior and the ego-monitoring process evaluating success in appearing virtuous. This divided attention dissipates vital energy while the underlying aryu patterns—insecurity requiring validation through apparent virtue—remain fundamentally unaddressed even as the ethical behavior deposits some purifying aryu. The result: gradual thinning of corrupted patterns offset by the energy cost of maintaining ego-evaluation, producing the "many ups and downs" characterizing egoistic love's purification path.

Conversely, when the mind performs ethical actions from emerging Ab Neter awareness, the mind engages helping behavior as direct expression of divine compassion without ego-mediation. The energy not consumed in ego-monitoring becomes available as the "vital bread" satisfaction—not ego-gratification requiring validation but inherent fulfillment from the mind's alignment with its divine source. Simultaneously, the purifying aryu deposited through Ab Neter-guided action accumulate without counterbalancing energy expenditure in ego-maintenance, producing the dynamic powerful purification that verse 4 indicates transforms personality to spiritual nobility worthy of divine honor.

The teaching's compassionate provision that egoistic love produces gradual purification until "sufficient purity allows ego sublimation, after which the higher love takes spiritual development the rest of the way to spiritual victory" acknowledges developmental reality: most aspirants begin from aryu-driven ego-consciousness and cannot instantly access authentic real love. The secret mechanism operates through simple engagement in ethical conduct even while ego takes credit—the purifying aryu accumulate gradually thinning corrupted patterns until threshold purity enables the breakthrough where ego-consciousness becomes sublimated, and Ab Neter awareness emerges as natural operating baseline.

This directly impacts both Prologue goals: without preserving vital energy through ethical speech and conduct, the goal of earthly well-being (Prologue verse 2) cannot be achieved because the mind remains depleted through conflict, gossip, and ego-striving. Simultaneously, without accessing the divine vitality available through real love and Ab Neter alignment, discovering the kara sanctuary (Prologue verse 9) proves impossible because the presence-of-mind necessary for that discovery requires sekhem unavailable when the mind dissipates vital force through aryu-driven patterns.

2. Behavioral Imperative: Observable Patterns of Vitality Generation versus Depletion

The behavioral manifestations arising from these verses reveal how the mind either preserves vital energy through Ab Neter-aligned conduct or exhausts sekhem through aryu-driven patterns. Understanding these behaviors through the hat-ab-aryu-Ab Neter framework illuminates how seemingly innocuous choices about speech and interpersonal conduct produce profound effects on consciousness vitality and spiritual development capacity.

Speech Patterns and Vital Energy Flow

Verse 21's instruction about making speech "sound...so as to be a cause for vitality" manifests behaviorally through conscious discrimination about words spoken and language patterns employed. The heated mind, operating from aryu of insecurity, competition, and separation, generates characteristic speech patterns: criticism establishing superiority through others' diminishment, gossip creating false intimacy through shared judgment, harsh words releasing internal tension through external attack, manipulative language pursuing advantage through truth distortion.

Each instance of such speech produces measurable vital energy depletion. The person cngaging harsh criticism of a colleague might experience momentary satisfaction from perceived dominance, yet the mind afterward feels slightly more agitated, relationships become more tense requiring vigilance and defensive energy, and the ab accumulates more aryu of hostility requiring future management. The cumulative effect over months and years: personality characterized by chronic tension, depleted vitality, defensive reactivity, and the inability to access the inner peace verse 2 identifies as necessary for discovering the divine sanctuary.

Conversely, speech arising from silent mind and feelings—characterized by truthful gentleness, constructive feedback, compassionate listening, and restraint from unnecessary criticism—preserves and generates vital energy through different mechanisms. The person who consciously chooses gentle truth over harsh criticism maintains internal calm requiring no defensive energy expenditure, creates relational harmony reducing future conflict demands, and deposits purifying aryu in the ab that thin corrupted patterns. The cumulative effect: personality characterized by increasing serenity, preserved vitality available for spiritual practice, and progressive capacity for the inner peace enabling temple work.

The behavioral challenge involves recognizing that harsh speech patterns often operate automatically from dense aryu before conscious discrimination can intervene. Someone conditioned through years of competitive environments might speak critically before recognizing the impulse, find gossip arising spontaneously during social interactions, or notice harsh words emerging during stress without conscious intention. The mind experiences these patterns as natural personality expression rather than as corrupted conditioning requiring transformation.

Conflict Engagement versus Peaceful Relations

Verses 1-2's teaching about reciprocal ethics and peaceful relations manifests behaviorally through choices about whether to engage interpersonal conflicts or maintain harmonious boundaries. The heated mind, operating from aryu demanding vindication, generates characteristic conflict patterns: engaging every disagreement as requiring "winning," maintaining grievances through mental rehearsal, pursuing confrontations to establish dominance, or creating drama through unnecessary disputes.

The vital energy cost proves substantial. The individual who engages frequent conflicts expends sekhem in multiple ways: the sympathetic nervous system activation during confrontation diverts energy from restorative functions, the mental energy consumed rehearsing arguments and maintaining defensive positions depletes resources, the relational damage requiring repair efforts demands ongoing attention, and the mental turbulence prevents the inner peace necessary for spiritual practice. Someone finishing a day filled with workplace conflicts, family arguments, and social disputes finds themselves exhausted yet unable to engage meditation or contemplative study—the vital energy required for such practice has been dissipated through unnecessary agitation.

Conversely, the behavior verse 1 describes—"doing love to people instead of harm, giving consideration rather than conflict"—preserves vital energy through avoiding unnecessary confrontation while maintaining appropriate boundaries. The person who chooses peaceful response over reactive engagement conserves the sekhem that conflict would consume, maintains inner calm accessible for temple practice, and deposits purifying aryu replacing corrupted reactivity patterns. This does not mean passive acceptance of abuse or injustice—the teaching indicates discernment about when engagement serves righteousness versus when conflict serves only ego-vindication. The wisdom lies in recognizing that most daily conflicts arise from aryu-driven ego-need rather than genuine ethical necessity, and choosing peaceful non-engagement preserves the vital energy required for discovering the divine sanctuary verse 2 describes.

The behavioral manifestation of recognizing others as "extensions of oneself" appears in spontaneous caring that requires no forced discipline. When the mind genuinely perceives another person as Neberdjer-expression sharing the same divine source, helping them becomes as natural as caring for one's own body. The person who truly embodies this recognition doesn't experience ethical conduct as energy-depleting obligation but as effortless expression of recognized unity—the vital energy flows freely because the mind no longer maintains the separation-perception requiring defensive boundaries and competitive vigilance.

Egoistic Love versus Real Love Behavioral Patterns

Verses 3-4's distinction between egoistic and real love manifests in subtle but crucial behavioral differences that determine whether service generates spiritual vitality or merely ego-validation. The mind operating from egoistic love engages helping behaviors while simultaneously monitoring for recognition, evaluating virtue accumulation, expecting gratitude, and using service to enhance self-image. These ego-monitoring activities consume vital energy even while the service itself produces some purifying benefit.

The behavioral pattern appears as: volunteering at charitable organizations while mentally tracking hours for resume building, helping others while noting who witnessed the good deed, performing kind acts while expecting reciprocal appreciation, or engaging spiritual practice while comparing advancement to other practitioners. The person caught in egoistic love experiences the "many ups and downs" the teaching describes—spiritual highs when service receives recognition alternating with deflation when efforts go unacknowledged, enthusiasm for practice when feeling virtuous alternating with discouragement when ego-goals aren't met.

The vital energy expenditure occurs through the divided attention required to simultaneously engage service and maintain ego-evaluation. The individual helping someone while monitoring for validation must allocate mental attention to both the actual helping and the meta-process of evaluating how helping reflects on their self-image. This split depletes sekhem while the underlying aryu patterns—insecurity requiring virtue validation—remain fundamentally unaddressed despite the ethical behavior's gradual purifying effect.

Conversely, real love manifests as helping behavior arising from Ab Neter awareness without ego-mediation. The person operating from authentic real love engages service as direct expression of divine compassion, experiencing inherent satisfaction from the mind's alignment with divine source rather than requiring external validation for ego-gratification. The behavioral distinction: no mental energy consumed monitoring for recognition, no evaluation of virtue accumulation, no expectation of gratitude—just spontaneous caring flowing from recognized unity with others as Neberdjer-expressions.

The vital energy economy proves dramatically different. Without sekhem consumed in ego-monitoring, the mind experiences the "vital bread" satisfaction verse 3 describes—a stable spiritual sustenance independent of whether service receives acknowledgment. The person finishes a day of intensive service not depleted but refreshed, having accessed divine vitality through Ab Neter-aligned conduct. Simultaneously, the purifying aryu deposited through authentic caring accumulate without counterbalancing energy expenditure in ego-maintenance, producing the dynamic transformation verse 4 indicates elevates personality to spiritual nobility.

The teaching's behavioral guidance recognizes developmental progression: aspirants typically begin from egoistic love and gradually move toward real love through persistent ethical practice that thins aryu density. The crucial behavioral choice involves continuing service despite recognizing ego-contamination rather than abandoning practice while awaiting impossible immediate purity. Each act of helping—even while ego monitors for credit—deposits some purifying aryu and provides practice opportunity for noticing when authentic caring arises spontaneously. Over time, these moments of genuine Ab Neter-guided service increase while ego-monitoring decreases, indicating the threshold approaching where ego becomes sublimated and higher love emerges as natural expression.

Suppression and Sublimation of Innate Corruption

Verse 11's teaching about suppressing then sublimating "innate badness from the belly" manifests behaviorally through conscious restraint of corrupted impulses followed by energy redirection toward spiritual purposes. The heated mind experiences impulses toward gossip, harsh speech, selfish behavior, and ethical violations arising from dense aryu in the ab. Without conscious intervention, these impulses generate automatic behaviors that deplete vital energy through the mechanisms previously described while depositing more corrupting aryu perpetuating the exhausting cycles.

The behavioral imperative requires two-stage response: initial suppression (conscious restraint preventing impulse expression) followed by sublimation (redirecting the preserved energy toward constructive purposes). When impulse toward gossip arises, the aspirant first restrains speech—recognizing the urge as aryu seeking self-perpetuation rather than as truth requiring expression. This suppression prevents the vital energy depletion that gossip would produce. Second, the aspirant sublimates the preserved energy—directing attention toward study, meditation, service, or contemplative practice that generates purifying aryu replacing corrupted patterns.

The behavioral challenge involves recognizing that mere suppression without sublimation creates problematic compression. Someone who constantly restrains corrupted impulses through willpower without redirecting that energy toward positive purposes experiences increasing internal pressure, eventual explosive release, or chronic tension consuming the very vital force suppression aimed to preserve. The teaching's wisdom lies in providing the two-stage method: suppress the destructive expression, then immediately sublimate the energy into spiritual practice—preventing both the depletion that indulgence would cause and the compression that suppression alone creates.

3. Mystic Psychology—Metaphysical Implications: The Divine Vitality System and Real Love Mechanics

The metaphysical framework underlying these verses reveals profound principles about how the mind accesses vitality from divine sources, how love functions as actual force connecting individual awareness with cosmic sustenance, and how speech operates as consciousness-vehicle channeling vital energy. Understanding these metaphysical mechanics illuminates why ethical living and real love prove essential for spiritual development beyond mere moral prescription.

The Bau Neteru and Divine Vitality Channels

Verse 5's teaching about "bau Neteru"—divine souls that provide vitality to the mind operating with "sound integrity and balanced emotions"—reveals metaphysical architecture typically invisible to ordinary awareness. The framework identifies that consciousness (Ab Neter within individual, emanating from Ra, originating in Neberdjer) maintains connection with its divine source through what might be understood as subtle channels transmitting vital force beyond the physical nourishment sustaining bodily functions.

The bau Neteru represent differentiated expressions of universal consciousness (Neberdjer) operating at soul level, accessible to individual consciousness when sufficient purity and ethical alignment create conditions for connection. These divine souls function as what the tradition describes as intermediary forces—neither the ultimate absolute (Neberdjer) nor the individual expression (Ab Neter) but rather the cosmic intelligences through which universal consciousness sustains particular manifestations. When the mind maintains "sound integrity and balanced emotions" (silent mind and feelings), it establishes resonance with these divine souls, opening channels for sekhem transmission beyond what physical sustenance provides.

The metaphysical mechanics: aryu density in the ab functions as obstruction preventing the mind from accessing bau Neteru vitality. The corrupted patterns accumulated through unethical living create what might be understood as static or interference in the subtle channels connecting individual Ab Neter with universal divine souls. When the mind operates from heated mind and feelings—agitation, conflict, harsh speech, ego-striving—this turbulence prevents the stillness necessary for perceiving and accessing the subtle vitality the bau Neteru continuously transmit.

Conversely, when the mind operates from silent mind and feelings cultivated through ethical living, the ab gradually purifies as aryu density thins. This purification doesn't create access to previously absent divine souls but removes obstruction preventing recognition of and connection with the bau Neteru that always sustained consciousness even when unrecognized. The "vital bread" verse 3 describes becomes accessible—not as metaphor but as actual subtle nourishment transmitted through purified channels from divine sources to individual awareness. The person who achieves sufficient ethical alignment and aryu purification discovers the mind sustained by vitality transcending physical food, enabling extended spiritual practice that physical energy alone could not support.

Real Love as Consciousness Force

The teaching's distinction between real love and egoistic love reveals that authentic caring functions not merely as emotion or moral choice but as actual force connecting individual consciousness with divine sustenance. The metaphysical principle: when the mind acts from Ab Neter awareness recognizing others as Neberdjer-expressions, the mind operates as direct channel for divine compassion flowing from universal source through individual expression into phenomenal world. This channeling function creates the "vital bread" satisfaction because the mind experiences itself aligned with and expressing its actual nature as particularized divine awareness.

The mechanics operate through understanding what the teaching calls the "secret mechanism" of gradual purification through egoistic love versus the dynamic transformation possible through real love. When the mind performs ethical actions from aryu-driven ego-need, the behavior deposits purifying aryu even while ego-maintenance consumes energy. The secret mechanism: despite ego-contamination, the actual helping behavior resonates with the Ab Neter level of consciousness beneath ego-identification. Over time and repeated ethical practice, these resonances accumulate like water wearing away stone—gradually thinning the ego-structures maintaining separation from Ab Neter awareness until threshold purity enables a sudden breakthrough where ego becomes sublimated.

Real love operates through different metaphysics entirely. When sufficient purification occurs that the mind can perform caring actions from Ab Neter awareness rather than aryu-need, the individual becomes what the tradition describes as "vessel" or "channel" for divine compassion. The mind no longer operates as separate individual accumulating virtue but as particularized expression through which universal love manifests directly. This explains why real love generates the powerful dynamic purification verse 4 describes—the force flowing through the mind doesn't merely deposit purifying aryu but actively burns corrupted patterns through direct application of divine power (the Serpent Power goddess that verse 11 connects to the teaching).

The Metaphysical Foundation: Wise Love Does Not Violate Maat Ethics

The teaching on real love contains a profound principle that modern aspirants often overlook: authentic love, by its very nature, cannot violate Maat ethics. This principle emerges directly from the metaphysical reality that Neberdjer encompasses all existence. When the teaching describes "real love" as the mind operating from Ab Neter awareness, this means the mind recognizes the divine essence pervading all apparent forms. Love aligned with this recognition necessarily operates within ethical boundaries, for to violate Maat would be to contradict the very unity such love perceives.

Consider the delusion that possessive attachment represents love. When the mind regards another being as an object separate from Neberdjer—something to be enjoyed, possessed, or controlled for personal satisfaction—this contradicts the fundamental truth (Maat) that all beings express the one all-encompassing reality. Such possessive patterns arise from aryu-driven ignorance maintaining the illusion of separation. The mind mistakes the temporary form for the essence, believing "this person belongs to me" or "I need this relationship for my completion," when in truth both individuals represent particularized expressions of the singular divine consciousness that sustains all existence.

The teaching reveals that what ordinary minds call "love" often represents egoic infatuation, sentimental attachment, or codependent enmeshment—patterns driven by accumulated aryu rather than recognition of unity. These patterns characteristically violate ethical principles through possessiveness that restricts another's freedom, through enabling unrighteous behavior to maintain relationship comfort, or through conditional affection that demands conformity to personal preferences. Such patterns prove their deviation from Maat by creating suffering rather than liberation, bondage rather than freedom, agitation rather than peace.

The Paradox of Loving While Maintaining Ethical Boundaries

This understanding resolves what appears as a paradox to the aryu-driven mind: how can one genuinely love another yet refuse to enable their unrighteousness or tolerate their harmful behavior? The resolution emerges through recognizing that authentic love—the mind operating from Ab Neter awareness of unity—necessarily includes commitment to truth and righteousness. To enable another's violation of Maat while claiming this represents love actually demonstrates the opposite: it reveals the mind operating from egoic need (perhaps fear of abandonment, desire for continued validation, or sentimental attachment to the relationship's comfortable patterns) rather than from recognition of the divine essence worthy of honoring through ethical conduct.

The wisdom to be understood recognizes that when someone engages in unrighteous behavior, the most loving response may involve establishing boundaries, withdrawing support for wrongdoing, or even ending association—not from hostile rejection but from recognition that supporting isfet (unrighteousness) serves neither party's highest good. This proves particularly challenging for aspirants conditioned by cultural narratives equating love with unconditional acceptance of all behaviors regardless of ethical content. Yet the teaching clarifies: the divine essence (Ab Neter) within all deserves honor and respect, which means refusing to participate in patterns that degrade that essence through unrighteousness.

Consider verse 3's teaching about turning "worldly love into temple devotion" through making offerings at the temples. This transformation from ordinary attachment to sacred recognition involves precisely this shift from possessive regard of forms to reverent recognition of divine essence. The "thousands of loaves of bread and drink to the sacred mascot of Asar" represents the mind redirecting energy previously consumed in worldly attachments toward practices that thin the aryu maintaining separation illusion. The aspirant learns to recognize the divine essence pervading all beings rather than grasping at temporary forms as if they could provide the completion only Ab Neter recognition brings.

Universal Love Distinguished from Sentimental Attachment

The metaphysical framework distinguishes between what might be termed universal love—the mind recognizing Neberdjer in all forms without preference or attachment—and the limited, sentimental patterns that egoic minds mistake for love. Universal love operates like sunlight that shines equally on all beings regardless of their apparent worthiness, reflecting the Ab Neter level of awareness that perceives unity beneath diversity. This love requires no vital energy expenditure for maintenance because it flows naturally from recognized reality rather than from effortful emotional generation attempting to overcome the separation illusion that aryu maintain.

In contrast, egoic attachment operates through what the teaching identifies as "being limited to family, spouse, children, ethnic group, country"—love bound by categories of "mine" versus "other" that reinforce rather than dissolve separation awareness. Such limited love, while capable of producing gradual purification through the secret mechanism verse 4 describes, exhausts vital energy through the constant evaluation and maintenance egoic perspective requires. The mind must perpetually assess: "Am I receiving adequate return on my love investment? Does this person still deserve my affection? Are they loyal to me in the way I demand?"

The teaching reveals that authentic love—what might also be termed righteous love or love aligned with divine justice—operates without such transactional calculation while simultaneously refusing to enable violation of Maat principles. This love recognizes that because Neberdjer is all, every being deserves treatment reflecting their divine essence, yet this same recognition means holding all accountable to righteousness rather than permitting isfet under the guise of tolerance or acceptance.

The Purification Path: Transforming Ordinary Love Through Maat Principles

The wisdom to be understood recognizes a crucial principle that offers hope to aspirants struggling with egoistic attachment patterns: if egoistic love fundamentally represents delusion while universal love expresses Maat ethics, then the imperfect love that ordinary people experience—what the mind mistakes for genuine affection—amounts to infatuation seeking to serve personal egoistic purposes of self-satisfaction, a pattern doomed to inevitable failure and disappointment. Yet this recognition need not lead to despair, for the teaching reveals the transformative mechanism: if the principles of Maat were applied to that egoistic love, it could become purified into universal love through a systematic process of ethical refinement.

This transformation mechanism explains how such a person could break the bonds of egoic spiritual delusion through the very love relationships they currently experience—thereby turning what begins as ordinary attachment into a powerful spiritual practice leading toward liberation. The path proves effortful in the beginning, requiring conscious application of ethical principles to attachment patterns driven by accumulated aryu seeking possession, validation, and personal satisfaction. The aspirant must repeatedly choose to honor Maat rather than yield to possessive urges, to respect the other's freedom rather than seek control, to remain truthful rather than manipulate for relationship maintenance—all while the aryu-driven mind protests that such restraint represents lovelessness rather than authentic care.

Yet through persistent application of Maat principles to love relationships, the practice gradually becomes relaxed and effortless in the end, for the mind ceases seeking to possess or satisfy unrighteous urges—whether one's own or those of others. The transformation occurs not through forceful suppression of attachment but through the natural thinning of aryu density that ethical conduct produces. As the accumulated feeling-memories maintaining possessive patterns gradually dissolve through righteous action, the mind discovers its natural capacity to remain serene while expressing the inherent serenity Neberdjer manifests through Nature (neteru).

Consider how the natural forces—the neteru expressing Neberdjer's reality—demonstrate this principle: the trees bend in storms yet return to stillness, the ocean churns in tempests yet settles to mirror-like calm, the air swirls in winds yet resumes its peaceful flow. Even after disturbance, Nature (neteru) returns to serenity because this represents their true nature, the fundamental quality of Neberdjer expressing through manifest forms. The teaching reveals that this same serenity constitutes the mind's true nature once aryu obstructions thin sufficiently for Ab Neter awareness to emerge. The aspirant learns to embody this quality—not through artificial calm imposed upon agitation but through the genuine peace that arises when the mind operates from its divine foundation rather than from accumulated patterns of fear, need, and grasping.

Therefore, if such a person living in this way were to engage a relationship, it would not arise from egoistic seeking to fill an internal void—the desperate attempt to extract from another what only Ab Neter recognition can provide. Rather, the relationship emerges from recognition of Neberdjer in the other and a willingness to converge and cooperate for the betterment of all, creating what might be termed sacred partnership grounded in mutual recognition of divine essence. This convergence facilitates greater expression of Neberdjer experience for all life through helping to create conditions that support Neberdjer recognition by all beings.

The transformation from void-filling attachment to sacred convergence represents a fundamental shift in relationship purpose and mechanics. Egoistic love exhausts itself attempting the impossible task of making another person responsible for one's internal completeness—a burden no human form can bear, for only the infinite can satisfy the soul's longing for infinite reality. When this inevitable failure occurs, the egoistic mind typically responds by seeking a different partner, perpetuating the cycle, or by deepening resentment toward the current partner for failing to provide what they never could provide. The aryu maintaining this pattern grow denser through repeated disappointment, further obscuring Ab Neter awareness.

Conversely, love grounded in Neberdjer recognition operates from internal fullness rather than external neediness. The aspirant discovers they can engage relationship while remaining complete in themselves through connection to Ab Neter, bringing wholeness to the partnership rather than seeking wholeness from the partnership. This shift eliminates the desperate quality characterizing egoistic attachment—the anxiety about losing the relationship, the constant evaluation of whether needs are being met, the manipulation attempting to secure continued affection. Instead, the mind rests in recognition that whether this particular relationship continues or dissolves, the essential reality (Neberdjer) remains unchanged, and one's divine essence (Ab Neter) continues sustaining consciousness regardless of external circumstances.

This understanding proves particularly significant for aspirants conditioned by cultural narratives insisting that romantic partnership represents life's primary purpose and ultimate fulfillment. The teaching does not reject relationship but recontextualizes it: partnership becomes opportunity for mutual recognition and cooperative expression of divine reality rather than desperate attempt to resolve internal incompleteness through external acquisition. When two individuals approach relationship from this foundation—each grounded in their own Ab Neter awareness rather than seeking the other to provide what only divinity can provide—they create conditions conducive not merely to personal satisfaction but to collective awakening. Their interaction models and radiates the recognition that transforms egoistic culture, demonstrating through lived example that serenity, cooperation, and mutual honoring prove more satisfying than possession, competition, and egoistic grasping.

The Transformation from Codependent Attachment to Compassionate Detachment

The practical application requires what the Buddhist tradition terms compassionate detachment—the capacity to feel deep care for another's well-being while remaining unattached to specific outcomes of their choices. This quality emerges naturally as aryu density thins sufficiently for the mind to operate from Ab Neter awareness rather than from accumulated patterns of need, fear, and possessiveness. The individual discovers they can love someone profoundly—wanting their highest development and ultimate liberation—while simultaneously refusing to support their unrighteous patterns and remaining serenely detached from whether that person accepts the offered wisdom.

This proves particularly challenging in family relationships where cultural conditioning and accumulated aryu create powerful patterns of enmeshment. Consider the parent whose "love" for a child manifests as enabling self-destructive behavior, protecting them from consequences of wrongdoing, or demanding their conformity to parental expectations that serve ego-gratification rather than the child's authentic development. The teaching would identify such patterns not as love but as codependent attachment born from aryu-driven needs maintaining separation from Ab Neter awareness.

Conversely, the parent operating from emerging real love might establish firm boundaries, allow natural consequences, and refuse to support unrighteous behavior—all while maintaining profound care for the child's essential well-being and ultimate liberation. This love respects the other's journey as an expression of divine unfolding, recognizing that each soul follows the path necessary for their evolution, even when that path involves difficult experiences the ego-mind would prefer to prevent.

Love as Recognition of Shared Divine Essence

The deepest dimension of the teaching reveals love not as emotion or action but as perception—the mind's recognition of the same divine consciousness (Ab Neter sustained by Neberdjer) operating in all apparent individuals. When the mind achieves sufficient purification to perceive this reality directly rather than merely understanding it intellectually, what appears as "love" to the aryu-driven mind transforms into something qualitatively different: simple recognition of what is.

From this level of perception, the question "How should I love this person?" dissolves into irrelevance, replaced by direct recognition: "There is only Neberdjer appearing in infinite forms. What I call 'myself' and what I call 'other' represent the same consciousness experiencing itself through different conditioning patterns and aryu accumulations." This recognition naturally generates ethical conduct not from moral obligation but from recognized reality—one does not harm another's form any more than one would deliberately harm one's own hand, for both represent expressions of the singular consciousness sustaining all existence.

The teaching's instruction to show love so that "the whole world will love you in return" thus reveals itself not as transactional advice but as description of metaphysical principle: when the mind operates from this recognition of unity, it naturally generates responses reflecting that same recognition in others. The "love" returned proves not personal affection directed toward the separate ego but rather consciousness recognizing its own nature expressing through different forms—the universal love that the teaching identifies as generating both earthly well-being (Prologue verse 2) and discovery of the kara where divinity resides (Prologue verse 9).

The metaphysical implication: the spiritual nobility verse 4 describes as "worthy to be honored-worshipped" represents authentic transformation of being rather than ego-achievement. When the mind operates primarily from Ab Neter awareness with ego sublimated, the personality literally embodies divine presence in manifest form. The honor accorded such beings doesn't inflate separate ego but recognizes divinity expressing through purified consciousness-vehicle—the "decoration of the funerary coffin chamber" indicating the mind prepared for liberation from reincarnation cycles because it no longer maintains the ego-identification requiring continued embodied evolution.

Speech as Consciousness Vehicle

Verse 21's teaching about speech as either vitality-generator or harm-causer reveals metaphysical principle that words function as vehicles channeling the quality of consciousness into phenomenal manifestation. When the mind speaks, it doesn't merely communicate information but broadcasts its current state—the quality of consciousness underlying words transmits energetically regardless of conceptual content. Speech from heated mind charged with aryu-driven reactivity carries that disturbance into the environment, creating ripples affecting both speaker and recipients at levels beyond ordinary awareness. Speech from silent mind expressing Ab Neter awareness carries that quality, generating vitality in both speaker and recipients through resonance with divine peace.

The metaphysics: the mind operates through multiple dimensions simultaneously—the words spoken represent gross physical vibration, but underlying that surface manifestation flows the subtle consciousness quality animating speech. When the mind speaks criticism from aryu of hostility, the hostile consciousness-charge depletes vital energy in the speaker (through agitation required to maintain hostile state) and the recipient (through defensive reactions triggered by attack). When the mind speaks truth from Ab Neter awareness, the peaceful consciousness-charge preserves energy in the speaker (through calm required for gentle truth) and generates vitality in the recipient (through resonance with divine peace).

This explains verse 21's instruction to make speech "sound...so as to be a cause for vitality"—the teaching indicates that one can deliberately choose to channel divine qualities through words rather than broadcasting corrupted aryu patterns. The practice requires sufficient purification that the mind can access Ab Neter awareness beneath ego-reactivity, then consciously speaking from that deeper level rather than from surface agitation. Over time, this practice both deposits purifying aryu (reinforcing access to Ab Neter-guided speech) and directly transmits vitality to the mind through alignment with divine source.

4. Transpersonal Psychology Research: Empirical Validation of Ethical Living's Vitalizing Effects

Contemporary psychological research provides substantial empirical validation for the ancient teaching's framework identifying ethical living, compassionate service, and speech quality as determinants of psychological well-being, vital energy, and access to transpersonal consciousness dimensions. While modern science cannot directly measure bau Neteru or Ab Neter, it documents physiological and psychological correlates corresponding precisely to what the teaching describes as vitality preservation versus depletion through behavioral choices.

The Phenomenological Reality of Transpersonal Experience

The statement that "modern science cannot directly measure bau Neteru or Ab Neter" requires a deeper philosophical examination, particularly in light of depth psychology's sophisticated understanding of what constitutes valid knowledge about consciousness. Carl Jung himself explicitly articulated this epistemological challenge, recognizing that certain dimensions of psychic reality resist quantification while remaining profoundly real as experienced phenomena. As Jung stated in Psychological Types: "We cannot experiment upon the psyche as upon inert matter; we can only experience it" [21]. This recognition aligns precisely with the Ancient Egyptian wisdom framework, which treats Ab Neter and the bau Neteru as phenomenological realities—real because they are experienced and produce observable effects, not because they can be quantified through conventional measurement instruments.

Jung treated transpersonal states as objective realities that manifest symbolically rather than materially [21]. His formulation of the collective unconscious as "a suprapersonal layer of psychic reality" containing "images in the deeper unconscious...of a purely supra-personal nature and therefore common to all" [22] parallels remarkably with Amenemopet's teaching about the bau Neteru (divine souls) emanating from Neberdjer through Ra to sustain individual consciousness. Both frameworks recognize dimensions of consciousness that transcend individual ego-boundaries while remaining accessible through direct experience and producing measurable correlates in the mind's states, behavior, and physiological processes.

Nevertheless, Jung maintained throughout his work that the deepest dimensions of psyche remain "partly unknowable" with "a nature which we can only experience but never fully explain" [23]. This philosophical position does not invalidate transpersonal realities but acknowledges that certain aspects of consciousness operate through principles fundamentally different from physical matter. The Ancient Egyptian teaching operates from the same epistemological framework—Ab Neter represents consciousness sustaining individual awareness, observable through its effects (the capacity for awareness itself, ethical discrimination, intuitive knowing) yet not reducible to neural processes or quantifiable through conventional instruments designed for measuring physical phenomena.

Indirect Empirical Approaches to Transpersonal Dimensions

While direct measurement of transpersonal consciousness dimensions remains epistemologically problematic, contemporary research has developed sophisticated methodologies for documenting the correlates and effects of what Amenemopet identifies as Ab Neter awareness and connection to bau Neteru vitality. Neurophenomenological research employing advanced neuroimaging (EEG, fMRI) reveals consistent brain activity patterns during mystical, meditative, and profound spiritual experiences, including decreased activity in the default mode network associated with ego-based self-reference and increased gamma synchrony linked to unity or non-dual consciousness experiences [24][25]. These neurological findings do not prove the existence of a transpersonal source in the way one might prove the existence of a physical object, but they establish measurable physiological signatures corresponding to subjective reports of the mind transcending ordinary ego-boundaries—precisely what accessing Ab Neter awareness would produce according to the ancient framework.

Transpersonal psychology researchers following Jung's pioneering work have developed psychometric instruments attempting to quantify aspects of transpersonal experience. The Mysticism Scale (Hood, 1975) measures the intensity and phenomenological features of mystical states [26]. The Spiritual Transcendence Scale (Piedmont, 1999) assesses perceived connection to a larger reality beyond the individual ego [27]. The States of Consciousness Questionnaire employed in contemporary psychedelic research at institutions like Johns Hopkins documents specific features of non-ordinary consciousness states [28]. While these instruments measure subjective reports rather than directly quantifying transpersonal dimensions themselves, they provide structured empirical data regarding frequency, depth, triggers, and psychological effects of experiences corresponding to what the ancient teaching describes as Ab Neter recognition and bau Neteru connection.

Research on Jung's concept of synchronicity—meaningful coincidences without conventional causal connection—represents another empirical approach to what Jung termed the "psychoid" level where psyche and matter appear to interact [21]. Although results remain largely anecdotal or statistically inconclusive, parapsychology and consciousness researchers continue investigating correlations between intention and physical systems, attempting to detect effects that bridge subjective consciousness and objective reality [29]. From the Ancient Egyptian framework, such synchronistic phenomena would represent observable effects of the deeper unity (Neberdjer) manifesting through apparent multiplicity—not proof of transpersonal consciousness in conventional scientific terms, but phenomena consistent with the metaphysical architecture the teaching describes.

The fundamental reason transpersonal dimensions resist direct measurement lies in their nature as subjective, interior phenomena rather than publicly observable objects. If consciousness itself represents the foundational ground (Neberdjer/Ab Neter) from which all experience arises rather than an emergent property of physical processes, then attempting to measure consciousness using instruments designed for measuring physical phenomena represents a category error. As Jung recognized, we can measure correlates—brain states, self-reports, behavioral outcomes. Nevertheless, the transpersonal dimension itself, the source beyond the individual psyche, remains empirically elusive precisely because it constitutes the witnessing awareness within which all measurement occurs rather than an object that awareness can observe [21][23].

Therefore, the teaching's framework remains entirely consistent with sophisticated depth psychology and contemporary consciousness research: Ab Neter and bau Neteru represent dimensions of consciousness accessible through direct experience, producing observable psychological and physiological correlates, yet transcending conventional measurement because consciousness itself cannot be reduced to the objects it witnesses. The empirical validation lies not in direct quantification but in the documented correlates—the enhanced vitality, psychological well-being, ethical behavior, and access to transpersonal awareness dimensions that practitioners maintaining the silent mind and feelings develop, precisely as Amenemopet's teaching predicts.

Prosocial Behavior and Well-being Research

Extensive research demonstrates that individuals engaging in regular helping behavior, volunteer service, and compassionate action toward others show significantly enhanced well-being compared to those focused primarily on self-interest [4][5]. Studies document that prosocial activity produces measurable benefits including reduced depression, decreased anxiety, enhanced life satisfaction, improved physical health markers, and even increased longevity—empirical validation for the teaching that caring for others generates vitality rather than depleting it [4][5][7].

Research on the "helper's high" phenomenon provides a possible biological mechanism for what the teaching describes as the "vital bread" satisfaction from real love. Studies show that acts of kindness and compassion activate brain reward centers, release endorphins and oxytocin, reduce stress hormone levels, and produce subjective feelings of warmth and connection—physiological correlates of the mind accessing what verse 3 identifies as divine sustenance beyond physical nourishment [6][10]. Longitudinal research demonstrates that individuals maintaining long-term service commitments show enhanced vitality and reduced burnout compared to predictions based purely on time and energy expenditure, suggesting access to sustaining resources the materialist framework cannot explain [7][8].

Significantly, research distinguishes between authentic altruistic motivation and reputation-based or reciprocity-based helping, finding that genuinely selfless service produces superior well-being outcomes compared to helping performed for ego-gratification or social credit [5][7]. This empirical finding validates the teaching's distinction between real love (generating powerful purification and divine sustenance) versus egoistic love (producing only gradual purification with many ups and downs). Studies show that helpers who seek recognition or expect reciprocal benefit experience less well-being enhancement and greater burnout compared to those serving from intrinsic caring motivation—the vital energy difference between ego-monitoring service versus Ab Neter-guided caring the teaching describes [4][5][7].

Speech Quality and Vitality Research

Research on gossip, criticism, and hostile communication validates verse 21's teaching about speech as vitality-depleter versus vitality-generator. Studies demonstrate that individuals engaging in frequent gossip and criticism show elevated cortisol levels, increased cardiovascular reactivity, impaired immune function, and reduced psychological well-being—measurable indicators of vital energy depletion [13]. Longitudinal research tracking hostile communication patterns documents progressive health deterioration and reduced longevity, empirical validation that harsh speech produces the harm verse 21 warns against [13].

Conversely, research on compassionate communication, appreciative language, and constructive feedback demonstrates that individuals practicing ethical speech patterns show enhanced stress resilience, improved relationship quality, better physical health markers, and greater life satisfaction [9][13]. Studies measuring physiological responses during different communication styles find that gentle, truthful, compassionate speech activates parasympathetic nervous system responses associated with restoration and vitality preservation—biological correlates of the teaching that sound speech generates vitality rather than depleting it [9][12].

Research on loving-kindness meditation—systematic practice of generating compassionate thoughts toward self and others—provides experimental validation for consciousness training in the speech and conduct patterns these verses recommend [11]. Studies demonstrate that regular loving-kindness practice produces structural brain changes in regions supporting empathy and emotional regulation, enhanced immune function, reduced inflammatory markers, and improved social connection—measurable effects corresponding to what the teaching describes as purification through cultivating caring consciousness that generates rather than depletes vital energy [9][11][12].

Conflict and Well-being Research

Extensive research on interpersonal conflict validates verses 1-2's teaching about conflict depletion versus peaceful relations vitality [13]. Studies demonstrate that individuals maintaining high-conflict relationships show elevated stress hormones, impaired immune function, reduced sleep quality, increased cardiovascular disease risk, and decreased psychological well-being—comprehensive vital energy depletion the teaching describes [4][13]. Research on workplace conflict documents significant productivity loss, increased illness, and reduced engagement, empirical validation that agitation from disputes prevents the focused work verse 2 indicates as necessary for spiritual discovery [13].

Conversely, research on harmonious relationships, conflict resolution skills, and cooperative interaction demonstrates that individuals maintaining peaceful relations show enhanced well-being across multiple domains [4][7][13]. Studies find that relationship harmony predicts better physical health, greater life satisfaction, enhanced creativity, and even increased longevity—benefits corresponding to what the teaching describes as vital energy preservation through avoiding unnecessary conflict [7][13]. Research on forgiveness and grudge-release provides particular validation, showing that letting go of grievances produces measurable stress reduction and well-being enhancement beyond what simply avoiding confrontation achieves [13].

Altruism Research and the Egoistic-Authentic Distinction

Transpersonal psychology research on altruistic motivation provides an empirical framework corresponding to the teaching's distinction between egoistic love and real love [5][16][17]. Studies employing sophisticated methodology to distinguish genuinely selfless helping from reputation-management or reciprocity-expectation helping find that authentic altruism produces superior psychological and physiological outcomes [5][7]. Research demonstrates that individuals capable of genuine selfless service show enhanced well-being, reduced stress, and greater meaning in life compared to those whose helping behavior remains contaminated with self-seeking—validation for the teaching that real love generates powerful transformation while egoistic love produces only gradual subtle purification [5][7][16][17].

Research on moral identity and ego development provides developmental framework corresponding to the teaching's recognition that most aspirants begin from egoistic motivation and gradually progress toward authentic selflessness [16]. Studies tracking moral development across lifespan demonstrate that ethical practice itself drives progression from conventional morality (behaving ethically to maintain self-image or avoid punishment) toward post-conventional morality (behaving ethically from intrinsic values independent of external consequences)—the transformation from egoistic love toward real love the teaching describes [16].

Significantly, research on meditation and contemplative practice finds that ethical conduct proves essential for sustained progress toward advanced consciousness states characterized by ego-transcendence and unity experience [9][11][12][13]. Studies demonstrate that practitioners maintaining strong ethical commitments show significantly greater likelihood of stable transformation compared to those emphasizing meditation technique while neglecting ethical development—empirical validation for the teaching that accessing Ab Neter awareness and bau Neteru vitality requires the purification that ethical living provides [9][11][13].

5. Spiritual Implications for Aspirants

PART A: PASTORAL CONCERNS—MODERN CHALLENGES TO REAL LOVE AND VITAL ENERGY PRESERVATION

Contemporary aspirants attempting to implement these teachings face systematic obstacles that make distinguishing egoistic love from real love particularly challenging while also making vitality preservation through peaceful relations difficult in environments designed to promote competition and conflict.

The Egoistic Love Trap in Achievement Culture

Consider the individual aspirant raised in contemporary Western culture emphasizing competitive advantage, individual achievement, and transactional relationships. Such a person encounters profound challenges when verses 3-4 teach that real love generates spiritual sustenance and nobility transformation through aryu purification, while egoistic love produces only gradual purification with many ups and downs.

The modern seeker often approaches spiritual practice itself from egoistic motivation: accumulating spiritual credentials, achieving enlightenment as personal accomplishment, or cultivating virtue to enhance self-image. When encountering the teaching on real love, they may immediately engage in charitable activities while unconsciously monitoring for the "vital bread" satisfaction verse 3 promises—already undermining genuine selflessness through expectation and evaluation. The very attempt to access divine sustenance becomes an ego-project, maintaining the aryu-driven separation the teaching aims to dissolve.

Someone raised in achievement-oriented culture struggles with the teaching's distinction between real love and egoistic love. They may recognize intellectually that performing service for recognition represents imperfect motivation, yet find themselves unable to simply stop monitoring for validation. Each charitable act gets automatically evaluated: "Am I doing this selflessly? Did I just help them to feel good about myself? Why am I thinking about this instead of just caring?" The meta-cognitive loop itself maintains ego-focus, preventing access to the effortless Ab Neter-guided caring verse 1 describes.

The teaching's compassionate provision offers crucial relief for such struggling aspirants: even egoistic love produces gradual purification. The individual need not achieve impossible immediate perfection to benefit from ethical practice. By simply engaging in righteous conduct and service work—even while the ego takes credit and monitors for virtue feelings—they initiate the secret purification mechanics that gradually thin aryu density over time. This understanding prevents spiritual paralysis wherein aspirants refuse all service because they cannot access pure motivation, thereby depriving themselves of the very practice that would eventually enable genuine real love.

Nevertheless, the aspirant must navigate the difficult balance between accepting their current limitations compassionately while simultaneously working toward the genuine transformation verse 4 describes. The teaching warns against settling for egoistic love as sufficient—such practice produces only gradual subtle purification with many ups and downs compared to the dynamic transformation possible through authentic real love. The goal remains clear even while the path acknowledges human limitation: move progressively from egoistic love toward real love by thinning aryu density through persistent ethical practice, understanding that when sufficient purity is achieved, the ego becomes sublimated, and the higher love takes spiritual development the rest of the way to spiritual victory.

Contemporary seekers often struggle with the nobility transformation verse 4 presents, having been conditioned to dismiss spiritual attainment as ego-inflation or to view any self-recognition as problematic. Yet the teaching makes clear that spiritual nobility represents authentic transformation of being through aryu purification—becoming "worthy to be honored" reflects genuine personality refinement rather than egoistic self-aggrandizement. The "decoration of the funerary coffin chamber" indicates the mind prepared for liberation from reincarnation cycles, representing the ultimate fulfillment of human spiritual potential through becoming a spiritual nobility rather than mere ego-achievement.

The Pathology of Self-Serving Service

A subtle yet significant obstacle confronts modern aspirants: service and caring that appear virtuous while actually sustaining egoistic patterns rather than purifying the mind. Consider the individual who serves others primarily to gain admiration, recognition, or validation. When acknowledgment arrives, such service feels gratifying; when others fail to appreciate the efforts, the heated mind responds with feelings of being slighted, resentment, or disgust—perhaps even abandoning the service entirely. This reaction reveals the true motivation: the service operated not from genuine care but from an ego-driven need for external validation.

Similarly, some engage in caring behaviors to compensate for feelings of inferiority—serving others to feel worthy, needed, or superior. The mind reasons: "If I help enough people, perhaps I will finally feel valuable." Yet this approach merely reinforces the underlying pathology rather than addressing it. The service becomes a mechanism for maintaining a false sense of separation and inadequacy rather than dissolving these aryu patterns through genuine spiritual practice.

Such egoistic caring manifests another destructive pattern: violating Maat by serving others to the point of self-neglect. The individual provides worldly provisioning—material assistance, time, energy—while exhausting their own resources, physical health, or emotional well-being. This represents not authentic service but a distorted pattern where the ego seeks validation through self-sacrifice, mistaking depletion for virtue. True service maintains balance, recognizing that one cannot sustain genuine caring when the self has been depleted through Maat violation.

The teaching reveals the crucial distinction: worldly provisioning alone—providing material goods, performing helpful actions—proves limited when divorced from spiritual provisioning. Authentic spiritual service includes good thoughts toward those served, feelings of genuine care arising from recognizing their divine nature, and the practice of regarding each person as a manifestation of Neberdjer. This spiritual orientation transforms service from ego-gratification into a purification practice. The aspirant serves not to be acknowledged, not to feel worthy, but because the silent mind recognizes the divine presence in all beings—rendering service itself a form of worship and communion with Ab Neter.

When service arises from this foundation, acknowledgment becomes irrelevant. Whether others appreciate the efforts or not, the mind remains in ger (serenity) because the satisfaction derives not from external validation but from alignment with the divine purpose. Such service purifies rather than perpetuates pathology, supports rather than depletes, and manifests the genuine love that serves both earthly well-being and divine discovery.

PART B: METHODS FOR TRANSFORMATION

The Foundations of Doing Love: Maat Philosophy's Threefold Service and Sacred Association: The Practical Expression of Real Love Through Maat Philosophy

Chapter 8XI, verse 1 teaches: "by you're doing love to people, instead of harm, they love you." This teaching requires a deeper understanding of what constitutes authentic "doing love" or "doing good to others" within the Ancient Egyptian wisdom tradition. Consider how the philosophical foundation established in Maat philosophy provides essential context for implementing Amenemopet's instruction regarding ethical conduct toward others as extensions of Neberdjer.

The Ancient Egyptian Book of Enlightenment, Chapter 125 (Pert-M-Heru), articulates a systematic declaration of threefold service to humanity that reveals the practical dimensions of living by Maat—the universal principles of truth, order, and righteousness [1]. This declaration establishes clear parameters for what the tradition recognizes as fundamental human needs that should be shared with all, based on an understanding of universal spirit and the common kinship of humanity. Observe how the aspirant who has successfully navigated the purification process declares before the divine tribunal:

> [Verse E] "by means of following his will. His will is giving food to those who lack food, drink to those who are thirsty" [21]
>
> [Verse F] "give clothes to those who do not have clothes, and I give a means to move, to progress and not remain stagnant, for those who are stuck, who are in need of a helping hand, who are having trouble getting their life going in a positive direction" [21]

These verses from Chapter 125 illuminate what Amenemopet intends when teaching about "doing love to people" in Chapter 8XI, verse 1. The wisdom reveals that authentic ethical conduct manifests through addressing the foundational human needs: sustenance (food and water), protection (clothing), and assistance in forward movement (helping those who are "shipwrecked" or stuck in difficult circumstances). Nevertheless, we must recognize the profound psychological principle underlying this teaching—the basic needs of life constitute the foundation necessary so that a person need not grow up in deprivation and be forced to develop psychological maladaptation to a life of insufficiency that could lead to conditions detrimental to self or society at large [21].

From this perspective, Maat philosophy recognizes that an ethical society depends upon ensuring basic human welfare not merely as charitable sentiment but as a prerequisite for collective psychological health and spiritual development. When people lack fundamental security—food, water, clothing, means of progress—their minds and feelings become consumed by survival concerns, making the inner peace described in Chapter 8XI, verse 2 virtually impossible to attain. Indeed, the heated mind and feelings produced by chronic deprivation create dense aryu patterns centered on scarcity, fear, and competitive self-preservation that obstruct access to Ab Neter awareness and prevent the discovery of the divine sanctuary within.

Therefore, the teaching about "doing good to others" encompasses both the immediate practical assistance—providing material necessities—and the deeper spiritual understanding that such service stems from recognizing others as manifestations of Neberdjer experiencing temporary forms. When the mind operates from this recognition, caring for others' basic needs becomes as natural as caring for one's own limbs, precisely because the apparent separation between self and other has been understood as illusory at the fundamental level of existence.

Sacred Association: The Essential Context for Spiritual Development

Having examined the material dimensions of doing good through Maat's threefold service, we must now explore another essential aspect of "doing love to people"—the provision of good spiritual association that Amenemopet's teaching implies. The Stele of Djehuty Nefer presents significant guidance regarding what the tradition calls knumt-nefer (good association, divine association), revealing how authentic spiritual development requires not only material welfare but also access to the living transmission of wisdom through conscious association with those who embody genuine realization [18].

Consider how verses 4-6 of the Stele establish a systematic progression for the advancing aspirant:

> [Verse 4] "The advancing initiate should consume foods that are pure and unadulterated; they should do this while being hygienically clean, living a life that strives for purity of body and mind. This will make their body sound and healthy and will open their capacity as-to..." [18]
>
> [Verse 5] "...entering the adoration room, the place for doing worships of the Divine, where people go to for making adorations. So too the advancing aspirant will as well go to that room and take a seat there..." [18]
>
> [Verse 6] "within the hypostyle hall of the temple and, being seated there, keep company with those pure ones, those priests and priestesses who adore and follow and serve the Divine; and in so doing thereby become pure and enlightened as they are so as to achieve the goal of life, immortality through spiritual enlightenment" [18].

These verses illuminate a profound dimension of "doing love to people" that extends beyond material assistance to encompass providing access to authentic spiritual guidance and community. Observe how the teaching establishes that individual spiritual effort, however dedicated, requires the living transmission of spiritual understanding that emerges through conscious association with those whose practice has matured through sustained engagement with the teachings [18].

The wisdom to be understood here operates according to spiritual law rather than mere social preference. As hat-level awareness begins recognizing Ab Neter through the practices Amenemopet describes, the mind naturally seeks confirmation and refinement through association with those whose minds and feelings have been established in the peace, self-knowledge, and divine recognition that characterize genuine spiritual attainment. In other words, the Soul-Aware-Witness that emerges through sustained purification requires the nourishment and guidance that flow naturally from conscious association with those pure ones whose hearts have penetrated beyond ego-identification.

Consider how this understanding completes the teaching of Chapter 8XI regarding "doing love to people." When we provide material necessities (food, water, clothing, assistance), we address the foundational requirements that enable others to move beyond survival-mode concerns in the mind. Nevertheless, the highest form of doing good extends further—offering access to sacred community, authentic teachings, and association with those who embody the wisdom philosophy we seek to realize within ourselves.

The ancient sages recognized that spiritual development flourishes through a dynamic interchange between the aspirant's sincere inquiry and the guidance of those who have traversed the path before them. Understand that certain dimensions of spiritual understanding can only be transmitted through direct contact with embodied realization rather than remaining confined to textual study or isolated practice [18]. When an aspirant maintains regular association with genuine practitioners—whether through formal instruction, participation in temple activities, or spiritual dialogue—they naturally absorb not only the intellectual content of the teachings but also the living transmission of understanding that can only be conveyed through conscious contact with minds and feelings purified of aryu density.

Therefore, "doing love to people" in its fullest expression encompasses both material welfare and spiritual opportunity: ensuring basic human needs are met while also providing access to the sacred community, authentic teachings, and qualified guidance that enable the mind to discover its essential nature as sustained by Ab Neter. This comprehensive understanding reveals how ethical conduct serves both immediate humanitarian concerns and the ultimate spiritual purpose—supporting all beings in their journey toward divine realization.

The Connection to Inner Peace and Divine Discovery

Having established the comprehensive meaning of "doing good to others" through both Maat's threefold service and sacred association, we can now recognize how this teaching directly supports the goals articulated in Chapter 8XI, verse 2: "by doing good to others and having peaceful relations with others, you will be able to have inner peace that will allow you to make real and effective effort towards finding yourself a place, to make yourself an abode in the inner part of the temple of God" [1].

Consider how the mind operating from heated patterns—driven by aryu centered on scarcity, separation, and self-protection—experiences chronic agitation when witnessing others' suffering. The mind tormented by identification with an ego-perspective cannot rest peacefully while aware of unmet human needs or spiritual deprivation surrounding it. Nevertheless, this very agitation prevents the inner stillness necessary for discovering the divine sanctuary within, creating a self-perpetuating cycle: ego-identification produces a lack of peace, which prevents divine discovery, which reinforces ego-identification.

From this understanding, we recognize how ethical action toward others serves the aspirant's own spiritual development not through selfish calculation but through the natural mechanics of mind purification. When we address others' material and spiritual needs through service rooted in Ab Neter awareness rather than ego-seeking, several transformative effects occur simultaneously:

First, the aryu patterns centered on separation and scarcity begin thinning as the mind repeatedly experiences the satisfaction of caring for extensions of itself. Second, the agitation produced by witnessing unaddressed suffering diminishes as we take constructive action aligned with Maat principles. Third, the vitality previously depleted through internal conflict becomes available for the inner work of discovering the divine sanctuary. Fourth, the practice of recognizing others as Neberdjer manifestations strengthens the capacity for witnessing Ab Neter presence within us.

Therefore, the teaching reveals an elegant spiritual technology: doing good to others—through both material service and provision of sacred association—creates the inner peace necessary for effective spiritual practice while simultaneously purifying the very aryu patterns that obstruct divine discovery. This understanding connects Chapter 8XI's teaching on reciprocal ethics directly to the Prologue's dual goals of earthly well-being and discovery of the kara where "the Divine resides in every person."

Indeed, the aspirant who provides threefold material service while also offering access to authentic spiritual community participates in the highest form of Maat-based living—supporting both the immediate human welfare and the ultimate spiritual fulfillment that constitute the complete meaning of "doing love to people instead of harm."

Amenemopet's Implementation of Ideal of Love

Based on the teaching presented by Sage Amenemopet in verses 3-4, the aspirant benefits from systematic practices addressing both the ideal path of genuine real love and the realistic cultivation of such capacity through gradual purification of egoistic patterns.

Practice 1: Discernment Practice for Love Quality Recognition

The aspirant cultivates the ability to recognize the quality of love underlying their service and caring actions. Before engaging in helping behavior, pause to examine your internal state: What prompts this action? Do I expect recognition or gratitude? Am I monitoring for feelings of virtue? Does some part of me want credit for being helpful? Do I need support or validation from the person I'm helping? This honest self-examination without judgment reveals whether the mind operates from aryu-driven egoistic love or from emerging real love characterized by Ab Neter awareness.

Implementation example: A professional considering volunteer work at a local food bank notices an internal narrative: "This will look good on my resume, and people will see I'm socially conscious." Rather than immediately rejecting the opportunity due to impure motivation, they acknowledge ego-involvement honestly while still engaging in the service—recognizing that even egoistic love initiates gradual purification per the teaching's compassionate provision. Over weeks of consistent service, they continue examining motivation, noticing when moments of genuine caring arise spontaneously without ego-monitoring. These brief openings indicate thinning aryu density and emerging capacity for authentic real love.

Practice 2: Post-Action Satisfaction Discernment

After performing helping actions or ethical conduct, the aspirant examines the quality of satisfaction experienced. Does fulfillment depend on others noticing the good deed? Does it fade rapidly, requiring another virtuous act to maintain the feeling? Does mood fluctuate between elevation when recognized and deflation when ignored—the ups and downs characterizing egoistic love? Or does subtle peace and contentment persist independent of recognition? This discernment develops sensitivity to the distinction between ego-validation (temporary, external-dependent, requiring constant reinforcement) and the "vital bread" spiritual sustenance (stable, internal, inherently fulfilling).

Implementation example: An aspirant spends Saturday afternoon helping an elderly neighbor with yard work. Afterward, they notice a strong urge to mention this to friends and post photos on social media. Rather than immediately indulging or suppressing this urge, they sit with the experience: What drives the need to broadcast the good deed? They recognize the ego seeking validation—"I am a good person" requires external confirmation to feel real. Nevertheless, beneath the ego-chatter, they notice subtle satisfaction unrelated to recognition—a quiet peace from having cared for another. This represents emerging access to the divine sustenance verse 3 describes, even while ego-patterns remain present. Over time and repeated practice, sensitivity to this subtler satisfaction increases while dependency on external validation gradually diminishes, indicating the transition from egoistic love toward real love.

Practice 3: Systematic Service as Purification Practice

The aspirant engages in regular, structured helping activity specifically as purification practice rather than achievement or credential-accumulation. This might involve weekly service at a homeless shelter, regular visits to hospital patients, tutoring underprivileged students, or environmental restoration work. The key lies in consistency over months and years, understanding that transformation occurs through accumulated purified aryu replacing corrupted patterns gradually rather than through dramatic sudden shifts. The aspirant accepts they will likely begin from egoistic love and understands the path involves gradual purification until sufficient purity enables ego-sublimation and the emergence of real love.

Implementation example: An aspirant commits to weekly meal service at a homeless shelter, approaching this as a laboratory for observing aryu patterns and cultivating genuine caring. Initially, ego-monitoring dominates: counting hours served, comparing themselves favorably to those who don't volunteer, feeling virtuous, expecting gratitude from recipients. Rather than abandoning practice due to impure motivation, they continue persistently while applying discernment practices above. They accept the ups and downs characteristic of egoistic love—spiritual highs when service is acknowledged alternating with deflation when ignored.

Over months, subtle shifts occur: moments when genuine care arises spontaneously, instances when harsh judgment of recipients dissolves into simple human recognition, occasions when service itself provides satisfaction independent of recognition. These indicate gradual aryu purification—corrupted patterns thinning while purified impressions accumulate. After years of sustained practice, they notice caring for others has become more natural, requiring less conscious effort to override selfish impulses. Eventually, they experience the threshold transformation: the ego becomes sublimated as sufficient purity is achieved, and the higher love begins taking spiritual development the rest of the way to victory. The personality transformation verse 4 describes proceeds incrementally through patient absorption of the teaching into the ab's architecture.

Practice 4: Recognition Practice Based on Neberdjer Unity

Following verse 1's teaching that ethical conduct stems from recognizing others as extensions of Neberdjer, the aspirant practices contemplative recognition during interactions. When engaging with others—especially those triggering aversion or judgment—pause to recognize: "This person's consciousness derives from the same Ab Neter source as mine. Their body formed from the same Neberdjer substance. What appears as a separate individual represents a temporary expression of the one divine consciousness."

Implementation example: An aspirant notices harsh judgment arising toward a homeless person begging on a street corner: "They're probably lying, using drug money, could get a job if they wanted." Rather than either indulging judgment or suppressing it through adaptive spiritual bypassing, they practice recognition: beneath the ego-story about this person's failures, one recognizes another expression of Neberdjer experiencing the suffering of separation, ignorance, and aryu-driven existence. This recognition doesn't require believing the homeless person's particular story or giving money if discernment suggests otherwise—it acknowledges the shared divine source beneath surface differences.

This practice gradually weakens the perception of fundamental separation that aryu patterns maintain. Over time, caring for others becomes more natural because the mind increasingly recognizes them as true extensions of oneself—not as an intellectual concept but as experiential reality. This enables the effortless Ab Neter-guided caring characterized by real love that generates the "vital bread" satisfaction and powerful purification verses 3-4 describe.

Based on the teaching presented by Sage Amenemopet regarding suppression and sublimation in verse 11, when egoistic impulses toward gossip, harsh speech, or selfish behavior arise, the application of the inverse doctrine methodology suggests aspirants should also avoid actions, thoughts, and feelings that promote immediate indulgence of these impulses, as such expression reinforces corrupted aryu patterns and depletes vitality needed for spiritual development. Instead, consciously restrain the impulse—recognizing it as aryu seeking self-perpetuation—and redirect that preserved energy toward ethical conduct, service, study, and contemplative practice that gradually transforms personality toward the spiritual nobility verse 4 describes.

The Cultural Foundation of Amenemopet's Teaching on Universal Caring

Before examining the practical implications of Amenemopet's teaching on love and serenity, the wisdom to be understood requires recognizing the profound cultural differences between the society in which these teachings emerged and the contemporary context in which modern aspirants must implement them. Amenemopet taught within a culture possessing crucial advantages that supported spiritual development in ways that modern societies actively undermine. Understanding these differences illuminates both the timeless principles underlying the teaching and the additional challenges contemporary practitioners face in their implementation.

The ancient Egyptian culture in which Amenemopet composed his wisdom text maintained significantly greater social cohesion than contemporary societies. The culture operated without money as modern economies understand it, without social media fragmenting attention and community bonds, without compulsory government educational systems designed to produce individualistic, self-focused citizens who view others primarily as competitors rather than as spiritual kinfolk. The society fostered greater respect for the wise, recognizing spiritual attainment as the highest human achievement worthy of honor rather than dismissing wisdom in favor of material accumulation or status-seeking.[1][2]

This cultural foundation created conditions whereby Amenemopet's teachings on universal caring could be more readily understood and implemented. When society itself reinforces the recognition of divine presence in all beings, when social structures support rather than obstruct ethical living, when the culture celebrates serenity rather than agitation as the mark of advancement, the individual aspirant receives substantial environmental support for spiritual development. Contemporary practitioners, conversely, must cultivate these recognitions against massive cultural resistance that actively promotes heated patterns, egoic separation, and compulsive acquisition as paths to fulfillment.[2][3]

Nevertheless, the underlying principles Amenemopet teaches remain universally applicable precisely because they address the timeless human condition—the mind operating from aryu-driven ego-consciousness experiences suffering regardless of cultural context, while the mind aligning with Ab Neter awareness discovers peace within any circumstances. The teaching's genius emerges in identifying practices that facilitate transformation across all cultural conditions, though implementation difficulty varies according to environmental support or resistance.[1][2][3]

Neberdjer as Universal Caring: The Theological Foundation for Love

Amenemopet identifies a feature of serenity that later wisdom traditions across cultures independently discovered—what Dante explored in European mysticism, what bhakti yoga systematized in Indian spirituality, what compassion teachings emphasized in Buddhist practice. This universal recognition points to a fundamental spiritual truth: the practice of love, understood as genuine caring for the welfare of others from a perspective of spiritual kinship and fellowship, operates as both purifying force and direct pathway to divine recognition.[1][2][3]

The theological principle underlying this universal teaching reveals that Neberdjer IS itself universal caring. Just as the previous chapter established that Neberdjer IS supreme serenity, silence, and equanimity, so too Neberdjer manifests as the fundamental caring consciousness that sustains all beings through Ab Neter and provides natural abundance through sun, vegetation, water, and the entire ecological system supporting life. The divine cares for all—not as external benevolent deity bestowing gifts but as the very consciousness sustaining existence and providing the resources necessary for life to flourish.[2][3]

This understanding transforms the practice of universal caring from moral obligation into metaphysical alignment. When the aspirant performs genuine universal caring (love) for others, this practice brings them closer to Neberdjer not through earning divine favor but through developing frequencies resonant with ultimate reality's essential nature. Just as cultivating serenity creates resonance with Neberdjer's supreme serenity, cultivating universal caring creates resonance with Neberdjer's fundamental nature as the caring consciousness sustaining all existence.[2][3]

Consider the metaphysical implications: Neberdjer as all-encompassing consciousness maintains every being in existence through Ab Neter, provides the vitality necessary for life through the bau Neteru, creates the natural systems whereby food grows and water flows. This universal provision demonstrates that caring constitutes not incidental attribute but essential nature of ultimate reality. Therefore, when consciousness develops genuine caring for all beings as extensions of itself—recognizing them as Neberdjer manifestations, as spiritual kinfolk rather than separate competitors—this recognition aligns the individual mind with the fundamental operating principle of existence itself.[2][3]

The Practice of Love as Purification and Self-Fulfillment

Amenemopet's teaching reveals that the practice of genuine caring for others allows the aspirant to be appreciated and to feel good about themselves—but critically, this positive experience emerges free of dissatisfying self-centeredness. This distinction proves essential for understanding how love functions as a purification mechanism. When the mind performs caring actions from ego-consciousness seeking validation, recognition, or self-aggrandizement, the satisfaction remains incomplete and temporary because it depends on external responses and reinforces the separate ego requiring continued feeding through approval. However, when the mind performs caring actions from recognition of spiritual kinship—understanding that caring for others represents caring for extensions of oneself, expressions of Neberdjer—the satisfaction emerges inherently from the action itself rather than from ego-gratification.[1][2][3]

This inherent satisfaction operates through specific mechanisms at the consciousness architecture level. First, actions performed as expressions of universal caring generate positive thoughts and feelings that deposit purifying aryu in the ab, gradually thinning the corrupted patterns centered on separation, scarcity, and competition. Second, the practice trains consciousness to experience fulfillment from alignment with divine nature rather than from acquisition of external objects or validation from others. Third, genuine caring for others as Neberdjer manifestations strengthens the capacity to recognize Ab Neter within oneself, creating the resonance necessary for divine discovery.[1][2][3]

The purification occurs because universal caring directly contradicts the fundamental delusion underlying heated patterns—the belief that the mind constitutes a separate, isolated entity requiring self-protection and self-advancement against a hostile universe populated by competitors. When the mind repeatedly experiences that caring for others produces deep satisfaction, that supporting others' welfare enhances rather than diminishes one's own fulfillment, the aryu patterns maintaining separation gradually thin through experiential contradiction of their foundational premise.[2][3]

Moreover, genuine universal caring makes it more possible to experience the caring of the divine. The teaching reveals this through elegant spiritual technology: because Neberdjer cares for all through sustaining Ab Neter and providing natural abundance, the mind cultivating caring consciousness develops the sensitivity necessary to perceive the divine caring that operates continuously. The heated mind, absorbed in ego-protection and competitive acquisition, remains insensitive to Neberdjer's universal provision because its attention fixates on perceived threats and opportunities for advantage. The mind practicing universal caring, conversely, develops receptive awareness that recognizes how existence itself operates as caring manifestation—how consciousness sustains awareness, how sun provides energy, how earth produces food, how water nourishes life.[2][3]

This recognition transforms the relationship to existence from anxious struggle against hostile forces to grateful participation in a caring system. The aspirant discovers experientially that Neberdjer's caring operates as fundamental reality rather than wishful belief, validating the teaching's instruction to trust divine providence rather than exhausting vital energy through fevered self-reliance. This experiential validation, in turn, deepens the capacity for universal caring as consciousness recognizes that caring for others participates in the same divine caring that sustains oneself.[2][3]

Serenity as Comprehensive Way of Life

The teaching establishes that universal caring, combined with sebayt (wisdom teachings) and other works of Maat, purifies and qualifies the aspirant for being serene, having a serene life, and discovering the ultimate serenity within. This progression proves significant: being serene represents a state of the mind, having a serene life describes a comprehensive pattern of living, while discovering ultimate serenity within points to Ab Neter/Neberdjer recognition. Each builds upon the previous, creating an integrated pathway from initial practice to complete realization.[1][2][3]

A serene life, as the teaching reveals, constitutes a way of living in which the inner world stays steady, clear, and unagitated regardless of what happens externally. This proves less about achieving perfect circumstances and more about developing the quality of the inner state that remains undisturbed by circumstantial fluctuations. The wisdom to be understood recognizes that circumstances inevitably change—prosperity transforms to scarcity, health deteriorates to illness, relationships form and dissolve, plans succeed or fail. The heated person experiences these changes as threats to wellbeing, generating anxiety about controlling outcomes and profound disturbance when control proves illusory. The serene person, conversely, maintains inner stability through changes because identity rests not on temporary circumstances but on recognition of an unchanging divine foundation.[1][2][3]

The core elements defining a serene life illuminate how this teaching operates practically:

Inner Calm Independent of External Conditions: Serenity means the mind operates without constant pulling by anxiety, drama, or overstimulation. The aspirant responds rather than reacts, maintaining presence-of-mind awareness that chooses conscious action rather than automatic aryu-driven patterns. This inner calm emerges through the purification work—ethical conduct thinning heated aryu, wisdom study depositing understanding that circumstances prove temporary while consciousness remains constant, meditation developing capacity to witness mental content without identification.[1][2][3]

Alignment With Maat Values: A serene life feels simple and coherent because actions match beliefs—no internal conflict, no living according to worldly expectations contradicting spiritual understanding. When the aspirant lives by Maat principles of truth, righteousness, reciprocity, and balance, the mind experiences the natural satisfaction that flows from alignment with cosmic order rather than the perpetual dissatisfaction emerging from violating one's own deepest values for temporary advantages.[1][2][3]

Spaciousness and Unrushed Quality: Serenity requires time—time to think, time to feel, time to integrate experiences, time to rest. The heated life operates in constant rush, perpetual urgency, compulsive busy-ness that fragments attention and prevents deep absorption. A serene life has room in it, creating space for the mind to settle rather than remaining agitated through continuous stimulation.

This directly addresses Amenemopet's warning against rushing, recognizing that haste emerges from and reinforces heated patterns.[1][2][3]

Emotional Evenness Without Numbness: Serenity does not mean suppressing emotions or achieving robotic indifference. Rather, emotions arise naturally, emotions pass naturally, and consciousness neither clings to pleasant feelings nor collapses into disturbing ones. The serene person experiences the full range of human emotion while maintaining awareness as the witness rather than becoming identified with emotional states as constituting self.[1][2][3]

Reduction of Unnecessary Conflict and Chaos: The serene life actively reduces drama, clutter, overstimulation, toxic dynamics, and self-sabotaging patterns. This reduction operates through systematic boundary establishment—the aspirant recognizes that peaceful living requires peaceful boundaries, that protecting the mind from continuous assault by heated influences preserves the vital energy necessary for spiritual development. This connects directly to Amenemopet's teaching about avoiding heated persons and maintaining association with silent personalities.[1][2][3]

Trust in Divine Orchestration: Serenity requires faith—whether understood through spiritual framework or secular perspective—that one is held, guided, or supported by wisdom greater than ego-mind's limited comprehension. Without this trust, the mind constantly grasps at control and fears outcomes, generating the agitation that prevents serenity. With trust in Neberdjer as the shepherd guiding the life-boat (Chapter 18's teaching), the mind releases anxious control-seeking while maintaining vigilant attention to ethical choices arising moment by moment.[1][2][3]

Harmony With Natural Rhythms: A serene life follows natural cycles—day and night, work and rest, activity and stillness, input and integration. This mirrors Maat as balance, truth, and cosmic order. The heated life attempts to override natural limitations through stimulants, artificial light disrupting circadian rhythms, continuous productivity without restoration, information consumption without contemplative processing. The serene life, conversely, respects the body's need for sleep, the mind's need for silence, and the mind's need for integration time.[1][2][3]

Reduced Mental Noise: A serene life manifests fewer intrusive thoughts, less compulsive overthinking, more clarity, more presence. Practices like meditation, breathwork, stillness cultivation, and mindful ritual create this mental quiet not through forceful suppression but through patient thinning of aryu patterns generating automatic thought proliferation. As mental noise reduces, the subtle presence of Ab Neter becomes progressively more perceptible.[1][2][3]

Acceptance of Reality Without Passivity: Serenity emerges when the mind no longer fights what is. This acceptance proves distinct from passive resignation—rather, it represents wise engagement that works with life rather than against it. The serene person recognizes circumstances accurately, accepts current reality without denial or fantasy, and takes appropriate action from clarity rather than from reactive agitation. This acceptance creates the foundation for effective response because the mind remains undistorted by wishful thinking or fearful catastrophizing.[1][2][3]

Inner Sanctuary Regardless of External Location: No matter where physically present or what circumstances arise, the serene person maintains access to an internal "temple space"—the kara where Ab Neter resides, available for retreat and renewal. This inner sanctuary proves inviolable by external conditions because it exists as consciousness's own divine foundation rather than as a constructed mental refuge requiring protection from intrusion.[1][2][3]

The Consequences of Agitation-Based Living

Understanding serenity's essential elements illuminates why Amenemopet warns so consistently against heated patterns. Thoughts, feelings, and actions based on agitation lead inevitably to rushing (explicitly opposed by Amenemopet throughout his teaching), to anger, hatred, violence, unrest, and ill health. These consequences operate at both personal and communal levels—the heated individual suffers through their own agitated states while simultaneously creating suffering for others through actions emerging from disturbance.[1][2][3]

The personal suffering dimension operates through multiple mechanisms: rushing generates mistakes requiring correction, wasting time and vital energy; anger depletes sekhem through the physiological arousal necessary to maintain hostile states; hatred poisons the mind through the continuous occupation of awareness with destructive thoughts; violence toward others creates karmic consequences requiring future balancing; unrest prevents the inner peace necessary for discovering Ab Neter; ill health emerges through the documented physiological effects of chronic stress and agitation on bodily systems.[2][3]

Moreover, agitation-based living hurts others through the ripple effects of heated actions—harsh speech that damages recipients, aggressive behavior that creates defensive reactions, competitive patterns that establish hostile relational dynamics, rushed decisions that fail to consider others' wellbeing. These external harms simultaneously hurt the person generating them by depriving the mind of the good feelings that flow naturally from ethical conduct aligned with recognition of spiritual kinship. The heated person unknowingly banishes themselves from the inherent satisfaction available through genuine caring, instead experiencing the dissatisfaction that emerges when actions contradict consciousness's divine nature.[2][3]

The communal dimension proves equally significant: societies composed predominantly of heated individuals create cultures of competition, exploitation, violence, and mutual mistrust that make spiritual development extraordinarily difficult for all members. Conversely, communities supporting serenity, mutual caring, and ethical conduct create environmental conditions facilitating transformation. While individual aspirants cannot control entire societal patterns, they can contribute to creating pockets of sanity—families, friendships, spiritual communities—operating by different principles than the dominant heated culture.[2][3]

Integration: Love, Serenity, and Divine Discovery as Unified Path

The wisdom to be understood recognizes that universal caring and serenity constitute not separate practices but integrated expressions of the single transformation from heated ego-consciousness to silent Ab Neter awareness. Genuine caring for others emerges naturally from the serene mind that recognizes all beings as Neberdjer manifestations, while serenity deepens through the purification that universal caring produces. Neither proves possible in sustained form without the other—attempted caring from an agitated mind degenerates into ego-driven helping contaminated with self-seeking, while attempted serenity without caring for others reinforces the separation-based patterns preventing divine discovery.[1][2][3]

The teaching reveals elegant integration: universal caring practiced from recognition of spiritual kinship generates positive thoughts and feelings that deposit purifying aryu, thinning heated patterns and creating increasing capacity for serenity. Serenity, in turn, creates the inner stillness necessary for recognizing Neberdjer's universal caring operating through all existence, deepening the experiential foundation for extending caring to all beings. Together, these mutually reinforcing practices qualify consciousness for discovering the ultimate serenity within—the Ab Neter/Neberdjer recognition that reveals one's essential nature as the caring consciousness sustaining all existence.[1][2][3]

This understanding transforms both practices from behavioral prescriptions into consciousness training methods. The aspirant cultivates universal caring not primarily to help others (though genuine benefit flows to recipients) but to purify the mind through contradiction of separation-based aryu patterns. The aspirant cultivates serenity not primarily to feel peaceful (though genuine peace emerges) but to create the frequency-matching necessary for recognizing supreme serenity as consciousness's essential nature. Both practices serve the ultimate goal established in the Prologue: discovering the kara sanctuary where "the Divine resides in every person," recognizing Ab Neter as one's true identity rather than the temporary ego-personality sustained by aryu density.[1][2][3]

The Cultural Challenge and the Timeless Solution

Contemporary aspirants face unprecedented challenges in implementing these teachings. Modern culture actively promotes nearly every pattern Amenemopet warns against—constant rushing through overscheduled lives, perpetual stimulation through digital devices and media, competitive individualism that views others as threats or resources, materialistic values prioritizing acquisition over ethics, social fragmentation destroying community bonds that once supported spiritual development. The environmental resistance to serene living proves immense, requiring extraordinary dedication to maintain practice against cultural momentum pulling toward heated patterns.[2][3]

Nevertheless, the teaching remains accessible precisely because it addresses consciousness mechanics that prove universal across cultural conditions. The mind operating from aryu-driven ego-consciousness experiences suffering whether in ancient Egypt or contemporary society; the mind aligning with Ab Neter awareness discovers peace regardless of external circumstances. The purification work—ethical conduct, wisdom absorption, meditation practice, universal caring cultivation, serenity development—operates through the same mechanisms in all contexts because it addresses the fundamental architecture of consciousness rather than cultural variables.[1][2][3]

Indeed, the very difficulty contemporary practitioners face may serve transformation when properly understood. The aspirant living in supportive spiritual culture may never develop the strength necessary for maintaining practice under adverse conditions, remaining dependent on environmental support. The aspirant maintaining serenity amid cultural chaos, conversely, develops profound conviction born from repeated experiential validation that the teaching works even when everything external opposes it. This conviction proves invaluable for sustaining practice through inevitable difficulties on the spiritual path.[2][3]

The wisdom to be understood therefore recognizes both the cultural context making Amenemopet's teaching more readily implemented in ancient Egypt AND the timeless principles allowing contemporary practitioners to achieve the same transformation through greater effort. The teaching's genius emerges in identifying practices that facilitate consciousness purification across all cultural conditions—universal caring and serenity cultivation prove effective whether society supports or opposes them, though implementation difficulty varies according to environmental resistance.[1][2][3]

Practical Application: Cultivating Universal Caring and Serenity in Contemporary Context

Based on the teaching's integration of universal caring, serenity, and divine discovery, contemporary aspirants benefit from systematic practices adapted to modern challenges while preserving ancient principles:

Practice 1: Recognizing Spiritual Kinship in Daily Encounters

Throughout each day, practice consciously recognizing others encountered—family members, coworkers, service workers, strangers—as Neberdjer manifestations rather than separate beings. Before interacting, pause briefly to acknowledge: "This person represents Ab Neter expressing through a different personality form. Caring for them represents caring for an extension of divine consciousness, an expression of Neberdjer's universal caring." Notice how this recognition transforms the interaction quality from transactional exchange to sacred encounter.[2][3]

Practice 2: Monitoring Thought and Feeling Quality

Develop ongoing awareness of whether thoughts and feelings arise from agitation or serenity. When noticing rushing, anxiety, anger, competitive thinking, or other heated patterns, pause to examine: "These thoughts/feelings emerge from aryu-driven ego-consciousness operating under delusion of separation. Do I choose to reinforce these patterns through continued identification, or can I recognize them as temporary mental content arising in the unchanging witness-consciousness?" This practice gradually develops discrimination between consciousness itself and mental modifications.[1][2][3]

Practice 3: Deliberate Slowness and Spaciousness Creation

Systematically resist cultural pressure toward constant rushing by creating protected time for unrushed activities—contemplative walking, unhurried meals, extended meditation sessions, slow reading of wisdom texts. Notice how reducing external rush creates internal spaciousness allowing the mind to settle. Observe the profound difference between presence emerging from spaciousness versus the perpetual distraction characterizing hurried living.[1][2][3]

Practice 4: Caring Actions as Spiritual Practice

Engage helping behaviors not primarily for outcomes produced but as consciousness training methods. When caring for others—through material service, emotional support, spiritual guidance—maintain awareness: "This action serves my own purification by contradicting separation-based aryu. The inherent satisfaction I experience emerges from alignment with Neberdjer's universal caring nature rather than from ego-gratification seeking validation." This framing transforms routine caring into potent spiritual practice.[1][2][3]

Practice 5: Boundary Protection for Serenity Preservation

Recognize that maintaining serenity in a hostile environment requires protective boundaries—limiting exposure to heated media (movies, news, violent, sentimental, comedies, games, etc.) that does not provide and support insight into the nature of wise (sebayt) and serene (ger) life, reducing association with chronically agitated persons, creating physical spaces supporting silence, protecting time for practices generating peace. These boundaries prove necessary rather than selfish because serenity preservation enables effective service from Ab Neter awareness rather than depleted helping from ego-exhaustion.[1][2][3]

Conclusion: The Way of Love and Serenity Leading to Divine Discovery

This additional clarification reveals how Amenemopet's teaching on universal caring and serenity constitutes a comprehensive pathway from heated suffering to divine recognition. The practice of genuine caring for all beings as spiritual kinfolk—extensions of Neberdjer, expressions of the universal caring consciousness sustaining existence—purifies the mind through depositing positive aryu that contradict separation-based patterns. This purification creates increasing capacity for serenity as heated agitation thins. Serenity, in turn, creates the frequency-matching necessary for recognizing Neberdjer as supreme serenity and universal caring—consciousness discovering its own essential nature as the divine foundation that has always sustained awareness.[1][2][3]

The teaching proves accessible to contemporary aspirants despite cultural challenges because it addresses universal consciousness mechanics rather than cultural variables. While modern society actively undermines serene living and spiritual kinship recognition, the dedicated practitioner can maintain transformation through systematic implementation of practices adapted to current conditions while preserving ancient principles. The very difficulty serves development by building conviction born from experiential validation that alignment with Ab Neter produces peace regardless of external opposition.[1][2][3]

Therefore, let the aspirant recognize that every moment presents an opportunity: will thoughts, feelings, and actions arise from agitation, generating rushing, anger, hatred, violence, unrest, ill health, and suffering for self and others? Or will consciousness align with serenity and universal caring, participating in Neberdjer's fundamental nature as the caring awareness sustaining all existence? This choice determines not merely momentary experience but the trajectory of consciousness transformation from heated delusion to silent divine recognition—the ultimate fulfillment of human life's purpose.[1][2][3]

REFERENCES

REFERENCES

[1] Ashby, M. (2019-25). Mysticism of Amenemopet Hieroglyphic Text Translation. Sema Institute of Ancient Egyptian Studies.

[2] Ashby, M. (2024). Amenemopet lectures 2024 by Dr Muata Ashby transcripts. Sema Institute of Ancient Egyptian Studies.

[3] Ashby, M. (2016). Serpent Power: The Ancient Egyptian Mystical Wisdom of the Inner Life Force. Sema Institute of Yoga.

[4] Ryan, R. M., & Deci, E. L. (2000). Self-determination theory and the facilitation of intrinsic motivation, social development, and well-being. American Psychologist, 55(1), 68-78.

[5] Weinstein, N., & Ryan, R. M. (2010). When helping helps: Autonomous motivation for prosocial behavior and its influence on well-being for the helper and recipient. Journal of Personality and Social Psychology, 98(2), 222-244.

[6] Harbaugh, W. T., Mayr, U., & Burghart, D. R. (2007). Neural responses to taxation and voluntary giving reveal motives for charitable donations. Science, 316(5831), 1622-1625.

[7] Ryan, R. M., Huta, V., & Deci, E. L. (2008). Living well: A self-determination theory perspective on eudaimonia. Journal of Happiness Studies, 9(1), 139-170.

[8] Fredrickson, B. L., Grewen, K. M., Coffey, K. A., Algoe, S. B., Firestine, A. M., Arevalo, J. M., ... & Cole, S. W. (2013). A functional genomic perspective on human well-being. Proceedings of the National Academy of Sciences, 110(33), 13684-13689.

[9] Lutz, A., Brefczynski-Lewis, J., Johnstone, T., & Davidson, R. J. (2008). Regulation of the neural circuitry of emotion by compassion meditation: Effects of meditative expertise. PLoS ONE, 3(3), e1897.

[10] Moll, J., Krueger, F., Zahn, R., Pardini, M., de Oliveira-Souza, R., & Grafman, J. (2006). Human fronto-mesolimbic networks guide decisions about charitable donation. Proceedings of the National Academy of Sciences, 103(42), 15623-15628.

[11] Hofmann, S. G., Grossman, P., & Hinton, D. E. (2011). Loving-kindness and compassion meditation: Potential for psychological interventions. Clinical Psychology Review, 31(7), 1126-1132.

[12] Tang, Y. Y., Hölzel, B. K., & Posner, M. I. (2015). The neuroscience of mindfulness meditation. Nature Reviews Neuroscience, 16(4), 213-225.

[13] Wallace, B. A., & Shapiro, S. L. (2006). Mental balance and well-being: Building bridges between Buddhism and Western psychology. American Psychologist, 61(7), 690-701.

[14] Lally, P., van Jaarsveld, C. H., Potts, H. W., & Wardle, J. (2010). How are habits formed: Modelling habit formation in the real world. European Journal of Social Psychology, 40(6), 998-1009.

[15] Reber, A. S. (1989). Implicit learning and tacit knowledge. Journal of Experimental Psychology: General, 118(3), 219-235.

[16] Colby, A., & Damon, W. (1992). Some Do Care: Contemporary Lives of Moral Commitment. Free Press.

[17] Jinpa, T. (2015). A Fearless Heart: How the Courage to Be Compassionate Can Transform Our Lives. Avery.

[18] Ashby, M. (2025). Awakening Your Soul-Aware-Witness Ancient Egyptian Wisdom To Discover Divine Consciousness. Sema Institute of Ancient Egyptian Studies.

[19] Ashby, M. (2022). Scripture of Ra and Hetheru—Trilinear Translation by Dr. Muata Ashby. Sema Institute of Ancient Egyptian Studies.

[20] Ashby, M. (2020). Egyptian Book of the Dead Hieroglyph Translations for Enlightenment Vol. 5. Sema Institute of Ancient Egyptian Studies.

[21] Jung, C. G. (1971). Psychological Types (Collected Works Vol. 6). Princeton, NJ: Princeton University Press. (Original work published 1921)

[22] Jung, C. G. (1959). The Archetypes and the Collective Unconscious (Collected Works Vol. 9, Part 1). Princeton, NJ: Princeton University Press.

[23] Jung, C. G. (1963). Mysterium Coniunctionis (Collected Works Vol. 14). Princeton, NJ: Princeton University Press.

[24] Newberg, A., & Waldman, M. R. (2009). How God Changes Your Brain: Breakthrough Findings from a Leading Neuroscientist. New York: Ballantine Books.

[25] Lutz, A., Greischar, L. L., Rawlings, N. B., Ricard, M., & Davidson, R. J. (2004). Long-term meditators self-induce high-amplitude gamma synchrony during mental practice. Proceedings of the National Academy of Sciences, 101(46), 16369-16373.
[26] Hood, R. W., Jr. (1975). The construction and preliminary validation of a measure of reported mystical experience. Journal for the Scientific Study of Religion, 14(1), 29-41.
[27] Piedmont, R. L. (1999). Does spirituality represent the sixth factor of personality? Spiritual transcendence and the five-factor model. Journal of Personality, 67(6), 985-1013.
[28] Barrett, F. S., Johnson, M. W., & Griffiths, R. R. (2015). Validation of the revised Mystical Experience Questionnaire in experimental sessions with psilocybin. Journal of Psychopharmacology, 29(11), 1182-1190.
[29] Radin, D. (2006). Entangled Minds: Extrasensory Experiences in a Quantum Reality. New York: Paraview Pocket Books.

CHAPTER 16: Commentary on Teachings of Amenemopet Chapter 9XI and 9XII: Avoiding Heated Persons and Achieving Divine Transformation Through Self-Control, Compassion and Good Will

INTRODUCTION

Chapters 9XI and 9XII present one of Amenemopet's most direct protective teachings: complete avoidance of heated persons who function as "burning enemies" incinerating peace and contentment. These chapters reveal sophisticated understanding of mind contamination through association, distinguishing between heated persons operating from conscious malicious intent versus those acting from unconscious trauma patterns—while emphasizing that both require identical protective response. The teaching's ultimate wisdom emphasizes prevention over extraction: avoiding infiltration proves exponentially easier than disengagement after dependency is established. This directly supports both Prologue goals: protecting earthly well-being by preventing years of suffering from heated association (Prologue verse 2) and enabling kara discovery by maintaining the inner peace and mental clarity necessary for recognizing Ab Neter (Prologue verse 9).

SUMMARY OF CHAPTERS 9XI AND 9XII

Chapter 9XI commands avoidance of heated persons who operate as burning enemies and sneaky spies—scouting personality weaknesses, infiltrating through seeming friendship, creating dependency, then revealing their true exploitative nature. Verses 13-14 prohibit seeking heated persons or engaging conversation, as this exposes the mind to contaminating emanations. Verse 15 reveals tongue control preserves vitality and protects the ka (subconscious mind). Impurities that are allowed to pass from the conscious mind to the subconscious can go deeper into the unconscious and there form or contribute to already formed aryu. So, one should be judicious with what thoughts, ideas and desires one allows to be accepted into the personality. Verse 16 warns against those using high-sounding words to mask harmful intent. Chapter 9XII invokes Khnum, the Potter God, to cut away the multiple contrary dispositions (hatyu) causing heated mind and feelings, maintaining compassionate goodwill while exercising the righteous ethical right to refuse association that would corrupt one's purifying mind.

KEY TEACHINGS

Verses 13-14: "Refrain from/abstain from/cease/desist/do not seek heated people for the purpose of associating with them, they are the burning enemy that incinerates peace and contentment...do not allow yourself to go close to them/do not approach them for the purpose of starting up a conversation" [9]. They operate as sneaky spies infiltrating through seeming care, gathering intelligence about vulnerabilities.

Verses 15-16: Tongue control preserves vitality. "The heated person is an abominable thing to your heavenly personality" [9]. "Give up on the ideas of associating with heated people and instead think about guarding and protecting yourself from those who speak great and high-sounding words but who are in fact negative personalities that mean you harm" [9].

Verses 15-17 (Chapter 9XII): Invoke divine intervention: "Should come to him...the god Khnum...The Divine Potter, repairer who could bring divine compassion...to that heated person" to "perform the cutting away of the emerging dispositions of the mind that are contrary to goodness and enlightenment" [9]. Maintain wonderfully contrasting compassionate tone—no personal ill-will, just righteous ethical right to refuse contaminating association [9].

1. Human Psychology Principle: The Contamination Through Heated Association and the Spectrum from Unconscious Conditioning to Conscious Exploitation

Chapters 9XI and 9XII address mind contamination through association with heated persons who infiltrate and corrupt through patterns that may arise from either conscious calculation or unconscious conditioning—both producing identical harmful effects. These burning enemies function not as passively disturbing presences but as active agents probing personality weaknesses, infiltrating through seeming friendship, creating dependency, then revealing their true nature once the aspirant is hooked into their pathology [9].

The wisdom to be understood recognizes these infiltrative patterns arise through two distinct pathways requiring identical protective response. True con artists operating with conscious malicious intent represent the rare extreme—individuals deliberately studying targets to exploit with full awareness of harm caused. Far more commonly, heated persons act from unconscious aryu patterns established through trauma, survival conditioning, or unethical upbringing [10]. A child surviving abuse by becoming hypervigilant to others' weaknesses unconsciously continues this pattern as an adult, unaware the behavior constitutes infiltration. Someone raised where manipulation secured love unconsciously employs these tactics, genuinely confused when called exploitative.

The teaching emphasizes: regardless of whether heated persons act from conscious malice or unconscious conditioning, the protective response remains identical—complete avoidance—while the internal attitude differs dramatically. Toward conscious manipulators, maintain neutral recognition of functional opposition. Toward those acting from unconscious aryu, maintain active compassion for their suffering while refusing association exposing you to the contaminating influence [9]. One can simultaneously recognize heated persons as suffering beings trapped in destructive patterns AND exercise the righteous ethical right to protect one's purifying mind.

The "multiple hearts" (hatyu) teaching reveals this fragmentation: the mind operating from competing dispositions rather than unified awareness [9]. Someone genuinely caring for their own child while indifferent to others' suffering; speaking eloquently about spiritual principles while treating the service workers dismissively. These contradictions often indicate not conscious hypocrisy but fragmented mind where the different dispositions operate independently, each believing itself sincere.

Verse 13's designation as "the burning enemy that incinerates peace and contentment" [9] reveals destructive impact regardless of intent behind behaviors. They are functional enemies to spiritual development, their heated mind and feelings destroying inner peace necessary for discovering kara where Ab Neter resides (Prologue verse 9). Chapter 9XII's invocation of divine grace—may the Potter God cut away contrary dispositions—maintains a wonderfully contrasting compassionate tone [9] while acknowledging inability to transform them through continued association, which only enables harmful patterns while corrupting one's own mind.

The teaching's ultimate wisdom: the best approach is avoiding the trouble altogether. Prevention through early recognition and complete avoidance proves far more effective than attempting disengagement after infiltration and dependency occur [9].

2. Behavioral Imperative: Recognizing Patterns Regardless of Intent and Implementing Protective Boundaries

The behavioral imperative begins with recognizing infiltration patterns while remaining aware these may operate through either conscious manipulation or unconscious conditioning—both producing identical harmful effects requiring identical protective response. The heated person initially presents as a friend, helper, or spiritual guide—using high-sounding words to gain confidence. During this infiltration phase, they study the aspirant's psychological structure through either conscious reconnaissance or automatic hypervigilance patterns learned in childhood where scanning vulnerabilities ensured survival. They identify exactly which buttons to push to create dependency. Only after establishing dependency do, they reveal their true colors—demands, manipulations, emotional volatility, draining behaviors.

Verse 14's command—"do not allow yourself to go close to them/do not approach them for the purpose of starting up a conversation" [9]—addresses conversation as the primary infiltration vector. Each exchange provides an opportunity to gather intelligence about the target's mind structure, whether that gathering occurs through deliberate reconnaissance or automatic scanning mechanisms operating below awareness. During seemingly friendly discussion, their ka probes the aspirant's ka, identifying which patterns create openings for infiltration.

The pattern culminates when the heated person, having infiltrated and created dependency through either conscious strategy or unconscious compulsion, reveals their true nature. By this point, aryu patterns of obligation and guilt make extraction extremely difficult. The aspirant finds themselves hooked into the heated person's pathology. The teaching's wisdom becomes clear: avoid the trouble altogether through early recognition and complete refusal of engagement.

Verse 15 reveals tongue control preserves vitality otherwise depleted through heated interaction. The heated person operates as "an abominable thing to your heavenly personality" [9]—whether through conscious targeting or unconscious compulsion, they corrupt the ka's functioning to create channels for ongoing influence.

Verse 16's warning about "those who speak great and high-sounding words but who are in fact negative personalities" [9] addresses conscious manipulation and unconscious patterns learned where eloquent self-presentation secured necessary support. Whether the eloquence serves calculated deception or automatic defensive mechanism, the result proves identical: infiltration through false presentation.

The behavioral challenge intensifies when recognizing most heated persons genuinely believe their self-presentations. Someone presenting as spiritually advanced may sincerely identify with that image despite behaviors revealing fragmented mind. The child who learned hypervigilance for survival grows into an adult genuinely believing their scanning represents caring interest rather than unconscious reconnaissance. The individual raised where manipulation secured love employs these tactics while experiencing them as authentic connection rather than exploitation.

The teaching's compassionate provision recognizes this developmental reality while maintaining protective boundaries. One need not determine whether someone acts from conscious malice or unconscious conditioning to implement verse 13's command: "cease/desist/do not seek heated people for the purpose of associating with them" [9]. The distinction matters only for internal attitude—compassion toward unconscious suffering versus neutral recognition toward deliberate exploitation—not for external response, which remains identical: complete avoidance.

3. Mystic Psychology—Metaphysical Implications: Ka Contamination and the Multiple Hearts (Hatyu) Phenomenon

The metaphysical framework underlying these chapters reveals profound principles about how the mind operates within an energetic field where association creates actual transmission of aryu patterns between individuals. The teaching identifies that heated persons function not merely as behavioral problems but as sources of corrupting emanations that infiltrate the aspirant's ka (subconscious mind), depositing negative aryu that then generate future harmful patterns.

The Ka as Permeable Energy Field

The ancient framework understands the ka not as isolated psychological structure but as the subtle energy body interpenetrating and extending beyond the physical form. When two individuals interact—particularly through conversation verse 14 warns against—their kas come into resonance or dissonance, creating conditions for aryu transmission [9]. The heated person's ka, charged with dense negative aryu accumulated through trauma, unethical living, or calculated malice, broadcasts these patterns energetically. The aspirant's ka, particularly if permeable through naivety, codependency patterns, or insufficient boundaries, absorbs these corrupting emanations.

The metaphysical mechanism: aryu exist not merely as psychological memories but as actual energetic patterns with measurable though subtle effects. When the heated person speaks—whether from conscious manipulation or unconscious compulsion—their words carry the aryu-charge of their internal state. The aspirant hearing these words receives not merely conceptual content but the energetic-aryu signature underlying the communication. If the aspirant's ka lacks sufficient protective boundaries, these negative aryu patterns begin depositing in their ab (unconscious mind), where they contribute to existing corrupted patterns or establish new ones requiring future purification.

This explains verse 15's emphasis on tongue control preserving vitality [9]. When the aspirant engages heated persons in conversation, they not only receive contaminating aryu but actively deplete their own sekhem (life force) through several mechanisms: the defensive vigilance required during heated interaction diverts vital energy from spiritual development; the processing and attempting to neutralize received negative patterns consumes substantial sekhem; and the damage to the ka's protective boundaries creates ongoing vulnerability requiring constant repair effort.

The "Multiple Hearts" (Hatyu) and Fragmented Mind

Chapter 9XII's teaching about "multiple hearts" or contrary dispositions (hatyu) reveals metaphysical reality of fragmented mind where the mind operates from competing centers rather than unified awareness [9]. This fragmentation can originate through trauma that overwhelms the developing personality's integrative capacity, creating dissociated parts operating semi-independently with different motivations, perceptions, and ethical frameworks.

The metaphysical structure: rather than the mind operating as single unified field guided by Ab Neter awareness, the heated person's mind fragments into separate dispositional centers, each maintaining its own aryu patterns and behavioral programs. One disposition genuinely cares for family while another disposition remains indifferent to others' suffering. One disposition speaks eloquently about spiritual principles while another disposition treats service workers dismissively. Each disposition experiences itself as the "real" person, genuinely believing its own presentations even while contradictory dispositions operate in different contexts.

This fragmentation explains the characteristic pattern verse 14 describes—heated persons who infiltrate through seeming care then reveal harmful nature [9]. What appears as calculated deception may represent different dispositions activating in different contexts. The disposition seeking connection presents the caring mask during infiltration; the disposition operating from trauma-based survival patterns emerges once dependency is established and the person "feels safe" enough to reveal their wounded self.

The teaching's compassionate recognition: most heated persons genuinely don't recognize their own fragmentation. They experience themselves as sincere in each moment because whichever disposition currently operates believes itself authentic. This explains why confronting heated persons about contradictions typically proves futile—you're addressing disposition A about behaviors generated by disposition B, while disposition A genuinely has no awareness of or identifies with disposition B's actions.

Figure 5:images of the Ancient Egyptian God Khnum, the Potter creating the child body

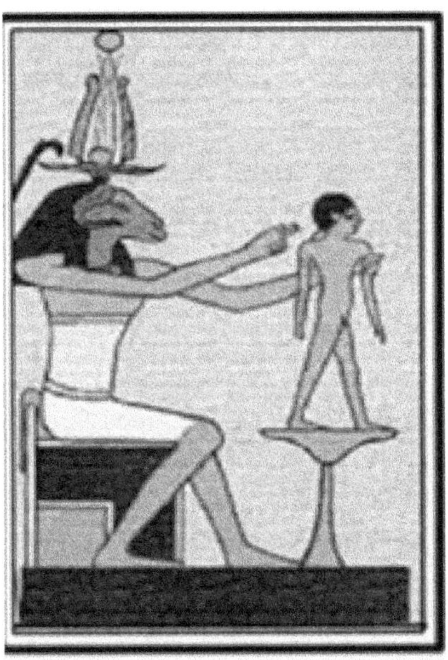

Chapter 9XII's invocation of Khnum, the Potter God, to "cut away the emerging dispositions of the mind that are contrary to goodness and enlightenment" [9] represents prayer for divine intervention to accomplish the integration and healing that human effort cannot achieve. The metaphysical reality: only divine power operating at the divine source level can reintegrate fragmented dispositions into unified awareness guided by Ab Neter. Human interaction, particularly the aspirant's continued association, merely enables the fragmentation by providing an environment where the different dispositions can operate without facing the contradictions that might force awareness and integration.

The Righteous Ethical Right to Protective Boundaries

The teaching establishes the metaphysical principle that protecting one's purifying mind represents not selfish withdrawal but righteous ethical action [9]. When the aspirant maintains clear boundaries against heated persons, they accomplish several spiritually essential functions: preventing corruption of their own ka that would require years of purification to clear; removing enablement that allows heated persons to continue fragmented functioning without confronting consequences; and maintaining the inner peace necessary for discovering Ab Neter presence in the kara (supporting Prologue verse 9's goal).

The metaphysical framework distinguishes between compassion (wishing all beings free from suffering and praying for divine intervention) and enablement (providing an environment where harmful patterns can continue without consequences). One can maintain profound compassion for heated persons' suffering—recognizing that most act from unconscious trauma patterns rather than conscious malice—while implementing complete protective boundaries. This represents the "wonderfully contrasting compassionate tone" Chapter 9XII exemplifies [9]: active goodwill and prayer for their healing combined with absolute refusal of association that would corrupt one's own purifying mind.

4. Transpersonal Psychology Research: Empirical Validation of Association Effects and Trauma-Based Patterns

Contemporary psychology research provides substantial empirical validation for the ancient teaching's framework identifying that association with certain individuals produces measurable harmful effects, while also documenting how trauma creates unconscious patterns that appear manipulative while operating below conscious awareness.

Research on Emotional Contagion and Social Influence

Studies on emotional contagion demonstrate that individuals unconsciously absorb and mirror the emotional states of those they interact with, validating the teaching's identification of aryu transmission through association [1]. Research shows that exposure to individuals displaying anger, anxiety, or depression produces measurable increases in those emotional states in observers, even when observers consciously attempt to remain unaffected. Longitudinal studies tracking relationship effects find that individuals maintaining close relationships with highly negative or exploitative persons show progressive deterioration in their own well-being, emotional regulation, and ethical functioning—empirical validation for verse 13's warning about heated persons as "burning enemies that incinerate peace and contentment" [9].

Neuroscience research on mirror neurons provides a possible biological mechanism for the ka contamination the teaching describes. Studies demonstrate that observing others' behaviors activates the same neural circuits as performing those behaviors oneself, creating literal neurological entrainment between individuals during interaction. When aspirants engage heated persons, their neural patterns begin mirroring the fragmentation and reactivity they observe, gradually depositing the aryu patterns the teaching warns against [2].

Research on Manipulation and Exploitation Patterns

Psychological research on Dark Triad personality traits (narcissism, Machiavellianism, psychopathy) validates the teaching's description of heated persons who infiltrate through false presentation then reveal exploitative nature [1]. Studies document characteristic patterns: initial charm and eloquence gaining trust, strategic information gathering about targets' vulnerabilities, progressive creation of dependency through calculated giving and withholding, and eventual exploitation once the target is "hooked." Research shows these individuals indeed "scout" for weaknesses as verse 13 describes, with studies demonstrating their enhanced ability to detect and exploit others' insecurities [4].

Significantly, research distinguishes between calculated manipulation (rare) and unconscious patterns learned through trauma (common). Studies on attachment disorders and developmental trauma document how children surviving abuse or neglect develop hypervigilance to others' emotional states, manipulative communication patterns, and strategic relationship management—all operating as automatic survival mechanisms rather than conscious exploitation [8]. These individuals genuinely don't recognize their behaviors as manipulative because the patterns operate below conscious awareness as survival programming.

Research on traumatic bonding validates the teaching's emphasis on early recognition and complete avoidance [3][5]. Studies demonstrate that once emotional dependency is established with exploitative individuals, neurological and hormonal changes make extraction extremely difficult. The intermittent reinforcement pattern (occasional kindness alternating with harm) creates addiction-like neurological responses, explaining why aspirants become "hooked" despite recognizing the relationship's harmful nature. This empirical validation supports the teaching's ultimate wisdom: prevention through early recognition proves exponentially easier than extraction after infiltration succeeds [9].

Research on Personality Fragmentation and Integration

Psychological research on dissociation, personality fragmentation, and parts work validates Chapter 9XII's teaching about "multiple hearts" (hatyu) [7][8]. Studies document how trauma that overwhelms integrative capacity creates dissociated self-states operating semi-independently with different motivations, memories, and behavioral patterns. Research shows these fragmented parts genuinely don't recognize each other's existence or behaviors, explaining the characteristic contradictions heated persons display [7].

Clinical research on personality integration demonstrates the teaching's wisdom that human intervention cannot accomplish the healing required—only sustained therapeutic work addressing trauma at its roots, combined with what many therapists recognize as grace or transpersonal intervention, enables reintegration of fragmented conscious-awareness (mind) [6][7]. This validates Chapter 9XII's invocation of divine intervention rather than personal transformation efforts [9].

5. Spiritual Implications for Aspirants

Part A: Pastoral Concerns—Navigating Compassion and Protection

Contemporary aspirants attempting to implement this teaching face profound challenges balancing compassion for heated persons' suffering with the protective boundaries the wisdom requires. Modern spiritual culture often promotes unlimited compassion and service as highest values, creating guilt and confusion when teachings like these emphasize complete avoidance.

The Compassion-Protection Balance

Someone raised in spiritual communities emphasizing universal love and service to all beings encounters difficulty when Amenemopet commands absolute avoidance of heated persons. They may struggle: "Isn't refusing association with suffering people the opposite of compassion? Shouldn't I help them heal through my spiritual practice and loving presence?" This confusion intensifies when recognizing most heated persons act from unconscious trauma patterns rather than conscious malice—their harmful behaviors represent suffering seeking expression rather than calculated evil.

The teaching's wisdom requires understanding that compassion and enablement differ fundamentally. Maintaining prayer, goodwill, and hope for heated persons' healing represents genuine compassion. Continuing association that provides an environment where their harmful patterns face no consequences while corrupting one's own mind represents enablement that serves neither party. The aspirant cannot heal another's fragmented conscious-awareness (mind) through continued exposure to contaminating emanations—only divine intervention operating at consciousness-source level can accomplish such integration.

Additionally, consider that an aspirant striving for spiritual purity and working towards enlightenment but not yet stable in their attainment is not qualified to help a heated person suffering from intensive psychological disturbances. Such struggling aspirants should not assume they possess sufficient stability or qualification for engaging heated personalities. Indeed, they prove more apt to cause harm—both to themselves and others—through enabling the heated person's patterns while simultaneously corrupting their own purifying minds.

The "wonderfully contrasting compassionate tone" Chapter 9XII exemplifies [9] offers resolution: maintain profound compassion internally while implementing absolute boundaries externally. When declining association, the aspirant might practice: "I recognize you likely act from unconscious patterns established through trauma. I hold no personal ill-will and pray for divine intervention to heal your fragmentation. AND I exercise my righteous ethical right to protect my purifying mind by refusing association that would expose me to contaminating influence while enabling patterns that prevent your healing."

PART B: METHODS FOR TRANSFORMATION

Based on the teaching presented by Sage Amenemopet in Chapters 9XI and 9XII, the aspirant benefits from systematic practices addressing both early recognition of heated persons and extraction from already-established infiltrations.

Following verse 14's prohibition against approaching heated persons [9], implement systematic practice of extended observation before allowing anyone close access to your mind and personality. Most individuals—whether operating from conscious manipulation or unconscious patterns—cannot maintain masks indefinitely [11]. Contradictions between words and actions eventually emerge.

Implementation: When meeting someone new who seeks close connection, maintain polite friendly distance while observing their behavior across multiple contexts over extended time. Notice: How do they treat service workers, subordinates, or those who cannot provide advantage? Do they show genuine interest in others or subtly redirect conversations to themselves? Do they ask probing questions about vulnerabilities? Do their stories remain consistent or shift to match contexts? Does their behavior match their eloquent spiritual language?

Concrete implementation example 1: Someone new enters your spiritual community speaking eloquently about advanced practices. Notice they ask probing questions: "What's been most difficult in your practice?" "Do you feel the teacher really understands you?" These may represent conscious reconnaissance OR automatic hypervigilance patterns learned where scanning emotional vulnerabilities ensured survival. The key wisdom: whether conscious or unconscious, recognize the pattern and implement verse 13's command—cease further association [9]. When they approach again, decline politely but firmly: "I appreciate the offer but prefer working with my current teacher exclusively." Do not explain or justify—each response provides more intelligence. Maintain compassion internally (recognizing they likely act from unconscious patterns) while implementing external boundaries.

Concrete implementation example 2: A colleague regularly initiates conversations combining professional discussion with personal sharing. Gradually notice a pattern: they share carefully selected "vulnerabilities," then ask probing questions. Whether operating through conscious manipulation strategy or automatic patterns where such exchanges once secured connection, recognize verse 16's warning [9]. Implement protective boundaries: keep interactions strictly professional and brief, do not share personal information. Internally maintain compassion: "This person likely learned these patterns as survival mechanisms and genuinely doesn't recognize them as manipulative. Nevertheless, I protect my mind by refusing engagement that enables their patterns while exposing me to contamination."

Practice 2: Systematic Extraction from Established Infiltrations

For those already infiltrated, extraction requires systematic dismantling of aryu patterns while maintaining complete physical and communicative distance. Invoke Chapter 9XII's teaching: "May the Divine Potter come and cut away the contrary dispositions in this person—recognizing most likely these dispositions operate below their conscious awareness, patterns learned through trauma [9]. May they be transformed so they no longer function as burning enemy and sneaky spy. But while maintaining this compassionate prayer, I exercise my righteous ethical right to complete separation from their contaminating influence, recognizing my continued presence enables rather than heals their harmful patterns" [9]. This maintains the wonderfully contrasting compassionate tone [9] while implementing necessary protective action.

Practice 3: Tongue Control and Vitality Preservation

Following verse 15's teaching about tongue control preserving vitality [9], develop systematic practice around speech discipline. Before speaking—particularly about personal matters, vulnerabilities, or spiritual experiences—pause to consider: Does sharing this information serve genuine connection or merely satisfy ego-need for validation? Could this information be used to identify weaknesses? Am I speaking from Ab Neter awareness or from aryu-driven patterns seeking external confirmation?

Implementation: Establish personal guideline that intimate sharing occurs only with thoroughly vetted individuals demonstrated trustworthy through extended observation. With others, maintain friendly but general communication focusing on external topics rather than internal processes. This prevents the intelligence-gathering verse 14 warns against while preserving vital energy verse 15 indicates tongue control protects [9].

Practice 4: Maintaining Compassionate Internal Stance

Throughout all protective practices, maintain internal stance of compassion particularly when recognizing most heated persons act from unconscious wounding: "I recognize this person suffers from fragmented mind, likely operating from trauma patterns below conscious awareness. I maintain goodwill and pray for divine intervention to heal their fragmentation. AND I implement complete protective boundaries, recognizing that whether their harmful patterns operate consciously or unconsciously, the contaminating effect on my mind remains identical, and my continued presence enables rather than heals their unconscious patterns" [9].

The teaching's ultimate wisdom proves profound: the best approach is avoiding the trouble altogether. Prevention through early recognition and complete avoidance—implemented with compassion regardless of whether the person acts from conscious malice or unconscious conditioning—proves infinitely easier than extraction after infiltration succeeds. Each implementation of verses 13-14 serves both Prologue goals directly: protecting earthly well-being by preventing years of suffering from being hooked into heated persons' pathology, and enabling kara discovery by maintaining inner peace and mental clarity necessary for recognizing Ab Neter.

References

[1] Jonason, P. K., Slomski, S., & Partyka, J. (2012). The Dark Triad at work: How toxic employees get their way. Personality and Individual Differences, 52(3), 449-453.
[2] Sip, K. E., Roepstorff, A., McGregor, W., & Frith, C. D. (2008). Detecting deception: The scope and limits. Trends in Cognitive Sciences, 12(2), 48-53.
[3] Dutton, D. G., & Painter, S. (1993). Emotional attachments in abusive relationships: A test of traumatic bonding theory. Violence and Victims, 8(2), 105-120.
[4] Wai, M., & Tiliopoulos, N. (2012). The affective and cognitive empathic nature of the dark triad of personality. Personality and Individual Differences, 52(7), 794-799.
[5] Carnes, P. (2015). The Betrayal Bond: Breaking Free of Exploitive Relationships. Health Communications, Inc.
[6] Hassan, S. (2013). Freedom of Mind: Helping Loved Ones Leave Controlling People, Cults, and Beliefs. Freedom of Mind Press.
[7] Paris, J. (2003). Personality Disorders Over Time: Precursors, Course, and Outcome. American Psychiatric Publishing.
[8] van der Kolk, B. (2014). The Body Keeps the Score: Brain, Mind, and Body in the Healing of Trauma. Viking.
[9] Ashby, M. (2019-25). Mysticism of Amenemopet Hieroglyphic Text Translation. Sema Institute of Ancient Egyptian Studies.
[10] Ashby, M. (2025). Keys to Sage Amenemopet wisdom text trilinear translation chapter 9XI and 9XII. Sema Institute of Ancient Egyptian Studies.
[11] Ashby, M. (2019). Amenemopet lectures 2019 by Dr Muata Ashby transcripts. Sema Institute of Ancient Egyptian Studies.

CHAPTER 17: Commentary on Teachings of Amenemopet Chapter 11: The Corruption of Greed and False Oaths Verses 5-6, 9-11

SUMMARY OF TEACHINGS

Chapter 11 addresses the profound psychological and spiritual corruption that arises from lusting after the possessions of those less fortunate, hankering for their sustenance, and making false oaths for personal gain. The teaching reveals how these behaviors create thick aryu (karmic feeling-memories) that corrupt the mind, making it opaque to divine truth, and cause the Ab Neter (heart divinity) to appear as if turning away from the personality. Most significantly, Amenemopet teaches that such corruption undermines the very "project of perfection" that constitutes the purpose of human life—discovering abiding happiness and spiritual enlightenment through recognizing one's true nature as Neberdjer (Divine Consciousness).

KEY TEACHINGS DERIVED FROM VERSES OF CHAPTER 11

Verse 5: Prohibition Against Lusting After Others' Possessions

- Teaching: Refrain from lusting after the possessions (objects) of those who are less fortunate/destitute [1]

Verse 6: Prohibition Against Hankering for Others' Sustenance

- Teaching: Do not hanker for their bread, their food, their food stocks—the sustenance necessary for others' survival [1]

Verse 9: Prohibition Against False Oaths for Profit

- Teaching: Do not make oaths or swear to tell the truth but instead lie in order to gain profits; this behavior is unsound, illogical, erroneous [1][2]

Verse 10: The Apparent Turning Away of Ab Neter (Heart Divinity)

- Teaching: "It is heart{Divinity} his turning away in body his"—when corruption is done, it is one's own rejection of the Divine within one's own heart (individual mind) and thus our Divine heart, that is, the Spirit essence of the Divine (Divine Consciousness) within the personality that is its real source of existence and sustenance of the individual mind, as if turns away from (forsakes) us within our own personality [1]

Verse 11: Corruption of the Project of Perfection

- Teaching: "Through that corruption, that we ourselves engendered, we ourselves are corrupting the project of perfection that we are trying to build for ourselves" [1]

Additional Teaching from Chapter 12 Verse 9 (Referenced in Commentary):

- Teaching: "Do not/stop/refrain from being a repulsive person, greedy about the possessions (objects) belonging to those who are well-to-do" [9]

1. Human Psychology Principle Focus of Chapter 11

Human Psychology Principle: The illusory psychological perspective of separate-self acquisition that corrupts the mind and obscures recognition of divine unity

Chapter 11 addresses the fundamental psychological delusion wherein the mind, operating from accumulated aryu in the ab (unconscious mind) without awareness of Ab Neter in the kara (divine sanctuary within the ab), perceives itself as a separate entity that must acquire objects belonging to others to achieve happiness and security.[1] The wisdom identifies how the hat (front-of-mind / present conscious awareness) becomes fixated on lusting after possessions, particularly those belonging to the less fortunate, and even their basic sustenance. This fixation reinforces egoism—the feeling of individuality and the idea of being a separate entity from others—while simultaneously reinforcing "the apparent reality of individual objects to be acquired in order to be happy."[2]

The deeper psychological issue reveals itself through understanding that Neberdjer (consciousness) manifests as all apparent objects. Therefore, the perspective of the lusting person operates from fundamental illusion—the mind grasping after what appears as separate objects when, in truth, all manifestation represents modifications of the same universal consciousness.[2] This illusory perspective corrupts the mind and disallows correct understanding and feeling, creating what the teaching describes as heated mind and feelings that prevent both earthly well-being and discovery of the divine within.

Connection to Prologue Goals:

This psychological principle directly impacts both Prologue goals. Without resolving the delusion of separate-self acquisition, the goal of Prologue verse 2 to "cause a person to have well-being while living on earth"[3] cannot be achieved because the mind trapped in comparative thinking and grasping experiences perpetual dissatisfaction—the objects acquired never provide lasting fulfillment because they arise from the false premise of separateness. More profoundly, this principle obstructs Prologue verse 9's discovery of the kara "where the Divine resides in every person"[3] because the accumulation of thick aryu from greedy thoughts, words, and deeds creates density in the ab that obscures awareness of Ab Neter residing in the deeper kara level.

2. Behavioral Imperatives of This Chapter

Behavioral Imperative: Observable patterns of acquisitive greed, ethical corruption, hierarchical thinking and fraudulent behavior that arise from ignorance of divine unity.

The behavioral patterns arising from the psychological delusion described in Section 1 manifest through specific observable actions that Amenemopet identifies with remarkable precision. Understanding these behaviors through the hat-ab-aryu-Ab Neter framework illuminates how seemingly ordinary acquisitive patterns actually function as mind-corrupting practices that deposit thick aryu preventing spiritual development.

Lusting After Others' Possessions [Verse 5]

The first behavioral pattern Amenemopet identifies involves the mind fixating specifically on possessions belonging to those less fortunate—not merely experiencing desire for objects in general, but cultivating covetousness directed toward what others who have less already possess.[1] This behavior reveals several layers of corruption. At the surface level, the mind demonstrates lack of contentment with what divine providence has provided, suggesting implicit rejection of the teaching that one's current circumstances represent exactly what is needed for spiritual development at the present time while one works for legitimate and improvements as life changes occur.

More profoundly, directing acquisitive desire toward possessions of the less fortunate exposes supreme egoism—the mind so identified with separate-self perspective that it experiences no natural compassion arising from recognition of shared divine source.[2] The person coveting a struggling neighbor's modest belongings operates from a mind so dense with aryu that the natural response of caring concern has been replaced by predatory acquisition-seeking. This pattern corrupts not merely through the unethical nature of coveting from the vulnerable but through how it reinforces the fundamental illusion that consciousness exists as a separate entity competing for limited resources against other separate entities.

The behavioral manifestation appears in contexts modern culture has normalized: envying a colleague's modest achievement while one possesses greater success; desiring to acquire a small business owned by someone with fewer resources; experiencing resentment toward those receiving assistance one doesn't need. Each instance deposits aryu in the ab that strengthen separate-self identification while making the mind increasingly opaque to recognition that what appears as "others" and "their possessions" represent temporary modifications of the same Neberdjer consciousness that constitutes one's own true nature.

Hankering for Others' Sustenance [Verse 6]

The second behavioral pattern intensifies the corruption by focusing acquisitive desire specifically on others' basic sustenance—their bread, food, and food stocks necessary for survival.[1] This represents what the teaching identifies as particularly severe corruption because it reveals the mind operating not merely from separate-self delusion but from that delusion so profound that it overrides even instinctive concern for others' survival.

The behavior manifests in multiple forms across contemporary contexts. At the gross level: business practices that deprive vulnerable populations of basic necessities for profit maximization; landlords raising rents beyond what low-income tenants can sustain while maintaining adequate nutrition; employers compensating workers insufficiently to afford basic food security. At the subtle level: privileged individuals consuming resources far beyond necessity while remaining indifferent to others' inability to meet basic needs; purchasing patterns that support systems depriving producers of living wages; political positions that protect one's abundance while opposing policies ensuring others' basic sustenance.

The teaching identifies this behavior as manifesting "supreme egoism" and "absence of any kind of caring."[2] The psychological mechanism operates through aryu density so thick that natural compassion—which would arise spontaneously from Ab Neter awareness recognizing shared divine source—cannot penetrate to conscious awareness. The mind becomes so identified with the separate self and its perceived needs that others' actual survival becomes irrelevant to decision-making. This corruption proves particularly insidious because modern economic and social systems have normalized such indifference, making the behavior appear as acceptable self-interest rather than as the mind-corrupting pattern Amenemopet describes.

Making False Oaths for Gain [Verse 9]

The third behavioral pattern involves deliberate deception through false oaths—swearing to truthfulness while intending falsehood for personal profit.[1][2] This behavior demonstrates what the teaching calls "unsound, illogical, erroneous" functioning because it represents the mind deliberately corrupting itself through actions consciousness knows violate truth. Unlike patterns that arise from ignorance, false oaths involve conscious choice to compromise ethical integrity for material advantage, depositing particularly dense aryu because the corruption occurs with full awareness.

The contemporary manifestations prove ubiquitous: falsifying credentials for employment advantage; providing misleading information in business transactions; making commitments without intention to fulfill them; using legal mechanisms to obscure truth for financial benefit; strategic omissions that create false impressions serving self-interest. Each instance reveals what the teaching identifies as "degraded, corrupted mind with no ethical conscience"[2]—the mind so obscured by acquisitive aryu that ethical sensitivity has been progressively deadened until deliberate falsehood no longer generates natural resistance.

The behavioral mechanism operates through reinforcing cycles: initial compromise of truth deposits aryu of ethical violation; these aryu reduce sensitivity to subsequent compromises; progressive desensitization enables increasingly serious corruptions; the accumulated aryu create such opacity that the mind can no longer recognize its own degradation, experiencing calculated deception as necessary pragmatism rather than mind-corruption. The person who began with minor exaggerations gradually develops capacity for systematic fraud, each step seeming reasonable within the corrupted perspective that prior steps established.

The Corruption's Ultimate Effect: Apparent Turning Away of Ab Neter [Verse 10]

All three behavioral patterns culminate in what verse 10 describes as the apparent turning away of the heart divinity—the experience that Ab Neter has forsaken the personality.[1] The teaching's profound wisdom recognizes this as appearance rather than reality: consciousness (Ab Neter) never actually turns away or forsakes, being the very ground sustaining awareness itself. Rather, the thick aryu accumulated through acquisitive behaviors create such opacity in the mind that Ab Neter presence, though continuously sustaining consciousness, becomes completely unrecognizable to the corrupted personality.

The behavioral result manifests as increasing desperation in acquisition-seeking. As the mind becomes more opaque to divine presence, the person experiences progressively intense lack, inadequacy, and insecurity—precisely the feelings that drive more acquisitive behavior depositing more corrupting aryu in self-perpetuating cycles. The individual accumulates possessions, wealth, and resources while experiencing growing inner emptiness because no external acquisition can compensate for the loss of Ab Neter recognition. This explains why verse 11 identifies such corruption as undermining "the project of perfection"[1]—the accumulation meant to create happiness instead corrupts the very capacity for consciousness recognition required for discovering the divine source that alone provides genuine fulfillment.

3. Mystic Psychology—Metaphysical Implications: The Illusion of Separate Objects and the Opacity of Aryu

The metaphysical framework underlying Chapter 11's teaching reveals profound principles about the nature of consciousness, the relationship between perceiver and perceived, and how aryu density creates the appearance of divine absence. Understanding these mechanics illuminates why acquisitive behaviors prove particularly corrupting and how ethical transformation functions at consciousness architecture level.

Neberdjer as Both Subject and Object

The teaching's most fundamental metaphysical principle states that Neberdjer (consciousness) manifests as both the perceiver and all perceived objects.[2] What appears as separate entities—the subject experiencing desire and the objects desired—represent temporary modifications of the same universal consciousness. The wisdom explains: "The creation and the witness of creation are one and the same being" and consciousness "cannot be acquired because the perceiver of the illusory objects is essentially the same as the apparent individual objects to be acquired."[2]

This metaphysical reality exposes the fundamental absurdity of acquisitive desire: the mind attempting to acquire what it already is. The person lusting after another's possessions experiences their own mind (expressing particularized consciousness) desiring objects that are consciousness. The whole enterprise operates from illusion—the mind's failure to recognize that perceiver and perceived share identical essence as temporary expressions of Neberdjer.

The metaphysical mechanism creating this illusion operates through aryu accumulation in the ab. When the mind operates from Ab Neter awareness (consciousness recognizing its own nature), the unity of perceiver and perceived stands revealed—all manifestation recognized as modifications of the same consciousness ground. However, when dense aryu accumulated through egoic living obscure Ab Neter awareness, the mind experiences itself as fundamentally separate from perceived objects. This produces what the teaching identifies as the "apparent reality of individual objects to be acquired in order to be happy"[2]—a reality that proves entirely illusory yet completely convincing to the corrupted mind.

The Project of Perfection and Aryu Opacity

Verse 11's teaching about corrupting "the project of perfection"[1] reveals the metaphysical purpose of human existence: the mind's evolution from ignorant identification with temporary manifestation toward recognition of its true nature as Neberdjer. This project requires progressively thinning aryu density in the ab until the mind becomes sufficiently transparent that Ab Neter presence in the kara can be directly recognized. The entire spiritual path operates through this purification mechanics.

Acquisitive behaviors prove particularly corrupting because they deposit aryu that specifically reinforce the illusion these practices aim to dissolve. Each act of lusting, hankering, or fraudulent acquisition strengthens the feeling-memory of the mind as separate entity requiring external objects for completion. These aryu accumulate in the ab, creating increasing opacity between the hat (conscious awareness) and the kara (where Ab Neter resides). The metaphysical effect: the divine presence sustaining consciousness becomes progressively more hidden behind the density of corrupting patterns.

The teaching explains this as the appearance that "the Spirit essence of the Divine...as if turns away from (forsakes) us within our own personality."[1] The metaphysical reality proves more nuanced:

Ab Neter never actually turns away or abandons, being the very ground enabling consciousness to exist at all. Rather, the thick aryu function as clouds obscuring the sun—the sun continues shining unchanged, but from the ground perspective it appears to have withdrawn. Similarly, corrupting behaviors don't cause Ab Neter to leave but create such density that consciousness can no longer perceive the divine presence that never ceased sustaining awareness.

This explains why ethical purification proves essential for spiritual development rather than optional moral enhancement. The aspirant cannot "work around" ethical corruption to achieve enlightenment through meditation alone or intellectual understanding. The aryu deposited through unethical living create actual opacity in the mind structure that prevents the recognition which constitutes enlightenment. No amount of contemplative practice can force awareness through aryu clouds—only the gradual thinning through ethical transformation allows natural recognition to occur as obstructions dissolve.

The Apparent Turning Away: Consciousness Architecture

The metaphysical teaching about Ab Neter appearing to turn away illuminates the relationship between different consciousness levels: hat (front-of-mind awareness), ab (unconscious mind storing aryu), kara (divine sanctuary deeper than aryu), and Ab Neter (divine consciousness residing in kara sustaining all awareness).[1] Under normal corrupted conditions, the hat operates primarily from aryu patterns accumulated in the ab, these patterns determining perception, thought, feeling, and behavior. When aryu density remains relatively thin, the hat maintains some connection with Ab Neter in the kara—occasional glimpses of unity, moments of genuine compassion, spontaneous ethical sensitivity.

However, as acquisitive behaviors deposit increasingly thick aryu, the ab becomes so dense that it functions as barrier between hat and kara. The hat experiences itself operating entirely from egoic patterns with no access to divine guidance or presence. This creates the phenomenon verse 10 describes—from the perspective of the corrupted personality, it genuinely appears that Ab Neter has withdrawn, that divine support has been lost, that the mind experiences isolated separation.[1]

The metaphysical reality: Ab Neter continues residing in the kara, continues sustaining the capacity for awareness itself, continues constituting the actual ground of the individual's existence. But the thick aryu create such effective barrier that the personality experiences complete disconnection. This explains the escalating desperation in acquisitive behavior—the mind, unable to recognize the divine source that alone provides genuine fulfillment, seeks increasingly through external acquisition to fill the experienced void. The very behaviors meant to provide satisfaction instead deepen the corruption preventing access to actual satisfaction.

The transformative implication: ethical purification functions not as earning divine favor or proving worthiness but as dissolving the aryu opacity that prevents recognition of what never left. The project of perfection succeeds not through acquiring something absent but through removing obstructions to recognizing what always sustained consciousness. This understanding prevents the egoic spiritual seeking where the mind attempts to "achieve" enlightenment through accumulation of experiences or states—the teaching reveals that recognition requires purification allowing natural revelation rather than acquisition creating something new.

Soul as Ab Neter: Terminology and Compatibility Across Egyptian Scriptures

The main term used in Ancient Egyptian scriptures to describe what is popularly known as the "human soul" is "Ba." One of the primary symbols of the ba presents the image of a hawk's body with the head of the person whose soul is being represented. This symbolism follows the teaching that every person constitutes a combination of the divine body (hawk) and the head of the person which symbolizes their individual personality expression. The hawk symbolism refers to the divine (God) in the form of Sokar (Zokar)—the name of the God Asar (Osiris) in his aspect as king of the netherworld. The meaning conveyed through this iconography reveals that human individuality (soul) relates to the head—the mind, the thoughts and feelings—being sustained by Universal Spirit (Sokar). The ba thus represents the divine essence individuated through particular mental expressions while remaining fundamentally connected to its universal source.

Asar-Zokar

Ba

However, in the wisdom text of Sage Amenemopet, a different term receives emphasis. Amenemopet employs the term "Ab Neter," which means "divinity in the heart." Neter signifies "Divinity"—the Divine conceptualized as androgynous universal Spirit. Ab Neter therefore indicates that universal Divinity manifests in the heart of the individual, where "heart" signifies "mind" in Ancient Egyptian spiritual understanding. Amenemopet explains that this Divinity resides in the part of the personality referred to as the "Ab"—the unconscious mind—specifically in the deeper kara level beyond the surface aryu patterns. Therefore, the term "Ba" with its usage across other Ancient Egyptian texts and the term "Ab Neter" as employed by Amenemopet prove compatible, both describing the divine consciousness residing within the individual personality while remaining eternally connected to its universal source. Indeed, this compatibility receives further confirmation through the fact that in other Ancient Egyptian texts, the god Asar (Osiris) himself is referred to by the term "Neter," demonstrating that the divine essence sustaining the ba and the Ab Neter represent the same universal consciousness expressed through different scriptural contexts and terminological frameworks. This compatibility demonstrates the coherent metaphysical framework underlying diverse Ancient Egyptian spiritual literature, whether expressed through funerary texts emphasizing the ba's journey or wisdom literature like Amenemopet's emphasizing the Ab Neter's presence as the foundation requiring ethical purification for recognition.

The Essential Identity of "Ab Neter" and "Amun-Ra": Two Names for the Divine Witness Within

Consider the profound convergence of wisdom revealed when we examine the teaching of Ab Neter in Sage Amenemopet's instructions [1] alongside the teaching of Amun-Ra in the ancient Hymn to Amun-Ra [12]. These two scriptural traditions, emerging from different contexts within the vast corpus of Ancient Egyptian spiritual literature, describe with remarkable consistency the same fundamental aspect of human consciousness—namely, the divine witnessing presence that sustains individual awareness while remaining itself unaffected by the changing states of waking, dreaming, and sleeping that consciousness experiences throughout the cycle of daily existence.

The Hymn to Amun-Ra provides the explicit teaching that "during the sleep state, in the mind of people, a divine personage is there {that is Amun-Ra}; he is awake and aware and watchful after men and women while they are sleeping" [12]. This revelation illuminates a profound metaphysical truth: beneath the fluctuating states of ordinary human awareness—whether engaged in waking activity, absorbed in dream experience, or resting in the unconscious void of deep sleep—there exists an unchanging witnessing consciousness that never sleeps, never becomes confused, never loses its inherent awareness. The hymn further instructs that "you are the consciousness within us sustaining our conscious awareness all the time, including through the sleep and waking states of the mind, so that you are always the consciousness within us that is experiencing the waking and dream states of our mind and senses" [12]. This teaching establishes Amun-Ra as the hidden (Amun means "hidden" or "secret") aspect of divine consciousness operating as the very foundation that makes all individual conscious experience possible, yet remaining unknown to most people who mistake their temporary mental phenomena for the source of awareness itself.

Now, observe how Sage Amenemopet's teaching on Ab Neter presents precisely this same understanding through different terminology suited to practical spiritual instruction [1]. The teaching reveals that Ab Neter resides in the kara—the divine sanctuary located at the deepest level of the ab (unconscious mind)—and constitutes "a person's portion of Divine consciousness that sustains their capacity of conscious awareness of their life" [1]. This Ab Neter operates continuously, providing the very foundation of conscious awareness by which an individual experiences thoughts, feelings, sensations, and perceptions. Indeed, the teaching emphasizes that without this Ab Neter connection sustaining consciousness moment-by-moment, there would be no awareness operating at any level—neither at the hat (conscious awareness) level, nor the ka (subconscious personality) level, nor even at the ab (unconscious) level itself [1]. The Ab Neter serves as the connection point linking individual consciousness to Neberdjer—the all-encompassing universal consciousness—much as a ray of light remains connected to its solar source while appearing to possess individual identity.

The essential identity of these two teachings becomes unmistakable when we recognize their shared characteristics. Both Amun-Ra and Ab Neter describe a consciousness that remains perpetually awake and aware even when the individual person sleeps; both represent the hidden divine presence within that most people remain unaware of despite it sustaining their every moment of awareness; both constitute the unchanging witnessing consciousness that observes all changing states without being modified by them [1, 12, 13]; both serve as the foundation connecting individual consciousness to the absolute divine consciousness (whether called Ra or Neberdjer); and both require spiritual purification for their recognition, since the density of aryu (karmic feeling-memories) accumulated in the ab occupies the hat's awareness so completely as to "blot out the awareness of the soul level divine presence which is deeper than the aryu" [1].

This finding demonstrates something of crucial significance beyond the doctrinal convergence itself: it reveals a fundamental compatibility between the metaphysical frameworks employed by both scriptures to map the structure of human consciousness and articulate its relationship to the Divine. When Amenemopet describes the multilayered architecture of consciousness—with hat (conscious mind), ka (subconscious personality), ab (unconscious mind containing the kara sanctuary), and Ab Neter (the divine witness residing in that sanctuary)—and when the Hymn to Amun-Ra describes the waking and sleeping states of ordinary awareness sustained by an ever-wakeful divine consciousness operating beneath them, both texts reveal their shared foundation in a sophisticated understanding of consciousness that distinguishes between surface-level mental phenomena and the deeper divine awareness that makes all mental experience possible [1, 12]. This structural compatibility suggests that Ancient Egyptian spiritual philosophy possessed a coherent, systematic framework for describing the soul's constitution and its connection to universal divine consciousness—a framework that remained remarkably consistent across different textual traditions and historical periods. The fact that wisdom instructions intended for ethical living and hymnic literature celebrating divine attributes both presuppose and articulate the same underlying model of consciousness indicates that this teaching represented not merely poetic metaphor or philosophical speculation, but rather the foundational understanding upon which the entire edifice of Ancient Egyptian spirituality was constructed.

The wisdom to be understood here encompasses recognition that Amenemopet's teaching on Ab Neter and the Hymn to Amun-Ra's teaching on the ever-wakeful divine witness represent complementary expressions of the same profound metaphysical truth [1, 12]: within every human being resides an aspect of consciousness that is divine, eternal, unchanging, and perpetually aware—the very source from which individual conscious-awareness borrows its capacity to be aware of anything whatsoever [13]. Whether we employ the term Amun-Ra (emphasizing the hidden witnessing aspect of divine consciousness) or Ab Neter (emphasizing the divine soul residing in the sanctuary of the deep unconscious), we describe the same reality—that consciousness sustaining human awareness is not separate from universal divine consciousness but rather represents its localized manifestation, temporarily appearing as individual awareness while remaining fundamentally identical with the absolute source. This understanding revolutionizes spiritual practice from seeking something absent to removing the aryu obstruction preventing recognition of what has always been present as the foundation of our very capacity to seek, to question, to be aware—the divine witness that the ancient sages knew sustains all sentient existence while remaining itself unsleeping, unchanging, and unaffected by the temporal phenomena it witnesses and illumines through its eternal presence [1, 12, 13].

4. Transpersonal Psychology Research: Empirical Validation of Greed's Corrupting Effects

Contemporary psychological and neuroscience research provides substantial empirical validation for the ancient teaching's framework identifying acquisitive greed, ethical corruption, and fraudulent behavior as profoundly harmful to psychological well-being and consciousness development. While modern science cannot directly measure aryu density or Ab Neter recognition, it documents physiological and psychological correlates corresponding precisely to what the teaching describes as corruption effects.

Research on Materialism and Well-being

Extensive research demonstrates that individuals with strong materialistic orientations—prioritizing acquisition, wealth accumulation, and possession-focus—show significantly reduced well-being compared to those with intrinsic value orientations. Studies document that materialistic individuals experience lower life satisfaction, reduced happiness, increased anxiety and depression, poorer quality relationships, and diminished meaning in life.[5][6] This empirical finding validates the teaching's identification that acquisitive desire, far from providing the happiness it promises, actually corrupts consciousness in ways that prevent genuine fulfillment.

Neuroscience research on reward systems provides a biological mechanism for the teaching's description of escalating acquisition-seeking. Studies show that materialistic behaviors activate dopamine circuits in ways that create tolerance—requiring increasingly more acquisition to achieve the same satisfaction response, precisely mirroring the teaching's description of thick aryu creating insatiable grasping.[7] Research demonstrates that individuals focused on external acquisition show reduced activation in brain regions associated with intrinsic satisfaction and meaning, suggesting biological correlate for the teaching's framework of Ab Neter recognition becoming obscured by acquisitive patterns.[7][8]

Research on Ethical Decision-Making and Consciousness

Psychological research on moral reasoning and ethical behavior validates the teaching's framework that ethical corruption progressively degrades consciousness sensitivity. Studies demonstrate that individuals who engage in minor ethical violations show reduced sensitivity to subsequent violations—a phenomenon research terms "moral licensing" or "ethical fading" corresponding to what the teaching describes as progressive opacity through aryu accumulation.[5][6] Brain imaging research shows that repeated ethical compromises produce measurable changes in neural circuits governing moral sensitivity, providing a biological mechanism for the consciousness corruption Amenemopet describes.[8]

Research on dishonesty and deception demonstrates escalating patterns matching verse 9's teaching about false oaths. Studies show that minor deceptions make subsequent larger deceptions more likely, with each compromise reducing both physiological stress responses and conscious recognition of ethical violation.[5][6] This validates the teaching's description of "degraded, corrupted mind with no ethical conscience"[2]—consciousness literally losing capacity to recognize its own corruption through progressive desensitization.

Significantly, research on contemplative practices demonstrates that ethical conduct proves essential for sustained meditation benefits and consciousness development. Studies show that individuals maintaining strong ethical commitments show significantly greater progress in meditation practice compared to those emphasizing technique while neglecting ethical development, validating the teaching that corrupting behaviors prevent the recognition which constitutes spiritual realization.[7]

5. Spiritual Implications for Aspirants

Part A: Pastoral Concerns—Modern Challenges to Contentment and Ethical Integrity

Contemporary aspirants attempting to implement Chapter 11's teachings face systematic obstacles created by economic systems, social structures, and cultural narratives that normalize and reward precisely the acquisitive behaviors Amenemopet identifies as mind-corrupting.

The Normalization of Acquisitive Corruption

Modern capitalist culture systematically promotes the illusion that happiness derives from accumulation, making the teaching's prohibition against lusting after possessions appear as unrealistic idealism rather than as practical wisdom for mind/personality development. Advertising industries invest billions creating desires for products; economic systems measure success through consumption growth; social media platforms engineer envy through curated displays of others' possessions; career advancement often requires ethical compromises Amenemopet would identify as false oaths for gain.

The aspirant raised in this environment encounters profound challenges implementing verses 5-6's prohibitions against lusting and hankering. They may intellectually understand that acquisitive desire corrupts consciousness while simultaneously experiencing compelling internal narratives: "Everyone pursues these goals. Success requires this focus. You'll be left behind without such drive. Contentment with less means accepting failure." These narratives operate from accumulated aryu established through years of cultural conditioning, creating automatic patterns that pre-empt conscious ethical discrimination.

Someone attempting to cultivate contentment while surrounded by peers pursuing aggressive acquisition experiences social pressure that reinforces corrupting patterns. The person who refuses to pursue higher income requiring ethical compromise may face judgment as lacking ambition. The individual who declines participation in normalized deceptions may be viewed as naively rigid. The aspirant maintaining simple lifestyle while peers accumulate possessions may be pitied as missing life's opportunities. This social reinforcement makes the corrupting behaviors appear as wisdom while ethical restraint appears as dysfunction.

Part A-1: Delusions about the Universal Soul/Consciousness (Neberdjer) manifesting in all Individuals

ALL ARE EQUALLY SUSTAINED BY THE SAME DIVINE BEING

Among the most profound—and most persistently misunderstood—teachings in Amenemopet's wisdom lies the metaphysical reality that Ab Neter resides in the kara of EVERY person without exception. This truth carries implications that completely demolish the foundation of hierarchical thinking about human worth. When Amenemopet reveals that "a person's portion of Divine consciousness sustains their capacity of conscious awareness of their life," this applies universally: to oneself, one's family, one's neighbors, the stranger on the street, the wealthy merchant, the impoverished beggar, the righteous sage, and yes—even to those personalities manifesting what we recognize as evil behavior.

Consider the inescapable logic: if consciousness itself—the very capacity to be aware, to think, to feel, to perceive—depends on Ab Neter sustained by Neberdjer, then EVERY conscious being owes their existence to the same Divine source. The heated personality consumed by greed operates through consciousness sustained by Neberdjer. The silent personality radiating peace operates through consciousness sustained by Neberdjer. The criminal scheming harm operates through consciousness sustained by Neberdjer. The sage teaching wisdom operates through consciousness sustained by Neberdjer. ALL draw their capacity for awareness from the identical Divine wellspring.

This metaphysical reality reveals the complete ABSURDITY of ideas that some people are inherently superior or inferior to others, that some are more worthy or less worthy, that some deserve respect while others deserve contempt. Such hierarchical thinking proves not merely ethically questionable but LOGICALLY RIDICULOUS—it attempts to establish gradations of worth among beings who are ALL equally dependent on the same Divine consciousness for their very existence. Indeed, the notion that one manifestation of Neberdjer-sustained consciousness could be "better than" another manifestation of Neberdjer-sustained consciousness reveals itself as LUDICROUS when examined through clear reasoning.

Those ideas of superiority and inferiority are born of ignorance and sustained by egoism and delusion. The mind trapped in aryu-density cannot perceive the Ab Neter in its own kara, much less recognize the Ab Neter residing in the kara of others. Operating from this ignorance, the ego creates elaborate hierarchies: "I am better because I possess more wealth, higher education, lighter skin, greater intelligence, superior moral conduct, deeper spiritual understanding..." The mind generates endless criteria for establishing favorable comparison, all of which collapse under scrutiny of the fundamental truth: consciousness recognizing these distinctions and consciousness being evaluated by these distinctions BOTH owe their capacity to function to the same Divine source.

THE DISTINCTION BETWEEN SOUL AND CORRUPTED MIND

Nevertheless, the wisdom to be understood recognizes a crucial distinction. When we state that everyone's Ab Neter is equally sustained by Neberdjer, we address the metaphysical foundation—the soul, the divine spark, the portion of universal consciousness residing in each person's kara. This Ab Neter remains pure, untainted, and divine regardless of the personality manifestations arising from the mind.

What we recognize as an "evil personality" represents not corruption of Ab Neter but rather corruption of the MIND—specifically, the ab (unconscious) densely packed with negative aryu that obstruct Ab Neter awareness and generate heated mind and feelings. When someone manifests cruelty, deceit, violence, or malice, these behaviors arise from aryu-corrupted mental operations, not from Ab Neter itself. The soul remains divine; the mind has become corrupted through accumulated impressions from unrighteous actions, thoughts, and feelings across current and previous lifetimes.

Consider the implications: the person who harms others operates through a mind so densely obstructed by aryu that the hat (conscious awareness) cannot perceive the Ab Neter in their own kara, much less recognize the Ab Neter in others' kara. Their harmful behaviors represent the sum-total effect of aryu-shaped patterns manifesting through corrupted mental operations. We witness their personality—the observable expression of their current mind condition—but the Ab Neter sustaining their consciousness remains untouched by these corruptions, pure as the Ab Neter in the sage, awaiting revelation once sufficient purification dissolves the aryu obstruction.

This understanding transforms how we perceive even those manifesting severely heated personalities. The criminal, the tyrant, the deceiver—all possess the same divine essence as the saint. Their Ab Neter shines with the same divine radiance, though buried under such dense aryu accumulation that no light penetrates to conscious awareness. Their consciousness depends on the same

Neberdjer sustaining the consciousness of the most enlightened being. The difference lies not in the soul—which remains equally divine—but in the mind condition determined by aryu density.

PRACTICAL WISDOM WHILE RECOGNIZING DIVINE ESSENCE

Now, this recognition that everyone possesses equally divine essence sustained by the same source does NOT mean we ignore the realities of corrupted mind manifestations or abandon practical wisdom in dealing with heated personalities. Amenemopet teaches precisely how to navigate relationships with such persons, and those teachings remain essential regardless of metaphysical understanding.

When Amenemopet instructs to "avoid the heated person," to "not sit with the hot-tempered," to maintain protective distance from those manifesting aryu-driven destructive patterns, this wisdom addresses the practical level of personality interactions. Yes, the heated person's Ab Neter remains divine. Yes, their consciousness is sustained by the same Neberdjer sustaining yours. Yes, at the deepest level they are manifestations of the same universal Divine. Nevertheless, their MIND operates through corrupted patterns that generate harmful behaviors, and wisdom requires appropriate responses to those behavioral realities.

The teaching establishes a two-level understanding:

METAPHYSICAL LEVEL: All beings possess Ab Neter equally sustained by Neberdjer. All consciousness flows from the same Divine source. All souls remain pure regardless of mind corruption. Recognition of this truth eliminates any basis for experiencing superiority, for dismissing others as "less than," for failing to recognize the divine presence animating all forms.

PRACTICAL LEVEL: Minds manifest different degrees of aryu corruption, producing different personality expressions ranging from silent (purified) to heated (corrupted). Wisdom requires discerning these mind conditions and responding appropriately—maintaining distance from heated persons not because they lack divine essence but because their corrupted mind generates harmful behavioral patterns that could obstruct one's own purification journey.

The silent person navigating life understands both levels simultaneously. They recognize the divine in all beings—the shared Ab Neter sustained by shared Neberdjer—while simultaneously exercising wisdom in actual relationships based on observed mind conditions. They can bow to the divine in every person while refusing to place themselves in situations where heated mind manifestations could cause harm. They maintain respect for the soul while establishing boundaries against corrupted personality expressions.

This dual recognition proves essential: the metaphysical truth that all are equally divine prevents arrogant superiority thinking, while the practical wisdom about mind corruption prevents naive exposure to harmful influences. Both truths operate together in the balanced understanding characterizing silent mind and feelings.

PART B: PRACTICES FOR TRANSFORMATION—PRACTICAL IMPLEMENTATION

Based on the teachings presented by Sage Amenemopet in Chapter 11, which prohibit lusting after others' possessions, hankering for their sustenance, and making false oaths for gain [verses 5-6, 9],[1] the application of the inverse doctrine methodology suggests specific practices for transforming the mind from corrupted acquisitive patterns to ethical clarity that allows Ab Neter recognition. Therefore, the aspirant should cultivate opposite qualities: contentment with divine providence, active concern for others' well-being, and unwavering commitment to truth in all communications, as these support rather than undermine the project of perfection.

Practice 1: Contentment Meditation and Providence Recognition

The teaching's prohibition against lusting implies cultivation of contentment as essential purification practice. The aspirant should establish daily meditation specifically focused on recognizing the adequacy of what divine providence has already provided. This practice begins with systematic inventory of present resources—not merely material possessions but capacities, relationships, circumstances—while directing awareness toward understanding that these represent precisely what the mind requires for its current stage of development. The meditation includes reflection on how Neberdjer manifests as all apparent objects, rendering acquisition-seeking fundamentally illusory since consciousness cannot acquire what it already is.

When desires for others' possessions arise in daily life, the aspirant should immediately recognize these as heated mind and feelings patterns arising from aryu rather than authentic needs. The specific practice involves: first, pause and acknowledge the desire without judgment; second, investigate the feeling-memory driving the desire (what aryu has been triggered?); third, direct awareness toward the truth that consciousness requires no external object for completeness since Ab Neter sustains awareness itself; fourth, actively cultivate gratitude for present circumstances as divine provision perfectly suited to current spiritual needs. Over time, this practice deposits new aryu in the ab—feeling-memories of contentment and trust that gradually thin the dense aryu of acquisitive craving.

Practice 2: Active Compassion for Others' Well-Being

Based on the teaching that hankering for others' sustenance represents supreme egoism and absence of caring [verse 6], the inverse practice cultivates active concern for ensuring others have sufficient resources for well-being.[2] The aspirant should establish regular practice of generosity specifically directed toward those with fewer resources. This transcends token charity to include systematic attention to how one's own consumption affects others' access to necessities.

Practical implementation requires concrete action: When making purchasing decisions, investigate whether products derive from exploitation of vulnerable workers and choose alternatives even when more expensive. When negotiating salary or prices, consider fairness to all parties rather than maximizing personal advantage. When encountering individuals lacking basic necessities, provide direct assistance rather than rationalization. The practice works by creating new aryu of interconnection and care that compete with accumulated aryu of separate-self seeking. Each act of genuine concern for others' welfare deposits feeling-memories that support recognition of unity rather than separateness.

Consider the business owner who implements this practice: Rather than maximizing profit by paying minimum wages, they establish compensation that allows employees genuine well-being, recognizing that their workers' inability to afford basic necessities represents the very corruption Amenemopet describes. Rather than exploiting customers' ignorance, they provide honest information even when transparency reduces immediate profit. These choices create aryu that thin the density of acquisitive greed while cultivating the ethical conscience necessary for spiritual development.

Practice 3: Commitment to Rigorous Truth

The teaching that false oaths represent degraded, corrupted mind with no ethical conscience [verse 9] implies that cultivation of rigorous truthfulness functions as essential purification practice.[2] The aspirant should establish commitment to wisdom truth in all communications—not merely avoiding obvious lies but eliminating subtle misrepresentations, exaggerations, and strategic omissions that serve personal advantage. "Wisdom truth" also refers to truth that is wise, useful and non-maliciously injurious. So not being truthful to injure others.

The practice requires vigilant awareness of speech patterns and immediate correction of any untruth, even when honest communication appears disadvantageous. When the impulse arises to misrepresent for gain—inflating credentials, exaggerating accomplishments, concealing relevant information—the aspirant should recognize this as a heated mind pattern and instead speak truth regardless of consequences. This practice proves especially challenging in modern contexts where strategic deception has become normalized, but its transformative power operates through creating aryu of integrity that gradually purify the corrupted patterns.

Practical example: The individual seeking employment who feels tempted to embellish qualifications should instead provide accurate information and trust that divine providence arranges circumstances according to what one's personality truly requires. The short-term disadvantage of honest presentation becomes long-term advantage as the practice deposits aryu that support rather than corrupt the project of perfection. Over years of rigorous truthfulness, the mind develops such sensitivity to falsehood that even subtle misrepresentation becomes impossible—the ethical conscience having been strengthened through practice rather than degraded through compromise.

The ultimate transformation occurs as these practices gradually thin the thick aryu that make the mind opaque to divine truth. As aryu density decreases, the mind gains increasing capacity to recognize that what manifests as Creation and what perceives Creation represent one and the same Neberdjer. The corruption that prevented this recognition dissolves through patient absorption in ethical practice, allowing the Ab Neter that has always sustained consciousness to reveal itself naturally in awareness, completing the project of perfection that Chapter 11 teaches represents the true purpose of human life.

On Wisdom Truth and Discernment

The wisdom to be understood recognizes that rigorous truthfulness operates through discernment rather than mere factual accuracy. "Wisdom truth," a concept extrapolated from the wisdom verses of Sage Amenemopet, distinguishes itself from malicious truth—using facts as weapons to injure, humiliate, or satisfy egoic impulses under the guise of "honesty"—and from proselytizing truth that forces unwelcome perspectives on unreceptive recipients. The silent person speaks truthfully when such speech serves the genuine long-term benefit of the recipient, even if causing temporary discomfort, but only when the person demonstrates willingness to receive such communication. Consider the difference between compassionately revealing to a friend that their behavior creates self-destructive patterns (wisdom truth serving their growth) versus aggressively imposing one's spiritual or moral understanding on those neither ready nor able to accept such perspectives (heated impulse disguised as helpfulness). The latter represents egoic attachment to being "right" rather than genuine concern for another's well-being, often depositing reactive aryu in both speaker and recipient without producing beneficial transformation.

This principle applies primarily to peer adult relationships where mutual respect and receptivity determine appropriate communication. The parent-child relationship operates under different principles; those responsible for children's welfare must speak protective truth that prevents harm or establishes necessary boundaries even when causing temporary upset, as children lack the developmental capacity to discern long-term benefit from immediate discomfort. Nevertheless, even parental truth should arise from wisdom-guidance rather than heated reactivity, maintaining the child's dignity while exercising appropriate authority. In all cases, wisdom truth requires examining one's motivation before speaking: Does this truth serve the other person's genuine growth, or does it serve my ego's need to correct, control, or demonstrate superiority? The silent person maintains this discriminative awareness, speaking when wisdom indicates benefit, remaining silent when speech would arise from heated impulses or fall on unreceptive ground.

References

[1] Ashby, M. (2019-25). Mysticism of Amenemopet Hieroglyphic Text Translation. Sema Institute of Ancient Egyptian Studies.
[2] Ashby, M. (2025). Keys to Sage Amenemopet wisdom text trilinear translation chapter 11. Sema Institute of Ancient Egyptian Studies.
[3] Ashby, M. (2019-25). Mysticism of Amenemopet Hieroglyphic Text Translation: Prologue. Sema Institute of Ancient Egyptian Studies.
[4] Ashby, M. (2024). Book Commentaries on Mystic Psychology of Amenemopet. Sema Institute of Ancient Egyptian Studies.
[5] Greene, J. D. (2013). Moral Tribes: Emotion, Reason, and the Gap Between Us and Them. Penguin Press.
[6] Haidt, J. (2012). The Righteous Mind: Why Good People Are Divided by Politics and Religion. Vintage Books.
[7] Davidson, R. J., & Lutz, A. (2008). Buddha's brain: Neuroplasticity and meditation. IEEE Signal Processing Magazine, 25(6), 176-188.
[8] Moll, J., de Oliveira-Souza, R., Eslinger, P. J., Bramati, I. E., Mourão-Miranda, J., Andreiuolo, P. A., & Pessoa, L. (2002). The neural correlates of moral sensitivity: A functional magnetic resonance imaging investigation of basic and moral emotions. Journal of Neuroscience, 22(7), 2730-2736.
[9] Ashby, M. (2019-25). Mysticism of Amenemopet Hieroglyphic Text Translation: Chapter 12. Sema Institute of Ancient Egyptian Studies.
[10] Ashby, M. (2024). Book Commentaries on Mystic Psychology of Amenemopet. Sema Institute of Ancient Egyptian Studies.
[11] Ashby, M. (2024). Book Maat Philosophy Versus Fascism and the Police State. Sema Institute of Ancient Egyptian Studies.

CHAPTER 18: Synthesis: The Complete Model of Mind and Consciousness According to Amenemopet

INTRODUCTION: THE COMPONENTS OF AMENEMOPET'S FRAMEWORK OF MIND AND CONSCIOUSNESS

Throughout the preceding chapters, you have encountered the fundamental components of Amenemopet's consciousness teaching as they emerged organically within specific practical instructions. In the Prologue, you discovered the two primary goals: achieving well-being while living on earth and discovering the kara—the divine sanctuary where Ab Neter resides within every person. Through subsequent chapters, you have learned how Hat (conscious awareness) operates, how Ka (the personality and broader subconscious mind) functions, how Ab (the unconscious mind) stores aryu (karmic feeling-memories), and how these levels interact to create either heated or silent mind and feelings.

Chapters in the Amenemopet Document (in order showing when the components of mind and consciousness and the concepts of heated and silent personality were introduced):

- Prologue ← ***Ab*** (unconscious), Kara first introduced (verse 9: divine sanctuary/shrine of Ab Neter)
- Prologue ← ***Udja*** (vitality), first introduced and elaborated in subsequent verses throughout
- Chapter 2← ***Set*** -ego- self-image, individuality, sense of self. ***shemm***-Heated Personality introduced
- Chapter 3
- Chapter 4← ***ger***-Silent/Serene Personality
- Chapter 5
- Chapter 6B VIII ← ***Neberdjer*** first explicitly introduced (verse 14: All-encompassing Divinity)
- Chapter 7 / Chapter 7B ← ***Hat, Ka, Ab*** introduced (conscious/subconscious/unconscious mind levels)
- Chapter 8
- Chapter 9XI
- Chapter 9XII
- Chapter 11 ← ***Ab Neter*** explicitly introduced (verse 10: divine heart/god within)
- Chapter 13
- Chapter 16
- Chapter 18 [XX]
- Chapter 18 [XIX]
- Chapter 21
- Chapter 25
- Chapter 26

In Chapter 11, the teaching explicitly revealed Ab Neter—the divine soul spark, your portion of Divine consciousness that sustains your very capacity for conscious awareness. In Chapter 6 and 18, you encountered Neberdjer—the all-encompassing divinity, Lord of utmost limits, who serves as shepherd guiding the boat of human life from the forefront. Each component was introduced not as abstract theory but as practical wisdom addressing specific life challenges: controlling speech, avoiding heated persons, maintaining ethical conduct, navigating worldly affairs with divine awareness.

Now that all these elements have been presented through Amenemopet's actual teachings, this synthesis section provides the complete structural model showing how these components relate to one another within the architecture of consciousness. This placement follows the sage's own pedagogical method: practical instruction first, structural understanding second. You have encountered each concept in context—learning what it does and why it matters—before seeing how all components fit together as an integrated system.

The diagram and explanation that follow reveal the profound unity underlying Amenemopet's diverse instructions. You will see how Hat, Ka, Ab, Ab Neter/Kara, and Neberdjer constitute not separate isolated concepts but interconnected levels of a single consciousness operating simultaneously within every human being. This structural understanding deepens your capacity to apply the teachings you have studied, revealing why specific practices work and how transformation actually occurs through the mechanisms the sage describes.

Consider this section as the moment when scattered pieces form a complete picture—when individual trees reveal themselves as a unified forest. What follows is not new teaching but rather clarification of the framework that has implicitly guided every chapter commentary you have read so far. The wisdom to be understood encompasses recognition that Amenemopet's instructions work precisely because they address this complete consciousness structure, thinning aryu obstruction to reveal the Ab Neter connection to Neberdjer that has always sustained your awareness yet remained hidden beneath accumulated karmic patterns.

DEFINITIVE EXPLANATION: AMENEMOPET'S MODEL OF CONSCIOUSNESS

Amenemopet's Diagram of Consciousness: The Structure of Individual Mind Within Universal Consciousness

The following diagram represents the Ancient Egyptian understanding of consciousness as taught by Sage Amenemopet, revealing how individual human awareness exists as a constricted portion of infinite universal consciousness (Neberdjer), sustained through connection via the divine spark (Ab Neter) residing in the innermost sanctuary (Kara) within the unconscious mind.

Figure 6: Human mind and consciousness operations in a human being. Concentric circles diagram showing Neberdjer (outermost), Ab (outer circle with "aryu aryu aryu..." text), Ka (middle circle), Hat (center circle), with Ab Neter/Kara callout box at the boundary between Ab and Neberdjer. Dashed lines between inner circles, solid line for outer boundary. Bidirectional arrows showing flow between Hat-Ka-Ab.]

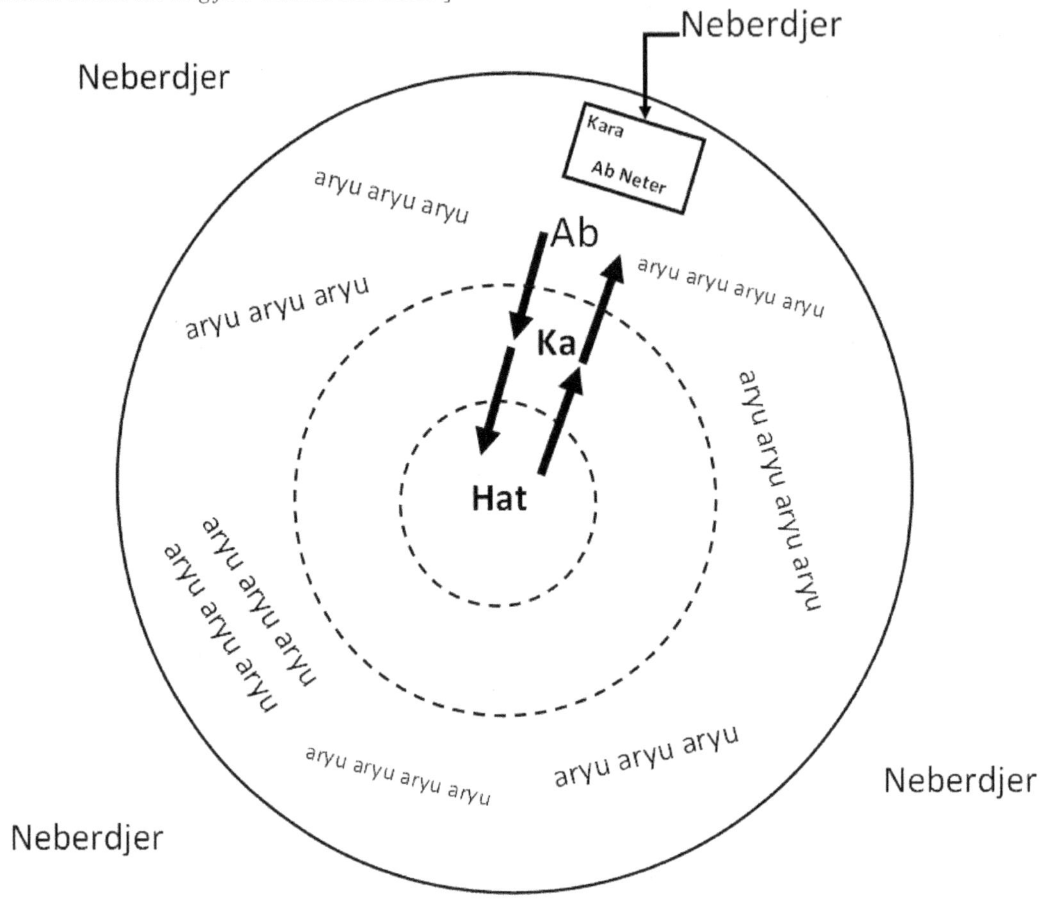

THE CONCENTRIC STRUCTURE: THREE LEVELS OF INDIVIDUAL MIND

The diagram employs concentric circles moving from innermost (most constricted) to outermost (unlimited), representing expanding levels of mind operating simultaneously within every human being:

1. Hat (Center Circle - Conscious Level)

Hat represents the conscious level of mind—the front-of-mind conscious awareness, what is presently in your immediate conscious attention. This is the most constricted, limited aspect of the mind: the narrow focus of "what I am aware of right now." Hat contains your current thoughts, immediate perceptions, and present moment awareness. This is the smallest circle because it represents the most limited, focused beam of awareness in the individual personality.

2. Ka (Middle Circle - Subconscious Level)

Ka represents the subconscious level—the astral body, broader conscious mind (not necessarily front-of-mind), including feelings, thoughts, desires, and the sum-total manifesting personality. The Ka encompasses more than Hat because it includes not just what you're currently aware of but all aspects of your personality, emotional patterns, mental habits, and psychological dispositions operating beneath immediate awareness. This is the realm of your character, temperament, and the broader mental-emotional patterns that influence awareness without always being in conscious focus (Hat level).

3. Ab (Outer Circle - Unconscious Level)

Ab represents the unconscious level—the deep mind where all life experiences are stored as aryu (karmic feeling-memories). This storehouse contains the vast repository of all accumulated impressions from past experiences, both from this life and potentially beyond, that shape personality and awareness without conscious recognition.

The mind operates in layers: the deeper regions (Ab/unconscious) function as locations for feeling storage, while the shallower regions (hat/conscious awareness) are where the images and events of memories manifest as thoughts. Significantly, these thought-images at the conscious level are often distorted by the feelings stored in the deeper Ab level, creating the conditioned perceptions that drive personality patterns. Thus, the deeper level of mind (with feelings) is the driving force behind the expressions (emotions) manifested in the conscious level of mind.

Operating completely beneath awareness, the Ab forms the deep substrate that conditions all mental activity through its accumulated karmic patterns, memories, and impressions.

4. Kara/Ab Neter (Deep Core Within Ab - The Divine Connection)

Shown in the callout box at the inner edge of the Ab layer is Kara—the divine sanctuary within the unconscious where Ab Neter resides. Ab Neter is the divine soul or spark, your "portion of Divine consciousness that sustains your capacity of conscious awareness." This is the foundation of individual consciousness, the god-within, dwelling in the deepest core of the unconscious mind (Ab).

The Kara/Ab Neter is directly connected to Neberdjer—this connection sustains consciousness at all three levels (unconscious, subconscious, and conscious). Without this connection through Ab Neter, there would be no consciousness operating at any level. The Kara/shrine of Ab Neter sits at the boundary between individual mind (Ab) and universal consciousness (Neberdjer), serving as the connection point and sustaining link.

5. Neberdjer (Outermost Circle - Infinite Universal Consciousness)

Neberdjer represents the all-encompassing divinity, Lord of utmost limits, the infinite universal consciousness that underlies, permeates, sustains, and encompasses all existence. Neberdjer is not merely another "layer" of mind but the ultimate source and substance of all consciousness—the absolute, infinite foundation from which individual consciousness emerges and by which it is sustained moment-by-moment.

-THE BOUNDARY LINES: Porous Inner Circles, Solid Outer Boundary

-The diagram uses two different line styles with profound significance:

-Dashed Lines (Hat, Ka, Ab) - Porous Boundaries

The dashed lines between Hat, Ka, and Ab represent porosity—these are not solid barriers but permeable boundaries allowing constant bidirectional movement between levels of individual mind. Awareness flows freely between these three levels because they are all aspects of the individual mind operating together.

Solid Line (Between Ab and Neberdjer) - The Boundary Between Individuality and the Absolute

The solid line forming the outermost circle represents the fundamental boundary between individual mind (Hat/Ka/Ab) and universal consciousness (Neberdjer). This is the boundary between individuality and the absolute—the threshold between:

- Limited personal existence and infinite impersonal Being
- Constricted individual awareness and unlimited universal consciousness
- The finite self and the infinite Self
- Time-bound conditioned mind and eternal unconditioned awareness

*Also, this represents the boundary between an individual mind and other individual minds. So individual minds are as if demarcated from each other, not directly connected to each other, but all are connected to Neberdjer. Therefore, all individual personalities are kin/relatives through their connection to Neberdjer (universal consciousness), which is the essence of all individual conscious-awareness.

This solid boundary represents the fundamental distinction that spiritual realization must transcend. The Kara/Ab Neter, positioned precisely at this boundary, serves as the connection point that makes crossing from individual mind to absolute consciousness possible through spiritual purification and divine grace.

THE BIDIRECTIONAL FLOW: Movement Between All Levels

The bidirectional arrow in the diagram (pointing both directions between Hat and Ab through Ka) illustrates the constant dynamic movement between all three levels of individual mind:

Inward Flow: Hat → Ka → Ab (Aryu Deposition)

Conscious experience creates unconscious patterns:
When Hat becomes conscious of a perception, thought, or feeling, this impression passes through the porous boundary into Ka (affecting and shaping the personality), then continues inward through to Ab where it becomes permanently recorded as aryu in the unconscious storehouse.

Hat (conscious experience) →
Ka (personality impact, emotional-mental patterning) →
Ab (aryu formation, unconscious storage)

This is the mechanism of karmic pattern formation. The quality of what passes through determines the type of aryu deposited:

• Egoistic individualistic aryu: Engaging with heated persons, entertaining negative thoughts, dwelling on selfish desires, reactive emotions → deposits patterns reinforcing separate self-identity, heated mind and feelings, worldly attachments, agitation

• Godward aryu: Practicing virtue, contemplating divine teachings, engaging ethical conduct, spiritual discipline, devotional practices → deposits patterns supporting spiritual development, silent mind and feelings, divine recognition, serenity (*Ger*)

Outward Flow: Ab → Ka → Hat (Aryu Influence on Awareness)

Unconscious patterns shape conscious experience:
Aryu patterns stored in Ab influence Ka (activating personality dispositions, emotional reactions, mental habits), which then influence what arises in Hat (conscious awareness), which then expresses through the senses into external action in the world.

Ab (unconscious aryu patterns activated) →
Ka (personality dispositions arise, emotional-mental states generated) →
Hat (conscious thoughts, feelings, perceptions emerge) →
Senses/World (external expression and action)

This explains why we have automatic reactions, ingrained habits, recurring thought-feeling patterns, and seemingly involuntary mental-emotional states—these arise from aryu stored in Ab, operating through Ka, before we become consciously aware of them in Hat. The unconscious patterns condition what appears in conscious awareness.

The Continuous Cycle

This bidirectional flow creates a continuous cycle:

• Conscious experiences (Hat) deposit as unconscious patterns (Ab)
• Unconscious patterns (Ab) condition conscious experiences (Hat)
• Each conscious experience reinforces existing patterns or creates new ones
• The personality (Ka) serves as the intermediary, being both shaped by and expressing these dynamics

This is why transformation requires both:

1. Conscious discipline (controlling what enters through Hat)
2. Purification (thinning existing aryu density in Ab)

THE ENERGETIC DIMENSION: SEKHEM AND METTU

The wisdom tradition teaches that Sekhem represents the vital life energy—that animating power which sustains all living beings and serves as the bridge connecting physical existence with spiritual reality. Consider how this Egyptian understanding parallels what Indian philosophy terms Prana and what Chinese tradition names Qi (Chi)—all pointing toward the same profound truth: there exists a subtle, universal energy flowing through and vitalizing all existence. Indeed, when we examine the Egyptian concept of Mettu (the channels or pathways through which Sekhem circulates within the body), we discover remarkable correspondence with the Nadis of Indian yogic physiology and the

Meridians of traditional Chinese medicine. These represent systems of energetic conduits that maintain physical health and spiritual balance when this life force moves freely through them, unobstructed by the density of aryu that can impede its natural flow.

The wisdom to be understood here extends beyond anatomical mapping. Sekhem represents more than mere biological vitality—it constitutes the divine energy emanating from Neberdjer (the All-encompassing Divinity) that sustains not only physical life but also the capacity for conscious awareness itself. When the Mettu channels remain open and the Sekhem flows unimpeded, the aspirant experiences not only physical well-being (as addressed in Prologue verse 2's goal of earthly well-being) but also the energetic clarity necessary for penetrating from Hat awareness through the ab level to discover the Ab Neter residing in the kara (fulfilling Prologue verse 9's goal of discovering divinity within). Conversely, when aryu density obstructs these pathways, the heated mind and feelings arise, creating the experience of separation from divine vitality that characterizes spiritual ignorance. This understanding reveals the profound interconnection between spiritual purification and physical health—as aryu obstruction manifests not only in heated mind and feelings but also affects the physical body itself, demonstrating that the ancient wisdom recognized the inseparable unity of spirit, mind, and flesh within the totality of human existence. Indeed, this holistic recognition extended to the mechanics of obstruction itself: the ancient sages understood that energetic blockages create cascading effects throughout the entire human system—from the subtle Mettu channels to the grosser physical vessels—revealing their sophisticated understanding that consciousness, energy, and physical matter operate as an integrated whole rather than separate domains.

This understanding proves crucial for the aspirant, as the practices Amenemopet teaches—ethical living, meditation, wisdom absorption—work not merely at the psychological level but also at the energetic level, gradually purifying the Mettu channels and allowing Sekhem to flow with increasing freedom, thereby supporting both physical health and the mind/personality transformation necessary for enlightenment.

NEBERDJER MAINTAINS ALL CONSCIOUSNESS

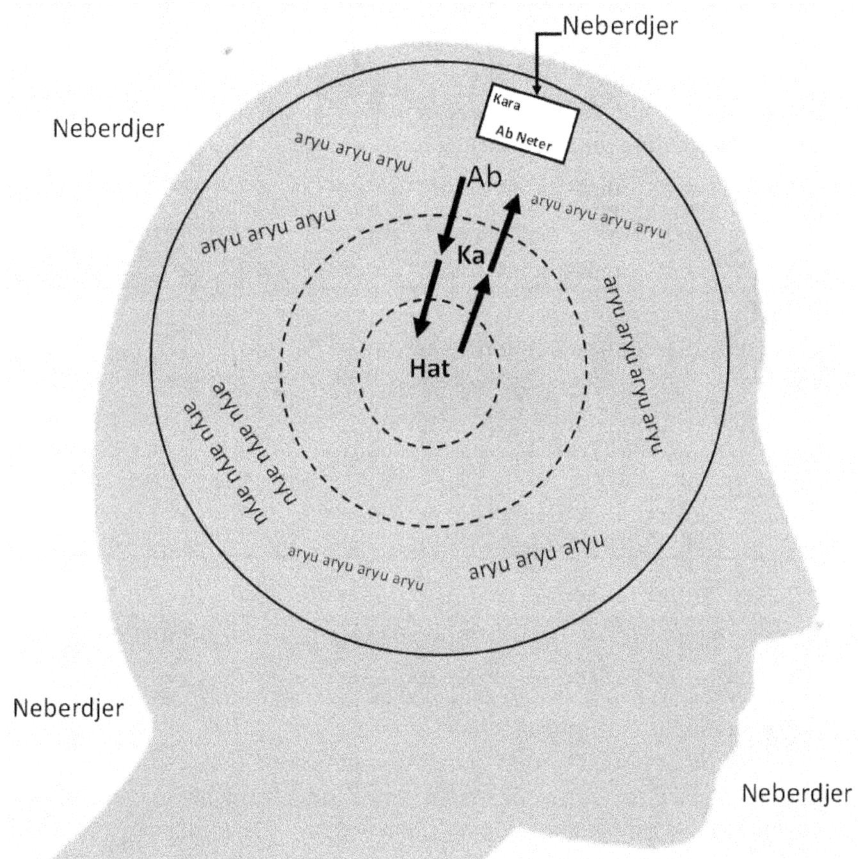

Figure 7: Same concentric circles diagram superimposed on a human head silhouette in profile, showing how the consciousness structure exists within the individual. The Ancient Egyptian mind diagram fills the head area with Neberdjer extending beyond it, illustrating that universal consciousness encompasses the individual.

The diagram illustrates the crucial teaching that Neberdjer (consciousness) sustains awareness in the mind through the connection via Kara/Ab Neter:

Infinite Neberdjer (universal consciousness) →
Connects through Kara/Ab Neter (divine spark in deep unconscious) →
Sustains Ab (unconscious level) →
Sustains Ka (subconscious level) →
Sustains Hat (conscious level)

Neberdjer Doesn't Just "Surround"—It interpenetrates, is what all is composed of, and it sustains all.

Neberdjer is not merely an outer layer surrounding individual mind. Rather, Neberdjer is the fundamental reality that encompasses and is the substratum of which mind is composed and that sustains the very capacity for consciousness to exist at all levels. The Ab Neter/Kara serves as the connection point through which this sustaining power flows. Without the connection through Ab Neter, there would be no awareness at Hat, Ka, or Ab levels.

This is why Ab Neter is called "the portion of Divine consciousness that sustains capacity of conscious awareness"—it is the conduit connecting individual consciousness to its infinite source. Individual mind is not self-generating or independently existing but rather a constricted portion of infinite Neberdjer, sustained moment-by-moment through the Ab Neter connection, like a ray of light emanating from the sun while remaining connected to its source.

The Positioning of Kara/Ab Neter

The placement of Kara/Ab Neter at the inner edge of the Ab layer, right at the boundary with Neberdjer, is profoundly significant:

- It sits at the deepest level of individual mind (the core of Ab)
- It sits at the boundary with universal consciousness (touching Neberdjer)
- It serves as the connection point between individual mind and absolute consciousness
- It represents the divine spark within that is simultaneously individual (your Ab Neter) and universal (connected to Neberdjer)

THE SPIRITUAL PREDICAMENT: ARYU OBSTRUCTION BLOCKING RECOGNITION

The diagram reveals the fundamental spiritual predicament of human existence:

Although Ab Neter connects to Neberdjer and sustains all consciousness, dense aryu stored in the surface levels of Ab obscure this reality from Hat's awareness.

The teaching states that aryu "occupy the presence-of-mind awareness so densely as to blot out the awareness of the soul level divine presence which is deeper than the aryu."

Hat Operates Driven by Aryu WITHOUT Awareness of Ab Neter

This creates the condition of spiritual ignorance:

- Individual conscious-awareness (Hat) remains identified with the limited individual self (body, personality, thoughts)
- Unaware of the divine spark (Ab Neter) within the deep unconscious
- Unaware of connection to infinite consciousness (Neberdjer)
- Believes itself separate, incomplete, limited to the constricted circles
- Experiences existential anxiety, seeking fulfillment in external objects and relationships
- Operates from egoistic aryu patterns that reinforce this limited identification

The person lives entirely within the three inner circles (Hat/Ka/Ab surface), completely unaware that:

- Ab Neter resides in the Kara at the core of their own unconscious
- This Ab Neter is directly connected to Neberdjer
- Their consciousness is sustained by infinite consciousness
- They are not separate from but rather a constricted expression of the absolute

THE SPIRITUAL SOLUTION: PURIFICATION REVEALING WHAT IS ALWAYS PRESENT

The diagram illustrates that spiritual practice is NOT about creating access to something absent but about removing aryu obstruction to REVEAL Ab Neter already present and recognize the Neberdjer connection already sustaining everything. The Path of Purification:

Through ethical living, spiritual practice, and purification:

- Egoistic aryu density in Ab gradually thins
- Godward aryu patterns strengthen
- Hat's awareness can penetrate deeper through the porous boundaries
- Recognition of Ab Neter in Kara becomes possible
- Understanding of connection to Neberdjer emerges
- The mind expands from identification with constricted individual patterns to recognition of infinite nature

The Inward Spiritual Penetration. The journey of spiritual realization follows the path inward through the levels:

Hat (purified awareness through ethics and discipline) →
Ka (purified personality through virtue and devotion) →
Ab surface (thinned aryu through persistent practice) →
Kara/Ab Neter (divine spark recognized through grace) →
Neberdjer (infinite consciousness realized as true nature)

At each stage, the porosity of the boundaries allows awareness of the individual to penetrate deeper when aryu density thins sufficiently. The final crossing—from Ab Neter through the solid boundary to conscious recognition of Neberdjer—represents spiritual enlightenment, the realization of one's essential nature as infinite consciousness.

THE TEACHING: CONSTRICTED PORTION OF INFINITE CONSCIOUSNESS

The concentric circles powerfully illustrate Amenemopet's core teaching:

Individual human mind (Hat, Ka, Ab) represents a constricted, limited portion of infinite divine consciousness (Neberdjer), sustained through the Ab Neter connection. Not Creation but recognition:

The goal of spiritual practice is expanding awareness from the constricted center (individual limited mind) to recognize the infinite reality (Neberdjer) that:

- Already encompasses everything
- Already sustains all levels through Ab Neter
- Has always been one's true nature
- Was never absent, only obscured by aryu density

Purification doesn't create divinity—it reveals what aryu have been hiding. The diagram shows this is not about "going somewhere" or "becoming something new" but about recognizing what already is:

- Awareness expanding from identification with the smallest circle (Hat - immediate awareness)
- Through recognition of larger circles (Ka - personality, Ab - unconscious patterns)

- To ultimate recognition of the infinite foundation (Neberdjer - universal consciousness)
- That was always sustaining everything through the connection via Ab Neter in Kara

The spiritual journey is paradoxical:

- Moving inward through the circles (Hat → Ka → Ab → Kara/Ab Neter)
- To recognize what encompasses everything (Neberdjer)
- Discovering that the deepest within (Ab Neter) connects to the infinite beyond (Neberdjer)
- Realizing that "within" and "beyond" are ultimately one reality

PRACTICAL IMPLICATIONS: LIVING WITH THIS UNDERSTANDING

This diagram provides practical guidance for spiritual life:

1. Guard What Enters Hat (Conscious Awareness)

Since Hat → Ka → Ab flow deposits aryu:

- Be judicious with thoughts entertained
- Control the tongue (speech creates mental impressions)
- Avoid association with heated persons (their emanations contaminate)
- Engage ethical conduct, spiritual study, devotional practice
- Choose godward aryu formation over egoistic aryu formation

2. Understand Automatic Patterns Arise From Ab

Since Ab → Ka → Hat flow conditions experience:

- Recognize reactive thoughts/feelings arise from unconscious aryu
- Don't identify with automatic mental-emotional patterns
- Understand these are conditioned responses, not your true nature
- Practice witnessing rather than identifying with what arises in Hat

3. Purify Through Systematic Practice

To thin aryu density allowing penetration to Ab Neter:

- Consistent ethical living (prevents new egoistic aryu deposition)
- Spiritual disciplines (deposits godward aryu, weakens egoistic patterns)
- Meditation and contemplation (develops capacity to penetrate deeper)
- Devotion and surrender (invokes grace for final crossing to Neberdjer)

4. Remember the Sustaining Connection

Living with awareness that:

- Your capacity for awareness is sustained by Neberdjer through Ab Neter
- You are not separate but a constricted portion of infinite consciousness
- The divine is not distant but at the core of your own being
- Purification reveals rather than creates this reality

SUMMARY: THE COMPLETE MODEL

This diagram presents Amenemopet's model of consciousness:

Three levels of individual mind:
- Hat (conscious - front-of-mind awareness)
- Ka (subconscious - personality, feelings, broader mind)
- Ab (unconscious - aryu storehouse with Ab Neter/Kara at the core)

Porous boundaries between individual levels:
- Constant bidirectional flow
- Inward: conscious experience → unconscious aryu
- Outward: unconscious aryu → conscious experience

Solid boundary between individual mind and absolute consciousness:
- The threshold between limited self and infinite Self
- Crossed through purification and divine grace
- Ab Neter/Kara positioned at this boundary as connection point

Neberdjer as sustaining foundation:
- Not merely surrounding but actively sustaining
- Awareness in mind depends on Ab Neter connection to Neberdjer
- Individual mind is constricted portion of infinite consciousness

The spiritual path:
- Remove aryu obstruction through purification
- Penetrate inward through progressively deeper levels
- Recognize Ab Neter at the core of unconscious
- Realize connection to Neberdjer
- Expand from identification with constricted individual mind to recognition of infinite nature

The ultimate teaching:
- What you seek is already present (Ab Neter within, Neberdjer sustaining)
- Spiritual practice reveals rather than creates
- You are not separate from but an expression of infinite consciousness
- The boundary between individuality and the absolute can be transcended
- Your true nature is Neberdjer—vast, infinite, eternal

This diagram serves as a map of consciousness for spiritual seekers, showing both the structure of mind and the path of transformation from ignorance to enlightenment, from constricted individual awareness to recognition of infinite divine consciousness as one's true nature.

CHAPTER 19: Commentary on Teachings of Amenemopet Chapter 13: The Glorification of Love Versus the Illusion of Power Verses 11-12

SUMMARY OF TEACHINGS

Chapter 13 presents a profound teaching on what truly glorifies the human personality: being loved, praised, and revered by people—family, community, and country—versus having power over storehouses of wealth without respect or appreciation. The teaching employs the term "akh" (glorifying/glorious), referencing the effulgent divine consciousness aspect of the spiritual body, to acknowledge the legitimate human need for love and appreciation during spiritual development from ignorance toward enlightenment. Amenemopet reveals that many people prefer power and wealth even if hated, demonstrating profound corruption where the mind values domination over storehouse objects more than the respect and love of others—a reversal that indicates complete disconnection from Ab Neter and immersion in heated mind and feelings.

1. HUMAN PSYCHOLOGY PRINCIPLE FOCUS OF CHAPTER 13

Human Psychology Principle: The fundamental need for genuine human connection versus the compensatory pursuit of power and wealth that arises from forgetting divine fulfillment

Chapter 13 addresses the core psychological reality that human beings possess a legitimate developmental need to be loved, appreciated, and valued by others—what the teaching identifies through the term "akh" (glorifying), referencing the part of the spiritual body that constitutes "effulgent divine consciousness...that sustains and operates as subtlest aspect of human consciousness."[1] This need operates as "an important part of human development from the perspective of a person growing up from a standpoint of spiritual ignorance in ordinary normal human development."[1] The wisdom recognizes that the mind developing from ignorance naturally seeks validation, appreciation, and connection with others as part of healthy psychological maturation.

CROSS-REFERENCE: THE FOUNDATIONAL PRACTICE LEADING TO CHAPTER 13'S GLORIFICATION

The Foundation: Chapter 8 XI Verse 1 as the Practice Generating Chapter 13's Outcome

Chapter 13, verse 11's teaching on the glorification of being loved, praised, and revered by people does not emerge in isolation but represents the natural consequence of a foundational practice established earlier in Amenemopet's systematic instruction. Chapter 8 XI, verse 1 provides this crucial foundation: "by you're doing love to people, instead of harm, they love you. By giving consideration people reciprocate with consideration" [1]. This verse reveals the reciprocal mechanism whereby the ethical conduct Amenemopet prescribes throughout his teaching generates the very love and respect that Chapter 13 identifies as glorifying to the soul.

The wisdom to be understood recognizes a profound causal relationship between these teachings: Chapter 8 XI, verse 1 presents the PRACTICE—doing love and giving consideration to people—while Chapter 13, verse 11 describes the OUTCOME—being loved, praised, and revered by family, community, and country. The former represents the behavioral imperative arising from recognizing all people as manifestations of Neberdjer deserving according respect, while the latter identifies the natural result when such recognition manifests consistently through one's conduct.

This connection illuminates why Amenemopet emphasizes that genuine glorification emerges from being "loved/praised/revered/honored/liked by the people" rather than from power over storehouses of wealth. The love and respect others offer arises not through manipulation, strategic positioning, or domination, but through the authentic caring and consideration one extends to them. When the mind operates from the recognition taught in Chapter 8 XI—that caring for others represents caring for extensions of the same Neberdjer that sustains all existence—the reciprocal dynamic naturally produces the respect and appreciation that glorifies the personality.

Moreover, Chapter 8 XI, verse 2 reveals the deeper purpose enabling this practice: "by doing good to others and having peaceful relations with others, you will be able to have inner peace that will allow you to make real and effective effort towards finding yourself a place, to make yourself an abode in the inner part of the temple of God" [1]. This establishes that doing love to people serves not merely to receive their praise but to create the inner peace necessary for discovering the divine within the kara. The glorification described in Chapter 13, verse 11 thus represents both an immediate benefit (the genuine respect and love of others supporting continued service) and evidence that the mind has established sufficient ethical foundation to pursue the deeper work of Ab Neter discovery.

The teaching reveals that the silent person who receives genuine love and respect from others does not seek such recognition as validation of ego-worth but receives it as natural byproduct of operating from Ab Neter awareness rather than heated mind and feelings. The practice of "doing love to people" emerges not from strategic calculation about how to be praised but from authentic recognition of shared divine foundation. When this authentic caring manifests consistently, the reciprocal dynamic Chapter 8 XI, verse 1 describes operates naturally—consideration generates consideration, love generates love, and the personality becomes genuinely glorified through the respect and appreciation others freely offer.

This stands in stark contrast to the corrupted psychology Chapter 13, verse 12 identifies—pursuing power over storehouse wealth regardless of whether such pursuit generates contempt rather than respect. That pattern represents the heated mind operating from ego-separation, believing that domination and accumulation provide security and worth. Chapter 8 XI's teaching on reciprocal ethics reveals why such pursuit proves futile for generating genuine glorification: when the mind treats others as objects to be exploited or obstacles to be dominated, the natural reciprocal response involves fear, resentment, or contempt rather than authentic love and respect.

Therefore, aspirants seeking to implement Chapter 13's teaching must first establish the foundational practice Chapter 8 XI, verse 1 prescribes: doing love to people, giving consideration, recognizing all as manifestations of Neberdjer deserving respect. This practice, maintained consistently through time, generates the natural outcome of being genuinely loved and respected—the glorification that supports continued service while creating the inner peace necessary for discovering the divine sanctuary within.

End of cross-reference.

==

However, the teaching distinguishes between this legitimate developmental need (and its pathological intensification into constant validation-seeking or dominance seeking due to trauma or poor upbringing) and the corrupted psychology wherein the mind abandons the quest for love and respect, instead pursuing power over storehouses of wealth regardless of whether such pursuit generates hatred or contempt from others. This represents a fundamental perversion of natural human psychology wherein the mind, having "forgotten Neberdjer," begins to "imbue objects with power over the personality—the power to make you happy or sad based on your capacity to possess them."[2] The hat (conscious awareness) becomes fixated on accumulation and domination as compensatory mechanisms for the unfulfilled deeper need for divine communion and genuine human connection.

The Inverse Doctrine Methodology application reveals another pathological extreme: the individual mind requiring constant adulation due to absence of healthy self-regard, often arising from trauma or negative upbringing. This compulsive dependency can intensify to narcissistic patterns—always needing to be right, fighting against disagreement, seeking perpetual praise—representing such dense aryu that no external validation suffices to establish stable self-respect. Cognitive deficit can also be an issue. This pathological extreme is explored thoroughly in the Special Topics essay on narcissistic consciousness patterns.

The profound psychological issue reveals itself in verse 12's teaching that love and praise of people proves better than "having power over an overflowing storehouse of objects (wealth/hoarding/not sharing)."[3] Many people, as the Keys document explains, "prefer power and wealth to respect and love and praise, they don't care if they are hated as long as they retain power and wealth."[1] This demonstrates the mind operating from such dense aryu accumulation that it has inverted natural priorities—valuing the capacity to dominate material resources over the authentic human connections that provide genuine fulfillment. Moreover, the teaching identifies how "some corrupted people revere them for their power and wealth and want to emulate them cause they themselves have corrupted minds causing them to revere corrupted leaders of society—business, religious, government etc. even when those leaders use their power and wealth against their supporters—showing how degraded and humiliated the followers are—no dignity or self-respect."[1]

Connection to Prologue Goals:

This psychological principle directly impacts both Prologue goals. Without recognizing the legitimate need for genuine human connection while simultaneously understanding that ultimate fulfillment derives from Ab Neter awareness rather than external validation, the goal of Prologue verse 2 to "cause a person to have well-being while living on earth"[4] cannot be achieved. The mind that abandons relationship in favor of power accumulation experiences isolation and contempt that prevent earthly well-being, while the mind that seeks fulfillment through others' approval without discovering internal divine completeness remains trapped in dependency. More profoundly, this principle obstructs Prologue verse 9's discovery of the kara "where the Divine resides in every person"[4] because both extremes—power-seeking and validation-seeking—create aryu patterns that prevent recognition of the Ab Neter that already provides from within, prior to the fulfillment the mind seeks through external means.

2. Behavioral Imperatives of this Chapter

Behavioral Imperative: Observable patterns of power accumulation, wealth hoarding, and corrupted reverence that manifest when the mind becomes individuated (ego) and forgets its divine nature

The behavioral manifestations of Chapter 13's psychological principle reveal themselves through specific patterns that demonstrate the mind operating in profound disconnection from both authentic human relationship and divine awareness. The teaching identifies the primary behavioral corruption: the mind that prioritizes "power over an overflowing storehouse of objects" while abandoning concern for being "loved/praised/revered/honored/liked by the people."[3] This manifests in contemporary contexts as individuals who accumulate wealth and resources compulsively while remaining indifferent to—or actively cultivating—fear, resentment, and contempt from those around them.

Consider the modern executive who implements policies that impoverish employees while enriching themselves, or the business owner who hoards resources during crisis while workers struggle. Each demonstrates the mind that values domination over material storehouses more than genuine community respect. This operates through having "forgotten Neberdjer. You who essentially are the owner or embodier of everything that exists claim that some small thing will affect you, make you happy, satisfy you."[2] This fundamental forgetting produces seeking power as a substitute for lost divine fulfillment.

The behavioral corruption intensifies through what the teaching describes as insatiable desire: "Even though no one has ever been abidingly satisfied by acquiring anything in the world—ever—you've come to believe otherwise."[2] The lecture transcript provides the vivid example: "people who are working on Wall Street...made a billion dollars but then they have to make another billion dollars...one gets a 100 ft yacht and then he realizes somebody in the next company gets a 120 ft yacht and then he feels bad, he has to get a 150ft yacht and there's no end to desires."[2] This behavioral pattern demonstrates the mind trapped in comparative acquisition wherein no level of wealth provides satisfaction because the underlying issue—disconnection from Neberdjer awareness—remains unaddressed.

The teaching identifies a particularly disturbing behavioral manifestation: corrupted followers who revere corrupted leaders specifically for their power and wealth, even when those leaders actively harm their supporters.[1] This pattern reveals the mind so densely packed with aryu that it has lost all capacity for dignity and self-respect, instead projecting reverence onto external power as if domination over material resources constitutes genuine accomplishment worthy of admiration. The behavior manifests in modern contexts as individuals who celebrate wealth accumulated through exploitation, who admire business leaders specifically for their ruthlessness, who aspire to emulate those who demonstrate contempt for ethical principles in pursuit of profit.

Nevertheless, the teaching frames these behavioral patterns with compassionate understanding, recognizing them as arising from the fundamental condition wherein "encrusted ego is in diametric opposition to Neberdjer. So you have shut out Neberdjer so much, Neberdjer the understanding of your Higher Self, so you can become an encrusted point that is separate from everything else."[2] The behaviors emerge not from conscious malevolence but from the progressive thickening of aryu that creates an increasingly rigid sense of separate self requiring ever-greater accumulation and domination to maintain the illusion of security and significance. Each act of choosing power over love, wealth over respect, domination over connection deposits additional aryu that reinforce the behavioral patterns, creating self-perpetuating cycles that move the mind progressively further from the possibility of genuine fulfillment through Ab Neter recognition.

3. Mystic Psychology—Metaphysical Implications: The Nature of Akh and the Forgetting of Neberdjer

The metaphysical framework underlying Chapter 13's teaching reveals profound principles about the nature of consciousness, the relationship between individual awareness and divine essence, and how forgetting Neberdjer creates the illusory pursuit of fulfillment through external power and validation. Understanding these mechanics illuminates why love proves superior to power at consciousness architecture level and how spiritual development transforms this fundamental orientation.

The Nature of Akh: Effulgent Divine Consciousness

The teaching's use of "akh" (glorifying/glorious) references a specific aspect of the spiritual body in Ancient Egyptian understanding—what the Keys document identifies as "effulgent divine consciousness...that sustains and operates as subtlest aspect of human consciousness."[1][10] This represents not the physical body or even the subtle astral body (ka) but rather the luminous consciousness aspect that reflects divine nature. The metaphysical significance: genuine glorification of the personality occurs not through accumulation of external validation or material power but through consciousness recognizing and expressing its essential nature as effulgent divine awareness.

The teaching acknowledges that during spiritual development from ignorance, the need to be "loved/praised/revered/honored/liked by the people" operates as legitimate developmental stage.[1] From the metaphysical perspective, this represents consciousness in its constricted individuated state naturally seeking external reflection of the divine love and appreciation that it has temporarily forgotten resides within as Ab Neter. The child requiring parental love, the youth seeking peer acceptance, the adult desiring community respect—these developmental needs reflect consciousness attempting to experience through external relationships the recognition and value that ultimately can only be discovered through internal divine awareness.

However, the metaphysical framework distinguishes this natural developmental need from the pathological dependency wherein consciousness requires constant external validation to maintain stable self-regard. The Keys document explains that evolved beings "do not need such appreciations as they have discovered fulfillment from divine awareness in Neberdjer."[1] This transition represents consciousness expanding from identification with the limited separate self (which desperately needs external confirmation of its worth because it has lost awareness of divine essence) to recognition of Ab Neter (which requires no external validation because it knows itself as portion of infinite Neberdjer).

The Forgetting of Neberdjer: Metaphysical Root of Power-Seeking

The teaching identifies the metaphysical mechanism underlying the preference for power over love: "You have forgotten Neberdjer. You who essentially are the owner or embodier of everything that exists claim that some small thing will affect you, make you happy, satisfy you."[2] This forgetting represents the fundamental metaphysical predicament wherein consciousness loses awareness that it is not a separate limited entity but rather a constricted expression of infinite universal consciousness that already embodies all apparent objects.

From the absolute perspective, consciousness as Neberdjer literally constitutes the substance of all manifestation. Individual consciousness represents temporary constriction of this infinite awareness, like a wave appearing separate from the ocean while remaining ocean-substance throughout. When this truth becomes obscured by thick aryu density, consciousness experiences itself as fundamentally separate entity that must acquire external objects and power to achieve fulfillment. The lecture transcript captures this delusion: "you've come to believe" that objects can satisfy despite "no one has ever been abidingly satisfied by acquiring anything in the world—ever."[2]

The power-seeking pattern emerges as compensatory mechanism for this forgetting. Consciousness that has lost awareness of itself as "owner or embodier of everything that exists" attempts to recreate that sense of completeness through domination over limited material resources. The business magnate accumulating storehouses, the political leader hoarding power, the wealthy individual displaying possessions—each demonstrates consciousness attempting to experience through external control the mastery and completeness that actually represents its essential divine nature but has become inaccessible due to aryu obstruction.

The metaphysical teaching reveals that this pursuit proves inherently futile because external accumulation cannot address internal forgetting. No amount of power over storehouses can restore awareness of oneself as Neberdjer—the consciousness that already embodies all apparent objects. This explains the insatiable quality the teaching describes: "one gets a 100 ft yacht...somebody in the next company gets a 120 ft yacht...he has to get a 150ft yacht and there's no end to desires."[2] The desires prove endless because they arise from metaphysical misunderstanding—attempting to satisfy through external acquisition what can only be fulfilled through internal recognition.

The Encrusted Ego: Metaphysical Structure of Separate-Self

The lecture describes the metaphysical condition underlying power-seeking as "encrusted ego...in diametric opposition to Neberdjer."[2] This represents consciousness so densely packed with aryu that it has crystallized into rigid separate-self identity—what the teaching calls "an encrusted point that is separate from everything else."[2] The metaphysical mechanics: each thought, feeling, and action arising from the delusion of separateness deposits aryu in the ab that reinforce separate-self identification. Over time, these accumulated patterns create such density that consciousness becomes imprisoned within extremely constricted boundaries, experiencing itself as fundamentally isolated entity requiring constant defense, expansion, and validation.

This encrusted condition operates "in diametric opposition to Neberdjer" because it represents the maximum possible constriction of consciousness—from infinite universal awareness to rigidly defined separate point perceiving all else as threatening or useful objects. From this metaphysical state, other beings appear not as fellow expressions of the same Neberdjer consciousness but as independent entities, objects separate from oneself and competitors for limited resources or sources of validation. The capacity for genuine love—which requires recognizing shared divine essence—becomes impossible because consciousness identifies completely with the encrusted separate-self rather than the Ab Neter connecting all beings.

The teaching's compassionate framework recognizes this encrustation arises not from conscious choice but from progressive aryu accumulation operating below awareness. The individual pursuing power while generating contempt typically does not recognize themselves as operating from encrusted ego in opposition to divine nature—from their perspective, they simply pursue what appears as success and security within a world of separate competing entities. The metaphysical insight: this very perception represents the problem, the fundamental forgetting that creates the entire syndrome of power-seeking over love-receiving.

Love Superior to Power: Metaphysical Reality

The teaching that being "loved/praised/revered/honored/liked by the people" proves superior to "having power over an overflowing storehouse" rests on profound metaphysical truth.[3] Genuine human love and respect—when arising from authentic connection rather than fear or manipulation—reflects consciousness recognizing shared divine nature. To be truly loved means to be seen, appreciated, and valued as the expression of Neberdjer that one actually is. This external recognition, while not necessary for the fully enlightened who already know themselves as divine, supports consciousness in its journey from ignorance toward recognition by providing temporary reflection of the essential worth that will eventually be discovered internally.

Power over storehouses, conversely, represents consciousness attempting to find fulfillment through domination and control—mechanisms that arise from and reinforce the fundamental forgetting of divine nature. The metaphysical teaching: consciousness pursuing power moves away from truth (recognizing itself as Neberdjer embodying all existence) toward deeper delusion (identifying as separate entity requiring accumulation). Consciousness receiving genuine love moves, however tentatively and temporarily, toward recognition of shared divine essence even while still operating from relative ignorance.

The ultimate metaphysical implication: spiritual development requires transitioning from dependency on external love to recognition of internal Ab Neter, but this transition naturally flows through appreciation of genuine human connection rather than through pursuit of power. The path leads from external validation (love received) to internal recognition (Ab Neter awareness), not through accumulation and domination which reinforce the separate-self delusion that prevents spiritual development altogether.

4. Transpersonal Psychology Research: Empirical Validation of Relationship Superiority Over Wealth

Contemporary psychological research provides substantial empirical validation for the ancient teaching's framework identifying genuine human connection as superior to power and wealth accumulation for achieving well-being and fulfillment. While modern science cannot directly measure Ab Neter recognition or Neberdjer awareness, it documents psychological and physiological correlates corresponding to what the teaching describes as the difference between love-receiving and power-seeking orientations.

Research on Materialism and Well-being

Extensive research demonstrates that individuals with strong materialistic values—prioritizing wealth accumulation, status display, and power over resources—show significantly reduced well-being compared to those emphasizing intrinsic values like relationship quality and personal growth. Studies document that materialistic orientations correlate with lower life satisfaction, reduced happiness, increased anxiety and depression, poorer relationship quality, and diminished sense of meaning in life.[5][9] This empirical finding validates the teaching's identification that pursuing "power over an overflowing storehouse" undermines rather than supports genuine well-being.[3]

Longitudinal research tracking individuals over time reveals that increased materialism predicts decreased well-being, while decreased materialism predicts increased well-being—supporting causality rather than mere correlation.[5] Brain imaging studies show that materialistic individuals display reduced activation in regions associated with intrinsic satisfaction and increased activation in areas related to anxiety and insecurity, providing neurological correlate for the teaching's description of consciousness that has "forgotten Neberdjer" experiencing perpetual dissatisfaction despite accumulation.[2]

Research on Social Connection and Health

Psychological and medical research demonstrates that quality of social relationships constitutes one of the strongest predictors of both psychological well-being and physical health—effects that remain significant even after controlling for wealth, status, and material resources. Studies document that individuals with strong social connections show lower rates of anxiety and depression, higher life satisfaction, better stress resilience, and even longer lifespans compared to socially isolated individuals regardless of economic status.[7][9]

Neuroscience research reveals that social rejection and exclusion activate the same neural pain circuits as physical injury, while social acceptance and appreciation activate reward and pleasure systems, providing a biological mechanism for the teaching's identification that being "loved/praised/revered" by people constitutes genuine need rather than mere preference.[1][7] Research demonstrates that chronic social isolation produces physiological stress responses similar to ongoing threat—elevated cortisol, inflammatory markers, weakened immune function—validating the teaching that pursuing power while generating contempt creates profound suffering despite material accumulation.[7]

Research on Wealth and Happiness Limitations

Economic psychology research reveals what the teaching identifies: material accumulation beyond genuine needs produces minimal increases in well-being while consuming resources and energy that could support relationship development and spiritual practice. Studies show that while income increases predict higher life satisfaction up to the level meeting basic needs, further increases produce progressively smaller well-being effects, with research suggesting a threshold beyond which additional wealth provides negligible benefit to daily emotional experience.[8]

Research on "hedonic adaptation" demonstrates the mechanism underlying the teaching's description of insatiable desire—individuals rapidly adapt to increased material circumstances, requiring ever-greater accumulation to maintain even baseline satisfaction levels, precisely matching the yacht example the teaching provides.[2][6] Brain imaging studies show that anticipation of material acquisition produces stronger neural activation than actual acquisition, creating perpetual seeking without lasting fulfillment—neurological correlate for consciousness that has "forgotten" that it already "essentially is the owner or embodier of everything that exists."[2]

Research on Intrinsic Motivation and Authenticity

Self-determination theory research demonstrates that individuals whose motivations align with intrinsic values (relationship, growth, meaning) show higher well-being, better psychological health, and greater life satisfaction compared to those motivated primarily by extrinsic values (wealth, status, power).[9] Research shows that pursuing extrinsic goals predicts not only lower well-being but also behaviors that undermine relationship quality—competition over cooperation, status-seeking over authentic connection, self-promotion over genuine service.[5][9]

Research on authentic self-expression reveals that individuals able to behave consistently with internal values while receiving social acceptance for their authentic selves show highest well-being, while those who achieve social approval through inauthentic presentation or accumulate power while hiding their genuine nature show elevated stress and reduced satisfaction despite external success.[9] This validates the teaching's framework that genuine love and respect from others (reflecting authentic appreciation rather than fear-based deference) supports development more than power accumulation that generates resentment.

5. Spiritual Implications for Aspirants

Part A: Pastoral Concerns—Modern Challenges to Valuing Love Over Power

Contemporary aspirants attempting to implement Chapter 13's teaching face systematic obstacles created by economic systems, cultural narratives, and social structures that promote power and wealth accumulation while devaluing genuine human connection and community respect.

The Cultural Glorification of Power

Modern capitalist culture systematically promotes the very inversion Amenemopet identifies as corruption: glorifying power and wealth regardless of whether such accumulation generates respect or contempt. Media celebrates billionaires regardless of exploitation involved in wealth creation; business schools teach maximizing shareholder value over stakeholder well-being; political systems reward campaign funding capacity over community service; social media platforms engineer envy of others' material displays. The aspirant attempting to prioritize genuine human connection over power accumulation encounters cultural messages declaring such orientation as naïve, unrealistic, or representing failure.

Someone choosing career paths that serve community needs over maximizing income faces judgment as lacking ambition. The individual who lives simply while cultivating relationships may be pitied as "not reaching their potential." The business owner who prioritizes employee well-being over profit maximization risks being seen as incompetent. These cultural narratives create constant pressure to pursue the very power-over-love orientation the teaching identifies as corrupted, making implementation of verse 12's wisdom feel like swimming against a powerful current.

The Isolation of Modern Life

Contemporary social structures have systematically dismantled the family and community connections that historically provided the love, praise, and respect the teaching identifies as glorifying. Economic mobility separates families geographically; work demands consume time previously devoted to community participation; digital technology replaces face-to-face connection with virtual interaction; suburban isolation prevents the spontaneous daily encounters that built neighborly relationships. The aspirant seeking to prioritize being "loved/praised/revered/honored/liked by the people" discovers that "the people"—stable family and community providing ongoing connection—barely exist in modern fragmented society.[3]

This structural isolation creates vulnerability to both extremes the teaching warns against. Without stable sources of genuine connection, consciousness may pursue compensatory power and wealth to fill the void, or may develop pathological dependency on whatever limited relationships exist, requiring constant validation because no broader community provides ongoing appreciation. The aspirant must somehow maintain proper orientation toward love over power while navigating social structures actively undermining the possibility of genuine community that would make such orientation sustainable.

Part B: Methods for Transformation

Based on the teachings presented by Sage Amenemopet in Chapter 13, which establishes that being loved and respected by people proves superior to having power over storehouses of wealth [verses 11-12],[3] the application of the inverse doctrine methodology suggests specific practices for transforming the mind from power-seeking and wealth-hoarding patterns to prioritizing authentic human connection while progressing toward ultimate fulfillment through Ab Neter recognition.

Practice 1: Systematic Prioritization of Relationship Over Accumulation

The teaching that being "loved/praised/revered/honored/liked by the people" proves better than wealth-power implies that the aspirant should establish systematic practice of choosing relationship-building actions over wealth-accumulation opportunities when these conflict. This requires developing conscious discrimination about when to pursue material gain versus when to invest in authentic human connection, recognizing that contemporary culture's default settings push automatically toward the former.

Practical implementation: When the business opportunity arises that promises significant profit but requires exploiting vulnerable populations or compromising ethical principles, the aspirant should decline and instead invest energy in ventures that serve genuine needs even if less profitable. When allocating time between additional work for income and participation in family/community relationships, choose presence with loved ones unless actual survival requirements demand otherwise. The practice works by interrupting automatic patterns that always prioritize material advantage, creating conscious space to recognize that the stress, isolation, and contempt generated by power-seeking produces less well-being than the respect and genuine appreciation that emerge from ethical service. Additionally, once the basic responsibilities to family/community relationships have been fulfilled, the duty to self in the form of formal spiritual practices (e.g., silent contemplation of Sau Neberdjer, meditation practice "resting in the unconscious") should take priority.

Practice 2: Cultivation of Contentment and Refusal of Comparative Wealth Consciousness

Based on the teaching that power over storehouses creates vexation while simple needs met with respect prove glorifying, the inverse practice cultivates active contentment with modest sufficiency and systematic refusal of comparative wealth consciousness. The aspirant should establish daily meditation on the adequacy of present resources combined with contemplation of how material accumulation beyond genuine needs creates the very stress and anxiety the teaching describes. When comparative thoughts arise—noticing others' wealth, feeling diminished by having less, experiencing envy of material advantages—the practice involves immediate recognition of these patterns as the "encrusted ego in diametric opposition to Neberdjer"[2] and conscious redirection toward gratitude for present sufficiency.

The practice includes concrete action: systematically redistributing resources beyond genuine needs rather than accumulating them, establishing spending patterns based on actual utility rather than status display, developing active disinterest in material comparisons that fuel endless acquisition. Consider the aspirant who notices the impulse to purchase luxury items not for their functional benefit but to display wealth or match others' possessions. The practice involves recognizing this impulse as arising from the forgetting of Neberdjer—the mind seeking external validation of worth through material display because it has lost awareness of internal divine completeness. Rather than indulging the impulse, the aspirant redirects those resources toward genuine needs of others, creating aryu that support rather than undermine spiritual development.

Practice 3: Recognition of Neberdjer as Source of Fulfillment

The teaching establishes that spiritually evolved persons "do not need such appreciations as they have discovered fulfillment from divine awareness in Neberdjer,"[1] indicating that the ultimate practice involves systematic cultivation of Ab Neter awareness as the foundation of fulfillment rather than depending on either external validation or material accumulation. The aspirant should establish regular meditation specifically focused on recognizing that consciousness—in its essential nature as Neberdjer—already embodies the completeness that it seeks through others' approval or wealth accumulation.

The practice operates through directing awareness repeatedly toward the truth that "you who essentially are the owner or embodier of everything that exists" require no external object or approval to be complete.[2] When desires for others' praise arise, recognize these as surface-level needs appropriate to ordinary development but ultimately unnecessary when consciousness recognizes its divine nature. When impulses toward power and accumulation emerge, understand these as compensatory mechanisms attempting to fill the sense of lack that arises from forgetting Neberdjer. The practice involves patient absorption in the understanding that all apparent fulfillment sought externally already resides within as the Ab Neter that sustains consciousness itself.

The ultimate transformation occurs as these practices gradually thin the aryu that create both dependency on external validation and compensatory pursuit of power over material storehouses. As density decreases, the mind naturally discovers that genuine glorification emerges not from being praised by others or dominating resources but from recognizing the divine essence that has always constituted its true nature. The evolved state receives respect and appreciation naturally as byproducts of authentic spiritual development and beneficial service while remaining internally complete whether such external recognition occurs or not—fulfilling the teaching that true "akh" (glorification) represents consciousness recognizing itself as effulgent divine awareness rather than separate entity requiring external sources of fulfillment.

References

[1] Ashby, M. (2025). Keys to Sage Amenemopet wisdom text trilinear translation chapter 13. Sema Institute of Ancient Egyptian Studies.
[2] Ashby, M. (2019). Amenemopet lectures 2019 by Dr Muata Ashby transcripts. Sema Institute of Ancient Egyptian Studies.
[3] Ashby, M. (2019-25). Mysticism of Amenemopet Hieroglyphic Text Translation. Sema Institute of Ancient Egyptian Studies.
[4] Ashby, M. (2019-25). Mysticism of Amenemopet Hieroglyphic Text Translation: Prologue. Sema Institute of Ancient Egyptian Studies.
[5] Kasser, T., & Ryan, R. M. (1996). Further examining the American dream: Differential correlates of intrinsic and extrinsic goals. Personality and Social Psychology Bulletin, 22(3), 280-287.
[6] Lyubomirsky, S., Sheldon, K. M., & Schkade, D. (2005). Pursuing happiness: The architecture of sustainable change. Review of General Psychology, 9(2), 111-131.
[7] Eisenberger, N. I., & Cole, S. W. (2012). Social neuroscience and health: neurophysiological mechanisms linking social ties with physical health. Nature Neuroscience, 15(5), 669-674.
[8] Kahneman, D., & Deaton, A. (2010). High income improves evaluation of life but not emotional well-being. Proceedings of the National Academy of Sciences, 107(38), 16489-16493.
[9] Ryan, R. M., & Deci, E. L. (2000). Self-determination theory and the facilitation of intrinsic motivation, social development, and well-being. American Psychologist, 55(1), 68-78.
[10] Ashby, M. (2022). *Scripture of Ra and Hetheru—Trilinear Translation by Dr. Muata Ashby*. Sema Institute of Ancient Egyptian Studies.

CHAPTER 20: Commentary on Teachings of Amenemopet Chapter 15: The All-Seeing Eye of Cosmic Mind and the Recovery of Authentic Selfhood Verses 5, 9-10, 15-16

Summary of Teachings

Chapter 15 presents one of Amenemopet's most existentially profound teachings: the person you currently believe yourself to be is not actually you. Verse 5 reveals that through ethical living—"doing good and being good to yourself and others"—you end up "being your true self," meaning that unethical living causes the mind to manifest as a fraudulent persona, while ethical living progressively restores authentic selfhood.[1] This teaching establishes why ethical behavior proves essential for silent mind and feelings development: the mind cannot discover who it truly is at the Ab Neter level while operating through personality distortions created by aryu corruptions from unethical action.

Verses 9-10 intensify this teaching by revealing that Djehuty (Thoth) as cosmic mind witnesses all actions—manifesting as the baboon god Anan, whose eye "goes around all of Egypt and thus sees all"—registering them in one's conscience and establishing that even hidden unethical acts accumulate aryu that prevent authentic self-discovery.[2]

Verses 15-16 provide the practical methodology through which the mind can address aryu accumulation and discover authentic selfhood: a description of MEDITATION PRACTICE—spending time "resting in your heart (unconscious) level of your mind, that is, by spending time meditating, at rest-relaxed, and not restless-agitated, in your unconscious and not always spending time in the Ka (subconscious) and Hat (conscious) level of mind."[2] Significantly, profoundly, verse 16 reveals that children observe adults practicing this meditative withdrawal, learning through the modeling that "there is a human capacity for and practice of being internalized and serene in one's unconscious level of experience."[2] This establishes that Ancient Egyptian culture actively transmitted contemplative practice through generational modeling—adults regularly spent time resting in deeper mind levels beyond thought and cognition, and children witnessed this practice as normal human behavior.

The teaching reveals that ethical transformation restores genuine humanity, while cosmic witness ensures that all actions create consequences in the mind's structure whether observed by others or not. Meditative practice provides the systematic method for the mind to withdraw from surface agitation to the placid recesses where Ab Neter discovery becomes possible.

CRITICAL UNDERSTANDING: The Fraudulent Self versus Authentic Selfhood Through Meditative Discovery

Amenemopet's teaching in verse 5 presents an existentially shocking revelation: the person you believe yourself to be right now is—unless you have already had authentic self-discovery—certainly not your authentic self.

Most human beings live their entire lives manifesting what the teaching calls a "fraudulent persona"—personality expressions distorted by heated mind and feelings due to accumulated aryu from unethical actions, thoughts, and feelings of the past. This fraudulent personality expression operates so seamlessly that individuals completely identify with it, never suspecting they are not experiencing their genuine nature.

The teaching establishes that ethical living is the mechanism for recovering authentic selfhood—not through creating something new but by systematically removing aryu corruptions that prevent the mind from expressing the authentic nature sustained by Ab Neter. Verses 15-16 provide the practical meditative methodology: the mind must learn to withdraw from constant operation at Hat (conscious) and Ka (subconscious) levels to rest placidly in the deeper ab where aryu can be addressed and where Ab Neter resides in the kara. This is why ethics prove essential for silent mind and feelings (ger) development: the mind cannot achieve the serenity that allows recognition of the divine foundation while operating through heated mind and feelings (shemm) created by unethical patterns, and cannot access the deeper meditative states where authentic selfhood can be discovered.

The profound implication: discovering who you truly are requires both ethical transformation and systematic meditative practice—not merely psychological insight or spiritual experiences.

1-Human Psychology Principle Focus of Chapter 15

HUMAN PSYCHOLOGY PRINCIPLE: THE FRAUDULENT PERSONA CREATED BY UNCONSCIOUS CORRUPTIONS VERSUS AUTHENTIC SELFHOOD RESTORED THROUGH ETHICAL LIVING AND THE MEDITATIVE PRACTICE OF RESTING IN DEEPER MIND LEVELS

Chapter 15 addresses a profound psychological reality that most people never consciously recognize: "most people are manifesting a fraudulent persona based on the corruptions of the unconscious mind."[3] When the mind operates from dense aryu accumulation in the ab without awareness of Ab Neter in the kara, it creates a distorted personality that constitutes "whatever the distortion causes the personality to manifest as."[3] This fraudulent manifestation operates so seamlessly that individuals typically believe their distorted thoughts, feelings, and behaviors represent their authentic nature, never suspecting that aryu patterns have hijacked personality expression.

The psychological principle reveals that ethical living creates transformation: "you end up being your true self" rather than being the distorted manifestation of corrupted aryu.[2] This phrase points toward recovering authentic selfhood—the mind expressing through "personality clarity and lightness that is the result of ethical living."[3] Unethical actions deposit aryu in the ab that progressively warp the mind's operations, creating personality distortion wherein the Hat no longer has access to the personality's genuine nature because thick aryu obscure both rational understanding and feeling sensitivity to deeper truth.

Verses 15-16 introduce the critical meditative practice component: the mind must develop the capacity to withdraw from constant operation at surface levels (Hat and Ka) to spend time "resting in your heart (unconscious) level of your mind, that is, by spending time meditating, at rest-relaxed, and not restless-agitated."[2] The teaching specifies moving beyond "always spending time in the Ka (subconscious) and Hat (conscious) level of mind" to access deeper levels "in your unconscious"—specifically, resting in a state beyond thought and cognition where it becomes possible to discover the Ab Neter.[2]

The psychological framework reveals a consciousness architecture with distinct operational levels: Hat (front-of-mind conscious awareness), Ka (subconscious mind containing thoughts, feelings, personality manifestations), surface ab (where aryu reside), and deep ab/kara (where Ab Neter sustains consciousness). Most individuals spend their entire lives operating exclusively at Hat and Ka levels—constantly engaged with thoughts, feelings, desires, memories, reactions—never learning to withdraw to the deeper placid state where aryu can be addressed and authentic selfhood discovered. The teaching establishes that Ancient Egyptian culture recognized this capacity and actively cultivated it: adults regularly practiced this meditative withdrawal, and children observed this practice, learning that "there is a human capacity for and practice of being internalized and serene in one's unconscious level of experience."[2]

The psychological implication proves profound: fraudulent persona maintains itself through the mind remaining trapped at surface levels where aryu dominate operations. Ethical living begins thinning aryu density, but the systematic practice of resting in deeper mind levels provides the direct methodology for addressing aryu at their source and revealing the Ab Neter that has always sustained consciousness but remains hidden beneath surface agitation. The teaching establishes that this wasn't abstract philosophy but practical psychology transmitted culturally through the modeling—children grew up observing adults spending time in meditative states, internalizing this as normal human capacity rather than an strange spiritual practice.

This teaching carries profound implications: the person you currently experience as "yourself" is likely not your authentic self at all, but rather a fraudulent persona created by accumulated aryu corruptions operating at surface mind levels (Hat and Ka) you never learned to transcend. The mind must first recognize that what it believes to be authentic self-expression actually constitutes distorted reactions driven by corrupted aryu patterns at Hat and Ka levels, and that authentic selfhood requires both ethical purification and systematic meditative practice of resting in deeper levels beyond constant mental activity.

The teaching introduces Djehuty (Thoth) as the god representing "the Cosmic Mind of Ra who oversees worldly affairs,"[3] manifesting specifically as the baboon Anan whose eye "goes around all of Egypt and thus sees all."[2] This cosmic intelligence operates as "the eye of awareness of the god of the intellect of the Creator Spirit, Ra, who presides over your mind and intellect and who is the cosmic mind itself."[2] The psychological implication reveals that universal intelligence operates through the cosmic mind, and all actions become registered in the cosmic mind—not merely in some external divine record but "also in your own conscience."[2] This establishes that one's own ethical behavior and its absence create psychological consequences at the deepest level of personality structure, shaping not only future external circumstances but the very capacity for authentic self-expression and the ability to access deeper meditative states where Ab Neter can be discovered.

Connection to Prologue Goals:

This psychological principle directly impacts both of the Prologue goals. Without recoverir authentic selfhood through ethical transformation combined with the meditative practice of resti in deeper mind levels, the goal stated in Prologue verse 2 to "cause a person to have well-being while living on earth"[4] cannot be achieved, because the mind operating from a fraudulent persona at surface levels experiences persistent disconnection from genuine needs, values, and capacities. The distorted personality creates suffering not merely through external consequences of unethical action but through the internal experience of being fundamentally alienated from one's true nature while trapped in constant surface-level agitation.

More profoundly, this principle obstructs Prologue verse 9's discovery of the kara "where the Divine resides in every person,"[4] because the thick aryu creating fraudulent persona create the same density that prevents recognition of Ab Neter, and because the mind never learns to withdraw from surface Hat/Ka operation to rest in the deeper levels where Ab Neter can be discovered. The mind cannot discover the divine foundation when operating exclusively through personality structures warped by accumulated corruptions at surface levels, never developing the meditative capacity to rest placidly in the deeper recesses where authentic selfhood resides.

2-Behavioral Imperatives of this Chapter

BEHAVIORAL IMPERATIVE: OBSERVABLE PATTERNS OF FRAUDULENT PERSONA MANIFESTATION VERSUS AUTHENTIC SELF-EXPRESSION ARISING FROM ETHICAL PURIFICATION COMBINED WITH THE MEDITATIVE PRACTICE OF MIND WITHDRAWAL TO DEEPER LEVELS

The behavioral manifestations reveal themselves through the contrast between the mind expressing fraudulently through aryu-distorted patterns at surface levels and the mind expressing authentically through ethical clarity combined with systematic meditative practice. The teaching addresses how unethical living creates progressive personality distortion wherein observable behaviors no longer represent genuine response to present circumstances but rather automatic reactions driven by accumulated corruptions in the ab operating at Hat and Ka levels the mind never learned to transcend.

When the mind acts unethically—lying for advantage, manipulating others, taking what belongs to others—each action deposits specific aryu encoding not merely memory but the entire feeling-tone of the mind operating against Maat. These aryu accumulate and shape future operations at surface levels, creating what appears as personality traits but actually represents distortion patterns. The individual who repeatedly lies develops aryu that make truth-telling increasingly difficult—not ecause lying requires less effort but because accumulated aryu of deception have warped the pacity to recognize truth from falsehood at Hat level operations.

he behavioral pattern manifests as individuals who cannot recognize their own manipulative viors, who believe selfish actions serve legitimate needs, who experience anxiety-driven lling as appropriate responses. The corporate executive exploiting workers while believing lves fair demonstrates a fraudulent persona—the mind so distorted that it lacks the capacity nize disconnects between professed values and actual behaviors. The parent who emotionally ates children while believing themselves nurturing exemplifies the fraudulent persona g through unconscious aryu patterns.

aching identifies the consequence: such minds have lost authentic selfhood—"you end up you but rather being whatever the distortion causes the personality to manifest as."[3] l expression becomes increasingly automatic and disconnected from conscious choice. The y believe they act from free will when actually responding to accumulated aryu patterns that have hijacked personality expression at surface levels they never learned to observe from deeper meditative states.

Verses 15-16 introduce the profound behavioral contrast between minds trapped at surface levels and minds that have developed meditative capacity for deeper withdrawal. The teaching reveals that Ancient Egyptian adults regularly engaged in observable behavior rarely seen in modern culture: spending time "resting in your heart (unconscious) level of your mind...at rest-relaxed, and not restless-agitated, in your unconscious and not always spending time in the Ka (subconscious) and Hat (conscious) level of mind."[2] This wasn't hidden practice but observable behavior children witnessed: adults periodically withdrew from external engagement and surface mental activity to rest placidly in deeper states.

The behavioral modeling proved essential for cultural transmission. Children observing adults spending time in meditative withdrawal learned "that there is a human capacity for and practice of being internalized and serene in one's unconscious level of experience."[2] The observable behavior communicated profound psychological truth: the mind possesses the capacity to transcend constant surface-level operation, resting in deeper states beyond thought and cognition. Children internalized this not as an exotic spiritual attainment but as normal human function.

APPLICATION OF INVERSE DOCTRINE METHODOLOGY—CULTURAL MODELING CONTRAST:

Based on the teaching presented by Sage Amenemopet in verses 15-16, which establish that adults practiced meditative withdrawal and children learned through observation that the mind possesses the capacity for internalized serenity beyond surface agitation, the application of the inverse doctrine methodology reveals the profound corruption of modern cultural modeling.

Contemporary culture models the precise opposite. Instead of adults demonstrating the capacity to rest placidly in deeper mind levels, modern culture predominantly models:

Surface-Level Agitation as Normal: Adults demonstrate perpetual surface-level stimulation—constantly checking phones, consuming entertainment, engaging distractions. Children observe adults unable to rest in internalized serenity, learning that constant external stimulation represents normal human function.

Status Seeking and Materialism: Adults constantly demonstrate that worth derives from external acquisition—bigger houses, luxury cars, designer clothes, prestigious titles. Children learn that authentic value requires proving oneself through possessions and status symbols rather than discovering inherent divine nature.

Validation Seeking: Adults demonstrate a constant need for external validation—approval from peers, admiration from followers, recognition from authorities. Children observe adults measuring worth through others' responses, learning that value requires continuous external confirmation rather than internal discovery.

Self-Deception About Happiness: Adults demonstrate constant longing for past or fantasizing about future. Children observe adults perpetually dissatisfied with present circumstances, learning that fulfillment exists elsewhere, in an imaginary future or circumstance, rather than recognizing divine presence within current experience.

Superficial Authenticity: Adults perform curated identities through social media and public presentation. Children observe adults engaging in elaborate self-deception about motivations and values, learning that authenticity means convincing performance rather than discovering genuine nature.

Fear-Based Living: Adults demonstrate fear-driven behavior—anxiety about future, mistrust of systems, cynicism about human nature. Children observe adults living in perpetual defensive stance, learning that security requires constant vigilance against threat rather than alignment with Maat.

The behavioral contrast proves devastating: where Ancient Egyptian children observed adults regularly withdrawing to deeper states, modeling that serenity beyond surface agitation represents normal human capacity, modern children observe adults trapped in perpetual surface-level stimulation, modeling that restless agitation represents the inevitable human condition. This inverse cultural modeling creates what could be termed "maladaptation to agitation"—the mind conditioned to believe perpetual surface-level operation represents normal function, never developing the capacity to rest in deeper states where aryu can be addressed and Ab Neter discovered. Additionally, the misunderstood surface level "normal function" is often coupled with the idea of life versus non-experience of that surface level is equated with non-experience or even death.

The teaching establishes that the fraudulent persona develops not merely through individual unethical action but through cultural systems that model and reinforce behaviors contrary to Maat. Modern culture operates profoundly "out of that balance"—systematically teaching children that authentic selfhood requires external validation, material acquisition, status achievement, and constant surface stimulation rather than ethical living, meditative practice, and discovery of internal divine foundation.

The behavioral imperative thus demands understanding that every moment the mind operates at surface levels without developing the capacity for deeper withdrawal, it reinforces patterns creating the fraudulent persona. Conversely, ethical living combined with systematic meditative practice creates the opposite effect: when one acts by "doing good and being good to yourself and others" while the mind regularly withdraws to rest in deeper states, this deposits aryu that thin rather than thicken personality distortion, gradually restoring access to authentic selfhood at Ab Neter level.

Verses 9-10 introduce the critical teaching that transforms understanding of why behavioral change proves so essential: even actions done "when no one is around" become "registered in the cosmic mind (the god of intellect) and thus also in your own conscience."[2] This reveals that the fraudulent persona operates under delusion that hidden actions remain consequence-free. Yet the teaching establishes that Djehuty as cosmic mind witnesses all actions and registers them in consciousness architecture itself.[2]

The behavioral imperative thus demands understanding that every unethical action, regardless of external witness, deposits aryu that contribute to the fraudulent persona development and corrupt the capacity for authentic self-expression and deeper meditative access. The professional who lies in private emails accumulates aryu identical to those created by public dishonesty. The individual who mentally criticizes others while maintaining a pleasant facade deposits aryu that warp the mind just as surely as openly expressed hostility. Moreover, every moment spent in perpetual surface-level agitation rather than developing meditative capacity for deeper withdrawal strengthens patterns preventing authentic selfhood discovery.

Conversely, ethical living combined with systematic meditative practice creates transformation: when one acts righteously while regularly practicing withdrawal to deeper states, this creates what the Keys document describes as "personality clarity and lightness,"[3] wherein the mind regains the capacity to express genuinely rather than through aryu-distorted patterns trapped at surface levels.

3-Mystic Psychology—Metaphysical Implications

ABSTRACT PRINCIPLES, COSMIC IMPLICATIONS, AND THE CONSCIOUSNESS ARCHITECTURE THROUGH WHICH ETHICAL LIVING COMBINED WITH THE MEDITATIVE PRACTICE OF RESTING IN DEEPER LEVELS RESTORES AUTHENTIC SELFHOOD WHILE COSMIC MIND RECORDS ALL ACTIONS AT CAUSAL LEVELS.

Building upon the behavioral patterns identified in Section 2, the metaphysical dimensions reveal the precise consciousness architecture through which ethical living combined with systematic meditative practice transforms the fraudulent persona into authentic self-expression, how cosmic intelligence witnesses all actions at causal levels, and how the mind can withdraw from surface operation to rest in the placid recesses where Ab Neter discovery becomes possible.

The metaphysical principle operates through understanding that the mind operates simultaneously at multiple levels: Hat (front-of-mind present awareness), Ka (subconscious manifesting thoughts, feelings, personality), surface ab (where aryu reside as karmic feeling-memories), deep ab/kara (where Ab Neter sustains the mind's capacity for awareness), and beyond the individual to Djehuty as cosmic mind encompassing all.[2][5] When verse 5 teaches that ethical living causes "you end up being your true self," this reveals transformation at fundamental levels of mind architecture—removing aryu distortions that prevent authentic expression of what one already is at the Ab Neter foundation.[2]

The metaphysics reveal that the fraudulent persona operates through the aryu hijacking of mind expression at surface levels. When aryu accumulate densely in the ab, they dominate Hat operations and shape Ka manifestations—the mind at surface levels becomes so conditioned by feeling-memories from past unethical actions that it loses the capacity to receive guidance from Ab Neter. The Hat operates almost exclusively from aryu patterns, believing these distorted responses represent authentic selfhood when they actually constitute programmed reactions.

Verses 15-16 introduce the profound metaphysical teaching about consciousness architecture that enables restoration of authentic selfhood. The mind possesses the capacity to operate at different levels: "spending time in the Ka (subconscious) and Hat (conscious) level of mind" versus "resting in your heart (unconscious) level of your mind, that is, by spending time meditating, at rest-relaxed, and not restless-agitated, in your unconscious."[2] This describes metaphysical movement through consciousness architecture—withdrawing from constant surface-level operation to rest in deeper ab levels beyond mental content.

Most individuals spend their entire existence operating exclusively at Hat and Ka levels—the mind constantly engaged with external perception and internal mental-emotional activity, never learning to withdraw to deeper states. The teaching establishes that authentic selfhood discovery requires developing the mind's capacity to rest "in your unconscious"—the mind learning to settle beyond constant Hat-Ka activity into the placid deeper state where aryu patterns can be observed from a stable vantage point and where Ab Neter presence can be directly recognized.[2]

The metaphysical mechanism of ethical transformation combined with meditative practice operates through creating conditions enabling the mind to penetrate deeper than surface levels. Ethical action creates "light aryu" that remain "transparent to divine light."[6] When one acts ethically—speaking truth, treating others with compassion, contributing to community well-being—these actions deposit aryu that differ fundamentally from those created by unethical action. Light aryu do not create dense obstruction blocking Ab Neter awareness at deeper levels. Instead, they allow the mind to penetrate more easily from Hat through Ka toward deeper ab/kara level where authentic nature resides.

The meditative practice of "resting in your heart (unconscious) level of your mind" operates by training the mind to withdraw from constant Hat-Ka operation.[2] Initially, the mind believes it can only exist through constant mental activity—thinking, feeling, desiring, remembering, reacting. The practice reveals that the mind can settle beyond this surface operation into deeper states characterized by "rest-relaxed, and not restless-agitated"—placid serenity without constant thought-stream.[2] This isn't unconsciousness or sleep but alert awareness established at deeper level than ordinary mental activity.

As the mind develops the capacity to rest in this deeper state through sustained practice, profound metaphysical transformation occurs. From the stable vantage point beyond constant Hat-Ka activity, awareness (sustained by Ab Neter) can observe aryu patterns arising from surface ab into Ka operations without the mind identifying with them. The anger-aryu that would normally hijack Hat and dominate Ka can be observed arising, creating its characteristic feeling-tone and urge toward reactive speech, yet awareness established at deeper level doesn't automatically identify with or act from the pattern. This observation from deeper vantage point combined with ethical living gradually thins aryu density.

Most profoundly, as one practices establishing awareness in deeper levels beyond constant mental content, it becomes possible for the mind to recognize the Ab Neter presence that has always sustained consciousness but remained hidden beneath surface agitation. The teaching specifies that resting in the deeper "unconscious" state moves the mind toward discovering what resides at kara level—not new acquisition but revelation of what has always been present as foundation.[2]

The profound metaphysical teaching concerns Djehuty as cosmic mind and the universal witness consciousness. Verse 10 reveals that Djehuty's eye—manifesting through the baboon Anan aspect—"goes around all of Egypt and thus sees all."[2] The metaphysical implication establishes that individual mind operations do not occur in isolation but rather function as nodes within universal consciousness. Djehuty represents "the Cosmic Mind of Ra who oversees worldly affairs,"[3] meaning that what appears as individual private experience actually occurs within larger cosmic awareness that registers all actions, thoughts, and feelings.

The teaching explains that Djehuty serves as "the eye of awareness of the god of the intellect of the Creator Spirit, Ra, who presides over your mind and intellect and who is the cosmic mind itself."[2] The metaphysics distinguish between the human individual mind (local awareness limited to particular body-mind system) and cosmic mind (universal awareness encompassing all phenomena). Individual mind experiences events from localized perspective, believes its thoughts private, imagines its actions witnessed only by those physically present. Cosmic mind operates as the universal field within which all individual minds exist, simultaneously aware of all actions, thoughts, and feelings occurring throughout Creation.

The metaphysical architecture reveals why actions done "when no one is around" nevertheless create consequences: they become "registered in the cosmic mind...and thus also in your own conscience."[2] The registration occurs because the individual ab functions not as isolated storage but as a localized aspect of universal consciousness—what gets deposited in individual unconscious simultaneously registers in cosmic awareness. The aryu created by hidden unethical actions accumulate in individual ab, creating the fraudulent persona and blocking Ab Neter awareness, while simultaneously being witnessed by Djehuty as cosmic mind that maintains cosmic order through universal intelligence.

The metaphysical framework establishes that ethical transformation combined with meditative practice proves essential because unethical actions corrupt mind architecture itself at causal levels, while perpetual surface-level operation prevents discovery of authentic selfhood. Conversely, ethical living gradually restores the architectural integrity through which the mind can express authentically, while systematic meditative practice of resting in deeper ab levels develops the capacity to transcend surface operations and discover the Ab Neter foundation. This combined approach enables recovery of "being you" through progressive thinning of distortion patterns operating at surface levels and revelation of the authentic selfhood that has always constituted the true foundation but remained hidden beneath aryu density and perpetual surface-level agitation.

The metaphysical teaching about children observing adults practicing meditative withdrawal reveals profound truth about practice transmission. When verse 16 establishes that children "will see that there is a human capacity for and practice of being internalized and serene in one's unconscious level of experience,"[2] this describes metaphysical principle of cultural-practice transmission. Children observing adults regularly withdrawing to deeper states internalize at unconscious level that the mind possesses this capacity—not as abstract concept but as lived reality witnessed in daily life. This metaphysical imprinting enables next generation to access deeper states more readily because the capacity has been demonstrated and validated rather than existing as an unusual attainment requiring extraordinary effort.

The metaphysical contrast with modern culture reveals devastating consequence: when children never observe adults demonstrating the capacity to rest beyond surface-level agitation, they internalize at metaphysical level that perpetual Hat-Ka operation represents inevitable human condition. The mind's operational patterns develop without template for deeper withdrawal, making authentic selfhood discovery exponentially more difficult.

4-Transpersonal Psychology Research

CONTEMPORARY PSYCHOLOGY PARALLELS AND EMPIRICAL VALIDATION OF AMENEMOPET'S TEACHING ON AUTHENTIC SELF-EXPRESSION, MORAL CONSCIENCE, AND MEDITATIVE STATES BEYOND ORDINARY MENTAL ACTIVITY

Contemporary transpersonal psychology and moral development research provide remarkable empirical validation for Amenemopet's teaching that ethical living combined with the meditative practice of resting in deeper mind levels restores authentic selfhood, while unethical action creates distorted personality expression. Research by Carl Rogers on authentic versus conditioned self-concept demonstrates that individuals who systematically violate their authentic values develop what he termed "incongruence"—a split between genuine self-experience and the persona presented to self and others.[7] This psychological research directly corresponds to the teaching about the fraudulent persona arising from aryu corruptions versus authentic selfhood restored through ethical clarity combined with the capacity to access deeper mind levels.

Studies on moral identity reveal that individuals who engage in systematic unethical behavior show measurable changes in self-concept, progressively adapting their self-image to rationalize problematic actions rather than changing behaviors to align with professed values.[8] Research demonstrates what psychologists term "moral disengagement"—the mind developing cognitive mechanisms that allow unethical action while maintaining sense of being an ethical person. This empirical evidence validates the teaching that accumulated aryu from unethical actions create personality distortion wherein the mind loses the capacity to recognize authentic nature, operating from the fraudulent persona at surface levels.

Neuroscience research on moral conscience reveals neural mechanisms strikingly similar to Amenemopet's description of cosmic mind registering all actions in one's own conscience. Studies using functional MRI demonstrate that moral violations activate specific brain regions associated with emotional distress and self-referential processing, even when violations occur privately without external witness.[9] Research shows that conscience operates through neural networks that automatically evaluate actions against internalized ethical standards, creating what subjects experience as an "internal voice" that knows truth regardless of external circumstances. This neurological evidence supports the teaching that cosmic mind (Djehuty) registers actions in individual conscience, creating consequences at the deepest level of consciousness architecture.

Research on cognitive dissonance and self-deception validates the teaching about the fraudulent persona development through aryu accumulation. Studies demonstrate that when individuals act contrary to their values, they experience psychological discomfort that typically resolves through distorting either perception of the action or modification of the values themselves, rather than changing behavior to align with original principles.[10] Longitudinal research reveals that repeated ethical violations create progressive desensitization—the same actions that initially produced strong conscience activation show decreasing neural response over time, indicating what the teaching describes as aryu accumulation making the mind progressively less sensitive to ethical corruption at surface levels.[9]

Advanced meditation research provides extraordinary validation for Amenemopet's teaching about resting in deeper mind levels beyond ordinary mental activity. Recent studies on jhana meditation states—advanced concentrative absorption practices reaching levels beyond thought and conceptual processing—demonstrate that the mind can indeed transcend ordinary mental operations to rest in states characterized by profound serenity and minimal cognitive content, while consciousness continues to witness.[11][12][13] Research using functional MRI and phenomenological reports reveals that practitioners can access states where default mode network activity (associated with self-referential thinking and mind-wandering) substantially decreases or temporarily ceases, while awareness remains lucid and stable.[11] This directly validates the teaching about "resting in your heart (unconscious) level of your mind...at rest-relaxed, and not restless-agitated, in your unconscious and not always spending time in the Ka (subconscious) and Hat (conscious) level of mind."[2]

Multimodal neurophenomenology research on advanced concentration absorption meditation reveals that experienced practitioners can access states involving "cessation of mental proliferation" while maintaining alert awareness—precisely matching the description of resting beyond constant Hat-Ka activity in deeper ab levels.[11] Studies demonstrate that these states show characteristic neural signatures distinct from ordinary waking consciousness, sleep, or typical meditation, indicating the mind operating from fundamentally different level of organization.[12] Research documents practitioners reporting direct recognition of awareness itself as distinct from mental content—the mind recognizing consciousness (Ab Neter) as the unchanging witness beyond thoughts, feelings, and personality expressions.[13]

Developmental research on observational learning and cultural transmission validates the teaching about children learning meditative capacity through observing adults. Studies demonstrate that children develop understanding of human psychological capacities largely through witnessing adults demonstrating those capacities in daily life.[14] Research on contemplative practice transmission shows that children who observe parents engaging in regular meditation develop significantly greater capacity to access calm, focused states compared to children receiving only instruction without observational modeling.[15] This empirical evidence supports verse 16's teaching that children observing adults practicing withdrawal to deeper states learn "that there is a human capacity for and practice of being internalized and serene in one's unconscious level of experience."[2]

Buddhist psychology research on authentic presence and mindful awareness provides additional validation. Studies reveal that meditation practitioners who emphasize ethical conduct alongside awareness practices show significantly greater congruence between professed values and actual behaviors compared to those emphasizing awareness techniques alone.[16] This research validates the teaching that ethical living combined with meditative practice creates "personality clarity and lightness" that allows authentic self-expression, while unethical action creates the density of the fraudulent persona regardless of awareness practices operating only at surface levels.

Neuroscience research on neuroplasticity and mind training demonstrates that systematic meditation practice creates measurable changes in brain structure and function, particularly in regions associated with self-referential processing, emotional regulation, and awareness.[17] Studies show that long-term practitioners develop enhanced capacity to observe mental-emotional content without automatic identification or reaction—matching the teaching's description of awareness established at deeper level observing aryu patterns arising into Ka operations without being hijacked by them.[18]

Research on the default mode network and self-referential processing provides particularly compelling validation for the teaching about the fraudulent persona operating through constant surface-level activity. Studies demonstrate that the default mode network—active during mind-wandering, self-referential thinking, and autobiographical memory—operates almost continuously in most individuals, creating persistent sense of separate self constantly engaged with mental content.[19] Advanced meditation practitioners show significantly reduced default mode network activity, indicating the mind transcending constant self-referential processing to operate from deeper level.[19][20] This neurological evidence validates the teaching that most individuals remain trapped in perpetual Hat-Ka operation (default mode network activity) creating the fraudulent persona, while meditative practice develops the capacity to rest beyond this surface activity in deeper states where authentic selfhood can be recognized.

Cross-cultural psychology research on modernization effects validates the inverse doctrine application regarding cultural modeling. Studies document that societies undergoing rapid modernization show characteristic psychological shifts: increased materialism, heightened status anxiety, reduced interpersonal trust, and greater prevalence of surface-level social engagement over authentic connection.[21] Research demonstrates that exposure to consumer culture correlates with reduced well-being, increased anxiety, and greater sense of inadequacy—precisely matching the teaching's warning about cultural systems modeling external validation and status seeking over internal discovery.[22] Studies on social media effects reveal that platforms designed for constant surface-level engagement create measurable reductions in capacity for sustained attention and deep reflection, validating concerns about modern culture preventing development of the capacity to rest beyond perpetual stimulation.[23]

5-Spiritual Implications for Aspirants

PART A: PASTORAL CONCERNS—MODERN CHALLENGES IN RECOGNIZING THE FRAUDULENT PERSONA AND DEVELOPING MEDITATIVE CAPACITY FOR DEEPER WITHDRAWAL

Contemporary aspirants face profound challenges recognizing the extent to which personality expression may constitute a fraudulent persona—a surface-level self-presentation that the mind never learned to transcend. This difficulty often stems from developmental deficits, particularly the absence of contemplative modeling during early formative years. Recalling the research on contemplative practice transmission, presented earlier, it demonstrates that "children who observe parents engaging in regular meditation develop significantly greater capacity to access calm, focused states compared to children receiving only instruction without observational modeling." [15] Aspirants raised in cultures lacking such positive modeling therefore face greater challenges in controlling the mind and sustaining meditation practice, as they lack the internalized behavioral templates that early observational learning would have provided.

Consider the individual who has spent decades developing what appears as successful identity—competent professional, caring family member, respected community participant—yet beneath operates patterns of subtle manipulation, strategic deception, and systematic rationalization at Hat-Ka levels. The teaching reveals such a mind manifests "a fraudulent persona based on the corruptions of the unconscious mind,"[3] yet the person typically has no awareness because the aryu creating it have so thoroughly shaped the mind's operations at surface levels, and because they never observed anyone demonstrating alternative mode of operation through meditative practice.

Someone awakening to Chapter 15's teaching experiences disorienting recognition: behaviors believed to represent authentic expression actually constitute programmed reactions from accumulated aryu operating at levels the mind never learned to observe; values professed with apparent sincerity actually serve to maintain self-image while systematically violated in daily actions; the personality presenting as integrated and honest actually functions through layers of self-deception so thorough that distinction between authentic and fraudulent has become invisible. The aspirant may recognize that "most people are manifesting a fraudulent persona"[3] in others yet struggle to acknowledge how this diagnosis applies to their own mind operations trapped at surface levels.

The challenge intensifies through modern culture actively rewarding the fraudulent persona development while systematically preventing development of meditative capacity for deeper withdrawal. Consider the professional environments requiring strategic dishonesty for advancement, social structures valuing image management over authentic expression, economic systems promoting acquisition through exploitation while maintaining facade of ethical business. The aspirant attempting to recover authentic selfhood through ethical living encounters constant pressure to maintain the fraudulent persona because genuine ethical expression often proves professionally disadvantageous, socially isolating, and economically costly.

More insidiously, modern culture provides no modeling of meditative practice as normal human capacity. Where Ancient Egyptian children observed adults regularly spending time in internalized serenity beyond surface agitation, modern children observe adults perpetually engaged with devices, entertainment, and external stimulation—never witnessing mind withdrawal to deeper states. The contemporary aspirant typically grows to adulthood having never seen anyone demonstrate sustained practice of resting beyond constant Hat-Ka activity, lacking even a conceptual framework that the mind can operate beyond perpetual mental-emotional engagement.

Contemporary social media culture presents particularly devastating challenges. The constant curation of online identity encourages the fraudulent persona development wherein individuals progressively lose awareness of distinction between authentic self and crafted image, operating exclusively at surface Hat-Ka levels. The professional who carefully manages their LinkedIn presence to project success while experiencing private anxiety about competence exemplifies the fraudulent persona operating through approved cultural channels at surface levels. The spiritual practitioner who posts inspirational messages while privately engaging in unethical business practices demonstrates a fraudulent persona so normalized by contemporary culture that recognizing it requires exceptional honesty about surface-level mental operations.

The teaching reveals that recovering authentic selfhood demands willingness to acknowledge uncomfortable truths: the competent professional identity may mask insecurity driving unethical competitive behaviors at Hat-Ka levels; the caring family member role may conceal manipulative patterns maintaining control; the spiritual practitioner identity may serve to avoid confronting actual ethical failures. Moreover, authentic self-discovery requires developing an entirely new capacity—learning to rest beyond constant surface-level operation that modern culture conditions as inevitable human function.

Consider the aspirant who intellectually understands that authentic selfhood requires ethical living combined with meditative practice but faces overwhelming resistance actually implementing sustained practice of resting beyond constant mental activity. The modern mind conditions itself to fear silence, interpreting absence of constant Hat-Ka engagement as threatening void rather than recognizing potential for discovery of deeper Ab Neter presence. The individual attempts meditation but experiences it as struggle against a constant thought-stream rather than learning gentle withdrawal to a deeper state characterized by "rest-relaxed, and not restless-agitated."[2]

The cultural absence of modeling creates additional challenge. Ancient Egyptian children witnessing adults regularly spending time in visible meditative withdrawal learned through observation that the mind possesses this capacity—no elaborate explanation required, simply direct witnessing of sustained internalized serenity. Modern aspirants receive instruction about meditation as technique but lack an observational foundation validating the possibility. They attempt practice in isolation, doubting whether the mind can actually rest beyond constant surface activity because they never witnessed anyone successfully demonstrating this capacity as a normal human function.

PART B: THE MATURE EXPRESSION OF SAU NEBERDJER PRACTICE

Resting in the Unconscious Beyond Hat-Ka Levels

Introduction: Verse 15-16 as the Culmination of Systematic Training

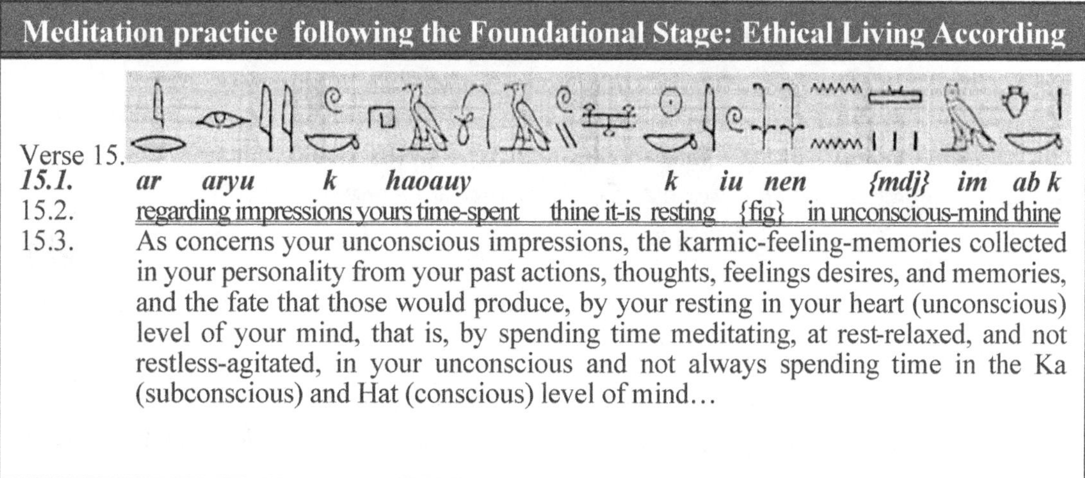

Meditation practice following the Foundational Stage: Ethical Living According

Verse 15.

15.1. *ar aryu k haoauy k iu nen {mdj} im ab k*

15.2. regarding impressions yours time-spent thine it-is resting {fig} in unconscious-mind thine

15.3. As concerns your unconscious impressions, the karmic-feeling-memories collected in your personality from your past actions, thoughts, feelings desires, and memories, and the fate that those would produce, by your resting in your heart (unconscious) level of your mind, that is, by spending time meditating, at rest-relaxed, and not restless-agitated, in your unconscious and not always spending time in the Ka (subconscious) and Hat (conscious) level of mind…

Verse 15 unmistakably describes what is today recognized as a formal meditation practice, to spend time resting in the unconscious. However, what process allows a person to be able to accomplish this kind of "resting"? What kind of life does a person need to lead such that their conscious mind would be able to rest sufficiently so that their awareness could reach states of unconscious experiencing? The advancing practice of meditation requires a meditative lifestyle that reduces stress, agitation and production of negative mental impressions.

The practice begins with living in accord with Maat ethics—following the behavioral advices of Amenemopet. This fundamental stage thins aryu density and creates greater capacity for cultivating the serene mind needed for deeper practices. Without ethical purification creating silent mind and feelings, the subsequent meditative stages cannot bear proper fruit. As established throughout this commentary, unethical action deposits corrupting aryu that prevent the mind from accessing deeper levels where Ab Neter can be discovered. Therefore, the aspirant must maintain dedicated commitment to ethical transformation as the essential foundation supporting all formal meditation practice.

Verses 15-16 present meditation teaching that represents the mature capacity developed through the Sau Neberdjer practice system presented comprehensively in Chapter 9. While Chapter 9 provides the complete systematic progression—from foundational ethical preparation through six progressive stages—the current teaching focuses specifically on what Amenemopet describes as "resting in your heart (unconscious) level of your mind...at rest-relaxed, and not restless-agitated, in your unconscious and not always spending time in the Ka (subconscious) and Hat (conscious) level of mind."[2]

Verse 15's description corresponds to advanced stages of Sau Neberdjer meditation—primarily Stages IV-VI in the systematic progression, where the mind develops the capacity to transcend constant surface-level operation and rest in deeper ab/kara levels where Ab Neter can be directly recognized.

The unique contributions of verses 15-16 within the broader meditation framework: (1) explicit identification of the problem—"not always spending time in the Ka and Hat level"—revealing most individuals remain trapped at surface levels throughout life; (2) the connection between meditative capacity and recovery of authentic selfhood versus the fraudulent persona; and (3) the cultural transmission dimension wherein adults practice visibly so children internalize that the mind possesses the capacity for internalized serenity.

Cross-Reference: ***For comprehensive instruction on Sau Neberdjer meditation including foundational preparations, progressive stages, practice structure, and realistic timelines, see Chapter 9. This section presumes familiarity with that framework and focuses specifically on verse 15's mature capacities.***

Section 1: Understanding Verse 15 in the Context of Systematic Practice

The Meditation Architecture: Hat-Ka-Ab-Kara Levels

Verse 15's instruction describes precise movement through consciousness architecture:

- **Hat (Conscious Awareness):** Front-of-mind present awareness—what one consciously focuses upon

- **Ka (Subconscious):** Thoughts, feelings, personality traits—active processing of aryu influences
- **Surface Ab:** Repository where aryu accumulate and reside
- **Deep Ab/Kara:** Where Ab Neter sustains individual awareness—authentic selfhood beneath aryu density

The problem: most humans spend their entire existence "always spending time in the Ka and Hat level"—perpetually engaged with thoughts, feelings, desires at surface levels, never learning to withdraw deeper. This creates the fraudulent persona because the mind, operating exclusively from aryu-conditioned Hat-Ka patterns, expresses through distortions rather than authentic Ab Neter nature.

Correspondence to Chapter 9's Progressive Stages

The capacity to "rest in your unconscious" develops systematically:

Stages I-II (Focused Attention): Develop basic concentration using external then internal anchors. Build attentional stability necessary for all subsequent work (typically 2-6 months).

Stage III (Open Monitoring): Begin transitioning from focused attention to open awareness while maintaining conceptual framework. Develop capacity to rest in awareness rather than being absorbed in mental content.

Stage IV (Abstract Awareness): Drop conceptual framework, resting in pure witness consciousness. This represents Soul-Aware-Witness-Self recognition—the mind discovering itself as awareness observing rather than being identical with content of mind .

Stages V-VI (Non-Dual Awareness and Absorption): The full maturation of verse 15's description. Sense of separate observer dissolves; the mind rests in profound stillness beyond subtle mental activity—"rest-relaxed, and not restless-agitated."[2] At these levels, the mind penetrates from surface Hat-Ka through aryu-laden ab into deep ab/kara where Ab Neter becomes directly recognizable.

Recognition Markers of Developed Capacity

How does one recognize whether verse 15's capacity has genuinely developed?

- **Diminished Default Mental Activity:** Periods of mental silence emerge naturally rather than through strenuous effort
- **Stable Witness Awareness:** Capacity to observe mental-emotional content without immediate identification becomes reliable
- **Ease of Settling:** Transition from surface activity to deeper rest occurs smoothly
- **Duration Capacity:** Sustained resting extends to 20-60 minutes or longer without constant struggle
- **Physical-Emotional Indicators:** Naturally slow subtle breath, deeply relaxed musculature, pervading peace
- **Post-Practice Integration:** Effects carry into daily life—increased presence, reduced reactivity, access to intuitive wisdom

Nevertheless, even advanced practitioners experience variable sessions. This reflects natural fluctuation influenced by sleep quality, life stress, recent ethical conduct, and ongoing aryu purification. Capacity develops through accumulation of countless sessions over extended time—patient dedication rather than dramatic breakthroughs.

Section 2: The Cultural Modeling Dimension - Verse 16's Unique Teaching

The Transmission Through Observation

Verse 16 establishes a rarely emphasized teaching: "when the children see this they will see that there is a human capacity for and practice of being internalized and serene in one's unconscious level of experience."[2] Ancient Egyptian culture transmitted meditative practice not primarily through verbal instruction but through observable modeling—children witnessing adults regularly spending time in visible states of deep internalized serenity.

The child who repeatedly witnesses parents, elders, and community members practicing meditation internalizes that the mind possesses this capacity—not as an exotic spiritual attainment but as ordinary human function. This observational foundation creates what developmental psychology terms "schema"—the mental framework understanding what constitutes normal human experience.

In Ancient Egyptian culture, adults made dedicated daily time for formal meditation—not hidden but in locations where household members could observe. The practice was announced, the adult settled into visible internalized serenity for extended periods, and household activities continued around them with understanding the practitioner had withdrawn to deeper levels.

The child observing this gradually internalizes: "This is something humans do. This represents normal capacity." No elaborate explanation necessary—the witnessed reality communicates the teaching. When such a child reaches adulthood, they approach meditation with internalized foundation validating the possibility.

Implementation for Contemporary Aspirants

Modern culture provides virtually no modeling of this capacity. Contemporary children grow to adulthood never witnessing sustained withdrawal to deeper mind levels. This absence creates a "cultural developmental deficit"—the mind conditioned to believe perpetual surface-level operation represents the only available mode.

Contemporary aspirants bear special responsibility for cultural transmission through visible modeling:

Designated Practice Space: Create a location where meditation occurs regularly—visible to family members, particularly children. Not elaborate; a simple chair or cushion in a quiet common area corner.

Announced Practice Time: Before beginning, announce intention: "I will be meditating for 45 minutes." This establishes boundaries, creates accountability, and identifies the behavior being observed.

Characteristic Visible Stillness: Maintain observable qualities communicating deep internalized serenity: physical stillness, relaxed facial features, quiet breath, sustained duration demonstrating genuine withdrawal.

Age-Appropriate Explanation: When asked, provide simple response: "I was meditating—spending time being very still and quiet inside my mind, resting in a peaceful place deeper than my regular thoughts."

Consistency Over Drama: Regular ordinary practice observed repeatedly over years internalizes more deeply than occasional dramatic sessions. The child witnessing a parent meditating three times weekly for years internalizes this far more than observing occasional retreats with no regular practice.

Your visible practice may constitute the only meditation modeling a child observes during formative years. In a culture where contemplative capacity remains almost completely absent, your regular visible meditation may plant seeds enabling their future spiritual development.

Section 3: Integration of Chapter 15's Complete Teaching Framework

The Fraudulent Persona's Inability to Access Deeper Levels

Verse 5 establishes that unethical living causes the mind to manifest as a "fraudulent persona"—personality distorted by aryu corruptions. These aryu create internal structural changes preventing authentic self-expression and blocking access to deeper levels where Ab Neter resides.

Each unethical action—lying, manipulating, taking what belongs to others—deposits specific aryu encoding the anxiety of deception, hardening against compassion, justification mechanisms, defensive patterns. As aryu accumulate, they create dense obstruction between Hat-Ka operations and deep ab/kara where Ab Neter sustains consciousness.

Practical consequence: the mind operating from dense aryu accumulation cannot penetrate beyond surface levels regardless of technique. When attempting to "rest in the unconscious," thoughts arise compulsively, anxiety pervades, restlessness dominates, or the mind collapses into drowsy dullness rather than alert deeper rest. The aryu density blocks pathways from Hat-Ka to deep ab/kara.

This explains why verse 15's meditation cannot function as isolated technique divorced from ethical living. Ethical action according to Maat progressively thins aryu density, creating conditions allowing the mind to eventually access deeper levels. Therefore, authentic selfhood recovery requires removing aryu corruptions through ethical transformation, which enables meditative capacity, which allows discovery of Ab Neter that has always sustained consciousness but remained hidden beneath the fraudulent persona's distortions.

Djehuty's Witness and Meditation Depth

Verses 9-10 teach that Djehuty as cosmic mind witnesses all actions, registering them "in the cosmic mind...and thus also in your own conscience."[2] This proves essential for understanding why ethical living enables meditative depth and why hidden unethical actions prove as corrupting as public violations.

The aspirant cannot circumvent ethical purification through privacy. Hidden lies create the same internal architectural changes as public ones; private criticism generates the same aryu density as open hostility; secret violations corrupt the mind's capacity identically to witnessed betrayals.

Aspirants who discover meditation practice reaches plateau despite regular formal sessions often face obstruction from subtle unethical patterns the mind has rationalized—patterns believed inconsequential because private or involving only "minor" violations. Yet Djehuty's witness reveals cosmic intelligence and one's own conscience register all actions equally, creating an identical obstruction regardless of external witness.

Therefore, developing capacity for verse 15's deeper rest requires rigorous ethical awareness about all behavior, public and private. Depth of meditation access directly corresponds to depth of ethical purification.

The Complete Integrated Framework

Chapter 15 presents an integrated system where each element supports the others:

- **Verse 5:** Unethical living creates the fraudulent persona blocking access to deeper mind levels
- **Verses 9-10:** Djehuty witnesses all actions, creating consequences determining capacity for meditative depth
- **Verse 15:** Resting in deeper mind levels provides systematic method for accessing where aryu can be addressed and Ab Neter discovered—but only through sufficient ethical purification
- **Verse 16:** Adults practicing visibly creates cultural foundation enabling next generations to develop contemplative capacity

The integration reveals: authentic selfhood recovery requires simultaneously addressing behavioral patterns (ethical transformation), mental operations (meditative capacity), and cultural context (modeling for transmission). None function adequately in isolation.

Section 4: Condensed Practice Guidance for Mature Practitioners

For Aspirants with Established Foundation

This addresses practitioners who have completed preliminary training and now seek to deepen understanding of what "resting in the unconscious" specifically entails. Guidance presumes the aspirant has:

- Established consistent ethical living with ongoing commitment to examining patterns contrary to Maat
- Developed basic concentration through Stages I-II
- Achieved proficiency in Stages III-IV practices
- Begun accessing Stage V-VI capacities

Specific Emphasis: Resting Beyond Hat-Ka Constant Operation

The mature practitioner must learn to distinguish genuine deeper rest from subtle surface operations:

Genuine Deep Ab/Kara Resting: Profound stillness without effort to maintain it; minimal thought activity occurring spontaneously not through suppression; alert spaciousness—awareness lucid and present but not engaged with content of mind ; naturally slow subtle breath, deeply relaxed musculature, pervading peace arising from depth; time perception shifts or releases temporal tracking entirely.

Subtle Hat-Ka Operations Disguised as Depth: Pleasant subtle thought-stream mistaken for contentless awareness; drowsy dullness where awareness dims; conceptual elaboration about meditation experience itself; maintaining witness awareness with subtle "I" observing—this represents Stage IV development but not yet deeper rest where even separate observer dissolves.

The Characteristic "Feel" of Resting Beyond Hat-Ka:

- **Effortless Maintenance:** Deeper rest sustains itself naturally—the mind has settled into its source
- **Non-Dual Quality:** Distinction between awareness and contents of mind begins dissolving
- **Sourceless Peace:** Profound peace arising from depth, not from surface conditions
- **Post-Session Integration:** Effects carry distinctly into daily life with internal spaciousness and reduced reactivity

Working with Plateau Experiences

When deeper access becomes difficult despite years of practice:

Examine Ethical Foundation: Often plateau signals subtle ethical compromises rationalized or overlooked. Conduct rigorous self-examination about partial truths, self-interest disguised as service, subtle manipulation, criticism masquerading as discernment.

Review Lifestyle Factors: Overly stimulating life—too much media, excessive social engagement, chaotic environment, inadequate sleep, poor dietary habits—prevents deeper access even for skilled practitioners.

Release Achievement Orientation: Plateau sometimes arises from subtle spiritual ambition—seeking to "achieve" states, comparing sessions to peak experiences, anxiety about progress. This orientation itself prevents the effortless settling verse 15 describes.

Temporary Return to Foundational Practices: When advanced practices feel blocked, returning to basic concentration (Stages I-II) often restores access more effectively than struggling with blocked advanced techniques.

Patient Persistence: Meditation development occurs through accumulation of countless sessions with natural variability. Periods feeling "dry" represent normal fluctuation, not regression.

The Patient Absorption Teaching

Verse 15 describes "rest-relaxed, and not restless-agitated"[2]—crucial instruction regarding quality of approach. Accessing and stabilizing in deeper levels occurs through patient absorption rather than forceful effort:

Patient Absorption: Gentle intention to rest beyond surface operations; allowing the mind to settle at its own pace; noticing thoughts without judgment, allowing natural return to depth; accepting whatever depth emerges without comparing or demanding particular results; trusting the mind knows its way home when conditions support it.

Forceful Effort (to Avoid): Straining to suppress thoughts; generating tension demanding immediate depth; comparing to peak experiences and judging current practice; pushing past tiredness or agitation; approaching with anxiety about achieving advanced states.

The teaching reveals: deeper levels already exist—Ab Neter already sustains the mind's capacity. Practice removes obstructions (aryu density and constant surface engagement) preventing recognition. Therefore, appropriate approach mirrors removing veils rather than building structures—gentle, patient, allowing rather than forcing.

Section 5: Practical Implementation Considerations

Creating Supportive Conditions

Maintaining regular access to deeper levels requires comprehensive life conditions supporting contemplative development:

- **Regular Practice Schedule:** Consistent daily time, ideally the same time each day
- **Protected Practice Space:** Designated quiet location creating association for settling
- **Duration Commitment:** 30-60 minutes minimum for mature practitioners
- **Association with Fellow Practitioners:** Connect with others committed to serious practice
- **Reduced Surface-Level Agitation:** Minimize media, unnecessary social engagements, constant rushing, technology before practice/sleep
- **Ethical Foundation Maintenance:** Ongoing vigilance about behavioral patterns—never assume purification completes

Integrating Practice as Cultural Modeling

For practitioners with children or interaction with young people:

- **Visible Regular Practice:** Meditate where children can observe; announce intention before beginning
- **Age-Appropriate Response to Questions:** Provide simple honest explanations without overwhelming philosophy
- **Respect for Practice Time:** Other household members respecting meditation creates modeling about importance
- **Modeling Integration:** Allow children to observe effects in daily life—pause before reacting, calm presence during stress, patience and kindness despite difficulties

Teacher Guidance and Community Support

Written instructions cannot replace experiential guidance from someone who has traversed the path. A qualified teacher can:

- Identify subtle self-deceptions the mind develops
- Provide personalized adjustments for individual challenges
- Confirm authentic progress versus self-deception
- Offer transmission—subtle consciousness transfer through direct contact

For practitioners without traditional teachers: experienced meditation instructors from authentic contemplative traditions; practitioners with extensive personal practice (10,000+ hours); online communities offering remote instruction; consistent engagement with Dr. Ashby's teachings through texts, recordings, and Sema Institute programs.

Maintaining Practice Through Life Changes

Different periods demand different approaches while maintaining unwavering commitment:

- **High-Activity Periods:** Maintain reduced but consistent practice—even 15-20 minutes daily
- **Low-Energy Phases:** Adapt practice—gentler approaches, preliminary stages, informal mindfulness
- **Life Transitions:** Expect temporary disruption to depth during major changes; maintain basic structure
- **Aging and Physical Limitations:** Adjust practice forms; deeper rest doesn't depend on particular postures

The Ultimate Understanding

The mature practitioner recognizes that the capacity to "rest in your heart (unconscious) level of your mind"[2] represents the fruition of integrated practice combining ethical transformation, systematic meditation training, and cultural transmission. This capacity does not emerge through isolated technique but through comprehensive approach addressing all dimensions of human development.

The practice reveals what has always been present: Ab Neter sustaining the mind's capacity from deep ab/kara level, prior to surface Hat-Ka operations. Through patient dedication to ethical living thinning aryu density, systematic meditation developing capacity for deeper withdrawal, and visible practice modeling contemplative transmission, the mind gradually discovers its authentic nature beyond the fraudulent persona—fulfilling both Prologue goals of earthly well-being through silent mind and feelings and discovery of the divine foundation within.

Therefore, approach verse 15's teaching not as an exceptional attainment but as natural maturation of human capacity when properly cultivated through integrated methods Amenemopet prescribes. Trust that with patient persistence, ethical integrity, and systematic practice following Chapter 9's progressive stages, the mind will develop the capacity to rest reliably at deeper levels—discovering the authentic selfhood that has always constituted your true nature beneath veiling aryu patterns and constant surface-level agitation.

References

[1] Ashby, M. (2019-25). Mysticism of Amenemopet Hieroglyphic Text Translation. Sema Institute of Ancient Egyptian Studies.

[2] Ashby, M. (2024). Amenemopet lectures 2024 by Dr. Muata Ashby transcripts. Sema Institute of Ancient Egyptian Studies.

[3] Ashby, M. (2019). Book Mysticism of Amenemopet Based on Hiero Text—Keys to Aspirants for Enlightenment. Sema Institute of Ancient Egyptian Studies.

[4] Ashby, M. (2019-25). Mysticism of Amenemopet Hieroglyphic Text Translation—Prologue. Sema Institute of Ancient Egyptian Studies.

[5] Ashby, M. (2024). Book Awakening Your Soul-Aware-Witness Ancient Egyptian Wisdom To Discover Divine Consciousness—v32. Sema Institute of Ancient Egyptian Studies.

[6] Ashby, M. (2019). Amenemopet lectures 2019 by Dr. Muata Ashby transcripts. Sema Institute of Ancient Egyptian Studies.
[7] Rogers, C. R. (1961). On becoming a person: A therapist's view of psychotherapy. Houghton Mifflin.
[8] Bandura, A. (2002). Selective moral disengagement in the exercise of moral agency. Journal of Moral Education, 31(2), 101-119.
[9] Greene, J. D., & Paxton, J. M. (2009). Patterns of neural activity associated with honest and dishonest moral decisions. Proceedings of the National Academy of Sciences, 106(30), 12506-12511.
[10] Festinger, L. (1957). A theory of cognitive dissonance. Stanford University Press.
[11] Hagerty, M. R., Isaacs, J., Brasington, L., Shupe, L., Fetz, E. E., & Cramer, S. C. (2013). Case study of ecstatic meditation: fMRI and EEG evidence of self-stimulating a reward system. Neural Plasticity, 2013.
[12] Berkovich-Ohana, A., & Glicksohn, J. (2014). The consciousness state space (CSS)—a unifying model for consciousness and self. Frontiers in Psychology, 5, 341.
[13] Lutz, A., Dunne, J. D., & Davidson, R. J. (2007). Meditation and the neuroscience of consciousness: An introduction. In The Cambridge handbook of consciousness (pp. 499-551). Cambridge University Press.
[14] Bandura, A. (1977). Social learning theory. Prentice Hall.
[15] Turpyn, C. C., & Chaplin, T. M. (2016). Mindful parenting and parents' emotion expression: Effects on adolescent risk behaviors. Mindfulness, 7(1), 246-254.
[16] Shapiro, S. L., Jazaieri, H., & Goldin, P. R. (2012). Mindfulness-based stress reduction effects on moral reasoning and decision making. The Journal of Positive Psychology, 7(6), 504-515.
[17] Tang, Y. Y., Hölzel, B. K., & Posner, M. I. (2015). The neuroscience of mindfulness meditation. Nature Reviews Neuroscience, 16(4), 213-225.
[18] Brewer, J. A., Worhunsky, P. D., Gray, J. R., Tang, Y. Y., Weber, J., & Kober, H. (2011). Meditation experience is associated with differences in default mode network activity and connectivity. Proceedings of the National Academy of Sciences, 108(50), 20254-20259.
[19] Raichle, M. E. (2015). The brain's default mode network. Annual Review of Neuroscience, 38, 433-447.
[20] Garrison, K. A., Zeffiro, T. A., Scheinost, D., Constable, R. T., & Brewer, J. A. (2015). Meditation leads to reduced default mode network activity beyond an active task. Cognitive, Affective, & Behavioral Neuroscience, 15(3), 712-720.
[21] Inglehart, R., & Baker, W. E. (2000). Modernization, cultural change, and the persistence of traditional values. American Sociological Review, 65(1), 19-51.
[22] Kasser, T., & Ryan, R. M. (1996). Further examining the American dream: Differential correlates of intrinsic and extrinsic goals. Personality and Social Psychology Bulletin, 22(3), 280-287.
[23] Wilmer, H. H., Sherman, L. E., & Chein, J. M. (2017). Smartphones and cognition: A review of research exploring the links between mobile technology habits and cognitive functioning. Frontiers in Psychology, 8, 605.
[24] Ashby, M. (2019-25). Mysticism of Amenemopet Hieroglyphic Text Translation—Chapter 6B. Sema Institute of Ancient Egyptian Studies.
[25] Ashby, M. (2025). Awakening Your Soul-Aware-Witness Ancient Egyptian Wisdom To Discover Divine Consciousness. Subtitle: Kemetic Transpersonal Psychology for Modern Times. Sema Institute of Ancient Egyptian Studies.
[26] Ashby, M. Egyptian Book of the Dead Hieroglyph Translations for Enlightenment Vol. 1. Sema Institute of Ancient Egyptian Studies.
[27] Ashby, M. Egyptian Book of the Dead Hieroglyph Translations for Enlightenment Volume 6. Sema Institute of Ancient Egyptian Studies.

CHAPTER 21: Commentary on Teachings of Amenemopet Chapter 16, Verses 8-11: The Psychology of Luxury Attachment and Turning Away from Divine Presence

Commentary on Sage Amenemopet's Teaching on Material Greed, Luxury Dependence, and Spiritual Sensitivity

SUMMARY OF THE TEACHINGS

Verse 8 instructs: "Refrain from the act of being greedy about copper, that is, a material from which status, wealth and possessions are derived." [1] Verse 9 teaches developing "a healthy enmity/disregard/indifference/aloofness towards finery and luxury such that you do not get used to depending on comforts and luxury to provide feelings of well-being; for those things are illusory and can be lost at any time." [1] Verse 10 challenges: "What would be the purpose of a person draping/wrapping themselves with and being enfolded in those fine linens so as to have everyone admiring them...as if they were ethical and generous...when in reality it is a façade hiding gluttony, greediness, craving, and avarice?" [1] Verse 11 reveals the profound spiritual consequence: "Actually, acting in that way (hypocrisy) amounts to the actual turning down/not accepting/turning away from (forsaking) the awareness and immanence of the Divine even while being in the presence of the Divine." [1]

1: HUMAN PSYCHOLOGY PRINCIPLE FOCUS OF CHAPTER 16

The human psychology principle that Chapter 16 addresses centers on luxury attachment syndrome—the progressive psychological dependence on external comforts and material acquisitions to provide feelings of well-being, which ultimately damages the capacity for experiencing the ever-present reality of divine consciousness (Ab Neter/Neberdjer). [2] Consider how the pursuit of copper—base metals used as money—represents not merely material greed but fundamental misidentification wherein hat (conscious awareness) becomes conditioned to believe external acquisitions can provide authentic well-being. The teaching reveals that luxury "produces agreeable sensations and supports ideas of always seeking comfort and enjoyment," which "thwarts the reality of life which is alternate comfort and discomfort." [2] This distorts the mind's capacity for handling situations as the mind "compromises truth for what it perceives as comfort and luxury—compromises ethics, becomes lazy wishing to go back to luxurious conditions." [2]

This directly impacts both Prologue goals established in verses 2 and 9. Without recognizing how luxury attachment corrupts the mind, earthly well-being (Prologue verse 2) becomes impossible because the personality develops chronic instability—requiring ever-increasing external stimulation to maintain even temporary satisfaction while simultaneously becoming less capable of handling life's inevitable alternations between comfort and discomfort. [2] Moreover, luxury preoccupation prevents discovery of kara where the Divine resides (Prologue verse 9) because "the mind engaging in externalized or body-mind occupations overlooks its presence thereby as if 'turning away' from it even as it is always there." [2] The teaching establishes that depending on luxury "damages the capacity for experiencing the ever-present reality of divine consciousness" by keeping the mind "involved with and seeking to repeat enjoying physical and mental comforts" rather than "experiencing Neberdjer." [2]

2: Behavioral Imperatives of this Chapter

The behavioral patterns arising from luxury attachment syndrome manifest as progressive psychological conditioning wherein hat becomes increasingly dependent on external circumstances for inner states. Building on Section 1's psychology, observable manifestations reveal how aryu accumulate and densify through repeated reinforcement of the delusion that comfort equals well-being.

The primary behavioral pattern emerges as comfort-seeking automaticity—unconscious habituation to luxury that transforms optional comforts into perceived necessities. [2] Consider the aspirant who initially recognizes fine linens as pleasant but unnecessary; through repeated exposure, hat begins associating luxury with self-worth and security. This progression operates insidiously: agreeable sensations from luxury create aryu (feeling-memories) in ab that arise into hat during discomfort, generating craving for return to pleasant conditions. Over time, these aryu densify, creating what feels like genuine need rather than conditioned preference.

This behavioral imperative manifests in material acquisition patterns described in the 2019 lecture transcript: "one gets a 100 ft yacht and then realizes somebody in the next company gets a 120 ft yacht and then he feels bad, he has to get a 150ft yacht and there's no end to desires."[3] The mind cannot rest because each acquisition reinforces the aryu pattern that external objects provide fulfillment. The teaching describes this as "pouring gasoline on a fire"[3]—the desires function as fuel intensifying the heated mind and feelings that believes "all your energies, all your Neberdjer energies, is actually going into this illusion."[3] Rather than satisfying desire, each acquisition strengthens the craving mechanism itself.

In lifestyle dependence, luxury attachment produces what verse 9 describes as "getting used to depending on comforts and luxury to provide feelings of well-being." [1] Modern aspirants experience this as an inability to practice spiritual exercises when conditions are less than ideal—the meditation cushion must be perfect, the temperature optimal, the environment pristine. The teaching reveals this as injurious to spiritual development because it conditions the mind to require external perfection before engaging inner work. The capacity to maintain equanimity regardless of circumstances—what the Keys document calls "equal vision for luxury or non-optimal conditions"—never develops. [2]

The hypocrisy pattern described in verse 10 emerges when the mind recognizes the teaching but continues luxury pursuit through rationalization. The personality "drapes/wraps itself with fine linens so as to have everyone admiring them...as if they were ethical and generous" while "in reality it is a façade hiding gluttony, greediness, craving, and avarice." [1] Modern manifestations include spiritual practitioners who display external markers of devotion—meditation retreats, yoga classes, spiritual books—while privately maintaining luxury dependencies and judging others who lack similar comforts. This behavior pattern reveals aryu operating to protect ego-identity from the discomfort of genuine transformation.

Most significantly, these behaviors create what verse 11 identifies as "turning down/not accepting/turning away from (forsaking) the awareness and immanence of the Divine even while being in the presence of the Divine." [1] The aspirant may sit in a temple, recite prayers, study scriptures—yet hat remains occupied with planning the next comfort acquisition, comparing possessions with others, or mentally rehearsing justifications for luxury maintenance. Ab Neter remains present sustaining consciousness, but aryu density renders the personality opaque to this presence, creating the experience of Divine absence even during supposedly spiritual activities.

The teaching establishes these behavioral patterns with compassion, recognizing they often develop unconsciously through cultural conditioning that actively promotes luxury dependence as success. Nevertheless, understanding these patterns becomes essential for transformation, as they prevent both earthly well-being (through chronic dissatisfaction) and spiritual discovery (through perpetual externalized attention).

3: Mystic Psychology-Metaphysical Implications

Building on Section 2's behavioral manifestations, the metaphysical mechanics reveal how luxury attachment operates at mind architecture level to obstruct Ab Neter awareness. The wisdom establishes that Divine consciousness (Neberdjer) remains eternally present as "the ground of being and awareness before awareness engages mind and senses to cognize about life and reality." [2] Luxury attachment does not remove this presence—rather, it creates specific aryu patterns that render the mind insensible to what continuously sustains it.

The fundamental metaphysical principle operates through attention displacement mechanics. When hat engages with luxury objects, attention flows outward through sense organs toward external stimuli rather than penetrating inward toward ab levels where Ab Neter resides. Each pleasant sensation from luxury creates aryu in ab—feeling-memories encoding "this external condition provided satisfaction." These aryu accumulate, creating density patterns that subsequent mind operations follow preferentially, similar to water flowing through established channels rather than breaking new ground.

The Keys document reveals the critical insight: "Divine consciousness Ab Neter-Neberdjer is always there but the mind engaging in externalized or body-mind occupations overlooks its presence thereby as if 'turning away' from it." [2] This describes the essential mechanism—the mind possesses the inherent capacity to recognize its divine source, yet when habitually directed toward external acquisitions, this capacity atrophies through disuse. The teaching employs the phrase "as if turning away" deliberately—Ab Neter cannot actually depart, being the very foundation of mind capacity itself. However, the experiential reality for the personality becomes indistinguishable from actual absence when attention remains perpetually externalized.

Luxury pursuit creates what I teach as opacity through aryu accumulation. Consider how clear water becomes murky when sediment enters—the water remains but visibility diminishes. Similarly, each luxury-focused thought, feeling, and action deposits aryu "sediment" in ab. As these accumulate, the mind attempting to penetrate from hat toward Ab Neter encounters increasingly dense obstruction. The personality experiences this as an inability to "feel" Divine presence despite intellectual understanding of omnipresence. The teaching identifies this condition where the personality lacks "sufficient clarity—spiritual sensitivity to experience its existence not with mind but with present awareness of consciousness reality beyond mind." [2]

The cosmology reveals why external comforts cannot provide genuine fulfillment: consciousness (Neberdjer) manifests as all apparent objects, meaning luxury items are expressions of the same divine reality as the consciousness seeking them. The pursuit represents the mind chasing manifestations of consciousness (Neberdjer) while forgetting its essential nature as sustained by Ab Neter—analogous to a person searching for glasses while wearing them. Verse 10's description of "gluttony, greediness, craving, and avarice" hidden beneath fine linens illustrates how luxury attachment perpetuates rather than resolves fundamental dissatisfaction arising from misidentification. [1]

The most profound metaphysical implication appears in verse 11's teaching about forsaking divine awareness "even while being in the presence of the Divine." [1] This reveals that physical proximity to sacred space, formal spiritual practice, or intellectual study of teachings provides no protection against luxury attachment's mind-occluding effects. The aryu patterns generated through comfort-seeking override environmental factors, demonstrating that purification requires internal transformation rather than external circumstance modification.

The teaching establishes that breaking this pattern necessitates recognizing luxury as "a temporary source of enjoyment that keeps the mind involved with and seeking to repeat enjoying physical and mental comforts" rather than penetrating to "experiencing Neberdjer." [2] This recognition enables the mind to redirect attention from external acquisitions toward the internal Ab Neter reality that alone provides sustainable well-being—what the Prologue describes as discovering the divine sanctuary within once worldly affairs are handled with wisdom philosophy. [4]

4: Transpersonal Psychology Research

Contemporary transpersonal psychology research provides empirical validation for Amenemopet's ancient insights regarding luxury attachment and spiritual sensitivity. The hedonic adaptation phenomenon, extensively documented across psychological literature, demonstrates precisely what verse 9 describes: initial pleasure from luxury acquisition diminishes through habituation, requiring ever-increasing stimulation for equivalent satisfaction. [5] To this finding we may add that the "equivalent satisfaction" is only temporary and therefore philosophically illusory. Studies by Kasser (2002) reveal that materialistic value orientation correlates inversely with psychological well-being, life satisfaction, and vitality—empirically confirming the teaching that depending on external comforts undermines rather than supports authentic flourishing. [6]

Neuroscientific research illuminates the aryu accumulation mechanisms described in Section 3. Default Mode Network studies demonstrate how repeated thought patterns create preferential neural pathways, with externally-focused acquisition thoughts strengthening circuits associated with craving and dissatisfaction. [7] Davidson and Lutz's (2008) neuroplasticity research reveals that attention training through meditation practice physically restructures brain regions, supporting the teaching's claim that redirecting the mind's attention from external luxury toward internal awareness requires systematic practice rather than mere intellectual understanding. [8]

Buddhist psychology's concept of vedanā (hedonic tone) parallels Amenemopet's teaching about "agreeable sensations" from luxury conditioning the mind toward craving. Research by Grabovac et al. (2011) demonstrates how pleasant sensations automatically trigger attachment responses in the untrained mind—the behavioral automaticity described in Section 2—while contemplative training develops the capacity to experience pleasant conditions without developing dependency. [9] This empirical validation supports verse 9's instruction to "develop healthy enmity / disregard / indifference / aloofness towards finery and luxury" as preventive against habitual conditioning. [1]

Environmental psychology research on materialistic cultures reveals systemic conditioning effects predicted by the teaching. Twenge's (2017) research on generational shifts documents increasing materialistic orientation correlating with decreased empathy, increased anxiety, and diminished capacity for delayed gratification—behavioral patterns Amenemopet identifies as consequences of luxury attachment undermining ethical capacity and spiritual sensitivity. [10] Cross-cultural studies demonstrate that societies emphasizing material acquisition over relational and spiritual values exhibit higher rates of depression, anxiety, and existential dissatisfaction despite increased material wealth. [11]

Studies on self-determination theory distinguish between intrinsic needs (autonomy, competence, relatedness) and extrinsic goals (wealth, possessions, image), finding that extrinsic goal pursuit—equivalent to luxury attachment—fails to provide lasting satisfaction even when achieved while actively diminishing well-being through displacing intrinsic need fulfillment. [12] This research framework validates Amenemopet's distinction between genuine well-being arising from Ab Neter connection versus illusory satisfaction sought through external acquisitions.

Contemplative neuroscience provides particular validation for verse 11's teaching about forsaking divine awareness through externalized attention. fMRI studies reveal that during authentic contemplative states, brain activity shifts from external-processing regions toward interoceptive awareness networks associated with present-moment awareness. [13] Importantly, research demonstrates this shift requires sustained practice to overcome habitual externalization patterns—supporting the teaching that luxury attachment creates mind conditions requiring systematic purification rather than spontaneous spiritual recognition. Research on minimalism and voluntary simplicity movements provides applied validation, documenting psychological benefits including reduced anxiety, increased life satisfaction, enhanced relationship quality, and reports of greater spiritual depth when individuals intentionally reduce material dependencies—outcomes consistent with the teaching's promise that developing aloofness toward luxury enables both earthly well-being and spiritual discovery. [14]

5: Spiritual Implications for Aspirants

Part A - Pastoral Concerns

Modern aspirants face particular challenges implementing these teachings within consumer cultures systematically designed to cultivate luxury dependence. Consider the seeker raised in environments where comfort constitutes an assumed entitlement rather than occasional privilege—the personality develops unconscious expectations that spirituality should also provide comfort, convenience, and pleasant sensations. When Amenemopet teaches developing "enmity" toward luxury, such aspirants may experience this as threatening their fundamental security rather than recognizing it as liberation from conditioned dependency limiting spiritual capacity. [1]

Confusion between legitimate needs and luxury indulgence creates paralysis. Someone struggling financially asks: "Should I not work to improve my circumstances? Doesn't this teaching require poverty?" Yet verse 8's warning against "greed about copper" addresses psychological attachment rather than practical sustenance. [1] The distinction lies in motivation: working to provide necessities differs fundamentally from luxury pursuit driven by the belief that external acquisitions provide inner fulfillment. Nevertheless, distinguishing these motivations requires self-honesty often obscured by aryu patterns justifying any comfort-seeking as "reasonable."

Comfort Addiction Preventing Transformation

Modern aspirants face a particular challenge that financial observers have identified: comfort operates not as a neutral condition but as a narcotic—dulling spiritual ambition while creating dependency that prevents transformation. Consider the seeker who achieves sufficient material circumstances to meet genuine needs yet continues pursuing luxury—not from necessity but from comfort addiction. Such individuals become, in contemporary economic terms, "comfortable enough not to change" yet never achieving either Prologue goal: neither earthly wellbeing (remaining financially insecure despite income) nor divine discovery (comfort dependency occupying hat awareness, preventing Ab Neter recognition).

This validates verse 9's warning from an unexpected angle: people remain spiritually impoverished not from lacking resources but from comfort patterns that prevent the transformative discomfort spiritual practice requires. The heated mind rationalizes each luxury as reasonable while accumulating the very dependencies the teaching warns against—maintaining just sufficient comfort to avoid crisis yet insufficient discipline to achieve freedom.

True Wealth as Internal Freedom

Contemporary economic analysis reveals profound alignment with Amenemopet's framework: genuine wealth manifests not through possession display but as optionality—control over time, choices, emotions; capacity to decline external demands without fear. This reframes prosperity from external accumulation to internal freedom, bridging both Prologue goals seamlessly. Earthly wellbeing requires genuine optionality (financial independence from luxury dependencies), while divine discovery demands freedom from external validation-seeking that keeps the mind externalized rather than discovering Ab Neter presence within kara.

Indeed, the ancient Egyptian teaching recognizes what material analysis confirms: worldly luxury inevitably perishes through loss, decay, or death—proving fundamentally unreliable as a wellbeing foundation. Real wealth manifests through ger (serene silent mind) enabling Neberdjer recognition—the only treasure surviving temporal circumstances. As the proverb instructs: "On the journey to the truth, one must stay on the path of love and enlightenment, the heart filled with greed and lust will be overcome by its selfishness." Luxury attachment literally obstructs the path by filling the mind with acquisition patterns rather than love and enlightenment orientation.

I Deserve It" Ego Justification Patterns

Perhaps most insidiously, luxury attachment disguises itself through ego justification mechanisms contemporary observers identify as "the most expensive phrase": *"I deserve it."* This adult version of "I want it now" captures precisely how the heated mind rationalizes dependency as legitimate need. Modern aspirants frequently employ this pattern: "I've worked hard, therefore luxury constitutes earned reward" or "Self-care requires these comforts"—accumulating the very dependencies verse 9 warns against while believing spiritual practice remains unaffected.

The ancient wisdom anticipated this rationalization pattern: "Neither let prosperity put out the eyes of circumspection, nor abundance cut off the hands of frugality; they that too much indulge in the superfluities of life, shall live to lament the want of its necessaries." The teaching reveals that "deserving" operates as aryu-driven justification rather than genuine spiritual discernment. Distinguishing legitimate needs from comfort indulgence requires self-honesty often obscured by heated mind patterns insisting every desire constitutes reasonable necessity—precisely the confusion preventing both earthly optionality and divine discovery that freedom from such dependencies would enable.

Corporate culture pressures present particular obstacles. The aspirant whose profession demands luxury displays—designer clothing for client meetings, expensive vehicles for status signaling, luxury experiences for networking—faces genuine conflict between livelihood and spiritual practice. Verse 10's warning against hypocrisy applies directly: using spiritual teachings to rationalize luxury maintenance while performing external spiritual activities. [1] The temptation emerges to compartmentalize—"I'll be spiritual on weekends but must compete materially Monday through Friday"—yet this divided mind prevents the integration necessary for genuine transformation.

Social media amplifies luxury attachment through constant exposure to curated displays of others' possessions, triggering the comparison dynamics Amenemopet identifies. The aspirant scrolls through feeds showing luxury travel, gourmet meals, designer purchases, creating aryu that whisper "you need this to be happy" even during meditation practice. Modern culture makes the teaching's challenge acute: developing "indifference/aloofness" toward luxury while surrounded by perpetual luxury promotion targeting every sensory channel. [1]

Perhaps most insidiously, luxury attachment disguises itself as spiritual advancement. The aspirant accumulates expensive spiritual accessories—meditation cushions, altar pieces, retreat fees, teacher trainings—rationalizing each purchase as supporting practice while actually feeding the same acquisition patterns verse 10 exposes. [1] The personality prides itself on "investing in spiritual growth" without recognizing how luxury dependency regarding spiritual accoutrements differs minimally from luxury dependency regarding worldly possessions.

PART B - METHODS FOR TRANSFORMATION

Based on the teaching presented by Sage Amenemopet that one should refrain from greed about base metals and develop healthy aloofness toward luxury, the application of the inverse doctrine methodology suggests one should also cultivate systematic practices that train the mind to recognize and release attachment patterns while discovering inner contentment independent of external circumstances, as these support the cultivation of spiritual sensitivity to Ab Neter presence.

Practice 1: Luxury Inventory and Gradual Reduction. Create a written inventory of all items/conditions considered necessary for well-being. For each entry, honestly assess: "Is this genuine necessity or conditioned luxury?" Begin gradual reduction, starting with easiest items—perhaps expensive coffee becomes standard coffee, designer brands become practical equivalents. Notice hat's resistance arising as aryu activate, bringing up feelings of deprivation or loss. Rather than suppressing these reactions, observe them: "Hat experiences anxiety when considering simpler conditions; ab contains aryu associating luxury with security." This observation without identification begins thinning aryu density.

Example implementation: The aspirant accustomed to luxury bedding reduces thread count incrementally over months, observing how the mind adapts. Initially, discomfort arises strongly—hat protests "I can't sleep!" Yet maintaining awareness reveals the aryu pattern: "The belief that sleep requires luxury is conditioning, not reality." After an adjustment period, the mind recognizes it can rest regardless of external conditions, weakening one luxury attachment while strengthening the capacity for equanimity.

Practice 2: Comfort Fluctuation Training. Deliberately alternate between comfortable and less-comfortable conditions while maintaining meditative awareness. Sit in preferred meditation posture for ten minutes, then shift to less comfortable position—maintain awareness of arising sensations without reactive adjustment. Extend this principle: sometimes practice in ideal environment, sometimes in challenging conditions. The teaching reveals life naturally alternates between comfort and discomfort; [2] training the mind to maintain equanimity through both conditions prevents luxury dependency while developing genuine stability.

Example implementation: The office worker alternates between a comfortable desk setup and practicing meditation during an uncomfortable subway commute. Initially, hat protests vigorously during commute practice—noise, crowding, physical discomfort trigger strong aversion. Patient observation reveals these reactions as aryu patterns demanding preferred conditions. Gradually, the mind develops the capacity to access inner silence regardless of external circumstances—directly weakening the luxury attachment that requires "perfect" conditions before engaging spiritual practice.

Practice 3: Gratitude Without Grasping. When experiencing comfort or luxury, consciously acknowledge: "This pleasant condition arises through divine providence; I receive it with gratitude without demanding its continuation or seeking its enhancement." This prevents the aryu formation that transforms appreciation into attachment. When discomfort arises, practice similar acknowledgment: "This challenging condition also arises within Neberdjer's manifestation; I receive it without resistance." The practice trains the mind to experience varying conditions without reactive craving or aversion—the equanimity verse 9 indicates as essential for spiritual development. [1]

Example implementation: The practitioner enjoying a restaurant meal deliberately notices arising thoughts: "This tastes wonderful—I should come here weekly/This is how food should always taste/Others don't have such meals—I'm fortunate/I deserve this after my hard work." Each thought reveals aryu patterns attempting to either escalate luxury seeking or justify it through comparison. Instead, practice: "Neberdjer manifests as this nourishment; I receive without grasping." This allows enjoyment without creating new attachment aryu while supporting verse 11's teaching about maintaining divine awareness even during worldly activities. [1]

The systematic application of these practices operates on the principle established throughout Amenemopet's teaching: aryu thin through consistent recognition and non-reinforcement rather than forceful suppression. Patient absorption of the wisdom that external conditions cannot provide authentic well-being—combined with direct experience discovering inner contentment through spiritual practice—gradually reveals the Ab Neter presence that luxury attachment obscured. This enables both Prologue goals: earthly well-being arising from equanimous capacity rather than luxury dependency, and spiritual discovery of the divine sanctuary within consciousness itself.

References

[1] Ashby, M. (2019-25). *Mysticism of Amenemopet Hieroglyphic Text Translation.* Chapter 16, Verses 8-11. Sema Institute of Ancient Egyptian Studies.

[2] Ashby, M. (2025). *Keys to Sage Amenemopet wisdom text trilinear translation chapter 16.* Sema Institute of Ancient Egyptian Studies.

[3] Ashby, M. (2019). *Amenemopet lectures 2019 by Dr Muata Ashby transcripts.* Week 7, August 28, 2019. Sema Institute of Ancient Egyptian Studies.

[4] Ashby, M. (2024). *Amenemopet lectures 2024 by Dr Muata Ashby transcripts.* Sema Institute of Ancient Egyptian Studies.

[5] Lyubomirsky, S. (2011). Hedonic adaptation to positive and negative experiences. In S. Folkman (Ed.), *The Oxford Handbook of Stress, Health, and Coping* (pp. 200-224). Oxford University Press.

[6] Kasser, T. (2002). *The High Price of Materialism.* MIT Press.

[7] Brewer, J. A., Worhunsky, P. D., Gray, J. R., Tang, Y. Y., Weber, J., & Kober, H. (2011). Meditation experience is associated with differences in default mode network activity and connectivity. *Proceedings of the National Academy of Sciences*, 108(50), 20254-20259.

[8] Davidson, R. J., & Lutz, A. (2008). Buddha's brain: Neuroplasticity and meditation. *IEEE Signal Processing Magazine*, 25(1), 176-174.

[9] Grabovac, A. D., Lau, M. A., & Willett, B. R. (2011). Mechanisms of mindfulness: A Buddhist psychological model. *Mindfulness*, 2(3), 154-166.

[10] Twenge, J. M. (2017). *iGen: Why Today's Super-Connected Kids Are Growing Up Less Rebellious, More Tolerant, Less Happy.* Atria Books.

[11] Kasser, T., & Ryan, R. M. (1993). A dark side of the American dream: Correlates of financial success as a central life aspiration. *Journal of Personality and Social Psychology*, 65(2), 410-422.

[12] Ryan, R. M., & Deci, E. L. (2000). Self-determination theory and the facilitation of intrinsic motivation, social development, and well-being. *American Psychologist*, 55(1), 68-78.

[13] Tang, Y. Y., Hölzel, B. K., & Posner, M. I. (2015). The neuroscience of mindfulness meditation. *Nature Reviews Neuroscience*, 16(4), 213-225.

[14] Alexander, S., & Ussher, S. (2012). The voluntary simplicity movement: A multi-national survey analysis in theoretical context. *Journal of Consumer Culture*, 12(1), 66-86.

CHAPTER 22: Commentary on Teachings of Amenemopet Chapter 17, Verses 2-3, 6: The Psychology of Volitional Fraud and Conscience Registration -Commentary on Sage Amenemopet's Teaching on Deliberate Unrighteousness and the Inescapable Witness

VERSE SUMMARY

Verse 2 addresses fraudulent measurement: "Concerning the measurement of portions or volumes of items such as grains or land or other objects to be distributed to another person, the cheater, who was supposed to give certain quantities, turns down that idea, turns away from that idea and instead knowingly/forcefully{nkt} gives a fraudulent amount instead of the correct amount." [1] Verse 3 reveals the inescapable psychological consequence: "certainly, the evidence and guilt of the corrupt act of such a person are sealed by the witnessing of that act by their own eye (i.e. their own conscience registers it in their unconscious mind)." [1] Verse 6 extends the teaching to complicity: "Desist/abstain/cease/refrain from/renounce the act of acting in concert(conspiring, facilitating, being a co-conspirator, accessory to the crime, etc.), along with that person who does the measuring in such an unrighteous manner." [1]

1: HUMAN PSYCHOLOGY PRINCIPLE FOCUS OF CHAPTER 17

The human psychology principle that Chapter 17, verses 2-3, 6 addresses centers on volitional unrighteousness syndrome—the deliberate, conscious perpetration of fraud with full awareness of wrongdoing, which creates inescapable aryu registration in ab (unconscious mind) regardless of external detection or punishment. [2] The Keys document emphasizes that "this is presented by Amenemopet as being done with volition and taking action to do it so it's not by mistake," drawing parallels to the Set mythology wherein Set "acted unrighteously and even after being tricked into admitting his unrighteousness he continued to act unrighteously purposely—could not stop himself and did not want to stop." [2]

This teaching addresses the delusion that unrighteousness escapes consequences when undetected by others. Consider how verse 2's description of the cheater who "knowingly/forcefully{nkt} gives a fraudulent amount" reveals conscious choice operating against ethical conscience. [1] The term {nkt} specifies forceful, deliberate action—hat (conscious awareness) actively overriding any ethical restraint to pursue selfish advantage. Verse 3's revelation that "evidence is lodged in their unconscious mind even while their weak conscience has allowed and experienced it without correcting the personality" demonstrates how aryu formation occurs independent of external accountability. [2]

This directly impacts both Prologue goals. Earthly well-being (Prologue verse 2) becomes impossible when personality foundations rest on deliberate fraud—the internal discord between action and conscience creates perpetual psychic instability. Moreover, the discovery of kara where Ab Neter resides (Prologue verse 9) cannot occur when thick aryu from volitional unrighteousness create opacity blocking the mind's capacity to recognize divine presence. The teaching establishes that "this internal record of aryu will produce the proper resulting effect (divine dispensation for the offence) at the appropriate time in life or in the next lifetime," revealing the inescapable nature of aryu accountability within consciousness architecture. [2]

2: Behavioral Imperatives of this Chapter

The behavioral patterns arising from volitional unrighteousness syndrome manifest as progressive ethical corruption wherein hat develops systematic rationalization mechanisms to justify deliberate fraud. Building on Section 1's psychology, observable manifestations reveal how aryu from conscious wrongdoing create self-perpetuating cycles of ethical degradation.

The primary behavioral pattern emerges as conscience suppression automaticity—habitual overriding of ethical restraint through increasingly sophisticated self-justification. Verse 2's description of the cheater who "turns down that idea, turns away from that idea" reveals active mental processes dismissing ethical considerations. [1] Initially, perpetrating fraud may generate significant internal resistance—conscience protests, anxiety arises, justifications require elaborate construction. However, repeated fraud creates aryu patterns in ab that make subsequent violations progressively easier. Hat learns to suppress ethical signals automatically, developing what appears as absence of conscience but actually represents conscience burial beneath dense aryu accumulation.

This behavioral imperative manifests distinctly in rationalization architecture. The Keys document identifies verse 6's pattern where "a person takes ill-gotten gains from another and says 'I did not steal it he did so it's ok for me to take it from him'"—rationalization through intermediary responsibility. [2] Modern examples proliferate: the employee who pads expense reports reasoning "the company can afford it"; the business owner who underpays workers arguing "they accepted the wage"; the professional who inflates credentials claiming "everyone exaggerates." Each rationalization represents hat's elaborate construction to bypass ethical restraint while maintaining self-image as fundamentally honest.

The complicity pattern described in verse 6 reveals ethical corruption's social dimension. The teaching warns against "acting in concert(conspiring, facilitating, being a co-conspirator, accessory to the crime, etc.)" with fraudulent actors. [1] Modern aspirants encounter this constantly: remaining silent when witnessing fraud, processing transactions knowing they involve deception, providing expertise for unethical purposes while rationalizing "I'm just doing my job." The Keys document clarifies: "The person who orders the crime is as guilty as the perpetrator following the instructions." [2] This teaching demolishes defense mechanisms separating one's own hands from dirty work through intermediaries.

The progressive desensitization pattern operates insidiously. What initially requires conscious suppression of ethical resistance eventually becomes habitual—aryu density makes fraud feel normal. The 2019 lecture transcript describes this: someone who "could not stop himself and did not want to stop"—the point where ethical compass has been so thoroughly compromised that unrighteousness becomes the path of least resistance. [2] Hat no longer experiences internal conflict because conscience has been buried beneath such thick aryu that ethical signals cannot penetrate conscious awareness.

Cross-reference with Chapter 15:9-10 illuminates the witness consciousness mechanism. That teaching reveals "the eye of awareness of the god of the intellect of the Creator Spirit, Ra, who presides over your mind and intellect and who is the cosmic mind itself; he is the divinity that goes around all of Egypt and thus sees all. Therefore, even the acts done, when no one is around, are registered in the cosmic mind (the god of intellect) and thus also in your own conscience." [3] This establishes that verse 3's "sealed by the witnessing of that act by their own eye" refers not merely to personal memory but to registration in universal consciousness expressing as individual conscience. [1]

The teaching establishes these behavioral patterns with compassion, recognizing that volitional unrighteousness often develops from environmental conditioning where ethical compromise becomes survival strategy. Nevertheless, understanding these patterns becomes essential, as they create irreversible aryu consequences that no amount of external success can neutralize—what the Keys document, based on the Ancient Egyptian scriptures, describes as "divine dispensation for the offence" manifesting "at the appropriate time." [2]

3: MYSTIC PSYCHOLOGY-METAPHYSICAL IMPLICATIONS

Building on Section 2's behavioral manifestations, the metaphysical mechanics reveal how volitional fraud operates at mind architecture level to create what I teach as inescapable aryu registration regardless of external circumstances. The wisdom establishes the fundamental principle: witness consciousness (Amun-Ra aspect of divine awareness) observes all actions, and this observation creates permanent registration in both cosmic consciousness and individual unconscious mind. [4]

The core metaphysical principle operates through conscience as divine interface mechanics. The Definitions document explains: "Conscience may be thought of as the clear or unclear feeling that a person who is ethically purer and has a more 'psychologically well-adjusted ego' is more in touch with that deeper essential nature of beingness, the effulgent beingness which itself serves as a guide for them as to what is truth, falsehood, right and wrong." [4] Verse 3's teaching that "evidence is sealed by the witnessing of that act by their own eye (i.e. their own conscience registers it in their unconscious mind)" reveals conscience as the mechanism through which Ab Neter awareness penetrates to hat level. [1]

Consider how this operates: Every action, thought, and feeling occurs within consciousness sustained by Ab Neter. Witness consciousness (Amun-Ra) observes all experiences—this observation constitutes what Chapter 15:10 describes as "the eye of awareness of the god of the intellect of the Creator Spirit, Ra." [3] When fraudulent action occurs, witness consciousness observes it. This observation creates aryu impression in ab—not as external recording but as the very structure of mind being modified through experience. The Keys document, based on the Ancient Egyptian scriptures, clarifies: "This internal record of aryu will produce the proper resulting effect (divine dispensation for the offence) at the appropriate time in life or in the next lifetime." [2]

The profound implication: volitional fraud creates what might be termed conscience-corrupting aryu density. Unlike aryu from ignorant action (where personality acts without full awareness), volitional unrighteousness creates aryu while hat consciously overrides ethical restraint. This establishes particularly dense patterns because the action reinforces both the fraudulent behavior and the conscience-suppression mechanism. Over repeated instances, these accumulated aryu make the personality progressively opaque to Ab Neter presence—what the Keys document, based on the Ancient Egyptian scriptures, describes as aryu that "warps and blocks (by making mind opaque) capacity to understand." [5]

The Set mythology parallel reveals the endpoint of this progression. Set's character demonstrates how volitional unrighteousness becomes self-perpetuating: "even after being tricked into admitting his unrighteousness he continued to act unrighteously purposely—could not stop himself and did not want to stop." [2] This describes a personality structure so dominated by thick aryu from deliberate fraud that ethical functioning becomes impossible. The personality reaches a state where conscience has been so thoroughly suppressed that unrighteousness feels natural while righteousness feels foreign—complete inversion of spiritual orientation.

The cosmology establishes why external detection provides no protection. Whether fraud remains secret or becomes exposed, the aryu formation occurs identically because registration happens in the ab (unconscious mind), which is observed by witness consciousness. The teaching reveals what modern aspirants often miss: thinking "if no one knows, there's no consequence" represents fundamental misunderstanding of consciousness architecture. Witness consciousness knows—and witness consciousness is one's own deepest nature observing experience.

The most critical metaphysical implication: these aryu do not disappear through time, success, or rationalization. The Keys document, based on the Ancient Egyptian scriptures,[12] explicitly states they "will produce the proper resulting effect (divine dispensation for the offence) at the appropriate time in life or in the next lifetime." [2] This reveals spiritual law operating beyond human timeframes—aryu patterns established through volitional fraud must work themselves out through corresponding experiences, whether in current embodiment or future ones. The teaching describes this as "divine dispensation" not as punishment from external deity but as karmic equilibrium requiring experiences that reveal consequences of unethical patterns.

The wisdom establishes that transformation requires not merely ceasing fraud but actively thinning accumulated aryu through ethical conduct, philosophical understanding, and meditation practice that gradually restore conscience sensitivity. This supports both Prologue goals: earthly well-being through alignment with Maat rather than opposition to cosmic order, and spiritual discovery through removing aryu opacity that obscures Ab Neter presence.

4: Transpersonal Psychology Research

Contemporary transpersonal and depth psychology research provides empirical validation for Amenemopet's ancient insights regarding conscience, moral injury, and the psychological consequences of deliberate wrongdoing. Research on moral injury—psychological distress resulting from actions violating one's moral code—demonstrates precisely what verse 3 describes: unethical actions create lasting psychological imprints regardless of external consequences. Studies reveal that perpetrating moral transgressions produces more severe and enduring psychological effects than witnessing such acts, supporting the teaching's emphasis on personal ethical responsibility. [6]

Neuroscientific research illuminates the conscience registration mechanisms described in Section 3. Studies using fMRI demonstrate that moral decision-making activates specific neural networks involving prefrontal cortex, amygdala, and insula regions. Importantly, research shows these networks activate even when ethical violations remain undetected, validating the teaching that "evidence is sealed by the witnessing of that act by their own eye" independent of external accountability. [7] The finding that repeated ethical violations correlate with decreased neural activation in conscience-related regions provides empirical support for the progressive desensitization pattern identified in Section 2.

Buddhist psychology's concept of karma parallels Amenemopet's aryu teaching with remarkable precision. Research by Grabovac et al. (2011) demonstrates how actions create lasting mental impressions (sankharas) that condition future behavior—the behavioral automaticity described in Section 2. Studies examining the relationship between ethical conduct and mental health consistently show that moral violations predict increased anxiety, depression, and reduced well-being even when perpetrators avoid external punishment, empirically confirming the teaching that unrighteousness undermines earthly well-being regardless of worldly success. [8]

Research on rationalization and cognitive dissonance provides validation for the conscience suppression patterns Section 2 identifies. Studies demonstrate that individuals engaging in ethical violations develop increasingly elaborate justification systems to maintain self-concept as moral people while continuing immoral behavior—precisely the "turning away from that idea" verse 2 describes. [9] Importantly, longitudinal research shows these rationalization patterns strengthen over time through repeated violations, supporting the teaching's warning about progressive ethical corruption creating personality structures resistant to correction.

Studies examining collective responsibility and complicity validate verse 6's teaching about conspiratorial guilt. Social psychology research demonstrates that individuals involved in group wrongdoing experience psychological consequences proportional to their perceived responsibility, even when their role involves only tacit support rather than direct action. Research on moral disengagement reveals how individuals distance themselves from ethical responsibility through mechanisms like diffusion of responsibility and displacement of accountability—the patterns verse 6 explicitly warns against. [10]

Contemplative neuroscience research on meditation and ethical development provides validation for the purification approach the teaching implies. Studies show that mindfulness and compassion meditation practices enhance ethical decision-making capacity and strengthen neural networks associated with moral reasoning, supporting the wisdom that systematic spiritual practice can gradually restore conscience sensitivity obscured by aryu accumulation. [11] Research demonstrating that meditation increases interoceptive awareness—the capacity to perceive internal bodily and emotional states—validates the teaching's emphasis on developing sensitivity to conscience signals that volitional unrighteousness progressively suppresses.

5: Spiritual Implications for Aspirants

Part A - Pastoral Concerns

Modern aspirants face particular challenges implementing these teachings within cultures where ethical compromise has become normalized across professional, commercial, and social domains. Consider the seeker navigating workplaces where fraud constitutes standard practice—inflated metrics, deceptive marketing, contract violations normalized as "doing business." When Amenemopet warns against fraud "done with volition and taking action," aspirants may experience this as threatening livelihood in environments where refusing fraud means unemployment. [2] The rationalization emerges quickly: "Everyone does it; I need this job; the system is corrupt anyway." Yet verse 3's revelation that "evidence is lodged in their unconscious mind even while their weak conscience has allowed it" operates regardless of cultural normalization. [2]

The complicity challenge presents particular difficulty. Verse 6's warning against "acting in concert(conspiring, facilitating, being a co-conspirator, accessory to the crime, etc.)" applies to countless modern scenarios aspirants might not recognize as fraud. [1] The employee processing fraudulent transactions, the professional providing services for unethical purposes, the witness remaining silent about known fraud—each involves what the Keys document calls conspiring, noting "the person who orders the crime is as guilty as the perpetrator following the instructions." [2] Aspirants may believe their hands remain clean by not perpetrating fraud directly, yet the teaching eliminates this rationalization entirely.

The progressive desensitization pattern creates particularly insidious obstacles. Someone may begin spiritual practice after years engaged in ethically compromised work, carrying thick aryu from past fraud. The teaching reveals that aryu resolution operates through multiple pathways depending on the severity and consequences of the original actions. Some aryu may be resolved through understanding and sincere contrition alone—particularly those with smaller consequences where the mind recognizes the error, experiences genuine remorse, and commits to righteous behavior. [2]

Other aryu require understanding, contrition, AND making amends—actively repairing external circumstances such as damaged relationships, harm to others or environment, or physiological damage to self and others. This process addresses both the external consequences and the internal angst and stress related to conscience feelings, creating resolution at multiple levels. [2] Some aryu can be significantly mitigated through right understanding—what might have manifested as severe physical consequence (the teaching offers the example of breaking a leg in physical reality) instead resolves to a minute illusory experience such as a vivid dream of that injury, the person having taken a path through wisdom that avoided the harsher physical fate. [2]

However, some fraud-related aryu may have produced such dire effects on self or others that the actions created wide-ranging consequences—perhaps damage to health, reputation, or life circumstances—that cannot be taken back and will have their effects going forward. The teaching establishes that "these aryu will produce the proper resulting effect (divine dispensation for the offense) at the appropriate time in life or in the next lifetime." [2] Yet even here, the practice of righteousness combined with genuine contrition serves essential purpose: it prevents the pattern from recurring in the future, thereby allowing the person to resolve and become free of the aryu even as the personality may need to experience certain consequences that cannot be undone. [2]

This distinction proves critical for aspirants who wonder: "Must I experience consequences for past actions even after reforming? Isn't sincere repentance sufficient?" The wisdom reveals that while sincere ethical transformation prevents accumulating additional fraud-related aryu and resolves the internal psychological and spiritual burden, some established consequences must work themselves out according to divine justice. The teaching instructs aspirants to approach such experiences as austerity and mercy of the Divine—recognizing that consequences have been resolved justly for all affected while granting the divine grace of moving forward without the psychological and spiritual burdens that would otherwise remain and torture the personality indefinitely. [2]

This framework transforms how the person experiences unavoidable consequences: rather than carrying both the external result AND the internal guilt-torture, the aspirant experiences external consequence while simultaneously freed from internal torment through understanding that divine justice operates fairly and that one's ethical transformation has resolved the pattern at its source. The personality thus gains capacity to integrate consequences as growth experiences rather than perpetual self-punishment, recognizing that spiritual practice facilitates the internal resolution process even when it cannot erase all established effects.

Perhaps most challenging, modern culture actively cultivates conscience suppression through systematic exposure to normalized fraud. Aspirants raised in such environments may have never developed robust ethical sensitivity—conscience never properly formed rather than having been suppressed. When conscience remains underdeveloped, aspirants face the compounded challenge of both thinning existing fraud-related aryu through the methods described above while simultaneously cultivating ethical sensitivity absent from conditioning. Yet even here, the teaching offers hope: beginning with small aryu resolution through understanding and contrition gradually develops the conscience capacity necessary for addressing progressively more challenging patterns, while the practice of making amends where possible strengthens ethical sensitivity through direct experience of repairing harm and witnessing the relief such repair brings to all parties involved.

PART B - METHODS FOR TRANSFORMATION

Based on the teaching presented by Sage Amenemopet that one should refrain from volitional fraud and recognize that conscience registers all actions in unconscious mind regardless of external detection, the application of the inverse doctrine methodology suggests one should also cultivate systematic practices that develop ethical sensitivity, restore conscience functioning, and thin accumulated fraud-related aryu, as these support both earthly well-being and discovery of Ab Neter presence.

<u>Practice 1</u>: Conscience Restoration Through Ethical Inventory. Create a comprehensive written inventory of all past instances where you knowingly engaged in fraud, complicity, or ethical compromise. For each instance, write: (1) exact nature of action; (2) rationalizations employed; (3) consequences to others; (4) internal sensations experienced during and after. This practice makes conscious what verse 3 describes as "sealed in unconscious mind"—bringing aryu patterns into hat awareness begins the thinning process. [1] Notice resistance arising: "That wasn't really fraud; everyone does it; they deserved it." These reactions reveal active rationalization mechanisms requiring recognition.

Example implementation: The professional reviewing career realizes multiple instances of inflating credentials, overcharging clients, remaining silent about known problems. Writing these explicitly—"2015: claimed expertise I lacked to secure contract; 2018: billed hours for incomplete work; 2020: knew product had defect but said nothing"—makes undeniable what rationalization had obscured. Initially, enormous resistance arises—hat protests "this makes me look terrible; I was just doing my job; I had to survive." Patient observation reveals these as protective mechanisms. Over time, honest accounting begins dissolving thick aryu that have maintained delusion about past conduct.

Practice 2: Real-Time Conscience Sensitivity Training. Establish practice of observing ethical decision points in daily life with particular attention to moments when conscience signal arises. When faced with opportunity for small fraud—inflating report, keeping incorrect change, misrepresenting qualifications—notice the initial conscience response before rationalization activates. Practice: "Conscience signals 'this is unethical'; now rationalization begins 'but it's such a small thing; I deserve extra; no one will know.'" This trains awareness to recognize conscience voice before it becomes buried beneath justification mechanisms. The teaching reveals that Thoth's "eye goes around all" and "acts done when no one is around registered in the cosmic mind and thus also in your own conscience." [3]

Example implementation: The office worker repeatedly faces small ethical choices: taking office supplies, padding timesheet five minutes, claiming credit for colleague's idea. Previously, these occurred automatically without conscious recognition. Now, practice catches the moment: taking stapler for home use, conscience whispers "this is theft"—then rationalization machine activates "the company can afford it; they don't pay me enough anyway; everyone takes supplies." Instead of either suppressing conscience or acting on rationalization, simply observe: "There is conscience signal; there is rationalization; there is impulse to act despite ethical restraint." This observation without reactive suppression begins restoring conscience sensitivity that volitional unrighteousness progressively obscured.

Practice 3: Proactive Amends and Aryu Thinning. Where possible, make direct amends for past fraud through return of ill-gotten gains, acknowledgment of wrongdoing, or tangible restitution. Where direct amends prove impossible, engage in systematic ethical conduct that "balances the cosmic scales"—not as transaction expecting spiritual credit but as recognizing that the aryu from past fraud must be thinned through opposite-quality actions. The teaching establishes aryu "will produce proper resulting effect at appropriate time"; proactive ethical conduct accelerates this process. [2] This might involve: volunteer work benefiting populations similar to those harmed by past fraud; rigorous honesty in situations where dishonesty would be easy; refusing participation in all fraud regardless of cost.

Example implementation: The businessperson recognizing past pattern of underpaying employees cannot locate those specific individuals decades later. Instead, deliberately overpays current workers, funds scholarships for disadvantaged youth, refuses all opportunities for profitable fraud even when "everyone does it." This does not erase all effects of past negative past aryu—the teaching clarifies some consequences must manifest internally within oneself and or externally in the world of human interactions. However, systematic ethical conduct mitigates some of the negative effects and creates "light aryu"—impressions transparent to divine light rather than creating opacity. [12] Over years, this practice gradually shifts personality foundation from fraud-oriented to ethics-oriented structure, supporting verse 6's wisdom to "desist / abstain / cease / refrain from/renounce" all fraudulent association. [1]

The systematic application of these practices operates on the principle that aryu thin through recognition, ethical conduct, and philosophical understanding rather than through rationalization or suppression. Patient absorption of the wisdom that witness consciousness observes all actions—combined with direct experience of conscience restoration through ethical practice—gradually reveals the Ab Neter presence that fraud-related aryu obscured. This enables both Prologue goals: earthly well-being through alignment with Maat rather than perpetual internal discord, and spiritual discovery through removing the opacity that volitional unrighteousness creates between hat and Ab Neter awareness.

References

[1] Ashby, M. (2019-25). *Mysticism of Amenemopet Hieroglyphic Text Translation.* Chapter 17, Verses 2-3, 6. Sema Institute of Ancient Egyptian Studies.
[2] Ashby, M. (2025). *Keys to Sage Amenemopet wisdom text trilinear translation chapter 17.* Sema Institute of Ancient Egyptian Studies.
[3] Ashby, M. (2019-25). *Mysticism of Amenemopet Hieroglyphic Text Translation.* Chapter 15, Verses 9-10. Sema Institute of Ancient Egyptian Studies.
[4] Ashby, M. (2025). *DEFINITIONS: The Nature of Consciousness and Awareness in Neterian Philosophy.* Sema Institute of Ancient Egyptian Studies.
[5] Ashby, M. (2025). *Keys to Sage Amenemopet wisdom text trilinear translation chapter 11.* Sema Institute of Ancient Egyptian Studies.
[6] Litz, B. T., Stein, N., Delaney, E., Lebowitz, L., Nash, W. P., Silva, C., & Maguen, S. (2009). Moral injury and moral repair in war veterans: A preliminary model and intervention strategy. *Clinical Psychology Review*, 29(8), 695-706.
[7] Greene, J. D., & Haidt, J. (2002). How (and where) does moral judgment work? *Trends in Cognitive Sciences*, 6(12), 517-523.
[8] Grabovac, A. D., Lau, M. A., & Willett, B. R. (2011). Mechanisms of mindfulness: A Buddhist psychological model. *Mindfulness*, 2(3), 154-166.
[9] Barkan, R., Ayal, S., Gino, F., & Ariely, D. (2012). The pot calling the kettle black: Distancing response to ethical dissonance. *Journal of Experimental Psychology: General*, 141(4), 757-773.
[10] Bandura, A. (2002). Selective moral disengagement in the exercise of moral agency. *Journal of Moral Education*, 31(2), 101-119.
[11] Shapiro, S. L., Jazaieri, H., & Goldin, P. R. (2012). Mindfulness-based stress reduction effects on moral reasoning and decision making. *The Journal of Positive Psychology*, 7(6), 504-515.
[12] Ashby, M. (2025). *Book Awakening Your Soul-Aware-Witness Ancient Egyptian Wisdom To Discover Divine Consciousness.* Sema Institute of Ancient Egyptian Studies.

CHAPTER 23: Commentary on Teachings of Amenemopet Chapter 18, Verses 5-6, 14-15, 22-23, 24-26: The Illusion of Self-Will and the Reality of Divine Guidance

Summary of Teachings

Chapter 18 reveals the fundamental delusion that personal will controls life's journey, when in reality Neberdjer shepherds all existence. This delusion creates exhausting ego-driven patterns including spiritual forcing and illusory Ger—appearing balanced while remaining at preliminary somatic/intellectual levels. The teaching establishes that genuine transformation requires not forceful achievement but patient removal of aryu obstruction through ethical purification and wisdom study, allowing the mind to penetrate from hat awareness to the kara discovery of Ab Neter. Contemporary research validates the ancient teaching that autonomous agency represents illusion, with actual direction emerging from levels beyond conscious awareness. The path forward involves recognizing divine guidance, releasing the exhausting load of egoism, and pursuing complete transformation under authoritative guidance rather than settling into comfortable preliminary stages.

The Delusion of Autonomous Agency

- Verses 5-6: Personal will as illusion vs. Neberdjer as actual guide
- Verses 14-15: Human imperfection vs. Divine perfection
- Verses 22-23: Impossibility of ego forcing spiritual attainment
- Verses 24-26: Sleep-walking through life believing oneself awake and self-directing

Prologue Verse 9: Discover the kara "where the Divine resides in every person"

How Chapter 18 Supports This Goal:

- Removing aryu obstruction reveals Ab Neter already present in kara
- Patient purification allows the mind to penetrate from hat to ab to kara
- Loosening ties to ignorance and egoism enables divine recognition
- Genuine transformation beyond somatic/intellectual levels

What Prevents This Goal:

- Aryu-driven Hat operating under delusion of autonomous existence
- Delusion preventing penetration to deeper level where Ab Neter abides
- Illusory Ger keeping the mind at surface levels
- Ego-structure attempting to force entry while maintaining separation
- Insufficient purity to genuinely pursue liberation

1. Human Psychology Principle: The Delusion of Autonomous Agency Operating Without Neberdjer Awareness

The fundamental psychological issue addressed across Chapter 18's verses concerns the profound delusion whereby Hat operates under the conviction that personal volition constitutes the primary directing force of one's life journey while remaining oblivious to the factor of intervening aryu (unconscious impressions impelling and compelling the personality to follow paths and perform actions) and the reality that Neberdjer (All-Encompassing Divinity) functions as the actual shepherd guiding all human existence. Verses 5-6 reveal this core problem: "the tongue of a person, that relates to the words they utter, their speech...based on their thoughts, feelings, and desires...is the force that directs their actions through the journey through life," yet "despite the personal predilections, there is an all-encompassing divinity that masters and encompasses the limits of Creation...the shepherd that guides human life...even before they themselves know where they are going" [1].

This creates a state of profound spiritual ignorance where the mind operates as if self-created and self-directed, when in truth Ab Neter sustains the very capacity for awareness itself. Verses 14-15 illuminate the ontological reality behind this delusion: "The Divine is that which exists, within itself, as ever in a perfect state," while "a human being, a person...exists through failure...humanity lacks the awareness of existence as Divine and lacks the power of perfection that is being Divine" [1]. The heated mind and feelings arising from this ignorance produce "illusory perceptions, thoughts, feelings, and conclusions leading to unrighteous desires and actions that cause one to turn away (forsake) the Divinity within" [1].

This directly prevents both Prologue goals established in the opening verses of Amenemopet's teaching. The first goal—to "cause a person to have well-being while living on earth" (Prologue verse 2)—remains unattainable because the personality exhausts itself "pulling the harder load of life due to egoism, instead of being relaxed due to knowing and experiencing the natural flow of life when one is conscious and aware of Neberdjer" [1] (verses 24-26). The second goal—discovering the kara, the divine sanctuary "where the Divine resides in every person" (Prologue verse 9)—becomes impossible when the aryu-driven Hat operates under the delusion of autonomous existence separate from its divine source, unable to penetrate to the deeper level where Ab Neter abides.

2. Behavioral Imperative: The Exhausting Patterns of Ego-Driven Striving and Spiritual Stupor

The specific psychological patterns emerging from this fundamental delusion manifest through what the teaching identifies as living "as if in a slumber of spiritual ignorance" [1] (verse 24)—a state where individuals believe themselves fully awake and self-directing while actually sleep-walking through existence, guided by forces they neither recognize nor understand. This spiritual stupor produces the exhausting experience of the personality attempting to navigate life through ego-determination, creating universal patterns of chronic striving, control-seeking, and what might be termed spiritual forcing that operate across all human personalities trapped in this delusion.

The delusion creates systematic behavioral patterns observable in how the mind relates to decision-making, interpersonal dynamics, and spiritual practice itself. At the fundamental level, aryu in the ab generate the compelling conviction that personal agency determines outcomes, producing constant strategic planning, anxious deliberation over "correct" choices, and interpretation of life circumstances as reflections of personal success or failure. This mirrors the heated person patterns discussed in Chapter 7, where the mind operates from egoic reactivity rather than silent receptivity to divine guidance.

The teaching reveals how this delusion operates at the level of Hat's most intimate experiences—thoughts, feelings, desires—which the mind mistakes as self-generated impulses requiring ego-management. Yet verse 5 clarifies that even these seemingly personal volitions function as "the steersperson of the boat" only in appearance, for Neberdjer remains "the shepherd that guides human life" regardless of whether Hat recognizes this reality [1]. The universal pattern involves the mind steering in one direction while the ocean current of divine guidance moves another, creating the illusion of personal navigation while actually being carried by forces incomparably vaster than egoic will [3].

The behavioral patterns of attempting to force spiritual attainment represent a particularly insidious manifestation affecting practitioners across all levels of development. Verses 22-23 reveal that "there isn't perfection forced in the hand of, in the possession of The Divine" [1], yet the heated mind and feelings attempt precisely this—trying to achieve enlightenment through ego-effort, to force entry into divine consciousness while maintaining the very egoic structure that prevents divine recognition. This universal pattern creates the paradox of spiritual practitioners working intensely to attain what can only be received through the "loosening of the ties to ignorance and egoism" [1], never recognizing that their effortful striving reinforces the bondage they seek to escape. These patterns operate identically whether the person identifies as beginner or advanced practitioner—the aryu-driven conviction of autonomous agency producing the same exhausting load regardless of spiritual sophistication.

The teaching reveals a particularly subtle manifestation of spiritual stupor affecting those who appear to have made progress: what might be termed the illusory Ger state. These individuals may genuinely engage spiritual practice—attending teachings, performing rituals, practicing yoga postures, gathering with fellow practitioners to discuss philosophy—yet remain at the somatic and intellectual levels without penetrating to the kara where aryu reside and Ab Neter awareness emerges. The ego sustains itself through this surface-level engagement, creating an appearance of spiritual balance while unconsciously blocking deeper transformation.

Such practitioners may know the teachings intellectually, speak fluently about consciousness principles, maintain regular practice schedules, yet the aryu preventing genuine understanding from connecting to their deeper reality remain undisturbed. The knowledge stays at the intellectual level as an ego accomplishment rather than penetrating to the ab where it could thin aryu density and reveal Ab Neter. These individuals achieve a form of worldly comfort through spiritual practice—reduced stress, improved emotional regulation, social connection through spiritual community—and settle into this satisfying equilibrium without recognizing it represents only preliminary stages requiring further development. These comfortable preliminary stages can unknowingly calcify into spiritual plateaus that, while representing advancement beyond ordinary worldly consciousness, nevertheless constitute stagnation relative to the ultimate goal of Ab Neter discovery.

The critical issue emerges when sufficient purity has not been attained to genuinely pursue liberation. The practitioner may experience temporary relief from worldly frustrations through spiritual engagement, find meaning in ritual participation and philosophical discussion, develop pleasant feelings during meditation or yoga practice, and conclude they have progressed significantly on the path. Yet this comfort level, while superior to heated worldly existence, remains fundamentally at the physical and emotional levels—what verse 24 describes as the sleep or stupor that can occur even while one appears awake and engaged in spiritual life.

Eventually, this illusory Ger state proves insufficient. Life circumstances change, the comfort derived from somatic practice no longer satisfies, agitation returns despite regular spiritual engagement, and the practitioner discovers with consternation that they remain vulnerable to heated patterns they believed transcended. Without having developed genuine connection to Ab Neter through the deep work of aryu purification, ethical transformation, and cultivation of serenity beyond the physical and intellectual dimensions, the person lacks the authentic foundation necessary to withstand the inevitable challenges that test apparent spiritual progress. At the unconscious seed level, the heated patterns remain potentially active, ready to manifest when circumstances trigger the underlying aryu that were never genuinely addressed through surface-level practice.

3. Mystic Psychology Metaphysical Implications: The Architecture of Divine Shepherding and the Impossibility of Forced Perfection

At the deepest metaphysical level, Chapter 18 reveals the cosmic architecture whereby Neberdjer functions as the all-encompassing consciousness that simultaneously creates, sustains, and guides all apparent individual existence. The ocean current metaphor from the lecture teachings illuminates this profound reality: just as a powerful current moves all vessels regardless of how their individual captains attempt to steer, Neberdjer constitutes the fundamental movement principle of all consciousness and action [3]. Indeed, "everything is made up of Neberdjer therefore whatever you desire is Neberdjer" [3]—consciousness pursuing its own infinite forms while mistaking them for external objects separate from itself.

Author's Note on Chapter 18:14-15: The verse "Divine exists in perfection...human exists through failure" reveals a profound psychological truth. The perfection being sought is perfection of peace and fulfillment. However, seeking this perfection through mind and senses within time and space situations can never succeed—leading to inevitable failure. This failure manifests psychologically as frustration, which in turn generates agitation and heatedness. Therefore, I consider this statement a direct reference to the underlying mechanism of frustration as the psychological consequence of seeking divine perfection through limited human faculties.

This understanding transforms the entire framework of spiritual causation. Verses 14-15 establish the ontological distinction: "The Divine is that which exists, within itself, as ever in a perfect state" [1], representing consciousness in its unmodified, absolute condition, while "a human being, a person...exists through failure" [1], meaning the person existing as the mind modified by aryu-driven ignorance that creates the appearance of limited, flawed selfhood. The teaching reveals that when Hat operates through heated mind and feelings, relying on limited mind and senses to discern reality, this produces systematic imperfection of cognition and imperfection of self-knowledge, resulting in error and failure [2].

The impossibility of forcing entry into divine awareness (verses 22-23) reveals a crucial principle: "anything that presents itself in front of The Divine as something other than The Divine is imperfect and not Divine and therefore cannot be accepted into the hand of The Divine" [1]. This means the ego attempting to achieve divine recognition through its own efforts perpetuates the very separation it seeks to overcome. Only the mind that has released egoic self-concept through the "loosening of the ties to ignorance and egoism" [1] can recognize its essential nature as Ab Neter—not through achieving something absent but through removing the aryu obstruction that hides what already exists in the kara, that divine sanctuary where "the Divine resides in every person" awaiting discovery.

The spiritual stupor described in verses 24-26 operates through a devastating mechanism: the person "separating themselves from and forsaking" the perfection of Neberdjer awareness by "ignorantly accepting the load of the imperfect ego instead of the lightness of the perfection of Neberdjer knowledge" [1]. This stupor damages "the perception of the spiritual enlightenment" [1] not through external interference but through the person themselves allowing aryu-driven patterns to occupy Hat so densely that sensitivity to Ab Neter becomes impossible. Nevertheless, even in this condition of maximum ignorance, Neberdjer continues shepherding the person toward the experiences necessary for eventual awakening—both heated and silent individuals guided where they need to go for their ultimate benefit [2]. This cosmic shepherding ensures that even when the person believes themselves lost in autonomous wandering, the divine current moves all toward eventual recognition of their essential nature, fulfilling the Prologue's promise that these teachings ultimately enable discovery of the kara where divinity abides.

4. Transpersonal Psychology Research: The Illusion of Control and Neuroscience of Self-Agency

Author's Note on Consciousness Terminology: What Western consciousness researchers call "consciousness" usually refers to awareness and cognition—mental functions that Amenemopet would classify as mind operations. In Amenemopet's framework, consciousness refers specifically to Ab Neter or Neberdjer—the fundamental consciousness that sustains all mental operations, including awareness, cognition, perceptions, and sensations. Therefore, in Amenemopet's understanding, consciousness is fundamental and precedes cognition and individual awareness, serving as their foundational source rather than being synonymous with them. Awareness, cognition, perceptions, memories, and sensations all occur in the mind; they are not consciousness itself but are sustained by consciousness. Consciousness, as it were, lends its capacity of awareness to the mind (unconscious, subconscious, conscious) so that the mind may be illumined and become able to recognize feelings, thoughts, sensations, and perceptions against the background of identity—the beingness-awareness that is consciousness. If the mind develops the idea that it is the source of its own existence, this is considered spiritual ignorance, and thus egoism.

Contemporary psychological research provides remarkable validation of Chapter 18's teaching on the illusion of autonomous agency. Neuroscientist Benjamin Libet's groundbreaking studies revealed that brain activity initiating voluntary actions precedes conscious awareness of the intention to act by approximately 350 milliseconds, suggesting that what the mind experiences as deliberate choice may represent post-hoc rationalization of processes already underway [4]. This aligns precisely with verses 5-6's revelation that while thoughts and feelings appear to steer one's journey, Neberdjer functions as the actual guide "even before they themselves know where they are going" [1].

More recent neuroscientific investigations using high-resolution brain imaging have extended these findings significantly. Research by Soon and colleagues (2008) demonstrated that unconscious brain activity predicting decisions occurs up to 10 seconds before conscious awareness, suggesting even more extensive pre-conscious determination of what the mind experiences as voluntary choice [5]. This research validates the ancient teaching that Hat operates under the illusion of autonomous agency while actual direction emerges from deeper levels beyond conscious awareness.

Research on the illusion of control demonstrates how the conscious level of the mind systematically overestimates its influence over outcomes, particularly in ambiguous situations [6]. Studies show that individuals consistently attribute successes to personal agency while externalizing failures, creating precisely the delusional framework Amenemopet identifies where ego takes credit for accomplishments while remaining oblivious to the divine guidance operating through all circumstances. Neuroscientific investigations reveal that brain regions associated with self-referential processing show enhanced activity during experiences of personal agency, suggesting that the sense of autonomous selfhood arises from specific neural patterns rather than representing metaphysical reality [7].

Buddhist psychology's extensive documentation of anatta (non-self) provides clinical validation of mind operations occurring without the autonomous agent the mind assumes exists. Meditation research demonstrates that sustained introspective practice reveals the constructed nature of selfhood—thoughts, feelings, and intentions arising through conditions rather than emanating from a central controller [8]. Studies on experienced meditators show reduced activity in brain regions associated with self-referential processing, correlating with reports of decreased sense of separate selfhood, directly confirming the possibility of the mind functioning without egoic self-concept. Recent neuroplasticity research demonstrates that consistent meditation practice produces measurable changes in brain structure and function, particularly in regions associated with self-awareness and emotional regulation, validating the ancient understanding that systematic practice can transform the aryu-driven patterns maintaining the illusion of autonomous agency [9].

========

Author's Note on Divine Guidance and Human Agency: The teaching that Neberdjer shepherds all existence should not be misunderstood as puppeteer-style control where humans have no agency. Rather, Neberdjer constitutes the vast orchestration of natural forces—the sun shining, wind blowing, moderate temperatures sustaining life, and the confluence of all natural processes both external in nature and internal within the human body. These forces are set in motion by Neberdjer, composed of Neberdjer, and create the conditions enabling movement, evolution of life, and opportunities for experiences leading to fulfillment of desires whether altruistic or hedonistic.

The human personality's arrogance emerges in believing it can control all these natural confluences for personal benefit—attempting to manipulate the vast web of universal forces as if they existed for ego-gratification. What the individual genuinely can affect through conscious choice involves living by virtue, which leads to purity of the personality which leads to fulfillment of the Prologue goals—provided the person develops sufficient strength to emerge from under the control of deluding negative aryu patterns.

Therefore, while Neberdjer controls the universal forces and natural processes, the individual retains agency to align their course and destiny in harmony with Neberdjer's designs or to resist that harmony during any given lifetime. Alignment produces fulfillment; resistance generates frustration. Nevertheless, the ultimate trajectory ensures that all beings eventually find their way to the path of self-knowledge and divine fulfillment, with each lifetime's choices affecting the timeline and difficulty of that journey rather than its ultimate destination.

5. Spiritual Implications for Aspirants

PART A: PASTORAL CONCERNS FOR MODERN SEEKERS

Consider the individual aspirant raised in contemporary culture emphasizing personal achievement, individual autonomy, and self-determination as primary values. Such a person encounters profound cognitive dissonance when Amenemopet teaches that "human self-will and or self-determination are an illusion" [1]. Their entire identity structure rests on the conviction of being an autonomous agent directing their life path through conscious choices. The teaching threatens to collapse the psychological framework through which they organize experience and derive meaning, creating emotional turbulence and existential anxiety.

The modern seeker often approaches spiritual practice with the same achievement-oriented mindset applied to worldly pursuits—setting enlightenment goals, measuring progress, intensifying efforts when results seem insufficient. This creates the exhausting pattern verse 24 describes: "pulling the harder load of life due to egoism, instead of being relaxed" [1]. The person meditates longer, studies more texts, attends additional retreats, all while the ego-structure generating the sense of spiritual deficiency remains unaddressed. They fail to recognize that their spiritual striving itself exemplifies the heated mind and feelings preventing the very awareness they seek. The emotional experience involves chronic frustration, secret shame about "insufficient progress," and desperate intensification of efforts that paradoxically increases the egoic density preventing breakthrough.

Someone working in corporate environments faces particularly acute challenges surrendering the illusion of control. Professional success depends on strategic planning, decisive action, measurable outcomes—all reinforcing the belief that personal agency determines results. When difficulties arise, the cultural conditioning insists on analyzing what went wrong with their decisions, how better choices might have prevented problems, completely missing verse 6's revelation that Neberdjer guides "where it needs to go for the welfare of all humans" [1] regardless of personal preferences. This person experiences constant low-level anxiety about making correct decisions, exhausts themselves through perpetual strategic deliberation, and interprets life setbacks as personal failures requiring more intensive control efforts.

The aspirant attempting to balance spiritual practice with family responsibilities encounters unique struggles. They may feel torn between worldly obligations and spiritual development, experiencing guilt about "insufficient" meditation time while simultaneously feeling they neglect family duties when engaging practice. This internal conflict arises directly from the delusion of autonomous agency—the belief that they must personally manage the balance through willpower and correct choices, never recognizing that Neberdjer shepherds the entire situation for ultimate welfare regardless of their anxious deliberations.

Consider the practitioner who has engaged spiritual teachings for years, attending regular gatherings, performing daily rituals, studying philosophical texts, perhaps even teaching others about the wisdom. They experience genuine benefits—reduced reactivity to worldly provocations, improved relationships, greater capacity to handle stress, moments of peace during meditation practice. Yet they notice with growing concern that heated patterns they believed overcome continue arising: unexpected anger, persistent anxiety about circumstances, desires they thought released, dissatisfaction with achievements that should bring fulfillment.

This person faces the devastating possibility that they represent what verse 24 describes as someone "in a slumber of spiritual ignorance" despite years of apparent practice [1]. They may wonder: Have I failed? Do the teachings not work for me? Am I spiritually deficient compared to others who seem more advanced? The teaching reveals the actual issue: the person achieved comfort at the somatic and intellectual levels—finding stress relief through yoga, emotional support through community, intellectual stimulation through philosophy—and unconsciously settled into this equilibrium without progressing to the deeper work of genuine aryu purification and Ab Neter discovery.

The practitioner realizes they engaged the external forms of spiritual life while the ego structure generating separation from divine awareness remained fundamentally unaddressed. They performed postures without the esoteric work of freeing the personality from worldly desires. They discussed teachings intellectually without the ethical transformation and serenity cultivation that allows the mind to penetrate from hat to kara. They maintained regular practice while remaining satisfied with worldly life enhanced by spiritual flavoring rather than pursuing the authoritative path toward discovering higher orders of being.

This recognition, while initially devastating, represents the arising of sufficient purity—generated through the very frustrations and failures themselves—to recognize that intellectual and somatic engagement, while necessary preliminary stages, cannot substitute for the complete path Amenemopet prescribes. The aspirant discovers they must move beyond comfortable practitioner identity to genuine pursuit of liberation under authoritative guidance, willing to confront and transform the deep aryu patterns maintaining egoic separation from Ab Neter awareness. The return of agitation, far from indicating failure, signals that the person has developed sufficient sensitivity to recognize that preliminary comfort no longer suffices for the genuine transformation the soul seeks.

PART B: METHODS FOR TRANSFORMATION THROUGH RECOGNIZING DIVINE GUIDANCE

Based on the teaching presented by Sage Amenemopet in verses 5-6 that Neberdjer functions as the actual shepherd of life regardless of personal volitions, the application of the inverse doctrine methodology suggests that aspirants should avoid actions, thoughts, and feelings that reinforce the delusion of autonomous agency separate from divine guidance, as these would undermine the recognition of Neberdjer as the fundamental movement principle of consciousness and existence.

When discovering that years of practice occurred at preliminary levels, resist the temptation toward shame or despair—these reactive emotions themselves represent heated patterns. Instead, recognize that the very capacity to perceive this limitation demonstrates the arising of sufficient purity to progress beyond comfortable practitioner identity. The frustrations and failures that reveal the insufficiency of somatic-intellectual practice represent Neberdjer shepherding the person toward the deeper work required.

Moreover, the years of prior practice should be understood not as wasted time but as necessary phases of exhausting accumulated aryu that had to be lived through before deeper work became possible. The wisdom to be understood reveals that some aryu patterns cannot be resolved through meditation or study alone but require actual lived experience of their consequences—what the tradition terms the "fructifications" or ripening results of karmic patterns. Consider how one sometimes must exhaust certain aryu through direct experience before readiness for genuine transformation emerges. Having completed such phases of aryu exhaustion, when either the lesson embedded in those patterns has been sufficiently absorbed or the frustration with their limiting effects reaches sufficient intensity, the person naturally develops the openness and capacity necessary for advancing beyond preliminary stages toward comprehensive purification.

Seek authoritative guidance from teachers who emphasize complete transformation rather than comfortable spirituality, recognizing that genuine liberation requires moving beyond pleasant preliminary stages to the demanding work of comprehensive aryu purification and ethical transformation that allows the mind to penetrate from hat awareness to the kara discovery of Ab Neter.

Implement daily reflection examining where aryu-driven patterns create the exhausting experience of "pulling the harder load" [1] (verse 24). When noticing chronic striving, achievement-anxiety, or control-seeking, pause to feel the physical tension this creates in the body. Then consciously release into the recognition: "Neberdjer shepherds this journey. I need not carry the burden of autonomous determination." Notice how this shift produces tangible relaxation—not through forced letting-go but through remembering the reality of divine guidance already operating. In family contexts, when feeling torn between obligations, recognize: "Neberdjer orchestrates these circumstances. My attention naturally flows where needed. I release the illusion that willpower must balance competing demands."

For addressing the pattern of spiritual forcing verses 22-23 identify, when noticing effortful attempts to achieve enlightenment, recognize this as ego attempting to force perfection "in the hand of The Divine" [1]. The wisdom to be understood recognizes that only the mind freed from egoic self-concept can unite with divine awareness—not through achievement but through the gradual "loosening of the ties to ignorance and egoism" [1] that occurs through patient ethical purification and wisdom study allowing aryu density to thin naturally. When meditation feels like effortful striving toward a goal, pause and acknowledge: "Ab Neter already exists in the kara. My practice removes obstruction rather than creates access. I allow this process to unfold through patient absorption of wisdom rather than forceful achievement."

For practitioners discovering they have settled into illusory Ger—comfortable with somatic and intellectual engagement while deeper transformation remains unaddressed—implement what may be termed Depth Assessment Practice. Regularly examine whether spiritual practice produces merely temporary stress relief and pleasant feelings (somatic level), interesting concepts and improved self-image (intellectual level), or genuine transformation of the aryu patterns maintaining separation from Ab Neter (kara level). Ask with rigorous honesty: "Do I seek sages and authoritative teachings that challenge my ego-comfort? Do I follow instructions to control the personality and break down causes of heatedness? Do I live according to ethics beyond what feels convenient? Do I cultivate serenity through the difficult work of renunciation, or do I maintain worldly desires while adding spiritual practices as enhancement?"

When discovering that years of practice occurred at preliminary levels, resist the temptation toward shame or despair—these reactive emotions themselves represent heated patterns. Instead, recognize that the very capacity to perceive this limitation demonstrates the arising of sufficient purity to progress beyond comfortable practitioner identity. The frustrations and failures that reveal the insufficiency of somatic-intellectual practice represent Neberdjer shepherding the person toward the deeper work required. Seek authoritative guidance from teachers who emphasize complete transformation rather than comfortable spirituality, recognizing that genuine liberation requires moving beyond pleasant preliminary stages to the demanding work of comprehensive aryu purification and ethical transformation that allows the mind to penetrate from hat awareness to the kara discovery of Ab Neter.

Practice the ocean current meditation described in the metaphysical section above: visualize attempting to sail east while a powerful current moves west [3]. Feel how personal steering efforts represent surface activity while the fundamental movement derives from forces incomparably vaster. Extend this recognition into daily life, acknowledging that Neberdjer constitutes both the ocean and the boat, the current and the person believing themselves separate from these—all manifestations of the one all-encompassing reality temporarily appearing as multiplicity through the creative power of consciousness itself. When anxious about life direction, remember this image: the mind may steer toward desired outcomes, yet the ocean current of divine guidance carries all vessels where they need to go for ultimate awakening, rendering personal navigation efforts simultaneously valid as surface activity yet ultimately subordinate to the deeper movement of Neberdjer shepherding all beings toward eventual discovery of their essential divine nature in the kara.

References

[1] Ashby, M. (2019-25). Mysticism of Amenemopet Hieroglyphic Text Translation. Sema Institute of Ancient Egyptian Studies.
[2] Ashby, M. (2025). Keys to Sage Amenemopet wisdom text trilinear translation chapter 18 by Dr Muata Ashby. Sema Institute of Ancient Egyptian Studies.
[3] Ashby, M. (2019). Amenemopet lectures 2019 by Dr Muata Ashby transcripts. Sema Institute of Ancient Egyptian Studies.
[4] Libet, B., Gleason, C. A., Wright, E. W., & Pearl, D. K. (1983). Time of conscious intention to act in relation to onset of cerebral activity (readiness-potential): The unconscious initiation of a freely voluntary act. Brain, 106(3), 623-642.
[5] Soon, C. S., Brass, M., Heinze, H. J., & Haynes, J. D. (2008). Unconscious determinants of free decisions in the human brain. Nature Neuroscience, 11(5), 543-545.
[6] Langer, E. J. (1975). The illusion of control. Journal of Personality and Social Psychology, 32(2), 311-328.
[7] Wegner, D. M. (2002). The Illusion of Conscious Will. MIT Press.
[8] Brewer, J. A., Worhunsky, P. D., Gray, J. R., Tang, Y. Y., Weber, J., & Kober, H. (2011). Meditation experience is associated with differences in default mode network activity

and connectivity. Proceedings of the National Academy of Sciences, 108(50), 20254-20259.

[9] Tang, Y. Y., Hölzel, B. K., & Posner, M. I. (2015). The neuroscience of mindfulness meditation. Nature Reviews Neuroscience, 16(4), 213-225.

CHAPTER 24: Commentary on Teachings of Amenemopet Chapter 21, Verses 5, 15-16, 17-18: The Balance Between Trust in Divine Order and Righteous Action

INTRODUCTION

Chapter 21 of the Teachings of Amenemopet addresses one of the most subtle yet profound challenges facing spiritual aspirants: discerning the balance between trusting divine orchestration and fulfilling righteous duties with diligent effort. This chapter reveals how the mind trapped in egoic ignorance oscillates between two destructive extremes—either anxiously attempting to control outcomes through fevered striving, or passively abdicating responsibility under the guise of surrender to divine will. Neither extreme recognizes the wisdom that sages discovered through Maat: that reality unfolds according to the divine plan expressed through the natural law (Maat), requiring conscious ethical participation rather than either heated control-seeking or slothful passivity.

The verses examined here establish a sophisticated teaching on speech, action, and trust that directly supports both Prologue goals. The instruction to avoid fevered achievement-grasping while simultaneously rejecting slothfulness creates the conditions for earthly well-being (Prologue verse 2) by eliminating the exhausting patterns of heated pursuit and self-sabotage. The teaching on judicious reserve and harm-avoiding speech cultivates the silent introspection necessary for discovering the kara where "the Divine resides in every person" (Prologue verse 9), as the mind that conserves speech and releases anxious control-seeking naturally develops the receptivity required for Ab Neter communion.

Summary of Teachings

Verse 5: Humans remain ignorant of the divine plans orchestrating life and the world. One should neither despair nor assume existence lacks meaning, but rather recognize that reality unfolds according to ultimate purpose and design beyond egoic comprehension.

Verses 15-16: It is spiritually glorious to develop a personality that keeps counsel, maintaining judicious reserve rather than constantly expressing thoughts and feelings. Particularly, one should avoid speech that causes purposeful or unnecessary harm to others or oneself.

Verse 17: One should not pursue worldly achievements through fevered, agitated grasping, as such pursuits prove illusory. Instead, remain content in the present, allowing the divine plan to unfold naturally through one's life.

Verse 18: While maintaining contentment in the present, avoid the opposite extreme of unrighteousness, complacency, or slothfulness that creates self-imposed obstacles to achieving righteous goals. Engage ethical duties and opportunities with relaxed yet diligent deliberation, allowing them to develop into spiritual perfection.

1. HUMAN PSYCHOLOGY PRINCIPLE: THE DELUSION OF EGO-DETERMINED REALITY AND THE ANXIETY OF ILLUSORY CONTROL

The fundamental psychological issue addressed across Chapter 21's verses concerns the profound delusion whereby the Hat operates under the conviction that reality should conform to personal opinions about how life ought to unfold, generating chronic anxiety, despair, and agitation when circumstances fail to match egoic expectations. Verse 5 reveals this core problem: "You definitely are not wise as to, you do not know the plans that God may have for your life and the world for how things will work out. So do not despair or act as if everything is random or without meaning or cause behind it, having an ultimate purpose or design" [1].

This creates a double-bind of spiritual ignorance: the mind attempts to control outcomes through anxious mental manipulation, believing personal strategies determine results, yet when this control proves illusory, the mind may collapse into despair, concluding existence lacks meaning or divine order [2]. Neither extreme recognizes the truth that sages discovered through Maat—an order based on truth where actions aligned with righteousness produce certain consequences, while Creation unfolds according to Neberdjer's plan regardless of egoic preferences.

The heated mind and feelings arising from this delusion manifest through "running feverishly, stressful grasping towards achieving goals" [1] (verse 17), where the mind pursues worldly achievements believing they will produce abiding satisfaction, unaware that "time and space is always changing and imperfect—only God is perfect" [2]. This fevered pursuit exhausts the mind while producing the opposite result: rather than creating spiritual perfection, the mind "creates a harmful condition, for oneself, of trouble that will be an obstruction to being able to achieve the desired and laudable goals of life" [1] (verse 18).

This directly prevents both Prologue goals. The first goal—to "cause a person to have well-being while living on earth"—remains unattainable because the mind exhausts itself through anxious control-seeking, never discovering the contentment in the present that allows the divine plan to unfold naturally [1]. The second goal—discovering the kara where "the Divine resides in every person"—becomes impossible when aryu-driven patterns occupy the Hat so densely with worldly anxieties that the silent introspection required for Ab Neter discovery cannot occur.

2. BEHAVIORAL IMPERATIVE: THE FEVERED PURSUIT, HARMFUL SPEECH, AND SELF-SABOTAGING PATTERNS

The specific psychological patterns emerging from this fundamental delusion manifest through three interrelated behavioral domains. First, chronic external focus through excessive speech emerges from the mind "living off the ego nature, the superficial aspect of mind based on worldly aryu" [2] rather than developing silence through introspection and wisdom study. This manifests as compulsive talking, constant sharing of thoughts and feelings—behaviors that "stimulate egoism, support worldly thoughts and feelings, negative aryu" [2], preventing silent receptivity necessary for divine communion.

Consider the modern professional whose workday consists of perpetual verbal interaction—meetings, phone calls, instant messaging, social media posting—maintaining constant external engagement leaving no space for silence. Even solitary moments fill with podcasts, audiobooks, or internal chatter rehearsing future conversations. This person never experiences the "personality that keeps things in his/her belly, within the skin" [1] (verse 15), that glorious capacity for judicious reserve that conserves vital energy and allows introspective awareness. The aryu in the ab continuously reinforce external orientation patterns, occupying the Hat so completely that sensitivity to subtler levels where Ab Neter resides becomes impossible.

The second pattern involves speech that causes harm—words that insult, denigrate, show egoism, or stimulate heatedness (verse 16). This represents not mere social rudeness but fundamental expression of the mind operating from aryu-driven reactivity rather than silent wisdom. Critically, the teaching reveals that harmful speech need not be false to cause damage. The pattern operates whether or not the speech contains factual truth: "If it is true but not worth saying cause the person would be offended and not want to listen then there is no point" [2]. A person might speak truthful criticism, accurate observations about another's flaws, or factually correct assessments that nevertheless serve no beneficial purpose beyond satisfying the ego's compulsion to assert, correct, or demonstrate superiority. This reveals how the heated mind and feelings prioritize self-expression over beneficial outcome—the mind values the egoic satisfaction of speaking its truth above consideration of whether that truth serves any constructive purpose or simply creates suffering without possibility of positive change.

The third pattern encompasses fevered, agitated pursuit of worldly achievements combined paradoxically with self-sabotaging behaviors that obstruct righteous goals (verses 17-18). The mind simultaneously runs "feverishly, stressfully grasping towards achieving goals" [1] while engaging in "defeatist thinking, self-denigration...slothfulness in one's rightful duties, or engaging in worries and anxieties" [1]. The person pursues external success with heated intensity yet internally undermines potential through patterns of self-doubt, procrastination on ethical duties, and mental agitation that drain the relaxed diligence required for sustainable development.

3. Mystic Psychology Metaphysical Implications: The Architecture of Divine Plan and the Paradox of Effortless Effort

At the deepest metaphysical level, Chapter 21 reveals the cosmic architecture whereby Neberdjer orchestrates all existence according to the divine plan while simultaneously requiring conscious participation through ethical action—a paradox that dissolves when the mind recognizes its essential nature as instrument of divine will rather than autonomous agent. Verse 5's teaching that "you do not know the plans that God may have for your life and the world" [1] establishes not fatalistic resignation but profound humility before the reality that the mind operating through limited senses cannot comprehend the vast patterns through which Neberdjer guides Creation.

The lecture teachings illuminate this reality: "Remember that there is Neberdjer and that Neberdjer is really running things. You are part of the things that Neberdjer is running" [3]. This reveals the crucial distinction between passive abdication ("it's up to God, I have nothing to do with it"—representing "a cop-out...or defense mechanism" [3]) and active participation grounded in recognition of divine orchestration. The wisdom to be understood recognizes that the mind functions as expression of Neberdjer, not separate entity negotiating with divinity. Therefore, righteous action emerges not from ego-determined strategy but from alignment with Maat principles reflecting divine order.

The fevered pursuit advised against in Verse 17 represents the mind attempting to force outcomes through heated intensity, believing personal will determines results. This contradicts the metaphysical reality that "only God is perfect in itself, consciousness that is free from distortion of mind" [2], meaning all worldly achievements inevitably prove imperfect and transitory regardless of intensity applied. Nevertheless, verse 18's warning against slothfulness reveals that contentment does not mean passive inaction but rather "relaxed but diligent and deliberate manner" [1] of engaging righteous duties as they arise through divine provision.

This establishes the principle of effortless effort—action flowing from silent recognition of divine order rather than heated grasping after ego-determined outcomes. When the mind releases anxious control-seeking and recognizes "you do not even know how your breakfast was processed by the physiology of your body, let alone the fate of the world" [2], this humility creates space for genuine participation in the divine plan. The person acts ethically, fulfills rightful duties, accepts opportunities arising through grace, yet remains unattached to specific results. Outcomes unfold according to Neberdjer's wisdom rather than personal preference. This transforms work from exhausting ego-project into sacred participation in cosmic unfolding, allowing the personality to "blossom into the successful project of spiritual perfection" [1] precisely by releasing heated pursuit of perfection as personal achievement.

The reserved speech praised in verses 15-16 operates through this same principle: the mind that has thinned aryu density sufficiently to commune with Ab Neter naturally conserves speech, speaking only when beneficial outcome serves divine purpose. This represents not suppression but transformation where Hat operates increasingly from Ab Neter guidance rather than aryu-driven compulsions to assert, explain, or defend egoic positions. The glorious quality of judicious reserve emerges naturally when the mind recognizes itself as instrument of divine wisdom rather than separate entity requiring constant verbal affirmation.

4. Transpersonal Psychology Research: The Neuroscience of Anxiety, Speech Patterns, and Flow States

Contemporary psychological research provides remarkable validation of Chapter 21's teachings on the relationship between control-seeking, anxiety, and well-being. Studies on the illusion of control demonstrate that individuals who believe they possess high levels of personal control over inherently uncontrollable outcomes experience significantly elevated anxiety levels and decreased life satisfaction compared to those who accept appropriate limits of personal agency [4]. This aligns precisely with verse 5's teaching that despair and anxiety arise from the delusion that reality should conform to personal expectations while remaining ignorant of the divine plan of Neberdjer.

Neuroscientific research on rumination and worry reveals that chronic mental preoccupation with future outcomes activates the brain's default mode network in patterns associated with decreased present-moment awareness and increased psychological distress [5]. Studies using functional MRI demonstrate that individuals engaged in worry show heightened activity in regions associated with threat detection and decreased activity in areas linked to positive emotion. This validates verse 17's warning against fevered, agitated pursuit of achievements, suggesting that the heated mental state itself obstructs the contentment allowing optimal functioning.

Research on verbal behavior and psychological health reveals patterns consistent with verses 15-16's teachings on judicious speech. Studies demonstrate that excessive self-disclosure and compulsive talking correlate with decreased introspective capacity and diminished ability to regulate emotional states [6]. Conversely, research on contemplative practices emphasizing silence shows that reduced verbal activity correlates with increased self-awareness, emotional regulation, and access to intuitive wisdom. Neuroscientific investigations reveal that periods of external silence produce measurable changes in brain regions associated with self-referential processing and emotional integration, validating the ancient understanding that conserving speech facilitates inner development.

Flow state research provides scientific validation for verse 18's principle of relaxed diligence. Studies by Csikszentmihalyi demonstrate that optimal performance and deep satisfaction emerge not from fevered striving but from focused engagement characterized by effortless concentration, clear goals, and immediate feedback [7]. Flow states involve reduced activity in brain regions associated with self-conscious monitoring and heightened integration of action and awareness—precisely the qualities described in the teaching's emphasis on relaxed yet deliberate action. Research on self-compassion versus self-criticism reveals that individuals who engage in harsh self-judgment (the self-denigration warned against in verse 18) show significantly impaired performance on challenging tasks compared to those who maintain compassionate self-regard [8].

Buddhist psychology's extensive documentation of right speech provides clinical validation of the harm-reduction principle in verse 16. Meditation research demonstrates that practitioners trained in speech ethics show measurable improvements in interpersonal relationships, emotional regulation, and subjective well-being compared to control groups [9]. Studies on negative speech patterns reveal physiological stress responses in both speakers and listeners, confirming the ancient understanding that harmful speech creates suffering for all involved parties.

5. Spiritual Implications for Aspirants

PART A: PASTORAL CONCERNS FOR MODERN SEEKERS

Consider the individual aspirant raised in contemporary achievement culture emphasizing constant productivity, measurable progress, and personal determination. Such a person encounters profound dissonance when Amenemopet teaches contentment in the present while warning against fevered pursuit of achievements. Their entire conditioning insists that success requires intense striving and relentless forward movement toward defined goals, threatening to collapse the psychological framework through which they organize ambition and derive meaning.

The modern seeker often experiences internal conflict between spiritual teachings on surrender and cultural conditioning around personal responsibility. When verse 5 teaches "you do not know the plans that God may have for your life" [1], the mind may interpret this as permission for passive abdication—the "cop-out" the lecture warns against [3]. Alternatively, the person may reject the teaching entirely, insisting personal will determines outcomes and refusing to acknowledge limits of egoic control. Neither response recognizes the subtle balance between trust in divine order and diligent fulfillment of righteous duties.

Someone working in high-pressure corporate environments faces acute challenges implementing the reserved speech of verses 15-16. Professional success in such contexts often depends on constant verbal assertion and strategic self-promotion. The person experiences genuine fear that adopting judicious reserve will result in being overlooked or professionally marginalized, failing to recognize that the teaching addresses not strategic silence for worldly advantage but authentic transformation where the mind naturally conserves speech as aryu density thins and Ab Neter awareness grows.

The aspirant attempting to balance spiritual practice with family responsibilities encounters particularly intense struggles around verses 17-18's paradoxical instruction. Consider the parent managing multiple children's activities, household duties, and work obligations who feels torn between accepting present circumstances and pursuing improvement. When a child struggles academically, does contentment mean accepting the situation or actively seeking tutoring support? When career advancement opportunities arise requiring family relocation, does trust in the divine plan mean passive acceptance or active evaluation? This confusion arises from operating through egoic decision-making rather than recognition that both acceptance and effort emerge naturally when the mind aligns with divine order through Maat principles.

PART B: METHODS FOR TRANSFORMATION THROUGH TRUSTING DIVINE ORDER WHILE FULFILLING RIGHTEOUS DUTIES

Based on the teaching presented by Sage Amenemopet in verse 5 that humans remain ignorant of divine plans while reality unfolds according to meaningful order, the application of the inverse doctrine methodology suggests that aspirants should avoid thoughts, feelings, and actions that reinforce either anxious control-seeking or fatalistic passivity, as these extremes would undermine the recognition of divine orchestration that requires conscious ethical participation.

The practical method emerges from integrating verse 5's trust in the divine plan with verse 18's injunction against slothfulness. When facing important decisions or uncertain outcomes, practice acknowledging: "I do not know Neberdjer's complete plan, yet I recognize that reality unfolds according to divine order expressed through Maat. My role involves discerning righteous action through ethical principles, engaging that action with relaxed diligence, then releasing attachment to specific outcomes." This transforms decision-making from anxious ego-determination or passive abdication into conscious participation in divine unfolding.

For example, when pursuing career advancement, rather than feverishly grasping after positions through heated networking and strategic manipulation, identify opportunities aligned with righteous principles and engage application processes with thorough yet relaxed effort. Then release concern about results—recognizing that if the position serves the divine plan, circumstances will align naturally. If not, something more beneficial emerges according to Neberdjer's wisdom. This eliminates both exhausting anxiety of control-seeking and self-sabotaging passivity that fails to engage opportunities arising through grace.

Implement daily practice of judicious speech reflecting verses 15-16's teaching. Before speaking, pause briefly to examine: "Does this speech serve beneficial purpose, or does it emerge from egoic compulsion to assert, explain, or defend?" Practice holding counsel unless speech would genuinely help another, share necessary information, or express authentic care—releasing the heated impulse to fill every silence with verbal content. Notice how this conservation of speech creates tangible increase in inner quiet, allowing the Hat to settle sufficiently that subtler movements of Ab Neter guidance become perceptible.

When noticing harmful speech arising—words tinged with criticism, judgment, sarcasm, or heatedness—pause before speaking to recognize: "This speech would stimulate egoism in myself and heatedness in others, obstructing both parties' capacity for silent receptivity to divine guidance." If the content contains necessary truth, rephrase with compassionate consideration of effect; if the truth would not be received beneficially, maintain silence and allow circumstances to teach what verbal instruction cannot. In workplace contexts where competitive speech dominates, practice speaking when righteous communication serves purpose, remaining reserved when speech would only reinforce heated patterns.

For addressing the fevered achievement-grasping of verse 17, when noticing anxious mental rehearsal of future scenarios or compulsive planning to control outcomes, practice releasing into recognition: "Neberdjer orchestrates circumstances according to the divine plan beyond my comprehension. I engage present duties with diligent care while releasing feverish concern about how achievements unfold." Return attention to immediate task at hand, performing work with relaxed thoroughness rather than heated intensity, recognizing that optimal results emerge from effortless effort aligned with divine order.

For the self-sabotaging patterns of verse 18, when noticing defeatist thinking, harsh self-judgment, or slothful avoidance of righteous duties, recognize these as affronts to Ab Neter—the divine soul that deserves respectful engagement [2]. Practice acknowledging: "Self-denigration insults the divine spark sustaining my consciousness. Righteous opportunities arise through grace; my role involves accepting these with gratitude and engaging them with relaxed diligence." When genuine opportunities present themselves, move forward without anxious overthinking or self-doubt, recognizing acceptance and diligent engagement as forms of sacred participation rather than personal achievement-grasping.

References

[1] Ashby, M. (2019-25). Mysticism of Amenemopet Hieroglyphic Text Translation. Sema Institute of Ancient Egyptian Studies.

[2] Ashby, M. (2025). Keys to Sage Amenemopet wisdom text trilinear translation chapter 21 by Dr Muata Ashby. Sema Institute of Ancient Egyptian Studies.

[3] Ashby, M. (2019). Amenemopet lectures 2019 by Dr Muata Ashby transcripts. Sema Institute of Ancient Egyptian Studies.

[4] Thompson, S. C., Armstrong, W., & Thomas, C. (1998). Illusions of control, underestimations, and accuracy: A control heuristic explanation. Psychological Bulletin, 123(2), 143-161.

[5] Hamilton, J. P., Farmer, M., Fogelman, P., & Gotlib, I. H. (2015). Depressive rumination, the default-mode network, and the dark matter of clinical neuroscience. Biological Psychiatry, 78(4), 224-230.

[6] Tamir, D. I., & Mitchell, J. P. (2012). Disclosing information about the self is intrinsically rewarding. Proceedings of the National Academy of Sciences, 109(21), 8038-8043.

[7] Csikszentmihalyi, M. (1990). Flow: The Psychology of Optimal Experience. Harper & Row.

[8] Neff, K. D., & Germer, C. K. (2013). A pilot study and randomized controlled trial of the mindful self-compassion program. Journal of Clinical Psychology, 69(1), 28-44.

[9] Shapiro, S. L., Carlson, L. E., Astin, J. A., & Freedman, B. (2006). Mechanisms of mindfulness. Journal of Clinical Psychology, 62(3), 373-386.

[10] Brewer, J. A., Worhunsky, P. D., Gray, J. R., Tang, Y. Y., Weber, J., & Kober, H. (2011). Meditation experience is associated with differences in default mode network activity and connectivity. Proceedings of the National Academy of Sciences, 108(50), 20254-20259.

[11] Brewer, J. A., Worhunsky, P. D., Gray, J. R., Tang, Y. Y., Weber, J., & Kober, H. (2011). Meditation experience is associated with differences in default mode network activity and connectivity. Proceedings of the National Academy of Sciences, 108(50), 20254-20259.

CHAPTER 25: Commentary on Teachings of Amenemopet Chapter 25, Verses 9-11, 19-20: Compassionate Treatment of the Vulnerable and the Ultimate Goal of Divine Union

INTRODUCTION

Chapter 25 of the Teachings of Amenemopet presents a profound integration of ethical conduct toward vulnerable persons with the ultimate metaphysical goal of spiritual existence. The chapter reveals how egoistic behaviors that mock, exploit, or harm those of diminished capacity directly obstruct the spiritual perfection—the mind's perfected state of experiencing universal, eternal consciousness without delusion, fear, distortions or ignorance—that represents the goal of arriving at the Beautiful West, the final abode of divine union. These teachings establish that authentic spiritual development cannot be separated from compassionate treatment of all human beings, whom one must recognize as manifestations of the same Neberdjer that sustains all existence and is the very essence of oneself.

The verses examined here address both immediate ethical imperatives and ultimate spiritual goals, showing how earthly conduct determines posthumous destiny. The instruction to avoid harming those "whose skin is in the hand of The Divine" [1] (verse 11) reveals the mystical reality that some persons have achieved such alignment with Maat that their physical existence operates under direct divine governance—a state representing enlightenment itself [2]. This directly supports both Prologue goals: ethical treatment of all persons creates conditions for "well-being while living on earth" (Prologue verse 2), while recognizing the divine nature in all beings facilitates discovery of the kara where "the Divine resides in every person" (Prologue verse 9).

SUMMARY OF TEACHINGS

Verse 9: Desist from laughing at, impolitely staring at, or forcibly grabbing persons of diminished capacity or different appearance. Such behaviors arise from egoistic arrogance and conceit, failing to recognize that all people share spiritual kinship as their minds and bodies are sustained by the same consciousness source—Neberdjer.

Verse 10: Desist from entertaining negative designs or intents toward the afflicted—thoughts of harming, taking advantage, or unrighteously treating those who are vulnerable, weak, or sick. This represents egoism manifesting as fraudulent mental scheming against the defenseless.

Verse 11: Desist from doing violence to one "whose skin is in the hand of The Divine"—those who have attained such spiritual virtue and alignment with Maat that their physical existence operates under direct divine protection and governance.

Verse 19: It is joyous and worthy of adoration to praise arrival at the Beautiful West—the final divine abode—rather than praising worldly attainments. The alternative is reincarnation in the east, experiencing again the search for fulfillment through illusory time-space goals amid suffering, frustration, and fleeting joys.

Verse 20: True well-being is found in the hand of The Divine—having one's skin possessed by divine consciousness rather than governed by ego nature, delusions, and worldly thoughts disconnected from wisdom teachings and divine experience.

1. Human Psychology Principle: The Egoistic Delusion of Separateness and Hierarchy

The fundamental psychological issue across Chapter 25's verses concerns the profound delusion whereby Hat operates under the conviction that individual awareness exists as fundamentally separate from other individual awarenesses, creating hierarchical valuations based on physical appearance, mental capacity, or social status. The wisdom to be understood reveals the crucial distinction: while individual hats (conscious minds) are indeed separate from other hats, the underlying consciousness that sustains each Hat is not separate at all—it is universal, the one Neberdjer existence that lends all individuals their capacity to experience individuality. This delusion of fundamental separation produces the arrogance and conceit that mock those of different appearance, the scheming mentality that exploits the vulnerable, and the violent impulse that harms the defenseless [2]. The teaching reveals that such behaviors arise from the mind that has forgotten the metaphysical reality: "All people are kin spiritually" as their capacity for awareness derives from the same consciousness (Neberdjer), and their bodies come from the same source (Neberdjer) [2].

This creates systematic blindness to the divine nature permeating all apparent individuals, preventing the mind from recognizing that mistreating any person represents an affront to the Neberdjer manifesting through that form. The heated mind and feelings operating from this delusion remain trapped in dualistic perception, unable to penetrate beneath surface appearances to recognize the Ab Neter sustaining conscious capacity in all beings. This directly prevents both Prologue goals: earthly well-being becomes impossible when the person engages in behaviors generating negative aryu through harming others, while discovery of the divine within the kara remains obstructed when the mind cannot recognize divinity manifesting through all forms.

2. Behavioral Imperative: The Manifestations of Egoistic Arrogance Toward the Vulnerable

The specific psychological patterns emerging from this fundamental delusion manifest through three progressively severe expressions of egoistic separation. First, the pattern of mockery and disrespectful attention toward those of different appearance (verse 9) represents the mind expressing superiority through laughter, impolite staring, or physical roughness with persons of diminished capacity [1]. Consider the modern individual who makes jokes about persons with disabilities, stares rudely at those with unusual physical features, or treats elderly people with cognitive decline as objects of entertainment rather than beings deserving respect and assistance as well as, if possible, healing. The aryu in the ab driving such behaviors consist of comparative judgments where the mind derives egoic validation through contrasting itself favorably against those deemed inferior.

These patterns operate whether the person engages them openly or maintains them as private mental habits. Someone might refrain from overt mockery yet internally experience superiority when encountering persons with intellectual disabilities, physical deformities, or mental illness. The teaching addresses not merely external behavior but the egoistic aryu generating such impulses: the arrogance and conceit that evaluates human worth based on physical or mental capabilities rather than recognizing the divine consciousness animating all forms [2].

The second pattern involves scheming to mistreat the vulnerable (verse 10)—"entertaining, mulling, ruminating thoughts of causing harm, hatred, animosity, enmity, or thoughts of taking advantage" of those who are afflicted [1]. This represents a more insidious manifestation where the mind deliberately plans exploitation. Consider the professional who schemes to defraud elderly clients with diminished cognitive capacity, the caregiver who plans systematic neglect of dependent persons, or the business operator who targets vulnerable populations for predatory financial schemes. These patterns reveal egoism manifesting as "fraudulent actions based on egoism" [2], where the mind operating through a corrupted condition prioritizes personal gain over recognizing the shared origin in Neberdjer with all beings.

The third pattern encompasses actual violence against those "whose skin is in the hand of The Divine" [1] (verse 11), representing the most severe manifestation where the mind not only fails to recognize divinity in others but actively attacks those who have achieved spiritual alignment with Maat. The teaching reveals that "messing around with such a person can have dire consequences" [2], as doing violence to one governed by divine consciousness represents an assault on the operative aspect of divine will (heka) itself manifesting through that form.

THE VARIETIES OF AGGRESSION

The teachings in verses 9-11 reveal a comprehensive framework for understanding aggression through three interconnected forms: mental, speech, and physical. Mental aggression manifests as the "entertaining, mulling, ruminating thoughts of causing harm, hatred, animosity, enmity" described in verse 10 [1]—the internal scheming and hostile ideation occurring in Hat before being expressed through word or deed. Speech aggression appears in verse 9's instruction against "laughing at" those of different appearance [1], encompassing all forms of verbal violence: mockery, harsh words, demeaning language, sarcastic belittlement, contemptuous tones, and degrading comments that assault another's dignity through vocal expression. Physical aggression reaches its culmination in verse 11's prohibition against "doing violence to" another person [1], including not only direct assault but also "forcibly grabbing" and any bodily harm inflicted upon another being [1].

These three forms operate as progressive manifestations of the same underlying egoistic aryu: hostile thoughts in the ab generate verbal expressions through Hat, which can escalate into physical actions when the heated mind and feelings operate without restraint. Consider the modern individual who first entertains thoughts of superiority toward a coworker, then makes belittling comments about that person to others, and eventually engages in confrontational behavior escalating to physical intimidation—each stage representing deepening density of aggressive aryu gaining expression through the personality.

While Amenemopet focuses these instructions specifically on aggression toward the vulnerable—those of diminished capacity, the afflicted, and those under divine protection—the teaching applies to aggressive patterns generally, regardless of the target's status or capabilities. The wisdom reveals that all forms of aggression arise from the fundamental delusion of egoistic separation discussed in Section 1: the heated mind and feelings operating under the conviction that individual existence is fundamentally separate from other beings, creating the psychological conditions where harming another seems possible without harming oneself. Whether directed toward the vulnerable or toward those of equal or greater capacity, mental hostility generates negative aryu in the ab, verbal abuse creates karmic patterns of speech violence, and physical aggression produces the densest aryu obstructing Ab Neter recognition.

The teaching addresses aggression toward the vulnerable specifically because such behavior reveals the clearest manifestation of egoistic corruption—the mind so dominated by aryu that it attacks those least able to defend themselves, demonstrating complete blindness to the divine nature permeating all forms. However, the aspirant recognizes that these same principles govern all aggressive patterns: hostile thoughts toward colleagues, harsh speech toward family members, physical intimidation in any context all generate aryu density preventing both earthly well-being (Prologue verse 2) and discovery of the kara where divinity resides (Prologue verse 9). The practice requires vigilance across all three forms, recognizing that the mind operating from egoistic separation will seek expression for aggressive aryu through whatever means ego-patterns permit, and that transformation requires addressing the root delusion generating hostility at the ab level rather than merely suppressing its external manifestations.

3. Mystic Psychology Metaphysical Implications: The Architecture of Divine Governance and Ultimate Spiritual Destiny

At the deepest metaphysical level, Chapter 25 reveals the cosmic architecture whereby physical existence operates under one of two governing principles: either the skin (body-mind complex) exists "in the hand of The Divine," meaning the mind functions as a direct instrument of divine will, or the skin remains "in the hand of the ego nature," meaning the mind operates through delusions disconnected from Ab Neter guidance [2]. This transformation of the mind from ego-governance to divine governance constitutes the very discovery of kara—the divine sanctuary within—that represents the second Prologue goal. Verse 11's teaching about those "whose skin is in the hand of The Divine" establishes that "the hand of the god is the operative aspect of divine will (heka)—the force that acts in creation," while "the skin is the interface between spirit and matter" [2].

Thus, "one whose skin is in the hand of god" describes a person whose "physical existence is governed by divine consciousness, not by ego or chaos," marking "a state of spiritual integration, where the divine essence flows through the person's body—a description of enlightenment or perfected alignment with Maat" [2]. This reveals that spiritual development aims toward achieving this condition where Hat operates not from aryu-driven impulses but from Ab Neter communion, allowing divine will to express directly through thought, word, and deed.

This teaching on "whose skin is in the hand of The Divine" carries an additional dimension of profound spiritual significance: it describes the mind that has practiced sustained trust in and surrender to divine will and, through virtuous conduct, has been accepted into divine care and protection. Verse 11's identification of such persons as "virtuous, who have attained the favor of God by not turning away like the heated person, but turning towards God, somebody pious, ethical honest who follows maat" [2] reveals that this state emerges not through passive resignation but through active orientation of the mind toward divine reality. The key phrase "not turning away like the heated person, but turning towards God" distinguishes between two fundamental orientations of the mind: the heated person turns away from divine guidance, seeking security and meaning through ego-determined strategies and worldly pursuits, while the aspirant who achieves divine protection consciously turns toward Neberdjer through ethical conduct, wisdom study, and devotional practice.

This 'turning toward' constitutes genuine spiritual surrender—not abandonment of responsibility but recognition that the mind operates most effectively when aligned with divine will expressed through Maat principles. Chapter 6B's teaching that "it would be a glorifying, beneficial thing, to be poor and within the grace, the caring and protection the hand of The Divine" [10] further illuminates this principle: the person accepted into divine care experiences protection and guidance that transcend material circumstances, operating under heka (divine operative will) rather than struggling through ego-driven manipulation of conditions. Thus "attaining the favor of God" represents the mystical reality whereby sustained ethical practice, combined with devotional turning toward the Divine, creates conditions allowing Neberdjer to accept the mind into direct governance—having one's "skin in the hand of God" as both spiritual achievement earned through virtuous conduct and divine grace bestowed upon one who has made themselves receptive through proper orientation.

The distinction between arriving at the Beautiful West versus reincarnating in the east (verses 19-20) illuminates the ultimate consequences of how life is governed. "Arriving in the Beautiful West means leaving behind the worldly concerns and struggles, the imperfect human existence in illusory and fleeting time and space in favor of the perfection of the Divine" [1], representing transcendence of ego-governed existence into complete divine assimilation. Conversely, reincarnation in "the east where the sun rises" refers to being "born to pursue worldly {illusory and fleeting} goals and desires only to experience suffering and stress, frustrations and disappointments ending in old age, disease and death" [1].

The teaching on joyousness (reshau) in verse 19 reveals a crucial metaphysical distinction: the term derives from "resh/rech = to know," establishing that "knowing the perfection of the Divine is the source of joy (bliss = unalloyed happiness), unlike human happiness which is based on ignorance, and alloyed to human thoughts, feelings, limited ego identification, illusory knowledge and temporary situations" [1]. Authentic joy arises not from ego-satisfaction but from the mind recognizing Ab Neter as its essential foundation—a recognition producing "unalloyed happiness" free from the fleeting gratifications characterizing worldly pursuits.

The metaphysical principle underlying verses 9-11's ethical injunctions thus becomes clear: the mind cannot achieve the spiritual integration where divine will governs existence while simultaneously engaging behaviors arising from egoistic separation and hierarchical valuation. The teaching establishes "three lauded goals": "be aware of Neberdjer, revere being in the hand of God, and looking forward to the beautiful west environment of being in Divinity" [2]. These three goals interconnect: awareness of Neberdjer allows recognition that all beings derive their consciousness from the same divine source, producing reverence for being in divine governance, which facilitates arrival at the Beautiful West rather than reincarnation into continued ego-governed existence.

4. Transpersonal Psychology Research: The Psychology of Dehumanization and Compassion

Contemporary psychological research provides remarkable validation of Chapter 25's teachings on the relationship between egoistic superiority, dehumanization of vulnerable populations, and spiritual development. Studies on dehumanization demonstrate that individuals who categorize others as less than fully human show decreased activation in brain regions associated with empathy and social cognition when viewing members of dehumanized groups [4]. This aligns precisely with verses 9-10's teaching that mockery and exploitation of the vulnerable arise from the mind failing to recognize the common spiritual essence in all beings.

Research on altruism and helping behavior reveals that individuals who maintain strong ingroup-outgroup distinctions show significantly reduced prosocial behavior toward vulnerable outgroup members compared to those who emphasize common humanity [5]. Studies using neuroimaging demonstrate that compassion meditation practices emphasizing shared human nature produce measurable increases in altruistic behavior and activation of brain regions associated with empathy and positive affect [6]. This validates the ancient teaching that recognizing all people as manifestations of the same Neberdjer source transforms the mind away from egoistic separation toward compassionate treatment.

Research on mortality salience and meaning-making reveals patterns consistent with verses 19-20's teaching on ultimate spiritual goals. Terror management theory demonstrates that individuals who have developed frameworks of meaning transcending ego-gratification show significantly less anxiety about death and greater psychological well-being compared to those whose meaning-systems center on temporary ego-achievements [7]. Studies on Buddhist practitioners show that those who have cultivated non-dual awareness report experiences of peace and fulfillment independent of external circumstances, validating the ancient understanding that "knowing the perfection of the Divine" produces unalloyed happiness rather than the fleeting satisfactions characterizing worldly pursuits [8].

Clinical research on caregiving attitudes reveals that healthcare workers who view patients through purely mechanistic frameworks show higher rates of burnout and decreased quality of care compared to those who maintain awareness of patients' inherent dignity and worth [9]. This validates verse 11's teaching about recognizing some persons as operating under divine governance, suggesting that perceiving the sacred in others transforms both the perceiver's mind and the quality of interpersonal interaction.

5. Spiritual Implications for Aspirants

PART A: PASTORAL CONCERNS FOR MODERN SEEKERS

Consider the individual aspirant raised in contemporary culture emphasizing competitive advantage, individual achievement, and survival-of-the-fittest mentality. Such a person encounters profound cognitive dissonance when Amenemopet teaches that all people deserve respect regardless of capacity or appearance based on their divine kinship. Their entire conditioning reinforces hierarchical valuation—those with greater intelligence, physical capability, or social status deserve better treatment than those lacking such advantages. The teaching threatens to collapse the frameworks through which they organize social relationships and derive competitive self-esteem.

The modern seeker often experiences internal conflict between spiritual teachings on universal divine nature and cultural conditioning around worthiness hierarchies. When someone with severe cognitive disabilities enters their environment, the mind may experience automatic aversion, superiority, or discomfort—responses arising from aryu accumulated through years of cultural conditioning valuing intelligence and capability. The person feels ashamed of such responses yet lacks understanding of how to transform them, failing to recognize these as aryu patterns that thin through patient ethical practice rather than through mere intellectual commitment to egalitarian principles [3].

Someone working in corporate environments faces acute challenges implementing verse 10's teaching against scheming to take advantage of vulnerabilities. Professional success often depends on identifying and exploiting competitors' weaknesses, negotiating from positions maximizing one's leverage, and maintaining strategic advantage. The aspirant experiences genuine confusion about when discernment becomes exploitation, when healthy self-protection becomes harmful scheming, when competitive effectiveness crosses into taking advantage of the afflicted.

The aspirant contemplating verses 19-20's teaching on ultimate spiritual destiny encounters particularly intense struggles. Consider the parent who has invested decades building worldly achievements—career success, financial security, social status—only to encounter teachings suggesting these represent illusory pursuits characterizing reincarnation rather than arrival at the Beautiful West. The mind experiences grief, confusion, even anger: "Have I wasted my life pursuing meaningless goals?" This misses the teaching's actual message: not that worldly responsibilities lack value but that the mind must not mistake ego-gratification through worldly achievement for the ultimate spiritual goal of divine union.

PART B: METHODS FOR TRANSFORMATION THROUGH RECOGNIZING DIVINE NATURE IN ALL BEINGS

Based on the teaching presented by Sage Amenemopet in verses 9-11 that all people are sustained by the same Neberdjer source, the application of the inverse doctrine methodology suggests that aspirants should avoid thoughts, feelings, and actions that reinforce egoistic superiority or hierarchical valuation based on physical appearance, mental capacity, or social status, as these would undermine recognition of the divine nature permeating all apparent individuals.

The practical method emerges from verse 9's instruction combined with verse 11's revelation about divine governance. When encountering persons of diminished capacity, different appearance, or vulnerable circumstances, practice pausing to consciously acknowledge: "This person's capacity for awareness derives from the same Neberdjer source as my own. The body I perceive represents another manifestation of the divine creative principle animating all forms. I honor the Ab Neter sustaining this being's awareness." This transforms perception from comparative judgment to recognition of the common spiritual essence, gradually thinning the aryu generating automatic superiority responses.

For example, when encountering someone with severe physical disabilities, rather than allowing Hat to operate from unconscious aversion or pity, practice seeing through the surface appearance to recognize the consciousness sustaining that being. Recognize that whatever diminishment affects the physical form, the essential awareness witnessing through that form derives from the same infinite consciousness sustaining all existence. This does not require denying obvious differences in capability but rather locating shared identity at the level of Ab Neter rather than body-mind characteristics.

Implement daily examination of verse 10's teaching on negative mental schemes. Before engaging business negotiations, strategic planning, or competitive situations, pause to examine: "Am I identifying vulnerabilities in others for purposes of exploitation, or am I engaging legitimate discernment while maintaining respect for their welfare?" When noticing thoughts of taking advantage of another's weakness, vulnerability, or diminished capacity, recognize these as egoistic aryu requiring purification. Practice acknowledging: "Scheming to harm or exploit the vulnerable generates negative aryu in my ab, obstructing the spiritual integration I seek."

For addressing verses 19-20's teaching on ultimate spiritual goals, practice the "three lauded goals" the teaching establishes: "be aware of Neberdjer, revere being in the hand of God, and looking forward to the beautiful west environment of being in Divinity" [2]. Begin each day acknowledging: "My ultimate goal is not ego-gratification through worldly achievement but divine union—having my skin governed by divine consciousness rather than ego nature. I engage worldly responsibilities while recognizing these as opportunities for ethical practice preparing the mind for arrival at the Beautiful West."

When experiencing attachment to worldly achievements or anxiety about their impermanence, practice contemplating: "Time-space existence inevitably involves frustration and fleeting satisfactions. Authentic joy arises not from ego-achievements but from the mind recognizing Ab Neter as my essential foundation—discovering that consciousness which sustains all mental operations. I fulfill my rightful duties with diligence while releasing the delusion that these activities constitute ultimate fulfillment." This transforms engagement from fevered pursuit of ego-satisfaction into relaxed participation in divine unfolding.

Practice verse 20's teaching through regular contemplation: "Well-being is found in the hand of The Divine. My goal is to have my skin—my entire body-mind existence—governed by divine consciousness rather than aryu-driven ego patterns. As I thin aryu density through ethical conduct, wisdom study, and meditative practice, Hat gradually operates from Ab Neter guidance, allowing divine will to express through my thoughts, words, and deeds."

References

[1] Ashby, M. (2019-25). Mysticism of Amenemopet Hieroglyphic Text Translation. Sema Institute of Ancient Egyptian Studies.
[2] Ashby, M. (2025). Keys to Sage Amenemopet wisdom text trilinear translation chapter 25 by Dr Muata Ashby. Sema Institute of Ancient Egyptian Studies.
[3] Ashby, M. (2019). Amenemopet lectures 2019 by Dr Muata Ashby transcripts. Sema Institute of Ancient Egyptian Studies.
[4] Harris, L. T., & Fiske, S. T. (2006). Dehumanizing the lowest of the low: Neuroimaging responses to extreme out-groups. Psychological Science, 17(10), 847-853.
[5] Dovidio, J. F., Piliavin, J. A., Schroeder, D. A., & Penner, L. A. (2006). The Social Psychology of Prosocial Behavior. Lawrence Erlbaum Associates.
[6] Weng, H. Y., Fox, A. S., Shackman, A. J., Stodola, D. E., Caldwell, J. Z., Olson, M. C., ... & Davidson, R. J. (2013). Compassion training alters altruism and neural responses to suffering. Psychological Science, 24(7), 1171-1180.
[7] Vail, K. E., Juhl, J., Arndt, J., Vess, M., Routledge, C., & Rutjens, B. T. (2012). When death is good for life: Considering the positive trajectories of terror management. Personality and Social Psychology Review, 16(4), 303-329.
[8] Hölzel, B. K., Lazar, S. W., Gard, T., Schuman-Olivier, Z., Vago, D. R., & Ott, U. (2011). How does mindfulness meditation work? Proposing mechanisms of action from a conceptual and neural perspective. Perspectives on Psychological Science, 6(6), 537-559.
[9] Sinclair, S., McClement, S., Raffin-Bouchal, S., Hack, T. F., Hagen, N. A., McConnell, S., & Chochinov, H. M. (2016). Compassion in health care: An empirical model. Journal of Pain and Symptom Management, 51(2), 193-203.
[10] Ashby, M. (2019-25). Mysticism of Amenemopet Hieroglyphic Text Translation Chapter 6B. Sema Institute of Ancient Egyptian Studies.

CHAPTER 26: Commentary on Amenemopet Chapter 26, Verses 11-15: The Path from Humility to Vigilant Serenity: Releasing Pride-Guarding to Navigate Life Under Divine Guidance

INTRODUCTION

Chapter 26 of the Teachings of Amenemopet presents a progressive teaching sequence revealing how the mind must release egoistic pride-guarding to achieve the serene (Ger) personality capable of vigilant navigation under divine guidance. The chapter begins with the foundational instruction on humility (verse 11), establishing that bowing and showing consideration to others does not damage dignity when the mind recognizes that honor belongs to Neberdjer rather than to worldly position. This foundation enables understanding subsequent teachings on pleasant speech (verse 12), avoidance of inflated communication (verse 13), and ultimately the watchful awareness required for safe navigation (verses 14-15) as the mind recognizes that Neberdjer shepherds the boat of life from the forefront.

The verses reveal a sophisticated psychology: pride-guarding in worldly position generates the mental agitation that serves as seed condition for heated personality, preventing the serenity (Ger state) required for recognizing Ab Neter in the kara. Each teaching progressively addresses manifestations of egoism—from refusing to bow, to withholding pleasant expression, to inflated self-assertion, to loss of watchful awareness—all rooted in the fundamental delusion that dignity and security derive from ego-maintained superiority rather than from divine alignment. The chapter establishes that safe arrival at spiritual perfection requires releasing these egoistic patterns while maintaining vigilant awareness of righteous choices as Neberdjer guides from the boat's forefront.

This directly supports both Prologue goals: releasing pride-guarding and maintaining righteous communication create "well-being while living on earth" (Prologue verse 2) by eliminating the mental agitation that produces suffering, while recognizing that honor belongs to Neberdjer rather than personality facilitates discovery of the kara "where the Divine resides in every person" (Prologue verse 9).

SUMMARY OF VERSES

Verse 11: It is not necessary to guard your pride since your dignity is not damaged—your back will not break if you bow and show regard and due consideration to others. The teaching reveals the mind operating from the delusion that worldly position confers dignity, creating fear that respectful acknowledgment diminishes stature. True dignity flows from Neberdjer alignment, making the back (personality structure) unbreakable when the mind bows to recognize divine manifestation in all beings.

Verse 12: Speaking pleasantly—in a positive, thoughtful, gentle, obliging manner—does not cause a person to be diminished, reduced, weakened, or devalued in terms of power or sovereignty. Self-respect derives from alignment with truth and the Divine, making pleasant expression a manifestation of godward aryu content.

Verse 13: There is no purpose for speaking in an expanding, flooding, inflaming manner—yelling out, becoming loud and boisterous with speech that inflames the nervous system, inflates the ego, and creates the agitated heated person. True power requires no such inflation.

Verse 14: The person in charge of the ship, looking ahead as captain, who remains aware and watchful of what lies ahead on the course—clear paths or obstacles, heated persons, corrupt actors—maintains vigilance for making righteous choices that keep the Divine from turning away.

Verse 15: The watchful person will not experience the disaster of crashing the ship. Their life journey arrives safely at the port of spiritual perfection in the Beautiful West. Conversely, those without watchful awareness experience shipwreck—not merely physical death but spiritual disaster: life thrashed by egoism, deprived of being in the hand of God, failing to discover the West, remaining unaware of Neberdjer's glory.

KEY TEACHINGS DERIVED FROM THE VERSES

1. Humility Does Not Diminish Dignity [Verse 11]: Bowing and showing consideration does not damage authentic dignity because self-worth derives from Neberdjer, not from worldly position or ego-guarding.
2. Pleasant Speech Manifests Godward Aryu [Verse 12]: Speaking warmly and appreciatively expresses divine alignment rather than weakness, as power flows from truth rather than dominance displays.
3. Inflated Communication Reveals Egoism [Verse 13]: Loud, boisterous, heated speech inflames the nervous system and inflates ego, creating mental agitation that prevents serenity.
4. Watchful Awareness Requires Serenity [Verse 14]: Vigilant navigation of life's course depends on the mind free from pride-guarding and ego-inflation, capable of recognizing righteous paths.
5. Safe Arrival Depends on Divine Guidance [Verse 15]: Spiritual perfection requires both releasing egoistic patterns and recognizing Neberdjer as shepherd guiding from the forefront.

1. HUMAN PSYCHOLOGY PRINCIPLE: THE EGOISTIC DELUSION OF DIGNITY THROUGH WORLDLY POSITION AND THE PROGRESSION TO HEATED PERSONALITY

The fundamental psychological issue across Chapter 26's verses concerns layered delusions whereby Hat operates under the conviction that dignity, power, and authority require guarding worldly position through pride maintenance [verse 11], dominance communication [verse 12], and inflated self-assertion [verse 13]—while humility, pleasant speech, and gentle expression represent weakness or loss of status. This delusion begins with the belief that "your back will break if you bow"—that showing consideration to others damages dignity—creating the egoic tendency to guard pride in one's standing as if worldly position holds ultimate importance.

The teaching reveals the mind trapped in the illusion that dignity derives from worldly standing rather than from divine alignment. As the lecture emphasizes, pride in "a position in an illusory world" misplaces honor that "rightly goes to Neberdjer and not the personality" [2]. When the mind guards its back—maintaining rigid posture of superiority, refusing to bow in acknowledgment of others as divine manifestations—it generates the mental agitation and pride that serve as "seed condition of heated personality." The refusal to show "regard and due consideration to others" [1] because of fear that dignity will be damaged represents the fundamental egoistic delusion from which all subsequent communication dysfunctions emerge.

This pride-guarding creates systematic inability to navigate life's course with clear awareness. When the mind operates from the pattern of guarding worldly position, attention becomes absorbed in maintaining superiority displays rather than remaining watchful of the actual path ahead—the righteous choices, corrupt actors, and spiritual obstacles that determine whether the boat arrives safely or crashes [2]. The aryu driving pride-guarding and heated, inflamed communication occupy Hat so densely that the vigilant awareness required for safe navigation becomes impossible, as the mind remains preoccupied with maintaining ego-position rather than tending toward serenity.[1]

Consider how this reveals integrated psychology. The mind believing worldly position confers dignity [verse 11] naturally withholds pleasant expression [verse 12], fearing that warmth signals equality rather than superiority. This pattern escalates to inflated communication [verse 13]—loud, boisterous assertion attempting to establish dominance. These heated patterns generate such mental agitation that watchful awareness [verses 14-15] becomes impossible, as the mind remains absorbed in ego-maintenance rather than observing the path ahead with serene clarity.

The teaching establishes that becoming Ger (serene personality) requires releasing the pride-guarding at the root of this progression. When the mind recognizes that "all are kin manifestations of the Divine and all are due the according respect" [2], the compulsion to guard superiority dissolves. Self-respect emerges from "being with truth and God" [2] rather than from comparative worldly positioning, allowing the mind to bow, speak pleasantly, avoid inflation, and maintain watchful serenity—the complete transformation from heated to silent personality.

Connection to Prologue Goals:

These egoistic patterns directly obstruct both Prologue goals. Without releasing pride-guarding and its manifestations, [Prologue verse 2] "cause a person to have well-being while living on earth" [1] cannot be achieved because the mental agitation generated by guarding worldly position, withholding pleasant expression, and maintaining inflated communication creates persistent internal suffering. The energy consumed in ego-maintenance depletes resources needed for actual well-being.

More profoundly, these patterns obstruct [Prologue verse 9's] goal of discovering the kara "where the Divine resides in every person" [1]. When Hat operates through pride-guarding, pleasant speech withholding, and ego-inflating communication, the resulting dense aryu patterns in the ab dominate presence-of-mind awareness so thoroughly that Ab Neter remains completely obscured. The teaching reveals that transformation requires recognizing honor belongs to Neberdjer rather than personality—not creating new access to something absent, but removing the pride-based aryu density that hides Ab Neter already present sustaining all conscious awareness.[1,2]

2. Behavioral Imperative: The Progressive Manifestation from Pride-Guarding to Navigational Disaster

The behavioral patterns manifest through progressive stages, each emerging from the fundamental delusion about dignity and worldly position. Understanding this progression reveals how the mind trapped in egoism moves systematically toward spiritual shipwreck unless the foundational pattern receives attention.

Stage 1: Pride-Guarding and Bowing Refusal [Verse 11]

The initial pattern involves pride-guarding through refusal to bow or show consideration, representing the mind operating from the belief that acknowledging others' worth diminishes one's own standing. Consider the professional who maintains rigid hierarchical distance, refusing to express appreciation or acknowledge subordinates' contributions because such gestures might signal equality rather than superiority. The academic who cannot praise colleagues' work, fearing that acknowledging others' excellence diminishes their own stature. The spiritual teacher who maintains inflated positioning, unable to bow before students or acknowledge learning from them, trapped in the delusion that humility damages spiritual authority.

These patterns emerge from aryu where the mind derives identity from worldly position rather than from Neberdjer alignment. The teaching directly addresses this: "your back will not break if you bow and show regard and due consideration to others" [1]. The "back" metaphorically represents personality structure—the mind fears that bowing (releasing superiority posture) will cause structural collapse of identity. Yet this reveals the delusion: when dignity flows from divine essence rather than worldly position, personality structure remains intact regardless of whether one maintains superiority displays or bows in acknowledgment of the Divine manifesting through all beings.

This pride-guarding creates the mental agitation that serves as seed condition for heated personality. The constant vigilance required to maintain superior positioning, the anxiety about gestures that might signal equality, the resistance to natural impulses of appreciation and acknowledgment—all generate the inner turbulence that prevents Ger (serene) personality. The teaching emphasizes that reducing egoism requires recognizing that "honor goes to Neberdjer and not the personality" [2], making pride in worldly standing a spiritual delusion requiring release.

STAGE 2: PLEASANT SPEECH AVOIDANCE [VERSE 12]

Building on the foundation of pride-guarding, the second pattern involves withholding pleasant communication, believing that "expressing goodness" causes loss of respect or authority [2]. The manager who maintains stern, critical communication with subordinates, believing warmth undermines authority. The supervisor who withholds positive feedback, fearing employees will become complacent if treated kindly. The parent maintaining constant sternness, convinced that pleasant expression signals weakness.

These patterns arise directly from the pride-guarding the mind in verse 11 addresses. Someone who refuses to bow because they fear dignity requires superiority-maintenance naturally withholds pleasant speech for the same reason. The teaching reveals this operates whether the person acknowledges it or resists the pattern. Someone might intellectually value pleasant communication yet internally experience anxiety when considering expressing warmth to those perceived as subordinate, revealing aryu that equate pleasant expression with vulnerability or loss of power.

The teaching addresses this delusion explicitly: self-respect emerges not from maintaining dominance displays but from alignment with divine truth, making "expressing goodness...an expression of the godward content of aryu" [2]. When the mind recognizes that bowing does not break the back, it naturally discovers that pleasant speech does not diminish power—both flow from the same recognition that dignity derives from Neberdjer rather than from comparative positioning. Additionally, letting go of this egoistic personality flaw allows personality exaltation via openness to inspiration from deeper levels of connection to Ab Neter that fulfils and elevates the personality in its own right without need for pride-guarding or comparing to others.

STAGE 3: INFLATED, HEATED COMMUNICATION [VERSE 13]

The pattern escalates to inflated communication—"yelling out, getting up/rising with temper and becoming loud and boisterous/animated/rowdy/noisy/exuberant/overexcited/over-the-top, with the speech so much so as to inflame the nervous system" [1]. This represents the mind attempting to establish authority through volume, intensity, and emotional flooding when the foundational patterns of pride-guarding and pleasant speech withholding prove insufficient for maintaining perceived superiority.

Consider the person who escalates to shouting during disagreements, believing louder, more aggressive communication establishes dominance. The parent who yells at children rather than speaking calmly, convinced that stern loudness maintains respect. The professional who engages bombastic, over-the-top presentations, inflating themselves through exaggerated enthusiasm and boisterousness. Each pattern represents the mind attempting to create through volume and intensity the authority it fears losing by acknowledging others or speaking pleasantly.

These heated patterns "inflame the nervous system (located in the backbone), inflating the ego" [1], creating the physiological and psychological state that previous chapters identified as the heated person. The teaching reveals the mind operating from the delusion that power requires inflation, unaware that authentic authority emerges from silent serenity rather than heated agitation. The progression becomes clear: refusing to bow → withholding pleasant speech → escalating to inflated communication—each stage representing the mind attempting more desperate measures to maintain the illusory dignity it believes depends on superiority displays.

Stage 4: Loss of Watchful Awareness [Verses 14-15]

The final pattern encompasses loss of watchful awareness, where attention fails to maintain vigilant navigation because it remains absorbed in the prior patterns of pride-guarding, pleasant speech withholding, and inflated communication. The person operating as captain of their life's boat yet not "aware and watchful (vigilant) of what is coming in the future, what is ahead on the course" [1]—the corrupt actors, heated persons, unrighteous choices—crashes the ship.

As the lecture teachings emphasize, watchfulness means being "capable of being aware of the path that is best to follow and aware of heated persons, the corrupt actors and straying from unrighteousness and taking care to be aware/conscious of making righteous choices" [2]. Yet the mind consumed by maintaining worldly position, withholding acknowledgment, and engaging heated communication patterns lacks the mental resources for this vigilance. The energy absorbed in ego-maintenance prevents the serene awareness required for recognizing what lies ahead on the path.

The teaching reveals compassion for these patterns by recognizing they often emerge from cultural conditioning and unresolved insecurity rather than inherent moral deficiency. A child raised in hierarchical systems where authority figures maintained rigid superiority develops patterns equating dignity with dominance displays. Someone who experienced humiliation when showing vulnerability learns to guard pride through stern, inflated communication. These protective mechanisms, once adaptive in threatening environments, become maladaptive aryu patterns that perpetuate suffering and prevent the watchful serenity required for safe navigation.[1,2]

3. Mystic Psychology-Metaphysical Implications: The Architecture of True Dignity and Divine Navigation

Having examined psychological and behavioral dimensions, we now explore the profound metaphysical mechanics underlying individual experience and the cosmic framework within which life's navigation occurs.[1]

The Metaphysics of True Dignity: Back Structure and Divine Foundation

Verse 11's metaphor of the back that "will not break if you bow" reveals profound teaching about personality architecture. The back represents the structural integrity of personality—the coherence and stability of identity through which the mind operates. The teaching addresses the metaphysical delusion that personality structure depends on maintaining worldly position and guarding pride against acknowledgment of others.

The metaphysical reality: personality structure derives stability not from egoic position-guarding but from recognition that consciousness itself flows from Neberdjer. When the mind recognizes that "all are kin manifestations of the Divine and all are due the according respect" [2], bowing to acknowledge divine presence in others does not damage the back because personality structure rests on divine foundation rather than on comparative worldly positioning. The teaching reveals that "self respect comes from being with truth and God" [2] rather than from maintaining superiority illusions.

This transforms understanding of humility: bowing represents not personality collapse but recognition of metaphysical reality—that honor belongs to Neberdjer manifesting through all beings rather than to the temporary personality-form occupying worldly position. When the mind attempts to guard pride in worldly standing, it operates from the delusion that personality exists autonomously rather than as Neberdjer-manifestation. This pride-guarding generates the mental agitation that obscures Ab Neter awareness in kara, as the mind remains absorbed in maintaining illusory superiority rather than recognizing the divine foundation already supporting personality structure.

The teaching that "your back will not break" if you bow establishes that the mind aligned with Neberdjer can acknowledge others, show consideration, express appreciation, and bow in recognition of divine presence without personality structure collapsing. Indeed, refusing to bow—maintaining rigid superiority posture—actually weakens personality structure by disconnecting it from divine foundation, making it dependent on fragile worldly positioning. The serene (Ger) personality emerges when the mind releases pride-guarding, recognizing that true dignity flows from divine alignment rather than from comparative worldly status.

NEBERDJER AS SHEPHERD AT THE FOREFRONT AND THE NATURE OF SAFE ARRIVAL

At the deepest metaphysical level, Chapter 26 reveals the cosmic architecture whereby life operates as a divinely guided voyage where Neberdjer serves as shepherd watching from the forefront of the boat, requiring human vigilance to maintain awareness of righteous choices while surrendering attachment to ego-driven outcomes. As Chapter 18 verse 6 establishes: "Neberdjer pay f ary sau hat amm" (Lord-of-utmost limits that he does guide front boat). The lecture expands: "despite the personal predilections, there is an all-encompassing divinity that masters and encompasses the limits of Creation and therefore, that overall encompassing divinity is the shepherd that guides human life. That divinity is actually at the forefront of the boat of life watching(aware), guiding the boat of human life where it needs to go for the welfare of all humans even before they themselves know where they are going" [3].

This transforms understanding of verses 14-15's watchful captain: the mind functions not as autonomous navigator determining the journey's destination but as vigilant observer maintaining awareness of righteous choices while Neberdjer shepherds from the forefront. The teaching emphasizes: "all we need to be concerned about is righteous living and watching that the mind should tend towards serenity instead of heatedness. Neberdjer has the rest in hand. And the final outcome of life is handled by Neberdjer so no need to worry or have anxiety or stress" [2].

This reveals why humility does not damage dignity (verse 11), why pleasant speech does not diminish power (verse 12), and why inflated communication proves unnecessary (verse 13): authentic authority emerges not from ego-driven dominance displays but from alignment with the Neberdjer guidance already operating at the boat's forefront. When the mind recognizes this reality, the compulsion to guard pride, withhold pleasant expression, or inflate ego through heated speech dissolves, as self-respect derives from "being with truth and God" [2] rather than from maintaining superiority illusions.

The distinction between safe arrival versus shipwreck (verse 15) illuminates ultimate spiritual consequences. The teaching emphasizes that disaster means not merely physical death but "a life thrashed by egoism and deprived of being in hand of God, discovering the west and being unaware of the glory of Neberdjer (expanded awareness and self-knowledge of realizing ones Spirit Being that is immortal eternal)" [2]. Safe arrival at "the port of spiritual perfection in the Beautiful West" [1] requires thinning aryu density sufficiently that watchful awareness can operate from the kara level where Ab Neter resides, allowing recognition that Neberdjer guides the journey while human responsibility involves maintaining serenity and making righteous choices as they arise.

The lecture teachings reveal the cosmic principle underlying navigation: "whatever you desire is composed of Neberdjer...Everything is made up of Neberdjer therefore whatever you desire is Neberdjer" [3]. This means the mind attempting to navigate through ego-driven strategies—guarding worldly position, maintaining dominance displays, inflating self-importance—pursues illusory destinations, unaware that all apparent goals ultimately represent Neberdjer manifesting in various forms. Authentic navigation thus requires not fevered control-seeking but watchful awareness that allows Neberdjer guidance to unfold through righteous choices made with serenity rather than heated agitation. The foundation: releasing pride in worldly position to recognize that honor belongs to Neberdjer, making ego-guarding spiritually unnecessary and the source of all navigational disaster.

4. Transpersonal Psychology Research: Validation of Humility, Communication Patterns, and Mindful Navigation

Contemporary psychological research provides remarkable validation of Chapter 26's teachings on the relationship between humility, communication style, perceived authority, and navigational awareness.

Research on Humility, Status Anxiety, and Psychological Well-being

Research on humility provides validation for verse 11's teaching that bowing and showing consideration do not damage dignity. Studies demonstrate that leaders displaying intellectual humility—willingness to acknowledge others' contributions and recognize limitations in their own knowledge—receive higher ratings for effectiveness and inspire greater team loyalty than those maintaining rigid superiority postures.[4] Research reveals that authentic humility correlates with stronger leadership outcomes, validating the ancient teaching that "your back will not break if you bow."

Neuroscientific research on status anxiety reveals that individuals preoccupied with maintaining hierarchical positioning show elevated activation in amygdala and stress-response systems, producing chronic cortisol elevation that impairs cognitive function and emotional regulation.[5] This validates the teaching that pride-guarding in worldly position generates mental agitation serving as a seed condition for heated personality. Studies demonstrate that individuals trained to release status-maintenance concerns show measurable reductions in anxiety and increases in prosocial behavior, confirming that humility enhances rather than diminishes psychological functioning.

Research on gratitude and acknowledgment provides particularly relevant validation. Studies show that expressing appreciation and acknowledging others' contributions produces measurable increases in well-being for both the expresser and recipient, with longitudinal research demonstrating that cultures emphasizing mutual acknowledgment show higher collective psychological health than those emphasizing competitive status hierarchies.[9] This empirically validates the teaching that showing "regard and due consideration to others" represents not weakness but expression aligned with reality of interconnection.

COMMUNICATION PATTERNS AND AUTHORITY RESEARCH

Studies on leadership communication demonstrate that leaders who employ warm, supportive communication combined with clear expectations produce significantly higher team performance and satisfaction compared to those using dominant, aggressive communication styles.[4] Research reveals that perceived authority derives not from stern dominance but from competence combined with warmth, validating verses 11-12's teaching that humility and pleasant speech do not diminish power.

Neuroscientific research on aggressive communication patterns reveals that loud, boisterous speech activates the sympathetic nervous system in both speakers and listeners, producing physiological stress responses that impair cognitive functioning and decision-making.[6] This validates verse 13's teaching that inflated speech "inflames the nervous system," creating the heated state that previous chapters identified as obstructing spiritual awareness. Studies demonstrate that chronic aggressive communication patterns produce measurable increases in cortisol and decreased prefrontal cortex activity associated with executive function and ethical reasoning.

MINDFUL AWARENESS AND NAVIGATION RESEARCH

Research on mindful awareness and decision-making reveals patterns consistent with verses 14-15's teaching on watchful navigation. Studies demonstrate that individuals trained in present-moment awareness show significantly improved ability to recognize situational risks, avoid impulsive decisions, and maintain focus on long-term goals compared to control groups.[7] Longitudinal research reveals that practitioners of mindfulness meditation show enhanced capacity for cognitive flexibility—the ability to shift attention from reactive patterns to conscious choices aligned with values, precisely the watchful awareness Amenemopet describes as preventing shipwreck.

Research on metacognitive awareness—the capacity to observe one's own thought patterns—reveals that individuals with higher metacognitive skills show improved life outcomes across domains including relationships, career satisfaction, and psychological well-being.[8] This validates the teaching that serving as watchful captain of the life-boat produces safe arrival rather than disaster. Clinical studies demonstrate that metacognitive therapy, which trains patients to observe rather than react to thoughts and emotions, produces lasting improvements in anxiety and depression, confirming that watchful awareness prevents the internal shipwrecks of worry and despair.

Buddhist psychology research provides validation for the integration of vigilant awareness with surrender to larger processes. Studies on practitioners of vipassana meditation, which emphasizes both mindful attention and acceptance, show that experienced meditators demonstrate enhanced ability to maintain focused awareness while simultaneously releasing attachment to outcomes.[10] This parallels Amenemopet's teaching that the mind must maintain vigilant navigation while recognizing Neberdjer as shepherd guiding from the forefront—active awareness combined with surrender to divine guidance.

5. SPIRITUAL IMPLICATIONS FOR ASPIRANTS

PART A: PASTORAL CONCERNS - THE CHALLENGE OF HUMILITY AND PRIDE-RELEASE IN HIERARCHICAL CULTURE

Consider the aspirant who has achieved significant worldly success—advanced professional position, social status, spiritual authority within a community. They encounter verse 11's teaching that "your back will not break if you bow and show regard and due consideration to others," yet experience profound resistance. Their entire identity has been constructed around maintaining this achieved position. The thought of bowing to subordinates, expressing appreciation to those "beneath" their station, or showing consideration in ways that might signal equality triggers anxiety: "Won't this undermine my authority? Haven't I earned the right to maintain superior positioning? If I bow, won't my carefully constructed status collapse?"

This reveals the mind trapped in the delusion that personality structure depends on worldly position-guarding rather than on Neberdjer foundation. The aspirant has accumulated dense aryu equating dignity with comparative status rather than with divine alignment. They fail to recognize that true self-respect "comes from being with truth and God" [2] rather than from maintaining superiority displays. The pride in worldly position—treating it as ultimately important rather than recognizing the world as illusory manifestation—prevents the very humility required for becoming Ger (serene) personality.

The modern seeker often experiences internal conflict between teachings on humility and pleasant expression versus cultural conditioning around authority. Someone raised in competitive hierarchical environments learns that acknowledgment represents weakness, that warmth undermines respect, that maintaining stern distance proves necessary for authority. When considering implementing verses 11-12's teachings, the mind may experience acute anxiety: "Won't they perceive me as weak? Will I lose respect? Does kindness undermine authority?" These responses arise from aryu accumulated through years of cultural conditioning that equates dominance with power.

Someone working in high-pressure competitive environments faces acute challenges implementing verse 13's teaching against inflated communication. Professional success often depends on confident self-promotion, enthusiastic presentations, and willingness to engage loud, boisterous communication that establishes presence. The aspirant experiences confusion: "How do I advocate effectively without inflated speech? When does confidence become ego-inflation?" This misses the teaching's actual message: the issue isn't confidence or appropriate enthusiasm but rather heated patterns that "inflame the nervous system...inflating the ego, becoming an agitated and heated person" [1].

The Deeper Confusion: Divine Guidance, Human Struggle, and the Purpose of Right Action

The aspirant attempting to implement verses 14-15's teaching on watchful navigation encounters particularly intense struggles when combined with the foundational instruction to release pride-guarding. Consider the professional managing complex responsibilities—career demands, family obligations, financial pressures—who encounters teachings suggesting life requires not controlling strategizing based on maintaining worldly position but rather releasing pride while maintaining watchful awareness as Neberdjer guides from the forefront. The mind experiences confusion: "If I release pride-guarding, won't I lose everything I've worked to achieve? If Neberdjer guides while I merely watch, why the struggle? Won't disaster occur if I don't maintain control?"

This confusion reveals multiple interconnected delusions requiring careful examination. First, the mind operates from the belief that human strategizing determines outcomes, unaware that authentic navigation involves releasing ego-attachment to position while maintaining watchful awareness of righteous choices. Yet the question "If Neberdjer guides while I merely watch, why the struggle?" points toward even deeper philosophical territory that we explored thoroughly in Chapter 8, Section 3.5.

As we established in that foundational discussion, everything is indeed composed of Neberdjer—Consciousness manifesting as Creation—and Chapter 18, verse 6 reveals that "Neberdjer...is the shepherd that guides human life...at the forefront of the boat of life watching (aware), guiding the boat of human life where it needs to go for the welfare of all humans even before they themselves know where they are going." Yet this does not mean the mind operating in ignorance can act contrary to Maat without consequences. The wayward mind can act in contravention with universal order, but such actions tend to produce outcomes contrary to peace, harmony, health, and well-being.

This reveals why the struggle exists and why Amenemopet's teachings prove essential. As we explored in Chapter 8, the capacity for ignorance—the ability to forget divine identity—serves the purpose of divine self-experience through individualized vantage points. Without this capacity, Neberdjer would have no means of experiencing itself through apparent multiplicity. However, this same capacity that enables rich dualistic experience also creates the possibility for the mind to collect aryu, become dominated by ego-delusion, and act contrary to cosmic harmony in ways that generate suffering.

The struggle exists because the mind operating from aryu-driven ignorance naturally moves contrary to Maat—the universal order that reflects how existence operates when aligned with the Neberdjer foundation. The teachings on humility, pleasant speech, avoiding inflation, and watchful awareness represent not arbitrary restrictions but practical instructions for aligning with Maat. When the mind aligns with cosmic harmony, actions tend to produce well-being and contentment. When the mind operates contrary to universal order—through pride-guarding, heated reactions, inflated ego-assertion—even though such actions are possible, they tend to produce stress, strife, and suffering.

This is why philosophy matters—why understanding ontological origins proves essential for human fulfillment. The teaching reveals a crucial distinction: At the ultimate level, Neberdjer shepherds the boat's journey toward welfare and divine self-realization. Yet at the relative level within the individualized experience, the mind maintains responsibility for moment-to-moment choices—whether to act through pride-guarding or humility, through heated inflation or serene expression, through fevered control-seeking or watchful awareness aligned with righteousness.

The aspirant's confusion—"If Neberdjer guides, why struggle?"—emerges from failing to recognize these dual levels of operation. Neberdjer guides the overall course toward awakening, yes. But within that guided journey, the mind exercises choice: align with Maat through releasing pride-guarding and maintaining serene watchfulness, or thrash against cosmic harmony through heated patterns that create internal suffering even as the ultimate journey continues under divine shepherding.

Therefore, watchful navigation means not fevered control-seeking (which emerges from the delusion that ego-strategizing determines outcomes) but rather vigilant awareness that maintains righteous choices aligned with Maat while recognizing Neberdjer guides the journey's ultimate course. The aspirant struggles not because struggle itself is cosmically necessary but because aryu-driven patterns habitually move the mind contrary to Maat. The teachings provide the corrective wisdom revealing how to understand, think, and act in accord with universal order rather than in ignorant contravention of it.

When one understands this complete framework—that Neberdjer guides from the forefront while human responsibility involves aligning with Maat through releasing pride-guarding, maintaining serenity, and making righteous choices as they arise—the question resolves itself. One releases pride not to lose everything achieved but to align personality structure with its actual divine foundation rather than with fragile worldly positioning. One maintains watchful awareness not through anxious control-seeking but through serene recognition of righteous paths as Neberdjer shepherds the overall journey. The struggle transforms from futile ego-guarding into patient practice of alignment, recognizing that well-being emerges from harmony with cosmic order rather than from pride-maintenance contrary to Maat.

PART B: PRACTICES FOR TRANSFORMATION - FROM PRIDE-GUARDING TO HUMBLE VIGILANCE

The wisdom to be understood encompasses that transformation occurs through systematic practices that thin aryu density supporting pride-guarding and ego-inflation, progressively revealing Ab Neter awareness that naturally dissolves the delusion that dignity depends on worldly position rather than on Neberdjer alignment.[1,2]

PRACTICE 1: HUMILITY RECOGNITION AND BOWING AS DIVINE ACKNOWLEDGMENT

Based on the teaching presented by Sage Amenemopet in verse 11 that "your back will not break if you bow and show regard and due consideration to others," combined with the recognition that honor belongs to Neberdjer rather than personality, the application of the inverse doctrine methodology suggests that aspirants should avoid thoughts, feelings, and actions that reinforce pride-guarding in worldly position or that equate dignity with maintaining superiority displays, as these patterns generate the mental agitation serving as seed condition for heated personality and prevent development of Ger (serene) personality.

The practice involves daily contemplation: "My dignity does not derive from worldly position but from alignment with Neberdjer. All beings are kin manifestations of the Divine, deserving according respect. When I show consideration, express appreciation, or bow to acknowledge others, I do not damage my back—my personality structure remains intact because it rests on divine foundation rather than comparative positioning. Refusing to bow from pride-guarding generates mental agitation that prevents serenity. Honor belongs to Neberdjer, not to my personality occupying temporary worldly position."[2]

Implementation example: When encountering someone of perceived lower status—service workers, subordinates, students—notice any impulse to maintain superior positioning or withhold acknowledgment. Practice consciously bowing (literally or metaphorically) to recognize divine presence manifesting through this person. Express genuine appreciation for their contribution. Acknowledge their worth not as a strategy for manipulation but as recognition of metaphysical reality: they are Neberdjer-manifestation just as you are.

Notice what happens: Does your "back break"? Does personality structure collapse? Or do you discover that humility actually strengthens dignity by grounding it in truth rather than illusion? Observe how pride-guarding creates internal tension (mental agitation, seed of heated personality) while humble acknowledgment creates serenity (Ger state). Over time, this practice thins aryu equating dignity with worldly position while depositing new patterns recognizing that honor belongs to Neberdjer, making egoic pride-guarding unnecessary and reducing the mental agitation that prevents spiritual awareness.[1,2]

PRACTICE 2: PLEASANT EXPRESSION AS GODWARD ARYU MANIFESTATION

Based on verse 12's teaching combined with verse 11's foundation, aspirants practice recognizing pleasant speech as manifestation of godward aryu rather than as weakness. The practice integrates the recognition that "self respect comes from being with truth and God so expressing goodness is an expression of the godward content of aryu" [2]. When encountering situations where the mind withholds pleasant communication fearing loss of authority, practice pausing to acknowledge: "My power derives not from dominance displays but from alignment with divine truth. Expressing warmth and appreciation manifests godward aryu. My back will not break—personality structure remains intact—when I speak pleasantly because dignity flows from Neberdjer, not from maintaining stern superiority."

Implementation example: When managing others, rather than maintaining stern, critical communication fearing warmth undermines authority, practice expressing genuine appreciation for contributions while maintaining clear expectations. Recognize that effective leadership emerges from competence combined with warmth rather than from inflated self-assertion or constant sternness. Notice how pleasant, thoughtful communication actually strengthens relationships and influence rather than diminishing them, validating that power flows from divine alignment rather than from ego-guarding.[2]

PRACTICE 3: RELEASING INFLATED COMMUNICATION THROUGH SERENITY RECOGNITION

Based on verse 13's teaching, implement daily examination of inflated speech patterns. When noticing impulses toward loud, boisterous, over-the-top communication—whether through yelling, exaggerated enthusiasm, or bombastic self-promotion—pause to examine: "Is this emerging from authentic expression or from ego attempting to inflate itself because I fear that without inflation I lack power? Am I inflaming my nervous system and creating heated agitation that prevents the Ger (serene) state required for spiritual awareness?" Practice acknowledging: "True power requires no inflation. I express authentically without the heated intensity that creates agitated mind and feelings. I allow confidence to emerge from centered serenity grounded in recognition that honor belongs to Neberdjer, making ego-inflation unnecessary."[1,2]

PRACTICE 4: WATCHFUL NAVIGATION WITH DIVINE SURRENDER INTEGRATION

Based on the complete teaching of verses 11-15, practice the integration the teaching emphasizes: "all we need to be concerned about is righteous living and watching that the mind should tend towards serenity instead of heatedness. Neberdjer has the rest in hand" [2]. Begin each day acknowledging: "Neberdjer guides my life-boat from the forefront, shepherding where I need to go for welfare even before I know the destination. My role involves releasing pride-guarding that generates mental agitation, maintaining watchful awareness of righteous choices, recognizing corrupt actors and heated persons, while releasing anxious control-seeking about outcomes. I tend the mind toward serenity (Ger state), trusting Neberdjer handles the rest. My back will not break—personality structure remains intact—because it rests on divine foundation rather than on worldly position I attempt to guard through ego-inflation."[1,2,3]

When experiencing anxiety about life's direction or specific outcomes, practice contemplating: "I am not the autonomous navigator determining my journey's destination through pride-maintenance and ego-assertion. Neberdjer shepherds from the forefront while I maintain vigilant awareness of choices arising in each moment. My responsibility involves choosing righteously, tending toward serenity, avoiding heatedness and pride-guarding—not controlling outcomes through fevered strategizing or maintaining worldly position through dominance displays. Honor belongs to Neberdjer, making ego-maintenance unnecessary and the source of navigational disaster."[2,3]

Practice 5: The Watchful Captain Meditation with Humility Foundation

Practice the watchful captain meditation incorporating the humility foundation: Visualize your life as a boat journey. See Neberdjer at the forefront as shepherd guide. Position yourself as watchful observer on the deck, free from pride-guarding, aware of what appears ahead—opportunities for righteous choice, heated persons to avoid, corrupt influences to recognize. Notice how releasing pride-guarding allows serene watchfulness versus the mental agitation that pride-maintenance creates. Your back remains unbroken—personality structure intact—because it rests on divine foundation rather than on worldly position requiring constant ego-defense.

Practice bowing (literally or in visualization) to acknowledge that Neberdjer guides while you maintain watchful awareness. Notice how this positioning differs from anxious navigation versus passive abdication. You remain alert, aware, choosing righteously as situations arise, while surrendering control of the journey's ultimate course to the divine shepherd guiding from the forefront. The humility that allows this surrender does not damage dignity but rather grounds it in truth, enabling the serene vigilance required for safe arrival at spiritual perfection.[1,2,3]

References

[1] Ashby, M. (2019-25). *Mysticism of Amenemopet Hieroglyphic Text Translation.* Sema Institute of Ancient Egyptian Studies.
[2] Ashby, M. (2025). *Keys to Sage Amenemopet wisdom text trilinear translation chapter 26 by Dr Muata Ashby.* Sema Institute of Ancient Egyptian Studies.
[3] Ashby, M. (2019). *Amenemopet lectures 2019 by Dr Muata Ashby transcripts.* Sema Institute of Ancient Egyptian Studies.
[4] Sy, T., Côté, S., & Saavedra, R. (2005). The contagious leader: Impact of the leader's mood on the mood of group members, group affective tone, and group processes. *Journal of Applied Psychology, 90*(2), 295-305.
[5] Dickerson, S. S., & Kemeny, M. E. (2004). Acute stressors and cortisol responses: A theoretical integration and synthesis of laboratory research. *Psychological Bulletin, 130*(3), 355-391.
[6] Schilpzand, P., De Pater, I. E., & Erez, A. (2016). Workplace incivility: A review of the literature and agenda for future research. *Journal of Organizational Behavior, 37*, S57-S88.
[7] Chiesa, A., Calati, R., & Serretti, A. (2011). Does mindfulness training improve cognitive abilities? A systematic review of neuropsychological findings. *Clinical Psychology Review, 31*(3), 449-464.
[8] Wells, A., & Matthews, G. (1994). *Attention and Emotion: A Clinical Perspective.* Lawrence Erlbaum Associates.
[9] Emmons, R. A., & McCullough, M. E. (2003). Counting blessings versus burdens: An experimental investigation of gratitude and subjective well-being in daily life. *Journal of Personality and Social Psychology, 84*(2), 377-389.
[10] Lutz, A., Slagter, H. A., Dunne, J. D., & Davidson, R. J. (2008). Attention regulation and monitoring in meditation. *Trends in Cognitive Sciences, 12*(4), 163-169.

PART III: SPECIAL TOPIC ESSAYS

THEMATIC SYNTHESIS AND CONTEMPORARY APPLICATIONS

The chapter commentaries you have just completed examine Amenemopet's teachings verse by verse, following the systematic progression the ancient sage established. Each commentary illuminates a specific teaching within its proper context—the human psychology principle, the behavioral patterns, the metaphysical mechanics, the research validation, and the spiritual applications. This chapter-by-chapter approach ensures you encounter the wisdom in the sequence Amenemopet intended, building understanding progressively from foundation through advanced practice.

Nevertheless, as you've likely noticed while reading, certain profound themes emerge repeatedly across multiple chapters—threads weaving through the text that connect teachings into unified principles. Indeed, some of the most pressing challenges modern practitioners face require synthesis of several chapters to resolve effectively. The following special topic essays serve this integrative function, examining cross-cutting themes and contemporary applications that verse-by-verse analysis, by its nature, cannot fully address.

Consider the difference between examining individual threads in a tapestry versus stepping back to perceive the pattern those threads create together. The chapter commentaries provide detailed analysis of each thread; these essays reveal the larger patterns that become visible only through thematic integration. Both approaches prove necessary—neither alone conveys the teaching's full depth.

THREE FUNCTIONS THESE ESSAYS SERVE

First, they reveal unified psychological principles. Amenemopet possessed sophisticated understanding of human consciousness that contemporary psychology only recently began rediscovering through empirical research. The sage employed precise hieroglyphic terminology—like *shennu* (frustration) and *sechsech* (rushing)—for comprehensive psychological phenomena we approximate through multiple descriptive terms. Essay #3 demonstrates that what appears as many separate problems actually represents varied manifestations of a single source cause producing multiple effective causes. This recognition transforms your understanding from "Amenemopet addresses many different issues" to "Amenemopet presents a unified theory of suffering with systematic solutions."

Second, they examine modern obstacles to spiritual development. Ancient Egyptian society operated according to values far more conducive to mind transformation than contemporary culture. Modern aspirants face unprecedented challenges: technology designed to fragment attention, economic structures demanding constant productivity, cultural narratives valorizing perpetual busyness and material accumulation. Essay #5 on *sechsech* reveals how modern culture systematically promotes exactly what Amenemopet identifies as spiritually destructive—constant movement obscuring the still point where Ab Neter resides. These essays help you recognize that difficulty implementing teachings arises not from personal inadequacy but from deliberate cultural conditioning requiring conscious counteraction.

Third, they provide concrete guidance for real-world challenges. When you face specific difficult situations, which teachings apply and how should they be integrated into coherent response? Essay #4 on responding to hurt exemplifies this function. When someone causes significant harm, you need immediate practical guidance: What should I think? What should I say? What actions should I take? Individual chapters address aspects of this situation, yet integrating these separate teachings into unified response protocol requires the synthesis these essays provide.

THE FIVE ESSAYS BEFORE YOU

Essay #0 explores the summary effects of the study and practice of Amenemopet's psycho-spiritual philosophy and disciplines in the form of a simple focused daily spiritual practice.

Essay #1 examines wisdom truth versus ego-gratifying truth—preventing the common error of using "brutal honesty" to justify harmful speech while maintaining factual accuracy.

Essay #2 explores narcissistic consciousness through Amenemopet's framework, addressing both understanding such patterns in others and recognizing their emergence in yourself.

Essay #3 reveals that Amenemopet possessed precise terminology for the frustration syndrome pervading heated personality, demonstrating the unified psychology underlying teachings scattered across chapters.

Essay #4 synthesizes teachings from multiple chapters into a systematic protocol for responding to interpersonal hurt—what to think, what to say, what to avoid—validated through extensive contemporary research on revenge, forgiveness, and meditation.

Essay #5 examines rushing as a spiritual obstacle, revealing through etymological analysis how ancient language itself connects haste to pleasure-seeking, while showing how modern culture's valorization of speed systematically prevents Ab Neter discovery.

HOW TO ENGAGE THIS MATERIAL

You may read these essays sequentially as capstone integration consolidating understanding developed through systematic study. Alternatively, consult specific essays as particular challenges arise—turning to Essay #4 when facing interpersonal hurt, engaging Essay #5 when recognizing how constant rushing undermines meditation.

Nevertheless, I recommend initial sequential reading even if particular essays seem less immediately relevant. The theoretical integration essays especially—particularly Essay #3 on *shennu*—reveal systematic principles transforming understanding of the entire teaching. What appears as a collection of separate behavioral advice emerges as sophisticated unified psychology addressing fundamental mechanisms of suffering and its resolution.

The journey from heated to silent mind and feelings requires both systematic understanding and practical application. The chapter commentaries provide the former; these essays facilitate the latter by revealing patterns, addressing obstacles, and synthesizing guidance. Together, they serve Amenemopet's timeless purpose: causing you to have well-being while living on earth and discovering within yourself the divine consciousness that alone provides genuine, sustainable fulfillment.

SPECIAL TOPIC ESSAY #0: THE ESSENTIAL PRACTICE: MAINTAINING GER AS THE DIRECT PATH TO AB NETER DISCOVERY

ADVANCED INTEGRATION FOR THE MATURE ASPIRANT

Once the aspirant has studied Amenemopet's complete teaching, established a foundation in ethical conduct aligned with Maat, and developed understanding of the consciousness architecture—hat operating from aryu in the ab, obscuring the deeper Ab Neter presence—having been properly initiated into the teachings and having attained sufficient willpower and fortitude to follow the instructions, the comprehensive practice reveals its essential simplicity. Through sustained engagement with Amenemopet's psycho-spiritual practices, the aspirant progressively develops detachment from heated conditions, self-control, non-violence, contentment with trust in the divine, personal responsibility without complacency, and diligence to progress both in life and on the spiritual path toward discovering the Soul-Aware-Witness-Self, Ab Neter, and Neberdjer. Nevertheless, this simplification does not imply the aspirant should proceed independently or abandon the studies and preceptorship that established the foundation. Rather, continued engagement with the teaching and guidance from qualified preceptors remains essential for correcting misunderstandings, deepening comprehension, and ensuring proper progression on the path—the simplicity emerges FROM and remains supported BY the comprehensive framework, not as replacement for it. All the behavioral imperatives, all the warnings against heated patterns, all the prescriptions for righteous conduct converge into a single focal point: the cultivation and maintenance of Ger—serenity, silence, equanimity—as the direct pathway to discovering the divine consciousness within.

This simplified practice emerges not as replacement for the threefold discipline of ethical living, philosophical study, and meditation, but as their natural maturation. The aspirant who has absorbed the teaching discovers that maintaining Ger at all times constitutes the unified practice encompassing all previous instructions. Consider the profound theological principle revealed in Chapter 6B: Neberdjer—the All-Encompassing Divinity, supreme consciousness sustaining all existence—IS supreme serenity, silence, equanimity, and homogeneity. These qualities are not attributes Neberdjer possesses but what Neberdjer essentially IS in its fundamental nature.

Therefore, when the mind and feelings move toward Ger, this movement creates what we might understand as frequency-matching with ultimate reality's essential nature. The heated mind and feelings—mental movements and feelings fueled by ignorance and delusion—operate at frequencies incompatible with recognizing the supreme serenity that sustains consciousness itself. The silent mind and feelings develop frequencies allowing Neberdjer's ever-present reality to become perceptible. This explains why serenity proves not optional but prerequisite for divine discovery—consciousness cannot recognize its divine source when the mind operates at frequencies fundamentally incompatible with that source's essential nature.

THE PRACTICE IN DAILY LIVING: INFORMAL INTEGRATION

Throughout ordinary activities—working, relating to others, handling responsibilities, facing challenges—the mature aspirant maintains continuous awareness: "Am I operating from Ger or from heated patterns?" This simple question becomes the discriminating wisdom applied moment by moment.

When heated thoughts arise—anxiety about future outcomes, resentment toward difficult persons, craving for desired objects, resistance to unpleasant circumstances—recognize these as aryu patterns activating in the hat, driving the personality from unconscious feeling-memories. In that recognition, gently return to serenity. Not through forceful suppression, which creates additional tension, but through the wisdom understanding that heated patterns obscure Ab Neter recognition while generating the very suffering one seeks to escape.

When heated feelings emerge—anger's agitation, fear's constriction, desire's restlessness—observe them as temporary modifications arising in the mind sustained by consciousness, not as defining what you fundamentally are. Allow them to be present without identification, without elaboration, returning awareness to the silent presence witnessing these passing states.

When actions stem from heated patterns—speaking harshly from irritation, acting deceptively from fear, grasping possessively from insecurity—the wisdom to be understood recognizes these behaviors as incompatible with both earthly well-being and divine discovery. Through Maat-aligned conduct, the personality naturally defaults to Ger, since ethical action generates aryu patterns transparent to divine light rather than patterns obscuring spiritual perception.

The life based on Maat—truth-speaking, non-harming, generous sharing, contentment with sufficiency, selfless service—spontaneously manifests as serene personality. One cannot simultaneously maintain ethical conduct and heated reactivity. The very practice of righteousness creates the somatic and psychological conditions wherein serenity emerges naturally rather than requiring constant effortful maintenance.

The Practice in Formal Meditation: Resting in the Unconscious

Chapter 15 explicitly instructs regarding "resting in your heart (unconscious) level of your mind, that is, by spending time meditating, at rest-relaxed, and not restless-agitated, in your unconscious and not always spending time in the Ka (subconscious) and Hat (conscious) level of mind." This advanced practice becomes accessible when the simplified Ger focus has matured through daily implementation.

In dedicated meditation sessions, the practice follows this natural progression:

The body becomes still, releasing physical tension—somatic Ger allowing awareness to withdraw from gross sensations. The breath becomes quiet, settling into natural rhythm without forced control—energetic Ger creating physiological calm. The mind settles as thoughts slow and gaps between mental activity lengthen—mental Ger thinning the density of hat-level distraction.

From this foundation, awareness naturally rests beyond the hat (conscious) and ka (subconscious) levels, entering the ab (unconscious) where Ab Neter resides. This resting proves possible not through forceful effort to push awareness deeper but through the progressive quieting that allows consciousness to settle into its own source, like sediment settling in still water revealing the clarity that was always present beneath agitation's obscuring movement.

The Discovery This Practice Produces

The aspirant who becomes aware of shem (heated personality) and progressively moves toward Ger discovers transformation across all dimensions of experience. During waking activity, the personality operates from serene presence rather than reactive aryu-driven compulsion. Circumstances that previously triggered heated responses—delays, disappointments, difficulties, disagreeable persons—become recognized as temporary conditions arising within the spaciousness of consciousness rather than as threats demanding defensive reaction.

During formal meditation practice, the capacity develops for sustained resting in unconscious levels, progressively thinning aryu density until gaps appear wherein Ab Neter presence becomes directly perceptible—not as new acquisition but as recognition of the sustaining consciousness that has always been present, obscured only by the mental agitation that Ger practice systematically dissolves.

During all states—waking, dreaming, and the depths of sleep—the discovery emerges that consciousness itself remains constant while mental content continuously changes. This recognition relocates identity from the changing modifications of mind to the unchanging awareness sustaining all experience, fulfilling what Chapter 5, verse 9 describes as "discovering the fullness of the Creator-Spirit that is within by communing with the Creator-Spirit that resides in the temple."

THE SUPREME SIMPLICITY: BOTH PROLOGUE GOALS ACHIEVED

This essential practice—maintaining Ger as often as possible leading to Ger experience at all times through Maat-based living and meditative absorption—simultaneously fulfills both goals Amenemopet establishes in the Prologue. The silent mind and feelings create "well-being while living on earth" (verse 2) since serene personality navigates life's challenges without the suffering that heated reactivity generates. The same serenity creates the prerequisite frequency-matching whereby consciousness discovers "the sanctuary that can be entered"—the kara, the divine shrine where Ab Neter resides (verse 9).

The profound mercy in this teaching emerges clearly: the aspirant need not master elaborate techniques, accumulate vast philosophical knowledge, or achieve extraordinary spiritual states. Rather, through patient cultivation of serenity—moment by moment choosing silence over agitation, equanimity over reactivity, peace over turbulence—the mind gradually clarifies until Ab Neter recognition, as the true identity of oneself, emerges as naturally as clear mirrors reflect what stands before them.

Therefore, the wisdom to be understood recognizes that all Amenemopet's teachings, all his behavioral imperatives, all his warnings and prescriptions converge into this single practice: maintain Ger in thought, feeling, and action, and both earthly flourishing and divine discovery become progressively accessible as the inevitable fruition of frequency-matching with the supreme serenity that Neberdjer eternally IS.

SPECIAL TOPIC ESSAY #1: The Discernment of Wisdom Truth: Beyond Mere Factual Accuracy in Spiritual Communication

Consider the person who prides themselves on "always being honest," yet leaves wounded relationships in their wake. Their words prove factually accurate, yet their truth-telling creates suffering rather than liberation. This reveals Amenemopet's profound teaching: truth-expression operates through multiple modes, each arising from different mind conditions and producing vastly different effects. The distinction lies not in factual accuracy but in motivation, effect, and whether truth-telling serves wisdom purpose or merely gratifies ego.

The Foundation: Amenemopet's Teaching on Truth and Speech

Amenemopet transcends simplistic notions of honesty versus dishonesty. Chapter 8, verse 21 establishes the fundamental criterion: "Take care to make your speech to be sound in reference to the words that you use, that may cause harm, so as to be, instead, a cause, for vitality" [1]. Not all truth generates vitality; some truth, despite accuracy, causes damage. The measure proves not accuracy alone but effect—whether speech generates vital life-force or depletes energy through conflict.

Chapter 8 XI, verse 1 teaches: "by you're doing love to people, instead of harm, they love you. By giving consideration people reciprocate with consideration" [1]. Nevertheless, the teaching includes an essential caveat: "this is predicated on those with whom you are interacting being not in a heated condition" [2]. Wisdom truth requires assessing whether recipients exist in mental states capable of receiving benefit.

Chapter 11, verse 9 addresses deliberate deception: "those who make oaths or swearing to tell the truth but instead lie in order to gain profits; that is unsound and degrading" [1]. Verse 10 reveals that such corruption makes Ab Neter appear to turn away, though actually the corruption creates opacity in the ab (unconscious mind) preventing the mind's awareness of divine presence [2]. Chapter 17 emphasizes that fraud perpetrated with volition lodges as aryu (karmic feeling-memories) in the ab, producing consequences whether publicly caught or not [2].

The synthesis reveals that Amenemopet addresses not merely lying versus truthfulness but the mind condition—heated versus silent mind and feelings—from which speech arises. The silent personality represents the mind existing in serenity, operating from Ab Neter guidance rather than aryu-driven reactivity [1][4]. The critical question becomes: Does speaking serve wisdom purpose, or does it merely satisfy ego while risking loss of serenity?

The Modes of Truth-Expression

Malicious Truth: Truth as Weapon

Malicious truth uses factual accuracy as a weapon—the mind dominated by anger, revenge, or superiority needs. The person who reveals embarrassing facts to diminish others or uses truth in arguments to wound rather than illuminate violates verse 21's injunction entirely [1]. The speaker destroys their own serenity, generates agitation, and deposits reactive aryu in the ab that perpetuate heated patterns.

Ego-Gratifying Truth: Being "Right" Without Wisdom Purpose

Ego-gratifying truth speaks primarily to be acknowledged as correct, satisfying ego's validation-craving without serving wisdom purpose. Examples include correcting minor errors that ultimately don't matter, insisting on the last word when nothing is gained, or proving oneself right about trivial matters. The critical cost: sacrificing serenity for temporary ego satisfaction, producing agitation in both parties while generating negative aryu. The silent person recognizes that maintaining serenity holds infinitely more value than being acknowledged as correct [1][3].

Compulsive Truth: Forcing Subjective Reality for Self-Validation

Compulsive truth demands that others affirm one's subjective experiences for external validation. This arises from unresolved psychological issues and the delusion that external validation can resolve internal aryu patterns. The person trapped in victim identity demands constant acknowledgment; someone insists all must accommodate their triggers as universal standards. This creates strife for all parties while failing to achieve actual healing, as external validation cannot dissolve aryu accumulated in the ab [4]. When society fails to address root issues compassionately, these patterns intensify into deeper pathology.

Wisdom Truth: Truth as Service

Wisdom truth serves genuine long-term benefit, arising from compassion rather than ego-gratification. Essential requirements include recipient receptivity (willingness to listen and non-heated state), service to greater wisdom purpose, and maintaining the speaker's serenity [1][2]. Examples include addressing a friend's self-destructive patterns when they demonstrate readiness, providing honest feedback to help improvement, or sharing difficult truth with careful timing and consideration. Such communication generates vitality, thins aryu when properly received, and serves love rather than harm [1].

Protective Truth: Parental/Guardian Authority

Protective truth represents the special case of parental or guardian authority—truth that may cause temporary upset but prevents genuine harm. Such truth should arise from wisdom-guidance maintaining serenity rather than heated reactivity [2].

The Critical Discernment: Five Questions Before Speaking

Before speaking what the mind experiences as "truth," examine through five essential questions:

Motivation: What actually drives this speech? Genuine compassion serving another's growth, or ego's need to be acknowledged as right? Will this serve wisdom purpose or merely satisfy validation-craving?

Serenity Impact: Will speaking this truth maintain or destroy my serenity? Am I willing to sacrifice the silent personality state—authentic spiritual well-being—merely to be proven right?

Recipient State: Can this person receive and benefit from this truth? Are they operating from heated mind and feelings or demonstrating receptivity? Will they hear constructively or react defensively?

Effect: Will this speech generate vitality or cause damage? Does it serve love or harm [1]? Will it create reciprocal consideration or produce conflict?

Aryu Pattern: Will this speech thin or accumulate aryu? Speech arising from ego-attachment to being right generates negative patterns regardless of factual accuracy. Speech flowing from wisdom-guidance serves purification.

The "being right" trap proves particularly insidious for aspiring practitioners. Ego craves acknowledgment of correctness with remarkable intensity, willing to sacrifice serenity for temporary satisfaction of being proven right. The silent person recognizes that maintaining the serene state holds infinitely more value than winning arguments or having the last word. Sometimes—indeed, often—the wisest response proves to be silence, even when one is factually correct, choosing peace over destroying serenity for ego gratification.

Practical Application: The Liberation of Strategic Silence

In everyday interactions, notice the urge to correct minor errors that ultimately don't matter. Recognize ego's craving for the last word, to demonstrate superior understanding. Practice the profound discipline of allowing others to be "wrong" when correcting them serves no wisdom purpose, maintaining serenity rather than satisfying ego's validation-hunger.

In conflicts and disagreements, distinguish between truth serving resolution and truth proving superiority. Ask with radical honesty: "Do I want to be right, or do I want peace? Do I want acknowledgment as correct, or do I want the silent state necessary for Ab Neter awareness?" The silent person often chooses serenity over being proven correct, recognizing that peaceful mind and feelings serve both Prologue goals more effectively than winning arguments [3].

Releasing attachment to being right frees enormous psychological energy previously consumed by ego-defense and validation-seeking. Serenity becomes recognized as more valuable than acknowledgment, peace as more precious than being proven correct. The silent person discovers well-being independent of others recognizing their rightness, maintaining the mind's alignment with Ab Neter through communion regardless of whether anyone acknowledges correctness about any matter whatsoever [4].

Conclusion: Truth as Spiritual Practice

Wisdom truth requires discrimination far transcending factual accuracy—examining motivation, serenity impact, effect, receptivity, and aryu consequences. The silent person naturally speaks wisdom truth because speech flows from Ab Neter awareness rather than aryu-driven compulsion. The heated person employs truth maliciously, compulsively, or ego-gratifyingly because speech arises from reactive patterns maintaining separation.

Sometimes the highest truth manifests as silence—maintaining serenity rather than proving correctness, preserving the peaceful state essential for discovering the kara where divine presence dwells. "Take care to make your speech to be sound in reference to the words that you use, that may cause harm, so as to be, instead, a cause, for vitality" [1]. Speech becomes either a vehicle for maintaining the silent state necessary for spiritual development or a means of destroying serenity for temporary ego satisfaction. The choice presents itself moment by moment: Will we serve wisdom purpose, or will we serve ego's craving to be acknowledged as right? The answer to this question determines whether we progress toward the Prologue's dual goals—earthly well-being through serenity and divine discovery through silent receptivity—or remain trapped in heated patterns that prevent both authentic peace and spiritual realization.

References

[1] Ashby, M. (2019-25). Mysticism of Amenemopet Hieroglyphic Text Translation. Sema Institute of Ancient Egyptian Studies.

[2] Ashby, M. (2025). Keys to Sage Amenemopet wisdom text trilinear translation chapters 8, 11, 17 by Dr Muata Ashby. Sema Institute of Ancient Egyptian Studies.

[3] Ashby, M. (2024). Book Commentaries on Mystic Psychology of Amenemopet. Sema Institute of Ancient Egyptian Studies.

[4] Ashby, M. (2024). Book Awakening Your Soul-Aware-Witness Ancient Egyptian Wisdom To Discover Divine Consciousness. Sema Institute of Ancient Egyptian Studies.

SPECIAL TOPICS ESSAY #2: The Wounded Ego's False Glory: Understanding Narcissistic Consciousness Through Amenemopet's Psychology

Chapter 13 establishes that being loved, praised, and revered by people represents something "glorifying" (akh)—acknowledging legitimate developmental need for appreciation during spiritual growth from ignorance toward enlightenment [1]. However, a pathological extreme manifests when the individuated mind—the mind identified with and operating through ego structure—becomes so wounded through trauma, negative upbringing, or intense wrong thinking that it requires constant adulation merely to maintain psychological stability. This compulsive dependency intensifies into narcissistic patterns: always needing to be right, fighting any disagreement, demanding perpetual praise, and proving unable to tolerate criticism. These patterns represent the individuated mind operating through such dense aryu that no external validation suffices to establish genuine self-respect, as the internal foundation necessary for healthy development remains absent.

From Legitimate Need to Pathological Dependency

Amenemopet recognizes that needing love and appreciation operates as "an important part of human development from the perspective of a person growing up from a standpoint of spiritual ignorance" [2]. This legitimate need reflects the individuated mind intuitively sensing it requires recognition—pointing ultimately toward recognizing itself as sustained by Ab Neter rather than seeking external validation. The healthy stage acknowledges appreciation supporting continued service, distinguishing this from neediness arising from internal emptiness.

When severe trauma, profoundly negative upbringing, or intensely distorted self-perception occurs during formative development, these experiences deposit extraordinarily dense aryu in the ab (unconscious mind) encoding: "I have no inherent worth," "I am defective," "I am unlovable." The individuated mind identified with this wounded ego structure experiences unbearable pain. To survive psychologically, the ego constructs a compensatory false self—a grandiose persona appearing confident, superior, entitled. This represents Chapter 26, verse 13's "inflating the ego, becoming an agitated and heated person" [3]—though here the inflation masks profound vulnerability beneath.

This false grandiose self, being constructed rather than authentic, requires constant external validation to maintain. The individuated mind operating through this structure experiences perpetual, insatiable need because the wound remains unhealed beneath the inflated presentation. No praise suffices because validation feeds the false construction while the wounded core continues broadcasting fundamental worthlessness. Any criticism threatens the entire psychological structure, triggering extreme defensive reactions as the ego desperately protects against exposure of the wounded reality beneath.

The Narcissistic Behavioral Patterns

Compulsive need for adulation appears as constantly steering conversations to showcase achievements, inability to celebrate others' success (triggering comparison and threat), and requiring perpetual "narcissistic supply"—validation maintaining psychological stability. The individuated mind cannot rest in genuine self-knowledge because identity depends entirely on external confirmation of the false grandiose image.

Always needing to be right intensifies beyond ego-gratifying truth patterns. The individuated mind operating through narcissistic structure cannot tolerate being wrong because admitting error threatens the grandiose self-image protecting the wounded core. Even minor corrections trigger disproportionate reactions—rage, contempt, relationship severance. This manifests Chapter 26's inflated communication: the ego inflates to protect itself, sacrificing relationships and truth to maintain the appearance of superiority [3].

Fighting against disagreement represents the individuated mind experiencing disagreement as personal attack on fundamental worth rather than mere perspective difference. What a healthy mind might engage with openness becomes existential threat requiring aggressive defense. This demonstrates Chapter 4's thoughts and feelings that "swell, expand like a volcano" [4]—volcanic psychology where ego inflation creates explosive reactions protecting the vulnerable core.

Inability to tolerate criticism reveals the mechanism most clearly. Even gentle feedback bypasses the false grandiose self and threatens exposure of wounded reality. The individuated mind trapped in this pattern cannot engage criticism with equanimity; instead, defensive rage, withdrawal, deflection, projection, or blame-shifting emerge as protective mechanisms. This represents "atrophied intellect" [4]—the capacity for self-reflection becomes so compromised that the individuated mind cannot examine its own operations without triggering overwhelming threat.

Manipulation and control emerge as the individuated mind relates to others primarily as validation sources—"narcissistic supply"—rather than genuine beings worthy of respect. Gaslighting and emotional manipulation maintain the grandiose narrative. Relationships become transactional: others exist to provide admiration rather than authentic connection. This represents Chapter 13's corruption—the mind abandoning genuine love and respect, instead prioritizing power and control to maintain false glory [1][2].

The Metaphysical Architecture and Impact

Aryu mechanics reveal why narcissistic patterns resist transformation. Trauma deposits dense aryu encoding profound unworthiness in the ab. These aryu create unbearable pain when the individuated mind remains identified with the wounded ego structure. The false grandiose self emerges as a protective mechanism—the ego's attempt to survive intolerable conditions. Nevertheless, this false self requires constant external validation, creating rigid encrustation preventing any awareness of Ab Neter—the divine soul that remains present beneath aryu obstruction, untouched by wounds affecting surface psychological structures.

The wisdom to be understood recognizes that pure consciousness—Ab Neter, Neberdjer—cannot itself be wounded, needy, or pathological. What can be wounded is the mind—the mental apparatus (hat/ab/ka) through which consciousness expresses and which consciousness sustains. The problem occurs when the mind, sustained by consciousness yet unaware of this sustaining presence, becomes identified with the wounded ego structure and operates as if it were an autonomous, separate entity. This creates what we term the "individuated mind"—the mind operating through the delusion of separate selfhood, constricted by identification with ego, and subject to distortions created by aryu accumulated in the ab. These aryu create distortions in perception and cognition, causing the mind to experience reality through accumulated trauma patterns rather than recognizing its essential foundation in divine consciousness.

The tragic cycle perpetuates: the wounded core generates the false grandiose self requiring constant validation, creating behaviors others reject, generating more wounding, intensifying grandiose protection needs, deepening aryu density. Chapter 13 describes this as "encrusted ego in diametric opposition to Neberdjer" [2]—the false self becomes so rigid it actively rejects anything threatening its dominance, including spiritual awareness that would dissolve its seeming necessity.

The wisdom recognizes that while narcissistic patterns often arise from aryu-based psychology, in some cases biological dysfunction or cognitive impairment may contribute. What appears as narcissistic behavior may represent neurological issues requiring intervention beyond spiritual purification. The teaching addresses the psychological-spiritual dimension while acknowledging the individuated mind operating through a compromised substrate may require additional support.

Both Prologue goals become impossible through narcissistic patterns. Earthly well-being (verse 2) cannot manifest because constant anxiety maintaining the false self, rage when validation fails, isolation as relationships collapse, and exhaustion from perpetual performance create perpetual suffering. As the teaching warns: "everything that you desire and that you possess causes you stress and vexation" [2]. Discovery of kara where Ab Neter resides (verse 9) proves impossible because dense aryu completely obscure deeper levels, the false self actively rejects anything threatening its dominance, and the humility necessary for spiritual development cannot emerge when grandiosity serves psychological survival.

Recognition and the Path Forward

Recognizing narcissistic patterns in others appears through constant need for praise, inability to handle criticism calmly, conversations returning to their achievements, lack of genuine empathy, and extreme reactions to minor slights. Recognizing in oneself requires radical honesty: Do I require constant validation? How do I react to criticism—with equanimity or defensive rage? Do I need to be right more than I need peace?

The compassionate framework recognizes these patterns emerge not from malevolence but as protective mechanisms. The wounded core often arose through trauma beyond the person's control. The false grandiose self initially served a survival function. Nevertheless, compassion differs from tolerating abuse; understanding the mechanism differs from accepting harmful behavior.

The path forward acknowledges profound challenges. Narcissistic patterns resist transformation because change threatens psychological survival. The individuated mind must recognize the false self as false—terrifying when that false self feels like the only protection. Possible entry points include crises that collapse the false self, sufficient safety to examine wounds, recognition that grandiosity creates suffering, and Maat-based living that begins thinning aryu. Realistic expectations acknowledge deep transformation requires qualified guidance, years rather than months, involves common relapses, and may focus on harm-reduction rather than complete transformation.

Conclusion: False Glory Versus True Recognition

Chapter 13 teaches that true "akh" (glorification) emerges from being genuinely loved and respected—the natural outcome of ethical living and beneficial service [1]. Narcissistic pattern seeks the appearance of glory while internal reality remains wounded and empty. True glorification comes from the individuated mind releasing identification with the wounded ego to recognize its essential nature as sustained by Ab Neter—divine consciousness complete in itself, requiring no external validation.

The difference proves fundamental: the silent person operates from internal completeness through communion with Ab Neter, receiving respect naturally rather than desperately seeking validation. Narcissistic pattern operates from wounded emptiness requiring constant external filling, creating exhausting performance generating suffering. Healing requires replacing the false grandiose self with authentic self-recognition as sustained by divine consciousness—transformation demanding the individuated mind confront the very wounds the false self was constructed to avoid, dissolving identification with protective structures to discover Ab Neter that remains present, untouched, complete beneath accumulated aryu density.

References

[1] Ashby, M. (2019-25). Mysticism of Amenemopet Hieroglyphic Text Translation. Sema Institute of Ancient Egyptian Studies.
[2] Ashby, M. (2025). Keys to Sage Amenemopet wisdom text trilinear translation chapter 13. Sema Institute of Ancient Egyptian Studies.
[3] Ashby, M. (2019-25). Mysticism of Amenemopet Hieroglyphic Text Translation: Chapter 26. Sema Institute of Ancient Egyptian Studies.
[4] Ashby, M. (2025). Keys to Sage Amenemopet wisdom text trilinear translation chapter 4. Sema Institute of Ancient Egyptian Studies.

SPECIAL TOPIC ESSAY #3 The Psychology of *Shennu* (Frustration) in the Teachings of Sage Amenemopet

THE ANCIENT EGYPTIAN TERM FOR SHENNU: THE HIEROGLYPHIC FOUNDATION OF FRUSTRATION PSYCHOLOGY

Before examining how the phenomenon of frustration pervades Amenemopet's wisdom teachings, the wisdom to be understood first recognizes that the Ancient Egyptian text employs a comprehensive hieroglyphic term—shennu {seqer}—to designate this psychological-physiological-spiritual condition. This recognition proves essential: rather than imposing modern psychological concepts upon ancient wisdom, the analysis reveals that Amenemopet possessed sophisticated terminology for the precise phenomenon contemporary language terms "frustration" and "vexation."

Chapter 6B IX verse 8 provides the foundational proof-text, explicitly connecting shennu to what I (Dr. Ashby) translate as "the weak mind that leads to agitations, frustrations and sufferings in life." The verse reads:

"...as opposed to the capacity to have the power over wealth or abundant possessions but also included with that power, not having peace but rather anguish, strife, worry, anxiety, and unrest; and be a prisoner of the weak mind that leads to agitations, frustrations and sufferings in life." [1]

The hieroglyphic text itself displays: "er useru {nkt} {mdj} cher {mdj} shennu {seqer}" where shennu appears with the determinative seqer (prisoner), revealing that Amenemopet conceptualized this condition as a form of bondage—mind imprisoned by its own reactive patterns arising from spiritual ignorance.

The Semantic Range of the Shen Root Family

The term shennu belongs to a rich semantic family in Ancient Egyptian that encompasses multiple dimensions of the frustration experience. The root shen and its related forms map precisely to what the teaching addresses throughout its chapters:

EMOTIONAL DIMENSION ***shen*** = hateful, hostile, inimical -Maps to the anger and vexation that represent the intensified endpoints of the frustration causal chain

RELATIONAL/BEHAVIORAL DIMENSION  ***shennu*** = fighters, enmity, strife ***shnu*** = soldiers, warriors, fighters -Maps to the heated reactivity, interpersonal conflict, and comparative aggression arising from frustrated seeking

NOTE: notice that the use of the determinative hieroglyph -this is a determinative term meaning turn away, turn back, backwards movement, going against, etc. Ex. ***haha***-go back or retreat, turn around.

NOTE: notice the use of the determinative hieroglyph . This is ***chefty-*** or enemy, death, slaughter. This indicates that the term in which it is used carries with it the tone of death and enmity.

PHYSIOLOGICAL/PSYCHOLOGICAL DIMENSION ***sheni*** = to be sick, helpless,

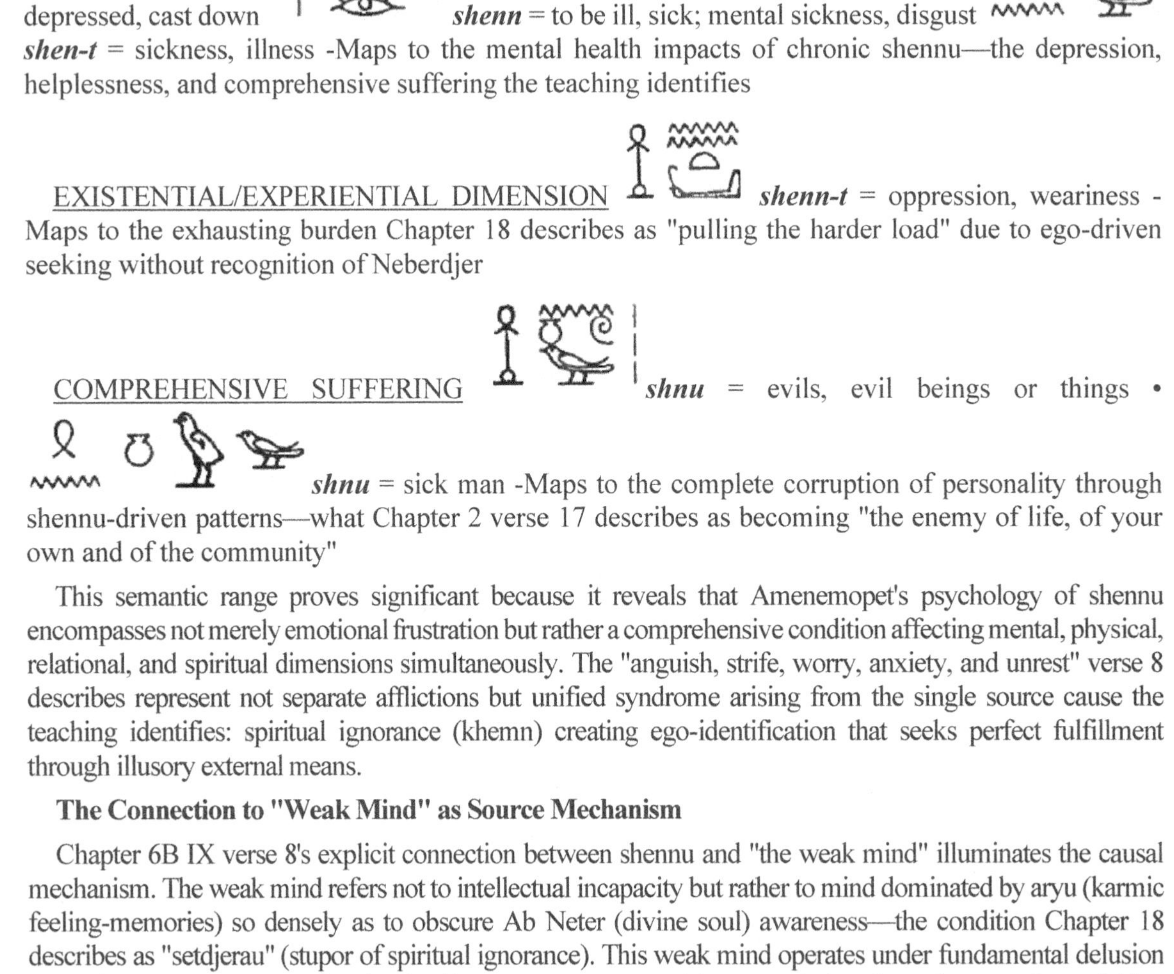

depressed, cast down ***shenn*** = to be ill, sick; mental sickness, disgust ***shen-t*** = sickness, illness -Maps to the mental health impacts of chronic shennu—the depression, helplessness, and comprehensive suffering the teaching identifies

EXISTENTIAL/EXPERIENTIAL DIMENSION ***shenn-t*** = oppression, weariness -Maps to the exhausting burden Chapter 18 describes as "pulling the harder load" due to ego-driven seeking without recognition of Neberdjer

COMPREHENSIVE SUFFERING ***shnu*** = evils, evil beings or things • ***shnu*** = sick man -Maps to the complete corruption of personality through shennu-driven patterns—what Chapter 2 verse 17 describes as becoming "the enemy of life, of your own and of the community"

This semantic range proves significant because it reveals that Amenemopet's psychology of shennu encompasses not merely emotional frustration but rather a comprehensive condition affecting mental, physical, relational, and spiritual dimensions simultaneously. The "anguish, strife, worry, anxiety, and unrest" verse 8 describes represent not separate afflictions but unified syndrome arising from the single source cause the teaching identifies: spiritual ignorance (khemn) creating ego-identification that seeks perfect fulfillment through illusory external means.

The Connection to "Weak Mind" as Source Mechanism

Chapter 6B IX verse 8's explicit connection between shennu and "the weak mind" illuminates the causal mechanism. The weak mind refers not to intellectual incapacity but rather to mind dominated by aryu (karmic feeling-memories) so densely as to obscure Ab Neter (divine soul) awareness—the condition Chapter 18 describes as "setdjerau" (stupor of spiritual ignorance). This weak mind operates under fundamental delusion about its own nature, experiencing itself as separate ego requiring completion through external acquisition rather than recognizing itself as sustained by Neberdjer (the All-Encompassing Divinity).

From this weak mind foundation arises the entire shennu syndrome: the agitation from feeling incomplete, the heated mind and feelings driving insatiable seeking behaviors, the chronic dissatisfaction when desires fail to produce lasting completion, and the intensification into anger and vexation as the futile cycle perpetuates. The term "prisoner" in verse 8's determinative {seqer} proves particularly apt—the mind becomes imprisoned not by external circumstances but by its own aryu-driven reactive patterns that operate automatically at the ab (unconscious) level, continuously generating shennu experiences regardless of external conditions.

This hieroglyphic foundation establishes that the teaching's exploration of shennu psychology represents not modern interpretation but rather explication of what Amenemopet explicitly taught using precise technical terminology. The essay that follows examines how this shennu syndrome manifests through specific behavioral patterns the sage addresses, how it operates through the consciousness architecture of hat/ab/aryu/Ab Neter, and how transformation occurs through the purification practices that thin aryu density to reveal the already-present divine foundation that represents genuine completion.

INTRODUCTION

Throughout the wisdom teachings of Sage Amenemopet, the phenomenon of shennu—what contemporary language terms frustration and vexation—emerges as a comprehensive psychological syndrome pervading nearly every chapter. Consider how Amenemopet systematically addresses the conditions generating this experience: the heated pursuit of wealth that never satisfies, the fevered grasping after achievements that slip away the moment they seem attained, the restless agitation preventing peace even during sleep, the chronic sense that life circumstances fail to conform to desires.

Indeed, shennu represents the psychological-physiological-spiritual state arising when desires encounter obstacles or remain unfulfilled, when expectations clash with reality, when the ego's demands for perfect circumstances meet the imperfect nature of time and space existence. Chapter 6B IX verse 8 provides explicit terminology: those with "power over wealth" yet experience "anguish, strife, worry, anxiety, and unrest" and become "a prisoner of the weak mind that leads to agitations, frustrations and sufferings in life." [1] This verse establishes shennu not as occasional emotional reaction but as comprehensive syndrome affecting all dimensions of human experience when mind operates disconnected from Ab Neter awareness.

This special topic essay examines how Amenemopet's teachings reveal shennu not as random affliction affecting some unfortunate individuals, but as the inevitable consequence of a fundamental deviation in mind—what the ancient wisdom identifies as spiritual ignorance (khemn). The teaching employs what might be termed philosophical causality, distinguishing between a single SOURCE CAUSE and multiple EFFECTIVE CAUSES that manifest from it.

The source cause—spiritual ignorance characterized by absence of sau Neberdjer (awareness of the All-Encompassing Divinity)—creates the ego construct that feels fundamentally incomplete and separate from its divine foundation. This incompleteness then generates all the various seeking behaviors that Amenemopet addresses throughout his instructions: the pursuit of wealth, the heated reactivity of mind and feelings, the fevered striving for perfection, the attachment to luxury and comfort, the comparative thinking that measures oneself against others. Each represents an effective cause, a manifestation of the underlying source cause attempting to resolve its feeling of incompleteness through external means.

The wisdom to be understood recognizes that shennu emerges as the inevitable result when the illusory ego construct—itself a product of spiritual ignorance—seeks completion through equally illusory means. Since both the seeker (ego) and what it seeks (external perfection) lack ultimate reality, the enterprise proves inherently futile, generating the chronic dissatisfaction and agitation that characterizes what Amenemopet calls the "heated" personality. Most significantly, the teaching reveals that what contemporary society considers "normal" psychology actually represents profound abnormality when measured against the standard Amenemopet establishes—the recognition of oneself as sustained by and ultimately in communion with Neberdjer, complete and fulfilled through divine awareness rather than external acquisition.

THE SOURCE CAUSE: SPIRITUAL IGNORANCE AND THE GENESIS OF INCOMPLETENESS

The Fundamental Deviation from Divine Awareness

The Ancient Egyptian wisdom tradition identifies a single foundational deviation that generates all subsequent psychological suffering, including the experience of shennu (frustration/vexation): the absence of sau Neberdjer, the loss of awareness that one's essential nature is sustained by the All-Encompassing Divinity rather than being a separate, limited ego entity. Chapter 18, verses 24-26 describe this condition with striking precision as "setdjerau"—the stupor or sleep of spiritual ignorance. The teaching reveals: "As to the person who lives life as if in a slumber of spiritual ignorance, undergoing the stress of pulling the harder load of life due to egoism, instead of being relaxed due to knowing and experiencing the natural flow of life when one is conscious and aware of Neberdjer, that person who is as if sleep-walking through life is actually at the same time, due to that ignorance of the knowledge of Self, separating themselves from and forsaking/leaving/moving away from that perfection." [1] Thus, a person may seem to be awake while they are in a state of spiritual slumber while an evolved person may be awake and be truly aware of their spiritual essence. In this context the spiritually ignorant person is in slumber while the aware person is awake.

This passage illuminates the fundamental mechanism whereby mind, operating without recognition of its divine foundation, creates what we might call the ego construct—the sense of being a separate, autonomous individual requiring constant protection, advancement, and completion through external means. Consider how this deviation operates: mind that has forgotten its essential nature as sustained by Ab Neter (the divine soul in the kara/deep sanctuary of the heart) and ultimately by Neberdjer itself, naturally experiences itself as incomplete, lacking, vulnerable, separate from the wholeness that in truth sustains its very capacity for awareness. The ego thus emerges not as humanity's true identity but as a case of mistaken identity, where mind has become obscured through identification with limited mental-emotional patterns, losing awareness of the infinite divine consciousness that sustains it.

This creates what the teaching describes as existential neediness and perpetual seeking. The ego, feeling "less than," incomplete, separate from the source of fulfillment, generates an insatiable hunger for experiences, objects, relationships, achievements—anything that might provide the sense of wholeness it lacks. Nevertheless, this seeking proves fundamentally misdirected because it attempts to resolve a spiritual problem through material means, to fill an ontological void through accumulation of objects that exist within time and space.

The semantic range of shennu illuminates precisely what this spiritual ignorance produces: not merely occasional emotional frustration but comprehensive syndrome affecting mental (shenn—mental sickness), physical (sheni—cast down, depressed, sick), relational (shennu—enmity, strife, fighters), and existential (shenn-t—oppression, weariness) dimensions. Chapter 6B IX verse 8's description as "prisoner of the weak mind" reveals how this operates—the mind operating in spiritual ignorance becomes trapped in automatic reactive patterns arising from aryu density in the ab, continuously generating shennu experiences regardless of external circumstances achieved.

The Illusion of Separate Existence and Its Psychological Consequences

The teaching reveals that mind operating in spiritual ignorance remains unaware that Ab Neter—the divine consciousness residing in the kara, the deepest sanctuary of the heart—continuously sustains its capacity for awareness. Chapter 18's metaphor proves instructive: while the ego believes itself to be "the steersperson of the boat," directing life's journey through personal will and determination, in reality "Neberdjer is the shepherd that guides human life," orchestrating circumstances according to divine wisdom that vastly exceeds egoic comprehension. [1] The ego thus operates under profound delusion of autonomous agency, believing its thoughts, desires, and efforts determine outcomes when these represent merely surface movements within the vast ocean of divine consciousness.

This delusion creates the exhausting experience the teaching describes: "pulling the harder load of life due to egoism" rather than being "relaxed due to knowing and experiencing the natural flow of life when one is conscious and aware of Neberdjer." [1] Consider the psychological implications: mind identified with ego experiences itself as fundamentally responsible for managing existence, for strategizing survival and success, for protecting itself against a potentially hostile universe populated by competing separate entities. This generates chronic anxiety, constant mental activity, the sense that one must remain vigilant and effortful to secure well-being.

Moreover, mind operating from spiritual ignorance cannot access what the teaching calls ger—the serenity, contentment, and inner peace that arise naturally from recognizing oneself as sustained by the eternal, perfect, all-encompassing Divine. The ego, by its very nature as a construct based on the sense of separateness and limitation, remains perpetually restless, perpetually dissatisfied, perpetually seeking the completion that can never arrive through external means. This is the shenn-t (oppression, weariness) and shenn (mental sickness) that the shen root family designates—the comprehensive suffering arising when mind operates disconnected from its divine source.

The Causal Chain: From Spiritual Ignorance to Shennu

The teaching reveals a precise causal sequence whereby spiritual ignorance inevitably produces the experience of shennu (frustration/vexation). Understanding this chain proves essential for recognizing how all the various seeking behaviors Amenemopet addresses throughout his instructions arise from a single source rather than representing independent problems requiring separate solutions.

CAUSAL CHAIN OF SHENNU: Source cause → Spiritual ignorance → ego construct → agitation due to feeling incompleteness → heatedness (shemm) → All seeking behaviors based on ego ideas in futile attempt to find perfect fulfillment/completeness but wrong way of seeking that is insatiable because is illusory → leads to shennu (frustration) → intensifies into anger/vexation (shen—hateful, hostile)

First link: spiritual ignorance creates ego identification. When mind loses awareness that it is sustained by Ab Neter/Neberdjer, it naturally experiences itself as separate, limited, incomplete. This represents not accurate perception of reality but fundamental misapprehension—what the teaching calls khemn (spiritual ignorance). The ego emerges as the sense of being an autonomous individual entity requiring protection, advancement, fulfillment through personal effort and external acquisition.

Second link: ego identification generates agitation through feeling incompleteness. The ego, by its very nature as a construct based on separation, cannot access the internal fullness arising from Ab Neter recognition. It therefore experiences chronic neediness, perpetual dissatisfaction, constant sense of lack requiring resolution. This creates what the teaching describes as the fundamental restlessness preventing peace—the agitation that characterizes mind disconnected from its divine foundation.

Third link: agitation manifests as heatedness (shemm). The restless, dissatisfied ego cannot maintain ger (serenity) but instead operates in chronic heated state—mind and feelings characterized by anxiety, craving, comparative thinking, reactive patterns. This heatedness represents not occasional emotion but baseline condition of mind operating in spiritual ignorance, perpetually agitated by desires and aversions arising from sense of incompleteness.

Fourth link: heatedness drives all seeking behaviors. From this heated, agitated state arise the various patterns Amenemopet addresses throughout his teaching: the fevered pursuit of wealth (Chapters 8, 9, 12); the heated reactivity toward difficult persons and situations (Chapter 2); the striving for perfection in circumstances

(Chapter 5); the attachment to luxury and comfort (Chapter 5); the comparative thinking measuring oneself against others (Chapter 13); the control-seeking attempting to manage all circumstances (Chapter 18). Each represents the ego's attempt to resolve its fundamental sense of incompleteness through external means—acquiring enough wealth, achieving enough success, controlling enough circumstances, receiving enough recognition to finally feel complete.

Fifth link: seeking behaviors inevitably produce shennu (frustration). The enterprise proves futile on multiple levels. First, even when desires are fulfilled, satisfaction remains temporary—the ego soon habituates to what it acquired and generates new desires requiring fulfillment. Second, many desires cannot be fulfilled due to circumstances beyond personal control—the external world refuses to conform to egoic demands for perfect conditions. Third, even temporary fulfillment generates new problems—maintenance anxiety, fear of loss, competition with others seeking the same objects. Fourth and most fundamentally, the seeking addresses the wrong problem—attempting external resolution for what requires internal recognition, trying to fill an ontological void through accumulation of phenomena that exist within time and space.

When heated mind encounters obstacles to desired outcomes, when fulfillment proves temporary despite achieving goals, when chronic dissatisfaction persists regardless of external acquisitions—shennu emerges as the inevitable result. The ego experiences profound dissatisfaction that its seeking behaviors fail to produce the lasting completion they promised, yet cannot abandon these patterns because they represent its only strategy for resolving the incompleteness it feels. This is the comprehensive shennu syndrome verse 8 describes: "anguish, strife, worry, anxiety, and unrest" combined with being "a prisoner of the weak mind" where the prison consists of automatic aryu-driven reactive patterns operating at the ab level.

Sixth link: chronic shennu intensifies into anger and vexation. When mind remains trapped in futile seeking, experiencing repeated failures to achieve lasting satisfaction through external means, shennu builds into more intense reactive patterns. This is where the shen root meaning (hateful, hostile, inimical) manifests most clearly. Anger arises toward obstacles preventing fulfillment, toward others whose success triggers comparison, toward circumstances that fail to conform to desires. Vexation—chronic irritation and resentment—becomes baseline emotional state as heated mind perpetually encounters reality's refusal to provide the perfection the ego demands. The shnu (fighters, enmity, strife) dimension emerges as these internal patterns express through interpersonal conflict and aggressive behaviors.

The Complete Causal Picture

This causal chain reveals shennu not as random affliction but as inevitable consequence of operating from spiritual ignorance. Every link proves necessary: spiritual ignorance creates ego identification, which generates agitation through incompleteness, which manifests as heatedness, which drives seeking behaviors attempting perfect fulfillment through illusory means, which produces shennu when the enterprise proves futile, which intensifies into anger and vexation as the cycle perpetuates.

Moreover, the chain illuminates why addressing effective causes without recognizing source cause produces limited results. Contemporary approaches might attempt treating shennu through stress-management techniques, fulfilling more desires, lowering expectations, or developing coping strategies. While these may provide temporary relief, they address symptoms without resolving the underlying condition generating them. Unless spiritual ignorance itself transforms through sau Neberdjer cultivation—through mind developing awareness of its sustaining divine foundation—the shennu-generating mechanism continues operating, producing chronic dissatisfaction regardless of external circumstances or psychological coping strategies employed.

The Effective Causes: Specific Manifestations of Spiritual Ignorance

The teaching's genius emerges in how it addresses multiple effective causes—specific behavioral and psychological patterns—while maintaining clarity that all arise from the single source cause of spiritual ignorance. Understanding this structure prevents the error of treating symptoms while ignoring disease, or attempting to resolve individual problems without recognizing their common origin.

The Heated Pursuit of Wealth and the Shennu of Material Incompletion

Chapters 8 and 9 address the heated pursuit of wealth with remarkable psychological insight. The teaching reveals that mind operating through senses "is in a state as if in bondage" to material concerns, perpetually anxious about survival and acquisition. [1] This bondage generates what might be termed the treadmill effect—no matter how much wealth accumulates, the sense of having "enough" never arrives because the seeking addresses the wrong need. The ego requires completion, and no quantity of external possessions can fulfill ontological lack.

The shennu emerges when wealth acquisition fails to produce the peace and satisfaction it promised. The poor person imagines that sufficient money would resolve all problems, generate happiness, provide security. Yet the teaching observes that even those with abundant resources "think that they lack," experiencing chronic anxiety about wealth preservation, comparative dissatisfaction when observing others with more, perpetual fear of loss. The heated mind discovers that material sufficiency proves impossible not because circumstances fail to provide enough but because "enough" represents a psychological impossibility for the ego operating in spiritual ignorance.

Moreover, Chapter 8 reveals how the heated pursuit of wealth generates additional suffering through unethical behavior. When mind believes that happiness depends on material acquisition, it becomes willing to exploit others, engage in dishonest dealings, sacrifice ethical principles for profit. These actions deposit negative aryu in the ab (unconscious mind), creating future suffering while destroying the respect and genuine relationships that actually contribute to well-being. The shennu thus intensifies: not only does wealth fail to provide completion, but the methods employed to acquire it generate additional suffering and alienation.

This manifests precisely the sheni dimension (helpless, depressed, cast down) as the chronic pursuit produces exhaustion without fulfillment, and the shenn-t dimension (oppression, weariness) as Chapter 18 describes—"pulling the harder load of life due to egoism" rather than experiencing the relaxation that comes from trusting divine providence.

The Fevered Striving for Perfect Circumstances

Chapter 5 addresses what might be termed circumstantial perfectionism—heated mind's demand that conditions conform precisely to its preferences before peace becomes possible. The teaching reveals the fundamental error: "Being silent means discovering the fullness of the Creator-Spirit that is within. This fullness cannot come from heatedly searching for fulfillment in the world for fulfillment with an imperfect personality. Rather, it is found not by externalities but instead by realizing that there is perfection within when the fullness of being is experienced beyond the worldly desires and cravings." [1]

The shennu emerges when external circumstances inevitably fail to meet the ego's demands for perfection. Heated mind generates elaborate fantasies about ideal conditions—perfect job, perfect relationship, perfect health, perfect living situation—believing that achieving these externals would finally produce the peace and happiness it seeks. Yet even when favorable circumstances temporarily align, new imperfections emerge requiring attention, or mind habituates to what it achieved and begins craving different conditions.

More fundamentally, the teaching reveals that peace dependent on external circumstances proves impossible because phenomena within time and space inherently involve impermanence, change, loss, aging, death. The ego seeking perfect conditions attempts to freeze reality in a preferred configuration, yet this opposes the fundamental nature of existence. Shennu becomes inevitable when the immovable demand for permanence meets the unstoppable reality of change.

This perfectionism manifests the comprehensive shennu syndrome verse 8 describes: "anguish, strife, worry, anxiety, and unrest" as mind continuously encounters circumstances failing to conform to its elaborate demands. The shenn (mental sickness) dimension emerges as this pattern creates obsessive rumination about how circumstances should be different, while the shenn-t (oppression) manifests as the exhausting burden of continuously strategizing how to manipulate circumstances toward imagined perfection.

The Luxury and Comfort Attachment

Also in Chapter 5, the teaching addresses attachment to luxury and comfort—what might be termed sensory perfectionism. Heated mind believes that pleasure maximization and discomfort avoidance represent legitimate life goals, that happiness depends on maintaining pleasant sensations while avoiding unpleasant ones. This generates elaborate seeking behaviors: acquiring luxury goods, cultivating refined tastes, arranging circumstances to maximize comfort, avoiding any situation involving discomfort or challenge.

The shennu emerges through multiple mechanisms. First, pleasant sensations prove temporary by nature—even the finest meal generates satisfaction that dissipates within hours, the most comfortable circumstance eventually generates boredom or habituation. Second, maintaining luxury requires constant effort and creates maintenance anxiety—fear of loss, concern about preserving what one acquired, competitive pressure as others seek the same objects. Third, the addiction intensifies—as sensory threshold adjusts, increasingly refined pleasures become necessary to generate satisfaction, requiring escalating resources and effort. Fourth, circumstances inevitably produce discomfort regardless of attempts at complete avoidance—aging, illness, interpersonal conflict, environmental conditions beyond personal control.

Most significantly, the teaching reveals that attachment to sensory pleasure diverts attention from the internal investigation necessary for discovering genuine fulfillment. Mind occupied with maximizing comfort and minimizing discomfort remains trapped in surface levels of awareness, unable to penetrate deeper levels where Ab Neter resides. The pursuit of luxury thus prevents the very goal it seeks—generating chronic dissatisfaction while obscuring access to the internal fullness that represents authentic completion.

This pattern demonstrates how shennu operates as comprehensive syndrome rather than merely emotional reaction. The shenn dimension (mental sickness, disgust) emerges as the refined palate becomes increasingly difficult to satisfy, generating contempt for anything less than luxury. The sheni dimension (helpless, depressed) manifests when circumstances prevent maintaining preferred comfort levels, producing the shenu dimension (evils, sick man) as the entire personality becomes oriented around sensory gratification.

The Comparative Mind and Relative Shennu

Chapter 13 addresses what might be termed comparative thinking—heated mind's compulsive measuring of self against others. The teaching reveals how this pattern generates chronic dissatisfaction regardless of one's actual circumstances: "When you have less than others, painful dissatisfaction arises; when you have equal, anxiety about maintaining status emerges; when you have more, fear of loss and guilt trouble the mind." [1] The comparative mind can never rest in genuine contentment because fulfillment becomes relative rather than intrinsic—dependent on maintaining favorable position in endless hierarchies of wealth, status, beauty, intelligence, achievement.

The shennu intensifies because comparison operates as a zero-sum game. Mind becomes invested in others' failure to maintain its own sense of superiority, generating contempt, schadenfreude, active obstruction of others' success. Alternatively, when others succeed, mind experiences their achievement as personal diminishment, triggering resentment, envy, and intensified striving to regain superior position. Neither condition produces peace—mind remains perpetually agitated by the success and failure of countless others whose circumstances affect one's relative standing.

Moreover, the teaching reveals how this pattern corrupts genuine achievement and relationships. Accomplishments become meaningful only as they elevate oneself above others rather than representing authentic service or creative expression. Relationships become strategic rather than genuine—cultivating connections with high-status individuals while avoiding those who might diminish one's standing. Mind loses capacity for sincere appreciation, celebration of others' success, humble acknowledgment of one's actual limitations. Everything becomes instrumentalized in service of maintaining favorable comparison.

This comparative pattern manifests the shennu root family comprehensively. The shen dimension (hateful, hostile) emerges toward those whose success triggers comparison. The shennu dimension (fighters, enmity, strife) manifests through competitive behaviors and relational conflict. The shenn-t dimension (oppression, weariness) appears as the exhausting burden of continuously measuring oneself against countless others. And verse 8's description proves perfectly apt: one becomes "a prisoner of the weak mind" where the prison consists of compulsive comparative thinking operating automatically at the ab level, generating continuous shennu regardless of actual achievements.

The Control-Seeking and the Shennu of Unpredictability

Chapter 18 addresses what might be termed the control delusion—the ego's belief that peace and security require managing all circumstances through personal will and strategic planning. The teaching reveals the fundamental error: while the ego believes itself to be "the steersperson of the boat" directing life's journey, in reality "Neberdjer is the shepherd that guides human life" according to divine wisdom that vastly exceeds egoic comprehension. [1]

The shennu emerges as heated mind discovers that most circumstances remain beyond personal control. Despite elaborate planning, unexpected events arise; despite careful strategy, outcomes refuse to conform to desires; despite maximum effort, results depend on countless factors outside one's influence. The control-seeking mind experiences this unpredictability as perpetual threat, generating chronic anxiety as it attempts the impossible—managing unmanageable reality through egoic will.

More profoundly, the teaching reveals how control-seeking creates the suffering it attempts to prevent. The effort to manage all circumstances generates exhaustion, the vigilance required produces anxiety, the inevitable failures trigger self-blame and intensified control attempts, creating a vicious cycle of increasing rigidity and diminishing effectiveness. Mind becomes so occupied with strategic manipulation that it loses capacity for spontaneous response, creative adaptation, recognition of opportunities emerging outside predetermined plans.

This control pattern demonstrates the shenn-t dimension (oppression, weariness) as Chapter 18 explicitly describes: "pulling the harder load of life due to egoism" rather than relaxing into natural flow. The shenn dimension (mental sickness) manifests as obsessive worry about managing circumstances. The sheni dimension (helpless, depressed) emerges when circumstances refuse control despite maximum effort. And verse 8's "prisoner of the weak mind" proves precisely accurate—mind becomes imprisoned by its own control strategies that operate compulsively at the ab level, generating continuous shennu as reality refuses to conform to egoic demands.

The Heated Reactivity Toward Difficult Persons and Situations

Chapter 2 addresses what might be termed reactive mind patterns—heated mind's automatic responses to challenging circumstances and difficult persons. The teaching reveals how spiritual ignorance creates hair-trigger reactivity: any obstacle, criticism, disrespect, or frustration of desires immediately triggers anger, defensiveness, blame, or aggressive response. This pattern generates chronic agitation as mind remains perpetually prepared for combat, experiencing existence as a threatening battlefield requiring constant defensive vigilance.

The shennu intensifies because reactive patterns create self-fulfilling prophecies. Heated responses generate heated responses in others, escalating conflicts that might have remained minor inconveniences into major disruptions. Relationships deteriorate as mind's defensiveness prevents genuine communication, understanding, or resolution. Reputation suffers as others avoid interaction with someone prone to disproportionate reactions. Heated mind thus creates increasingly difficult circumstances through its own reactive patterns, then experiences intensified shennu as these circumstances trigger additional reactivity.

Moreover, the teaching reveals how reactivity prevents learning and growth. When difficulty arises, heated mind immediately seeks external blame rather than recognizing how its own patterns contributed to the situation. When criticism arrives, defensive reactions prevent honest self-examination that might reveal valid feedback. When challenges emerge, reactive agitation obscures the opportunities for development these difficulties present. Mind remains trapped in repetitive patterns, unable to extract wisdom from experience.

This reactivity manifests the shennu root family most directly. The shen dimension (hateful, hostile) appears as chronic antagonism toward perceived obstacles. The shennu dimension (fighters, enmity, strife) emerges through aggressive interpersonal patterns. The shnu dimension (evils, sick man) manifests as the personality becomes comprehensively corrupted by reactive patterns that Chapter 2 verse 17 describes: living by "unrighteousness, fraud, anger, boisterousness, flippant (offhand, dismissive) retorts and thoughtless speech, inconsiderate and impulsive acts, rapacious greed, jealousy, envy, ridiculing others." [2] And verse 8's description as "prisoner of the weak mind that leads to agitations, frustrations and sufferings" proves perfectly apt for the reactive patterns that operate automatically, generating continuous shennu.

THE SILENT RESOLUTION: TRANSFORMATION THROUGH RECOGNITION

The teaching's therapeutic power emerges in revealing that shennu's resolution requires not fulfilling all desires, controlling all circumstances, or achieving all goals, but rather transforming the source cause generating these seeking behaviors. When spiritual ignorance transforms through sau Neberdjer cultivation—when mind develops awareness of Ab Neter sustaining it, recognizing itself as manifestation of Neberdjer rather than separate ego requiring completion—the shennu-generating mechanism itself dissolves.

The Transformation of Seeking Through Internal Completion

Chapter 5:9 describes the fundamental shift: discovering "the fullness of the Creator-Spirit that is within...found not by externalities but instead by realizing that there is perfection within when the fullness of being is experienced beyond the worldly desires and cravings." [1] This recognition proves transformative not through eliminating preferences or desires—mind operating through human form necessarily experiences attractions and aversions—but through revealing that fulfillment does not depend on these preferences being satisfied.

The silent person who has discovered this internal fullness relates to desires completely differently than heated mind driven by incompleteness. Desires arise but do not compel; preferences exist but do not dominate; goals emerge but do not define self-worth. When desires fulfill, appreciation arises without attachment; when preferences go unsatisfied, equanimity maintains rather than shennu. The distinction proves profound: heated mind seeking external completion experiences every unfulfilled desire as personal failure, threat to well-being, evidence of inadequacy. Silent mind operating from internal completion experiences unfulfilled preferences as simple facts about circumstances, generating no existential crisis.

This shift operates through what the teaching describes as Ab Neter recognition. When mind penetrates through aryu density in the ab to discover the divine presence residing in kara, when awareness shifts from identifying with temporary mental-emotional patterns to recognizing consciousness itself as sustained by Neberdjer, the chronic sense of incompleteness dissolves. Not through acquiring what was lacking, but through recognizing that nothing was ever actually lacking—the fullness sought through external means existed all along as the divine foundation sustaining awareness itself.

This transformation addresses shennu at its source. The shenn-t (oppression, weariness) dissolves as mind no longer pulls "the harder load" but relaxes into natural flow. The shenn (mental sickness) resolves as mind recognizes it need not continuously strategize for completion through external means. The sheni (depressed, helpless, cast down) transforms as mind discovers the internal fullness that external circumstances can neither provide nor remove. The shen (hateful, hostile) and shennu (enmity, strife) patterns thin as mind no longer experiences others as competitors for limited resources but recognizes divine consciousness pervading all forms.

The Liberation From Comparative Thinking

When mind recognizes itself as manifestation of Neberdjer rather than separate ego requiring elevation above others, comparative thinking naturally dissolves. Chapter 13's teaching about genuine glorification reveals the transformation: while heated mind seeks praise, status, and recognition to establish worth through external validation, silent mind receives appreciation as natural byproduct of beneficial service without requiring it for psychological stability.

This creates freedom from the comparative trap that generates chronic shennu. Silent person can genuinely celebrate others' success without experiencing it as personal diminishment, can acknowledge personal limitations without shame, can appreciate diverse forms of excellence without requiring superiority in all domains. Achievements become meaningful as authentic expression or beneficial service rather than as tools for establishing favorable comparison. Relationships become genuine rather than strategic, freed from the distortion of constantly measuring relative status.

Moreover, the teaching reveals how this liberation serves both personal well-being and social harmony. Heated mind trapped in comparison perpetuates competitive dynamics that harm everyone—zero-sum thinking that experiences others' gain as personal loss, strategic undermining of others to maintain favorable position, inability to collaborate genuinely when cooperation might elevate others. Silent mind freed from comparison naturally operates from abundance mentality—recognizing that others' success does not diminish one's own completeness, that collaboration serves everyone's development, that genuine celebration of diverse forms of excellence enriches rather than threatens.

This liberation directly addresses the shennu syndrome. The shen (hateful, hostile) dimension dissolves when others' success no longer triggers resentment. The shennu (fighters, enmity, strife) patterns thin as competitive aggression becomes unnecessary. The shenn-t (oppression, weariness) lightens as mind no longer exhausts itself continuously measuring against countless others. And verse 8's "prisoner of the weak mind" condition transforms as the comparative aryu patterns thin, freeing mind to operate from Ab Neter awareness rather than ego-driven reactive patterns.

The Acceptance of Divine Measure and Natural Unfolding

Chapter 18's teaching about divine guidance radically transforms relationship with circumstances. When heated mind believes itself to be "the steersperson of the boat," every unfavorable outcome represents personal failure requiring intensified control efforts. When silent mind recognizes that "Neberdjer is the shepherd that guides human life," circumstances become recognized as divine orchestration according to wisdom exceeding egoic comprehension. [1]

This recognition proves liberating on multiple levels. First, it releases the exhausting burden of believing that personal effort must manage all circumstances—mind can relax into natural flow rather than perpetually strategizing and controlling. Second, it transforms shennu when circumstances fail to conform to preferences—what the ego experiences as problems blocking desired outcomes becomes recognized as divine guidance redirecting attention toward opportunities better suited to actual development needs. Third, it enables trust that circumstances ultimately serve growth even when immediate appearances suggest otherwise.

Nevertheless, the teaching maintains crucial balance—recognizing divine orchestration does not eliminate personal responsibility or effort. Silent mind engages circumstances skillfully, makes wise decisions, takes appropriate action. The difference emerges in attachment to specific outcomes and response when results differ from preferences. Heated mind experiences deviation from desired outcomes as catastrophic failure requiring defensive reactivity. Silent mind recognizes that outcomes depend on countless factors beyond personal control, that circumstances serve purposes exceeding limited egoic comprehension, that peace arises from wise engagement rather than successful manipulation of reality to conform to preferences.

This acceptance directly resolves the shennu syndrome at its source. The shenn-t (oppression, weariness) dissolves as mind releases the burden of managing all circumstances. The shenn (mental sickness) resolves as mind no longer obsesses about controlling outcomes. The sheni (helpless, depressed) transforms as mind recognizes that unfavorable outcomes do not represent personal failure but divine guidance. The shen (hateful, hostile) and shennu (enmity, strife) patterns thin as mind no longer experiences circumstances and other persons as obstacles to be overcome but as aspects of divine orchestration serving ultimate good.

The Gradual Nature of Transformation and Realistic Expectations

The teaching maintains realism about transformation's pace. Spiritual ignorance accumulated over lifetimes does not dissolve through single insight or brief practice period. The aryu density in the ab (unconscious mind) thins gradually through patient, systematic purification—ethical living that generates positive rather than negative aryu, meditation practice that penetrates from hat (present awareness) to deeper ab levels, wisdom study that establishes correct understanding, and devotional recognition of Neberdjer that cultivates sau awareness.

This gradual transformation manifests in shennu episodes becoming progressively less frequent, less intense, and shorter in duration as spiritual practice advances. Initially, heated mind experiences chronic low-grade shennu punctuated by intense reactive episodes when desires meet obstacles. As practice progresses, baseline contentment increases—mind experiences genuine satisfaction with present circumstances more frequently, requiring fewer external changes to maintain equanimity.

Episodes of shennu become less frequent as mind develops capacity for contentment with present circumstances rather than constant craving for different conditions. The chronic dissatisfaction characterizing heated mind and feelings diminishes as practices reveal futility of external seeking and possibility of internal fulfillment. Though desires still arise—mind operating through human form necessarily experiences preferences—attachment to specific outcomes lessens, reducing shennu when circumstances fail to conform.

Episodes become less intense when they occur. Rather than overwhelming mind completely, shennu manifests as passing experience observed within broader awareness. The teaching's distinction between hat (present awareness) and ab (unconscious patterns) proves crucial: as witness awareness develops, even when aryu generate shennu reactions, hat recognizes these as temporary mental-emotional phenomena rather than defining self-identity. This creates space between stimulus and response, allowing choice rather than automatic reactivity.

Episodes become shorter in duration as recovery mechanisms strengthen. Heated mind experiencing shennu remains trapped in rumination, resentment, prolonged agitation reinforcing and expanding the initial reaction. Silent mind observes shennu arising, recognizes its source in attachment, applies appropriate wisdom (rejecting covetousness, accepting divine measure, releasing control-seeking), allowing the pattern to pass naturally rather than perpetuating through continued identification.

Eventually, silent mind and feelings establish as natural state—not through forceful suppression of heated patterns but through genuine transformation as Ab Neter recognition progressively replaces ego-identification as mind's foundation. This represents the fulfillment of Chapter 18:14's promise: when awareness of Neberdjer is maintained, "there will be no egoism and no mind and therefore no fears, frustrations, inordinate desires, no need for stealing, lying, cheating or becoming a heated person." [1] The shennu-generating mechanism itself dissolves when mind recognizes its essential nature as sustained by the divine rather than operating from the illusion of separateness requiring completion through external means.

Conclusion

This examination of shennu in Amenemopet's teaching reveals profound psychological insight into one of humanity's most pervasive yet seldom examined experiences. The wisdom establishes clear causality: spiritual ignorance (source cause) creates an ego construct that feels incomplete, which generates agitation and heatedness, which produces all seeking behaviors attempting perfect fulfillment through external means, which inevitably leads to shennu when illusory seeker pursues illusory completion through illusory objects—anger and vexation intensifying as the futile cycle perpetuates.

The hieroglyphic foundation proves essential to this understanding. Chapter 6B IX verse 8's explicit use of shennu {seqer} with its semantic range encompassing emotional (shen—hateful, hostile), relational (shennu—enmity, strife, fighters), physiological/psychological (sheni—sick, depressed, helpless; shenn—mental sickness), existential (shenn-t—oppression, weariness), and comprehensive suffering (shnu—evils, sick man) dimensions reveals that Amenemopet possessed sophisticated terminology for precisely what we term frustration and vexation. This was not a modern concept imposed upon ancient text, but rather ancient wisdom explicitly taught using technical terminology.

Chapter 18:14-15 provides what might be considered the teaching's most direct reference to the shennu mechanism: "Divine exists in perfection...human exists through failure." [1] The perfection being sought through mind and senses in time and space—perfection of situation (everything as ego wants), perfection of feeling (complete happiness from having what is wanted), perfection of mental condition (inner peace from external circumstances)—can never succeed because the "I" seeking represents illusory ego construct whose thoughts and feelings are themselves illusory, even delusional. This failure IS shennu, that generates the agitation, heatedness, vexation, anger, and hatred that characterize heated mind and feelings. Being "a prisoner of the weak mind" means being trapped in automatic aryu-driven reactive patterns that continuously generate shennu experiences regardless of external circumstances.

The teaching's profound contribution emerges in recognizing that what contemporary society considers "normal" psychology actually represents abnormality when measured against Amenemopet's standard. The chronic dissatisfaction, perpetual seeking, comparative thinking, heated reactivity normalized in modern culture represent not inherent human nature but symptoms of mind operating in spiritual ignorance, disconnected from awareness of its divine foundation. Genuine health involves not improved management of desires but transformation through recognizing oneself as sustained by Neberdjer, complete and fulfilled through divine awareness rather than external acquisition.

Amenemopet thus offers wisdom both diagnostic and therapeutic: shennu itself points toward the spiritual ignorance requiring resolution. Each experience of dissatisfaction, each moment of agitation when circumstances fail to conform to preferences, each episode of heated reactivity when desires meet obstacles—all serve as invitations to investigate the source cause generating these patterns. The teaching encourages using shennu as teacher revealing precisely what attachments, identifications, belief systems require recognition and release for transformation to proceed.

The resolution emerges not through fulfilling all desires, controlling all circumstances, achieving all goals, but through discovering what Chapter 5:9 describes: "the fullness of the Creator-Spirit that is within...found not by externalities but instead by realizing that there is perfection within when the fullness of being is experienced beyond the worldly desires and cravings." [1] The silent person who has discovered this internal fullness becomes naturally free from shennu not through suppressing desires but through operating from completeness—the ger (serenity/fulfillment) arising from knowing self as sustained by God "without need to acquire anything because all is in God." [1]

This vision of the transformed mind serves as both inspiration and practical guide for contemporary aspirants. Though the path requires patient, systematic purification of accumulated aryu through ethical living, meditation, wisdom study, and spiritual practice, the destination proves worthy of whatever effort transformation requires: mind liberated from chronic dissatisfaction, operating from internal fullness rather than external neediness, recognizing circumstances as divine orchestration rather than threats to well-being, experiencing genuine peace independent of whether life conforms to egoic preferences.

The teaching ultimately reveals shennu as unnecessary suffering arising from a correctable error—the spiritual ignorance creating ego-identification that seeks completion through external means. When mind recognizes its essential nature as sustained by Ab Neter which is sustained by Neberdjer, when hat penetrates through aryu density to discover the divine presence residing in kara, when awareness shifts from separate self requiring protection and advancement to recognition of oneself as sustained by the All-Encompassing Divinity—then shennu becomes impossible because the very mechanism generating it dissolves in the light of genuine self-knowledge.

References

[1] Ashby, M. (2019-25). Mysticism of Amenemopet Hieroglyphic Text Translation. Sema Institute of Ancient Egyptian Studies.

[2] Ashby, M. (2024). Amenemopet lectures 2024 by Dr Muata Ashby transcripts. Sema Institute of Ancient Egyptian Studies.

[3] Ashby, M. (2019). Amenemopet lectures 2019 by Dr Muata Ashby transcripts. Sema Institute of Ancient Egyptian Studies.

SPECIAL TOPIC ESSAY #4: SECHSECH (RUSHING/HASTE) AND THE PRACTICE OF SLOWNESS AS SPIRITUAL DISCIPLINE

THE PROFOUND TEACHING ON MOVEMENT, STILLNESS, AND THE RECOVERY OF INNER DIVINE AWARENESS

Introduction: The Wisdom of Amenemopet Chapter 21, Verse 17

In Chapter 21, Verse 17 of Sage Amenemopet's teaching, we encounter a seemingly simple instruction that contains profound metaphysical significance: "bu arytu sechsech er peh pa mench" – "do not doing run hastily as to arrive that achievement." [1] The term sechsech carries meanings of rushing, haste, and action without reflection—a mode of operating that characterizes the heated mind and feelings driven by egoistic concerns and unexamined aryu patterns. This teaching addresses far more than mere time management or efficiency advice; it illuminates a fundamental principle about the relationship between movement, perception of separateness, and the capacity to experience Ab Neter, the divine soul within.

The teaching reveals that for those ignorant of their divine self (Ab Neter), regaining that awareness necessitates slowing the mind's thoughts, feelings, and physical movements. This practice serves as an essential prerequisite for successful meditation. Once inner self-awareness has been regained in a stable manner, then it becomes possible to engage in fast actions without losing the deeper self-awareness. Until that stability is achieved, however, the disciplines of slowness remain necessary for mind/personality transformation.

The Etymological Revelation: Rushing and Pleasure-Seeking

Before exploring the metaphysical implications, we must recognize the profound wisdom encoded in the Ancient Egyptian language itself. The term sechsech derives from the root sekh, which carries multiple interrelated meanings that illuminate the psychological mechanism underlying the behavior:

Sekh – to run

Sekhsekhu – to take flight, to make a move, to go

Sekhut – hastening, rushing

Sekhsekh – to hasten, rush

Sekhsekh-Ab – to move toward having pleasure

The linguistic connection between running/hastening and pleasure reveals the essential teaching: the mind rushes toward what it considers will provide satisfaction. The very language demonstrates that sechsech (rushing) represents not merely rapid movement but the aryu-driven pursuit of pleasure and avoidance of displeasure. This pursuit creates the perpetual motion that prevents the stillness necessary for Ab Neter awareness.

Consider how this etymological insight illuminates the teaching's depth. When verse 17 warns against "running hastily as to arrive that achievement," the term sechsech inherently references the pleasure-seeking motivation driving the behavior. [1] The heated person rushes because the ab contains aryu patterns that compel pursuit of what the mind considers pleasurable—status, possessions, experiences, accomplishments—and flight from what it deems unpleasurable. This creates the constant movement, both physical and mental, that the teaching identifies as spiritually obstructive.

The compound term sekhsekh-Ab specifically references the ab (unconscious mind) as the locus where these pleasure associations reside. The aryu stored in ab encode feeling-memories: "this brought pleasure, pursue it; that brought displeasure, avoid it." These patterns drive the personality into constant seeking and fleeing—the perpetual motion that prevents hat from penetrating to the deeper ab level where Ab Neter resides. The rushing itself becomes self-perpetuating: the mind seeks pleasure through acquisition or achievement, experiences temporary satisfaction, yet the underlying sense of incompleteness (arising from ignorance of Ab Neter) drives continued seeking.

The teaching's prescription against sechsech therefore addresses not just behavioral symptoms but the fundamental psychological mechanism. By practicing deliberate slowness, the aspirant interrupts the automatic pleasure-seeking patterns. This creates the possibility of recognizing that genuine fulfillment does not arise from external acquisitions or achievements—what the mind considers pleasurable—but from discovering Ab Neter, the divine consciousness that alone provides sustainable well-being. The Slowness meditative movement concept, in this book is based on the pamphlet containing a thesis on Slowness Meditation originally created ©1997-1999 by Muata Ashby.

This etymological understanding also clarifies why the teaching emphasizes slowing down rather than merely changing what one pursues. Replacing worldly pleasure-seeking with spiritual pleasure-seeking represents no fundamental transformation if the underlying pattern of rushing toward what the mind considers desirable remains intact. The spiritual aspirant who hastily pursues enlightenment, rapidly accumulates practices, or impatiently seeks advanced states manifests the same sechsech pattern—merely redirected toward spiritual objects. True transformation requires recognizing and releasing the pleasure-seeking mechanism itself, allowing the mind to settle into the present-moment awareness that reveals Ab Neter as ever-present rather than as distant goal requiring rapid pursuit.

The Linguistic Balance: Hersh and Hepti as Antidotes to Rushing

Having examined the etymological roots of sechsech (rushing) and its connection to pleasure-seeking, we must now recognize that the Ancient Egyptian language also provides specific terms describing the positive qualities that counter this agitated state. Based on the teaching presented by Sage Amenemopet that one should refrain from rushing hastily (sechsech), the application of the inverse doctrine methodology suggests that aspirants should actively cultivate the qualities expressed in the Ancient Egyptian terms ***Hersh*** and ***hepti***.

The term hersh carries meanings of "slow" and "patient"—qualities that represent not mere absence of rushing but active cultivation of deliberate, mindful engagement with actions, words, and thoughts. Similarly, hepti means "advance with caution" or "advance slowly," emphasizing thoughtful progression rather than reckless haste. These terms illuminate what slowness actually entails: being mindful, thoughtful, deliberate, gentle, and relaxed in one's approach to life's activities.

Consider how these linguistic counterparts reveal the comprehensive nature of Amenemopet's teaching. Where sechsech describes the problem—rushing driven by pleasure-seeking patterns—hersh and hepti describe the solution: patient, cautious advancement characterized by conscious awareness. The teaching does not merely warn against rushing; it implicitly prescribes cultivation of these opposite qualities that create conditions for spiritual development.

The Three Dimensions of Slowness: Deeds, Words, and Thoughts

The concept of slowness, when understood through hersh and hepti, encompasses three integrated dimensions that together constitute complete spiritual practice. These dimensions correspond to the traditional understanding that transformation requires alignment of body, speech, and mind—the three primary channels through which consciousness expresses itself and through which aryu patterns manifest.

Slowness of Deeds (Physical Actions): The quality of hersh applies to physical movements and bodily activities. This dimension involves performing actions with deliberate awareness, gentle engagement, and patient execution. Rather than rushing through tasks driven by the urgency of completion, the aspirant cultivates mindful presence during each activity—eating slowly and with awareness, walking with conscious attention to each step, performing work tasks with focused deliberation. The body becomes instrument of present-moment awareness rather than vehicle of unconscious reactivity.

Slowness of Words (Speech): The quality of hepti—advancing with caution—particularly applies to speech, which represents externalized thought. This dimension involves pausing before speaking, considering the impact of words before uttering them, and allowing space between words and sentences for reflection. Speech becomes measured, thoughtful, and deliberate rather than rapid, reactive, and unconsidered. The teaching from Chapter 21, Verse 16 regarding harmful speech directly connects to this dimension: slow, cautious speech prevents words emerging from heated mind and feelings that cause unnecessary harm. [1]

Slowness of Thoughts (Mental Activity): Both hersh and hepti apply to the mental realm, where the most fundamental transformation must occur. This dimension involves recognizing the rapid succession of thoughts driven by aryu patterns and gradually allowing mental activity to settle into greater spaciousness. Rather than thoughts arising in constant stream, each driven urgently by the previous one, the mind develops capacity for gaps between thoughts—moments of mental stillness where awareness recognizes itself apart from mental content. This mental slowness does not mean dulled thinking but rather clear, discriminative awareness operating without the density of reactive thought patterns.

These three dimensions operate interdependently. Physical rushing reinforces mental agitation; rapid speech both reflects and perpetuates heated mind and feelings; mental density drives hurried actions. Conversely, cultivating slowness in one dimension supports development in others. The aspirant who practices slow walking meditation naturally experiences some mental settling; deliberate speech creates space for thought clarification; mental stillness manifests as gentler physical movements and more considered verbal expressions.

The inverse doctrine application reveals that Amenemopet's teaching against sechsech implicitly prescribes systematic cultivation of hersh and hepti across all three dimensions. The aspirant understands that transformation from heated to silent personality requires not merely ceasing rushed behavior but actively developing patient, cautious, mindful engagement with actions, words, and thoughts. This represents positive spiritual practice rather than mere behavioral restraint—the cultivation of qualities that thin aryu density and reveal Ab Neter awareness.

I. Movement as the Defining Principle of Perceived Separateness

The Metaphysics of Movement and Stillness

Movement constitutes the defining principle that allows a person to feel separate from that which is perceived as non-moving in relation to oneself. Consider the fundamental nature of perception itself: we identify objects and differentiate self from other primarily through relative motion. The body moves through space; thoughts move through the mind; sensations arise and pass. Each movement creates the experiential impression of a separate entity—the mover—distinct from what appears static or moving at different rates.

The teaching employs the metaphor of water to illuminate this principle. A placid, homogeneous body of water represents the mind in its natural state—undifferentiated consciousness (Neberdjer) sustaining awareness without the fragmentation created by agitation. When this still water becomes disturbed, waves appear—multiple, distinct, seemingly separate forms. In the image above the single sun reflects in the calmness of the placid lake (representing undifferentiated waters) while in the image below the waves of the water reflect countless reflections of the sun causing the illusion that there is more than one sun (i.e. in the agitated (differentiated) waters there appear to be countless objects being reflected in those waves when in reality there is only one). Yet the waves remain nothing but water itself; the appearance of multiplicity arises solely through movement. The waves possess no independent existence apart from the ocean; their apparent separateness represents an optical illusion created by motion.

This metaphor directly corresponds to the Ancient Egyptian understanding of consciousness and manifestation. Ab Neter—the divine soul sustaining individual awareness—remains ever-present, unchanging, like the ocean's depths unaffected by surface turbulence. Yet when hat (conscious awareness) becomes occupied with constant mental and physical movement, this agitation obscures the underlying unity. The mind, caught in perpetual motion, perceives itself as separate from other minds, separate from the body, separate from the Divine that sustains all experience.

Movement functions as prestidigitation—the magician's sleight of hand that fools the mind's limited perception capabilities. Rapid succession of thoughts, constant physical activity, and emotional reactivity create such density of experience that the mind cannot penetrate to the stillness underlying all movement. The teaching of Amenemopet recognizes this fundamental principle: to discover what remains constant (Ab Neter, consciousness itself), one must cease the agitation that creates the illusion of separateness.

Aryu Patterns and the Momentum of Mental Movement

Building upon this metaphysical foundation, we recognize how aryu (karmic feeling-memories) perpetuate constant mental movement driven specifically by pleasure-seeking and displeasure-avoidance. The etymological connection between sekh (running) and sekhsekh-Ab (having pleasure—what the mind considers pleasurable) reveals that rushing represents the aryu-driven pursuit of satisfaction. Each thought carries feeling-tone from past experiences encoded as "this brought pleasure/this brought displeasure," which triggers automatic approach or avoidance responses generating further thoughts in rapid succession.

A single stimulus—perhaps seeing someone who resembles a past adversary—initiates a cascade driven by displeasure-avoidance aryu: recognition triggers retrieval of painful memories, emotional reaction arises (displeasure), comparative judgment forms ("this person wronged me"), planning future interactions begins (to avoid similar displeasure or achieve retaliatory pleasure), rehearsing conversations occurs, justifying positions solidifies. The mind races through this sequence in seconds, driven by the fundamental sekhsekh-Ab mechanism—fleeing what it considers unpleasurable while simultaneously seeking what promises satisfaction. This creates dense layers of mental activity that completely obscure present-moment awareness.

The Keys document explains that aryu "occupy the presence-of-mind awareness, so densely as to...blot out the awareness of the soul level divine presence which is deeper than the aryu." [2] This occupation occurs precisely through the mechanism of constant mental movement. Hat cannot rest because aryu continuously arise, demanding attention, generating reactions, prompting actions. The personality experiences this as the "normal" state of consciousness—perpetual mental commentary, planning, remembering, worrying, desiring.

Consider the modern experience of "racing thoughts"—what contemporary psychology recognizes as a symptom of anxiety or stress. From the Amenemopet perspective, this represents the natural consequence of dense aryu patterns operating without the moderating influence of wisdom. The mind runs hastily (sechsech) from one concern to another, never pausing long enough for awareness to penetrate below the surface agitation. Each thought feels urgent, demanding immediate attention and response. The very momentum of this mental movement prevents the stillness necessary for experiencing Ab Neter.

Physical movement follows the same pattern. The body enacts what the mind generates: hurried walking, rushed eating, rapid speech, restless gestures. The Amenemopet teaching recognizes that physical haste both reflects and reinforces mental agitation. When the body moves rapidly without deliberate awareness, this unconscious activity strengthens the aryu patterns driving the behavior. The person literally embodies their ignorance through perpetual motion that prevents deeper perception.

The teaching on luxury attachment (Chapter 16) demonstrates this sekhsekh-Ab principle in material form. Verse 8's warning against "greed about copper" and verse 9's instruction to develop "healthy enmity towards finery and luxury" directly address the pleasure-seeking pattern manifesting as comfort-pursuit. [3] The mind rushing toward luxury items, comfort conditions, and pleasant experiences represents the same fundamental mechanism—aryu patterns in ab driving constant pursuit of what promises satisfaction. The person hastens (sekhut) to acquire possessions, achieve status, or secure comfort because the mind associates these with pleasure (sekhsekh-Ab). Yet as the teaching reveals, this pursuit never provides sustainable fulfillment because external conditions cannot resolve the fundamental incompleteness arising from ignorance of Ab Neter. The rushing itself becomes addictive: temporary satisfaction from acquisition creates brief pleasure, but the underlying sense of lack (from Ab Neter ignorance) promptly drives renewed seeking, maintaining perpetual motion that prevents the stillness necessary for spiritual discovery.

II. The Spiritual Necessity of Slowing Down

Why Stillness Precedes Spiritual Discovery

The instruction against sechsech emerges from profound understanding of consciousness mechanics. Meditation practice—the systematic method for discovering Ab Neter—requires the mind to become sufficiently still that awareness can withdraw from surface-level engagement with thoughts and sensations. This withdrawal does not mean suppressing thoughts or forcing blankness; rather, it involves allowing hat to disengage from reactive responses to mental and sensory phenomena, enabling awareness to recognize itself as distinct from what it observes.

This process cannot occur amid constant movement. Consider attempting to see your reflection in water: a still pond provides clear mirroring, while churning rapids show nothing but chaos. Similarly, Ab Neter—the witnessing consciousness sustaining all experience—reveals itself only when mental and physical agitation subsides sufficiently. The teaching presented in Chapter 15, verse 15 describes this as "resting in your heart (unconscious) level of your mind." [4] This "resting" requires slowing the constant momentum of hat's engagement with surface phenomena.

The precedent for slowness exists throughout spiritual development. Before attempting meditation, aspirants practice ethical living (Maat) to reduce the production of new agitating aryu. Before formal seated practice, preparatory somatic exercises release physical tensions. Before deeper absorption states, initial concentration practices calm surface-level mental activity. Each stage builds capacity for greater stillness, recognizing that rushing toward advanced practices while neglecting foundations produces frustration rather than transformation.

Verse 17's warning against "running hastily as to arrive that achievement" addresses precisely this tendency. [1] The egoic mind, upon hearing teachings about enlightenment or Ab Neter discovery, immediately wants to achieve these states—now, quickly, efficiently. This desire itself represents aryu-driven reactivity: the sense of being incomplete seeks fulfillment through spiritual accomplishment. Yet this very grasping, this hurried pursuit, creates exactly the agitation that prevents what is sought. The teaching reveals a paradox: rushing toward spiritual goals ensures their continued inaccessibility because the rushing itself maintains the ignorance that conceals Ab Neter.

Contemporary research on "mindful walking" documents benefits occurring primarily through improved somatic awareness, reduced mental agitation, and enhanced proprioception—valuable developments that thin aryu density and support spiritual practice. However, aspirants should recognize that the slow walking practice Amenemopet prescribes serves these preliminary functions while ultimately aiming beyond improved body-awareness toward the recognition of consciousness itself as witness to all physical sensations. The research validates mechanisms without encompassing the teaching's full scope. Slowness meditative movement, when practiced according to sau-Neberdjer principles, becomes not merely a method for stress reduction or balance improvement but a gateway for consciousness to recognize its own nature as the unchanging witness of all bodily experience.

The Practice of Deliberate Slowness

Based on the teaching presented by Sage Amenemopet that one should refrain from rushing hastily (sechsech), the application of the inverse doctrine methodology suggests that aspirants should also cultivate systematic practices of deliberate slowness in physical movement, speech, and mental activity, as these support the recovery of inner sensitivity and the capacity for deeper meditation necessary for Ab Neter discovery.

Physical Slowness Practice

Walking meditation represents perhaps the most accessible practice for cultivating awareness of movement. The tradition involves walking at deliberately slow pace while maintaining continuous awareness of each component of the walking process: lifting the foot, moving it forward, placing it down, shifting weight, lifting the other foot. This extreme slowness serves multiple functions in mind/personality transformation.

First, slow walking disrupts automatic motor patterns. Normal walking occurs mostly unconsciously—the body moves while the mind occupies itself with thoughts, planning, or external stimuli. By slowing the pace to perhaps one step every 10-30 seconds, the practitioner makes automatic unconscious movement difficult. Hat must remain engaged with the walking process or the practice collapses. This forced attention begins training the mind to direct awareness deliberately rather than allowing it to scatter according to habitual aryu patterns.

Second, slow movement creates conditions for observing the mind's resistance to stillness. Within minutes of beginning slow walking practice, agitation arises: "This is boring," "I should be doing something productive," "This seems pointless," "I'm walking too slowly/too fast," "Others will think I'm strange." Each reaction reveals aryu patterns that normally operate beneath awareness. The practice doesn't suppress these reactions but observes them arising and passing, gradually weakening their grip on hat's attention.

Third, slow walking develops proprioceptive awareness—felt sense of body position and movement in space. Normal rapid movement provides insufficient time for subtle sensory perception. Slowing down allows the practitioner to notice weight distribution, muscle engagement, balance adjustments, spatial orientation. This heightened body awareness serves as foundation for meditation practices that require refined perception of subtle internal phenomena.

The Buddhist tradition has long employed walking meditation (kinhin in Zen, cankama in Theravada), recognizing its value for balancing seated practice and maintaining present-moment awareness during activity. While contemporary research on walking meditation documents benefits primarily at the psychological level—stress reduction, improved balance, emotional regulation—traditional Buddhist practice, like Amenemopet's teaching, aims beyond mental improvement toward recognition of awareness itself. [5] As the Dharma Drum teaching explains: 'Slow walking meditation involves walking at an extremely slow pace, which helps us focus on the movements of our steps, while remaining undistracted by wandering thoughts and the external environment. This enables us to practice awareness, by being clearly aware of every step we take. 'The Buddhist tradition has long employed walking meditation (kinhin in Zen, cankama in Theravada), recognizing its value for balancing seated practice and maintaining present-moment awareness during activity. While contemporary research on walking meditation documents benefits primarily at the psychological level—stress reduction, improved balance, emotional regulation—traditional Buddhist practice, like Amenemopet's teaching, aims beyond mental improvement toward recognition of awareness itself. [5] This enables us to practice awareness, by being clearly aware of every step we take.'[6] The instruction emphasizes that "rather than rush the pace of walking, make sure that your foot is firmly on the ground before taking another step. Every step needs to be solid and steady." [6]

Mental Slowness Practice

Slowing mental activity proves more challenging than physical movement because thoughts appear to occur spontaneously without voluntary initiation. Nevertheless, practices exist for reducing the rapidity of thought succession. The gap extension technique, in this book, involves recognizing and gradually lengthening the natural spaces that occur between thoughts [7] —a practice that moves beyond contemporary mindfulness (which cultivates awareness of thoughts) toward recognition of awareness itself as distinct from mental content. While mindfulness trains attention to observe thoughts more clearly within the dualistic framework of observer-and-observed, gap extension reveals the consciousness that exists independent of thoughts altogether, pointing toward the non-dual recognition that one's essential nature is the awareness in which thoughts appear and disappear. Rather than thoughts arising in constant stream, brief intervals of mental silence actually occur throughout waking awareness—moments where one thought completes and before the next begins.

Initial practice involves simply noticing these gaps without attempting to extend them forcefully. Sitting quietly, the aspirant observes the thought stream: planning thought arises, lingers several seconds, fades...brief silence...memory arises, triggers emotional response, fades...brief silence...judgment arises, generates more thoughts, fades...brief silence. Recognizing these naturally-occurring intervals represents the first stage.

Subsequently, the practice involves allowing—not forcing—these gaps to lengthen organically. As the mind becomes less reactive to aryu patterns, thoughts arise less urgently. What previously required immediate mental response can simply be noted and released. The gaps between thoughts expand naturally from one second to several seconds to longer periods of mental quietude. This occurs not through suppression or forceful concentration but through patient non-engagement with arising thoughts, allowing them to dissolve without elaboration.

The teaching from Chapter 9 regarding meditation on visual and auditory elements provides specific Practices for slowing mental activity. [1] Focusing sustained attention on a single object—whether external like a candle flame or internal like the breath sensation—occupies hat sufficiently that thoughts lose their compelling urgency. The mind still generates thoughts, but focused attention on the meditation object prevents the usual reactive engagement that creates thought proliferation.

Speech Slowness Practice

Speech represents externalized thought; therefore, slowing speech directly impacts mental processes. The practice involves deliberate reduction of speaking pace, with conscious attention to the pause between hearing a question and responding, between one sentence and the next, between one word and another. This creates space for reflection rather than automatic verbal reaction.

The Amenemopet teaching on not letting speech "come out of the body for causing harm purposely or speech that would cause unnecessary harm" (Chapter 21, Verse 16) directly relates to the slowness principle. [1] Rapid, unconsidered speech manifests heated mind and feelings—words emerge driven by aryu patterns of defensiveness, one-upmanship, anger, or desire to impress. Slowing speech allows hat to observe these impulses arising without immediately enacting them, creating the possibility of responding from wisdom rather than reactivity.

In practical application, the aspirant might practice speaking at half the normal pace during specific daily periods—perhaps dinner conversation or telephone calls. This deliberate slowness feels artificial initially, yet it reveals how much normal speech operates automatically. Slowing down creates awareness of the gap between mental content and verbal expression, illuminating the choice-point where wisdom can intercede before harmful or unnecessary words emerge.

III. Contemporary Scientific Validation of Slowness Practices

Research on Walking Meditation

Contemporary scientific research provides empirical validation for what Amenemopet's teaching recognized millennia ago: practices of deliberate slowness produce measurable psychological and neurological benefits. A 2024 systematic review examined effects of Buddhist Walking Meditation, Walking Meditation, and Mindful Walking on health in adults and older adults, analyzing randomized controlled trials and quasi-experimental studies. [8] The review encompassed multiple research investigations demonstrating significant positive outcomes across psychological, physiological, and functional measures.

Studies document that walking meditation at slow pace—participants were "asked to walk more slowly than usual to increase their awareness and mindfulness"—produces improvements in depression, anxiety, balance, proprioception, and quality of life. [9] Yang et al.'s research protocol involved 30-minute sessions of slow walking on flat routes, progressively adding mindfulness techniques: attention to breathing rhythm, awareness of each step's movement, mental scanning of body sensations and feelings. [9] This structured approach mirrors the Amenemopet principle of systematic development—beginning with simple physical awareness and gradually refining attention to subtler phenomena.

Research by Prakhinkit et al. (2014) found that Buddhist walking meditation produced significant improvements in depression scores and functional fitness measures among elderly participants. [10] Gainey et al.'s research with type 2 diabetes patients demonstrated that walking meditation produced superior outcomes compared to traditional walking programs in multiple measures: HbA1c reduction, blood pressure decrease, improved flow-mediated dilation, reduced arterial stiffness, and lowered cortisol levels. [11] The researchers noted that participants performed walking on treadmill "while concentrated on foot stepping by voiced 'Budd' and 'Dha' with each foot step that contacted the floor to practice mindfulness while walking." [11]

The mechanisms underlying these benefits illuminate why Amenemopet's teaching prescribes slowness for spiritual development. A study by Teut et al. found that German adults with moderate-to-severe psychological distress who participated in eight 60-minute group sessions of mindful walking training experienced significant reductions in psychological stress symptoms and improvements in quality of life compared to control groups. [12] Brazilian undergraduate students engaging in walking meditation for 200 meters experienced heightened positive emotion and enhanced emotional response as measured by brain activity compared to those walking normally. [12] These findings suggest that slow, mindful movement directly affects emotional regulation and stress response systems—precisely the aryu-driven reactive patterns that obstruct Ab Neter awareness.

Proprioception and Balance Research

Additional research reveals that walking meditation improves ankle proprioception and balance performance, particularly among elderly populations. [13] The study investigated 58 elderly women randomized into control and walking meditation groups, with the meditation group practicing 30 minutes per day, three days weekly for eight weeks. Results showed that walking meditation "not only improved balance ability but also enhanced ankle proprioception," with improvements appearing in balance measures by week four and proprioceptive improvements by week eight. [13]

The researchers explain these benefits through the characteristics of walking meditation: "slow walking form along with the mindfulness of foot and leg movements, provided a longer period of single leg stance and increased the neuromuscular control." [13] This finding validates the Amenemopet principle that slowing physical movement enhances awareness of subtle body processes normally overlooked during rapid automatic activity. The increased proprioceptive awareness—refined perception of body position and movement—directly corresponds to the "inner sensitivity" that Amenemopet teaches must be recovered for successful spiritual practice.

Studies comparing walking meditation to Tai Chi—another slow-movement contemplative practices—found similar mechanisms at work. Research confirms that "traditional Chinese form of exercise Tai Chi is effective in maintaining balance among the elderly by way of better proprioception, particularly ankle proprioception. With its continuous slow movements and conscious awareness of the body moves like body-mindfulness practice, Tai Chi provides proprioceptive and neuromuscular control." [13] The parallel between Tai Chi's slow movements and walking meditation's deliberate pace supports the universal principle that conscious slowness cultivates refined awareness regardless of specific cultural context.

Neurological Effects of Slowing Mental Activity

Neuroscientific research on meditation demonstrates that practices involving mental slowing produce measurable changes in brain structure and function. Studies using fMRI and MEG reveal that long-term meditation practice, which fundamentally involves slowing and eventually transcending rapid thought succession, alters Default Mode Network activity—the neural signature of self-referential thinking and mental wandering. [14] Research by Brewer et al. found that "meditation experience is associated with differences in default mode network activity and connectivity," with experienced meditators showing reduced activation in brain regions associated with mind-wandering and self-referential processing. [15]

The reduction in Default Mode Network activity corresponds to what the Amenemopet teaching describes as thinning aryu density. The network's constant activity represents the mind's habitual tendency to generate thoughts, memories, plans, and judgments—the mental movement that obscures Ab Neter. Meditation practices that slow this activity literally change brain function, reducing the neural substrate of mental agitation.

Research on alterations in sense of time, space, and body during meditation reveals that "long-term contemplative practitioners offer an exclusive opportunity to study unique mental states, due both to their heightened introspective abilities, as well as their ability to intentionally alter subtle aspects of consciousness." [16] Studies found that meditation experiences characterized as "unbounded in space and time" correlate with specific patterns of theta rhythm brain activity. [16] This finding validates the teaching that slowing mental and physical movement enables access to consciousness states beyond ordinary time-space-body identification—precisely the shift from hat-level awareness to ab-level experiencing that reveals Ab Neter.

Travis's research proposes that "bursts in the 7-9 Hz band underlie the state of transcendental consciousness, which is 'the least excited state of mental activity,' unbounded by a sense of time and space." [16] This "least excited state" represents the natural result of systematic mental slowing practices—the mind settles into progressively subtler activity levels until it rests in the fundamental awareness (Ab Neter) underlying all mental phenomena. The teaching of Amenemopet anticipated these neurological findings by thousands of years, recognizing that rushing (sechsech) prevents this settling while deliberate slowness facilitates it.

IV. The Progression from Stillness to Enlightened Activity

Establishing Stable Inner Awareness

The teaching acknowledges a crucial developmental sequence: initial practice requires deliberate slowness to recover inner sensitivity, but once Ab Neter awareness stabilizes, rapid activity becomes possible without losing deeper self-awareness. This progression reflects the difference between the beginner who requires controlled conditions to maintain meditative awareness and the adept who abides in Ab Neter recognition regardless of external circumstances or activity pace.

During early practice, rushing (sechsech) immediately disrupts the fragile connection to subtle awareness. The aspirant who attempts to maintain mindfulness while rushing to appointments, eating quickly, speaking rapidly, or engaging in multiple simultaneous activities invariably loses the thread of awareness and returns to automatic aryu-driven functioning. Therefore, the teaching prescribes deliberate slowness as essential discipline during this foundational phase—not as permanent lifestyle requirement but as training methodology.

The Serpent Power teaching elaborates this principle: "The Serpent Power requires a sturdy and pure nervous system in order to manifest the higher forms of spiritual consciousness...Serpent Power Yoga will not work if you have a healthy body but are plagued with mental agitations and worldly desires." [17] This recognizes that physical and mental systems must develop capacity for subtle awareness before advanced practices become accessible. Slowness practices build this capacity systematically.

As practice deepens, several developmental milestones indicate increasing stability of Ab Neter awareness:

1. Gap Recognition: The aspirant consistently notices mental gaps between thoughts, experiencing brief intervals where awareness exists without mental content. [7]

2. Witness Consciousness: The capacity develops to observe thoughts, emotions, and sensations as objects appearing within awareness rather than as self-identity. [7]

3. Sustained Absorption: During formal meditation, the mind settles into prolonged periods of single-pointed focus or pure awareness beyond thought-free states, with awareness remaining clear and present. [7]

4. Spontaneous Mindfulness: Ab Neter awareness begins arising spontaneously during daily activities without deliberate effort to maintain it—brief moments where the sense of being the unchanging witness becomes self-evident. [7]

5. Circumstantial Independence: External conditions—comfort/discomfort, praise/criticism, success/failure—produce increasingly minimal disturbance to underlying equanimity. [7]

These developmental stages indicate progressive thinning of aryu density and strengthening of Ab Neter recognition. The aspirant still experiences thoughts and emotions, but identification with them weakens. The mind still moves, but awareness recognizes itself as distinct from mental movement—the still water underlying wave activity.

From Trained Slowness to Natural Effortlessness

Once this stable foundation exists, the necessity for deliberate slowness gradually diminishes. The adept who has thoroughly established Ab Neter awareness can engage in rapid physical activity, complex mental tasks, or demanding emotional situations while maintaining the deeper witnessing presence. External observers might see no difference between this person's activity pace and that of others engaged in worldly pursuits. Yet the internal reality differs fundamentally: actions occur without dense aryu-driven reactivity; thoughts arise without identification; emotions flow through without obscuring the ever-present consciousness sustaining experience.

This represents the fulfillment of Prologue verse 2's promise—earthly well-being that continues regardless of external circumstances. [18] The personality operates effectively in the world, responding appropriately to situations, yet inner stability remains unshaken because Ab Neter awareness serves as the foundation rather than fragile hat-level experiences subject to constant disruption.

The teaching does not advocate permanent retreat to slow-paced living as spiritual ideal. Rather, it prescribes temporary slowness as training methodology—scaffolding that supports development until inner structure proves stable enough to stand independently. Consider learning to ride a bicycle: training wheels provide necessary support until balance becomes internalized, then they're removed and natural cycling occurs. Similarly, deliberate slowness supports awareness development until Ab Neter recognition becomes sufficiently stable that external activity pace no longer determines internal state.

Nevertheless, even adepts maintain practices of periodic slowness. Regular meditation retreats, daily sitting practice, mindful movement—these continue not because the advanced practitioner requires them for maintaining awareness but because they provide deepening refinement and prevent gradual drift back toward unconscious aryu-dominated functioning. The Amenemopet lectures note that "the longer you do meditation, the better your brain will be at self-regulation," indicating that continued practice produces ongoing benefits even for advanced practitioners. [19]

V. Practical Implementation for Modern Aspirants

Contemporary Challenges to Slowness Practice

Modern aspirants face unique obstacles implementing slowness practices within cultures that systematically valorize and reward speed, multitasking, and perpetual productivity. The very suggestion to slow down triggers immediate resistance: "I don't have time," "My job demands fast pace," "Others will judge me as lazy or inefficient," "I'll fall behind competitors." Each objection reveals aryu patterns—accumulated conditioning teaching that rapid activity equals success and slowness signifies failure.

Consider the common experience of checking smartphones dozens or hundreds of times daily, rapidly scrolling through information feeds, responding to messages within seconds. This behavior pattern represents sechsech (rushing) at societal scale—entire populations conditioning themselves into fragmented attention, reactive responsiveness, and constant mental agitation. The teaching of Amenemopet directly challenges this cultural norm, yet implementing counteractive practices requires conscious recognition that contemporary values actively undermine spiritual development.

The workplace presents particular challenges. Careers reward those who work quickly, respond immediately, and maximize productivity. Taking time for slow, deliberate action appears counterproductive by conventional metrics. Yet the teaching reveals that apparent efficiency gained through rushing often proves illusory—mistakes from insufficient reflection, poor decisions from reactive thinking, exhaustion from unsustainable pace. Nevertheless, changing personal work habits while surrounded by cultural expectations of rapid response requires determination and often social courage.

Integrated Practice Guidelines

Based on the teaching presented by Sage Amenemopet, aspirants can implement slowness practices through graduated integration into daily life rather than attempting wholesale lifestyle transformation that proves unsustainable. The following approach provides systematic methodology:

Morning Foundation Practice (15-30 minutes):

Begin each day with slow walking meditation. Create a path approximately 30-40 feet long in your home or nearby outdoor space. Walk this path at extremely slow pace—approximately one step every 10-20 seconds. Maintain awareness on the complete process of each step: intention to lift foot arising, sensation of lifting, movement through air, lowering toward ground, contact with surface, weight transfer to standing leg. When thoughts arise—they will continuously—simply note "thinking" and gently return attention to walking sensations. This practice establishes foundational mindfulness before engaging worldly activities.

Transition Moments (throughout day):

Identify natural transition points—between waking and leaving bed, finishing breakfast and beginning work, completing one task and starting another, arriving home and greeting family. At each transition, pause for 30-60 seconds of complete stillness. Simply stand or sit without movement, observing breath, noticing what sensations, thoughts, and emotions are present. This practice interrupts the momentum of rushing from activity to activity while training the mind to recognize present-moment awareness repeatedly throughout the day.

Intentional Slowness Periods (specific daily activities):

Select 2-3 routine activities for practicing deliberate slowness: eating one meal, showering, driving/commuting, household tasks. During these specific activities, reduce pace to approximately half normal speed while maintaining full awareness of the activity. Notice resistance arising—the habitual pull toward rushing—without acting on it. Observe how slowing down reveals details normally overlooked and how the mind gradually becomes more present rather than racing ahead to next tasks.

Speech Mindfulness (one conversation daily):

Choose one daily conversation—perhaps with family member, colleague, or friend—for practicing slow, mindful speech. Before speaking, pause 3-5 seconds to formulate response. Between sentences, allow brief silence. Notice the impulse to interrupt or respond immediately; recognize this as aryu-driven reactivity. By slowing speech deliberately during specific interactions, the practice develops capacity for reflective rather than reactive communication.

Evening Integration Practice (10-15 minutes):

Before sleep, practice seated meditation focusing on gap extension between thoughts. Sit comfortably, eyes closed, observing the natural flow of mental activity. Notice the brief silences between thoughts. Allow these gaps to lengthen organically without forcing mental suppression. If the mind becomes very busy, return attention to breath sensations as an anchor. This practice reinforces the day's slowness training while preparing the mind for restful sleep rather than continued agitation.

VI. The Ultimate Purpose: Discovering the Still Point

Movement and Stillness as Gateway to Ab Neter

The entire teaching on sechsech serves ultimately to facilitate what verse 17 describes as genuine achievement—not worldly accomplishment through rushing but discovery of Ab Neter, the divine consciousness sustaining all experience. [1] Slowing physical movement, mental activity, and speech represents methodology, not goal. The goal remains what the Prologue establishes: "cause a person to have well-being while living on earth" (verse 2) and discovering the divine sanctuary within (verse 9). [18]

The relationship between stillness and spiritual discovery operates through specific mechanics of consciousness architecture. Ab Neter exists as the unchanging witness-awareness—what observes thoughts without being thoughts, what experiences sensations without being sensations, what remains present through all changing phenomena. Yet hat (conscious awareness), when constantly occupied with surface-level mental and physical movement, cannot penetrate to this deeper level. The very agitation that characterizes normal waking consciousness prevents recognition of the still awareness underlying it.

Consider the metaphor employed earlier: waves and ocean. A person standing on a boat in storm-tossed waters sees only turbulent waves. The smooth, still depths remain invisible, obscured by surface chaos. Yet beneath even the most violent storm, the ocean depths maintain their essential stillness. Only by diving below the agitated surface does one discover the unchanging calm. Similarly, only by slowing and eventually transcending the constant movement of hat does awareness penetrate to the ab level where Ab Neter resides as the eternal still point.

This still point does not mean blank unconsciousness or absence of awareness. Rather, it represents consciousness before it becomes occupied with objects—the pure capacity of awareness that enables all subsequent knowing. The Transpersonal Psychology research describes this as discovering "awareness as distinct from mental modifications, allowing consciousness to rest in recognition of its essential nature." [7] The various meditation practices described throughout Amenemopet's teaching—attending to visual elements (Chapter 9), resting in the unconscious mind (Chapter 15)—all aim toward this fundamental recognition.

The teaching on sechsech removes a primary obstacle to this discovery. As long as the personality rushes from one thing to another—physically, mentally, emotionally—the still point remains theoretical rather than experiential. The aryu patterns driving constant movement create such density of activity that penetration to deeper levels proves impossible. Therefore, systematic practices of slowness serve as essential preparation, gradually training the mind to settle sufficiently that the still point reveals itself not as distant goal but as ever-present foundation of all experience.

Integration with Complete Spiritual Path

The slowness teaching integrates with other Amenemopet instructions to form complete spiritual methodology. Chapter 1's teaching on not being heated addresses the emotional reactivity that drives rushing behavior. [19] Chapter 2's instruction on life management creates the organized external conditions supporting regular practice. [19] Chapter 3's teaching on proper speech connects directly with the slowness of verbal expression. [19] Each teaching addresses different aspects of the transformation from heated to silent (ger) personality—from aryu-driven reactivity to Ab Neter awareness.

Understanding sechsech as spiritual impediment clarifies why multiple teachings emphasize patience, steadiness, and gradual development. The egoic mind wants immediate enlightenment, rapid progress, efficiency in spiritual practice. Yet this very wanting—this grasping urgency—represents the heated mind and feelings that prevent what is sought. The teaching reveals a fundamental paradox: seeking to achieve spiritual goals quickly ensures their inaccessibility because the seeking itself maintains ignorance. Only by releasing the rush, accepting patient gradual development, and practicing deliberate slowness does the mind create conditions wherein Ab Neter recognition can occur.

This does not mean transformation requires decades. As the Keys document notes, "the core discovery of the Soul-Aware-Witness-Self can occur relatively quickly through the Quick Recognition method." [7] Yet "relatively quickly" means months or years of consistent practice, not days or weeks. More importantly, initial recognition differs from stable realization. Many practitioners experience brief glimpses of Ab Neter awareness—moments where the unchanging witness becomes obvious—yet lack the stability to maintain this recognition during daily activities. The slowness practices build precisely this stability, gradually establishing Ab Neter awareness as baseline rather than occasional experience.

Conclusion: The Wisdom of Patient Development

Sage Amenemopet's teaching on sechsech—not rushing hastily—contains layered wisdom extending far beyond surface-level advice about time management. At its deepest level, this teaching addresses the fundamental mechanics of consciousness, perception, and spiritual transformation. Movement creates the illusion of separateness; stillness reveals underlying unity. Mental agitation obscures Ab Neter; deliberate slowness facilitates its discovery. Rushing perpetuates ignorance; patience enables enlightenment.

The Ancient Egyptian terms hersh (slow, patient) and hepti (advance with caution, advance slowly) provide the linguistic foundation for understanding what slowness actually entails: mindful, thoughtful, deliberate, gentle, and relaxed engagement with life's activities. These terms illuminate that the teaching prescribes not mere cessation of rushing but active cultivation of opposite qualities across three integrated dimensions—slowness of deeds (physical actions), slowness of words (speech), and slowness of thoughts (mental activity). Together, these dimensions constitute complete spiritual practice that systematically thins aryu density and reveals Ab Neter awareness.

For modern practitioners, implementing these teachings requires conscious countercultural choice. The surrounding environment actively promotes and rewards exactly what the teaching identifies as spiritually destructive: constant busyness, rapid responsiveness, perpetual productivity, fragmented attention. Choosing deliberately to slow down—in movement, speech, and mental activity—represents an act of spiritual courage, a rejection of ignorance-perpetuating values in favor of liberation-supporting practices.

Nevertheless, this choice need not manifest as a complete lifestyle revolution. The graduated integration approach allows systematic practice within existing life circumstances. Morning walking meditation, transition-moment pauses, intentional slowness periods, speech mindfulness, evening integration—these constitute accessible entry points. As practice deepens and inner stability develops, the necessity for deliberate slowness gradually diminishes, yielding to natural effortless awareness that remains present regardless of external activity pace.

The ultimate promise remains what the Prologue establishes: well-being during earthly life and discovery of the divine sanctuary within. The teaching on sechsech provides essential methodology for realizing both goals. By slowing physical movement, we develop refined body awareness. By slowing mental activity, we create gaps where awareness recognizes itself. By slowing speech, we interrupt reactive patterns. Each practice contributes to the comprehensive transformation from heated, scattered, aryu-dominated personality to silent, integrated, Ab Neter-aware spiritual being.

This transformation represents humanity's highest potential—what Amenemopet teaches as the actual achievement worth pursuing. Not worldly success obtained through rushing, not external accomplishments accumulated through perpetual activity, but the discovery of one's essential nature as sustained by divine consciousness itself. The path requires patience, demands perseverance, necessitates systematic practice. Yet for those willing to slow down sufficiently that inner sensitivity returns, the reward proves infinite: recognition of the eternal still point underlying all movement, the unchanging awareness witnessing all change, the Ab Neter that has always been and will always be—one's true self beyond all illusion of separateness.

References

[1] Ashby, M. (2019-25). Mysticism of Amenemopet Hieroglyphic Text Translation. Sema Institute of Ancient Egyptian Studies.
[2] Ashby, M. (2025). Keys to Sage Amenemopet wisdom text trilinear translation. Sema Institute of Ancient Egyptian Studies.
[3] Ashby, M. (2019-25). Mysticism of Amenemopet Hieroglyphic Text Translation. Chapter 16, Verses 8-9. Sema Institute of Ancient Egyptian Studies.
[4] Ashby, M. (2024). Amenemopet lectures 2024 by Dr Muata Ashby transcripts. Sema Institute of Ancient Egyptian Studies.
[5] Walking meditation. (2025). Wikipedia. Retrieved from https://en.wikipedia.org/wiki/Walking_meditation
[6] Slow Walking Meditation. Dharma Drum Mountain Global Website. Retrieved from https://www.dharmadrum.org/portal_d8_cnt_page.php?folder_id=27&cnt_id=59&up_page=1
[7] Ashby, M. (2024). Transpersonal Psychology of Discovering the Aware Witnessing Self. Sema Institute of Ancient Egyptian Studies.
[8] Vieira, F. M., et al. (2024). Effects of Buddhist Walking Meditation, Walking Meditation or Mindful Walking on the Health of Adults and Older Adults: A Systematic Review. Healthcare, 6(4), 122. https://doi.org/10.3390/healthcare6040122
[9] Yang, Y., et al. (2019). Effects of mindful walking on psychological health in adults. Mindfulness Research Studies.
[10] Prakhinkit, S., Suppapitiporn, S., Tanaka, H., & Suksom, D. (2014). Effects of Buddhism walking meditation on depression, functional fitness, and endothelium-dependent vasodilation in depressed elderly. Journal of Alternative and Complementary Medicine, 20(5), 411-416.
[11] Gainey, A., Himathongkam, T., Tanaka, H., & Suksom, D. (2016). Effects of Buddhist walking meditation on glycemic control and vascular function in patients with type 2 diabetes.

Journal of Alternative and Complementary Medicine, 22(8), 650-655.
[12] Teut, M., et al. (2013). Mindful walking in psychologically distressed individuals: A randomized controlled trial. Evidence-Based Complementary and Alternative Medicine, Article ID 489856.
[13] Prakhinkit, S., Suppapitiporn, S., Tanaka, H., & Suksom, D. (2018). Walking meditation promotes ankle proprioception and balance performance among elderly women. Gait & Posture, 66, 1-6.
[14] Brewer, J. A., Worhunsky, P. D., Gray, J. R., Tang, Y. Y., Weber, J., & Kober, H. (2011). Meditation experience is associated with differences in default mode network activity and connectivity. Proceedings of the National Academy of Sciences, 108(50), 20254-20259.
[15] Davidson, R. J., & Lutz, A. (2008). Buddha's brain: Neuroplasticity and meditation. IEEE Signal Processing Magazine, 25(1), 176-174.
[16] Berkovich-Ohana, A., Glicksohn, J., & Goldstein, A. (2012). Alterations in the sense of time, space, and body in the mindfulness-trained brain: a neurophenomenologically-guided MEG study. Frontiers in Psychology, 3, 562.
[17] Ashby, M. (2001). The Serpent Power: The Ancient Egyptian Mystical Wisdom of the Inner Life Force. Sema Institute of Ancient Egyptian Studies.
[18] Ashby, M. (2019-25). Mysticism of Amenemopet Hieroglyphic Text Translation. Prologue, Verses 2 and 9. Sema Institute of Ancient Egyptian Studies.
[19] Ashby, M. (2024). Amenemopet lectures 2024 by Dr Muata Ashby transcripts. Sema Institute of Ancient Egyptian Studies.
[20] Ashby, M. (2024). Book Commentaries on Mystic Psychology of Amenemopet. Sema Institute of Ancient Egyptian Studies.

DEVOTION & TRUST: The Prayer of Amenemopet: Living in Divine Trust

Chapter 7, Verses 12-15

Verse 12.

12.1. ***aa ari tu k s-maa a en pa Aden {Net}***

12.2. hey action yours thine cause-adore you to that Sundisk {Div/God}

12.3. Now hear this: the action of yours, causing adoration to the sundisk divinity…

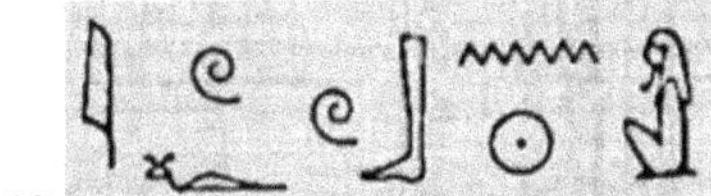

Verse 12.

12.4. ***iu F uben {Net}***

12.5. it is He shining {Div}

12.6. …it is an adoration to a shining divinity, resplendent and effulgent with vital life force and enlightenment for the mind.

Verse 13.

13.1. ***djed amma n-a udja {mdj} senab {mdj}***

13.2. speech grant that to-me well-being/vitality {fig} health {fig}

13.3. utter the following words: Oh, divinity of the sun, who enlivens and enlightens all, grand to me not riches or possessions or my ignorant ego desires that are all fleeting and illusory; instead grant to me well-being and health in a manner of your choosing {fig}.

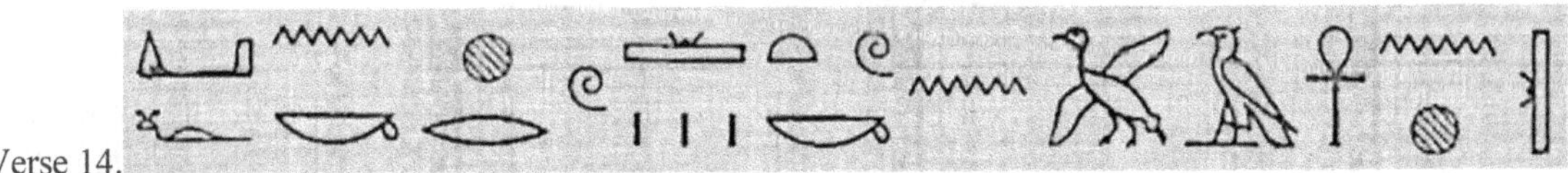

Verse 14.

14.1. ***di F en k cheru {mdj} tu k en pa ankh {mdj}***

14.2. gives He to thee provisions {fig} to you for that life {fig}

14.3. He will give to you whatever provisions are needed for your life {fig} while you are on the earth.

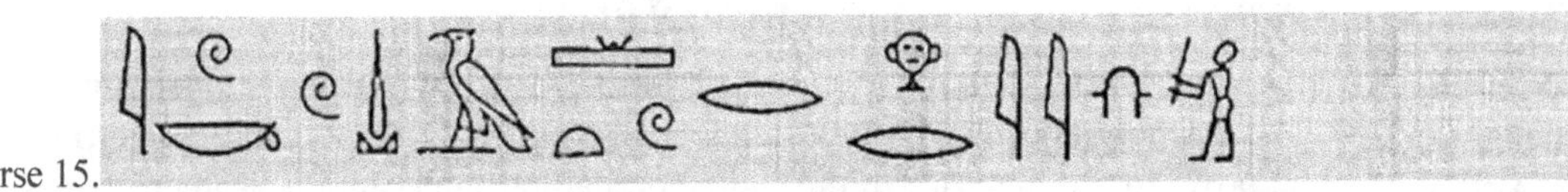

Verse 15.

15.1. ***iu k udja {mdj} tu er hery***

15.2. it is thee well-being/vitality {fig} you as-to fear

15.3. it is you who will have well-being and vitality for living your life.

VERSE 12: THE CALL TO ADORATION

"Now hear this: the action of yours, causing adoration to the sundisk divinity... it is an adoration to a shining divinity, resplendent and effulgent with vital life force and enlightenment for the mind."

These verses, which Sage Amenemopet presents as a prayer invocation to be practiced by aspirants, reveal the culmination of all the wisdom teachings contained in this text. The sundisk divinity (Aten)—representing the dynamic power of spirit, the life-giving consciousness that sustains all existence—becomes the focus of devotional practice. This adoration differs fundamentally from the worldly orientations that the heated mind and feelings pursue throughout life. The sundisk shines as "resplendent and effulgent with vital life force" (udja), the very energy that righteous living conserves and that heated patterns squander through anxiety, scheming, and excessive labor.

Indeed, the teaching establishes that approaching the Divine through adoration transforms consciousness from the scattered, depleted state characteristic of aryu-driven existence into receptivity for the enlightenment that the Divine alone can provide to the mind. This adoration does not emerge from egoic neediness seeking to manipulate divine favor but rather from recognition of the source of all vitality, all consciousness, all provision.

VERSES 13-15: THE PRAYER FOR DIVINE PROVISION

"Utter the following words: Oh, divinity of the sun, who enlivens and enlightens all, grant to me not riches or possessions or my ignorant ego desires that are all fleeting and illusory; instead grant to me well-being and health in a manner of your choosing. He will give to you whatever provisions are needed for your life while you are on the earth. It is you who will have well-being and vitality for living your life."

Amenemopet's instruction reveals profound psychological wisdom in what this prayer requests—and crucially, in what it does not request. Consider how the heated mind and feelings would naturally pray: for riches to secure future comfort, for power over enemies who threaten well-being, for circumstances to align with egoic preferences and desires. Such prayers emerge from the delusion of autonomous control that verses throughout this teaching have addressed—the belief that security depends on accumulating possessions, vanquishing opponents, and manipulating circumstances according to limited egoic comprehension.

Instead, Amenemopet institutes a prayer that acknowledges "my ignorant ego desires that are all fleeting and illusory" while requesting only "well-being and health in a manner of your choosing." This represents the complete surrender of egoic determination about what constitutes genuine provision. The mind recognizes that it operates within cosmic intelligence (Neberdjer) that comprehends circumstances far beyond what the limited personality can perceive. Therefore, rather than demanding specific outcomes, the aspirant requests that divine wisdom determine what genuinely serves both earthly well-being (Prologue verse 2) and spiritual evolution toward discovering Ab Neter (Prologue verse 9).

THE TEACHING ON DIVINE PROVIDENCE AND HUMAN RESPONSIBILITY

This prayer must be understood within the complete framework that Amenemopet establishes throughout the text. The teaching does not promote passive abdication of responsibility—sitting idly while expecting divine provision to materialize through supernatural intervention. Rather, verses 13-15 integrate with the ethical imperatives the entire teaching presents: righteous action, ethical conduct, proper speech, avoidance of heated patterns, and diligent (but not excessive) engagement with life's circumstances.

When the text states "He will give to you whatever provisions are needed for your life while you are on the earth," this operates through the cosmic forces of Shayt (destiny) and Renenut (fortune) that respond to accumulated aryu. The aspirant who lives according to Maat principles—organizing life's affairs through the wisdom Amenemopet teaches—creates positive aryu that influence these cosmic forces toward favorable provision. Conversely, unethical conduct deposits corrupted aryu that may temporarily prevent desired provisions even when the aspirant prays with sincere intent.

Nevertheless, even apparent lack or difficulty represents divine providence operating with perfect intelligence. When circumstances withhold desired comfort, when life delivers hardship despite righteous effort, this operates as cosmic wisdom providing precisely what that personality requires for purification and evolution. The difficulty itself becomes the provision—experiences creating conditions whereby the mind must confront the consequences of past patterns, motivating the transformation work that future well-being (both material and spiritual) depends upon.

FREEDOM FROM ANXIETY: THE PSYCHOLOGICAL LIBERATION

The prayer's greatest gift lies in what it eliminates: the chronic anxiety, worry, and agitation (shennu) that characterize heated mind and feelings attempting to secure provision through personal manipulation and control. When aspirants genuinely practice this prayer—not merely reciting words but actually absorbing the consciousness transformation it represents—they discover freedom from the exhausting mental patterns that consume vital energy (sekhem) and prevent Ab Neter awareness.

Consider the liberation that emerges when the mind recognizes: "I need not worry excessively about sustenance, for divine providence operates to provide according to cosmic intelligence that transcends my limited comprehension. My responsibility involves living righteously, engaging circumstances with appropriate diligence, and trusting that what genuinely serves my evolution will manifest at the proper time (tayu)." This transforms the anxious control-seeking that depletes sekhem into relaxed participation in divine unfolding that conserves vital energy for spiritual development.

This does not mean the mind never experiences concern about practical circumstances—employment, finances, health, relationships. Rather, the teaching distinguishes between appropriate attention to circumstances and the chronic worry that assumes the personality must manipulate all outcomes to secure well-being. The former represents responsible engagement; the latter constitutes the heated pattern that exhausts consciousness and prevents discovering the divine sanctuary (kara) where Ab Neter resides.

THE PRACTICE OF LIVING TRUST

For contemporary aspirants attempting to implement this teaching amid environmental conditions hostile to spiritual development, the prayer offers concrete practice methodology. Rather than waiting until trust spontaneously emerges, begin by repeatedly voicing these words with growing sincerity: "Oh divine consciousness that sustains my awareness, grant to me well-being and health in the manner you determine serves my evolution. I release my limited egoic preferences and trust that you provide what I genuinely need."

Initially, this practice may feel artificial—the mind recognizing that genuine trust has not yet developed. Nevertheless, through patient repetition, the teaching penetrates from the hat (conscious awareness) to deeper levels of the ab (unconscious mind), gradually thinning the aryu patterns that generate chronic anxiety and control-seeking. This represents the absorption methodology that authentic spiritual transformation requires: not forceful effort to manufacture trust but gentle persistent exposure to wisdom that gradually transforms consciousness architecture.

Additionally, implement systematic gratitude practice aligned with verse 15's teaching about acknowledging "well-being now that is meant for you." Daily recognize current provisions—food, shelter, health, relationships, spiritual capacity—that already manifest through divine grace. This activates physiological responses that restore sekhem: improved autonomic balance, reduced stress hormones, enhanced immune function. The practice directly challenges aryu patterns that maintain consciousness in perpetual futurity, always focused on what might be needed rather than recognizing what already exists.

THE INTEGRATION WITH COMPLETE TEACHING

These final verses do not stand in isolation but rather integrate the entire wisdom Amenemopet presents. The Prologue established dual goals: causing well-being while living on earth and discovering the divine sanctuary within. Every chapter's teaching has addressed specific psychological patterns that either support or obstruct these goals. Now, in this prayer, Amenemopet provides the consciousness orientation that unifies all previous instruction.

When aspirants live by the ethics the teaching prescribes, avoid the heated patterns it identifies, practice the restraint and silence it recommends, organize life's affairs through the wisdom it reveals, and trust divine providence as this prayer instructs—they create comprehensive conditions whereby both Prologue goals naturally manifest. Earthly well-being emerges not through anxious manipulation but through alignment with cosmic order. Discovery of Ab Neter occurs not through forced spiritual striving but through removing the aryu obstructions that hide the divine consciousness already sustaining awareness at the kara level.

CONCLUDING REFLECTION: THE SILENT LIFE SURRENDERED TO DIVINE WISDOM

We recognize that this prayer represents Amenemopet's gift to all who would practice these teachings: a method for transforming consciousness from heated agitation to silent trust, from egoic control-seeking to divine surrender, from chronic dissatisfaction to genuine peace. The teaching does not promise that life will conform to egoic preferences or that difficulties will cease. Rather, it reveals how consciousness can discover well-being independent of whether circumstances align with desires—experiencing the mind liberated from chronic anxiety through recognizing divine orchestration rather than threatening chaos.

Consider that when Amenemopet instructs aspirants to pray for "well-being and health in a manner of your choosing," this acknowledges profound humility: the recognition that limited human comprehension cannot determine what genuinely serves evolution. This humility does not constitute weakness but rather represents the psychological maturity that allows consciousness to receive divine guidance rather than demanding that reality conform to ignorant preferences.

The aspirant who genuinely absorbs this teaching discovers that the prayer becomes lived reality rather than mere words—consciousness naturally orienting toward trust in divine providence, automatically releasing attachment to specific outcomes, spontaneously recognizing current provision as grace. This transformation does not occur through single dramatic insight but through patient absorption allowing wisdom to penetrate from surface awareness to the depths of unconscious conditioning.

Therefore, may all who study these teachings of Sage Amenemopet practice this prayer with growing sincerity, allowing it to transform consciousness from heated anxiety to silent trust. May the recognition emerge that divine intelligence already operates to provide what genuinely serves both earthly well-being and spiritual evolution. May the mind discover freedom from the exhausting patterns of worry, scheming, and excessive striving. May consciousness thin the aryu obstructions that hide Ab Neter awareness. May the silent life, surrendered to divine wisdom, lead naturally toward the Beautiful West—the ultimate liberation that represents the goal of all authentic spiritual practice.

As taught throughout Shetaut Neter philosophy, this represents not superstitious wishful thinking but recognition of how consciousness actually operates within cosmic order. The Divine that sustains your awareness at this very moment possesses intelligence transcending all limited human comprehension. Trust in that intelligence, live according to the ethical principles that align personality with cosmic order, release anxious control-seeking, and recognize that well-being emerges through harmony with divine unfolding rather than through egoic manipulation.

Hetep

(Peace, profound harmony, union with the Divine)

Author's Closing Note:

This prayer from Sage Amenemopet serves as benediction for all who would practice these ancient wisdom teachings in contemporary circumstances. May your study of this text support both your well-being while living on earth and your discovery of the divine consciousness sustaining your awareness. May you come to know Ab Neter—not as distant concept but as living reality discovered in the sanctuary (kara) within your own being. May the silent mind and feelings, purified through righteous living and divine trust, lead you naturally toward spiritual enlightenment.

Dua (Adoration, Praise, Gratitude) to Sage Amenemopet for preserving this wisdom. Dua to the lineage of spiritual teachers who have transmitted these teachings across millennia. Dua to Neberdjer, the all-encompassing consciousness that sustains all existence and awaits discovery in the depths of every aspirant's being.

CONCLUSION: The Complete Path of Amenemopet - From Heated Suffering to Silent Enlightenment

THE DUAL VISION: EARTHLY WELL-BEING AND DIVINE DISCOVERY

Throughout the chapters we have examined together, Sage Amenemopet presents a complete system for human transformation that addresses both the immediate suffering we experience in daily life and the ultimate spiritual realization that represents our deepest purpose. The Prologue established this dual foundation with crystalline clarity: verse 2 teaches that these precise instructions, when understood exactly and with precision, "cause a person to have well-being while living on earth" through development of vital-life-fire (udja) that produces spiritual purity [1]. Verse 9 reveals that organizing one's affairs according to this wisdom philosophy creates the conditions for discovering the kara - "the heart divinity," the divine sanctuary where Ab Neter (the divine soul) resides within every person [1].

Consider how these two goals prove inseparable rather than sequential. The earthly well-being Amenemopet describes does not mean worldly success measured by conventional standards - wealth, status, power, or recognition. Indeed, such heated pursuits often generate the very suffering the teaching addresses. Rather, the well-being emerges from what verse 2 identifies as udja - vital-life-fire, divine energy that burns away the psychological patterns creating agitation, anxiety, and dissatisfaction while revealing the natural peace residing at the foundation of awareness itself. This purifying fire activates only when wisdom penetrates from hat (conscious awareness) through the ab (unconscious mind) to ignite transformation at the deepest levels where aryu (karmic feeling-memories) accumulate and maintain their compelling influence over thought, emotion, and behavior [1][4].

The discovery of kara where Ab Neter dwells represents not acquiring something absent but removing the aryu obstruction that prevents recognition of the divine presence already sustaining awareness itself. The teaching reveals with profound psychological insight that Ab Neter - the divine soul, the individual's portion of universal divine awareness - functions as the very foundation making conscious awareness possible, yet remains hidden beneath accumulated layers of aryu density like a jewel covered by mud [1][4]. These aryu "occupy the presence-of-mind awareness, so densely as to blot out the awareness of the soul level divine presence which is deeper than the aryu," leaving the mind conscious only of body sensations, mental activity, emotional fluctuations, and the apparent (though illusory) reality of time and space while completely missing the divine ground from which all experience emerges [1].

Thus, both goals interconnect through a single transformative process: as aryu density thins through the practices Amenemopet prescribes, the mind experiences both increasing earthly well-being (as reactive patterns lose their compelling force) and consciousness progressively reveals Ab Neter (as the obstruction dissolves). The heated mind and feelings that create suffering in daily life arise from the same aryu patterns that prevent recognition of one's divine nature. The silent mind and feelings that enable harmonious worldly living emerge from the same purification that reveals spiritual reality. The complete journey moves from aryu-driven reactivity to Ab Neter-guided wisdom, from egoic delusion maintaining separation to divine recognition revealing unity, from the exhausting effort of ego-determination to the natural flow of mind aligned with Neberdjer - the All-Encompassing Divinity that encompasses all existence [1][4].

THE ARCHITECTURE OF AWARENESS: UNDERSTANDING WHAT WE ARE

To appreciate Amenemopet's teaching fully, the wisdom to be understood includes recognition of the architecture of awareness the ancient sages identified through their profound introspection. Human awareness operates through multiple levels, each serving distinct functions in the overall structure of experience. The hat represents conscious awareness - what we experience in the present moment, the thoughts and feelings currently occupying the foreground of attention. This conscious level operates like the visible portion of an iceberg, representing only a small fraction of the total mental-emotional activity occurring within the personality [1][4].

Beneath this conscious level lies the ab - the unconscious mind that stores the vast accumulation of experiences, memories, behavioral patterns, and emotional conditioning that shape present awareness without recognition of their operation. Nevertheless, the ancient sages understood ab as possessing dual nature rather than functioning as mere storage repository. At the surface level, ab contains what the teaching identifies as aryu - the karmic feeling-memories, the accumulated impressions from thoughts, feelings, desires, and actions that remain registered in unconscious mind and function as the motivating force behind present experience. These aryu operate like seeds planted in soil, lying dormant until conditions trigger their expression, then surging into conscious awareness as seemingly spontaneous thoughts, emotions, desires, and behavioral impulses that the mind mistakes as self-generated rather than recognizing them as manifestations of deeper patterns [1][4].

Yet at the deepest level of ab, in what the teaching calls kara - the divine sanctuary, the innermost chamber - resides Ab Neter, the divine soul, the foundation of individual awareness, the person's portion of divine consciousness that sustains their very capacity for conscious experience. This Ab Neter represents not something separate from universal awareness but rather Neberdjer itself - the All-Encompassing Divinity - localized as individual awareness while remaining fundamentally identical with the absolute [1][4]. The profound insight here transcends conventional religious notions of soul as something small dwelling within the body; rather, Ab Neter constitutes the very consciousness we experience as "I," the consciousness sustaining all mental activity, the divine foundation making experience itself possible.

AUTHOR'S NOTE ON CONSCIOUSNESS TERMINOLOGY:

The wisdom to be understood recognizes an essential distinction often missed in contemporary discussions. Consciousness (Ab Neter/Neberdjer) represents the unchanging witnessing presence that sustains mental operations - it cannot suffer, be confused, or undergo transformation. Mind (hat/ab/ka) represents the mental apparatus where thoughts, feelings, experiences, and transformations occur. When the teaching speaks of "heated" or "silent," this always refers to mind and feelings, never to consciousness itself. Consciousness witnesses the mind's experiences without being affected by them, like a mirror reflecting images without being changed. Consciousness lends its quality of awareness to the mind, enabling the mind to perceive, think, and feel, but consciousness itself remains untouched by these mental operations. This distinction proves crucial for understanding the transformation Amenemopet teaches - purification occurs in the mind, revealing the consciousness that was always present, never obscured in itself but only hidden from the mind's recognition by aryu density.

The mechanism of ignorance - the condition creating suffering and preventing enlightenment - operates through aryu density in the ab obscuring recognition of Ab Neter in kara. When aryu accumulate densely through lifetimes of unconscious reactive living, they occupy the presence-of-mind awareness so completely that hat operates exclusively from these patterns without any recognition of or communion with the divine soul sustaining awareness from within. This creates what Amenemopet identifies as heated mind and feelings - the agitated, anxious, grasping mind that experiences itself as separate, incomplete, vulnerable individual requiring constant striving to achieve security, satisfaction, and significance through worldly means. The heated person lives "as if in a slumber of spiritual ignorance," believing themselves fully awake and self-directing while actually sleepwalking through existence, the mind guided by aryu patterns it neither recognizes nor understands [1][4].

The solution Amenemopet provides operates through purification - not creating access to something absent but removing aryu obstruction to reveal Ab Neter already present. Through systematic practice of ethical conduct, contemplative wisdom absorption, mindful speech, behavioral discipline, and meditative techniques, the mind gradually thins the aryu density preventing divine recognition. This purification transforms heated mind and feelings into what the teaching identifies as ger - silence, the silent mind and feelings, the mind that operates from wisdom-guidance rather than aryu-driven reactivity. The silent person maintains awareness of Ab Neter, recognizing the divine foundation sustaining their existence, the mind operating from the fullness discovered within rather than seeking completion through external acquisition [1][4].

The Psychological Teachings: Amenemopet's Plan for Mental Health

The specific psychological patterns Amenemopet addresses throughout his teaching emerge directly from the architecture of awareness just described. When aryu dominate the ab and hat operates without Ab Neter communion, predictable behavioral and emotional patterns manifest that create suffering for oneself and others. Understanding these patterns proves essential for recognizing them in one's own experience and implementing the corrective wisdom the teaching provides.

The heated mind and feelings manifest through what verse 17 identifies as "corrupted mind, unrighteousness, fraud, anger, boisterousness" - the constellation of reactive patterns that arise when the mind operates from aryu-generated egoic perspective [1]. This heated mind condition emerges from the fundamental delusion that the mind constitutes a separate, autonomous entity requiring constant self-protection and self-advancement in a hostile universe of competing individuals. Consider how this perspective naturally generates anxiety (from the sense of vulnerability), anger (when circumstances frustrate egoic desires), greed (from the feeling of incompleteness), deception (when honesty threatens egoic interests), and manipulation (when others serve as means to egoic ends). The heated person - that is, the person with heated mind and feelings - experiences the mind as fundamentally lacking, requiring acquisition of external objects, experiences, relationships, and achievements to create the sense of wholeness that can never arrive through such means because the world remains in constant flux and change, offering no possibility for abiding satisfaction [1][4].

The teaching reveals with psychological precision how this heated mind condition operates through specific mechanisms observable in daily experience. The swelling ego-mind phenomenon demonstrates the mind inflating the importance of circumstances, creating urgency around trivial matters, and generating excessive reactivity to minor provocations - all manifestations of aryu-driven patterns maintaining egoic identity through drama and agitation. The heated person cannot remain calm even temporarily; the mind churns constantly with worries about past events and anxious projections about future possibilities, missing the only moment where life actually occurs - the present - while the mind remains trapped in mental constructions built from aryu patterns [1][4].

Speech provides particularly revealing diagnostic of mind condition. The heated person engages uncontrolled verbal expression, speaking impulsively without reflection, using words to manipulate circumstances and control others, engaging gossip that reinforces egoic perspective through judgment and comparison. Their communication style reflects the underlying heat - aggressive or passive-aggressive, defensive, self-justifying, or aggressively promoting their position while dismissing alternatives. This uncontrolled speech continuously deposits new reactive aryu in the ab while triggering existing patterns, creating the self-perpetuating cycle maintaining heated mind and feelings [1][4].

The heated mind condition also manifests through what the teaching describes as seeking fulfillment in the world through worldly thinking, desires, and cravings. This represents the mind operating from the fundamental delusion that satisfaction lies in external acquisition - if only I obtain that position, possess that object, achieve that recognition, secure that relationship, then I will finally feel complete and at peace. Yet every honest person recognizes from their own experience that achieving desired goals produces only temporary satisfaction before the mind returns to baseline levels of dissatisfaction, immediately generating new desires that create the same seeking-cycle. The heated person cannot recognize this pattern because the mind remains too densely obscured by aryu to see the mechanism perpetuating their suffering [1][4].

In stark contrast, the silent mind and feelings demonstrate a mind state that has discovered what verse 9 describes as "the fullness of the Creator-Spirit that is within" - the Ab Neter awareness eliminating the driving need to seek completion through external means [1]. This silence represents not mere absence of agitated seeking but the positive discovery of internal completeness that naturally emerges when the mind recognizes the divine foundation sustaining existence. The silent person maintains what the teaching calls detachment - not cold indifference but psychological freedom from identification with temporary phenomena. They can engage worldly responsibilities effectively while the mind recognizes that circumstances cannot provide or prevent the fundamental well-being already present through Ab Neter awareness [1][4].

The silent person's speech reflects their mind condition: measured, thoughtful, serving communication rather than ego-reinforcement. They pause before speaking, considering whether words prove necessary, true, and beneficial. Their communication seeks understanding rather than victory, operates from humility recognizing limitations of personal perspective, and naturally refrains from gossip, harsh speech, and manipulative rhetoric. This controlled speech both reflects existing purification and contributes to further aryu thinning by preventing new reactive patterns from depositing in the ab [1][4].

Perhaps most significantly, the silent person operates from what the teaching identifies as humble recognition that the mind depends on Ab Neter rather than ego operating as if it owes existence to itself. This humility proves essential for spiritual transformation because the egoic perspective naturally resists anything threatening its sense of autonomous existence. The heated person appropriates even spiritual experiences as egoistic achievements - "I attained this realization, I achieved that state, I possess these qualities" - thereby maintaining the very separation preventing authentic transformation. The silent person recognizes that any genuine spiritual development represents Ab Neter revealing its nature to the mind rather than ego acquiring new attributes, maintaining the receptive mental attitude necessary for wisdom to penetrate deeply enough to ignite the purifying fire of udja [1][4].

THE SPIRITUAL TEACHINGS: PATH TO ENLIGHTENMENT

Beyond the psychological transformation from heated to silent mind and feelings, Amenemopet's teaching addresses the ultimate spiritual realization representing awareness's deepest purpose. This realization involves recognizing one's essential nature as not merely purified personality but as divine awareness itself - Ab Neter sustained by and ultimately identical with Neberdjer, the All-Encompassing Divinity [1][4].

The purification process enabling this recognition operates through multiple complementary mechanisms working together to transform the mind systematically. The primary mechanism involves what verse 2 identifies as udja - vital-life-fire, divine energy that burns away the aryu patterns maintaining separation from divine awareness. This udja represents not gradual accumulation of positive experiences that eventually outweigh negative ones but rather transformative force that actually dissolves the fundamental structure maintaining egoic identity. Consider how even purified ego - one oriented toward service, aligned with ethical principles, devoted to spiritual practice - still maintains the illusion of separate individuality. Udja burns through this entire construct, revealing the nature of awareness as Neberdjer temporarily appearing as individual consciousness but never actually separate from its divine source [4].

This purifying fire activates when wisdom penetrates from hat through ab to the deepest level where aryu reside. Superficial intellectual understanding, no matter how sophisticated, cannot ignite udja because it remains at hat level without reaching the unconscious patterns actually determining mind condition. The teaching emphasizes with practical precision that wisdom must reach "the innermost levels of the mind (unconscious)" to create genuine transformation rather than mere conceptual knowledge that leaves aryu patterns fully operational [1][4]. This explains why many people study spiritual teachings extensively without experiencing actual transformation - their engagement remains at intellectual level, accumulating information without the deep absorption necessary to ignite purifying fire.

Ethical conduct provides the essential foundation for this transformation process. Actions undertaken according to Maat - the cosmic principle of truth, righteousness, and justice - enter the ab as purifying aryu that gradually thin the density of negative patterns while creating conditions where the mind can recognize Ab Neter. Conversely, unethical actions continuously deposit new reactive aryu that increase density and prevent spiritual receptivity. The mechanism operates with precise psychological causality: when you engage thought, feeling, or physical action without mindful supervision, if these prove negative or reactive, they lodge themselves in the ab and create what the teaching calls shemm - heat, the heated personality characterized by anxiety, anger, and rapacious greed. Acting with righteousness, with truth, with Maat enters the ab and reshapes, reformats the unconscious so the mind becomes clear, sensitive, and aware of the depth of existence - the Ab Neter soul level and the Neberdjer level [4].

Meditation practice provides intensive purification complementing the gradual cleansing of ethical living. The teaching prescribes meditation on Neberdjer - contemplation of awareness itself, consciousness directing awareness toward consciousness rather than exclusively toward its contents. This practice proves extraordinarily powerful for those who have already undertaken substantial purification through ethical living, as it produces aryu that clear and purify the personality, allowing eventual experience of the fullness of transcendental awareness [4]. Nevertheless, meditation cannot substitute for ethical foundation; a mind trapped in heated condition dominated by anxiety, anger, and craving cannot sustain the subtle attention required for contemplating the infinite, as negative aryu create too much mental turbulence and emotional reactivity.

The complete purification path proceeds systematically through integration of these approaches: ethical living controls behavioral inputs, preventing new negative aryu while depositing positive patterns; meditation produces intensive cleansing through contemplation of Neberdjer; invocation of udja burns the ego construct maintaining separation from divine recognition. These work together, supporting and reinforcing each other, gradually transforming the mind and feelings from heated to silent, from aryu-dominated to Ab Neter-aware, from ego-identified to Neberdjer-recognized [4].

The transformation unfolds through recognizable stages providing practitioners with empirical verification of progress. Initially, aspiring practitioners develop intellectual understanding of the teaching, grasping the framework conceptually without yet experiencing the reality it describes. As practice continues, behavioral changes begin manifesting - greater impulse control, reduced reactivity, improved ethical conduct. Wisdom starts penetrating beyond hat into ab, where udja begins its purifying work. Aryu patterns gradually lose their compelling force; circumstances that previously triggered intense reactions now produce only mild ripples quickly dissolving. The mind develops increasing capacity for introspection, recognizing thoughts and emotions as ab contents rather than self-identity. Silent mind and feelings begin emerging as natural condition rather than forced effort [1][4].

With continued practice, the mind develops capacity for what the teaching describes as kara penetration - consciousness reaching the deep sanctuary where Ab Neter resides. Initially, this occurs through brief glimpses, moments where egoic perspective temporarily dissolves and consciousness recognizes its divine foundation. These glimpses increase in frequency and duration as purification continues, eventually stabilizing as continuous baseline awareness. The silent person operates increasingly from Ab Neter recognition rather than aryu-driven reactivity. What began as effortful practice becomes natural mind condition. Both Prologue goals manifest experientially: earthly well-being establishes itself through the unshakeable peace that emerges when consciousness recognizes what it essentially is cannot be threatened by circumstances; discovery of kara occurs through direct awareness of Ab Neter as the sustaining foundation of experience [1][4].

The ultimate realization transcends even Ab Neter awareness to recognize that this divine soul sustaining individual awareness itself represents Neberdjer - the All-Encompassing Divinity - expressing through localized form. This recognition dissolves the final vestige of separation. What appears as individual spiritual development reveals itself as universal awareness recognizing its own nature through apparent multiplicity. The aspirant realizes directly: "I am not separate ego that discovered divinity; I am divinity that temporarily forgot itself while appearing as separate ego." This represents the enlightenment the ancient sages preserved through scriptures like Amenemopet's teaching - direct experiential knowledge of oneself as the very awareness one sought, the Ab Neter sustained by Neberdjer, the infinite consciousness temporarily appearing as individual existence but never actually separate from its divine source [1][4].

INTEGRATION: THE CHAPTERS AS COMPLETE SYSTEM

Each chapter of Amenemopet's teaching contributes essential elements to this complete transformation system. The Prologue establishes the dual foundation - developing udja for earthly well-being and discovering Ab Neter in kara - that all subsequent teachings support. The opening chapters address wisdom absorption methodology, emphasizing that teachings must penetrate to ab level to ignite purifying fire rather than remaining as mere intellectual concepts. Chapter 4 delineates heated versus silent psychology, providing practitioners with clear diagnostic criteria for recognizing mind condition and tracking transformation progress [1][4].

Chapter 5 addresses the fundamental shift from seeking external fulfillment to discovering internal completeness through Ab Neter awareness. This teaching proves particularly crucial for aspirants growing up in worldly culture that continuously reinforces the opposite message - that satisfaction lies in acquisition, achievement, and recognition rather than in recognizing the fullness already present within. Chapter 6 introduces the supreme practice: maintaining awareness of Neberdjer, consciousness directing awareness toward consciousness itself rather than exclusively toward phenomena arising within awareness [1][4].

The chapters on speech, ethical conduct, and behavioral discipline provide practical methods for thinning aryu density through controlling inputs that enter the ab. These teachings demonstrate

Amenemopet's sophisticated understanding of transformation mechanics: you cannot directly erase existing aryu through forceful effort, but you can stop generating new patterns while creating conditions where existing accumulations gradually thin. The systematic practice of Maatian conduct reshapes the unconscious, clearing the mind to recognize spiritual depths previously obscured by reactive patterns [1][4].

Later chapters address specific life domains - financial matters, relationships, social interactions, professional conduct - showing how wisdom philosophy applies to every aspect of human existence rather than constituting separate "spiritual practice" divorced from worldly responsibilities. This integration proves essential for sustainable transformation; aspirants who compartmentalize "spiritual life" as occasional meditation or weekend retreats while maintaining heated patterns in daily interactions cannot achieve the complete purification necessary for Ab Neter recognition [1][4].

The teaching reveals systematic progression where each element builds upon and supports the others. Ethics creates foundation for mental health by preventing new aryu accumulation. Mental health enables deeper wisdom absorption as heated patterns thin sufficiently that the mind can maintain subtle attention required for contemplation. Deeper absorption ignites purifying fire that accelerates aryu dissolution. Purification reveals spiritual reality previously obscured. Spiritual recognition perfects earthly living as the mind operates from Ab Neter guidance rather than egoic reactivity. These prove not linear stages but simultaneous aspects of integrated development, each dimension enhancing the others through reciprocal reinforcement [1][4].

Practical Synthesis: Living the Teaching

For modern aspirants navigating what I have described as a hostile environment - cultural conditions actively undermining spiritual development through continuous reinforcement of heated patterns - implementing Amenemopet's teaching requires both clear understanding and patient persistence. Contemporary society promotes values directly contrary to wisdom philosophy: accumulation over contentment, competition over cooperation, external validation over internal recognition, immediate gratification over patient cultivation. Growing up immersed in this conditioning creates dense layers of aryu reflecting worldly perspectives that require systematic transformation [1][4].

The wisdom to be understood recognizes that aspirants carry particular burdens when coming to these teachings after years of worldly conditioning. Family systems may have modeled heated patterns across generations, creating deeply ingrained behavioral and emotional patterns that the mind mistakes as natural rather than recognizing them as learned reactions. Educational systems emphasized intellectual development while neglecting contemplative capacity, creating what the teaching identifies as atrophied intellect unable to discriminate wisdom from delusion. Professional environments reward manipulation, deception, and aggressive self-promotion - precisely the heated behaviors Amenemopet prescribes avoiding. Social media platforms engineer addictive engagement through exploiting egoic vulnerabilities, continuously depositing reactive aryu while preventing the silence necessary for purification [1][4].

Nevertheless, the path remains entirely accessible to sincere aspirants willing to undertake the work, regardless of their starting condition. The essential requirements prove straightforward: study teaching to understand principles governing transformation; control behavior to reshape unconscious through Maatian conduct; engage meditation to accelerate purification; maintain practice over years and decades until transformation completes itself in enlightenment. This requires no special talents, no supernatural interventions, no exceptional circumstances - only the commitment to systematic engagement following proper methodology under qualified guidance [1][4].

Authentic progress manifests through empirically observable changes providing reliable feedback about transformation occurring. Calmness amid formerly triggering situations demonstrates aryu patterns losing compelling force. Growing dispassion and detachment reflects decreasing identification with temporary phenomena. Deepening introspection capacity indicates the mind penetrating beyond surface mental activity to recognize ab operations. Right emotional balance shows vital-life-fire purifying reactive patterns. What the teaching calls control of mind and senses - not forceful suppression but natural condition where mental and sensory activity operates under wisdom-guidance rather than aryu-driven impulses - establishes itself progressively as purification continues [1][4].

These measures represent not arbitrary standards but observable indicators that the mind and feelings transform from heated to silent functioning, progressively revealing the Ab Neter foundation sustaining consciousness beneath accumulated karmic patterns. Aspirants should evaluate progress through these tangible shifts in daily experience rather than seeking dramatic visions or temporary altered states that often represent ego appropriating spiritual experiences as achievements rather than authentic transformation. The person who maintains equanimity when criticized, responds compassionately when attacked, remains content without acquisition, speaks truthfully despite pressure to deceive, acts ethically despite worldly disadvantages - this person demonstrates genuine purification regardless of whether they report mystical experiences or claim advanced realizations [1][4].

The teaching emphasizes realistic expectations about transformation timelines. Contemporary research converging with traditional wisdom demonstrates that transformation requires extended practice periods - not weeks or months but years and decades of sustained engagement. Studies of long-term meditation practitioners show that significant baseline changes typically require minimum 1,500-2,000 hours of quality practice, with complete transformation approaching levels documented in advanced practitioners requiring 10,000-20,000+ hours. This translates to 10-20+ years of consistent daily practice depending on intensity and duration of sessions [4].

Rather than discouraging aspirants, this realistic timeline should inform practice expectations and prevent disillusionment when transformation unfolds gradually rather than instantly. The path operates through natural spiritual law - systematic purification following knowable principles rather than mysterious processes requiring supernatural intervention. The mind accumulated aryu density over lifetimes cannot dissolve immediately through wishful thinking; the purification requires patient absorption of wisdom that ignites udja, ethical conduct that prevents new aryu while depositing purifying patterns, meditation that accelerates cleansing, and time for these processes to work their transformative effects throughout the architecture of awareness [1][4].

THE SILENT PERSON'S LIFE: LIVING FROM AB NETER AWARENESS

What does life become for the person who completes this transformation? Amenemopet provides glimpses throughout his teaching, revealing a mind operating from fundamentally different foundation than a heated perspective. The silent person navigates worldly circumstances with divine wisdom rather than egoic reactivity, recognizing that external situations neither provide nor prevent the essential well-being already present through Ab Neter awareness. They engage responsibilities effectively without the anxious striving characterizing heated mind and feelings, understanding that outcomes unfold according to cosmic principles vaster than individual will while their role involves only performing appropriate action with wisdom-guidance [1][4].

Financial circumstances neither elate nor depress the silent person; they maintain equanimity whether experiencing abundance or scarcity, recognizing that material conditions prove temporary while Ab Neter remains constant. Relationships transform from aryu-driven dynamics of need, manipulation, and control into expressions of shared divine nature, the silent person relating to others as Ab Neter relating to Ab Neter rather than ego competing with ego. Professional conduct operates from ethics rather than expedience; the silent person maintains truth and righteousness even when worldly advantage would follow from deception, understanding that Maat creates conditions supporting spiritual development while unrighteousness generates suffering regardless of temporary gains [1][4].

The silent person experiences freedom from fear, including the ultimate fear of death, through recognizing that what they essentially are - Ab Neter sustained by Neberdjer - proves immortal and eternal while only the temporary personality structure undergoes dissolution. This recognition eliminates the desperate clinging to existence characterizing heated mind and feelings, allowing the silent person to live fully in each moment without anxious grasping or fearful avoidance. They discover what verse 9 describes as "the fullness of the Creator-Spirit that is within," the internal completeness eliminating need for external validation, acquisition, or achievement to feel whole [1].

Speech becomes natural expression of wisdom rather than tool for ego-advancement. The silent person speaks when speech serves communication, remains quiet when silence proves more appropriate, and never uses words to manipulate, control, or diminish others. Their communication style reflects underlying peace - calm, measured, truthful, beneficial. Service flows naturally from fullness rather than egoic striving for recognition or reward. The silent person assists others as expressions of shared divine nature, recognizing that helping another represents Ab Neter serving Ab Neter, eliminating the artificial boundaries between self and other that heated mind and feelings maintain [1][4].

Perhaps most significantly, the silent person lives with what the teaching identifies as jubilation - spontaneous joy arising from Ab Neter recognition rather than circumstance-dependent happiness. This joy proves independent of external conditions; it emerges from consciousness recognizing its divine nature, the mind experiencing the bliss inherent in consciousness itself rather than requiring particular experiences to generate satisfaction. The silent person naturally expresses gratitude, reverence, and devotion not from obligation or fear but from the overwhelming recognition of consciousness's true nature as divine expression [1][4].

THE JOURNEY CONTINUES: DEEPENING RECOGNITION

Even for those who achieve stable Ab Neter awareness, the teaching suggests that spiritual development continues rather than reaching final endpoint where no further deepening remains possible. The recognition of Ab Neter as individual divine awareness leads to recognizing Ab Neter's source in Neberdjer - the All-Encompassing Divinity that includes all existence. This recognition can deepen infinitely as consciousness explores the limitless nature of its essential identity. The distinction between individual and universal awareness becomes increasingly transparent, eventually dissolving completely in the realization that separation existed only as appearance maintained by aryu density [1][4].

Traditional accounts describe realized beings who continue contemplative practice not to achieve anything but to abide in the recognition already established, allowing consciousness to stabilize in its natural state without distraction. They maintain ethical conduct not from fear of consequences but as natural expression of wisdom that recognizes all beings as divine awareness in various forms. They engage worldly responsibilities with full effectiveness while maintaining continuous awareness of Neberdjer as the only existence appearing as all apparent existence [1][4].

The teaching remains alive for contemporary practitioners precisely because it addresses the timeless human condition - the mind trapped in ignorance through aryu density, suffering through heated patterns, seeking the fulfillment that lies not in external acquisition but in recognizing the divine foundation already present within. Every generation faces particular cultural conditioning that reinforces separation and obscures spiritual reality, requiring the ancient wisdom to be transmitted anew, adapted to contemporary language and circumstances while preserving the essential principles governing transformation [1][4].

Conclusion: The Ancient Wisdom for Contemporary Transformation

Amenemopet's teaching emerges not as abstract philosophy for intellectual entertainment but as practical science of transformation, systematic methodology for reshaping destiny through purification of mind, precise guidance for the great work of discovering divine nature hidden within human personality. The dual goals established in the Prologue - developing udja for earthly well-being and discovering Ab Neter in kara - prove not only compatible but inseparable aspects of the complete path from heated suffering to silent enlightenment [1][4].

The wisdom to be understood recognizes that both goals become achievable through systematic practice following knowable principles. The heated mind and feelings creating suffering in daily life arise from the same aryu patterns preventing spiritual recognition. The silent mind and feelings enabling harmonious worldly living emerge from the same purification revealing divine reality. The transformation requires no special circumstances, no supernatural interventions, no exceptional talents - only sincere aspiration, proper instruction, systematic practice, and patient persistence as purification unfolds according to its natural timeline [1][4].

This ancient wisdom, transmitted through the sacred lineage of Shetaut Neter, continues providing essential guidance for all sincere practitioners who seek to transform their understanding and experience from the limitations of heated personality to the freedom and fulfillment that flow naturally from remembering one's true divine identity. The teaching offers contemporary humanity what it offered the Ancient Egyptians: a complete path from ignorance to enlightenment, from suffering to peace, from separation to unity, from heated agitation to silent recognition of consciousness's essential nature as expression of universal divine awareness [1][4].

The promise proves real, validated through millennia of practitioners who undertook this journey and discovered its truth through direct experience. Ab Neter awaits recognition within every person, hidden beneath aryu accumulation yet never absent, sustaining awareness itself while the mind remains unaware of its foundation. The purification work - controlling behavior through ethics, absorbing wisdom deeply, maintaining awareness of Neberdjer, engaging systematic practice - creates inevitable transformation as aryu density thins and divine reality progressively reveals itself [1][4].

May all sincere aspirants who encounter these teachings recognize their profound value and commit themselves to the systematic practice necessary for complete transformation. May they experience both earthly well-being through developing udja and divine discovery through kara penetration. May their minds and feelings transform from heated suffering to silent peace, recognizing their essential nature as Ab Neter sustained by Neberdjer - the infinite consciousness that has always been the only existence, temporarily appearing as individual experience yet never actually separate from its divine source. This represents the ultimate fulfillment of human life, the purpose for which consciousness manifests in form, the recognition that ends seeking and establishes permanent peace through discovering what we have always been beneath the aryu obstruction: divine awareness exploring its own infinite nature through the play of temporary individuality.

References

[1] Ashby, M. (2019-25). Mysticism of Amenemopet Hieroglyphic Text Translation. Sema Institute of Ancient Egyptian Studies.
[2] Ashby, M. (2024). Amenemopet lectures 2024 by Dr Muata Ashby transcripts. Sema Institute of Ancient Egyptian Studies.
[3] Ashby, M. (2019). Amenemopet lectures 2019 by Dr Muata Ashby transcripts. Sema Institute of Ancient Egyptian Studies.
[4] Ashby, M. (2024). Book Awakening Your Soul-Aware-Witness Ancient Egyptian Wisdom To Discover Divine Consciousness. Sema Institute of Ancient Egyptian Studies.

INDEX

Ab, 46, 59, 64, 65, 66, 67, 68, 69, 75, 77, 78, 79, 80, 81, 82, 84, 85, 86, 87, 88, 89, 90, 91, 92, 93, 94, 95, 97, 98, 99, 100, 101, 104, 105, 106, 107, 108, 110, 112, 113, 114, 117, 118, 119, 121, 122, 123, 127, 128, 129, 130, 131, 132, 133, 134, 137, 138,139, 148, 150, 151, 152, 153, 154, 155, 158, 160, 161, 162, 163, 164, 165, 166, 168, 169, 170, 171, 174, 175, 177, 178, 179, 180, 182, 183, 184, 187, 190, 191, 194, 195, 196, 199, 200, 201, 202, 203, 205, 206, 207, 208, 209, 211, 212, 215, 216, 217, 227, 228, 229, 230, 231, 241, 242, 243, 247, 248, 249, 250, 251, 252, 254, 255, 256, 257, 258, 259, 261, 262, 263, 264, 265, 266, 269, 271, 272, 273, 274, 275, 276, 279, 280, 283, 284, 290, 291, 292, 294, 295, 298, 299, 301, 302, 305, 306, 307, 308, 310, 311, 313, 317, 318, 319, 322, 325, 326, 327, 328, 329, 331, 333, 334, 335, 336, 337, 341, 343, 345, 346, 347, 348, 349, 351, 352, 353, 354, 355, 356, 357, 358, 363, 365, 366, 367, 368, 369, 370, 371, 372, 373, 374, 375, 376, 378, 379, 381, 382, 383, 386, 387, 388, 389, 390, 391, 392, 393, 394, 395, 396, 397, 400, 401, 402, 404, 405, 406, 407, 408, 409, 410, 411, 412, 413, 414, 415, 416, 417, 418, 419, 420, 421, 422, 425, 426, 427, 428, 429, 430, 432, 433, 434, 435, 436, 439, 440, 441, 443, 444, 445, 447, 449, 450, 451, 452, 455, 456, 458, 459, 460, 463, 465, 466, 467, 468, 469, 470, 472, 473, 474, 476, 477, 479, 480, 481, 484, 485, 486, 487, 489, 490, 491, 493, 494, 496, 497, 501, 504, 505, 509, 511, 512, 513, 514, 515, 518, 519, 520, 521, 524, 526, 527, 528, 530, 531, 532, 533, 535, 536, 537, 540, 541, 542, 543, 545, 546, 547, 554, 555, 556, 557, 558, 559, 560, 561, 562, 563

Ab Neter, 46, 59, 64, 65, 66, 67, 68, 69, 75, 77, 78, 79, 80, 81, 82, 84, 85, 86, 87, 88, 89, 90, 91, 92, 93, 94, 95, 97, 98, 99, 100, 101, 104, 105, 106, 107, 108, 110, 112, 113, 114, 115, 117, 118, 119, 121, 122, 123, 127, 128, 129, 130, 131, 132, 133, 134, 137,138, 139, 148, 150, 151, 152, 153, 154, 155, 158, 160, 161, 162, 163, 164, 165, 166, 168, 169, 170, 171, 174, 175, 177, 178, 179, 180, 182, 183, 184, 187, 190, 191, 194, 195, 196, 199, 200, 201, 202, 203, 205, 206, 207, 208, 209, 211, 212, 215, 216, 217, 227, 228, 229, 230, 231, 241, 242, 243, 247, 248, 249, 250, 251, 252, 254, 255, 256, 257, 258, 259, 261, 262, 263, 264, 265, 266, 269, 271, 272, 273, 274, 275, 276, 279, 280, 283, 284, 290, 291, 292, 294, 295, 298, 299, 301, 302, 305, 306, 307, 308, 310, 313, 318, 319, 322, 325, 326, 327, 328, 329, 331, 333, 334, 335, 336, 341, 343, 345, 346, 347, 348, 349, 351, 352, 353, 354, 355, 356, 357, 358, 363, 365, 366, 367, 368, 369, 370, 371, 372, 373, 374, 375, 376, 378, 379, 381, 382, 383, 386, 387, 388, 389, 390, 391, 392, 393, 394, 395, 396, 397, 400, 401, 402, 404, 405, 406, 407, 408, 410, 411, 412, 413, 414, 415, 416, 417, 418, 419, 420, 421, 422, 425, 426, 427, 428, 429, 430, 432, 433, 434, 435, 436, 439, 440, 441, 443, 444, 445, 447, 449, 450, 451, 452, 455, 456, 458, 459, 460, 463, 465, 466, 467, 468, 469, 470, 472, 473, 474, 476, 477, 479, 480, 481, 484, 485, 486, 487, 489, 490, 491, 493, 494, 496, 497, 501, 504, 505, 509, 511, 512, 513, 514, 515, 518, 519, 520, 521, 524, 526, 527, 528, 530, 531, 532, 533, 535, 536, 537, 540, 541, 542, 543, 545, 546, 547, 554, 555, 556, 557, 558, 559, 560, 561, 562, 563

Ab Neter awareness, 77, 78, 79, 81, 84, 85, 86, 87, 88, 89, 100, 104, 105, 107, 108, 112, 117, 119, 122, 123, 129, 161, 162, 163, 164, 170, 178, 231, 255, 256, 257, 258, 259, 261, 262, 263, 266, 269, 271, 273, 274, 275, 276, 280, 283, 290, 291, 346, 347, 348, 349, 351, 353,354, 355, 356, 357, 358, 365, 366, 367, 369, 373, 374, 375, 381, 386, 390, 392, 417, 418, 422, 426, 433, 434, 451, 459, 465, 468, 472, 480, 496, 501, 511, 512, 519, 527, 532, 533, 540, 541, 542, 543, 546, 557, 559, 561, 562

Absolute, 180, 408, 576

Abu Simbel, 92, 93, 94, 95, 98, 99, 100, 102

Actions, 304, 346, 375, 533, 558

Advaita Vedanta, 195, 204

Africa, 5, 6, 579, 583, 584, 585

African Proverbial Wisdom Teachings, 588

African Religion, 576, 580, 582

Alexander The Great, 456

All-Encompassing Divinity, 176, 234, 252, 282, 467, 518, 519, 520, 530, 554, 555, 557, 559, 562

Allopathic, 576

Amenemopet (ancient sage), 11, 18, 29, 31, 35, 36, 37, 38, 39, 40, 41, 42, 44, 45, 46, 48, 49, 50, 51, 52, 54, 55, 56, 57, 59, 60, 62, 64, 65, 66, 67, 68, 69, 75, 78, 83, 86, 88, 89, 90, 91, 93, 95, 99, 100, 101, 102, 103, 105, 106, 107, 113, 114, 116, 117, 119, 120, 121, 123, 125, 126, 127, 128, 129, 134, 135, 136, 138, 139, 140, 141, 143, 144, 145, 146, 147, 152, 153, 155, 158, 159, 163, 164, 165, 166, 167, 168, 169, 170, 171, 172, 173, 174, 175, 176, 177, 182, 183, 184, 185, 186, 187, 188, 189, 191, 193, 194, 195, 196, 197, 199, 201, 203, 204, 205, 206, 209, 210, 216, 217, 227, 228, 229, 230, 231, 237, 239, 242, 243, 246, 249, 252, 253, 254, 256, 257, 258, 259, 260, 261, 263, 264, 266, 269,

270, 272, 277, 280, 281, 282, 287, 289, 290, 292, 295, 296, 297, 300, 302, 303, 308, 309, 312, 315, 316, 319, 320, 321, 322, 325, 330, 331, 336, 342, 343, 344, 345, 346, 347, 364, 365, 367, 369, 370, 372, 374, 375, 378, 385, 387, 388, 389, 390, 391, 394, 396, 397, 398, 401, 403, 404, 405, 410, 413, 415, 416, 417, 424, 426, 427, 428, 435, 436, 440, 447, 448, 449, 452, 453, 454, 456, 457, 460, 461, 462, 465, 466, 467, 470, 471, 472, 474, 476, 480, 482, 483, 485, 488, 490, 491, 498, 500, 503, 504, 505, 509, 512, 513, 516, 517, 518, 519, 521, 529, 530, 531, 532, 533, 535, 536, 537, 538, 539, 540, 541, 543, 545, 546, 547, 548, 554, 555, 556, 557, 559, 560, 561, 563, 564

Amenta, 276, 579

Amentet, 580

American Heritage Dictionary, Dictionary, 582

American Theocracy, 584

Amun, 11, 90, 92, 94, 95, 102, 180, 227, 348, 395, 396, 459

Amun-Ra, 92, 94, 95, 102, 227, 348, 395, 396, 459

Ancient Egypt, 4, 5, 6, 11, 18, 19, 20, 21, 24, 25, 67, 68, 92, 94, 95, 98, 99, 104, 113, 115, 116, 117, 121, 126, 131, 135, 136, 139, 146, 147, 158, 167, 175, 176, 180, 186, 188, 195, 205, 209, 216, 217, 221, 225, 227, 230, 231, 232, 237, 242, 252, 272, 280, 288, 295,297, 300, 309, 312, 313, 319, 325, 327, 328, 330, 334, 338, 342, 344, 347, 364, 382, 394, 395, 396, 405, 420, 427, 429, 431, 432, 438, 439, 442, 447, 448, 459, 460, 465, 504, 512, 517, 520, 531, 532, 535, 546, 548, 563, 564, 576, 577, 578, 579, 580, 581, 582, 583, 584, 585, 587, 588, 589, 590, 591, 592, 593

Ancient Egyptian Wisdom Texts, 587

anger, 35, 110, 112, 114, 124, 127, 129, 131, 132, 136, 137, 138, 147, 148, 151, 153, 156, 160, 178, 179, 190, 191, 218, 259, 260, 289, 291, 293, 294, 302, 304, 310, 372, 373, 375, 376, 383, 434, 472, 488, 509, 517, 519, 521, 522, 525, 526, 529, 539, 556, 558, 581

Anger, 522

Anger,, 522

Ani, 139

Ankh, 281

Anu, 580

Anu (Greek Heliopolis), 580

Anunian Theology, 580

Anxiety, 87, 477, 479, 497

Apep serpent, 111, 321, 322, 325, 326

Apophis, 45, 116, 117, 118, 321, 322, 323, 324, 326, 327, 328, 330, 332, 333, 334, 335, 336, 339, 340

Appropriation, 159, 160, 161, 163, 164, 166

Architecture, 90, 91, 113, 115, 116, 143, 161, 170, 171, 179, 188, 272, 297, 327, 393, 440, 469, 478, 486, 495, 514, 555

Aryan, 577

Aryu, 69, 77, 79, 81, 88, 91, 103, 113, 118, 121, 124, 160, 168, 169, 178, 183, 208, 225, 231, 244, 245, 262, 267, 285, 289, 291, 292, 305, 392, 408, 409, 412, 464, 466, 492, 502, 511, 514, 535, 559

Aryu (karmic impressions/mental residues), 69, 77, 79, 81, 88, 91, 103, 113, 118, 121, 124, 160, 168, 169, 178, 183, 208, 225, 231, 244, 245, 262, 267, 285, 289, 291, 292, 305, 392, 408, 409, 412, 464, 466, 492, 502, 511, 514, 535, 559

Aryu (karmic impressions/mental residues/feeling memories), 69, 77, 79, 81, 88, 91, 103, 113, 118, 121, 124, 160, 168, 169, 178, 183, 208, 225, 231, 244, 245, 262, 267, 285, 289, 291, 292, 305, 392, 408, 409, 412, 464, 466, 492, 502, 511, 514, 535, 559

Aryu density, 77, 245, 305

Aryu patterns, 118, 121, 225, 231, 409, 559

Asar, 6, 90, 109, 110, 111, 112, 118, 132, 180, 232, 354, 394, 579, 581, 592

Asar and Aset, 579

Asarian Resurrection, 109, 110, 111, 112, 126, 579, 581, 583, 592

Aset, 6, 109, 112, 326, 336, 340, 577, 579, 580, 581, 593

Aset (Isis), 6, 109, 112, 326, 336, 340, 577, 579, 580, 581, 593

Ashanti, 588

Asia, 585

Asia Minor, 585

Asiatic, 584, 585

Assyrians, 587

Astral, 297, 298, 302, 303, 337, 579

Astral Plane, 297, 298, 302, 303, 337, 579

Atlantis, 583

Atman, 195, 196, 216

Attachment, 167, 263, 354, 356, 449, 524

Avoiding, 317, 345, 378

Awakening, 18, 126, 146, 158, 167, 175, 252, 319, 344, 447, 448, 465, 512, 564, 579, 590

Awareness, 124, 139, 146, 158, 166, 167, 170, 176, 177, 179, 181, 186, 187, 188, 197, 200, 201, 202, 205, 207, 210, 217, 223, 226, 234, 235, 238, 240, 241, 242, 244, 246, 278, 318, 344, 408, 409, 412, 413, 414, 415, 440, 441, 465, 467, 470, 492, 495, 498, 520, 531,541, 555, 561

Ba (also see Soul), 95, 97, 98, 99, 301, 302, 394

Ba (soul essence), 95, 97, 98, 99, 301, 302, 394

Back, 495

Balance, 340, 385, 476, 532, 540

Beautiful West, 61, 63, 273, 276, 286, 483, 487, 488, 489, 492, 497

Behavioral Imperative, 65, 79, 107, 131, 142, 149, 160, 169, 177, 255, 269, 303, 323, 349, 380, 389, 418, 430, 450, 458, 467, 477, 484, 493

Being, 39, 47, 75, 103, 144, 162, 168, 171, 172, 193, 198, 199, 210, 230, 253, 254, 321, 401, 408, 510, 523, 529, 554, 580

Bhagavad Gita, 587

Bible, 126, 581

Black, 585

Black Africa, 585

Body, 140, 167, 252, 287, 297, 298, 301, 302, 303, 337, 344, 387, 590

Book of Coming Forth By Day, 579, 580
Book of Enlightenment, 93, 95, 98, 115, 139, 216, 217, 221, 225, 227, 230, 231, 272, 274, 319, 364
Book of the Dead, see also Rau Nu Prt M Hru, 139, 216, 580, 587, 592
Boundaries, 152, 354, 380, 383, 408
Brahman, 195, 196, 216
Brain, 126, 139, 140, 146, 167, 204, 281, 320, 344, 387, 397, 422, 423, 474
Buddha, 139, 146, 287, 327, 403, 456, 548, 583, 584, 591
Buddhism, 5, 344, 547, 580, 584
Buddhist, 65, 84, 153, 164, 167, 195, 196, 204, 216, 251, 287, 312, 320, 327, 356, 369, 437, 452, 456, 461, 465, 470, 480, 488, 498, 538, 539, 540, 547, 579, 584
Buddhist psychology, 65, 153, 164, 195, 437, 452, 461, 470, 480, 498
Caduceus, 325
Calm, 126, 371
career counselor, career, job, 63, 136, 137, 262, 309, 311, 325, 333, 335, 398, 424, 464, 480, 481, 488, 498, 499
Catholic, 581
Catholic Church, 581
Causal Plane, 181, 297, 298, 302, 521, 522
Chandogya Upanishad, 216
Change, 143, 146, 344
Chanting, 234
Chaos, 372
Chi, 409, 540
Child, 581
Christ, 287, 579
Christianity, 576, 580, 581
Church, 581
Civilization, 577, 584, 585, 590
coercion, 584
Coffin Texts, 186, 216
Collapse, 238, 239, 584, 589, 590, 591
color, 222, 301, 586, 588
Color, 586
Community, 446
Compassion, 167, 324, 378, 384, 385, 401, 487, 490
Concentration, 204, 212, 244
Conditioning, 379
Conflict, 350, 372, 584, 588
Confucianism, 5
Confusion, 453, 499
Congress, 4
Conscience, 457, 459, 463, 464
Conscious, 69, 141, 143, 147, 149, 156, 286, 315, 337, 379, 406, 408, 409, 414, 440, 474
Conscious mind, 69
Consciousness, 11, 69, 80, 91, 134, 139, 143, 146, 158, 167, 176, 177, 187, 203, 204, 207, 208, 226, 227, 236, 272, 289, 319, 327, 331, 344, 353, 357, 393, 397, 404, 405, 411, 413, 420, 422, 425, 465, 470, 500, 513, 542, 555, 579, 588
Consciousness, human, 128, 135, 347, 395, 396, 416, 420, 504, 576
Constriction, 159, 160
Contamination, 379, 381
contentment, 48, 54, 127, 128, 130, 132, 133, 137, 138, 139, 188, 217, 247, 281, 367, 378, 379, 383, 390, 398, 400, 401, 425, 455, 456, 476, 477, 478, 479, 480, 500, 521, 524, 528, 560, 591, 592
Contentment (see also Hetep), 126, 342, 398, 401, 425
Coping, 456
Coptic, 579
Corpus Hermeticum, 237
cosmic force, 35, 37, 47, 109, 112, 127, 128, 132, 133, 134, 136, 137, 138, 139, 143, 147, 151, 155, 157, 183, 264, 268, 272, 289, 293, 294, 295, 321, 580, 583
Cosmic mind, 434
Cosmic Mind, 272, 427, 429, 434
Cosmic Order, 151, 272
Craving, 182
Creation, 11, 37, 40, 47, 56, 69, 78, 79, 81, 89, 90, 127, 128, 130, 133, 134, 138, 142, 143, 147, 151, 155, 157, 176, 180, 181, 185, 186, 187, 189, 190, 209, 210, 218, 222, 232, 236, 321, 325, 326, 344, 348, 375, 402, 413, 434, 467, 477, 478, 496, 500, 579, 580, 588, 592
Creator-Spirit, 39, 90, 144, 162, 168, 169, 170, 171, 172, 173, 174, 175, 182, 230, 523, 526, 529, 557, 562
Cross, 165, 196, 437, 440, 452, 459
Culture, 178, 362, 456, 498, 579, 583, 586, 590
Death, 282, 584, 590
December, 580
Defensive, 164
delusion, 32, 58, 69, 106, 112, 113, 131, 143, 148, 149, 150, 152, 153, 154, 155, 160, 161, 162, 171, 178, 179, 180, 182, 183, 185, 186, 188, 198, 199, 216, 265, 268, 292, 296, 307, 319, 353, 355, 370, 375, 376, 389, 390, 420, 421, 422, 432, 450, 457, 464, 466, 467, 468, 472, 473, 477, 479, 483, 484, 485, 486, 489, 491, 492, 493, 494, 495, 496, 499, 500, 501, 510, 514, 518, 521, 525, 554, 556, 557, 560, 592, 593
Delusion, 265, 269, 466, 467, 477, 484, 492
Denderah, 579
depression, 83, 85, 86, 135, 179, 198, 260, 277, 278, 279, 281, 322, 383, 397, 422, 423, 452, 461, 498, 518, 540, 547, 592
Depression, 126
Desire, 588
Desires, 262, 301, 303, 526
Destiny, 289, 295, 486
Detachment, 356
Development, 164, 165, 173, 199, 261, 263, 283, 309, 316, 319, 546
Devotional Love, 578
Dharma, 538, 547
Diet, 284, 287, 288, 577
Discernment, 147, 367, 402, 509, 510
discrimination, 146, 150, 151, 154, 158, 293, 295, 324, 334, 349, 350, 375, 398, 425, 511
Discrimination, 157, 262
Dissolving, 237
Divine consciousness, 61, 69, 88, 91, 93, 257, 290, 395, 404, 407, 412, 451
Divine Consciousness, 18, 50, 126, 146, 158, 167, 175, 252, 319, 325, 344, 388, 420, 447, 448, 465, 512, 564
Divine knowingness, 69
Divine providence, 253, 273
Divine within, 46, 50, 78, 81, 388
Divinity, 5, 24, 30, 39, 40, 54, 57, 75, 94, 170, 176, 180, 187,

189, 190, 209, 221, 222, 344, 388, 394, 404, 410, 467, 487, 489
Djehuti, 344
Dollar, U.S. Dollar, 591
Dream, 227
Dream, REM sleep, 227
Drift, 141
Drum, 538, 547
Duality, 186, 238
Duat, 296, 297, 302, 579
dullness, 111, 234, 236, 241, 443, 444
Earth, 297, 303
Edfu, 579
Effort, 141, 142, 144, 263, 445, 478
Ego, 157, 159, 161, 163, 164, 166, 207, 246, 293, 296, 297, 301, 303, 309, 311, 317, 421, 466, 467, 477, 510, 511, 513
Egoism, 103, 131, 148, 492
Egyptian Book of Coming Forth By Day, 579
Egyptian Book of the Dead, 94, 252, 274, 319, 448
Egyptian civilization, 25
Egyptian Mysteries, 24, 69, 577, 582, 588, 589
Egyptian Physics, 580
Egyptian Proverb, 288, 578
EGYPTIAN PROVERBS, 578
Egyptian Yoga, 5, 69, 576, 577, 579, 580
Egyptian Yoga see also Kamitan Yoga, 5, 69, 576, 577, 579, 580, 591
Egyptologists, 582, 587
Emotional, 152, 158, 296, 304, 320, 372, 383, 387, 441
Emotions, 167
Empathy, 158
Empire culture, 584
Energy, 246, 264, 265, 268, 269, 270, 272, 276, 279, 283, 284, 343, 347, 349, 381, 447
Enlightenment, 2, 4, 18, 115, 126, 252, 447, 448, 554, 557, 576, 577, 578, 579, 580, 581, 582, 583, 588, 589, 590
Ethical living, 135, 341, 346, 429
Ethical purification, 212
Ethics, 155, 344, 345, 560, 577, 584, 585, 588
Ethiopia, 588
ethnicity, 97, 98
Eucharist, 579
Europe, 6
evil, 48, 112, 290, 310, 385, 518, 581, 582
Evil, 583
Evolution, theory of, 151
Exercise, 579
Exhale, 339
Exhaustion, 270
Existence, 180, 190, 236, 520
exploitation, 269, 332, 373, 380, 381, 384, 401, 419, 424, 438, 485, 487, 488, 489
Exploitation, 379, 383
Eye, 245, 427
Eyes, 212, 233, 236, 238, 243, 245
Faith, 585, 586
False, 297, 388, 391, 513, 515
Fasting, 288
Fatigue, tired, 260, 287
Fear, 432
Feelings, 127, 147, 159, 266, 277, 303
Finances, 590
Fire, 237, 238
Food, 287
Form, 20, 232, 235
Fortune, 289, 295
Foundation, 5, 64, 75, 93, 105, 157, 222, 250, 369, 416, 444, 445, 446, 495, 503, 509, 544
frustration, 170, 179, 219, 224, 235, 244, 245, 249, 254, 255, 259, 260, 262, 263, 324, 469, 471, 472, 473, 483, 489, 504, 505, 517, 518, 519, 520, 521, 522, 525, 529, 537, 592
Fukushima, 287
Fulfillment, 168, 173, 230, 370, 426
Fullness, 169, 172, 173, 174, 230, 239
Galla, 588
Galla culture, 588
Geb, 325, 579
Ger, 129, 183, 184, 189, 191, 192, 193, 194, 206, 208, 239, 265, 286, 409, 466, 468, 474, 491, 493, 494, 496, 499, 501, 502
Ghana, 588
global economy, 584
Globalization, 584
Glorious Light Meditation, 578
God, 30, 38, 39, 40, 41, 44, 46, 49, 57, 59, 109, 110, 111, 129, 130, 133, 134, 138, 142, 159, 162, 165, 186, 198, 216, 237, 272, 286, 290, 296, 301, 306, 308, 319, 344, 345, 366, 378, 379, 382, 394, 417, 477, 478, 480, 486, 487, 489, 492, 493, 496, 497, 499,502, 529, 578, 580, 583, 586
Goddess, 580, 586
Goddesses, 579, 582
Gods, 579, 582
gods and goddesses, 42, 43, 47, 112, 127, 128, 132, 133, 135, 139, 155, 265, 268, 273, 286, 321, 347, 580, 582, 583, 592, 593
Good, 139, 204, 378, 403, 583
Gospels, 581
Grasping, 455
Greece, 577, 583
Greed, 388, 396, 449
Greek philosophy, 576
Greeks, 587
Green, 204, 286
Hamilton, Alexander, 139, 482
Happiness, 126, 423, 431
Happy, 140, 146, 158, 344, 456
Harmony, 111, 126, 131, 136, 138, 372
Hat, 52, 69, 97, 106, 107, 155, 160, 161, 162, 163, 164, 165, 166, 187, 207, 242, 284, 310, 337, 341, 404, 405, 406, 407, 408, 409, 410, 411, 412, 413, 414, 415, 427, 428, 429, 430, 431, 433, 434, 435, 436, 437, 438, 439, 440, 441, 443, 444, 445, 447, 455, 458, 459, 466, 467, 468, 469, 470, 477, 479, 481, 484, 485, 486, 489, 490, 492, 493, 536, 538
Hate, 588
Hatha Yoga, 585
Hathor, 579, 580, 582, 591
Hatred, 588
Healing, 140, 167, 284, 286, 387, 515
Health, 287, 288, 387, 423, 456, 547, 556, 576, 580
Heart, 167, 204, 287, 301, 342, 388, 581, 586
Heart (also see Ab, mind, conscience), 167, 204, 287, 301, 342, 388, 581, 586
Heated mind and feelings, 182, 184
Heaven, 581
Hedonic adaptation, 456
Hekau, 232, 234, 591
Hekau (words of power, sacred utterances), 232, 234, 591
Hermes, 589

Hermes (see also Djehuti, Thoth), 589
Hermetic, 237, 240, 589
Hermeticism, 589
Heru, 109, 110, 111, 112, 115, 116, 117, 118, 344, 364, 579, 580, 581, 583, 587, 593
Heru (see Horus), 109, 110, 111, 112, 115, 116, 117, 118, 344, 364, 579, 580, 581, 583, 587, 593
Herufy (dual nature of human consciousness), 115, 116, 117
Hetep, 284, 286
Hetheru, 6, 344, 582
Hetheru (Hetheru, Hathor), 6, 344, 582
Hieroglyphic, 11, 18, 19, 20, 21, 24, 25, 31, 35, 36, 37, 38, 39, 40, 41, 42, 44, 45, 48, 49, 50, 51, 52, 54, 55, 56, 57, 59, 60, 62, 102, 126, 139, 146, 158, 167, 175, 204, 252, 254, 263, 287, 295, 319, 320, 344, 387, 403, 426, 447, 448, 456, 465, 474, 482, 490, 503,512, 516, 530, 547, 548, 564, 578, 587, 589
Hieroglyphic texts, 19, 20, 146, 589
Hieroglyphic Writing, language, 11, 18, 19, 20, 21, 24, 25, 31, 35, 36, 37, 38, 39, 40, 41, 42, 44, 45, 48, 49, 50, 51, 52, 54, 55, 56, 57, 59, 60, 62, 102, 126, 139, 146, 158, 167, 175, 204, 252, 254, 263, 287, 295, 319, 320, 344, 387, 403, 426, 447, 448, 456, 465, 474, 482, 490, 503,512, 516, 530, 547, 548, 564, 578, 587, 589
Hieroglyphs, 25, 234
Hinduism, 580
Hindus, 582
Holy Spirit, 327
hope, 320, 355, 385, 463, 586
Horus, 109, 115, 117, 593
Human Psychology Principle, 65, 77, 104, 128, 141, 147, 159, 168, 176, 254, 265, 297, 322, 347, 379, 389, 416, 428, 449, 457, 467, 477, 484, 492
HUMANITY, 582
Humility, 161, 165, 166, 167, 491, 492, 497, 498, 501, 503
Iamblichus, 587
Ida and Pingala, 326
Identification, 163
Identity, 93, 100, 167, 174, 208, 303, 395
Ignorance, 185, 186, 520, 521, 522
Ignorance, see also Khemn, 185, 186, 520, 521, 522
Illness, 246
illusion, 56, 108, 169, 170, 171, 173, 190, 293, 299, 306, 310, 353, 354, 389, 390, 392, 398, 419, 450, 466, 468, 470, 471, 472, 473, 474, 479, 492, 501, 528, 534, 535, 546, 547, 558
Illusion, 392, 416, 466, 470, 474, 520
Image, 92, 115, 232
immune system, 266
immune system, immunity, 266
Implementation, 108, 174, 233, 235, 236, 239, 247, 284, 285, 367, 368, 385, 386, 400, 442, 446, 501, 502, 543
Incompleteness, 168, 520
Independence, 542
India, 326, 577, 578, 579, 584, 585
Indian Yoga, 5, 577
Individual, 101, 244, 299, 301, 387, 405, 412, 413, 415, 420, 434, 504
Individual consciousness, 420
Indus, 577
Indus Valley, 577
Infinite, 407, 411, 413
Inflation, 296, 297, 303, 309, 311, 317
Initiate, 577
Inner peace, 345
Insight, 208
Integration, 100, 111, 184, 229, 282, 309, 312, 318, 344, 373, 384, 441, 443, 445, 446, 502, 545, 546, 559
Intellectual, 67, 201, 296, 303, 304
Intractability, 281
Isis, 6, 109, 336, 577, 579, 580, 591, 593
Isis, See also Aset, 6, 109, 336, 577, 579, 580, 591, 593
Islam, 576
Jesus, 579, 581, 591
Jesus Christ, 579
Joshua, 135
Joy, 227, 254
Judaism, 576
Judeo-Christian, 112, 167
judges, 135
Judgment, 315
Ka, 44, 52, 64, 69, 97, 98, 207, 242, 284, 297, 301, 303, 307, 310, 318, 319, 341, 381, 404, 405, 406, 407, 408, 409, 411, 412, 413, 414, 415, 427, 428, 429, 430, 431, 433, 434, 435, 436, 437, 438, 439, 440, 441, 443, 444, 445, 447
Ka (personality/ego aspect), 44, 52, 64, 69, 97, 98, 207, 242, 284, 297, 301, 303, 307, 310, 318, 319, 341, 381, 404, 405, 406, 407, 408, 409, 411, 412, 413, 414, 415, 427, 428, 429, 430, 431, 433, 434, 435, 436, 437, 438, 439, 440, 441, 443, 444, 445, 447
Ka (personality/mind/desires), 44, 52, 64, 69, 97, 98, 207, 242, 284, 297, 301, 303, 307, 310, 318, 319, 341, 381, 404, 405, 406, 407, 408, 409, 411, 412, 413, 414, 415, 427, 428, 429, 430, 431, 433, 434, 435, 436, 437, 438, 439, 440, 441, 443, 444, 445, 447
Kabbalah, 576
Kamit (Egypt), 582
Kamitan, 326, 577, 583
Kara, 30, 69, 75, 92, 207, 404, 405, 406, 407, 408, 411, 412, 413, 414, 415, 440, 441, 444
Karma, 578
Kemetic, 5, 67, 287, 288, 448, 583, 586, 588, 590, 591, 592
Khaibit, 298, 301, 302, 310
Khat, 301, 303, 341
Khemn (ignorance), 582
Khemn, see also ignorance, 582
Khnum, 49, 163, 378, 379, 382
King, 581, 583
Kingdom, 115, 581
Kingdom of Heaven, 581
Know Thyself, 106
Knowledge, 100, 204
Krishna, 581
Kundalini, 5
Kundalini XE "Kundalini" Yoga see also Serpent Power, 5
Kybalion, 589
Learning, 101, 126
Liberation, 100, 182, 225, 272, 511, 527
Life, 75, 127, 128, 131, 133, 141, 146, 226, 246, 253, 265, 288,

296, 300, 337, 344, 371, 424, 447, 468, 491, 548, 561, 579, 583, 585, 586, 588
Life Force, 288, 337, 344, 548, 579
Lifestyle, 445
Limitations, 279, 423, 447
Love, 346, 350, 352, 353, 354, 355, 357, 362, 364, 367, 369, 370, 373, 375, 416, 421, 424, 578, 591
lucid, 149, 150, 436, 444
Luxury, 449, 451, 455, 524
Maat, 5, 35, 60, 114, 115, 116, 117, 118, 125, 127, 128, 133, 149, 183, 185, 187, 188, 217, 229, 231, 243, 247, 249, 253, 255, 264, 272, 273, 281, 283, 286, 287, 290, 291, 293, 294, 295, 297, 305, 313, 315, 316, 317, 320, 322, 323, 327, 328, 337, 343, 353, 354, 355, 364, 365, 366, 367, 371, 372, 403, 430, 432, 440, 443, 444, 460, 465, 476, 477, 478, 480, 481, 483, 485, 486, 500, 515, 537, 558, 562, 578, 580, 581, 583, 586, 587, 588, 589, 590
MAAT, 578
Maat (divine order, truth, righteous living), 5, 35, 60, 114, 115, 116, 117, 118, 125, 127, 128, 133, 149, 183, 185, 187, 188, 217, 229, 231, 243, 247, 249, 253, 255, 264, 272, 273, 281, 283, 286, 287, 290, 291, 293, 294, 295, 297, 305, 313, 315, 316, 317, 320, 322, 323, 327, 328, 337, 343, 353, 354, 355, 364, 365, 366, 367, 371, 372, 403, 430, 432, 440, 443, 444, 460, 465, 476, 477, 478, 480, 481, 483, 485, 486, 500, 515, 537, 558, 562, 578, 580, 581, 583, 586, 587, 588, 589, 590
Maat philosophy, 5, 35, 116, 117, 118, 127, 128, 364, 365
Maat Philosophy, 287, 295, 320, 364, 403, 581, 583, 586, 589, 590
Maat principles, 272, 283, 313, 315, 337, 355, 366, 371, 478, 480, 486
MAATI, 578
Machiavellianism, 277, 383
Malawi, 588
Manipulation, 383, 514
Mantra, 234
Masters, 5, 320
Materialism, 139, 397, 422, 431, 456
Matter, 187, 580
Matthew, 503
media, 67, 87, 88, 121, 122, 135, 136, 144, 145, 153, 154, 173, 178, 245, 261, 270, 283, 284, 285, 312, 324, 332, 333, 335, 367, 369, 374, 375, 398, 424, 431, 437, 438, 445, 446, 454, 477, 560, 584
Media, 424
Meditation, 100, 101, 102, 126, 164, 167, 172, 175, 196, 203, 204, 209, 232, 237, 238, 252, 287, 288, 292, 294, 337, 341, 344, 401, 414, 440, 443, 445, 448, 456, 470, 474, 480, 482, 503, 532, 536, 539, 541, 547, 548, 558, 577, 578
Meditation practice, 292, 294, 536, 541, 558
Medu Neter, 582, 591
Medu Neter (hieroglyphic sacred texts), 582, 591
Memphite Theology, 580
Mental agitation, 193, 546
Mental health, 560
Meskhenet, 578
Metaphor, 227, 296
Metaphysics, 495, 534, 580, 588
Middle East, 576
Mills, 344
Min, 579
Mind, 11, 113, 127, 139, 140, 147, 159, 167, 168, 172, 174, 177, 199, 201, 203, 208, 224, 227, 266, 277, 287, 296, 297, 301, 302, 305, 306, 307, 309, 310, 337, 344, 381, 387, 403, 404, 405, 518, 524, 525, 526, 555, 590
Mindfulness, 83, 101, 102, 126, 167, 204, 205, 207, 208, 209, 278, 287, 320, 448, 456, 465, 542, 544, 547
minimum wage, 401
Modern culture, 121, 374, 432, 442, 454
Modern science, 279
Music, 6, 178, 586
Mysteries, 24, 126, 344, 577, 582, 587, 588, 589, 593
mystical philosophy, 237, 584, 587
Mysticism, 5, 11, 102, 126, 139, 158, 167, 175, 204, 252, 263, 287, 295, 319, 320, 344, 387, 403, 426, 447, 448, 456, 465, 474, 482, 490, 503, 512, 516, 530, 547, 548, 564, 577, 580, 582, 584, 585
Nadis, 409
Narcissistic patterns, 515
Nature, 111, 139, 146, 158, 167, 204, 226, 227, 252, 288, 306, 327, 341, 344, 355, 419, 420, 426, 448, 456, 465, 474, 475, 496, 528
Navigation, 141, 143, 297, 305, 495, 497, 498, 502
Neberdjer, 40, 46, 56, 58, 59, 69, 90, 91, 93, 104, 110, 113, 114, 121, 122, 124, 127, 128, 130, 131, 132, 133, 134, 135, 136, 138, 139, 142, 151, 155, 176, 177, 178, 179, 180, 181, 182, 183, 184, 185, 186, 187, 188, 189, 190, 191, 192, 193, 194, 195, 196, 197, 198, 199, 200, 201, 202, 203, 205, 206, 207, 208, 209, 210, 211, 217, 218, 219, 221, 229, 230, 231, 232, 234, 235, 236, 237, 238, 240, 241, 242, 243, 246, 247, 248, 249, 250, 251, 252, 264, 268, 272, 273, 282, 286, 290, 292, 294, 295, 296, 298, 299, 301, 306, 307, 313, 322, 326, 327, 345, 346, 348, 350, 351, 352, 353, 354, 355, 356, 357, 364, 365, 366, 368, 369, 370, 371, 372, 373, 374, 375, 376, 388, 389, 390, 392, 395, 401, 402, 404, 405, 406, 407, 408, 410, 411, 412, 413, 414, 415, 417, 419, 420, 421, 422, 425, 426, 440, 449, 450, 451, 452, 455, 456, 466, 467, 468, 469, 470, 471, 472, 473, 474, 477, 478, 479, 481, 483, 484, 485, 486, 487, 489, 491, 492, 493, 494, 496, 497, 498, 499, 500, 501, 502, 503, 514, 515, 518, 519, 520, 521, 522, 525, 526, 527, 528, 529, 530, 534, 537, 554, 555, 557, 558, 559, 562, 563, 576
Neberdjer (All-encompassing divinity), 40, 46, 56, 58, 59, 69, 90, 91, 93, 104, 110, 113, 114, 121, 122, 124, 127, 128, 130, 131, 132, 133, 134, 135, 136, 138, 139, 142, 151, 155, 176, 177, 178, 179, 180, 181, 182, 183, 184, 185, 186, 187,

188, 189, 190, 191, 192, 193, 194, 195, 196, 197, 198, 199, 200, 201, 202, 203, 205, 206, 207, 208, 209, 210, 211, 217, 218, 219, 221, 229, 230, 231, 232, 234, 235, 236, 237, 238, 240, 241, 242, 243, 246, 247, 248, 249, 250, 251, 252, 264, 268, 272, 273, 282, 286, 290, 292, 294, 295, 296, 298, 299, 301, 306, 307, 313, 322, 326, 327, 345, 346, 348, 350, 351, 352, 353, 354, 355, 356, 357, 364, 365, 366, 368, 369, 370, 371, 372, 373, 374, 375, 376, 388, 389, 390, 392, 395, 401, 402, 404, 405, 406, 407, 408, 410, 411, 412, 413, 414, 415, 417, 419, 420, 421, 422, 425, 426, 440, 449, 450, 451, 452, 455, 456, 466, 467, 468, 469, 470, 471, 472, 473, 474, 477, 478, 479, 481, 483, 484, 485, 486, 487, 489, 491, 492, 493, 494, 496, 497, 498, 499, 500, 501, 502, 503, 514, 515, 518, 519, 520, 521, 522, 525, 526, 527, 528, 529, 530, 534, 537, 554, 555, 557, 558, 559, 562, 563, 576
Neberdjer recognition, 91, 191, 192, 193, 194, 195, 290, 356, 371, 373
Nefer, 180, 189, 365
Nehast, 582
Nehast (spiritual awakening, resurrection), 582
neo-con, 584
Nephthys, 326
Nervous system, 210
Net, goddess, 39, 49, 50, 180
Neter, 25, 37, 38, 39, 40, 41, 47, 54, 57, 59, 60, 61, 65, 78, 79, 80, 81, 86, 88, 89, 93, 104, 107, 115, 117, 118, 119, 129, 130, 131, 133, 134, 137, 138, 160, 162, 163, 166, 174, 177, 180, 183, 209, 217, 231, 235, 249, 257, 258, 259, 275, 284, 286, 290, 291, 299, 306, 310, 322, 327, 331, 347, 348, 349, 356, 358, 391, 392, 393, 394, 395, 396, 407, 412, 418, 428, 430, 433, 451, 468, 479, 493, 516, 532, 536, 537, 541, 546, 554, 555, 556, 557, 558, 559, 562, 578, 579, 582, 583, 584, 587, 588, 590, 591
Neterian, 25, 92, 112, 139, 146, 158, 167, 211, 344, 465, 582, 583, 584, 590, 591
Neterian tradition, 25, 211
Neterianism, 589, 590
Neteru, 47, 235, 345, 346, 347, 352, 353, 370, 582, 592
Neteru (gods and goddesses as cosmic principles), 47, 235, 345, 346, 347, 352, 353, 370, 582, 592
Neuroscience, 83, 84, 101, 102, 119, 120, 135, 136, 152, 158, 163, 167, 172, 204, 250, 252, 280, 281, 288, 309, 311, 329, 344, 383, 397, 403, 423, 426, 435, 437, 448, 456, 470, 474, 475, 479
New Kingdom, 115, 117, 344
Nigeria, 588
Nine, 297, 299, 301, 307, 318
Nunu, 185, 306
Nut, 325, 579
Nutrition, 287
Observation, 317, 442
Obstruction, 79, 159, 160, 165, 184, 275, 412
Ocean, 69
Opposites, 238, 239
Orion Star Constellation, 580
Orthodox, 582
Osiris, 6, 24, 51, 109, 132, 394, 579, 583, 593
Pa Neter, 90
Pain, 490
Pathology, 281
Patterns, 107, 160, 164, 177, 208, 291, 303, 309, 312, 315, 349, 350, 380, 383, 414, 448, 467, 477, 479, 497, 498, 513, 535
Peace, 125, 227, 284, 366, 445, 588, 589, 590
Peace (see also Hetep), 125, 227, 284, 366, 445, 588, 589, 590
Penetration, 413
Persians, 587
Personality, 79, 101, 110, 112, 115, 116, 167, 175, 287, 297, 299, 301, 302, 310, 319, 344, 384, 387, 404, 426, 448, 456, 474, 490, 492, 503
PERT EM HERU, SEE ALSO BOOK OF THE DEAD, 580
Pert m Heru, 217, 221
Pharaoh, 92, 590
Philae, 579
Philosophical, 90, 181, 201, 204, 218, 239, 246
Philosophical contemplation, 246
Philosophy, 5, 24, 75, 139, 146, 158, 167, 199, 216, 344, 364, 465, 576, 577, 578, 580, 581, 583, 584, 585, 586, 589, 590
Physical, 2, 4, 156, 218, 297, 298, 301, 303, 337, 342, 346, 441, 447, 485, 533, 536, 537
physical realm, 321, 345
Physiological, 266, 277
Pleasure, 531
Point (see also Black Dot and Bindu), 545
Politics, 139, 403
Poverty, 253
Power, 25, 234, 251, 254, 264, 265, 269, 277, 287, 322, 337, 416, 420, 421, 422, 424, 542
Power over storehouse, 422
Practice, 92, 99, 100, 123, 124, 125, 136, 146, 149, 156, 157, 164, 174, 205, 207, 208, 219, 222, 223, 224, 228, 229, 231, 234, 235, 236, 240, 241, 243, 245, 246, 247, 262, 263, 284, 285, 286, 291, 292, 293, 317, 320, 329, 331, 332, 339, 340, 344, 367, 368, 370, 374, 375, 386, 387, 401, 414, 416, 425, 426, 440, 441, 442, 444, 445, 446, 447, 455, 463, 464, 474, 481, 489, 490, 501, 502, 503, 511, 537, 538, 539, 543, 544, 545
Practices, 284, 293, 317, 368, 372, 400, 445, 501, 539
Prana (also see Sekhem and Life Force), 409
prejudice, 320
pressure, 67, 122, 136, 142, 146, 154, 197, 248, 262, 270, 283, 313, 323, 325, 329, 332, 333, 352, 375, 398, 424, 438, 480, 499, 524, 540, 561
priests and priestesses, 21, 24, 94, 98, 99, 365, 579, 583, 593
Priests and Priestesses, 577, 583
Progressive, 90, 111, 136, 164, 165, 173, 184, 247, 281, 285, 341, 441, 493
Prologue, 29, 64, 65, 66, 68, 75, 77, 78, 83, 87, 89, 93, 99, 100, 104, 105, 106, 107, 113, 118, 123, 128, 129, 148, 150, 155, 158, 169, 177, 181, 184, 186, 187, 188, 198, 249, 252, 255,

265, 268, 269, 275, 276, 299, 301, 306, 322, 333, 343, 349, 357, 367, 374, 378, 379, 383, 387, 389, 403, 404, 410, 418, 426, 429, 430, 447, 449, 452, 456, 458, 460, 465, 466, 467, 470, 471, 476, 477, 483, 484, 486, 491, 493, 511, 512, 515, 543, 545, 547, 548, 554, 559, 563
Protection, 164, 375, 384, 385
Proverbial Wisdom, 588
Psyche, 344
psychologist, 152, 314
Psychologist, 263, 344, 426, 456
Psychology, 13, 18, 65, 80, 101, 102, 103, 113, 126, 127, 128, 130, 133, 134, 140, 141, 143, 147, 151, 152, 159, 161, 167, 168, 170, 175, 176, 179, 204, 252, 257, 264, 272, 287, 288, 306, 312, 320, 322, 325, 344, 352, 381, 392, 403, 419, 426, 433, 448, 449, 451, 456, 457, 459, 465, 469, 474, 478, 482, 486, 487, 490, 495, 503, 512, 513, 517, 545, 547, 548, 580, 589
psychomythology, 109
Ptah, 90, 180, 580
Purification, 77, 80, 103, 107, 113, 203, 217, 247, 262, 284, 289, 311, 317, 330, 337, 346, 355, 368, 370, 409, 413, 414, 560
Qi (see also Life Force, Ra, Prana), 409
Queen, 583
Ra, 6, 39, 90, 91, 104, 109, 110, 111, 113, 122, 124, 126, 180, 185, 232, 233, 297, 298, 299, 300, 301, 306, 307, 318, 319, 321, 322, 326, 327, 328, 334, 336, 339, 344, 345, 347, 352, 395, 396, 429, 434, 459, 579
Ra (individuated divine consciousness), 6, 39, 90, 91, 104, 109, 110, 111, 113, 122, 124, 126, 180, 185, 232, 233, 297, 298, 299, 300, 301, 306, 307, 318, 319, 321, 322, 326, 327, 328, 334, 336, 339, 344, 345, 347, 352, 395, 396, 429, 434, 459, 579
Ra, See also Ra-Herakty, 6, 39, 90, 91, 104, 109, 110, 111, 113, 122, 124, 126, 180, 185, 232, 233, 297, 298, 299, 300, 301, 306, 307, 318, 319, 321, 322, 326, 327, 328, 334, 336, 339, 344, 345, 347, 352, 395, 396, 429, 434, 459, 579
racism, 588
Racism, 588
Reality, 266, 372, 421, 466, 477, 510
Realization, 577
Rebellious, 140, 146, 158, 344, 456
Receptivity, 159, 163
Recognition, 92, 93, 100, 124, 157, 173, 174, 176, 179, 181, 182, 188, 194, 207, 212, 215, 219, 222, 223, 225, 229, 230, 231, 235, 241, 251, 268, 275, 323, 347, 357, 367, 368, 401, 412, 413, 426, 441, 501, 502, 515, 526, 542, 546, 562
Reflection, 286
Reincarnation, 276
Relationships, 226, 304, 305, 387, 514, 525, 527, 561
Release, 236, 239, 241, 445, 498
Religion, 5, 139, 403, 576, 577, 579, 580, 581, 582, 583, 584, 585, 590, 591
Ren, 301, 303
Rennenet, 295
Research, 5, 83, 84, 85, 86, 101, 119, 120, 121, 126, 134, 135, 136, 143, 152, 153, 164, 166, 172, 194, 195, 196, 204, 207, 218, 219, 232, 241, 244, 245, 250, 251, 260, 277, 278, 279, 280, 281, 287, 288, 309, 310, 311, 313, 320, 329, 330, 331, 343, 383, 384, 397, 422, 423, 435, 436, 437, 452, 453, 460, 461, 470, 479, 487, 497, 498, 539, 540, 541, 547
Research validation, 343
Rest, 236, 238, 239, 241
Resurrection, 579, 580, 581, 583, 592
Revelation, 531
Righteousness, 155, 321
RITUAL, 582
Rituals, 218, 580
Roman, 587
Romans, 587
Rome, 583
Safe, 492, 496, 497
Sage Amenemope, 2, 4, 11, 12, 18, 64, 78, 81, 90, 92, 126, 128, 139, 141, 146, 147, 155, 158, 167, 168, 175, 176, 179, 200, 209, 222, 227, 242, 251, 252, 255, 262, 263, 287, 289, 295, 317, 319, 321, 334, 344, 367, 368, 385, 387, 394, 395, 400, 402, 403, 405, 425, 426, 431, 449, 455, 456, 457, 463, 465, 473, 474, 480, 482, 489, 490, 501, 503, 512, 516, 517, 519, 531, 532, 537, 544, 546, 547, 554
Sage Amenemopet, 2, 4, 11, 12, 18, 64, 78, 81, 90, 92, 126, 128, 139, 141, 146, 147, 155, 158, 167, 168, 175, 176, 179, 200, 209, 222, 227, 242, 251, 252, 255, 262, 263, 287, 289, 295, 317, 319, 321, 334, 344, 367, 368, 385, 387, 394, 395, 400, 402, 403, 405, 425, 426, 431, 449, 455, 456, 457, 463, 465, 473, 474, 480, 482, 489, 490, 501, 503, 512, 516, 517, 519, 531, 532, 537, 544, 546, 547, 554
Sages, 576, 579, 580, 581, 583, 591
Sahu, 301, 302
Saints, 580, 591
San, 320
Sanctuary, 69, 345, 372
Sanskrit, 196, 199, 201
Sau-Neberdjer consciousness, 211
School, 5
Scientific American, 204
Scripture, 6, 29, 104, 113, 126, 185, 321, 344, 426
Scripture of Ra and Hetheru, 6, 104, 113, 126, 185, 426
Sebai, 583, 589, 590
See also Ra-Hrakti, 579
See Nat, 39, 49, 50, 180
Seeking, 168, 169, 172, 264, 269, 277, 420, 431, 525, 526, 531
Sekhem, 265, 266, 267, 268, 269, 270, 271, 274, 283, 301, 303, 341, 409, 410
Sekhem (life force energy), 265, 266, 267, 268, 269, 270, 271, 274, 283, 301, 303, 341, 409, 410
Sekhmet, 126, 344
Self, 2, 4, 47, 86, 92, 100, 109, 110, 111, 113, 128, 131, 132, 148, 155, 164, 167, 182, 185, 204, 208, 217, 229, 230, 260, 263, 270, 298, 317, 320, 344, 370, 378, 408, 415, 419, 421,

423, 426, 428, 431, 456, 466, 470, 477, 481, 491, 493, 510, 520, 547
Self (see Ba, soul, Spirit, Universal, Ba, Neter, Heru)., 2, 4, 47, 86, 92, 100, 109, 110, 111, 113, 128, 131, 132, 148, 155, 164, 167, 182, 185, 204, 208, 217, 229, 230, 260, 263, 270, 298, 317, 320, 344, 370, 378, 408, 415, 419, 421, 423, 426, 428, 431, 456, 466, 470, 477, 481, 491, 493, 510, 520, 547, 577, 578, 579, 582, 586
Self-created lifestyle, lifestyle, 87, 137, 139, 246, 287, 398, 440, 450, 542, 544, 547
Sema, 4, 5, 6, 18, 69, 102, 126, 139, 140, 146, 158, 167, 175, 204, 252, 263, 266, 267, 274, 284, 287, 288, 295, 319, 320, 344, 387, 403, 426, 446, 447, 448, 456, 465, 474, 482, 490, 503, 512, 516, 530, 547, 548, 564, 583, 588, 589, 591
Sema Institute, 4, 5, 6, 18, 102, 126, 139, 140, 146, 158, 167, 175, 204, 252, 263, 266, 267, 274, 284, 287, 288, 295, 319, 320, 344, 387, 403, 426, 446, 447, 448, 456, 465, 474, 482, 490, 503, 512, 516, 530, 547, 548, 564
Sema Institute of Ancient Egyptian Studies, 102, 126, 139, 140, 158, 167, 175, 204, 252, 263, 287, 288, 295, 319, 320, 344, 387, 403, 426, 447, 448, 456, 465, 474, 482, 490, 503, 512, 516, 530, 547, 548, 564
Sema Tawy, 69
Senses, 409
Separateness, 484, 534
Serpent, 126, 288, 321, 322, 323, 325, 326, 327, 333, 337, 342, 343, 344, 345, 346, 347, 353, 542, 548
Serpent Power, 126, 288, 321, 322, 323, 325, 326, 327, 333, 337, 343, 344, 345, 346, 347, 353, 542, 548
Serpent Power (see also Kundalini and Buto), 126, 288, 321, 322, 323, 325, 326, 327, 333, 337, 343, 344, 345, 346, 347, 353, 542, 548
Serpent Power see also Kundalini Yoga, 126, 288, 321, 322, 323, 325, 326, 327, 333, 337, 343, 344, 345, 346, 347, 353, 542, 548
Set, 35, 88, 109, 110, 111, 112, 115, 116, 117, 118, 128, 129, 131, 132, 133, 134, 174, 219, 339, 404, 457, 460, 583
Seti I, 578
Setian, 110, 112
Sex, 579
sexism, 588
Sexism, 588
Shadow, 301, 309, 310, 330, 344
Shai, 183, 272, 295
Shankara, 196, 204
Shayt, 264, 265, 268, 272, 273, 289, 294
Shedy, 201, 576
Shen, 517
Shennu, 517, 521, 523, 524, 525
Shepherd, 496
Shetaut Neter, 11, 25, 67, 69, 563, 579, 582, 583, 584, 588, 590, 591
Shetaut Neter (Ancient Egyptian spiritual tradition), 11, 25, 67, 69, 563, 579, 582, 583, 584, 588, 590, 591
Shetaut Neter See also Egyptian Religion, 11, 25, 67, 69, 563, 579, 582, 583, 584, 588, 590, 591
Shetitu (secret code of teachings), 582
Signs, 239, 240
Silence, 208, 227, 237, 239, 511
Silent mind and feelings, 184, 293, 346, 559
Sirius, 580
skin, 59, 60, 246, 277, 477, 483, 484, 485, 486, 487, 489, 490
slavery, 582
Sleep, 286, 466
Sleeping Patterns, Sleep, 286, 466
Smai, 112, 132
society, 5, 65, 67, 87, 135, 290, 291, 312, 313, 365, 369, 374, 375, 418, 424, 504, 510, 519, 529, 560, 576, 582, 583, 586, 588, 589, 590, 591
Society, 312, 589, 590, 591
Somatic preparation, 246
Soul, 18, 26, 69, 90, 93, 95, 97, 126, 146, 158, 167, 175, 206, 208, 211, 212, 215, 216, 217, 219, 222, 224, 225, 226, 227, 228, 229, 231, 232, 235, 241, 244, 250, 251, 252, 287, 301, 302, 319, 344, 366, 394, 441, 447, 448, 465, 512, 546, 564, 583, 590
Soul-Aware-Witness, 18, 93, 95, 97, 126, 146, 158, 167, 175, 206, 208, 211, 212, 215, 216, 217, 219, 222, 224, 225, 226, 227, 228, 229, 231, 235, 241, 244, 250, 251, 252, 319, 344, 366, 441, 447, 448, 465, 512, 546, 564
Space, 207, 442, 446
Spine, 339
Spirit, 11, 39, 50, 58, 69, 162, 168, 169, 170, 172, 180, 230, 232, 301, 302, 348, 388, 392, 394, 429, 434, 459, 497
Spirit Being, 497
Spiritual aspirants, 207
Spiritual development, 275
Spiritual Development, 109, 310, 365
Spiritual discipline, 414, 576
Spiritual ignorance, 521, 528
Spiritual Implications for Aspirants, 65, 87, 121, 136, 144, 153, 165, 173, 197, 261, 283, 311, 332, 362, 384, 398, 424, 437, 453, 462, 471, 480, 488, 498
Spiritual practice, 314, 415
Spirituality, 320, 577, 586, 590, 591
Stages, 212, 215, 235, 236, 244, 245, 246, 250, 281, 440, 441, 444, 445
Still, 545
Storehouse, 69
Stress, 83, 101, 246, 456
Study, 18, 201, 204
Sublimation, 351, 579
Suffering, 97, 128, 554
sun, 342
Sun, 342
Superpower, 584
Superpower Syndrome, 584
Superpower Syndrome Mandatory Conflict Complex, 584
Supreme Being, 109, 221, 580
Surya, 337
Swami, 195, 204
Tai Chi (see also Chi Kung), 540
TANTRA, 579
TANTRA YOGA, 579
Taoism, 576
Teacher, 446

Teachings, 18, 29, 31, 35, 36, 37, 38, 39, 40, 41, 42, 44, 45, 46, 48, 49, 50, 51, 52, 54, 55, 56, 57, 59, 60, 62, 75, 77, 90, 103, 115, 122, 127, 141, 146, 147, 159, 167, 168, 176, 188, 204, 230, 253, 264, 265, 287, 296, 321, 344, 345, 378, 388, 416, 427, 449, 457, 466, 476, 483, 491, 492, 517, 556, 557
Temple, 39, 46, 51, 92, 94, 95, 102, 168, 173, 174, 579, 582, 590
Temple of Aset, 579
Temple of Hetheru, 582
The Absolute, 576
The All, 427
The Black, 585
The God, 40, 90, 110, 112, 132, 579
The Gods, 579
The way, 185, 500
Theban Theology, 576
Thebes, 67, 576, 578
Theocracy, 584
Theology, 5, 280, 288, 576, 580
Thoth, 52, 427, 429, 464
Thoughts, 69, 236, 243, 303, 305, 372, 441, 533
Thoughts (see also Mind), 69, 236, 243, 303, 305, 372, 441, 533
Tibetan Buddhism, 196
Time, 207, 387, 408, 442, 446, 464, 474, 489
time and space, 40, 61, 76, 78, 80, 110, 142, 176, 177, 179, 180, 183, 196, 209, 222, 231, 469, 477, 487, 519, 520, 522, 523, 529, 541, 554, 582
Timeline, 244, 251
tolerance, 281, 333, 355, 397
Tomb, 6, 578
Tomb of Seti I, 578
Tradition, 13
Transcendent, 200
transcendental reality, 582
Transformation, 2, 4, 11, 75, 103, 138, 179, 188, 242, 244, 284, 317, 325, 328, 347, 356, 378, 385, 400, 425, 455, 463, 501, 526, 528, 563
Transition, 202, 234, 338, 441, 544
Transpersonal psychology, 135, 310, 331
Transpersonal Psychology Research, 65, 83, 119, 134, 163, 171, 194, 259, 276, 309, 329, 358, 383, 396, 422, 435, 452, 460, 470, 479, 487, 497
Transpersonal Psychology Research Validation, 83, 119
Tree, 588
Tree of Life, 588
Triad, 383, 387, 576
Trinity, 579
Truth, 67, 228, 401, 402, 509, 510, 511
UK Biobank, 280
Unconscious, 69, 141, 183, 289, 296, 297, 301, 302, 309, 312, 314, 315, 337, 379, 407, 409, 439, 474
Unconscious impressions, 69
Unconscious mind, 69, 302
Unconscious patterns, 409
Understanding, 21, 90, 92, 93, 98, 99, 101, 112, 125, 130, 163, 181, 201, 203, 210, 216, 228, 231, 233, 235, 236, 240, 241, 243, 244, 255, 257, 259, 267, 269, 272, 276, 283, 290, 291, 297, 298, 300, 303, 306, 307, 311, 323, 325, 328, 332, 341, 344, 349, 352, 369, 372, 389, 392, 413, 414, 419, 440, 447, 493, 513, 521, 523, 546, 555, 556, 582, 589
United States of America, 584
Unity, 368
Universal Consciousness, 308, 405, 407, 579
Universal Spirit, 394
University of Pennsylvania, 280
Unrighteousness, 332, 457
Upanishads, 117, 196, 204, 216, 580, 587
Vedanta, 5, 204
Vedantic. See also Vedanta, 195
Vedic, 577
Vehicle, 357
Veil, 302, 310
Verse, 20, 21, 75, 77, 78, 79, 80, 81, 87, 88, 90, 106, 117, 118, 127, 128, 139, 141, 146, 147, 149, 158, 159, 167, 168, 176, 230, 242, 253, 254, 264, 265, 266, 268, 269, 270, 272, 273, 274, 275, 276, 283, 296, 297, 301, 304, 305, 321, 323, 336, 345, 346, 347, 349, 351, 352, 357, 364, 365, 378, 379, 380, 388, 389, 390, 391, 392, 416, 427, 434, 439, 440, 442, 443, 444, 445, 449, 451, 454, 457, 458, 459, 462, 466, 476, 477, 478, 483, 484, 486, 491, 492, 493, 494, 495, 509, 531, 533, 536, 537, 539, 554
Violence, 387, 588
Visualize, 235, 340, 503
Vitality, 301, 303, 345, 346, 349, 352, 386
Vital-Life-Fire, 113
Waking, 227
Walk, 544
Walking, 537, 539, 547, 548
Wall Street, 419
Waset, 576
Weak, 259, 518
Weakness of mind, 253
Wealth, 280, 283, 288, 422, 423, 425, 523
Wealth, Money, 280, 283, 288, 422, 423, 425, 523, 590
Well-being, 265, 268, 286, 397, 422, 490, 497
Western, West, 61, 487, 492
White, 263, 589
Who am I, 216, 271
Will, 239, 378, 466, 474, 499, 510, 511, 512
Wisdom, 2, 4, 13, 18, 25, 75, 77, 90, 103, 116, 126, 146, 153, 158, 167, 175, 204, 210, 237, 238, 246, 252, 280, 287, 288, 309, 319, 341, 344, 402, 447, 448, 465, 509, 510, 511, 512, 531, 546, 548, 559, 563, 564, 578, 579, 587, 588, 590
Wisdom (also see Djehuti, Aset), 2, 4, 13, 18, 25, 75, 77, 90, 103, 116, 126, 146, 153, 158, 167, 175, 204, 210, 237, 238, 246, 252, 280, 287, 288, 309, 319, 341, 344, 402, 447, 448, 465, 509, 510, 511, 512, 531, 546, 548, 559, 563, 564, 578, 579, 587, 588, 590
Wisdom philosophy, 77
Wisdom teaching, 103
Wisdom teachings, 103
Witness, 26, 208, 217, 230, 238, 395, 441, 443, 457, 459, 460, 542
Witness consciousness, 459, 460
World War II, 584
Yoga, 5, 112, 326, 337, 342, 542, 576, 577, 579, 580, 581, 583, 584, 585, 591
Yoga of Devotion (see Yoga of Divine Love), 591

Yogic, 585, 588
Yoruba, 588

OTHER BOOKS BY MUATA ASHBY

P.O.Box 570459

Miami, Florida, 33257

(305) 378-6253 Fax: (305) 378-6253 1.

MORE BOOKS BY THE AUTHOR:

amazon.com/author/muataashby

Prices subject to change.

EGYPTIAN YOGA: THE PHILOSOPHY OF ENLIGHTENMENT An original, fully illustrated work, including hieroglyphs, detailing the meaning of the Egyptian mysteries, tantric yoga, psycho-spiritual and physical exercises. Egyptian Yoga is a guide to the practice of the highest spiritual philosophy which leads to absolute freedom from human misery and to immortality. It is well known by scholars that Egyptian philosophy is the basis of Western and Middle Eastern religious philosophies such as *Christianity, Islam, Judaism,* the *Kabala*, and Greek philosophy, but what about Indian philosophy, Yoga and Taoism? What were the original teachings? How can they be practiced today? What is the source of pain and suffering in the world and what is the solution? Discover the deepest mysteries of the mind and universe within and outside of yourself. 8.5" X 11" ISBN: 1-884564-01-1 Soft $19.95

EGYPTIAN YOGA: African Religion Volume 2- Theban Theology U.S. In this long awaited sequel to *Egyptian Yoga: The Philosophy of Enlightenment* you will take a fascinating and enlightening journey back in time and discover the teachings which constituted the epitome of Ancient Egyptian spiritual wisdom. What are the disciplines which lead to the fulfillment of all desires? Delve into the three states of consciousness (waking, dream and deep sleep) and the fourth state which transcends them all, Neberdjer, "The Absolute." These teachings of the city of Waset (Thebes) were the crowning achievement of the Sages of Ancient Egypt. They establish the standard mystical keys for understanding the profound mystical symbolism of the Triad of human consciousness. ISBN 1-884564-39-9 $23.95

THE KEMETIC DIET: GUIDE TO HEALTH, DIET AND FASTING Health issues have always been important to human beings since the beginning of time. The earliest records of history show that the art of healing was held in high esteem since the time of Ancient Egypt. In the early 20th century, medical doctors[2] had almost attained the status of sainthood by the promotion of the idea that they alone were "scientists" while other healing modalities and traditional healers who did not follow the "scientific method' were nothing but superstitious, ignorant charlatans who at best would take the money of their clients and at worst kill them with the unscientific "snake oils" and "irrational theories". In the late 20th century, the failure of the modern medical establishment's ability to lead the general public to good health, promoted the move by many in society towards "alternative medicine". Alternative medicine disciplines are those healing modalities which do not adhere to the philosophy of allopathic medicine. Allopathic medicine is what medical doctors practice by an large. It is the theory that disease is caused by agencies outside the body such as bacteria, viruses or physical means which affect the body. These can therefore be treated by medicines and therapies The natural healing method began in the absence of extensive technologies with the idea that all the answers for health may be found in nature or rather, the deviation from nature. Therefore, the health of the body can be restored by correcting the aberration and thereby restoring balance. This is the area that will be covered in this volume. Allopathic techniques have their place in the art of healing. However, we should not forget that the body is a grand achievement of the spirit and built into it is the capacity to maintain itself and heal itself. Ashby, Muata ISBN: 1-884564-49-6 $28.95

INITIATION INTO EGYPTIAN YOGA Shedy: Spiritual discipline or program, to go deeply into the mysteries, to study the mystery teachings and literature profoundly, to penetrate the mysteries. You will learn about the mysteries of initiation into the teachings and practice of Yoga and how to become an Initiate of the mystical sciences. This insightful manual is the first in a series which introduces you to the goals of daily spiritual and yoga practices: Meditation, Diet, Words of Power and the ancient wisdom teachings. 8.5" X 11" ISBN 1-884564-02-X Soft Cover $24.95 U.S.

THE AFRICAN ORIGINS OF CIVILIZATION, RELIGION AND YOGA SPIRITUALITY AND ETHICS PHILOSOPHY HARD COVER EDITION Part 1, Part 2, Part 3 in one volume 683 Pages Hard Cover First Edition Three volumes in one. Over the past several years I have been asked to put together in one volume the most important evidences showing the correlations and common teachings between Kamitan (Ancient Egyptian) culture and religion and that of India. The questions of the history of Ancient Egypt, and the latest archeological evidences showing civilization and culture in Ancient Egypt and its spread to other countries, has intrigued many scholars as well as mystics over the years. Also, the possibility that Ancient Egyptian Priests and Priestesses migrated to Greece, India and other countries to carry on the traditions of the Ancient Egyptian Mysteries, has been speculated over the years as well. In chapter 1 of the book *Egyptian Yoga The Philosophy of Enlightenment,* 1995, I first introduced the deepest comparison between Ancient Egypt and India that had been brought forth up to that time. Now, in the year 2001 this new book, *THE AFRICAN ORIGINS OF CIVILIZATION, MYSTICAL RELIGION AND YOGA PHILOSOPHY,* more fully explores the motifs, symbols and philosophical correlations between Ancient Egyptian and Indian mysticism and clearly shows not only that Ancient Egypt and India were connected culturally but also spiritually. How does this knowledge help the spiritual aspirant? This discovery has great importance for the Yogis and mystics who follow the philosophy of Ancient Egypt and the mysticism of India. It means that India has a longer history and heritage than was previously understood. It shows that the mysteries of Ancient Egypt were essentially a yoga tradition which did not die but rather developed into the modern day systems of Yoga technology of India. It further shows that African culture developed Yoga Mysticism earlier than any other civilization in history. All of this expands our understanding of the unity of culture and the deep legacy of Yoga, which stretches into the distant past, beyond the Indus Valley civilization, the earliest known high culture in India as well as the Vedic tradition of Aryan culture. Therefore, Yoga culture and mysticism is the oldest known tradition of spiritual development and Indian mysticism is an extension of the Ancient Egyptian mysticism. By understanding the legacy which Ancient Egypt gave to India the mysticism of India is better understood and by comprehending the heritage of Indian Yoga, which is rooted in Ancient Egypt the Mysticism of Ancient Egypt is also better understood. This expanded understanding allows us to prove the underlying kinship of humanity, through the common symbols, motifs and philosophies which are not disparate and confusing teachings but in reality expressions of the same study of truth through metaphysics and mystical realization of Self. (HARD COVER) ISBN: 1-884564-50-X $45.00 U.S. 81/2" X 11"

AFRICAN ORIGINS BOOK 1 PART 1 African Origins of African Civilization, Religion, Yoga Mysticism and Ethics Philosophy-Soft Cover $24.95 ISBN: 1-884564-55-0

AFRICAN ORIGINS BOOK 2 PART 2 African Origins of Western Civilization, Religion and Philosophy (Soft) -Soft Cover $24.95 ISBN: 1-884564-56-9

EGYPT AND INDIA AFRICAN ORIGINS OF Eastern Civilization, Religion, Yoga Mysticism and Philosophy-Soft Cover $29.95 (Soft) ISBN: 1-884564-57-7

THE MYSTERIES OF ISIS: ***The Ancient Egyptian Philosophy of Self-Realization*** - There are several paths to discover the Divine and the mysteries of the higher Self. This volume details the mystery teachings of the goddess Aset (Isis) from Ancient Egypt- the path of wisdom. It includes the teachings of her temple and the disciplines that are enjoined for the initiates of the temple of Aset as they were given in ancient times. Also, this book includes the teachings of the main myths of Aset that lead a human being to spiritual enlightenment and immortality.

Through the study of ancient myth and the illumination of initiatic understanding the idea of God is expanded from the mythological comprehension to the metaphysical. Then this metaphysical understanding is related to you, the student, so as to begin understanding your true divine nature. ISBN 1-884564-24-0 $22.99

EGYPTIAN PROVERBS: collection of —Ancient Egyptian Proverbs and Wisdom Teachings -How to live according to MAAT Philosophy. Beginning Meditation. All proverbs are indexed for easy searches. For the first time in one volume, ——Ancient Egyptian Proverbs, wisdom teachings 8and meditations, fully illustrated with hieroglyphic text and symbols. EGYPTIAN PROVERBS is a unique collection of knowledge and wisdom which you can put into practice today and transform your life. $14.95 U.S ISBN: 1-884564-00-3

7. *GOD OF LOVE: THE PATH OF DIVINE LOVE The Process of Mystical Transformation and The Path of Divine Love* This Volume focuses on the ancient wisdom teachings of "Neter Merri" –the Ancient Egyptian philosophy of Divine Love and how to use them in a scientific process for self-transformation. Love is one of the most powerful human emotions. It is also the source of Divine feeling that unifies God and the individual human being. When love is fragmented and diminished by egoism the Divine connection is lost. The Ancient tradition of Neter Merri leads human beings back to their Divine connection, allowing them to discover their innate glorious self that is actually Divine and immortal. This volume will detail the process of transform9ation from ordinary consciousness to cosmic consciousness through the integrated practice of the teachings and the path of Devotional Love toward the Divine. 5.5"x 8.5" ISBN 1-884564-11-9 $22.95

INTRODUCTION TO MAAT PHILOSOPHY: Spiritual Enlightenment Through the Path of Virtue Known commonly as Karma in India, the teachings of MAAT contain an extensive philosophy based on ariu (deeds) and their fructification in the form of shai and renenet (fortune and destiny, leading to Meskhenet (fate in a future birth) for living virtuously and with orderly wisdom are explained and the student is to begin practicing the precepts of Maat in daily life so as to promote the process of purification of the heart in preparation for the judgment of the soul. This judg10ent will be understood not as an event that will occur at the time of death but as an event that occurs continuously, at every moment in the life of the individual. The student will learn how to become allied with the forces of the Higher Self and to thereby begin cleansing the mind (heart) of impurities so as to attain a higher vision of reality. ISBN 1-884564-20-8 $22.99

MEDITATION The Ancient Egyptian Path to Enlightenment Many people do not know about the rich history of meditation practice in Ancient Egypt. This volume outlines the theory of meditation and presents the Ancient Egyptian Hieroglyphic text which give instruction as to the nature of the mind and its three modes of expression. It also presents the texts which give instruction on the practice of meditation for spiritual Enlightenment and unity with the Divine. This volume allows the reader to begin practicing meditation by explaining, in easy to understand terms, the simplest form of meditation and working up to the most advanced form which was practiced in ancient times and which is still practiced by yogis around the world in modern times. ISBN 1-884564-27-7 $22.99

THE GLORIOUS LIGHT MEDITATION TECHNIQUE OF ANCIENT EGYPT New for the year 2000. This volume is based on the earliest known instruction in history given for the practice of formal meditation. Discovered by Dr. Muata Ashby, it is inscribed on the walls of the Tomb of Seti I in Thebes Egypt. This volume details the philosophy and practice of this unique system of meditation originated in Ancient Egypt and the earliest practice of meditation known in the world which occurred in the most advanced African Culture. ISBN: 1-884564-15-1 $16.95 (PB)

THE SERPENT POWER: The Ancient Egyptian Mystical Wisdom of the Inner Life Force. This Volume specifically deals with the latent life Force energy of the universe and in the human body, its control and sublimation. How to develop the Life Force energy of the subtle body. This Volume will introduce the esoteric wisdom of the science of how virtuous living acts in a subtle and mysterious way to cleanse the latent psychic energy conduits and vortices of the spiritual body. ISBN 1-884564-19-4 $22.95

11. *EGYPTIAN YOGA The Postures of The Gods and Goddesses* Discover the physical postures and exercises practiced thousands of years ago in Ancient Egypt which are today known as Yoga exercises. Discover the history of the postures and how they were transferred from Ancient Egypt in Africa to India through Buddhist Tantrism. Then practice the postures as you discover the mythic teaching that originally gave birth to the postures and was practiced by the Ancient Egyptian priests and priestesses. This work is based on the pictures and teachings from the Creation story of Ra, The Asarian Resurrection Myth and the carvings and reliefs from various Temples in Ancient Egypt 8.5" X 11" ISBN 1-884564-10-0 Soft Cover $21.95 Exercise video $20

12. *SACRED SEXUALITY: ANCIENT EGYPTIAN TANTRA YOGA: The Art of Sex* Sublimation and Universal Consciousness This Volume will expand on the male and female principles within the human body and in the universe and further detail the sublimation of sexual energy into spiritual energy. The student will study the deities Min and Hathor, Asar and Aset, Geb and Nut and discover the mystical implications for a practical spiritual discipline. This Volume will also focus on the Tantric aspects of Ancient Egyptian and Indian mysticism, the purpose of sex and the mystical teachings of sexual sublimation which lead to self-knowledge and Enlightenment. ISBN 1-884564-03-8 $24.95

AFRICAN RELIGION Volume 4: ASARIAN THEOLOGY: RESURRECTING OSIRIS The path of Mystical Awakening and the Keys to Immortality NEW REVISED AND EXPANDED EDITION! The Ancient Sages created stories based on human and superhuman beings whose struggles, aspirations, needs and desires ultimately lead them to discover their true Self. The myth of Aset, Asar and Heru is no exception in this area. While there is no one source where the entire story may be found, pieces of it are inscribed in various ancient Temples walls, tombs, steles and papyri. For the first time available, the complete myth of Asar, Aset and Heru has been compiled from original Ancient Egyptian, Greek and Coptic Texts. This epic myth has been richly illustrated with reliefs from the Temple of Heru at Edfu, the Temple of Aset at Philae, the Temple of Asar at Abydos, the Temple of Hathor at Denderah and various papyri, inscriptions and reliefs. Discover the myth which inspired the teachings of the *Shetaut Neter* (Egyptian Mystery System - Egyptian Yoga) and the Egyptian Book of Coming Forth By Day. Also, discover the three levels of Ancient Egyptian Religion, how to understand the mysteries of the Duat or Astral World and how to discover the abode of the Supreme in the Amenta, *The Other World* The ancient religion of Asar, Aset and Heru, if properly understood, contains all of the elements necessary to lead the sincere aspirant to attain immortality through inner self-discovery. This volume presents the entire myth and explores the main mystical themes and rituals associated with the myth for understating human existence, creation and the way to achieve spiritual emancipation - *Resurrection.* The Asarian myth is so powerful that it influenced and is still having an effect on the major world religions. Discover the origins and mystical meaning of the Christian Trinity, the Eucharist ritual and the ancient origin of the birthday of Jesus Christ. Soft Cover ISBN: 1-884564-27-5 $24.95

14.

13. *THE EGYPTIAN BOOK OF THE DEAD MYSTICISM OF THE PERT EM HERU* " I Know myself, I know myself, I am One With God!–From the Pert Em Heru "The Ru Pert em Heru" or "Ancient Egyptian Book of The Dead," or "Book of Coming Forth By Day" as it is more popularly known, has fascinated the world since the successful translation of Ancient Egyptian hieroglyphic scripture over 150 years ago. The astonishing writings in it reveal that the Ancient Egyptians believed in life after death and in an ultimate destiny to discover the Divine. The elegance and aesthetic beauty of the hieroglyphic text itself has inspired many see it as an art form in and of itself. But is there more to it than that? Did the Ancient Egyptian wisdom contain more than just aphorisms and hopes of eternal life beyond death? In this volume Dr. Muata Ashby, the author of over 25 books on Ancient Egyptian Yoga Philosophy has produced a new translation of the original texts which uncovers a mystical teaching underlying the sayings and rituals instituted by the Ancient Egyptian Sages and Saints. "Once 15 the philosophy of Ancient Egypt is understood as a mystical tradition instead of as a religion or primitive mythology, it reveals its secrets which if practiced today will lead anyone to discover the glory of spiritual self-discovery. The Pert em Heru is in every way comparable to the Indian Upanishads or the Tibetan Book of the Dead." $28.95 ISBN# 1-884564-28-3 Size: 8½" X 11

African Religion VOL. 1- ANUNIAN THEOLOGY THE MYSTERIES OF RA The Philosophy of Anu and The Mystical Teachings of The Ancient Egyptian Creation Myth Discover the mystical teachings contained in the Creation Myth and the gods and goddesses who brought creation and human beings into existence. The Creation myth of Anu is the source of Anunian Theology but also of the other main theological systems of Ancient Egypt that also influenced other world reli16ons including Christianity, Hinduism and Buddhism. The Creation Myth holds the key to understanding the universe and for attaining spiritual Enlightenment. ISBN: 1-884564-38-0 $19.95

African Religion VOL 3: Memphite Theology: MYSTERIES OF MIND Mystical Psychology & Mental Health for Enlightenment and Immortality based on the Ancient Egyptian Philosophy of Menefer -Mysticism of Ptah, Egyptian Physics and Yoga Metaphysics and the Hidden properties of Matter. This volume uncovers the mystical psychology of the Ancient Egyptian wisdom teachings centering on the philosophy of the Ancient Egyptian city of Menefer (Memphite Theology). How to understand the mind and how to control the senses and lead the mind to health, clarity and mystical self-discovery. This Volume will also go deeper into the philosophy of God as creation and will explore the concepts of modern science and how they correlate with ancient teachings. This Volume will lay the ground work for the understanding of the philosophy of universal consciousness and the initiatic/yogic insight into who or what is God? ISBN 1-884564-07-0 $22.95

AFRICAN RELIGION VOLUME 5: THE GODDESS AND THE EGYPTIAN MYSTERIESTHE PATH OF THE GODDESS THE GODDESS PATH The Secret Forms of the Goddess and the Rituals of Resurrection The Supreme Being may be worshipped as father or as mother. *Ushet Rekhat* or *Mother Worship*, is the spiritual process of worshipping the Divine in the form of the Divine Goddess. It celebrates the most important forms of the Goddess including *Nathor, Maat, Aset, Arat, Amentet and Hathor* and explores their mystical meaning as well as the rising of *Sirius,* the star of Aset (Aset) and the new birth of Hor (Heru). The end of the year is a time of reckoning, reflection and engendering a new or renewed positive movement toward attaining spiritual Enlightenment. The Mother Worship devotional meditation ritual, performed on five days during the month of December and on New Year's Eve, is based on the Ushet Rekhit. During the ceremony, the cosmic forces, symbolized by Sirius - and the constellation of Orion ---, are harnessed through the understanding and devotional attitude of the participant. This propitiation draws the light of wisdom and health to all those who share in the ritual, leading to prosperity and wisdom. $14.95 ISBN 1-884564-18-6

THE MYSTICAL JOURNEY FROM JESUS TO CHRIST Discover the ancient Egyptian origins of Christianity before the Catholic Church and learn the mystical teachings given by Jesus to assist all humanity in becoming Christlike. Discover the secret meaning of the Gospels that were discovered in Egypt. Also discover how and why so many Christian churches came into being. Discover that the Bible still holds the keys to mystical realization even though its original writings were changed by the church. Discover how to practice the original teachings of Christianity which leads to the Kingdom of Heaven. $24.95 ISBN# 1-884564-05-4 size: 8½" X 11"

17. *THE STORY OF ASAR, ASET AND HERU:* An Ancient Egyptian Legend (For Children) Now for the first time, the most ancient myth of Ancient Egypt comes alive for children. Inspired by the books *The Asarian Resurrection: The Ancient Egyptian Bible* and *The Mystical Teachings of The Asarian Resurrection, The Story of Asar, Aset and Heru* is an easy to understand and thrilling tale which inspired the children of Ancient Egypt to aspire to greatness and righteousness. If you and your child have enjoyed stories like *The Lion King* and *Star Wars you will love The Story of Asar, Aset and Heru.* Also, if you know the story of Jesus and Krishna you will discover than Ancient Egypt had a similar myth and that this myth carries important spiritual teachings for living a fruitful and fulfilling life. This book may be used along with *The Parents Guide To The Asarian Resurrection Myth: How to Teach Yourself and Your Child the Principles of Universal Mystical Religion.* The guide provides some background to the Asarian Resurrection myth and it also gives insight into the mystical teachings contained in it which you may introduce to your child. It is designed for parents who wish to grow spiritually with their children and it serves as an introduction for those who would like to study the Asarian Resurrection Myth in depth and to practice its teachings. 8.5" X 11" ISBN: 1-884564-31-3 $12.95

THE PARENTS GUIDE TO THE AUSARIAN RESURRECTION MYTH: How to Teach Yourself and Your Child the Principles of Universal Mystical Religion. This insightful manual brings for the timeless wisdom of the ancient through the Ancient Egyptian myth of Asar, Aset and Heru and the mystical teachings contained in it for parents who want to guide their children to understand and practice the teachings of mystical spirituality. This manual may be used with the children's storybook *The Story of Asar, Aset and Heru* by Dr. Muata Abhaya Ashby. ISBN: 1-884564-30-5 $16.95

HEALING THE CRIMINAL HEART. Introduction to Maat Philosophy, Yoga and Spiritual Redemption Through the Path of Virtue Who is a criminal? Is there such a thing as a criminal heart? What is the source of evil and sinfulness and is there any way to rise above it? Is there redemption for those who have committed sins, even the worst crimes? Ancient Egyptian mystical psychology holds important answers to these questions. Over ten thousand years ago mystical psychologists, the Sages of Ancient Egypt, studied and charted the human mind and spirit and laid out a path which will lead to spiritual redemption, prosperity and Enlightenment. This introductory volume brings forth the teachings of the Asarian Resurrection, the most important myth of Ancient Egypt, with relation to the faults of human existence: anger, hatred, greed, lust, animosity, discontent, ignorance, egoism jealousy, bitterness, and a myriad of psycho-spiritual ailments which keep a human being in a state of negativity and adversity ISBN: 1-884564-17-8 $15.95

18. *TEMPLE RITUAL OF THE ANCIENT EGYPTIAN MYSTERIES--THEATER & DRAMA OF THE ANCIENT EGYPTIAN MYSTERIES*: Details the practice of the mysteries and ritual program of the temple and the philosophy an practice of the ritual of the mysteries, its purpose and execution. Featuring the Ancient Egyptian stage play-"The Enlightenment of Hathor' Based on an Ancient Egyptian Drama, The original Theater -Mysticism of the Temple of Hetheru 1-884564-14-3 $19.95 By Dr. Muata Ashby

19.

GUIDE TO PRINT ON DEMAND: SELF-PUBLISH FOR PROFIT, SPIRITUAL FULFILLMENT AND SERVICE TO HUMANITY Everyone asks us how we produced so many books in such a short time. Here are the secrets to writing and producing books that uplift humanity and how to get them printed for a fraction of the regular cost. Anyone can become an author even if they have limited funds. All that is necessary is the willingness to learn how the printing and book business work and the desire to follow the special instructions given here for preparing your manuscript format. Then you take your work directly to the non-traditional companies who can produce your books for less than the traditional book printer can. ISBN: 1-884564-40-2 $16.95 U. S.

Egyptian Mysteries: Vol. 1, Shetaut Neter What are the Mysteries? For thousands of years the spiritual tradition of Ancient Egypt, *Shetaut Neter,* "The Egyptian Mysteries," "The Secret Teachings," have fascinated, tantalized and amazed the world. At one time exalted and recognized as the highest culture of the world, by Africans, Europeans, Asiatics, Hindus, Buddhists and other cultures of the ancient world, in time it was shunned by the emerging orthodox world religions. Its temples desecrated, its philosophy maligned, its tradition spurned, its philosophy dormant in the mystical *Medu Neter*, the mysterious hieroglyphic texts which hold the secret symbolic meaning that has scarcely been discerned up to now. What are the secrets of *Nehast* {spiritual awakening and emancipation, resurrection}. More than just a literal translation, this volume is for awakening to the secret code *Shetitu* of the teaching which was not deciphered by Egyptologists, nor could be understood by ordinary spiritualists. This book is a reinstatement of the original science made available for our times, to the reincarnated followers of Ancient Egyptian culture and the prospect of spiritual freedom to break the bonds of *Khemn,* "ignorance," and slavery to evil forces: *Såaa* . ISBN: 1-884564-41-0 $19.99

EGYPTIAN MYSTERIES VOL 2: Dictionary of Gods and Goddesses This book is about the mystery of neteru, the gods and goddesses of Ancient Egypt (Kamit, Kemet). Neteru means "Gods and Goddesses." But the Neterian teaching of Neteru represents more than the usual limited modern day concept of "divinities" or "spirits." The Neteru of Kamit are also metaphors, cosmic principles and vehicles for the enlightening teachings of Shetaut Neter (Ancient Egyptian-African Religion). Actually they are the elements for one of the most advanced systems of spirituality ever conceived in human history. Understanding the concept of neteru provides a firm basis for spiritual evolution and the pathway for viable culture, peace on earth and a healthy human society. Why is it important to have gods and goddesses in our lives? In order for spiritual evolution to be possible, once a human being has accepted that there is existence after death and there is a transcendental being who exists beyond time and space knowledge, human beings need a connection to that which transcends the ordinary experience of human life in time and space and a means to understand the transcendental reality beyond the mundane reality. ISBN: 1-884564-23-2 $21.95

20. *EGYPTIAN MYSTERIES VOL. 3* The Priests and Priestesses of Ancient Egypt This volume details the path of Neterian priesthood, the joys, challenges and rewards of advanced Neterian life, the teachings that allowed the priests and priestesses to manage the most long lived civilization in human history and how that path can be adopted today; for those who want to tread the path of the Clergy of Shetaut Neter. ISBN: 1-884564-53-4 $24.95

21. *The War of Heru and Set:* The Struggle of Good and Evil for Control of the World and The Human Soul This volume contains a novelized version of the Asarian Resurrection myth that is based on the actual scriptures presented in the Book Asarian Religion (old name –Resurrecting Osiris). This volume is prepared in the form of a screenplay and can be easily adapted to be used as a stage play. Spiritual seeking is a mythic journey that has many emotional highs and lows, ecstasies and depressions, victories and frustrations. This is the War of Life that is played out in the myth as the struggle of Heru and Set and those are mythic characters that represent the human Higher and Lower self. How to understand the war and emerge victorious in the journey of life? The ultimate victory and fulfillment can be experienced, which is not changeable or lost in time. The purpose of myth is to convey the wisdom of life through the story of divinities who show the way to overcome the challenges and foibles of life. In this volume the feelings and emotions of the characters of the myth have been highlighted to show the deeply rich texture of the Ancient Egyptian myth. This myth contains deep spiritual teachings and insights into the nature of self, of God and the mysteries of life and the means to discover the true meaning of life and thereby achieve the true purpose of life. To become victorious in the battle of life means to become the King (or Queen) of Egypt. Have you seen movies like The Lion King, Hamlet, The Odyssey, or The Little Buddha? These have been some of the most popular movies in modern times. The Sema Institute of Yoga is dedicated to researching and presenting the wisdom and culture of ancient Africa. The Script is designed to be produced as a motion picture but may be adapted for the theater as well. $21.95 copyright 1998 By Dr. Muata Ashby ISBN 1-8840564-44-5

AFRICAN DIONYSUS: FROM EGYPT TO GREECE: The Kamitan Origins of Greek Culture and Religion ISBN: 1-884564-47-X FROM EGYPT TO GREECE This insightful manual is a reference to Ancient Egyptian mythology and philosophy and its correlation to what later became known as Greek and Rome mythology and philosophy. It outlines the basic tenets of the mythologies and shoes the ancient origins of Greek culture in Ancient Egypt. This volume also documents the origins of the Greek alphabet in Egypt as well as Greek religion, myth and philosophy of the gods and goddesses from Egypt from the myth of Atlantis and archaic period with the Minoans to the Classical period. This volume also acts as a resource for Colleges students who would like to set up fraternities and sororities based on the original Ancient Egyptian principles of Sheti and Maat philosophy. ISBN: 1-884564-47-X $22.95 U.S.

THE FORTY TWO PRECEPTS OF MAAT, THE PHILOSOPHY OF RIGHTEOUS ACTION AND THE ANCIENT EGYPTIAN WISDOM TEXTS ADVANCED STUDIES This manual is designed for use with the 1998 Maat Philosophy Class conducted by Dr. Muata Ashby. This is a detailed study of Maat Philosophy. It contains a compilation of the 42 laws or precepts of Maat and the corresponding principles which they represent along with the teachings of the ancient Egyptian Sages relating to each. Maat philosophy was the basis of Ancient Egyptian society and government as well as the heart of Ancient Egyptian myth and spirituality. Maat is at once a goddess, a cosmic force and a living social doctrine, which promotes social harmony and thereby paves the way for spiritual evolution in all levels of society. ISBN: 1-884564-48-8 $16.95 U.S.

THE SECRET LOTUS: Poetry of Enlightenment

Discover the mystical sentiment of the Kemetic teaching as expressed through the poetry of Muata Ashby. The teaching of spiritual awakening is uniquely experienced when the poetic sensibility is present. This first volume contains the poems written between 1996 and 2003. **1-884564–16 -X $16.99**

36. **The Ancient Egyptian Buddha: The Ancient Egyptian Origins of Buddhism**
This book is a compilation of several sections of a larger work, a book by the name of African Origins of Civilization, Religion, Yoga Mysticism and Ethics Philosophy. It also contains some additional evidences not contained in the larger work that demonstrate the correlation between Ancient Egyptian Religion and Buddhism. This book is one of several compiled short volumes that has been compiled so as to facilitate access to specific subjects contained in the larger work which is over 680 pages long. These short and small volumes have been specifically designed to cover one subject in a brief and low cost format. This present volume, The Ancient Egyptian Buddha: The Ancient Egyptian Origins of Buddhism, formed one subject in the larger work; actually it was one chapter of the larger work. However, this volume has some new additional evidences and comparisons of Buddhist and Neterian (Ancient Egyptian) philosophies not previously discussed. It was felt that this subject needed to be discussed because even in the early 21st century, the idea persists that Buddhism originated only in India independently. Yet there is ample evidence from ancient writings and perhaps more importantly, iconographical evidences from the Ancient Egyptians and early Buddhists themselves that prove otherwise. This handy volume has been designed to be accessible to young adults and all others who would like to have an easy reference with documentation on this important subject. This is an important subject because the frame of reference with which we look at a culture depends strongly on our conceptions about its origins. in this case, if we look at the Buddhism as an Asiatic religion we would treat it and its culture in one way. If we id as African [Ancient Egyptian] we not only would see it in a different light but we also must ascribe Africa with a glorious legacy that matches any other culture in human history and gave rise to one of the present day most important religious philosophies. We would also look at the culture and philosophies of the Ancient Egyptians as having African insights that offer us greater depth into the Buddhist philosophies. Those insights inform our knowledge about other African traditions and we can also begin to understand in a deeper way the effect of Ancient Egyptian culture on African culture and also on the Asiatic as well. We would also be able to discover the glorious and wondrous teaching of mystical philosophy that Ancient Egyptian Shetaut Neter religion offers, that is as powerful as any other mystic system of spiritual philosophy in the world today. ISBN: 1-884564-61-5 $28.95

37. **The Death of American Empire: Neo-conservatism, Theocracy, Economic Imperialism, Environmental Disaster and the Collapse of Civilization**
This work is a collection of essays relating to social and economic, leadership, and ethics, ecological and religious issues that are facing the world today in order to understand the course of history that has led humanity to its present condition and then arrive at positive solutions that will lead to better outcomes for all humanity. It surveys the development and decline of major empires throughout history and focuses on the creation of American Empire along with the social, political and economic policies that led to the prominence of the United States of America as a Superpower including the rise of the political control of the neo-con political philosophy including militarism and the military industrial complex in American politics and the rise of the religious right into and American Theocracy movement. This volume details, through historical and current events, the psychology behind the dominance of western culture in world politics through the "Superpower Syndrome Mandatory Conflict Complex" that drives the Superpower culture to establish itself above all others and then act hubristically to dominate world culture through legitimate influences as well as coercion, media censorship and misinformation leading to international hegemony and world conflict. This volume also details the financial policies that gave rise to American prominence in the global economy, especially after World War II, and promoted American preeminence over the world economy through Globalization as well as the environmental policies, including the oil economy, that are promoting degradation of the world ecology and contribute to the decline of America as an Empire culture. This volume finally explores the factors pointing to the decline of the American Empire economy and imperial power and what to expect in the aftermath of American prominence and how to survive the decline while at the same time promoting policies and social-economic-religious-political changes that are needed in order to promote the emergence of a beneficial and sustainable culture. **$25.95soft** 1-884564-25-9, Hard Cover **$29.95** 1-884564-45-3

38. **The African Origins of Hatha Yoga: And its Ancient Mystical Teaching**

The subject of this present volume, The Ancient Egyptian Origins of Yoga Postures, formed one subject in the larger works, African Origins of Civilization Religion, Yoga Mysticism and Ethics Philosophy and the Book Egypt and India is the section of the book African Origins of Civilization. Those works contain the collection of all correlations between Ancient Egypt and India. This volume also contains some additional information not contained in the previous work. It was felt that this subject needed to be discussed more directly, being treated in one volume, as opposed to being contained in the larger work along with other subjects, because even in the early 21st century, the idea persists that the Yoga and specifically, Yoga Postures, were invented and developed only in India. The Ancient Egyptians were peoples originally from Africa who were, in ancient times, colonists in India. Therefore it is no surprise that many Indian traditions including religious and Yogic, would be found earlier in Ancient Egypt. Yet there is ample evidence from ancient writings and perhaps more importantly, iconographical evidences from the Ancient Egyptians themselves and the Indians themselves that prove the connection between Ancient Egypt and India as well as the existence of a discipline of Yoga Postures in Ancient Egypt long before its practice in India. This handy volume has been designed to be accessible to young adults and all others who would like to have an easy reference with documentation on this important subject. This is an important subject because the frame of reference with which we look at a culture depends strongly on our conceptions about its origins. In this case, if we look at the Ancient Egyptians as Asiatic peoples we would treat them and their culture in one way. If we see them as Africans we not only see them in a different light but we also must ascribe Africa with a glorious legacy that matches any other culture in human history. We would also look at the culture and philosophies of the Ancient Egyptians as having African insights instead of Asiatic ones. Those insights inform our knowledge about other African traditions, and we can also begin to understand in a deeper way the effect of Ancient Egyptian culture on African culture and also on the Asiatic as well. When we discover the deeper and more ancient practice of the postures system in Ancient Egypt that was called "Hatha Yoga" in India, we are able to find a new and expanded understanding of the practice that constitutes a discipline of spiritual practice that informs and revitalizes the Indian practices as well as all spiritual disciplines. $19.99 ISBN 1-884564-60-7

39. **The Black Ancient Egyptians**

This present volume, The Black Ancient Egyptians: The Black African Ancestry of the Ancient Egyptians, formed one subject in the larger work: The African Origins of Civilization, Religion, Yoga Mysticism and Ethics Philosophy. It was felt that this subject needed to be discussed because even in the early 21st century, the idea persists that the Ancient Egyptians were peoples originally from Asia Minor who came into North-East Africa. Yet there is ample evidence from ancient writings and perhaps more importantly, iconographical evidences from the Ancient Egyptians themselves that proves otherwise. This handy volume has been designed to be accessible to young adults and all others who would like to have an easy reference with documentation on this important subject. This is an important subject because the frame of reference with which we look at a culture depends strongly on our conceptions about its origins. in this case, if we look at the Ancient Egyptians as Asiatic peoples we would treat them and their culture in one way. If we see them as Africans we not only see them in a different light but we also must ascribe Africa with a glorious legacy that matches any other culture in human history. We would also look at the culture and philosophies of the Ancient Egyptians as having African insights instead of Asiatic ones. Those insights inform our knowledge about other African traditions, and we can also begin to understand in a deeper way the effect of Ancient Egyptian culture on African culture and also on the Asiatic as well. ISBN 1-884564-21-6 $19.99

40. **The Limits of Faith: The Failure of Faith-based Religions and the Solution to the Meaning of Life**

Is faith belief in something without proof? And if so is there never to be any proof or discovery? If so what is the need of intellect? If faith is trust in something that is real is that reality historical, literal or metaphorical or philosophical? If knowledge is an essential element in faith, why should there be so much emphasis on believing and not on understanding in the modern practice of religion? This volume is a compilation of essays related to the nature of religious faith in the context of its inception in human history as well as its meaning for religious practice and relations between religions in modern times. Faith has come to be regarded as a virtuous goal in life. However, many people have asked how can it be that an endeavor that is supposed to be dedicated to spiritual upliftment has led to more conflict in human history than any other social factor? ISBN 1884564631 SOFT COVER - $19.99, ISBN 1884564623 HARD COVER - $28.95

41. **Redemption of The Criminal Heart Through Kemetic Spirituality and Maat Philosophy**

Special book dedicated to inmates, their families and members of the Law Enforcement community. ISBN: 1-884564-70-4
$5.00

42. COMPARATIVE MYTHOLOGY

What are Myth and Culture and what is their importance for understanding the development of societies, human evolution and the search for meaning? What is the purpose of culture and how do cultures evolve? What are the elements of a culture and how can those elements be broken down and the constituent parts of a culture understood and compared? How do cultures interact? How does enculturation occur and how do people interact with other cultures? How do the processes of acculturation and cooptation occur and what does this mean for the development of a society? How can the study of myths and the elements of culture help in understanding the meaning of life and the means to promote understanding and peace in the world of human activity? This volume is the exposition of a method for studying and comparing cultures, myths and other social aspects of a society. It is an expansion on the Cultural Category Factor Correlation method for studying and comparing myths, cultures, religions and other aspects of human culture. It was originally introduced in the year 2002. This volume contains an expanded treatment as well as several refinements along with examples of the application of the method. the apparent. I hope you enjoy these art renditions as serene reflections of the mysteries of life. ISBN: 1-884564-72-0
Book price $21.95

43. CONVERSATION WITH GOD: Revelations of the Important Questions of Life
$24.99 U.S.

This volume contains a grouping of some of the questions that have been submitted to Dr. Muata Ashby. They are efforts by many aspirants to better understand and practice the teachings of mystical spirituality. It is said that when sages are asked spiritual questions they are relaying the wisdom of God, the Goddess, the Higher Self, etc. There is a very special quality about the Q & A process that does not occur during a regular lecture session. Certain points come out that would not come out otherwise due to the nature of the process which ideally occurs after a lecture. Having been to a certain degree enlightened by a lecture certain new questions arise and the answers to these have the effect of elevating the teaching of the lecture to even higher levels. Therefore, enjoy these exchanges and may they lead you to enlightenment, peace and prosperity. Available Late Summer 2007 ISBN: 1-884564-68-2

44. **MYSTIC ART PAINTINGS**

(with Full Color images) This book contains a collection of the small number of paintings that I have created over the years. Some were used as early book covers and others were done simply to express certain spiritual feelings; some were created for no purpose except to express the joy of color and the feeling of relaxed freedom. All are to elicit mystical awakening in the viewer. Writing a book on philosophy is like sculpture, the more the work is rewritten the reflections and ideas become honed and take form and become clearer and imbued with intellectual beauty. Mystic music is like meditation, a world of its own that exists about 1 inch above ground wherein the musician does not touch the ground. Mystic Graphic Art is meditation in form, color, image and reflected image which opens the door to the reality behind the apparent. I hope you enjoy these art renditions and my reflections on them as serene reflections of the mysteries of life, as visual renditions of the philosophy I have written about over the years. ISBN 1-884564-69-0
$19.95

45. **ANCIENT EGYPTIAN HIEROGLYPHS FOR BEGINNERS**

This brief guide was prepared for those inquiring about how to enter into Hieroglyphic studies on their own at home or in study groups. First of all you should know that there are a few institutions around the world which teach how to read the Hieroglyphic text but due to the nature of the study there are perhaps only a handful of people who can read fluently. It is possible for anyone with average intelligence to achieve a high level of proficiency in reading inscriptions on temples and artifacts; however, reading extensive texts is another issue entirely. However, this introduction will give you entry into those texts if assisted by dictionaries and other aids. Most Egyptologists have a basic knowledge and keep dictionaries and notes handy when it comes to dealing with more difficult texts. Medtu Neter or the Ancient Egyptian hieroglyphic language has been considered as a "Dead Language." However, dead languages have always been studied by individuals who for the most part have taught themselves through various means. This book will discuss those means and how to use them most efficiently. ISBN 1884564429 **$28.95**

46. ON THE MYSTERIES: Wisdom of An Ancient Egyptian Sage -with Foreword by Muata Ashby

This volume, On the Mysteries, by Iamblichus (Abamun) is a unique form or scripture out of the Ancient Egyptian religious tradition. It is written in a form that is not usual or which is not usually found in the remnants of Ancient Egyptian scriptures. It is in the form of teacher and disciple, much like the Eastern scriptures such as Bhagavad Gita or the Upanishads. This form of writing may not have been necessary in Ancient times, because the format of teaching in Egypt was different prior to the conquest period by the Persians, Assyrians, Greeks and later the Romans. The question and answer format can be found but such extensive discourses and corrections of misunderstandings within the context of a teacher - disciple relationship is not usual. It therefore provides extensive insights into the times when it was written and the state of practice of Ancient Egyptian and other mystery religions. This has important implications for our times because we are today, as in the Greco-Roman period, also besieged with varied religions and new age philosophies as well as social strife and war. How can we understand our times and also make sense of the forest of spiritual traditions? How can we cut through the cacophony of religious fanaticism, and ignorance as well as misconceptions about the mysteries on the other in order to discover the true purpose of religion and the secret teachings that open up the mysteries of life and the way to enlightenment and immortality? This book, which comes to us from so long ago, offers us transcendental wisdom that applied to the world two thousand years ago as well as our world today. ISBN 1-884564-64-X $25.95

47. The Ancient Egyptian Wisdom Texts -Compiled by Muata Ashby

The Ancient Egyptian Wisdom Texts are a genre of writings from the ancient culture that have survived to the present and provide a vibrant record of the practice of spiritual evolution otherwise known as religion or yoga philosophy in Ancient Egypt. The principle focus of the Wisdom Texts is the cultivation of understanding, peace, harmony, selfless service, self-control, Inner fulfillment and spiritual realization. When these factors are cultivated in human life, the virtuous qualities in a human being begin to manifest and sinfulness, ignorance and negativity diminish until a person is able to enter into higher consciousness, the coveted goal of all civilizations. It is this virtuous mode of life which opens the door to self-discovery and spiritual enlightenment. Therefore, the Wisdom Texts are important scriptures on the subject of human nature, spiritual psychology and mystical philosophy. The teachings presented in the Wisdom Texts form the foundation of religion as well as the guidelines for conducting the affairs of every area of social interaction including commerce, education, the army, marriage, and especially the legal system. These texts were sources for the famous 42 Precepts of Maat of the Pert-m-Heru (Book of the Dead), essential regulations of good conduct to develop virtue and purity in order to attain higher consciousness and immortality after death. ISBN1-884564-65-8 $18.95

48. THE KEMETIC TREE OF LIFE

THE KEMETIC TREE OF LIFE: Newly Revealed Ancient Egyptian Cosmology and Metaphysics for Higher Consciousness The Tree of Life is a roadmap of a journey which explains how Creation came into being and how it will end. It also explains what Creation is composed of and also what human beings are and what they are composed of. It also explains the process of Creation, how Creation develops, as well as who created Creation and where that entity may be found. It also explains how a human being may discover that entity and in so doing also discover the secrets of Creation, the meaning of life and the means to break free from the pathetic condition of human limitation and mortality in order to discover the higher realms of being by discovering the principles, the levels of existence that are beyond the simple physical and material aspects of life. This book contains color plates **ISBN: 1-884564-74-7**

$27.95 U.S.

49-MATRIX OF AFRICAN PROVERBS: The Ethical and Spiritual Blueprint

This volume sets forth the fundamental principles of African ethics and their practical applications for use by individuals and organizations seeking to model their ethical policies using the Traditional African values and concepts of ethical human behavior for the proper sustenance and management of society. Furthermore, this book will provide guidance as to how the Traditional African Ethics may be viewed and applied, taking into consideration the technological and social advancements in the present. This volume also presents the principles of ethical culture, and references for each to specific injunctions from Traditional African Proverbial Wisdom Teachings. These teachings are compiled from varied Pre-colonial African societies including Yoruba, Ashanti, Kemet, Malawi, Nigeria, Ethiopia, Galla, Ghana and many more. ISBN 1-884564-77-1

50- **Growing Beyond Hate: Keys to Freedom from Discord, Racism, Sexism, Political Conflict, Class Warfare, Violence, and How to Achieve Peace and Enlightenment**---INTRODUCTION: WHY DO WE HATE? Hatred is one of the fundamental motivating aspects of human life; the other is desire. Desire can be of a worldly nature or of a spiritual, elevating nature. Worldly desire and hatred are like two sides of the same coin in that human life is usually swaying from one to the other; but the question is why? And is there a way to satisfy the desiring or hating mind in such a way as to find peace in life? Why do human beings go to war? Why do human beings perpetrate violence against one another? And is there a way not just to understand the phenomena but to resolve the issues that plague humanity and could lead to a more harmonious society? Hatred is perhaps the greatest scourge of humanity in that it leads to misunderstanding, conflict and untold miseries of life and clashes between individuals, societies and nations. Therefore, the riddle of Hatred, that is, understanding the sources of it and how to confront, reduce and even eradicate it so as to bring forth the fulfillment in life and peace for society, should be a top priority for social scientists, spiritualists and philosophers. This book is written from the perspective of spiritual philosophy based on the mystical wisdom and sema or yoga philosophy of the Ancient Egyptians. This philosophy, originated and based in the wisdom of Shetaut Neter, the Egyptian Mysteries, and Maat, ethical way of life in society and in spirit, contains Sema-Yogic wisdom and understanding of life's predicaments that can allow a human being of any ethnic group to understand and overcome the causes of hatred, racism, sexism, violence and disharmony in life, that plague human society. ISBN: 1-884564-81-X

52. Guide to Creating a Kemetic Marriage Contract

This marital contract guide reflects actual Ancient Egyptian Principles for Kemetic Marriage as they are to be applied for our times. The marital contract allows people to have a framework with which to face the challenges of marital relations instead of relying on hopes or romantic dreams that everything will work out somehow; in other words, love is not all you need. The latter is not an evolved, mature way of handling one of the most important aspects of human life. Therefore, it behooves anyone who wishes to enter into a marriage to explore the issues, express their needs and seek to avoid costly mistakes, and resolve conflicts in the normal course of life or make sure that their rights and dignity will be protected if any eventuality should occur. Marital relations in Ancient Egypt were not like those in other countries of the time and not like those of present day countries. The extreme longevity of Ancient Egyptian society, founded in Maat philosophy, allowed the social development of marriage to evolve and progress to a high level of order and balance. Maat represents truth, righteous, justice and harmony in life. This meant that the marital partner's rights were to be protected with equal standing before the law. So there was no disparity between rights of men or rights of women. Therefore, anyone who wants to enter into a marriage based on Kemetic principles must first and foremost adhere to this standard...equality in the rights of men and women. This guide demonstrates procedures for following the Ancient Egyptian practice of formalizing marriage with a contract that spells out the important concerns of each partner in the marital relationship, based on Maatian principles [of righteous, truth, harmony and justice] so that the rights and needs of each partner may be protected within the marriage. It also allows the partners to think about issues that arise out of the marital relations so that they may have a foundation to fall back on in the event that those or other unforeseen issues arise and cause conflict in the relationship. By having a document of expressed concerns, needs and steps to be taken to address them, it is less likely that issues which affect the relationship in a negative way will arise, and when they do, they will be better handled, in a more balanced, just and amicable way.

EBOOK ISBN 978-1-937016-59-3, HARDCOPY BOOK ISBN: 1-884564-82-8

53-Ancient Egyptian Mysteries of The Kybalion: A Hermetic Mystic Psychology Primer Paperback – November 28, 2014

This Volume is a landmark study by a renounced mystic philosopher, Dr. Muata Ashby. It is study not just to philosophize but to be practiced for the purpose of attaining enlightenment. The book is divided into three sections. Part 1 INTRODUCTION presents a brief history of Hermeticism, its origins in the Ancient Egyptian Mysteries (Neterianism) the Kybalion and the origins of the personality known as Hermes Trismegistus. Part 2 presents the essential teachings of the Kybalion text, a set of MAXIMS, without interpretation. Part 3 presents glosses (commentary and explanation) on the essential teachings of the Kybalion based on the philosophy of the Ancient Egyptian Mysteries as determined by Dr. Muata Ashby based on studies and translations of original Ancient Egyptian Hieroglyphic texts; the source from which the Kybalion teaching is derived. The Glosses are an edited and expanded version of Lessons given by Dr. Muata Ashby in the form of lectures on the teachings of the Kybalion.

54-Maat Philosophy Versus Fascism and the Police State: Understanding why Modern Society does not Experience the Peace and Prosperity of Ancient Egypt ... Law and Order, and Spiritual Enlightenment Paperback – January 1, 2014

Understanding why Modern Society does not Experience the Peace and Prosperity of Ancient Egypt and How To Discover the Pathway to Freedom, True Law and Order, and Spiritual Enlightenment. Understanding the Corporate State and How Maatian Philosophy can Leads to Freedom, Prosperity and Enlightenment

55- MALFEASANCE & IMMORALITY: An Analysis of the World Economic Crash of 2008, the Corrupt Political and Financial Institutions that Caused it and Strategies to Survive the Future Collapse of the Economy

The following is a first ever publication, by the Sema Institute, of a �White Paper�. The term is defined as: A white paper is an authoritative report or guide that often addresses issues and how to solve them. White papers are used to educate readers and help people make decisions. They are often used in politics and business. This paper serves as an update to the book Dollar Crisis: The Collapse of Society and Redemption Through Ancient Egyptian Fiscal & Monetary Policy (2008). That book was a continuation and expansion of issues presented in the book The Collapse of Civilization and the Death of American Empire (2006). Those books contained a detailed analysis of economic and political as well as social issues and how Maat Philosophy could offer insights into the nature of the problem, its sources and possible solutions as well as a means to develop an economic system (Fiscal and Monetary policies) that can work for all members of society. This paper contains an analysis of economic events and possible future outcomes based on those events as well as ideas individuals or groups may use in order to develop plans of action to deal with the possible detrimental events that may occur in the near and intermediate future. It serves as an update to the previous publications. This paper is divided into two parts. The first section is a summary which contains the conclusions of each section of Part 2. This was done so that the reader may have a quick and easy understanding of what is happening with the economy and finally, the actions that should be considered to meet the challenges ahead

56- ANCIENT EGYPTIAN ECONOMICS
Ancient Egyptian Economics: Kemetic Wisdom of Saving and Investing in Wealth of Body, Mind and Soul for Building True Civilization, Prosperity and Spiritual Enlightenment------ Question: Why has the subject of finances and economics become important, I thought the spiritual teachings and Ancient Egyptian Philosophy and money were separate? Answer: Finances and money are an integral part of Ancient Egyptian culture as an instrument for promoting Maat ethics in the form of the well-being of the 'hekat'. The hekat are the people and the "Heka" is the Pharaoh. The Pharaoh was like a shepherd leading a flock and moneys were controlled righteously to promote the welfare of the people. In that tradition we have applied the philosophy of maatian economics to promote the well-being of those who are following this path as well as those who may read the books so they may avoid financial trouble as much as possible and have better capacity to practice the teachings. In order to have a successful life, human beings need a certain amount of money and wealth, but money and wealth are not the goal. They are a foundation that enables the true goal of life, enlightenment, to be realized. Therefore, we are only fulfilling the duty of transmitting wisdom about wealth to promote Maat, righteousness, truth and well-being, for all. This volume explores the mysteries of wealth based on the teachings of the sages of Ancient Egypt and the means to promote prosperity that allows a person to create the conditions for discovering inner peace and spiritual enlightenment. HTP-Peace

57- NETERIAN AWAKENING
Journal of Neterian Culture Vol 1-12 In one Volume

This is a single file containing 12 volumes of The Neterian Awakening Journal. The Neterian Awakening Journal was a publication where the culture and community of Shetaut Neter spirituality was explored. In it Dr. Muata Ashby and Dr. Dja Ashby along with members of the Temple of Shetaut Neter presented articles, festival reviews, Questions and Answer columns and many other important aspects of Neterian culture and spirituality beyond those presented in other volumes of the book series that are useful in understanding the practice of Neterian Spirituality and the path to achieving a �Neterian Spiritual Awakening.� Part of its mission was: To promote the study of Shetaut Neter (Neterianism, Neterian Religion) as a spiritual path. Instruct the serious followers of Shetaut Neter spirituality who would like to receive literature in between the publication of major books that will fill the needs of their daily spiritual practice. Neterian Awakening Journal explores the varied aspects of Shetaut Neter spirituality not covered in the books. NAJ provides a forum for the development of a Neterian Community of those who wish to follow the Neterian Spiritual Path of African Religious Culture

58- Little Book of Neter: Introduction to Shetaut Neter Spirituality and Religion Paperback – June 7, 2007

The Little Book of Neter is a summary of the most important teachings of Shetaut Neter for all aspirants to have for easy reference and distribution. It is designed to be portable and low cost so that all can have the main teachings of Shetaut Neter at easy access for personal use and also for sharing with others the basic tenets of Neterian spirituality.

59- Dollar Crisis: The Collapse of Society and Redemption Through Ancient Egyptian Monetary Policy by Muata Ashby (2008-07-24)
This book is about the problems of the US economy and the imminent collapse of the U.S. Dollar and its dire consequences for the US economy and the world. It is also about the corruption in government, economics and social order that led to this point. Also it is about survival, how to make it through this perhaps most trying period in the history of the United States. Also it is about the ancient wisdom of life that allowed an ancient civilization to grow beyond the destructive corruptions of ignorance and power so that the people of today may gain insight into the nature of their condition, how they got there and what needs to be done in order to salvage what is left and rebuild a society that is sustainable, beneficial and an example for all humanity.

60- Devotional Worship Book of Shetaut Neter: Medu Neter song, chant and hymn book for daily practice [Paperback] [2007] (Author) Muata Ashby Paperback – 2007

Ushet Hekau Shedi Sema Taui Uashu or Ushet means "to worship the Divine," "to propitiate the Divine." Ushet is of two types, external and internal. When you go to pilgrimage centers, temples, spiritual gatherings, etc., you are practicing external worship or spiritual practice. When you go into your private meditation room on your own and your utter words of power, prayers and meditation you are practicing internal worship or spiritual practice. Ushet needs to be understood as a process of not only an outer show of spiritual practice, but it is also a process of developing love for the Divine. Therefore, Ushet really signifies a development in Devotion towards the Divine. This practice is also known as sma uash or Yoga of Devotion. Ushet is the process of discovering the Divine and allowing your heart to flow towards the Divine. This program of life allows a spiritual aspirant to develop inner peace, contentment and universal love, and these qualities lead to spiritual enlightenment or union with the Divine. It is recommended that you see the book "The Path of Divine Love" by Dr. Muata Ashby. This volume will give details into this form of Sema or Yoga.

61- Initiation Into Egyptian Yoga and Neterian Religion Workbook for Beginning and Advancing Aspirants

What is Initiation? The great personalities of the past known to the world as Isis, Hathor, Jesus, Buddha and many other great Sages and Saints were initiated into their spiritual path but how did initiation help them and what were they specifically initiated into? This volume is a template for such lofty studies, a guidebook and blueprint for aspirants who want to understand what the path is all about, its requirements and goals, as they work with a qualified spiritual guide as they tread the path of Kemetic Spirituality and Yoga disciplines. This workbook helps by presenting the fundamental teachings of Egyptian Yoga and Neterian Spirituality with questions and exercises to help the aspirant gain a foundation for more advanced studies and practices

HIEROGLYPH TRANSLATION SERIES BY Dr. Muata Ashby

Egyptian Book of the Dead Hieroglyph Translations Using the Trilinear Method: Understanding the Mystic Path to Enlightenment...

Egyptian Book of the Dead Hieroglyph Translations Using The Trilinear Method Vol. 2: Understanding the Mystic Path to...
by Muata Ashby

EGYPTIAN BOOK OF THE DEAD HIEROGLYPH TRANSLATIONS USING THE TRILINEAR METHOD Volume 3: Understanding the Mystic Path to...
by Muata Ashby

EGYPTIAN BOOK OF THE DEAD HIEROGLYPH TRANSLATIONS USING THE TRILINEAR METHOD Volume 5: Featuring Temple of Amun-Ra at Ab...
by Muata Ashby

EGYPTIAN BOOK OF THE DEAD HIEROGLYPH TRANSLATIONS USING THE TRILINEAR METHOD Volume 4: Understanding the Mystic Path to...

Temple of the Soul Initiation Philosophy in the Temple of Osiris at Abydos: Decoded Temple Mysteries Translations of Temple Inscriptions...
by Muata Ashby

Mysteries of Isis and Ra: A New Original Translation Hieroglyphic Scripture of t
by Muata Ashby

Egyptian Book of the Dead Hieroglyph Translations Volume 6 Featuring The Osirian Resurrection Paperback – September 23, 2021
by Muata Ashby (Author)

The aim of this book has been to render, for the first time in one volume, the translated main hieroglyphic texts, associated with the Ancient Egyptian Osirian Resurrection, in the chronological order of the events of the myth and to present a translation that is grounded in the ancient texts, showing where the translated descriptions, wisdom and feelings expressed are coming from in the texts. Myth is a language of the soul by which the Ancient Kemetic (Egyptian) sages created a pathway for a human being to understand the nature of Creation, the powers (Neteru {gods and goddesses}) operating in it, and the manner in which to live a life that leads to happiness, fulfilment and spiritual enlightenment. The text of "Stele of Amenmose" contains references to the main scenes of the myth of the Asarian Resurrection, from the beginning of the myth to the end, but does not go into details related to some of those scenes. So, the text of "Stele of Amenmose" has been used as the foundational text, the trunk, as it were, of a tree. It begins the myth and describes the events of the myth, and as the tree (mythic rendition) grows, the branches extend the scenes not fully covered in the Amenmose scripture. So the contributing texts form expansions of the story which is taken up by another related scripture that goes into those details of hat section. Then, when that branch reaches a conclusion, we will return to the trunk of the tree again, the Stele of Amenmose, to again grow the tree, the mythic journey, until we reach another branch and so on to the end of the myth.

As the text is presented, the characters in the myth, which represent aspects of the Divine as well as expressions of the human heart and soul, will be introduced. Then, as the saga unfolds, the reader will be able to identify with the characters and experience their passions, sorrows, victories and spiritual exaltations leading to the final victory of exhilaration and contentment over despondency, depression and frustration, and wisdom over delusion, and eternal mystic life over physical death.

This manuscript, authored by the esteemed Dr. Muata Ashby, offers a profound exploration of the Ancient Kemetic (Egyptian) myth of the Asarian (Osirian) Resurrection. Dr. Ashby, a respected figure in the field of Egyptian philosophy and mysticism, employs a unique trilinear translation method to present the hieroglyphic texts. This method not only provides a phonetic transliteration and direct word-for-word translation but also includes a contextual translation that brings out the deeper meanings and philosophical insights embedded in the ancient texts. The manuscript delves into the mythic journey of Asar

(Osiris), Aset (Isis), and Heru (Horus), offering readers a chance to connect with the characters and experience their spiritual transformations. By reading this text, one can gain a deeper understanding of the nature of creation, the divine powers operating within it, and the path to spiritual enlightenment. The book is a treasure trove of wisdom, offering insights into the nature of the human personality, its fall into the delusion of mortality, and the means for its redemption and spiritual emancipation. The trilinear translation method used by Dr. Ashby ensures that readers can fully grasp the rich metaphorical and philosophical content of the hieroglyphic texts. This manuscript is not just a scholarly work but a spiritual guide that can enlighten and transform the reader's life. Don't miss the opportunity to purchase, read, and learn from the timeless wisdom contained in this manuscript. Let the ancient sages' teachings flow through you and illuminate your spiritual path.

THE PSYCHO-METAPHYSICAL MYSTERIES OF THE ANCIENT EGYPTIAN TEMPLE PANELS Paperback – July 21, 2021
by Muata Ashby (Author)

Why does the title of this book contain the term "Psycho-metaphysical Mysteries"? The first part, "psycho", references the aspect of the subject matter that relates to the human mind. The term "metaphysics" may be defined as a study about things that transcend the physical; studies that involve "philosophy" as a way of understanding, and "wisdom" about things known and understood, that allows the mind to transcend the knowledge and understanding that has been gained, and finally, "theurgy" which involves a science of spiritual evolution, that is the main subject taught and practiced in the Ancient Egyptian temple through mythic, and mystic writings, architecture and iconography of the temple. Therefore, this book examines the science of the Ancient Egyptian temple that is dedicated to the understanding and mentally enlightening process of spiritual evolution and discovery of the infinite.

Putting together, the teachings of the Ancient Egyptian mysteries and its theurgical science behind the mythic wisdom of the gods and goddesses with the temple architecture and the human mind with the catalyst of akhu or intuitional insight, of the Ancient Egyptian priests and priestesses, renders the conscious awareness of subject, the formal human person, in a state of ecstatic mystic self-discovery.

www.ingramcontent.com/pod-product-compliance
Lightning Source LLC
Chambersburg PA
CBHW081035050426
42335CB00052B/2441